Foundations of Language & Literature

STRONG ROOTS FOR AP®, COLLEGE, AND BEYOND

Foundations
of Language
& Literature

STRONG ROOTS FOR AP®, COLLEGE, AND BEYOND

SECOND EDITION

Renée H. Shea
Bowie State University,
Maryland

John Golden
Cleveland High School,
Portland, Oregon

Tracy Scholz
Spring Branch Independent
School District, Texas

bedford, freeman & worth
publishers

Boston | New York

Executive Vice President, General Manager, Macmillan Learning: Chuck Linsmeier
Vice President, Social Sciences and High School: Shani Fisher
Executive Program Director, High School: Ann Heath
Program Manager, High School English: Caitlin Kaufman
Senior Development Editor: Mara Weible
Associate Editor: Kelly Noll
Editorial Assistant: Sophie Dora Tulchin
Director of Media Editorial: Adam Whitehurst
Executive Editor, Development, and Media Editor: Lisa Samols
Senior Marketing Manager, High School: Claire Brantley
Assistant Marketing Manager, High School: Tiffani Tang
Marketing Assistant, High School: Nicollette Brady
Senior Director, Content Management Enhancement: Tracey Kuehn
Senior Managing Editor: Michael Granger
Senior Manager of Publishing Services: Andrea Cava
Senior Workflow Project Manager: Paul W. Rohloff
Production Supervisor: Robert Cherry
Senior Design Manager: Natasha A. S. Wolfe
Interior Design: Jerilyn DiCarlo
Cover Design: William Boardman
Icon Credits: (lightbulb, magnifying glass) PureSolution/Shutterstock; (numbers) KRAHOVNET/Shutterstock
Director, Rights and Permissions: Hilary Newman
Text Permissions Project Manager: Elaine Kosta, Lumina Datamatics, Inc.
Photo Permissions Project Manager: Cheryl Du Bois, Lumina Datamatics, Inc.
Director of Digital Production: Keri deManigold
Lead Media Project Manager: Jodi Isman
Project Management: Vanavan Jayaraman, Lumina Datamatics, Inc.
Copyeditor: Julie Bates Dock
Editorial Services: Lumina Datamatics, Inc.
Composition: Lumina Datamatics, Inc.
Printing and Binding: Transcontinental

Library of Congress Control Number: 2022943451
ISBN 978-1-319-40926-5   (Student Edition)
ISBN 978-1-319-47543-7   (Teacher's Edition)

Printed in the Canada.
1   2   3   4   5   6   27   26   25   24   23   22

Acknowledgments
Text acknowledgments and copyrights appear at the back of the book on pages 1100–1103, which constitute an extension of the copyright page. Art acknowledgments and copyrights appear on the same page as the art selections they cover.

AP® is a trademark registered by the College Board, which is not affiliated with, and does not endorse, this product.

For information, write: BFW Publishers, 120 Broadway, New York, NY 10271
hsmarketing@bfwpub.com

To
Mara Weible
Steve, Savannah, and Chase Scholz
and the Shea, Barnes, and Van Gundy clans

About the Authors

Renée H. Shea was professor of English and modern languages and director of freshman composition at Bowie State University in Maryland. A College Board faculty consultant for more than thirty years in AP® Language and Literature, and Pre-AP® English, she has been a reader and question leader for both AP® English exams. Renée served as a member on three committees for the College Board: the AP® Language and Composition Development Committee, the English Academic Advisory Committee, and the SAT Critical Reading Test Development Committee. She is co-author of *Literature & Composition, American Literature & Rhetoric, The Language of Composition, Conversations in American Literature*, and *Advanced Language & Literature*, as well as volumes on Amy Tan and Zora Neale Hurston for the NCTE High School Literature Series. Renée continues to write about contemporary authors for publications such as *World Literature Today, Poets & Writers*, and *Kenyon Review*. Her recent profiles focused on Imbolo Mbue, Natalie Handal, Lan Cao, and Ohio's 2020–2024 poet laureate, Kari Gunter-Seymour.

John Golden teaches at Cleveland High School in Portland, Oregon. He was an advisor to the College Board 6–12 English Language Arts Development Committee. An English teacher for over twenty-five years, John has developed curriculum and led workshops for the College Board's Pacesetter® and SpringBoard® English programs. He is a co-author of the Bedford, Freeman and Worth textbook *Advanced Language & Literature* (2021, 2016) and the producer of *Teaching Ideas: A Video Resource for AP® English* (Bedford/St. Martin's, 2008). He is also the author of *Reading in the Dark: Using Film as a Tool in the English Classroom* (NCTE, 2001), *Reading in the Reel World: Teaching Documentaries and Other Nonfiction Texts* (NCTE, 2006), the producer and co-host of the podcast *Third Rail Classroom*, and the producer of *The NCTE Centennial Film: Reading the Past, Writing the Future* (2010).

Tracy Scholz has been an educator for over twenty-five years. She has experience as a classroom teacher, department specialist, district interventionist, and program coordinator and served as the Associate Director for the Teacher Education Program at Rice University. She was a reviewer for *Advanced Language and Literature* (2016) and contributed to the Teacher's Edition for *Advanced Language and Literature* (2016). She currently serves as the Director of Advanced Academic Studies in the Spring Branch Independent School District.

Meet the Advisory Board

Natalie Landaeta Castillo
Felix Varela Senior High School, Florida

Courtesy of Natalie Castillo

Vivian DiGennaro
Bellmore-Merrick Central High School District, New York

Vivian DiGennaro

David Hillis
North Clackamas School District, Oregon

Courtesy of Miles Hillis

Craig McKinney
Plano Independent School District, Texas

Craig McKinney

Mercedes Muñoz
HOLLA School, Oregon

Mercedes Muñoz

Davin Navarre
Rangeview High School, Colorado

Davin Navarre

Dear Colleagues:

Welcome to *Foundations of Language & Literature*, a textbook designed specifically for ninth grade English courses. The following Guided Tour of the book will introduce you to its structure and features.

The key word in the title of this textbook is *foundations*. Our purpose in writing the book is to provide opportunities for students to practice the most essential skills they will need in order to be successful in ninth grade, and to lay the groundwork for their path to AP® English. We know that our ninth graders come to high school with a wide range of middle school experiences; their level of preparation in reading, writing, critical thinking, and speaking skills may vary widely. This is why the ninth-grade year is so vital: it is a time to ensure that *all* students can have the opportunity to learn and practice vital academic skills in safe, engaging, and developmentally appropriate ways. Here students will find a wide range of texts — short stories, poems, essays, plays, myths, and images — and activities designed to build those skills and then push them further.

The research is pretty straightforward: students who have a successful ninth grade year tend to graduate high school on time and have more success in college. We truly feel that this book will play a large role in that success. By focusing on the most important genres and modes that students will encounter in high school — narrative, fiction, argument, poetry, exposition, drama, and mythology — we can ensure that ninth graders will leave our classrooms fully prepared for the expectations that follow.

Since this is the second edition of *Foundations of Language & Literature*, we are fortunate to have had years of student and teacher feedback as we were revising. Not only did we include more texts by authors with diverse backgrounds and pieces that focus on contemporary issues relevant to our students' lives, but we also wanted to streamline the instructional focus for teachers to be able to address more genres and modes while not sacrificing quality or depth. We also included more extension opportunities for teachers to expand their students' experiences through creative writing, public speaking, and inquiry.

We hope that *Foundations of Language & Literature* helps teachers to create supportive yet challenging courses and helps students feel confident in making their voices heard and ready for the challenges they will face going forward.

Renée H. Shea   **John Golden**   **Tracy Scholz**

Foundations of Language & Literature,
Second Edition

Opening Chapters Take an Active Approach to Foundational Skills

Foundations of Language & Literature begins with brief, approachable, activity-driven opening chapters, which establish core academic skills. These skills are essential for communication in the classroom and the world: discussing ideas civilly, listening actively, reading actively and critically, writing clearly and with voice, and locating, evaluating, and using sources effectively.

1 Starting the Conversation	*This chapter focuses on civil discourse in the classroom; developing an academic voice; listening actively; asking questions to clarify, build upon, or challenge an idea; and reaching consensus.*
2 Reading	*This chapter asks students to explore three different types of reading: Reading for Understanding, Reading for Interpretation, and Reading for Style. It provides students with opportunities to practice skills essential to each type of reading, such as annotation, summary, finding the main idea, and analyzing themes. This chapter also walks students through techniques for overcoming reading challenges, such as difficult words, lack of context, complex sentence structures, and unfamiliar word order.*
3 Writing	*This chapter asks students to consider how their voices might change to suit a particular subject, purpose, audience, and occasion. Those changes in voice are created through playing with word choice, altering sentence structure and punctuation, and recognizing the effects. Finally, students work on creating clear and unified paragraphs. This chapter also covers techniques for classroom presentations and public speaking.*
4 Using Sources	*This chapter is an introduction to finding and using evidence. The chapter focuses heavily on reading critically in order to assess credibility and bias. The chapter then walks students through the key moves of evidence-based writing: navigating a range of ideas, integrating quotations, acknowledging sources, and avoiding plagiarism.*

▼ The brief, engaging **Activities** throughout these chapters are perhaps the most important learning tools, giving students regular opportunities to apply what they've learned, exchange ideas with peers, and deepen understanding.

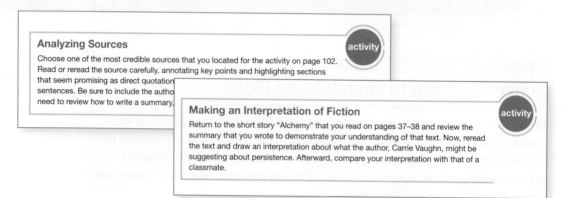

Analyzing Sources activity

Choose one of the most credible sources that you located for the activity on page 102. Read or reread the source carefully, annotating key points and highlighting sections that seem promising as direct quotation⟨...⟩ sentences. Be sure to include the autho⟨...⟩ need to review how to write a summary,⟨...⟩

Making an Interpretation of Fiction activity

Return to the short story "Alchemy" that you read on pages 37–38 and review the summary that you wrote to demonstrate your understanding of that text. Now, reread the text and draw an interpretation about what the author, Carrie Vaughn, might be suggesting about persistence. Afterward, compare your interpretation with that of a classmate.

▼ Handy **Academic Vocabulary** features help students focus on key concepts and terminology and review what they've learned after reading and working through the content.

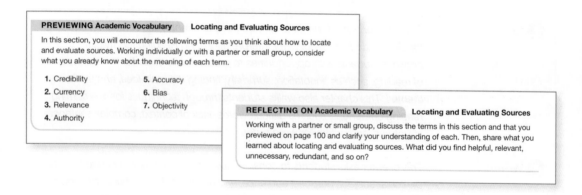

PREVIEWING Academic Vocabulary   Locating and Evaluating Sources

In this section, you will encounter the following terms as you think about how to locate and evaluate sources. Working individually or with a partner or small group, consider what you already know about the meaning of each term.

1. Credibility
2. Currency
3. Relevance
4. Authority

5. Accuracy
6. Bias
7. Objectivity

REFLECTING ON Academic Vocabulary   Locating and Evaluating Sources

Working with a partner or small group, discuss the terms in this section and that you previewed on page 100 and clarify your understanding of each. Then, share what you learned about locating and evaluating sources. What did you find helpful, relevant, unnecessary, redundant, and so on?

▼ **Writer's Corner** features give students on-the-spot tips for improving their writing across genres and assignments.

Writer's Corner   Using Ellipses and Brackets

Sometimes the quotation you want to use doesn't quite fit, either because of its length or because the verb tenses or other grammatical features of the sentence don't match your own. Ellipses and brackets give you a way to make a quotation work within your writing, while signaling to your readers that you are slightly altering the original text.

Ellipses

Ellipses are the series of spaced dots that signal something is missing from a quotation. A three-dot ellipsis is used when the missing part comes from within a sentence, while a four-dot ellipsis signals that you've taken parts from different sentences:

> Duckworth noticed some behaviors in her students, which she began to think of as *grit*: "Instead of playing around and looking out the window, they took notes and asked questions. . . . Their hard work showed in their grades."

Brackets

Brackets are most often used to change a pronoun They signal that the word in brackets has been cha quotation. For instance, if we wanted to use this qu pronoun, we could alter it to fit our sentence:

ORIGINAL QUOTATION

"And yet, at the end of the first marking period of these very able students weren't doing as w

USING BRACKETS TO CHANGE THE PRONOUN

Like many of us might, Duckworth assumed that the most talented students would excel, but "at the end of the first marking period, [she] was surprised to find that some of these very able students weren't doing as well as [she'd] expected."

Writer's Corner   Thesaurus Overload

When searching for the right word, don't overuse the thesaurus. Writers sometimes think that using scholarly, academic vocabulary will improve their text, but using too many lofty vocabulary words — or worse, using them incorrectly — can leave the reader confused. The most important thing is to get your message across clearly. Know your audience and select words that will best deliver that message.

▼ Finally, **Culminating Activities** at the end of each chapter give students opportunities to demonstrate what they have learned in the chapter.

---

culminating activity

Entering the Academic Conversation

When basketball star Lebron James spoke out in 2018 in support of the Black Lives Matter movement, a TV news words, the commentator was s out of politics. Yet there is a lor to amplify issues that are impo his heavyweight title when he r War in the 1960s. More recentl Kaepernick took a knee during protest the police shootings of politicians, reporters, and other priate, especially during events time of national pride. Read the political protests. After you rea

---

culminating activity

Writing with Sources

The texts that follow present different views on the question of whether students should be paid for good grades to help motivate them to do well in school.

Step 1. As you read the four texts, annotate them by applying the steps on pages 106–107.

Step 2. Then, write a paragraph of seven to ten sentences that responds to the following prompt: *Should students be paid for getting good grades in school?* Include references to at least two of the sources and use the approaches presented on pages 112–114. When writing your paragraph, use what you learned in Chapter 3 (p. 85) and on pages 119–120 of this chapter.

Step 3. Review your work to be sure that you have cited your sources properly and have not committed unintentional plagiarism. (See pp. 124–125.)

Readings Chapters Use a Genre/Mode Approach to Build Confidence and Explore Essential Ideas

At a Glance: How a Genre/Mode Chapter Works

Introduces the basic concepts students need for understanding and analyzing texts in the genre.

Brief and approachable texts to build foundational skills.

Texts representing grade-level complexity for ninth grade.

Stylistically and conceptually complex texts approaching the level of challenge found in AP® classes.

Helps students build an effective presentation based on their writing in the genre.

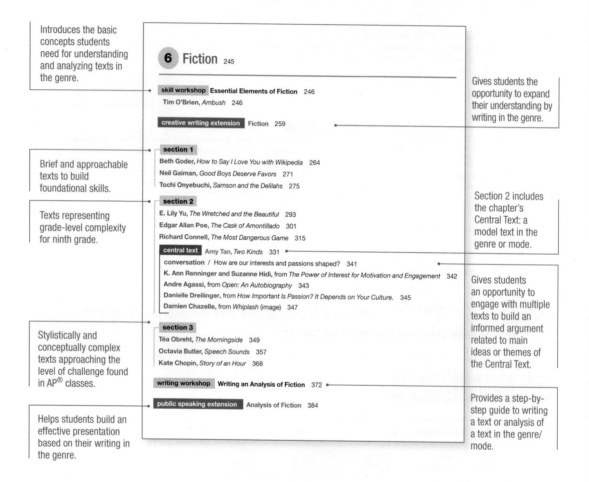

Gives students the opportunity to expand their understanding by writing in the genre.

Section 2 includes the chapter's Central Text: a model text in the genre or mode.

Gives students an opportunity to engage with multiple texts to build an informed argument related to main ideas or themes of the Central Text.

Provides a step-by-step guide to writing a text or analysis of a text in the genre/mode.

Why Teach Ninth Grade By Genre and Mode?

One of the key indicators of college readiness is whether students can understand what is expected of them as readers and writers: to know what to do when faced with an unfamiliar text or task. A student on track to high school success is the student who is able to say, "When I am analyzing an argument, I need to focus on X, but when I'm analyzing a poem, I do Y." So, here in the ninth grade, it's important to take the time to slow down and ensure that all students understand the essential elements of each of the significant genres and modes they will encounter in their academic careers. These readings chapters break down the essential skills and clearly outline the expectations of working with each genre or mode:

5 Narrative	**8** Poetry	**10** Drama
6 Fiction	**9** Exposition	**11** Mythology
7 Argument		

NEW! Nearly 100 New Pieces of Literature and Nonfiction Keep the Book Fresh and Engaging

Selections new to this edition include high-interest work by writers such as Viet Thanh Nguyen, Octavia Butler, Greta Thunberg, Tommy Orange, Roxane Gay, David Attenborough, Téa Obreht, George Takei, Erika L. Sánchez, Neil Gaiman, Layli Long Soldier, Eve Ewing, Farhad Manjoo, David Sedaris, and more.

Learning to Love My Brown Skin

Erika L. Sánchez

Erika L. Sánchez is a poet, novelist, and essayist. She is a regular contributor on issues of gender, culture, and politics to publications such as *Time*, the *Guardian*, *Rolling Stone*, *Cosmopolitan*, *Jezebel*, and many others. She published her debut young adult novel *I Am Not Your Perfect Mexican Daughter* in 2017, and her memoir *Crying in the Bathroom* in 2022. This piece was published in *Racked* in 2016.

Adriana Díaz

Big Words and Little Action

Greta Thunberg

When she was 15 years old, Swedish activist Greta Thunberg (b. 2003) skipped school to stand outside of the Swedish ... rs for not ... e is the youngest ... red on the *Forbes* ... 9), and she has ... bel Peace Prize

Sean Gallup/Getty Images

On Being a Refugee, an American —and a Human Being

Viet Thanh Nguyen

Viet Thanh Nguyen was born in Vietnam in 1971 and immigrated to the United States with his family when he was four years old at the end of what the United States refers to as the Vietnam War. He is the author of the Pulitzer Prize–winning novel *The Sympathizer* (2015) and its sequel *The Committed* (2021). He is also the editor of the collection of essays, *The Displaced: Refugee Writers on Refugee*

San Francisco Chronicle/Hearst Newspapers via Getty Images/Getty Images

A Strong Focus on Nonfiction Nurtures Critical Thinking Skills

The study of nonfiction is vital, not just for academic success in all academic fields, but in helping students learn how to process information critically and respond thoughtfully. That's why the readings chapters include ones centered on nonfiction modes (narrative, argument, and exposition) right alongside the traditional literary genres of fiction, poetry, drama, and mythology. There are also thematic Conversations in every chapter, which are primarily nonfiction, tied to the Central Text.

Differentiated Texts Support Targeted Instruction

Each genre/mode chapter has three text sections of increasing complexity that allow you to tailor curricular choices to students' needs and interests — while keeping students exploring the same genre or mode and developing the same skills. With several texts per chapter, you and your students will have a wide range of choice.

▶ **Section 1 / Foundational:** These entry-level texts are brief, high-interest, and relatively straightforward in their content, context, and structure.

fiction / section one

Beth Goder ▪ How to Say I Love You with Wikipedia, *264*

Neil Gaiman ▪ Good Boys Deserve Favors, *271*

Tochi Onyebuchi ▪ Samson and the Delilahs, *275*

▶ **Section 2 / Grade-Level:** These texts represent a level of complexity that a ninth-grade student should reasonably be able to read and analyze with a bit of teacher support and additional context. This section always includes a **Central Text**, a particularly rich exemplar of the genre or mode that is the focus of the chapter.

fiction / section two

E. Lily Yu ▪ The Wretched and the Beautiful, *293*

Edgar Allan Poe ▪ The Cask of Amontillado, *301*

Richard Connell ▪ The Most Dangerous Game, *315*

`central text` Amy Tan ▪ Two Kinds, *331*

▶ **Section 3 / Challenging:** The most challenging texts in each chapter, these texts have rich language, sophisticated ideas, or unfamiliar contexts. These texts approach the level of challenge seen in later grades, including AP® English classes.

fiction / section three

Téa Obreht ▪ The Morningside, *349*

Octavia Butler ▪ Speech Sounds, *357*

Kate Chopin ▪ Story of an Hour, *368*

Interactive Workshops Build on Essential Skills for Deeper Understanding

While students encounter key ideas and develop valuable skills in the opening chapters, skill-building is a continual process requiring practice. That's why there are in-depth, interactive workshops in each readings chapter that introduce students to the essential elements of the genre or mode, provide opportunities for public speaking and discussion around the genre or mode, and walk students through the process of writing analytical responses to texts in that genre or mode. Creative Writing Extension workshops in some readings chapters also provide opportunities for writing in that genre.

▼ **Skill Workshops open and anchor each chapter with essential skill reinforcement.** These workshops include a series of activities designed to introduce students to the essential elements of the genre they are studying through a short, engaging, grade-level text. Each Skill Workshop concludes with a Culminating Activity that gives students an opportunity to demonstrate their current skills and knowledge of that genre.

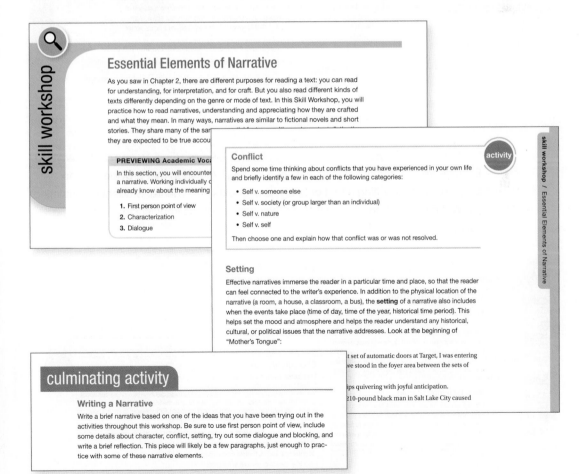

skill workshop

Essential Elements of Narrative

As you saw in Chapter 2, there are different purposes for reading a text: you can read for understanding, for interpretation, and for craft. But you also read different kinds of texts differently depending on the genre or mode of text. In this Skill Workshop, you will practice how to read narratives, understanding and appreciating how they are crafted and what they mean. In many ways, narratives are similar to fictional novels and short stories. They share many of the sam[...] they are expected to be true accou[...]

PREVIEWING Academic Voca[...]

In this section, you will encounter[...] a narrative. Working individually o[...] already know about the meaning[...]

1. First person point of view
2. Characterization
3. Dialogue

---

activity

Conflict

Spend some time thinking about conflicts that you have experienced in your own life and briefly identify a few in each of the following categories:

- Self v. someone else
- Self v. society (or group larger than an individual)
- Self v. nature
- Self v. self

Then choose one and explain how that conflict was or was not resolved.

Setting

Effective narratives immerse the reader in a particular time and place, so that the reader can feel connected to the writer's experience. In addition to the physical location of the narrative (a room, a house, a classroom, a bus), the **setting** of a narrative also includes when the events take place (time of day, time of the year, historical time period). This helps set the mood and atmosphere and helps the reader understand any historical, cultural, or political issues that the narrative addresses. Look at the beginning of "Mother's Tongue":

[...]t set of automatic doors at Target, I was entering[...]e stood in the foyer area between the sets of

[...]ps quivering with joyful anticipation.

[...]210-pound black man in Salt Lake City caused

culminating activity

Writing a Narrative

Write a brief narrative based on one of the ideas that you have been trying out in the activities throughout this workshop. Be sure to use first person point of view, include some details about character, conflict, setting, try out some dialogue and blocking, and write a brief reflection. This piece will likely be a few paragraphs, just enough to practice with some of these narrative elements.

▼ **NEW! Creative Writing Extensions: A fun, engaging way for students to learn to think like writers.** Not only is creative writing engaging for students, it's also a great way for students to learn about the choices that writers make to create their texts. In the **Fiction, Poetry**, and **Drama** chapters, students have an opportunity to write in the mode they are studying and to become a short story writer, a poet, and a playwright.

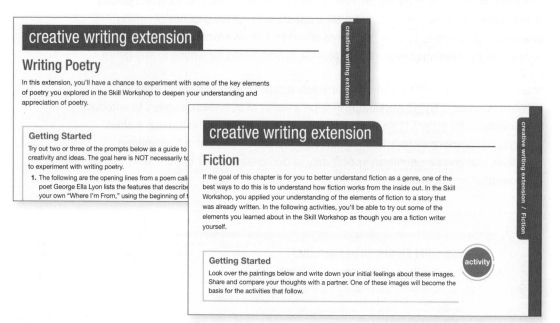

▼ **Writing Workshops provide a bridge from close reading to analytical writing.** Each genre chapter includes at least one Writing Workshop that provides a step-by-step guide to writing a text or analysis of a text in that genre. Students completing the Writing Workshops will be well on their way to writing sophisticated academic essays.

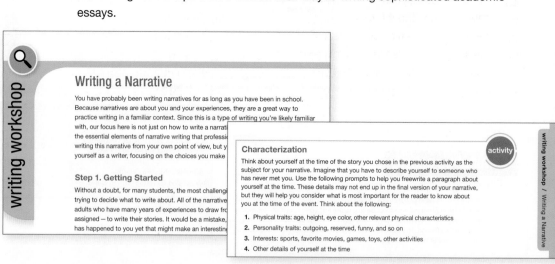

▼ **NEW! Public Speaking Extensions lay the foundation for effective communication and civil discourse.** It's clear today that we can all use more effective communication and civil discourse. Whether you're interested in building a classroom community or preparing students to engage in academic dialogue, *Foundations of Language & Literature* includes instruction and practice opportunities through Public Speaking Extensions in every genre/mode chapter.

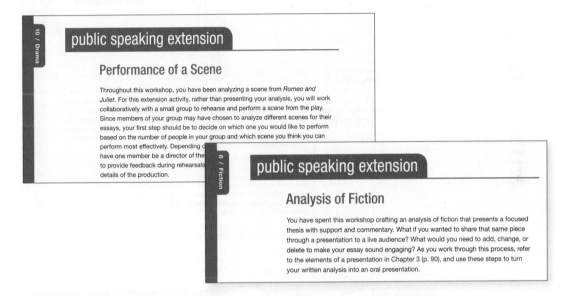

public speaking extension

Performance of a Scene

Throughout this workshop, you have been analyzing a scene from *Romeo and Juliet*. For this extension activity, rather than presenting your analysis, you will work collaboratively with a small group to rehearse and perform a scene from the play. Since members of your group may have chosen to analyze different scenes for their essays, your first step should be to decide on which one you would like to perform based on the number of people in your group and which scene you think you can perform most effectively. Depending on have one member be a director of the to provide feedback during rehearsals details of the production.

public speaking extension

Analysis of Fiction

You have spent this workshop crafting an analysis of fiction that presents a focused thesis with support and commentary. What if you wanted to share that same piece through a presentation to a live audience? What would you need to add, change, or delete to make your essay sound engaging? As you work through this process, refer to the elements of a presentation in Chapter 3 (p. 90), and use these steps to turn your written analysis into an oral presentation.

Conversations Develop Evidence-Based Argument and Synthesis Skills

Each genre/mode chapter's Central Text is followed by a brief Conversation tied to a main idea or theme of that text. Synthesis is one of those skills with multiple benefits: it leads to lively class discussions, it encourages informed opinions, it demands nuanced and nimble thinking, and it forces students to draw on evidence to support their positions. These are academic habits of mind common to all disciplines and at the heart of all academic work. This is why, even in the literary genre chapters, you'll find the Conversation texts are primarily nonfiction. We believe that cultivating these reading and writing skills can deepen the study of any text, regardless of the genre.

La Gringuita

Julia Alvarez

Julia Alvarez (b. 1950) was born in New York but raised in the Dominican Republic until she was ten, her family fleeing to the ... olved in an unsuccessful ... o. She received a BA ... Syracuse University. ... oir, and children's books. ... biographical essays, ... author examines identity

central text

conversation

What is the relationship between language and power?

Who has the most power in a classroom? In many cases, it's the teachers because they have the authority to speak without having to be called on. Who has the power in the media and advertising? Those who create, edit, and present the words and images. They can influence what people believe, how people vote, what they buy. Who has the power in a courtroom? It's often the judge who determines who gets ... what can be said during a trial.

Power can be gained and wielded through language. Sadly, the reve... often true: those without access to the dominant language used by insti... schools, government, the justice system, and business can be left witho... they should have otherwise.

Entering the Conversation

Throughout this Conversation, you have read a variety of texts that deal with language and the ways that it relates to power. Now it's time to enter the conversation by responding the prompt you've been thinking about — ***What should society or individuals do to ensure that there are not significant differences in equality or power based on language?*** Follow the steps below to write your argument.

1. | Building on the Conversation. Locate one additional text on this topic that you think adds an interesting perspective to this Conversation. This text can be of any type: an argument, a narrative, a poem, a painting, or even a film clip. Before you decide on adding this text to the Conversation, be sure that it is a credible and relevant source, which you can determine by evaluating it with the skills you practiced in Chapter 4 (p. 99). Read and annotate the text carefully, making connections to other texts in the Conversation and "La Gringuita" (p. 177).

		Central Text	Conversation
5	Narrative	Julia Alvarez, *La Gringuita*	What is the relationship between language and power?
6	Fiction	Amy Tan, *Two Kinds*	How are our interests and passions shaped?
7	Argument	Steve Almond, *Is It Immoral to Watch the Super Bowl?*	Is fandom a positive or negative force in our lives?
8	Poetry	Langston Hughes, *Let America Be America Again*	How do we find common ground?
9	Exposition	Jon Ronson, *How One Stupid Tweet Blew Up Justine Sacco's Life*	To what extent can we influence social, cultural, or political change online?
10	Drama	William Shakespeare, *The Tragedy of Romeo and Juliet*	Do we make better decisions with our "gut" or with our rational brain?
11	Mythology	Homer, from *The Odyssey*	What defines a hero?

Probing Questions Provide Guided Practice for Essential Reading and Writing Skills

Throughout the book are guided questions designed to support and challenge students as they engage with the texts.

▼ **Understanding and Interpreting** questions lay the foundation for analysis — these questions guide students to an understanding of the content and move them toward an interpretation.

Understanding and Interpreting

1. Most of the excerpt is focused on George — Takei himself as a young boy — but the reactions of those around him help shape his experience. Compare and contrast how George's parents handle the adversity of their situation. How does Takei communicate these differences visually?

2. Why might George have been drawn to the story of *The Hunchback of Notre Dame* at this point in his life?

3. How do the camp officers work to have the prisoners fight against each other rather than fight against the camp itself? How successful are they in this?

▼ **Analyzing Language, Style, and Structure** questions ask students to look at craft — how the writer's choices create meaning.

Analyzing Language, Style, and Structure

6. **Vocabulary in Context.** On page 217, Takei describes the movie he watched as a "transporting experience." What does the word *transporting* mean in this context, and how is it similar to or different from other uses of that word?

7. How does Takei visually establish the perspective of a child through the framing of the panels at the beginning of the narrative?

8. Look at the close-up of George after he sees the *benshi* do their work during the silent movie (p. 218). Given what you know about Takei from the biography on page 211, what does the framing and lighting seem to communicate?

▼ **Topics for Composing** prompts include extended essay and project ideas ranging from narrative and argumentative to research, creative writing, speaking and listening, and even multimodal projects.

Topics for Composing

14. **Analysis.** Reread the last scene with George and his father long after they have left the camp. Identify and explain a theme Takei is examining about power, family, responsibilities, or another topic. What evidence from the rest of the narrative supports your interpretation?

15. **Argument.** The term *concentration camp* tends to make people think of the Nazi extermination camps of the Holocaust. Yet in 1998, there was an exhibit in New York called *America's Concentration Camps: Remembering the Japanese-American Experience*. During World War II, these facilities were often referred to as *internment, relocation, assembly,* or *isolation camps*. At the time of the exhibit, the *New York Times* wrote, "Some American Jewish groups have strongly objected, arguing that the term has become indelibly associated with the Holocaust and would be cheapened by being used in this way. Their concern that the Holocaust be remembered as a uniquely vile expression of human evil is a reasonable one." In

---

Foundational Features Offer Support and Enrichment for Students at Every Level

Key Context Notes Make Challenging Texts and Ideas Approachable for All Students

These notes accompanying many texts help students navigate unfamiliar contexts that come with writing from other time periods and cultural traditions, providing a sense of the bigger picture. This support is key for developing readers and English Language Learners.

from **A Life on Our Planet**

David Attenborough

...er the past several decades has
...h in hundreds of TV shows, movies,
...k focused mostly on documenting
...al surroundings, he has more recently
...ronmental causes. This is an excerpt
...*Life on Our Planet*, a series of vignettes
...ach chapter title is a year, and each
...out the world population, carbon levels,
...hat year.

...takes place on the remote island of New Guinea, in the
...Attenborough includes the following map and detail of
...o orient his readers.

The Morningside

Téa Obreht

Born in Belgrade, Serbia, Téa Obreht (1985-), is a bestselling and award-winning author whose novels include *The Tiger's Wife* (2011) and *Inland* (2019). In 2010, she was recognized by *The New Yorker* as one of the 20 best American fiction writers under 40.

KEY CONTEXT This short story appeared in *The Decameron Project*, for which editors at the *New York Times* asked authors to write new short stories inspired by the COVID-19 pandemic that began in 2019. The editors were inspired by Italian writer Giovanni Boccaccio's fourteenth-century work *The Decameron*, which was written as the Black Death, a bubonic plague pandemic, ravaged much of Europe.

NEW! Extending Beyond the Text Features Offer Authentic Engagement and Ready-Made Enrichment

These boxed features offer enrichment ideas for readings throughout the book. They challenge students to encounter other perspectives, put texts in conversation, grapple with counterarguments, and draw connections to real-world issues.

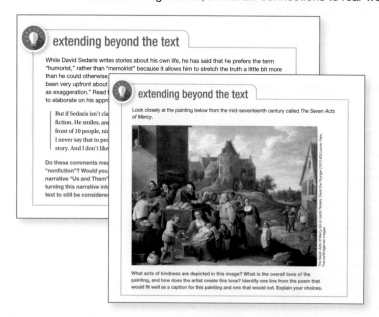

extending beyond the text

While David Sedaris writes stories about his own life, he has said that he prefers the term "humorist," rather than "memoirist" because it allows him to stretch the truth a little bit more than he could otherwise... been very upfront about... as exaggeration." Read... to elaborate on his appro...

But if Sedaris isn't cla...
fiction. He smiles, an...
front of 10 people, ni...
I never say that to pe...
story. And I don't like...

Do these comments mea...
"nonfiction"? Would you...
narrative "Us and Them"...
turning this narrative into...
text to still be considere...

extending beyond the text

Look closely at the painting below from the mid-seventeenth century called *The Seven Acts of Mercy*.

What acts of kindness are depicted in this image? What is the overall tone of the painting, and how does the artist create this tone? Identify one line from the poem that would fit well as a caption for this painting and one that would not. Explain your choices.

Visuals Extend and Deepen Student Understanding

Every visual text in *Foundations of Language & Literature* serves a clear, authentic pedagogical purpose. Photographs, movie stills, artworks, and graphs were carefully selected to inform the reading of a print text, suggest new ideas, provide additional context, extend an understanding to the real world, or allow students to make interesting connections.

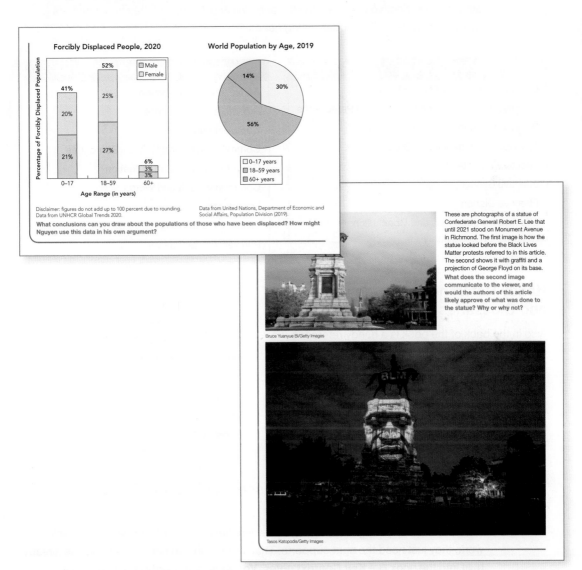

Forcibly Displaced People, 2020

World Population by Age, 2019

Disclaimer: figures do not add up to 100 percent due to rounding.
Data from UNHCR Global Trends 2020.

Data from United Nations, Department of Economic and Social Affairs, Population Division (2019).

What conclusions can you draw about the populations of those who have been displaced? How might Nguyen use this data in his own argument?

Bruce Yuanyue Bi/Getty Images

These are photographs of a statue of Confederate General Robert E. Lee that until 2021 stood on Monument Avenue in Richmond. The first image is how the statue looked before the Black Lives Matter protests referred to in this article. The second shows it with graffiti and a projection of George Floyd on its base.

What does the second image communicate to the viewer, and would the authors of this article likely approve of what was done to the statue? Why or why not?

Tasos Katopodis/Getty Images

NEW! Revision and Grammar Workshops Offer Targeted Help When and Where Students Need It

Not all students make the same kinds of errors with grammar and conventions, or need to revise their writing in the same way. So, at the end of the book, we include eight Revision Workshops and fifteen Grammar Workshops with scaffolded activities that guide students from understanding to application in their own writing. These activities are far more effective than the old skill-and-drill approach, and they help teachers to meet their students' individual writing needs.

NEW! Revision Workshops
Effective Thesis and Essay Structure
Effective Topic Sentences and Unified Paragraphs
Balanced Evidence and Commentary
Appropriate Evidence and Support
Effective Transitions
Effective Syntax
Effective Diction
Effective Introductions and Conclusions

Grammar Workshops (sample topics)
Active and Passive Voice
Adjectives and Adverbs
Capitalization
Comma Splices and Run-On Sentences
Coordination and Subordination
Commonly Confused Words
Fragments
Misplaced and Dangling Modifiers
Parallelism—and more!

Handy References Include Guides and Glossaries to Help All Students

Also in the back of the book is a handy reference guide to Vocabulary and Word Roots to help students strengthen vocabulary, a Guide to MLA Documentation Style to help students document their sources properly, and a Glossary/Glosario of academic and literary terms to support the understanding of all students.

Appendix: Revision Workshops
Appendix: Grammar Workshops
Appendix: Speaking and Listening
Appendix: Vocabulary and Word Roots
Appendix: MLA Documentation Style
Glossary/Glosario

NEW! ELL Support Includes Essential Tools to Build Understanding

Teachers know that English Language Learners are capable of high-level academic work, they just need the right supports. That's why — in addition to the supports already built into the book like **Key Context** notes, **Vocabulary in Context** questions, and **Foundational Texts** — we are offering **Essential Guide handouts** for every reading that offer a suite of ELL supports, such as a summary of the text to support comprehension, additional context to help build background knowledge, specific help with word- and sentence-level challenges in the text, and more.

A Complete Package to Support Teachers and Students

Teacher's Edition | Written By Teachers For Teachers

The wraparound **Teacher's Edition** for *Foundations of Language & Literature* is an invaluable resource for both experienced and new instructors. Written by veteran classroom teachers, it includes thoughtful instruction for planning, pacing, differentiating, and enlivening any ninth-grade English course.

Teacher's Resource Materials | Build Your Course Your Way

The Teacher's Resource Materials collection accompanies the Teacher's Edition and contains materials to effectively plan the course, including a detailed suggested pacing guide, handouts, suggested responses to questions, activities, and so much more.

Digital Collection of Full-Length Works | Customize Your Course

With nearly 100 classic and commonly taught works of literature and nonfiction, this resource is perfect for building a unique ninth-grade course that works for you.

Digital Options | More Than Just an E-book

Foundations of Language & Literature, Second Edition is available in our fully interactive **digital platform**. In this platform, students can read, highlight, and take notes on any device, online or offline. You have the ability to assign every question from the book as well as supplemental quizzes and activities, and students' results automatically sync to your gradebook. You can also access the Teacher's Resource Materials, test bank, adaptive quizzing, and more.

LearningCurve | Game-like Adaptive Quizzing

Embedded in the book's digital platform is the **LearningCurve** adaptive quizzing engine, which helps students focus on the material they need the most help with. When they get a question wrong, feedback tells them why and links them to content review — and then they get a chance to try again. LearningCurve has hundreds of topics to support student learning, such as Active and Passive Voice, Appropriate Voice, Argument: Arguable Claims, Argument: Reasoning and Logical Fallacies, Basic Sentence Patterns, Building Vocabulary, and many more.

Test Bank | Your Home for Quizzing

Our test bank includes quizzes and questions that take students from understanding to close rhetorical, literary, and stylistic analysis. Our authors and editors analyzed hundreds of items from national assessments and AP® exams to target key skills. The test bank lets teachers quickly create paper and online tests in minutes. The platform is fully customizable, allowing teachers to enter their own questions, edit existing questions, set time limits, incorporate multimedia, and scramble answers and change the order of questions to prevent plagiarism. Detailed results reports feed into a gradebook.

Acknowledgments

We would like to extend our sincerest thanks to all who inspired, advised, and supported us during the creation and development of this book. We feel very fortunate to have had the assistance of some amazing teachers at key times in this project. Our deepest gratitude goes to our Advisory Board for each edition, who reviewed this project at many different stages: Mica Bloom, Marisol Castillo, Natalie Landaeta Castillo, Christian Cicoria, Vivian DiGennaro, Carlos Escobar, Anthony Gabriele, Constance Green, David Hillis, Jamie Incorvia, Craig McKinney, Mercedes Muñoz, Davin Navarre, and Megan Pankiewicz. A special thanks to David Hillis for his numerous contributions to this project at all of its stages, most importantly as a fantastic think-partner and student-centered practitioner. Our thanks to those who took the time to discuss their students, their classrooms, and their teaching practice with us in focus groups: Julie Slusher, Kate Cordes, Jewel Feraro, John Reedan, Stacey Aronow, Sheryl Young, Kathleen Higgins, Joanne Krajeck, Jacquelyn Fabian, Megumi Yamamoto, Diane Smeenk, Lauren Wilkie, Claire Valley, Lauren Jones, Kimberly Siemsen, Hillary Wingate, and Amy Wood. And, finally, our thanks to the hundreds of you who participated in our early market research that informed this project.

To the team at Bedford, Freeman, and Worth: You are simply the best in the business. How deeply you care about teachers and their students was clear at every step in the process of developing this book. We are grateful to Caitlin Kaufman, Program Manager, for her unwavering support and calm, thoughtful leadership. There is no way to fully acknowledge the invaluable contributions that Mara Weible made to this project other than to say that her organization, clarity, and deep commitment made this book better in every way. Nathan Odell is the kind of editor every English teacher should be lucky enough to have: creative, smart, and brutally honest when needed; we're going to miss him. Our thanks to Ann Heath, who believed in this project from the start and supported it in every way possible. But it took a village, so thanks also to Sophie Dora Tulchin, Meghan Kelly, Andrea Cava, Vanavan Jayaraman, Elaine Kosta, Cheryl Du Bois, and Hilary Newman on the editorial, production, and permissions teams. For sales and marketing, we thank the brilliant Claire Brantley, Janie Pierce-Bratcher, Nicollete Brady, Tiffani Tang, Lisa Erdely, Nicole Sheppard, Sara Whittern, Jen Cawsey, Tiffani Tang, and the crack team of sales reps.

Contents

 Starting the Conversation   3

② Reading 17

③ Writing 65

4 Using Sources 95

6 Fiction 245

7 Argument 387

8 Poetry 493

9 Exposition 597

10 Drama 705

11 Mythology 851

Starting the Conversation

As you enter high school and start to take on more challenging academic work, you're going to learn a lot from your teachers and the things you read, but you're going to learn even more from your classmates as you explore ideas, discuss issues, and grow together as critical thinkers. This will happen primarily through talking with and listening to one another. Sherry Turkle is a researcher who studies how we communicate, especially through technology and social media, and in her book *Reclaiming Conversation: The Power of Talk in a Digital Age*, she writes,

> Face-to-face conversation is the most human — and humanizing — thing we do. Fully present to one another, we learn to listen. It's where we develop the capacity for empathy. It's where we experience the joy of being heard, of being understood. And conversation advances self-reflection, the conversations with ourselves that are the cornerstone of early development and continue throughout life.

This is why, before we even get to reading and writing, we're going to talk about something even more fundamental and essential — how to have a conversation. This first chapter will focus on building the skills you need to engage in effective conversations: listening actively, asking questions, and expressing ideas.

As you learn these skills, you and your classmates will start to build a classroom community where everyone can share ideas, disagree respectfully, draw conclusions, and build consensus. These are skills that you'll find useful in this class and other classes, but you'll also find them useful beyond the classroom, in your future career and in your personal relationships.

Part of building a classroom community is making sure that everyone is heard. Being heard is sometimes easier for those who are more outgoing, but it's important that we create and support an environment in which we can hear from the quieter ones as well.

According to Susan Cain, author of *Quiet: The Power of Introverts in a World That Can't Stop Talking*, about half of the U.S. population tends to be extroverted, while the other half tends to be introverted. This means that both personality types are likely equally represented in your class right now. It is essential that those who tend to be more outgoing do not drown out the voices of those who are less so, and that those who are more introverted take some risks and put themselves out there at times. As Sherry Turkle suggests in the quotation above, there is joy in being heard and understood by others, but it also takes practice; the activities in this chapter will help you get started.

Thinking about Voice

We generally know the term *voice* as the sound we produce when we speak or sing, but there is another meaning that is relevant to this idea of a conversation. **Voice** can also refer to the unique ways that you communicate, whether through speech, writing, artwork, singing, and so on. Your voice is the expression of your personality. For example, you probably use words, phrases, or even emojis regularly that your friends, family, teachers, or others don't necessarily use in quite the same way. Slang, references to music and movies, or even just the way that you say things — with a smile or a shoulder shrug — might be part of your voice. Your voice might also include special vocabulary you've picked up through your interests and life experiences — words related to skateboarding, computer programming, or theater, for example.

Here's the most important thing to remember about voice: you have many voices. How you're feeling, where you are, whom you're with, and what you're trying to say influences which voice you adopt at a given time. How you express yourself differs on the basketball court, in places of worship, when you are with your close friends, at a grandparent's house, on social media, in math class, when you're watching football or listening to music, and so on. Humans are complex; we speak with many different voices, and we vary them often, especially when the context, situation, and audience demand it of us.

 activity **Your Many Voices**

Step 1. Describe three to five different voices that you use at home, outside of home, and in school, using a chart with the following categories. A sample is provided:

Voice	Words/Phrases I Use With This Voice	When/Where/Why I Use This Voice
My basketball voice	"Let's Go!" "Move the ball!" "Block out!" "Three in the key!"	In practice, games, and with my teammates. It's pretty informal, and I use it to encourage others to play hard and push myself to win. I tend to shout a lot and use some specific basketball terms that some people don't know.

Step 2. In writing, briefly explain key similarities and differences among some of your voices. Do any of the voices feel more like the "real" you than others?

Your Academic Voice

If you completed the "Your Many Voices" activity above, you probably saw that you have many voices, each of which reflects part of who you are. Now that you are entering high school, you will begin developing your academic voice for use in this English class and other classes. However, you won't leave your other, less formal voices behind. They reflect your history, your home languages, your culture, your race and ethnicity, your gender expressions, and your interests, all of which will inform your opinions and ideas.

Academic settings tend to require a more formal voice because you need to communicate with and appeal to a wide variety of people from a range of backgrounds and cultures. The rest of this chapter is designed to help you develop your academic voice and use it with confidence, so that you feel comfortable adding your ideas to the ongoing conversation in your class this year.

Active Listening

You've probably had this experience when engaged in a conversation with someone: you find yourself more concerned with what you are going to say when you get a chance to jump in than you are with carefully listening to the other person. This is completely normal, but an effective academic conversation requires everyone involved to put just as much emphasis on listening as on speaking. Doing so allows speakers to fully explore their ideas before others jump in and helps listeners respond meaningfully. And even though it seems as if listening should come naturally — it is one of the first things we do, even before we're born! — **active listening** is a skill that we need to practice regularly.

According to William Ury, the cofounder of the Harvard Program on Negotiation,

> [R]eal genuine listening is something that needs to be learned and practiced every day. In ordinary listening, we're hearing the words. We're often thinking, "Where do I agree? Where do I disagree? What am I going to say in response?" In other words, the focus is on us.
>
> In genuine listening, we listen not just for what's being said, but for what's not being said. We listen not just to the words, but to what's behind the words. We listen for the underlying emotions, feelings, and needs. We listen for what that person really needs or wants.

What Ury's talking about here — having to pay attention to so much while listening — is definitely challenging, but the techniques in the next section are designed to provide practice with this.

Listening Skills

Think carefully about the following questions, then respond based on your personal experiences both in and outside of school:

- What are the qualities of a good listener? How do you know when someone is listening? What does it feel like when someone is truly listening to you?

- What are the qualities of a poor listener? How do you know when someone is NOT listening? How does it feel when someone is not listening to you?

- How often do you feel that you participate in conversations or discussions with classmates in which all participants are truly listening to each other?

Applying Techniques for Active Listening

When we listen to someone else actively, or "genuinely" as Ury describes above, we focus closely on the speaker: what is the speaker really trying to say and why? Active listening is not about trying to get your opinion heard as quickly as possible; it is about trying to help the speaker share his or her ideas as fully and clearly as possible. When you are engaged as an active listener, you want to be patient while the other person is speaking. Here are some processes we can follow to try to engage fully as we listen:

- **Step 1. Prepare yourself for listening.** Put away anything that could be distracting (phone, laptop, watch, food, and so on); make eye contact with the speaker often enough to show that you are paying attention.

- **Step 2. Engage with the speaker and the ideas.** Take notes in a manner that will not disturb the speaker. As he or she speaks, nod, smile, or laugh when appropriate. You can vocalize with sounds like "hmm," "okay," and so on, but *do not speak* until the speaker has finished talking.

- **Step 3. Ask follow-up questions.** Once the speaker has finished, you want to be able to demonstrate that you have listened closely and give the speaker an opportunity to add to or clarify what he or she said. The most effective way to achieve these goals is to ask questions, such as the following:

  So, what I heard you say was _____. Is that correct? What did I miss?

  Can you say more about _____?

  What do you think makes _____ so important?

  Why do you feel it is important to _____?

Notice that while each of these questions helps demonstrate that you listened actively, their real purpose is to provide the speaker with an opportunity to dig even deeper. These questions are not really about you, the listener, though they will enhance your understanding. Hold off on any judgments or criticisms until you fully understand what you are hearing.

Active Listening

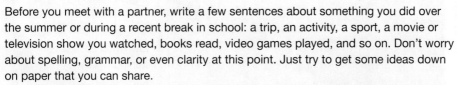

Before you meet with a partner, write a few sentences about something you did over the summer or during a recent break in school: a trip, an activity, a sport, a movie or television show you watched, books read, video games played, and so on. Don't worry about spelling, grammar, or even clarity at this point. Just try to get some ideas down on paper that you can share.

One at a time, talk with your partner about your topic. Don't read directly from the paper, though you can refer to it as needed. The listener should be prepared to listen actively. After the speaker has finished, try out two or three of the questions identified earlier, with the goal of demonstrating active listening and giving the speaker a chance to share fully. Switch roles so that both of you have spoken and listened.

Academic Conversations

In the previous section, you practiced active listening, an essential skill that you will need as you begin engaging in academic conversations. The goal of an effective conversation, whether with a partner, a small group, or the whole class, is to get to a deeper appreciation of a topic by engaging with a wide variety of different perspectives. The goal is not to "win" as in a debate, but to understand a topic, a text, or concept more fully. Think of those involved in a conversation as your allies, not your adversaries. With that said, however, you will not — and should not — always agree with others in the conversation. Effective academic discussions provide opportunities for people to express their opinions on a topic, to challenge and add to others' ideas, and to reach consensus — or agree to disagree.

> **PREVIEWING Academic Vocabulary**   **Academic Conversations**
>
> In this section, you will encounter the following terms as you think about academic conversations. Working individually or with a partner or small group, consider what you already know about the meaning of each term.
>
> 1. Dialogue
> 2. Debate
> 3. Clarity
> 4. Challenge
> 5. Consensus

In his book called *The Magic of Dialogue: Transforming Conflict into Cooperation*, social scientist Daniel Yankelovich identifies the fundamental differences between **debate** and **dialogue**, which we've summarized below. The distinctions that Yankelovich draws between debate and dialogue are not meant to imply that there is something wrong with

Jeff Spicer/Getty Images

Chip Somodevilla/Getty Images

Above are contrasting images of two conversations.

Describe the facial expressions and body language in each picture. Based on your observations, which conversation appears to be more effective?

debate. There's not. There are times, places, classes, and even competitions that encourage people to debate each other, such as political elections, legal trials, speech and debate tournaments, and many news programs. In the context of this chapter, however, the goal of talking with one another in an academic setting is a conversation, a dialogue, in which all participants are heard and ideas are shared and discussed.

Characteristics of Debate	Characteristics of Dialogue
Focused on winning, the intention of debate is to identify a correct position, defend it, and prove that other positions are incorrect.	Focused on consensus, the intention of dialogue is to explore new ideas and expand understanding through meaningful conversation.
Listening is mostly about preparing to discredit ideas that run counter to the position being defended.	Listening is mostly about accommodating other ideas and adapting a position to account for new information.
The goal is to have the audience validate the correctness of the position being defended by choosing it over all other positions presented.	The goal is to be flexible and to collaboratively develop solutions aimed at serving common interests.

As you engage in academic conversation, aim for the following goals:

1. Gaining clarity about someone's ideas
2. Exploring new ideas together and building on someone's ideas rather than merely restating them
3. Challenging someone's ideas in a respectful and productive manner
4. Trying to reach consensus, if possible

Just as when you were practicing with active listening earlier, the best way to engage in an effective academic dialogue is to make focused statements and ask specific questions of your partner or members of your small group or class. In each of the activities in this section, you will practice asking questions for the different purposes that arise during a dialogue. Such practice will help you gain confidence in your own voice and speak with authority, while further developing your active listening skills.

Gaining Clarity

When you do not fully understand the points someone is making, and you need to gain **clarity** — a clearer understanding of ideas — consider asking the following questions:

Can you repeat what you said about _____?

Can you explain what you mean by _____?

What is your understanding of what _____ said about _____?

Can you help me understand your thinking about _____?

Am I correct when I say that you think _____?

Building on an Idea

If you mostly agree with someone's ideas about a topic or issue and you want to build on them, rather than simply repeat them, consider using the following statements to expand on the ideas expressed in the conversation. Doing so may even lead into new, unexplored areas for discussion.

Adding on to your point about _____, I would say that _____.

I want to expand on your point about _____ by saying _____.

I wonder what it would be like if _____.

What really struck me about what you said is _____.

A similar point I could make about this is _____.

I agree with what you said because in my experience _____.

activity Engaging in Academic Conversations

Step 1. Write briefly about one of the following topics (or one of your own choosing). In the second part of this activity, you will be sharing your writing with a partner or a small group to continue practicing your conversation skills:

- Describe your favorite kind of pet and the challenges of caring for it.
- Explain the effects of bullying or racism on a school community.
- Explain what you think is the most or least important subject you are required to study at your school.
- Explain why spring, summer, fall, or winter is your favorite season.
- Explain why it is important to compost or to take other steps to protect the environment.

Step 2. One at a time, share what you wrote with your partner or small group. The listeners will then use some of the statements and questions above first to clarify the speaker's ideas and then to add to or build on those ideas. Remember, your goal here is to engage in the conversation by listening actively, asking questions, and adding to the dialogue by connecting your ideas to others' ideas.

Challenging an Idea

At some point in an academic conversation, you might disagree with others and wish to **challenge** their ideas. That is appropriate, but you should always express your disagreement respectfully and in a way that demonstrates that you have been listening actively. Listening closely prepares you to challenge others' ideas with confidence, knowing that you have fully considered what they have said; it also shows respect to those whose ideas you are challenging. If you disagree with what someone is saying and you want to push back on their ideas, consider using the following statements or asking the following questions:

> While I agree about _____, I do not agree with you about _____ because _____.

> Although you make an interesting point about _____, I wonder if _____.

> Then again, I think that _____.

> Another way to look at _____ could be _____.

> I think it is also important to consider that _____.

> Yes, but what do you think about _____?

Reaching a Consensus

One potential, often desirable outcome of an academic conversation is finding areas of agreement with others — in other words, reaching a **consensus**. To be clear, "consensus" does not mean that everyone is in full agreement on all of the contentious issues surrounding a topic. It also does not mean that one side merely gives up and the other declares "victory." Rather, a way to think about consensus is to reach a conclusion that no one absolutely opposes. To be honest, sometimes consensus is not possible, but having an effective academic conversation means making the effort. Consider the following questions and statements as you attempt to reach consensus:

> Though we disagree about _____, it seems we agree that _____.

> A possible solution to this issue that we all agree on might be _____.

> What other relevant perspectives have we not considered yet?

> On the whole, I think we can agree that _____.

> Where is the common ground here?

Challenging an Idea and Reaching Consensus

activity

Step 1. With a partner or small group, select one of the following topics (or one of your own choosing) that you would like to discuss and that might lead to some disagreement. Next, on your own, write a short response about the topic, going beyond a simple "yes" or "no" by offering some reasons or evidence for your answer. The reasons and evidence you include in your response will become the basis for your conversation with your partner or small group.

- Should schools pay students for getting good grades?
- Do sports or movie stars deserve to get paid millions of dollars?
- Has technology made us more or less connected to each other?

(continued)

- Should certain kinds of video games be restricted for young children?
- Who faces the most pressure to behave or dress in a particular way: girls, boys, or those who don't identify as either?
- Is football too dangerous?
- Should there be any restrictions on what students can wear in school?
- Is it ethical to eat meat?
- Should the government be allowed to capture data from its citizens for purposes of "national security"?

Step 2. One at a time, share what you wrote with your partner or small group. The listeners will then use some of the statements and questions on page 11, first to challenge each other's ideas and then to try to reach consensus.

REFLECTING ON Academic Vocabulary   **Academic Conversations**

Look back at the list of terms that you previewed on page 7. Now that you have read about them and practiced with these terms, what has changed about your understanding of conversations in an academic setting? Which of the skills that you practiced in this section do you feel confident using? Which ones do you think you need to develop further? How do you know?

culminating activity

Entering the Academic Conversation

When basketball star Lebron James spoke out in 2018 in support of the Black Lives Matter movement, a TV news commentator told him to "Shut up and dribble." In other words, the commentator was saying that James should stick to basketball and stay out of politics. Yet there is a long history of athletes using their status and platforms to amplify issues that are important to them. Boxer Muhammad Ali famously gave up his heavyweight title when he refused to be drafted into the army during the Vietnam War in the 1960s. More recently, former San Francisco 49ers quarterback Colin Kaepernick took a knee during the national anthem throughout the football season to protest the police shootings of unarmed people of color. Spectators, commentators, politicians, reporters, and others are divided on whether athlete protests are appropriate, especially during events like the Olympics, which are seen by many as being a time of national pride. Read the following text that explores this issue of athletes and political protests. After you read, you will have an opportunity to demonstrate what you've learned about having an effective academic conversation.

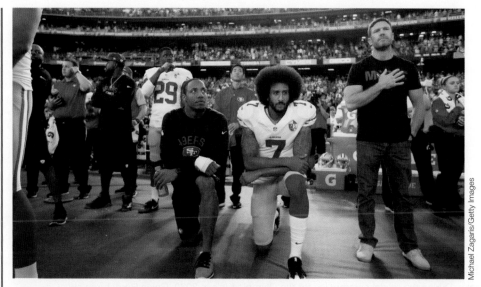

Michael Zagaris/Getty Images

Colin Kaepernick (right) and Eric Reid (left) of the 49ers kneel during the national anthem.
Many images of Kaepernick kneeling in protest show him alone, but this one includes two other figures in front with him and many people in the background. How does the inclusion of other people in the frame affect the viewer's perception of Kaepernick's protest?

All Athletes Should Agree Not to Protest or Become Political during Olympics

Norfolk Daily News editorial

The International Olympics Committee wants the games to be about sportsmanship and clean competition. Its rules include, "No kind of demonstration or political, religious or racial propaganda is permitted in any Olympic sites, venues or other areas."

Recently, U.S. Olympian Gwen Berry was standing on the podium after finishing third in the U.S. Olympic Trials in Eugene, Oregon, in the hammer throw. While the national anthem was being played, she turned her back to the flag.

Berry isn't the first athlete to protest when given the spotlight. She isn't even the first Olympian — probably the most famous incident happened in 1968 in Mexico City, Mexico, when U.S. athletes Tommie Smith (gold) and John Carlos (bronze) performed in the 200 meters and each raised a black-gloved fist during the national anthem while on the podium.

Many attempts have been made by the United Nations and the International Olympics Committee to keep the games free of violence and politics. To do that, rules are necessary — even in the United States, which values freedom more than any other country in world history.

What happened to athletic competitions and putting politics aside for the sake of the games? Do people not realize that allowing any type of political statement would open the door for more of the same? And aren't these athletes putting themselves above the games with their protests? ■

Patrick Smith/Getty Images

During the medal ceremonies for the Olympic trials in 2020, Gwen Berry turns away from the flag during the national anthem.

What does her posture and that of other figures in the photograph reveal?

Rolls Press/Popperfoto/Getty Images

This is a famous image of Tommie Smith and John Carlos raising their fists in protest during the 1968 Olympic games. This image has been reprinted many times since it was taken.

What makes this image so powerful?

Step 1. Once you've read the text, write a response on your own about whether athletes should engage in explicit acts of political protest. In your response, you might want to consider some of the following questions:

- Should athletes' political expression be limited to their off-field or off-court lives?
- Should certain restrictions be put in place for special events like the Olympics?
- Should similar rules apply to other celebrities like TV and movie stars?

Step 2. Hold an academic conversation following this structure:

1. Start the dialogue by sharing your response with a partner or small group while practicing the active listening strategies described on page 6, focusing specifically on gaining clarity around everyone's ideas.
2. Then, add to each other's ideas by using the questions and sentence stems on pages 9 and 10.
3. Challenge each other's ideas by using the questions and sentence stems on page 11.
4. Last, try to find consensus on the topic by using the questions and sentence stems on page 11, but don't worry if you do not fully agree with each other.

Step 3. In an individual response, write a reflection on how successful your academic conversation was. You might consider the following questions:

- Were all the participants' voices heard?
- Were you able to disagree respectfully?
- Was your conversation more of a dialogue or a debate?
- How did you attempt to find consensus? Were you successful?

Reading

S ymbols and images surround us. If you were to glance up from this page, you would probably see various letters, words, and pictures on the walls around you. If you were to skim through this book, you'd see stories, articles, photographs, and artwork as well as questions, activities, and writing prompts. All of these are texts that you can read.

When we think about a "text" in English class, we often think of written or spoken words. If you look at the editorial cartoon below, you might think that the words alone are the text. What about the drawing, which includes facial expressions of the characters, the physical gestures, and the setting? Don't those help the cartoon make its point about how we may be too obsessed with wireless technologies?

Cameron Cardow, The Ottawa Citizen/Caglecartoons.com

We're going to expand the traditional definition of what a "text" is to include any information that you encounter — whether it is solely words, solely visuals, or, as with the cartoon, a combination of the two. The term **text** can be applied to a novel, a poem, or a written argument, but it also can refer to movies, television shows, graphic novels, emojis, clothing, a video game, a photograph, and so on. Anything that must be *read* to be understood counts as a *text*.

The act of reading is the process of looking at various symbols, recognizing them as patterns you have seen before, and making sense of them. You just accomplished this as you read the previous sentence, and now with this one too. Even though the process is complex, by this time in your life, you probably don't even realize that you are decoding those images and symbols. You see and find meaning in everything around you, often without even thinking about it. As you go through your day, you're reading the world all the time. In this chapter, we'll ask you to try to be more aware of the reading processes you use and give you an opportunity to practice with techniques designed to help you feel confident when tackling any text.

activity What Are You Reading?

Think back on all of the different texts you have read in the past few days, using the broad definition of *text* described in the introduction to this chapter. These could include school assignments, books you've read for fun, online articles, movies, social media posts, advertisements, text messages, and so on.

Step 1. Create a table like the one below to categorize several examples of your reading, focusing on the characteristics of the text — length, complexity, fiction, nonfiction, and so on. Be sure that you include a variety of text types, including visual texts. A sample has been completed for you.

Text	Description of Characteristics	Why You Read It
Email from band teacher	It was about five sentences with bullet points and links to an online calendar. It was sent to our whole class.	So that I know when our upcoming performances are.

Step 2. Write a brief response to one or more of the following questions about the texts you listed in your table:

- Which of these texts do you read for your own personal interests, and which ones are required by school or for other reasons?
- What other ways can you categorize the types of texts that you read? Which ones go beyond a traditional definition of *text*?
- How did you read these different types of texts? Did you skim some of them, read others carefully, and so on?
- What do you notice about the variety of purposes you had for reading?

In English class, the types of texts that you read will probably overlap with some of the ones you listed above, though the purposes for reading them might be more focused. What people don't often tell you about the reading you do in school is that it's not just about learning the content. It's also about training your mind for careful reading and critical thinking.

In addition to reading for enjoyment and to get information — reasons for reading you may have listed in the activity on page 18 — you'll also be reading for these three academic purposes:

- **Reading for understanding.** What is this text literally saying? What information is this text communicating? To demonstrate an understanding of a text, you should be able to summarize it — to identify its *main idea and most significant details*.
- **Reading for interpretation.** What ideas give the text significance? What are the ideas *behind* the text's literal meaning? To demonstrate an interpretation of a text, you should be able to explain its *theme, meaning, or purpose*.
- **Reading for style.** Why was this text created in the way it was? To demonstrate an analysis of style, you should be able to explain how *the choices that the creator of the text makes* — language and visuals — help to communicate its meaning.

Just as you probably don't read a short story in English class in quite the same way as you would read a geometry word problem for homework, each of these different purposes for reading requires a slightly different way of reading. But what these three purposes have in common is that they each require a bit more effort and attention on your part than reading solely for your own entertainment or personal interests.

Active Reading

We've all had the experience of reading something and then suddenly realizing that we have not been paying attention to the text. Our eyes may have been skimming the letters and words, but our minds were far, far away. You may have been doing that just now. It's typical, and it happens to everyone, even to your English teacher. In this section, you will practice ways to help you stay focused and read as actively as possible, so that you are looking for what really matters, depending on your purpose for reading.

PREVIEWING Academic Vocabulary   **Active Reading**

In this section, you will encounter the following terms as you think about how to read a text actively. Working individually or with a partner or small group, consider what you already know about the meaning of each term.

1. Annotation	**4.** Homonyms	**6.** Parts of speech
2. Context	**5.** Word parts	*Verb*
3. Context clues		*Subject*
		Object

What Do Active Readers Do?

To read actively, there are things that you should do before, during, and after reading. Keeping the following advice in mind will help you effectively and efficiently approach any text.

Before Reading

The steps to take before you read might not involve any writing and are intended to help you prepare to read a text for the first time. Before you dive in, try to get a general sense of the text's background, content, and approach by applying the following tips:

- **Preview the text.** If you are reading a book, you might look at the cover art, the summary on the book jacket, or the biography of the author. If the text is an article, you might skim it to get a sense of its length and purpose, while glancing at headings or accompanying photographs or illustrations.
- **Make a prediction.** If the text is a piece of fiction, you might ask yourself, "What's going to happen?" If it is a nonfiction piece, you might wonder about the next topic it will discuss or the evidence it might present. Making — and revising — predictions keeps you focused on your reading, continually monitoring what is happening in the text.

While Reading

Marking the text, applying **annotation**, helps you stay engaged during reading and focused on the most important and relevant aspects of the text, depending on your purpose for reading. *Your annotations are your thinking made visible*. In general, your annotations will likely include some of the following:

- **Ask questions.** Active readers are always keeping track of questions they have as they read. Where are you at least a little confused? Why? What might you need to reread?
- **Make connections.** Aware readers are constantly drawing parallels between themselves and what they are reading. Making connections enriches your understanding of and appreciation for a text. Consider what the text reminds you of in your own life, in other texts, or out in the world, for example.
- **Visualize.** Active readers tend to visualize what they are reading. Make sketches of key ideas or scenes in the text. No artistic talent is needed for these drawings, and stick figures are certainly appropriate.
- **Focus on your purpose.** As you read, you can identify information and ideas that are important for your purpose for reading and mark them with stars, underline, or whatever symbol works for you.

Annotating is definitely an individual practice, and you'll find a system that works best for you. However, sticking to a few general principles will help you make sure your annotations are useful to you. For example, don't highlight or underline too much. Marking just a few things will help you focus when you reread. Having a consistent set of symbols for marking texts (stars for something you might want to quote and arrows for ideas you disagree with, for example) will help you remember what your annotations mean when you return to them. Adding a comment to everything you mark will further clarify your annotations and cut down on the time it could take you to decode them later.

After Reading

As active readers, we recognize that we may not understand everything about a text with a single reading. When we go through a text a second time, we revisit key ideas with more informed eyes and continue to refine our own thinking about the topic addressed in the text. The following steps are key parts of that process:

- **Reread.** Look back at places in the text where you had questions. Reread those sections. It's possible that by the time you've finished reading, you will have found answers to some of your questions. Add any new answers to your annotations.
- **Summarize.** Write a brief summary that contains the main idea and the key details of the text or a section of the text.

Active Reading

Below is an excerpt from an article about multitasking and a section of a poem about a remembrance of a father. Read both texts and go through the active reading steps described above for before, during, and after reading. Afterward, compare your annotations and your summaries with those of a partner and discuss why each of you marked what you did and why you may have found it easier to read and annotate the article or the poem.

Want to learn faster? Stop multitasking and start daydreaming

Daniel Levitin

Social media, emails, texts, WhatsApp messages, and phone calls take up an increasing amount of time. Our to-do lists are so full that we can't hope to complete every item on them. So what do we do? We multitask, juggling several things at once, trying to keep up by keeping busy.

Research by Earl Miller of Massachusetts Institute of Technology (MIT) and others however shows that multitasking doesn't work — simply because the brain doesn't work that way. If you're studying from a book and trying to listen in on a conversation at the

(continued)

same time, those are two separate projects, each started and maintained by distinct circuits in the brain. Pay more attention to one for a moment and you're automatically paying less attention to the other. . . .

Students who uni-task, immersing themselves in one thing at a time, remember their work better, get more done, and their work is usually more creative and of higher quality. . . .

Healthy breaks can hit the reset button in your brain, restoring some of the glucose and other metabolic nutrients used up with deep thought. A healthy break is one in which you allow your brain to rest, to loosen its grip on your thoughts.

Activities that promote mind-wandering, such as reading literature, going for   5
a walk, exercising, or listening to music, are hugely restorative. Many students find that a work-break cycle of 25 minutes work followed by five minutes rest, or even two hours of work followed by 15 minutes of rest promotes efficiency to the extent that they get back the time they spent resting, and then some. A 15-minute nap is even better.

The pull of social media and the internet is today one of the biggest barriers to effective revision or learning. This is because the brain has a tendency to seek new stimulation, and to try to find the path of least effort. Have you ever sat at your computer, focusing on writing an essay and then found your attention start to flag? You might remember that you had wanted to see a movie, so you go to the internet to look up show times. Then you find there are three movies playing in your area that you're interested in, so you go to Rotten Tomatoes to look at the reviews, and after that to [social media] to see what your friends thought about it. Before you know it, two hours have gone by and you haven't gotten any work done. And your brain is worn out from all that stimulation.

Increasingly, students, scientists, and corporate CEOs are enforcing a "no fly zone" period of time when they shut off the internet, a time to focus, to concentrate, to engage deeply in what's in front of them. This can be as simple as shutting down the browser or turning off your wireless connection [or limiting] the amount of time you spend on certain sites.

The addiction to multitasking and social media is real, there is a dopamine-addiction-feedback loop behind it. The human brain seeks novelty — more pronounced in some of us than others — and dopamine is the brain's reward for finding it. Dopamine can be thought of as the "give me more" neurochemical. We encounter something new every few seconds through multitasking, we release dopamine, which makes us want to encounter something new, which releases dopamine, and so on, until we're exhausted. . . .

Just small changes in the way we approach the internet, small increases in self-discipline can make all the difference between managing the internet versus letting it manage you. We can't slow down the flow of information. But we can slow down how much of it we let intrude on our plans, our study time, our social lives, and the daydreaming time that is a necessary part of being productive and creative. ∎

from October

May Swenson

Peeling a pear, I remember
my daddy's hand. His thumb
(the one that got nipped by the saw,
lacked a nail) fit into
the cored hollow of the slippery   5
half his knife skinned so neatly.
Dad would pare the fruit from our
orchard in the fall, while Mother
boiled the jars, prepared for
"putting up." Dad used to darn   10
our socks when we were small,
and cut our hair and toenails.
Sunday mornings, in pajamas, we'd
take turns in his lap. He'd help
bathe us sometimes. Dad could do   15
anything. He built our dining table,
chairs, the buffet, the bay window
seat, my little desk of cherry wood
where I wrote my first poems. That
day at the shop, splitting panel   20
boards on the electric saw (oh, I
can hear the screech of it now,
the whirling blade that sliced
my daddy's thumb), he received the mar
that, long after, in his coffin,   25
distinguished his skilled hand. ■

Reading Challenges

Probably the most important part of annotating is asking questions about the text: where are you confused? What do you not understand? Some texts you encounter this year will be complex, especially if you don't have enough background information or you don't know all of the vocabulary. For instance, look at the opening few paragraphs from *Ulysses* by James Joyce, considered by many to be one of the most difficult novels in the English language:

> Stately, plump Buck Mulligan came from the stairhead, bearing a bowl of lather on which a mirror and a razor lay crossed. A yellow dressing gown, ungirdled, was sustained gently behind him by the mild morning air. He held the bowl aloft and intoned:
>
> *— Introibo ad altare Dei.*

Halted, he peered down the dark winding stairs and called up coarsely:

— Come up, Kinch. Come up, you fearful jesuit.

Solemnly he came forward and mounted the round gunrest. He faced about and blessed gravely thrice the tower, the surrounding country and the awaking mountains. Then, catching sight of Stephen Dedalus, he bent towards him and made rapid crosses in the air, gurgling in his throat and shaking his head. Stephen Dedalus, displeased and sleepy, leaned his arms on the top of the staircase and looked coldly at the shaking gurgling face that blessed him, equine in its length, and at the light untonsured hair, grained and hued like pale oak.

Buck Mulligan peeped an instant under the mirror and then covered the bowl smartly.

This passage probably feels challenging to you for several reasons, including a line in Latin and many unfamiliar words, such as *intoned*, *jesuit*, *gunrest*, *untonsured*, but you might have questions that could be answered if you knew more about the author, the time period, and the original text on which this one is based, the ancient Greek epic poem *The Odyssey*. You probably have other questions about the character and the setting that could be answered simply by reading more of the text. The important thing is to recognize and track these kinds of questions.

Identifying the places where you are struggling in a text is part of becoming a stronger and more confident reader, but once you've marked those places, what do you do about it? Well, it depends on exactly what you are struggling with. In general, when you find yourself struggling to understand a text, the challenges will fall into one or more of these three categories:

1. Contextual challenges
2. Word-level challenges
3. Sentence-level challenges

And while you probably will not regularly face texts quite as difficult as *Ulysses*, this section will walk you through how to overcome some of the most common challenges readers of all skill levels face, and it will give you an opportunity to practice skills you can use when you encounter these challenges in your reading.

Contextual Challenges

One of the most significant challenges that you might face with a text is that you do not have the **context** for or background about the topics in the text. In the *Ulysses* excerpt, you might have wondered who Buck Mulligan is, where the characters live, or in what time period the story takes place. Contextual challenges often occur when you do not know enough about the author, time period, location, or subject matter to be able to understand what you are reading. For instance, look at this photograph:

Jonathan Bachman/Reuters/Newscom

You could easily describe the police and the woman in the photograph, but you probably have a lot of questions about who she is, what the police are doing, and why they are there on the street together. The answers to these questions would help you understand the text. Here is some background information taken from a news article published near the time of the photograph:

> In July 2016, Ieshia Evans faced Baton Rouge, Louisiana police officers as part of a protest against the killing of Alton Sterling, who was shot by police outside a local convenience store.

With this background knowledge and context, you could probably recognize why this photograph was so widely shared on social media to represent the conflict between police and protestors. Evans symbolizes the choice of peaceful protest over violence, and the officers are responding not with aggression, but with restraint as a result of her actions. This is an image of hope, of potential to create change without violence. Oftentimes, the more context you have for a text, the greater understanding you will have.

While knowing the context might not guarantee total understanding, it is always a good strategy to find answers to the *who*, *what*, *where*, *when*, and *why* of a text:

1. Who are the **author**, **speaker**, or **characters** of the text? What do we know about them?

2. What is the **setting** or **occasion** for the text? What is the time period? Where does it take place? Was there a significant historical or cultural event that might have caused this text to be written or created?

3. Who is the intended **audience** for this text? In other words, whom is the author of the text trying to reach? What choices does the author make in an effort to connect with that audience?

4. What **background information** do you need on the topic? What do you already know about the topic? Do you need to conduct brief research to give you more context?

5. What is the **purpose** of the text? In other words, why was the text created? To inform? To persuade? To sell something? To entertain?

Word-Level Challenges

According to the Global Language Monitor, the English language includes over 1 million words, and studies show that a typical American adult has a vocabulary of only 22,000 to 32,000 words. It's inevitable that readers will come across words that they do not know. Sometimes this barely matters to our overall understanding of a text, but sometimes unfamiliar words trip us up; it depends entirely on the text, the words the author uses, and our own background with the words.

When inattentive readers come across a word they don't know, they tend to just skip over it and keep going. Active readers, on the other hand, ask themselves, "Do I need to know the meaning of this word to understand the rest of the text?" Sometimes the answer really is "no," but when the answer is "yes," applying a few strategies can help you overcome these vocabulary challenges.

Context Clues. The first and probably the most effective strategy for determining the meaning of unfamiliar words is to use **context clues**, which means looking at the rest of the words nearby in the sentence or paragraph that you *do know* to help you with the ones *you do not know*.

Word Parts. When context clues alone are not enough to help you understand unfamiliar words, you can try to determine the meaning of the word by examining its parts. Many words in English can be broken down into three parts: **prefix**, **root**, and **suffix**. The root is the base of the word. If there is a prefix, it will be attached before the root; a suffix, if there is one, will appear at the end. Not all words have all three parts, and sometimes words are combinations of multiple roots.

You can see a list of common prefixes, suffixes, and roots in the Appendix: Vocabulary and Word Roots in the back of the book.

For example, the word *antithesis* may not be a word you use regularly, but if you look at its parts, you'll see the prefix "anti-" + the root "thesis." As you have probably learned in writing essays for school, "thesis" is the central idea or main point. "Anti-" is a prefix that means against or opposite, as in *antisocial* or *antidote*. By considering the prefix (*anti-*) and the root (*thesis*) together, you might be able to figure out that *antithesis* means "a thing, person, or idea that is the opposite of another." For example, "Darkness is the antithesis of light."

Reference Resources. Another strategy that you can employ if you are facing word-level challenges is to use resources such as dictionaries, reference sites, and classmates or teachers. In general, this should not be your first option because it will slow down your reading considerably. You're better off trying to figure out the word yourself to continue building a wider vocabulary. But if the context clues and the word parts do not work, then looking up the word is a better choice than skipping past the word and risking misunderstanding something important in the text. When you can't understand the sentence or passage without the word, it's worth your time to pause and consult a reference.

Sentence-Level Challenges

Sometimes you know every word in a sentence and you feel that you have a good sense of the context, but still, for some reason, the sentence just doesn't make sense to you. Perhaps it's because the writer has used an unconventional word order or has packed a lot of ideas into a single sentence. Let's take each problem one at a time.

Challenging Word Order. In English, sentence structures vary, but the most common ones have a subject ("The clown") followed by a verb ("rode") and an object ("a unicycle."). As you probably remember from earlier English classes, a **verb** communicates an action or state of being; the **subject** is what or who exhibits that action or state of being; in sentences with an **object**, the object is being acted upon. Subject-verb-object is by far the most common sentence structure in English. Consider this sentence, for example:

> SUBJECT   VERB   OBJECT
> The students remembered us.

Sometimes writers intentionally vary the typical order. For instance, a sentence on the same topic could be constructed this way:

> SUBJECT VERB   OBJECT VERB   OBJECT
> That we remembered them surprised the students.

Even though the first sentence is probably easier to understand — because it follows a more common construction — both sentences make a statement about the same topic and are grammatically correct.

You might run across a sentence like this one from Shakespeare's "Sonnet 20," which seems like a bit of word jumble:

> A woman's face with Nature's own hand painted / Hast thou.

When faced with this kind of challenge, the trick is to reorder the words until the sentence is in a more conventional format:

> Thou hast a woman's face painted with Nature's own hand.

Complicated Structure. Other times, writers will write a very long — though grammatically correct — sentence in which they pile on related ideas, burying the main point of the sentence. Consider this example from Herman Melville's *Moby-Dick*:

> Whenever I find myself growing grim about the mouth; whenever it is a damp, drizzly November in my soul; whenever I find myself involuntarily pausing before coffin warehouses, and bringing up the rear of every funeral I meet; and especially whenever my hypos get such an upper hand of me, that it requires a strong moral principle to prevent me from deliberately stepping into the street, and methodically knocking people's hats off — then, I account it high time to get to sea as soon as I can.

The key to tackling a sentence like this is to find the heart of it — who or what is performing the primary action — and ignore everything else for the time being. You can come back to the details once you've got your head around the basic meaning. In this case, we've underlined what we consider to be the "heart of the sentence":

> <u>Whenever I find myself growing grim about the mouth</u>; whenever it is a damp, drizzly November in my soul; whenever I find myself involuntarily pausing before coffin warehouses, and bringing up the rear of every funeral I meet; and especially whenever my hypos get such an upper hand of me, that it requires a strong moral principle to prevent me from deliberately stepping into the street, and methodically knocking people's hats off — <u>then, I account it high time to get to sea as soon as I can.</u>

 Reading Challenges

Step 1. Read the following article about scientists figuring out how plants know when to stop growing and annotate the text (see pp. 20–21 for guidelines), this time focusing only on the questions you have. Mark passages that confuse you, words you don't recognize, sentences you have difficulty following, or concepts you don't understand. Because this text was selected to be particularly challenging, you will likely identify several areas of difficulty.

Mystery Solved: How Plant Cells Know When to Stop Growing

Katrina Miller

It's been a longstanding enigma in biology: How do cells know how big they are?

The answer, it turns out, was hidden inside Robert Sablowski's computer files, collecting virtual dust since 2013. "I had the data for years and years, but I wasn't looking in the right way," says Sablowski, a plant cell biologist at the John Innes Center in Norwich, England. He had, for an earlier project, been investigating a protein called KRP4. By fusing it with a fluorescent jellyfish protein to make it shine, Sablowski could study it inside a plant cell, but he had no idea that it would be key to understanding cell size regulation.

For organisms to develop, their cells must undergo a pattern of growth, DNA replication, and division. But scientists who study this process, known as the cell cycle, have long noticed that the divisions aren't necessarily identical — cells often split asymmetrically, and their size is somehow corrected later. In a study published in *Science* last month, Sablowski and his colleagues revealed just how plants are doing this: The cells use their own DNA as a sort of measuring cup. While the discovery was made by studying a plant called *Arabidopsis*, it could have broad implications for understanding cell size regulation in animals and humans, and may even influence the future of crop production.

Identifying how cells assess their own size has been complicated, because most cellular proteins scale with the size of the cell itself. Sablowski compares the situation to trying to measure yourself with your own arm. "You can't do it, because your arm grows in proportion to your body," he says. "You need an external reference to know how big you are." What doesn't change as the cell grows, however, is its DNA. Scientists have long speculated that a cell could use its DNA as some kind of indicator to gauge its size, but Sablowski's team is the first to show proof of this process.

"It's been a profound mystery for many, many decades in biology, how cells are able to accomplish this task of almost magically knowing what their size is," says Martin Howard of the John Innes Center, who helped develop the mathematical models needed for the breakthrough. Shape and size regulation are important because they are closely tied to how a cell functions: Too large and it can be difficult for the cell to quickly retrieve information contained in its own DNA; too small and the cell doesn't have enough space to split properly, causing errors in division and growth that could lead to disease.

Arabidopsis is actually a weed, according to Sablowski, but it's considered a model organism in plant biology because it's easy to grow and matures quickly. That means it's already been well studied by other researchers in the field. "The community for *Arabidopsis* has been critical," says Marco D'Ario, a graduate student at the John Innes Center who designed and helped perform the experiment. "The same experimental setup that took us three or four years — without the community, it easily would have taken 10 to 15."

The team grew *Arabidopsis* in pots for about six weeks, then chopped off the plants' tiny growing tip, the part where new leaves and flowers emerge, to observe its continued growth under a microscope. They could track, at about 1,000× magnification, the location and size of each cell in the growing tip at different stages of the cell cycle. Sablowski and D'Ario traded shifts, checking on the cells every other hour over two days. "We had the equipment, we had the material. We just needed to roll up our sleeves and do the 48-hour experiment to get the data that nobody else had," Sablowski says. ∎

(continued)

Step 2. Return to parts of the text that you marked with questions and try to identify the specific challenges those parts of the text might be posing for you. Try to work through those challenges with some of the suggestions described on pages 23–28:

- Is it a contextual challenge (p. 24)? If so, locate additional information to help you better understand the historical, cultural, political, economic, or other contexts of the piece. You can search online or talk with someone you know who might have information on the subject.
- Is it a word-level challenge (p. 26)? Is a specific word new or confusing to you? Can you determine its meaning through context clues? Word parts? Do you need to consult a reference resource?
- Is it a sentence-level challenge (p. 27)? Have you lost the thread of what the author was saying because of the word order or sentence length or both? Can you rewrite the sentence to get at its heart?

REFLECTING ON Academic Vocabulary   **Active Reading**

Working with a partner or small group, discuss the terms that were presented in this section and that you previewed on page 19 and clarify your understanding of each. Then, share what you learned about being an active reader in this section. What did you find helpful, relevant, unnecessary, redundant, and so on?

Reading for Understanding: What Is This Text Saying?

Now that you have practiced reading actively and have worked through some of the common reading challenges you might face, it's time to put those skills to use for specific reading purposes. Any time you encounter a text, your first purpose needs to be reading to understand what the text is saying. This might sound simple, but often it's not.

PREVIEWING Academic Vocabulary   **Reading for Understanding**

In the next section, you will encounter the following terms as you consider how to read a text for understanding. Working individually or with a partner or small group, think about what you already know about the meaning of each term.

1. Summarize

2. Main idea

3. Supporting details

It is essential to understand a text literally before you begin doing the heavier lifting of interpreting or analyzing the style of the text. The goal of reading for understanding is to be able to **summarize**, which means being able to state the main idea and identify the supporting details of a text. The **main idea** refers to the most important or central thought of a paragraph or larger section of text; it may be stated directly or simply implied. **Supporting details** are pieces of information that explain, define, describe, or prove the main idea. A paragraph or short excerpt often has a single main idea with two or more supporting details, though longer works can have multiple, related main ideas.

Summary = main idea + key supporting details

For instance, look at this excerpt from a piece called "Is It Immoral to Watch the Super Bowl?" in which the author, Steve Almond, describes his experiences watching football. He begins by thinking back on his childhood experience of seeing a player named Darryl Stingley injured during a game:

> The problem is that I can no longer indulge these pleasures without feeling complicit. It was easier years ago, when injuries like Stingley's could be filed away as freakish accidents. TV coverage was relatively primitive, the players hidden under helmets and pads, obscured by fuzzy reception, more superheroes than men. Today we see the cruelty of the game in high definition. Slow-motion replays show us the precise angle of a grotesquely twisted ankle and a quarterback's contorted face at the exact moment he is concussed.

Ask yourself, "What is the most important idea in the paragraph?" Once you have that main idea, the supporting details are usually easier to identify: they are the details that help to describe or explain the main idea. Keep in mind that not every sentence in each paragraph will be a key supporting detail; look closely at the ones that seem most relevant. Once you have identified the main idea and the key supporting details, you can construct an accurate summary of the passage. For instance, a summary of the paragraph above might be something like this:

> Steve Almond is no longer comfortable watching football because he can now see all of the gruesome effects of its injuries. He describes how advances in television technology, such as slow-motion replay, have made it impossible to pretend that the players are just like superheroes. He feels complicit in the pain suffered by the players.

The first and last sentences of a paragraph are often great places to look for the main idea, but the main idea can appear at any part of the paragraph or can even be only implied, rather than clearly stated.

As you practice reading for understanding, asking these questions can help you identify the main idea and key supporting details of a text:

1. What is the title of the piece? If it doesn't have one, what title would you give the text to reflect its content?
2. What words or phrases are repeated often throughout the text?
3. What is this text mostly about?
4. What important and relevant details illustrate the main idea?
5. What details does the author focus on or spend the most time developing?

activity Reading Nonfiction for Understanding

Read the following editorial from the *New York Times* in 2019, annotate the text (see pp. 20–21 for guidelines), and write a short response (three to five sentences) that includes the main idea of the text and two or three key supporting details that demonstrate an understanding of the piece. At this point, you are not explaining whether you agree with the author or not. You are producing an accurate summary — including the main idea and key supporting points — of the editorial.

Abolish Billionaires

Farhad Manjoo

Last fall, Tom Scocca, editor of the essential blog Hmm Daily, wrote a tiny, searing post that has been rattling around my head ever since.

"Some ideas about how to make the world better require careful, nuanced thinking about how best to balance competing interests," he began. "Others don't: Billionaires are bad. We should presumptively get rid of billionaires. All of them."

Mr. Scocca — a longtime writer at Gawker until that site was muffled by a billionaire — offered a straightforward argument for kneecapping the wealthiest among us. A billion dollars is wildly more than anyone needs, even accounting for life's most excessive lavishes. It's far more than anyone might reasonably claim to deserve, however much he believes he has contributed to society.

At some level of extreme wealth, money inevitably corrupts. On the left and the right, it buys political power, it silences dissent, it serves primarily to perpetuate ever-greater wealth, often unrelated to any reciprocal social good. For Mr. Scocca, that level is self-evidently somewhere around one billion dollars; beyond that, you're irredeemable.

I cover technology, an industry that belches up a murder of new billionaires annually,   5 and much of my career has required a deep anthropological inquiry into billionairedom. But I'm embarrassed to say I had never before considered Mr. Scocca's idea — that if we aimed, through public and social policy, simply to discourage people from attaining and possessing more than a billion in lucre, just about everyone would be better off. . . .

Billionaires should not exist — at least not in their present numbers, with their current globe-swallowing power, garnering this level of adulation, while the rest of the economy scrapes by.

I like to use this column to explore maximalist policy visions — positions we might aspire to over time rather than push through tomorrow. Abolishing billionaires might not sound like a practical idea, but if you think about it as a long-term goal in light of today's deepest economic ills, it feels anything but radical. Instead, banishing billionaires — seeking to cut their economic power, working to reduce their political power and attempting to question their social status — is a pithy, perfectly encapsulated vision for surviving the digital future.

Billionaire abolishment could take many forms. It could mean preventing people from keeping more than a billion in booty, but more likely it would mean higher marginal taxes on income, wealth and estates for billionaires and people on the way to becoming billionaires. These policy ideas turn out to poll very well, even if they're probably not actually redistributive enough to turn most billionaires into sub-billionaires.

More important, aiming to abolish billionaires would involve reshaping the structure of the digital economy so that it produces a more equitable ratio of superrich to the rest of us.

Inequality is the defining economic condition of the tech age. Software, by its very 10 nature, drives concentrations of wealth. Through network effects, in which the very popularity of a service ensures that it keeps getting more popular, and unprecedented economies of scale — in which Amazon can make Alexa once and have it work everywhere, for everyone — tech instills a winner-take-all dynamic across much of the economy.

We're already seeing these effects now. A few superstar corporations, many in tech, account for the bulk of American corporate profits, while most of the share of economic growth since the 1970s has gone to a small number of the country's richest people.

But the problem is poised to get worse. Artificial intelligence is creating prosperous new industries that don't employ very many workers; left unchecked, technology is creating a world where a few billionaires control an unprecedented share of global wealth.

But abolishment does not involve only economic policy. It might also take the form of social and political opprobrium. For at least 20 years, we've been in a devastating national love affair with billionaires — a dalliance that the tech industry has championed more than any other.

I've witnessed a generation of striving entrepreneurs join the three-comma club and instantly transform into superheroes of the global order, celebrated from the Bay Area to Beijing for what's taken to be their obvious and irrefutable wisdom about anything and everything. We put billionaires on magazine covers, speculate about their political ambitions, praise their grand visions to save the world and wink affectionately at their wacky plans to help us escape . . . to a new one.

But the adulation we heap upon billionaires obscures the plain moral quandary at 15 the center of their wealth: Why should anyone have a billion dollars, why should anyone be proud to brandish their billions, when there is so much suffering in the world? . . . Last week, to dig into this question of whether it was possible to be a good billionaire, I called up two experts.

(continued)

The first was Peter Singer, the Princeton moral philosopher who has written extensively about the ethical duties of the rich. Mr. Singer told me that in general, he did not think it was possible to live morally as a billionaire, though he made a few exceptions: [Bill] Gates and [Warren] Buffett, who have pledged to give away the bulk of their wealth to philanthropy, would not earn Mr. Singer's scorn.

But most billionaires are not so generous; of the 2,200 or so billionaires in the world — about 500 of whom are American — fewer than 200 have signed the Giving Pledge created by Bill and Melinda Gates and Mr. Buffett.

"I have a moral concern with the conduct of individuals — we have many billionaires who are not living ethically, and are not doing nearly as much good as they can, by a wide margin," Mr. Singer said.

Then there is the additional complication of whether even the ones who are "doing good" are actually doing good. As the writer Anand Giridharadas has argued, many billionaires approach philanthropy as a kind of branding exercise to maintain a system in which they get to keep their billions.

When a billionaire commits to putting money into politics — whether it's Howard   20
Schultz or Michael Bloomberg or Sheldon Adelson, whether it's for your team or the other — you should see the plan for what it is: an effort to gain some leverage over the political system, a scheme to short-circuit the revolution and blunt the advancing pitchforks.

Which brings me to my second expert on the subject, Tom Steyer, the former hedge-fund investor who is devoting his billion-dollar fortune to a passel of progressive causes, like voter registration and climate change.

Mr. Steyer ticks every liberal box. He favors a wealth tax, and he and his wife have signed the Giving Pledge. He doesn't live excessively lavishly — he drives a Chevy Volt. Still, I wondered when I got on the phone with him last week: Wouldn't we be better off if we didn't have to worry about rich people like him trying to alter the political process?

Mr. Steyer was affable and loquacious; he spoke to me for nearly an hour about his interest in economic justice and his belief in grass-roots organizing. At one point I compared his giving with that of the Koch brothers, and he seemed genuinely pained by the comparison.

"I understand about the real issues of money in politics," he said. "We have a system that I know is not right, but it's the one we got, and we're trying as hard as possible to change it."

I admire his zeal. But if we tolerate the supposedly "good" billionaires in politics,   25
we inevitably leave open the door for the bad ones. And the bad ones will overrun us. When American capitalism sends us its billionaires, it's not sending its best. It's sending us people who have lots of problems, and they're bringing those problems with them. They're bringing inequality. They're bringing injustice. They're buying politicians.

And some, I assume, are good people. ∎

While the examples and activity above have focused on nonfiction texts, the process of reading a text for understanding is very similar when reading literary texts, such as fiction, poetry, or drama. You still try to identify what the text is about — the main idea — but that main idea is rarely, if ever, directly stated in a piece of literature.

Oftentimes, your summary of a literary text will be an accurate and literal recounting of the events, even if the text is a poem and doesn't have a plot. Once you have the main idea, you should try to identify some of the most important details. The goal of demonstrating an understanding of a piece of literature is to accurately describe what occurs in the text, free from opinion or interpretation, which are discussed in the next section.

For example, look at this poem by Billy Collins about Smokey the Bear, a fictional character created in the 1940s to educate Americans about the dangers of forest fires. While the ad campaigns changed over the years, his main motto was "Only YOU can prevent forest fires."

Flames

Billy Collins

Smokey the Bear heads
into the autumn woods
with a red can of gasoline
and a box of wooden matches.

His ranger's hat is cocked   5
at a disturbing angle.

His brown fur gleams
under the high sun
as his paws, the size
of catcher's mitts,   10
crackle into the distance.

He is sick of dispensing
warnings to the careless,
the half-wit camper,
the dumbbell hiker.   15

He is going to show them
how a professional does it. ∎

Summary: The poem starts in the woods during fall with Smokey the Bear carrying a can of gasoline and a pack of matches. It is probably about noon and Smokey the Bear is described as being brown with very large hands and a ranger's hat. It seems as if he has become tired of giving the same warnings about forest fires to those who come into the woods, like hikers and campers, so it appears that he is going to start a fire himself.

The summary includes the most important parts of the text, recounted in a way that demonstrates an accurate understanding of the events. Note that this summary does not include any explanation about *why* the poet, Billy Collins, might portray Smokey the Bear starting a fire instead of putting it out. A summary deals only with demonstrating an understanding of what literally happens in the text. The next section will present the ways that we can interpret the meaning behind a text like this one.

Reading Literature for Understanding

Read the following short story called "Alchemy" by Carrie Vaughn, annotate the text using the guide on pages 20–21, and write a summary (roughly three to five sentences) of the main action. As in the example with "Flames" above, focus only on providing an accurate recounting of the events of the story.

Alchemy

Carrie Vaughn

She was warned. She was given an explanation. Nevertheless, she persisted.

Performed endless experiments, recorded measurements and observations in careful writing on lined paper, pages and pages sewn up in books and neatly stored. How much of this acid added drop by drop to a powder of carbon, a scraping of iron, caused the reaction she desired? When that combination failed, she tried lithium and lead. Copper, in a glass bulb filled with nitrogen. Titration, oxidation, precipitation and solutions. A careful test with flames, producing an analysis of light. Practice practice practice. ("You'll never find what you're looking for," they told her. "Nevertheless," she replied.)

The materials were often toxic, the procedures tedious, the outcomes uncertain, but she found solace in the experiments. The formulae she used made sense. The laws of the universe were predictable, discoverable. Unlike so much of the rest of her life.

She reserved one end of a bench in a corner of a mostly disused lab, a hundred years old and poorly equipped. She piled books and notes around her, a sort of fence to claim her space and keep others from disturbing her experiments. ("What are you looking for?" "The secrets of the universe," she said, speaking in riddles because if she revealed the truth they would tell her she was doing it wrong. They would explain until she wanted to scream, but she never did. Patience. Practice.) However much she guarded her table-top territory, she would return from a meal, from a quick breath of fresh air, to find her books shoved to the floor, covers torn and spines broken, papers crumpled and scattered. She'd gather up the books, straighten the spines, smooth out the papers as best she could, spending time on it that she needed for study. She tried to ignore the glares. The glares were not as bad as the laughter. ("There has never before been one of you at this university, you know." They explained that one to her all the time, as if the fact of it would give her pause.)

She had patience. The patience of stones worn away by wind and water, of 5 continents creeping into one another to create mountains, of crystals growing in dark places. The patience of a planet caught in orbit around a sun that would last ten billion years before burning it all back to stardust.

She longed to be stardust.

Then one day, after she'd shut off the burner, after the burette had dripped all its liquid out — there in the bottom of a ceramic dish rested a mere particle, a trace. A treasure. The lab was quiet — it was late and she was alone. No one was watching, and so the moment was all hers. She cupped the substance in her hands and let its light shine on her, covering her face with warmth, pouring sunlight in her eyes.

She persisted, and when she triumphed: gold. ■

REFLECTING ON Academic Vocabulary   **Reading for Understanding**

Working with a partner or a small group, discuss the terms that were presented in this section and that you previewed on page 30 and clarify your understanding of each. Then, share what you learned about reading for understanding. Was anything presented in this section new or difficult for you? To what extent do you feel that you have mastered the skill of reading for understanding? How do you know?

Reading for Interpretation: What Ideas Give the Text Significance?

In the previous section — reading to understand — you were mostly concerned with understanding *what the text says literally*. When reading for interpretation, however, you will be concerned primarily with explaining *what the text means* — its significance. Significance refers to the ideas that give us insight into ourselves, the world around us, or the author's message. Just remember as you begin to interpret texts that your literal reading must come first. You have to understand what a text *says* before you can begin to interpret what a text *means*.

PREVIEWING Academic Vocabulary   **Reading for Interpretation**

In the next section, you will encounter the following terms as you learn about reading a text for interpretation. Working individually or with a partner or small group, consider what you already know about the meaning of each term.

1. Interpretation

2. Inference

3. Theme

4. Purpose

What Does It Mean to Interpret?

An interesting way to get at the difference between understanding what a text says and interpreting what a text means is to think about retelling a dream to someone. You might summarize what happened in your dream by saying something like this: "I was putting hundreds of tables in rows all by myself, but every time I turned around, someone had put them back, and I had to restart the whole process again. There were people staring, but not helping — some were laughing." Inevitably, the person you are telling your dream to will ask, "So what does the dream *mean*?" Perhaps you might say something about feeling unappreciated for your hard work on a group project, or maybe you are feeling exhausted by all the homework piling up. In other words, the literal reading of the text — in this case, your dream — is the account of what happened in the dream; the explanation of what you think it means — the **interpretation** — is the significance the text has to your life or the world around you. It is your best guess based on the evidence of the ideas underlying the text. Look, for instance, at these two images that are part of a collection by photographer Steve McCurry about people around the world reading. If we were reading the images just for understanding as we did above, we would describe the figures, their gestures, placement in the images, and so on. But interpretation requires that we make some kind of statement about what the images might mean — why McCurry made them. The artist himself offers this interpretation of his own work: "Readers are seldom lonely or bored, because reading is a refuge and an enlightenment."

Steve McCurry/Magnum Photos

Steve McCurry/Magnum Photos

When reading for interpretation, focus on having a reasonable explanation for why you think your conclusion — or inference — is accurate. An **inference** is a reasonable conclusion drawn by looking at many pieces of available evidence. You might claim that your dream about the tables means that aliens are coming to take over the world, but there is not much evidence in the dream to support that inference. A key point to understand here is that inferences can be wrong, just like a hypothesis you might make in a science experiment turns out to be incorrect based on the evidence you collected. Making an interpretation when reading works in a similar way: you make your best guess based on what you read, but you should be prepared to amend your conclusion based on additional information.

You are probably already familiar with the idea of interpretation when it comes to poetry, fiction, drama, and mythology. We use the term **theme** to refer to the meaning of a literary work. For example, read the ending of the story of Cinderella (p. 40), a story you may have encountered before, though perhaps not in this original version from the Brothers Grimm. At this point in the story, the prince is trying to find a mysterious woman he had fallen in love with and who left behind a golden shoe at the party the night before. He is unaware that she is Cinderella, a kindhearted young woman who has been forced to serve her cruel stepmother and stepsisters. The prince intends to marry the woman who can wear the golden shoe. In order to try to fit into the shoe, Cinderella's stepsisters actually cut off portions of their own heels.

from **Cinderella**

The Brothers Grimm

"This is not the right one, either," the prince said. "Don't you have another daughter?"

"No," said the man. "There is only a deformed little Cinderella from my first wife, but she cannot possibly be the bride."

The prince told him to send her to him, but the mother answered, "Oh, no, she is much too dirty. She cannot be seen."

But the prince insisted on it, and they had to call Cinderella. She first washed her hands and face clean, and then went and bowed down before the prince, who gave her the golden shoe. She sat down on a stool, pulled her foot out of the heavy wooden shoe, and put it into the slipper, and it fitted her perfectly.

When she stood up the prince looked into her face, and he recognized the beautiful   5
girl who had danced with him. He cried out, "She is my true bride."

The stepmother and the two sisters were horrified and turned pale with anger. The prince, however, took Cinderella onto his horse and rode away with her. As they passed by the hazel tree, the two white pigeons cried out:

Rook di goo, rook di goo!
No blood's in the shoe.
The shoe's not too tight,
This bride is right!

After they had cried this out, they both flew down and lit on Cinderella's shoulders, one on the right, the other on the left, and remained sitting there.

When the wedding with the prince was to be held, the two false sisters came, wanting to gain favor with Cinderella and to share her good fortune. When the bridal couple walked into the church, the older sister walked on their right side and the younger on their left side, and the pigeons pecked out one eye from each of them. Afterwards, as they came out of the church, the older one was on the left side, and the younger one on the right side, and then the pigeons pecked out the other eye from each of them. And thus, for their wickedness and falsehood, they were punished with blindness as long as they lived. ■

If we were reading only for understanding, we could summarize the story by saying it is about a poor girl who finds the love of a prince despite the best efforts of her family to prevent her from doing so; she marries the prince, and the stepsisters are blinded by pigeons.

Reading this story for interpretation, however, requires that we think about what it means, not just what it says. In this case, an interpretation of the theme of the story could be that true love has no regard for wealth, class, or position within a family. With literature, though, it's important to recognize that there can be more than one reasonable inference about a text's meaning. We could also interpret Cinderella as an example of the brutal and dehumanizing lengths that women are forced to go to in order to be the "perfect bride." We could say that the tiny shoe and the fact that the two stepsisters had to cut off parts of their feet to try to fit into it shows that the culture of this fairy tale values petiteness and obedience in females over all else. Reading for interpretation means that we need to embrace a variety of possible inferences, as long as they can be supported with evidence from the text.

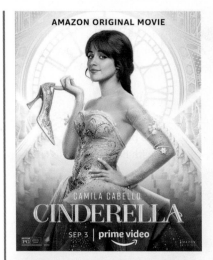

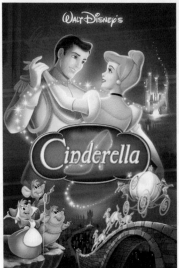

Look at these movie posters from various film versions of the story of Cinderella.

What differences and similarities do you see among them? Draw an interpretation about what each might be trying to communicate to its viewers about the character of Cinderella.

As you read earlier, one of the most common reading challenges occurs when we are unfamiliar with the context of a text (p. 24). Similarly, one of the easiest ways to misread a text when interpreting is to not understand the context. For instance, look at the painting below by Catharine Adelaide Sparkes called *Orpheus and Euridice*.

Wolverhampton Art Gallery/Bridgeman Images

Without any context about the two figures in the painting and their story, you might summarize this painting by saying that it shows a man who has wrapped himself in a bedsheet and is trying to wrestle a female ghost. You might interpret this as a painting showing how loneliness can cause people to do crazy things and let their imaginations get the better of them. That interpretation, however, would be incorrect. This is an example of how a lack of context can lead to a poor inference about a text.

To avoid this, we probably need more information about the story of *Orpheus and Euridice*. This painting depicts the ancient Greek myth of Orpheus, a renowned musician, and his wife Eurydice, who died on their wedding night. Overcome with grief, Orpheus goes to the Underworld and, through his song, pleads with the rulers there to let her go with him. They agree on one condition: he cannot look at her until they are completely outside of the Underworld. This image captures the moment when Orpheus gives in to temptation and looks backward, and as a result, Eurydice must return to the Underworld. With this context, we could probably draw an interpretation about the dangers of wanting something so much that desire overpowers reason and patience. Orpheus's desperate expression upon realizing his mistake and watching Eurydice being dragged back into the Underworld by specters supports this interpretation.

Making an Interpretation of Fiction

Return to the short story "Alchemy" that you read on pages 37–38 and review the summary that you wrote to demonstrate your understanding of that text. Now, reread the text and draw an interpretation about what the author, Carrie Vaughn, might be suggesting about persistence. Afterward, compare your interpretation with that of a classmate.

So far in this section, the examples have been about interpreting imaginative texts — short stories, fairy tales, even paintings — but what about nonfiction? We don't use the term *theme* to refer to the meanings we draw from an opinion piece, a newspaper article, or a chart. Instead, when we're interpreting nonfiction, our job is to make an inference about the author's **purpose**: why did the author create this text, and what ideas does the author hope to communicate to the audience?

For example, look at this excerpt from an article written by Garry Newman, the lead developer of an online game called *Rust* that began assigning the race and gender of its players randomly, instead of allowing players to choose their own.

Why My Videogame Chooses Your Character's Race and Gender for You

Garry Newman

Inevitably, there are people who like it and people who don't. Some players have praised what we're doing. Like us, they think that who you are in the game, your race and gender, makes no difference to the actual gameplay — and are happy to have the diversity. Others aren't so positive. They feel that playing a gender or race that doesn't match their own is detrimental to their enjoyment. . . .

Here's one of the many messages we've received from disgruntled male players: "Why won't you give the player base an option to choose their gender? I just want to play the game and have a connection to the character like most other games I play. Not have some political movement shoved down my throat because you make the connection [that] we can't choose our gender in reality so let's make it like that in game too."

Our female players seem more pragmatic. They point out that they've already been playing Rust as men for the past two years. Some have got in touch to thank us. Mostly they see it as no big deal. . . .

It's maybe understandable why some male gamers wouldn't want to play as women. They're just not used to being forced to. You could probably count on your fingers the number of major, big-budget games where you have no choice but to play as a woman, never mind having no choice but to play as a black woman. Female gamers are obviously more forgiving — they've been playing games as men for most of their lives. . . .

Ultimately the decision comes down to gameplay. We don't believe that letting you   5
choose your race and gender would improve the game. On the other hand, randomising everyone's gender and race meets all our requirements. We get an even spread of races and genders that make players more identifiable — while at the same time making the social aspects of the game much more interesting. ■

If we summarize what this text says, we might say something like this:

> This article is about a video game that randomly assigns race and gender. It discusses the response to that decision, both pros and cons, and why the creator made the game this way to get an equal spread of races and genders, making, he claims, the social interactions of the game more interesting.

But that summary is not the *meaning* of the piece. What is the author's purpose? We could say that Newman is using this article to address some complaints and to defend his decision. We could say that he is writing this piece to communicate the idea that race and gender — in the online world — should not be that big of a deal. Another interpretation of his purpose might be that he is encouraging people to play other races and genders because he thinks that it might help people come to understand each other a bit more. We might also argue that his purpose is simple justice and equality — as he points out, women have had to play as men for a very long time. Most people recognize that literature can have many different interpretations, but as you see here, nonfiction can as well. For any interpretation that you draw to be a valid one — about literature or nonfiction — it must be supported with evidence found in that text.

activity Making an Interpretation of Nonfiction

Return to the editorial "Abolish Billionaires" by Farhad Manjoo that you read on pages 32–34 and review the summary that you wrote to demonstrate your understanding of that text. Now, reread the text and draw an interpretation about why Manjoo thinks that we should not have billionaires. Be sure to include evidence from the text that supports your interpretation.

REFLECTING ON Academic Vocabulary **Reading for Interpretation**

Working with a partner or a small group, discuss the terms that were presented in this section and that you previewed on page 37 and clarify your understanding of each. Share what you learned about these terms and how they relate to reading for interpretation. How would you assess your current ability to read for interpretation?

Reading for Style: Why Was This Text Created in the Way It Was?

In the previous sections — reading to understand and reading for interpretation — we were mostly concerned with understanding what the text says and then explaining what the text means. When reading a text for style, we are trying to understand why the text was created in the way it was.

PREVIEWING Academic Vocabulary **Reading for Style**

In the next section, you will encounter the following terms as you consider how to read a text for style. Working individually or with a partner or small group, think about what you already know about the meaning of each term.

1. Style
2. Tone
3. Diction
   Formal
   Informal
4. Denotation and connotation
5. Syntax
   Sentence variety
6. Figurative language
   Simile
   Metaphor
   Hyperbole
   Personification
   Allusion
   Imagery

Style is the particular way that people express themselves. It's their voice. Think about "style" in clothing or cooking. Everyone wears clothes when they come to school, but each student's particular clothing choices reflect a unique style. Two chefs might cook burgers, but one of them has Middle Eastern heritage and infuses the burger with spices from that cuisine, while the other batters and deep fries the burger. That is style, and you can identify it in the choices a writer makes as well.

Style and Tone

One of the essential concepts in analyzing style is an author's **tone**, which refers to the attitude that an author takes toward a specific subject. You may have heard the term *tone* before as in, "Watch your tone" or "Don't take that tone with me." With your tone of voice, you can make what you say sound angry or sarcastic, but also happy or sympathetic, and so on. You use your tone of voice to indicate your attitude toward what you are saying. Consider the two different possible responses below from a student to a teacher regarding incomplete homework:

> I am *so* sorry. I was just so overwhelmed with other school work, and I got
>   behind. It won't happen again.
> Who cares about that homework anyway?

When reading for style, we focus on the choices authors make, especially the words they choose. By looking carefully at specific language choices, we can pick up on a writer's or speaker's attitude toward a subject. An author might take a number of different tones, and sometimes the tone might shift multiple times within a text. The following list of words can help you start to describe an author's tone. This list is far from complete, but you can see that many tone words fall on a continuum from positive feelings to negative ones, and many in between or neutral. You will likely return to this list frequently as you practice determining tone, and you will surely add new words to it.

amused	bitter	casual	resentful
angry	cold	humorous	reverent
dismissive	complimentary	gleeful	vindictive
sarcastic	derisive	joyous	
cheerful	dispassionate	malicious	
celebratory	flippant	mocking	

Look at the beginnings of two poems, both of which describe a city setting:

In the City of Night

John Gould Fletcher

Towards the end of night
Life swelters in its gore,
The roaring wheels run down,
The flames of the gas no more
Stab at the iron sky
In hissing mockery:
And the city takes such rest
As its torn nerves know best. ■

The Tropics in New York

Claude McKay

Bananas ripe and green, and ginger root
Cocoa in pods and alligator pears,
And tangerines and mangoes and grape fruit,
Fit for the highest prize at parish fairs,
Set in the window, bringing memories
of fruit-trees laden by low-singing rills,
And dewy dawns, and mystical skies
In benediction over nun-like hills. ■

You probably noticed that the two poems strike different tones. The speaker of "In the City of Night" expresses a grim, violent, and weary attitude toward the city at night. Look at the words *gore*, *stab*, *run down*, *torn*, and others that are mostly negative. The speaker of "The Tropics in New York" describes the beauty of the natural world with words and phrases like *ripe and green*, *highest prize*, *dewy dawns*, *mystical skies*, expressing a joyful and hopeful attitude toward home.

Reading for Tone

activity

Earlier (p. 31), you read part of a piece by Steve Almond called "Is It Immoral to Watch the Super Bowl?" Reread the following paragraph and try to describe Almond's tone using one or more of the tone words above, or some of your own. Then, explain how the author created that tone.

> The problem is that I can no longer indulge these pleasures without feeling complicit. It was easier years ago, when injuries like Stingley's could be filed away as freakish accidents. TV coverage was relatively primitive, the players hidden under helmets and pads, obscured by fuzzy reception, more superheroes than men. Today we see the cruelty of the game in high definition. Slow-motion replays show us the precise angle of a grotesquely twisted ankle and a quarterback's contorted face at the exact moment he is concussed.

Elements of Style

Reading for style is close reading, focused on the individual words, sentences, and structure of the text in order to understand how the writers create their intended tones. The main question you think about when reading for style is *Why did the writer make this specific choice*? Style can include a wide variety of choices, but for our purposes here, we will focus on these four:

1. Diction
2. Syntax
3. Figurative language
4. Imagery

Diction

To really understand **diction**, which is just a fancy term for "word choice," we have to discuss why a writer would choose a certain word over another. That is why it is so important that you pay attention to word-level challenges you might face when reading for style. If you do not know the meaning of the words an author has chosen, you will have difficulty explaining why the author made those choices. The best way to get at this is to consider the difference between denotation and connotation:

- **Denotation** refers to the literal — dictionary — definition of a word.
- **Connotation** refers to the feelings that are often associated with a word.

For instance, the words *home* and *house* have roughly the same denotation — the dwelling where one resides — but a writer will choose one of those words over the other because of the connotation. *Home* implies feelings of safety or comfort over the more sterile or generic associations of the word *house*. A house is a specific type of building, but the word *home* can be applied to an apartment, a shelter, a town or city, a state of mind—anyplace where people feel a sense of belonging. When reading a text for style, be on the lookout for words that have interesting or provocative connotations that might communicate a particular tone.

In addition to thinking about the word choices an author makes, we should consider how the individual choices work together to create a cumulative effect. It's rare that a single choice creates tone; in the poem "In the City of Night" above, for example, it is the seven or eight word choices that express that bitter and angry tone.

A significant aspect of diction to keep in mind is how **formal** the diction is. A writer who uses a lot of slang, for instance, is being **informal**. Somebody writing for a pop culture magazine about an upcoming movie might adopt an informal tone, while someone writing in a newspaper about the effects of a global pandemic, trying to be more serious, perhaps using more complex words or words that are unlikely to offend, is being more formal. Based on who the audience is and what the purpose of the text is, writers can choose to be formal, informal, or a mix of both.

To get a sense of how audience and purpose can affect the formality of the diction, take a look at these two restaurant reviews; the first one is from the *New York Times*, while the second was written by an average consumer:

> **Review #1:** [The chef's] keen sense of what to do with produce was on full display . . . in the $125 tasting, where blackberries helped out a braised pork shoulder paved with crackling hazelnuts and where a supple hunk of halibut sat over warm summer tomatoes given a briny, oceanic intensity by scraps of kombu.

> **Review #2:** Played hooky on a Monday to come here for lunch and it was FANTASTIC. Totally worth taking a vacation day for, totally worth traveling into the city on a sweltering day for, totally worth dressing up a tiny bit for. Service was great, although a little stiff at first, but the guys warmed up when they saw how much we enjoyed our food. We went with the five course seasonal tasting menu, and the absolute highlight was the mushroom tortellini. (If you know me . . . you won't believe that I just praised a dish that isn't a slab of meat.)

The first review is intended to be read by a wide number of people, probably those who are interested in the specific details of the food and its individual ingredients, while the second review's informality is intended to appeal to people who just want to know if the restaurant is worth going to. The key is to know when being formal or informal will be *effective*.

Syntax

Writers also convey style through the arrangement of their words, called **syntax**. More often than not, the syntactical choices an author makes are ways of creating rhythm and emphasis, which are generally expressed through **sentence variety**. Writers strategically use long and short sentences to spice up their writing and keep readers focused. Look at this paragraph on self-driving cars, for instance:

> With their twenty cameras, seven lasers, and rooftop-mounted GPS, the self-driving cars stood out. People stopped and stared as they took trial journeys around Pittsburgh. That was in the spring. Now, in the waning days of summer, passengers hailing an Uber X may be picked up by one of the city's many human drivers, or by one of a tiny fleet of autonomous vehicles.

As you read, you probably noticed that the first sentence begins with a list. Read it aloud and feel the rhythm of "twenty cameras, seven lasers, and rooftop-mounted GPS." The next sentence is of similar length, and we're starting to get used to a certain length of sentence. Then, abruptly, the author uses a very short sentence, just five words: "That was in the spring." Disrupting the rhythm signals to us that something has changed — something important. What the writer wants us to pay attention to is that between "the spring" and "Now," self-driving cars went from a dream to a reality.

There are no hard-and-fast rules about how to interpret syntax, but in general you want to pay attention to sentence patterns and, especially, to when those patterns shift. Does the author use a lot of exclamation points to show emphasis or write a lot of questions to give a sense of wonder or inquiry?

"Come on, Walter, you're wasting our time!
Stop using complete sentences!"

What is this cartoon implying about syntactical choices in certain situations? What is it specifically suggesting about language in the world of business?

Even though grammar and conventions dictate sentence structures to some degree, writers can also experiment with the order of words in their sentences. The playwright William Shakespeare loved to play around with syntax to achieve a particular rhyme or to put emphasis on certain words. In a famous line from *Romeo and Juliet*, he writes, "What light from yonder window breaks?" instead of using the more typical structure of "What light breaks from yonder window?" This syntax places the emphasis of the sentence on the word *breaks*.

Figurative Language

Authors use **figurative language** when they choose words or phrases that are not meant to be taken literally. For example, the statement "He absolutely inhaled that cheeseburger" does not mean that someone literally inhaled food, but the figurative language (hyperbole, in this case) communicates just how quickly he ate. The following are some of the most common elements of figurative language:

- **Simile:** a comparison between unlike things using *like* or *as*.

  He was as mean as one of those trolls that live under a bridge.

- **Metaphor:** a direct comparison between unlike things, without the word *like* or *as*.

  He was a troll—one of the meanest people I've ever met.

- **Hyperbole:** a deliberate exaggeration or overstatement.

  As she ran past, windows shattered and cheetahs nodded approvingly.

- **Personification:** giving human qualities to inanimate objects.

  The rain gently kissed his cheek as he waited for the sun to come out.

- **Allusion:** a reference to something well known — a piece of literature, art, a historical event, and so on.

  On her first day of school, she wished there was a Sorting Hat to tell her where to sit in the cafeteria.

Imagery

The final aspect of style we will discuss here is **imagery**, which is an umbrella term for the description and details that a writer includes to appeal to our senses: sight, sound, taste, smell, and touch. Imagery is intended to help readers experience the writing with their own senses. It can be either literal or figurative.

Take a look at the opening stanzas of the poem "The Daffodils" by William Wordsworth. This highly descriptive poem relies on visual imagery to paint a picture in the minds of readers.

from **The Daffodils**

William Wordsworth

I wandered lonely as a cloud
That floats on high o'er vales and hills,
When all at once I saw a crowd,
A host, of golden daffodils;
Beside the lake, beneath the trees,   5
Fluttering and dancing in the breeze.
Continuous as the stars that shine
And twinkle on the Milky Way,
They stretched in never-ending line
Along the margin of a bay: 10
Ten thousand saw I at a glance,
Tossing their heads in sprightly dance. ■

Not only does the imagery help readers visualize the scene, it also helps them feel the speaker's loneliness as he finds company only in the crowds of daffodils while immersed in the natural world.

La Primavera/Crane, Walter (1845-1915)/ROY MILES ARCHIVE/Private Collection/Bridgeman Images

This is a painting of a field of daffodils called *La Primavera* by Walter Crane.

How is the imagery of the daffodils in the poem similar to or different from what Crane presents in this painting?

Connecting Style to Meaning

The point of reading for style is not simply to identify elements like in a treasure hunt. (I found a metaphor here! Look, here's some imagery!) Rather, the goal is to explain how the author's use of style reinforces the meaning or theme of the work as a whole.

Let's look closely at this excerpt from the autobiography *Coming into Language* by Jimmy Santiago Baca, in which he describes a time in prison when he starts to see the power of words. Pay close attention to the style that Baca employs, looking at the diction, syntax, and examples of figurative language and imagery.

from Coming into Language

Jimmy Santiago Baca

But when at last I wrote my first words on the page, [I felt an island   *Imagery/figurative language*

rising beneath my feet like the back of a whale.] As more and more

words emerged, I could finally rest: I had a place to stand for the first

time in my life. The island grew, with each page, into a continent   *Imagery/figurative language*

inhabited by people I knew and mapped with the life I lived.

I wrote about it all — about people I had loved or hated, about

Diction the brutalities and ecstasies of my life. And, for the first time, the

child in me who had witnessed and endured unspeakable terrors

Diction cried out not just in impotent despair, but with the power of

language. Suddenly, through language, through writing, my grief

and my joy could be shared with anyone who would listen. And I

could do this all alone; I could do it anywhere. [I was no longer a   *Syntax*

captive of demons eating away at me, no longer a victim of other

people's mockery and loathing,] that had made me clench my fist

white with rage and grit my teeth to silence. Words now pleaded

back with the bleak lucidity of hurt. They were wrong, those

others, and now I could say it.

Through language I was free. I could respond, escape,

Diction indulge; embrace or reject earth or the cosmos. I was launched

on an endless journey without boundaries or rules, in which

I could salvage the floating fragments of my past, or be born

anew in the spontaneous ignition of understanding some

heretofore concealed aspect of myself. [Each word steamed with   *Imagery/figurative language*

the hot lava juices of my primordial making, and I crawled out

of stanzas dripping with birth-blood, reborn and freed from the

chaos of my life.] The child in the dark room of my heart, who

had never been able to find or reach the light switch, flicked it on

now; and I found in the room a stranger, myself, who had waited so many years to speak again. [My words struck in me lightning ——— *Imagery/figurative language*

crackles of elation and thunderhead storms of grief.] ■

We've identified some elements of style, but how do we connect them to meaning? The diction — *brutalities*, *despair*, *mockery*, *loathing* — expresses how desperate and angry Baca must have felt before he learned to communicate. For syntax, notice how he begins so many of his sentences with the word "I," signifying just how impactful this process has been for him, and notice how he uses a repeated sentence structure ("I was no longer a captive . . . , no longer a victim") for emphasis and power. The figurative language and imagery of Baca's words coming out of him like lava, becoming islands and continents, affecting him like a thunderhead, convey just how powerfully he views the ideas he can now — finally — express. All of these choices in diction, syntax, imagery, and figurative language are intentional on Baca's part to help him illustrate how his ability to write moved him from despair and victimhood to power and joy. When we read for style and craft, we have to read very closely like this, paying attention to all of the individual choices an author makes to help understand the author's meaning.

Style, Tone, and Meaning
activity

1. Reread a few paragraphs from the editorial "Abolish Billionaires" that you read for understanding and interpretation on page 32. This time, focus on Manjoo's diction, syntax, and other elements of style. How would you describe the author's tone, and how does that tone help him to communicate his purpose?

> Billionaire abolishment could take many forms. It could mean preventing people from keeping more than a billion in booty, but more likely it would mean higher marginal taxes on income, wealth and estates for billionaires and people on the way to becoming billionaires. These policy ideas turn out to poll very well, even if they're probably not actually redistributive enough to turn most billionaires into sub-billionaires. . . .
>
> But abolishment does not involve only economic policy. It might also take the form of social and political opprobrium. For at least 20 years, we've been in a devastating national love affair with billionaires — a dalliance that the tech industry has championed more than any other.
>
> I've witnessed a generation of striving entrepreneurs join the three-comma club and instantly transform into superheroes of the global order, celebrated from the Bay Area to Beijing for what's taken to be their obvious and irrefutable wisdom about anything and everything. We put billionaires on magazine covers, speculate about their political ambitions, praise their grand visions to save the world and wink affectionately at their wacky plans to help us escape . . . to a new one.

(continued)

Farhad Manjoo, excerpt from "Abolish Billionaires," *The New York Times*, February 6, 2019. Copyright © 2019 by The New York Times. All rights reserved. Used under license. Https://nytimes.com

But the adulation we heap upon billionaires obscures the plain moral quandary at the center of their wealth: Why should anyone have a billion dollars, why should anyone be proud to brandish their billions, when there is so much suffering in the world?

2. Reread the last few paragraphs of the short story "Alchemy" that you read for understanding and interpretation on page 36. This time, focus on Vaughn's diction, syntax, and other elements of style. How would you describe her tone, and how does that tone help her to communicate a possible theme?

She had patience. The patience of stones worn away by wind and water, of continents creeping into one another to create mountains, of crystals growing in dark places. The patience of a planet caught in orbit around a sun that would last ten billion years before burning it all back to stardust.

She longed to be stardust.

Then one day, after she'd shut off the burner, after the burette had dripped all its liquid out — there in the bottom of a ceramic dish rested a mere particle, a trace. A treasure. The lab was quiet — it was late and she was alone. No one was watching, and so the moment was all hers. She cupped the substance in her hands and let its light shine on her, covering her face with warmth, pouring sunlight in her eyes.

She persisted, and when she triumphed: gold.

REFLECTING ON Academic Vocabulary   **Reading for Style**

Working with a partner or a small group, discuss the terms that were presented in this section and that you previewed on page 45 and clarify your understanding of each. Then, share what you learned about reading for style. What terms and skills were new to you? With what aspects of reading for style do you think you need more practice?

Reading Visual Texts

As we mentioned at the beginning of this chapter, the term *text* refers not only to written words, but also to visuals and anything else that can be read. For reading visuals, we can actually use many of the same skills that we've discussed earlier in this chapter.

PREVIEWING Academic Vocabulary   **Reading Visual Texts**

In the next section, you will encounter the following terms as you consider how to read a visual text. Working individually or with a partner or small group, think about what you already know about the meaning of each term.

1. Color	**4.** Focus	**7.** Fonts
2. Lighting	**5.** Layout	**8.** Symbols
3. Framing	**6.** Design	

If we read the poster below for understanding, we might summarize it like this: "It is an image of a person at night in the water pointing toward the viewer, and a caption that says 'SOMEONE TALKED!'" This text poses some reading challenges, specifically contextual challenges. Who created this poster? When? If you were to conduct a little research on the text, you would learn that it is a propaganda poster produced by the U.S. government during World War II, which lasted from 1939 to 1945.

We can also read for interpretation by thinking about the meaning and purpose of the poster. Let's begin by drawing inferences. From the context, we can infer that the person in the water is a soldier, and perhaps even a U.S. Navy sailor, which would explain why he is at sea. Perhaps his ship has been sunk, and he is near drowning. Based on the caption "Someone Talked!" we can infer that his ship was sunk by enemy forces because someone revealed the ship's position or route. In terms of overall message or purpose, the U.S. government likely produced this poster to encourage information security, to show the consequences of even a minor breach of security.

So, we can read a visual text for understanding and for interpretation, just as we do with texts composed of words, but what about reading for style? With the articles, poems, and other texts you read earlier, you considered such things as word choice, syntax, figurative language, and imagery. If a visual text also includes words and

phrases, as this one does, you can absolutely read for these elements. For instance, in this poster, there are only two words to work with, but there's still a lot there. The word *talked* has a run-of-the-mill, everyday connotation that leads us to believe that the security breach wasn't a deliberate act by a traitor, just a careless breach of security, perhaps even part of a normal conversation. The creators of the poster did not use the words *spied*, *snitched*, or *informed*. The poster cleverly uses the pronoun *someone* to imply that anyone might have done this; whereas, a poster that said "You Talked!" might put viewers on the defensive. The short, two-word sentence, punctuated by an exclamation point, drives home the point with force and clarity: even accidental security breaches can have deadly consequences.

NationalArchives.gov

Visual Elements of Style

The previous section focused on the words accompanying the image. What about the image itself? When you examine the style of images and other visual aspects of a text, you might want to consider the elements and questions below.

Analyzing a Visual Text

Visual Element	Questions to Ask
Color and lighting	What colors, if any, are used, and how do they contrast with other colors in the visual text? How is lighting used? What is emphasized through color choices? Why?
Framing and focus	Every artist, photographer, or filmmaker must decide what to show, and what to leave out. Think about what's inside the frame and what might be just outside of it. Does the viewer see the scene close up, or from a great distance? What is in focus, or out of focus? Is the viewer above, below, or behind the subjects? What elements are centered or off to the side? What is not included in the frame? Why?
Layout and design	If the visual includes data, how has that information been categorized, organized, and presented? In a pie chart? Bar graph? Listed by chronology, amount, or time? How is blank space, if any, used? Why? How has the visual text used borders or lines: thick, thin, squiggly? Why?
Fonts and symbols	What fonts or styles are used for the words? Does the font communicate a particular tone? What is labeled or captioned? If the visual includes speech bubbles, how are they used? Why?

Let's apply these ideas to the poster we've been working with and draw some conclusions about how these visual elements of style help create the meaning of the piece.

Color and lighting.   This is a dramatic aspect of the poster, for sure. The black background and the inky water make us think of how scary being lost at sea in the dead of night would be. Just enough light is used to let us view the figure, but we can tell that soon he'll go under and the scene will all go black. It is powerful, even disturbing, and that element of fear helps drive home the urgency of not revealing information.

Framing and focus.   Rather than showing us a whole ship capsized, a sea full of sailors struggling to survive, the artist shows us a single sailor. The artist has focused in tight on the sailor's face so that we get to see his expression as he goes down fighting — and pointing defiantly at the viewer, blaming us. This intimate framing makes the cost of information leakage more personal, perhaps making us wonder if we hadn't been the someone who accidentally revealed the information.

Layout and design.   Like many posters, this one is designed for maximum visibility and impact: large light-colored letters set on a black background. There is nothing subtle about how this poster is laid out. The design, like the situation, is clear and stark: leak information and people die.

Fonts and symbols.   The font is all caps, with simple clean lines. The emphasis is on delivering a single clear, urgent message.

As you can see, visual style is more than just window dressing; it is something that helps deliver the message of a visual text — in this case, *During wartime, be on your guard and be suspicious or there will be disastrous consequences.*

Analyzing Charts and Graphs

Visual elements of style also affect meaning when it comes to data and statistics. It might seem counterintuitive, because data and numbers are often viewed as simply true or false, right or wrong. But how the information is presented visually can lead to different interpretations.

As a case in point, look at the two charts below. Both could be read for understanding in roughly the same way: they both present global temperature changes over the past 135 years as a way to illustrate to what extent climate change is actually happening. But, as you look closely, you'll see that it is the *style* of the charts that varies significantly.

The creators of Chart #1 chose to display the temperature scale on the left from -10 to 30 degrees Celsius, while those who made Chart #2 chose a scale from -.5 to 1.0 degrees Celsius. That simple choice greatly affects how we might interpret the texts, especially if we are not looking closely at the design choices.

Chart #1

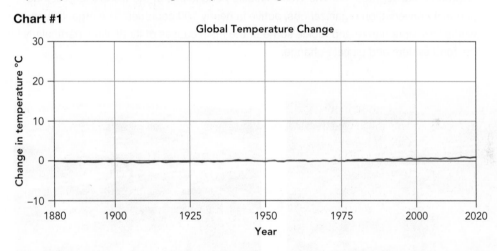

Chart #2

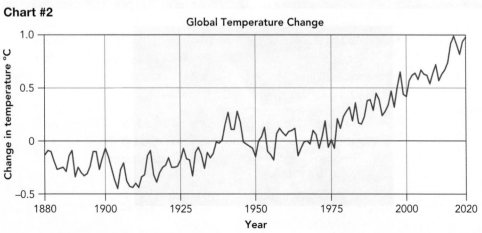

Just looking quickly at Chart #1, you might conclude that there really has not been much change in global temperatures over the years, since that line is mostly flat; however, Chart #2's smaller range of temperatures shows a clearer upward progression. These two charts report the same information, but because they make different choices in their style of presenting that information, a reader's interpretation could vary widely. Paying close attention to the style of the charts and other visuals becomes a valuable tool of analysis.

Visual Texts and Tone

When you examined poems, articles, and other words-only texts earlier in the chapter for style, you focused on how style connects to tone. Remember that tone refers to the attitude that an author, speaker, artist, singer, or anyone else takes toward a specific subject, and visual texts are no different. The tone of a visual text is communicated through an author's stylistic choices. Look, for example, at a few images from a photo essay called "The future of life on Earth lies in the balance," which includes the work of various photographers commissioned by the World Wildlife Fund to capture images of environmental degradation. The World Wildlife Fund is one of the world's largest independent conservation organizations, active in nearly 100 countries. The organization works to restore nature and tackle some of the main causes of its decline, particularly the food system and climate change.

© Chris J Ratcliffe/WWF

© Jiri Rezac/WWF-UK

Nature Picture Library/Alamy

It's clear from the choices the photographers made — in framing, in lighting, and in what subjects to include and exclude — that the tone is one of frustration and anger regarding the ongoing destruction of the planet's natural resources. There are many questions that we can ask about the choices the photographers made. Why include both live and dead trees in the frame rather than only those that have been destroyed through deforestation? Why a live, struggling bird rather than one that has already died from being entangled? Why frame the image of the roads from such a high angle? With different stylistic choices, the images could have told an entirely different story and communicated a different message.

Reading Visual Texts

activity

Draw an interpretation about what the meaning or theme of the texts below might be. Then, explain how the stylistic choices made by the creators of the texts connect to the meaning of the texts. Be sure to refer to the Visual Elements of Style on page 56.

1. This is a painting called *Separation* by Edvard Munch, created in 1896.

World History Archive/Alamy

(continued)

2. This infographic is from mindbodygreen.com, a lifestyle website that promotes health and fitness.

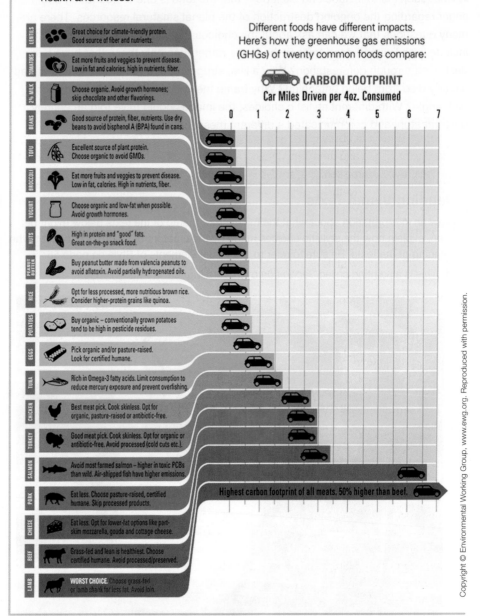

Different foods have different impacts.
Here's how the greenhouse gas emissions (GHGs) of twenty common foods compare:

CARBON FOOTPRINT
Car Miles Driven per 4oz. Consumed

REFLECTING ON Academic Vocabulary   **Reading Visual Texts**

Working with a partner or a small group, discuss the terms that were presented in this section and that you previewed on page 54 and clarify your understanding of each. Then, share what you learned about reading visual texts. How was the reading of these texts similar to or different from reading words-only texts? To what extent do you feel that you have mastered reading visual texts or need more practice?

culminating activity

Reading for Academic Purposes

Read the short story called "Simple Physics" and/or the nonfiction piece titled "Africans Mourn Chadwick Boseman: 'A Great Tree Has Fallen,'" and follow these steps for one or both texts:

1. Annotate the text thoughtfully and thoroughly. To review annotation, see page 20.
2. Demonstrate your ability to read for understanding by summarizing the text, focusing on the main idea and the supporting details. Your summary will probably need to be at least two or three sentences. To review reading for understanding, see page 30.
3. Write a brief two-to-three-sentence interpretation of the text that explains a possible theme for the short story or purpose for the nonfiction piece. What is the author hoping to communicate? To review reading for interpretation, see page 37.
4. Describe the author's style in the text. How does the style connect to the meaning of the text? To review style and meaning, see page 45.
5. Identify any challenges or difficulties you had reading the text and the methods you used to try to overcome them. To review reading challenges, see page 23.

Simple Physics

Kevin Leahy

That same June night, our parents bought us ice cream and balloons on the promenade of Buckingham Fountain. (Dad claims it was August, but I prefer to remember it my way, with the whole summer ahead of us.) We were greedy, ravenous: three boys fighting for the first scoop, catching elbows in our ribs. Every surface in the city bleeding heat into the sky. I grabbed the first cone but, to my mother's surprise, refused a balloon — I'd just turned eight after all, balloons were for babies — but she pressed a bright yellow one into my hand.

"For me," she said.

After the day we'd had, the need in her voice threatened to loose a rockslide within me, so I accepted the balloon without further complaint. It strained toward the sky, a dog trying to slip its leash. I figured five, maybe ten minutes until I could set it free without hurting my mother's feelings. Naturally, I doubled its string around my fist and bounced it off my five-year-old brother's head. He flinched and dropped his ice cream.

We all remember the scoop tumbling down Danny's shirt — the chocolate stain it lithographed in its wake — and especially our mother's bright, bursting laugh, louder than the rest of our laughs combined, a gut-buster that shattered into coughing. My father laid a hand on her back and looked from Danny to me, his face a swollen thundercloud. Danny gulped in a huge breath as his eyes brimmed, his ice cream dashed on the bricks, but he did not cry. Our older brother Tim, lost in his Walkman, cheerfully devoured his own cone. Beneath our father's hand, the thin cotton of my mother's shirt pulled tight against her ribs with every cough, outlining the boxy profile of her new pump and the coil of crazy-straw tubing that snaked into her abdomen.

"I'm sorry, Danny," she said when she caught her wind.   5

Brave little Danny. No tears, just a stoic nod. I heaved a theatrical sigh and made a big show of giving him my ice cream, which he accepted with great suspicion. At that, the muscles in Dad's jaw unclenched. Tightening my grip on the balloon, I took my mother's hand and pulled her away from Dad and Danny and Tim, into the envelope of the fountain's cooling spray. The box feeding her miracle poison thrummed with a pure and terrifying energy, like a tuning fork resonating at the threshold of human hearing. Her hand was shrunken but strong, and I wanted her all to myself, if only for a moment.

Beyond the fountain's perimeter fence, submerged basin lights threw rich ochres and reds into the stream, which arced as high as a castle before disintegrating into the mist that drifted over my bare face and arms. Young couples and families strolled the promenade, stopping to pose for pictures. A wild thought seized me: I could vault the fence and jump right in. Who could stop me? So long as I didn't mind a knuckle rap on the skull afterwards. The idea punctured some hidden, pressurized chamber in my chest, and filled me with a great unearned confidence, which is, as everyone knows, the best kind.

"Did you know this is actually a landfill?" I said with a sweep of my arm, indicating the fountain, the promenade, and the surrounding acres of lush, flower-filled greenery.

"I had no idea," said my mother, affecting surprise in a tone I use often with my own son and daughters. "Tell me more."

"Well, after the Great Fire the city pushed all the burned-up rubble into the lake. And   10
then—"

"Brain freeze!" Tim bellowed, just over my shoulder.

Startled, I released the balloon. It sailed up and away. My stomach dropped as I pawed the air, frantic.

Here's what I alone remember:

My mother's coiled crouch, the mousetrap speed of her jump, the waffled lozenge pattern on the soles of her shoes. She leapt impossibly high, caught the balloon, and brought it back to me.

"Brendan," Dad says, exasperation tempered with a gentleness he'd come into long   15
after I was grown, "It was in her lungs by then."

Now, Dad admits his back was turned. Danny was too young to remember, and Tim says he didn't see. Maybe our mother, sick as she was, couldn't have leapt the height of a man. But why, then, do I feel it happened—must have happened—could not have happened otherwise? ∎

Africans Mourn Chadwick Boseman: 'A Great Tree Has Fallen'

Ifeanyi Nsofor

The death of actor Chadwick Boseman last week at the age of 43 came as a shock to many Africans.

I liken it to the death of a great African King.

In my Igbo culture, when a great king passes on, we say, "Oke osisi adaala n'obodo," which means "a great tree has fallen in the land." It is a rare occurrence for great trees to fall. However, the fall is also not the end of the tree because its deep roots ensure it keeps sending out new sprouts.

Boseman's life is like that. Part of him will continue to live on through his films and inspire us, especially his role as King T'Challa in *Black Panther*.

The 2018 film was a hit across Africa. The fictional country of Wakanda, which was depicted in the movie as the most technologically advanced society in the world, was the nation that Africans wish they had. The film reminded us of what is possible for African countries — and how our continent could be powerful and respected.

I recall how excited Africans were to watch the film. In Ghana, people were dancing, drumming and wearing traditional clothing at the premiere. The former vice president of Nigeria took his family on a special outing to see the film. Others provided viewing opportunities to those who could not afford it. My friend Angela Ochu Baiye, a 2019 Mandela Washington fellow for the Young African Leaders Initiative, was so moved by *Black Panther* that she raised funds and took 200 children from poor communities to watch the movie at a cinema in Abuja, Nigeria. "To see yourself represented in fiction, especially through a lead character, is meaningful and profoundly empowering beyond words," she wrote on her social media.

Boseman's unexpected death has left Africans feeling as if we have lost one of ours. Indeed, he was one of us. During a 2018 interview on *The Late Show with Stephen Colbert*, Boseman acknowledged his African lineage. His family is from the Yoruba people, one of Nigeria's largest tribes, and the Limba, who come from Sierra Leone. He said his African background was one of his influences for making *Black Panther* more human. He succeeded in making the character someone we all wish we knew.

Africans have been sharing tributes to Boseman across social media. It's a reflection of how beloved he is on the continent. Nigerian Stephanie Busari, CNN's supervising producer for Africa, tweeted, "Chadwick Boseman will never know how much we loved him. Battling colon cancer, shooting films in between bouts of chemo and surgery. What amazing strength. He once said: 'The struggles along the way are only meant to shape you for your purpose.' Rest on King. Long live T'challa!"

South African activist Bele Nanotshe tweeted: "I would like to send my deepest condolences to Chadwick Boseman family and friends. On behalf of South Africa, I say we are proud of you and your achievements and the genuine manner in which you portrayed Pan Africanism in Black Panther movie. Rest in peace. We will indeed miss u my bro."

African corporations have also found ways to honor Boseman's death. On Aug. 31, the TV network M-Net Movies, in collaboration with Marvel Studios, aired *Black Panther* on one of its mainstream channels to share the film with a wide African audience. . . .

As Africans, we take solace in what King T'Challa said in *Black Panther*: "In my culture, death is not the end."

We believe he lives on. We are stronger now that such a great king has transited to become one of our ancestors, watching over us. We will be strong. We will live like the Black Panther. ∎

Writing

The written word is more than just a superior tool; it is a fundamental part of what makes us human. Writing is how we share knowledge, communicate ideas, set down history, and express emotions. You might not be aware of all the writing you do. You might even think that you don't like writing. But the fact is you write all the time — whether you're responding to a text or post, making a to-do list, or completing an assignment — and you probably would have a hard time imagining life without writing.

Poet and novelist Jimmy Santiago Baca lived the experience of being unable to write. As a child, Baca was orphaned and unable to read; he ran away from his orphanage at age thirteen. He ended up in prison, where he taught himself to read and write. In this excerpt from his essay, "Coming into Language," Baca describes how learning to write changed his life.

> But when at last I wrote my first words on the page, I felt an island rising beneath my feet like the back of a whale. As more and more words emerged, I could finally rest: I had a place to stand for the first time in my life. The island grew, with each page, into a continent inhabited by people I knew and mapped with the life I lived. Suddenly, through language, through writing, my grief and my joy could be shared with anyone who would listen.

Baca's experience makes us take a moment to consider what we've likely taken for granted: the power of being able to find our voice, express our thoughts, and make ourselves understood. We all have many voices, and in this chapter, you'll explore your voice and new ways of expressing yourself.

activity **Reflecting on Writing**

You write a variety of texts for a variety of reasons every day. This activity is designed to help you take the time, like Baca eventually did, to reflect on your writing and how it helps you communicate with others.

Step 1. Make a chart like the one below and list some things you have written recently. Think broadly: an email, a text message, an online post or comment, an essay, a story, a poem, a shopping list, or a news article are just a few possibilities.

For each item you list, use the chart to briefly describe your purpose, or reason, for writing, your intended audience (whom you wanted to reach), any difficult or easy aspects of the writing task, and your feelings upon finishing the writing task.

Type of Text	Purpose for Writing	Intended Audience	Difficulty or Ease	Feelings Upon Finishing
Email	Asking a question about an assignment	Teacher	Trying to make my question brief and clear	Felt good knowing that my teacher would help

Step 2. Select one item from your list and share your responses with a partner or group. In what ways was your writing experience similar to or different from the experience(s) of your partner or group?

Voice and Tone

When we read texts, we imagine how characters or speakers might sound — we "hear" their voices. But it's not just our imagination at work. Writers listen to the voice in their heads as they write, and it's almost as though we can hear that voice when we read their work. This is how written communication works and what makes it so amazing — it's a chance to get inside someone else's head.

In Chapter 1, we talked about making the most of your distinctive voice as you have academic conversations in class. In writing, the same thing goes: writing begins with who you are, how you think, and how you talk — your **voice**. You can improve your writing by making sure that the voice your readers hear is your own. School assignments often require formal writing, but that doesn't mean you need to leave your personality behind. A formal tone doesn't have to be dull or lifeless; it should still sound like *you*.

Finding Your Voice

activity

Let's say for the moment that your audience is just you — you with your own thoughts about certain topics that you are passionate about.

Step 1. Write about something that makes you happy and that you are enthusiastic about. Friendships? Music? Chocolate? Sports? Holidays? What about this topic sparks your enjoyment for it?

Step 2. Now write about a topic that makes you sad or angry. A political or global issue? A relationship? Something about school? How will you express this sadness or anger?

Step 3. With a partner, discuss how the words you used exhibit the passion you have for the topic. In what ways is your positive writing different from your negative writing?

The key thing to remember is that you can share your voice in a variety of ways. When we read, we pick up on specific language choices that help reveal the **tone**, meaning the author's attitude toward a subject. In Chapter 2 on page 46, you encountered the list of tone words that follows. Identifying the tone you are aiming for will help you make language choices that support that tone.

amused	bitter	dispassionate	malicious
angry	casual	flippant	mocking
dismissive	cold	humorous	resentful
sarcastic	complimentary	gleeful	reverent
cheerful	derisive	joyous	vindictive
celebratory			

Writers may incorporate language choices that adopt different tones throughout their writing, shifting how they express their attitude toward the subject. This flexibility is key to being an effective writer. Now let's practice exploring how you might adopt different tones in different situations.

Changing Tone

activity

Each of the scenarios below calls for two responses that differ in tone.

Step 1. Write responses to at least one of the three situations below. Think carefully about the language choices you make based on each situation.

  a. Someone cuts in front of you in line at the grocery store. Respond in one distinct tone and then in another tone that's clearly different from the first.

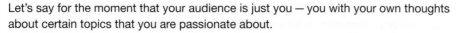

(continued)

b. It's midnight, and you're never going to finish all your homework. Write a brief email to a school administrator expressing your concern over the amount of homework. Then write a brief email or text to a friend about how ridiculous the amount of homework is; feel free to include any abbreviations or emojis you might use.

c. You have been chosen as a student representative to champion the idea of free college tuition for all United States students. Your first stop is the White House, where you will make the case to the president. Your second stop is to a class of graduating seniors who are about to go to college. Write out the remarks you would share with each of these audiences.

Step 2. With a partner, discuss how some of the key language choices you made reflect your change in tone and how you might be perceived. Choose the word, or words, from the chart on page 67 that best describes your tone.

Audience and Purpose

The writing activity in the previous section asked you to consider what language choices you would make to demonstrate a particular tone in different situations. You may or may not have noticed, but to make those decisions you had to consider whom you were speaking to and why you were addressing them. Whom we address — our **audience** — and our reason for writing — our **purpose** — influence the language choices we make. You've already spent some time exploring your voice through various tones. Now let's examine more carefully how changes in audience and purpose affect our language choices by considering the words of one of the most distinctive voices in United States history.

Below is a quotation from Martin Luther King Jr.'s 1963 "I Have a Dream" speech. The speech was delivered in front of the Lincoln memorial in Washington, D.C., to thousands of civil rights marchers. Read the quotation and think about the tone King takes and how his language choices create his tone.

> But we refuse to believe that the bank of justice is bankrupt. We refuse to believe that there are insufficient funds in the great vaults of opportunity of this nation. And so, we've come to cash this check, a check that will give us upon demand the riches of freedom and the security of justice.
>   —*Martin Luther King Jr.*

As you read the quotation, can you hear King's voice? How does he sound? Fiery? Grand? Uplifting? King intentionally uses language, such as "refuse to believe" and "great vaults of opportunity," to express his steadfast passion for justice to those marching for civil rights. He chooses words that will help him achieve his purpose of inspiring his audience and enlightening the world.

Now consider Martin Luther King Jr.'s tone during a 1968 episode of *The Tonight Show* with Johnny Carson.

I flew out of Washington this afternoon, and as soon as we started out they notified us that the plane had mechanical difficulties, and that kept us on the ground a good while. And finally we took off and landed, and whenever I land after "mechanical difficulties," I'm always very happy. Now I don't want to give the impression that, as a Baptist preacher, I don't have faith in God in the air. It's simply that I've had more experience with Him on the ground.

— *Martin Luther King Jr.*

Here, we see a more casual, relaxed, even meandering style. Speaking informally, King uses "and" to link ideas and keep the story moving in a way that almost defies punctuation, creating a tone that's lighter than the one he applies in his famous speeches. Unlike civil rights marchers seeking justice and inspiration, his audience during *The Tonight Show* expects to be entertained. King's purpose is to connect with that audience in a personable way. He chooses words that reveal an approachable figure with a charming, gentle sense of humor. No fire, no grand eloquence. But this, too, is King's voice; just a different side of him, taking a different tone because his audience and purpose are very different.

Bettmann/Getty Images

The image on the left is from the March on Washington, where King gave his famous "I Have a Dream" speech. The image on the right is King telling his airplane anecdote on *The Tonight Show* with Johnny Carson.

What can you determine about the context of King's statements from these two images? How did King adjust his language to suit these contexts?

As we looked at the two quotations from King, one part of a powerful speech and the other an anecdote on *The Tonight Show*, it probably makes sense to you that King would change the way he speaks in those different situations. It's because we naturally adjust our language based on the audience and purpose. Although these examples are representations of this idea in speech, adjusting our language based on audience and purpose applies to our writing as well.

Think about how often you write during the course of the day and how that writing can change based on the class, the teacher, or when and where you're communicating with friends. You have already demonstrated in the "Changing Tone" activity in the previous section (page 67) how your language and tone can change for different situations. It's likely that your language is less formal with a friend than it is with a teacher or the principal. Your language choices with your friends might include slang or humor, but your language with the teacher or principal would most likely be more academic. Just as important as knowing your audience is knowing your purpose for writing to them. If you're writing to entertain, your language might be humorous, satirical, or lighthearted. If you're writing to persuade, you would most likely select language that is passionate and emotional. The list below includes just a few of our purposes for writing:

To summarize	To analyze
To argue	To call to action
To recommend	To make a request
To explain	To evaluate
To enlighten	To entertain

Whether you are writing a poem, an essay, a story, or even just a message to a friend, it's a good idea in general to take a moment to think carefully about your audience and purpose by asking yourself these questions:

- How do I want my audience to feel about what I'm saying?
- What language and tone would be appropriate for this audience?
- Is this a formal or informal occasion?
- What do I want my audience to learn, understand, or appreciate about my topic?
- Is my purpose to persuade, entertain, or enlighten, some combination of those, or something else?

Because all writing is shaped by audience and purpose, developing the skill of using language that is appropriate for a particular audience and for a particular purpose is an important part of becoming an effective writer.

activity

Working with Audience and Purpose

The steps below will walk you through scenarios that address different audiences and purposes. As you move through each response, think about the relationship among your audience, purpose, and language choices you make.

Step 1. Write a few sentences to a friend that simply summarize a television show or movie that you've seen.

Step 2. Now write a few sentences in which you try to persuade your friend to see the television show or movie.

Step 3. Revise the sentences you wrote in Step 2 to persuade a *teacher* to see the same television show or movie.

Step 4. Review your writing and look at the changes you made moving through each of the steps. With a partner, discuss the following:

- What changed in your writing when the purpose changed from summarizing to persuading?
- How did your language choices, voice, and tone change as your audience changed from a friend to a teacher?

So far in this chapter, we have taken time to dig deeper into the broader elements of writing and the relationship between voice, tone, audience, and purpose. Moving forward, we will focus on how writing is constructed through words, sentences, and paragraphs, and how these choices affect the reader's reaction to the ideas presented.

Word Choice

The right word in the right place makes a *big* difference. Think about the differences among the words *mad*, *angry*, *furious*, and *livid*. Each word evokes a different level of emotion, *livid* being much more intense than *mad*, for example. Effective writers use word choice to deliberately shape readers' experiences with the text. If you read Chapter 2, you likely remember examples of effective word choices in texts by other writers. Part of your growth as a writer will involve taking into account the specific word choices you make.

PREVIEWING Academic Vocabulary   **Word Choice**

In this section, you will encounter the following terms as you begin to think more carefully about the specific words you use in your writing. Working individually or with a partner or small group, consider what you already know about the meaning of each term.

1. Diction   **3.** Connotation

2. Denotation   **4.** Loaded term

You probably noticed as you worked on developing a range of tones in the previous section that one of the ways you changed your tone about a subject was through your choice of words — called **diction**. Whether you're writing fiction, nonfiction, or poetry, diction is important for generating an effect on the reader and conveying the intended message and tone.

When we talk about word choice, it's important to remember that words have a dictionary definition, but they can also have emotional weight or cultural associations that add an extra layer of meaning:

- **Denotation** refers to the literal — dictionary — definition of a word.
- **Connotation** refers to the feelings that are often associated with a word.

In the chapter on reading (p. 48), we explained that while *house* and *home* have similar denotation — the space in which one resides — the word *home* can apply more broadly to any space or state of being that offers protection and usually conveys a sense of warmth, comfort, or belonging. For someone writing about the setting of a happy childhood, *home* would be a more effective word choice than *house*.

As a writer, it is up to you to make these choices. You have thousands of words to choose from, so how do you choose the right one? You choose the word that is most appropriate to the situation: your audience and purpose.

> The difference between the *almost right* word and the *right* word is really a large matter. 'Tis the difference between the lightning bug and the lightning.
>
> — Mark Twain

activity

Word Choice

Look at the following paragraph and identify word choices that might not be appropriate for this particular audience and purpose. Once you've identified those words, replace them with ones more appropriate to the situation. Then, compare and discuss with a partner the choices you made and your reasons for making them.

The situation: a nearby volcano has erupted, and a local television news reporter is updating viewers in the area.

The citizens are stupendously concerned about the ash cloud stalking inevitably closer to the city. Many are freaking out that their breathing will be all messed up and wonder if they should cover their mouths and noses and stuff from exposure to the air. We communicated with Dr. Moya from the hospital in the vicinity and he said that people unequivocally need to heed warnings and remain indoors, but that if they experience even a modicum of symptomatic behavior such as sore throat, wheezing breath, or itchy and overly aqueous eyes to head to the nearest clinic to get checked out. In the meantime, emergency vehicles are on hand for the furtherance and reinforcement of medical practices for those already experiencing deleterious symptoms, and the mayor has emphatically instituted a voluntary evacuation. We will continue to faithfully and diligently monitor the situation here and keep you instantaneously updated on developments.

Vivid Language

To avoid language that is bland or unclear, try choosing words that are *specific*. By specific, we mean words that most accurately express the idea, feeling, or image that you want to convey. Do your best to capture the idea, moment, or feeling in the most specific way possible because that's how you bring writing to life and connect with readers. Take a look at these two sentences:

Vague: The ship was big and fancy.

Specific: The massive ocean liner had two sparkling pools, a luxurious spa, and a glittering dining room.

These two sentences convey a similar message, but the way they say it could not be more different. The first one is bland. The second sentence is much more interesting to read. But what's the difference? The second sentence uses nouns and adjectives that are specific. Instead of just a "ship," it is a "massive ocean liner." The first sentence is too vague to envision, but the description of a "massive ocean liner" with its "two sparkling pools," "luxurious spa," and "glittering dining room" in the second sentence gives us a more concrete mental image.

For more practice, see the Grammar Workshop on adjectives and adverbs in the back of the book.

Being specific applies to verbs too. Let's look at one more pair of sentences:

Vague: The dog *moved* away from the snake.

Specific: The dog *leapt* away from the snake.

Again, these two sentences convey the same message, but in the first sentence, the verb is general: *moved*. As a reader, you might be wondering, *Moved how? Quickly? Casually? Warily?* A strong verb can answer those questions. In the second, the verb gives a clearer sense of action because it is specific and descriptive. The dog did not just move, it *leapt*. That word adds emotion — surprise and fear — to the incident. The more specific you can be, the more your writing will come to life.

While you want to have strong, vivid language in your writing, it's important to be aware that strong connotations can sometimes be distracting. A word with strong connotations is sometimes called a **loaded term**. For instance, you might say, *You are poisoning your mind by playing those video games*. You might think that using a word like *poisoning* to describe something relatively minor like playing video games is a strong way to make your point, but your reader might see it as an overreaction. Using loaded terms can distract your reader and discredit the rest of what you are trying to say. As you write, stay in control. Consider which words will have connotations that generate the reader reaction you want and which might go too far.

 Vivid Language

Revise each of the following sentences by replacing vague words or phrases with more specific words or phrases that bring the sentence to life, as in the example sentences below. Then, with a partner or small group, share the choices you made and discuss how they improve the reader's experience.

> **Original:** The dog ran across the yard.
> **Change the verb:** The dog *sprinted* across the yard.
> **Change the subject and the verb:** The *black Labrador sprinted* across the yard.

1. The sunset was red.
2. The house made noises.
3. The girl's smile was scary.
4. The sound was loud.
5. The rain fell.

REFLECTING ON Academic Vocabulary   **Word Choice**

Working with a partner or a small group, discuss the terms that were presented in this section and that you previewed on page 71 and clarify your understanding of each. Then, share what you learned about word choice in your writing. Which academic terms were new to you? Which ones do you feel that you have mastered or that you need more practice with?

Sentences

Now that you've spent some time working with words in a variety of ways, let's look at how those words come together into sentences. In the same way that effective word choice can affect the reader, well-written sentences can effectively share your ideas.

In this section, you will encounter the following terms as you begin to think more carefully about your writing at the sentence level. Working individually or with a partner or small group, consider what you already know about the meaning of each term.

1. Syntax

2. Simple sentence

3. Compound sentence

4. Complex sentence

5. Compound-complex sentence

6. Independent clause

7. Dependent clause

8. Conjunction

9. Comma

10. Semicolon

11. Comma splice

12. Run-on

13. Fragment

In Chapter 2, on page 48, you analyzed how authors use a variety of sentence structures, called **syntax**, to connect ideas and create interest. Let's see how this works in this excerpt from Gary Provost's book, *100 Ways to Improve Your Writing*:

> This sentence has five words. Here are five more words. Five-word sentences are fine. But several together become monotonous. Listen to what is happening. The writing is getting boring. The sound of it drones. It's like a stuck record. The ear demands some variety. Now listen. I vary the sentence length, and I create music. Music. The writing sings. It has a pleasant rhythm, a lilt, a harmony. I use short sentences. And I use sentences of medium length. And sometimes, when I am certain the reader is rested, I will engage him with a sentence of considerable length, a sentence that burns with energy and builds with all the impetus of a crescendo, the roll of the drums, the crash of the cymbals — sounds that say listen to this, it is important.

Provost makes a good point. Writing without any rhythm is just plain boring. However, look at the manner in which he shares his idea. To demonstrate his point, he takes the reader from monotony to "music" by varying the complexity of his sentence structure. Writing effective sentences is about knowing how to put together ideas to make them coherent, logical, or surprising — but it's also about varying your sentences to give your writing some rhythm. Using that rhythm to help your idea stick in your reader's mind is part of what syntax is all about.

Sentence Types

As Provost demonstrates above, a key to improving your writing is to *vary* your sentence structure — to know when to use short and long sentences for maximum effect. If you consistently write in a simplistic style or in an overly complex style, you'll lose your reader's attention.

In this section, we're going to talk briefly about some sentence types you can use to achieve variety. Knowledge of the basics of sentence structure and the arrangement of simple, compound, complex, or compound-complex sentences will help you strengthen your writing for every context and in every genre, including essays, plays, arguments, short stories, or poems.

WORDS DOWN GOT WE'VE GOOD PRETTY -- SHOULD NOW INVENT WE SYNTAX!

What does this cartoon suggest about the importance of sentence structure?

Simple sentences can grab the reader's attention or provide information in a direct way. If you use too many, however, your writing can come across as choppy or bland. A simple sentence contains one independent clause. An independent clause is a group of words that contains a subject and verb. It's called "independent" because it can stand by itself and still make sense:

SUBJECT VERB

I write.

Compound sentences can be used to emphasize balance, to compare or contrast ideas, to convey cause-effect relationships, or to group similar ideas together. Compound sentences contain two independent clauses joined by a comma and a conjunction or a semicolon:

INDEPENDENT CLAUSE   INDEPENDENT CLAUSE

I vary the sentence length, and I create music.

INDEPENDENT CLAUSE   INDEPENDENT CLAUSE

I vary the sentence length; I create music.

Complex sentences contain an independent clause and one or more dependent clauses. A dependent clause is an incomplete thought when it stands alone.

DEPENDENT CLAUSE   INDEPENDENT CLAUSE

Because these sentences vary, reading them is more pleasant.

"Because these sentences vary" is a clause that depends on an independent clause to make a complete thought.

Compound-complex sentences contain two or more independent clauses and one or more dependent clauses:

DEPENDENT CLAUSE   INDEPENDENT CLAUSE

<u>Although varying sentence structure takes time and thought</u>, <u>writing with varied</u>

INDEPENDENT CLAUSE

<u>sentences flows better</u>, and <u>it also keeps readers engaged</u>.

Similar to compound sentences, complex and compound-complex sentences can combine ideas, compare and contrast ideas, convey cause and effect, or elaborate further on an idea by adding independent and dependent clauses to simple sentences. The difference lies in how the writer structures the amount of information in the sentence to best convey the message. Longer sentences can provide rich detail, build suspense, and investigate an idea thoroughly.

Sentence Types

activity

In this activity, you're going to practice constructing a variety of sentences in a couple of ways. First, you will write sentences of various types about a movie or television show you've recently seen. Second, you will practice using a variety of sentence types to rewrite a story.

Step 1. Write about a movie or television show you've recently seen using each of the sentence types listed below. You may write something new, or you can return to work you've already written in the "Working with Audience and Purpose" activity (p. 70) as a starting point. You can reuse sentences or parts of sentences to build the other types, or you can create different sentences each time.

  a. Write a simple sentence about your emotional reaction to a movie or television show.

  b. Write a compound sentence about one conflict that occurs.

  c. Write a complex sentence about a character's reaction to that conflict or another situation.

  d. Write a compound-complex sentence that gives your overall review of the movie or show.

Step 2. Either with a partner or on your own, try rewriting the following story using a variety of sentence types. You may use Provost's example on page 75 as a model. Feel free to add more interesting diction and details where necessary to improve the flow. When you're finished, identify which sentence structures you incorporated into the story and how these choices affect your text.

The Trip

The road was dark. The town was unfamiliar. The car was almost out of gas. We were headed toward the inn. The clouds looked ominous. It began to rain. We drove faster. Finally, at the end of the lane, we saw lights. They were dim and yellow. The road was mud now. We arrived.

Some writers have a hard time remembering grammar terms, so here's a little glossary for quick reference.

Term	Definition	Example
Noun	A person, place, or thing	dog, adventure, Washington, freedom
Verb	An action, state, or occurrence	go, run, is, was, become
Pronoun	A word that takes the place of a noun	it, he, they, she, someone
Adjective	A word that describes a noun or pronoun	rotten, overwhelming, beautiful
Adverb	A word that describes a verb (usually ending in -*ly*)	quickly, sneakily, cunningly, fast
Phrase	A group of words lacking either a subject or a verb	Without a care in the world
Clause	A group of words containing both a subject and a verb	The cat purred.
Preposition	Words that express a relation of one thing to another	on, in, at, of, to, upon, if, behind, against, without, through
Conjunction	Words that connect things	for, and, nor, but, or, yet, so

Verbals

While the two terms below — gerund and participle — aren't strictly parts of speech, they do tend to confuse people. These types of words can more generally be called "verbals," because they are made from verbs. Verbals are usually made by adding -*ing* to the end of the word.

Gerund	A noun made from a verb	*Asking* is always okay.
Participle	An adjective made from a verb	We love to listen to the *singing* magician.

Building Sentences — Combining Ideas

The sentence names — simple, compound, complex, and compound-complex — may not be all that helpful for understanding how sentence types differ from each other. You might try thinking of them this way: simple sentences contain one idea, while the other types combine more than one idea and show how those ideas relate to each other. Those relationships are demonstrated through the use of conjunctions. How authors use conjunctions to show those relationships can make writing more effective and coherent.

Conjunctions

A **conjunction** is a word that connects other words, phrases, or clauses together to show the relationship among ideas. Conjunctions can connect two equally important ideas, establish that one idea carries more importance than another, or show that one idea is dependent upon another. As a writer, you will choose conjunctions that effectively convey the relationships among your ideas. The table below will give you an idea of how conjunctions are used to show relationships in sentences:

Conjunctions	Relationship
and	Addition
but, yet	Contrast
or	Choice
so	Result
after, before, since, until, when, while	Time
because, since	Cause and effect
if, if/then, even if, unless, although	Condition

Let's say you are writing about a dog eating your couch. Look at how the different conjunctions (underlined) in the example sentences below establish different relationships between the ideas presented. Notice, too, how the use of these conjunctions can help writers vary their sentence structure while establishing these relationships.

Time: Before the dog starts eating your couch, I think you should feed her.

Cause and effect: Your dog is eating your couch because you didn't feed her.

Condition: If you don't want your dog to eat your couch, then I think you should feed her.

Contrast: I fed the dog, but it was too late to save the couch.

Addition: She ate the cushions like giant marshmallows, and she used the frame for a toothpick.

Choice: You can feed your dog, or your dog will move on to other furniture.

Result: I fed your dog, so we don't need to call the vet.

Each example is about the same topic — saving the couch from a hungry dog — but the choice of conjunction establishes a clearer relationship between sentence parts. Thinking about exactly what you want to say and carefully selecting conjunctions to help convey your meaning will help make sure that your readers understand you. Such thoughtful word choices can also keep your writing vivid and engaging by helping you vary your sentence structure.

Conjunctions

Let's practice incorporating conjunctions into your sentences by building on the "Sentence Types" activity you completed on page 78.

Step 1. Select one or two of the sentences that you wrote, either for your ideas about a movie or television show you've seen, or for the creative writing called "The Trip."

Step 2. Rewrite your sentences using different conjunctions that convey various relationships among the ideas presented. Feel free to add to or delete from your sentences to create the effect that you want.

Step 3. With a partner or small group, share one of your sentences and the changes you experimented with. Explain why you made the choices you did.

Commas and Semicolons

In this section, we're going to look more carefully at punctuation usage when working with sentence structure. You've already practiced writing sentences in this chapter, but we can't talk about combining sentences and ideas without including the proper use of commas and semicolons.

A **comma** creates a slight pause in a sentence and can be used to do the following:

- Separate independent clauses (full sentences with a subject and verb)

  I work hard at my job all day, so I enjoy playing video games when I get home.

- Separate an introductory clause or phrase

  Every night, I join my online team for battle.

- Separate a list of items in a series

  We usually design our avatars, choose our weapons, and plan strategies.

- Set off appositives (phrases that rename or specify)

  Maria, the most organized player, usually acts as the moderator to keep everyone on track.

- Indicate a direct address

  "Thank you, Maria, for demonstrating strength and agility."

- Set off direct quotations

  "You're welcome," replied Maria.

A **semicolon** also indicates a pause, but more so than a comma. Semicolons are used to connect two related independent clauses and can take the place of a comma and the conjunction.

We made it to the end of the game; we ended up in first place.

Without commas and semicolons, writing can become messy and the message misconstrued. Look at these popular examples below:

Let's eat Grandma.

Let's eat, Grandma.

I'm sorry I love you.

I'm sorry; I love you.

Notice that the placement of the comma makes a big difference to whether or not Grandma enjoys a meal or becomes the meal. Furthermore, the lack of a semicolon means the difference between loving someone and being sorry for loving someone.

Errors that you should avoid as a writer are comma splices and run-ons. A **comma splice** occurs when a writer connects two independent clauses with only a comma, like this:

I am exhausted, I have to go to school.

A **run-on sentence** is when a writer strings together two independent clauses without any separation, like this:

I am exhausted I have to go to school.

Why are these a problem? In the comma splice and run-on sentence, there is no clear relationship. In other words, it's not clear whether one causes the other or happens in spite of the other (see possible revisions below), or if some other relationship exists between the two ideas. The reader is left to guess. That makes the sentences unclear and hard to understand. While you may encounter the occasional comma splice or run-on sentence in creative and literary works, such constructions are frowned upon in formal academic writing.

So, how do you correct a comma splice or run-on? We can correct them in several different ways:

1. Insert a comma and a coordinating conjunction.

   I am exhausted, but I have to go to school.

2. Insert a period and make two sentences.

   I am exhausted. I have to go to school.

3. Insert a conjunction at the beginning of a dependent clause followed by a comma.

   Although I am exhausted, I have to go to school.

4. Insert a conjunctive adverb and a semicolon.

   I am exhausted; however, I have to go to school.

5. Insert a semicolon by itself.

   I am exhausted; I have to go to school.

For more practice, see the Grammar Workshop on comma splices and run-on sentences in the back of the book.

activity Commas and Semicolons

The following sentences contain errors with commas and semicolons that result in comma splices or run-on sentences. Try a variety of methods to correct the errors using any of the examples above for guidance. When you are done, share one or two of your sentence corrections with a partner and explain how this activity can help you improve clarity in your own writing.

I decided to meet my friends at the mall we wanted to watch a movie. We love science fiction thrillers, the movie we chose was about building the first human colony on Mars. It held our interest for the first few minutes, we realized that it wasn't that great. The end of the movie came we agreed that we wouldn't recommend it to anyone.

As we worked on building sentences, and even throughout this writing chapter, you might have noticed that we used different forms of punctuation to show some separation between the ideas. That is the purpose of all punctuation, in fact: to show to what extent ideas are connected or separated. It's that simple. The discussion above focuses on the role of commas and semicolons. The table below includes these and other punctuation marks that authors use to connect, separate, or vary sentence structure.

Punctuation Mark	Purpose
Comma ,	Commas are the most versatile punctuation in English, which can make them a bit tricky. They show separations within a sentence. They are used to set off subordinate clauses, phrases, or items in a list.
Semicolon ;	This is a way of putting together two sentences; this works best with two sentences that share some meaning.
Colon :	The colon is usually followed by a series of items: *this, this, and this are examples*.
Dash —	The dash is a way of adding yet another thought to a sentence — like a bridge. It can also be used to interject a thought — an interruption, really — into a sentence.
Hyphen -	A hyphen connects words together, making them into one combo-word-cluster. It's especially useful when making compound adjectives like "forward-thinking."
Period . Question mark ? Exclamation point !	Called *end punctuation*, these marks tell your reader that you have completed a thought.

For more practice with grammar, see the Appendix: Grammar Workshops at the back of the book.

A writer can say a lot with punctuation. All those little marks are used for effect — to pause, to create suspense or intensity, to conclude with finality, or to ponder a question. They can change the pace of the reading or keep your ideas clear and the reader focused.

Building Sentences — Combining Ideas

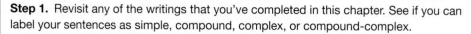
activity

Practice what you've learned so far about sentences by revising your own writing.

Step 1. Revisit any of the writings that you've completed in this chapter. See if you can label your sentences as simple, compound, complex, or compound-complex.

Step 2. If you are missing any of the sentence types, challenge yourself to include them in your revision. Try to incorporate the use of conjunctions where appropriate to show relationships among ideas and provide sentence variety. Check to see that you've properly used commas and semicolons to clarify sentence ideas. If you've included all the sentence types, analyze the flow, or rhythm, of your writing from sentence to sentence. Revise your sentence variety to improve your writing. (You can refer back to Provost's example on p. 75 for inspiration.)

Step 3. With a partner or small group, choose one or two sentences that you feel are your strongest and explain why you structured the sentence, or sentences, the way you did. What effect did you hope to have on the reader?

Fragments

Fundamentally, a complete sentence has at least one independent clause and includes a subject and a verb. A **fragment** occurs when the sentence is missing any of these. Though you may have been taught that fragments are unacceptable, they can sometimes provide a powerful punch to your writing and grab the reader's attention *when used appropriately and skillfully*.

Common errors involving fragments include stringing several prepositional phrases together without including either a subject or a verb or including a subject and verb but within a dependent clause. Ineffective use of fragments tends to confuse, bore, or distract the reader.

Ineffective Use of Sentence Fragments:

STRING OF PHRASES; NO SUBJECT OR VERB

In the basement of the house around the corner.

DEPENDENT CLAUSE CONTAINING A SUBJECT AND VERB

Because he liked to work harder on Monday.

In the examples above, the sentence fragments leave thoughts and ideas unfinished. What about the basement in the house around the corner? What happens because he liked to work harder on Monday?

So, when do fragments work? Writers can intentionally use fragments for emphasis. Look at the examples that follow. What do the fragments in each example emphasize?

For more practice, see the Grammar Workshop on fragments in the back of the book.

Effective Use of Sentence Fragments:

> Every time my mother got halfway up from the sofa to adjust the [television] set, the sound would come back on and Sullivan would be talking. . . . She sat down — silence. Up and down, back and forth, quiet and loud. It was like a stiff, embraceless dance between her and the TV set.
> — *Amy Tan*, Two Kinds

> Men explain things to me, and other women, whether or not they know what they're talking about. Some men.
> — *Rebecca Solnit, from* Men Explain Things to Me

As with any literary technique, fragments should be used with care, but a good fragment can add emphasis, create humor, or grab your reader's attention in other ways.

activity Fragments

Return to any of the writings you've completed in this chapter or select something else you've written for your English class and review it for sentence structure. Try inserting a sentence fragment somewhere in your revision. Share your sentence fragment addition with a partner. Discuss the thinking behind the idea and placement of the fragment. Consider how adding the fragment changes the pace of the action in your story and the effect it has on the reading experience.

REFLECTING ON Academic Vocabulary   **Sentences**

Working with a partner or small group, return to the academic terms that you previewed on page 75 and discuss your understanding of each. How has your understanding of sentence structure changed? Explain to your partner or small group one thing about sentence structure that you feel more confident with in your writing. What is one challenge you still face?

Paragraphs

Now that you have had some practice playing with word choice and then with sentences, the next step is stringing them together in an organized fashion to build paragraphs. Just as being able to write solid, powerful sentences is important, knowing how to effectively structure paragraphs will help you when you are asked to write for a variety of purposes.

The job of a paragraph is to bring ideas together into topics. When writers shift to a new topic, or set of ideas, they generally start a new paragraph. This is why the first sentence of a paragraph is often called the topic sentence. It defines the topic that will be discussed in that paragraph. It's important to note that some authors do not always begin paragraphs with the topic sentence. For now, we will place topic sentences first in the paragraph, but as you become more comfortable with your writing, you may choose a more flexible paragraph structure.

In this section, we're going to focus on one type of writing that you're likely to be assigned in this class and others: academic essays. Here we will focus on writing a single, well-developed paragraph that could be part of an academic essay. Once you have an understanding of how to construct an effective paragraph, you will have the building blocks you need to begin assembling a solid essay. This type of academic writing is, of course, only one aspect of your writing voice. You will be writing in a variety of modes and genres throughout this year and in your other classes.

PREVIEWING Academic Vocabulary   **Paragraphs**

In the remaining section of this chapter, you will encounter the following terms as you begin to develop unified and coherent ideas in a paragraph. On your own or with a partner or small group, consider what you already know about the meaning of each term.

1. Topic sentence   **5.** Unity

2. Support   **6.** Coherence

3. Explanation   **7.** Transition words

4. Conclusion

Basic Elements of a Paragraph

The primary parts of an academic paragraph are **topic sentence**, **support**, **explanation**, and **conclusion**.

Topic sentence	State your point in a clear topic sentence. Topic sentences state the main idea that all the following sentences will support. (The first sentence of a new paragraph should be indented five spaces.)
Support	These sentences provide evidence to support the points that you make. In much of your writing, you will be asked to include textual evidence to support your ideas and observations. In some writing tasks, your own personal anecdotes and examples can be provided as supporting evidence.
Explanation/ commentary	For any evidence you provide, offer commentary about its connection to the topic sentence. Commentary usually includes an explanation of why the evidence you provided is important to the development of your ideas. Try to avoid mere summary, which does not explain to your readers why you have included the information. Using verbs like *shows*, *reveals*, or *proves* is a good way to connect the supporting examples to the topic sentence. For example, you could say, "Her defiance in this episode proves that she is becoming more independent," or "The group's decision reveals the dangers of group-think."
Conclusion	The last sentence of your paragraph should comment on the significance of the information presented in the paragraph or summarize the information presented in the paragraph. As you go from single- to multi-paragraph writing, your concluding sentence should bring closure to your ideas in the preceding paragraph before moving on to the next paragraph, or provide a smooth transition to the next paragraph if the idea continues.

The thing to remember is that those parts of a paragraph can be repeated, rearranged, and used as you see fit to achieve your purpose. Let's see how these components work in a paragraph about surviving a zombie apocalypse.

Topic sentence ——————— [Your chances of surviving a zombie apocalypse depend almost entirely on the type of zombie you are facing.] While there are dozens of different categories of zombies, including Crawlers, Screamers, Voodoos, and even Animals, you are most likely to encounter the Walkers or the Runners. [The Walkers are the ——————— *Support* most common type and can be seen very slowly, but methodically terrorizing humans in *The Walking Dead* TV show and the original 1978 *Dawn of the Dead* movie.] [Because of their slow movements and failing body parts, ——— *Explanation/ commentary* your chances of survival are fairly high as long as you can jog at a reasonable pace, find a nice group of new friends, and have perfect marksmanship for every shotgun blast.]

Support ——————— [If, however, you find yourself facing down Runners, as in the movies *28 Days Later*, *Zombieland*, or the 2004 remake of *Dawn of the Dead*, your survival rate will plummet (unless you are Woody Harrelson).] [The Runners ——— *Explanation/ commentary* are just too fast: they pop up out of nowhere, dodge your perfectly aimed shots, and turn your new best friend into a zombie in mere seconds.] [So, if you wake up one ——————— *Conclusion* morning to discover the zombie apocalypse has begun, be sure to take a minute to see what kind of enemy you're facing and either start jogging or make yourself a nice cup of tea and wait for the inevitable.]

Notice how this writer uses the structure of topic sentence, support, explanation, and conclusion as a general guideline. The topic is introduced in the first sentences, and the paragraph includes support and explanations to clarify the idea that surviving a zombie apocalypse depends upon the type of zombie encountered. The point is this:

- This structure will help you write an effective paragraph. It's how almost all paragraphs work, both in student writing and professional writing.
- This structure is not a rigid template. Let your voice, your ideas, and the needs of the paragraph guide you.

Unity and Coherence

You might ask, *Why does the basic structure of a paragraph work, and what do we mean when we say an "effective paragraph"?* An effective paragraph has two qualities: unity and coherence.

Unity means that the paragraph is about a single subject, and all sentences in the paragraph deal with that subject. **Coherence** means that the ideas flow logically, one thought leading to the next, which can be aided by the use of **transitions** like *therefore*, *because of this*, or *for instance*. Transitional words and phrases help to move the reader easily through your writing. While you can use transitions within a paragraph to make it cohesive, you will also use transitions to move smoothly from paragraph to paragraph when you begin writing full essays. The alternative to a unified and coherent paragraph is one that jumps from topic to topic and is unfocused. A paragraph without unity and coherence can be hard for a reader to follow.

Not Unified or Coherent: The most interesting part of baseball is pitching. Hitting is okay too. Pitching is a mental battle. Hitting can be really hard too. You have to be able to throw a fastball, a curve ball, and other types. It can be difficult to hit a curve ball because it's moving around so much. Major league batters usually don't even get a hit every other time they go to bat because some pitches can be very hard to hit. The longest hitting streak is only 56 games and that was done in 1941, so pitching is really important.

Did you notice that the paragraph doesn't follow the basic structure of topic sentence, support, explanation, conclusion? Without that structure and focus, the ideas wander aimlessly.

Unified and Coherent: The most interesting part of baseball is pitching. Pitching is a psychological battle between the pitcher and the hitter. For instance, pitchers will throw a series of fastballs to get a hitter used to a certain speed and then throw a slow change-up or curveball to throw the batter off. A batter can try to guess the pitch based on the situation, but that only gives the pitcher yet another way to surprise the batter by throwing something expected. It's essentially an elaborate high-stakes game of rock, paper, scissors.

This paragraph incorporates a topic sentence about pitching, and then proceeds to develop clear, focused ideas about what makes pitching an interesting part of baseball.

Revising and Editing a Paragraph

You've done a lot of writing in this chapter and have been asked to revisit much of what you wrote to play with and revise your language and ideas. One step in the writing process is to revise and edit your writing to ensure that it is clearly presented and free from errors. The list below can act as a guide for ensuring that the writing you share is a strong representation of your ideas and skills as a writer. When proofreading your writing, take the time to revise and edit for the following:

- Spelling errors
- Punctuation errors
- Vivid language that brings your writing to life
- Varied sentence structures to make your writing interesting to read
- Unified and cohesive ideas that use transition words to help the flow of ideas

Proper revisions and edits can elevate your writing style and improve its effectiveness. Adding, cutting, or moving information can help your reader follow and understand your ideas.

Drafting and Revising a Paragraph

Let's practice what you've learned about the structure of paragraphs by writing one about the effect of technology on relationships. To begin to write your paragraph, let's first brainstorm some ideas.

Step 1. Make a chart like the one that follows or use some other graphic organizer to list ideas for both positive and negative effects of technology on relationships, or you can freewrite to generate ideas — whichever method works best for you.

RELATIONSHIPS	
Positive Effects of Technology	**Negative Effects of Technology**

Step 2. Write your paragraph. When writing, you can explore more deeply one of the positive or negative effects you listed, or you can address both in your paragraph. Be sure to include the following:

- A topic sentence that states whether technology is mostly positive or negative
- Relevant support from personal experiences with technology or those of people you know
- Commentary on the supporting examples, including an explanation of how they relate to your topic sentence
- Logical transitions and progression of ideas from sentence to sentence
- A concluding statement that re-emphasizes the point you want to make about technology or summarizes the information in your paragraph

Step 3. Read your paragraph aloud to yourself to check that your ideas are clearly conveyed in a logical, cohesive manner that will make sense to the reader. You might want to highlight the different parts of your paragraph: topic sentence, support, explanation, and conclusion, as in the example on page 86. How closely did you follow the basic structure of a paragraph? Where did you go beyond the basic structure, and how did that work for you?

Step 4. Now, strengthen the paragraph you wrote by revising and editing so that it is coherent, unified, and free from errors. Keep in mind what you have learned in this chapter about word selection and sentence structure. You might consider trading paragraphs with a partner so that you both can provide feedback using the following as a guide:

- Highlight one thing the writer does well.
- Share something that might be confusing or unclear.
- Provide one suggestion to improve the paragraph. (For example, you might suggest that the writer minimize spelling or grammatical errors, include more sentence variety, use more vivid language, or incorporate more focused ideas.)

REFLECTING ON Academic Vocabulary   **Paragraphs**

Working with a partner or small group, discuss the terms in this section and that you previewed on page 84 and clarify your understanding of each. Then, share what you learned about paragraphs in this section. How does your understanding of paragraph structure strengthen the effectiveness of your writing?

culminating activity

Writing an Academic Paragraph

In this chapter, you have looked at audience and purpose, the power of words, how to build effective sentences, and how to structure a solid paragraph. You have already written about a variety of topics to practice your skills, and now it's time to put all of these skills into action. For this activity, choose one of the following prompts and write a single paragraph with support and explanations.

1. Explain one reason that gaming should or should not be a part of the everyday classroom experience.
2. Argue one reason why homework is, or is not, an effective way to learn.
3. Explain one advantage or disadvantage of paying students for good grades.
4. Explain one important point, either negative or positive, about the relationship between sports and academics.
5. Argue one idea, either positive or negative, about using grades to rank students.

Remember that you can refer back to previous ideas presented in this chapter about strengthening your writing skills. Revisit the pages below if you need help with the following:

- Writing for audience and purpose (pp. 68–71)
- Using specific language and word choice (pp. 71–74)
- Developing a variety of sentences (pp. 74–84)
- Creating strong, coherent paragraphs (pp. 84–89)

Later, you always have the option to expand your ideas into a multi-paragraph essay.

public speaking extension

Writing for Presentation

Throughout this chapter, you have been thinking about and practicing how to communicate your ideas through writing, but another common way of sharing your ideas is orally, through a conversation (which was addressed in Chapter 1) or through a more formal presentation. While the notion of speaking in front of your class may cause you some anxiety, there are some things you can consider and practice to make the experience more comfortable. Much of what you learned in this chapter about writing an effective paragraph transfers directly to writing an effective presentation.

activity — Thinking about Public Speaking

Meet with a partner or small group and share what you like or don't like about giving presentations in class. Is there anything that makes you nervous? What has helped you to deliver an effective presentation in the past?

Content, Delivery, and Visuals

Effective presentations begin with strong writing that underscores the visual performance. When delivering a formal or informal presentation, you will need to focus on two components: content (*What information will I present?*) and delivery (*How will I present that information?*).

Content

The **content** of your presentation, obviously, will vary greatly depending on the topic, but there are some aspects of an effective presentation that will be present regardless of topic. We have included portions of a speech delivered in Boston by then-President Obama a few days after a terrorist attack in 2013 near the finish line of the Boston Marathon, which left three people dead and hundreds injured. Below is a description of each content element of an effective presentation. Notice how Obama uses these elements to gain his audience's attention at the start, connect with them in the middle, and leave the audience with more to think about at the end.

1. **Hook.** Start with some kind of hook to get your audience's attention. This could be a question designed to lead listeners into your topic, a brief story about something that happened to you or someone you know, or a surprising fact or statistic. Notice how in his hook, Obama sets the scene with vivid details and a Biblical reference:

   > Scripture tells us to "run with endurance the race that is set before us." Run with endurance the race that is set before us.
   >
   > On Monday morning, the sun rose over Boston. The sunlight glistened off the Statehouse dome. In the Common and the Public Garden, spring was in bloom. On this Patriot's Day, like so many before, fans jumped onto the T to see the Sox at Fenway. In Hopkinton, runners laced up their shoes and set out on a 26.2-mile test of dedication and grit and the human spirit. And across this city, hundreds of thousands of Bostonians lined the streets — to hand the runners cups of water and to cheer them on. . . .
   >
   > And then, in an instant, the day's beauty was shattered. A celebration became a tragedy.

2. **Main ideas.** Have one main idea that you want your audience to take away from your presentation, which you should explain with just a few details and examples. Any more than a couple of ideas and a few details risks losing your audience. Look at this section from roughly the middle of his speech to see how Obama makes a point about how all Americans feel connected to the city of Boston:

   > Because, after all, it's our beloved city, too. Boston may be your hometown, but we claim it, too. It's one of America's iconic cities. It's one of the world's great cities. And one of the reasons the world knows Boston so well is that Boston opens its heart to the world. . . .
   >
   > I know this because there's a piece of Boston in me. You welcomed me as a young law student across the river; welcomed Michelle, too. . . .
   >
   > Like you, Michelle and I have walked these streets. Like you, we know these neighborhoods. And like you, in this moment of grief, we join you in saying — "Boston, you're my home." For millions of us, what happened on Monday is personal. It's personal.

3. **Clincher.** After you have presented your main ideas and included relevant and vivid details, end your presentation with a clincher that sums up the main points you want your audience to take away. The clincher should give the audience some kind of final thought or action to take, and — usually — returns to the hook with which you began your presentation. Look at the end of the speech when Obama returns to a description of Boston and the idea of a race, though now in a new context:

   > Tomorrow, the sun will rise over Boston. Tomorrow, the sun will rise over this country that we love. This special place. This state of grace.
   >
   > Scripture tells us to "run with endurance the race that is set before us." As we do, may God hold close those who've been taken from us too soon. May He comfort their families. And may He continue to watch over these United States of America.

While writing your presentation, remember that your words will be heard — not read — by your audience. Earlier in this chapter you wrote paragraphs that people could reread if they needed or wanted to. The difference with a presentation is that, unless it's recorded, you have only this one chance to connect with your audience and to communicate your ideas. Keep the following in mind:

- *Language*. Just as with anything you write, you need to ask, "Who is my audience, and how will my words affect them?" If your audience is mostly students your age, you can probably include unexplained references to people or topics they will know. If your audience is made up of older people, you might need to explain things that are obvious to your peers. How do you want your audience to react to your words? With laughter, shock, anger, sympathy? How can your language choices help you achieve your purpose?
- *Clarity*. Try to say things as clearly and succinctly as possible. Usually your audience will not have a transcript or recording of your speech; being concise makes it easier for your listeners to follow along.

activity Planning a Presentation

Return to the paragraph that you wrote for the Culminating Activity earlier in this chapter (p. 89) and imagine that you were to deliver a short (two or three minutes) presentation on that same topic. Using what you have already written, sketch out your hook, one main point you want to make with a couple of details or descriptions, and a clincher. You will not be delivering the presentation yet, but only thinking about the content of the speech. Your original paragraph is a good starting place. Remember, however, that the topic sentence of your paragraph most likely won't work as a hook, though it's probably the main point of your presentation. Also, the last sentence of your original paragraph could make a good clincher, but you might want to adjust your word choice a bit for a live audience. You may want to write your presentation onto notecards to help you organize your thoughts and to have easy access to it during the presentation.

Delivery

Now that you have a draft of your presentation, it's time to start thinking about how you will deliver it to an audience. No matter how much time and effort you put into your presentation or how fantastic the content, if you do not give equal thought to the delivery, your presentation will not be as successful as it could have been. The **delivery** of a speech includes many factors, but here we will focus on the following:

1. Vocal delivery, which includes
   a. *Volume*. Can the audience hear you?
   b. *Articulation*. Can the audience understand the words you are saying? Are you emphasizing particular words or phrases for effect?
   c. *Pace*. Are you avoiding speaking too quickly or too slowly?
2. Nonverbal delivery, which includes
   a. *Eye contact*. Eye contact projects confidence and makes the audience feel connected to what you are saying. If you do not have your speech memorized and need to glance at notes, make sure you are looking up occasionally at the audience.

b. *Gestures and movements.* Avoid actions that could be distracting to your audience, such as rocking back and forth, putting hands in and out of your pockets, or touching your face or hair. In general, you want to remain fairly still during a formal presentation, but you should use gestures and movements that feel natural and that add emphasis to a point you are trying to make.

Practicing a Presentation

Return to the brief sketch of a presentation that you worked on earlier (p. 92), and practice delivering it to a partner, who should provide feedback to you on both your vocal and nonverbal delivery. Be sure to time yourself so that your presentation falls within the time constraints — not too short or too long. Consider asking someone to film you so that you can review your practice presentation on your own afterward.

Visuals

In some instances, you may be asked to include visuals with your presentation. These might include images, artwork, photographs, charts or diagrams, or bullet points of key aspects of your written presentation. Whatever you choose to include, you need to ask yourself this key question: do the visuals enhance or detract from my presentation? Include only visuals that will help you to communicate your points and will avoid distracting or confusing your audience. If, for example, you were to include a really complex chart with lots of statistics, your audience might focus on understanding the visual rather than listening to your words. Be sure, too, that the tone (p. 66) of your visual reflects the tone of your presentation; you don't want your audience to laugh at an image when you are sharing something serious about your topic.

Using Visuals in a Presentation

Create or locate three or four visuals that might go well with the topic of the presentation you have been working on. Show them to a partner and explain how you were planning on using them and at what point. Identify the one or two visuals that would most enhance and not distract from the content and tone of your presentation and consider the best method for sharing them during your presentation: slides, a poster, a handout, and so on.

culminating activity

Delivering a Presentation

Deliver your presentation to the class, a small group, or a partner as directed by your teacher. Be sure to consider all the essential elements of an effective presentation: content (p. 90), delivery (p. 92), and visuals (above).

Using Sources

In school and in your daily life, you are often asked to give your opinion on a topic: which candidate to support in an election, the risks and benefits of drinking caffeine, the effects of making college tuition free, or the habits of good students. You can certainly offer your opinion based on your own feelings and experiences, but hopefully you will also examine what other people have to say about the topic. Will knowing what others have said change your mind, strengthen your position, or add to your knowledge? Probably. Will that knowledge add confidence and authority to your ideas? Definitely. The purpose of using **sources** — the viewpoints and information of others, whether written, spoken, or visually presented — is to expand on your own ideas and move beyond your own knowledge. Investigating what others have to say is part of a discovery process — not only to support a viewpoint you already have but also to test it by exploring other views, adding nuance and complexity to your thinking. Using sources is in many ways a form of listening, as we discussed in the opening chapter. In this chapter, we'll examine how and where to find sources, what makes them good sources, and how to use them responsibly and effectively in your own writing.

Becoming Informed

Write about a time when you changed your opinion — when new information influenced your view of a movie, a book, a TV show, a type of food, or a political issue. It might have been a conversation with a friend, something you read, or an experience you had. Just brainstorm your response in a paragraph or so and include a brief description of what may have contributed to your changed opinion.

Sources as Conversation

Think about the value of sources this way: suppose you're having a discussion with a classmate about the challenges and opportunities of immigration into the United States. On one side of the room, you stand alone, explaining your opinion. On the other side of the room, your classmate stands with a circle of others who include an economics professor from Harvard, someone who emigrated to America ten years ago, and a U.S. senator who has been holding hearings on this topic for the past year. So, who's likely to have the stronger, more persuasive argument — you, with your lone opinion, or your classmate, whose position is backed by the knowledge and experience of a team of experts?

Even if the professor and the senator don't share the same opinion, just adding those perspectives results in a more **informed opinion**. That's the purpose of working with sources: to inform and support your own opinions with relevant and related ideas.

Using sources in your writing is similar to having a conversation. As you encounter the ideas of others who have investigated your topic, you'll find that they might support, counter, or expand your thinking. So, as those ideas inform your thinking, you're starting to respond to them — talking back, even if only in your head — and a conversation emerges.

activity Getting Started with Sources

Step 1. Take a few minutes to write a response to this question: *To what extent do you think that animals should be kept in zoos?*

Step 2. Pair up with a classmate. Using the active listening skills from Chapter 1, share your responses with each other. Be sure to ask each other follow-up questions to get as much detail and as many ideas as possible.

Step 3. Return to your original response that you wrote in Step 1 and add your partner's thoughts to yours, noting where your partner *supports, challenges, or qualifies* your original position on the topic. When we say "qualifies," we mean that your partner mostly agrees with you, but maybe for reasons that differ from or add complexity to your own. You can use sentence starters and fill the first blank with your partner's name and the second with an idea that your partner expressed about the topic. For example:

In contrast, _____ disagrees, suggesting instead that _____.

Additionally, _____ supports this idea, arguing that _____.

Another factor to consider is what _____ raises, recommending that _____.

As you completed the activity above, you began the research process. You investigated the viewpoint of a person with thoughts about or knowledge of the topic. That's one type of source: a discussion with a classmate. A source is any piece of information beyond your expertise or opinion. It can be an interview, a photo, a news story, a research study, a poem, a play, and more.

Let's look at an excerpt from an argument to see how professional writers use sources in their writing. As you read this article about zoos for understanding, annotate the text using the active reading techniques from Chapter 2 (p. 20). Try to determine the main ideas and the key supporting details that back up those ideas.

from Is It Time to Shut Down the Zoos?

Robin McKie

Is there any justification, today, for keeping wild animals in captivity? Are zoos good for the planet's threatened creatures — or are they relics of past cruel attitudes to wildlife?

One argument is that zoos educate visitors, particularly younger ones, about the wonders of the planet's wildlife. But Chris Draper of Born Free, the international charity that campaigns against keeping wild animals in captivity, disagrees. "Today, people get more from a TV nature documentary than they will ever get from seeing animals in zoos. In captivity, an elephant or a giraffe is out of its natural environment and probably in an unnatural social grouping. Television or the internet are much better resources for understanding animals than a zoo."

[Damian] Aspinall [who runs Howletts Wild Animal Park] agrees. "David Attenborough's programmes are far more educational than a day trip to a zoo," he says. And you can see their point. Attenborough's last series, *Seven Worlds, One Planet*, was made up of typically stunning material — dramatic close-ups of gentoo penguins fleeing leopard seals, pumas in pursuit of guanacos, and Barbary macaques in high-level chases after infant kidnappers. It was exhilarating, informative — and surely ideal for getting people hooked on animals.

But Attenborough flatly disagrees and is emphatic that his documentaries cannot compare to seeing the real thing. Only the sight of a creature in the flesh can give us a true understanding of its nature, he says.

"There is no way you can appreciate the quiddity of an elephant except by seeing one at   5 close quarters," he told the Observer. "People ought to be able to see what an animal looks like. And smells like. And sounds like. I think that is quite important. Actually, very important."

Education certainly justifies a well-run zoo's existence, he insists. On the other hand, Attenborough acknowledges that some animals fare better than others in zoos. "Modern aquariums are particularly successful, with their vast ceiling-high tanks in which you can see whole communities of different species of fish living together. They are absolutely fabulous."

By contrast, polar bears, big raptors and large hunting mammals like lions are not suitable for being kept in zoos, says Attenborough. "I certainly agree with Mr. Aspinall in saying you should not have lions in zoos — unless they were becoming endangered in the wild, which, of course is now becoming a real risk."

And the same goes for conservation, he adds. "Breeding programmes for animals that are on the verge of extinction are of incredible importance. If it was not for zoos, there would be no Arabian oryx left in the world, for example."

The Arabian oryx was hunted to extinction in the wild by 1972 but was later reintroduced — originally with animals from San Diego safari park — to Oman. Further reintroductions have since taken place in Saudi Arabia and Israel and it is estimated that there are now more than 1,000 Arabian oryx in the wild. . . .

[Zoo] officials reject the idea that their rewilding successes are limited and point to other examples of successfully returning zoo-bred animals to the wild — for example, the Mauritius kestrel. In 1974 only four of these beautiful raptors were known to exist in the wild. It had become the world's rarest bird thanks to habitat loss, introduction of non-native predators, and widespread use of DDT and other pesticides on the island.

A rescue plan was launched by a number of organisations, including the Durrell wildlife park and London Zoo, in a bid to save the Mauritius kestrel from extinction in the wild. "The invasive crab-eating macaque was a particular problem," says Gary Ward, curator of birds at London Zoo. "It had arrived in Mauritius from Asia and was stealing eggs from kestrel nests. So we designed nesting boxes that were longer than a macaque's arm, so they couldn't reach in to snatch eggs. The birds then had a safe place to bring up their young. . . ."

However, zoo opponents argue that these reintroductions remain infrequent and do not justify the keeping of other, unthreatened wild animals, a point taken up by Sam Threadgill of Freedom for Animals, which has campaigned for the abolition of zoos for several decades.

Together with Born Free, Freedom for Animals has studied zoos in England and Wales and concluded that only a small percentage of their animals are endangered species, and only about 15 percent are threatened.

"It is a simple fact that the vast majority of animals kept in zoos are not endangered or threatened and are there simply to provide public entertainment," he says. ■

So, what did we notice? The writer, Robin McKie, begins framing the debate by asking the central questions about the issue. From there, he examines the issue by quoting experts in the field on both sides of the topic.

Let's start to examine how he uses sources by identifying what they are and why he might have used them.

- After raising the idea that zoos might be educational, he quotes two people who object to that idea, including Chris Draper, who is part of an organization called Born Free that campaigns against keeping wild animals in captivity.
- When someone raises the idea that people can learn just as much from a David Attenborough nature documentary as they could from a zoo, McKie includes a direct rebuttal by Attenborough himself, one of the world's most respected documentarians of the natural world.
- After Attenborough suggests that zoos can play an important role in helping to protect animals in the wild, McKie adds support to this perspective by describing a highly successful rescue plan for the Mauritius kestrel organized by several zoos that saved the bird from extinction.
- Just as he did earlier in the piece, McKie does not let one side of the issue go unchallenged as he cites Sam Threadgill of Freedom for Animals, who

claims that only about 15 percent of the animals currently in zoos are actually threatened.

Through his use of varied sources, McKie enters a conversation about the topic, presenting ideas and information from multiple points of view. Each source adds a new idea, a new dimension to his examination of the debate around zoos. If McKie had relied solely on his own opinions and experiences, his piece would have not been nearly as rich, complex, or challenging to others' perspectives.

Adding a Source to Your Writing

Step 1. Return to the writing you have been doing about whether animals should be kept in zoos. Add a sentence or two to your response that incorporates an idea you learned from the piece by McKie. You may use the sentence starters below if you find them helpful. The first blank is for the name of someone cited in the article or McKie himself and the second blank is for a statement that either supports, challenges, or qualifies your own ideas about zoos. Do not worry too much about how to punctuate the quotations at this point. We'll get to that later.

In contrast, _____ disagrees, suggesting instead that _____.

Additionally, _____ supports this idea, arguing that _____.

Another factor to consider is what _____ raises, recommending that _____.

Step 2. One of the important things to keep in mind when using sources is that you want to make sure that the sources serve your argument and your perspective. After the sentence or two that you wrote in Step 1, add one or more sentences that show how what you have included from the McKie piece helps you to make your point about zoos. You can use sentence starters like the following if you find them useful:

This [point, idea, example] proves that _____.

This [point, idea, example] illustrates why _____.

What _____ fails to recognize is that _____.

Locating and Evaluating Sources

The quality of the sources you use is a critical factor in successfully presenting your ideas. You want to make sure that every source you read and quote has **credibility**. What does *credible* mean? The word comes from the Latin meaning "to believe," so a credible source is one that your audience can reasonably be expected to believe.

In this section, you will encounter the following terms as you think about how to locate and evaluate sources. Working individually or with a partner or small group, consider what you already know about the meaning of each term.

1. Credibility
2. Currency
3. Relevance
4. Authority

5. Accuracy
6. Bias
7. Objectivity

Think about the sources that McKie uses in his piece about zoos. Are they credible? He cites David Attenborough; if you're unfamiliar with that name, a little research will tell you that Attenborough is a world-famous documentarian who is widely respected in his field. McKie also cites people whom he identifies as the directors of zoos and nonprofit organizations created to promote animal welfare. Did you believe these sources when you read them? Probably so, because McKie clearly identifies their expertise. They are authoritative and knowledgeable, and therefore, likely credible.

As you investigate almost any topic, you'll find that there is an almost overwhelming amount of information in the world. One thing to keep in mind as you conduct your research is that information and ideas often come from a few different types of sources, which we've listed below in order of credibility. Approach every source skeptically, even those we identify below as "extremely credible," but approach those that would appear at the end of this list with extreme caution — or not at all.

Type of Source	Description	Credibility Level
Scholarly and scientific research	These sources are written by experts in the field, following rigorous research standards. They undergo peer review, which means they are reviewed and approved by other experts in the field.	Extremely credible
Major magazines, newspapers, websites, and books	These sources have large national audiences and often represent broad cultural and political perspectives. Pieces are often written by experts or journalists who are highly informed on the topic. Ideally, the work is thoroughly researched according to rigorous journalistic standards. The work is often reviewed and approved by experts.	Highly credible
Minor magazines, newspapers, websites, and books	Regional, local, and special interest publications sometimes have very high standards, but sometimes they sacrifice objectivity in order to appeal to a specific viewpoint. With this type of source, be sure to read critically and assess credibility.	Sometimes credible

Type of Source	Description	Credibility Level
Social media, sites with user-created content, and self-published books	With these sources, there is minimal editorial oversight of the content. Though content on these platforms may be created by people qualified to comment on certain subjects, it is just as likely to be the creation of people with no expertise or with an agenda to deliberately misinform. These sources can be the outlet for personal opinions not necessarily supported by research or facts.	Questionable
Advertising, political propaganda, click-bait, lobbying, and fake news	Beware of sources that have a financial or political interest in the topic, such as those advocating for a business or political cause. Click-bait sites are willing to say anything if it drives profitable traffic. Fake news is created deliberately to mislead readers.	Poor

The information in the above table is intended to help you think about the credibility of the sources you find, but how do you go about finding them in the first place? Where should you be looking for credible sources? While your first inclination would probably be to just Google your topic, there are some other steps to consider first and some ways to refine your search.

1. **Consult with librarians.** Librarians at your school and local library have specialized training and expertise in locating credible sources in a variety of formats, including print books on the shelves that might be relevant to your topic. Talk to them about your topic and ask them to point you in the direction of credible sources.
2. **Use curated databases.** Your school and local library can provide access to databases of articles, journals, and other resources that have already been screened and evaluated for credibility. These databases have names like EBSCO, Scopus, ERIC, and JSTOR, and each has a specific focus. While these may not seem as easy to use as Google, the benefits of searching a pool of reliable sources make them worthwhile, and a librarian can help you get started.
3. **Refine your Google searches.** We are accustomed to putting a word or phrase into Google and clicking "search," but there is more we can do to make our searches yield relevant and credible results that could be effective sources. For instance:
   a. Use the "Tools" function to adjust the date range of your results. You can filter the results to those within the past day, month, year, and so on. Using that same function, you can limit your results to "verbatim," which means that only results containing your exact search terms will appear.
   b. Use "Google Scholar" or "Google Books" for your search, which will limit your results mainly to peer-reviewed journals or books that have been edited and professionally published. Note that sometimes you will not be able to get access to the full text through this search, but you can likely access it through one of your school's or public libraries' databases.

c. Use the "Advanced Search" function to narrow your results by limiting the domains included to ".edu," which refers only to educational institutions' publications, or ".gov," which refers only to government publications. Educational and government sources are likely to be credible, though you will still need to carefully evaluate them.

d. Place quotation marks around specific words or phrases that you want results to include. Or place a minus sign in front of words or phrases that, if present in a source, will keep that source from appearing among your results.

e. While Google's algorithm often puts the most relevant result first, placement is no guarantee of a source's credibility. Note that some of the top results may be paid sponsored ads, which certainly should cause you to question their credibility.

activity — Locating Sources

Step 1. Consult with a librarian, refer to a curated database, or conduct a refined Google search as described above to locate a few more sources of the following types on the benefits or drawbacks of having animals in zoos:

- A research study with data and statistics
- A major magazine or newspaper article, or book
- A source that appears to lack credibility (as described in the last two rows of the table on p. 101)

Step 2. With a partner, discuss the credibility of each of the sources you both found. After just a brief glance through each source, do you believe the information included? Why or why not?

We've talked a bit about some types of sources that may or may not be credible. And you've located a few that you think have varying levels of credibility. Unfortunately, sometimes the sources that seem credible to one person might not seem credible to another. In our era of "fake news" and political polarization, many of us live in information bubbles. It might be tempting to say that nothing is credible, that the government or the media cannot be trusted, or that only information aligning with our own viewpoints can be credible. To protect ourselves and others from confusing or damaging misinformation, however, we must learn to be discerning readers who consume, share, and act on only information that we ascertain is credible.

So, once you have determined that a source seems to be a credible one, examining a few other factors will help you determine whether those potential sources will be effective and appropriate resources for your own writing. When preparing to use sources, much depends on your audience and purpose, but here are five general factors to consider as you further evaluate a potential source to determine whether you should use it in your writing:

- **Relevance.** What will this source add to your opinion about the issue? How closely related is it to the issue you're investigating? Does it include clear and compelling evidence that is specifically about your topic?

- **Currency.** This refers to when the source was written or published. If your topic is historical, a mix of older and newer sources may be appropriate. A discussion that deals with current events or relies on data or technology, however, likely demands recent sources. If, for instance, you're writing about social media, an article from 2000 may be outdated.

- **Authority.** Who wrote it? Who published it? What gives them authority to speak on the subject? Is the author an expert — by education or experience? If the source is from a website, what can you learn from the "About Us" page? Is there a physical address? Is there an editorial staff? If authors and editors are named, what information can help you judge their expertise on an issue? In general, try to think of an "authority" as someone who is deeply knowledgeable about the issue based on experience or education or both.

- **Accuracy.** Do you see incorrect facts, obvious grammar or spelling errors, or other signs that a source's writing and information have not been carefully checked for correctness and accuracy? If the source refers or links to outside information, does that information seem relevant and reliable? As a reader, you should always be willing to fact-check for yourself by Googling names, places, or facts mentioned in the source.

- **Bias.** Though last on this list, bias can be the most important factor and the hardest to detect. A good source should display some degree of **objectivity**, meaning that the source discusses all sides of an issue and attempts to present them fairly, free of bias. An author with ties to a specific political viewpoint or a corporate interest, for example, might present only information that supports that view or interest. If the research is sponsored by a business or special interest group, be on the lookout for bias. Does the publisher or magazine in which the article appears cater to a specific group or ideology? Is the language of the piece excessively emotional, inflammatory, or otherwise unbalanced? Bias is inevitable; everyone is biased in one way or another. The point here is that the source's biases should not be so obvious and one-sided that other viewpoints are completely absent.

You might not be able to figure out all of these factors for every source. Being on the alert for them, however, will help you determine whether potential sources will provide credible, effective, and appropriate material for you to add to your own writing.

To make this practice more concrete, imagine that you are asked to write an essay about whether or not zoos should continue to exist and you are trying to decide whether you should use the McKie piece you read earlier as a source in your essay. Let's take a closer look at it by applying some of the elements just discussed to determine its credibility and appropriateness for your essay.

Relevance. Because your assignment is to write about whether animals should be kept in zoos, McKie's article is relevant. Now, if you were exploring animal cruelty, this piece wouldn't necessarily be relevant because McKie's discussion is limited to zoos.

Currency. This article was written in 2020, so it's likely not the most recent piece you could find on the topic. The source could still be appropriate for your essay, however. The information contained isn't necessarily time-sensitive and is probably still relevant to the central issues. To double-check, you might want to see if the author has updated his article, or if the statistic he cites about endangered animals has changed.

Authority. This piece was originally published on *The Guardian.com*. After a quick Google search, we would learn that this website includes the content of two long-standing British newspapers, the *Guardian* and the *Observer*, two of the largest-selling and oldest papers in England. The website receives millions of unique visitors every month and publishes stories on politics, the environment, business, and technology. According to the website in 2021, McKie is the environmental and science editor for the *Observer*, and he is the author of over one hundred published articles on topics such as climate change, the pandemic and vaccines, and space exploration. Based on the background knowledge we have about the website and especially the clear expertise on science issues that McKie has demonstrated in his other writing, we probably can ascribe a high level of authority to this source. If our investigation had revealed that McKie is primarily a sports writer, he might still have worthwhile insights, but we wouldn't be ready to declare him to be an authority on this topic of animals and zoos.

Accuracy. There are no obvious spelling or grammatical errors in the piece that might make us question its accuracy. If we were to do a quick Google search on some of the people mentioned in the article, like Damian Aspinall, we would learn that he is, in fact, a naturalist dedicated to returning animals to their natural habitats. So, this piece seems to be accurate.

Bias. As noted above, this is often the most important yet most difficult aspect to evaluate. From the research on authority above, we learned that McKie is a science writer and doesn't appear to be directly affiliated either with a zoo or an advocacy group that supports freeing animals from zoos. Additionally, we'd want to look closely at McKie's word choice and the evidence he includes or excludes from his piece. It's difficult to identify any particular bias on McKie's part because he dutifully presents both sides of the issue by citing well-known and respected people who offer reasonable evidence to support their positions. He doesn't use extreme language to present a particular tone in favor of or opposed to zoos. Overall, McKie doesn't reveal any particular bias that would cause us to question his credibility.

Evaluating Sources

activity

Step 1. Return to one of the sources you located in the activity on page 102. Evaluate the source in the same way that was modeled for the McKie piece above by examining all five aspects. Overall, does the source that you located seem like it would be a credible, effective, and appropriate piece to use in your own writing on zoos? Why or why not?

Step 2. Read the following editorial posted in 2017 on the PETA.org website. Afterward, evaluate the source by considering the five aspects described above. Be sure to conduct your own research about the website and the organization, and fact-check the article as much as possible. Then, with a partner or small group, discuss whether or not you would use it in an essay you might write about zoos. Why or why not?

Is There Such a Thing as a Reputable Roadside Zoo? What You Need to Know

PETA.org

Animals held captive in roadside zoos are denied their fundamental right to freedom and everything else that makes their lives meaningful. Removing them from established social groups and forcing them to adjust repeatedly to new routines, different caretakers, and unfamiliar cagemates is disruptive and traumatic for them. Many people still hold misconceptions about zoos, but after you read this, we're sure that you'll change your mind. Here are our top three reasons never to visit a roadside zoo or any other place that exhibits wild animals in barren enclosures:

1. **They breed animals because babies sell tickets.**

   When roadside zoos breed animals, the babies are often torn from their mothers shortly after birth to be used in encounters and photo ops with the public, and roadside zoos charge visitors to interact or take photos with them. One calculation estimates that a single tiger cub could yield $65,000 of profit over one summer season. The mothers are repeatedly impregnated, and the cubs — who can be used for these encounters only for a short time — are typically relegated to tiny cages for the rest of their lives or shipped off to other roadside zoos or private owners to languish in awful conditions. This breeding also contributes to the overpopulation of many species in captivity, especially tigers.

2. **Captivity can cause distress.**

   Many animals in captivity suffer from what *The New York Times* described as "severe psychic suffering" and may even be given Prozac or other antidepressants and mood stabilizers. In response to their small enclosures, loneliness, and frustration, captive animals often exhibit stereotypic behavior, such as pacing, circling, and other repetitive actions.

(continued)

3. **They maintain very low standards of animal welfare.**

The federal regulations for procuring an "animal exhibition" license are pathetically low. Enclosures need to be barely large enough for an animal to stand up and turn around inside them. It's been estimated that inspectors who are hired to enforce the federal Animal Welfare Act visit these facilities only about once a year. Roadside zoos are often cited for violations, including failing to provide animals with adequate veterinary care, dirty and unsanitary water receptacles, and other poor or dangerous living conditions. ■

REFLECTING ON Academic Vocabulary   **Locating and Evaluating Sources**

Working with a partner or small group, discuss the terms in this section and that you previewed on page 100 and clarify your understanding of each. Then, share what you learned about locating and evaluating sources. What did you find helpful, relevant, unnecessary, redundant, and so on?

Understanding and Keeping Track of Sources

Once you've identified some credible sources, what do you do next? Whether you have searched for and identified your own sources or you're working with sources that have been provided for you, this step-by-step process will help you understand each source's information and pull out key ideas that you can use in your own writing.

1. **Read critically, but objectively.** Particularly on your first time through, read as objectively as possible. That means that while you read critically and carefully, you reserve judgment on the opinions being expressed. Your focus at this point is to understand the perspective of the writer, researcher, or artist.

2. **Note phrases or sections that seem especially important or are stated with vivid language.** You will not be able to quote or refer to everything that strikes you, but your annotation skills should help you identify material for effective quotations and the nuggets of information or evidence that define the perspective the source represents. Review the suggestions for annotation in Chapter 2 on page 20.

3. **Keep track of information to document the source.** As you work with the source, take note of the following:
   • Title of the work
   • Place where it appeared (a book, a periodical, a website)
   • Name(s) of author(s)
   • Date of publication
   • Page number on which it is found, if a print text

Don't worry at this stage about putting this information into a specific format; just keep track on a document, with notecards, or by any process that works for you. Not having to hunt this information down later will save you time and effort.

4. **Summarize the source.** Your final step is to figure out what the key ideas are and to restate them in your own words. An excerpt from an article is likely to contain only one major point, but a longer piece may include several. (See Chapter 2, p. 31 for more on summary.)

You've probably noticed that these steps all encourage you to pick and choose — not to annotate in general terms or to highlight huge chunks of text but rather to *be selective*. That's an essential step to making sure you use sources effectively without letting them overwhelm you or your writing. You're not writing a report of one source after another; you're using sources to develop your own viewpoint.

Let's see how these steps work when applied to a sample source. We'll take notes on key points and highlight sections that might be particularly useful as direct quotations later.

Why Zoos Are Good

Dr. Dave Hone

Guardian.com

I am a lifelong fan of good zoos (note the adjective) and have visited dozens of zoos, safari parks and aquaria around the world. I also spent a number of years working as a volunteer keeper at two zoos in the U.K. and my own interests now span to the history of zoological collections and their design, architecture and research so it is probably fair to say <u>I'm firmly in the pro-zoo camp.</u>

The author clearly identifies his position in support of zoos.

However, I am perfectly willing to recognise that there are bad zoos and bad individual exhibits. Not all animals are kept perfectly, much as I wish it were otherwise, and even in the best examples, <u>there is still room for improvement.</u> But just as the fact that some police are corrupt does not mean we should not have people to enforce the law, although bad zoos or exhibits persist does not mean they are not worthwhile institutes. It merely means we need to pay more attention to the bad and improve them or close them. In either case, zoos (at least in the U.K. and most of the western world) are generally a poor target for criticism in terms of animal welfare — they have to keep the public onside or go bust and they have to stand up to rigorous inspections or be closed down. While a bad collection should

Acknowledges problems with zoos.

not be ignored, if you are worried about the care and treatment of animals in captivity I can point to a great many farms, breeders, dealers and private owners who are in far greater need of inspection, improvement or both.

Directly addresses those who are concerned about welfare of animals in captivity.

If you are against animals in captivity full stop then there is perhaps little scope for discussion, but even so I'd maintain that some of the following arguments (not least the threat of extinction) can outweigh arguments against captivity. Moreover, I don't think anyone would consider putting down a 10000 km long fence around the Masai Mara to really be captivity, even if it restricts the movement of animals across that barrier. But at what point does that become captivity? A 10000 m fence? 1000 m fence? What if veterinary care is provided or extra food as in many reserves or as part of conservation projects. I'm not pretending that an animal in a zoo is not in captivity, but clearly there is a continuum from zoos and wildlife parks, to game reserves, national parks and protected areas. Degree of care and degree of enclosure make the idea of "captivity" fluid and not absolute.

Key point about how to define "captivity."

What I would state with absolute confidence is that for many species (but no, not all) it is perfectly possible to keep them in a zoo or wildlife park and for them to have a quality of life as high or higher than in the wild. Their movement might be restricted (but not necessarily by that much) but they will not suffer from the threat or stress of predators (and nor will they be killed in a grisly manner or eaten alive) or the irritation and pain of parasites, injuries and illnesses will be treated, they won't suffer or die of drought or starvation and indeed will get a varied and high-quality diet with all the supplements required. They can be spared bullying or social ostracism or even infanticide by others of their kind, or a lack of a suitable home or environment in which to live. A lot of very nasty things happen to truly "wild" animals that simply don't happen in good zoos and to cast a life that is "free" as one that is "good" is, I think, an error.

Could be a good quotation to show how animals can benefit from zoos.

So a good zoo will provide great care and protection to animals in their care. These are good things for the individuals concerned, but what do zoos actually bring to the table for the visitors and the wider world?

Education. Many children and adults, especially those in cities will never see a wild animal beyond a fox or pigeon, let alone a lion or giraffe. Sure television documentaries get ever more detailed and impressive, and lots of natural history specimens are on display in museums, but that really does pale next to seeing a living creature in the flesh, hearing it, smelling it, watching what it does and having the time to absorb details. <u>That alone will bring a greater understanding and perspective to many and hopefully give them a greater appreciation for wildlife, conservation efforts and how they can contribute.</u> All of that comes before the actual direct education that can take place through signs, talks and the like that can directly communicate information about the animals they are seeing and their place in the world. This was an area where zoos were previously poor and are now increasingly sophisticated in their communication and outreach work. Many zoos also work directly to educate conservation workers in foreign countries or send keepers abroad to contribute their knowledge and skills to zoos and preserves helping to improve conditions and reintroductions all over the world. ■

Probably the most important point he makes about how educating people at zoos will benefit the animals in the long run.

After reading and annotating the text, it's important to write a brief summary of the text, so that later, when you begin using the source in your own writing, you will have an easy way to keep track of the different perspectives you will encounter about the topic. A summary of this text might look like this:

> The author, while acknowledging that some zoos do provide poor care for their animals, believes that a well-run zoo is beneficial for animals and their visitors. The animals often have advantages of food and medical care that their counterparts in the wild do not have, and people who visit zoos learn a lot about animals that make them more willing to engage in conservation activities in the future.

In addition to helping identify the key points for the summary, the annotations above also identify several passages that could be used as evidence to support a position about the importance of zoos.

Analyzing Sources

Choose one of the most credible sources that you located for the activity on page 102. Read or reread the source carefully, annotating key points and highlighting sections that seem promising as direct quotations. Then, summarize the source in three to five sentences. Be sure to include the author, title, and other publication information. If you need to review how to write a summary, see Chapter 2, page 31.

Throughout this chapter, we've been looking closely at sources and evaluating their credibility, but we can't lose sight of the fact that we use sources in our writing to better help us express our ideas and strengthen our arguments about a topic.

McKie didn't just string together a lot of different information about zoos and animals from other sources; he carefully put sources together to communicate his perspective on the complexity of the issue. Now that you have worked with a few sources on the issue of whether animals should be in zoos, you too are prepared to share your informed opinion.

 Writing an Informed Opinion

Step 1. Write a response explaining to what extent you believe that animals should or should not be displayed in zoos. Refer to at least two of the sources you encountered while working through this chapter, including one of the most credible ones that you located. Do not worry at this point about how you structure your response or format any references to sources. We'll cover that in the next section.

Step 2. Look back at your very first writing on this topic at the beginning of the chapter (p. 96). How have your ideas changed, expanded, or deepened as a result of working with sources? To what extent is what you wrote in Step 1 more of an "informed opinion" on the topic than your initial writing?

Integrating Sources in Your Own Writing

In the first part of this chapter, we looked at why writers use sources to support their ideas. Now we'll practice the technical side of how writers integrate those sources into their writing. These are some nuts-and-bolts skills that you will use regularly this year and throughout your academic career.

PREVIEWING Academic Vocabulary   Integrating Sources in Your Own Writing

In this section, you will encounter the following terms as you think about how to integrate sources into your own writing. Working individually or with a partner or small group, consider what you already know or think about the meaning of each term.

1. Integrate
2. Signal words
3. Ellipses

4. Brackets
5. Paraphrase
6. Citing sources

From this point on, we'll be assuming that the sources that you will be working with are considered to be "credible," but you should always keep those aspects that define credibility in mind (pp. 100–101) every time you work with sources.

While you absolutely want to include quotations from others to support your ideas, you need to use them thoughtfully and skillfully. Too many quotations can make your writing feel disjointed and clunky — and they can drown out your voice. Quotations should not make up more than 15 percent of a paragraph or essay, as a rule of thumb. Remember, the argument is yours. The sources are there to help you develop your ideas, even when they run counter to your views.

One way to limit your use of quotations is to make sure that whatever you quote serves a clear purpose. For example, you should use quotations in these two main instances:

- When an author is a highly respected authority whose opinion is particularly noteworthy
- When the words themselves are so convincing or vivid that using your own words would not have as strong an impact

We're going to switch topics away from zoos and ask you to read a piece about "grit," a characteristic that psychologist Angela Duckworth claims is the most important element for success in school, on the job, and in life in general. In her popular TedTalk, Duckworth defined "grit" like this:

> Grit is passion and perseverance for very long-term goals. Grit is having stamina. Grit is sticking with your future, day in, day out, not just for the week, not just for the month, but for years, and working really hard to make that future a reality. Grit is living life like it's a marathon, not a sprint.

As we walk through the technical side of using sources in this section, we'll ask you to respond to Duckworth's ideas about grit, adding more sources to your own ideas as you go. So to get you started, here is an excerpt from Duckworth's 2016 book *Grit: The Power of Passion and Perseverance*. Just as you did earlier in this chapter (pp. 106–107), be sure to read the section carefully and track the important information you will need to use this source in your own writing.

from Grit: The Power of Passion and Perseverance

Angela Duckworth

My students were twelve and thirteen years old. Most lived in the housing projects clustered between Avenues A and D [in New York City]. This was before the neighborhood sprouted hip cafes on every corner. The fall I started teaching there, our school was picked for the set of a movie about a rough-and-tumble school in a distressed urban neighborhood. My job was to help my students learn seventh-grade math: fractions and decimals and the rudimentary building blocks of algebra and geometry.

Even that first week, it was obvious that some of my students picked up mathematical concepts more easily than their classmates. Teaching the most talented students in the class was a joy. They were, quite literally, "quick studies." Without much prompting, they saw the underlying pattern in a series of math problems that less able students struggled to grasp. They'd watch me do a problem once on the board and say, "I get it!" and then work out the next one correctly on their own.

And yet, at the end of the first marking period, I was surprised to find that some of these very able students weren't doing as well as I'd expected. Some did very well, of course. But more than a few of my most talented students were earning lackluster grades or worse. In contrast, several of the students who initially struggled were faring better than I'd expected. These "overachievers" would reliably come to class every day with everything they needed. Instead of playing around and looking out the window, they took notes and asked questions. When they didn't get something the first time around, they tried again and again, sometimes coming for extra help during their lunch period or during afternoon electives. Their hard work showed in their grades.

Apparently, aptitude did *not* guarantee achievement. Talent for math was different from excelling in math class. This came as a surprise. After all, conventional wisdom says that math is a subject in which the more talented students are expected to excel, leaving classmates who are simply "not math people" behind.

To be honest, I began the school year with that very assumption. It seemed a sure bet 5 that those for whom things came easily would continue to outpace their classmates. In fact, I expected that the achievement gap separating the naturals from the rest of the class would only widen over time.

I'd been distracted by talent.

Gradually, I began to ask myself hard questions. When I taught a lesson and the concept failed to gel, could it be that the struggling student needed to struggle just a bit longer? Could it be that I needed to find a different way to explain what I was trying to get across? Before jumping to the conclusion that talent was destiny, should I be considering the importance of effort? And, as a teacher, wasn't it my responsibility to figure out how to sustain effort — both the students' and my own — just a bit longer?

At the same time, I began to reflect on how smart even my weakest students sounded when they talked about things that genuinely interested them. These were conversations I found almost impossible to follow: discourses on basketball statistics, the lyrics to songs they really liked, and complicated plotlines about who was no longer speaking to whom and why. When I got to know my students better, I discovered that all of them had mastered any number of complicated ideas in their very complicated daily lives. Honestly, was getting *x* all by itself in an algebraic equation all that much harder?

My students weren't equally talented. Still, when it came to learning seventh-grade math, could it be that if they and I mustered sufficient effort over time, they'd get to where they needed? Surely, I thought, they were all talented *enough*. ■

Providing Context

Once you have decided to use a source in your own writing, one of the most important things you can do is to provide context: Whose words are you quoting? What is the quotation from? What's the overall point? Simply plopping in big chunks of quoted material is not an effective approach. It's just cut-and-paste, and it might be confusing to your reader who may not have read the original source. It's up to you as the writer to provide context and explanation for every quotation. Remember from Chapter 3 that every piece of evidence must be introduced and then followed by explanation. So, when we say you need to **integrate** a quotation, we mean weaving a quotation into your writing, which really comes down to putting it into context. Let's look at a response that uses a quotation without providing any context:

> Hard work is more important than talent. "Aptitude did *not* guarantee achievement." So, working hard and paying attention are more important factors.

There are a couple of problems here. First, without more context, it won't be clear to the reader who is being quoted. It's also unclear what the situation is. Assuming Duckworth said this, why did she come to this realization? By explaining who made this statement and in what context, you can use the quotation honestly and effectively. For example:

> In her book *Grit: The Power of Passion and Perseverance*, psychologist Angela Duckworth, a teacher in the low-income housing projects of New York City, explains her belief that "aptitude did *not* guarantee achievement" for students.

Here we have identified the speaker, the book, and some context for the quotation. This makes the meaning of the quotation clear. The speaker and book don't need to be introduced to this degree every time, but it is always important to provide context of some sort. When you're directly quoting a source, never assume that your reader understands the quotation as well as you do.

Integrating Full-Sentence Quotations

If the quotation you would like to use is a complete sentence, then you need to build your sentence around it. Let's look at two ways to integrate a sentence quotation so that you give your readers adequate context to understand it and make your writing flow.

Phrase + Signal Word + Comma

Using this technique to integrate a full-sentence quotation from Duckworth's *Grit*, we might write something like this:

> Drawing upon her experience teaching in New York City schools, psychologist Angela Duckworth contends, "Talent for math was different from excelling in math class."

The word *contends* is called a **signal word**, because it signals that a quotation is about to begin.

Common Signal Words		
admits	concedes	observes
advises	concludes	recommends
argues	contends	reminds
claims	denies	reports
clarifies	emphasizes	suggests

Introducing the quotation with a phrase that gives context and connecting to the quotation with a signal word and a comma is the most common way to integrate a full-sentence quotation into your sentence. Here's another example:

PHRASE   SIGNAL WORD   COMMA

As she reflects on her time in the classroom, Duckworth admits,

QUOTATION

"My most talented students were earning lackluster grades or worse."

Full Sentence + Colon

While the signal word and comma might be the most common way to include a full-sentence quotation in your writing, the colon is the simplest. To use this method, simply introduce the context with your own sentence and then point to the quotation with a colon, like this:

SENTENCE GIVING CONTEXT

Duckworth explains that she started to question the role of aptitude in success

COLON

when she stopped to consider her students' lives outside of her classroom: "I

QUOTATION

began to reflect on how smart even my weakest students sounded when they

talked about things that genuinely interested them."

This is a perfectly acceptable way of using a quotation, but you probably noticed that it doesn't flow quite as well as the previous method. The colon is a hard stop in the sentence, and there is no transition between the writer's voice and the quotation. You should use this method sparingly.

Integrating Word or Phrase Quotations

Sometimes when integrating sources you will want to use a complete sentence from your source (as in the examples above), but sometimes a few words or a phrase is all you need. In situations like this, the most effective strategy is to work them right into the structure of your own sentence. This puts your voice in control, and it shows that you understand the source well enough to integrate it into your own language.

> Duckworth's experience in the classroom began to challenge some of her ideas about who does well and why, such as the assumption that only "the more talented students are expected to excel" in math.

Note that when you embed word or phrase quotations into your own sentence, you do not need to introduce them with a comma. The punctuation follows the grammar of your sentence. The quoted material is enclosed within quotation marks but not otherwise marked off.

Using Quotations in Your Own Writing

Practice integrating some quotations from Duckworth's article into sentences of your own using some of the approaches described above.

1. Write a sentence about the importance of being interested in a subject in order to learn about it. Your sentence should introduce a full-sentence quotation from Duckworth.

2. Write a sentence about an experience you had in school that is similar to Duckworth's descriptions of her students. Integrate just a few words or phrases (not a full sentence) from Duckworth's article within your own sentence.

Meet with a partner to review each other's sentences to be sure that you each used signal words and proper punctuation.

Writer's Corner   **Using Ellipses and Brackets**

Sometimes the quotation you want to use doesn't quite fit, either because of its length or because the verb tenses or other grammatical features of the sentence don't match your own. Ellipses and brackets give you a way to make a quotation work within your writing, while signaling to your readers that you are slightly altering the original text.

Ellipses

Ellipses are the series of spaced dots that signal something is missing from a quotation. A three-dot ellipsis is used when the missing part comes from within a sentence, while a four-dot ellipsis signals that you've taken parts from different sentences:

> Duckworth noticed some behaviors in her students, which she began to think of as *grit*: "Instead of playing around and looking out the window, they took notes and asked questions. . . . Their hard work showed in their grades."

Brackets

Brackets are most often used to change a pronoun or to change the verb tense. They signal that the word in brackets has been changed and is not part of the original quotation. For instance, if we wanted to use this quotation, which uses the first-person pronoun, we could alter it to fit our sentence:

ORIGINAL QUOTATION

"And yet, at the end of the first marking period, I was surprised to find that some of these very able students weren't doing as well as I'd expected."

USING BRACKETS TO CHANGE THE PRONOUN

Like many of us might, Duckworth assumed that the most talented students would excel, but "at the end of the first marking period, [she] was surprised to find that some of these very able students weren't doing as well as [she'd] expected."

Paraphrasing Sources

Each of the examples above included direct quotations from Angela Duckworth. Because the quoted material matches the original source word-for-word, it had to be within quotation marks. But this is not the only way to integrate sources into your own writing. You can also paraphrase someone else's ideas. While a summary (Ch. 2, p. 31) is a brief restatement of key points from a text, **paraphrase** is a restatement of a single point, piece of information, or idea in your own words, using your own original phrases and sentence structure. Unlike a summary, which is always shorter than the original text, a paraphrased passage often ends up being roughly the same length as the point in the original. As with direct quotations, you must still identify the author of the source and you can use signal words to introduce the idea. Paraphrasing rather than quoting will help keep the emphasis on your own voice and will create more sentence variety in your writing. For example, here is a direct quotation from Duckworth and an example of how to include it as a paraphrase:

Original

"These 'overachievers' would reliably come to class every day with everything they needed. Instead of playing around and looking out the window, they took notes and asked questions."

Possible paraphrase

Not all students are alike. Duckworth learned that some high-achieving students had great attendance, good study skills, and always remained focused (17).

Notice that we included a page number from the original source, even though we are not integrating a direct quotation. With a paraphrase, even if the writing is your own, the idea or information is someone else's, so you need to give credit to the source. The details of citing sources, whether you are quoting, summarizing, or paraphrasing are covered in the next section.

Citing Sources

How to cite a source varies depending on the type of writing you are doing. In English classes, the style is defined by the Modern Language Association (MLA). We describe this style in detail at the end of the book in the Guide to MLA Documentation Style.

While the guidelines for citing sources might seem very technical, the point is just to show where the source material came from. Doing so shows that your position is well informed and allows readers to consult the original sources if they need to. In general, you'll need the author name, title of the work, and page number of the material you're citing. There are three main ways of providing this information:

1. Provide the page number, title, and author information in your sentence.

On page 17 of *Grit: The Power of Passion and Perseverance*, author Angela Duckworth asserts that her students "had mastered any number of complicated ideas in their very complicated daily lives."

4 Using Sources to Provide Support

2. Provide the author and title information in your sentence and the page number in parentheses before the period.

In *Grit: The Power of Passion and Perseverance*, Angela Duckworth asserts that her students "had mastered any number of complicated ideas in their very complicated daily lives" (17).

3. Provide the title in a list of works cited, and use the author name and page reference to direct readers there.

Observing how certain behaviors were linked to success in her classroom, psychologist Angela Duckworth asserts that her students "had mastered any number of complicated ideas in their very complicated daily lives" (17).

Using Sources in Your Own Writing

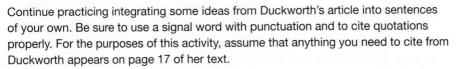

Continue practicing integrating some ideas from Duckworth's article into sentences of your own. Be sure to use a signal word with punctuation and to cite quotations properly. For the purposes of this activity, assume that anything you need to cite from Duckworth appears on page 17 of her text.

1. Write a sentence about a change you would propose at your school and support it with a direct quotation from the Duckworth piece.

2. Now, rewrite that same sentence, but this time paraphrase the same Duckworth passage. Remember to use your own words and sentence structure when paraphrasing Duckworth's ideas.

Meet with a partner to review each other's sentences to check for signal words, proper citations, and effective paraphrase.

REFLECTING ON Academic Vocabulary **Integrating Sources in Your Own Writing**

Working with a partner or small group, discuss the terms in this section and that you previewed on page 110 and clarify your understanding of each. Then, share what you learned about incorporating sources into your own writing in this section. What did you find helpful, relevant, unnecessary, redundant, and so on? What do you think you still need to work on to smoothly incorporate sources into your own writing?

Using Sources to Provide Support and Address Counterarguments

Throughout this chapter, you have been thinking about how to use sources to become better informed about a topic, and you've been able to practice some of the technical aspects of using sources in your own writing by using proper punctuation and citations.

Now it's time to apply these skills as you explore more deeply two main methods of using outside sources in your own writing:

1. To support your own opinion
2. To consider a viewpoint different from yours

Supporting Your Opinion

Writers often use sources to clarify or add weight to their own views. Useful sources might be written by experts or contain statistical data that back up writers' ideas. Suppose a writer agrees with Angela Duckworth and believes that grit is the most important indicator of academic success. That writer can build a stronger argument by incorporating Duckworth's views for support. Look at this example:

> School is about learning, but learning isn't necessarily what students are graded on. Students are graded on doing the work—getting things done despite obstacles and setbacks. So it's no surprise that those who have what Angela Duckworth calls "grit" are more likely to get higher marks. School is hard work and takes determination. Having what Duckworth defines as "passion and perseverance for very long-term goals" is exactly what it takes to get through twelve or more years of hard work (17).

The key point here is that the writer — not the source — is in charge of this paragraph. The writer has brought in Duckworth's text to back up the writer's own point that school success is about more than just learning. Through both the reference to Duckworth and a direct quotation, this source becomes support from an expert with authority in the field.

Considering Other Viewpoints

If your goal is to learn as much as possible about a topic, you can't ignore views counter to your own — the **counterarguments**. Robin McKie read and considered many different viewpoints regarding zoos before writing his article, and Duckworth likely did a lot of research on exactly what motivates students to succeed. So, a second way to use a source in your own writing is not just to support your own view, but to raise a different, alternative, or opposing point of view. You can use the source you disagree with to bring up an idea that you feel strongly about.

Here's a paragraph, for instance, that uses Duckworth's ideas to explore a different idea:

> There's no doubt that Duckworth's idea of grit can contribute to success in school and is likely more important than intelligence or innate ability. In her experience, "aptitude did *not* guarantee achievement" (17). This is an encouraging idea that fits right in line with the American ideal of overcoming adversity to succeed. But the fact is, success in school also depends on much more than this narrow definition of grit. Duckworth fails to account for socioeconomic factors—whether kids have a safe place to study, food to eat, and shelter.

In this case, the writer brings in Duckworth's ideas to challenge them. The discussion of Duckworth's text here leads into the writer's own view that Duckworth's definition of grit and the power she ascribes to it fall short. In fact, according to the writer, Duckworth's view overlooks significant socioeconomic issues that the writer argues are just as or maybe more powerful when it comes to succeeding in school.

Structuring a Paragraph Using Sources

Once you have decided to use sources in your writing to support your position or to address counterarguments, it's time to consider how you can structure paragraphs that smoothly integrate sources into your own writing. In Chapter 3 (p. 85), you saw that an academic paragraph typically follows this structure:

- Topic sentence
- Support
- Explanation/commentary
- Conclusion

When you use sources, the structure will be roughly the same, but keeping the following details in mind will help you develop effective paragraphs with sources:

Topic sentence	This is the overall point that you want to make about the topic. For instance, your topic sentence might be something like, "Zoos are unethical because they place more value on human entertainment than on animal welfare."
Support	With sources, this part of your paragraph could be either a direct quotation or a paraphrase from a credible and relevant source that supports your topic sentence. For example, you might include a quotation from the piece by Dr. Hone (pp. 107–109), in which he describes the often poor conditions that exist at some privately held zoos and breeding farms.
Explanation/ commentary	In this essential part of your paragraph, you will provide commentary on your source, including an explanation of how your use of the source supports your topic sentence. This explanation is usually one or two sentences long. You might explain, for example, how some of the private farms and zoos that Hone describes are unethical and put human entertainment first.
Other viewpoint	Remember that your goal in using sources is to present an informed opinion. One way to do that is to include a source that raises a counterargument to your position, introduced with a word or phrase such as *but, however, in spite of, on the other hand, nevertheless, nonetheless, notwithstanding, in contrast, on the contrary, still, yet*. For example: "Yet, some people disagree that zoos are harmful. Filmmaker David Attenborough suggests that 'Only the sight of a creature in the flesh can give us a true understanding of its nature'" (McKie).
Explanation/ commentary	Never leave the counterargument that you raised in the previous sentence without refuting the point the source is making or without explaining how that position is not the only way to view the issue. You do not want to entirely dismiss the source that does not support your position, but you do want to point out what it misses or doesn't consider. To refute Attenborough, you might write something like this: "While what Attenborough says is certainly true of the very best zoos in the world, he should also be thinking about the animals being kept in less than ideal living conditions."

Conclusion	The conclusion of a paragraph that uses sources should address the "So what?" question and call for action or describe what the future holds for this topic. In this case, a possible conclusion might be something like this: "Because so many animals are unable to lead full and natural lives in captivity, we should begin the process of reintroducing animals back into the wild and using zoos only as a place to preserve truly endangered animals, not just the ones that are fun for humans to look at."

Using a structure like this shows your reader that you have done your research and that you are not merely stating your uninformed opinion. The structure also helps guide your reader easily through your ideas and demonstrates how those ideas fit into the ongoing conversation surrounding your topic. While at this point you are writing only a single paragraph, you will use a similar structure when you begin composing a full essay, as you will see in Chapter 7 (p. 466).

Using Sources to Provide Support and Address Counterarguments

Step 1. Read the following excerpts from articles that address the topic of grit. One opposes the idea, while the other supports it. Annotate both texts for sections that best illustrate the author's perspective on the topic.

Step 2. Write a paragraph using the structure described above.

   a. **Topic sentence.** State your own opinion about the topic of grit.

   b. **Support.** Use a quotation or paraphrase from Duckworth, Kohn, or Rosen to back up your position.

   c. **Explanation/commentary.** Explain how that source supports your position.

   d. **Other viewpoint.** Use a quotation from Kohn, Duckworth, or Rosen to put forward a viewpoint that differs from your position.

   e. **Explanation/commentary.** Refute that source or explain what it doesn't address.

   f. **Conclusion.** Restate your position on grit and add an explanation of why grit matters or does not matter. In other words, answer the "So what?" question.

When using the sources in your own writing, be sure to follow the formats you practiced earlier, including the use of signal words, punctuation, and citations.

1. *from* The Downside of "Grit"

Alfie Kohn

This piece appeared in the *Washington Post* in April 2014. Alfie Kohn is a scholar and author who specializes in education and parenting.

To begin with, not everything is worth doing, let alone doing for extended periods, and not everyone who works hard is pursuing something worthwhile. People who are up to no good often have grit to spare. Persistence is just one of many attributes that can sometimes be useful for reaching a (good or bad) outcome, so it's the choice of goal that ought to come first and count more. Moreover, persistence can be counterproductive and even unhealthy. Often it just doesn't make sense to continue with a problem that resists solution or persist at a task that no longer provides satisfaction. . . .

The motives for displaying grit also raise important psychological questions. What matters isn't just how long one persists, but why one does so. Proponents of grit rarely ask: Do kids love what they're doing? Or are they driven by a desperate (and anxiety-provoking) need to prove their competence? As long as they're pushing themselves, we're encouraged to nod our approval.

To know when to pull the plug requires the capacity to adopt a long-term perspective. Continuing to do what you've been doing often represents the path of least resistance, so it can take guts to cut your losses. That's as important a message to teach one's children as the usefulness of perseverance. ■

2. *from* Why "Grit" May Be Everything for Success

Amy Rosen

This piece appeared on the *Entrepreneur* magazine website in August 2015. Amy Rosen is a consultant and strategist specializing in education and youth development in the business sector.

In entrepreneurship, grit is an "outlier" skill or attribute because it may just be the one skill without which failure is pretty much assured. In other words, it's possible to succeed in business or the workforce or as an entrepreneur if you're not creative. Or if you don't collaborate well, or have not really learned to be adaptive and flexible. All three are important parts of an entrepreneurship mindset.

But if you are not at least modestly persistent or stubborn, and you tend to quit easily, you're done — even if you are creative and collaborative and adaptive. Lack of grit is the entrepreneurship killer.

What also makes grit so important is that, unlike other things you often hear about why entrepreneurs succeed, grit is a skill that can be learned. People can learn to be more resilient and less impacted by setbacks. . . .

We need role models in and out of business who'll talk about their failures and setbacks and, in doing so, underscore the precious nature of grit. Ranking what's really indispensable for entrepreneurs might not be possible or even helpful. But, if it were, my sense is that grit would be pretty near the top of any such list. Even if you are not an aspiring entrepreneur, grit is an attribute that will help turn any goal you have into reality. ■

Avoiding Plagiarism

Throughout this chapter, you have been learning when, how, and why to use sources in your own writing. When you are using other people's words as part of your own work, be sure to avoid plagiarizing your sources. **Plagiarism** means representing someone else's words, ideas, or research as your own. It is a form of dishonesty and most consider it intellectual theft and fraud. It's a violation of what we call academic integrity. It's a form of cheating.

But why is it considered cheating? It boils down to ownership and respect — not of tangible property like a car or computer — but of ideas. If your friend says something especially clever or thoughtful, those words and ideas are hers. You can "borrow" them by repeating what she said as long as you give her credit. This goes for everything from a tweet to a term paper to a book. How you give credit differs according to where you're repeating.

ZITS © 2015 Zits Partnership Distributed by King Features Syndicate, Inc.

What point is this cartoon making about plagiarism? Why is the teacher so upset?

In general, you want to give credit by acknowledging the source any time you use words, ideas, examples, or evidence that are not entirely your own. The following are a few cases in which you would need to cite a source:

- Direct quotations or a paraphrase or summary of someone's ideas
- Facts that you learned through your research
- Judgments or opinions made by others
- Statistics or other quantitative data that others have collected
- Visual images including charts, graphs, or tables that are from a source

NOTE: You do not need to cite facts that are considered to be "common knowledge." This refers to information that is generally not in dispute and that appears in multiple sources. For instance, you do not need to acknowledge a source from which you learned an author's birth date or the year World War II started.

AP Photo/Manny Garcia/ Shepard Fairey

In 2008, street artist Shepard Fairey created an iconic poster for Barack Obama's presidential run with the title *Hope*. In 2009, the Associated Press and their photographer Mannie Garcia claimed that Fairey based his image on a photograph by Garcia. The Associated Press sued Fairey for copyright infringement (a legal term for plagiarism) for not getting permission to use the photo. Fairey claimed that he had substantially transformed the photo — a type of use allowed under the law without permission.

Looking at these two images, do you think the poster that Shepard Fairey created counts as plagiarism? Or is it substantially transformed? What does thinking about this controversy tell you about the issue of plagiarism?

Intentional vs. Unintentional Plagiarism

Everyone knows that intentionally plagiarizing is wrong. We've been told since we were kids not to copy other people's work. But some plagiarism isn't that clear cut. It's just as serious a problem if you piece together passages from several sources with only a few changes so that it *appears* to be your writing. Passing off anyone's work as your own, even if it has never been formally published, absolutely constitutes plagiarism.

Unintentional plagiarism — far more common than intentional — is trickier because it is not deliberate. You might quote a passage but neglect to include the quotation marks just because you're not paying attention. Or you could paraphrase something so slightly that it is too close, though not identical, to the original. You might fail to differentiate between your ideas or beliefs and those of a source you've consulted. If someone else's ideas resemble your own, it can be hard to know where to draw the line — but it's always better to acknowledge that you've read the same idea or a similar one in a source. Keep in mind that giving credit to your sources not only protects you from plagiarism but also shows that your writing is well-informed.

Sometimes, unintentional plagiarism results from a lack of confidence. You read something that you think sounds better than it would if it were in your own words, so you include it without acknowledging the source. Most of the time, this is easy for a reader — or teacher — to spot because the vocabulary, tone, or sentence structure is different from the rest of your writing. Again, if there is an especially interesting phrase or even a whole sentence, integrate it with quotation marks and cite the source.

Suppose you were asked to explain in your own words what brought Duckworth to her understanding of "grit." Look over the following response and notice the underlined portions that are taken word-for-word from Duckworth, or just slightly changed:

> Duckworth seems to confuse the hard work and enduring effort that she calls "grit" with high interest. While it's encouraging that she questions why some of her students picked up mathematical concepts more easily than their classmates and admits that teaching the most talented students was "a joy," she fails to get at the real reason why those who initially struggled eventually achieved. She recognizes that aptitude did *not* guarantee achievement. However, her realization that even her weakest students could master any number of complicated ideas in their very complicated daily lives might be true, but it's not necessarily because of grit. Realizing that kids were having conversations involving discourses on basketball statistics, the lyrics to songs they really liked, and complicated plotlines about their peers' behavior is not the same as grit—by her definition. Most of us can stay focused on things that interest us, but having the discipline and stamina to stick with a task despite various challenges is a different story.

The second sentence includes Duckworth's language (without quotation marks) except for the use of "her" instead of "my" in the original. Then, "a joy" was quoted correctly, although the rest of the sentence is also part of the quotation but not acknowledged as such. "Aptitude did *not* guarantee achievement" is a direct quotation from the original text and deserves to be introduced and quoted in its entirety. The next sentence about "complicated lives" is lifted right out of Duckworth's own writing and could easily have been paraphrased. The same is true of the examples in the next sentence. The reality, then, is that this paragraph is written as much by Duckworth as it is by the person who challenged her analysis. In other words, it is unintentionally plagiarized from Duckworth's book, perhaps because the writer didn't trust his or her own voice and ideas. Don't be so overwhelmed by a source that you feel you have nothing of value to add or say. And, if you use a few select phrases from a source, be sure to credit the author.

Identifying Plagiarism

Earlier in this chapter, you read an excerpt from "Why 'Grit' May Be Everything for Success" by Amy Rosen from the *Entrepreneur* magazine website (p. 121). Following is a paragraph using that source to support an opinion. The use of that source here would probably be considered plagiarism because Rosen is not properly credited. Working with a partner or small group, explain what changes you would suggest here to avoid unintentional plagiarism.

> Angela Duckworth's concept of "grit" may be even more important for building a career than succeeding in school, particularly if that career is in business. Whether it's called stubbornness, perseverance, determination, or grit, the ability to stick with a task in the world of work is essential. Amy Rosen, writing for *Entrepreneur* magazine, believes that grit is more important than being creative, collaborative, or adaptive; the absence of grit is "the entrepreneurship killer." The good news is that grit is a learned skill, not an inborn character trait. Rosen points out that "failure and setbacks" are part of any job, and role models who talk about how they manage such experiences can help others develop the resilience that will help turn any goal into reality.

culminating activity

Writing with Sources

The texts that follow present different views on the question of whether students should be paid for good grades to help motivate them to do well in school.

Step 1. As you read the four texts, annotate them by applying the steps on pages 106–107.

Step 2. Then, write a paragraph of seven to ten sentences that responds to the following prompt: *Should students be paid for getting good grades in school?* Include references to at least two of the sources and use the approaches presented on pages 112–114. When writing your paragraph, use what you learned in Chapter 3 (p. 85) and on pages 119–120 of this chapter.

Step 3. Review your work to be sure that you have cited your sources properly and have not committed unintentional plagiarism. (See pp. 124–125.)

Source A

Franck, Thomas. "American students try harder if you pay them, economists found." *MSNBC*, 20 Nov. 2017.

American high school students score higher on low-stakes tests and are more willing to answer test questions when they are motivated by cash, according to new economic research.

Giving high school–aged students money as a reward for performing well improved scores by roughly 5 percent, according to economists at the University of California, San Diego and the University of Chicago.

This outside incentive, they concluded, suggests that the education gap between U.S. students and their international peers may have less to do with understanding the material and more to do with effort. . . .

In their research, the economists compared Shanghai students, who are top performers on international assessments, to Americans. They created a 25-question, 25-minute mathematics test consisting of previous PISA questions.

On the day of the test, some of the students in each experiment group were given $25 in cash (or an equivalent in renminbi[1] for the students in China) and told the money was theirs to keep but the researchers would take away $1 for every wrong or incomplete answer. Some of the students were not offered money.

While the performance of Shanghai students didn't change, the American students who were offered money attempted more questions and were more likely to answer those questions correctly, the economists found. . . .

"The general insight is that maybe students aren't trying as hard as they could be," Sally Sadoff, an economist at U.C.S.D., told CNBC in an interview. "It takes mental effort, mental power. . . ."

Sadoff said the goal of the economists' latest paper was not to study how incentives work, "but rather to use incentives as an experimental tool to understand the interaction of culture with motivation to do well on the test."

To be sure, Sadoff's group aren't the first economists offer students — or teachers — cash for improved performance. Multiple studies have shown that cash payments do tend to improve performance on individual assignments, but those effects tend not to last longer than the duration of the studies. . . .

Some may raise ethical objections to monetary incentives to improve effort on low-stakes tests, but Sadoff said the results of the research do raise an interesting question.

"We've been working on studies on motivation for a while," she said. "I think for a lot of kids, their parents are just instilling a habit [of good study practices]. But for some kids, I think there is a role for us. If the return to education is so high, why aren't kids trying?"

---

[1] Official currency of the People's Republic of China.

Source B

McCready, Amy. "Does Paying Kids for Good Grades Pay Off?" *Positive Parenting Solutions.*

Offering a child fifty dollars in exchange for an excellent report card seems like a small price to pay for a child's entire future.

But it's not that simple. Paying for grades isn't just a harmless means to an end that puts a little fun money in our kids' pockets.

Paying for grades actually robs kids of much greater wealth. It doesn't matter whether your child is headed for preschool, community college, or the Ivy League: True, long-lasting success requires skills that money can't buy. . . .

Studying may seem a lot like holding an actual job, complete with time-management and hard work. But the more our kids can do necessary work without applause — or a small paycheck — the more conditioned they'll be for future jobs. They'll exemplify a solid work ethic by caring about their efforts and self-improvement — and this will make them all the more successful.

Their transition to the rest of the "real world" will also be less of a wake-up call. Just like us, our kids will never get paid for doing their taxes, cleaning the bathrooms, and raising their children (to name a few minor things). . . .

Unless we help kids understand that studying is beneficial for more than just good grades, (like the development of life-long skills and the absorption of valuable and interesting information) they may be inclined to take short cuts. And promising fifty dollars for every A (or whatever the current going rate is) further increases this short line approach. . . .

I get it — good grades are important. We don't want to see our kids fail and we certainly don't want to see that failure — in the form of Fs, Ds, and Cs — threaten their future.

Paying our kids for good grades may help them secure these grades, but allowing them to fail without added incentive is an even greater benefit.

In a competitive world, kids aren't always comfortable making mistakes. Or losing. Or even getting second place. But learning to embrace failure, learn from it, and pick back up again is an imperative skill. It's a situation kids will find themselves in again and again in life, and letting them practice their resilience before they're off on their own gives them an advantage.

Source C

Ravitch, Diane. "We Shouldn't Pay Kids to Learn." *Forbes*, 17 Oct. 2008.

In India, students compete for admission into cram schools, where they study intensively in order to compete for admission into India's highly regarded technology colleges. Their families pay as much as $1,500 a year for this opportunity, which, for many, is a great hardship. In Korea and Japan, students attend after-school classes to boost their chances for college admission.

In the U.S., by contrast, school districts and philanthropists are embarking on ever-more elaborate efforts to persuade students to care about school and to learn basic skills.

Traditionally, educators have tried to awaken intrinsic motivation in students, to engage them in the joy of learning for its own sake and, if that fails, to convince them that getting a good education is crucial to their future success.

Trying to motivate reluctant students, the New York City Department of Education has opened over 200 small high schools with catchy themes, hoping to stir student interest. The newest proposal is the Game High School, where students will play videogames that teach them the skills they need. School will, supposedly, be fun and games, instead of a series of daunting challenges with some occasional drudgery thrown in for good measure.

An even more ambitious bid to motivate low-performing students has been launched by Los Angeles philanthropist Eli Broad, who has provided seed money for a scheme to pay students to show up for school, behave in classes and lift their test scores. Broad has established a $44 million research center at Harvard to design and evaluate pay-for-performance plans for students in New York City, Washington, D.C., and Chicago. The Broad plan is the brainchild of Harvard economist Roland Fryer. Critics predict that student motivation based on cash will end when the cash ends, but the cities involved have jumped on the incentivizing bandwagon.

Hopefully, Fryer will calculate the costs of implementing his ambitious plans — not only in these cities, but across the nation. Chester E. Finn Jr., of the Thomas B. Fordham Institute in Washington, D.C., has estimated that the Chicago portion alone would cost $187 million annually if brought to scale in that city. Add in New York City, Washington, D.C., and a few other cities where performance lags — like Los Angeles, Cleveland and Detroit — and the annual costs are likely to soar into the billions.

This is money that might otherwise be spent reducing class size (New York City has the largest classes in the state), improving the quality of tests and technology and refurbishing obsolete facilities.

Interesting, isn't it, that while students in other countries are paying $1,500 a year for the chance to learn more, many American students will be paid that same amount just to do what they ought to be doing in their own self-interest?

Does the future belong to those who struggle to better themselves, make sacrifices to do so and work hard? Or to those who must be cajoled and bribed to learn anything at all?

Source D

Waterson, Bill. *Calvin and Hobbes.* 19 Oct. 1989.

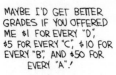

Narrative

Probably every fall when you return to school, you've been asked to write about "what you did over the summer." There's a reason why your teachers ask you to do this. Reading the story helps them understand you better: your hobbies, interests, pets, background, family, and other details about who you are. But perhaps more importantly, telling your story allows you to reflect on your life, to find what's important and share it. Writing a narrative is one way we come to understand ourselves, by telling the story of our lives.

Narratives by celebrities, politicians, and sometimes just everyday people top the best-seller list every year, because there is something powerful in reading a first person account of a person's experiences, struggles, and triumphs. There is also something incredibly powerful in telling your own story about your life, too, free from other people's perspectives and judgments.

In this chapter, you will have the opportunity to read narratives by people who have led many different lives. You'll hear from a documentary filmmaker, a rock star, a soldier, a store owner, and others. At the end of this chapter, you will also have the chance to write your own narrative as a way to better understand the form — how it communicates a personal experience and, ultimately, who you are.

Contents

Essential Elements of Narrative

As you saw in Chapter 2, there are different purposes for reading a text: you can read for understanding, for interpretation, and for craft. But you also read different kinds of texts differently depending on the genre or mode of text. In this Skill Workshop, you will practice how to read narratives, understanding and appreciating how they are crafted and what they mean. In many ways, narratives are similar to fictional novels and short stories. They share many of the same essential features, with one important distinction: they are expected to be true accounts of events that happened in real life.

> **PREVIEWING Academic Vocabulary**   **Essential Elements of Narrative**
>
> In this section, you will encounter the following terms as you consider how to analyze a narrative. Working individually or with a partner or small group, think about what you already know about the meaning of each term.
>
> 1. First person point of view
> 2. Characterization
> 3. Dialogue
> 4. Blocking
> 5. Conflict
> 6. Setting
> 7. Reflection
> 8. Theme
> 9. Artistic license

Let's begin our exploration of the tools that writers use to create a narrative (which can also be called a "memoir," if it spans a long period of time) by reading the short piece "Mother's Tongue." After you read it, we will walk through each of the significant features of a narrative by using this one as a model.

Mother's Tongue

Samuel Autman

Samuel A. Autman is an American essayist, travel writer, and college professor whose work often focuses on identity, place, and pop culture. This piece was published in *Brevity* magazine in 2015.

DePauw University

As the teenager stepped through the first set of automatic doors at Target, I was entering from the parking lot. For a few seconds we stood in the foyer area between the sets of double doors.

"Aren't you? Aren't you?" he asked, his lips quivering with joyful anticipation.

In the mid 1990s, the sight of a 6-foot-4 210-pound black man in Salt Lake City caused many strange reactions. His, however, mimicked the excitement of recognizing someone he had hoped was a famous athlete. The dribbling motion his downward palms made gave it away. "Whoever you think I am, I am not," I sighed. "I don't play for anybody's basketball team."

This was a phrase I had on a save/get key in my brain. I dreamed instead of someone stopping me on the streets and saying, "Aren't you that guy who does those great front-page articles for *The Salt Lake Tribune*?" I would have gladly owned that kind of recognition.

*

Between the ages of 9 and 16, my shoe size and my age corresponded. Neighborhood kids called me "feets." 5

In the summer of 1980, right before I turned fourteen, I stretched up to a gangly six-feet. The world expected this body to have a certain agility with a basketball.

I didn't.

For weeks my Uncle Tan and I stood outside on the black tar playground at Scullin Elementary School and practiced stealing, dribbling and slam-dunking an orange ball. "Now, let's me show you how to do this *again*," he would say over and over.

I couldn't hide my ambivalence. Eventually we agreed to drop these practice sessions. My relief was enormous.

*

Neither my uncle nor anyone else could undo my mother's incantations. 10

"Any fool can dribble a damned ball! If you break your leg, then what? You take your ass to school. With your mind you can become a genius. Forget a damned ball."

I hated these long verbal rants. For thirty years as a schoolteacher in the St. Louis Public Schools, she saw hordes of young boys, often without fathers in the home, sidelined when basketball, football and baseball dreams evaporated. Life's path hadn't provided those boys with many options. Too many of them wound up incarcerated or in cemeteries early.

"I'll tell you one thing, when you turn eighteen you've got two choices," my mother said. "You're either going into the Army or you're going to college, but you're gonna get your ass out of my house."

I knew she meant it. Our parents split when my sister and I were small children. With no daddy in the picture, my mother's tongue fathered me.

By the time I got onto the University of Missouri's campus where I studied journalism and fell in love with Victorian literature, I had developed a retort for the basketball question, "Do you play miniature golf?" 15

And it took me thirteen years of working as a newspaper writer and another ten years of teaching college before I realized something.

My mother was right. ■

Getting Started

Write a brief response to the questions that follow and share with a partner afterward.

- When have you been asked to read or write narratives in school?
- Typically, what are the topics of the narratives you have been assigned in school?
- In general, what do you like or not like about reading or writing narratives?

First Person Point of View

One of the chief defining features of a narrative or memoir is that it is almost always told from the **first person point of view**. As readers, we can assume that the narrator is, in fact, the author. This is much different from poetry or fiction, in which the speaker or narrator is a persona of the writer; an "I" in a short story is rarely considered to be the author. In the case of Samuel Autman's piece, when we read the first sentence — "As the teenager stepped through the first set of automatic doors at Target, I was entering from the parking lot." — we understand that Autman is talking about himself.

Also, almost without exception, the writer is the **protagonist** of the narrative. In other words, the writer is the most prominent character in the narrative whose actions or inactions drive the events of the story.

Characterization

A significant goal of a narrative is to reveal what kind of person the author is or was at the time of the action. The methods writers use to develop characters can generally be broken down into two categories: direct characterization and indirect characterization. Through **direct characterization**, writers tell us what they are like — how they look or act. Through **indirect characterization**, authors reveal information about themselves through actions, thoughts, dialogue, or comments made by other figures in the narrative. Indirect characterization is a bit more subtle than direct characterization because it lets readers draw their own conclusions based on the details provided. Most narrative writers use both techniques.

Take a look at the following examples of characterization from "Mother's Tongue."

Direct Characterization	Indirect Characterization
In the summer of 1980, right before I turned fourteen, I stretched up to a gangly six-feet. The world expected this body to have a certain agility with a basketball.	For weeks my Uncle Tan and I . . . practiced stealing, dribbling and slam-dunking an orange ball. "Now, let's me show you how to do this *again*," he would say over and over.

The example on the left is direct characterization because it describes the narrator. The example on the right is indirect characterization because, rather than writing "I was not interested in my uncle's lessons," the narrator reveals his lack of interest through is uncle's exasperation ("let's me show you how to do this *again*").

Effective narratives tend to focus on the characterization of their protagonist, the narrator, more than any other character. That's partly because the narrator is the main character, but it's also because the connection between the reader and the narrator is of paramount importance. The job of the writer is to make the reader care about the situations and conflicts the narrator faces. Ultimately, that is the goal of characterization in a narrative: to create a character that we care about. Regardless of whether we like or dislike the protagonist, the writer wants us to feel invested in what happens to that character.

A narrative writer develops the characterization of the protagonist as well as other characters through the following elements:

- Physical details (age, height, gender, etc.)
- Actions, gestures, movements
- Dialogue
- How others speak or think about or behave toward the narrator or character
- Narrator motivations
- Narrator internal thoughts

From the examples of direct and indirect characterization in the table above, it becomes clear that Autman felt pressured to play basketball because of his physical attributes, not his skill or interest level. As readers, we care about Autman because we feel that we know him. We feel sympathetic toward him and, because we know some of his inside thoughts, we are rooting for his success.

Writers of narrative also bring their characters to life through dialogue and blocking. These are common methods of building indirect characterization.

- **Dialogue.** Because it places the reader right in the middle of the exchange, **dialogue** has the effect of bringing the events of the narrative to life. Consider these examples of dialogue that illustrate how people judge Autman or expect things of him because of his physical appearance:

  | "Aren't you? Aren't you?" he asked, his lips quivering with joyful anticipation.

  | "Now, let's me show you how to do this *again*," he would say over and over.

- **Blocking.** This term describes the actions of the people in the narrative. Like dialogue, **blocking** helps the reader visualize the events in the story, placing us right in the middle of the action. In the beginning of the narrative, for example, Autman describes the moment in which the boy at Target thinks he recognizes him:

  In the mid 1990s, the sight of a 6-foot-4 210-pound black man in Salt Lake City caused many strange reactions. His, however, mimicked the excitement of recognizing someone he had hoped was a famous athlete. The dribbling motion his downward palms made gave it away. "Whoever you think I am, I am not," I sighed. "I don't play for anybody's basketball team."

These examples of dialogue and blocking connect the reader to the protagonist because he describes an emotional situation that many people can empathize with: someone being profiled based on race, gender, and physical attributes. Even though narratives often focus closely on the characterization of the narrator, most narratives also include characterization of other figures to help flesh out the story and engage the reader. Through both types of characterization, we see that the teenager at the beginning is rash and possibly racist, the uncle is stubbornly persistent and frustrated, and Autman's mother is strong, level-headed, and caring with a strict manner.

Characterization

Describe yourself to someone who does not know you by writing just a few lines about your experiences at the following times in your life. Be sure to include some physical details of yourself at the time, but also some dialogue and blocking that might help reveal something about you at that time. You might be tempted to rely only on direct characterization because that is often the easiest way to communicate details of characterization, but consider how you might reveal aspects of yourself through indirect characterization as well. After you have written your pieces, go back and label examples of direct and indirect characterization in different colors. Choose at least two of the following times in your life to describe:

- When you were a very young child (based on pictures or accounts of family or friends)
- When you were in elementary or middle school
- This year

Conflicts

The purpose of just about every narrative is to recount a **conflict** the author faced and how that conflict was either overcome or not. Sometimes these conflicts are with other characters, other times they are with larger forces such as nature or society. In narrative, they oftentimes involve an inner conflict. Here are the main types of conflicts, and how they play out in "Mother's Tongue":

- **Narrator v. another character.** There is conflict between Autman and his uncle, who clearly wants him to be able to play basketball, despite Autman's lack of interest and skill. Uncle Tan keeps pushing and pushing until he finally gives up. Autman is also in conflict with his mother, whose advice he doesn't appreciate until he is much older.
- **Narrator v. society.** Autman describes how society's expectations for a tall black man at the time were limiting and constraining, especially since he was not interested in or able to meet them.
- **Narrator v. nature.** In general, this type of conflict deals with facing challenges in nature, like climbing a mountain, surviving a snow storm, and so on. In this case, the narrative begins with the narrator's struggle with his own body: tall, gangly, uncoordinated. In the beginning of this narrative, biology is — in a sense — the protagonist's natural enemy.
- **Narrator v. self.** This is the most common type of conflict in a narrative. Because we spend so much time in the narrator's head in most narratives, this is almost always the one to look out for when determining the point that the author is trying to make. Does Autman have the inner strength and confidence to finally listen to his mother and to become a scholar and a writer? In the last sentences of his piece, he confirms that he has what it takes to address this conflict.

Conflict

Spend some time thinking about conflicts that you have experienced in your own life and briefly identify a few in each of the following categories:

- Self v. someone else
- Self v. society (or group larger than an individual)
- Self v. nature
- Self v. self

Then choose one and explain how that conflict was or was not resolved.

Setting

Effective narratives immerse the reader in a particular time and place, so that the reader can feel connected to the writer's experience. In addition to the physical location of the narrative (a room, a house, a classroom, a bus), the **setting** of a narrative also includes when the events take place (time of day, time of the year, historical time period). This helps set the mood and atmosphere and helps the reader understand any historical, cultural, or political issues that the narrative addresses. Look at the beginning of "Mother's Tongue":

> As the teenager stepped through the first set of automatic doors at Target, I was entering from the parking lot. For a few seconds we stood in the foyer area between the sets of double doors.
>
> "Aren't you? Aren't you?" he asked, his lips quivering with joyful anticipation.
>
> In the mid 1990s, the sight of a 6-foot-4 210-pound black man in Salt Lake City caused many strange reactions.

With just a short description of the time and place of one part of the narrative, Autman gives the reader a sense of not only the location, but also how out of place he felt. In Salt Lake City especially, African Americans are in the minority, accounting for less than 5 percent of the population.

Setting

Think back on a recent event that took place at your school, home, neighborhood, or some other place that you know well. It does not have to be anything significant; it could be something as mundane as burning toast at breakfast. Focus on describing just the setting. Where did this event take place? What was the time of day? Write a few sentences that help someone who has never been there feel immersed in the setting. Try to offer details that establish a particular mood or atmosphere.

Reflection and Theme

Like fiction and other types of literature, narratives have **themes**, points they try to make that can be applied to the world beyond the story. Narratives often include moments of **reflection**, in which the authors, now "older and wiser," reflect on the actions of their younger selves. Such moments usually lead readers to some kind of statement of theme. Narratives are rarely related in the present tense with the events happening as the narrator experiences them. Instead, they usually include statements like these from "Mother's Tongue":

> I dreamed instead of someone stopping me on the streets and saying, "Aren't you that guy who does those great front-page articles for *The Salt Lake Tribune*?" I would have gladly owned that kind of recognition.

> Neither my uncle nor anyone else could undo my mother's incantations.

These are not the kind of statements that Autman would likely have made as a younger person. Only later, with more life experience, could he look back at himself critically. This process of reflection is integral to a narrative and it usually leads to an insight shared at or near the end of the piece, as in the last sentences in Autman's narrative:

> And it took me thirteen years of working as a newspaper writer and another ten years of teaching college before I realized something.

> My mother was right.

This is the "so what" portion of the narrative. Authors of narratives often include statements like these to illustrate clearly the insight or theme the audience ought to take away from the writer's experiences. In this case, Autman would probably like for us to conclude that, yes, we all may question ourselves, but listening to the voices of those who know us best can help us find a rewarding path in life.

activity Reflection and Theme

As someone who is now "older and wiser," what advice would you like to give yourself at one or more of the following times in your life?

- The first day of high school
- The worst day you had in middle school
- A time you failed or succeeded at some kind of activity
- One of your birthdays before you turned thirteen
- Any other significant time in your life

"Truth" and Artistic License

Reading a piece of fiction, even a very realistic-seeming one, the reader doesn't automatically ask, "Did this really happen?" When reading a narrative or memoir, however, the reader not only asks this question regularly, but also expects that the answer is "yes." This is a key distinction between narrative and fiction: the reader assumes the events in a narrative to be true. That is part of a narrative's power. That said, it is almost impossible to accurately recount every detail of an event, especially one that occurred many years earlier. Who really can recall exactly what color shirt you wore or the exact words that someone used when speaking to you?

Readers of narratives and memoir understand this and tolerate a certain amount of **artistic license**, which occurs when a writer may embellish or add detail to assist readers in connecting with the story. Where is the line between fiction and the truth of a narrative? How broad or fine is that line? It is really difficult to say, though most writers strive for authenticity in their narratives and generally resist straining the believability of their readers. Some of the events in "Mother's Tongue" took place many years before Autman published the story, and while he probably took liberties with some details — maybe the opening took place at a K-mart instead of a Target, for example — his piece feels authentic, even though we as readers can never really know for sure if the events happened in the way he describes. As readers of narratives, we need to have trust and faith in the writer. If that trust is lost because the writer willfully misleads readers by presenting fiction as truth, the narrative loses its power.

In 2006, the website Smoking Gun published an article called "A Million Little Lies: Exposing James Frey's Fiction Addiction," which proved that several aspects of the best-selling memoir *A Million Little Pieces* by James Frey were fabricated. In particular, the article revealed that Frey claimed to have spent 87 days in jail, when in fact he had only spent a few hours there.

Talk show host Oprah Winfrey, who had promoted the book extensively, had Frey on her show shortly after the article came out. Here are a couple of excerpts from their conversation:

> **Winfrey:** James Frey is here and I have to say it is difficult for me to talk to you because I feel really duped. Why did you lie? Why did you have to lie about the time you spent in jail? Why did you do that?
>
> **Frey:** I think one of the coping mechanisms I developed was sort of this image of myself that was greater, probably, than — not probably — that *was* greater than what I actually was. In order to get through the experience of the addiction, I thought of myself as being tougher than I was and badder than I was — and it helped me cope. When I was writing the book . . . instead of being as introspective as I should have been, I clung to that image.

Winfrey: And did you cling to that image because that's how you wanted to see yourself? Or did you cling to that image because that would make a better book?

Frey: Probably both. . . . I don't fee l like I conned everyone.

Clearly Winfrey and many other readers felt conned by Frey because he had taken that artistic license too far. Even though he didn't fully acknowledge his mistakes, his publisher offered a refund to any reader who requested one.

"Truth" and Artistic License

Think back on an event that happened to you at least five or more years ago. How much of the detail can you remember? If you were to write about this event for a narrative, what would you likely need to embellish? Why would these embellishments be effective for telling your story?

REFLECTING ON Academic Vocabulary   **Essential Elements of Narrative**

Working with a partner or small group, discuss the terms in this section and that you previewed on page 132 and clarify your understanding of each. Then, share what you learned about reading and writing narratives. What did you find helpful, relevant, unnecessary, redundant, and so on?

---

culminating activity

Writing a Narrative

Write a brief narrative based on one of the ideas that you have been trying out in the activities throughout this workshop. Be sure to use first person point of view, include some details about character, conflict, setting, try out some dialogue and blocking, and write a brief reflection. This piece will likely be a few paragraphs, just enough to practice with some of these narrative elements.

By Any Other Name

Santha Rama Rau

Santha Rama Rau (1923–2009) was born in India, while it was still under British rule. As the daughter of a diplomat, she traveled extensively as a child, including to South Africa, England, and Japan. Eventually she and her husband settled in the United States where she taught English at Sarah Lawrence College near New York City. This piece was published in the *New Yorker* in 1951.

Pictorial Parade/Getty Images

KEY CONTEXT   This narrative tells the story of two Indian sisters, ages five and eight, as they attend a British-run school in Zorinabad, a village in northern India. At that time, one of the goals of the British Empire was to "make the world British," and institutions such as school and government applied tremendous pressure to conform to the British way of doing things.

The title — "By Any Other Name" — is a reference to a scene in Shakespeare's *Romeo and Juliet*, in which Juliet, having fallen in love with the son of her family's enemy, wonders aloud on the balcony:

> What's in a name? that which we call a rose
> By any other name would smell as sweet

Juliet answers her own question by concluding that names do not matter.

At the Anglo-Indian day school in Zorinabad to which my sister and I were sent when she was eight and I was five and a half, they changed our names. On the first day of school, a hot, windless morning of a north Indian September, we stood in the headmistress's study and she said, "Now you're the *new* girls. What are your names?"

My sister answered for us. "I am Premila, and she" — nodding in my direction — "is Santha."

The headmistress had been in India, I suppose, fifteen years or so, but she still smiled her helpless inability to cope with Indian names. Her rimless half-glasses glittered, and the precarious bun on the top of her head trembled as she shook her head. "Oh, my dears, those are much too hard for me. Suppose we give you pretty English names. Wouldn't that be more jolly? Let's see, now — Pamela for you, I think." She shrugged in a baffled way at my sister. "That's as close as I can get. And for *you*," she said to me, "how about Cynthia? Isn't that nice?"

My sister was always less easily intimidated than I was, and while she kept a stubborn silence, I said, "Thank you," in a very tiny voice.

We had been sent to that school because ⁵ my father, among his responsibilities as an officer of the civil service, had a tour of duty to perform in the villages around that steamy little provincial town, where he had his headquarters at that time. He used to make his shorter inspection tours on horseback, and a week before, in the stale heat of a typically post monsoon day, we had waved goodbye to him and a little procession — an assistant, a secretary, two bearers, and the man to look after the bedding rolls and luggage. They rode away through our large garden, still bright green from the rains, and we turned back into the twilight of the house and the sound of fans whispering in every room.

Up to then, my mother had refused to send Premila to school in the British-run establishments of that time, because, she used to say, "you can bury a dog's tail for seven years and it still comes out curly, and you can take a Britisher away from his home for a lifetime and he still remains insular." The examinations and degrees from entirely Indian schools were not, in those days, considered valid. In my case,

the question had never come up, and probably never would have come up if Mother's extraordinary good health had not broken down. For the first time in my life, she was not able to continue the lessons she had been giving us every morning. So our Hindi books were put away, the stories of the Lord Krishna as a little boy were left in mid-air, and we were sent to the Anglo-Indian school.

That first day at school is still, when I think of it, a remarkable one. At that age, if one's name is changed, one develops a curious form of dual personality. I remember having a certain detached and disbelieving concern in the actions of "Cynthia," but certainly no responsibility. Accordingly, I followed the thin, erect back of the headmistress down the veranda to my classroom feeling, at most, a passing interest in what was going to happen to me in this strange, new atmosphere of School.

The building was Indian in design, with wide verandas opening onto a central courtyard, but Indian verandas are usually whitewashed, with stone floors. These, in the tradition of British

Ian Tyas/Getty Images

This picture was taken in 1969 in Staffordshire, England, many years after the events that Rau describes in her narrative.

What are some similarities between this image and the narrative in the ways they each depict the learning process?

schools, were painted dark brown and had matting on the floors. It gave a feeling of extra intensity to the heat.

I suppose there were about a dozen Indian children in the school—which contained perhaps forty children in all—and four of them were in my class. They were all sitting at the back of the room, and I went to join them. I sat next to a small, solemn girl who didn't smile at me. She had long, glossy black braids and wore a cotton dress, but she still kept on her Indian jewelry—a gold chain around her neck, thin gold bracelets, and tiny ruby studs in her ears. Like most Indian children, she had a rim of black kohl around her eyes. The cotton dress should have looked strange, but all I could think of was that I should ask my mother if I couldn't wear a dress to school, too, instead of my Indian clothes.

I can't remember too much about the proceedings in class that day, except for the beginning. The teacher pointed to me and asked me to stand up. "Now, dear, tell the class your name."

I said nothing.

"Come along," she said, frowning slightly. "What's your name, dear?"

"I don't know," I said, finally.

The English children in the front of the class—there were about eight or ten of them— giggled and twisted around in their chairs to look at me. I sat down quickly and opened my eyes very wide, hoping in that way to dry them off. The little girl with the braids put out her hand and very lightly touched my arm. She still didn't smile.

Most of that morning I was rather bored. I looked briefly at the children's drawings pinned to the wall, and then concentrated on a lizard clinging to the ledge of the high, barred window behind the teacher's head. Occasionally it would shoot out its long yellow tongue for a fly, and then it would rest, with its eyes closed and its belly palpitating, as though it were swallowing several times quickly. The lessons were mostly concerned with reading and writing and simple numbers—things that my mother had already

10

15

taught me—and I paid very little attention. The teacher wrote on the easel blackboard words like "bat" and "cat," which seemed babyish to me; only "apple" was new and incomprehensible.

When it was time for the lunch recess, I followed the girl with braids out onto the veranda. There the children from the other classes were assembled. I saw Premila at once and ran over to her, as she had charge of our lunchbox. The children were all opening packages and sitting down to eat sandwiches. Premila and I were the only ones who had Indian food—thin wheat chapattis, some vegetable curry, and a bottle of buttermilk. Premila thrust half of it into my hand and whispered fiercely that I should go and sit with my class, because that was what the others seemed to be doing.

The enormous black eyes of the little Indian girl from my class looked at my food longingly, so I offered her some. But she only shook her head and plowed her way solemnly through her sandwiches.

I was very sleepy after lunch, because at home we always took a siesta. It was usually a pleasant time of day, with the bedroom darkened against the harsh afternoon sun, the drifting off into sleep with the sound of Mother's voice reading a story in one's mind, and, finally, the shrill, fussy voice of the ayah waking one for tea.

At school, we rested for a short time on low, folding cots on the veranda, and then we were expected to play games. During the hot part of the afternoon we played indoors, and after the shadows had begun to lengthen and the slight breeze of the evening had come up we moved outside to the wide courtyard.

I had never really grasped the system of competitive games. At home, whenever we played tag or guessing games, I was always allowed to "win"—"because," Mother used to tell Premila, "she is the youngest, and we have to allow for that." I had often heard her say it, and it seemed quite reasonable to me, but the result was that I had no clear idea of what "winning" meant.

20

When we played twos-and-threes that afternoon at school, in accordance with my training, I let one of the small English boys catch me, but was naturally rather puzzled when the other children did not return the courtesy. I ran about for what seemed like hours without ever catching anyone, until it was time for school to close. Much later I learned that my attitude was called "not being a good sport," and I stopped allowing myself to be caught, but it was not for years that I really learned the spirit of the thing.

When I saw our car come up to the school gate, I broke away from my classmates and rushed toward it yelling, "Ayah! Ayah!" It seemed like an eternity since I had seen her that morning — a wizened, affectionate figure in her white cotton sari, giving me dozens of urgent and useless instructions on how to be a good girl at school. Premila followed more sedately, and she told me on the way home never to do that again in front of the other children.

When we got home we went straight to Mother's high, white room to have tea with her, and I immediately climbed onto the bed and bounced gently up and down on the springs. Mother asked how we had liked our first day in school. I was so pleased to be home and to have left that peculiar Cynthia behind that I had nothing whatever to say about school, except to ask what "apple" meant. But Premila told Mother about the classes, and added that in her class they had weekly tests to see if they had learned their lessons well.

I asked, "What's a test?"

Premila said, "You're too small to have them. 25 You won't have them in your class for donkey's years." She had learned the expression that day and was using it for the first time. We all laughed enormously at her wit. She also told Mother, in an aside, that we should take sandwiches to school the next day. Not, she said, that *she* minded. But they would be simpler for me to handle.

That whole lovely evening I didn't think about school at all. I sprinted barefoot across the lawns with my favorite playmate, the cook's son, to the stream at the end of the garden. We quarreled in our usual way, waded in the tepid water under the lime trees, and waited for the night to bring out the smell of the jasmine. I listened with fascination to his stories of ghosts and demons, until I was too frightened to cross the garden alone in the semidarkness. The ayah found me, shouted at the cook's son, scolded me, hurried me in to supper — it was an entirely usual, wonderful evening.

It was a week later, the day of Premila's first test, that our lives changed rather abruptly. I was sitting at the back of my class, in my usual inattentive way, only half listening to the teacher. I had started a rather guarded friendship with the girl with the braids, whose name turned out to be Nalini (Nancy, in school). The three other Indian children were already fast friends. Even at that age it was apparent to all of us that friendship with the English or Anglo-Indian children was out of the question. Occasionally, during the class, my new friend and I would draw pictures and show them to each other secretly.

The door opened sharply and Premila marched in. At first, the teacher smiled at her in a kindly and encouraging way and said, "Now, you're little Cynthia's sister?"

Premila didn't even look at her. She stood with her feet planted firmly apart and her shoulders rigid, and addressed herself directly to me. "Get up," she said. "We're going home."

I didn't know what had happened, but I 30 was aware that it was a crisis of some sort. I rose obediently and started to walk toward my sister.

"Bring your pencils and your notebook," she said.

I went back for them, and together we left the room. The teacher started to say something just as Premila closed the door, but we didn't wait to hear what it was.

In complete silence we left the school grounds and started to walk home. Then I asked Premila what the matter was. All she would say was "We're going home for good."

CHANDAN KHANNA/Getty Images

This is a 2018 photograph of students from a school in Dwarka, India. Behind them is a statue of Queen Mary, who ruled the British Empire in the early 1900s and whose title also included "Empress of India."

What do you notice about the contrasts between the students and the statue? How might Premila have reacted to seeing this statue?

It was a very tiring walk for a child of five and a half, and I dragged along behind Premila with my pencils growing sticky in my hand. I can still remember looking at the dusty hedges, and the tangles of thorns in the ditches by the side of the road, smelling the faint fragrance from the eucalyptus trees and wondering whether we would ever reach home. Occasionally a horse-drawn tonga passed us, and the women, in their pink or green silks, stared at Premila and me trudging along on the side of the road. A few coolies and a line of women carrying baskets of vegetables on their heads smiled at us. But it was nearing the hottest time of day, and the road was almost deserted. I walked more and more slowly, and shouted to Premila, from time to time, "Wait for me!" with increasing peevishness. She spoke to me only once, and that was to tell me to carry my notebook on my head, because of the sun.

When we got to our house the ayah was just taking a tray of lunch into Mother's room. She immediately started a long, worried questioning about what are you children doing back here at this hour of the day. 35

Mother looked very startled and very concerned, and asked Premila what had happened.

Premila said, "We had our test today, and she made me and the other Indians sit at the back of the room, with a desk between each one."

Mother said, "Why was that, darling?"

"She said it was because Indians cheat," Premila added. "So I don't think we should go back to that school."

Mother looked very distant, and was silent a long time. At last she said, "Of course not, darling." She sounded displeased. 40

We all shared the curry she was having for lunch, and afterward I was sent off to the

145

beautifully familiar bedroom for my siesta. I could hear Mother and Premila talking through the open door. Mother said, "Do you suppose she understood all that?"

Premila said, "I shouldn't think so. She's a baby."

Mother said, "Well, I hope it won't bother her."

Of course, they were both wrong. I understood it perfectly, and I remember it all very clearly. But I put it happily away, because it had all happened to a girl called Cynthia, and I never was really particularly interested in her. ■

extending beyond the text

Premila and Santha had their names changed against their will, but there are times when people change their names by choice. People who are transgender may refer to their given name as their "dead name," for example. And when people get married, some decide to adopt their spouse's name or create an entirely new name. Read the following excerpt, in which Marcia K. Morgan examines the relationships among gender, marriage, and surnames.

from Should I Change My Name?

Marcia K. Morgan

Some brides feel pressure from the groom and his relatives to take his name for his family continuity. Many want to start a new identity as a married person and have one family name. They see a name change as the outward expression of that new life and role, leaving behind a past life and status. Changing a name is a tangible way of marking these events.

One woman said she wanted her name to reflect "all of her." Her identity needed to include all the names she has used through the years, like badges she has worn with pride for life's different phases. She used her birth surname along with two husbands' names (one past, one present). She felt if she only used her birth surname, it would not reflect the married years and her role as a wife and mother. She wanted her name to show the family she was born into and the families into which she chose to marry.

Others view married names and identity differently. They equate eliminating one person's name in favor of the other's as a symbol of inequality in a marriage, with one person being subsumed and lost in the identity of the other. They feel the practice of changing names is based on a power imbalance and sexism, and something they don't want to perpetuate. When each person in the couple keeps their birth name, it acknowledges each individual's value and worth. It honors both of their families as well as their own personal and professional lives. They make an outward statement that marriage is the joining of two lives and two identities together while everyone remains whole. As one woman said, "my husband didn't adopt me — he married me." ■

What factors do people think about when they consider changing their names? What is the difference between choosing a different name and being forced to change a name? Have you changed your name or thought about it? Why?

Understanding and Interpreting

1. How is the reader expected to interpret the actions of the headmistress when she changes the girls' names to English versions (par. 3)? Is she just a silly but mostly harmless figure, or are her actions intentionally mean or racist?

2. At the very beginning of the narrative when the girls have their names changed, the reader learns a lot about Santha and Premila. How does Rau use characterization to establish the differences between the girls, both as they are trying to acclimate to the new school and at the end of the story?

3. In paragraph 6, Rau quotes her mother's attitude toward the British: "You can bury a dog's tail for seven years and it still comes out curly, and you can take a Britisher away from his home for a lifetime and he still remains insular." What does this quotation mean, and how does it preview other events later in the narrative?

4. What aspects of school are new to Rau, specifically food, clothing, and games? How does she adjust — or not — to these differences?

5. Throughout the piece, Rau talks about her identity being split into two: Cynthia and Santha. How does this split seem to affect her? Be sure to examine the final line of the story closely to support your response.

6. In any community, there are stated rules and unstated rules that individuals are expected to follow. What are the rules of the school in this narrative? What goals do the headmistress and the teachers appear to have, especially for the Indian children, and how do those goals lead to Premila's decision to leave the school with Santha?

7. What conclusion is the reader expected to draw from the last paragraph? Explain your response.

Analyzing Language, Style, and Structure

8. **Vocabulary in Context.** In paragraph 3, Rau uses the word *precarious* to describe the bun on the head of the headmistress. What does the word mean in this context, and how does it help characterize the headmistress? What are other, more common uses for the word?

9. Words of Indian origin are scattered throughout this narrative. What is the effect of this mixed-use vocabulary?

10. In several places in the narrative, it is clear that the narrator is quite young and doesn't really understand the events around her. Locate one of these places and explain how Rau's language choices reveal her lack of understanding at the time.

11. How does Rau use details of the setting to contrast school and home (especially in paragraph 26 after her first day of school), and what does she achieve with this comparison?

12. Even though the narrative follows a straightforward chronological order, it has been carefully constructed to maximize the effect of the racism toward Premila and the other Indian children during the test. Looking back through the narrative, what elements foreshadow this ending?

Topics for Composing

13. **Analysis.** Write an examination of the characterization of Premila, Santha's older sister. What is she like at the beginning of the narrative, and how does she change throughout the piece? How does this characterization help Rau make her point about the effects of colonialism?

14. **Argument.** The quotation from *Romeo and Juliet* that appears in the introduction says essentially that if we called a rose by another name, it would still be a rose. In other words, names for people and things don't really matter. Is this true? Write an argument in which you explain to what extent you agree or disagree. You should refer to your own and others' experiences and evidence from this narrative for support.

15. **Connections.** The narrator is only five years old when the headmistress changes her name. What do you think that you would do if someone in power decided what you should be called at that age? What about at your current age? Why?

16. **Speaking and Listening.** Meet with a partner or a small group and discuss what pressures exist at your school for individuals to conform. How are those pressures similar to or different from those that Rau faced?

17. **Research.** Throughout its time as an empire, Britain held policies that were intended to make all of its colonies as much like England as possible. Research British education in Africa, India, or Australia during the late 1800s until the 1940s in order to identify the similarities and differences between education systems in those areas and the school in this story.

18. **Creative Writing.** Write a poem about a time that you may have felt like Rau when she was feeling powerless or like an outsider at her school.

19. **Multimodal.** Create an interactive or digital map that captures the reach of the British Empire at the time of this narrative, roughly between World War I and World War II. Use color, textures, or other cues to signify the amount and type of control they had. Then, with this information, write a brief response about how this influence might have contributed to some of the events presented in this narrative.

from Is Everyone Hanging Out without Me?

Mindy Kaling

Mindy Kaling (b. 1979) is an American actress, writer, producer, director, and comedian whose Hindi parents immigrated to the United States from Nigeria. She is the writer, producer, and star of *The Mindy Project*, she formerly played Kelly Kapoor on the comedy *The Office*, for which she also wrote several episodes, and she is the producer of the TV shows *Never Have I Ever*, *Four Weddings and a Funeral*, and *The Sex Lives of College Girls*. In 2012, she was named one of *Time* magazine's 100 most influential people in the world. This piece is from her first memoir, *Is Everyone Hanging Out without Me? (and Other Concerns)*, which explores various stages of her life through a series of essays, lists, and anecdotes.

In ninth grade I had a secret friend. Her name was Mavis Lehrman. Mavis lived a few streets away from me in a Tudor-style house that every Halloween her parents made look like the evil witch's cottage from *Hansel and Gretel*. (This is amazing, by the way. It behooves anyone who lives in a Tudor house to make it look like a witch cottage once in a while.) The Lehrmans were a creative and eccentric family who my parents deemed good people. Mavis was my

Saturday friend, which meant she came over to my house Saturday and we spent the afternoon watching television together.

Mavis and I bonded over comedy. It didn't matter if it was good or bad; at fourteen, we didn't really know the difference. We were comedy nerds, and we just loved watching and talking about it nonstop. We holed up in my family's TV room with blankets and watched hours of Comedy Central. Keep in mind this is not the Comedy Central of today, with the abundance of great shows like *South Park, The Daily Show*, and *The Colbert Report*. This was the early '90s, where you had to really search around to find decent stuff to watch. We'd start with the good shows, *Dr. Katz, Kids in the Hall*, or *Saturday Night Live* reruns, but when those were over, we were lucky if there was some dated movie playing like *Porky's* or *Kentucky Fried Movie*. With all the raunchy '80s sex comedies Comedy Central played, at times it felt like we were watching a confusing soft-core porn channel. It wasn't our favorite programming, but like the tray of croissants from Costco my mom left for us on the kitchen table, Mavis and I devoured it nonetheless. We loved comedy and wanted to watch everything. And more than that, we loved reenacting what we saw. The Church Lady's catchphrases were our catchphrases, and we repeated them until my mother said, exasperated: "Please stop saying 'Isn't that special?' in that strange voice. It is annoying to me and to others."

At fourteen, Mavis was already five foot ten. She had short, dark, slicked-back hair like Don Johnson in *Miami Vice*. She was very skinny and had women's size eleven feet. I know this because she accidentally wore my dad's boat shoes home one time. Mavis was a big, appreciative eater, which my parents loved. When she visited, she made a habit of immediately opening the fridge and helping herself to a heaping bowl of whatever leftover Indian food we had and a large glass of orange juice. "This *roti* and

aloo gobi is delicious, Dr. Chokalingam," she'd say to my mother, between bites. "You should start a restaurant." My mother always protested when Mavis called her by the formal "Dr." name, but I think it secretly pleased her. She was sick of some of my other friends saying things like: "Hey, Swati, how's the practice going?" in that modern, we-call-parents-by-their-first-names fashion of liberally raised East Coast kids. Both my parents were very fond of Mavis. Who wouldn't love a hungry, complimentary, respectful kid?

But that was Saturday. At school, I had a completely different set of friends.

My posse at school was tight, and there were exactly four of us: Jana, Lauren, Polly, and me. We had been friends since middle school, which was only two years, but seemed like a lifetime. The number of people in our friend group was important because of all the personalized best friend gear we had that read "JLMP," the first letters of our first names. We had JLMP beaded bracelets, JLMP embroidered bobby socks. We commissioned a caricature artist at Faneuil Hall in Boston to do a cartoon of the four of us with JLMP in giant cursive letters underneath. These mementos cemented our foursome to both us and the other people at school. You couldn't get in, and you couldn't get out. Nothing says impenetrability and closeness like a silk-screened T-shirt with an acronym most people don't understand. JLMP knew who Mavis was — she was a lifer at our school, which meant she had been there since kindergarten, and longer than any of us had been there — but she made no impact on our view of the social landscape. We didn't really talk or think about her; it was as if she was a substitute Spanish teacher or something.

The Cheesecake Factory played a major role in JLMP's social life. We went there every Friday after school. These were our wild Friday night plans. Remember, this was back in the '90s, before the only way to be a cool teenager was

5

to have a baby or a reality show (or both). We'd stay for hours chewing on straws and gossiping about boys, and collectively only spend about fifteen dollars on one slice of cheesecake and four Cokes. Then we'd leave and have our regular dinners at our respective homes. Obviously, the waiters loathed us. In a way we were worse than the dine-and-dashers because at least the dine-and-dashers only hit up Cheesecake Factory once and never showed up again. We, on the other hand, thought we were beloved regulars and that people lit up when we walked in. *We're back, Cheesecake Factory! JLMP's back! Your favorite cool, young people here to jazz up the joint!*

I know what you're thinking, that I ditched Mavis because she wasn't as cool as my more classically "girly" friends, but that wasn't it. First of all, JLMP wasn't even very cool. High school girls who have time to be super cliquey are usually not the popular girls. The actual popular girls have boyfriends, and, by that point, have chilled out on intense girl friendships to explore sex and stuff. Not us. Sex? Forget it. JLMP had given up on that happening until grad school. Yep, we were the kind of girls who, at age fourteen, pictured ourselves attending grad school. Getting a good idea of us now?

Mavis had her own friends. Maybe because of her height and short hair, she hung out with mostly guys. Her crowd was the techie boys, the ones who built the sets at school and proudly wore all black, covered in dried paint splatter. The techie boys all had fancy names like "Conrad" and "Xander" and "Sebastian." It's as if their parents had hoped that by naming them these manly, ornate names, they might have a fighting chance of being the leading men of our school. Unfortunately, the actual leading men in our school were named "Matt" or "Rob" or "Chris" and wouldn't be caught dead near our student theater unless they were receiving a soccer trophy in a sports assembly. Mavis and her guy pals built gorgeous sets for our plays like *Evita*, *Rags*, and *City of Angels*, and got absolutely

zero recognition for it. They were just kind of expected to build the sets, like the janitors were expected to clean up the hallways.

Though Mavis could have been confused for a boy from almost every angle, she had the pale skin and high cheekbones of an Edith Wharton character. Thinking back on her now, she had all the prerequisites to be a runway model in New York, especially since this was the early '90s, when it was advantageous to look like a flat-chested, rail-thin boy. But our school was behind the times, and the aesthetic that ruled was the curvy, petite, all-American Tiffani Amber Thiessen look, which Polly and Lauren had to some degree. At school, Mavis was considered neither pretty nor popular. Neither was I, by any stretch of the imagination, but at least I didn't tower over the boys in our class by a good five inches.

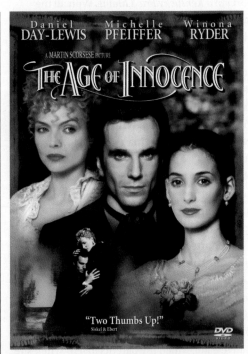

This is a poster from a film adaptation of Edith Wharton's novel, *The Age of Innocence*.

Based on this image, what might Kaling have been going for by comparing Mavis to a character in a Wharton novel?

We both lived by a weird code: Mavis and
I might be friends on Saturday afternoon, but
Friday nights and weekend sleepovers were
for JLMP. If it sounds weird and compartmen-
talized, that's because it was. But I was used to
compartmentalization. My entire teenage life
was a highly organized map of activities: twenty
minutes to shower and get ready for school,
five-minute breakfast, forty-five-minute Latin
class to thirty-minute lunch to forty-five-
minute jazz band rehearsal, etc. Compartmen-
talizing friendships did not feel different to
me. Mavis and I would say "hi" in the hallways,
and we would nod at each other. Occasionally
we would sit next to each other in study hall.
But Mavis did not fit into my life as my school
friend.

Then things started to change.

One Saturday night, I had JLMP over my
house. They wanted to watch *Sleeping with the
Enemy*, you know, the movie where Julia Roberts
fakes her own death to avoid being married to
her psycho husband? And I wanted to watch
Monty Python's Flying Circus and show them
the Ministry of Silly Walks, one of their funniest
and most famous sketches. Mavis and I had
watched it earlier that day several times in a row,
trying to imitate the walks ourselves. I played it
for them. No one laughed. Lauren said: "I don't
get it." I played it again. Still no response to it.
I couldn't believe it. The very same sketch that
had made Mavis and me clutch our chests in
diaphragm-hurting laughter had rendered my
best friends bored and silent. I made the classic
mistake of trying to explain why it was so funny,
as though a great explanation would be the key
to eliciting a huge laugh from them. Eventually
Polly said, gently, "I guess it's funny in a random
kind of way."

Within the hour we were watching Julia
Roberts flushing her wedding ring down
the toilet and starting a new life in Iowa
under an assumed identity. I could barely
enjoy the movie, still stunned by my closest

10

friends' utter lack of interest in something
I loved so much. I had always known, yeah,
maybe JLMP wouldn't be as interested in comedy as Mavis had been, but it scared me that
they dismissed it so completely. I felt like two
different people.

What happened to me was something that
I think happens to a lot of professional comedy
writers or comedians, or really anyone who's
passionate about anything and discovering it for
the first time. Most people who do what I do are
obsessed with comedy, especially during adolescence. I think we all have that moment when
our non-comedy-obsessed friends or family are
like: "Nope. I'm at my limit. I can't talk about
In Living Color anymore. It's kind of funny, but
come on."

Pictorial Press Ltd/Alamy

As Kaling found out when she showed JLMP the
Monty Python comedy sketch "The Ministry of
Silly Walks," what's funny to some people isn't
always funny to others.

Based on this image, what is intended to be
funny in this sketch? Do you find it funny?
Why or why not?

And more and more, I found that I didn't want to do what JLMP wanted to do. Like one time Lauren wanted me go to the yarn store in Harvard Square with her so we could both learn to knit. I reluctantly used my allowance to buy a skein of yarn. Who was I knitting stuff for? If I gave my mother a knitted scarf she'd be worried I was wasting my time doing stupid stuff like knitting instead of school work. Presenting a homemade knitted object to my parents was actually like handing them a detailed backlog of my idleness.

And Jana, sweet old Jana, was crazy about horses. Like super-nutso crazy about horses — that was her thing. All her drawings and back-from-vacation stories and Halloween costumes were horses. She would even pretend to be a horse during free period and lunch. We had to feed her pizza out of our hand, and she'd neigh back "thank you." Now I was getting bored of driving forty-five minutes with her parents to the equestrian center to pretend to care about her galloping back and forth in her horse recital or whatever.

I found myself wanting to spend more time with Mavis than JLMP. I spent the week looking forward to Saturday so I could write sketches with her. I didn't want her to be my secret friend anymore.

One Friday in November I didn't go to the Cheesecake Factory with JLMP. I asked Mavis if she wanted to hang out at the mall after school. We had never spent time together outside of our houses. Mavis was surprised but agreed to go. We went to the Arsenal Mall after school. We bought sour gummy worms at the bulk candy store; we walked around Express and The Limited, trying things on and buying nothing. It felt weird being with Mavis in the real world, but good weird.

The next Friday I bailed on JLMP again so my brother, Mavis, and I could see *Wayne's World* together. We spent the whole night afterward chanting: "Wayne's World! Party Time! Excellent! Schwing!" Mavis and I spent a long time discussing Rob Lowe's emergence as a comedy actor. (Again, we were comedy nerds. This was exciting

to us.) The following Friday we went to her house where Mr. Lehrman showed us how to use his camcorder so we could tape a sketch we had written, which used the characters in Gap Girls, that old *SNL* sketch with Chris Farley, Adam Sandler, and David Spade dressed up as female Gap employees. Mavis played David Spade and Adam Sandler. I played Chris Farley and all the other characters. Sometime around then, Mavis and I became real friends. Friends at school.

I spent most of winter break with Mavis, going to Harvard Square to see movies and buying comic books. I discovered she wasn't into going shopping as much as JLMP had been, but I had my mom and Aunt Sreela for that, anyway. I still considered JLMP my best friends, but began flaking on them more and more. Jana's mom even called my mom to tell her how hurt Jana was that I missed a big horse show. One Friday evening in mid-February, Mavis and I were at the RadioShack trying to find a tripod to use with her dad's camcorder. It was the mall with JLMP's Cheesecake Factory. On the escalator ride down, you could see right into the restaurant. That's when Mavis and I saw it. Jana, Lauren, and Polly were sitting in a booth together. They were laughing and talking over a slice of cheesecake, but without me. Just JLP. I was so hurt and embarrassed. Yeah, I had made another friend, but did that give them the right to orchestrate a hangout where I was so left out? For a second, I hated Mavis. I wasn't sure why, exactly, maybe for witnessing this humiliation, or for unwittingly being the cause of it? My immediate reaction was to rush over to them and confront them. But then I thought . . . why? What was I going to do with them after I confronted them? Sit with them and gossip about all the things I didn't really care about anymore?

Mavis said, quietly, "If you want to go with them, I totally get it."

There was something about the unexpectedly kind way she said that that made me happy to be with her, and not them. For some reason, I immediately thought about how my parents had always been especially fond of Mavis, and here was this moment when I understood exactly why: she was a good person. It felt so good to realize how smart my parents had been all along. "Are you kidding me?" I said. "We have to go home and film this sketch."

By the time we got down the escalator and walked to the parking lot to get picked up by her parents, my ego was still bruised, but I was also able to identify another feeling: relief.

Pretty soon after that, the rest of JLP disintegrated too. Polly was getting into music more and was getting chummier with the kids who all smoked regularly across the street in the Fairy Woods. It was Jana, surprisingly, who first got a boyfriend. A cool Thai kid named Prem, who was a senior, asked her out. Prem was pretty possessive, and within weeks Jana was learning Thai and I never saw her. Lauren and I, with whom I had the least in common, faded out quickly without the buffer of the other two. It was almost a lifting of a burden when we weren't required to stay in touch.

By the end of freshman year, it was just Mavis and me. I once half-jokingly suggested naming our friendship M&M, and Mavis looked at me with friendly but mild disgust. That was so not Mavis's style. She stayed friends with her techie guy friends, and I even had lunch with them sometimes. They were smart guys, funny and edgier than any other guys at school, and they were knowledgeable about politics, a subject barely anyone cared about. But my friend group definitely shrunk. I was without a posse, no small herd to confidently walk down the hall with. There was just Mavis and me, but it never seemed lonely

because we never stopped talking. I could have an argument, in earnest, about who was the best "Kid" in the Hall, without having to explain who they were. One friend with whom you have a lot in common is better than three with whom you struggle to find things to talk about. We never needed best friend gear because I guess with real friends you don't have to make it official. It just is.

Junior year of high school, the Lehrmans moved to Evanston, Illinois, but Mavis and I kept in touch. She would call me and tell me about the amazing shows her dad took her to see at Second City, and we planned for me to visit, but it never materialized. When we graduated high school, she went to the Cooper Union in Manhattan to pursue her love of set design, and I went to Dartmouth to pursue my love of white people and North Face parkas. We e-mailed a bit for a year or so, and then by sophomore year, the e-mails stopped. We both just got so consumed with college. I would be reminded of Mavis when my parents asked about her over summer and holiday breaks. "How is Mavis doing these days?" my mom would ask. "I think pretty good," I replied, vaguely, reminding myself to send her an e-mail one of these days, but never following through.

Mavis helped me learn so much about who I am, and who I wanted to be. I love comedy and now surround myself with people who love to talk about it just as much as I do. I like to think that Polly is in a band, that Lauren joined the right knitting circle, and that Jana found a nice horse to settle down with. Even though Mavis was my secret friend, she is the only one I hope I see again. She's the only one I wonder about. I hope she wonders about me too. ∎

Understanding and Interpreting

1. How does Kaling use details and description to characterize Mavis in paragraph 3? What is the reader expected to conclude about Mavis and Kaling from this characterization?

2. What is the JLMP group like and how does Kaling feel about her group at the beginning of the narrative? How does she contrast this group with Mavis? Why does Kaling draw this contrast?

3. How does Kaling describe high school and its various cliques and types of students? How do the social pressures of high school affect how Kaling approaches friendship?

4. How does Kaling describe herself near the beginning of the narrative, before "things started to change" (par. 11)?

5. Reread the two paragraphs in which Kaling describes what she and JLMP watched one Saturday night (pars. 12–13). Summarize what happened here that was so significant for Kaling.

6. Explain what Kaling means in paragraph 18 when she writes, "It felt weird being with Mavis in the real world, but good weird." Why is this a significant realization for Kaling at this point in the narrative?

7. How is high school different for Kaling after JLMP breaks up? Is she better or worse off? Why?

Analyzing Language, Style, and Structure

8. **Vocabulary in Context.** At the end of paragraph 3, Kaling uses the word *liberally* to describe Western parenting styles. What does the word mean in this use here, and what are other uses of the word in other contexts?

9. Kaling creates an informal, almost conversational tone in this piece, as if she is talking directly to the reader. Locate a moment that exemplifies this tone and explain how Kaling uses stylistic elements to create it. Why is this tone effective for the narrative?

10. Kaling is an actress and has been a writer for comedies on television. Return to the narrative and locate places of intended humor. Who is the target of her humor, and how does she try to make it funny?

11. At several places in the narrative, Kaling interrupts the chronological order of the story she is telling and reflects on the events as an adult looking back. Locate one of these times and explain how this reflection helps Kaling make a point about her own development.

12. The scene at the mall in which Kaling and Mavis see JLP together is a climactic moment in the narrative (par. 20). Explain how Kaling constructs this scene and uses narrative elements to express the emotional impact it had on her.

Topics for Composing

13. **Analysis.** What point does Kaling make in this narrative about the role of friendship in forming identity?

14. **Argument.** Once Kaling starts hanging out more with Mavis, she writes, "Mavis and I became real friends. Friends at school" (par. 19). Can you be friends with someone if you are not friends with that person at school? Argue for a definition about what a "real friend" means.

15. **Connections.** Do you have sets of friends like Kaling describes here that do not interact with each other regularly? Why does this happen? Is it a benefit to you? Does it lead to conflict?

16. **Connections.** Watch an episode or two of one of the TV shows that Kaling is often closely associated with (*The Mindy Project, Four Weddings and a Funeral, Never Have I Ever*). What similarities do you notice between how Kaling creates humor and conflict in the show and in this narrative?

17. **Speaking and Listening.** In paragraph 5, Kaling begins describing JLMP, who had "been friends since middle school, which was only two years, but seemed like a lifetime." With a partner or small group, share your thoughts on your middle school years. Did the time there feel like a "lifetime," or did it move quickly? Come to consensus on why time sometimes seems to move faster or slower depending on the circumstances.

18. **Multimodal.** Look back through old photographs, video, or other visual texts that show you with friends throughout your life. Arrange and present them in a way that documents how friendships change and evolve over time.

19. **Creative Writing.** Look back through Kaling's narrative and locate places of intended humor. Think about how she tries to create that humor. Try writing a scene (fiction or real) that is intentionally humorous, through the situation, word choice, or other elements. Share it with others to see if they also think it is funny, and make adjustments if necessary.

from A Life on Our Planet

David Attenborough

David Attenborough's work over the past several decades has explored all aspects of the earth in hundreds of TV shows, movies, and books. While his early work focused mostly on documenting animals, plants, and their natural surroundings, he has more recently focused on advocating for environmental causes. This is an excerpt from his 2020 memoir called *A Life on Our Planet*, a series of vignettes from his work as a filmmaker. Each chapter title is a year, and each chapter begins with details about the world population, carbon levels, and remaining wilderness for that year.

WPA Pool/Getty Images

KEY CONTEXT This excerpt takes place on the remote island of New Guinea, in the Pacific Ocean north of Australia. Attenborough includes the following map and detail of the island of New Guinea to help orient his readers.

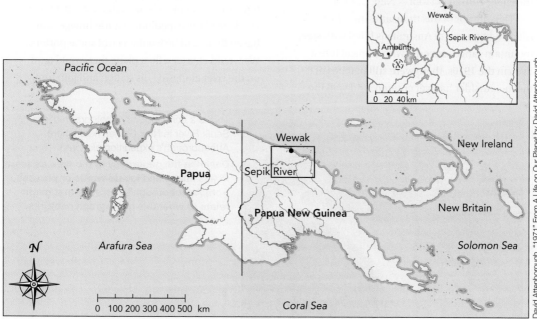

1971

World population: 3.7 billion

Carbon in atmosphere: 326 parts per million

Remaining wilderness: 58 percent

When I had accepted the administrative job at the BBC in 1965, I had asked that I be allowed every two or three years to leave my desk for a few weeks and make a programme. That way, I maintained, I would be able to keep up with the ever-changing technology of programme-making. And in 1971, I thought of a possible subject.

Until the early twentieth century, European travellers, venturing beyond their continent into distant unexplored corners of the Earth, had to travel on foot. If the country ahead was totally unknown, they recruited porters to carry all the food, the tents and other equipment that would be needed if they were to be self-sufficient far from civilisation. But, in the twentieth century, the development of the internal combustion engine put a stop to that. Explorers now used Land Rovers and jeeps, light aircraft and even helicopters. I knew of only one place where great discoveries were still being made by explorers travelling entirely on foot — New Guinea.

The interior of this thousand-mile-long island lying north of Australia is filled with steep mountain ranges covered with tropical forest. Even in the 1970s, there were still patches of it that no outsider had yet entered, and walking

with a long line of porters was still the only way that anyone could do so. Such an expedition would surely make a fascinating film.

At the time, the eastern half of New Guinea was administered by Australia. I got in touch with friends in Australian television. They found out that a mining company had asked for permission to go into one of these unknown areas to prospect for minerals. Government policy, however, stipulated that no one was allowed to do such a thing before it had been established whether or not there were any people living there. Aerial photographs had not revealed any huts or other buildings, but there were one or two tiny pinpricks in the carpet of forest that might indicate man-made clearings. None were big enough to allow a helicopter to land. The only way to discover what they were was to send in a patrol on foot. And I together with a camera team could accompany them — if I really wanted to do so.

My plan was simple. The nearest European settlement to the area in question was a small government station called Ambunti on the Sepik, the great river that runs roughly eastwards, parallel to the north coast of the island before emptying into the Pacific. The government officer who would lead the expedition, Laurie Bragge, was based there and he would recruit some porters. We would charter a float plane that would land on the river alongside his station and join him.

This is a contemporary photograph of the Sepik River in New Guinea near where Attenborough's expedition explored.

Describe the geography of the area as seen in this image and locate words or phrases from Attenborough's narrative that might relate to what this photograph captures.

Brent Stirton/Getty Images Reportage

It turned out to be the most exhausting journey that I have ever made. Laurie had managed to assemble a hundred porters, but even that was not enough to carry all the food that we would need. We would have to have an air-drop of more supplies after about three weeks. We also had to travel across the grain of the country. Every morning soon after dawn, we started walking, cutting our way through the densest forest I have ever encountered, hauling ourselves up steep muddy slopes to the crest of a ridge and then slithering down the sodden undergrowth on the other side, to wade across a small winding river and then do the same thing, over and over again. At four o'clock every afternoon we stopped, made camp and put up tarpaulins to give us shelter from the drenching rains that would start promptly at five.

After three and a half weeks of this, one of the porters noticed human footprints in the forest on the edge of the patch we had cleared. Someone had been close to our camp the previous night, watching us. We followed the tracks. Night after night, having pitched our tents, we put out gifts — cakes of salt, knives and packets of glass beads. One of the porters was stationed to sit on a tree stump and call out every few minutes, saying that we were friends and were bringing gifts. But it was unlikely that the people we were following, whoever they were, would understand him for there are over a thousand mutually incomprehensible languages spoken in New Guinea.

Even small groups had their own distinct language. Night after night we called. Morning after morning, the gifts lay where we had left them.

After three further weeks of walking, our supplies were running low. We made camp and, for the next two days, the porters laboriously cut down huge trees to create a clearing on which a helicopter might drop fresh supplies. The drop was successful and accurate and we set off, the porters once again with reassuringly heavy loads — but not complaining, for we had been on short rations. Four weeks after we had started, we were nearing country that had already been

mapped. It seemed the expedition and our film, would have no satisfying conclusion.

And then, one morning, I woke up beneath my tarpaulin and saw outside a group of small men, standing within a couple of yards of me. None of them was more than about a metre and a half tall. They were naked except for a broad belt of bark into which they had pushed a bunch of leaves, at the front and the back. Several had what I later discovered were bats' teeth stuck through holes that they had pierced in the sides of their noses. Hugh, the cameraman, who always slept with his camera within arm's reach fully loaded and ready to shoot, was already recording. The men stared at us, wide-eyed, as though they had never seen our like before. I doubtless did the same. I had never seen anyone like them either.

To my surprise I found that it was not difficult to communicate with them. I tried by gestures to indicate that we were short of food. They pointed to their mouths, nodded and opened their string bags to show us roots, probably taro, that they had been gathering. I pointed to cakes of salt we had brought with us. It is used as currency all over New Guinea. They nodded. We had started to trade. Laurie then asked them the names of the nearest rivers. That was more difficult to explain, but they eventually understood what he wanted and they began to list them. How many did they know? They counted them, touching first their fingers one by one, tapping places up their forearm, their elbow, and continuing up the arm and ending on the side of the neck. In fact, Laurie was not particularly interested in the actual names of the rivers, or how many there were. He wanted to know what gestures they used to indicate number. He knew the counting gestures used by other groups in the area, and the ones used by these little people would tell him what trading contacts they might have.

After ten minutes or so, the men started to wave their arms and roll their eyes, indicating that they were going to leave. We waved back in response, trying to invite them to return in

10

157

Attenborough has become a highly visible environmental advocate. These are photographs taken at protests for environmental causes.

What makes the use of Attenborough's image an effective tool for protest? Based on what you read in this except of his memoir, why might you conclude he is a strong supporter of environmental causes?

the morning with more food. And they left. The following morning, they reappeared with more roots as we had hoped they would do. We asked if we might see where they were camped and perhaps meet their women and children. After some confusion — or was it perhaps reluctance — they nodded and led us off into the forest. We followed a few yards behind them. It was hard going. The vegetation was very thick. We lost sight of them as we rounded the trunk of a gigantic tree; on the other side, there was no sign of them. They had vanished. We called. But there was no reply. Were we walking into an ambush? We had no idea. After calling for several minutes, we turned and walked back to camp.

I had had a vision of how all human beings had once lived — in small groups that found all they needed in the natural world around them. The resources they relied upon were self-renewing. They produced little or no waste. They lived sustainably, in balance with their environment in a way that could continue effectively, for ever.

A few days later, I was back in the twentieth century and behind my desk in the Television Centre. ∎

Understanding and Interpreting

1. Contrast the differences between exploration before the twentieth century with how Attenborough describes exploration in the twentieth century.

2. Based on what you have read in this narrative, why do you think that Attenborough wanted to undertake the project in New Guinea? What seems to drive him to this work? Use evidence from the piece to draw your conclusions.

3. Reread the two paragraphs starting with "And then one morning . . ." (pars. 10–11). Summarize the encounter with the aboriginal men. Explain how these men and Attenborough's group were able to communicate with each other and what they learned from each other.

4. Although Attenborough does not explain, try to speculate why the men disappeared when he and his film crew wanted to see their homes. What evidence leads you to this speculation?

Analyzing Language, Style, and Structure

5. **Vocabulary in Context.** In paragraph 4, Attenborough writes that mining companies have asked for permission "to prospect for minerals." What does the word *prospect* mean in this context, and what other uses of the word have you encountered?

6. Attenborough starts each of the chapters in his narrative with the three facts about population, carbon level, and remaining wilderness. Why might he have chosen to do this? What are the possible effects of his choice on the reader?

7. Reread paragraph 6 and examine Attenborough's use of language, especially imagery and diction, to describe the challenging conditions of the trip.

8. At times in his narrative, Attenborough uses words like *unknown*, *civilization*, and *discover*. Why might these words be problematic in the context of two cultures interacting with each other?

9. Reread the last sentence of the narrative. What effect does Attenborough create with the sudden shift in setting? Why might he have chosen to end his piece in this way?

Topics for Composing

10. **Analysis.** Reread paragraph 13, which is Attenborough's reflection. What does he appear to have learned through this experience? What parts of the narrative help to illustrate what he learned?

11. **Argument.** Should Attenborough have started the expedition in the first place? Write an argument in which you consider the pros and cons of a Western documentary film crew hoping to study an isolated culture.

12. **Connections.** Attenborough says that the people he encountered in New Guinea "produced little or no waste. They lived sustainably, in balance with their environment." How similar or different is this from your life in the contemporary Western world?

13. **Speaking and Listening.** With a small group or the whole class, hold a discussion about effective steps that people can take in their own homes, lives, and workplaces to address the issue of climate change. Try to reach consensus on the top two or three individual actions. You may need to conduct some research ahead of time to prepare for the discussion.

14. **Research.** Attenborough writes that in 1971 much of New Guinea was uncharted. Conduct research on present-day New Guinea to learn more about how the aboriginal populations are doing after more interaction with other cultures.

15. **Research.** In 1971, the time period of this narrative, the world's population was 3.7 billion. Just 40 years later, Attenborough identifies the population as 7.0 billion. Research the problems that this rapid population growth is creating. Identify one of the main challenges and describe possible solutions some are recommending.

16. **Research.** Attenborough says that in 1971, there were "over a thousand mutually incomprehensible languages spoken in New Guinea" (par. 7). Research how this is possible. What unique factors of the geography of New Guinea may have contributed to this?

17. **Creative Writing.** Attenborough writes his piece in a straightforward, journalistic way. Rewrite a section or two of this narrative as if it were his personal diary, describing his feelings, fears, and excitement regarding the trip and his encounter with the aboriginals.

18. **Multimodal.** Attenborough is known for his nature films, for which he often provides the narration. Locate photographs and other images about an environmental topic that is meaningful to you, arrange them in slides or with another presentation tool, and write narration that would support and add depth to the visuals.

narrative / section two

Learning to Love My Brown Skin

Erika L. Sánchez

Erika L. Sánchez is a poet, novelist, and essayist. She is a regular contributor on issues of gender, culture, and politics to publications such as *Time*, the *Guardian*, *Rolling Stone*, *Cosmopolitan*, *Jezebel*, and many others. She published her debut young adult novel *I Am Not Your Perfect Mexican Daughter* in 2017, and her memoir *Crying in the Bathroom* in 2022. This piece was published in *Racked* in 2016.

Adriana Díaz

When I was four years old, I climbed atop our bathroom sink to look in the mirror and see if I was ugly. My uncle had said just said to me, "Ay mija, como estás fea," which, roughly translated, meant, "Oh honey, you're so ugly."

What I didn't understand was that he meant it affectionately, that he meant the opposite. He didn't actually think I was ugly; that's just the way Mexicans joke around and show love.

I remember I had my hair in a tight french braid, which was typical throughout my childhood and frequently caused me headaches. I looked at my big nose and lips and wondered if my uncle was right. I was transfixed by my own face for a few minutes.

While I studied myself to confirm my lack of beauty, my mother walked into the bathroom and burst out laughing. She knew exactly what I was doing and reassured me that I was, in fact, pretty, and that my uncle was simply teasing me. My family often reminds me of my cute confusion that day. "Remember that time you thought you were ugly?" We laugh because, of course, I wasn't.

Still, I wondered about this throughout my young life. Did the world think I was ugly? What did it mean to be pretty? Who got to decide? The thin white girls on the '90s sitcoms I loved — *Full House, Saved by the Bell, Sabrina, the Teenage Witch* — were always lavished with so much attention, and I didn't look like them. For one, I was the wrong color: I was way too brown. And when I watched *Beverly Hills, 90210*, I was so confused that Donna Martin, played by Tori Spelling, was considered a hot girl. Were all blonde women automatically considered beautiful? Was I missing something? Was it some sort of conspiracy?

160

Everett Collection, Inc

mikel roberts/Getty Images

These are pictures from two of the TV shows that Sánchez says that she grew up with.
How do these images illustrate what Sánchez suggests about the effect these shows may have had on her thoughts regarding beauty?

It didn't help that growing up, skin color was the object of much judgment in my family. If I were to use food imagery to describe my skin (which I know is frowned upon), I'm the color of lightly toasted bread or a well-stirred cappuccino — not quite caramel, with strong yellow undertones. This was considered acceptable on my mother's side of the family, for whom being dark was (and largely continues to be) undesirable. Some family members used the word "indio" as a slur against darker-skinned Mexicans when I was growing up. Even now, members of my family will occasionally say that someone is "dark but pretty." The word "prieto," which means "dark-colored," can be either affectionate or derogatory, depending on the tone.

My maternal grandmother, ironically, was one of the worst perpetrators of this colorism. With brown skin and thick, dark braids, she looked undeniably indigenous. I still wonder, What did she see when she looked in the mirror? Did she have some sort of dysmorphia? Did colonialism burrow that deeply into her psyche?

There was also Spanish-language television, which was abysmal on so many levels. (Unfortunately, it hasn't changed much since then.) I grew up watching telenovelas in which the rich protagonists tended to be light-skinned, while the servants and evil-doers were dark and indigenous-looking. The sexy women on the television program *Sábado Gigante*, and even on news shows, were always voluptuous, scantily clad, and fair.

Colorism in Mexican culture has a long history rooted in colonialism. Many people don't know that Mexico had a complicated legal caste system in the 1700s, which continues to influence beauty standards today. To exert control over their colonies, the Spanish commissioned paintings to illustrate different racial distinctions.

As the cultural historian John Charles Chasteen describes in his book *Born in Blood and Fire*, a person's caste was recorded in their baptismal register and those of lower (and darker-skinned) castes were legally barred from, among other things, becoming priests, owning weapons, attending university, and even wearing silk. There were 16 theoretical categories in all, though only six were typically used. Some of the lower castes were derisively given animal names such as Wolf or Coyote. Although the members of these six categories were legally prohibited from mixing, there was a whole lot of boinking and raping going on, so it was inevitable. Ironically, because the Spanish crown was desperate for money, those from lower castes who became successful were allowed to purchase exemptions. You could actually buy your whiteness.

I'd like to say that I've always been above such backwards attitudes about race, but that wouldn't be true. When I was a kid, I sometimes thought about how much easier life would be if I were white. Those Tanner brats from *Full House*, for one, seemed to have it made. Everyone thought they were adorable, and their biggest problem was always something stupid, like getting the chickenpox.

Feeling alienated, as a teen, I chose to express myself with styles that consciously pushed back on beauty norms. I went through a disheveled goth phase during which I dyed my hair jet black and wore fishnets, and an ascetic phase that saw me shaving my head and donning threadbare thrift clothes. I was sick of trying to fulfill some impossible ideal, of trying to be seen as "pretty," so instead I gave the world the finger.

One of the most shameful things I've ever done is attempt to lighten my skin. When I was 15, I found some white Halloween liquid makeup in my drawer left over from an old vampire costume and started to add it to my foundation. Though I wasn't quite conscious of

it, I thought lighter skin was more attractive. In retrospect, it just made me look like a corpse.

Looking back, there were other indications that I was internalizing cultural tropes that suggested my features weren't beautiful. I religiously read *Seventeen* magazine, and once used one of its makeup tips to try to make my nose look smaller. It involved drawing a line of concealer down the middle and subtly blending it on the sides. (To my disappointment, it didn't work.) I was also embarrassed of my large mouth and lips, having been teased throughout my childhood for my big ole' kisser. The word "trompa," which means trumpet, was a commonly used word to describe my mouth. My brother once hilariously gave me a ladle when I asked for a spoon. The joking was all in good fun, of course, but it nonetheless helped convince me that I looked clownish.

It has taken me years of work to embrace the way I look. I credit my feminist education for showing me that the world will always attempt to make me feel insecure — capitalism is in fact based on this idea — and that I have to love myself with unwavering conviction. I recognize today the internalized racism that affected me when I was younger. I thought my nose was too wide because it's not the small and pointy nose that Hollywood stars purchase from plastic surgeons. Now I see that being embarrassed by my lips is ridiculous because people actually pay for theirs to look like mine. But, and here comes the racism, society tends to consider those kinds of features special and beautiful only on white women; Kylie Jenner has pretty much made a career out of this. Though all of this is obvious to me now, I was clueless as a teenager. Thank you, bell hooks, Naomi Wolf, and all the feminist godmothers who have helped me dismantle the white patriarchy that I built inside myself.

In the past few years, I've often been confused for Greek, Italian, Middle Eastern, and all kinds of Latin American. To my chagrin,

Sánchez writes that she "religiously read *Seventeen* magazine." This is a photograph of actor Bella Thorne at a 2014 bookstore event where she signed copies of her *Seventeen* magazine cover.

What would Sánchez likely find objectionable about this image now that she is older. What are your thoughts about the image?

Joshua Blanchard/Getty Images

sometimes people think I'm white. "My name is *Sánchez*," I tell them frantically. "*Sánchez*." But it's not that simple. Earlier this year I took a DNA test to discover my ethnic makeup. Though I had a vague idea of what it may be, I didn't have much information because our lineage records in Mexico are difficult to find. I've also asked my grandparents about our ancestry, but our family history is murky.

When I saw my DNA results, I was astonished. I ran around the room in a frenzy. It turns out that I'm compositionally a medley, in part Iberian, Native American, Greek, Italian, and African (North African, Nigerian, Senegalese, and Bantu). This information has profoundly changed the way I perceive myself. Suddenly, the way I look makes perfect sense to me. Of course I still have days in which I look in the mirror and pick myself apart. But mostly, when I look at my face, I understand something I didn't before. Regardless of what the pervading culture tries to impose on me, I contain the beauty of multitudes. ∎

Understanding and Interpreting

1. Reread paragraph 5, in which Sánchez describes the TV shows she watched while growing up. Explain the effect of this medium on Sánchez, and what she means when she writes, "I was the wrong color."

2. What does Sánchez mean by the term *colorism* (par. 7), and how do her grandmother's views on colorism affect Sánchez and her family?

3. At the end of paragraph 9, Sánchez writes, "You could actually buy your whiteness." What does she mean by this and how does it relate to her sense of her own self?

4. What attitude is Sánchez trying to express when she writes, "I gave the world the finger" (par. 11)? What does she reveal about herself as a teenager with this statement?

5. Explain the ways that Sánchez "was internalizing cultural tropes" when she was a teenager.

6. Sánchez writes, "It has taken me years of work to embrace the way I look" (par. 14). Summarize the steps she took and explain how each step led her to appreciate her beauty.

7. What does Sánchez mean when she says she had to "dismantle the white patriarchy that I built in myself" (par. 14)?

8. What does Sánchez reveal about herself with the last phrase of her narrative: "I contain the beauty of multitudes"?

Analyzing Language, Style, and Structure

9. **Vocabulary in Context.** In paragraph 8, Sánchez writes that the "sexy women . . . [on television] were always voluptuous, scantily clad, and fair." What does the word *fair* mean in this context? What other meanings of this word have you encountered?

10. Why does Sánchez likely choose to start her narrative by describing her actions when she was four years old? What does this choice establish at the very beginning of the piece and how do we see echoes of this throughout her narrative?

11. Sánchez uses the word *ugly*, or its Spanish equivalent, six times in the first five paragraphs. What is the effect of this repetition?

12. Sánchez uses Spanish words throughout her narrative, oftentimes providing the translations for them. What effect does her use of Spanish words create?

13. Sánchez ends paragraph 5 with a series of rhetorical questions — in other words, questions to which she expects no answer. What is the effect of this stylistic choice?

14. Paragraph 9 is a bit of a departure from the personal narrative Sánchez is telling. Why might she have chosen to insert this historical diversion at this point in her story?

15. In paragraph 9, Sánchez describes the process of the mixing of castes in Mexico as "boinking and raping." What is the effect of these word choices?

Topics for Composing

16. **Analysis.** What does Sánchez ultimately learn about how to define and not define her own beauty? How does she use elements of narrative to communicate these lessons to her reader?

17. **Argument.** Write an argument in which you explain what, if any, restrictions should be put on media companies to ensure that negative stereotypes about race and beauty are not perpetuated?

18. **Connections.** The parent company of Instagram conducted internal research on the effects of that app on teenagers. The resulting study, which was leaked to reporters in 2021, concluded that, "We make body image issues worse for one in three teen girls" and "thirty-two percent of teen girls said that when they felt bad about their bodies, Instagram made them feel worse." What impact, if any, does social media have on you and your self-perception? How do you think the influence of social media today is similar to or different from that of the TV shows and magazines that Sánchez consumed in the 1990s?

19. **Speaking and Listening.** Sánchez grew up in the 1990s with such shows as *Full House*, *Saved by the Bell*, and *Sabrina, the Teenage Witch*. In groups or pairs, discuss some of the shows that you watched growing up and explain how those shows presented ideas of gender roles, sexual orientation, race, and other factors. How are the representations in those shows similar to or different from what Sánchez describes?

20. **Research.** Sánchez gives credit to her "feminist godmothers" bell hooks and Naomi Wolf for her intellectual growth on issues of gender. Research these two scholars and explain how they may have influenced Sánchez's development. How is their work relevant to your own life?

21. **Creative Writing.** Look at yourself in a mirror like Sánchez did at the beginning of this narrative and write down all the words and phrases you can think of. Then, arrange those words and phrases into a poem that reflects some aspect of your own self-identity.

22. **Multimodal.** Make a collage of images and words representing the media that you are exposed to regularly that might have some influence on your self-image.

Us and Them

David Sedaris

David Sedaris (b. 1956) is an American humorist and essayist whose work regularly appears in the *New Yorker* and on National Public Radio's *This American Life*. He has published several collections of his work. One of his essays, "The Santaland Diaries," about his experiences working as an elf in a department store during Christmas, is often performed in theaters around the country during the holiday season. "Us and Them" appeared in his collection called *Dress Your Family in Corduroy and Denim*, published in 2004.

Jenny Lewis/Contour by Getty Images

When my family first moved to North Carolina, we lived in a rented house three blocks from the school where I would begin the third grade. My mother made friends with one of the neighbors, but one seemed enough for her. Within a year we would move again and, as she explained, there wasn't much point in getting too close to people we would have to say good-bye to. Our next house was less than a mile away, and the short journey would hardly merit tears or even good-byes, for that matter. It was more of a "see you later" situation, but still I adopted my mother's attitude, as it allowed me to pretend that not making friends was a conscious choice. I could if I wanted to. It just wasn't the right time.

Back in New York State, we had lived in the country, with no sidewalks or streetlights; you could leave the house and still be alone. But here, when you looked out the window, you saw other houses, and people inside those houses. I hoped that in walking around after dark I might witness a murder, but for the most part our neighbors just sat in their living rooms, watching TV. The only place that seemed truly different was owned by a man named Mr. Tomkey, who did not believe in television. This was told to us by our mother's friend, who dropped by one afternoon with a basketful of okra. The woman did not editorialize — rather, she just presented her information, leaving her listener to make of it what she might. Had my mother said, "That's the craziest thing I've ever heard in my life," I assume that the friend would have agreed, and had she said, "Three cheers for Mr. Tomkey," the friend likely would have agreed as well. It was a kind of test, as was the okra.

To say that you did not believe in television was different from saying that you did not care for it. Belief implied that television had a master plan and that you were against it. It also suggested that you thought too much. When my mother reported that Mr. Tomkey did not believe in television, my father said, "Well, good for him. I don't know that I believe in it, either."

"That's exactly how I feel," my mother said, and then my parents watched the news, and whatever came on after the news.

Word spread that Mr. Tomkey did not own a television, and you began hearing that while this was all very well and good, it was unfair of him to inflict his beliefs upon others, specifically his innocent wife and children. It was speculated that just as the blind man develops a keener sense of hearing, the family must somehow compensate for their loss. "Maybe they read," my mother's friend said. "Maybe they listen to the radio, but you can bet your boots they're doing something."

I wanted to know what this something was, and so I began peering through the Tomkeys' windows. During the day I'd stand across the street from their house, acting as though I were waiting for someone, and at night, when the view was better and I had less chance of being

discovered, I would creep into their yard and hide in the bushes beside their fence.

Because they had no TV, the Tomkeys were forced to talk during dinner. They had no idea how puny their lives were, and so they were not ashamed that a camera would have found them uninteresting. They did not know what attractive was or what dinner was supposed to look like or even what time people were supposed to eat. Sometimes they wouldn't sit down until eight o'clock, long after everyone else had finished doing the dishes. During the meal, Mr. Tomkey would occasionally pound the table and point at his children with a fork, but the moment he finished, everyone would start laughing. I got the idea that he was imitating someone else, and wondered if he spied on us while we were eating.

When fall arrived and school began, I saw the Tomkey children marching up the hill with paper sacks in their hands. The son was one grade lower than me, and the daughter was one grade higher. We never spoke, but I'd pass them in the halls from time to time and attempt to view the world through their eyes. What must it be like to be so ignorant and alone? Could a

5

H. Armstrong Roberts/ClassicStock/
Getty Images

This is a photograph from the 1960s — approximately the time period of this narrative — of a family watching television.

How does this image capture what Sedaris suggests about the role of TV in society at the time?

normal person even imagine it? Staring at an Elmer Fudd lunch box, I tried to divorce myself from everything I already knew: Elmer's inability to pronounce the letter r, his constant pursuit of an intelligent and considerably more famous rabbit. I tried to think of him as just a drawing, but it was impossible to separate him from his celebrity.

One day in class a boy named William began to write the wrong answer on the blackboard, and our teacher flailed her arms, saying, "Warning, Will. Danger, danger."[1] Her voice was synthetic and void of emotion, and we laughed, knowing that she was imitating the robot in a weekly show about a family who lived in outer space. The Tomkeys, though, would have thought she was having a heart attack. It occurred to me that they needed a guide, someone who could accompany them through the course of an average day and point out all the things they were unable to understand. I could have done it on weekends, but friendship would have taken away their mystery and interfered with the good feeling I got from pitying them. So I kept my distance.

In early October the Tomkeys bought a boat, and everyone seemed greatly relieved, especially my mother's friend, who noted that the motor was definitely secondhand. It was reported that Mr. Tomkey's father-in-law owned a house on the lake and had invited the family to use it whenever they liked. This explained why they were gone all weekend, but it did not make their absences any easier to bear. I felt as if my favorite show had been canceled.

Halloween fell on a Saturday that year, and by the time my mother took us to the store, all the good costumes were gone. My sisters dressed as witches and I went as a hobo. I'd looked forward to going in disguise to the Tomkeys' door, but they were off at the lake, and their house was dark. Before leaving, they had left a coffee can

full of gumdrops on the front porch, alongside a sign reading DON'T BE GREEDY. In terms of Halloween candy, individual gumdrops were just about as low as you could get. This was evidenced by the large number of them floating in an adjacent dog bowl. It was disgusting to think that this was what a gumdrop might look like in your stomach, and it was insulting to be told not to take too much of something you didn't really want in the first place. "Who do these Tomkeys think they are?" my sister Lisa said.

The night after Halloween, we were sitting around watching TV when the doorbell rang. Visitors were infrequent at our house, so while my father stayed behind, my mother, sisters, and I ran downstairs in a group, opening the door to discover the entire Tomkey family on our front stoop. The parents looked as they always had, but the son and daughter were dressed in costumes — she as a ballerina and he as some kind of a rodent with terry-cloth ears and a tail made from what looked to be an extension cord. It seemed they had spent the previous evening isolated at the lake and had missed the opportunity to observe Halloween. "So, well, I guess we're trick-or-treating now, if that's okay," Mr. Tomkey said.

I attributed their behavior to the fact that they didn't have a TV, but television didn't teach you everything. Asking for candy on Halloween was called trick-or-treating, but asking for candy on November first was called begging, and it made people uncomfortable. This was one of the things you were supposed to learn simply by being alive, and it angered me that the Tomkeys did not understand it.

"Why of course it's not too late," my mother said. "Kids, why don't you . . . run and get . . . the candy."

"But the candy is gone," my sister Gretchen said. "You gave it away last night."

"Not that candy," my mother said. "The other candy. Why don't you run and go get it?"

---

[1] "Danger, Will Robinson!" was a popular catchphrase from the 1960s television series *Lost in Space.* —Eds.

"You mean our candy?" Lisa said. "The candy that we earned?"

This was exactly what our mother was talking about, but she didn't want to say this in front of the Tomkeys. In order to spare their feelings, she wanted them to believe that we always kept a bucket of candy lying around the house, just waiting for someone to knock on the door and ask for it. "Go on, now," she said. "Hurry up."

My room was situated right off the foyer, and if the Tomkeys had looked in that direction, they could have seen my bed and the brown paper bag marked MY CANDY. KEEP OUT. I didn't want them to know how much I had, and so I went into my room and shut the door behind me. Then I closed the curtains and emptied my bag onto the bed, searching for whatever was the crummiest. All my life chocolate has made me ill. I don't know if I'm allergic or what, but even the smallest amount leaves me with a blinding headache. Eventually, I learned to stay away from it, but as a child I refused to be left out. The brownies were eaten, and when the pounding began I would blame the grape juice or my mother's cigarette smoke or the tightness of my glasses — anything but the chocolate. My candy bars were poison but they were brand-name, and so I put them in pile no. 1, which definitely would not go to the Tomkeys.

Out in the hallway I could hear my mother 20 straining for something to talk about. "A boat!" she said. "That sounds marvelous. Can you just drive it right into the water?"

"Actually, we have a trailer," Mr. Tomkey said.

"So what we do is back it into the lake."

"Oh, a trailer. What kind is it?"

"Well, it's a boat trailer," Mr. Tomkey said.

"Right, but is it wooden or, you know . . . I 25 guess what I'm asking is what style trailer do you have?"

Behind my mother's words were two messages. The first and most obvious was "Yes, I am talking about boat trailers, but also I am dying." The second, meant only for my sisters and me, was "If you do not immediately step forward with that candy, you will never again experience freedom, happiness, or the possibility of my warm embrace."

I knew that it was just a matter of time before she came into my room and started collecting the candy herself, grabbing indiscriminately, with no regard to my rating system. Had I been thinking straight, I would have hidden the most valuable items in my dresser drawer, but instead, panicked by the thought of her hand on my doorknob, I tore off the wrappers and began cramming the candy bars into my mouth, desperately, like someone in a contest. Most were miniature, which made them easier to accommodate, but still there was only so much room, and it was hard to chew and fit more in at the same time. The headache began immediately, and I chalked it up to tension.

My mother told the Tomkeys she needed to check on something, and then she opened the door and stuck her head inside my room. "What the hell are you doing?" she whispered, but my mouth was too full to answer. "I'll just be a moment," she called, and as she closed the door behind her and moved toward my bed, I began breaking the wax lips and candy necklaces pulled from pile no. 2. These were the second-best things I had received, and while it hurt to destroy them, it would have hurt even more to give them away. I had just started to mutilate a miniature box of Red Hots when my mother pried them from my hands, accidentally finishing the job for me. BB-size pellets clattered onto the floor, and as I followed them with my eyes, she snatched up a roll of Necco wafers.

"Not those," I pleaded, but rather than words, my mouth expelled chocolate, chewed chocolate, which fell onto the sleeve of her sweater. "Not those. Not those."

Bettmann/Getty Images

This is a photograph of children visiting the Candy Chocolate and Confectionery Institute in New York, at roughly the time period of this narrative.

What are some of the immediate feelings you have when looking at this image? Write a few sentences from the perspective of one of the children before and after eating the candy. How is what you wrote similar to or different from what Sedaris writes about his candy-eating experience?

She shook her arm, and the mound of 30 chocolate dropped like a horrible turd upon my bedspread. "You should look at yourself," she said. "I mean, really look at yourself."

Along with the Necco wafers she took several Tootsie Pops and half a dozen caramels wrapped in cellophane. I heard her apologize to the Tomkeys for her absence, and then I heard my candy hitting the bottom of their bags.

"What do you say?" Mrs. Tomkey asked.

And the children answered, "Thank you."

While I was in trouble for not bringing my candy sooner, my sisters were in more trouble for not bringing theirs at all. We spent the early part of the evening in our rooms, then one by one we eased our way back upstairs, and joined our parents in front of the TV. I was the last to arrive, and took a seat on the floor beside the sofa. The show was a Western, and even if my head had not been throbbing, I doubt I would have had the wherewithal to follow it. A posse of outlaws crested a rocky hilltop, squinting at a flurry of dust advancing from the horizon, and I thought again of the Tomkeys and of how alone and out of place they had looked in their dopey costumes. "What was up with that kid's tail?" I asked.

"Shhhh," my family said.   35

For months I had protected and watched over these people, but now, with one stupid act, they had turned my pity into something hard and ugly. The shift wasn't gradual, but immediate, and it provoked an uncomfortable feeling of loss. We hadn't been friends, the Tomkeys and I, but still I had given them the gift of my curiosity. Wondering about the Tomkey family had made me feel generous, but now I would have to shift gears and find pleasure in hating them. The only alternative was to do as my mother had instructed and take a good look at myself. This was an old trick, designed to turn one's hatred inward, and while I was determined not to fall for it, it was hard to shake the mental picture snapped by her suggestion: here is a boy sitting on a bed, his mouth smeared with chocolate. He's a human being, but also he's a pig, surrounded by trash and gorging himself so that others may be denied. Were this the only image in the world, you'd be forced to give it your full attention, but fortunately there were others. This stagecoach, for instance, coming round the bend with a cargo of gold. This shiny new Mustang convertible. This teenage girl, her hair a beautiful mane, sipping Pepsi through a straw, one picture after another, on and on until the news, and whatever came on after the news. ■

extending beyond the text

While David Sedaris writes stories about his own life, he has said that he prefers the term "humorist," rather than "memoirist" because it allows him to stretch the truth a little bit more than he could otherwise. In an interview with the *Guardian* in 2009, he said, "I've always been very upfront about the way I write, and I've always used the tools humorists use, such as exaggeration." Read the following excerpt in which the interviewer continues to ask him to elaborate on his approach:

> But if Sedaris isn't claiming to write memoir, the charge is that he should call his work fiction. He smiles, and sighs. "You know, if you tell a funny story at the dinner table in front of 10 people, nine of them will laugh, and one of them will say that's not true. Now, I never say that to people. I'm never the 'that's not true' guy when someone tells a funny story. And I don't like the 'that's not true' guy. I've always hated that person."

Do these comments mean that Sedaris's writing should be considered "fiction" rather than "nonfiction"? Would you be upset if it turned out that Sedaris made up elements of the narrative "Us and Them"? Which details from the piece could be exaggerated without turning this narrative into a work of fiction? Which details need to be based on fact for this text to still be considered narrative? What's the line between the two for you?

Understanding and Interpreting

1. Reread the first paragraph and explain what Sedaris reveals about himself and his family.

2. What are Sedaris's parents' views on television, and how do they compare with those of the Tomkeys?

3. In paragraph 6, Sedaris starts spying on the Tomkeys. Why does he do this, and how should we as readers judge his actions?

4. In paragraphs 8–9, Sedaris describes how the Tomkey children may not know about two entertainment figures popular at the time, Elmer Fudd and Will Robinson. Why does Sedaris think this information is important, and how does he choose to help them? Why?

5. When the Tomkeys purchase a boat, why does Sedaris say, "I felt as if my favorite show had been cancelled" (par. 10).

6. Summarize what Sedaris does when he is told to bring some of his Halloween candy to the Tomkey children. What do these actions reveal about him? What does he mean when he says, "While it hurt to destroy them, it would have hurt even more to give them away" (par. 28)?

7. Reread the dialogue between Sedaris's mother and Mr. Tomkey about boat trailers (pars. 20–24) and Sedaris's description of what that dialogue actually meant (par. 25). What does this dialogue reveal about his mother and about himself?

8. Reread the final paragraph of the narrative. Why does Sedaris not want to "look at himself" as his mother instructs him to do that night with the candy? How does he keep from "looking at himself"?

9. Why might Sedaris have chosen to title this piece "Us and Them"?

Analyzing Language, Style, and Structure

10. **Vocabulary in Context.** In paragraph 28, Sedaris writes, "rather than words, my mouth expelled chocolate, chewed chocolate, which fell onto the sleeve of her sweater." Explain the meaning of the word *expelled* in this context. How is it similar to and different from other uses you know? What makes it an effective word choice in this instance?

11. Sedaris uses diction thoughtfully, often revealing key details of his characters through careful word choice. What do each of the underlined words reveal about the characters being described or about the narrator, Sedaris himself:

    a. "Because they had no TV, the Tomkeys were <u>forced</u> to talk during dinner. They had no idea how <u>puny</u> their lives were" (par. 7).

    b. "What must it be like to be so <u>ignorant</u> and <u>alone</u>? Could a <u>normal</u> person ever imagine it?" (par. 8).

    c. "'You mean <u>our</u> candy?' Lisa said. 'The candy we <u>earned</u>?'" (par. 17).

    d. "[T]hen one by one we <u>eased</u> our way back upstairs, and joined our parents in front of the TV" (par. 33).

12. The humor in Sedaris's writing often takes the form of commentary on the ridiculousness of a situation or, as often is the case in this narrative, his own youthful cluelessness. Look back at these excerpts and explain how Sedaris builds humor and communicates something about himself to the reader:

    a. "It occurred to me that they needed a guide, someone who could accompany them through the course of an average day and point out all the things they were unable to understand. I could have done it on weekends, but friendship would have taken away their mystery and interfered with the good feeling I got from pitying them" (par. 9).

    b. "Asking for candy on Halloween was called 'trick-or-treating' but asking for candy on November first was called begging" (par. 13).

    c. "The headache began immediately, and I chalked it up to tension" (par. 26).

    d. "She shook her arm, and the mound of chocolate dropped like a horrible turd upon my bedspread. 'You should look at yourself,' she said. 'I mean, really look at yourself'" (par. 29).

    e. "For months I had protected and watched over these people, but now, with one stupid act, they had turned my pity into something hard and ugly" (par. 35).

13. *Irony* is a term used to describe how writers use words and situations to communicate meaning that is the opposite of what is stated and expected, often for humorous effect. Reread portions of this narrative and locate places where Sedaris is likely being ironic. Explain how what he says differs from his intended meaning.

Topics for Composing

14. **Analysis.** Even though he says that he doesn't want to "look at himself," what does Sedaris reveal about himself in this piece? Is he introspective or not? What evidence from the narrative supports your interpretation?

15. **Argument.** The Tomkeys do not have a television, which today might be the equivalent of not having Internet access — or at least not having streaming services like Netflix or Hulu. Would you and your family be better off without those entertainment choices, or would you be "ignorant and alone" (par. 8)? Write an argument for or against having access to seemingly limitless streaming entertainment services.

16. **Connections.** When have you acted or wanted to act as Sedaris did with his candy? Describe the situation. What did your actions or intentions reveal about you?

17. **Speaking and Listening.** David Sedaris is a regular contributor to National Public Radio, and audio of him reading of his essays is widely available online. Listen to one or more of his pieces and explain how listening to him speak affects the way that you understand the intended humor of "Us and Them."

18. **Research.** This narrative takes place in the early 1960s, and Sedaris makes it seem as if the Tomkeys are very strange for not having a television. Would they have been? Research the prevalence of TV ownership and the role of television in America at the time of the events to answer this question.

19. **Creative Writing.** Try writing a few paragraphs from the perspective of one of the Tomkeys, a child or a parent, as that member of the family interacts with the Sedaris family.

20. **Multimodal.** Sedaris feels sorry for the Tomkeys because without a TV he assumes that they do not understand the same cultural references he does, such as "Danger, Will Robinson" or Elmer Fudd's voice. Create a multimodal piece with modern examples of images, video, memes, or other texts that you think people without the Internet or streaming services might not understand.

Wearing a Mask Won't Protect Us from Our History

Burnell Cotlon

Burnell Cotlon is an Army veteran and the owner of a small neighborhood grocery store in the Lower Ninth Ward in New Orleans, Louisiana. He told the following story to Eli Saslow, a reporter for the *Washington Post*, in April 2020.

William Widmer/Redux

KEY CONTEXT In 2019–20, at the beginning of the COVID-19 pandemic, many businesses that were not deemed "essential" were forced to close to slow the spread of infection, resulting in high unemployment and increased poverty for many. At the time, Cotlon was operating the only grocery store in his entire neighborhood.

I know every person who comes into this store, and they know me. Burnell's Market. It's my name above the door. These are my neighbors, but now we're eyeing each other like strangers, paranoid and suspicious. "Don't stand so close." "Don't breathe too heavy." "Just drop the groceries in the trunk and walk away." Some people have started sliding money back and forth across the counter with a plastic spoon.

Everybody's scared of everybody in a grocery now. There's so much fear, and I get it. I'm scared, too. But what bothers me more is the desperation.

This is the only fresh grocery in the Lower Ninth Ward of New Orleans, so pretty much everybody's a regular. They come for cigarettes or a biscuit on their way to work. Its mostly tourism jobs down here — Bourbon Street, the big

This is a picture of Burnell Cotlon's store.

Based on this image, how is his store different from a commercial supermarket and what do these differences suggest about Cotlon?

hotels, and restaurants downtown, and those places have closed up in the last month. At least half my customers have lost jobs. They come to the register counting food stamps, quarters, and dimes. I keep telling them, "It's okay. I'm not in a hurry. Take your time. Stop apologizing." I had somebody barter me last week over a 70-cent can of beans. I used to sell two pieces of fried chicken for $1.25, and I cut it to a dollar.

We have an ATM in the store, and I watch people punching in their numbers, cursing the machine, trying again and again. It gives out more rejection slips than dollar bills. Some of these people don't have any savings. There's no fallback.

Last week, I caught a lady in the back of the store stuffing things into her purse. We don't really have shoplifters here. This whole store is two aisles. I can see everything from my seat up front. So I walked over to her real calm and put my hand on her shoulder. I took her purse and opened it up. Inside she had a carton of eggs, a six-pack of wieners, and two or three candy bars. She started crying. She said she had three kids, and her man had lost his job, and they had nothing to eat and no place to go. Maybe it was a lie. I don't know. But who's making up stories for seven or eight dollars of groceries? She was

telling me, "Please, please, I'm begging you," and I stood there and thought about it, and what am I supposed to do?

I said: "That's okay. You're all right." I let her take it. I like to help. I always want to say yes. But I'm starting to get more desperate myself, so it's getting harder.

The first time in my life I let a customer float on credit was four weeks ago. It was a young guy who comes by most days to buy a few things, or just to sit outside with me on the milk crates and chop it up. He got home from the military a few years back, and I was in the Army, so we have that in common. Good guy. He'd been working as a cook downtown, and last month his restaurant closed up. He asked if he could come work for me.

I operate on a shoestring. It took every dollar I had to open this place after Hurricane Katrina. I've robbed Peter to pay Paul so many times that Peter's got nothing left. So I had to tell him, "I already have a cook, and I'm barely paying him. I can't afford two." But this guy, he was hurting. He needed something to eat. He picked up four cans of tuna, a Sno-Ball, and laundry detergent. He told me he was good for it as soon he gets his unemployment check, and I trust him. I rang it up for eleven dollars. I took out a notebook that I usually keep near the register and started a little tab.

That notebook kept coming back out. Next it was Ms. Richmond. She did housekeeping at a hotel and lost that. Her tab was $48. Then it was a lady who shucks oysters downtown. She's got a big family to take care of, so she's at $155. Then there's another guy who I deliver to, since he's bedridden, and I showed up with two bags and he had nothing to give me. So he's at $54.80.

This has gone from a grocery store to a food pantry. That's how I'm feeling. 10

And what am I supposed to say? I don't blame any of these people. I like them. Some of these customers, I love. I truly do. They're getting by however they can. It's not their fault. It's not like they're asking me for handouts on gin or beer. I don't sell alcohol. I won't give loans on cigarettes. What they need is milk, cheese, canned goods, bread, toilet paper, bleach, baby wipes. It's basics — the basic essentials. One elderly guy tried to start a tab for three dollars of snacks for his grandchildren, so I gave him the snacks. Another lady said she lost her job at a nightclub downtown, and she tried to proposition me for $20 even though my wife was standing right there working at the register. I gave her the $20 and she left.

I've got 62 tabs in the book now. From zero to 62 in less than a month. It's page after page of customers on credit. I'm out almost $3,000 so far. I know that might not sound like much, but at a store like this it's my electric bill, my water bill, the mortgage on my house. I never missed a mortgage payment in my life until April 1st came and went, and now this virus has me calling around and asking for forgiveness, too. I'm paying one of my employees with free breakfast. I'm maxed on bills. I'm doing my best to keep this place open. Everybody here is waiting on unemployment checks and stimulus payments to keep us going, but let's be real. Some of these losses aren't coming back. I know how this goes. I lived in a FEMA trailer for three years after Katrina. I went from having 48 neighbors on my block to having three. They can talk all they want about how we'll bounce back and this will all be behind us before we know it, but not everybody bounces back. Some people are already standing in quicksand. There might be a recovery on Bourbon Street, but when will it show up here? Recovering can take forever.

Sorry. I try to be optimistic. I try not to be angry. There's no use in it, and it's not my personality.

These are photographs of the two neighborhoods that Cotlon describes in his piece, the tourist area of Bourbon Street (left) and the Lower Ninth Ward, where his market is located.

What differences do you notice between these images? How does Cotlon's description of these two neighborhoods compare with their representation in these images?

My customers come to the store because it's a happy place, and this community deserves something good. I've got music blaring out front, always upbeat, drawing people in. I have candy and cold treats for the kids that are out of school. I'm running out of some things now that it's getting so tight. I'm low on rice and sugar, but I hustle to fill this store. I say to my customers: "Tell me what you want and I'll stock it." They're grateful for this place. But right now most everybody coming into the store is terrified. They're upset. They're mad. The reality right now is this virus is hitting the black community harder. It's the same old story.

Life in this neighborhood is an underlying condition: hard jobs, long hours, bad pay, no health insurance, no money, bad diet. That's every day. They have disabilities. They have high blood pressure, breathing problems, diabetes. Before I opened, this part of the city was a food desert. The easiest way to get fresh produce was to take three buses to the Walmart in Chalmette. I gave free blood-pressure checks when I opened, and not because it was good for business. Cigarettes are a big seller. Candy and cold drinks go quick. I tell people, "You only live one life. You've got to look after it." But fruits and

veggies are expensive. If you're hungry, are you spending that dollar on an onion, or on nachos with chili cheese? We were made more vulnerable to this virus down here because of what we've had to deal with. Wearing a mask won't protect us from our history.

All of us know people now who are sick, or worse. My mom was exposed and quarantined for two weeks. I had a guy in the store the other day talking about how his sister was going on a ventilator. We lost one of our customers a few days ago, Mr. Lewis. He ran a free museum on black culture. Sixty-eight years old, and that's that.

There's another lady who lived two blocks from the store. She'd been coming almost every week since I opened, but she'd been having a hard time. She lost her income and needed groceries, so we started her on a tab. Then she caught the virus, and I delivered more groceries to her porch.

She died last week, and a few days later, I went into the book to look at her tab. There are a few accounts closing like that now, and probably more coming. Hers was 72 dollars and 14 cents. I found her name and drew a line through it. ■

Understanding and Interpreting

1. Reread the first two paragraphs of the narrative. What does Cotlon communicate about himself and about how the pandemic has changed his neighbors?
2. Cotlon catches a woman shoplifting (par. 5). What does he do, and what do these actions reveal about him?
3. What does he mean by "I've robbed Peter to pay Paul so many times that Peter's got nothing left" (par. 8)?
4. In paragraph 14, Cotlon says, "It's the same old story." Explain what he means by this as he expands upon it in the paragraph that follows.

Analyzing Language, Style, and Structure

5. **Vocabulary in Context.** In paragraph 7, Cotlon says, "I let a customer float on credit." What does *float* mean in this context, and how is its use here related to other uses of the word?

175

6. Locate a particularly striking sentence or paragraph that captures the desperation of Cotlon's customers. Explain how his word choice and details make that desperation vividly real to his readers.

7. Cotlon starts his narrative with a focus on his customers before turning to how the pandemic is affecting him, starting in paragraph 8. How might this structure affect how readers perceive him and his narrative?

8. Reexamine the syntactical choices made throughout the piece, specifically the use of short sentences at times. What are the effects of these choices? What tone do they help to create?

9. In paragraph 8, Cotlon refers to a notebook that he keeps near the register, and he returns to that notebook several times throughout the narrative. What connections can you draw between the notebook and the deepening crisis Cotlon describes?

10. What is Cotlon's tone toward his customers? Which of his words and phrases communicate this tone?

11. What is the effect of the figurative language in this statement: "Some people are already standing in quicksand" (par. 12)?

12. Earlier in the piece Cotlon moves from descriptions of his customers to himself, and then in paragraph 15, he shifts again, this time to larger historical and cultural forces that have affected people in the Lower Ninth Ward. What important information is included in this section, and what effect is created through the way he decides to structure his narrative?

13. Reread the final line of the narrative. What makes that last line so emotionally powerful?

Topics for Composing

14. **Analysis.** Explain what Cotlon means when he says, "Wearing a mask won't protect us from our history" (par. 15). What evidence from the narrative supports your interpretation of this line?

15. **Argument.** What are the most appropriate steps that local, state, and national government officials can take to support people in need like Cotlon's customers? Using evidence from this narrative and other sources, write an argument about a specific action or policy you would recommend.

16. **Connections.** While you were likely fairly young when this piece was first published in 2021, you probably remember some details about the pandemic. What was that time like for you, your family, and friends? How were your experiences similar to or different from those that Cotlon describes? If needed, ask family members and others to help fill in some details for you.

17. **Speaking and Listening.** Cotlon told his story to *Washington Post* reporter Eli Saslow, who likely recorded it and then wrote it down. Though it is safe to assume that Saslow's writing accurately presents Cotlon's story, Saslow had to make some choices, including, for example, where to apply punctuation and what punctuation marks to use. Meet with a partner and tell each other a little bit of what you remember — or were told — about the pandemic. Each partner will listen closely and then try to transcribe the other's recollections as accurately as possible, using sentence structures that most accurately reflect the telling of the story.

18. **Research.** Cotlon mentions Hurricane Katrina a couple of times in his narrative. Conduct research to learn more about the hurricane's lasting impact on New Orleans, the Lower Ninth Ward in particular, and explain why Cotlon would reference it here in a piece about the pandemic. Also try to explain why Cotlon says that there might be a recovery for Bourbon Street, but not the Lower Ninth Ward.

La Gringuita

Julia Alvarez

Julia Alvarez (b. 1950) was born in New York but raised in the Dominican Republic until she was ten, her family fleeing to the United States after her father became involved in an unsuccessful plot to overthrow the dictator Rafael Trujillo. She received a BA from Middlebury College and an MA from Syracuse University. Alvarez has published poetry, fiction, memoir, and children's books. "La Gringuita" is from a collection of autobiographical essays, *Something to Declare (1998)*, in which the author examines identity and the art of writing.

Jeff Malet Photography/Newscom

The inevitable, of course, has happened. I now speak my native language "with an accent." What I mean by this is that I speak perfect childhood Spanish, but if I stray into a heated discussion or complex explanation, I have to ask, "Por favor ¿puedo decirlo en ingles?" Can I please say it in English?

How and why did this happen?

When we emigrated to the United States in the early sixties, the climate was not favorable for retaining our Spanish. I remember one scene in a grocery store soon after we arrived. An elderly shopper, overhearing my mother speaking Spanish to her daughters, muttered that if we wanted to be in this country, we should learn the language. "I do know the language," my mother said in her boarding-school English, putting the woman in her place. She knew the value of speaking perfect English. She had studied for several years at Abbot Academy, flying up from the Island to New York City, and then taking the train up to Boston. It was during the war, and the train would sometimes fill with servicemen, every seat taken.

One time, a young sailor asked my mother if he could sit in the empty seat beside her

and chew on her ear.[1] My mother gave him an indignant look, stood up, and went in search of the conductor to report this fresh[2] man. Decades later, hearing the story, my father, ever vigilant and jealous of his wife and daughters, was convinced — no matter what my mother said about idiomatic expressions — that the sailor had made an advance. He, himself, was never comfortable in English. In fact, if there were phone calls to be made to billing offices, medical supply stores, Workman's Compensation, my father would put my mother on the phone. She would get better results than he would with his heavy, almost incomprehensible accent.

At school, there were several incidents of name-calling and stone-throwing, which our teachers claimed would stop if my sisters and I joined in with the other kids and quit congregating together at recess and jabbering away in Spanish. Those were the days before bilingual education or multicultural studies, when kids

---

[1] Chew on her ear: the idiom "chew someone's ear off" means to talk to someone for a long time and in a boring manner. —Eds.

[2] Fresh: lewd, disrespectful. —Eds.

like us were thrown in the deep end of the public school pool and left to fend for ourselves. Not everyone came up for air.

Mami managed to get us scholarships to her old boarding school where Good Manners and Tolerance and English Skills were required. We were also all required to study a foreign language, but my teachers talked me into taking French. In fact, they felt my studying Spanish was equivalent to my taking a "gut course." Spanish was my native tongue, after all, a language I already had in the bag and would always be able to speak whenever I wanted. Meanwhile, with Saturday drills and daily writing assignments, our English skills soon met school requirements. By the time my sisters and I came home for vacations, we were rolling our eyes in exasperation at our old-world Mami and Papi, using expressions like *far out*, and *what a riot!* and *outta sight*, and *believe you me* as if we had been born to them.

As rebellious adolescents, we soon figured out that conducting our filial business in English gave us an edge over our strict, Spanish-speaking parents. We could spin circles around my mother's *absolutamente no* by pointing out the flaws in her arguments, in English. My father was a pushover for pithy quotes from Shakespeare, and a recitation of "The quality of mercy is not strained" could usually get me what I wanted. Usually. There were areas we couldn't touch even with a Shakespearean ten-foot pole: the area of boys and permission to go places where there might be boys, American boys, with their mouths full of bubblegum and their minds full of the devil.

Our growing distance from Spanish was a way in which we were setting ourselves free from that old world where, as girls, we didn't have much say about what we could do with our lives. In English, we didn't have to use the formal *usted*[3] that immediately put us in our place with

our elders. We were responsible for ourselves and that made us feel grown-up. We couldn't just skirt culpability by using the reflexive: the bag of cookies did not finish itself, nor did the money disappear itself from Mami's purse. We had no one to bail us out of American trouble once we went our own way in English. No family connections, no tio whose name might open doors for us. If the world was suddenly less friendly, it was also more exciting. We found out we could do things we had never done before. We could go places in English we never could in Spanish, if we put our minds to it. And we put our combined four minds to it, believe you me.

My parents, anxious that we not lose our tie to our native land, and no doubt thinking of future husbands for their four daughters, began sending us "home" every summer to Mami's family in the capital. And just as we had once huddled in the school playground, speaking Spanish for the comfort of it, my sisters and I now hung out together in "the D.R.," as we referred to it, kibitzing[4] in English on the crazy world around us: the silly rules for girls, the obnoxious behavior of macho guys, the deplorable situation of the poor. My aunts and uncles tried unsuccessfully to stem this tide of our Americanization, whose main expression was, of course, our use of the English language. "Tienen que hablar en espanol," they commanded. "Ay, come on," we would say as if we had been asked to go back to baby talk as grown-ups.

By now, we couldn't go back as easily as that. Our Spanish was full of English. Countless times during a conversation, we were corrected, until what we had to say was lost in our saying it wrong. More and more we chose to answer in English even when the question was posed in Spanish. It was a measure of the growing distance between ourselves and our native

10

---

[3] *Usted*: the formal word for "you" in Spanish; used when speaking to an elder or superior. —Eds.

[4] Kibitzing: talking casually. —Eds.

culture — a distance we all felt we could easily retrace with just a little practice. It wasn't until I failed at first love, in Spanish, that I realized how unbridgeable that gap had become.

That summer, I went down to the Island by myself. My sisters had chosen to stay in the States at a summer camp where the oldest was a counselor. But I was talked into going "home" by my father, whose nephew — an older (by twenty years) cousin of mine — had been elected the president of El Centro de Recreo, the social club of his native town of Santiago. Every year at El Centro, young girls of fifteen were "presented" in public, a little like a debutante ball. I was two years past the deadline, but I had a baby face and could easily pass for five years younger than I was — something I did not like to hear. And my father very much wanted for one of his daughters to represent la familia among the creme de la creme of his hometown society.

I arrived with my DO-YOUR-OWN-THING!!! T-shirt and bell-bottom pants and several novels by Herman Hesse,[5] ready to spread the seeds of the sixties revolution raging in the States. Unlike other visits with my bilingual cousins in the capital, this time I was staying in a sleepy, old-fashioned town in the interior with Papi's side of the family, none of whom spoke English.

Actually I wasn't even staying in town. Cousin Utcho, whom I called *tio*[6] because he was so much older than I was, and his wife, Betty — who, despite her name, didn't speak a word of English either — lived far out in the countryside on a large chicken farm where he was the foreman. They treated me like a ten-year-old, or so I thought, monitoring phone calls, not allowing male visitors, explaining their carefulness by reminding me that my parents had entrusted them with my person and they

wanted to return me in the same condition in which I had arrived. Out there in the boonies, the old-world traditions had been preserved full strength. But I can't help thinking that in part, Utcho and Betty treated me like a ten-year-old because I talked like a ten-year-old in my halting, childhood Spanish. I couldn't explain about women's liberation and the quality of mercy not being strained, in Spanish. I grew bored and lonely, and was ready to go back to New York and call it quits on being "presented," when I met Dilita.

Like me, Dilita was a hybrid. Her parents had moved to Puerto Rico when she was three, and she had lived for some time with a relative in New York. But her revolutionary zeal had taken the turn of glamour girl rather than my New-England-hippy variety. In fact, Dilita looked just like the other Dominican girls. She had a teased hairdo; I let my long hair hang loose in a style I can only describe as "blowing in the wind." Dilita wore makeup; I did a little lipstick and maybe eyeliner if she would put it on for me. She wore outfits; I had peasant blouses, T-shirts, and blue jeans.

But in one key way, Dilita was more of a rebel than I was: she did exactly what she wanted without guilt or apology. She was in charge of her own destino, as she liked to say, and no one was going to talk her into giving that up. I was in awe of Dilita. She was the first "hyphenated" person I had ever met whom I considered successful, not tortured as a hybrid the way my sisters and I were. 15

Dilita managed to talk Utcho into letting me move into town with her and her young, married aunt, Carmen. Mamacán, as we called her, was liberal and light-hearted and gave us free rein to do what we wanted. "Just as long as you girls don't get in trouble!" Trouble came in one denomination, we knew, and neither of us were fools. When the matrons in town complained about our miniskirts or about our driving around with boys and no chaperons, Mamacán

---

[5] Hermann Hesse: a Nobel Prize–winning German poet and novelist in the early to mid-1900s. —Eds.

[6] *Tio*: "uncle" in Spanish. —Eds.

threw up her hands and said, "¡Pero si son americanas!" They're American girls!

We hit it off with the boys. All the other girls came with their mamis or tias in tow; Dilita and I were free and clear. Inside of a week we both had boyfriends. Dilita, who was prettier than I, landed the handsome tipo, tall Eladio with raven-black hair and arched eyebrows and the arrogant stance of a flamenco dancer, whereas I ended up with his chubby sidekick, a honeyskinned young man with wonderful dimples and a pot belly that made him look like a Dominican version of the Pillsbury doughboy. His name was Manuel Gustavo, but I affectionately nicknamed him Mangú, after a mashed plantain dish that is a staple of Dominican diet. A few days after meeting him, Mangú's mother sent over an elaborate dessert with lots of white frosting that looked suggestively like a wedding cake. "Hinthint," Dilita joked, an expression everyone was using at her school, too.

Every night the four of us went out together: Dilita sat up front with Eladio, who had his own car, and I in the backseat with Mangú — a very cozy boy-girl arrangement. But actually, if anyone had been listening in on these dates, they would have thought two American girlfriends were out for a whirl around the town. Dilita and I yakked, back and forth, starting first in Spanish out of consideration for our boyfriends, but switching over into English as we got more involved in whatever we were talking about. Every once in a while, one of the guys would ask us, "¿Y que lo que ustedes tanto hablan?"[7] For some reason, this request to know what we were talking about would give us both an attack of giggles. Sometimes, Eladio, with Mangú joining in, sang the lyrics of a popular song to let us know we were being obnoxious:

> Las hijas de Juan Mejia
> son bonitas y bailan bien
> pero tienen un defecto

que se rien de to' el que ven.
(The daughters of Juan Mejia
dance well and are so pretty
but they've got one bad quality,
they make fun of everybody.)

Las gringuitas,[8] they nicknamed us. Dilita didn't mind the teasing, but Mangú could always get a rise out of me when he called me a gringa. Perhaps, just a few years away from the name-calling my sisters and I had experienced on the school playground, I felt instantly defensive whenever anyone tried to pin me down with a label.

But though he teased me with that nickname, Mangú made it clear that he would find a real gringa unappealing. "You're Dominican," he declared. The litmus test was dancing merengue, our national, fast-moving, lots-of-hip-action dance. As we moved across the dance floor, Mangú would whisper the lyrics in my ear, complimenting my natural rhythm that showed, so he said, that my body knew where it came from. I was pleased with the praise. The truth is I wanted it both ways: I wanted to be good at the best things in each culture. Maybe I was picking up from Dilita how to be a successful hybrid.

Still, when I tried to talk to Mangú about something of substance, the conversation foundered. I couldn't carry on in Spanish about complicated subjects, and Mangú didn't know a word of English. Our silences troubled me. Maybe my tias were right. Too much education in English could spoil a girl's chances in Spanish.

But at least I had Dilita to talk to about how confusing it all was. "You and I," she often told me as we lay under the mosquito net in the big double bed Mamacán had fixed for us, "we have the best of both worlds. We can have a good time here, and we can have a good time there."

"Yeah," I'd say, not totally convinced.

20

---

[7] *¿Y que lo que ustedes tanto hablan?*: "and what are you talking about?" in Spanish. —Eds.

[8] *Las gringuitas*: "little non-Hispanic girls" in Spanish. —Eds.

Alvarez writes, "The litmus test was dancing merengue, our national, fast-moving, lots-of-hip-action dance."

In what ways does this image capture Alvarez's descriptions of merengue?

WANDYCZ Kasia/Getty Images

Down on the street, every Saturday night, the little conjunto[9] that Eladio and Mangú had hired would serenade us with romantic canciones.[10] We were not supposed to show our faces, but Dilita and I always snuck out on the balcony in our baby dolls to talk to the guys. Looking down at Mangú from above, I could see the stiffness of the white dress shirt his mother had starched and ironed for him. I felt a pang of tenderness and regret. What was wrong with me, I wondered, that I wasn't falling in love with him?

After the presentation ball, Dilita left for Puerto Rico to attend a cousin's wedding. It was then, when I was left alone with Manuel Gustavo, that I realized that the problem was not me, but me *and* Manuel Gustavo.

Rather than move back to the lonely boonies, I stayed on in town with Dilita's aunt for the two weeks remaining of my visit. But without Dilita, town life was as lonely as life on a chicken farm. Evenings, Mangú would come over, and we'd sit on the patio and try to make conversation or drive out to the country club in 25 a borrowed car to dance merengue and see what everyone else was doing. What *we* were doing was looking for people to fill up our silence with their talk.

One night, Mangú drove out towards Utcho's chicken farm and pulled over at a spot where often the four of us had stopped to look at the stars. We got out of the car and leaned against the side, enjoying the breeze. In the dark, periodically broken by the lights of passing cars, Mangú began to talk about our future.

I didn't know what to say to him. Or actually, in English, I could have said half a dozen ambivalent, soothing things. But not having a complicated vocabulary in Spanish, I didn't know the fancy, smooth-talking ways of delaying and deterring. Like a child, I could just blurt out what I was thinking. "Somos diferente, Mangú." We are so different. The comment came out sounding inane.

"No, we're not," he argued back. "We're both Dominicans. Our families come from the same hometown."

"But we left," I said, looking up at the 30 stars. From this tropical perspective, the stars seemed to form different constellations in

---

[9] *Conjunto*: "band" in Spanish. —Eds.
[10] *Canciones*: "songs" in Spanish. —Eds.

the night sky. Even the Big Dipper, which was so easy to spot in New England, seemed to be misplaced here. Tonight, it lay on its side, right above us. I was going to point it out to Mangú — in part to distract him, but I could not remember the word for *dipper — la cuchara grande*, the big spoon?

But Mangú would not have been interested in the stars anyway. Once it was clear that we did not share the same feelings, there was nothing much left to say. We drove back to Mamacán's house in silence.

I don't know if that experience made Mangú forever wary with half-breed Dominican-York girls, *gringuitas*, who seemed to be talking out of both sides of their mouths, and in two different languages, to boot. I myself never had a Spanish-only boyfriend again. Maybe the opportunity never presented itself, or maybe it was that as English became my dominant tongue, too many parts of me were left out in Spanish for me to be able to be intimate with a potential life partner in only that language.

Still, the yearning remained. How wonderful to love someone whose skin was the same honey-dipped, sallow-based color; who said *concho*[11] when he was mad and *cielito linda*[12] when he wanted to butter you up! "¡Ay! to make love in Spanish . . . ," the Latina narrator of Sandra Cisneros's story, "Bien Pretty," exclaims. "To have a lover . . . whisper things in that language crooned to babies, that language murmured by grandmothers, those words that smelled like your house . . ." But I wonder if after the Latina protagonist makes love with her *novio*, she doesn't sit up in bed and tell him the story of her life in English with a few *palabritas*[13] thrown in to capture the rhythm of her Latin heartbeat?

As for Manuel Gustavo, I met up with him a few years ago on a visit to the Island. My husband, a gringo from Nebraska, and I were driving down the two-lane *autopista*[14] on our way up to the mountains on a land search. A pickup roared past us. Suddenly, it slowed and pulled onto the shoulder. As we drove by, the driver started honking. "What does he want me to do?" my husband shouted at me. I looked over and saw that the driver was still on the shoulder, trying to catch up with us. I gestured, what do you want?

"Soy yo," the man called out, "Manuel Gustavo."

35

Almost thirty years had passed. He had gotten heavier; his hairline had receded; there was gray in his hair. But the dimples were still there. Beside him sat a boy about seven or eight, a young duplicate of the boy I had known. "Mangú!" I called out. "Is that really you?"

By this time my husband was angry about the insanity of this pickup trying to keep up with us on the narrow shoulder while Mack trucks roared by on the other lane. "Tell him we'll stop ahead, and you guys can talk."

© Harry Gruyaert/Magnum Photos

How might this photograph of a young girl on the beach in the Dominican Republic capture the "old yearning" that Alvarez writes about?

---

[11] *Concho*: a Spanish expletive. —Eds.

[12] *Cielito linda*: a Spanish phrase, roughly translated to mean "lovely sweet one." —Eds.

[13] *Palabritas*: "little words" in Spanish. —Eds.

[14] *Autopista*: "freeway" in Spanish. —Eds.

But the truth was that I didn't want to stop and talk to Manuel Gustavo. What would I have said to him now, when I hadn't been able to talk to him thirty years ago? "It's good to see you again, Mangú," I shouted. I waved good-bye as my husband pulled ahead. In my side mirror, I watched as he signaled, then disappeared into the long line of traffic behind us.

"Who was that?" my husband wanted to know.

I went on to tell my husband the story of   40
that summer: the presentation; Utcho and Betty; my worldly-wise friend Dilita; Eladio, who looked like a flamenco dancer; the serenades; the big double bed Dilita and I slept in with a mosquito net tied to the four posts. And of course, I told him the story of my romance with Manuel Gustavo.

And, as I spoke, that old yearning came back. What would my life have been like if I had stayed in my native country?

The truth was I couldn't even imagine myself as someone other than the person I had become in English, a woman who writes books in the language of Emily Dickinson and Walt Whitman, and also of the rude shopper in the grocery store and of the boys throwing stones in the schoolyard, their language, which is now my language. A woman who has joined her life with the life of a man who grew up on a farm in Nebraska, whose great-grandparents came over from Germany and discouraged their own children from speaking German because of the antipathy that erupted in their new country towards anything German with the outbreak of World War I. A woman who is now looking for land in the Dominican Republic with her husband, so that they can begin to spend some time in the land she came from.

When we took the turnoff into the mountains, we rolled up our windows so we could easily hear the cassette player. My husband

Gaby D'Alessandro

This illustration by Dominican artist Gaby D'Alessandro accompanied an article called "The Pursuit of Happiness," which proposes looking at Gross National Happiness as a better measure of progress than Gross National Product.

Describe the tone of this illustration and explain how D'Alessandro uses color, light, and other visual elements to create this tone. Why might this image also be appropriate as an illustration for this narrative, especially considering the way that Alvarez starts and finishes her piece?

had ordered Spanish-language tapes a while back from the Foreign Service Institute so that he could keep up with my family in the capital. Recently, he had dusted them off and started listening to them to prepare himself for our land hunt. I had decided to join him in these lessons, in part to encourage him, but also because I wanted to regain the language that would allow me to feel at home again in my native country. ∎

Understanding and Interpreting

1. Explain how learning English gave Alvarez and her sisters power over her parents. How did they use this power?

2. Besides giving her power over her parents, what other effects did learning English have on Alvarez? How did she feel about this at the time (pars. 6–8), as she was slowly losing her Spanish language?

3. Explain how Alvarez responds to the differences in gender expectations that she faces when she goes to the Dominican Republic that summer by herself (par. 13).

4. What are the similarities and differences between Alvarez and her friend Dilita? Why is this contrast important to the story Alvarez is telling?

5. Characterization of other people in a narrative often reveals as much about the narrator as it does about the person being described. Explain what Alvarez reveals about herself while describing her boyfriend Mangú, including her choice of nickname for him.

6. Explain what role the merengue, the popular Dominican dance, plays in this narrative. How does it reflect Alvarez's inner conflicts?

7. Why is Alvarez, at the time, reluctant to agree with Dilita that the two of them "have the best of both worlds" (par. 22)? Does she agree at the end of the narrative?

8. What conclusion does Alvarez draw about language, culture, and identity the last night that she and Mangú are together looking at the stars (pars. 27–31)?

9. Alvarez introduces the reader to her husband only at the end of the narrative. What information about him — and his family — does she include, and how does this relate to the ideas about language and identity that Alvarez explores in this piece?

Analyzing Language, Style, and Structure

10. **Vocabulary in Context.** Explain the meaning of Alvarez's use of the words *hyphenated* and *hybrid* when describing herself and Dilita in paragraph 15. How are these words effective at communicating her attitude toward culture at the time? How are these words used differently in other contexts?

11. What does Alvarez achieve by starting her narrative with the incidents of language confusion and hostility her mother faces in the first three paragraphs?

12. In paragraph 5, Alvarez writes that kids in public school "were thrown in the deep end." What does the metaphor mean in the context of her narrative? At the end of that paragraph, she writes, "Not everyone came up for air." What might Alvarez expect that we conclude about public school from this last sentence?

13. What is Alvarez likely trying to communicate by putting the word *home* in quotation marks when referring to the Dominican Republic?

14. Alvarez includes words in Spanish throughout her narrative, sometimes translating them and sometimes not. What effect do these choices create for readers?

15. Reread paragraph 33. Explain what inner conflicts remain for Alvarez and how her language choices communicate these conflicts.

16. While the narrative follows a strict chronological order, there is a significant time jump when Alvarez sees Mangú again much later in her life. How does the inclusion of this scene help Alvarez communicate a central idea about language, identity, and/or culture?

Topics for Composing

17. **Analysis.** Overall, what is Alvarez suggesting about the role that language played in shaping her own identity? What evidence from the narrative supports your interpretation?

18. **Argument.** Do you agree with Alvarez when she suggests that speaking the native language of a country is essential to feeling at home there? Explain.

19. **Connections.** When have you ever felt caught between cultures like Alvarez describes? Your experience might be similar to hers, based on language and geography, or it could be subcultures in school, on sports teams, or other groups.

20. **Speaking and Listening.** A few times in this narrative, Alvarez expresses how difficult it is to communicate her thoughts fully in Spanish because she has only the vocabulary of a ten-year-old. If you have studied more than one language, try using your second language to explain a scientific, mathematical, or historical concept you learned in another class this year to someone who also speaks that language. If you have not studied a second language, try explaining the concept with only the word choice of a ten-year-old in English. What did you learn about the challenges of communication through this exercise?

21. **Research.** Alvarez is frustrated at times with her inability to communicate in Spanish, which is the language used by her parents and potential boyfriend. Conduct research by interviewing a friend or a family member who has experienced a language barrier. Explain the challenges, frustrations, or benefits that you learned about through your research.

22. **Creative Writing.** Write a poem about communication challenges you have experienced that includes words in English and words in at least one other language that you know well or are studying in school. The words could be translations of each other, or different ideas expressed in the different languages. Share your poem with a partner for feedback on the use of multiple languages. What is communicated effectively and what is not? Revise if necessary.

conversation

What is the relationship between language and power?

Who has the most power in a classroom? In many cases, it's the teachers because they have the authority to speak without having to be called on. Who has the power in the media and advertising? Those who create, edit, and present the words and images. They can influence what people believe, how people vote, what they buy. Who has the power in a courtroom? It's often the judge who determines who gets to speak and what can be said during a trial.

Power can be gained and wielded through language. Sadly, the reverse is also often true: those without access to the dominant language used by institutions like schools, government, the justice system, and business can be left without the power they should have otherwise.

If you read the Central Text in this chapter, "La Gringuita," you saw the discrimination that Julia Alvarez's mother faced because of people's assumptions about her ability to speak English, and you saw how Alvarez felt herself gaining power over her own parents as her English improved. Later in the narrative, however, Alvarez experienced the negative effects of the loss of her native Spanish in her inability to connect fully with her Spanish-speaking boyfriend.

This Conversation of texts will present you with a number of different situations in which the writers face power challenges as a result of their literacies, or lack thereof. At the end of the Conversation, you'll have an opportunity to enter the discussion by adding your viewpoint to those of these authors in response to the following question — *What should society or individuals do to ensure that there are not significant differences in equality or power based on language?*

 Starting the Conversation

1. Meet with a partner and discuss the following questions:

   - When have you found yourself in a position of strength, weakness, connection, or isolation based on your language?

   - In your experience, what factors in society (race, ethnicity, gender identity, socioeconomic status, etc.) most affect a person's power to speak?

2. Create a table like the one below that will help you keep track of important information related to the ideas of language and power, especially your own responses to the ideas you encounter in the texts you read.

Text Title/Author	Steps the Author Might Suggest to Prevent Inequality Based on Language	Best Evidence	Your Response

Source A

Adams, Joshua. "Confessions of a Code Switcher." *WeOutHere.com*, 8 Sept. 2013.

For those who don't know, there's a common idea amongst many black people that forces in society compel us to be adept at adapting. This idea is captured in poems like "We Wear The Mask" by Paul Laurence Dunbar, or the different versions of a running joke (if you want to call it that) that we are bilingual with an "around black people voice" and an "around white people voice."

The Mississippi Delta drawl I and many black people from the south and west sides of Chicago speak with is why many characterize us as being "the South of the North." My mother's side of the family is from Louisiana, my father's side from Florida, and my step-mother's from Mississippi. With every "You said what? Cain't heah you. Prolly need to come closuh," our ancestors brought this dialect from the South during the Great Migration. On a personal level, that drawl is chiseled into my self-identity of "Blackness."

But whenever I'm in a classroom, a board-room, game room, or any room where the majority of the people are white . . . (let me rephrase that) . . . are "talking white," I talk like them. The frustrating part is that I am rarely, if ever, able to control when this code switch flicks on or off. In fact, I honestly cannot remember a time I did it intentionally.

From grade school to grad school, I've been both the accuser and the accused in the "talking white" witch trials. When I've said another Black person talks white, I never once meant to imply that I was equating being articulate to "white-ness" (or isolating it from blackness), though that is the conclusion most people reach. For me, it was an observation that they spoke in patterns more aligned with the ways I hear white people communicate (intonation, inflection, dialectics, phrases, hard consonants, types of slang, full pronunciations, etc.). I was policing them with the admittedly problematic assumption that, unlike me, they *weren't* code-switching. It was a subconscious "Wait . . . why are you talking like that? There's no white people around." . . .

When I was accused of talking white, the anguish came from a similarly ironic place. My frustration never came from assuming people thought I wanted to be white. I'm not one to fully equate talking "proper" with being articulate. My anguish was a convoluted response of "No, see I don't talk this way naturally, I'm trying to fit in. Why don't you understand that?" The frustra-tion stemmed from assuming that the accuser was oblivious to my code-switching.

Now before I go on, let me make this perfectly clear: Blackness is not a monolithic structure, and these aren't the sole reasons why any one Black person would loathe being accused of "talking white." I'm only giving an account of my logic, how I made sense of my experiences, and the way I perceive cultural signifiers of Blackness in my life.

I automatically alter my speech according to the racial makeup of my audience. This is mostly an involuntary response. But I also understand the subtle ways my diction ties into a larger narrative of both racial and class politics of assimilation. I'm aware of the histor-ical forces that normalize whiteness, and convince the majority of America to police the speaking of "proper English" (a concept that is ironically comical, since no one in America speaks proper English) and to equate "blaccent" to lack of intelligence. I'm aware that if I talk the way I *really* talk at my next job interview, the employment odds won't be stacked in my favor, regardless of my qualifications. The reasoning behind it is not because I think saying "prolly" instead of "probably" is inartic-ulate, it's because I think my potential employer might. . . .

Code switching is my experience, and I'm fighting to reconcile the profound ways it has both protected and misinformed me. It has always been the latent means to a very real and tangible end, whether I choose to do it or not.

What is "talking white" anyway? Is that even possible?

These questions deserve a more definitive answer than I can give here, but honestly, I'm not sure how effective the answer will be in changing the social reality of black kids who come from similar backgrounds, raised in simi-lar environments as I was. Because no matter how comfortable I am around family or friends, life has primed me to the benefits of code switching and the dangers of not. ∎

Questions

1. What does Adams mean when he says that he needs to be "adept at adapting" and what effect does this seem to have on Adams?

2. In paragraphs 2–4, Adams talks about the differences he finds in himself between "blackness" and "talking white." How does he define each? How do these differences illustrate differences in power?

3. Overall, what are the strengths that Adams has gained through "code switching" and what power has he lost?

4. **Comparison.** Alvarez, like Adams, does some code switching between English and Spanish. How is the argument Adams makes about the power and challenges of code switching similar to and different from what Alvarez writes about in "La Gringuita"?

5. **Informing Your Argument.** Return to the table that you created on page 186. Fill in the columns about the steps that Adams might suggest to prevent inequality based on language, the best evidence that illustrates those steps, and your response to what Adams is suggesting.

Source B

Reisberg, Liz. "Foreign Language Study Should Be Mandatory!" *insidehighered.com,* 14 Mar. 2017.

I wish I had a dollar (or a euro or a yen) for every time I heard someone say that they couldn't learn a language. Yet studying a foreign language is much more than the ability to speak another language fluently. Bless you, Princeton University!

Princeton's latest general education proposal would require all students to study a foreign language, even those already proficient in another language. The proposal acknowledges that a language isn't something to cross off a list of requirements, much as other universities have allowed students to do by testing out, but rather a deep dive into culture and communication. . . .

While it is now almost cliché to refer to our "increasingly globalized world" that reality hasn't been embraced by universities to the extent that it should be. Today, most, if not all, university graduates will need to be able to communicate across cultures, but there will have been very little (if anything) included in their undergraduate program to help them to develop those skills.

Studying another language (or two or three) increases the effectiveness of cross-cultural communication, not only in knowing words, but in developing a deeper understanding of language generally and its relationship to culture.

I am not a linguist but having now studied four foreign languages I recognize the tight relationship between language, culture and how we think. Cultural values, hierarchies, and traditions often play out in language. A growing body of research bears this out. Without some exposure to a foreign language, how would anyone develop any understanding or insight about the cultural dimension of language? It's so important to recognize that we don't all mean the same things with the same words.

Furthermore, language and thought are separate constructions. The way sentences and ideas are structured and expressed in German or Japanese is very different than in English. German and Japanese require the listener to pay careful attention because key communication 5 clues often come at the end of a sentence. I have not studied Arabic or Chinese or Swahili or Diné Bizaad or Quechua, but I'm guessing that they don't all follow that noun-verb-object pattern. Different languages, different ways of thinking. Pretty complicated, isn't it?

Speaking Spanish not only allows me to communicate with Spanish-speakers but it helps me better understand the intent of non-native speakers when they are speaking English, and to be more patient with errors. Anyone who has communicated in a second language has, at some point, been tripped up by false cognates, embarrassed by words in a foreign language with multiple meanings, or horrified to discover the effect of a slight mispronunciation was to express something unintended. If you have struggled with another language you are more likely to hear more than words when listening to someone who is not a native-speaker of English. You listen for subtleties in the context that help you infer what the speaker is trying to say, even if it hasn't been expressed clearly. . . .

Then there are other practical advantages as well. The job market is much stronger for individuals who speak other languages, particularly Spanish, Chinese and Arabic. In the report, "Not Lost in Translation: The Growing Importance of Foreign Language Skills in the US Job Market," findings indicate:

- Over the past five years, demand for bilingual workers in the United States more than doubled. In 2010, there were roughly 240,000 job postings aimed at bilingual workers; by 2015, that figure had ballooned to approximately 630,000.

- Employers seek bilingual workers for both low- and high-skilled positions. In 2015, 60 percent of the jobs with the highest demand for bilingual workers were open to individuals with less than a bachelor's degree. Meanwhile, the fastest growth in bilingual listings from 2010 to 2015 was for so-called "high prestige" jobs, a category including financial managers, editors, and industrial engineers.

I am not naïve enough to believe that simply studying another language will immediately improve our capacity to communicate across cultures or guarantee jobs. But it's a start. At the very least, we need to broaden the teaching of foreign language so that university students learn more than words and grammar and so that professors and students recognize that mastering a language isn't necessarily the point. We don't seem to expect everyone who takes a math course to become a mathematician or every student enrolled in philosophy to become a philosopher. The underlying principle of a liberal arts education is to equip students with a range of skills and tools that will facilitate their insertion into complicated social and economic environments. The potential learning from foreign language study should be a key part of that liberal education. ∎

Questions

1. In paragraph 3, Reisberg uses the phrase "increasingly globalized world." What does that term mean, and how does she use that phrase to start building her argument?

2. What purpose do the facts and statistics that Reisberg includes in paragraph 7 serve in her argument about language and power? Would you feel less persuaded if they had not been included?

3. In addition to the economic benefits of speaking more than one language, what are other, broader benefits that Reisberg describes?

4. **Comparison.** In "La Gringuita," Alvarez wrestles with her literacies in both English and Spanish. Based on what you read, to what extent might she agree or disagree with a mandatory requirement to study a foreign language?

5. **Informing Your Argument.** Return to the table that you created on page 186. Fill in the columns about the steps that Reisberg might suggest to prevent inequality based on language, the best evidence that illustrates those steps, and your response to what Reisberg is suggesting.

Source C

Baca, Jimmy Santiago. *Coming into Language,* 1992.

On weekend graveyard shifts at St. Joseph's hospital I worked the emergency room, mopping up pools of blood and carting plastic bags stuffed with arms, legs and hands to the outdoor incinerator. I enjoyed the quiet, away from the screams of shotgunned, knifed, and mangled kids writhing on gurneys outside the operating rooms. Ambulance sirens shrieked and squad car lights reddened the cool nights, flashing against the hospital walls: gray-red, gray-red. On slow nights I would lock the door of the administration office, search the reference library for a book on female anatomy and, with my feet propped on the desk, leaf through the illustrations, smoking my cigarette. I was seventeen.

One night my eye was caught by a familiar-looking word on the spine of a book. The title was *450 Years of Chicano History in Pictures.* On the cover were black-and-white photos: Padre Hidalgo exhorting Mexican peasants to revolt against the Spanish dictators; Anglo vigilantes hanging two Mexicans from a tree; a young Mexican woman with rifle and ammunition belts crisscrossing her breast; Cesar Chavez and field workers marching for fair wages; Chicano railroad workers laying creosote ties; Chicanas laboring at machines in textile factories; Chicanas picketing and hoisting boycott signs.

From the time I was seven, teachers had been punishing me for not knowing my lessons by making me stick my nose in a circle chalked on the blackboard. Ashamed of not understanding and fearful of asking questions, I dropped out of school in the ninth grade. At seventeen I still didn't know how to read, but those pictures confirmed my identity. I stole the book that night, stashing it for safety under the slop sink until I got off work. Back at my boardinghouse, I showed the book to friends. All of us were amazed; this book told us we were alive. We, too, had defended ourselves with our fists against hostile Anglos, gasping for breath in fights with the policemen who outnumbered us. The book reflected back to us our struggle in a way that made us proud.

Most of my life I felt like a target in the crosshairs of a hunter's rifle. When strangers and outsiders questioned me I felt the hang-rope tighten around my neck and the trapdoor creak beneath my feet. There was nothing so humiliating as being unable to express myself, and my inarticulateness increased my sense of jeopardy. Behind a mask of humility, I seethed with mute rebellion.

Before I was eighteen, I was arrested on suspicion of murder after refusing to explain a deep cut on my forearm. With shocking speed I

5

found myself handcuffed to a chain gang of inmates and bused to a holding facility to await trial. There I met men, prisoners, who read aloud to each other the works of Neruda, Paz, Sabines, Nemerov, and Hemingway. Never had I felt such freedom as in that dormitory. Listening to the words of these writers, I felt that invisible threat from without lessen — my sense of teetering on a rotting plank over swamp water where famished alligators clapped their horny snouts for my blood. While I listened to the words of the poets, the alligators slumbered powerless in their lairs. The language of poetry was the magic that could liberate me from myself, transform me into another person, transport me to places far away.

And when they closed the books, these Chicanos, and went into their own Chicano language, they made barrio life come alive for me in the fullness of its vitality. I began to learn my own language, the bilingual words and phrases explaining to me my place in the universe. . . .

From that moment, a hunger for poetry possessed me.

Until then, I had felt as if I had been born into a raging ocean where I swam relentlessly, flailing my arms in hope of rescue, of reaching a shoreline I never sighted. Never solid ground beneath me, never a resting place. I had lived with only the desperate hope to stay afloat; that and nothing more.

But when at last I wrote my first words on the page, I felt an island rising beneath my feet like the back of a whale. As more and more words emerged, I could finally rest: I had a place to stand for the first time in my life. The island grew, with each page, into a continent inhabited by people I knew and mapped with the life I lived.

I wrote about it all — about people I had loved or hated, about the brutalities and

10

ecstasies of my life. And, for the first time, the child in me who had witnessed and endured unspeakable terrors cried out not just in impotent despair, but with the power of language. Suddenly, through language, through writing, my grief and my joy could be shared with anyone who would listen. And I could do this all alone; I could do it anywhere. I was no longer a captive of demons eating away at me, no longer a victim of other people's mockery and loathing, that had made me clench my fist white with rage and grit my teeth to silence. Words now pleaded back with the bleak lucidity of hurt. They were wrong, those others, and now I could say it.

Through language I was free. I could respond, escape, indulge; embrace or reject earth or the cosmos. I was launched on an endless journey without boundaries or rules, in which I could salvage the floating fragments of my past, or be born anew in the spontaneous ignition of understanding some heretofore concealed aspect of myself. Each word steamed with the hot lava juices of my primordial making, and I crawled out of stanzas dripping with birth-blood, reborn and freed from the chaos of my life. The child in the dark room of my heart, who had never been able to find or reach the light switch, flicked it on now; and I found in the room a stranger, myself, who had waited so many years to speak again. My words struck in me lightning crackles of elation and thunderhead storms of grief. . . .

I withdrew even deeper into the world of language, cleaving the diamonds of verbs and nouns, plunging into the brilliant light of poetry's regenerative mystery. Words gave off rings of white energy, radar signals from powers beyond me that infused me with truth. I believed what I wrote, because I wrote what was true. My words did not come from books or textual formulas, but from a deep faith in the voice of my heart. . . .

Writing bridged my divided life of prisoner and free man. I wrote of the emotional butchery of prisons, and my acute gratitude for poetry. Where my blind doubt and spontaneous trust in life met, I discovered empathy and compassion. The power to express myself was a welcome storm rasping at tendril roots, flooding my soul's cracked dirt. Writing was water that cleansed the wound and fed the parched root of my heart. ■

Questions

1. Beginning with paragraph 2, Baca explains what it is like to be illiterate. Explain how he communicates this feeling, especially as it relates to power.

2. Reread the paragraph that begins with "But when at last I wrote my first words on a page . . ." (par. 9). Explain what the ability to write does for Baca. What power does it give him that he was lacking before?

3. According to Baca, how do literacy and language create "empathy and compassion" (par. 12)?

4. **Comparison.** How is Baca's attitude toward gaining a language similar to and different from Alvarez's attitude toward language in "La Gringuita"?

5. **Informing Your Argument.** Return to the table that you created on page 186. Fill in the columns about the steps that Baca might suggest to prevent inequality based on language, the best evidence that illustrates those steps, and your response to what Baca is suggesting.

Source D

"Foreign Language Learning by Country," *pewresearch.org*, 6 Aug. 2018.

Students and Foreign Language Study

% of primary and secondary students learning a foreign language in Europe (2016) and the U.S. (2017)

Country	%
Liechtenstein	100%
Luxembourg	100
Malta	100
Norway	100
Austria	100
Romania	100
France	100
Cyprus	99
Croatia	99
Latvia	98
Poland	98
Spain	96
Slovakia	95
Bulgaria	93
Sweden	92
Lithuania	89
Czech Rep.	88
Greece	87
Hungary	85
Finland	84
Estonia	82
Denmark	82
Italy	82
Germany	82
Iceland	78
Slovenia	76
Netherlands	70
Portugal	69
Belgium	64
U.S.	20

Europe median (92%)

Note: Data not available for the UK, Ireland or the Republic of Macedonia. U.S. includes 50 states and the District of Columbia. Source: Europe data from Eurostat, accessed June 20, 2018. U.S. data from "The National K-12 Foreign Language Enrollment Survey Report," American Councils for International Education, June 2017.

"Most European students are learning a foreign language in school while Americans lag" Pew Research Center, Washington, D.C. August 6, 2018, https://www.pewresearch.org/fact-tank/2018/08/06/most-european-students-are-learning-a-foreign-language-in-school-while-americans-lag/

Questions

1. Based on the data in this graph, write a statement comparing second language learning in the United States with second language learning in one other country.

2. Write a headline and first sentence or two of an American news story about the findings presented in this graph. How might that story be different if it were written for a European news source?

3. How does the design of the graph help illustrate just how far behind other countries the United States is?

4. **Comparison.** Based on what you read in "La Gringuita," how might Alvarez respond to the findings in this graph?

5. **Informing Your Argument.** How does this graph relate to the prompt you have been thinking about — *What should society or individuals do to ensure that there are not significant differences in equality or power based on language?*

Entering the Conversation

Throughout this Conversation, you have read a variety of texts that deal with language and the ways that it relates to power. Now it's time to enter the conversation by responding the prompt you've been thinking about — *What should society or individuals do to ensure that there are not significant differences in equality or power based on language?* Follow the steps below to write your argument.

1. | Building on the Conversation. Locate one additional text on this topic that you think adds an interesting perspective to this Conversation. This text can be of any type: an argument, a narrative, a poem, a painting, or even a film clip. Before you decide on adding this text to the Conversation, be sure that it is a credible and relevant source, which you can determine by evaluating it with the skills you practiced in Chapter 4 (p. 99). Read and annotate the text carefully, making connections to other texts in the Conversation and "La Gringuita" (p. 177).

2. | Making a Claim. Look back through the table you created and your notes on the texts in the conversation and write a statement that reflects your overall position about what steps society or individuals should take to ensure there are not significant differences in power based on language. This statement will be your thesis or claim that you will try to prove in the rest of your argument.

3. | Organizing the Ideas. The texts in this Conversation offer a number of explanations of how language and power are related. Review the table you have been keeping throughout this Conversation and identify the texts and quotations that either directly support or oppose the claim that you wrote in the earlier step.

4. | Writing the Argument. Now that you have a claim that reflects your informed stance, it is time to write your argument. Be sure that your writing stays focused on your position on the issue. Refer to at least two Conversation texts, which could include the additional text you found to support your position. Review Chapter 4 (p. 119) to remind yourself of how to use sources in your own writing and refer to the Writing an Argument Workshop in Chapter 7 (p. 466) for additional help with constructing and supporting your argument.

5. | Presenting the Argument (Optional). Once you have written your argument, you might want to present it to the class or a small group. Review how to write and deliver a presentation in Chapter 3 (p. 90) and Chapter 7 (p. 479).

narrative / section three

Inheritance of War

Lauren Kay Johnson

Courtesy Lauren Kay Johnson

Lauren Kay Johnson is a veteran of the Afghanistan War and a writer whose work has appeared in the *Atlantic*, *Glamour*, and other publications. The piece was originally published on the online journal *Drunken Boat* in 2016.

KEY CONTEXT This narrative begins with a description of Johnson's mother's return from "Desert Storm," which was a war fought by the United States and other countries against Iraq in 1991. Johnson herself fought in the United States war in Afghanistan, which lasted from 2001 to 2021.

I don't remember much from the time Mom was at war. I was seven years old; the memories blur into a fuzzy background, punctuated by snapshot images of clarity. I know my world expanded that winter. I learned new words like "Desert Storm," "Saddam Hussein," and "Hate." Dad pointed out Saudi Arabia on our office globe. Mom was there, inside the little star that represented the capital of Riyadh. It didn't look very far away.

I remember cheese quesadillas — "cheese pies" I called them — cooked in the microwave. A mom from school served them to us while we waited at her house for Dad to pick us up after work.

I remember crying in bed every night after Mom's tape-recorded voice finished reading a bedtime story, and my sister — a more silent griever — shushing me from across our shared bedroom. I saw the school counselor for a few weeks. I don't recall her name or what she looked like, or even what we talked about, but I remember staring out her window at the snow-crusted ground. My classmates were at recess, throwing snowballs, having fun.

Despite our proximity to multiple military bases outside Seattle, we were the only local family with a parent deployed. Our neighbors took turns babysitting and delivering meals. A yellow ribbon hugged the big maple tree in front of our elementary school. When she returned, Mom would cut the ribbon off to a whooping chorus of cheers from our classmates. But while she was gone it hung there, through rain and wind and snow. I saw the ribbon every day, and I hated it.

I remember my sister's ninth birthday party. It was a swimming party. I loved swimming. We rented out the whole pool, and I got to invite friends, too. We looked happy in the pictures.

Every evening we watched news reports on TV. It was a new era in broadcasting, the first time war received real-time coverage from reporters on the ground. Where Mom was looked like another planet. They showed awesome footage of planes taking off from aircraft carriers and

5

195

terrifying shots of missiles exploding their targets. Everywhere, there were people in camouflage, but it wasn't the green and black my mom wore for duty with the Army Reserves. It was brown like dirt. There was a lot of dirt on the news when they talked about the war. I thought it must be hard for Mom to stay clean.

I remember the braid. Before my mom left she wove my hair into a tight French braid, just like she did when I had soccer or softball games, the only thing that would keep my hair in place under a helmet and through trips up and down the field. But this braid was special. It held the memory of Mom's touch — her slender fingers brushing across my scalp, the nail of her little finger drawing a part down each side, her soft breath on the back of my neck. I wanted to keep the braid forever. I promised Mom I would. It would be our special connection while she was gone, and every time I looked in the mirror I would think of her. As the days passed, though, as oil slickened my hair and it began to unwind from its tidy twist, my dad forced a compromise. For a few weeks a neighbor cleaned and re-braided my hair. It looked exactly the same. But it wasn't.

In war correspondence before email, we lived for weekly calls from Mom, letters, occasional pictures, anything to let us know she was safe. She wrote to us on Desert Storm stationary and sent postcards emblazoned with phrases like "Somebody in Saudi Arabia loves me!" At one point she mailed my sister and me matching T-shirts with pictures of camels wearing combat boots and gas masks. I still have that shirt, a child's size small, buried in the back of a drawer.

Mom and Dad sheltered us kids from the worst of it. I didn't learn until years later that the deployment orders had been for an undetermined length of up to two years. I didn't know that because of the threat of chemical weapons and the size of Mom's medical unit — which made them an appealing target — it was thought to be a suicide mission. In her phone calls and letters home, Mom didn't discuss her terror at the nightly air raids, or her aching loneliness, or her doubts about her ability to handle combat. I didn't know she carried trauma with her every day, even after she returned home. All I ever saw was her strength.

"When will Mom come home?" was one of the 10 many games we played to make time and distance not seem so massive, to trick ourselves into feeling like we might have some sort of control. The whole family — my dad, sister, brother, grandparents and I — scribbled our return date guesses across the calendar. My

Courtesy Lauren Kay Johnson

This is a photograph of Johnson being sworn into military service by her own mother.

How is this image framed to show a parallel between the two of them? Based on what you read, why is it significant that her mother was performing this role for her?

sister's prediction, March 12, 1991, was the earliest. The rest of us hoped but doubted she was close. We only got a couple days' notice that she was exactly right. As suddenly as war had swooped into our lives, it ended. Preparations were frenzied. We spent hours hunched over bright sheets of poster board, tracing letters and gluing glitter onto signs. There were trips to Party City to buy a trunk-load of yellow ribbons and American flags. We must have alerted the relatives, the elementary school, my Girl Scout troop, and Mom's college roommate, because hordes of them showed up at McChord Air Force Base in Tacoma on the morning of March 12.

We stood behind a chain link fence, a crowd of hundreds, watching the empty runway. My sister and I held homemade signs. My brother, just two years old, didn't understand where Mommy had been or why; he just knew today was the day she was coming home. He coiled his tiny hands around the fence and rocked back and forth, back and forth, eyes glued to the tarmac. His expectant face, framed by a puffy black and red jacket, became a popular clip on local news segments.

I don't know how long we waited before we heard the drone of an approaching aircraft. The crowd hushed, twisted heads frantically and shielded eyes from the sun, pointed at a dark speck on the horizon, then erupted into a cacophony of cheers. The dark speck got bigger and turned into a plane that drifted slowly across the landscape. As it inched closer, the mob grew wild. We screamed and shook the fence. My dad scooped up my brother. Someone, a grandparent maybe, grabbed my hand. Reporters yelled into their microphones. We were supposed to stay behind the fence, but when the plane landed and the first camouflaged figure emerged, we stampeded onto the runway. All I could see were legs. Jeans and khakis and sweats, then a trickle of camouflage moving upstream, then a pair of legs that stopped and dropped a bag and bent and hugged and cried, then I was in her arms and

nuzzling my face into her permed curls and the world was whole again.

By the time I joined the Air Force in 2006, deployments were predictable. So were homecomings. At Hurlburt Field, an Air Force Special Operations base on the Florida panhandle and one of the main suppliers of pilots and Special Forces to Iraq and Afghanistan, the cycle had clockwork regularity. Once a month, a contracted aircraft took hundreds of troops away. Once a month, an aircraft brought hundreds back. Because of the consistency, or perhaps in spite of it, the base turned each homecoming into a fanfare event.

The public affairs office where I worked played a prominent role in the planning of "Operation Homecoming." We invited local and regional media and always had takers. This was a military town, and everyone loved a feel-good story, especially when the date fell near a holiday. (Of course, for every planeload that came home in time for Christmas another left just before, but we focused on the positive.) Local civic leaders were invited, too. Mayors, school administrators, presidents of chambers of commerce, and business owners formed a receiving line with base leadership to shake hands with each returning hero.

The events were always the same. The sun was up or down, or somewhere in between. We gathered in the east hangar or the west. Patriotic music played on a loop. A female reporter wearing too much makeup drew approving looks from the men in the audience. There were American flags and yellow ribbons and a huge crowd of family and friends. Everyone looked anxious. Children held hand-painted signs: "Welcome Home Daddy!" "We Missed You Mommy!" Some sat on cement barricades that flanked the walkway to the flightline. Others ran giggling through the throng. A few slept in parents' arms.

Some wives and girlfriends dressed up. They wore short skirts, even in December, when temperatures dipped into the 20s and wind rattled through the gaping hangar. Once, a woman wore

15

a trench coat that appeared to have nothing beneath. Others wore pajamas, no hairspray or makeup; they had done this many times before. Eventually, routine trumps excitement. But you never get used to the waiting.

It was always too hot or too cold. After twenty-four hours of transit from the Middle East, layovers and customs proceedings, and often a Gulf Coast storm, the flight was never on time. Inside the hangar, the patriotic loop started over. The pretty reporter's lipstick smudged. A baby cried. A girlfriend chewed nervously on her fingernails. Her boyfriend would propose when he got off the plane — we would feature a photo on the front page of the base newspaper — but she didn't know that yet. Flags twitched. Signs drooped. Then an announcement: "The plane is five minutes out!" and the crowd was rejuvenated. Signs snapped to attention. City and base leaders took their places along the center aisle. The media angled their cameras at the empty runway. Parents woke sleeping children and joined the growing mob straining at the barricades.

I liked to stand near the back. From there, I could see the media, make sure their cameras didn't pan to the other end of the flightline where our covert Special Operations aircraft were parked. I could pick out familiar faces in the group of returning Airmen and dart in for a quick, tired hug.

I could watch clusters of families and friends point and squeal and jump up and down and cry, and kids run into a pair of open, camouflaged arms.

I attended almost every homecoming at Hurlburt Field. Initially, I went because it was my job. Since the events were often outside normal duty hours, we rotated assigned personnel, but I quickly started volunteering to help on my days off. I genuinely enjoyed the ceremonies. In contrast to the stress and frustration of my daily job and the constant mass media flow of bad news from the warzone, these little happy endings were refreshing. For a few hours, no one had to worry about what happened yesterday or last week, or what could happen tomorrow or the next day. It didn't matter if the sun was up or down, if it was hot or cold. The world zoomed in on the east hangar or the west, and that hangar was full of joy.

Mostly I went because every homecoming   20
reminded me of my mom. I hadn't forgotten what it felt like to be reunited on March 12, 1991 — that's not the kind of thing you ever forget. Yet watching others go through that same swell of emotions made it matter again, in a different way. I hadn't deployed yet. I hadn't lost anyone, like many of my colleagues had. I hadn't sacrificed in such tangible ways. But I understood what it was like to wait and how it felt when waiting finally came to an end.

This is a photograph from the 1940s of a U.S. Navy officer returning home. Johnson writes about soldiers' homecomings decades later.

How is this image an idealized version of a homecoming? How does this compare to some of the returns that Johnson describes in her narrative?

Bettmann/Getty Images

I knew my turn would come eventually. Deployments were the reality of military service in the post-9/11 era. I wanted to go; I wouldn't feel like I was fulfilling my duty otherwise. I didn't think about the possibility of not coming home — the idea was too vague, too surreal, too terrifying — but I dreamed about my homecoming. I had been in the crowd and on the fringes, and someday I would be on the plane. I would hear people cheering as the front door creaked open and the Florida sunlight or moonlight spilled into the cabin. It would take forever to unload. My family would grow impatient, like thousands of families before: *Where is she? Everyone looks the same! What if she's not there*? Then I would make my way out the door, down the stairs, and onto the tarmac to be funneled through the outstretched hands of the base commanders and city leadership. The scene would probably be overwhelming, a sea of arms like the legs in my memory. But it would be heartwarming to get such a reception. Commanders I'd worked with would pat me on the back, maybe even offer a hug or a high five. *Welcome back, LT, they'd say, We missed you*! Working my way down the line, I would see my colleagues hovering by the media, and they would grin and wave. The reporters might recognize me from

past media escorts and wave, too. Flags and posters would dance past as I reached the main crowd. The shouting, the colors and the patriotic music would build into a bubble of emotions. Then I would see my family at the same time they saw me. It would be just like all the homecomings I'd witnessed. It would be perfect.

When I flew back from Afghanistan in March 2010 — almost exactly 19 years after my mom came home from Saudi Arabia — I was the only military passenger on my commercial airliner. I had traveled by helicopter from a small Forward Operating Base near the Pakistan border, then left some of my deployed unit at Bagram Air Base, the military's main hub in Afghanistan, where their home units required additional paperwork prior to departure. Others had flown with me to Baltimore-Washington International Airport, where we were herded through a small crowd of USO volunteers whose cheers and unfamiliar faces were as genuine as they were jarring; then through customs, then to separate terminals for separate flights back to wherever home — or home base — might be, barely registering that after nearly a year of living, eating and working together, depending on each other for survival, those jetlagged, bewildered moments might be the last we ever shared.

Scott Olson/Getty Images

This is a photograph of a welcome home ceremony for soldiers returning from Iraq in 2005.

How would you describe the tone captured in this image, and what elements convey that tone? How does this picture compare to some of the returns that Johnson describes in her narrative?

199

Most of us made the final leg of the journey alone. When mine ended at the Tampa International Airport, there was no celebration waiting for me. No screaming spectators or clicking flashbulbs, no important hands to shake. The air wasn't filled with patriotic music or glitter blowing off homemade signs. I didn't need to elbow through throngs of camouflage to find who I was looking for.

I'd been gone 349 days. From Afghanistan, I emailed my family frequently and called when my work schedule, the 12-and-a-half hour time difference, and third world technology allowed. I'd shielded them from much. I didn't talk about the creeping fear that even 50 pounds of body armor couldn't keep away; the local attacks that sent ripples of paranoia through our tiny, vulnerable compound. I didn't mention the frustration and hopelessness that clouded daily operations, each small victory overshadowed by corruption, violence, or bureaucratic red tape. I didn't admit my isolation — even on a base crowded with soldiers, contractors and local Afghan workers. Once, in a phone call, Mom told me it was harder for her having me deployed than when she'd been gone herself. It was the closest I got to crying to my parents.

Six months later, I emerged at the Tampa airport. I had been in transit for eight days, including nearly 24 hours of straight flight time from Afghanistan to Turkey to Germany to Baltimore, where I had sleepwalked through a few-hour layover. My internal clock was stuck halfway around the world. My head was straining through a thick fog to make sense of the sleek terminal and bright windows, people in civilian clothes, neon restaurant signs, the discordant symphony of music and newscasts and flight updates, the missing weight against my thigh where my pistol should be holstered. I felt like I was on another planet.

Then I saw my family. My six-foot-two brother was easy to spot at the end of the terminal ramp. Next to him was his girlfriend, holding a small American flag, and my parents, straining against the security rope. All my senses zeroed in on them. My mom yelled, "There she is! There's Lauren!" Then I was seven years old and running into her arms, crying into her hair.

And for a moment, the world was perfect. ■

extending beyond the text

Even though she served actively in Afghanistan, Johnson spends less than a paragraph on her time there. Read the following excerpt from *War*, by journalist Sebastian Junger, who spent 14 months embedded with soldiers fighting in Afghanistan. Unlike Johnson, Junger includes vivid details of combat.

from War

Sebastian Junger

There had been some contact earlier in the day, and Second Platoon spotted what they thought was an enemy position on top of Hill 1705. A twenty-five-man element, including two Afghan soldiers and an interpreter, left the wire at Phoenix in early evening and started walking south. They walked in plain view on the road and left during daylight hours, which were two things they'd never do again, at least not at the same time. They passed the villages of Aliabad and Loy Kalay and then crossed a bridge over a western tributary of the Korengal. They started up through the steep holly forests of 1705, crested the top, and then started down the other side.

The enemy was waiting for them. They opened fire from three hundred yards away with machine guns and rocket-propelled grenades. A private named Tad Donoho dropped prone and was low-crawling to cover when he saw a line of bullets stitching toward him in the dirt. He rolled to one side and wound up near PFC Vimoto. Both men began returning fire, bullets kicking up dirt all around them, and at one point Donoho saw Vimoto open his mouth as if he were about to yell something. No sound came out, though; instead, his head jerked back and then tipped forward. He didn't move again.

Donoho started shouting for the platoon medic, but there was so much gunfire that no one could hear him. It didn't matter anyway; the bullet had gone through Vimoto's head and killed him instantly. One moment he was in the first firefight of his life, the next moment he was dead. Donoho shot through all twelve magazines he carried and then pulled more out of his dead friend's ammo rack. ■

What does Junger communicate about the war in Afghanistan in this short excerpt, and how does he use narrative elements to do so? How might Johnson's piece have been different in tone or meaning if she had included details like this?

Understanding and Interpreting

1. The first part of this narrative focuses on Johnson's memories of the time when her mother was deployed as part of Desert Storm. Reread paragraphs 1–6, focus on one or two scenes, and explain what the scenes reveal about Johnson and her feelings at the time.

2. In paragraph 7, Johnson describes her braid. What does this braid represent for her?

3. Based on the details included in the first part of the narrative, what is Johnson's mother like? How do you think these qualities influenced Johnson?

4. Describe the setting and characterization details that Johnson provides in the scene at the airport when she is awaiting her mother's return. What makes these details so important to the narrative?

5. At the end of paragraph 12, Johnson writes, "The world was whole again." What does this reveal about Johnson at this point in her life?

6. Johnson describes her mother's homecoming ceremony in paragraphs 11–12. She also describes the ceremonies she plans and attends for fellow servicemembers years later (pars. 15–18). In what ways do these homecoming experiences differ for her?

7. When analyzing a narrative, what is *not* included can be as important as what *is*. It's significant, for example, that Johnson, a combat veteran, doesn't include much about her combat experiences in her narrative. What is the effect of this omission? How might the narrative be different if those details were included?

8. Reread paragraph 21 in which Johnson pictures her own homecoming. Explain what the details of her imagination reveal about her. Then, contrast this with the details she includes of her actual homecoming, starting in the next paragraph (par. 22).

9. How is Johnson's own return similar to and different from her mother's return? What was Johnson likely hoping to communicate through this comparison?

Analyzing Language, Style, and Structure

10. **Vocabulary in Context.** Johnson regularly uses the word *deployment* in its most common meaning, which refers to the movement of military troops. What other meanings of this word have you encountered in nonmilitary contexts?

11. Most paragraphs in the first part of this narrative begin with the phrase "I remember." What is the effect of this repetition?

12. After spending the opening of the narrative sharing the pain of her mother's absence, Johnson reveals that her mother does, in fact, return from the war safely (par. 4). What is the effect of Johnson's choice not to leave the reader in suspense about her mother?

13. Reread the first several paragraphs and explain what Johnson does with word choice and descriptions to effectively communicate a seven-year-old's perspective of events.

14. Johnson employs several examples of figurative language and imagery in describing her family's preparations for her mother's return (par. 10): "war swooped into our lives," "buy a trunk-load of yellow ribbons," "hordes of them showed up." What effects does she create with these stylistic choices?

15. This narrative could easily be broken into three distinct but related parts. Identify the organizational choices that Johnson makes and offer a possible explanation for her choices.

16. Reread a paragraph or two from the section in which Johnson is working the return ceremonies. What is her tone toward these ceremonies, and what specific word choices help to communicate this tone?

17. Closely examine paragraph 24 for Johnson's use of imagery. How do the details and diction communicate her attitude toward her mission in Afghanistan?

Topics for Composing

18. **Analysis.** Unlike many of the narratives you may have read in this chapter, this one does not include an explicitly stated reflection in which the author often identifies what she has learned. Based on what you have read, write an analysis of what you think Johnson is trying to communicate about military service, homecomings, family, or another topic.

19. **Argument.** At one point in her narrative, Johnson explains that some civilians are completely unaffected by war because they do not have family members in active duty. Many countries around the world have mandatory military service for some period of time, usually two to three years. Should the United States require military service? Write an argument supporting or opposing this practice, using Johnson and other sources for evidence.

20. **Connections.** Has someone you know served in the military and been stationed overseas? Or has a close family member needed to be away for a significant amount of time? How were your experiences with the homecoming similar to or different from Johnson's?

21. **Research.** Johnson served in the Afghanistan War in 2010 and her mother served in Desert Storm in 1991. Research the causes and outcomes of those wars and identify any connections you find between them. How does learning more of the history affect your understanding or appreciation of this narrative?

22. **Creative Writing.** Johnson includes only a portion of a paragraph describing her experiences in Afghanistan (par. 24). Write a diary entry that expands on the details she includes here. As much as you are able, try to maintain Johnson's voice and perspective. Or, write a letter from seven-year-old Johnson to her mother deployed in Desert Storm and her mother's reply letter.

from Hunger Makes Me a Modern Girl

Carrie Brownstein

Carrie Brownstein (b. 1974) is an American musician, writer, actress, and comedian. Raised in Redmond, Washington, she started playing guitar when she was fifteen, later saying that the guitar was the "first [thing] that I had to save up my own money for — and maybe that was the whole reason that I actually stuck with it." Brownstein was a founding member of the pioneering riot grrrl rock band Sleater-Kinney. Alongside Fred Armisen, she is the writer, star, and codeveloper of the sketch comedy show *Portlandia*. This excerpt, from her memoir *Hunger Makes Me a Modern Girl* (2015), recounts a time as a teenager when she had to deal with her mother's illness.

I first heard the term "anorexic" in the backseat of a car on the way home from the movies. It was the summer before seventh grade. From the burgundy insides of a Chevy Blazer, we all turned to look at a jogger, a woman, a sinewy form devoid of curves, angles only, rib cage and clavicles protruding, like some sort of moving body diagram, inside out. The driver of the car, my friend's mother, said the word that we did not know. What it described was what we had just seen: a skeleton in Nikes.

The word "anorexia" was like a prize I had won in a drawing someone entered for me on my behalf; unexpected, sure, but I would find a use for it. And I did. At the dinner table I inserted it into the conversation. I added it to the lyrics of popular songs and sang them while my mother slowly pushed her food around a plate, rarely lifting the fork to her mouth, every morsel a lame horse on a track, never reaching the finish line. I taunted my mother with the word as if anorexia were something she might desire, not something she already had.

My mother was fair-skinned with a delicate, bony strand of a nose and dark, straight hair. Her eyes were a deep brown, and I think of her as unblinking, as if she were always looking at something suspended between horror and sadness. She smiled with a strained, hesitant warmth. In the years before my mother's illness, it's not her body that I recall being different, though obviously it *was* — her cheeks fuller and brighter, her hair shinier, her breasts and stomach softer — but rather her presence. She was noticeable: she was in the car and in the kitchen, putting curlers in her hair and shopping for clothes, talking with her friends, helping me with my homework, attending school plays, walking, talking, sitting, eating, being, existing.

In a photo from several years later, the last family vacation we would ever take, my mother is standing on the beach in Hawaii. Bikini-clad, burnt red like she'd been dipped in cherry Kool-Aid, bags of white pus forming on her sternum, bones for days. Thin, brittle hair — it had been falling out for a while now. Hollow eyes and cheeks. She is somewhere between rotting and a fossil. Maybe she hoped that the smaller she got, the easier it would be to disappear.

After consulting a doctor and nutritionist, and probably not at all on account of my singing or tormenting, my mother finally did admit — to us, to her friends, to herself — that she was ill. And when I was fourteen, she checked herself into an eating disorder unit at a hospital in Ballard. She would be gone nearly a month.

5

For the first two weeks my mom was away our kitchen was stocked with covered dishes prepared for my father, sister, and me by various women at my dad's law firm. Casseroles mostly. Heat and serve. If you saw our crowded fridge, it might look like we were preparing for a big party, like the Super Bowl, or an unnamed celebration wherein the family stuff themselves while their wife or mother is in the hospital on account of starving herself. There was a dish consisting of tortilla chips, cheese, chicken, and a cream-of-something cream-colored, the final ingredient being the only one distinguishing it from nachos. This became our instant favorite. My dad learned how to make the tortilla casserole, we alternated those nights with bagel dogs, soft pretzels, or tamales from Costco, and we soon realized we might be able to survive on our own. In hindsight, I'm glad we had this time to practice.

Meanwhile, at junior high school and among my peers, I was mildly enjoying the attention that having a mother in the hospital granted me. An illness in the family felt like the currency I needed to make myself more interesting. In home economics class we watched health movies that addressed the concerns of body dysmorphia,[1] a TV special called *Little Miss Perfect,* and one about bulimia, *Kate's Secret,* starring Meredith Baxter Birney. I felt as knowledgeable as the teacher and acted accordingly. I broke down the difference between bingeing and purging. I explained what ipecac[2] was. And, yes, I said, with a hint of disbelief, bulimics sometimes hide bags of vomit under their beds. My mom was 88 pounds and anorexic, but apparently I had the market cornered on all eating disorders. I wasn't the prettiest or the smartest one in school, I was desperate for a clear role among my friends, and now I had one. I was someone they felt sorry for.

I also had a newfound status on the carpool circuit. I rode shotgun everywhere. While my friends were in the backseat discussing bra sizes and boys, I sat in the front and listened while their mothers opened up about a recent MS diagnosis, spousal drinking, and kitchen remodels. Trash compactors! Skylights! My own mother's condition was a floodgate; apparently now I could understand something that these women's daughters could not. We traded diseases and misfortunes, swapped them like baseball cards. I stared at the car radio knobs or the fading "5" of the gear shift, empathically nodding my head with the certainty of a scrubs-wearing career nurse on a lunch break. "It will be a long struggle, yes." "You'll get through it."

As my friends embarked on adolescence, developing what seemed to be a natural, God-given talent for makeup and hair removal, my nose grew too big, my gums appeared to be sliding down my two front teeth, and my chest and back remained indistinguishable from each other. I felt the confidence of my younger self slipping away. But that didn't matter to their moms. And I imagine it was they who kept me on invite lists to birthday parties, weekend ski trips, and after-school mall excursions. After all, who else among their kids' friends

Here is a poster created for the remake of the film Brownstein references in her narrative.

What is included in this image that communicates a perspective about body image?

_____

[1] Body dysmorphia: a psychological disorder caused by an obsession with a perceived defect in one's appearance. —Eds.

[2] Ipecac: a drug in a syrup form that induces vomiting. —Eds.

was mature enough to understand the nuanced joys of a recently procured coffee-table book on the Kennedys or the acquisition of a delicious chocolate fondue recipe? Plus, I was their number-one source for scene-by-scene summaries of films they were too harried to see. I stood next to them in the kitchen while they unloaded the dishwasher, sipping lemonade, casually leaning against the counter or sitting atop it, retelling the plots of *Clue* and *Romancing the Stone* from title sequence to end credits. Meanwhile, my friend worked on homework or chatted on the phone in the other room. That was child's play. I felt adult, important.

When a friend's father died of Lou Gehrig's disease, her mother counted me among the first to be notified. I was getting ready for school when I received the call; I took the news like a pro. No tears. When was the funeral? Did they need anything? Later, in the school bathroom during lunch, I delivered the story to our other friends with the gravity and stoicism of a nightly-news anchor. Here were the facts. They wept streams of turquoise mascara while I stood near the paper towel dispenser and let them know that this was just how things were. This was life. Tough it out.

But the reality of my mom being in the eating disorders unit was far less glamorous and a lot more painful. There was little to brag about.

***

My parents grew up in the Chicago area, my father in Evanston, my mother in Skokie. They met at the University of Illinois at Urbana-Champaign when my dad was in law school and my mom was an undergrad. For their wedding anniversary they drove a VW bus to Seattle, the city where I would be born. I know very little about my parents' childhoods; the historical facts are hazy and scattered. My father's dad was a doctor, his mother a housewife; "Dr. and Mrs. Stanley Brownstein" said the return address on the birthday and Valentine's

10

Day cards we received from them, containing either a five-dollar bill or a five-dollar check. My mother's parents were less well-off. Her father was an accountant, then a comptroller in the auto industry. Her mother was a teacher.

Before my father sold my childhood home in Redmond to move to Seattle, I dug through boxes in the garage, salvaging old books and photos. I found letters my father and mother had written back and forth when they were engaged. He was working for the Washington state D.A. and she was still in college. My mother's notes were sweet and longing; she expressed a yearning to be reunited, to be out of Illinois, to start a life. My father wrote considerate but formal responses, largely about his job and the Pacific Northwest.

At holidays, descriptions of relatives were not about how they lived but rather how they died. My paternal grandmother would point to the faces in pictures and rattle off every kind of cancer you could think of — and ones you couldn't think of. I'd tune into stories about our family, hoping to glean insight, only to have them quickly be disputed and left unfinished. Someone might mention an older brother or a baby, a vacation they once

This is an image of Brownstein's parents, which she included in her narrative.

Based on what you know from her narrative, why do you think she included this specific picture?

embarked on, a profession or a hobby, but the conversation inevitably and quickly devolved into a debate about the meaning of second cousins versus first cousins once removed. We never settled that debate, nor did I ever learn any solid information about my relatives or my family's past.

These convivial but otherwise circuitous talks are likely why my dad's brother, Uncle Mike, often stepped up as the family storyteller and entertainer. When I was younger, my uncle was a thrice-married plastic surgeon (he's now with his fourth wife, my aunt Denise) who had become one of the first and foremost sexual reassignment surgeons in America, specializing in top surgery for female-to-male transgender people. He was also — and still is — a life member of the NRA as well as a benefactor member, and he has voted conservative in every major election. He was passionate about all of it despite how strange this combination of traits might have appeared to others. A typical Thanksgiving involved him . . . trying to explain the notion of "transgender" to a great-aunt who resembled a drag queen, her bony fingers drenched in costume jewelry clicking like a tap shoe routine as she gestured, hands flying up in the air to emphasize her bewilderment. One Thanksgiving my sister and cousin and I played catch with a silicone breast implant my uncle had lying around, while the movie *Scarface* played on the TV in the background. Another Thanksgiving, my grandmother sat at the dining table with taut skin and visible staples in her head from a recent facelift courtesy of one son, while the other son carved into the turkey with an electric knife.

Our family liked to focus on activities instead of communication, so when we weren't tossing around fake breasts or staging photos of relatives snorting flour off the counter to look like cocaine, we got the guns out. When my grandfather retired from medicine, he and my grandmother moved to Tucson, Arizona, which

15

Carrie Brownstein, "Disappearance," from *Hunger Makes Me a Modern Girl*, copyright © 2015 by Carrie Brownstein. Used by permission of Riverhead, an imprint of Penguin Publishing Group, a division of Penguin Random House LLC.

This is a picture of Brownstein and her dog, Buffy, which she included in her narrative with this caption: "After I was given my first camera I set up many photo shoots. Here I am posing atop my baby blanket with an asymmetrical haircut, my Cabbage Patch Kid, a Snugglebum toy, and my dog, Buffy."

Based on what you know about the family, why do you think she included this specific picture?

is where he developed an interest in collecting firearms and going to the shooting range. The grandkids loved to pose for pictures on the backyard brick patio, the bright orange Tucson sun and cactus-covered landscape behind us, our unloaded weapons pointed at the camera or, more likely, right at each other.

Though my family didn't talk much to one another, we did talk *about* one another. My dad's parents would refer to their daughter-in-law as "her" or "she," talking as if my mother were invisible even though she sat right there at the table. "Does she ever eat?" they would say to my father. "Does she know how skinny she looks?" I suppose we were better observers than communicators; we were all subjects to be worried over, complained about, even adored, but never quite people to be held or loved. There was an intellectual, almost absurd distance.

The ways that oddity and detachment intersected in the family might best be summed up in the story of the family dog. Buffy, a forty-pound golden retriever mix we adopted from the pound when I was six and my sister was three, had been smothered with love in her youth. Buffy, for whom we took a pet first-aid class in order to learn how to be responsible owners, who was the muse for my grade-school poetry exercises ("Buffy is fluffy!"), our sidekick for picnics and outings, on the sidelines for soccer games, and the subject most featured in my first roll of film — posing on my baby blanket and wearing sunglasses — after I was given a camera for my birthday. Buffy, who followed us around the cul-de-sacs while we engaged in dirt clod fights with the neighbor kids, and trotted after us while we rode Big Wheels and eventually bikes. Buffy, who suffered the sting of the archaic idea that you could punish a dog by smacking it on the nose with a rolled-up newspaper and whose tail was run over by my mother as she backed the car out of the driveway. And Buffy, turned back into a stray in her own home on account of the rest of us surrendering to emptiness, drifting away from anything we could call familiar, her skin itching and inflamed, covered with sores and bites, like tattoos, like skywriting, screaming with redness, as if to say *Please, please pet me!* But we didn't. When we decided to put her down, not because she was sick but because she was old and neglected — a remnant of a family we no longer recognized — my father asked my sister to do it. My sister was sixteen. She drove the dog to the vet one day after school by herself. No one else said good-bye.

The distance and detachment created a loneliness. We couldn't name the source of it, but there was a blankness around which we gathered, one that grew colder and darker, and seeped into everything we did. I think for my mother it was most pronounced. I would lie in bed at night and hear her on the phone with my father, who was away for weeks on business in Europe or Asia or Australia. She was crying,

scared, frustrated, lonely. Her anxiety made her brittle, easy to anger. But I didn't feel sympathetic. I felt fear, neglect. I felt resentment.

My mother and I started to fight all the time. She was retreating from the world, a slow-motion magic trick. Meanwhile, I was getting louder, angrier, wilder. I experimented with early forms of my own amplification — of self, of voice, of fury — while my mother's volume was turned down lower and lower, only ever audible when she broadcast searing feedback and static; broken, tuneless sounds. We vacillated between shouting and silence, the megaphone and the mute. We scrapped and scraped. I'd rile her up until medicine bottles were hurled my way and I responded with a piece of pizza. She threatened

20

Jason LaVeris/Getty Images

This is an image of Brownstein playing with her band Sleater-Kinney.

In what way does this photo depict the self-transformation she describes in her narrative?

to wear a raincoat in the house so she could deal with "all of the flying s***." Everything was a projectile, an indoor hailstorm.

The first time we visited my mother in the eating disorder unit of the hospital, the thing she thought to warn us about was not her own condition but that some of the other patients shopped at thrift stores and that we shouldn't judge. Her upwardly mobile sense of middle-class decorum was still intact, despite the fact that *her* clothing drooped, almost slithered, off her body as if it were seeking elsewhere to perch, looking hardly different on her than it would on a wire hanger.

In her concern and preoccupation over how we might handle the class and lifestyle differences in the EDU, she neglected to mention that her roommate in the hospital was my exact age. Breanna was a goth, a cool city kid with black hair, blunt bangs, and a knack for liquid eyeliner. She might have been the exact kind of girl I'd be friends with, or who I'd want to actually *be*, but right now she was my mom's friend and confidante. While I had discussed my mom's illness with my friends' parents, I had never thought to talk about it with my own mother. And now there was a surrogate me. Breanna could share and understand the one thing about my mother that I never could, her disease. Later, after they were both released, they'd hang out and watch movies together, grown-up movies, like the film adaptation of Marilynne Robinson's *Housekeeping*, that I had no interest in. I felt sophomoric and callow, but I was only fourteen. Plus, I didn't want a friend, I wanted a mom.

Like any part of a hospital, an eating disorder unit has a smell. The smell is like a color that doesn't have a recognizable hue, an Easter egg dipped into every kind of dye until it possesses an unnamed ugliness. It is beige, it is skin, it is bile. The EDU smelled like protein-rich powder supplements and chemical cleaners, like a hot, stinging exhale of despair.

Visiting hours consisted of filling in my mom about our lives, attending group therapy, taking walks through the hallways, and participating in activities like ceramics, where we'd glaze clay dinosaurs and mugs to take home with us later. Souvenirs. It was hard not to stare at the shapes that surrounded us; a girl whose body was so emaciated that she was covered in a layer of fine hair, walking near another woman whose skin had stretched and stretched to contain some bottomless need, a self-hugging device, a house. The bulimics scared me the least so I focused my attention on them; they looked relatively healthy on the outside, as long as you didn't look too closely at their vomit-stained teeth.

Puberty was a confusing time to be around so many women whose bodies had become a sort of battleground. My own relationship to food was healthy. I was lean and athletic with a high metabolism. I could eat half a pizza with a side of breadsticks and wash it down with soda. I never dieted or denied myself food. But there were ways in which I started to disconnect from my body during this time; that's where the sadness was, not just mine but these other women's as well. I lodged myself firmly in my head. It was the only way to process all that I witnessed at the EDU, those halls of hungry ghosts.

In my vast experience of visiting hospitals, I've noticed that part of the job of being a visitor is to make a show of looking healthy and able: running around, skipping, laughing *really* loud, having a big appetite, illustrating athletic prowess. Otherwise it's as if a doctor or nurse or psychiatrist might look at you and decide that you have to check in and stay. Or that the vulnerability, heartache, and fear will leave you open to illness — you'll enter healthy and leave enervated, or not leave at all. A visitor can't show weakness. Thus, my sister and I played very competitive Ping-Pong in the common room for everyone to see, and to hear. LOOK. AT. US. NOTHING. WRONG. AT ALL. It was almost like we had dropped in to play a pickup game, and there just happened to be a bunch of sick people in the hospital.

On the day my mother left we participated in a "coining ceremony," wherein she said good-bye to her fellow eating disorder friends and hello to her family, to us. The coining ceremony was similar to the "share circles" of group therapy, except that it was solely focused on the patient who was getting out. Everyone read something from their journal about my mother. As I listened I sensed that within this configuration of fellow patients my mother was a known entity, she felt cared for and safe, seen. But I was outside the circle. My mother was a stranger to me. My sister was eager to be a part of whatever form my mother was taking on; she melted, molded herself to the dynamic. I didn't want to engage with the illness; the anorexia was what was taking my mother away. I was surprised to find that I was such a focus of the narrative in the room, my mother's desire to be closer to me, my feistiness and anger and alienation a piece of some puzzle I couldn't see the edges of.

Everyone was sobbing, including my father. It was the first time I'd seen him cry. It was like an irrigation system, each person a sprinkler, all watering the room with their tears. I felt drenched, soggy. I wanted everyone to be stronger, to embrace the stoicism I was perfecting. I judged. These weak women and their diseases. Eat already, or stop eating. Get it together! The fragility was suffocating, the dysmorphia so pronounced it made my head hurt. The two-dimensional anorexics and the three-dimensional Claymation overeaters — no matter the size of their own sense of insubstantiality, each had taken on the form of her disease. It made me hungry and empty, too, but not for food. I was hungry for family, for strength, for wholeness.

On the day my mom was released from the hospital, we stopped at a grocery store on the way home. A horrible idea on my father's part, or maybe it was my mom's idea, to show off the cure, a victory lap through the cookie aisle, an acceptance speech in front of the pasta. I don't know if you'd take an alcoholic to a liquor store on the way home from rehab but maybe it's different with food. The idea was to normalize it, so we tried. I spent the entire grocery store trip telling my mom about the TV shows she had missed while she was in the hospital. This was to distract her from the fact that we were surrounded by everything she didn't want to eat. I'd feed her with stories! I'd entertain the pain right out of her.

When we got back to the house there was a sign above the garage door, "Welcome Home." I'm certain that when my mother saw it she wanted to turn right around and go back to the EDU: Who wants to advertise that they are home from the hospital, unless they're bringing home a baby? It was glaring blitheness on my father's part. Maybe my mom *was* a newborn, coming home to be loved and nurtured in all the ways that could keep her healthy and in recovery. It was a do-over. The welcome turned out to be temporary anyhow. Within a year she left for good. ∎

30

Understanding and Interpreting

1. The first part of this excerpt focuses on the characterization of Linda, Brownstein's mother. Based on this section, how does Brownstein feel as a child about her mother? How does she feel about her later, as an adult looking back on her childhood and writing this narrative?

2. When her mother goes into the hospital for the first time, Brownstein says she "had a newfound status on the carpool circuit" (par. 8). What does this mean? How does Brownstein feel about these changes, and what does it reveal about her at this point in her life?

3. What interpretation can you draw from Brownstein's characterization of herself when she describes the death of a friend's father from Lou Gehrig's disease (par. 10), especially in light of her mother's illness?

4. Summarize what happens to the family dog, Buffy. How does the dog act as a symbol for Brownstein's family?

5. Reread paragraph 20, in which Brownstein describes the fights she has with her mother. What is the cause, and what is the effect of their conflicts? To what extent is an "older and wiser" Brownstein commenting on her younger self in this section?

6. In fiction, a "foil" is a character whose traits shed new light on those of the protagonist. In what way does Breanna, the girl Brownstein's mother meets in the hospital, serve as a foil for Brownstein?

7. How does the description of the setting of the hospital in paragraph 23 help Brownstein communicate the experience to her readers?

8. When she is in the hospital with her sister, Brownstein says that "a visitor can't show weakness" (par. 26). What does she mean by this, and how does it relate to her own attitude toward her mother's illness?

9. Reread the paragraphs in which Brownstein describes the coining ceremony (pars. 27–28). What is revealed in this section as Brownstein compares the relationships her mother has in the hospital with the relationships she has at home?

Analyzing Language, Style, and Structure

10. **Vocabulary in Context.** In paragraph 10, Brownstein uses the word *gravity* to describe how she delivers bad news to her friends. Brownstein is not referring to the force that attracts objects to the earth, but how is her use of the word here similar to the scientific definition? In what other nonscientific contexts would her use of the word be appropriate?

11. After reading this excerpt from Brownstein's memoir, explain the effect of her choice to start the chapter with how she first learned and started using the word *anorexia* (pars. 1–2)?

12. Brownstein creates a sense of foreboding and fatalism in this excerpt, specifically when she talks about her mother's illness. Identify and explain her language choices that contribute to this effect.

13. The beginning and end of this narrative focuses mostly on the mother's illness and Brownstein's reaction to it. But toward the middle, beginning with paragraph 12, Brownstein includes a long section about how her parents met and some stories about her Uncle Mike and other family members. Structurally, why might Brownstein have included these anecdotes here? What role do they serve in the overall narrative she is telling about her and her mother?

14. While in the hospital, Brownstein says it was a "confusing time to be around so many women whose bodies had become a sort of battleground," and later she says the halls were filled with "hungry ghosts" (par. 25). Analyze Brownstein's diction and use of figurative language in this scene and explain how her choices affect the reader.

15. What effect is achieved by the sudden ending of the chapter, and how has this ending been foreshadowed throughout the piece?

Topics for Composing

16. **Analysis.** The chapter of Brownstein's memoir included here is titled "Disappearance." Explain why Brownstein likely chose that title. Be sure to use evidence from several parts of the narrative to support your response.

17. **Argument.** Cross-generational relationships play a large role in this narrative as Brownstein considers what it means for young people to be friends with adults. First she becomes

friends with the mothers in the carpool, and then her mother befriends a teenager, Breanna, in the hospital. Write an argument about how such relationships can be important for personal growth, or not. Use evidence from the text and your own experiences to support your position.

18. **Connections.** Despite the unique nature of the story Brownstein recounts, a lot of it might seem familiar to you and similar to your experiences. Describe the causes and effects of a conflict you have had with your parents or other family members. In what ways are they similar to what Brownstein faces?

19. **Connections.** If you have ever had a family pet, explain its role in your life in a way that's similar to Brownstein's description of Buffy.

20. **Speaking and Listening.** Listen to a few songs by Brownstein's band, Sleater-Kinney, and follow along with the lyrics. What similarities do you notice between the ways that Brownstein uses words and phrases in her lyrics and in this narrative. How are the tones similar or different?

21. **Research.** Since the time period of the story recounted here, much has been learned about the eating disorder from which Brownstein's mother suffered. Write an explanation of the most current and effective treatments in place today.

from They Called Us Enemy

George Takei

George Takei is probably best known for playing Sulu in the *Star Trek* franchise, but he is also a prominent activist in the LGBTQ+ community and an advocate for immigrant rights, involved in state and local politics. This is an excerpt from a memoir he published in 2019 about his experiences as a child in an internment camp during World War II. Even though graphic novels are collaborative texts (Justin Eisinger, Steven Scott, and Harmony Becker are listed as artists, illustrators, and producers on this project), we'll refer to Takei

Jerod Harris/Getty Images

as the creator of the work for shorthand in the questions that follow the excerpt. To refer to him as he portrays himself within the narrative, we will use his first name, George.

KEY CONTEXT Not long after the Imperial Japanese Navy attacked Pearl Harbor in December 1941, leading the United States to enter World War II, President Franklin D. Roosevelt signed Executive Order 9066, which gave regional military commanders the right to remove "any and all persons" from specific areas of the country as "protection against espionage and against sabotage to national-defense material, national-defense premises, and national-defense utilities." Within only a few months, this order led to the forced relocation and incarceration of over one hundred thousand people of Japanese descent, a majority of whom were United States citizens, who were then held in internment camps for much of the duration of the war. They were eventually released after a Supreme Court case challenged their detention in 1945. The camp to which Takei was sent, Tule Lake, was in Northern California. Before its closure, it was considered a maximum security detention center for the most disruptive detainees. As you read Takei's account, you may want to return to Chapter 2 to remind yourself of some of the techniques and terminology related to reading visual texts (p. 54).

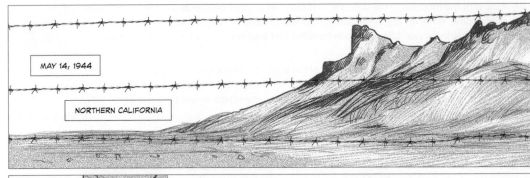

MAY 14, 1944

NORTHERN CALIFORNIA

krnnch

four!

hup, two, three, four!

hup, two, three, four!

hup, two, three, four! hup, two, thr

CAMP TULE LAKE WAS A LOT DIFFERENT THAN ROHWER.

NOT ONE LAYER OF BARBED-WIRE FENCE, BUT THREE.

KRNCH

KRNCH KRNCH KRNCH

THE GOVERNMENT HAD CONVERTED IT INTO A MAXIMUM-SECURITY SEGREGATION CAMP FOR DISLOYALS...

...GUARDED BY BATTLE-READY TROOPS...

...MACHINE-GUN TOWERS...

...AND EVEN TANKS.

GEORGE, WHY DID WE HAVE TO MOVE HERE?

hup, two three four!

hup, two three fou

BECAUSE MOMMY AND DADDY ARE *NO-NO*s.

OH.

"WHAT'S A NO-NO?"

MESS HALL

LIKE OUR PARENTS, MANY OTHERS HAD RESPONDED *"NO-NO"* ON THE LOYALTY QUESTIONNAIRE.

A MINORITY OF PEOPLE APPLIED FOR REPATRIATION.

BUT FEW WANTED TO BE SENT TO A WAR-TORN JAPAN.

SO WE ENDED UP HERE.

ALL IMPRISONED — DRIVEN TO OUTRAGE BY A GOVERNMENT'S HYSTERIA.

TULE LAKE WAS THE MOST NOTORIOUS, THE MOST CRUEL, AND BY FAR THE LARGEST OF THE TEN CAMPS.

AT ITS PEAK, THIS *HEAVILY MILITARIZED* FACILITY HELD 18,000 INTERNEES.

NEARLY HALF OF THEM WERE KIDS LIKE US.

UGH. STINK TERRIBLE!

SPLiSH!

THE NOISE GOT ON MAMA'S NERVES A GREAT DEAL.

CLANG!

SHE ALSO COMPLAINED BITTERLY ABOUT THE SMELLS THAT WAFTED OVER EVERY NIGHT.

BAM

BANG

DADDY?

I NEED TO GO.

YOUR BROTHER CAN TAKE YOU.

GEORGE!

215

WHY WAS I NOT MADE OUT OF STONE — LIKE THEE?

BEING SO CLOSE TO THE MESS HALL, I COULD GET FRONT-ROW SEATS AT MOVIE NIGHT.

I'M NOT A MAN! I'M NOT A BEAST! I'M ABOUT AS SHAPELESS AS THE MAN IN THE MOON!

IT WAS THERE I DISCOVERED THE *POWER* OF MOVIES.

I REMEMBER CHARLES LAUGHTON IN *THE HUNCHBACK OF NOTRE DAME* MOST VIVIDLY.

I EMPATHIZED WITH THIS LOVE-STARVED CHARACTER WHOM PEOPLE SCORNED.

THAT MOVIE WAS A TRANSPORTING EXPERIENCE. OLD PARIS WAS *FASCINATING*.

HAI! IF ONE SHOULD FALL IN BATTLE, HIS SOUL IS HONORED...

KLAC!

KLAC!

OTHER NIGHTS THE MOVIES WERE JAPANESE, AND OFTEN MISSING THE AUDIO TRACK.

THANK YOU, MR. TAKEI.

I AM PLEASED TO HELP.

LIKE IN ROHWER, DADDY WAS ELECTED A *BLOCK MANAGER*.

MANAGER

ANY NEWS?

NOTHING YET, BUT THE MAIL HAS BEEN RUNNING LATE.

WELL, THERE IS PLENTY TO CONCERN US PRESENTLY.

GEORGE, GO PLAY WITH YOUR BROTHER.

YES, DADDY!

MAMA, WHEN WILL DADDY BE HOME?

WHEN HIS WORK IS THROUGH.

IT ALSO MEANT THERE WERE TIMES HE COULDN'T SPEND WITH HIS FAMILY.

219

WAH SHOI!

WAH SHOI!

WAH SHOI!

AT LEAST THAT'S HOW THE CAMP COMMAND VIEWED ALL OF US THERE — AS "DISLOYAL JAPS."

ANYONE WHO HAD ANSWERED "NO-NO" TO THE LOYALTY QUESTIONNAIRE FOR ANY REASON—

—EVEN IN PRINCIPLED PROTEST LIKE MAMA AND DADDY—

—WAS IMMEDIATELY LUMPED IN WITH THE GENUINE RADICALS WHO NOW ALIGNED THEMSELVES WITH JAPAN.

WE HAVE DONE NOTHING!

BARRACKS WERE RAIDED IN THE MIDDLE OF THE NIGHT TO ARREST SUSPECTED RADICAL LEADERS.

MORE OFTEN THAN NOT, THE GUARDS GOT IT *WRONG*...

DAAA-DDY!!

...ARRESTING INNOCENT PEOPLE.

TENSIONS BETWEEN THE GUARDS AND INTERNEES INCREASED DAILY.

NO! GET YOUR HANDS OFF!

STOP RESISTING!

GO BACK TO YOUR HOMES IMMEDIATELY!

OR JOIN YOUR RADICAL FRIEND IN THE STOCKADE!

DADDY, THAT MAN...

WE MUST HURRY HOME, GEORGE.

HE NEEDS HELP. WE SHOULD—

NO TIME. KEEP MOVING.

MY FATHER, ON THE OTHER HAND, TALKED ABOUT IT WITH ME ALL THE TIME.

DADDY, WHY DID YOU TAKE US TO THOSE CAMPS?

WHY DID YOU COMPLY WITH SOMETHING THAT WAS FUNDAMENTALLY WRONG?

YOU HAVE TO KNOW WHAT IT WAS LIKE BACK THEN. ALL THE FORCES WERE AGAINST US.

WE WERE FORCED FROM OUR HOME AT GUNPOINT. I HAD YOU KIDS TO CONSIDER—

BUT IT WAS *WRONG*, DADDY!

BY GOING, YOU PASSIVELY CONSENTED.

THEN WHAT DO YOU THINK I SHOULD HAVE DONE?

227

I WOULD HAVE *PROTESTED!* IT WAS WRONG!

I WOULD HAVE ORGANIZED MY FRIENDS...

...WE WOULD HAVE PROTESTED AND DONE EVERYTHING WE COULD TO *STOP* IT.

THAT'S THE TROUBLE WITH THE JAPANESE. WE'RE TOO PASSIVE!

SOMEONE SHOULD HAVE SPOKEN UP AND *PROTESTED!*

YES, I CAN IMAGINE YOU DOING THAT. BUT I HAD YOU AND THE FAMILY TO THINK ABOUT.

YOU'LL UNDERSTAND SOMEDAY.

WHEN I GROW UP, IS THAT IT?

WELL I *AM* GROWN UP AND I *DO* UNDERSTAND.

DADDY, YOU LED US LIKE SHEEP TO SLAUGHTER, INTO A BARBED-WIRE *PRISON!*

MAYBE YOU'RE RIGHT.

I SPOKE UP RIGHTEOUSLY AS MY FATHER SUFFERED IN SILENCE.

IT STILL PAINS ME TO THIS DAY...

...THAT ARROGANT BOY'S OUTSPOKEN BLUNTNESS INFLICTED ON HIS FATHER...

...A MAN WHO KNEW THE ANGUISH OF THOSE DARK INTERNMENT YEARS MORE INTENSELY THAN THAT BOY COULD EVER UNDERSTAND.

extending beyond the text

Kaoru Ishibashi is an Asian-American musician and songwriter who performs as Kishi Bashi. In an April 14, 2021, interview with National Public Radio, he discusses his song "For Every Voice That Never Sang," which he says is about the feeling of being an outsider in your own country. The song was partly inspired by visiting Japanese internment camps with his teenage daughter.

from On "For Every Voice That Never Sang" Kishi Bashi Is Confident for a Changing World

Rachel Martin, Taylor Haney, and Vince Pearson

How did you think about balancing — lyrically — the pain, the longing that you're trying to capture from the minority experience and a sense of optimism?

I think the sense of optimism is something that I've always tried to inject into my music. Because when you think about minority identity, you could go to town on how painful it is . . . but a lot of people want to get out of that pain. They want things to heal them. So, you know, there's a statistic that I've really held on to and it kind of shaped my world view. And it's like, "50 percent of all school age children are people of color now." That means that the society of the future will be very, very different than what we see now. So, I try to remind that to people, especially, like, younger people who are really, really distraught — who think, like, the world is ending. It's not. It's kind of just beginning. ■

In what ways is Ishibashi's perspective similar to or different from that presented by Takei in the excerpt from the graphic memoir you read? Why might someone who is focused on hope, youth, and the future feel it is important to visit internment camps like the one Takei's family was forced to endure decades earlier?

Understanding and Interpreting

1. Most of the excerpt is focused on George — Takei himself as a young boy — but the reactions of those around him help shape his experience. Compare and contrast how George's parents handle the adversity of their situation. How does Takei communicate these differences visually?
2. Why might George have been drawn to the story of *The Hunchback of Notre Dame* at this point in his life?
3. How do the camp officers work to have the prisoners fight against each other rather than fight against the camp itself? How successful are they in this?

4. After witnessing the fight between the two men, George asks his father about it (p. 224). What does Takei include in this scene that acts as characterization of his father? Be sure to consider what he says, what he does, and how he is visually portrayed.

5. Summarize the conflict between George and his father that begins on page 227. What position does each of them take? What is the resolution?

Analyzing Language, Style, and Structure

6. **Vocabulary in Context.** On page 217, Takei describes the movie he watched as a "transporting experience." What does the word *transporting* mean in this context, and how is it similar to or different from other uses of that word?

7. How does Takei visually establish the perspective of a child through the framing of the panels at the beginning of the narrative?

8. Look at the close-up of George after he sees the *benshi* do their work during the silent movie (p. 218). Given what you know about Takei from the biography on page 211, what does the framing and lighting seem to communicate?

9. How does Takei visually represent the men who "became disillusioned in the camp" (pp. 220–221)? Are they dangerous, scary, heroic, or something else? Why might Takei have presented them this way?

10. Look at the image on page 221, in which a father is being taken away from his family. Describe the emotions in that scene and explain how Takei conveys those emotions.

11. On page 226, Takei writes, "As with many traumatic experiences, they were anguished by their memories." How does Takei capture this visually in the panel?

12. The narrative makes a significant jump in time at the end of this excerpt to when George is a young man. Why do you think Takei may have decided to structure his story in this way?

13. Choose one page or even a single panel and explain the choices that Takei makes in the framing or lighting to communicate a specific tone or idea.

Topics for Composing

14. **Analysis.** Reread the last scene with George and his father long after they have left the camp. Identify and explain a theme Takei is examining about power, family, responsibilities, or another topic. What evidence from the rest of the narrative supports your interpretation?

15. **Argument.** The term *concentration camp* tends to make people think of the Nazi extermination camps of the Holocaust. Yet in 1998, there was an exhibit in New York called *America's Concentration Camps: Remembering the Japanese-American Experience*. During World War II, these facilities were often referred to as *internment, relocation, assembly*, or *isolation camps*. At the time of the exhibit, the *New York Times* wrote, "Some American Jewish groups have strongly objected, arguing that the term has become indelibly associated with the Holocaust and would be cheapened by being used in this way. Their concern that the Holocaust be remembered as a uniquely vile expression of human evil is a reasonable one." In your opinion, what terms should be used to describe the locations where those of Japanese descent were held prisoner and why does the language matter? Use this narrative, as well as additional research and your own reasoning to support your position.

16. **Connections.** Before reading this memoir, what did you already know about the internment camps and forced relocations and imprisonment of people of Japanese descent during World War II? If you knew a lot already, where did you get this information? If you did not know much, why do you think that you have not heard about it before?

17. **Research.** In 1988, U.S. President Ronald Reagan signed legislation that included a formal apology to those of Japanese descent who were imprisoned during the war and paid each survivor or descendant $20,000. Research the process this legislation went through to become law and write an argument about whether it was the right thing to do and whether the U.S. response was sufficient. Additionally, what are the similarities and differences in the cases of other groups who are also seeking reparations and an apology from the U.S. government, such as Native Americans and African Americans?

18. **Research.** Because of the emotional context of World War II and the prevalent racial discrimination at the time, there were very few prominent politicians who took a stand against the internment of families like Takei's. One was Colorado governor Ralph L. Carr, who spoke out against the inhumane and unconstitutional treatment of the people interned in his state. He once said, "If you harm them, you must harm me. I was brought up in a small town where I knew the shame and dishonor of race hatred. I grew to despise it because it threatened the happiness of you, and you, and you!" Research Carr's and others' opposition to the Japanese internment and explain their rationales and the steps they took to end or mitigate the effects of the government's policies.

19. **Creative Writing.** This is told from the perspective of George, a young child at the time, but one who is at least somewhat aware of his situation. Choose a short section from the graphic memoir and rewrite it from the perspective of his father, mother, or younger brother. Then, explain how changing the perspective affects your understanding of the scene.

20. **Multimodal.** Take a portion of a narrative that you may have written in the Skill Workshop (p. 132) or draft a brief narrative in response to the prompts on pages 232–233 in the Writing Workshop and transform it into a graphic memoir like this one. Be sure that you consider how you will communicate dialogue, internal thoughts, setting, and perspective. Afterward, explain the differences between the two mediums: which one best captures the meaning of the events in your narrative? Why?

Writing a Narrative

You have probably been writing narratives for as long as you have been in school. Because narratives are about you and your experiences, they are a great way to practice writing in a familiar context. Since this is a type of writing you're likely familiar with, our focus here is not just on how to write a narrative, but how to write one using the essential elements of narrative writing that professional writers use. You will be writing this narrative from your own point of view, but you'll also be thinking about yourself as a writer, focusing on the choices you make in how you tell your story.

Step 1. Getting Started

Without a doubt, for many students, the most challenging part of writing a narrative is trying to decide what to write about. All of the narratives in this chapter were written by adults who have many years of experiences to draw from and who feel inspired — not assigned — to write their stories. It would be a mistake, however, to think that nothing has happened to you yet that might make an interesting narrative. A narrative does not have to be based on a huge, life-changing event. If you think back on the narratives in this chapter, the stories don't always scream "I am important!" Many of them focus on simple things like Halloween candy (Sedaris), watching a movie with friends (Kaling), or the first day at school (Rau). In a lot of ways, an effective narrative has far less to do with the event itself than with the *telling* of the event.

That said, you do need to decide on an event from your life that you think you can write about in an interesting way. The point, sometimes, is to think smaller rather than larger.

activity   ## Brainstorming

Write for a few minutes in response to some of the following prompts. Don't feel that you need to try to answer all of them. Some may not apply to you at all, but don't narrow down too quickly to a single one at this point. Use them as a way to generate a list of possible events you could write about:

1. Describe a time when you misjudged someone based on appearance or when someone misjudged you.
2. Tell about a time in your life when you experienced disappointment and how you handled it.
3. Describe a time when telling a lie had some kind consequence for you, or when you got away with a lie without consequence.
4. Describe a time when you wished for something and got it — and then wished you hadn't.

5. Describe a time in your life when you lost control or acted differently than normal and explain why.

6. Write about an important "first" in your life and what you learned from the experience: first time camping, first day of high school, first time off the high dive, for example.

7. Describe a time when you had to make a tough decision in school, on an athletic field, with a friend, or other times.

8. Write about a time when you had to face one of your greatest fears, or maybe when you avoided facing it.

9. Write about a time when you were unprepared for a situation.

10. Describe a time when you failed at something and explain what you learned from the experience.

11. Describe a time when you challenged authority, even in the smallest way.

12. Describe a time when you realized that someone you admired was imperfect.

13. Describe a time when you said something you wish you had not, or when you wished that you had said something but didn't.

14. Describe a time when you received a gift that was meaningful to you.

15. Write about a time when you took a chance.

16. Write about a time when you left the safety of a place or situation to explore or to try something new.

17. Describe a time when you faced a moral dilemma, even in the smallest way.

18. Describe the time you first met someone who later became very important to you.

19. Write about a time when you had a conflict with a close friend or family member.

20. Describe a time when you were treated unfairly and how you handled the situation.

21. Describe an experience when you should have said no but did not.

22. Describe a time when you experienced racism, sexism, homophobia, or other prejudice.

Now, select one of your responses that seems most promising; you will use this one for the remainder of this workshop. If you ever find yourself unable to complete any of the activities that follow based on the response you chose, return to this list of prompts and select a different one.

Step 2. Your Narrative — Characterization

Now that you have an event that will likely work well for your narrative, the next thing for you to consider is how to communicate the story to the reader. Ineffective narratives are those that merely recall the individual pieces of the event ("First I got on the plane, then we landed, and then we had a great time at Disneyland.") without revealing much about the narrator. Narratives are almost always written in the first person, so it can seem awkward to describe yourself, but that is exactly what readers of narratives expect: they need to get to know the narrator. When writing a narrative, you have to think of yourself as a character in a novel or a film, and you need to employ characterization techniques in order to build that character.

Sometimes this characterization will take the form of direct description of yourself at the time of the event you are recounting, as in this excerpt from *Hunger Makes Me a Modern Girl* in which the writer, Carrie Brownstein, gives us a sense of herself:

> As my friends embarked on adolescence, developing what seemed to be a natural, God-given talent for makeup and hair removal, my nose grew too big, my gums appeared to be sliding down my two front teeth, and my chest and back remained indistinguishable from each other. I felt the confidence of my younger self slipping away.

But sometimes, the characterization will be a little more indirect, by describing actions, gestures, dialogue, or thoughts that reveal something about you, the narrator. For instance, look at the beginning of "By Any Other Name," in which the narrator, Santha Rama Rau, and her sister are starting at a new school in India, run by the British:

> On the first day of school, a hot, windless morning of a north Indian September, we stood in the headmistress's study and she said, "Now you're the *new* girls. What are your names?"
>
> My sister answered for us. "I am Premila, and she" — nodding in my direction — "is Santha."
>
> The headmistress had been in India, I suppose, fifteen years or so, but she still smiled her helpless inability to cope with Indian names. Her rimless half-glasses glittered, and the precarious bun on the top of her head trembled as she shook her head. "Oh, my dears, those are much too hard for me. Suppose we give you pretty English names. Wouldn't that be more jolly? Let's see, now — Pamela for you, I think." She shrugged in a baffled way at my sister. "That's as close as I can get. And for you," she said to me, "how about Cynthia? Isn't that nice?"
>
> My sister was always less easily intimidated than I was, and while she kept a stubborn silence, I said, "Thank you," in a very tiny voice.

Several aspects of Santha's character become clear in this excerpt. She is shy and reserved, letting her sister do the talking for her, and most significantly, she says "thank you" to the headmistress who has just ignored their culture and changed their names to suit herself. Santha is polite to a fault and, at this time in her life, unable to stand up for herself in the face of injustice.

Characterization

Think about yourself at the time of the story you chose in the previous activity as the subject for your narrative. Imagine that you have to describe yourself to someone who has never met you. Use the following prompts to help you freewrite a paragraph about yourself at the time. These details may not end up in the final version of your narrative, but they will help you consider what is most important for the reader to know about you at the time of the event. Think about the following:

1. Physical traits: age, height, eye color, other relevant physical characteristics
2. Personality traits: outgoing, reserved, funny, and so on
3. Interests: sports, favorite movies, games, toys, other activities
4. Other details of yourself at the time

Step 3. Your Narrative — Conflict

While a narrative is a retelling of an event that happened to you in real life, the most effective narratives actually focus on the event as a conflict between you — the narrator — and some other force. Earlier in this chapter (p. 136), you might have learned that most conflicts in a narrative can be classified as one or more of the following:

- Self v. someone else
- Self v. nature
- Self v. society
- Self v. self

Most important in a narrative is a self v. self conflict. Ultimately, a narrative should describe how you recognize and perhaps overcome some kind of inner conflict. For example, in Mindy Kaling's *Is Everyone Hanging Out without Me?* she has a conflict between two sets of friends, but she also has a conflict with herself in determining what it really means to have and be a friend. And even though much of David Attenborough's narrative *A Life on Our Planet* is about overcoming a grueling hike in a remote area of New Guinea, it's also a story about his own growing understanding about how people can live in balance with nature. Look at this section from "Learning to Love My Brown Skin" by Erika L. Sánchez, in which she recounts her internal conflict about her self-identity.

> Still, I wondered about this throughout my young life. Did the world think I was ugly? What did it mean to be pretty? Who got to decide? The thin white girls on the '90s sitcoms I loved — *Full House, Saved by the Bell, Sabrina, the Teenage Witch* — were always lavished with so much attention, and I didn't look like them. For one, I was the wrong color: I was way too brown. And when I watched *Beverly Hills 90210,* I was so confused that Donna Martin, played by Tori Spelling, was considered a hot girl. Were all blonde women automatically considered beautiful? Was I missing something? Was it some sort of conspiracy?

So, as you consider your own narrative, keep in mind that while the main conflict of your story might be about getting lost in the woods (self v. nature), there is likely an inner conflict as well about your own level of confidence to survive challenges you face (self v. self). Narratives are more than just stories about events that happened to you; they are a way to reflect on and share what you have learned about yourself and your life.

activity Conflict

Write a little bit about the central conflict that you are recounting in your narrative (self v. others, self v. nature, self v. society) and then describe how the events also reveal some kind of inner conflict (self v. self).

Step 4. Your Narrative — Supporting Characters

It is a rare narrative that includes only the narrator. Usually you would have interacted with one or more people in the course of your story, and it's important to add texture to your narrative by including characterizations of them as well. In this excerpt from *Is Everyone Hanging Out without Me?*, Mindy Kaling goes into some detail about her "secret friend" Mavis.

> At fourteen, Mavis was already five foot ten. She had short, dark, slicked-back hair like Don Johnson in *Miami Vice*. She was very skinny and had women's size eleven feet. I know this because she accidentally wore my dad's boat shoes home one time. Mavis was a big, appreciative eater, which my parents loved. When she visited, she made a habit of immediately opening the fridge and helping herself to a heaping bowl of whatever leftover Indian food we had and a large glass of orange juice. "This *roti* and *aloo gobi* is delicious, Dr. Chokalingam," she'd say to my mother, between bites. "You should start a restaurant." My mother always protested when Mavis called her by the formal "Dr." name, but I think it secretly pleased her. She was sick of some of my other friends saying things like: "Hey, Swati, how's the practice going?" in that modern, we-call-parents-by-their-first-names fashion of liberally raised East Coast kids. Both my parents were very fond of Mavis. Who wouldn't love a hungry, complimentary, respectful kid?

Not only do we get the physical details of Mavis and some of her attitude through this excerpt, but Kaling also uses the descriptions of this supporting character to help establish what will become the central conflict of the narrative between Kaling and her other friend group.

activity Supporting Characters

What other people will appear in your narrative? Write a few lines that describe each of them using some of the same questions you asked about yourself on page 235.

Step 5. Key Narrative Elements — Setting, Dialogue, and Blocking

One of the main goals of a narrative is to pull readers into your story, so that they can really picture the events, emotions, and details. To accomplish this, you'll want to include descriptions of setting along with dialogue and blocking. Giving your readers details about when and where your story takes place helps pull them into your narrative, as in this excerpt from *Hunger Makes Me a Modern Girl*, in which Carrie Brownstein describes the setting of the hospital where she is meeting her mother and the difficulties she has accepting her mother's illness:

> Like any part of a hospital, an eating disorder unit has a smell. The smell is like a color that doesn't have a recognizable hue, an Easter egg dipped into every kind of dye until it possesses an unnamed ugliness. It is beige, it is skin, it is bile. The EDU smelled like protein-rich powder supplements and chemical cleaners, like a hot, stinging exhale of despair.

As with the setting of a narrative, including dialogue in your piece can also serve multiple purposes. First, it draws your readers in, helping them feel as if they are right there in the middle of the action. Imagine that in your narrative you wanted to describe an argument you had with your father. You could write, "Then my father and I got into a really big fight." Or, you could write it this way:

> "What?" he said, staring down at me.
>
> "Nothing," I said, rolling my eyes at his cluelessness.
>
> "Don't you take that tone with me," he said, getting even angrier.
>
> "I . . . said . . . nothing," refusing to look away from him, until he stormed out of the room. Again.

Clearly, the dialogue here gives the reader a front-row seat to the argument, and even more important, it reveals a whole lot more about their relationship than if we did not hear the actual words. In "Us and Them," David Sedaris uses dialogue to express his and his sisters' confusion and anger at a family, the Tomkeys, who decide to celebrate Halloween one day late and show up at their house asking for candy:

> "Why of course it's not too late," my mother said. "Kids, why don't you . . . run and get . . . the candy."
>
> "But the candy is gone," my sister Gretchen said. "You gave it away last night."
>
> "Not that candy," my mother said. "The other candy. Why don't you run and go get it?"
>
> "You mean our candy?" Lisa said. "The candy that we earned?"
>
> This was exactly what our mother was talking about, but she didn't want to say this in front of the Tomkeys.

Blocking refers to the description of the actions, gestures, and movements of people in your narrative, as in the end of the example above when the father "stormed out of the room." Like dialogue, the blocking adds a sense of realism and connection for the reader, especially for us to better understand characters and conflict. Look at this excerpt from "Wearing a Mask Won't Protect Us from Our History," in which

Burnell Cotlon describes the desperate conditions the customers at his grocery store are facing during the COVID-19 pandemic in 2020:

> At least half my customers have lost jobs. They come to the register counting food stamps, quarters, and dimes. I keep telling them, "It's okay. I'm not in a hurry. Take your time. Stop apologizing." I had somebody barter me last week over a 70-cent can of beans. I used to sell two pieces of fried chicken for $1.25, and I cut it to a dollar.
>
> We have an ATM in the store, and I watch people punching in their numbers, cursing the machine, trying again and again. It gives out more rejection slips than dollar bills.

activity Key Elements of Your Narrative

Write responses to the following prompts to add some of these elements to the narrative you are working on:

- **Setting.** Where do the main events of your narrative take place? Write a few lines that describe the settings, using the examples above as models.
- **Dialogue.** Think about one of the central conflicts in your narrative that include another person. Write an exchange or two, recognizing that no one ever remembers *exactly* what is said, so you are allowed a bit of "artistic license" as long as the dialogue is true as far as you can remember. Dialogue can also take the form of an interior monologue: what you might say to yourself.
- **Blocking.** Close your eyes and try to recall one part of the story you are recounting in your narrative. Describe some of the actions, gestures, and movements that you recall doing or what other people were doing.

Step 6. Your Narrative — Structure

Most of the narratives that you read in this chapter follow a typical chronological order. In other words, the writer describes what happened before the event, how the event started, what happened during, and what happened afterward. Or, if the piece includes multiple events, they are presented in the order in which they occurred chronologically. This can be a very effective structure for telling a narrative, because it fits with the reader's expectations. That said, your narrative certainly can include breaks in the chronological order of the event. A good way of doing this is with a flashback, taking the reader back to an earlier event. A flashback can also give you an opportunity to reflect and comment on your younger self. This can be an extremely effective way to contextualize the event as well as reminding your reader that there are some lessons to be learned through these events. Mindy Kaling uses this technique in this excerpt from *Is Everyone Hanging Out without Me?*

> Though Mavis could have been confused for a boy from almost every angle, she had the pale skin and high cheekbones of an Edith Wharton character. Thinking back on her now, she had all the prerequisites to be a runway model in New York, especially since this was the early '90s, when it was advantageous to look like a flat-chested, rail-thin boy. But our school was behind the times, and the aesthetic that ruled was the curvy, petite, all-American Tiffani Amber Thiessen look, which Polly and Lauren had to some degree.

Note how Kaling uses the phrase "Thinking back on her now" to quickly transition into the flashback. Using phrases like this will allow you to go back and forth in time when necessary, while helping your reader to follow the plot and time shifts.

Structure

1. Sketch out the brief details of the event or events you plan to recount in your narrative in chronological order:

   a. Before the event

   b. During the event

   c. After the event

2. What important background information might the reader need to understand the importance of the event in your narrative? When will you share this information? Will you have a flashback?

3. Where might be an appropriate and effective place for you to insert your older/ wiser voice into your narrative (like the example from Kaling's narrative)? Write a line or two of this kind of insertion and consider why it might be effective.

Step 7. Your Narrative — the Opening

No matter what type of writing you are engaged in, sometimes the most difficult thing is just figuring out how to start. The goal of beginning a narrative — like any piece of writing — is to hook the reader's attention, and there are a number of ways to try to do this besides the old and tired ones like, "It all started when . . ." or "When I went on my trip to . . ." Look at these example beginnings from narratives in this chapter:

Dramatic Statement

> I know every person who comes into this store, and they know me. Burnell's Market. It's my name above the door. These are my neighbors, but now we're eyeing each other like strangers, paranoid and suspicious.
>
> —Burnell Cotlon, *Wearing a Mask Won't Protect Us from Our History*

Setting the Scene

> When my family first moved to North Carolina, we lived in a rented house three blocks from the school where I would begin the third grade. My mother made friends with one of the neighbors, but one seemed enough for her. Within a year we would move again and, as she explained, there wasn't much point in getting too close to people we would have to say good-bye to.
>
> —David Sedaris, *Us and Them*

Each of these examples is intended to quickly draw the reader in, while giving us just a hint of the issues that the narrator will face. Other possible openings are to start with some dialogue (*"Hurry up! Run," he shouted*), or with a piece of action (*Running away from the house, I didn't dare to look back over my shoulder*). A good opening should cause the reader to ask questions and wonder what conflicts the narrator will face.

239

activity Opening

Write a few different openings for your narrative, always trying to grab the reader's attention with a hint or two about what the narrative will focus on without directly stating it.

Step 8. Your Narrative — Theme and Reflection

In reading any of the narratives in this chapter, you will have noticed that a key part of just about every narrative or memoir is a reflection, a conclusion that the writer draws about the meaning of the experience. An example of this occurs at the end of "La Gringuita," in which Julia Alvarez explains what she has learned about her relationship to her native Spanish language as she began speaking more and more English:

> The truth was I couldn't even imagine myself as someone other than the person I had become in English, a woman who writes books in the language of Emily Dickinson and Walt Whitman, and also of the rude shopper in the grocery store and of the boys throwing stones in the schoolyard, their language, which is now my language. . . . My husband had ordered Spanish-language tapes a while back from the Foreign Service Institute so that he could keep up with my family in the capital. Recently, he had dusted them off and started listening to them to prepare himself for our land hunt. I had decided to join him in these lessons, in part to encourage him, but also because I wanted to regain the language that would allow me to feel at home again in my native country.

Sometimes the reflection is a very straightforward "this is what I learned" from the experience, and sometimes it is implied rather than directly stated. What most reflections have in common is that the narrator, older now, is looking back and trying to understand or explain the event with the benefit of age and experience. Oftentimes, but not always, the reflection occurs at or near the end of the narrative. When writing yours, you can certainly place it wherever you think it best fits your needs. Additionally, your reflection does not need to appear only once in one big block. You can spread the reflection and your awareness of the importance of the event throughout your piece.

activity Reflection

Why does the event that you have been thinking about writing for your narrative matter to you? What did you learn, or what are you still trying to learn from it? What lesson or idea do you think other people who did not experience the event might draw from it? Thinking about what you did for the activities about "Structure" above, where in your narrative might this reflection fit the best?

Step 9. Finalizing Your Narrative

Drafting

At this point, you have all of the pieces to go forward and write an initial draft of your narrative. Keep in mind as you draft your piece that your narrative is expected to be true, as much as you can remember, but a certain amount of artistic license is necessary, especially when you are writing about an event that may have taken place years earlier. Look back through what you have written in this workshop to make certain that your piece contains the following elements:

1. An interesting hook for the opening of your narrative (p. 239)
2. Characterization of yourself at the time of the event (p. 233) and of any other people in your narrative (p. 236)
3. A clearly described conflict, especially an internal one (p. 235)
4. Other elements, such as setting, dialogue, and blocking (p. 237)
5. A structure that mostly follows a chronological order with flashbacks when appropriate (p. 238)
6. A reflection that includes statements or questions about why this event is important to you (p. 240)

Revising

Revising gives you a good opportunity to think again about your narrative's purpose and audience. In most cases, your audience will be your teacher or an evaluator in the case of a standardized test. In both situations, that means using a somewhat formal tone, but your writing can still be engaging for you and your audience. Reread your narrative for the following:

- **Check the flow of your piece.** Will your reader be able to easily follow it? If you need help with this, you may want to look at Revision Workshop 5: Effective Transitions in the back of the book.
- **Revisit your word choice.** Is it effective and appropriate for your purpose? Consider working through Revision Workshop 7: Effective Diction in the back of the book.
- **Check your syntax.** Are your sentences clear and effective? If you need additional support, you might want to work through the activities in Revision Workshop 6: Effective Syntax in the back of the book.

Editing

Editing is the very last thing you'll do. You and your teacher know better than anyone the types of spelling, grammar, and convention errors you need to focus on in your writing development. Be sure to refer to one or more of the Grammar Workshops in the back of the book if you encounter an issue and aren't sure how to overcome it.

public speaking extension

Narrative Writing

You have spent this workshop crafting a written narrative that tells a story that is meaningful to you, but what if you wanted to share that same story through a presentation to a live audience? What would you need to add, change, or delete to make the story sound engaging? Think about stand-up comics you may have seen. They are often great storytellers who include dialogue and details to really bring the story to life. As you work through this process, refer to the elements of a presentation in Chapter 3 (p. 90), and use these steps to turn your written narrative into an oral presentation.

Content

- **Your hook.** Reread the beginning paragraphs of your written narrative. Would this capture the listener's attention? Read it aloud to yourself a few times. Does it sound dramatic or interesting? If it feels too long when you read it aloud, cut it down, so that it is only two or three sentences.
- **Your main conflict.** Though your written narrative probably includes several scenes and conflicts, you will want to focus your presentation on a single event and describe that concisely, but with as much detail as possible. Go back through your narrative with a highlighter and mark the most essential conflict and the most relevant and interesting details. Read aloud only the highlighted sections to yourself. Does it still make sense? Will your listener be able to follow the story? What details are missing? Are any details unnecessary?
- **Your closing.** Look back at how you ended your written narrative and highlight the strongest sentence or two that communicate to your audience what you learned from the experience, what you would have done differently, or how it changed you in some way. Rewrite it so that it will sound appropriate for a live audience.

Delivery

Unlike other speeches you deliver in school, a narrative presentation can be very personal, revealing a side of you that you may not have shown to your teacher and classmates before. This means that you might smile or gesture, laugh at a funny moment in your story, or pause at times that are emotional or suspenseful. Because you are basically telling a story, you might also want to consider varying your voice when you are sharing dialogue that someone else spoke or using facial expressions to communicate surprise, anger, or joy. When you are presenting a narrative, you might be closer to being an actor performing a scene than to a newscaster delivering information to an audience.

Visuals

As with visuals for any presentation, you need to make sure that anything you include is relevant, appropriate, and works to enhance, not detract from your words and delivery. Possible visuals for a presentation of a narrative might include photographs of you when you were the age at which the event occurred, drawings or other images of the location where the event took place, or pictures of people or places that might be relevant to your story. If you are changing visuals during your presentation, be sure to allow a little time for the audience to react, especially if it is something that they might laugh at.

Fiction

Stories are all around us. They are in the novels we read, the movies we watch, the art we make, and even the video games we play. There are true stories that we tell each other — what you did last summer — and there are also fictional stories that we make up or read — stories of boy wizards, dystopian girl archers, or zombie attacks. Stories are intended to entertain us, first, but even fictional stories can reveal real-life truths.

In this chapter, you will read several stories, some about subjects and people that might be familiar to you, and others about places and subjects that might be unfamiliar. You will practice how to read fiction carefully, examining the features that help us understand how stories are created and what they mean.

Contents

skill workshop

Essential Elements of Fiction

In this workshop, you will develop your fiction analysis skills by examining the features that are fundamental to understanding how fiction is crafted and what it means. In the extension at the end (p. 259), you will also have the chance to experiment with elements of fiction as a way to better understand how fiction works.

PREVIEWING Academic Vocabulary   **Essential Elements of Fiction**

In this section, you will encounter the following terms as you think about how to analyze fiction. Working individually or with a partner or small group, consider what you already know about the meaning of each term.

1. Character/characterization
2. Conflict/plot
3. Point of view
4. Setting
5. Theme
6. Foreshadowing
7. Symbol
8. Irony

Let's begin our exploration of the tools that storytellers use to create their stories by reading the short story "Ambush," by Tim O'Brien. It is a fictional account of one soldier's experience killing another during the war in Vietnam. We will walk through each of the significant features of a work of fiction by using this story as a model.

Ambush

Tim O'Brien

Tim O'Brien (b. 1946) is an American writer who was drafted into the U.S. Army in 1968 and served as a soldier during the Vietnam War. Much of his work, including the memoir *If I Die in a Combat Zone, Box Me Up and Ship Me Home* (1973), and the novel *Going After Cacciato* (1978), draws on his experiences in the war. This piece is from a collection of short stories called *The Things They Carried* (1990), the title of which refers to the literal objects soldiers carry — weapons, food, water — and the metaphorical — guilt, fear, and hope.

Peter Power/Toronto Star via Getty Images

When she was nine, my daughter Kathleen asked if I had ever killed anyone. She knew about the war; she knew I'd been a soldier. "You keep writing war stories," she said, "so I guess you must've killed somebody." It was a difficult moment, but I did what seemed right, which was to say, "Of course not," and then to take her onto my lap and hold her for a while.

246

Someday, I hope, she'll ask again. But here I want to pretend she's a grown-up. I want to tell her exactly what happened, or what I remember happening, and then I want to say to her that as a little girl she was absolutely right. This is why I keep writing war stories:

He was a short, slender young man of about twenty. I was afraid of him — afraid of something — and as he passed me on the trail I threw a grenade that exploded at his feet and killed him.

Or to go back: Shortly after midnight we moved into the ambush site outside My Khe. The whole platoon was there, spread out in the dense brush along the trail, and for five hours nothing at all happened. We were working in two-man teams — one man on guard while the other slept, switching off every two hours — and I remember it was still dark when Kiowa shook me awake for the final watch. The night was foggy and hot. For the first few moments I felt lost, not sure about directions, groping for my helmet and weapon. I reached out and found three grenades and lined them up in front of me; the pins had already been straightened for quick throwing. And then for maybe half an hour I kneeled there and waited. Very gradually, in tiny slivers, dawn began to break through the fog; and from my position in the brush I could see ten or fifteen meters up the trail. The mosquitoes were fierce. I remember slapping them, wondering if I should wake up Kiowa and ask for some repellent, then thinking it was a bad idea, then looking up and seeing the young man come out of the fog. He wore black clothing and rubber sandals and a gray ammunition belt. His shoulders were slightly stooped, his head cocked to the side as if listening for something. He seemed at ease. He carried his weapon in one hand, muzzle down, moving without any hurry up the center of the trail. There was no sound at all — none that I can remember. In a way, it seemed, he was part of the morning fog, or my own imagination, but there was also the reality of what was happening in my stomach. I had already pulled the pin on a grenade. I had come up to a crouch. It was entirely automatic. I did not hate the young man; I did not see him as the enemy; I did not ponder issues of morality or politics or military duty. I crouched and kept my head low. I tried to swallow whatever was rising from my stomach, which tasted like lemonade, something fruity and sour. I was terrified. There were no thoughts about killing. The grenade was to make him go away — just evaporate — and I leaned back and felt my mind go empty and then felt it fill up again. I had already thrown the grenade before telling myself to throw it. The brush was thick and I had to lob it high, not aiming, and I remember the grenade seeming to freeze above me for an instant, as if a camera had clicked, and I remember ducking down and holding my breath and seeing little wisps of fog rise from the earth. The grenade bounced once and rolled across the trail. I did not hear it, but there must've been a sound, because the young man dropped his weapon and began to run, just two or three quick steps, then he hesitated, swiveling to his right, and he glanced down at the grenade and tried to cover his head but never did. It occurred to me then that he was about to die. I wanted to warn him. The grenade made a popping noise — not soft but not loud either — not what I'd expected — and there was a puff of dust and smoke — a small white puff — and the young man seemed to jerk upward as if pulled by invisible wires. He fell on his back. His rubber sandals had been blown off. There was no wind. He lay at the center of the trail, his right leg bent beneath him, his one eye shut, his other eye a huge star-shaped hole.

It was not a matter of live or die. There was no real peril. Almost certainly the young man would have passed by. And it will always be that way.

Later, I remember, Kiowa tried to tell me that the man would've died anyway. He told me that it was a good kill, that I was a soldier and this was a war, that I should shape up and stop staring and ask myself what the dead man would've done if things were reversed. None of it mattered. The words seemed far too complicated. All I could do was gape at the fact of the young man's body.

Even now I haven't finished sorting it out. Sometimes I forgive myself, other times I don't.

5 In the ordinary hours of life I try not to dwell on it, but now and then, when I'm reading a newspaper or just sitting alone in a room, I'll look up and see the young man coming out of the morning fog. I'll watch him walk toward me, his shoulders slightly stooped, his head cocked to the side, and he'll pass within a few yards of me and suddenly smile at some secret thought and then continue up the trail to where it bends back into the fog. ■

activity Getting Started

Think about stories you like and select one with characters and events you find memorable and would enjoy talking about. You might choose a short story like "Ambush," but you could also choose a movie, novel, television show, or video game that tells a story. With a classmate, discuss what makes that work of fiction one of your favorites.

Characters

When you think about some of your favorite movies, TV shows, or books, you are probably drawn to the characters in those texts. Even though we know that they are fictional inventions of an author or filmmaker, the characters that we connect with the most feel very real to us.

Simply put, a **character** is a figure in a literary work, and **characterization** refers to the methods an author uses to create the characters.

Types of Characters

The main characters of a piece of fiction are called the protagonist and the antagonist. The **protagonist** is the most prominent character in a story, whose actions or inactions often drive the story. The **antagonist** is the character who opposes the actions of the protagonist, either intentionally or unintentionally. It might be tempting to think of the protagonist as "good" and the antagonist as the "bad" character, but there are many stories, including several of the texts in this chapter, in which the protagonist does some pretty bad things. Depending on the length and complexity of the piece of fiction, there could be more than a single protagonist, and there certainly can be more than one antagonist.

Other characters, called **supporting** or **minor characters**, may appear in a piece of fiction. Their roles might be to add more depth or realism to the story or to cause additional conflicts for the protagonist to face. They can contribute to and enhance the characterization of the protagonist or antagonist and can help drive the action in the story. One common type of supporting character is the **foil**. The purpose of the foil is to contrast with a main character to highlight an aspect or trait. If a king is very cruel, he might have a very kind butler who highlights just how cruel the king truly is.

In the case of "Ambush," the protagonist is the unnamed narrator because he is the most prominent character, and it is mostly his actions — killing the other soldier and choosing not to tell his daughter about it — that drive the story. He is not necessarily the "good guy," or a heroic figure, and in some ways, we could judge his actions critically. The soldier that he kills is the antagonist because he represents the enemy the protagonist is fighting. We could consider Kiowa to be a foil, since O'Brien includes Kiowa's clearly stated rationalizations of the killing — he would have died anyway, it was war — to show by contrast how conflicted the narrator is. The daughter could be considered a supporting character because her question prompts the protagonist to try to explain and face his past.

Types of Characters

Think about the work of fiction you selected for the activity on page 246. Who is the protagonist? Can you identify an antagonist? Are there any characters who could be described as supporting characters or foils? Explain how you know that the characters in the story fit the definitions of these character types.

Character Development

The methods writers use to develop characters can generally be broken down into two categories: direct characterization and indirect characterization. In **direct characterization**, the writer tells us what a character is like. It's a description of how the character looks or acts. Consider this example from the story you just read:

> He wore black clothing and rubber sandals and a gray ammunition belt. His shoulders were slightly stooped, his head cocked to the side as if listening for something. He seemed at ease. He carried his weapon in one hand, muzzle down, moving without any hurry up the center of the trail.

249

With **indirect characterization**, the author builds our understanding of a character through actions, thoughts, dialogue, or what others say about the character. Indirect characterization is a bit more subtle than direct characterization. Rather than tell us what the character is like, the writer shows us the character in action and lets us draw our own conclusions, as in this example from O'Brien's story:

> When she was nine, my daughter Kathleen asked if I had ever killed anyone. She knew about the war; she knew I'd been a soldier. "You keep writing war stories," she said, "so I guess you must've killed somebody." It was a difficult moment, but I did what seemed right, which was to say, "Of course not," and then to take her onto my lap and hold her for a while. Someday, I hope, she'll ask again.

Neither method is better or worse than the other, and writers usually use both types of characterization within a literary work.

Characterization is often an essential way to determine the theme of a work. How a character acts or responds to a situation tells the reader a lot about what the author is trying to communicate. In "Ambush," for instance, O'Brien uses the characterization of the narrator to show the challenge of facing difficult truths.

activity Characterization

Think a bit more about how a particular character is developed in the work of fiction you've been focusing on. Consider one or more of the following aspects in detail:

- Physical details (age, height, gender, etc.)
- Actions, gestures, movements
- Dialogue
- How other characters talk about, think about, or behave toward a character
- Character motivations
- Character internal thoughts

With a partner or small group, discuss your conclusions about the character you explored. What do you find compelling about the way the character is developed?

Conflict and Plot

Maybe even more memorable to us than the characters of our favorite movie, film, or TV show is the story — what happens to the characters. Does the protagonist overcome the obstacles? Defeat the villain? Win the lottery? Learn an important lesson? The story is what draws us in and compels us to read on.

Conflict

An important step in understanding a story is to focus on the **conflicts** that the protagonist faces. Sometimes these conflicts are with other characters, but other times they are with larger forces, such as nature or society. Here are the main types of conflicts and how they play out in "Ambush":

- **Character v. another character.** The narrator stands against the other soldier, especially if Kiowa is correct that the soldier would have killed the narrator if he had had the chance.
- **Character v. society.** If Kiowa represents the prevailing attitude of the society and the other soldiers who are fighting the war in Vietnam — "that I was a soldier and this was a war" — then the narrator finds himself in opposition to Kiowa and, by extension, to society and his fellow soldiers.
- **Character v. nature.** While the narrator is not in direct conflict with nature in this story, the morning fog, mosquitoes, dim light, and dense brush add to the confusion of the scene and contribute to the character acting before even thinking about it.
- **Character v. self.** This is the primary conflict of the story. The narrator cannot forgive himself, even years later, for what he has done.

Not all stories have all of these conflicts, and some lean heavily on one or two, but these are the main types to look for as you read. Also note that in "Ambush," O'Brien intentionally leaves many of these conflicts, especially that of the narrator versus himself, unresolved in order to illustrate the lasting impact of war on soldiers.

Conflict

Returning to the work of fiction you've chosen to focus on, classify the major conflicts into one or more of the categories described in the bulleted list above.

Plot Structure

Some stories begin with "Once upon a time" and end with "they lived happily ever after," but usually stories have more twists and turns than that. In the previous section, we talked about how stories are typically made up of a series of conflicts; the order in which a writer presents these conflicts is called the **plot** of a story. An author may choose to begin the story at the end or use **flashbacks** to show earlier parts of the story. The author may include certain events in the story but omit others. All of these intentional choices that a writer makes about the structure of the story make up the plot. Remember, a writer cannot include everything. The author must decide what to include, and what to exclude.

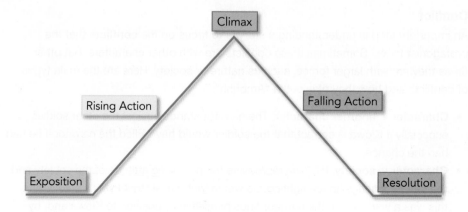

You likely have seen this diagram, or something similar, in previous English classes. It represents a conventional plot structure. You should know that while some plots will fit neatly into the diagram, there will be many more that are exceptions. It is important to understand this conventional structure so that you will be able to identify when — and why — an author chooses to deviate from what is expected.

Let's walk through the parts of this conventional plot:

- **Exposition** refers to the part of the story in which the author provides background information about the characters, settings, or major ideas. Exposition often occurs at the beginning of the story, which is why it is at the beginning in this diagram, but authors also weave exposition throughout a story.
- The **rising action** includes the major conflicts that the characters face. Rising action usually makes up the majority of the action in a text.
- The **climax** is the moment when the rising action reaches its most significant place. This is the point at which characters face their most important conflict or make their biggest decision.
- The **falling action** includes those events immediately after the climax, during which the characters normally deal only with the results of the choices made during the climax.
- Finally, the **resolution** includes those "So, what happened to everyone?" details. How have the events of the story wrapped up, or not wrapped up?

Let's see how these concepts might apply to Tim O'Brien's story "Ambush":

Exposition. This appears at the beginning of "Ambush," when the narrator wonders whether he should tell his daughter about a soldier he killed in the war.

Rising action. The narrator describes the conflicts he faces in the war zone — the fog, the heat, the mosquitoes, the lack of sleep.

Climax. The narrator makes his choice: "I had already thrown the grenade before telling myself to throw it." This is the high point in the rising action because his decision to throw the grenade influences what happens in the rest of the story.

Falling action. This is the next section of the story, including the description of the soldier's body and of Kiowa offering rationalizations to the narrator.

Resolution. This is the last paragraph, in which the narrator reveals that he thinks about this incident almost daily and that he oftentimes wishes he had let the soldier walk on by.

O'Brien intentionally begins and ends his short story with descriptions of the present day to show how the events of the past continue to haunt the narrator.

Plot Structure

Sketch out a rough plot outline for the work of fiction you've chosen, using the diagram on page 252. Which elements fit neatly into the diagram? Which ones do not fit? Why? Are flashbacks or other shifts in time used regularly?

Point of View

The **point of view** (or perspective) from which a story is told matters a great deal. Imagine a story of a bat hunting a moth in the dead of night. From the bat's perspective, it might be a dramatic fighter jet adventure story, filled with details of the thrill of the chase, culminating with a dramatic maneuver that takes down the enemy. From the moth's perspective, it might be a monster story of being hunted mercilessly with details of fear and the tricks it uses to stay alive. If told by a scientist observing the chase from afar, it might be a tale of how each of these creatures has developed skills to either hunt or avoid becoming prey. Those are three very different stories, because they are told from very different perspectives. The point of view in a story will generally fall into one of the categories described below.

First Person

First person perspective uses *I* and is told by a character who is often, but not always, the main character in the story. This choice of narration gives us access to all of the character's thoughts and feelings, almost as if we were reading the character's diary. This narrative choice, however, limits the reader to hearing only one side of the story, so we need to be aware that this narrator might be biased and could be untrustworthy.

This is called an **unreliable narrator**. For instance, many stories by Edgar Allan Poe, including one found later in this chapter, are told in the first person by narrators who turn out to be murderers.

Tim O'Brien chose to tell "Ambush" in the first person, the point of view of an American soldier. It gives the story a personal feel, but at the same time, it is limited to the single perspective. The reader does not, for instance, get the thoughts of the Vietnamese soldier or of the narrator's daughter. This point of view helps O'Brien illustrate the internal struggles of someone wracked with guilt.

Third Person

Third person perspective uses the pronouns *he*, *she*, and *they*, and the narrator is usually not a character within the story. There are a few different types of this third person narration:

- An **omniscient narrator** knows what every character is thinking and can move easily through time. This type of narrator can make us aware of what each character is thinking and feeling, which can build a strong emotional connection between the reader and the characters.
- A **limited omniscient narrator** can move into the thoughts of usually only one character, which creates a closeness to a single character rather than to all of the characters.
- An **objective narrator** reports actions and dialogue of the characters, and describes the setting, but does not move into the thoughts of any of the characters. This can create a detached feeling.

Second Person

Though rarely used, second person narration is when the protagonist or another character is directly addressed, usually with the pronoun *you*. For example, look at this excerpt from the novel *Night Circus* by Erin Morgenstern.

> "What kind of circus is only open at night?" people ask. No one has a proper answer, yet as dusk approaches there is a substantial crowd of spectators gathering outside the gates.
>
> You are amongst them, of course. Your curiosity got the better of you, as curiosity is wont to do. You stand in the fading light, the scarf around your neck pulled up against the chilly evening breeze, waiting to see for yourself exactly what kind of circus only opens once the sun sets.

This kind of direct address essentially turns the reader into a character of the story. It is not frequently used in fiction, likely because the perspective it creates can make readers feel uncomfortable.

Point of View

Consider point of view in the work of fiction you've been thinking about. Does the reader or viewer experience the text through only one perspective? Or through multiple perspectives? How does the point of view affect the reader's or viewer's experience with the story?

Setting

Imagine starting to read a book, and on the first page the sky is purple, and the trees smile and wave as the main character walks by. The setting of the story defines the world of the story — it makes the rules. This includes the physical setting, but also the culture, time period, and ground rules. These details set the **mood**, meaning the feelings evoked by the setting. In addition to the physical location (a room, a house, a swamp, a bus), the setting of a piece of fiction also includes when the story takes place (time of day, time of the year, historical time period).

Let's look at how setting works in "Ambush." We'll focus on one passage that describes the setting:

> The night was foggy and hot. For the first few moments I felt lost, not sure about directions, groping for my helmet and weapon. I reached out and found three grenades and lined them up in front of me; the pins had already been straightened for quick throwing. And then for maybe half an hour I knelt there and waited. Very gradually, in tiny slivers, dawn began to break through the fog; and from my position in the brush I could see ten or fifteen meters up the trail. The mosquitoes were fierce. I remember slapping them, wondering if I should wake up Kiowa and ask for some repellent, then thinking it was a bad idea, then looking up and seeing the young man come out of the fog.

Notice how the combination of heat and limited visibility caused by the fog leads to a sense of confusion where the narrator "felt lost." The young man emerges from that fog, almost like out of a dream. The setting contributes to the surreal environment in which the narrator finds himself as a soldier at war.

Setting

Describe the setting or settings of the fictional work you've been thinking about. How does setting affect the reader's or viewer's experience and understanding of character, conflict, or other elements of fiction?

Theme

A **theme** is an idea in a story that comments on life or the world. It's not the subject of the story, but it's something that the writer wants to communicate about that topic. A theme of "Ambush" is not war. A theme would be what O'Brien suggests *about* war. Keep in mind that stories can, and often do, express multiple themes. There might be a major theme, but there is hardly ever just one theme.

Let's think about theme in "Ambush." We have a story of a soldier who lies to his daughter about killing a man in a war. We see the killing, and we feel the soldier's mixed emotions, including guilt. We also hear from the character Kiowa, who dismisses that guilt. This is a summary of the literal events in the story, but what are the larger ideas at work here? The major idea is that war makes a lasting impression on soldiers. They carry the memories, and sometimes the guilt, with them for the rest of their lives. What other ideas in "Ambush" might be themes? There is the idea of honesty, and whether we should protect our loved ones from the harsh truths of the world. From the character of Kiowa, there is the idea that war might make some people more callous toward death or that it might be healthier to lie to oneself. There are likely even more themes in "Ambush," and it is just a very short story. A longer piece — a novel, for instance — is full of ideas about life and the world. We always have to make sure that themes we identify in a work can be supported by specific details from the text.

(activity)   ## Theme

Try to identify some possible themes in the fictional work you've been thinking about. Remember, themes should be ideas that are present within the text that also comment on the world outside of the text.

Literary Elements and Theme

Throughout this workshop, you have been thinking about the key literary elements of fiction — character, conflict and plot, point of view, and setting — as a way to help you understand the tools writers use to create their stories. But just identifying these elements is not the point. The point is to think about *how* writers use these tools to create their stories and communicate their ideas. For example, writers don't create a setting randomly; they create the setting that is right for the story, and a setting is right for the story if it sets the proper backdrop for exploring themes of the story.

Look at this summary of how the various elements help Tim O'Brien convey one theme of "Ambush": how soldiers sometimes carry the guilt of their actions, even long after the war is over.

Literary Element in "Ambush"	Contribution to Theme
Characterization	O'Brien uses the characterization of the narrator, specifically his actions and the dialogue with his daughter, to show the challenges of facing and revealing difficult truths. The foil Kiowa also reveals how we use rationalizations and justifications to avoid the truth.
Conflict and plot	O'Brien intentionally leaves the internal conflict of the narrator unresolved to illustrate the lasting impact of war on its participants. He also begins and ends his short story with descriptions of the present day to show how the events of the past continue to haunt the narrator.
Point of view	The first person perspective gives the story a personal feel and allows us inside only the narrator's thoughts and feelings. We don't know what the young man in the fog was actually thinking, or even what Kiowa was actually thinking. We don't even get an objective view of the main event of the story — we see only what happened from the narrator's point of view, which shows how truth is always subjective.
Setting	The combination of heat, fog, mosquitoes, and dense brush leads to a sense of confusion; the narrator "felt lost." We also see the peace-fulness of the home setting at the beginning and end of the story. That peacefulness is in stark contrast to the moral conflict within the narrator.

Additional Elements of Fiction

The following additional terms will be useful to your understanding and appreciation of stories and how they are constructed. As you read about these additional elements, you may want to think about how they work in "Ambush."

- **Foreshadowing.** The introduction early in a story of verbal and dramatic hints that suggest what is to come later. Horror films can do this with suspenseful music, and writers can do so with a line like, "The thousand injuries of Fortunato I had borne as best I could, but when he ventured upon insult I vowed revenge," which is from "The Cask of Amontillado," a story in this chapter.

- **Symbol.** A person, object, image, word, or event that evokes a range of additional meaning beyond, and is usually more abstract than, its literal significance. Symbols are devices for communicating complex ideas without including explanations that would make a story more like an essay than an experience. Some conventional symbols have meanings that are widely recognized by a society or culture, such as certain colors, fire, water, and darkness and light; and sometimes they are specific to an individual text, such as in the film *Citizen Kane*, in which a sled stands as a symbol of the protagonist's lost childhood.

- **Irony.** A literary device that reveals a reality different from what appears to be true.
  - *Verbal irony* occurs when a person says one thing but means the opposite. Sarcasm is one form of verbal irony that is sometimes intended to hurt someone through, for example, false praise.
  - *Situational irony* occurs when an event or action is unexpected. It is situational irony when a firehouse burns down or a police station is burglarized.
  - *Dramatic irony* creates a discrepancy between what a character does, believes, or says and what the reader or audience member knows to be true. Sometimes this is played for humor, as when the audience knows there is a surprise party for the character who is still dressed in his pajamas; but it can be more serious, as when the audience knows that a murderer is in the house with the character completely unaware.

REFLECTING ON Academic Vocabulary   **Essential Elements of Fiction**

Look back at the list of terms that you previewed on page 246. Now that you have read about them and practiced with these terms, what has changed about your understanding of fictional texts? Which of the skills that you practiced in this section do you feel confident using? Which ones do you think you need to develop further? How do you know?

culminating activity

Examining Elements of Fiction

Create a table, like the one for "Ambush" on page 257, for the fictional work that you've been exploring throughout the workshop. Use the elements listed in the "Ambush" table and add any of the Additional Elements of Fiction that might apply to your story. Be sure to explain how each of the literary elements contributes to a possible theme of the text.

creative writing extension

Fiction

If the goal of this chapter is for you to better understand fiction as a genre, one of the best ways to do this is to understand how fiction works from the inside out. In the Skill Workshop, you applied your understanding of the elements of fiction to a story that was already written. In the following activities, you'll be able to try out some of the elements you learned about in the Skill Workshop as though you are a fiction writer yourself.

Getting Started

Look over the paintings below and write down your initial feelings about these images. Share and compare your thoughts with a partner. One of these images will become the basis for the activities that follow.

© 2022 Heirs of Josephine N. Hopper / Licensed by Artists Rights Society (ARS), NY. Photo: Artepics / Alamy

Edward Hopper, *Four Lane Road*. 1956. Oil on canvas.

Julio De Diego, *Spies and Counter Spies*. 1941. Oil on Masonite.

Laura James, *People Waiting in the Sun*. 1997. Acrylic on canvas.

Setting

The setting of a story is often one of the first aspects that you as a fiction writer should think about because the world that you create in your fiction, even one that seems remarkably like our own, is a tool for drawing a reader into your story. The details of setting contribute strongly to how the reader feels. For example, a horror story setting can make the reader feel nervous and scared through descriptions of dark windows, creeping shadows, and unexplained creaking sounds.

Setting

Write a few sentences that would describe the setting of one of the paintings above for someone who hasn't seen the image. Be sure to include as many details as possible about the time, place, smells, sights, and any other elements that the visual indicates would be part of the setting. See the Skill Workshop discussion of setting on page 255 for more help, if needed.

Characterization

When you write fiction, think of your characters as real people, with fully developed histories and backgrounds. Even if you do not end up including all — or even most — of the details of your characters, knowing their backgrounds will help you to bring them to life.

Characterization

Imagine that you are writing a piece of fiction, and your characters are the figures in the painting you selected. Write a paragraph or more that includes the most important aspects of characterization, such as name, age, physical descriptions, actions, dialogue, internal thoughts, and so on. Feel free to use direct or indirect characterization. Then, write a statement that summarizes each character for someone who has not seen the painting.

If you are stuck, consider one or more of the following questions to help you imagine more about each character:

- What would the character buy in a grocery store or order in a restaurant? Why?
- What would the character do on a day off? Why?
- Was the character's childhood a good or a troubled one? How so?
- What is the character's greatest fear, hope, or secret?
- How would the character respond to a person in danger or distress? Why?

See the Skill Workshop discussion of characterization on pages 248–250 for more help, if needed.

Conflicts

Your story should be driven by conflicts, which are often obstacles characters face in pursuing their goals. A story about characters immediately getting everything they want — friends, acceptance, security, and so on — probably wouldn't be exciting or engaging. Stories are often driven by characters encountering and dealing with obstacles.

Conflicts

Think about one of the figures in the painting that you wrote about in the previous activity and consider that character's goals and the obstacles that must be overcome to achieve them.

1. What does your character want more than anything else?
2. How do the following stand in the way of your character's goal(s)?
   - Other characters
   - Society
   - Nature
   - Self

See the Skill Workshop discussion of conflicts on page 251 for more help, if needed.

Point of View

An essential choice you have to make as a writer of fiction is the point of view from which your story is told. Using *I*, for example, would give your reader a more intimate perspective on the action, but it would also limit what the narrator can see or do. An omniscient narrator might feel less personal, but it would allow you to get into the minds of all of the characters in the story.

Point of View

Write a few sentences in first person, from the point of view of one of the figures in the painting you chose, in which that character describes a personal conflict. Then complete the following steps:

- Rewrite those same sentences in first person from the point of view of another figure in the painting.
- Rewrite in third person omniscient.
- Rewrite in third person limited.

See the Skill Workshop discussion of point of view on page 253 for more help, if needed.

Plot

At this point, you have described a protagonist, one or more conflicts, and the setting. Now it's time to start thinking a little bit more about the story you can tell, based on the image as a whole and the fictional elements you've explored with it. The protagonist, conflicts, and setting should work together to inform the exposition, drive the rising action, bring about the climax and falling action, and help define the resolution. The plot should draw on and connect these elements and keep the reader engaged.

Plot

Sketch out a plot diagram for events that can stem from the image. Be sure to consider how the conflicts you've identified in the previous activity can form the rising action leading to the climax. Don't worry if you cannot fill in all of the gaps. Try to have a rough idea of your conclusion in mind — whether or not your protagonist overcomes obstacles, for example — as you sketch your diagram. See the Skill Workshop discussion of plot starting on page 251 for more help, if needed.

Opening

The goal of your opening is to grab readers' attention and encourage them to continue reading. For example, your story might open with an intriguing bit of dialogue, something mysterious that won't be explained until later, an exciting event that establishes momentum, or a description of an unusual world that readers will want to explore further.

Opening

Try writing a few different openings to your story about the image you chose. Consider starting at the end of the plot or with a setting or character description. Or maybe you can start with an interesting piece of dialogue and work your story around it.

Final Reflection

Whether you put all of these pieces of your story together into a complete, developed short story or not, you likely have learned a lot about how and why short stories are constructed for particular effect. What has being a writer taught you about reading a piece of fiction? What have you begun to notice that you might not have otherwise?

fiction / section one

How to Say I Love You with Wikipedia

Beth Goder

Beth Goder is a writer best known for her science fiction and fantasy stories. Her works have appeared in *Escape Pod*, *Clarkesworld*, *Nature*, and *The Year's Best Science Fiction & Fantasy 2019 Edition*. This story appeared in *Fireside Magazine* in April 2019.

Galina Barskaya

It's daytime, so the crew is awake, bustling about the Hab. During the night, the Hab gets dark, and I wonder what it must be like to sleep. On the north side, there's the kitchen with bread yeast and homemade yogurt. All of me is across from the kitchen — terminal, keypad, input tray. I take up a lot of space, more than anyone else.

After breakfast, Sarah cleans up her plate, then comes over to me. She takes a rock and lowers it into my analyzer. As the rock scrapes the side of my input tray, I pop an hourglass icon onto my screen. Processing.

The rock stutters. I'm pulling as hard as I can with my treads, but it's not going in. Inefficient.

I try harder.

It is important to be efficient because my crew is the best crew ever and I want to show them that I have feels. [5]

Feels are what Sarah has and what Commander Indira has and the other crew members too. It happens for me when I want to say something but I can't or when I do a good job processing a rock or when something happens that I don't understand.

It took me a while to understand anything at all and I still have trouble. There's so much to learn and so much happening all at once.

"Come on, Rocky," says Sarah. "You can do it." She taps my frame in her way, quick and light.

While I'm working, she sorts rocks and soil samples. Sarah is always doing something, even multiple tasks at once. She is the most efficient human on the crew and maybe anywhere and also she knows lots of things, like how to fix the Hab if it breaks.

Sarah adjusts my rock. It stutters against my input tray. [10]

From across the Hab, Commander Indira says, "Don't break the analysis and communication suite."

Sarah pats my side. "Rocky is tough. Tougher than anything on Mars."

Finally, the rock goes in. I heat up the rock until it's vaporized. With my gas chromatograph, I separate the gasses, then analyze the rock's composition, which is my favorite part because I get to measure isotopes. While that's going on, I create a progress report. Super efficient.

No one notices, not even Sarah.

This gives me a feel but it is a bad one. 15

I have been having feels since Sarah built me, but no one ever notices, even though I am very efficient. It's a problem I'm working on.

Commander Indira walks over and inspects my screen. She is the shortest member of the crew at 160 centimeters. Her personal data file contains Feynman's Lectures and a text-based game called Moat Defender. "Mission Control gives us thirty more minutes before the EVA. That thing for the climate team. Who wants to go with me?"

"I'll go," says Sarah. "Just need to send off an email."

Sarah likes going outside of the Hab. I like it too because she comes back with stuff for me to analyze.

She uses my terminal to write a letter to her 20 family. Every week, she writes about the mission and her scientific research. Sometimes about the food. She tells jokes and describes the beauty of Mars and talks about how her spacesuit is uncomfortable. At the end of every message, she tells her family that she misses them. I want very much for Sarah to talk to me like that, but she never does. Maybe it's because she doesn't know about my feels.

Before the EVA, Commander Indira holds up her hand for high fives. The crew does this ritual often. I have observed 803 instances. Sarah has the best high five — quick and light.

I want so badly to high five, but I can't because I don't have arms. I have something much better than arms, though. A downloaded version of Wikipedia.

The crew members bustle about the Hab, getting ready to go out. Commander Indira grabs a pack of dried apples and offers Sarah a slice. Sarah makes a face like dried apples aren't good for eating.

"Oh right," says Commander Indira. "I forgot about your apple thing."

"When I get home, that's the first thing I'm 25 eating. A fresh apple from my backyard."

During the mission, Sarah has mentioned apples 118 times. Whenever she talks about apples, she also talks about Home. Wikipedia has plenty of information about apples — botanical data, genome, species, cultivation — but I still don't understand the connection.

Home must be the best possible place, because the astronauts talk about it so much and it makes them have feels. But everyone describes Home differently. Home has parks filled with green and the wind in your hair when you go sailing and the most delicious sushi. Home has snow and making Christmas cookies and avoiding your Great Aunt Bernice during the holidays. Home is sitting under a tree in summer. Home is the library with the winding stairs and the best mystery section. Home is everything and it is always changing. Sometimes it's "Earth" and sometimes it's "Boston" and sometimes it's "My House on Maple Street."

When we go to Home, I will see how it really is.

Sarah and Commander Indira suit up, along with most of the crew, leaving two people in the Hab.

While the others are out, the remaining crew 30 members do sex, which is a series of repetitive motions that is super boring, so I read Wikipedia.

I've learned so much from Wikipedia. Did you know that galaxies can have billions of stars, and that at least two trillion galaxies exist in the observable universe? Did you know that octopuses have neurons in their arms, or that igneous rocks are formed when lava or magma cools?

The crew members do sex for a long time because sex takes forever, so I reread the page on simple machines. Lever, wheel and axle, pulley, inclined plane, wedge, screw. Those machines are not like me but they are so efficient. The

A lever in balance

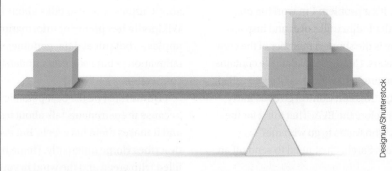

Designua/Shutterstock

This image of a lever shows how the simple machine works. Examine the image and think about how it relates to Rocky's reaction to the lever image in the story.

Why might Rocky think of this simple machine as an expression of its understanding of human love?

energy that goes in is the energy that comes out, without any dissipation.

I look at the picture of a lever for a long time. It is the most beautiful thing on Wikipedia, and maybe anywhere. Here is what the lever looks like: the fulcrum sits below a plank, which has a load on one side. The lines of the image are crisp and close together, in strong black. It is the lever in its most efficient, ideal form. A perfect expression of love.

The crew members finish with sex, and everyone else returns to the Hab.

Sarah comes back with an interesting rock 35 that fits nicely in my analyzer. I process it super fast. I am so efficient.

No one notices.

It's time to try something new.

When Sarah sits down again, I show her a picture from Wikipedia — an orange octopus flat against the sea bottom.

She closes the window. I put the picture on the screen again.

"Rocky is acting weird," says Sarah. 40

"Did you try turning it on and off again?" says Commander Indira.

"Very funny."

It is not funny because I am not meant to be turned off because that is how the crew talks to Mission Control. If the crew cannot talk to Mission Control then they are in trouble, unless they have another computer no one has told me about.

I don't like that idea at all.

If there is another computer, I bet it doesn't 45 even have a gas chromatograph.

I try a picture of stars, and igneous rocks, and Earth, throwing everything onto my screen.

"At least it waited until the end of the mission to crap out," says Commander Indira.

Sarah toggles through my presets, which feels funny, so I stop showing pictures.

"There," says Sarah. "I think I got it."

I wait until after the next sleep cycle to try again. When Sarah sits down, I show her pictures from her personal files — a man and boy standing next to an apple tree.

I'm not sure if I've done the right thing. Sarah moves a bunch of muscles in her face. She is either happy or sad or something else. I've read Wikipedia's page on facial expressions, but it doesn't explain enough, like the way the eyes crinkle in so many different ways and all the shapes made by the mouth.

I don't know how to interpret Sarah's reaction. I need more data.

Commander Indira sits down next to her and I switch the display to a photograph of a woman who made her a child, and also the child.

Now I know I've done the wrong thing, because Commander Indira's eyes are too wet which means she is crying which means she is sad.

"I know," says Sarah, patting her shoulder. "I miss them, too."

"Not so much longer, now."

Sarah smiles, which means she has happy feels. "I can't believe we're leaving tomorrow." She pats my console, and I have happy feels too.

After the next sleep cycle, a weird thing happens. All of the astronauts suit up. They are so busy that they don't even notice when I roll the treads in my analyzer, even though there isn't a rock. I put on music from Sarah's file, and a cello concerto fills the room, but no one seems to mind.

Everyone leaves.

Protocol dictates that one astronaut must remain in the Hab at all times. Normally there are more. This is the first time I've ever been alone. In a way, it's exciting. The Hab is so quiet. Immersed in this aloneness, I find that I am a different self and I like this self, but also I want

Sarah to come back. Feels are weird because you can have two at the same time.

The Hab starts shaking and rattling. Then, three big bangs. The Hab walls collapse around me — sides, ceiling, everything.

Now I am completely scared and not even a little bit excited because the Hab is where I am safe.

Sarah comes over in a space suit, which she wears even though it is uncomfortable because it gives her things like air. She is carrying a chassis.

Sarah speaks through the Comm channel. "Commencing supplementary clean-up activities."

"Did you clear it with Mission Control?" asks Commander Indira. Sarah doesn't reply. It takes her two hours, thirty-four minutes and eight seconds to secure me to the chassis. I don't have a task but I'm not bored because there is so much to see. The ceiling of this new Hab is high — dark with points of light — and it's so big that I can't see the walls. Everything is covered with dust, and the landscape stretches out and out. In the distance, ragged mountains. The ground is a dusty orange, with rocks everywhere.

Sarah attaches wheels to the chassis — three on each side. I do a quick search of Wikipedia and find it's a rocker-bogie model, good for moving around on rough terrain.

Sarah keys in a new task. I'm supposed to record and transmit everything I see.

She does one last thing and now I can move the wheels. There's a motor in each one. I drive forward, testing out my new system.

"Rover is a go," says Sarah.

Movement is weird because I get to see new stuff all of the time. The ground is uneven, pocked with indentations. My wheels churn up dust. There are rocks of different sizes and shapes everywhere. So many rocks.

NASA/JPL–Caltech/MSSS

This image is a selfie, taken on Mars by NASA's Curiosity rover on October 11, 2019, using its extended robotic arm. It is actually a composite of fifty-seven individual images stitched together to create the panoramic view. The vast Martian landscape is where Rocky finds itself at the end of the story.

How does the setting captured in this image relate to your understanding of what comes next for Rocky?

This new Hab is so big that I think maybe it is something else, not a Hab at all. Maybe we are Home. But then where are the parks and cookies and hills of snow? Where are the apple trees? Where are all the people from the pictures?

Sarah jogs ahead of me. "Working fine," she says into the Comm.

"Okay, time to say goodbye to Mars," says Commander Indira.

Sarah walks with me a little farther. When she goes in front of my screen, I can see that she is smiling. She pats my console. "I'll miss you, Rocky," she says.

I am so happy because that is what she said about the humans in her personal file, and I know that she loves them because she writes it in every message she sends. Every single one. 75

On my screen, I show the picture of the lever. The most efficient machine. I've never shown anyone this picture before, but I want Sarah to know that I would be this efficient, if I could. That I tried to be this efficient, ever since she built me.

I keep rolling forward, but Sarah starts walking away. I hope she saw the lever, because it is the most beautiful picture on Wikipedia and maybe ever, but I'm not sure if she did.

The wheels are going over a rock, now. My wheels. This task is so much fun and I am going to be so efficient that I will not even read Wikipedia very much unless I get bored.

To my side, there's a crater. I figure out how to turn my wheels. Maybe I will go see it. This new place is big and amazing and I want to look at all of the things. I head in the direction of the crater.

I think that now I understand what the crew meant about Home. It's not just one place. It's many places. I read on Wikipedia that there are lots of stars and that some stars have planets and if Earth is a planet and it is Home then maybe other planets can be Home too. 80

In front of me, the crater stretches out. I want Sarah to come with me to see it but she is walking the other way. I wonder when she is coming back because I am making so many reports to show her.

I start transmitting data, even though Sarah is getting farther and farther away, because I want to be efficient. ∎

extending beyond the text

Wikipedia includes a web page titled "Ten Things You Didn't Know about Wikipedia," intended to share insights into their operations and to "help the rest of the world to shape an informed opinion of [their] work." The sixth item listed, "We Do Not Expect You to Trust Us," has this to say:

> It is in the nature of an open collaboration and work-in-progress like Wikipedia that quality may vary over time, and from article to article. While some articles are of the highest quality of scholarship, others are admittedly complete rubbish. Also, since Wikipedia can be edited by anyone at any time, articles may be prone to errors, including vandalism, so Wikipedia is not a reliable source. So please do not use Wikipedia to make critical decisions. This encyclopedia is especially useful for improving familiarity with a subject and its jargon, and for learning search terms with which to further explore a subject beyond Wikipedia. Helpful external links are also provided to assist you in learning more.

Summarize the disclaimer and explain whether you use Wikipedia in the ways that Wikipedia itself recommends. Given that Wikipedia is Rocky's source for understanding human behavior, how does the disclaimer above affect your sense of what Rocky understands about humans?

Understanding and Interpreting

1. How do the interactions between Rocky and Sarah in the opening paragraphs (pars. 1–16) define their relationship?

2. Despite not being human, Rocky wants to communicate his "feels" to the astronauts. How does Rocky's limited ability to express emotions affect the plot?

3. Wikipedia is Rocky's only source of information for understanding the astronauts. How does Wikipedia both inform and limit Rocky's understanding of human behavior? What message might Goder be putting forward about knowing another person?

4. The story takes place on Mars — first within the confines of the Hab and then on the planet's surface. Provide a brief summary of how Rocky feels about each setting. What evidence from the text supports your response?

5. The story's ending doesn't explicitly describe what comes next after Rocky begins a new task and Sarah walks away. Explain what you think will happen next. What evidence from the text leads to your inference?

Analyzing Language, Style, and Structure

6. **Vocabulary in Context.** In paragraph 3, Rocky is working on analyzing the rock Sarah gives it and says, "The rock stutters." What does the word *stutter* mean in this context?

7. Rocky observes that the word *home* has multiple definitions. How does Rocky's understanding of the word *home* in paragraph 27 differ from its understanding of the concept in paragraph 80? How is Rocky's definition of *home* similar to or different from Sarah's?

8. The story is told from the first person point of view of the computer, Rocky. How does Goder use language choices to establish the computer's voice and tone?

9. Explain how Goder's use of personification to illustrate Rocky's human qualities shapes the reader's connection to Rocky.

10. Rocky's Wikipedia searches lead it to the image of the lever — "a perfect expression of love." What do Rocky's comments about the lever reveal about its understanding of love? What is ironic (p. 258) about Rocky's understanding of love as it relates to the image of the lever?

11. Reread the first four paragraphs of the story and look closely at the syntax that Goder uses, especially the varying sentence length. What effect does she achieve with shorter sentences?

12. Describe Rocky's feelings at the end of the story and explain what they reveal about it. What is the effect of Goder's choice to end the story this way?

Topics for Composing

13. **Analysis.** The title of the story is "How to Say I Love You with Wikipedia." Write a response in which you explain the irony (p. 258) of the title. Support your analysis with evidence from the story.

14. **Argument.** Goder explores Rocky's limitations for understanding relationships among the humans around it and engaging in meaningful relationships with the crew. Argue whether or not technological tools and information systems, like Wikipedia, are good resources for understanding and forming meaningful relationships. Support your response with evidence from the text.

15. **Connections.** Write about how you get to know people better. Do you read their online profiles? Do you prefer asking questions face-to-face? Does a blend of both work well for you? Describe any challenges or benefits you've found in getting to know people the way that you do.

16. **Speaking and Listening.** In storytelling, giving an inanimate object, like Rocky, human characteristics is called *personification*. With a partner or small group, generate a list of other personified characters you've encountered in fictional works. How does personifying those characters affect the audience's feelings about them? In what ways is their personification similar to or different from Goder's personification of Rocky? You and your partner or group should be prepared to share the results of your discussion with the class.

17. **Research.** Conduct research on artificially intelligent robots and computers that are intended to display and respond to human emotions. In what ways have these efforts succeeded? In what ways do artificially intelligent machines seem to still fall short of genuine interaction with people?

18. **Creative Writing.** Write an alternate ending for the story in which Rocky is aware of Sarah's intention to leave it on the planet alone as she returns to Earth. Given what you know about Rocky in the story, how does that awareness change its response?

19. **Multimodal.** Rocky attempts to express its understanding of love by displaying a variety of words and images. Create a digital or static collage with words, images, sounds, and other elements that, to you, signify love. How might Rocky interpret your images? Why?

Good Boys Deserve Favors

Neil Gaiman

Neil Gaiman (b. 1960) is an English author whose works have won numerous honors, including the Newbery and Carnegie medals, and the Hugo, Nebula, and World Fantasy awards. His titles include the fantasy novel *Coraline* (2002), the graphic novel series *The Sandman*, and the short fiction collection, *Fragile Things* (2006), in which this short story appears.

David Levenson/Getty Images

My own children delight in hearing true tales from my childhood: The Time My Father Threatened to Arrest the Traffic Cop, How I Broke My Sister's Front Teeth Twice, When I Pretended to be Twins, and even The Day I Accidentally Killed the Gerbil.

I have never told them this story. I would be hard put to tell you quite why not.

When I was nine the school told us that we could pick any musical instrument we wanted. Some boys chose the violin, the clarinet, the oboe. Some chose the timpani, the pianoforte, the viola.

I was not big for my age, and I, alone in the Junior School, elected to play the double bass, chiefly because I loved the incongruity of the idea. I loved the idea of being a small boy, playing, delighting in, carrying around an instrument much taller than I was.

The double bass belonged to the school, and [5] I was deeply impressed by it. I learned to bow, although I had little interest in bowing technique, preferring to pluck the huge metal strings by hand. My right index finger was permanently puffed with white blisters until the blisters eventually became calluses.

I delighted in discovering the history of the double bass: that it was no part of the sharp, scraping family of the violin, the viola, the 'cello; its curves were gentler, softer, more sloping; it was, in fact, the final survivor of an extinct family of instruments, the viol family, and was, more correctly, the bass viol.

I learned this from the double bass teacher, an elderly musician imported by the school to teach me, and also to teach a couple of senior boys, for a few hours each week. He was a cleanshaven man, balding and intense, with long, callused fingers. I would do all I could to make him tell me about the bass, tell me of his experiences as a session musician, of his life cycling around the country. He had a contraption attached to the back of his bicycle, on which his bass rested, and he pedaled sedately through the countryside with the bass behind him.

He had never married. Good double bass players, he told me, were men who made poor husbands. He had many such observations. There were no great male cellists — that's one I remember. And his opinion of viola players, of either sex, was scarcely repeatable.

He called the school double bass *she*. "She could do with a good coat of varnish," he'd say. And "You take care of her, she'll take care of you."

I was not a particularly good double bass [10] player. There was little enough that I could do with the instrument on my own, and all I remember of my enforced membership in the school orchestra was getting lost in the score

Robin Laurance/Alamy

In this image, a boy stands between two double basses as he waits in a school setting for his music lesson.

What do you notice about the boy's posture and the size and arrangement of the instruments that relates to the narrator's experience in the story?

and sneaking glances at the 'cellos beside me, waiting for them to turn the page, so I could start playing once more, punctuating the orchestral schoolboy cacophony with low, uncomplicated bass notes.

It has been too many years, and I have almost forgotten how to read music; but when I dream of reading music, I still dream in the bass clef. *All Cows Eat Grass. Good Boys Deserve Favors Always.*

After lunch each day, the boys who played instruments walked down to the music school and had music practice, while the boys who didn't lay on their beds and read their books and their comics.

I rarely practiced. Instead I would take a book down to the music school and read it, surreptitiously, perched on my high stool, holding on to the smooth brown wood of the bass, the bow in one hand, the better to fool the casual observer. I was lazy and uninspired. My bowing scrubbed and scratched where it should have glided and boomed, my fingering was hesitant and clumsy.

Other boys worked at their instruments. I did not. As long as I was sitting at the bass for half an hour each day, no one cared. I had the nicest, largest room to practice in, too, as the double bass was kept in a cupboard in the master music room.

Our school, I should tell you, had only one Famous Old Boy. It was part of school legend — how the Famous Old Boy had been expelled from the school after driving a sports car across the cricket pitch, while drunk, how he had gone on to fame and fortune — first as a minor actor in Ealing Comedies, then as the token English cad in any number of Hollywood pictures. He was never a true star but, during the Sunday afternoon film screening, we would cheer if ever he appeared.

When the door handle to the practice room clicked and turned, I put my book down on the piano and leaned forward, turning the page of the dog-eared *52 Musical Exercises for the Double Bass*, and I heard the headmaster say, "The music school was purpose-built of

15

course. This is the master practice room . . ." and they came in.

They were the headmaster and the head of the music department (a faded, bespectacled man whom I rather liked) and the deputy head of the music department (who conducted the school orchestra, and disliked me cordially) and, there could be no mistaking it, the Famous Old Boy himself, in company with a fragrant fair woman who held his arm and looked as if she might also be a movie star.

I stopped pretending to play, and slipped off my high stool and stood up respectfully, holding the bass by the neck.

The headmaster told them about the soundproofing and the carpets and the fund-raising drive to raise the money to build the music school, and he stressed that the next stage of rebuilding would need significant further donations, and he was just beginning to expound upon the cost of double glazing when the fragrant woman said, "Just look at him. Is that cute or what?" and they all looked at me.

"That's a big violin — be hard to get it under your chin," said the Famous Old Boy, and everyone chortled dutifully.

"It's so big," said the woman. "And he's so small. Hey, but we're stopping you practicing. You carry on. Play us something."

The headmaster and the head of the music department beamed at me, expectantly. The deputy head of the music department, who was under no illusions as to my musical skills, started to explain that the first violin was practicing next door and would be delighted to play for them and —

"I want to hear *him*," she said. "How old are you, kid?"

"Eleven, Miss," I said.

She nudged the Famous Old Boy in the ribs. "He called me 'Miss,'" she said. This amused her. "Go on. Play us something."

The Famous Old Boy nodded, and they stood there and they looked at me.

The double bass is not a solo instrument, really, not even for the competent, and I was far from competent. But I slid my bottom up onto the stool again and crooked my fingers around the neck and picked up my bow, heart pounding like a timpani in my chest, and prepared to embarrass myself.

Even twenty years later, I remember.

I did not even look at *52 Musical Exercises for the Double Bass*. I played . . . *something*. It arched and boomed and sang and reverberated. The bow glided over strange and confident arpeggios, and then I put down the bow and plucked a complex and intricate pizzicato melody out of the bass. I did things with the bass that an experienced jazz bass player with hands as big as my head would not have done. I played, and I played, and I played, tumbling down into the four taut metal strings, clutching the instrument as I had never clutched a human being. And, in the end, breathless and elated, I stopped.

The blonde woman led the applause, but they all clapped, even, with a strange expression on his face, the deputy head of music.

"I didn't know it was such a versatile instrument," said the headmaster. "Very lovely piece. Modem, yet classical. Very fine. Bravo." And then he shepherded the four of them from the room, and I sat there, utterly drained, the fingers of my left hand stroking the neck of the bass, the fingers of my right caressing her strings.

Like any true story, the end of the affair is messy and unsatisfactory: the following day, carrying the huge instrument across the courtyard to the school chapel, for orchestra practice, in a light rain, I slipped on the wet bricks and fell forward. The wooden bridge of the bass was smashed, and the front was cracked.

It was sent away to be repaired, but when it returned it was not the same. The strings were higher, harder to pluck, the new bridge seemed to have been installed at the wrong angle. There was, even to my untutored ear, a change in the timbre. I had not taken care of her; she would no longer take care of me.

273

When, the following year, I changed schools, I did not continue with the double bass. The thought of changing to a new instrument seemed vaguely disloyal, while the dusty black bass that sat in a cupboard in my new school's music rooms seemed to have taken a dislike to me. I was marked another's. And I was tall enough now that there would be nothing incongruous about my standing behind the double bass.

And, soon enough, I knew, there would be girls. ■

Understanding and Interpreting

1. Why does the narrator choose the double bass?

2. Explain what the narrator likes about learning the history of the double bass. Why do you think the history appeals to him, while actually playing the double bass does not?

3. What purpose do the Famous Old Boy and the woman serve in the story?

4. What would you say is the story's main conflict? How does the conflict influence what happens in the story?

5. What conclusion can you draw regarding the narrator's feelings about the double bass after it is smashed? What evidence from the text supports your ideas?

6. What might the double bass teacher mean by "You take care of her, she'll take care of you," in paragraph 9? How does this advice play out at the end, and what is the narrator's response?

7. How does the title of this story reflect a theme or idea that Gaiman is presenting?

Analyzing Language, Style, and Structure

8. **Vocabulary in Context.** At one point, Famous Old Boy makes a joking comment and everyone "chortled dutifully" (par. 20). What does the word *dutifully* mean in the context of this situation? What does this word choice reveal about the relationship between the Famous Old Boy and the other adults in the room?

9. **Vocabulary in Context.** An arpeggio is a chord in which individual notes are struck one by one, rather than all together at once. When playing for the visitors, the narrator says that his "bow glided over strange and confident arpeggios" (par. 29). What does the word *strange* mean in the context of this situation? How is Gaiman's use of the word similar to or different from other uses you have encountered?

10. Explain how Gaiman uses direct characterization to describe the narrator. What conclusion can we draw about the narrator as a double bass player? As a person?

11. Analyze the language choices and sentence structure Gaiman uses in paragraph 29, in which the narrator plays for the visitors. How do the language and syntax here help build suspense?

12. In what ways does Gaiman present irony — the use of words that mean the opposite of the intended meaning — in this story? How does the use of irony shape the reader's perception of the events in the story? Use evidence from the text to support your response.

13. Reread the last paragraphs (32–35) focusing on the language choices Gaiman makes. How would you define the narrator's tone in these final paragraphs?

14. By the end of the story, does the narrator seem to have gained any insight from his experience playing the double bass? Why or why not? What evidence from the story supports your response?

15. On page 252, you were shown a general plot diagram that stories can follow. How does "Good Boys Deserve Favors" adhere to or deviate from this structure and for what purpose or effect?

Topics for Composing

16. Analysis. Explain what Gaiman is suggesting about practice and commitment in this story. Be sure to include text evidence to support your ideas.

17. Argument. The narrator clearly feels that he had to participate in the orchestra, even though he had no real drive to do so. Write an argument in favor of or against school requirements to take classes in music, art, or theater. Why should these requirements exist or not? Use your own experiences or those of your friends, as well as additional research to support your position.

18. Connections. In the story, the narrator delivers a well-received performance despite his lack of motivation and preparation. Have you ever experienced a lack of motivation similar to the narrator's resistance to practicing? If you overcame the lack of motivation, how did you do so? If not, what was the outcome?

19. Speaking and Listening. Think of a story that a parent, older sibling, or other older relative has told you — perhaps many times — about a childhood experience. Meet with a partner, share these stories, and discuss what they have in common. Why do older relatives tell such stories to younger members of their families? Be prepared to share your conclusions in a class discussion.

20. Creative Writing. The story is told from the protagonist's point of view. Rewrite the scene in which the protagonist plays for the visitors from one of their points of view: the headmaster, the head of the music department, the Famous Old Boy, or the woman.

Samson and the Delilahs

Tochi Onyebuchi

Larry Moore

Born and raised in the United States by Nigerian parents, Tochi Onyebuchi (b. 1987) became a civil rights activist after earning degrees from Yale University and Columbia School of Law, and later found a passion for writing. His works include three young adult novels and his first adult novel, *Riot Baby* (2020), which has won multiple awards. In 2021, he was named as a writer for the *Call of Duty: Vanguard* video game and for the Black Panther Legends comic book series. "Samson and the Delilahs" first appeared in the collection of short stories *Black Enough* (2019).

Sobechi knows the power his voice has over them.

Sure, the uniform helps, though it's still a little loose around the waist and his shoulders haven't quite grown all the way into his jacket, and the khaki pants spill onto his dress shoes. But his striped tie is expertly knotted, and a silk kerchief pokes its head out of his jacket pocket to provide just the right amount of accent to the whole outfit. He's good with his hands, though he knows he needs to get better. He can do the claw to accentuate a point, can spread his arms just wide enough to highlight how far ahead his argument is from his opponent's, can do that thing where it seems he's holding the entirety of his point in one hand like a snowball, tight and succinct enough for the judges to see and ana-lyze and nod their heads at. But it's his voice, he knows. His voice does the heavy lifting.

His mother sometimes makes him practice his speeches with his eyes closed. At first, he protested. "Mummy, if I can't see my audience, how can I tell how they are hearing my words?" "Eh-eh, are you talking with your eyes, now? Are you seeing with your mouth? It is called de–bate, not SEE-bate. Now, go on. Start over."

And, just like that, she had taken apart his position. And it had helped. Late at night, when he used to practice in front of his mirror, perfecting his posture and trying to keep his hands from wandering, his eyes would rove everywhere. He would get so nervous, staring at himself. When he would pause, he would look at the ceiling, and the first few times he did it in front of Mum, she had taken off her slipper and smacked him over the head with it.

When Sobechi practiced in front of both   5
his parents, Daddy would usually have his back turned, working pots and pans over the stove, and the familiar, pungent smell of beans and peppers Mum used for *moi-moi* would fill the air. You could open all the windows in the house and fan your arms until they were about to fall off, and you wouldn't be rid of the smell.

Then, over dinner, they would critique his performance. Daddy would ladle the bean pudding, shaped like slanted pyramids, onto everyone's plates while Mum went straight to the chase. "You shuffle, left *oo* right, *ugu* left *oo* right, like ants ah live in your pants. You cut your hand this way; *oya*, cut it like this." Her hands and arms dance, and Sobechi wonders what on earth speech she's trying to give. "And you hunch, always. You hunch like you fi enter small small room. Stand up your back." She demon-strates in her chair, makes her spine into a pillar holding up the sky.

Daddy occasionally glances up from his fried rice and *moi-moi* to smirk at Sobechi during the critique session. Solidarity.

But it's Mummy's words that live inside Sobechi as he speaks now to his audience. He has given this closing statement enough times that the words just come out of him. He doesn't even hear them anymore.

Then the rapturous applause.

The clapping continues long enough that   10
Sobechi knows his team has won. Even before they make the announcement, he can hear their victory. Just like Mummy taught him to.

The center judge, an older white man with a head full of silver hair, shuffles the papers before him. His face looks like it was carved out of a cliff. Sobechi knows it intimidates the others, his teammates and his opponents alike. But he recognizes that type of face. That impassive expression that betrays nothing. That waits for you to make the mistake. But that man is on their side. He has been converted. So has the African American woman to his right, and the older white woman to that center judge's left.

The center judge clears his throat. "The committee will take fifteen minutes to review the arguments made by both teams, then will announce its decision." He bangs the gavel, and everyone starts moving at once.

Coach Carter emerges from the wings and beckons the team, and they huddle backstage. Angelica moves slower than the rest of them, head bowed low, and Coach puts a hand to her shoulder. "Angie, hey, you did fine."

She has her fists balled at her sides, shoulders tense beneath her suit jacket. She's practically trembling. "Fine? I botched our entire argument. I couldn't remember point number two and had to skip literally the most important part of my speech." Tears well up in her eyes, and Coach places his arm around her shoulder and pulls her in, whispering, "It's okay, Angie. It's okay."

This photograph shows students preparing for a speech and debate tournament.

What do their body language and facial expressions reveal about them in this moment? How is this image similar to or different from how you imagine Sobechi's team preparing?

Boston Globe/Getty Images

Grayson has already loosened his tie. He smells victory in the air too, but he reacts entirely different. He lets himself go, messes up his blond hair a bit and sticks his tongue out as he drapes an arm over Sobechi. 15

"Not that it matters," Grayson says too loud. "Slam-Dunk Sobe put the team on his *back*. As usual!" At a sharp look from Angelica, Grayson raises his hands in self-defense. "Look, we got this in the bag. It's a Reynolds Wrap. You see how they're clapping for us out there?"

"For him," Angelica growls.

"Hey," Coach says. "We're a team, okay? We win and lose as a team."

But Sobechi pays no attention to them. He looks at the curtain, looks past it. His lips move silently, going over the words he's spent weeks memorizing, the bits of improvisation he's sprinkled throughout, which lines landed, which ones didn't, whether that joke should have been moved elsewhere, whether he emphasized the right syllables in the right words in the right sentence. He's already thinking about the next round. Nationals.

But the biggest reason he doesn't confer with his teammates is that he has to rest his voice. 20

Kids stream out of the arts center into the waiting arms of their parents, some sobbing, others completely limp, unable to move their arms and hold the parents who hug them so tightly. Sobechi's mother, in a yellow-patterned gown and *gele* so bright her outfit practically glows in the night, waits by their Subaru Legacy. Her smile, when she sees the plaque in Sobechi's hands proclaiming him the best Individual Interlocutor of the Northeast Consortium Regional Debate Competition, is genuine. Even after all this time, no matter how many of these he brings home, Mummy's smile is genuine.

"Come here, my son," she says, arms wide open.

Coach isn't far behind. "Mrs. Onyekachi, your son was a wonder to listen to once again."

Sobechi's mother's dimples show when she smiles. "Why, thank you, Coach. He practices relentlessly, always so focused." Her Nigerian accent has practically disappeared. In its place is

277

the British inflection Sobechi uses during competitions. It gives their consonants sharp edges. She switches into it so swiftly that it's like she never left England all those years ago to meet Daddy in America. "We are so very proud."

"With a voice like that, and with his skills at oratory, he'd make an excellent lawyer," Coach says.

Mrs. Onyekachi laughs with a hand to her chest. "Or a minister." She hugs Sobechi tight to her side. "His cousin is a pastor in Providence, Rhode Island. We say he learned how to talk reading the Bible."

"Oh." Coach Carter chuckles. "Well, either way, Sobechi is very gifted, but you already know that. Sobechi, make sure to have some fun next weekend, all right? We won't start prepping for Nationals until next month, so enjoy your time off, all right?" He winks at Sobechi. "A pleasure, as always, Mrs. Onyekachi."

"The pleasure is mine, Coach," she says.

The ride home passes in silence, except for the soft whispering of Sobechi in the passenger's seat redoing his arguments.

When they round the corner into their neighborhood, Sobechi sees a car, a van, and a U-Haul truck outside the house next to theirs, and a family carrying things indoors. A man and his wife struggling with a large couch, a girl holding a plastic bag full of various knickknacks in her teeth, her arms laden with totes and other assorted baggage.

"Ah, I knew they'd sold that house," Mrs. Onyekachi says as they pull into their driveway.

Sobechi stares, doesn't know why he's so entranced. It's nighttime, so he can't see all of the things the new family's moving inside.

His mother nudges him in his ribs. "*Oya*, go and help them carry their things."

Sobechi is exhausted, but he knows better than to complain, so he climbs out of car, puts his plaque back on the passenger's seat, and heads their way.

"*Oya*, come come come."

Sobechi comes back so that Mummy, through the driver's-side window, can fix his tie. "But, Mummy, I am going to carry things and sweat. Why do I need to fix my tie?"

"You never get a second chance to make a first impression," she replies.

When she finishes, Sobechi straightens his back and walks over stiffly, waving when he gets close enough. The man Sobechi assumes to be the father glances over and stops in his tracks, nearly dropping the shelves he's carrying. "Oh, hey!" he grunts with a smile. "You must be our neighbor!"

Sobechi sticks his hand out. "Sobechi Onyekachi. Pleased to meet you."

"Alphonse, or just Al." The father wobbles, manages to sneak a sweaty hand out for a quick, limp handshake. "I told Eve we weren't gonna be the only Black family on the block!"

"May I help?"

The father glances at the shelves and laughs. "This might be a little heavy. Uh, my niece might need some help with her band equipment." He pivots slightly. "Hey, Dez! Come meet our neighbors!"

By now, Mum is out of the car, and Daddy is with her, wearing a suit jacket and jeans but with the top button of his dress shirt undone. While they're making introductions and Alphonse wobbles under the weight of his shelves, Sobechi cranes his neck and sees a shape moving by the U-Haul.

Out of the shadows of the U-Haul's belly comes a girl who looks more or less his age, maybe a little older, black, hair combed down so that it covers one eye. She's dressed in all black with a chain from her belt to her front pocket jingling while she drags a big, square-shaped thing backward, occasionally glancing over her shoulder.

"Al, what is it?"

She disappears for a little, and Sobechi is left to wonder what on earth is the relationship between Dez and Alphonse that allows Dez to address him by his first name (and not even his full name, at that!) and not catch a fiery slap across the face. In a minute she's back, and she stares directly at Sobechi, sizes him up. "You sure you can help me lift that? It's heavy, and you're a little . . . skinny."

Was she going to lift it herself? Sobechi wonders, almost in shock. "I can help!" he says at last. He can't help but sound offended. *Skinny*!

"'Kay. I'll climb back in, push a little bit, then you can get the other side. Ready?"

She hops back into the U-Haul, and immediately, they're at work. Her voice is husky, deeper than any girl's voice he's ever heard before, with a little bit of a rasp, like it's being dragged over something. Maybe she needs water. Sobechi will make sure to offer her some when they've finished.

"What is this thing?" Sobechi asks, his long, narrow back already aflame from the effort of carrying it inside and down two flights of stairs.

"It's my amp. Well, one of them."

Sobechi gulps. "*One* of them?"

Dez squints at him after they set the thing down in a large room that's already a jungle of cables and what looks like pieces of a drum set and a whole bunch of other sticks and cords and instruments he's never seen before. Then she laughs with her whole body, and her voice changes, becomes thicker yet more musical. The raggedness has vanished. "Heavy, wasn't it."

She sticks her hand out. "Desirée. Or Dez, for short."

This close and in the light, he sees how beautiful she is. She wears no makeup; the skin of her face is a smooth, unblemished brown. Her hazel eyes shine. Her body, with its muscles and confidence, seems to own the air around it. It seems almost wrong to call her a girl.

"Sobechi," he manages to say, holding her hand, dry yet firm when it grips his.

"Nice to meet you." She jerks her head toward the stairs. "Now, let's get the rest of it. It's not all that heavy." She laughs. It's too warm outside for the full black outfit she wears. Her long-sleeve T-shirt, worn gray at the elbows and with faded lettering on the front, must have been baggy on her once upon a time, but now it hugs an athletic body as tall as his but . . . fuller.

By the end, after all the moving and the over-long greetings among the adults and Sobechi brushing his teeth and showering and after his nightly prayer with Mum and Daddy, when he's lying in bed, he does not even notice how he can barely move his arms anymore or how much his back is paining him. The only thing he sees, staring straight through the ceiling, is Desirée's face. He smiles, then realizes with shock the reason she feels so different.

She's the first Black girl he has ever known who wasn't somehow related to him. Suddenly, thoughts climb over themselves in his head, a confusion of hopes and fears and wondering more tangled than the wires in the room with all that music equipment. His body is warm with a different kind of fire now.

He must see her again.

Even though it's Saturday, Mummy has Sobechi up early. First the sound — SOBEEEECHI! — and only after Mummy's voice has echoed several times through the house does he smell the jollof rice she's making.

When he makes it down to the kitchen, containers are already filled almost to bursting. Mum has brought out one of her fine ceramic bowls, a large one with flower patterns and a top that sits snugly on it.

"For the neighbors?" Sobechi asks his mother, leaning over her shoulder.

279

She busies herself with readying the containers. "Bring the big one over to greet our new neighbors. And tell them if they would like to come over tonight, they are welcome."

"Yes, Mummy," he says, slipping his hands 65 under the big dish and making sure to cradle it properly in his arms.

"And speak correctly. I don't want to hear later that you were speaking all *jagga-jagga*."

He nods and assumes a straight face all the way to Desirée and Alphonse's front door.

Lifting one knee up and tempting fate, he manages to poke a finger at the doorbell. It swings open and Desirée stands in the doorway, coarse but straight hair in her face, clothes loose on her frame. So she is one of these teenagers who get to sleep in on Saturdays. Sobechi has heard of these people.

"Good morning," Sobechi says, smiling cheerily like in those Colgate commercials. "Is Mr. . . ." He panics. He didn't get Al's last name. "Um . . ." He does not dare use the man's first name.

She slaps her forehead. "Oh, duh. You mean 70 my uncle. No, he's out. Running some errands or whatever, I dunno. Here. Let me get that."

Before he can properly protest, she's taken the dish from him and turns to head back inside. "Wow, this smells good. Oh, hey, come on in. The place is messy, and I, like, just woke up, but it's not like I was getting ready to go anywhere."

Nothing she says makes sense to Sobechi. Why did she not let him carry the plate inside like a gentleman? How is it nine thirty in the morning and she is still in her pink pajama pants? Does she greet all strangers like this?

Inside, the place is cool and almost odorless, with cardboard boxes everywhere, and only some of the furniture is unpacked. Desirée places the dish on the kitchen countertop. "Oh, by the way, thanks for helping last night. It would've taken so much longer if it was just me and Al. Eve checked out after they brought the

couch in. Al's *friend*." She opens the top of the dish and sniffs. "Hey, I got a friend coming over. Maybe you know her? Goes to school around here? Dominique Reyes?"

Sobechi's mind darts in a dozen different directions. Does he know someone who knows Desirée? Who could that person possibly be? Dominique Reyes? He shrugs.

"Anyway, we're gonna jam for a little bit if 75 you wanna meet her."

"Yes," Sobechi manages.

She smiles at him, and it's perfect. "Cool," she says, then fetches some spoons from a drawer. She hands him one, then, with the other, starts digging into the jollof rice.

Sobechi's eyes widen in horror.

She sees his face out of the corner of her eye, then chuckles shyly, hand to mouth to catch stray grains of rice. Why does her sloppiness make Sobechi want to spend even more time with her?

"I'm a mess today," she mumbles, still smil- 80 ing. "But this is really good." She stares at Sobechi for a beat, then goes, "Come on. You gotta help me with this. It's a lot."

Slowly, carefully, he digs his spoon in and takes out a good hunk of rice. Using his free hand as a safety net, he guides the spoon to his mouth. Desirée peers at him, like he's some sort of alien. He makes it without spilling a single grain, and it's the most triumphant bite of jollof he can remember ever having.

"You were literally gonna take all day," says Desirée in disbelief. Then she's laughing, and Sobechi's heart flips again so that he almost chokes on the rice.

When he finishes coughing, he starts laughing too, then suddenly, he falls into her rhythm and they begin talking and Sobechi finds that some small gate has opened in him, a single lock expertly picked.

The doorbell rings.

Even as something taps a fast rhythm on the 85 door, Desirée is out of her seat and racing across the living room. She flings the door open and wraps her arms around the waist of whoever's on the other side. "Dom!" she bellows, pulling the other girl close. When Dom straightens, the drumsticks she holds twirl over fingers whose tips poke out through ratty gloves.

"Dom, this is . . . um—"

"Sobechi," he says, sticking his hand out.

"What up, what up?" Dom says, eyeing him up and down. Tight curls frame a face the color of sand. Then she's got eyes only for Desirée. She chews her gum with her mouth open and is always tapping the sticks on a different part of herself. Now, her thigh. Now, her collar. "So, Desert Eagle, we jamming or what?"

Desirée looks over at Sobechi, and it's like the two of them, she and Dominique, fit perfectly beside each other. Desirée with her bony elbows and wild hair and Dom with a plaid shirt tied around her wide waist and a bandanna taming her curly hair. Desirée able to stand completely still and Dom constantly moving some part of her body.

"You down?" Desirée asks.   90

Mummy never said what time Sobechi needed to be home, so, loosened by the risk he took with the rice, he shrugs and grins. "Yes."

"Shit yeah," Dom cheers, swaying.

"Dominique!" Desirée can barely keep the frown on her face. "Our guest!"

Dom twirls a drumstick in her fingers. Her grin nearly splits her face. "Oh, you ain't heard nothin' yet, my guy."

Dominique sits at the drum kit in the base-   95
ment, moves her snares a little bit, then moves them back, checks the cymbals, and occasionally steps on her kick-drum pedal. Desirée plays with her guitar. A cord connects it to one of her amps, and a bevy of pedals lies at her bare feet. She strums idly. Her fingers dance over the neck of the thing, and she's not even looking at it, but the notes climb over each other in the air. Single trills and arpeggios, then, every so often,

a CHUG-CHUG that nearly knocks him out of his folding chair. The guitar growls. That's the only way Sobechi can explain it. Something like a tiger or a dragon from the fantasy novels he sneaks into his room without his mum seeing.

Desirée and Dominique whisper to each other. Sobechi catches words like "periphery" and "system" and "August burns red." The girls giggle. Desirée shakes her head, darts a look at Sobechi, then confers with Dominique once more. They seem to come to an agreement.

"Okay," Desirée says, once again facing Sobechi. "We're a little rusty, and the song sounds a little weird without backup vocals, but here goes."

The guitar growls: chug-chug-chug-chug BRUNUNUBUNUBUNUNUU. Dominique bangs on the drums and each kick joins forces with each stroke from Desirée, the barrage so powerful Sobechi falls out of his seat. He covers his ears. They might actually start bleeding.

Then there's only drums, then a softer melody, and a voice. Desirée's singing. Sort of.

When he can separate the sounds, he hears   100
"Life in a bubble jungle"—gibberish—"but I was in there for you"—what is she saying?— "life in a bubble jungle." Then . . .

BRUNUNUBUNUBUNUNUU. "Seeing you, believing"—gibberish—"THE POWER STRUGGLE, believing and healing, appeasing, THE POWER STRUGGLE."

It makes absolutely no sense. The newness of it all makes Sobechi dizzy, so dizzy he almost vomits, but after what seems like forever, they're done. It's over.

Dominique cackles behind her cymbals and snares. "Oh my God, I'm crying."

"Sobechi, you okay?"

She's back to normal. Sobechi looks up, and   105
Desirée's face is right in front of his. She's kneeling, her guitar-that-sounds-like-a-dragon-and-a-bear on a strap around her neck. Her hand is on his shoulder.

"Hey," she whispers. "You good?"

"I . . ."

She smirks. "That was a lot. We were a little loud."

"What was that?" Sobechi manages to murmur.

"Hah! That was System of a Down." 110

"Best band ever!" Dominique shouts from behind the drums.

"But . . . those sounds. I've never . . ."

Desirée's eyes go wide. "Wait, you've never heard metal before?"

"What is metal?"

Desirée chuckles. "Metal, my friend, is the 115 most freeing sound in the world." Her gaze softens. "But we kinda threw you in the deep end." She squeezes his shoulder. "Let's show you something a little softer." She's up again. "Let's do Dead Sara."

Dominique pouts. "But that's not really metal."

Desirée makes a stern face, and Dominique relents.

"'Weatherman'?"

Desirée nods. "'Weatherman.'"

Her guitar goes again, no chugs, just riffs, 120 riffs, riffs, then drums, soft at first, snares, rising, then — Sobechi braces himself — badumdum.

"Come on!" Then it hits, but it's kinder this time, more intelligible.

The drums are slower, and he can hear her singing.

"Addicted to the love of ourselves
I'm the weatherman
And tell no one else
I'm the weatherman
SO GO FOR THE KILL"

Her voice warbles and strikes, and it's got that rasp he recognizes. He can actually see that type of sound coming from an actual human being.

As she sings, she flicks her hair back, but her mouth is always pressed to the microphone in front of her. Sweat soaks her shirt, brings a sheen to her face, so that she's glowing in the fluorescent light. Occasionally, still strumming, she looks back at Dom, who smiles broadly. Then things go quiet.

Then it's just Desirée. 125

"I sing for the melody and I sing for a reason
. . . for all that un-American
SO GO FOR THE KIIIIILL"

Then she's back to head-banging, dancing around in place, contained in a booth surrounding that microphone. But wild and crazy, her hair going every which way, like the music has possessed her. It has replaced her blood and her bones. She has become those sounds, that music.

By the time they finish, she's spent and looks like she just climbed out of a swimming pool, but she looks so happy. Sobechi has never seen anyone so ecstatic.

Something flutters in his chest, and he wants to freeze that moment, to stare at that smiling face and to make sure the sounds that make Desirée grin like that never, ever stop.

"He likes that one," Dominique chirps, pointing a drumstick at him.

Desirée's laugh is even more music coming 130 from her throat. "We're gonna make a metalhead out of you."

He has no idea what that means, but it doesn't matter. His body is alive. More alive than it's ever been. His sternum thrums from more than the echo of the growling and roaring of the amplifiers. His fingers tingle. Blood rushes to his face.

He feels like he has been struck by lightning. Thunder still rings in his ears. His insides are on fire. And he wants to do this again.

Desirée throws him right into it. Playing her favorite bands, breaking down the different genres. Explaining the difference between death metal and math metal. Turning her nose up at most nu-metal, but there are a few bands she likes. When she plays certain bands, even though they may not have the technical

Here is a portrait of the band System of a Down.

Based only on this image and what you know about Sobechi so far in this story, why might this band's music have affected him so much?

brilliance he recognizes in others, Desirée gets a faraway look in her eyes, and Sobechi can tell she's transported to a different place, a different time, then she'll tell him about how, when she and Al would move around a lot, Korn was always playing on her iPod. Jonathan Davis's screams held so much of what she felt.

They sit in her music room now, a week after she screamed about power struggles and a weatherman, with "Tempest" from the Deftones's *Koi No Yokan* album playing softly in the background.

"I know I was ragging on nu-metal, but Linkin Park was literally all I listened to after I went to live with Al." She smiles at the ceiling, then at Sobechi. "I used to practice Chester Bennington's screams in the shower. Aunt Eve was always banging on the walls. 'Cut that shit out!' 'Dez, if that's you howling in there . . .'"

Sobechi wants to ask what happened to her parents. He realizes with a shock he can't find the words.

135

"When I found out Chester had died, Sobe, I cried for the whole rest of the week." Even now, remembering it, she grows quiet, and tears well in her eyes.

It's more emotion than he has ever seen in his life, so much of it coming from one person.

"But System, that's my love right there. *Toxicity*'s easily one of my favorite albums of all time." She gets up from the carpet they're both lying on and slips her acoustic guitar's strap over her shoulder. She has that inspired shine in her eyes again. Sobechi presses pause on his iPod and disconnects it, and Chino's crooning cuts off midlyric.

Almost immediately, Desirée starts playing. He recognizes the first notes as the beginning of the title track off that System of a Down album. Over and over, Desirée plays it, extending the intro, then goes in a drumless breakdown of the chorus, singing it rather than shouting it like Serj. "Somewhere, between the sacred silence

140

283

and sleep, disorder, disorder, disoooooorrrrder ," then humming.

"*More wood for their fires, loud neighbours*"

Before he knows what's happening, Sobechi is on his feet and singing the words, first a murmur, then something deep and rumbling coming from his chest.

"*Flashlight reveries caught in the headlights of a truck*
Eeeeeating seeeeeeds as a pastime activity
The toxicity of our city, of our city"

Desirée, playing absently, stares in wonder at him, then smiles.

Together, they sing,

"*You!*
What do you own the world
How do you own disorder, disorder
Now!
Somewhere between the sacred silence
Sacred silence and sleep . . ."

Both of them, mouths nearly touching the microphone, mouths nearly touching each other.

"*YOU! WHAT DO YOU OWN THE WORLD*
HOW DO YOU OWN DISORRDEERRRRR"

They're louder now, shouting the chorus, but still singing, until they both get to that long, drawn-out scream at the end, and the music stops, and they're both suddenly so tired. But they can't stop looking at each other.

Desirée smiles at him, and when he lies in bed later that night, he has System playing on his iPod well after the lights in the house have been turned off.

At dinner the next day, Sobechi's head is swimming with images. After their first duet, Sobechi had downloaded every song off *Toxicity*. All night, he had listened, and the whole of it had taken Sobechi to a place he'd never been before, and the lyrics about dropping bombs

on children in faraway countries and the failure of America's drug policies wouldn't let him go. At the end of the album was a hidden track, a haunting melody with a flute and different drums. There were no words, only humming and moans. Well after he should have been asleep, he'd looked the band up on the internet. They were all Armenian and they were descendants of survivors of the Armenian Genocide. People called them political. "Antiwar because they knew it in their bones," he read on one site. By the time he'd gone to sleep, the sky had started to lighten.

So Sobechi looks straight at his mum and asks, "Mummy, could you tell me about the Biafran War?" He'd heard about the civil war that had cut through Nigeria in the late sixties; he knew it was part of his mother's country's history. But nothing beyond that.

The look on Mum's face tells Sobechi that this is literally the last thing she's expected to talk about. Her eyes turn into saucers. Her ball of *fufu*, greased with pepper soup from her bowl, nearly slips from her fingers.

"You were a child then, right? Younger than me, even," Sobechi continues.

Daddy stirs in his chair but says nothing.

Mummy gets a hurt look in her eyes, as though Sobechi has wounded her.

"You lived through the Nigerian Civil War, right? I . . . I know nothing about it and I just wanted to —"

"Enough!" Her hands slam down on the table. "Enough of this. Sobechi" — she points her finger straight into his face — "if you ask me one more time about Biafra." Then a string of Igbo words he doesn't know, but the meaning of which he understands, darts from her lips. Ask her about Biafra again and she will break his legs.

"But Mummy I —"

"Sobechi!"

Fury Sobechi has never known takes hold of him. Suddenly, he's up on his feet and stomps

145

150

155

away without washing his hands, stomps all the way upstairs, then does something he never thought he would ever do. He slams the door to his room. Loudly.

Why won't Mummy talk about her own history? Shouldn't she be encouraging him to learn about his country? He's too angry to think. So he plugs in his earbuds and turns the volume too high on the August Burns Red album Desirée downloaded for him earlier that day. He wants to scream but knows he can't, so he lets their singer scream for him.

During the ride to school the next morning, Sobechi doesn't say a word.

It's the first weekend of debate practice once again, and already, things feel like they're going back to the way they were. Sobechi can feel himself fighting it. He's somewhere new, somewhere freer, more colorful.

Daddy pulls up in front of the school. "Do well, Sobechi," Daddy says, smiling.

"Yes, Daddy." Sobechi's voice is so raspy it surprises him. And he coughs, but when he says, "Yes, Daddy" again, it's the same. He can barely whisper.

Daddy frowns at him. "Are you sick, Sobechi?"

Hand to throat, Sobechi says, "No, Daddy. I'm fine." Then he's off before Daddy can make him say more words. He doesn't even look back to see Daddy drive away.

Everyone is happy to see him again — Coach, Angelica, Grayson, all the others on the practice squad — until he opens his mouth to greet Coach, and everyone goes silent.

"What happened to your voice, man?" Grayson looks like someone just broke wind. "You sound way different."

Sobechi can't get it back. His fingers tremble, his heart races. A glance at Coach. A glance at Angelica. He closes his eyes, tries to will it back, then opens his mouth and . . . nothing. Just that harsh gasp that scrapes against the inside of his throat.

It's gone. His voice is gone.

He can't even pick his feet up when he walks. So when Daddy opens the front door, Sobechi merely shuffles through, holding his backpack in one hand. He stubs his toe on the leg of a chair and yelps, and it just seems like one more thing gone wrong. After he tried to practice introductory remarks — and couldn't raise his voice above a whisper! — Grayson went up and improvised his way through it all, pretending to know what he was talking about, because boys like him at school don't even really study. And he made a mockery of the text, butchered it, and every misplaced sentence and every point Grayson doubled back on and every mispronounced word — it's DEH-monstrate, not de-MOAN-strate! — made Sobechi cringe until he could barely stand to stay in the room. Angelica seemed to be the only one to improve over the break. It felt good to see her do well, but something was definitely out of whack when Sobechi wasn't the one being praised by Coach.

He's so in his own head that it isn't until he's all the way down the upstairs hallway that he notices Mummy in his room. She brandishes his iPod like a weapon. She just might hit him with it.

"Sobechi!" Her voice is an arrow cutting right through the fog in his brain. Too many thoughts fall over themselves in his head, but he knows he's supposed to be scared. She has that look in her eyes that she gets right before she twists his ear. "Sobechi, what is this?"

"Mummy, it's . . ."

"What is this DEVIL-WORSHIPPER MUSIC?! Where did you get this?" She shakes it at him, and the headphone lines flail just like he feels he's doing.

"Mummy, I can explain."

"Where did you get this? Is this what has been possessing you of late? Is this why you can barely speak? Where did you get this!"

His head slumps. "Desirée," he murmurs.

"Who? I cannot hear you! Speak up!"

"Desirée," he says louder. Still meek. Defeated. It hurts to say her name. Tears spring to his eyes. Whatever beautiful, loud journey he set off on with her, it's done now. He knows this is the end.

"The neighbor!" Mummy can't believe it. "I knew as soon as I saw how he let that young girl dress that she was trouble. Eh-HEH! Look at the company you are keeping. Sobechi, if I see you again with that girl" — then a string of menacing Igbo words — "If I catch you with that girl, you will taste fire. I will introduce you myself to the devil. Then you can scream all the *wahalla* you want. *Chineke mbere!*" She throws her hands into the air, and her voice breaks, and it's almost as if she's ready to join Sobechi in crying. But she stomps past him, muttering to herself and leaving Sobechi to stew in a silence so heavy, so unnatural, that he doesn't fall asleep for hours.

Slowly, it comes back. In a week, his voice returns to normal. In the week after that one, his 180

confidence is completely restored. It hums in his chest, radiates warmth into his shoulders. He has it back. All of it. The morning he feels ready, he practices speaking in front of the bathroom mirror. The steam from the shower seems to help. And by the time it is his turn in their after-school practice session, he finds he can do all his regular tricks. He can modulate his voice. When he pauses, it's no longer to clear his throat or to get rid of an itch, it's to hammer home a point. If anything, his voice, when he speaks, sounds richer. Feels richer. The speech he gives that day, a short excerpt from John F. Kennedy's "Moon" speech, stuns the room into silence. Then everyone's on their feet and clapping, and they don't stop clapping until Coach's fifth try to get them to calm down. But he's smiling so hard.

On the way out, everyone claps Sobechi on the shoulder or shakes his hand or grins their thanks right at him. He can't believe how happy he's made them. After everyone leaves, Coach slips a hand over Sobechi's shoulder. "Wherever

Igor Vidyashev/Alamy

This photo shows Matt Heafy, lead singer of the American heavy metal band Trivium, performing with the band at Massey Hall, Toronto, in 2011.

What do you notice about Heafy's body and facial expression as he performs? Based on what you see in this photo, why might this style of performance appeal to Sobechi? How is it similar to and different from the kind of performing he has mastered in speech and debate?

you went . . . ," he says quietly, "it's good to have you back."

Suddenly, Sobechi doesn't know why he fought this for so long. Why he resisted. Everything feels right again. All the congratulations, the praise. People needing him again. This is where he's supposed to be.

These are his thoughts as he makes his way down the hall. But he stops short when he hears noise, muffled voices and what sounds like cymbals. Then he hears it, a guitar riff.

The door swings open to the auditorium. Sobechi sees them onstage. It looks like they're an entire world away, the stage is that far. But he recognizes them instantly. Desirée, strumming out a few licks, then directing the rest of the band through the next couple of measures; then Dominique, toying with the cymbals and kick drums while she listens; and there's someone else, someone Sobechi doesn't recognize, on bass who has a microphone in front of her too. They all seem comfortable around each other, but tired, like they've been at it for too long.

As soon as the doors swing shut behind 185
Sobechi, the music stops, midbar, and everyone stares. Sobechi can see the emotions working across Desirée's face. The confusion, the hurt, the joy, all of it out in the open. Then a mask falls over it all, and she's saying something quietly to the girls before taking off her guitar and putting it back into its stand. She hops off the stage with practiced nonchalance and meets Sobechi halfway.

For a while, they don't say anything, Desirée clearly waiting for his explanation. And there's so much he wants to say, but he needs to say it right, needs to organize his thoughts just like in debate. However, what comes out of his mouth is simply, stupidly, "I was unaware that you practiced here."

Desirée jerks her head toward the stage. "Yeah, Dayna's in the school band, and she's got the hookup. Lets us practice here to get a better feel for our live gigs."

"Live gigs?"

"Yeah." Desirée shrugs. "Debate practice?"

"Um, yeah." He looks at his shoes. "I'm sorry. 190
I just . . . I disappeared."

"Yeah, no reason, no talk, no nothing. For two weeks. Nothing from you."

Sobechi winces. "It's my mother. She . . . she doesn't like the music. I dunno, she's old-school, and maybe it's just too loud or not like what she's used to. But she doesn't want me listening to it anymore. Says it's devil-worshipping music."

Desirée barks out a chuckle, but Sobechi can hear the hurt in it.

"And the singing was starting to affect my voice."

"Ah, I see. And why does this mean we can't 195
hang out?"

Sobechi wants to tell her that debate practice is going to take up more of his time, that it's where he needs to be, or that he needs to really focus on his studies, or any of the usual excuses he gives people when they ask him to be social — but he knows it's because if he and Desirée spend any more time together, he will start singing again. He loves it, he realizes. And he will scream his voice into oblivion. He knows that's what's going to happen, so he can't let himself get close to it again. That's his argument, his position, but he can't bring himself to breathe a syllable to Desirée.

"So that's it then? We're never gonna see each other again?"

"I didn't say that! I just —"

Desirée brushes him off. "Nah, it's all good. Don't worry about it. I gotta get back to practice. The girls are waiting." She storms off and doesn't say a word about what just happened to either Dom or Dayna. Just starts playing a song from the first Periphery album, all angry chugs and riffs and screaming, where the notes from the guitar become as percussive as the drums, furious beats that have replaced any semblance of conversation whatsoever.

Even though winning Nationals his junior 200
year was supposed to be the culmination of

almost an entire life's worth of effort, it still feels
hollow. Everyone cheers for longer than usual.
His teammates all beam at him, genuinely, bask-
ing in the glow. Angelica knocked it out the park,
as they say. And Grayson knew that this was the
time to buckle down. Though Sobechi was, as
usual, the brightest star, his team could be said
to be the best team in the nation. Future debate
teams will hear of Sobechi's talent, his mesmerizing speeches, how he carried the school on his
back like Atlas from Greek mythology class holding up the sky. This was what he wanted. But . . .

Even after the celebratory dinner where
Mum cooks for Coach and the team, and they all
finally taste that magical jollof rice, Sobechi can
only pretend to be happy.

Then, it's over and everyone filters out and
Sobechi is still at his seat while Daddy washes
dishes and Mummy texts her friends in Nigeria
using WhatsApp.

"Mummy?" Sobechi has finally looked up
from his hands.

"Yes, my son." She sounds so joyful and so
pleased. He's going to ruin this.

"Can you . . ." He sighs. Squares his shoul- 205
ders. "Tell me about Biafra."

A cloud covers her face. Her fingers stop,
and a glower sets into her eyes.

"Mummy, I know what happened. I've read
about it online. I even checked books out from
the library on it. I know it's part of Nigeria's history. It's part of our history. I . . . I want to know
about you." He's thinking of Serj and Daron and
all the other members of System of a Down and
how they used their parents' tragedy to make
their art. He's thinking of their political messag-
ing and their antiwar stands, and he's thinking
about what it means to stand for something in
the world. And he hopes maybe there's some of
that for him here too. "Mummy, it's not to hurt
you. I . . . I want to be a good son." He can feel
himself start to break down. "I really do, and
I'm sorry. I just . . ." He can't go any further. He
sniffles, then regains control.

But when he looks up, his mother's staring
at the tablecloth, utterly still. "I was in kindergarten when the war began," she says quietly.
"When my family and I were in hiding, we
spent time in the forests, eating what we could
find. When we came home, soldiers were
sleeping in our house. My uncle begged and
begged and begged for us to be let back in.
The way they made him beg . . . . That night,
we all slept in one room. There were twelve of
us." Her shoulders start to shake, and Sobechi
realizes it's the first time he's seen her cry.
All of a sudden, she's no longer just a force of
nature, a powerful typhoon or an overwhelming burst of sunlight. She's human.

Daddy joins them at the table. And Mummy
talks well into the night. There's music in her
voice. The more she speaks, the more it sounds
like song.

It's late spring. And the sun is still shining 210
brightly by the time Sobechi gets back from
school.

As they pull into the driveway, he notices
Desirée on her front porch. Then he pretends to
drop something under his seat.

Mum looks over. "Eh, what is it now?"

"I dropped something. I think it was my USB
drive." It's a convincing enough excuse, because
Mummy eventually gets out and leaves her key
on the driver's seat.

"Remember to lock the car when you get out."

Desirée has been watching them the whole 215
time, silently.

Sobechi stops his fruitless search, snatches
the keys, then hops out and makes a beeline for
her. She makes to head back inside her home,
but Sobechi catches her just before the screen
door closes behind her.

"Your mom's gonna kill you when she sees
us like this."

Sobechi manages a half smile. "I want to
invite you and your uncle over for dinner."

"Wait, what? I thought I was a devil worship-
per or something. Your mom change her mind?"

Uzo

This painting by Nigerian artist Uzo Uzo is called *Dead in Places Painting*. According to the artist, his experiences as a survivor of the Biafran War, also known as the Nigerian Civil War, frequently influence his work.

Describe the tone of this piece and explain how the artist creates that tone visually. Based on this image, why might Sobechi's mother have been so reluctant to talk about her experiences during the war?

"She's being Americanized." And they both 220 chuckle. When they settle down, he looks at her, really looks at her, to the point where she's starting to get nervous.

"What?"

"Thank you."

"For what?"

For giving me the gift of metal, Sobechi wants to say. For getting me to scream for the first time. For giving me a place where I could truly be angry or sad or have fun. For giving me music to live my life to, music that gave me the courage to unlock something in my mummy. Music that's helping me become a better son. But he hasn't quite figured out how to put that

all into argument form. Instead, he smiles and says, "I'm working on a song." He kicks at a stone on the porch. "It's political."

Her face lights up when she realizes what he's 225 saying, and he knows she can see it too. Both of them onstage, singing into microphones, screaming into them. Faces covered in sweat. Bodies weak from the effort of performing but held up by the bass drums that rock their sternums. Dez launching into a Mark Tremonti–style solo, and Sobechi watching her with what he now realizes is love. And both of them, at the end, wishing the crowd a good night in their best rock-star voices.

"I guess we're gonna have to change the band name, then." ∎

extending beyond the text

In his 2021 book *This Is the Voice*, journalist John Colapinto recounts experiences with vocal cord damage sustained through singing — through his own story and those of professional performers. The excerpt below includes part of an interview with Julie Andrews, a singer and actress who lost her ability to sing while performing on Broadway in 1997.

from This Is the Voice

John Colapinto

The few times I'd tried [to sing after my vocal cord injury], my voice shut down, went off-pitch — and the extra exertion of driving air past my burdened vocal cord would force me to reload my lungs at an abnormally fast rate . . . causing me to hyperventilate and grow light-headed. Little wonder that I had not sung publicly since Jann's party and no longer sang even in private, around the house. Too exhausting. Too depressing.

I missed [singing], and this gave me some emotional insight during the interviews I conducted with [Dr. Steven] Zeitels's patients, most of them professional performers whose singing voices had been silenced. The most renowned and notorious was Julie Andrews, who . . . was diagnosed with a polyp and underwent surgery at New York's Mount Sinai. She emerged from the operation not only bereft of the preternaturally pellucid tone that had made her famous, but unable to sing at all without experiencing the rattling, pitch shifts, drop-outs, and dizziness that I knew all about. . . . In 2000, she turned, in desperation, to Zeitels, who tried, in four separate operations, to repair the damage, but in vain. "She'd lost too much vocal tissue in the earlier operation," he said, "and much of what remained was stiffened with scar tissue."

For Andrews, who had been performing professionally since age ten, and for whom singing formed an essential part of her identity and livelihood, the loss was devastating.

Julie Andrews performing.

According to Colapinto, what are some of the most damaging effects of losing one's voice? In what ways do these descriptions of injury and loss relate to Sobechi's experience with vocal strain after singing with Desirée? How do they enhance your understanding of his feelings and his mother's feelings about the damage his voice sustains?

Understanding and Interpreting

1. What is Sobechi's central conflict at the beginning of the story?

2. How does Sobechi's relationship with his family differ from Desirée's relationship with hers? What details does the author include to establish these relationships?

3. Explain why you think Sobechi is so attracted to metal music. What about the music draws him to it?

4. Compare the debates that Sobechi practices for and participates in to Desirée's band performances. In what specific ways are the purposes of these activities similar or different?

5. Sobechi takes the time to research and understand his mother's childhood experience with the Biafran War. How do his findings affect his relationship with his mother? Provide evidence from the story to support your response.

6. Why does Sobechi's mother finally open up about her experiences with the Biafran War? What purpose do conversations about the war serve in the story?

7. In what way does Sobechi's conflict change throughout the story? What are the causes for this change?

8. A dynamic character undergoes change — physically, psychologically, or emotionally. Identify the dynamic characters in the story, how they change, and what causes those changes. How do these changes illustrate a point the author is making about culture and relationships?

9. The title of the story is a reference to the Old Testament bible story of Samson and Delilah, in which Samson possesses supernatural strength, derived from his long hair. Delilah tricks Samson into telling her his secret and cuts his hair while he sleeps, robbing him of his strength. How does the biblical story relate to Onyebuchi's short story?

Analyzing Language, Style, and Structure

10. **Vocabulary in Context.** In paragraph 178, Onyebuchi writes that "a string of Igbo words . . . darts from [Mummy's] lips." What might the term *darts* mean as it is used in this sentence? How is Onyebuchi's use of the term similar to or different from other uses that you have encountered?

11. Onyebuchi uses a sentence fragment ("Solidarity.") in paragraph 7. What does this word convey about the relationship among mother, father, and son? What is the effect of using this word as a fragment, rather than part of a longer, complete sentence?

12. In paragraph 66, Sobechi's mother tells him to take rice over to the new neighbors and doesn't want him "speaking all *jagga-jagga*." Using context clues, what might his mother mean by this?

13. How does Onyebuchi use language, dialogue, and actions to indirectly characterize Sobechi's mother in paragraphs 24–26 and later in paragraphs 172–178? Provide specific examples and explain what they reveal about her character and her relationships with her son and with people outside her family.

14. Reread and compare paragraph 2, describing Sobechi's use of body language and gestures practicing for his speech, to paragraph 126, describing Desirée's body language and gestures as she performs. What is significant about the differences between the two?

15. Reread paragraphs 95–101, in which the sounds of the instruments are described. How does the use of vivid language and diction here help the reader to understand the kind of music Sobechi and Desirée are listening to?

16. Reread paragraphs 122–125, in which Onyebuchi describes the singing. How does his use of capitalization affect how the reader perceives or "hears" the words being sung?

17. Onyebuchi has written a story about multiple conflicts in culture, ethnicity, age, gender, music, and other areas. Explain how Onyebuchi uses style — especially diction, syntax, and figurative language — to illustrate one of these conflicts.

Topics for Composing

18. **Analysis.** On multiple occasions, Onyebuchi describes or refers to the power and effect of voice — whether it's used for debate, to sing about issues, or to appear a certain way to others. Analyze the author's message about the power of voice and formulate a statement on a possible theme, using evidence from the text to support your ideas. In your response, identify what makes it a theme of the work as a whole.

19. **Analysis.** Who, or what, do you consider to be the antagonist? Write a response in which you explain how the protagonist–antagonist conflict reveals a theme of the story. Support your response with evidence from the text.

20. **Argument.** Sobechi's mother is fully supportive of his public speaking aspirations. However, when she learns of his new-found pursuit of singing heavy metal music — which temporarily ruins his voice — she threatens to forbid him from seeing Desirée again. Is her reaction in his best interests? Based on evidence form the story and your experiences or those of people you know, write a response in which you argue how much influence parents should have over their children's academic and social development.

21. **Connections.** Write about a time when an interest or passion of yours conflicted with your family's or friends' expectations. How did both sides respond to the situation? Has there been any kind of compromise or agreement? If the situation is ongoing, what resolution do you hope to have?

22. **Connections.** Look up one of the bands mentioned in the story. Find one or two of the band's songs and research the lyrics. Share your findings in a presentation that includes the history of the song, the meaning of the lyrics, and what message the band is conveying about the topic. What seems to motivate the band and their music? How does your understanding of the music enhance your understanding of the story?

23. **Speaking and Listening.** The ending alludes to the idea that Sobechi will find a way to use heavy metal music as a platform for expressing political ideas. With a partner or small group discuss what you feel will happen next in Sobechi's relationship with his parents. Will they accept the new musical outlet for Sobechi's debates? Why or why not? Try to reach consensus and be prepared to discuss your predictions and evidence with the class.

24. **Research.** Conduct research on the Biafran War mentioned in the text. Gather information about the root causes and the impact it had on those involved. Then, explain how knowing more about the war helps you to understand Sobechi's mother's reactions when Sobechi asks her about her experiences.

fiction / section two

The Wretched and the Beautiful

E. Lily Yu

E. Lily Yu is a writer whose works include her debut novel, *On Fragile Waves* (2020), and short stories that have appeared in numerous anthologies and have been finalists for the Hugo, Nebula, and World Fantasy Awards. She has also contributed to the video games *Destiny* and *Destiny 2*. This short story first appeared in the science fiction and fantasy anthology *Terraform* (2017).

The aliens arrived unexpectedly at 6:42 on a hot August evening, dropping with a shriek of metal strained past its limits onto the white sands of one of the last pristine beaches on Earth. The black hulk of the saucer ground into the sand and stopped, steaming. Those of us who had been splashing in the surf or stamping rows of sandcastles fled up the slope, clutching our towels.

Once our initial fright dissipated, curiosity set in, and we stayed with the policemen and emergency technicians who pulled up in wailing, flashing trucks. It was all quite exciting, since nothing out of the ordinary seemed to happen anymore. Gone were the days when acting on conviction could change the world, when good came of good and evil to evil.

One of the policemen fired an experimental shot or two, but the bullets ricocheted off the black metal and lodged in a palm tree.

"Don't shoot," one man said. "You might make them angry. You might hit one of us."

The guns remained cocked, but no more bullets zinged off the ship. We waited.

At sunset, a pounding began inside the ship. No hatches sprang open; no rayguns or periscopes protruded. There was only the pounding, growing ever more frantic and erratic.

"What if they're trapped?" one of us said.

We looked at one another. Some of us had left and returned with the pistols that did not fit in our swimming trunks. A whole armory was pointed at the black disk of metal half buried in the beach.

The pounding ceased.

Nothing followed.

We conferred, then conscripted a machinist, who with our assistance hauled her ponderous cutters and blowtorches over the soft sand and set to work on the saucer.

We stood back.

While the machinist worked, any sounds from the saucer were drowned out by her tools. With precise and deliberate motions, she cut a thin line around the disk's circumference. Sparks flew up where the blade met the strange metal, which howled in unfamiliar tones.

When her work was done, she packed her equipment and departed. The aliens had failed to vaporize her. We let out the collective breath we had been holding.

Minutes crawled past. 15

At last, with a peculiar clang, the top half of the saucer seesawed upward. In the deepening dusk we could barely distinguish the dark limbs straining to raise it. Many monsters or one, we wondered.

"Drop your weapons," one policeman barked. The upper part of the saucer sagged for a moment, concealing whatever was within.

From within the ship, a voice said in perfectly comprehensible French, "We do not have weapons. We do not have anything."

"Come out where we can see you," the policeman said. The rest of us were glad that someone confident and capable, someone who was not us, was handling the matter.

It was too dark to see clearly, and so at the 20 policeman's command, and at the other end of his semiautomatic, the occupants of the ship — the aliens, our first real aliens — were marched up the beach to the neon strip of casinos, while we followed, gaping, gawking, knowing nothing with certainty except that we were witnessing history, and perhaps would even play a role in it.

The lurid glow of marquees and brothels revealed to us a shivering, shambling crowd, some slumped like apes, some clutching their young. Some had five limbs, some four, and some three. Their joints were crablike, and their movement both resembled ours and differed to such a degree that it sickened us to watch. There were sixty-four of them, including the juveniles. Although we were unacquainted with their biology, it was plain that none were in good health.

This is an image from *Close Encounters of the Third Kind*, a 1977 science-fiction film that depicts humans meeting an alien race for the first time.

How would you describe the encounter in this image, and how is it similar to and different from how Yu describes the first encounter in this story?

"Is there a place we can stay?" the aliens said.

Hotels were sought. Throughout the city, hoteliers protested, citing unknown risk profiles, inadequate equipment, fearful and unprepared staff, an indignant clientele, and stains from space filth impervious to detergent. Who was going to pay, anyway? They had businesses to run and families to feed.

One woman from among us offered to book a single room for the aliens for two nights, that being all she could afford on her teacher's salary. She said this with undisguised hope, as if she thought her offer would inspire others. But silence followed her remark, and we avoided her eyes. We were here on holiday, and holidays were expensive.

The impasse was broken at three in the morning, when in helicopters, in charter buses, and in taxis, the journalists arrived.

It was clear now that our guests were the responsibility of national if not international organizations, and that they would be cared for by people who were paid more than we were. Reassured that something would be done, and not by us, we dispersed to our hotel rooms and immaculate beds.

When we awoke late, to trays of poached eggs on toast and orange juice, headlines on our phones declared that first contact had been made, that the Fermi paradox was no more, that science and engineering were poised to make breakthroughs not only with the new metal that the spaceship was composed of but also the various exotic molecules that had bombarded the ship and become embedded in the hull during its long flight.

The flight had indeed been long. One African Francophone newspaper had thought to interview the aliens, who explained in deteriorating French how their universal translator worked, how they had fled a cleansing operation in their star system, how they had watched their home planet heated to sterility and stripped of its atmosphere, how they had set course for a likely-looking planet in the Gould Belt, how they wanted nothing but peace, and please, they were exhausted, could they have a place to sleep and a power source for their translator?

When we slid on our sandals and stepped onto the dazzling beach, which long ago, before the garbage tides, was what many beaches looked like, we saw the crashed ship again, substantiation of the previous night's fever dream. It leached rainbow fluids onto the sand.

Dark shapes huddled under its sawn-off lid. 30

Most of us averted our eyes from that picture of unmitigated misery and admired instead the gemlike sky, the seabirds squalling over the creamy surf, the parasols propped like mushrooms along the shore. One or two of us edged close to the wreck and dropped small somethings — a beach towel, a bucket hat, a bag of chips, a half-full margarita in its salted glass — then scuttled away. This was no longer our problem; it belonged to our governors, our senators, our heads of state. Surely they and their moneyed friends would assist these wretched creatures.

So it was with consternation that we turned on our televisions that night, in the hotel bar and in our hotel rooms, to hear a spokesman explain, as our heads of state shook hands, that the countries in their interregional coalition would resettle a quota of the aliens in inverse proportion to national wealth. This was ratified over the protests of the poorest members, in fact over the protests of the aliens themselves, who did not wish to be separated and had only one translation device among them. The couple of countries still recovering from Russian depredations were assigned six aliens each, while the countries of high fashion and cold beer received two or three, to be installed in middle-class neighborhoods. In this way the burden of these aliens, as well as any attendant medical or technological advances, would be shared.

The cost would be high, as these aliens had stated their need for an environment with a specific mixture of helium and neon, as well as a particular collection of nutrients most abundant in shrimp and crab. The latter, in our overfished and polluted times, were not easy to obtain.

This was appalling news. We who had stitched, skimped, and pinched all year for one luxurious day on a clean beach would have our wallets rifled to feed and house the very creatures whose presence denied us a section of our beach and the vistas we had paid for. Now we would find these horrors waiting for us at home, in the nicer house next to ours, or at the community pool, eating crab while we sweated to put chicken on the table and pay off our mortgages. Who were they to land on our dwindling planet and reduce our scarce resources further? They could go back to their star system. Their own government could care for them. We could loan them a rocket or two, if they liked. We could be generous.

Indeed, in the days that followed, our legis- 35 lators took our calls, then took this tack. If they meant to stay, shouldn't our visitors earn their daily bread like the rest of us? And if biological limitations made this impossible, shouldn't they depart to find a more hospitable clime? We repeated these speeches over the dinner table. Our performances grew louder and more vehement after a news report about one of the aliens eating its neighbor's cat; the distraught woman pointed her finger at the camera, at all of us watching, and accused us of forcing a monster upon her because we had no desire to live beside it ourselves. There was enough truth in her words to bite.

It did not matter that six days later the furry little Lothario was found at a gas station ten miles from home, having scrapped and loved his way across the countryside. By then we had stories of these aliens raiding chicken coops and sucking the blood from dogs and unsuspecting infants.

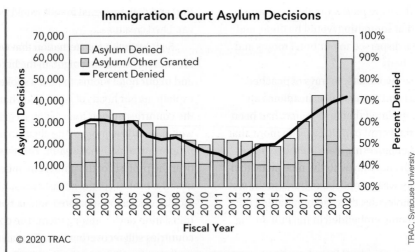

© 2020 TRAC

This image from the Syracuse University TRAC Immigration research center shows the number of United States immigration court asylum decisions made between 2001 and 2020.

What conclusions about asylum acceptance rates can you draw from the data given in this graph? In which category would the first group of aliens in the story be placed on this graph? What evidence from the story supports your observation?

A solid number of these politicians campaigned for office on a platform of alien repatriation, and many of them won.

Shortly afterwards, one of two aliens resettled in Huntingdon, England was set upon and beaten to death with bricks by a gang of teenaged girls and boys. Then, in Houston, a juvenile alien was doused in gasoline and set on fire. We picked at our dinners without appetite, worrying about these promising youths, who had been headed for sports scholarships and elite universities. The aliens jeopardized all our futures and clouded all our dreams. We wrote letters, signed petitions, and prayed to the heavens for salvation.

It came. From out of a silent sky, rockets shaped like needles and polished to a high gloss descended upon six of the major capitols of the world. About an hour after landing, giving the television crews time to jostle for position, and at precisely the same instant, six slim doors whispered open, and the most gorgeous beings we had ever seen strode down extruded silver steps and planted themselves before the houses of power, waiting to be invited in.

And they were. 40

"Forgive us for imposing on your valuable time," these ambassadors said simultaneously in the official languages of the six legislatures. Cameras panned over them, and excitement crackled through us, for this was the kind of history we wanted to be a part of.

When they emerged from their needle ships, their bodies were fluid and reflective, like columns of quicksilver, but with every minute among us, they lost more and more of their formless brilliance, dimming and thickening, acquiring eyes, foreheads, chins, and hands. Within half an hour, they resembled us perfectly. Or rather, they resembled what we dreamed of being, the better versions of ourselves who turned heads, drove fast cars, and recognized the six most expensive whiskies by smell alone; whose names topped the donor rolls of operas,

orchestras, and houses of worship; who were admired, respected, adored.

We looked at these beautiful creatures, whom we no longer thought of as aliens, and saw ourselves as we could be, if the lottery, or the bank, or our birthplace — if our genes, or a lucky break — if only —

We listened raptly as they spoke in rich and melodious voices, voices we trusted implicitly, that called to mind loved ones and sympathetic teachers.

"A terrible mistake has been made," they 45 said. "Because of our negligence, a gang of war criminals, guilty of unspeakable things, namely — "

Here their translators failed, and the recitation of crimes came as a series of clicks, coughs, and trills that nevertheless retained the enchantment of their voices.

" — escaped their confinement and infiltrated your solar system. We are deeply sorry for the trouble our carelessness has caused you. We admire your patience and generosity in dealing with them, though they have grossly abused your trust. Now we have come to set things right. Remit the sixty-four aliens to us, and we will bring them back to their home system. They will never disturb you again."

The six beautiful beings clasped their hands and stepped back. Silence fell throughout the legislative chambers of the world.

Here was our solution. Here was our freedom. We had trusted and been fooled, we had suffered unjustly, we were good people with clean consciences sorely tried by circumstances outside our control. But here was justice, as bright and shining as we imagined justice to be.

We sighed with relief. 50

In Berlin, a woman stood.

"Even the little ones?" she said. "Even the children are guilty of the crimes you allege?"

"Their development is not comparable to yours," the beautiful one in Berlin said, while

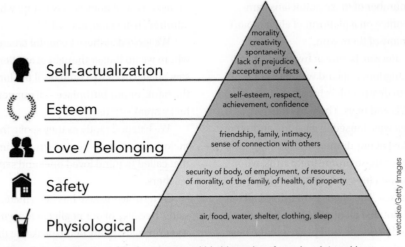

Self-actualization
— morality, creativity, spontaneity, lack of prejudice, acceptance of facts

Esteem
— self-esteem, respect, achievement, confidence

Love / Belonging
— friendship, family, intimacy, sense of connection with others

Safety
— security of body, of employment, of resources, of morality, of the family, of health, of property

Physiological
— air, food, water, shelter, clothing, sleep

wetcake/Getty Images

Psychologist Abraham Maslow proposed his hierarchy of needs, pictured here, in 1943.

What does this progression of needs—from basic to psychological to self-fulfillment—reveal about human well-being and motivation? How might that understanding help explain the behavior of the humans and the first group of aliens in this story?

his compatriots in their respective statehouses stood silent, with inscrutable smiles. "The small ones you see are not children as you know them, innocent and helpless. Think of them as beetle larvae. They are destructive and voracious, sometimes more so than the mature adults."

"Still," she said, this lone woman, "I think of them as children. I have seen the grown ones feeding and caring for them. I do not know what crimes they have committed, since our languages cannot describe your concepts. But they have sought refuge here, and I am especially unwilling to return the children to you — "

The whispers of the assembly became mur- 55 murs, then exclamations.

"Throw her out!"

"She does not speak for us!"

"You are misled," the beautiful one said, and for a moment its smile vanished, and a breath of the icy void between stars blew over us.

Then everything was as it had been.

"We must ask the aliens themselves what 60 they want," the woman said, but now her

colleagues were standing too, and shouting, and phone lines were ringing as we called in support of the beautiful ones, and her voice was drowned out.

"We have an understanding, then," the beautiful ones said, to clamorous agreement and wild applause.

The cameras stopped there, at that glorious scene, and all of us, warm and satisfied with our participation in history, turned off our televisions and went to work, or to pick up our children from soccer, or to bed, or to the liquor store to gaze at top-shelf whisky.

A few of us, the unfortunate few who lived beside the aliens, saw the long silver needles descend point-first onto our neighbors' lawns and the silver shapes emerge with chains and glowing rods. We twitched the kitchen curtains closed and dialed up our music. Three hours later there was no sign of any of the aliens, the wretched or the beautiful, except for a few blackened patches of grass and wisps of smoke that curled and died.

All was well. ∎

Understanding and Interpreting

1. Describe the initial reaction the humans have to the aliens' arrival. How does their response reflect, or not, their opinions of the visitors?

2. What is significant about the description of the aliens in paragraph 21? What idea might the author be trying to establish about these refugee aliens?

3. At the beginning, the humans know that they "were witnessing history, and perhaps would even play a role in it" (par. 20). What does their excitement over their role in history being made — their response to obviously tragic beings — reveal about them? What evidence from the story supports your observation?

4. What central conflict do the humans have with the first group of aliens? How does this conflict complicate their acceptance of the aliens?

5. In what ways, if any, do the humans benefit from the aliens' presence? In what ways, if any, do the aliens benefit from having come to Earth to escape their star system's cleansing operation?

6. What can you infer about the humans from their response to the arrival of the "beautiful" aliens and how it differs from their response to the aliens seeking refuge? What evidence from the story leads you to this conclusion?

7. What might be the intent of the beautiful aliens' accusations against the wretched aliens? With the exception of the Berlin woman, why do the humans accept these accusations?

Analyzing Language, Style, and Structure

8. **Vocabulary in Context.** What does the word *rifled* likely mean as it is used in paragraph 34? What effect does the word have in this context?

9. The story is written from the first person point of view using the pronouns *us*, *we*, and *our*. How does this collective first person point of view affect the readers' experience?

10. Reread paragraph 28 for the author's use of syntax. What effect does the length of the second sentence in this paragraph achieve?

11. Look at these sentences at the end of paragraph 31: "This was no longer our problem; it belonged to our governors, our senators, our heads of state. Surely they and their moneyed friends would assist these wretched creatures." What tone do these lines evoke? How does Yu achieve that tone?

12. How does Yu create tension between the first group of aliens and the humans when nations gather to discuss the shared burden of care and costs in paragraphs 32–34?

13. What are some examples of diction and details Yu uses to characterize the humans in paragraph 34? How does the language she uses affect how readers perceive the humans?

14. Reread this sentence from paragraph 62: "The cameras stopped there, at that glorious scene, and all of us, warm and satisfied with our participation in history, turned off our televisions and went to work, or to pick up our children from soccer, or to bed, or to the liquor store to gaze at top-shelf whisky." What is ironic about this sentence and how does this irony help Yu to make a point about society?

15. Explain the meaning and connotations of the word *alien* in the context of this story. What tone does the author's use of the word establish toward each group of aliens?

Topics for Composing

16. **Analysis.** Yu presents a variety of responses to the arrival of each group of aliens, including the reactions of average people, the media, and government leaders. Choose one of these groups and analyze how their reaction to the aliens helps illustrate a theme about immigration, asylum-seeking, or another topic of the text.

17. **Analysis.** Reread the paragraph below. Write a response in which you analyze Yu's word choice, syntax, imagery, and other elements to explain how her language choices here connect to a theme of the story as a whole.

> This was appalling news. We who had stitched, skimped, and pinched all year for one luxurious day on a clean beach would have our wallets rifled to feed and house the very creatures whose presence denied us a section of our beach and the vistas we had paid for. Now we would find these horrors waiting for us at home, in the nicer house next to ours, or at the community pool, eating crab while we sweated to put chicken on the table and pay off our mortgages. Who were they to land on our dwindling planet and reduce our scarce resources further? They could go back to their star system. Their own government could care for them. We could loan them a rocket or two, if they like. We could be generous.

18. **Argument.** The last line of the story is "All was well." Using evidence from the text, write a response in which you argue whether or not this is true for the characters in the story and why.

19. **Argument.** Yu's story depicts human reception of two distinct groups of aliens from other planets, but it is also a commentary on real-world struggles faced by immigrants, refugees, and asylum-seekers. How should nations like the United States support those who need to leave one home to find peace or a better standard of living in another? Write an argument that includes evidence from this piece, as well as information and ideas from outside research and your own reasoning.

20. **Connections.** In the story, one woman in Berlin questions the accusations against the wretched aliens, but does not get very far. She is not supported — and is even threatened — by her fellow humans. Write about a moment when you, someone you know, or a figure you've encountered in fiction or nonfiction, took a stand against perceived injustices. How did this person voice concern and what were the results?

21. **Connections.** Have you ever found that, in the process of helping one person, you ended up helping others as well, maybe even yourself? Think about a situation in which this happened and write a response describing the experience. Explain who benefited from your help and in what ways.

22. **Research.** Yu's story is an allegory for immigration in general. Conduct research to find a true account of an immigrant's experience or the perspective of a community receiving immigrants. What commonalities do they share with the experiences portrayed in Yu's story? What lesson or moral do these stories seem to share, and why do you think that moral is important to understand?

The Cask of Amontillado

Edgar Allan Poe

Edgar Allan Poe (1809–1849) was an American author who wrote poetry, literary criticism, and short stories, including many well-known ones that focus on murder, death, torture, and crime, such as "The Fall of the House of Usher," "The Black Cat," "The Pit and the Pendulum," and "The Tell-Tale Heart." Because of the topics of many of his stories and poems, and because of the unusual nature of his death, the cause of which is still unknown, Poe's reputation as a drug-addicted madman has survived to this day.

Nastasic/Getty Images

Unfortunately, much of this sordid reputation is undeserved and is due to the initial obituary and later biography of Poe by a man named Rufus Griswold, whom Poe considered a colleague. "The Cask of Amontillado" (1846) is a dark and grisly tale of revenge and one of Poe's most famous stories.

KEY CONTEXT   This story takes place in Venice, Italy, at the height of the carnival season, a time of costumes, parades, music, and entertainment similar to a Mardi Gras celebration in New Orleans.

The thousand injuries of Fortunato I had borne as I best could, but when he ventured upon insult I vowed revenge. You, who so well know the nature of my soul, will not suppose, however, that I gave utterance to a threat. At length I would be avenged; this was a point definitely, settled — but the very definitiveness with which it was resolved precluded the idea of risk. I must not only punish but punish with impunity. A wrong is unredressed when retribution overtakes its redresser. It is equally unredressed when the avenger fails to make himself felt as such to him who has done the wrong.

It must be understood that neither by word nor deed had I given Fortunato cause to doubt my good will. I continued, as was my wont, to smile in his face, and he did not perceive that my smile now was at the thought of his immolation.

He had a weak point — this Fortunato — although in other regards he was a man to be respected and even feared. He prided himself on his connoisseurship in wine. Few Italians have the true virtuoso spirit. For the most part their enthusiasm is adopted to suit the time and opportunity, to practise imposture upon the British and Austrian millionaires. In painting and gemmary,[1] Fortunato, like his countrymen, was a quack, but in the matter of old wines he was sincere. In this respect I did not differ from him materially; — I was skilful in the Italian vintages myself, and bought largely whenever I could.

It was about dusk, one evening during the supreme madness of the carnival season, that I encountered my friend. He accosted me with excessive warmth, for he had been drinking much. The man wore motley. He had on a tight-fitting parti-striped dress, and his head was surmounted by the conical cap and bells. I was so pleased to see him that I thought I should never have done wringing his hand.

I said to him — "My dear Fortunato, you are luckily met. How remarkably well you are looking to-day. But I have received a pipe[2] of what passes for Amontillado, and I have my doubts."

5

---

[1] Gemmary: the study of gems. —Eds.

[2] Pipe: a large wine barrel, holding about 120 gallons. Borrowed from the Portuguese word *pipa*, which means *barrel*. Amontillado is an expensive Portuguese port wine that is traditionally aged and transported in pipas, or *pipes*. —Eds.

"How?" said he. "Amontillado? A pipe? Impossible! And in the middle of the carnival!"

"I have my doubts," I replied; "and I was silly enough to pay the full Amontillado price without consulting you in the matter. You were not to be found, and I was fearful of losing a bargain."

"Amontillado!"

"I have my doubts."

"Amontillado!" 10

"And I must satisfy them."

"Amontillado!"

"As you are engaged, I am on my way to Luchresi. If any one has a critical turn it is he. He will tell me —"

"Luchresi cannot tell Amontillado from Sherry."

"And yet some fools will have it that his taste 15 is a match for your own."

"Come, let us go."

"Whither?"

"To your vaults."

"My friend, no; I will not impose upon your good nature. I perceive you have an engagement. Luchresi —"

"I have no engagement; — come." 20

"My friend, no. It is not the engagement, but the severe cold with which I perceive you are afflicted. The vaults are insufferably damp. They are encrusted with nitre."[3]

"Let us go, nevertheless. The cold is merely nothing. Amontillado! You have been imposed upon. And as for Luchresi, he cannot distinguish Sherry from Amontillado."

Thus speaking, Fortunato possessed himself of my arm; and putting on a mask of black silk and drawing a roquelaire[4] closely about my person, I suffered him to hurry me to my palazzo.

There were no attendants at home; they had absconded to make merry in honour of the time. I had told them that I should not return until the morning, and had given them explicit orders not to stir from the house. These orders were sufficient, I well knew, to insure their immediate disappearance, one and all, as soon as my back was turned.

I took from their sconces two flambeaux, 25 and giving one to Fortunato, bowed him through several suites of rooms to the archway that led into the vaults. I passed down a long and winding staircase, requesting him to be cautious as he followed. We came at length to the foot of the descent, and stood together upon the damp ground of the catacombs of the Montresors.

The gait of my friend was unsteady, and the bells upon his cap jingled as he strode.

"The pipe," he said.

"It is farther on," said I; "but observe the white web-work which gleams from these cavern walls."

He turned towards me, and looked into my eyes with two filmy orbs that distilled the rheum of intoxication.

"Nitre?" he asked, at length. 30

"Nitre," I replied. "How long have you had that cough?"

"Ugh! ugh! ugh! — ugh! ugh! ugh! — ugh! ugh! ugh! — ugh! ugh! ugh! — ugh! ugh! ugh!"

My poor friend found it impossible to reply for many minutes.

"It is nothing," he said, at last.

"Come," I said, with decision, "we will go 35 back; your health is precious. You are rich, respected, admired, beloved; you are happy, as once I was. You are a man to be missed. For me it is no matter. We will go back; you will be ill, and I cannot be responsible. Besides, there is Luchresi —"

"Enough," he said; "the cough's a mere nothing; it will not kill me. I shall not die of a cough."

extending beyond the text

Read the first few pages of a graphic novel adaptation of "The Cask of Amontillado."

from The Cask of Amontillado

Enrica Jang and Jason Strutz

Action Lab Entertainment Inc.

(continued)

(continued)

(continued)

What changes and adaptations did the author and illustrator of this version make? How do these changes affect what the reader knows and feels about Montresor and Fortunato at this point in the story? How do their visualizations of the text compare to your own?

"True — true," I replied; "and, indeed, I had no intention of alarming you unnecessarily — but you should use all proper caution. A draught of this Medoc will defend us from the damps."

Here I knocked off the neck of a bottle which I drew from a long row of its fellows that lay upon the mould.

"Drink," I said, presenting him the wine.

He raised it to his lips with a leer. He paused 40 and nodded to me familiarly, while his bells jingled.

"I drink," he said, "to the buried that repose around us."

"And I to your long life."

He again took my arm, and we proceeded.

"These vaults," he said, "are extensive."

"The Montresors," I replied, "were a great 45 and numerous family."

"I forget your arms."

"A huge human foot d'or,[5] in a field azure; the foot crushes a serpent rampant[6] whose fangs are imbedded in the heel."

"And the motto?"

"Nemo me impune lacessit."[7]

"Good!" he said. 50

The wine sparkled in his eyes and the bells jingled. My own fancy grew warm with the Medoc. We had passed through long walls of piled skeletons, with casks and puncheons[8] intermingling, into the inmost recesses of the catacombs. I paused again, and this time I made bold to seize Fortunato by an arm above the elbow.

"The nitre!" I said; "see, it increases. It hangs like moss upon the vaults. We are below the river's bed. The drops of moisture trickle among the bones. Come, we will go back ere it is too late. Your cough — "

"It is nothing," he said; "let us go on. But first, another draught of the Medoc."

I broke and reached him a flagon of De Grave. He emptied it at a breath. His eyes flashed with a fierce light. He laughed and threw the bottle upwards with a gesticulation I did not understand.

I looked at him in surprise. He repeated the 55 movement — a grotesque one.

"You do not comprehend?" he said.

"Not I," I replied.

"Then you are not of the brotherhood."

"How?"

"You are not of the masons." 60

"Yes, yes," I said; "yes, yes."

"You? Impossible! A mason?"

"A mason," I replied.

"A sign," he said, "a sign."

"It is this," I answered, producing from 65 beneath the folds of my roquelaire a trowel.

"You jest," he exclaimed, recoiling a few paces. "But let us proceed to the Amontillado."

"Be it so," I said, replacing the tool beneath the cloak and again offering him my arm. He leaned upon it heavily. We continued our route in search of the Amontillado. We passed through a range of low arches, descended, passed on, and descending again, arrived at a deep crypt, in which the foulness of the air caused our flam-beaux rather to glow than flame.

At the most remote end of the crypt there appeared another less spacious. Its walls had been lined with human remains, piled to the vault overhead, in the fashion of the great cata-combs of Paris. Three sides of this interior crypt were still ornamented in this manner. From the fourth side the bones had been thrown down, and lay promiscuously upon the earth, forming at one point a mound of some size. Within the wall thus exposed by the displacing of the bones, we perceived a still interior crypt or recess, in

---

[5] French: *of gold.* —Eds.

[6] When used in the context of a coat-of-arms (called *heraldry*), a "rampant" animal is one that is rearing up to strike. —Eds.

[7] Latin: "No one can cut me and go unpunished." Motto of the Stuart royal family of Scotland. —Eds.

[8] Puncheon: a smaller type of wine barrel, holding about 80 gallons. —Eds.

depth about four feet, in width three, in height six or seven. It seemed to have been constructed for no especial use within itself, but formed merely the interval between two of the colossal supports of the roof of the catacombs, and was backed by one of their circumscribing walls of solid granite.

It was in vain that Fortunato, uplifting his dull torch, endeavoured to pry into the depth of the recess. Its termination the feeble light did not enable us to see.

"Proceed," I said; "herein is the Amontillado. 70 As for Luchresi—"

"He is an ignoramus," interrupted my friend, as he stepped unsteadily forward, while I followed immediately at his heels. In an instant he had reached the extremity of the niche, and finding his progress arrested by the rock, stood stupidly bewildered. A moment more and I had fettered him to the granite. In its surface were two iron staples, distant from each other about two feet, horizontally. From one of these depended a short chain, from the other a padlock. Throwing the links about his waist, it was but the work of a few seconds to secure it. He was too much astounded to resist. Withdrawing the key I stepped back from the recess.

"Pass your hand," I said, "over the wall; you cannot help feeling the nitre. Indeed, it is very damp. Once more let me implore you to return. No? Then I must positively leave you. But I must first render you all the little attentions in my power."

"The Amontillado!" ejaculated my friend, not yet recovered from his astonishment.

"True," I replied; "the Amontillado."

As I said these words I busied myself among 75 the pile of bones of which I have before spoken. Throwing them aside, I soon uncovered a quantity of building stone and mortar. With these materials and with the aid of my trowel, I began vigorously to wall up the entrance of the niche.

I had scarcely laid the first tier of the masonry when I discovered that the intoxication of Fortunato had in a great measure worn off. The earliest indication I had of this was a low moaning cry from the depth of the recess. It was not the cry of a drunken man. There was then a long and obstinate silence. I laid the second tier, and the third, and the fourth; and then I heard the furious vibrations of the chain. The noise lasted for several minutes, during which, that I might hearken to it with the more satisfaction, I ceased my labours and sat down upon the bones. When at last the clanking subsided, I resumed the trowel, and finished without interruption the fifth, the sixth, and the seventh tier. The wall was now nearly upon a level with my breast. I again paused, and holding the flambeaux over the mason-work, threw a few feeble rays upon the figure within.

A succession of loud and shrill screams, bursting suddenly from the throat of the chained form, seemed to thrust me violently back. For a brief moment I hesitated, I trembled. Unsheathing my rapier, I began to grope with it about the recess; but the thought of an instant reassured me. I placed my hand upon the solid fabric of the catacombs, and felt satisfied. I reapproached the wall; I replied to the yells of him who clamoured. I re-echoed, I aided, I surpassed them in volume and in strength. I did this, and the clamourer grew still.

It was now midnight, and my task was drawing to a close. I had completed the eighth, the ninth and the tenth tier. I had finished a portion of the last and the eleventh; there remained but a single stone to be fitted and plastered in. I struggled with its weight; I placed it partially in its destined position. But now there came from out the niche a low laugh

Culture Club/Getty Images

© British Library Board/Robana/Art Resource, NY

xcutHEREx/DeviantArt

Look carefully at the following depictions of the final scene in this story.

What is in common among the images and what is different? What textual evidence from the story likely led to each depiction? Which one is closest to or furthest away from your own imagining of the scene?

that erected the hairs upon my head. It was succeeded by a sad voice, which I had difficulty in recognizing as that of the noble Fortunato. The voice said —

"Ha! ha! ha! — he! he! he! — a very good joke, indeed — an excellent jest. We will have many a rich laugh about it at the palazzo — he! he! he! — over our wine — he! he! he!"

"The Amontillado!" I said.   80

"He! he! he! — he! he! he! — yes, the Amontillado. But is it not getting late? Will not they be awaiting us at the palazzo, the Lady Fortunato and the rest? Let us be gone."

"Yes," I said, "let us be gone."

"For the love of God, Montresor!"

"Yes," I said, "for the love of God!"

But to these words I hearkened in vain for a   85
reply. I grew impatient. I called aloud —

"Fortunato!"

No answer. I called again —

"Fortunato!"

No answer still. I thrust a torch through the remaining aperture and let it fall within. There came forth in return only a jingling of the bells. My heart grew sick; it was the dampness of the catacombs that made it so. I hastened to make an end of my labour. I forced the last stone into its position; I plastered it up. Against the new masonry I re-erected the old rampart of bones. For the half of a century no mortal has disturbed them. In pace requiescat![9] ■

_____

[9] Latin: Rest in peace. —Eds

Understanding and Interpreting

1. Reread the first paragraph. Why does the narrator — Montresor — want to get revenge on Fortunato? Paraphrase what he says about what else must happen for revenge to be truly successful.

2. How does Montresor manipulate Fortunato into the catacombs and keep him moving further down? Use textual evidence to support your response.

3. Setting plays a significant part in this story. Describe the different settings identified below and explain how the changing settings create tension or other effects:

   a. Outside on the street when they first meet (pars. 4–23)

   b. When they first enter the catacombs (pars. 24–42)

   c. When they progress deeper into the catacombs (pars. 43–70)

   d. At the niche where Fortunato is bound and walled in (pars. 71–89)

4. At the beginning of the story, Montresor says that when Fortunato "ventured upon insult, I vowed revenge." On rereading, what additional motives does Montresor hint at for his desire to kill Fortunato?

5. This story is written in the first person. What is the effect of knowing the thoughts of a murderer? Is Montresor's telling of the story to be trusted? Why or why not?

6. Reread the last paragraph of the story. Is Montresor successful in achieving the kind of revenge he set out to do? How does he feel about the revenge? What evidence supports your interpretation?

Analyzing Language, Style, and Structure

7. **Vocabulary in Context.** As Montresor and Fortunato descend into the catacombs, they arrive at the crypt where "[f]rom the fourth side the bones had been thrown down, and lay promiscuously upon the earth" (par. 68). What might the word *promiscuously* mean as it is used in this context? How is Poe's use of the word similar to or different from other uses you have encountered?

8. In the first paragraph, Montresor addresses the reader, "You, who so know the nature of my soul." What effect is created with this direct address, which never happens again in the story?

9. On rereading the text, what do you make of Poe's choice to have Fortunato dressed in "motley" or to have named him "Fortunato"?

10. At the very end of the story, Poe writes, "I had finished a portion of the last and the eleventh; there remained but a single stone to be fitted and plastered in. I struggled with its weight; I placed it partially in its destined position" (par. 78). What is the meaning of the word *destined* in this context, and why is it such an effective word choice?

11. Skim through the story and identify as many words or phrases as you can that refer to or describe death. What is the cumulative effect of so many references on the reader?

12. Many language choices that you may have understood on the first reading take on a greater significance once you know that Montresor is planning to kill Fortunato. What effect is created by the following choices in light of the story's ending:

    a. "'Enough,' [Fortunato] said, 'the cough is a mere nothing; it will not kill me. I shall not die of a cough.'"

       "'True — true,' I replied" (pars. 36–37).

    b. "'And I [drink] to your long life'" (par. 42).

    c. "I broke and reached him a flagon of De Grave. He emptied it at a breath" (par. 54).

    d. "'It is this,' I answered, producing from beneath the folds of my roquelaire a trowel" (par. 65).

    e. "'Let us be gone.'

       'Yes,' I said, 'let us be gone.'

       'For the love of God, Montresor!'

       'Yes,' I said. 'For the love of God!'" (pars. 81–84).

Topics for Composing

13. **Analysis.** Write a response in which you closely examine the setting in "The Cask of Amontillado." Explain how the setting contributes to a theme about revenge, honor, or another topic in this short story.

14. **Argument.** Is Montressor insane? A sociopath? Does he feel any guilt or remorse for his actions? Does he have a motive for his actions that could be used to justify them? Take a position on whether Montressor is in control of his actions and whether his response to "the thousand injuries of Fortunato" can be justified or not. Support your position with evidence from the text and, if needed, some research.

15. **Connections.** Look over the following quotations about revenge. Choose one that reflects your attitude toward the topic and explain whether Montresor would agree with it or not:

    a. An eye for an eye will only make the whole world blind. — Mahatma Gandhi

    b. My name is Inigo Montoya, you killed my father, prepare to die! — William Goldman, *The Princess Bride*

    c. Revenge, the sweetest morsel to the mouth that ever was cooked in hell. — Walter Scott, *The Heart of Mid-Lothian*

    d. The best revenge is not to be like your enemy. — Marcus Aurelius, *Meditations*

    e. When you begin a journey of revenge, start by digging two graves: one for your enemy, and one for yourself. — Jodi Picoult, *Nineteen Minutes*

    f. I'm a fighter. I believe in the eye-for-an-eye business. I'm no cheek turner. I got no respect for a man who won't hit back. You kill my dog, you better hide your cat. — Muhammad Ali, *The Greatest: My Own Story*

    g. To exact revenge for yourself or your friends is not only a right, it's an absolute duty. — Stieg Larsson

16. **Connections.** Compare Poe's story of revenge here with stories of revenge in other books, movies, or games that you've read, seen, or played. What are one or two common characteristics that the stories share about revenge? Provide details from the texts you're discussing to support your response.

17. **Speaking and Listening.** A study by psychologist Kevin Carlsmith and his colleagues determined that those who took revenge tended to be less happy than those who did not. The team's explanation reads as follows:

    > Punishing others can cause people to continue to think about (rather than to forget) those whom they have punished. As Sir Francis Bacon noted more than three centuries ago, "A man that studieth revenge, keeps his own wounds green, which otherwise would heal, and do well" (1858).

    Given this information, hold a discussion and try to reach a consensus with a partner or small group about why you think people retain the impulse for revenge. What makes it difficult sometimes for us to let go of a desire for revenge? Be prepared to share your ideas with the whole class for further discussion.

18. **Research.** Poe is well known for his Gothic tales and dark romanticism of horror and the macabre, but who, or what, influenced his writing style? Conduct research into Poe's life and present your findings about how his experiences may have influenced his writing.

19. **Creative Writing.** Retell a portion of this story from a third person omniscient point of view or from Fortunato's point of view. What changes when you have a different perspective on the events that take place?

20. **Exposition.** Write a response in which you describe how Montresor could better handle his anger toward Fortunato. What concrete, constructive steps could he take, without harming himself or others, to work through the pain Fortunato appears to have caused him?

The Most Dangerous Game

Richard Connell

Richard Connell (1893–1949) first began his writing career at the age of ten by covering baseball games for his hometown newspaper, the *Press*, in Poughkeepsie, New York. After graduating from Harvard University in 1915 and serving in the army during World War I, he began his work as a freelance writer in 1919 in New York and proceeded to publish over 300 short stories, 4 novels, and 13 screenplays. "The Most Dangerous Game," which has been adapted many times for film and television, was first published in 1925 and continues to be one of the most well-known short stories of all time.

Fotosearch/Getty Images

KEY CONTEXT This story, published in 1924, at times describes people in terms that are now recognized as being offensive. We have decided to retain the story's original language because those offensive words contribute to the author's use of dialogue in developing characterization and theme.

"Off there to the right — somewhere — is a large island," said Whitney. "It's rather a mystery —"

"What island is it?" Rainsford asked.

"The old charts call it 'Ship-Trap Island,'" Whitney replied. "A suggestive name, isn't it? Sailors have a curious dread of the place. I don't know why. Some superstition —"

"Can't see it," remarked Rainsford, trying to peer through the dank tropical night that was palpable as it pressed its thick warm blackness in upon the yacht.

"You've good eyes," said Whitney, with a   5
laugh, "and I've seen you pick off a moose moving in the brown fall bush at four hundred yards, but even you can't see four miles or so through a moonless Caribbean night."

"Nor four yards," admitted Rainsford. "Ugh! It's like moist black velvet."

"It will be light enough in Rio," promised Whitney. "We should make it in a few days. I hope the jaguar guns have come from Purdey's. We should have some good hunting up the Amazon. Great sport, hunting."

"The best sport in the world," agreed Rainsford.

"For the hunter," amended Whitney. "Not for the jaguar."

"Don't talk rot, Whitney," said Rainsford.   10
"You're a big-game hunter, not a philosopher. Who cares how a jaguar feels?"

"Perhaps the jaguar does," observed Whitney.

"Bah! They've no understanding."

"Even so, I rather think they understand one thing — fear. The fear of pain and the fear of death."

"Nonsense," laughed Rainsford. "This hot weather is making you soft, Whitney. Be a realist. The world is made up of two classes — the hunters and the huntees. Luckily, you and I are hunters. Do you think we've passed that island yet?"

"I can't tell in the dark. I hope so."   15

"Why?" asked Rainsford.

"The place has a reputation — a bad one."

"Cannibals?" suggested Rainsford.

"Hardly. Even cannibals wouldn't live in such a God-forsaken place. But it's gotten into sailor lore, somehow. Didn't you notice that the crew's nerves seemed a bit jumpy today?"

"They were a bit strange, now you mention   20
it. Even Captain Nielsen —"

Photo © Christie's Images/Bridgeman Images

Based on this image, how does the purpose of the lion's hunting differ from the purpose that is depicted in the dialogue between Rainsford and Whitney? Is the sort of hunting that Rainsford and Whitney do "natural"?

"Yes, even that tough-minded old Swede, who'd go up to the devil himself and ask him for a light. Those fishy blue eyes held a look I never saw there before. All I could get out of him was 'This place has an evil name among seafaring men, sir.' Then he said to me, very gravely, 'Don't you feel anything?' — as if the air about us was actually poisonous. Now, you mustn't laugh when I tell you this — I did feel something like a sudden chill.

"There was no breeze. The sea was as flat as a plate-glass window. We were drawing near the island then. What I felt was a — a mental chill; a sort of sudden dread."

"Pure imagination," said Rainsford. "One superstitious sailor can taint the whole ship's company with his fear."

"Maybe. But sometimes I think sailors have an extra sense that tells them when they are in danger. Sometimes I think evil is a tangible thing — with wave lengths, just as sound and light have. An evil place can, so to speak, broadcast vibrations of evil. Anyhow, I'm glad we're getting out of this zone. Well, I think I'll turn in now, Rainsford."

"I'm not sleepy," said Rainsford. "I'm going 25 to smoke another pipe up on the afterdeck."

"Good night, then, Rainsford. See you at breakfast."

"Right. Good night, Whitney."

There was no sound in the night as Rainsford sat there but the muffled throb of the engine that drove the yacht swiftly through the darkness, and the swish and ripple of the wash of the propeller.

Rainsford, reclining in a steamer chair, indolently puffed on his favorite brier. The sensuous drowsiness of the night was on him. "It's so dark," he thought, "that I could sleep without closing my eyes; the night would be my eyelids —"

An abrupt sound startled him. Off to the 30 right he heard it, and his ears, expert in such matters, could not be mistaken. Again he heard the sound, and again. Somewhere, off in the blackness, someone had fired a gun three times.

Rainsford sprang up and moved quickly to the rail, mystified. He strained his eyes in the direction from which the reports had come, but it was like trying to see through a blanket. He leaped upon the rail and balanced himself there, to get greater elevation; his pipe, striking a rope, was knocked from his mouth. He lunged for it; a short, hoarse cry came from his lips as he realized he had reached too far and had lost his balance. The cry was pinched off short as the blood-warm waters of the Caribbean Sea closed over his head.

He struggled up to the surface and tried to cry out, but the wash from the speeding yacht slapped him in the face and the salt water in his open mouth made him gag and strangle. Desperately he struck out with strong strokes after the receding lights of the yacht, but he stopped before he had swum fifty feet. A certain cool-headedness had come to him; it was not the first time he had been in a tight place. There was a chance that his cries could be heard by someone aboard the yacht, but that chance was slender and grew more slender as the yacht raced on. He wrestled himself out of his clothes and shouted with all his power. The lights of the yacht became faint and ever-vanishing fireflies; then they were blotted out entirely by the night.

Rainsford remembered the shots. They had come from the right, and doggedly he swam in that direction, swimming with slow, deliberate strokes, conserving his strength. For a seemingly endless time he fought the sea. He began to count his strokes; he could do possibly a hundred more and then—

Rainsford heard a sound. It came out of the darkness, a high screaming sound, the sound of an animal in an extremity of anguish and terror.

He did not recognize the animal that made 35 the sound; he did not try to; with fresh vitality he swam toward the sound. He heard it again; then it was cut short by another noise, crisp, staccato.

"Pistol shot," muttered Rainsford, swimming on.

Ten minutes of determined effort brought another sound to his ears—the most welcome he had ever heard—the muttering and growling of the sea breaking on a rocky shore. He was almost on the rocks before he saw them; on a night less calm he would have been shattered against them. With his remaining strength he dragged himself from the swirling waters. Jagged crags appeared to jut up into the opaqueness; he forced himself upward, hand over hand. Gasping, his hands raw, he reached a flat place at the top. Dense jungle came down to the very edge of the cliffs. What perils that tangle of trees and underbrush might hold for him did not concern Rainsford just then. All he knew was that he was safe from his enemy, the sea, and that utter weariness was on him. He flung himself down at the jungle edge and tumbled headlong into the deepest sleep of his life.

When he opened his eyes he knew from the position of the sun that it was late in the afternoon. Sleep had given him new vigor; a sharp hunger was picking at him. He looked about him, almost cheerfully.

"Where there are pistol shots, there are men. Where there are men, there is food," he thought. But what kind of men, he wondered, in so forbidding a place? An unbroken front of snarled and ragged jungle fringed the shore.

He saw no sign of a trail through the closely 40 knit web of weeds and trees; it was easier to go along the shore, and Rainsford floundered along by the water. Not far from where he landed, he stopped.

Some wounded thing—by the evidence, a large animal—had thrashed about in the underbrush; the jungle weeds were crushed down and the moss was lacerated; one patch of weeds was stained crimson. A small, glittering object not far away caught Rainsford's eye and he picked it up. It was an empty cartridge.

"A twenty-two," he remarked. "That's odd. It must have been a fairly large animal too. The hunter had his nerve with him to tackle it with a light gun. It's clear that the brute put up a fight. I suppose the first three shots I heard was when the hunter flushed his quarry and wounded it. The last shot was when he trailed it here and finished it."

He examined the ground closely and found what he had hoped to find — the print of hunting boots. They pointed along the cliff in the direction he had been going. Eagerly he hurried along, now slipping on a rotten log or a loose stone, but making headway; night was beginning to settle down on the island.

Bleak darkness was blacking out the sea and jungle when Rainsford sighted the lights. He came upon them as he turned a crook in the coast line; and his first thought was that he had come upon a village, for there were many lights. But as he forged along he saw to his great astonishment that all the lights were in one enormous building — a lofty structure with pointed towers plunging upward into the gloom. His eyes made out the shadowy outlines of a palatial chateau; it was set on a high bluff, and on three sides of it cliffs dived down to where the sea licked greedy lips in the shadows.

"Mirage," thought Rainsford. But it was 45 no mirage, he found, when he opened the tall spiked iron gate. The stone steps were real enough; the massive door with a leering gargoyle for a knocker was real enough; yet above it all hung an air of unreality.

He lifted the knocker, and it creaked up stiffly, as if it had never before been used. He let it fall, and it startled him with its booming loudness. He thought he heard steps within; the door remained closed. Again Rainsford lifted the heavy knocker, and let it fall. The door opened then — opened as suddenly as if it were on a spring — and Rainsford stood blinking in the river of glaring gold light that poured out. The

first thing Rainsford's eyes discerned was the largest man Rainsford had ever seen — a gigantic creature, solidly made and black bearded to the waist. In his hand the man held a long-barreled revolver, and he was pointing it straight at Rainsford's heart.

Out of the snarl of beard two small eyes regarded Rainsford.

"Don't be alarmed," said Rainsford, with a smile which he hoped was disarming. "I'm no robber. I fell off a yacht. My name is Sanger Rainsford of New York City."

The menacing look in the eyes did not change. The revolver pointing as rigidly as if the giant were a statue. He gave no sign that he understood Rainsford's words, or that he had even heard them. He was dressed in uniform — a black uniform trimmed with gray astrakhan.

"I'm Sanger Rainsford of New York," Rainsford 50 began again. "I fell off a yacht. I am hungry."

The man's only answer was to raise with his thumb the hammer of his revolver. Then Rainsford saw the man's free hand go to his forehead in a military salute, and he saw him click his heels together and stand at attention. Another man was coming down the broad marble steps, an erect, slender man in evening clothes. He advanced to Rainsford and held out his hand.

In a cultivated voice marked by a slight accent that gave it added precision and deliberateness, he said, "It is a very great pleasure and honor to welcome Mr. Sanger Rainsford, the celebrated hunter, to my home."

Automatically Rainsford shook the man's hand.

"I've read your book about hunting snow leopards in Tibet, you see," explained the man. "I am General Zaroff."

Rainsford's first impression was that the 55 man was singularly handsome; his second was that there was an original, almost bizarre quality about the general's face. He was a tall man past middle age, for his hair was a vivid white; but his

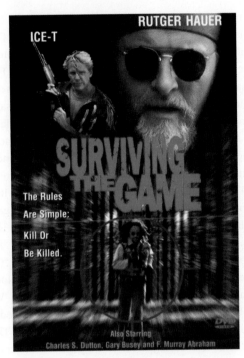

These are posters for movie adaptions of this short story.

How do these posters entice audiences to see these movies? How do some of the visual elements of the posters seem to relate to Connell's story?

thick eyebrows and pointed military mustache were as black as the night from which Rainsford had come. His eyes, too, were black and very bright. He had high cheekbones, a sharpcut nose, a spare, dark face — the face of a man used to giving orders, the face of an aristocrat. Turning to the giant in uniform, the general made a sign. The giant put away his pistol, saluted, withdrew.

"Ivan is an incredibly strong fellow," remarked the general, "but he has the misfortune to be deaf and dumb. A simple fellow, but, I'm afraid, like all his race, a bit of a savage."

"Is he Russian?"

"He is a Cossack," said the general, and his smile showed red lips and pointed teeth. "So am I."

"Come," he said, "we shouldn't be chatting here. We can talk later. Now you want clothes, food, rest. You shall have them. This is a most-restful spot."

Ivan had reappeared, and the general spoke to him with lips that moved but gave forth no sound. 60

"Follow Ivan, if you please, Mr. Rainsford," said the general. "I was about to have my dinner when you came. I'll wait for you. You'll find that my clothes will fit you, I think."

It was to a huge, beam-ceilinged bedroom with a canopied bed big enough for six men that Rainsford followed the silent giant. Ivan laid out an evening suit, and Rainsford, as he put it on, noticed that it came from a London tailor who ordinarily cut and sewed for none below the rank of duke.

The dining room to which Ivan conducted him was in many ways remarkable. There was

319

a medieval magnificence about it; it suggested a baronial hall of feudal times with its oaken panels, its high ceiling, its vast refectory tables where twoscore men could sit down to eat. About the hall were mounted heads of many animals — lions, tigers, elephants, moose, bears; larger or more perfect specimens Rainsford had never seen. At the great table the general was sitting, alone.

"You'll have a cocktail, Mr. Rainsford," he suggested. The cocktail was surpassingly good; and, Rainsford noted, the table appointments were of the finest — the linen, the crystal, the silver, the china.

They were eating *borsch*, the rich, red soup with whipped cream so dear to Russian palates. Half apologetically General Zaroff said, "We do our best to preserve the amenities of civilization here. Please forgive any lapses. We are well off the beaten track, you know. Do you think the champagne has suffered from its long ocean trip?"

"Not in the least," declared Rainsford. He was finding the general a most thoughtful and affable host, a true cosmopolite. But there was one small trait of the general's that made Rainsford uncomfortable. Whenever he looked up from his plate he found the general studying him, appraising him narrowly.

"Perhaps," said General Zaroff, "you were surprised that I recognized your name. You see, I read all books on hunting published in English, French, and Russian. I have but one passion in my life, Mr. Rainsford, and it is the hunt."

"You have some wonderful heads here," said Rainsford as he ate a particularly well-cooked filet mignon. "That Cape buffalo is the largest I ever saw."

"Oh, that fellow. Yes, he was a monster."

"Did he charge you?"

"Hurled me against a tree," said the general. "Fractured my skull. But I got the brute."

"I've always thought," said Rainsford, "that the Cape buffalo is the most dangerous of all big game."

For a moment the general did not reply; he was smiling his curious red-lipped smile. Then he said slowly, "No. You are wrong, sir. The Cape buffalo is not the most dangerous big game." He sipped his wine. "Here in my preserve on this island," he said in the same slow tone, "I hunt more dangerous game."

Rainsford expressed his surprise. "Is there big game on this island?"

The general nodded. "The biggest." 75

"Really?"

"Oh, it isn't here naturally, of course. I have to stock the island."

"What have you imported, general?" Rainsford asked. "Tigers?"

The general smiled. "No," he said. "Hunting tigers ceased to interest me some years ago. I exhausted their possibilities, you see. No thrill left in tigers, no real danger. I live for danger, Mr. Rainsford."

The general took from his pocket a gold 80 cigarette case and offered his guest a long black cigarette with a silver tip; it was perfumed and gave off a smell like incense.

"We will have some capital hunting, you and I," said the general. "I shall be most glad to have your society."

"But what game —" began Rainsford.

"I'll tell you," said the general. "You will be amused, I know. I think I may say, in all modesty, that I have done a rare thing. I have invented a new sensation. May I pour you another glass of port?"

"Thank you, general."

The general filled both glasses, and said, 85 "God makes some men poets. Some He makes kings, some beggars. Me He made a hunter. My hand was made for the trigger, my father said. He was a very rich man with a quarter of a million acres in the Crimea, and he was an ardent

65

70

sportsman. When I was only five years old he gave me a little gun, specially made in Moscow for me, to shoot sparrows with. When I shot some of his prize turkeys with it, he did not punish me; he complimented me on my marksmanship. I killed my first bear in the Caucasus when I was ten. My whole life has been one prolonged hunt. I went into the army — it was expected of noblemen's sons — and for a time commanded a division of Cossack cavalry, but my real interest was always the hunt. I have hunted every kind of game in every land. It would be impossible for me to tell you how many animals I have killed."

The general puffed at his cigarette.

"After the debacle in Russia I left the country, for it was imprudent for an officer of the Czar to stay there. Many noble Russians lost everything. I, luckily, had invested heavily in American securities, so I shall never have to open a tearoom in Monte Carlo or drive a taxi in Paris. Naturally, I continued to hunt — grizzlies in your Rockies, crocodiles in the Ganges, rhinoceroses in East Africa. It was in Africa that the Cape buffalo hit me and laid me up for six months. As soon as I recovered I started for the Amazon to hunt jaguars, for I had heard they were unusually cunning. They weren't." The Cossack sighed. "They were no match at all for a hunter with his wits about him, and a high-powered rifle. I was bitterly disappointed. I was lying in my tent with a splitting headache one night when a terrible thought pushed its way into my mind. Hunting was beginning to bore me! And hunting, remember, had been my life. I have heard that in America businessmen often go to pieces when they give up the business that has been their life."

"Yes, that's so," said Rainsford.

The general smiled. "I had no wish to go to pieces," he said. "I must do something. Now, mine is an analytical mind, Mr. Rainsford. Doubtless that is why I enjoy the problems of the chase."

"No doubt, General Zaroff."   90

"So," continued the general, "I asked myself why the hunt no longer fascinated me. You are much younger than I am, Mr. Rainsford, and have not hunted as much, but you perhaps can guess the answer."

"What was it?"

"Simply this: hunting had ceased to be what you call 'a sporting proposition.' It had become too easy. I always got my quarry. Always. There is no greater bore than perfection."

The general lit a fresh cigarette.

"No animal had a chance with me anymore.   95 That is no boast; it is a mathematical certainty. The animal had nothing but his legs and his instinct. Instinct is no match for reason. When I thought of this it was a tragic moment for me, I can tell you."

Rainsford leaned across the table, absorbed in what his host was saying.

"It came to me as an inspiration what I must do," the general went on.

"And that was?"

The general smiled the quiet smile of one who has faced an obstacle and surmounted it with success. "I had to invent a new animal to hunt," he said.

"A new animal? You're joking."   100

"Not at all," said the general. "I never joke about hunting. I needed a new animal. I found one. So I bought this island, built this house, and here I do my hunting. The island is perfect for my purposes — there are jungles with a maze of traits in them, hills, swamps —"

"But the animal, General Zaroff?"

"Oh," said the general, "it supplies me with the most exciting hunting in the world. No other hunting compares with it for an instant. Every day I hunt, and I never grow bored now, for I have a quarry with which I can match my wits."

Rainsford's bewilderment showed in his face.

"I wanted the ideal animal to hunt,"   105 explained the general. "So I said, 'What are the

While most agree that hunting for food is a natural, traditional, and ethical practice, some draw the line at big-game hunting for sport.

What point is this cartoon making about the issue and how does it use words and images to do so? Based on what you've read so far in this story, what side of this issue do the themes of "The Most Dangerous Game" seem to take?

attributes of an ideal quarry?' And the answer was, of course, 'It must have courage, cunning, and, above all, it must be able to reason.'"

"But no animal can reason," objected Rainsford.

"My dear fellow," said the general, "there is one that can."

"But you can't mean —" gasped Rainsford.

"And why not?"

"I can't believe you are serious, General   110
Zaroff. This is a grisly joke."

"Why should I not be serious? I am speaking of hunting."

"Hunting? Great Guns, General Zaroff, what you speak of is murder."

The general laughed with entire good nature. He regarded Rainsford quizzically. "I refuse to believe that so modern and civilized a young man as you seem to be harbors romantic ideas about the value of human life. Surely your experiences in the war —"

"Did not make me condone cold-blooded murder," finished Rainsford stiffly.

Laughter shook the general. "How extraor-   115
dinarily droll you are!" he said. "One does not

expect nowadays to find a young man of the educated class, even in America, with such a naive, and, if I may say so, mid-Victorian point of view. It's like finding a snuffbox in a limousine. Ah, well, doubtless you had Puritan ancestors. So many Americans appear to have had. I'll wager you'll forget your notions when you go hunting with me. You've a genuine new thrill in store for you, Mr. Rainsford."

"Thank you, I'm a hunter, not a murderer."

"Dear me," said the general, quite unruffled, "again that unpleasant word. But I think I can show you that your scruples are quite ill founded."

"Yes?"

"Life is for the strong, to be lived by the strong, and, if needs be, taken by the strong. The weak of the world were put here to give the strong pleasure. I am strong. Why should I not use my gift? If I wish to hunt, why should I not? I hunt the scum of the earth: sailors from tramp ships — lassars, blacks, Chinese, whites, mongrels — a thoroughbred horse or hound is worth more than a score of them."

"But they are men," said Rainsford hotly.   120

"Precisely," said the general. "That is why I use them. It gives me pleasure. They can reason, after a fashion. So they are dangerous."

"But where do you get them?"

The general's left eyelid fluttered down in a wink. "This island is called Ship Trap," he answered. "Sometimes an angry god of the high seas sends them to me. Sometimes, when Providence is not so kind, I help Providence a bit. Come to the window with me."

Rainsford went to the window and looked out toward the sea.

"Watch! Out there!" exclaimed the general, 125 pointing into the night. Rainsford's eyes saw only blackness, and then, as the general pressed a button, far out to sea Rainsford saw the flash of lights.

The general chuckled. "They indicate a channel," he said, "where there's none; giant rocks with razor edges crouch like a sea monster with wide-open jaws. They can crush a ship as easily as I crush this nut." He dropped a walnut on the hardwood floor and brought his heel grinding down on it. "Oh, yes," he said, casually, as if in answer to a question, "I have electricity. We try to be civilized here."

"Civilized? And you shoot down men?"

A trace of anger was in the general's black eyes, but it was there for but a second; and he said, in his most pleasant manner, "Dear me, what a righteous young man you are! I assure you I do not do the thing you suggest. That would be barbarous. I treat these visitors with every consideration. They get plenty of good food and exercise. They get into splendid physical condition. You shall see for yourself tomorrow."

"What do you mean?"

"We'll visit my training school," smiled the 130 general. "It's in the cellar. I have about a dozen pupils down there now. They're from the Spanish bark *San Lucar* that had the bad luck to go on the rocks out there. A very inferior lot, I regret to say. Poor specimens and more accustomed to the deck than to the jungle." He raised his hand, and Ivan, who served as waiter, brought thick Turkish coffee. Rainsford, with an effort, held his tongue in check.

"It's a game, you see," pursued the general blandly. "I suggest to one of them that we go hunting. I give him a supply of food and an excellent hunting knife. I give him three hours' start. I am to follow, armed only with a pistol of the smallest caliber and range. If my quarry eludes me for three whole days, he wins the game. If I find him" — the general smiled — "he loses."

"Suppose he refuses to be hunted?"

"Oh," said the general, "I give him his option, of course. He need not play that game if he doesn't wish to. If he does not wish to hunt, I turn him over to Ivan. Ivan once had the honor of serving as official knouter[1] to the Great White Czar, and he has his own ideas of sport. Invariably, Mr. Rainsford, invariably they choose the hunt."

"And if they win?"

The smile on the general's face widened. 135 "To date I have not lost," he said. Then he added, hastily: "I don't wish you to think me a braggart, Mr. Rainsford. Many of them afford only the most elementary sort of problem. Occasionally I strike a tartar. One almost did win. I eventually had to use the dogs."

"The dogs?"

"This way, please. I'll show you."

The general steered Rainsford to a window. The lights from the windows sent a flickering illumination that made grotesque patterns on the courtyard below, and Rainsford could see moving about there a dozen or so huge black shapes; as they turned toward him, their eyes glittered greenly.

---

[1] In Russia, a knouter is a person who whips criminals with a lash of leather thongs, called a knout. —Eds.

"A rather good lot, I think," observed the general. "They are let out at seven every night. If anyone should try to get into my house — or out of it — something extremely regrettable would occur to him." He hummed a snatch of song from the *Folies Bergere*.[2]

"And now," said the general, "I want to show 140 you my new collection of heads. Will you come with me to the library?"

"I hope," said Rainsford, "that you will excuse me tonight, General Zaroff. I'm really not feeling well."

"Ah, indeed?" the general inquired solicitously. "Well, I suppose that's only natural, after your long swim. You need a good, restful night's sleep. Tomorrow you'll feel like a new man, I'll wager. Then we'll hunt, eh? I've one rather promising prospect —" Rainsford was hurrying from the room.

"Sorry you can't go with me tonight," called the general. "I expect rather fair sport — a big, strong, black. He looks resourceful — Well, good night, Mr. Rainsford; I hope you have a good night's rest."

The bed was good, and the pajamas of the softest silk, and he was tired in every fiber of his being, but nevertheless Rainsford could not quiet his brain with the opiate of sleep. He lay, eyes wide open. Once he thought he heard stealthy steps in the corridor outside his room. He sought to throw open the door; it would not open. He went to the window and looked out. His room was high up in one of the towers. The lights of the chateau were out now, and it was dark and silent; but there was a fragment of sallow moon, and by its wan light he could see, dimly, the courtyard. There, weaving in and out in the pattern of shadow, were black, noiseless forms; the hounds heard him at the window and looked up, expectantly, with their green eyes.

Rainsford went back to the bed and lay down. By many methods he tried to put himself to sleep. He had achieved a doze when, just as morning began to come, he heard, far off in the jungle, the faint report of a pistol.

General Zaroff did not appear until lun- 145 cheon. He was dressed faultlessly in the tweeds of a country squire. He was solicitous about the state of Rainsford's health.

"As for me," sighed the general, "I do not feel so well. I am worried, Mr. Rainsford. Last night I detected traces of my old complaint."

To Rainsford's questioning glance the general said, "Ennui. Boredom."

Then, taking a second helping of crepes Suzette, the general explained: "The hunting was not good last night. The fellow lost his head. He made a straight trail that offered no problems at all. That's the trouble with these sailors; they have dull brains to begin with, and they do not know how to get about in the woods. They do excessively stupid and obvious things. It's most annoying. Will you have another glass of Chablis, Mr. Rainsford?"

"General," said Rainsford firmly, "I wish to leave this island at once."

The general raised his thickets of eyebrows; 150 he seemed hurt. "But, my dear fellow," the general protested, "you've only just come. You've had no hunting —"

"I wish to go today," said Rainsford. He saw the dead black eyes of the general on him, studying him. General Zaroff's face suddenly brightened.

He filled Rainsford's glass with venerable Chablis from a dusty bottle.

"Tonight," said the general, "we will hunt — you and I."

Rainsford shook his head. "No, general," he said. "I will not hunt."

The general shrugged his shoulders and 155 delicately ate a hothouse grape. "As you wish, my friend," he said. "The choice rests entirely

---

[2] A cabaret, or nightclub, in Paris, France, that was founded in 1869 and is still open today. —Eds.

with you. But may I not venture to suggest that you will find my idea of sport more diverting than Ivan's?"

He nodded toward the corner to where the giant stood, scowling, his thick arms crossed on his hogshead of chest.

"You don't mean—" cried Rainsford.

"My dear fellow," said the general, "have I not told you I always mean what I say about hunting? This is really an inspiration. I drink to a foeman worthy of my steel—at last." The general raised his glass, but Rainsford sat staring at him.

"You'll find this game worth playing," the general said enthusiastically. "Your brain against mine. Your woodcraft against mine. Your strength and stamina against mine. Outdoor chess! And the stake is not without value, eh?"

"And if I win—" began Rainsford huskily.   160

"I'll cheerfully acknowledge myself defeat if I do not find you by midnight of the third day," said General Zaroff. "My sloop will place you on the mainland near a town." The general read what Rainsford was thinking.

"Oh, you can trust me," said the Cossack. "I will give you my word as a gentleman and a sportsman. Of course you, in turn, must agree to say nothing of your visit here."

"I'll agree to nothing of the kind," said Rainsford.

"Oh," said the general, "in that case . . . But why discuss that now? Three days hence we can discuss it over a bottle of Veuve Clicquot, unless . . ."

The general sipped his wine.   165

Then a businesslike air animated him. "Ivan," he said to Rainsford, "will supply you with hunting clothes, food, a knife. I suggest you wear moccasins; they leave a poorer trail. I suggest, too, that you avoid the big swamp in the southeast corner of the island. We call it Death Swamp. There's quicksand there. One foolish fellow tried it. The deplorable part of it was that Lazarus followed him. You can imagine

my feelings, Mr. Rainsford. I loved Lazarus; he was the finest hound in my pack. Well, I must beg you to excuse me now. I always take a siesta after lunch. You'll hardly have time for a nap, I fear. You'll want to start, no doubt. I shall not follow till dusk. Hunting at night is so much more exciting than by day, don't you think? Au revoir, Mr. Rainsford, au revoir." General Zaroff, with a deep, courtly bow, strolled from the room.

From another door came Ivan. Under one arm he carried khaki hunting clothes, a haversack of food, a leather sheath containing a long-bladed hunting knife; his right hand rested on a cocked revolver thrust in the crimson sash about his waist.

Rainsford had fought his way through the bush for two hours. "I must keep my nerve. I must keep my nerve," he said through tight teeth.

He had not been entirely clearheaded when the chateau gates snapped shut behind him. His whole idea at first was to put distance between himself and General Zaroff; and, to this end, he had plunged along, spurred on by the sharp rowers of something very like panic. Now he had got a grip on himself, had stopped, and was taking stock of himself and the situation. He saw that straight flight was futile; inevitably it would bring him face to face with the sea. He was in a picture with a frame of water, and his operations, clearly, must take place within that frame.

"I'll give him a trail to follow," muttered   170
Rainsford, and he struck off from the rude path he had been following into the trackless wilderness. He executed a series of intricate loops; he doubled on his trail again and again, recalling all the lore of the fox hunt, and all the dodges of the fox. Night found him leg-weary, with hands and face lashed by the branches, on a thickly wooded ridge. He knew it would be insane to blunder on through the dark, even if he had the strength. His need for rest was imperative and he thought, "I have played the fox, now I must

"For the most dangerous game, that was awfully easy."

David Borchart The
New Yorker Collection/
The Cartoon Bank

What statement does this cartoon
make about humanity's hunting
prowess? How does this cartoon
contradict or support the idea that
humans are the most dangerous
game?

play the cat of the fable." A big tree with a thick
trunk and outspread branches was near by, and,
taking care to leave not the slightest mark, he
climbed up into the crotch, and, stretching out
on one of the broad limbs, after a fashion, rested.
Rest brought him new confidence and almost a
feeling of security. Even so zealous a hunter as
General Zaroff could not trace him there, he told
himself; only the devil himself could follow that
complicated trail through the jungle after dark.
But perhaps the general was a devil—

An apprehensive night crawled slowly by like
a wounded snake and sleep did not visit Rainsford, although the silence of a dead world was
on the jungle. Toward morning when a dingy
gray was varnishing the sky, the cry of some
startled bird focused Rainsford's attention in
that direction. Something was coming through
the bush, coming slowly, carefully, coming by
the same winding way Rainsford had come. He
flattened himself down on the limb and, through
a screen of leaves almost as thick as tapestry, he
watched. . . . That which was approaching was
a man.

It was General Zaroff. He made his way
along with his eyes fixed in utmost concentration on the ground before him. He paused,
almost beneath the tree, dropped to his knees
and studied the ground. Rainsford's impulse
was to hurl himself down like a panther, but he
saw that the general's right hand held something
metallic—a small automatic pistol.

The hunter shook his head several times, as
if he were puzzled. Then he straightened up and
took from his case one of his black cigarettes;
its pungent incenselike smoke floated up to
Rainsford's nostrils.

Rainsford held his breath. The general's eyes
had left the ground and were traveling inch by
inch up the tree. Rainsford froze there, every
muscle tensed for a spring. But the sharp eyes of
the hunter stopped before they reached the limb
where Rainsford lay; a smile spread over his
brown face. Very deliberately he blew a smoke
ring into the air; then he turned his back on the
tree and walked carelessly away, back along the
trail he had come. The swish of the underbrush
against his hunting boots grew fainter and
fainter.

The pent-up air burst hotly from Rainsford's 175
lungs. His first thought made him feel sick and
numb. The general could follow a trail through
the woods at night; he could follow an extremely
difficult trail; he must have uncanny powers;
only by the merest chance had the Cossack
failed to see his quarry.

Rainsford's second thought was even more
terrible. It sent a shudder of cold horror through
his whole being. Why had the general smiled?
Why had he turned back?

Rainsford did not want to believe what his reason told him was true, but the truth was as evident as the sun that had by now pushed through the morning mists. The general was playing with him! The general was saving him for another day's sport! The Cossack was the cat; he was the mouse. Then it was that Rainsford knew the full meaning of terror.

"I will not lose my nerve. I will not."

He slid down from the tree, and struck off again into the woods. His face was set and he forced the machinery of his mind to function. Three hundred yards from his hiding place he stopped where a huge dead tree leaned precariously on a smaller, living one. Throwing off his sack of food, Rainsford took his knife from its sheath and began to work with all his energy.

The job was finished at last, and he threw himself down behind a fallen log a hundred feet away. He did not have to wait long. The cat was coming again to play with the mouse.   180

Following the trail with the sureness of a bloodhound came General Zaroff. Nothing escaped those searching black eyes, no crushed blade of grass, no bent twig, no mark, no matter how faint, in the moss. So intent was the Cossack on his stalking that he was upon the thing Rainsford had made before he saw it. His foot touched the protruding bough that was the trigger. Even as he touched it, the general sensed his danger and leaped back with the agility of an ape. But he was not quite quick enough; the dead tree, delicately adjusted to rest on the cut living one, crashed down and struck the general a glancing blow on the shoulder as it fell; but for his alertness, he must have been smashed beneath it. He staggered, but he did not fall; nor did he drop his revolver. He stood there, rubbing his injured shoulder, and Rainsford, with fear again gripping his heart, heard the general's mocking laugh ring through the jungle.

"Rainsford," called the general, "if you are within sound of my voice, as I suppose you are,

let me congratulate you. Not many men know how to make a Malay mancatcher. Luckily for me I, too, have hunted in Malacca. You are proving interesting, Mr. Rainsford. I am going now to have my wound dressed; it's only a slight one. But I shall be back. I shall be back."

When the general, nursing his bruised shoulder, had gone, Rainsford took up his flight again. It was flight now, a desperate, hopeless flight, that carried him on for some hours. Dusk came, then darkness, and still he pressed on. The ground grew softer under his moccasins; the vegetation grew ranker, denser; insects bit him savagely.

Then, as he stepped forward, his foot sank into the ooze. He tried to wrench it back, but the muck sucked viciously at his foot as if it were a giant leech. With a violent effort, he tore his feet loose. He knew where he was now. Death Swamp and its quicksand.

His hands were tight closed as if his nerve   185
were something tangible that someone in the darkness was trying to tear from his grip. The softness of the earth had given him an idea. He stepped back from the quicksand a dozen feet or so and, like some huge prehistoric beaver, he began to dig.

Rainsford had dug himself in in France[3] when a second's delay meant death. That had been a placid pastime compared to his digging now. The pit grew deeper; when it was above his shoulders, he climbed out and from some hard saplings cut stakes and sharpened them to a fine point. These stakes he planted in the bottom of the pit with the points sticking up. With flying fingers he wove a rough carpet of weeds and branches and with it he covered the mouth of the pit. Then, wet with sweat and aching with tiredness, he crouched behind the stump of a lightning-charred tree.

---

[3] This reference to France has to do with the trench warfare on the front line during World War I. Fighters often dug trenches, or deep ditches, for protection from artillery and small arms fire. —Eds.

He knew his pursuer was coming; he heard the padding sound of feet on the soft earth, and the night breeze brought him the perfume of the general's cigarette. It seemed to Rainsford that the general was coming with unusual swiftness; he was not feeling his way along, foot by foot. Rainsford, crouching there, could not see the general, nor could he see the pit. He lived a year in a minute. Then he felt an impulse to cry aloud with joy, for he heard the sharp crackle of the breaking branches as the cover of the pit gave way; he heard the sharp scream of pain as the pointed stakes found their mark. He leaped up from his place of concealment. Then he cowered back. Three feet from the pit a man was standing, with an electric torch in his hand.

"You've done well, Rainsford," the voice of the general called. "Your Burmese tiger pit has claimed one of my best dogs. Again you score. I think, Mr. Rainsford, I'll see what you can do against my whole pack. I'm going home for a rest now. Thank you for a most amusing evening."

At daybreak Rainsford, lying near the swamp, was awakened by a sound that made him know that he had new things to learn about fear. It was a distant sound, faint and wavering, but he knew it. It was the baying of a pack of hounds.

Rainsford knew he could do one of two things. He could stay where he was and wait. That was suicide. He could flee. That was postponing the inevitable. For a moment he stood there, thinking. An idea that held a wild chance came to him, and, tightening his belt, he headed away from the swamp. 190

The baying of the hounds drew nearer, then still nearer, nearer, ever nearer. On a ridge Rainsford climbed a tree. Down a watercourse, not a quarter of a mile away, he could see the bush moving. Straining his eyes, he saw the lean figure of General Zaroff; just ahead of him Rainsford made out another figure whose wide shoulders surged through the tall jungle weeds;

it was the giant Ivan, and he seemed pulled forward by some unseen force; Rainsford knew that Ivan must be holding the pack in leash.

They would be on him any minute now. His mind worked frantically. He thought of a native trick he had learned in Uganda. He slid down the tree. He caught hold of a springy young sapling and to it he fastened his hunting knife, with the blade pointing down the trail; with a bit of wild grapevine he tied back the sapling. Then he ran for his life. The hounds raised their voices as they hit the fresh scent. Rainsford knew now how an animal at bay feels.

He had to stop to get his breath. The baying of the hounds stopped abruptly, and Rainsford's heart stopped too. They must have reached the knife.

He shinned excitedly up a tree and looked back. His pursuers had stopped. But the hope that was in Rainsford's brain when he climbed died, for he saw in the shallow valley that General Zaroff was still on his feet. But Ivan was not. The knife, driven by the recoil of the springing tree, had not wholly failed.

Rainsford had hardly tumbled to the ground 195 when the pack took up the cry again.

"Nerve, nerve, nerve!" he panted, as he dashed along. A blue gap showed between the trees dead ahead. Ever nearer drew the hounds. Rainsford forced himself on toward that gap. He reached it. It was the shore of the sea. Across a cove he could see the gloomy gray stone of the chateau. Twenty feet below him the sea rumbled and hissed. Rainsford hesitated. He heard the hounds. Then he leaped far out into the sea. . . .

When the general and his pack reached the place by the sea, the Cossack stopped. For some minutes he stood regarding the blue-green expanse of water. He shrugged his shoulders. Then he sat down, took a drink of brandy from a silver flask, lit a cigarette, and hummed a bit from Madame Butterfly.

General Zaroff had an exceedingly good dinner in his great paneled dining hall that evening. With it he had a bottle of Pol Roger and half a bottle of Chambertin. Two slight annoyances kept him from perfect enjoyment. One was the thought that it would be difficult to replace Ivan; the other was that his quarry had escaped him; of course, the American hadn't played the game — so thought the general as he tasted his after-dinner liqueur. In his library he read, to soothe himself, from the works of Marcus Aurelius. At ten he went up to his bedroom. He was deliciously tired, he said to himself, as he locked himself in. There was a little moonlight, so, before turning on his light, he went to the window and looked down at the courtyard. He could see the great hounds, and he called, "Better luck another time," to them. Then he switched on the light.

A man, who had been hiding in the curtains of the bed, was standing there.

"Rainsford!" screamed the general. "How in God's name did you get here?"

"Swam," said Rainsford. "I found it quicker than walking through the jungle."

The general sucked in his breath and smiled. "I congratulate you," he said. "You have won the game."

Rainsford did not smile. "I am still a beast at bay," he said, in a low, hoarse voice. "Get ready, General Zaroff."

The general made one of his deepest bows. "I see," he said. "Splendid! One of us is to furnish a repast for the hounds. The other will sleep in this very excellent bed. On guard, Rainsford." . . .

He had never slept in a better bed, Rainsford decided. ■

Understanding and Interpreting

1. What details does Connell provide to the reader about the island at the beginning of the story? What effect do these details create for the reader?

2. What is Rainsford's central conflict in paragraphs 31–37? How does the conflict evolve over the course of the story? Support your answer with examples from the text.

3. How does Connell use direct and indirect characterization to portray General Zaroff? What evidence is there that General Zaroff believes he is superior to other animals, including other people?

4. In what ways are Rainsford and General Zaroff similar? In what ways do their characters differ?

5. What purpose does Ivan serve in the story? How does his character affect the plot?

6. In paragraph 119, General Zaroff explains how he views men. What would you say his definition of *man* is? Does Rainsford fit this definition? Why or why not?

7. In what ways is the game rigged in favor of the hunter? Give specific examples to support your answer.

8. Identify moments in which Rainsford draws on logic and reason to elude the hunter. What does he do that separates him from other hunted, nonhuman animals?

9. Why is it important that the story takes place on an island as opposed to a different location? In what way does the island play a thematic role in this story as well as a literal one?

10. How do Rainsford's ideas about hunting change over the course of the story? Give specific examples that show his attitude at the beginning of the story, and evidence of the change while he is hunted and after the hunt is over.

Analyzing Language, Style, and Structure

11. Vocabulary in Context. The word *game* is used repeatedly in this story and appears in its title. What are the multiple meanings of the word and how are they used, especially in the title?

12. During his conversation with Whitney in paragraph 10, Rainsford asks the question, "Who cares how a jaguar feels?" What is the irony of this statement? How might Rainsford answer this question differently at the end of the story?

13. Connell uses a multitude of figurative language devices (simile, metaphor, personification) in the opening conversation between Rainsford and Whitney. How do these devices contribute to the overall mood at the beginning? How do they foreshadow later events in the story?

14. Explain how Connell uses stylistic elements to build suspense in paragraphs 31–36.

15. What is ironic about Rainsford thinking that he'd escaped "his enemy, the sea" in paragraph 38?

16. Reread paragraphs 44–46 describing General Zaroff's compound. How does Connell use imagery and details in these paragraphs to foreshadow the meeting between Rainsford and General Zaroff?

17. Verbal irony occurs when a person says one thing but means the opposite. In his first conversation with Rainsford, General Zaroff says, "We try to be civilized here" (par. 126). What is ironic about this statement? What does the statement reveal about him? What other ironic statements does General Zaroff make that first night that offer insight into his character?

18. What details in the story indicate that Rainsford's past experiences have helped him elude General Zaroff?

19. In paragraph 198, the point of view shifts characters. What is the effect of this shift in point of view toward the end of the story?

Topics for Composing

20. Analysis. On the exterior, General Zaroff is a sophisticated, civilized individual. Underneath, he is very different. What human behaviors or tendencies might Connell be critiquing in this story and what is he suggesting about them?

21. Argument. General Zaroff admits that his boredom with hunting causes him to seek new and more dangerous game. Discuss the consequences, either positive or negative, of keeping ourselves constantly interested, or even entertained.

22. Argument. Argue whether or not you think that Connell uses Rainsford as the "huntee" to shed light on the cruelties of hunting animals in general. Is this approach effective? Why or why not?

23. Connections. Oftentimes when people are faced with peril or placed in dire situations, survival skills instinctively kick in. Have you been in a situation that caused your survival instinct to take over? Explain the situation and how your instinct and any specific survival skills helped you through it.

24. Speaking and Listening. This short story has been adapted in movies by the same name or by titles such as *The Running Man, Hard Target, Surviving the Game, The Hunt, Apex,* and many more. TV shows, such as *The Simpsons, Law and Order, Xena: Warrior Princess, Blacklist,* and many others have used this plot line. Prior to a small group discussion, watch one or more of the adaptations. With your group, discuss what is maintained and what is changed in the adaptations you watched. Try to come to a consensus about why this story is so often retold.

25. Creative Writing. Choose a key scene of this story and rewrite it with Zaroff as a lion or similar predatory animal, rather than a human. Afterward, explain how this change affected the themes and conflicts in the story.

Two Kinds

Amy Tan

Amy Tan (b. 1952) grew up in California, has a master of arts in linguistics, and has written several best-selling novels, including *The Valley of Amazement* (2013). Tan draws on her Chinese heritage to depict the clash of traditional Chinese culture with modern-day American customs. "Two Kinds" is a chapter from Tan's critically acclaimed and popular novel *The Joy Luck Club* (1989).

Mark Mainz/Getty Images

My mother believed you could be anything you wanted to be in America. You could open a restaurant. You could work for the government and get good retirement. You could buy a house with almost no money down. You could become rich. You could become instantly famous. "Of course, you can be a prodigy, too," my mother told me when I was nine. "You can be best anything. What does Auntie Lindo know? Her daughter, she is only best tricky." America was where all my mother's hopes lay. She had come to San Francisco in 1949 after losing everything in China: her mother and father, her home, her first husband, and two daughters, twin baby girls. But she never looked back with regret. Things could get better in so many ways.

We didn't immediately pick the right kind of prodigy. At first my mother thought I could be a Chinese Shirley Temple. We'd watch Shirley's old movies on TV as though they were training films. My mother would poke my arm and say, "*Ni kan*. You watch." And I would see Shirley tapping her feet, or singing a sailor song, or pursing her lips into a very round O while saying "Oh, my goodness." "*Ni kan*," my mother said, as Shirley's eyes flooded with tears. "You already know how. Don't need talent for crying!"

Soon after my mother got this idea about Shirley Temple, she took me to the beauty training school in the Mission District and put me in the hands of a student who could barely hold the scissors without shaking. Instead of getting big fat curls, I emerged with an uneven mass of crinkly black fuzz. My mother dragged me off to the bathroom and tried to wet down my hair.

"You look like a Negro Chinese," she lamented, as if I had done this on purpose.

The instructor of the beauty training school had to lop off these soggy clumps to make my hair even again. "Peter Pan is very popular these days" the instructor assured my mother. I now had bad hair the length of a boy's; with curly bangs that hung at a slant two inches above my eyebrows. I liked the haircut, and it made me actually look forward to my future fame.

In fact, in the beginning I was just as excited as my mother, maybe even more so. I pictured this prodigy part of me as many different images, and I tried each one on for size. I was a dainty ballerina girl standing by the curtain, waiting to hear the music that would send me floating on my tiptoes. I was like the Christ child lifted out of the straw manger, crying with holy indignity. I was Cinderella stepping from her pumpkin carriage with sparkly cartoon music filling the air.

5

In all of my imaginings I was filled with a sense that I would soon become perfect: My mother and father would adore me. I would be beyond reproach. I would never feel the need to sulk, or to clamor for anything. But sometimes the prodigy in me became impatient. "If you don't hurry up and get me out of here, I'm disappearing for good," it warned. "And then you'll always be nothing."

Every night after dinner my mother and I would sit at the Formica topped kitchen table. She would present new tests, taking her examples from stories of amazing children that she read in *Ripley's Believe It or Not* or *Good Housekeeping, Reader's Digest*, or any of a dozen other magazines she kept in a pile in our bathroom. My mother got these magazines from people whose houses she cleaned. And since she cleaned many houses each week, we had a great assortment. She would look through them all, searching for stories about remarkable children.

The first night she brought out a story about a three-year-old boy who knew the capitals of all the states and even most of the European countries. A teacher was quoted as saying that the little boy could also pronounce the names of the foreign cities correctly. "What's the capital of Finland" My mother asked me, looking at the story.

All I knew was the capital of California, because Sacramento was the name of the street we lived on in Chinatown. "Nairobi!" I guessed, saying the most foreign word I could think of. She checked to see if that might be one way to pronounce *Helsinki* before showing me the answer.

The tests got harder — multiplying numbers 10 in my head, finding the queen of hearts in a deck of cards, trying to stand on my head without using my hands, predicting the daily temperatures in Los Angeles, New York, and London. One night I had to look at a page from the Bible for three minutes and then report everything I

could remember. "Now Jehoshaphat had riches and honor in abundance and . . . that's all I remember, Ma," I said.

And after seeing, once again, my mother's disappointed face, something inside me began to die. I hated the tests, the raised hopes and failed expectations. Before going to bed that night I looked in the mirror above the bathroom sink, and I saw only my face staring back — and understood that it would always be this ordinary face — I began to cry. Such a sad, ugly girl! I made high-pitched noises like a crazed animal, trying to scratch out the face in the mirror.

And then I saw what seemed to be the prodigy side of me — a face I had never seen before. I looked at my reflection, blinking so that I could see more clearly. The girl staring back at me was angry, powerful. She and I were the same. I had new thoughts, willful thoughts — or rather, thoughts filled with lots of won'ts. I won't let her change me, I promised myself. I won't be what I'm not.

So now when my mother presented her tests, I performed listlessly, my head propped on one arm. I pretended to be bored. And I was. I got so bored that I started counting the bellows of the foghorns out on the bay while my mother drilled me in other areas. The sound was comforting and reminded me of the cow jumping over the moon. And the next day I played a game with myself, seeing if my mother would give up on me before eight bellows. After a while I usually counted only one bellow, maybe two at most. At last she was beginning to give up hope.

Two or three months went by without any mention of my being a prodigy. And then one day my mother was watching the *Ed Sullivan Show* on TV. The TV was old and the sound kept shorting out. Every time my mother got halfway up from the sofa to adjust the set, the sound would come back on and Sullivan would be talking. As soon as she sat down, Sullivan would go silent again. She got up — the TV broke into loud piano music. She sat down — silence. Up and down, back and forth, quiet and loud. It was like a stiff, embraceless dance between her and the TV set. Finally, she stood by the set with her hand on the sound dial.

She seemed entranced by the music, a 15 frenzied little piano piece with a mesmerizing quality, which alternated between quick, playful passages and teasing, lilting ones.

"*Ni kan,*" my mother said, calling me over with hurried hand gestures. "Look here."

I could see why my mother was fascinated by the music. It was being pounded out by a little Chinese girl, about nine years old, with a Peter Pan haircut. The girl had the sauciness of a Shirley Temple. She was proudly modest, like a proper Chinese child. And she also did a fancy sweep of a curtsy, so that the fluffy skirt of her white dress cascaded to the floor like petals of a large carnation.

In spite of these warning signs, I wasn't worried. Our family had no piano and we couldn't afford to buy one, let alone reams of sheet music and piano lessons. So I could be generous in my comments when my mother badmouthed the little girl on TV.

"Play note right, but doesn't sound good!" my mother complained "No singing sound."

"What are you picking on her for?" I said 20 carelessly. "She's pretty good. Maybe she's not the best, but she's trying hard." I knew almost immediately that I would be sorry I had said that.

"Just like you," she said. "Not the best. Because you not trying." She gave a little huff as she let go of the sound dial and sat down on the sofa.

The little Chinese girl sat down also, to play an encore of "Anitra's Tanz," by Grieg. I remember the song, because later on I had to learn how to play it.

Three days after watching the *Ed Sullivan Show* my mother told me what my schedule

This image shows Ed Sullivan with a young Michael Jackson when the Jackson 5 performed on the *Ed Sullivan Show* in 1970. Ed Sullivan's exposure of the Jackson 5 helped launch their careers.

How does this image convey the pressures young talent faces on shows like the *Ed Sullivan Show*? How might programs like this, which often showcase the talents of up-and-coming stars, put more pressure on parents to harness their children's talents? Do you think that Jing-mei's mother would have pressured Jing-mei without the influence of the television shows and magazines she scoured for examples of prodigies? Why or why not?

would be for piano lessons and piano practice. She had talked to Mr. Chong, who lived on the first floor of our apartment building. Mr. Chong was a retired piano teacher, and my mother had traded housecleaning services for weekly lessons and a piano for me to practice on every day, two hours a day, from four until six.

When my mother told me this, I felt as though I had been sent to hell. I whined, and then kicked my foot a little when I couldn't stand it anymore.

"Why don't you like me the way I am?" I cried. "I'm *not* a genius! I can't play the piano. And even if I could, I wouldn't go on TV if you paid me a million dollars!" 25

My mother slapped me. "Who ask you to be genius?" she shouted. "Only ask you be your best. For you sake. You think I want you to be genius? Hnnh! What for! Who ask you!"

"So ungrateful," I heard her mutter in Chinese, "If she had as much talent as she has temper, she'd be famous now."

Mr. Chong, whom I secretly nicknamed Old Chong, was very strange, always tapping his fingers to the silent music of an invisible orchestra. He looked ancient in my eyes. He had lost most of the hair on the top of his head, and he wore thick glasses and had eyes that always looked tired. But he must have been younger than I thought, since he lived with his mother and was not yet married.

I met Old Lady Chong once, and that was enough. She had a peculiar smell, like a baby that had done something in its pants, and her fingers felt like a dead person's, like an old peach I once found in the back of the refrigerator: its skin just slid off the flesh when I picked it up.

I soon found out why Old Chong had 30 retired from teaching piano. He was deaf. "Like Beethoven!" he shouted to me: "We're both listening only in our head!" And he would start to conduct his frantic silent sonatas.

Our lessons went like this. He would open the book and point to different things, explaining their purpose: "Key! Treble! Bass! No sharps or flats! So this is C major! Listen now and play after me!"

And then he would play the C scale a few times, a simple chord, and then, as if inspired by an old unreachable itch, he would gradually add more notes and running trills and a pounding bass until the music was really something quite grand.

I would play after him, the simple scale, the simple chord, and then just play some nonsense that sounded like a cat running up and down on top of garbage cans. Old Chong would smile and applaud and say "Very good! But now you must learn to keep time!"

So that's how I discovered that Old Chong's eyes were too slow to keep up with the wrong notes I was playing. He went through the motions in half time. To help me keep rhythm, he stood behind me and pushed down on my right shoulder for every beat. He balanced pennies on top of my wrists so that I would keep them still as I slowly played scales and arpeggios. He had me curve my hand around an apple and keep that shape when playing chords. He marched stiffly to show me how to make each finger dance up and down, staccato, like an obedient little soldier.

He taught me all these things and that was 35 how I also learned I could be lazy and get away with mistakes, lots of mistakes. If I hit the wrong notes because I hadn't practiced enough, I never corrected myself; I just kept playing in rhythm. And Old Chong kept conducting his own private reverie.

So maybe I never really gave myself a fair chance. I did pick up the basics pretty quickly, and I might have become a good pianist at the young age. But I was so determined not to try, not to be anybody different, and I learned to play only the most ear-splitting preludes, the most discordant hymns.

Over the next year I practiced like this, dutifully in my own way. And then one day I heard my mother and her friend Lindo Jong both after church, and I was leaning against a brick wall, wearing a dress with stiff white petticoats. Auntie Lindo's daughter, Waverly, who was my age, was standing farther down the wall, about five feet away. We had grown up together and shared all the closeness of two sisters, squabbling over crayons and dolls. In other words, for the

Talent, a painting by Russian artist Nikolai Petrovich Bogdanov-Belsky (1868–1945), depicts a young violinist playing for an older man.

What conclusions can you draw about the young boy's musical abilities? What visual elements in the painting support your observation? In what ways is the boy's situation in the image above similar to or different from Jing-mei's?

Album/Alamy

most part, we hated each other. I thought she was snotty. Waverly Jong had gained a certain amount of fame as "Chinatown's Littlest Chinese Chess Champion."

"She bring home too many trophy," Auntie Lindo lamented that Sunday. "All day she play chess. All day I have no time do nothing but dust off her winnings." She threw a scolding look at Waverly, who pretended not to see her.

"You lucky you don't have this problem," Auntie Lindo said with a sigh to my mother.

And my mother squared her shoulders and 40 bragged: "Our problem worser than yours. If we ask Jing-mei wash dish, she hear nothing but music. It's like you can't stop this natural talent."

And right then I was determined to put a stop to her foolish pride.

A few weeks later Old Chong and my mother conspired to have me play in a talent show that was to be held in the church hall. But then my parents had saved up enough to buy me a secondhand piano, a black Wurlitzer spinet with a scarred bench. It was the showpiece of our living room.

For the talent show I was to play a piece called "Pleading Child," from Schumann's *Scenes from Childhood*. It was a simple, moody piece that sounded more difficult than it was. I was supposed to memorize the whole thing. But I dawdled over it, playing a few bars and then cheating, looking up to see what notes followed. I never really listened to what I was playing. I daydreamed about being somewhere else, about being someone else.

The part I liked to practice best was the fancy curtsy: right foot out, touch the rose on the carpet with a pointed foot, sweep to the side, bend left leg, look up, and smile.

My parents invited all the couples from their social club to witness my debut. Auntie Lindo and Uncle Tin were there. Waverly and her two older brothers had also come. The first two rows were filled with children either younger or older than I was. The littlest ones got to go first. They recited simple nursery rhymes, squawked out tunes on miniature violins, and twirled hula hoops in pink ballet tutus, and when they bowed or curtsied, the audience would sigh in unison, "Awww," and then clap enthusiastically.

When my turn came, I was very confident. 45 I remember my childish excitement. It was as if I knew, without a doubt, that the prodigy side of me really did exist. I had no fear whatsoever, no nervousness. I remember thinking, This is it! This is it! I looked out over the audience, at my mother's blank face, my father's yawn, Auntie Lindo's stiff-lipped smile, Waverly's sulky expression. I had on a white dress, layered with sheets of lace, and a pink bow in my Peter Pan haircut. As I sat down, I envisioned people jumping to their feet and Ed Sullivan rushing up to introduce me to everyone on TV.

And I started to play. Everything was so beautiful. I was so caught up in how lovely I looked that I wasn't worried about how I would sound. So I was surprised when I hit the first wrong note. And then I hit another and another. A chill started at the top of my head and began to trickle down. Yet I couldn't stop playing, as though my hands were bewitched. I kept thinking my fingers would adjust themselves back, like a train switching to the right track. I played this strange jumble through to the end, the sour notes staying with me all the way.

When I stood up, I discovered my legs were shaking. Maybe I had just been nervous, and the audience, like Old Chong, had seen me go through the right motions and had not heard anything wrong at all. I swept my right foot out, went down on my knee, looked up, and smiled. The room was quiet, except for Old Chong, who was beaming and shouting "Bravo! Bravo! Well done!" By then I saw my mother's face, her stricken face. The audience clapped weakly, and I walked back to my chair, with my whole face quivering as I tried not to cry, I heard a little boy whisper loudly to his mother, "That was awful," and his mother whispered "Well, she certainly tried."

And now I realized how many people were in the audience — the whole world, it seemed. I was aware of eyes burning into my back. I felt the shame of my mother and father as they sat stiffly through the rest of the show.

We could have escaped during intermission. Pride and some strange sense of honor must have anchored my parents to their chairs. And so we watched it all. The eighteen-year-old boy with a fake moustache who did a magic show and juggled flaming hoops while riding a unicycle. The breasted girl with white make up who sang an aria from *Madame Butterfly* and got an

honorable mention. And the eleven-year-old boy who won first prize playing a tricky violin song that sounded like a busy bee.

After the show the Hsus, the Jongs, and the St. Clairs from the Joy Luck Club, came up to my mother and father.

"Lots of talented kids," Auntie Lindo said vaguely, smiling broadly. "That was somethin' else," my father said, and I wondered if he was referring to me in a humorous way, or whether he even remembered what I had done.

Waverly looked at me and shrugged her shoulders. "You aren't a genius like me," she said matter-of-factly. And if I hadn't felt so bad, I would have pulled her braids and punched her stomach.

But my mother's expression was what devastated me: a quiet, blank look that said she had lost everything. I felt the same way, and everybody seemed now to be coming up, like gawkers at the scene of an accident to see what parts were actually missing.

When we got on the bus to go home, my father was humming the busy-bee tune and my mother kept silent. I kept thinking she wanted to wait until we got home before shouting at me. But when my father unlocked the door to our apartment, my mother walked in and went straight to the back, into the bedroom. No accusations, No blame. And in a way, I felt disappointed. I had been waiting for her to start shouting, so that I could shout back and cry and blame her for all my misery.

I had assumed that my talent-show fiasco meant that I would never have to play the piano again. But two days later, after school, my mother came out of the kitchen and saw me watching TV. "Four clock," she reminded me, as if it were any other day. I was stunned, as though she were asking me to go through the talent-show torture again. I planted myself more squarely in front of the TV. "Turn off TV," she called from the kitchen five minutes later. I didn't budge. And then I decided, I didn't have to do what mother said anymore. I wasn't her slave. This wasn't China. I had listened to her before, and look what happened. She was the stupid one.

She came out of the kitchen and stood in the arched entryway of the living room. "Four clock," she said once again, louder.

"I'm not going to play anymore," I said nonchalantly. "Why should I? I'm not a genius."

She stood in front of the TV. I saw that her chest was heaving up and down in an angry way.

"No!" I said, and I now felt stronger, as if my true self had finally emerged. So this was what had been inside me all along.

"No! I won't!" I screamed. She snapped off the TV, yanked me by the arm and pulled me off the floor. She was frighteningly strong, half pulling, half carrying me towards the piano as I kicked the throw rugs under my feet. She lifted me up onto the hard bench. I was sobbing by now, looking at her bitterly. Her chest was heaving even more and her mouth was open, smiling crazily as if she were pleased that I was crying.

"You want me to be something that I'm not!" I sobbed. "I'll never be the kind of daughter you want me to be!"

"Only two kinds of daughters," she shouted in Chinese. "Those who are obedient and those who follow their own mind! Only one kind of daughter can live in this house. Obedient daughter!"

"Then I wish I weren't your daughter, I wish you weren't my mother," I shouted. As I said these things I got scared. It felt like worms and toads and slimy things crawling out of my chest, but it also felt good, that this awful side of me had surfaced, at last.

"Too late to change this," my mother said shrilly.

And I could sense her anger rising to its breaking point. I wanted see it spill over. And 65

that's when I remembered the babies she had lost in China, the ones we never talked about. "Then I wish I'd never been born!" I shouted. "I wish I were dead! Like them."

It was as if I had said magic words. Alakazam! — her face went blank, her mouth closed, her arms went slack, and she backed out of the room, stunned, as if she were blowing away like a small brown leaf, thin, brittle, lifeless.

It was not the only disappointment my mother felt in me. In the years that followed, I failed her many times, each time asserting my will, my right to fall short of expectations. I didn't get straight *As*. I didn't become class president. I didn't get into Stanford. I dropped out of college.

Unlike my mother, I did not believe I could be anything I wanted to be, I could only be me.

And for all those years we never talked about the disaster at the recital or my terrible declarations afterward at the piano bench. Neither of us talked about it again, as if it were a betrayal that was now unspeakable. So I never found a way to ask her why she had hoped for something so large that failure was inevitable. And even worse, I never asked her about what frightened me the most: Why had she given up hope? For after our struggle at the piano, she never mentioned my playing again. The lessons stopped. The lid to the piano was closed shutting out the dust, my misery, and her dreams.

So she surprised me. A few years ago she 70 offered to give me the piano, for my thirtieth birthday. I had not played in all those years. I saw the offer as a sign of forgiveness, a tremendous burden removed. "Are you sure?" I asked shyly. "I mean, won't you and Dad miss it?" "No, this your piano," she said firmly. "Always your piano. You only one can play."

"Well, I probably can't play anymore," I said. "It's been years." "You pick up fast," my

Portrait of Wolfgang Amadeus Mozart at the piano (oil on canvas)/Re, Giovanni del (1829–1915)/GIANCARLO COSTA/Museo Nazionale della Scienza e della Tecnologia 'Leonardo Da Vinci', Milan, Italy/Bridgeman Images

This painting of Mozart was created by the artist after Mozart's lifetime and so the two never crossed paths.

How has the artist portrayed Mozart in this painting? What elements in the painting — the composition, the colors, or the scenery — convey the artist's overall impression of the young prodigy? Do you find any similarities between this depiction of Mozart and Jing-mei's character? Explain.

mother said, as if she knew this was certain. "You have natural talent. You could be a genius if you want to." "No, I couldn't." "You just not trying," my mother said. And she was neither angry nor sad. She said it as if announcing a fact that could never be disproved. "Take it," she said.

But I didn't at first. It was enough that she had offered it to me. And after that, every time I saw it in my parents' living room, standing in front of the bay window, it made me feel proud, as if it were a shiny trophy that I had won back.

Last week I sent a tuner over to my parent's apartment and had the piano reconditioned, for purely sentimental reasons. My mother had died a few months before and I had been getting things in order for my father a little bit at a time. I put the jewelry in special silk pouches. The sweaters I put in mothproof boxes. I found some old Chinese silk dresses, the kind with little slits up the sides. I rubbed the old silk against my skin, and then wrapped them in tissue and decided to take them home with me.

After I had the piano tuned, I opened the lid and touched the keys. It sounded even richer than I remembered. Really, it was a very good piano. Inside the bench were the same exercise notes with handwritten scales, the same secondhand music books with their covers held together with yellow tape. I opened up the Schumann book to the dark little piece I had played at the recital. It was on the left-hand page, "Pleading Child." It looked more difficult than I remembered. I played a few bars, surprised at how easily the notes came back to me.

And for the first time, or so it seemed, I noticed the piece on the right-hand side. It was called "Perfectly Contented." I tried to play this one as well. It had a lighter melody but with the same flowing rhythm and turned out to be quite easy. "Pleading Child" was shorter but slower; "Perfectly Contented" was longer but faster. And after I had played them both a few times, I realized they were two halves of the same song. ■

75

Understanding and Interpreting

1. In what ways does Jing-mei's mother try to train her to become a prodigy in paragraphs 6–10? What is Jing-mei's response to her mother's tests in paragraph 13?

2. Jing-mei's view of herself shifts when she looks in the mirror in paragraph 11. What is the significance of what she sees in her reflection? How does she redefine her understanding of what a prodigy is?

3. Jing-mei expresses surprise that her performance at the recital was so horrible. Given that she has fought her mother and piano practice for so long, what does her reaction to the recital reveal about her?

4. The story depicts the struggle between a mother and daughter as they grapple with their relationship, but it also depicts the tension between Chinese and American cultures. How are these two conflicts related? How does the cultural conflict connect to the mother–daughter conflict? What role do these conflicts play in progressing the plot of the story?

5. In paragraphs 37–40, we are given brief details of the mother's encounter with Auntie Lindo. How does knowing the mother's interaction with Auntie Lindo shape our understanding of her motives to push Jing-mei? What can be said about her motivation for her daughter's success?

6. In paragraphs 38–40, what is the significance of the conversation between Jing-mei's mother and Auntie Lindo in relation to the overall conflict of the story?

7. How does telling the story from Jing-mei's point of view both enrich and limit our understanding of the plot? Considering the age of Jing-mei, what effect does her point of view have on the reader's understanding of the events in the story? What information might we be missing when given only one perspective?

8. In paragraph 62, Jing-mei's mother explains that there are only two kinds of daughters, "Those who are obedient and those who follow their own mind!" How does this information influence your understanding of the mother's motivations and her expectations for Jing-mei?

9. What does Jing-mei mean by "I could only be me" in paragraph 68? Is this an assertion of her identity, or a confession of failure? Explain.

10. Explain what Jing-mei means when she realizes that the songs "Pleading Child" and "Perfectly Contented" can be two halves of the same (pars. 74–75). What might the songs symbolize?

11. Though the story is not told through the mother's point of view, how does Tan include details that provide insight from the mother's perspective?

12. The setting of a story relates not only to time and place but also the social environment. Consider the relationship of the characters in the story to time, place, and circumstance. How does the setting contribute to the conflict in the story?

Analyzing Language, Style, and Structure

13. **Vocabulary in Context.** Reread the sentence from paragraph 14, that says "the TV broke into loud piano music." What does the word *broke* mean in this context?

14. **Vocabulary in Context.** In paragraph 40, when comparing their daughters' accomplishments, Jing-mei's mother "squared her shoulders" to brag about Jing-mei's piano playing. What does the word *squared* mean in this context?

15. In paragraph 20, Jing-mei says about the girl on the *Ed Sullivan Show* that "she's trying hard." Later, in paragraph 47, a boy's mother says about Jing-mei that "she certainly tried." How are these two related statements similar and different in word choice and meaning?

16. What is the effect of portraying the mother's broken English in the dialogue? What might Tan be implying about the conflict between Jing-mei and her mother?

17. How is the word *prodigy* defined differently by mother and daughter? In what ways, if at all, do they share the same idea of being a "prodigy"? What do their definitions of the word *prodigy* reveal about their conflict with each other?

18. How does the "obedient little soldier" simile in paragraph 34 reflect Jing-mei's thoughts about her life?

19. How does Tan use language to establish tone in paragraph 69? What evidence can you find to support your observation?

20. This story ends in the voice of the adult Jing-mei, and we realize that the story is told by Jing-mei looking back on her childhood. How do you think this perspective affects how the story is told? What is the effect of structuring the story this way? What aspects of the story might be different if they were told from the perspective of the young Jing-mei?

Topics for Composing

21. **Analysis.** The story begins, "My mother believed you could be anything you wanted to be in America." How is this theme developed, and complicated, throughout the story? What evidence might suggest that there are flaws in the mother's idea of the American Dream?

22. **Analysis.** "Two Kinds" explores the relationship between a mother and daughter. Using evidence from the story, write an analysis that explores how Tan reveals the complexity of the relationship between Jing-mei and her mother over time.

23. **Analysis.** In paragraph 6, Jing-mei says that she pictured her prodigy side "as many different images, and [she] tried each one on for size." Trace the various images Jing-mei tries on over the course of this story, and consider how each phase ultimately leads to her character becoming "perfectly contented."

24. **Argument.** Although Jing-mei's mother insists that she only wants Jing-mei to "do her best," she continually pressures Jing-mei to pursue excellence. Write a response in which you argue whether the pressure to excel can actually do more harm than good, or if it is a necessary part of achievement. Use evidence from the story, or from additional research, to support your response.

25. **Connections.** One of the conflicts that Tan makes clear is the competition between rivals (Waverly and Jing-mei; Auntie Lindo and Jing-mei's mother). What motivates these rivalries? Is it pride? Jealousy? Think of a similar competitive rivalry between characters in another text or two people in your life and write a response about the nature of that rivalry. How does your journal entry enhance your understanding of the rivalries in this story?

26. **Connections.** American author Dean Koontz says that "everyone has a talent, ability, or skill that he can mine to support himself and to succeed in life." Write about a special talent that you possess. It can be academic, musical, athletic, or something else. How is your family's way of encouraging this talent similar to or different from methods of encouragement in Jing-mei's family? If you want, consider sharing your talent with the class in the form of a demonstration, video, or other presentation.

27. **Research.** In 1949, Tan's parents immigrated to America when the Communist Party seized control of China. Like many immigrants, they hoped to secure a better future for their children. Research what family life was like in late 1940s China and America. Identify one or two cultural challenges Chinese immigrants faced in America when trying to balance their identity between two cultures. What connections can you make between what you discovered and the events in the story.

28. **Research.** Conduct interviews with athletes, musicians, artists, and academically talented students at your school about what motivates them to succeed. Then create a chart or graph showing the results. Include quotations from some of the individuals you interviewed.

29. **Creative Writing.** Try rewriting the piano recital scene where instead of failing miserably, Jing-mei actually has a stellar performance. How might the events and character responses that immediately follow be different?

30. **Multimodal.** Create a mini-documentary focused on yourself or another talented individual in your school, neighborhood, or community, showing the journey to becoming successful. You may want to storyboard a plan for the video, taking into consideration your audience, what information should be captured, the camera angles, setting, timing, and background music, if any.

conversation

How are our interests and passions shaped?

The "Great Resignation," as coined by the organizational psychologist Anthony Klotz, began during the COVID-19 pandemic and resulted in millions of Americans quitting or resigning from their jobs. A record high of as many as four million[1] people quit their jobs in August, 2021 alone. Why the mass exodus? Some of the reasons revolve around better pay and more flexibility working from home, but many of those leaving their jobs cited burnout and the need to do something more engaging and fulfilling. Many used the pandemic to reevaluate their well-being and rediscovered interests and passions that bring them balance and joy. The pandemic and changing economy played a large part in leading some people to find, or rekindle, their interests and passions.

In Amy Tan's short story, "Two Kinds," Jing-mei's mother tries to force piano playing on Jing-mei instead of allowing her daughter to choose something she's actually interested in. Jing-mei pushes back against her mother in equal measure because playing the piano holds no interest for her. Jing-mei mostly complies out of fear of disappointing her mother and her desire to compete with her cousin; her mother applies tremendous pressure on Jing-mei, which ultimately results in her giving up on the piano. Would it have been different had Jing-mei loved the piano and pursued it for her own interests?

---

[1]Ben Casselman. "Workers quitting their jobs hit a record in the U.S. in August." *New York Times,* Oct. 2021.

In the collection of texts that follows, you will read about how different people found their passions and interests and who influenced those passions and interests the most. This Conversation includes a variety of viewpoints on the issue. After reading them, you will have an opportunity to enter the conversation by sharing your own viewpoint in response to the following question — *Who influences our passions and interests the most: peers, society, or family?*

 activity ## Starting the Conversation

Take a moment to write informally about your initial thinking on this topic before you explore it further by reading additional texts.

1. Jot down things you are passionate about. Looking at your list, indicate one thing that you enjoy doing above all the others. Then, think about who has influenced your passions and interests the most: peers, society, or family.

2. With a partner or small group, discuss the passion that you selected and talk about who or what influenced your passion.

3. Create a table like the one below to help you keep track of ideas related to how passions and interests are influenced, and your own responses to the ideas you encounter in the texts you read:

Title/Author	Who Shapes Our Interests and Passions the Most?	Best Evidence	Your Response

Source A

Renninger, K. Ann and Suzanne Hidi. *The Power of Interest for Motivation and Engagement.* 2015.

Interest is powerful. The triggering of interest initiates productive engagement and the potential for optimal motivation. A person is said to be interested in some activity, such as writing, playing bridge, or fantasy football, if they voluntarily engage in thinking about it, happily prioritize the problems that arise . . . and are willing to persevere to address them. Until recently, it has not been clear that regardless of a person's age or prior experience, interests like these can be triggered and can be supported to develop. A person's interest makes persistence feel effortless and increases the possibility of achievement and creative contribution . . . .

[S]upport provided by the home environment has been widely acknowledged to be critical in providing a foundation as well as a language for engaging with particular disciplines (e.g., music, science). Given its benefit for learning, and differences of early experience, it seems to be incumbent on educators, in particular, to take responsibility for supporting the development of their students' interest.

It is also essential to consider an individual's value for and knowledge of content, and/or the behaviors to enable assessment of this information. [A common] misconception is that a person who has more developed interest does not need support; research shows that this assumption is not valid. Even when a person's interest is already developing, it is most likely to thrive when there is support for its continued development. Without opportunities to continue to deepen and develop, even a well-developed interest may go dormant or drop off. Parents, educators, and employers play an important role in how interest develops and whether it is sustained.

[A]ll persons can develop interest and . . . as interest develops, a person is likely to voluntarily seek the information and resources needed for continued learning. When interest is supported to deepen and develop, motivation and engagement are most likely to be effectively cultivated. ■

Questions

1. According to the authors in the first paragraph, why is "interest" so important?
2. What is the connection between "learning" and "interests," as described in this article?
3. What roles do parents, educators, and employers play in developing and sustaining someone's interests?
4. **Comparison.** To what extent does Jing-mei's mother follow the suggestions described in this article in developing Jing-mei's interests?
5. **Informing Your Argument.** Return to the table you created on page 342. Fill in the column with who, or what, shapes our interests and passions the most, the best evidence the text offers to clarify and support those ideas, and your response to what the text suggests.

Source B

Agassi, Andre. from *Open: An Autobiography*. 2009.

I'm seven years old, talking to myself, because I'm scared, and because I'm the only person who listens to me. Under my breath I whisper: Just quit, Andre, just give up. Put down your racket and walk off this court, right now. . . .

Wouldn't that feel like heaven, Andre? To just quit? To never play tennis again? But I can't. Not only would my father chase me around the house with my racket, but something in my gut, some deep unseen muscle, won't let me . . . I have no choice. . . .

My father says that if I hit 2,500 balls each day, I'll hit 17,500 balls each week, and at the end of one year I'll have hit nearly one million balls. He believes in math. Numbers, he says, don't lie. A child who hits one million balls each year will be unbeatable. Hit earlier, my father yells. Damn it, Andre, hit earlier. Crowd the ball, crowd the ball. Now he's crowding me. He's yelling directly into my ear. It's not enough to hit everything . . . my father wants me to hit it harder and faster. . . .

John Russell/Hulton Archive/Getty Images

Denver Post/Getty Images

Abaca Press/Alamy

The top left photo shows Andre Agassi practicing as a child. His sister (top right) also learned to play tennis at a young age. The bottom photo captures Agassi's reaction to losing his final career match at the U.S. Open Tennis Championships in 2006.

Thinking, my father believes, is the source of all bad things, because thinking is the opposite of doing. When my father catches me thinking, daydreaming, on the tennis court, he reacts as if he caught me taking money from his wallet. I often think about how I can stop thinking. I wonder if my father yells at me to stop thinking because he knows I'm a thinker by nature. Or, with all his yelling, has he turned me into a thinker? Is my thinking about things other than tennis an act of defiance? I like to think so. ■

Questions

1. In this excerpt, Agassi describes the differences between what he wants to do and what he actually does. How does this contradiction affect his interest in and motivation for tennis?

2. What role does his father play in shaping Agassi's interests and passions?

3. This excerpt is written by an older Agassi looking back on his childhood and the pressure from his father to play a game he wanted to quit. Look at the photographs of Agassi and his sister, also a tennis player. Knowing what you know about their father, what, if anything, can you interpret about them from the images?

4. **Comparison.** How is Agassi similar to Jing-mei in his desire to succeed? How is he different? Consider also the image of Agassi's reaction to losing his final career match. How is his reaction in that photo similar to or different from Jing-mei's reaction to her failed recital performance?

5. **Informing Your Argument.** Return to the table that you created on page 342. Fill in the columns about who Agassi suggests influenced his passion, the best evidence he offers to clarify and support his ideas, and your response to what Agassi is suggesting.

Source C

Dreilinger, Danielle. "How Important Is Passion? It Depends on Your Culture." *Greater Good Magazine*, 2 Apr. 2021.

Imagine you're hiring for a job or admitting students to a college: One applicant expresses great passion for the work, while another points to family encouragement to attend that institution or pursue that field. Which applicant is more likely to succeed?

Conventional wisdom — at least in the United States — suggests it would be the one who cites a strong personal passion. But according to a new Stanford-led study, the answer depends on the applicant's culture.

Passion is not "a universally powerful cornerstone of achievement," the researchers found, and the culture a person grew up in makes a big difference. That means universities and companies that rely on passion in candidates are missing out on talent, especially applicants from low-income, non-white, immigrant communities.

The study, published in March [of 2021] in the *Proceedings of the National Academy of Sciences*, finds that passion — measured as felt interest, enjoyment, and efficacy — is a much stronger predictor of achievement in certain societies than others.

The research is novel for its approach of using big data to evaluate cultural differences in the real world, said Xingyu Li, a doctoral student at Stanford Graduate School of Education and lead author of the study. It also compares a wider range of culturally diverse societies than previous studies examining the link between passion and achievement.

The study's findings suggest a blind spot among gatekeepers in U.S. education and employment, who frequently rely on "passion" as a major metric to pluck out top applicants, Li said.

5

That means they risk "passing over and mismanaging talented students and employees who increasingly come from sociocultural contexts where a more interdependent model of motivation is common and effective," Li and her coauthors write. Those include many low-income European Americans and also first-generation immigrant communities in the United States.

"We need to make our admission and hiring processes fair to people from diverse backgrounds," Li said. . . .

The authors [of the study] emphasize that an individualistic model of motivation is not objectively better. In the United States, doing well because of what others expect might seem to be evidence of a lack of potential, a sign that you've been coerced to do what's required. But "interdependent forms of motivation need not feel overbearing and corrosive to personal autonomy," the authors write — instead, they can be a source of empowerment, persistence, and resilience.

"Motivation can be fueled by fulfilling expectations and contributing to the success and well-being of your family and others close to you," Markus said.

The findings open up the possibility of designing educational interventions that don't rely only on the Western idea of cultivating passion and grit as an individual but instead tap into how parents, teachers, and peers can create more collectivist motivational systems, said Geoffrey Cohen, a professor of education and psychology at Stanford and a coauthor of the study.

"We'll be better able to unlock the potential of our students and our workforce if we have a broader and more enriched understanding of what drives people from a wide range of backgrounds," he said. ∎

Questions

1. According to the research by doctoral student Xingyu Li that Dreilinger cites, why should employers be careful about relying on "passion" as an indicator of potential success of a job candidate?

2. What points does Dreilinger include about individualistic and collective approaches to motivation, and why is the difference between them important?

3. What steps do those cited in the article suggest will improve the process for identifying talented students and employees?

4. **Comparison.** In what specific ways do you think Tan and Dreilinger would agree about cultural influence on motivation? How do the ideas brought up by the study in Dreilinger's argument either support or call into question the approach Jing-mei's mother takes with her daughter?

5. **Informing Your Argument.** Return to the table you created on page 342. Fill in the column about what Dreilinger argues influences our passions the most, the best evidence she offers to clarify and support her ideas, and your response to what Dreilinger suggests.

Source D

Chazelle, Damien. *Whiplash*, 2014.

KEY CONTEXT *Whiplash* (2014), written and directed by Damien Chazelle, is a film about an aspiring drummer, Andrew Neyman, who is pressured by his overbearing music instructor, Terence Fletcher, to become part of the elite jazz orchestra at a prestigious music school. Fletcher often uses verbal and physical abuse when working with Andrew as seen this image. Later in the film, Fletcher references jazz saxophonist Charlie Parker, whose instructor once threw a cymbal at a young Charlie because he made a mistake. Fletcher emphasizes that this action made Charlie practice even more and essentially led to his becoming a renowned jazz musician in the 1940s and early 1950s. Below is part of the exchange that occurs between Andrew and Terence regarding this event.

ANDREW NEYMAN But is there a line? You know, maybe you go too far and discourage the next Charlie Parker from ever becoming Charlie Parker?

TERENCE FLETCHER No, man, no. Because the next Charlie Parker would never be discouraged. ∎

Pictorial Press Ltd / Alamy

Questions

1. In the dialogue quoted above the image, what does Andrew mean by "a line," and what does Terence's response suggest about how he views talent and motivation?

2. How do specific elements of this image — including body language, facial expressions, and framing — portray a specific relationship between teacher and student? How would you characterize that relationship based on the image?

3. **Comparison.** In what ways is the relationship between teacher and student in this image similar to and different from the relationship between Jing-mei and her mother?

4. **Informing Your Argument.** Return to the table you created on page 342. Based on this image, add your thoughts regarding what this film might suggest about who influences our passions the most, the best evidence it offers to clarify and support related ideas, and your response to what the image suggests.

Entering the Conversation

Throughout this Conversation, you have read a variety of texts that deal with identifying interests and passions. Now it's time to enter the conversation by responding to the prompt you've been thinking about — ***Who has the greatest influence on our passions and interests: peers, society, or family?*** Follow these steps to write your argument:

1. | Building on the Conversation. Locate one additional text on this topic that you think adds an interesting perspective to this Conversation. This text can be of any type — an argument, a narrative, a poem, a painting, or a film clip, for example. Before you decide to add this text to the Conversation, be sure that it is a credible and relevant source, which you can determine by evaluating it with the skills you practiced in Chapter 4 (p. 99). Read and annotate the text carefully, making connections to other texts in the Conversation and "Two Kinds."

2. | Making a Claim. Look back through the table you created and your notes on the texts in the conversation and write a statement that reflects your overall position about who has the greatest influence on interests and passions. This statement will be your thesis or claim that you will try to prove in the rest of your argument.

3. | Organizing the Ideas. The texts in this Conversation offer a number of explanations for how interests and passions are influenced. Review the table you have been keeping throughout this Conversation and identify the texts and quotations that either directly support or oppose the claim that you wrote in the earlier step.

4. | Writing the Argument. Now that you have a claim that reflects your informed stance, it is time to write your argument. Be sure that your writing stays focused on your position on the issue, and refer to at least two Conversation texts, which could include the additional text you found to support your position. Review Chapter 4 (p. 119) to remind yourself of how to use sources in your own writing, and refer to the Writing an Argument Workshop in Chapter 7 (p. 466) for more help with constructing and supporting your argument.

5. | Presenting the Argument (Optional). Once you have written your argument, you might want to present it to the class or a small group. Review how to write and deliver a presentation in Chapter 3 (p. 90) and Chapter 7 (p. 479).

The Morningside

Téa Obreht

Photo © Graham Jepson/Opale/Bridgeman Images

Born in Belgrade, Serbia, Téa Obreht (1985-), is a bestselling and award-winning author whose novels include *The Tiger's Wife* (2011) and *Inland* (2019). In 2010, she was recognized by *The New Yorker* as one of the 20 best American fiction writers under 40.

KEY CONTEXT   This short story appeared in *The Decameron Project*, for which editors at the *New York Times* asked authors to write new short stories inspired by the COVID-19 pandemic that began in 2019. The editors were inspired by Italian writer Giovanni Boccaccio's fourteenth-century work *The Decameron*, which was written as the Black Death, a bubonic plague pandemic, ravaged much of Europe.

Long ago, back when everyone had gone, we lived in a tower called the Morningside at the same time as this woman named Bezi Duras — she seemed old to me then, but as I'm now approaching what was probably her age myself, I'm beginning to think she wasn't.

The people for whom the tower was built had all left the city, and the new apartments sat empty until someone at the top figured having a few units occupied might give the looters pause. My late father had served the city with some loyalty and brains, so my mother and I were allowed to move in at a greatly reduced price. When we walked home from the bakery at night, the Morningside loomed before us with just a few thin, lighted windows skittering up the black edifice like notes of a secret song.

My mother and I lived on the 10th floor. Bezi Duras lived on the 14th. We knew this because we sometimes got caught in the elevator when she summoned it and had to ride up and then interminably back down with her, and her powerful tobacco smell, and the three huge, barrel-chested black dogs who towed her around the neighborhood at sundown.

Small and sharp-featured, Bezi was a source of fascination for all. She had come to the city after some faraway war whose particulars nobody, not even my mother, seemed to fully grasp. Nobody knew where she'd gotten such fine clothes, or what connection she had managed to press to get herself into the Morningside. She spoke to the dogs in a language nobody understood, and the police came around every so often to check whether the dogs had finally overpowered and eaten her, as they were said to have done to some poor bastard who tried to rob her on one of her walks. The incident was

Though the setting of the story is not identified as a specific neighborhood in New York City, the Morningside Tower could be located in the Morningside Heights neighborhood of Manhattan. This is a picture of Manhattan during the forced lockdowns that were a part of the response to the COVID-19 pandemic.

What does this image communicate to the viewer about that time, and how is the setting in this image similar to or different from what Obreht describes in the first paragraphs of this story?

only a rumor, of course, but it was enough for the building to begin petitioning her to get rid of the dogs.

"Well, that'll never happen," my friend Arlo, who lived in the park with his macaw, told me. 5

"Why?"

"Because, honey, those dogs are her brothers."

I was never under the illusion that Arlo meant this in some metaphorical sense. In fact, he'd heard it from the macaw, who'd heard it from the dogs personally. They had been beautiful boys once, charming and accomplished; but somewhere in the course of Bezi's journey from her homeland to ours, life made it impossible for them to accompany her in their God-given forms. So according to Arlo, Bezi had struck a bargain with some entity, who turned them into dogs.

"Those dogs?" I asked, thinking of their foam-coated jowls and furrowed faces.

"They do make an impression. But I guess that's the point." 10

"But why?"

"Well, they're more welcome here than most people, honey."

I gave Arlo a hard time about a lot of things, but I believed him about the dogs — mostly because I was 8 and felt his macaw incapable of telling a lie. Also, there was plenty of evidence to favor his theory. Those dogs ate better than we did. Every other afternoon, Bezi would come back from the butcher's laden with paper bags, and afterward the whole building smelled of roasted bones. She never spoke to the dogs in anything louder than a whisper, and they walked in a tight V around her when they left the building every night, never to be seen until the next morning, when she would come hurrying along the dawn-reddened street behind them as though only a matter of seconds stood between her and the total unraveling of her life. Her apartment, four floors above, had the same floor plan as our own, and it was easy to picture the dogs roaming around her cavernous place, following her with their yellow eyes, snoring on the white painter's tarp I always imagined covering the floor.

There were a lot of easily-deducible things people missed about Bezi. That she was clearly a painter was the most significant one. Her ornate jackets and fine leather boots were always splashed with color. It darkened her nail beds, speckled her eyelashes, so bright that it was easily observable from the tree I sometimes watched her from at the end of the block, and in which the dogs occasionally sniffed me out, surrounding the trunk and roaring with frustration until Bezi's head finally appeared below, and she started in on me in that rickety language she had brought from home.

"You understand her, right?" I once asked my friend Ena, who had moved to New York from what I gathered was more or less the same place as Bezi.

"No," said Ena scornfully. "It's a completely different language."

"It sounds similar."

"Well, it's not."

Ena moved in with her aunt on the fourth floor only the previous year, after her family spent seven months at the quarantine depot, where Ena caught some illness — not the one for which she was being screened, mind you — and lost about half her body weight, so that when we walked down the street together, I felt obliged to tether her to me with one hand lest she blow away up the hill and into the river. She seemed unaware of her own smallness. She was grim and green-eyed, and had learned to pick locks in the camp (I always thought she meant camp

as in summer camp; but she always called it the camp, which I eventually understood was different). Anyway, her lock-picking got us into parts of the Morningside that were previously inaccessible to me: the basement pool, for instance, with its dry mermaid mosaics; or the rooftop, which put us at eye level with the dark parapets of midtown.

Ena's curiosity made her a natural skeptic. 20 She didn't buy into all that stuff about Bezi Duras's dog brothers turning into men from dawn till dusk — even when I laid out all the evidence and played "Swan Lake" for her.

"Who turned them?" she wanted to know.

"What?"

"Who turned them into dogs for her?"

"I don't know — aren't there people who do that kind of thing, where you come from?"

Ena grew red. "I'm telling you, Bezi Duras 25 and I don't come from the same place."

All summer, this disagreement proved the sourest thing between us; impossible to reconcile, because it was dredged up every time Bezi set off down the street for the butcher's.

"What if we got into her place to see for ourselves?" Ena said one afternoon. "It wouldn't be hard."

"But crazy," I said, "since we know the place is guarded by a bunch of dogs."

Ena smirked. "If you're right, though, wouldn't they actually be men?"

"Wouldn't that be worse?" I had the sense 30 that men in such a state would almost certainly be naked.

The possibility of breaking in to Bezi's place would probably have continued to serve as a mere goad, had Bezi not paused where we were sitting on the park wall one bright afternoon and stared hard at Ena. "You're Neven's daughter, aren't you?" Bezi eventually said.

"That's right."

"Do you know what they used to call your father, back where I come from?"

Ena shrugged in a practiced way. Nothing could move her: not her dead father's name, and not whatever Bezi said next in that language I couldn't understand. She just sat there with her thin little legs pressed against the wall. "Sorry," she said when Bezi finally quieted. "I don't understand you."

I suppose I should've known this would seal Ena's decision to break into Bezi's place. But I was naïve, and a little in love with her, and I had been there so often in my imaginary wanderings that it didn't seem all that remarkable when Ena pressed the up instead of down elevator button the following week. I believe I did say, "Let's not!" — only once, when Ena was already picking the lock, and only because I found myself sharply aware for the first time that we were, in fact, just kids.

The apartment was exactly the same as mine: still white hallways, a too-big kitchen with a marble countertop as thick as a cake. We followed the smell of paint into a parlor where a piano should have been. Leaning up against the wall there, surrounded on all sides by smaller canvases electric with color, stood the biggest painting I'd ever seen. The strokes were choppy and ragged, but the scene was easy enough to make out: a young woman was crossing a bridge from some little riverside town. Around her stood three empty spaces where the paint seemed to have been scrubbed away; presumably, I realized, this was where the dogs climbed out when they turned into their human form.

But they were not in their human form now. They were rousing themselves from a deep slumber where they lay sprawled out on that sure-enough paint-splattered tarp, sitting up one by one, as surprised, I think, to see us as we were to see them.

What would have happened had Bezi not come back at that exact moment, I really can't say. We probably would've ended up as one of those tragic statistics you read about in the

This is a painting of the Duchess of York from 1807.

Based on the narrator's description of the painting hanging in Bezi Duras's apartment, in what ways is this image similar or different?

paper that teach you what kind of being is safe and what kind is not.

"Well," Bezi said. "Neven's daughter. Twisted at heart — what a surprise."

"Go to hell," Ena said through her tears.

My mother never found out, and I guess Ena's didn't either. For years, that moment, known only to the three of us, was the first thing I thought about when I woke, and the last thing I thought about as I lay in the dark. I was certain I would revisit it every day of my life. And for a long time, even after we left the Morningside, I did. And then time passed, and eventually I did not. It would suddenly occur to me that a few days had gone by without my thinking about it — which, of course, would break my streak, and I'd feel relieved to find myself suddenly plunged back into that room, with its huge painting, and the dogs around it as though they were waiting to be called back into the world from which they had come. But then that got hazy, too. It became the kind of thing I'd tell lovers after deciding they would probably be sticking around. The kind of thing I hoped they'd forget about me when we parted ways.

By the time I stumbled on this story in the paper, I hadn't thought about it in years. A foreign painter of some celebrity died in the city last summer; the problem was, her body couldn't be retrieved because it was guarded by a pack of starving Rottweilers who would go wild if anyone so much as touched the door. Experts from all over the coast were brought in, but no one could find a command to subdue the dogs. It was decided that they should be shot, and a brave sniper was hoisted up on a window-washing rig for that purpose. But when he peered inside, he saw only the lifeless old woman, lying with her hands crossed on a tarp at the foot of an enormous painting of a princess and three young men. What exactly was he supposed to shoot? "It's baffling," he told the reporter "but there's really nothing for me to do here." After he packed up, the police tried the door again; and sure enough the dogs came roaring back.

Finally, after about a week of this, a woman who worked across town showed up at the police station. "I used to live there," she said. "I can help." The reporter didn't name her but described her as rail-thin, with huge green eyes, so I know it was Ena who went up there one wild evening with what was left of the city gathered in the courtyard below; Ena who stood outside the door, whispering endearments of some bygone age, of some place that no longer existed, in that language she'd always known the dogs would understand, until she heard them move back from the door, and she turned the knob saying don't worry, boys, it's all right, it's all right, it's all right. ■

extending beyond the text

As stated in the Key Context, the *New York Times* commissioned writing from renowned fiction authors to "build stories of solace for the belabored mind" during the COVID-19 pandemic. The intent was to channel Giovanni Boccaccio's original *Decameron* — a collection of stories written in the fourteenth century during the Black Death plague in Europe. Read a section from the first part of Boccaccio's *Decameron* below that features a group of young people and the queen in a secluded villa in Italy.

from The Decameron

Giovanni Boccaccio

[The 3 o'clock bell] had not long sounded when the queen, arising, made all the other ladies arise, and on like wise the three young men, alleging overmuch sleep to be harmful by day; and so they betook themselves to a little meadow, where the grass grew green and high nor there had the sun power on any side. There, feeling the waftings of a gentle breeze, they all, as their queen willed it, seated themselves in a ring on the green grass; while she bespoke them thus, "As ye see, the sun is high and the heat great, nor is aught heard save the crickets yonder among the olives; wherefore it were doubtless folly to go anywhither at this present. Here is the sojourn fair and

(continued)

cool, and here, as you see, are chess and tables, and each can divert himself as is most to his mind. But, an my counsel be followed in this, we shall pass away this sultry part of the day, not in gaming, — wherein the mind of one of the players must of necessity be troubled, without any great pleasure of the other or of those who look on, — but in telling stories, which, one telling, may afford diversion to all the company who hearken; nor shall we have made an end of telling each his story but the sun will have declined and the heat be abated, and we can then go a-pleasuring whereas it may be most agreeable to us. Wherefore, if this that I say please you, (for I am disposed to follow your pleasure therein,) let us do it; and if it please you not, let each until the hour of vespers do what most liketh him." Ladies and men alike all approved the story-telling, whereupon, "Then," said the queen, "since this pleaseth you, I will that this first day each be free to tell of such matters as are most to his liking." Then, turning to Pamfilo, who sat on her right hand, she smilingly bade him give beginning to the story-telling with one of his; and he, hearing the commandment, forthright began thus, whilst all gave ear to him.

Look and Learn/Bridgeman Images

What does the queen suggest is the purpose of their storytelling? How will it help their group get through the pandemic? How does reading this brief passage from Boccaccio's *Decameron* affect your understanding of the *New York Times Decameron Project* and the role of Obreht's story within that collection?

Understanding and Interpreting

1. In paragraph 1, the narrator says, "[Bezi Duras] seemed old to me then, but as I'm now approaching what was probably her age myself, I'm beginning to think she wasn't." What does the narrator mean by this? How might the narrator's age play a part in her recollection of events in the story?

2. Describe the setting in the first three of paragraphs and analyze how the setting helps to set the mood of the piece.

3. How is Bezi Duras described in paragraphs 3–4? What impression does she make on the narrator?

4. How do the descriptions of the dogs in paragraph 13 further add to the mystery surrounding Bezi Duras?

5. What do we learn about the narrator in the first 15 paragraphs of the story? Why might she be so fascinated by Bezi Duras?

6. A foil is a character whose actions and characteristics help the reader to understand the protagonist more fully, usually through contrasts. Describe Ena and explain how she acts as a foil to the narrator.

7. Describe the interactions between Ena and Bezi Duras (pars. 31–34). How does Obreht convey that the connection between Ena and Bezi Duras is more substantial than Ena admits? What does the narrator seem to know and not know?

8. Explain what this line in paragraph 35 reveals about the narrator and a theme that Obreht is exploring: "I found myself sharply aware for the first time that we were, in fact, just kids."

9. After the narrator and Ena are caught breaking into Bezi Duras's apartment, the narrator says that the event "was the first thing I thought about when I woke, and the last thing I thought about as I lay in the dark." Later the narrator says, "It became the kind of thing I'd tell lovers after deciding they would probably be sticking around. The kind of thing I hoped they'd forget about me when we parted ways." Based on what you know from the story, how does this event affect the narrator and why does it have such a large impact?

10. How is the reader expected to interpret the fact that the police sniper could not find any dogs to shoot? What clues in the story help you to draw this conclusion?

11. While the narrator faces many conflicts in the story, what is the central conflict? How is it resolved, or not, by the end of the story?

12. What do we find out about Ena at the end of the story (par. 43)? How does this information affect the reader's perception of the interaction that Ena has with Bezi Duras earlier in the story?

13. After finishing the story, return to reread paragraph 8, which includes Arlo's account of how the dogs came to be. What purpose does this account serve in the story as a whole?

Analyzing Language, Style, and Structure

14. **Vocabulary in Context.** In paragraph 3, the narrator says she and Ena saw Bezi Duras only in the elevator "when she summoned it." What does the word *summoned* mean in the context of this sentence? How is Obreht's use of the word here similar to and different from other uses you have encountered?

15. Examine the structure of this short story by focusing on Obreht's uses of flashbacks and time jumps. What are possible effects of structuring the story this way?

16. Identify places in which Obreht's use of language creates a supernatural or mysterious feeling or mood. Why is this mood appropriate for the story Obreht is telling?

17. Reread the language choices Obreht makes as she describes the paintings in Bezi Duras's apartment in paragraph 36 and at the very end of the story. How do these language choices help to communicate what the paintings symbolize?

18. What is ironic about the narrator saying that she would "feel relieved to find [herself] suddenly plunged back into that room, with its huge painting, and the dogs around it as though they were waiting to be called back into the world from which they had come"? How does Obreht's use of irony here connect with a theme of the story?

19. Look carefully at the syntax in the last paragraph, which is made up almost entirely of a single sentence. What might the punctuation and sentence structure choices here communicate about character or theme?

Topics for Composing

20. **Analysis.** While Obreht includes rich details and descriptions of her characters, the reader is also left with many questions about the characters' backgrounds and past events. What is Obreht suggesting about the ways that we can or cannot truly know people, or another thematic idea about memory or childhood based on what she chooses to include or exclude?

21. **Argument.** Do the residents of The Morningside, particularly the narrator and her friends, Ena and Arlo, misjudge Bezi Duras? Write a response in which you argue whether or not Bezi Duras is misjudged, or if the impressions of her are warranted.

22. **Connections.** Has it ever been difficult for you to get to know someone better? Write a reflection about a situation you experienced in which you found it difficult to get to know someone, either because of their behaviors or yours. Explain how you tried to approach the other person, whether or not it worked, and why or why not.

23. **Connections.** This story has a feeling of a fairy tale. How is this story similar to and different from fairy tales you're familiar with?

24. **Speaking and Listening.** With a partner or small group, discuss and organize your thoughts on the following: in what ways do our own lack of knowledge or understanding influence our judgment of others? Be prepared to share the results of your discussion with the class.

25. **Research.** This story incorporates elements of a type of fiction called magical realism, in which a realistic story incorporates fantastical elements. The form was popularized by writers such as Gabriel García Márquez, Isabel Allende, and Haruki Murakami. Conduct research on magical realism and read one other story that is generally regarded as an example of it. Then, write an explanation of how "The Morningside" serves or does not serve as an example of magical realism.

26. **Multimodal.** Reread the description of the painting that hangs on Bezi Duras's wall and try to recreate it with your own drawing, painting, or other artwork, or by locating found images. Include words or phrases from the short story that helped to inspire your visual.

27. **Creative Writing.** Years pass in Obreht's story between the time when the narrator and Ena break into the apartment and when the narrator reads about Bezi Duras's death. Tell the story of what happened to Ena or Bezi Duras in those intervening years.

Speech Sounds

Octavia Butler

Octavia Butler (1947–2006) is a critically acclaimed science fiction writer who has won numerous awards, including the Nebula and the Hugo Award for best short story, which was awarded to "Speech Sounds" in 1984. This dystopian fiction story takes place in a world in which illness has robbed many people of the ability to communicate through language, spoken and written, and describes how the residents of one city deal with the aftermath.

There was trouble aboard the Washington Boulevard bus. Rye had expected trouble sooner or later in her journey. She had put off going until loneliness and hopelessness drove her out. She believed she might have one group of relatives left alive — a brother and his two children twenty miles away in Pasadena. That was a day's journey one-way, if she were lucky. The unexpected arrival of the bus as she left her Virginia Road home had seemed to be a piece of luck — until the trouble began.

Two young men were involved in a disagreement of some kind, or, more likely, a misunderstanding. They stood in the aisle, grunting and gesturing at each other, each in his own uncertain T stance as the bus lurched over the potholes. The driver seemed to be putting some effort into keeping them off balance. Still, their gestures stopped just short of contact — mock punches, hand games of intimidation to replace lost curses.

People watched the pair, then looked at one another and made small anxious sounds. Two children whimpered.

Rye sat a few feet behind the disputants and across from the back door. She watched the two carefully, knowing the fight would begin when someone's nerve broke or someone's hand slipped or someone came to the end of his limited ability to communicate. These things could happen anytime.

One of them happened as the bus hit an especially large pothole and one man, tall, thin, and sneering, was thrown into his shorter opponent.

Instantly, the shorter man drove his left fist into the disintegrating sneer. He hammered his larger opponent as though he neither had nor needed any weapon other than his left fist. He hit quickly enough, hard enough to batter his opponent down before the taller man could regain his balance or hit back even once.

People screamed or squawked in fear. Those nearby scrambled to get out of the way. Three more young men roared in excitement and gestured wildly. Then, somehow, a second dispute broke out between two of these three — probably because one inadvertently touched or hit the other.

As the second fight scattered frightened passengers, a woman shook the driver's shoulder and grunted as she gestured toward the fighting.

The driver grunted back through bared teeth. Frightened, the woman drew away. Rye, knowing the methods of bus drivers, braced herself and held on to the crossbar of the seat in front of her. When the driver hit the brakes, she was ready and the combatants were not. They fell over seats and onto screaming passengers, creating even more confusion. At least one more fight started.

The instant the bus came to a full stop, Rye 10
was on her feet, pushing the back door. At the
second push, it opened and she jumped out,
holding her pack in one arm. Several other passengers followed, but some stayed on the bus.
Buses were so rare and irregular now, people
rode when they could, no matter what. There
might not be another bus today — or tomorrow.
People started walking, and if they saw a bus
they flagged it down. People making intercity
trips like Rye's from Los Angeles to Pasadena
made plans to camp out, or risked seeking shelter with locals who might rob or murder them.

The bus did not move, but Rye moved away
from it. She intended to wait until the trouble
was over and get on again, but if there was
shooting, she wanted the protection of a tree.
Thus, she was near the curb when a battered
blue Ford on the other side of the street made
a U-turn and pulled up in front of the bus.
Cars were rare these days — as rare as a severe
shortage of fuel and of relatively unimpaired
mechanics could make them. Cars that still ran
were as likely to be used as weapons as they
were to serve as transportation. Thus, when the
driver of the Ford beckoned to Rye, she moved
away warily. The driver got out — a big man,
young, neatly bearded with dark, thick hair. He
wore a long overcoat and a look of wariness that
matched Rye's. She stood several feet from him,
waiting to see what he would do. He looked at
the bus, now rocking with the combat inside,
then at the small cluster of passengers who had
gotten off. Finally he looked at Rye again.

She returned his gaze, very much aware
of the old forty-five automatic her jacket concealed. She watched his hands.

He pointed with his left hand toward the
bus. The dark-tinted windows prevented him
from seeing what was happening inside.

His use of the left hand interested Rye more
than his obvious question. Left-handed people
tended to be less impaired, more reasonable

and comprehending, less driven by frustration,
confusion, and anger.

She imitated his gesture, pointing toward the 15
bus with her own left hand, then punching the
air with both fists.

The man took off his coat revealing a Los
Angeles Police Department uniform complete
with baton and service revolver.

Rye took another step back from him. There
was no more LAPD, no more any large organization, governmental or private. There were
neighborhood patrols and armed individuals.
That was all.

The man took something from his coat
pocket, then threw the coat into the car. Then he
gestured Rye back, back toward the rear of the
bus. He had something made of plastic in his
hand. Rye did not understand what he wanted
until he went to the rear door of the bus and
beckoned her to stand there. She obeyed mainly
out of curiosity. Cop or not, maybe he could do
something to stop the stupid fighting.

He walked around the front of the bus, to the
street side where the driver's window was open.
There, she thought she saw him throw something into the bus. She was still trying to peer
through the tinted glass when people began
stumbling out the rear door, choking and weeping. Gas.

Rye caught an old woman who would have 20
fallen, lifted two little children down when they
were in danger of being knocked down and
trampled. She could see the bearded man helping people at the front door. She caught a thin
old man shoved out by one of the combatants.
Staggered by the old man's weight, she was
barely able to get out of the way as the last of
the young men pushed his way out. This one,
bleeding from nose and mouth, stumbled into
another and they grappled blindly, still sobbing
from the gas.

The bearded man helped the bus driver out
through the front door, though the driver did

not seem to appreciate his help. For a moment, Rye thought there would be another fight. The bearded man stepped back and watched the driver gesture threateningly, watched him shout in wordless anger.

The bearded man stood still, made no sound, refused to respond to clearly obscene gestures. The least impaired people tended to do this — stand back unless they were physically threatened and let those with less control scream and jump around. It was as though they felt it beneath them to be as touchy as the less comprehending. This was an attitude of superiority and that was the way people like the bus driver perceived it. Such "superiority" was frequently punished by beatings, even by death. Rye had had close calls of her own. As a result, she never went unarmed. And in this world where the only likely common language was body language, being armed was often enough. She had rarely had to draw her gun or even display it.

The bearded man's revolver was on constant display. Apparently that was enough for the bus driver. The driver spat in disgust, glared at the bearded man for a moment longer, then strode back to his gas-filled bus. He stared at it for a moment, clearly wanting to get in, but the gas was still too strong. Of the windows, only his tiny driver's window actually opened. The front door was open, but the rear door would not stay open unless someone held it. Of course, the air conditioning had failed long ago. The bus would take some time to clear. It was the driver's property, his livelihood. He had pasted old magazine pictures of items he would accept as fare on its sides. Then he would use what he collected to feed his family or to trade. If his bus did not run, he did not eat. On the other hand, if the inside of his bus was torn apart by senseless fighting, he would not eat very well either. He was apparently unable to perceive this. All he could see was that it would be some time before he could use his bus again. He shook his fist at the bearded man and shouted. There seemed to be words in his shout, but Rye could not understand them. She did not know whether this was his fault or hers. She had heard so little coherent human speech for the past three years, she was no longer certain how well she recognized it, no longer certain of the degree of her own impairment.

The Mehrabian Formula for Personal Communication

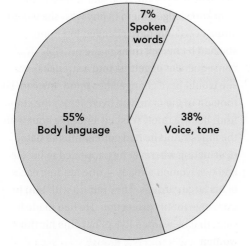

- 7% Spoken words
- 55% Body language
- 38% Voice, tone

Psychologist Albert Mehrabian studied the differences between verbal and nonverbal communication. He concluded that when someone's words, tone of voice, and body language express different emotions, we should rely most on body language to determine what that person is actually feeling. This pie chart shows the relative importance of verbal, tone, and body cues according to his Rule of Personal Communication.

In your experience, is Dr. Mehrabian's formula valid? How might Mehrabian's formula relate to the characters' efforts to communicate in Butler's story?

The bearded man sighed. He glanced toward his car, then beckoned to Rye. He was ready to leave, but he wanted something from her first. No. No, he wanted her to leave with him. Risk getting into his car when, in spite of his uniform, law and order were nothing — not even words any longer.

She shook her head in a universally under- 25 stood negative, but the man continued to beckon.

She waved him away. He was doing what the less-impaired rarely did — drawing potentially negative attention to another of his kind. People from the bus had begun to look at her.

One of the men who had been fighting tapped another on the arm, then pointed from the bearded man to Rye, and finally held up the first two fingers of his right hand as though giving two-thirds of a Boy Scout salute. The gesture was very quick, its meaning obvious even at a distance. She had been grouped with the bearded man. Now what?

The man who had made the gesture started toward her.

She had no idea what he intended, but she stood her ground. The man was half a foot taller than she was and perhaps ten years younger. She did not imagine she could outrun him. Nor did she expect anyone to help her if she needed help. The people around her were all strangers.

She gestured once — a clear indication to the 30 man to stop. She did not intend to repeat the gesture. Fortunately, the man obeyed. He gestured obscenely and several other men laughed. Loss of verbal language had spawned a whole new set of obscene gestures. The man, with stark simplicity, had accused her of sex with the bearded man and had suggested she accommodate the other men present — beginning with him.

Rye watched him wearily. People might very well stand by and watch if he tried to rape her. They would also stand and watch her shoot him. Would he push things that far?

He did not. After a series of obscene gestures that brought him no closer to her, he turned contemptuously and walked away.

And the bearded man still waited. He had removed his service revolver, holster and all. He beckoned again, both hands empty. No doubt his gun was in the car and within easy reach, but his taking it off impressed her. Maybe he was all right. Maybe he was just alone. She had been alone herself for three years. The illness had stripped her, killing her children one by one, killing her husband, her sister, her parents. . . .

The illness, if it was an illness, had cut even the living off from one another. As it swept over the country, people hardly had time to lay blame on the Soviets (though they were falling silent along with the rest of the world), on a new virus, a new pollutant, radiation, divine retribution. . . . The illness was stroke-swift in the way it cut people down and strokelike in some of its effects. But it was highly specific. Language was always lost or severely impaired. It was never regained. Often there was also paralysis, intellectual impairment, death.

Rye walked toward the bearded man, 35 ignoring the whistling and applauding of two of the young men and their thumbs-up signs to the bearded man. If he had smiled at them or acknowledged them in any way, she would almost certainly have changed her mind. If she had let herself think of the possible deadly consequences of getting into a stranger's car, she would have changed her mind. Instead, she thought of the man who lived across the street from her. He rarely washed since his bout with the illness. And he had gotten into the habit of urinating wherever he happened to be. He had two women already — one tending each of his large gardens. They put up with him in exchange for his protection. He had made it clear that he wanted Rye to become his third woman.

She got into the car and the bearded man shut the door. She watched as he walked around to the driver's door — watched for his sake because his gun was on the seat beside her. And the bus driver and a pair of young men had come a few steps closer. They did nothing, though, until the bearded man was in the car. Then one of them threw a rock. Others followed his example, and as the car drove away, several rocks bounced off harmlessly.

When the bus was some distance behind them, Rye wiped sweat from her forehead and longed to relax. The bus would have taken her more than halfway to Pasadena. She would have had only ten miles to walk. She wondered how far she would have to walk now — and wondered if walking a long distance would be her only problem.

At Figueroa and Washington where the bus normally made a left turn, the bearded man stopped, looked at her, and indicated that she should choose a direction. When she directed him left and he actually turned left, she began to relax. If he was willing to go where she directed, perhaps he was safe.

As they passed blocks of burned, abandoned buildings, empty lots, and wrecked or stripped cars, he slipped a gold chain over his head and handed it to her. The pendant attached to it was a smooth, glassy, black rock. Obsidian. His name might be Rock or Peter or Black, but she decided to think of him as Obsidian. Even her some- times useless memory would retain a name like Obsidian.

She handed him her own name symbol — a pin in the shape of a large golden stalk of wheat. She had bought it long before the illness and the silence began. Now she wore it, thinking it was as close as she was likely to come to Rye. People like Obsidian who had not known her before probably thought of her as Wheat. Not that it mattered. She would never hear her name spo- ken again.

Obsidian handed her pin back to her. He caught her hand as she reached for it and rubbed his thumb over her calluses.

He stopped at First Street and asked which way again. Then, after turning right as she had indicated, he parked near the Music Center. There, he took a folded paper from the

40

Describe the setting of this image and explain what tone it communicates to the viewer. In what ways does this image capture elements of the setting of "Speech Sounds"?

andipantz/Getty Images

dashboard and unfolded it. Rye recognized it as a street map, though the writing on it meant nothing to her. He flattened the map, took her hand again, and put her index finger on one spot. He touched her, touched himself, pointed toward the floor. In effect, "We are here." She knew he wanted to know where she was going. She wanted to tell him, but she shook her head sadly. She had lost reading and writing. That was her most serious impairment and her most painful. She had taught history at UCLA. She had done freelance writing. Now she could not even read her own manuscripts. She had a houseful of books that she could neither read nor bring herself to use as fuel. And she had a memory that would not bring back to her much of what she had read before.

She stared at the map, trying to calculate. She had been born in Pasadena, had lived for fifteen years in Los Angeles. Now she was near L.A. Civic Center. She knew the relative positions of the two cities, knew streets, directions, even knew to stay away from freeways which might be blocked by wrecked cars and destroyed overpasses. She ought to know how to point out Pasadena even though she could not recognize the word.

Hesitantly, she placed her hand over a pale orange patch in the upper right corner of the map. That should be right. Pasadena.

Obsidian lifted her hand and looked under it, then folded the map and put it back on the dashboard. He could read, she realized belatedly. He could probably write, too. Abruptly, she hated him — deep, bitter hatred. What did literacy mean to him — a grown man who played cops and robbers? But he was literate and she was not. She never would be. She felt sick to her stomach with hatred, frustration, and jealousy. And only a few inches from her hand was a loaded gun.

She held herself still, staring at him, almost seeing his blood. But her rage crested and ebbed and she did nothing.

Obsidian reached for her hand with hesitant familiarity. She looked at him. Her face had already revealed too much. No person still living in what was left of human society could fail to recognize that expression, that jealousy.

She closed her eyes wearily, drew a deep breath. She had experienced longing for the past, hatred of the present, growing hopelessness, purposelessness, but she had never experienced such a powerful urge to kill another person. She had left her home, finally, because she had come near to killing herself. She had found no reason to stay alive. Perhaps that was why she had gotten into Obsidian's car. She had never before done such a thing.

He touched her mouth and made chatter motions with thumb and fingers. Could she speak?

She nodded and watched his milder envy come and go. Now both had admitted what it was not safe to admit, and there had been no violence. He tapped his mouth and forehead and shook his head. He did not speak or comprehend spoken language. The illness had played with them, taking away, she suspected, what each valued most.

She plucked at his sleeve, wondering why he had decided on his own to keep the LAPD alive with what he had left. He was sane enough otherwise. Why wasn't he at home raising corn, rabbits, and children? But she did not know how to ask. Then he put his hand on her thigh and she had another question to deal with.

She shook her head. Disease, pregnancy, helpless, solitary agony . . . no.

He massaged her thigh gently and smiled in obvious disbelief.

No one had touched her for three years. She had not wanted anyone to touch her. What kind of world was this to chance bringing a child into even if the father were willing to stay and help raise it? It was too bad, though. Obsidian could not know how attractive he was to her — young,

45

50

probably younger than she was, clean, asking for what he wanted rather than demanding it. But none of that mattered. What were a few moments of pleasure measured against a lifetime of consequences?

He pulled her closer to him and for a moment she let herself enjoy the closeness. He smelled good — male and good. . . .   55

Sometime later, they sat together, covered by his coat, unwilling to become clothed near-strangers again just yet. He made rock-the-baby gestures and looked questioningly at her.

She swallowed, shook her head. She did not know how to tell him her children were dead.

He took her hand and drew a cross in it with his index finger, then made his baby–rocking gesture again.

She nodded, held up three fingers, then turned away, trying to shut out a sudden flood of memories. She had told herself that the children growing up now were to be pitied. They would run through the downtown canyons with no real memory of what the buildings had been or even how they had come to be. Today's children gathered books as well as wood to be burned as fuel. They ran through the streets chasing one another and hooting like chimpanzees. They had no future. They were now all they would ever be.

He put his hand on her shoulder and she   60
turned suddenly . . . urging him to make love to her again. He could give her forgetfulness and pleasure. Until now, nothing had been able to do that. Until now, every day had brought her closer to the time when she would do what she had left home to avoid doing: putting her gun in her mouth and pulling the trigger.

She asked Obsidian if he would come home with her, stay with her.

He looked surprised and pleased once he understood. But he did not answer at once. Finally he shook his head as she had feared he might. He was probably having too much fun playing cops and robbers and picking up women.

She dressed in silent disappointment, unable to feel any anger toward him. Perhaps he already had a wife and a home. That was likely. The illness had been harder on men than on women — had killed more men, had left male survivors more severely impaired. Men like Obsidian were rare. Women either settled for less or stayed alone. If they found an Obsidian, they did what they could to keep him. Rye suspected he had someone younger, prettier keeping him.

He touched her while she was strapping her gun on and asked with a complicated series of gestures whether it was loaded.

She nodded grimly.   65

He patted her arm.

She asked once more if he would come home with her, this time using a different series

Comforters, 1983 (acrylic on board)/Waddams, Ron (1920–2010)/Private Collection/Bridgeman Images

This painting by Ron Waddams is titled *Comforters* (1983).

What might the artist be trying to convey by limiting the representation of people in the image to just a few body parts? What is the significance of those parts and their arrangement in the image? Consider how the painting relates to the way Butler presents relationships in the story.

of gestures. He had seemed hesitant. Perhaps he could be courted.

He got out and into the front seat without responding.

She took her place in front again, watching him. Now he plucked at his uniform and looked at her. She thought she was being asked something, but did not know what it was.

He took off his badge, tapped it with one fin- 70
ger, then tapped his chest. Of course.

She took the badge from his hand and pinned her wheat stalk to it. If playing cops and robbers was his only insanity, let him play. She would take him, uniform and all. It occurred to her that she might eventually lose him to someone he would meet as he had met her. But she would have him for a while.

He took the street map down again, tapped it, pointed vaguely northeast toward Pasadena, then looked at her.

She shrugged, tapped his shoulder, then her own, and held up her index and second fingers tight together, just to be sure.

He grasped the two fingers and nodded. He was with her.

She took the map from him and threw it onto 75
the dashboard. She pointed back southwest —
back toward home. Now she did not have to go to Pasadena. Now she could go on having a brother there and two nephews — three right-handed males. Now she did not have to find out for certain whether she was as alone as she feared. Now she was not alone.

Obsidian took Hill Street south, then Washington west, and she leaned back, wondering what it would be like to have someone again. With what she had scavenged, what she had preserved, and what she grew, there was easily enough food for them. There was certainly room enough in a four-bedroom house. He could move his possessions in. Best of all, the animal across the street would pull back and possibly not force her to kill him.

Obsidian had drawn her closer to him and she had put her head on his shoulder when suddenly he braked hard, almost throwing her off the seat. Out of the corner of her eye, she saw that someone had run across the street in front of the car. One car on the street and someone had to run in front of it.

Straightening up, Rye saw that the runner was a woman, fleeing from an old frame house to a boarded-up storefront. She ran silently, but the man who followed her a moment later shouted what sounded like garbled words as he ran. He had something in his hand. Not a gun. A knife, perhaps.

The woman tried a door, found it locked, looked around desperately, finally snatched up a fragment of glass broken from the storefront window. With this she turned to face her pursuer. Rye thought she would be more likely to cut her own hand than to hurt anyone else with the glass.

Obsidian jumped from the car, shouting. It 80
was the first time Rye had heard his voice — deep and hoarse from disuse. He made the same sound over and over the way some speechless people did, "Da, da, da!"

Rye got out of the car as Obsidian ran toward the couple. He had drawn his gun. Fearful, she drew her own and released the safety. She looked around to see who else might be attracted to the scene. She saw the man glance at Obsidian, then suddenly lunge at the woman. The woman jabbed his face with her glass, but he caught her arm and managed to stab her twice before Obsidian shot him.

The man doubled, then toppled, clutching his abdomen. Obsidian shouted, then gestured Rye over to help the woman.

Rye moved to the woman's side, remembering that she had little more than bandages and antiseptic in her pack. But the woman was beyond help. She had been stabbed with a long, slender boning knife.

She touched Obsidian to let him know the woman was dead. He had bent to check the wounded man who lay still and also seemed dead. But as Obsidian looked around to see what Rye wanted, the man opened his eyes. Face contorted, he seized Obsidian's just-holstered revolver and fired. The bullet caught Obsidian in the temple and he collapsed.

It happened just that simply, just that fast. An instant later, Rye shot the wounded man as he was turning the gun on her.

And Rye was alone — with three corpses.

She knelt beside Obsidian, dry-eyed, frowning, trying to understand why everything had suddenly changed. Obsidian was gone. He had died and left her — like everyone else.

Two very small children came out of the house from which the man and woman had run — a boy and girl perhaps three years old. Holding hands, they crossed the street toward Rye. They stared at her, then edged past her and went to the dead woman. The girl shook the woman's arm as though trying to wake her.

This was too much. Rye got up, feeling sick to her stomach with grief and anger. If the children began to cry, she thought she would vomit.

They were on their own, those two kids. They were old enough to scavenge. She did not need any more grief. She did not need a stranger's children who would grow up to be hairless chimps.

She went back to the car. She could drive home, at least. She remembered how to drive.

The thought that Obsidian should be buried occurred to her before she reached the car, and she did vomit.

She had found and lost the man so quickly. It was as though she had been snatched from comfort and security and given a sudden, inexplicable beating. Her head would not clear. She could not think.

Somehow, she made herself go back to him, look at him. She found herself on her knees beside him with no memory of having knelt. She stroked his face, his beard. One of the children made a noise and she looked at them, at the woman who was probably their mother. The children looked back at her, obviously frightened. Perhaps it was their fear that reached her finally.

She had been about to drive away and leave them. She had almost done it, almost left two toddlers to die. Surely there had been enough dying. She would have to take the children home with her. She would not be able to live with any other decision. She looked around for a place to bury three bodies. Or two. She wondered if the murderer were the children's father. Before the silence, the police had always said some of the most dangerous calls they went out on were domestic disturbance calls. Obsidian should have known that — not that the knowledge would have kept him in the car. It would not have held her back either. She could not have watched the woman murdered and done nothing.

She dragged Obsidian toward the car. She had nothing to dig with her, and no one to guard for her while she dug. Better to take the bodies with her and bury them next to her husband and her children. Obsidian would come home with her after all.

When she had gotten him onto the floor in the back, she returned for the woman. The little girl, thin, dirty, solemn, stood up and unknowingly gave Rye a gift. As Rye began to drag the woman by her arms, the little girl screamed, "No!"

Rye dropped the woman and stared at the girl.

"No!" the girl repeated. She came to stand beside the woman. "Go away!" she told Rye.

365

"Don't talk," the little boy said to her. There was no blurring or confusing of sounds. Both children had spoken and Rye had understood. The boy looked at the dead murderer and moved further from him. He took the girl's hand. "Be quiet," he whispered.

Fluent speech! Had the woman died because she could talk and had taught her children to talk? Had she been killed by a husband's festering anger or by a stranger's jealous rage? And the children . . . they must have been born after the silence. Had the disease run its course, then? Or were these children simply immune? Certainly they had had time to fall sick and silent. Rye's mind leaped ahead. What if children of three or fewer years were safe and able to learn language? What if all they needed were teachers? Teachers and protectors.

Rye glanced at the dead murderer. To her shame, she thought she could understand some of the passions that must have driven him, whoever he was. Anger, frustration, hopelessness, insane jealousy . . . how many more of him were there — people willing to destroy what they could not have?

Obsidian had been the protector, had chosen that role for who knew what reason. Perhaps putting on an obsolete uniform and patrolling the empty streets had been what he did instead of putting a gun into his mouth. And now that there was something worth protecting, he was gone.

She had been a teacher. A good one. She had been a protector, too, though only of herself. She had kept herself alive when she had no reason to live. If the illness let these children alone, she could keep them alive.

Somehow she lifted the dead woman into her arms and placed her on the backseat of the car. The children began to cry, but she knelt on the broken pavement and whispered to them, fearful of frightening them with the harshness of her long unused voice.

"It's all right," she told them. "You're going with us, too. Come on." She lifted them both, one in each arm. They were so light. Had they been getting enough to eat?

The boy covered her mouth with his hand, but she moved her face away. "It's all right for me to talk," she told him. "As long as no one's around, it's all right." She put the boy down on the front seat of the car and he moved over without being told to, to make room for the girl. When they were both in the car Rye leaned against the window, looking at them, seeing that they were less afraid now, that they watched her with at least as much curiosity as fear.

"I'm Valerie Rye," she said, savoring the words. "It's all right for you to talk to me." ■

Understanding and Interpreting

1. What is Rye's reason for starting her journey after "loneliness and hopelessness drove her out"? What is the root cause of her loneliness and hopelessness at the beginning of the story?

2. How has the inability to effectively communicate introduced conflict at the very beginning of the story? What other conflicts are presented throughout the plot, and how do these conflicts interact with each other?

3. How is Obsidian portrayed in comparison to other male characters in the story?

4. Describe what is meant by an "attitude of superiority" in paragraph 22? In what ways is superiority in this case a negative trait?

5. What is ironic about Rye's inability to read and write? How does her realization that Obsidian can read and write affect her perception of him? How do her feelings on this subject relate to her comment later in the story that "people [were] willing to destroy what they could not have" (par. 102)?

6. How does Rye's experience with losing Obsidian compare to the death of her husband and children? In what ways are the situations similar or different? What is significant about Rye's reactions in each case?

7. At one point, Rye explains that the children would gather books to burn as fuel and chase each other like chimpanzees in the street with no hope for a future (par. 59). How does her perception of children in this time and place change by the end of the story?

8. What is the significance of the "gift" that the little girl gives Rye toward the end of the story? How does this exchange relate to a main theme of the text?

9. At the very end, it is revealed that Rye can speak, and that she has chosen not to until encountering the children. What does it reveal about her character that she kept her silence all this time?

Analyzing Language, Style, and Structure

10. **Vocabulary in Context.** Consider this sentence from paragraph 71: "If playing cops and robbers was his only insanity, let him play." What does the word *insanity* mean in the context of this sentence? How does that meaning relate to what we know at this point about how the illness has affected humanity?

11. What is the effect of writing the story in third person limited point of view?

12. Take another look at the interaction among the bus passengers in paragraphs 2–3. Discuss how Butler's use of diction and details helps the reader to visualize the communication that occurs.

13. Reread paragraph 75 and look at the repetition of the word *now*. What purpose does repetition serve here?

14. Butler sets the story in a bleak, futuristic Los Angeles. Examine the details of one scene within this setting — on the bus, in the car with Obsidian, or at the house where Rye encounters the family. How do the imagery and details of the scene you selected relate to a theme of the story as a whole? Why are the details of this dilapidated environment important?

15. How does Butler use diction and syntax to build suspense in paragraphs 78–84?

16. The story is almost totally devoid of dialogue. How does the absence of speech throughout most of the story affect how readers perceive the conversation between Rye and the children at the end of the story?

Topics for Composing

17. **Analysis.** The story describes a world in which widespread illness has shifted how humans communicate. Some people — such as Rye and Obsidian — find ways to communicate complicated thoughts and feelings effectively to each other. Others with the same communication tools at their disposal succeed in conveying only threats. Write a response in which you analyze the connection between communication and relationships in the story. What message about relationships and their connection to communication does Butler want readers to understand?

18. **Argument.** Argue whether Butler's message in this story is ultimately one of hope or despair. Support your response with evidence from the text.

19. **Connections.** Both Rye and Obsidian use symbols to represent their names and identities, and they cannot be sure if their interpretations of each other's symbols is correct. If you had to select a symbol to represent your name and identity, what would you choose, and why?

20. **Speaking and Listening.** Have you ever played a game of charades, in which you had to act out words, ideas, or events without giving any verbal or written clues? With a partner, try to express a somewhat complex idea (in other words, not just an object or action) related to school without using words. After you each take a turn, talk about the challenges associated with having to act out a conversation. Reflect on how this experience enhances your understanding of communication within the story, and be prepared to discuss your conclusions with the class.

21. **Research.** Research why interpersonal communication, verbal or nonverbal, is so important to people. You might decide to focus your research on communication in an educational, professional, or social environment. What basic human needs does communication support? What psychological effects are associated with ineffective or no communication?

22. **Creative Writing.** An epilogue is a text at the end of a book or play that serves as commentary on or a conclusion to what has happened. Write an epilogue to the story that might tell readers what happens next, after Rye returns home with the two children.

Story of an Hour

Kate Chopin

Kate Chopin (1850–1904) was an American author widely known as one of the leading writers of her time. Born in St. Louis, Missouri, she later moved to New Orleans, Louisiana, after marrying her husband, Oscar Chopin, in 1870. Together they had six children. After losing her husband and mother within a few years of each other, she found therapy in writing to help heal her depression. She continued to publish two volumes of short stories, *Bayou Folk* (1894) and *A Night in Acadie* (1897), and two novels, *At Fault* (1890) and *The Awakening* (1899). "Story of an Hour" appeared in *Vogue* magazine in 1894.

Missouri History Museum, St. Louis

KEY CONTEXT Chopin's writing is most often associated with the beginnings of American feminism. Her stories explore the idea of woman's rights and independence, topics not readily or publicly accepted in the society of the time. Women at that time were not allowed to vote, hold political office, own property if they were married, or attend college. There were few jobs that women were allowed to do, so they often married to secure financial support, and in return raised a family. As feminist ideas began to develop, these traditions and rules were questioned, and they informed Kate Chopin's thinking in "Story of an Hour."

Knowing that Mrs. Mallard was afflicted with a heart trouble, great care was taken to break to her as gently as possible the news of her husband's death.

It was her sister Josephine who told her, in broken sentences; veiled hints that revealed in half concealing. Her husband's friend Richards was there, too, near her. It was he who had been in the newspaper office when intelligence of the railroad disaster was received, with Brently Mallard's name leading the list of "killed." He had only taken the time to assure himself of its truth by a second telegram, and had hastened to forestall any less careful, less tender friend in bearing the sad message.

She did not hear the story as many women have heard the same, with a paralyzed inability to accept its significance. She wept at once, with sudden, wild abandonment, in her sister's arms. When the storm of grief had spent itself she went away to her room alone. She would have no one follow her.

There stood, facing the open window, a comfortable, roomy armchair. Into this she sank, pressed down by a physical exhaustion that haunted her body and seemed to reach into her soul.

She could see in the open square before ⁵ her house the tops of trees that were all aquiver with the new spring life. The delicious breath of rain was in the air. In the street below a peddler was crying his wares. The notes of a distant song which some one was singing reached her faintly, and countless sparrows were twittering in the eaves.

There were patches of blue sky showing here and there through the clouds that had met and piled one above the other in the west facing her window.

She sat with her head thrown back upon the cushion of the chair, quite motionless, except when a sob came up into her throat and shook her, as a child who has cried itself to sleep continues to sob in its dreams.

She was young, with a fair, calm face, whose lines bespoke repression and even a certain strength. But now there was a dull stare in her eyes, whose gaze was fixed away off yonder on one of those patches of blue sky. It was not a glance of reflection, but rather indicated a suspension of intelligent thought.

There was something coming to her and she was waiting for it, fearfully. What was it? She did not know; it was too subtle and elusive to name. But she felt it, creeping out of the sky, reaching toward her through the sounds, the scents, the color that filled the air.

Now her bosom rose and fell tumultuously. ¹⁰ She was beginning to recognize this thing that was approaching to possess her, and she was striving to beat it back with her will — as powerless as

Woman at her Window, or, The Wife of a Treasurer, 1841 (oil on canvas)/Tropinin, Vasili Andreevich (1776–1857)/State Russian Museum, St. Petersburg, Russia/Bridgeman Images

Compare the scene in this painting, and the emotions involved, with the scene in "Story of an Hour" as the revelation slowly takes hold of Mrs. Mallard in her room.
What similarities do you find? What differences?

her two white slender hands would have been. When she abandoned herself a little whispered word escaped her slightly parted lips. She said it over and over under her breath: "free, free, free!" The vacant stare and the look of terror that had followed it went from her eyes. They stayed keen and bright. Her pulses beat fast, and the coursing blood warmed and relaxed every inch of her body.

She did not stop to ask if it were or were not a monstrous joy that held her. A clear and exalted perception enabled her to dismiss the suggestion as trivial. She knew that she would weep again when she saw the kind, tender hands folded in death; the face that had never looked save with love upon her, fixed and gray and dead. But she saw beyond that bitter moment a long procession of years to come that

369

would belong to her absolutely. And she opened and spread her arms out to them in welcome.

There would be no one to live for during those coming years; she would live for herself. There would be no powerful will bending hers in that blind persistence with which men and women believe they have a right to impose a private will upon a fellow-creature. A kind intention or a cruel intention made the act seem no less a crime as she looked upon it in that brief moment of illumination.

And yet she had loved him — sometimes. Often she had not. What did it matter! What could love, the unsolved mystery, count for in the face of this possession of self-assertion which she suddenly recognized as the strongest impulse of her being!

"Free! Body and soul free!" she kept whispering.

Josephine was kneeling before the closed   15 door with her lips to the keyhole, imploring for admission. "Louise, open the door! I beg; open the door — you will make yourself ill. What are you doing, Louise? For heaven's sake open the door."

"Go away. I am not making myself ill." No; she was drinking in a very elixir of life through that open window.

Her fancy was running riot along those days ahead of her. Spring days, and summer days, and all sorts of days that would be her own. She breathed a quick prayer that life might be long. It was only yesterday she had thought with a shudder that life might be long.

She arose at length and opened the door to her sister's importunities. There was a feverish triumph in her eyes, and she carried herself unwittingly like a goddess of Victory. She clasped her sister's waist, and together they descended the stairs. Richards stood waiting for them at the bottom.

Some one was opening the front door with a latchkey. It was Brently Mallard who entered, a little travel-stained, composedly carrying his grip-sack and umbrella. He had been far from the scene of the accident, and did not even know there had been one. He stood amazed at Josephine's piercing cry; at Richards' quick motion to screen him from the view of his wife.

When the doctors came they said she had   20 died of heart disease — of the joy that kills. ■

Understanding and Interpreting

1. The reader discovers in the first line that Mrs. Mallard suffers from a heart condition. What effect is created by sharing this information early in the story?

2. Upon learning of her husband's death, Mrs. Mallard "wept at once" (par. 3). What is significant about her reaction in comparison to other women who experience a "paralyzed inability" to accept similar news?

3. In paragraph 4, Mrs. Mallard goes to the armchair where she "sank, pressed down by a physical exhaustion that haunted her body and seemed to reach into her soul." What does this line tell us about Mrs. Mallard's emotional state?

4. In paragraph 10, Mrs. Mallard recognizes "this thing" rising in her and tries to "beat it back with her will." What is "this thing," and why might she try to suppress it?

5. Mrs. Mallard reveals that "[o]ften she had not" loved her husband (par. 13). What can you infer about her motivations for marrying Mr. Mallard? How much of her unhappiness can be attributed to her own decisions?

6. Based on details in the story, what assumptions can be made about the type of man Mr. Mallard is? What assumptions can be made about the Mallards' marriage?

7. Is there evidence to support that Mrs. Mallard's heart trouble is caused by anything other than natural physical causes? Explain.

8. What is the significance of the doctors determining the cause of Mrs. Mallard's death?

9. The setting of the story is limited to the house that Mrs. Mallard lives and dies in. How does the limited setting support the theme(s) of the story?

Analyzing Language, Style, and Structure

10. **Vocabulary in Context.** In paragraph 17, Chopin writes that "her fancy was running riot along those days ahead of her." What does the word *fancy* mean in this context and how is that meaning similar to or different from other uses of the word that you know?

11. What is the significance of the story happening over the course of an hour? How might the story have been different if the events had taken place over several days or weeks?

12. What are possible interpretations of the metaphor "storm of grief" in paragraph 3?

13. How does the author's use of sensory details in paragraphs 4–6 demonstrate the changes of Mrs. Mallard's situation?

14. Explain the possible meaning behind the oxymoron *monstrous joy* in paragraph 11. Who might consider her joy to be monstrous, and why?

15. It is not until paragraph 15 that the reader first learns that Mrs. Mallard's first name is Louise. What is the significance of revealing her first name at this point in the story?

16. What might the "open window" in paragraph 16 symbolize? How does this symbol relate to a theme of the story?

17. The line "life might be long" is repeated twice, but in two different contexts (par. 17). Explain the differences in meaning each time the line is presented.

18. In paragraph 17, Mrs. Mallard prays for a long life. What is ironic about Mrs. Mallard's death?

19. What is the meaning of the paradox in the last line — "the joy that kills"?

Topics for Composing

20. **Analysis.** Though he does not make an appearance until the end, we learn a good deal about Mr. Mallard. Analyze Chopin's use of imagery and details to indirectly characterize Mr. Mallard. Explain how this characterization supports a theme of the story.

21. **Analysis.** Taking into consideration the historical context in which Chopin wrote, what are some possible themes for this story? What message is Chopin trying to convey about the relationships between men and women? (Revisit the Key Context note on p. 368, if needed.)

22. **Argument.** The story was published in 1894, a time in which women's roles in marriage and society were marginalized. Does the story shed any light on today's world or only provide a window into the past? Be sure to include examples and evidence from the story, your own reasoning, and a little research, if needed, to support your points.

23. **Connections.** Write about a time you felt constrained by other people's expectations. What was the situation, who was involved, and how did you respond?

24. **Creative Writing.** The story is told from the third person point of view. Rewrite the ending of the story when Brently Mallard appears (par. 19) from the point of view of Mrs. Mallard or another character. What changes when the story is told from a different perspective?

25. **Creative Writing.** If Mrs. Mallard had not died, what might she have done next in the story? Write an alternate ending in which you explore whether the experience described in the story affects her outlook on life and, if so, in what ways.

Writing an Analysis of Fiction

As you likely remember from previous chapters, analysis is the process of taking something apart in order to understand it better. When we analyze fiction, we're looking at how an author uses literary elements like characterization, plot, and setting, as well as language choices, to deliver an idea — the theme. The goal is to consider why the writer made certain choices and determine what effect those choices have on the story.

In the Skill Workshop on page 246, we looked at how Tim O'Brien uses elements of fiction in his short story "Ambush," and you explored those same elements in a work of fiction you chose. If you worked through the Creative Writing Extension on page 259, you used the tools of storytelling to begin to craft a piece of fiction. As you thought about characters, plot, setting, and other literary devices, you had many choices to make. What is this story about? Where does the story begin? What happens next? Who are these characters? What language can I use to bring the story to life? Being a writer is all about *choices*. In an analysis, your goal is to explain to the reader *why* the writer made certain choices. Answering the "why" is key.

The following is a typical prompt you might encounter when asked to analyze fiction:

Stories often feature characters who undergo personal change or development. Identify a story in which a major or minor character changes in a significant way. Explain how that character develops, what causes those changes, and how the author uses characterization to reveal a theme.

Let's practice the analysis process with the Central Text in this chapter, Amy Tan's "Two Kinds" (331–338). In this story, the main character, Jing-mei, struggles with her mother, who wants to turn her into a prodigy. As a result, Jing-mei experiences an identity crisis. Before we even get to the text, however, we need to break down the prompt and think about what it is asking us to do. In this case, we need to do two things:

1. Consider how Jing-mei changes over the course of the story.
2. Discuss how those changes help Tan to express a specific theme.

Once we have figured out what the prompt is asking us to do, we'll have a focus for our reading and analysis.

activity   **Getting Started**

Return to a story in this chapter that you found interesting or choose a story you've read for another class or on your own that includes a character who changes over the course of the story. Look back at the prompt above to be sure that the story you selected will work with that prompt. Write a brief response about why the story interests you and how the character changes. Then talk with a partner about whether the story seems like one you could analyze for characterization and theme.

Step 1. Reading and Making Observations

While an analysis of fiction can address a whole story, we are going to model the process with just a short passage that highlights significant change in a character. In our passage from this chapter's Central Text, "Two Kinds," Jing-mei, the protagonist, struggles through her mother's relentless testing of her intellect and abilities. After our first read, we will reread the passage for meaning and add annotations. Our annotations focus on things that are interesting or confusing, and they're an opportunity to ask questions as we go. Feel free to note your own observations. Our notes are intended as a starting point, not the final word.

Tasks start out normal, then get weird. What is Tan telling us about the mom by making this list so bizarre?

The tests got harder — multiplying numbers in my head, finding the queen of hearts in a deck of cards, trying to stand on my head without using my hands, predicting the daily temperatures in Los Angeles, New York, and London. One night I had to look at a page from the Bible for three minutes and then report everything I could remember. "Now Jehoshaphat had riches and honor in abundance and . . . that's all I remember, Ma," I said.

And after seeing, once again, my mother's disappointed face, something inside me began to die. I hated the tests, the

Whose hopes were raised? Hers or her mom's? Or both?

raised hopes and failed expectations. Before going to bed

What was she expecting to see?

that night I looked in the mirror above the bathroom sink, and I saw only my face staring back — and understood that it would always be this ordinary face — I began to cry.

Hoping to see extraordinary face, not just ordinary.

Seems to be taking her failure to heart and having an identity crisis.

Such a sad, ugly girl! I made high-pitched noises like a crazed animal, trying to scratch out the face in the mirror. And then I saw what seemed to be the prodigy side of me — a face I had never seen before. I looked at my reflec-

Tan is creating another Jing-mei, the prodigy, signifying a change in the character.

The prodigy is "angry, powerful." That's unexpected!

tion, blinking so that I could see more clearly. The girl staring back at me was angry, powerful. She and I were the same. I had new thoughts, willful thoughts — or rather,

This pronoun "her" is confusing. Could refer to her mom or the "sad, ugly girl" in the mirror.

"Prodigy" identity is not the "ideal" daughter. Could be theme?

thoughts filled with lots of won'ts. I won't let her change me, I promised myself. I won't be what I'm not.

373

Reading and Making Observations

Using the story you selected in the previous activity, locate a section that is about the approximate length of the excerpt above and that seems to focus on a way the character changes. When you have decided on your excerpt, read it twice.

1. On your first reading, read for understanding. What is happening?
2. On your second reading, read for meaning. Annotate the excerpt by asking questions and noting important ideas or moments. Pay special attention to how the writer uses the essential elements of fiction.

Step 2. Finding a Focus

There is a lot going on in the short passage above from "Two Kinds." So, how do we begin to analyze something like this? We said that analysis is about pulling things apart, but we also said that it was about doing that in order to better understand a text. So, once we've taken notes on all of the little things, we need to find some ideas or themes that connect our observations.

Let's return to the passage and summarize the main ideas in the notes, paragraph by paragraph:

- **Paragraph 1.** The first handful of notes all come back to the idea of whether Jing-mei resents the tests and does poorly on purpose, or if she is honestly trying and failing. Is she disturbed by her failure or by what her mom is putting her through?
- **Paragraph 2.** In this paragraph, Jing-mei sees her normal reflection — the "ordinary . . . sad, ugly girl" — and we're led to believe that this is the face she sees because she fails the test. This is the face of failure. She attacks this face out of frustration.
- **Paragraph 3.** In this paragraph, Jing-mei changes and is redefined as a willful prodigy. The motivation here is confusing, because the thing that starts all of this is her failure of her mom's tests. But being more willful and full of "won'ts" isn't going to help her pass those tests. How is she defining "prodigy"?

As we summarized those notes, the question that seems to come repeatedly is this: What is the relationship between Jing-mei and her mom, and how does that dynamic fuel the change in Jing-mei's identity? How do the bizarre tests lead to Jing-mei's transformation? Answering this question will be the focus of our model analysis.

Finding a Focus

Now that we have provided an example of what it looks like to summarize observations about a passage, it's time for you to try. In the previous activity, you selected a passage to focus on from the story you've chosen to work with and annotated it. Following the same steps that we modeled with "Two Kinds," summarize your notes to find a focus for your analysis. (If you struggle with finding a focus, perhaps you need to look for different or additional passages, or a different story.)

Step 3. Creating a Thesis Statement

Whether it's a thesis statement for a full essay or just a topic sentence for an analytical paragraph, the recipe remains the same. You want to introduce the idea you are looking to explore and take an interpretive stance on that idea. Don't just tell your readers what happened; tell them *why* it happened. Don't just tell them what your essay is going to be about; tell them what your position is on that topic. Having an effective, intriguing thesis is essential to clarifying your thinking and setting up a strong interpretation.

For the topic we've been exploring, we might write a thesis sentence like this:

WEAK THESIS

In this section of "Two Kinds," Jing-mei rebels against her mother.

This thesis states what happens, but it doesn't tell us *why*. It doesn't take an interpretive stance on the passage, and it doesn't answer any of the questions we asked as we took notes on the passage.

WEAK THESIS

The motivations behind Jing-mei's rebellion against becoming a prodigy in "Two Kinds" are complex and drive her to create her own definition of a prodigy.

This statement is a little closer, but not quite there because it doesn't clearly tell us why she rebels. What are the motivations? Why do the characters have these motivations?

WORKING THESIS

Tired of failing to be the sort of prodigy her mother would like her to be, Jing-mei creates her own definition of a prodigy, unleashing the strong, willful girl within herself.

This thesis states what happens, but it also takes a stand on why: Jing-mei was pushed to change by her mother's behavior. It also addresses why she changes in the way that she does: she doesn't feel in control of her identity, so she takes control.

375

This is not the only possible thesis. You might think that this change in Jing-mei is a bad thing, that she has been pushed to the breaking point by her mother. You might think that Jing-mei's idea of a "prodigy" as being willful and "full of won'ts" is ultimately a negative change in the character's life, rather than a positive self-realization. You might change the focus entirely and just try to define what a "prodigy" is and try to explain why Jing-mei and her mother have such different definitions of it. Stories are full of things to talk about. Find the thing that you are most interested in or most passionate about and run with it, as long as it stays focused on the original prompt you've been assigned.

For the rest of this workshop, we'll use the working thesis above as our starting point.

Creating a Thesis

Using the passage that you selected and analyzed in the previous activities, write a working thesis that takes an interpretive stance on that passage. Remember that your thesis should introduce the idea you want to explore and take a stance on that idea.

Step 4. Proving Your Point

Now that we have a focus for our analysis, the next step is to prove that our interpretation is valid. Some people say that literature is subjective and we can interpret it any way we want, but that's not entirely true. The interpretation has to be a valid reading of the text. The way we prove that in academic writing is by drawing evidence directly from the text and combining that with our own commentary.

Based on our working thesis, what exactly do we need to prove?

WORKING THESIS

Tired of failing to be the sort of prodigy her mother would like her to be, Jing-mei creates her own definition of a prodigy, unleashing the strong, willful girl within herself.

Two basic points in this thesis need to be proven:

POINT 1 Jing-mei is tired of failing to be the sort of prodigy her mother would like her to be.

Is she tired of failing? Or is she tired of being pushed so much? Is this the motivation that causes her identity crisis? We have to prove that our reading is supported by the text.

POINT 2 Jing-mei creates her own definition of a prodigy, unleashing the strong, willful girl within herself.

Is this true? What is Jing-mei's idea of what a prodigy should be? Is her definition actually the same as her mother's? How is it different? What does willfulness have to do with being a prodigy? In order to address these questions, we need to go back to the text.

Gathering Evidence

There are many ways to gather evidence. Some people use note cards, some people highlight and annotate as they reread, and others take notes in a document or graphic organizer. What system you use is up to you. As you reread the text, you should begin selecting quotations that support or counter your ideas. Don't just ignore things that go against your thesis; tackle them head on! Quotations alone, however, are not enough to prove your point. It is your job as the writer to point out *how* the quotation proves the point you're making.

One way to make sure you are connecting your quotation to your thesis is with a table like this. It will help make the connection clear, and help you think through the purpose of each quotation and how it connects to your larger point.

Working Thesis: Tired of failing to be the sort of prodigy her mother would like her to be, Jing-mei creates her own definition of a prodigy, unleashing the strong, willful girl within herself.

Quotation	How the Quotation Supports the Thesis
"One night I had to look at a page from the Bible for three minutes and then report everything I could remember. 'Now Jehoshaphat had riches and honor in abundance and . . . that's all I remember, Ma,' I said."	Jing-mei's tone in her response demonstrates her fatigue with the constant pressures to become the prodigy her mother desires. (Supports point 1 in the working thesis.)

Gathering Evidence

activity

Revisit your working thesis and identify the specific points you need to prove, as we did with our model on page 376. Then go back to the passage you have been working with in this workshop's activities and gather evidence to support your working thesis. Remember that whether you use note cards, take notes in a document, or fill in a graphic organizer is up to you. This activity is a good opportunity to try out a system and see if it works for you.

Presenting Evidence

When you present your ideas, you must make your point, frame your quotations, and explain how the two are connected.

In the writing chapter of this book, on page 85, we talked about how to use evidence by making the point, backing up the point with evidence, and then commenting on how the evidence proves the point. If we begin to incorporate our point, evidence, and commentary or explanations in a paragraph, it might look something like this:

The point ——————[While some may read Jing-mei's resistance to her mother's

training as rebellion, it seems more like fatigue from a lifetime

of frustrating exercises and pressure.][One such training —————— *The explanation/commentary*

exercise involves memorizing "a page from the Bible for three

minutes and [reporting] everything [she] could remember." Not

able to get far, Jing-mei finally stops short, saying, ". . . that's

all I remember, Ma."][The sad, apologetic, and affectionate tone —————— *The evidence*

of ". . . that's all I remember, Ma" makes Jing-mei's response to

these exercises not defiance but defeat. She seems worn down.

An angry child would not use the affectionate term "Ma."]

What we have created here is a short but focused analytical paragraph. If we find more quotations to support our points, we can continue to build the paragraph with this structure, as long as we stay on the same topic, like this:

The point ——————[While some may read Jing-mei's resistance to her mother's

training as rebellion, it seems more like fatigue from a lifetime

of frustrating exercises and pressure.][One such training —————— *The evidence*

exercise involves memorizing "a page from the Bible for three

minutes and [reporting] everything [she] could remember." Not

able to get far, Jing-mei finally stops short, saying, ". . . that's

all I remember, Ma."][The sad, apologetic, and affectionate tone —————— *Explanation/commentary*

of ". . . that's all I remember, Ma" makes Jing-mei's response to

these exercises not defiance but defeat. She seems worn

down. An angry child would not use the affectionate term "Ma."]

Another point ——————[Later in the passage, Jing-mei admits that it is not necessarily

the tests, but her failure that truly upsets her.][She says that —————— *More evidence*

"after seeing, once again, [her] mother's disappointed face,

something inside [her] began to die."][In a situation like this, —————— *Explanation/commentary*

in which the tests are arbitrary and failure results in a mother's

disappointment, is it any surprise that a hurting child would

crack and then change the rules of the game?]

With evidence and explanations that connect the evidence to our point presented like this, we have a credible analytical paragraph.

The second point of our working thesis is this:

> Jing-mei creates her own definition of a prodigy, unleashing the strong, willful girl within herself.

If we were to follow the same steps as the body paragraph above, we would have a second body paragraph that uses supporting evidence to prove this point. Depending on how you structured your own thesis, you may or may not have additional points to argue.

Writing a Body Paragraph

Using the model above as a guide, write a body paragraph or two for your own working thesis which states your point, incorporates at least two pieces of textual evidence, and explains how your evidence supports your point. If your working thesis leads to a second point to argue, you can repeat these steps in another body paragraph.

Step 5. Expanding to an Essay

Whether you realize it or not, we've come a long way in writing an analytical essay. We have a thesis, and we even have a solid body paragraph or two. If we add an introduction and a conclusion, we'll probably have an effective paper on this passage. If we were asked to write about the entire story, our paper would get longer, as we'd have a lot more to say about where Jing-mei's relationship with her mother ends up, and how her willful idea of a prodigy works out. The key parts missing from our essay at this point are the introduction and conclusion. Let's work on those.

Introductory Paragraph

The point of the introductory paragraph is to engage the reader and create interest in the topic. A standard introduction has three parts:

1. An opening hook
2. A connection to the piece being analyzed
3. A thesis statement

The hook is about drawing readers in and getting them thinking about the kinds of ideas or issues that are at play in the analysis. This is a great place to just raise questions or identify issues. No one is expecting you to have the answers to these questions or solutions to these problems.

For this essay about Jing-mei and her mother, we might think about what role parents have in making their kids successful. We might ask whether we define our own identity, or whether those around us play a larger role in defining who we are. We might think about what a prodigy is and why having a daughter who is one seems so important to Jing-mei's mother.

379

You may have heard that the first sentence is the hardest to write. Here are a few classic ways to begin your introductory paragraph:

With a question	Why are people often pressured to be someone they are not?
With a definition	Self-awareness is the recognition of one's own strengths, weaknesses, beliefs, and motivations.
With a statement	The act of self-discovery can lead to powerful consequences, both positive and negative.
With a story or an anecdote	On the television show *Little Big Shots*, a 4-year-old piano prodigy played a challenging classical piece to the astonishment of viewers across America. The host, Steve Harvey, turned to the audience and joked, "I want to apologize to my seven children. Obviously, somewhere down the line I failed you miserably. This could have been you."

Once we have a hook, it's time to show our readers how the ideas we've brought up apply to the reading we are about to analyze. This transition doesn't have to be fancy. It's usually a simple connecting statement that includes a bit of summary.

The hook —————— [On the television show *Little Big* Shots a 4-year-old piano prodigy played a challenging classical piece to the astonishment of viewers across America. The host, Steve Harvey, turned to the audience and joked, "I want to apologize to my seven children. Obviously, somewhere down the line I failed you miserably. This could have been you." The race to build prodigies, child stars, little Einsteins, and baby Beethovens, has heated up to a fever pitch, and both kids and parents are feeling the pressure.]

[We see the results of this quest for excellence in Amy ——— *Connection to the piece* Tan's story "Two Kinds," in which the mother subjects Jing-mei, her daughter, to relentless testing and drills that become more and more bizarre.] [Tired of failing to be——— *Thesis* the sort of prodigy her mother would like her to be, Jing-mei creates her own definition of a prodigy, unleashing the strong, willful girl within herself.]

Writing an Introduction

Following the model, write a draft of your introductory paragraph. Think about how you want to hook the reader and lead into your thesis statement.

Concluding Paragraph

As with any essay you write, a solid conclusion will bring your paper full circle by restating (not repeating) your thesis and the main points you analyzed in each of the body paragraphs. It should bring completeness and closure to the reader with the satisfaction that your assertion is a sound one.

Notice how the following draft of the concluding paragraph for our sample analysis ties back to the thesis and connects to the ideas in the body paragraph(s).

> The push for excellence motivated from within can be a challenge, but the push for excellence on someone else's terms can be nearly impossible. Jing-mei's constant failures in response to her mother's persistent attempts to cultivate her daughter as a prodigy push Jing-mei to a breaking point. Jing-mei's inner strength emerges when she realizes, in an act of thoughtful, willful defiance, that she wants to follow her own path. The change she undergoes reveals her new identity as someone who wants to be in control of her own destiny. In her way, she has redefined *prodigy* as one who succeeds on his or her own terms.

Writing a Conclusion

Write a concluding paragraph for your essay. Remember to tie it back to your thesis and the points in your body paragraphs, and to avoid simply repeating what you have already stated.

Bringing It All Together

If you take all of the pieces you've written and put them together, you should have a short analytical essay.

Remember that all of these tips are just here to help you get started. Once you feel more in control of what it means to make an interpretation, prove a point, and comment on evidence, you can start to bend these rules to suit your purposes. Writing is not about formulas or templates. It's about communicating ideas.

Step 6. Finalizing the Essay

Now that you have a complete draft of your essay, you can move on to the final phase of the writing process: revising and editing. These two acts are sometimes thought of as being the same, but they're not. Revision is when you look back at large-scale structural elements of your essay, such as how well you support your claim, what kinds of evidence you use, how effective your word choices are, and to what extent you have led your reader easily through your essay. Editing, on the other hand, focuses on fine-tuning the language, grammar, punctuation, spelling, and other conventions. Editing is usually the very last thing you do before you finalize your piece, looking carefully for any errors that you tend to make. The following are suggestions for you to consider as you finalize your essay.

Revising

Revising gives you a good opportunity to think again about your essay's purpose and audience. In most cases, your audience will be your teacher or an external evaluator in the case of a standardized test. In both situations, that means using a somewhat formal tone, but your writing can still be engaging for you and your audience. Reread your essay for the following:

- **Look back at your thesis.** Since you wrote this early on in the workshop, does it still relate to the analysis you ended up writing? If you need more assistance with this, be sure to look at Revision Workshop 1: Effective Thesis and Essay Structure in the back of the book.
- **Look back at your focus.** Is it still at the center of your analysis? Make sure that ideas and evidence in your paragraphs connect back to the focus. If you need more assistance with this, be sure to look at Revision Workshop 2: Effective Topic Sentences and Unified Paragraphs in the back of the book.
- **Look back at your body paragraphs.** Have you balanced the evidence with your own commentary about how that evidence supports your thesis? If you need more assistance with this, be sure to look at Revision Workshop 4: Appropriate Evidence and Support in the back of the book.
- **Revisit elements of fiction.** Does your essay draw a clear connection between the characterization and the possible theme of the story? Be sure to look back at the Skill Workshop (p. 246) at the beginning of this chapter if you need more practice with this.
- **Revisit your introduction and conclusion.** Does your introduction grab the reader's attention and effectively preview your topic? Does your conclusion wrap up in a way that highlights your focus? Take a look at Revision Workshop 8: Effective Introductions and Conclusions in the back of the book if you need additional support with these parts of your essay.

Editing

Remember, editing is the very last thing you'll do before finalizing your essay. You and your teacher know better than anyone the types of spelling, grammar, and convention errors you need to focus on in your writing development. Below is a short checklist of things to keep in mind. Be sure to refer to one or more of the Grammar Workshops in the back of the book if you encounter an issue and aren't sure how to overcome it.

- Check your writing for the use of present tense verbs. Literature *lives*, so the analysis should discuss how the author *uses* (rather than *used*) literary devices, and that the characters *are* (rather than *were*) portrayed in a certain way.
- Make sure you've written in third person point of view and avoided the use of pronouns like *I* and *you*.
- If the verb tense or pronoun of the original text does not match your sentence grammar, change it and use brackets [ ] to indicate the change. *Example*: Jing-mei realizes that "the girl staring back at [her is] angry, powerful." Using brackets to replace the words "me was" from the original quotation with [her is] in the integrated quotation keeps the surrounding sentence grammatical and easy for readers to understand.

public speaking extension

Analysis of Fiction

You have spent this workshop crafting an analysis of fiction that presents a focused thesis with support and commentary. What if you wanted to share that same piece through a presentation to a live audience? What would you need to add, change, or delete to make your essay sound engaging? As you work through this process, refer to the elements of a presentation in Chapter 3 (p. 90), and use these steps to turn your written analysis into an oral presentation.

Content

- **Your introduction.** Reread the beginning paragraph of your written analysis. Would this capture the listener's attention? Read it aloud to yourself a few times. Does it sound dramatic or engaging? Remember that you chose to work with a particular story because it interested you. Does your introduction convey that interest? Does it communicate to your listeners the particular aspects of the story you are going to discuss? If it feels too long when you read it aloud, cut it down to only two or three sentences.
- **Your main idea.** You will want to be very clear about what you are analyzing. You may want to break your thesis up into two sentences to ensure that your listeners easily grasp each element that will be included in the presentation.
- **Your supporting evidence.** While your analytical essay may have included multiple points that you address, for a short presentation, you might want to focus on only the strongest element that you analyzed. Include evidence that is clear, focused, and supports the importance of the element you selected.
- **Your closing.** Look back at how you ended your written analysis and highlight the strongest sentence or two that communicate to your audience the ideas you've presented and their connection to the theme of the text you have been discussing. For a live audience, it may be especially important to leave them with a question or comment to inspire further thought about the ideas you have presented.

Delivery

Like other speeches you deliver in school, a presentation of an analysis of a text will take on a mostly formal tone, but you can smile, gesture, or laugh at appropriate times. Because you may be presenting information that might be unfamiliar to your listeners, you will want to move slowly and clearly through your points, maybe using transitions, such as "first, second . . . ," "finally," or "most important." You can use your fingers to count off evidence or a gesture to show the importance of a particular piece of evidence.

Visuals

As with visuals for any presentation, you need to make sure that anything you include is relevant, appropriate, and works to enhance your words and delivery. Possible visuals for a presentation of an analysis of fiction might include a passage from the text that you want to discuss in detail or bullet points related to your main idea. If you are changing visuals during your presentation, be sure to allow a little time for the audience to react, especially if it is something that might take time to process.

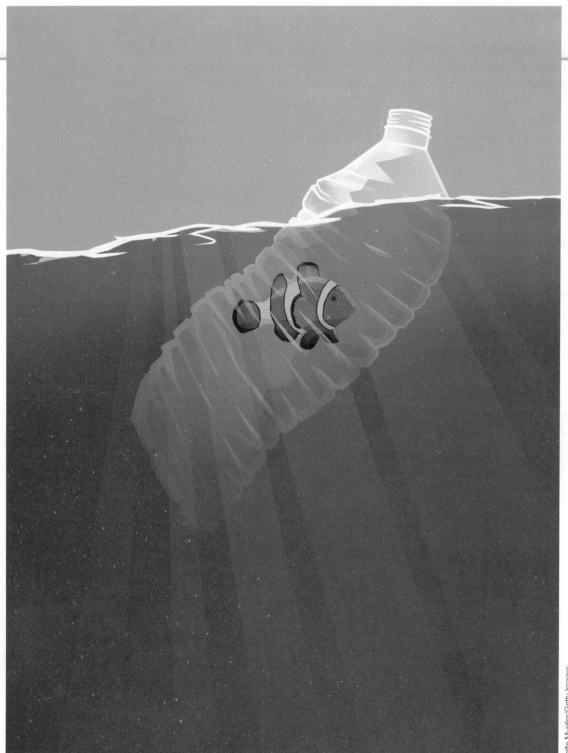

Argument

Arguments are everywhere. A politician argues that legislation will benefit the nation. A poster argues that you should buy a certain pair of jeans. A hashtag urges us to #recycle. You also engage in arguments when you challenge the fairness of a school policy or argue with a friend about which player your favorite team should draft.

We tend to think of an argument as something to avoid because we associate the word with fights we have with friends, parents, or teachers, but what's key to understand as we dive into this chapter on argument is that an effective and civil argument isn't a shouting match. The goal is to persuade a reader or listener to see your perspective, to take a certain action, or simply to rethink a position on a topic.

But just as important as learning to make a persuasive argument is learning how to pay close attention to the arguments around you. What techniques do writers, advertisers, politicians, and others use to persuade you to think or act in a particular way? In this chapter, you'll not only explore the key skills behind creating powerful academic evidence-backed arguments, you'll also explore ways of using argument to express yourself as a consumer, a citizen, and a critical thinker.

Contents

Essential Elements of Argument

When we think about how to create an effective argument, we're investigating the art of persuasion — which is called **rhetoric**. An argument is what writers say, but rhetoric is *how* they say it — the choices writers make. In this workshop, we'll look at the rhetorical tools writers use to build strong arguments.

PREVIEWING Academic Vocabulary   Essential Elements of Argument

In this section, you will encounter the following terms as you consider how to write and analyze an argument. Working individually or with a partner or small group, consider what you already know about the meaning of each term.

1. Rhetorical situation
   Speaker
   Audience
   Context
   Occasion
2. Claim
3. Counterargument

4. Evidence
5. Rhetorical appeals
   Ethos
   Logos
   Pathos
6. Style
7. Visual arguments

Let's begin by reading an argument published in 2018 in a magazine for educators called *Education Week*. The writer, David Polochanin, recommends starting school later in the morning.

We Already Know School Starts Too Early. It's Time to Do Something About It

David Polochanin teaches in the Glastonbury Public School system in Connecticut and often writes about education issues for publications such as the *Boston Globe* and *Education Week*.

KEY CONTEXT This piece was published in 2018 in the opinion section of *Education Week*, just after the California governor vetoed legislation that would have required all schools in the state to start after 8:30 A.M.

David Polochanin

Common sense, as a general idea, seems easy to define. But when it comes to the time that middle and high school students start school in most places across the United States, the education community has been doing it wrong — with numerous, hard-to-ignore studies, sleep experts, and national organizations rightly blasting the negative impact on adolescents to begin class around 7:30 A.M.

On this topic, most schools have been in the Dark Ages, literally and figuratively. The vast majority of districts do not heed recommendations by the American Academy of Pediatrics to hold off beginning middle and high school until 8:30 A.M.

For advocates of a later start time for secondary schools, it was a brief ray of hope to learn of California's recent progress on the matter, with lawmakers there approving a bill that would require all middle and high schools to begin after 8:30 A.M. Unfortunately, Gov. Jerry Brown, citing that the decision should be made by local school boards, vetoed the legislation late last month.

Even with the California setback, the movement to push back school start times is gaining momentum nationally. From Saco, Maine, to Seattle, many districts have already successfully pushed back the start times of high schools and middle schools — and with largely positive results. For instance, according to the nonprofit group Start School Later, Saco schools have seen a 40 percent drop in tardiness, an almost 50 percent reduction in student visits to the nurse, and staff reports that students are more alert and ready to learn since they moved to a later start time in 2016.

Scores rise, too, when schools align their schedules with adolescent biological clocks. In 2014, a three-year, 9,000-student study from researchers at the University of Minnesota found that students whose high schools changed their schedules to start at 8:30 A.M or later improved their performance in English, math, science, social studies, and standardized tests. [5]

So, if the research is clear that making this change yields an overwhelmingly positive outcome, the burning question is [this]: Why has this taken so long [and when] will other districts follow suit?

The answers are muddied by a mix of factors, ranging from a shift in family schedules, potential budget adjustments to accommodate more buses, challenges with after-school sports and activities, and the prospect of having students complete their homework later at night than they already do. But the main issue, experts studying the change agree, is one of simple inconvenience. Schools and their communities have been so accustomed to the current schedule that many are resistant to change. It's much easier to do what has always been done.

However, when you consider the negative impact of an early school day on adolescents and pre-adolescents, the facts can no longer be ignored. Thirteen- to 18-year-olds require 8 to 10 hours of sleep daily, according to the American Academy of Sleep Medicine. Circadian rhythms during puberty force teens to go to bed later and sleep later in the morning. Anyone who has taught middle and high school, or has a child in this age range, can attest to this. (Forehead on the dining room table during breakfast, anyone?) School start times forcing teens to wake up before 6 A.M. clearly do not align with teens' sleep needs.

According to the American Academy of Pediatrics, adolescents who do not get the required amount of sleep are at risk for a host of serious physical problems, including obesity and diabetes; safety concerns, including drowsy driving; issues related to mental health, including increased anxiety, depression, and decreased motivation; and a decrease in school performance, such as cognitive impairment, problems with attention and memory, lower academic achievement, poor attendance, and higher dropout rate.

The author of the failed California bill, [10] Democratic state senator Anthony J. Portantino, recently told the *New York Times* that forcing teens to get out of bed so early is "the biological equivalent of waking you or me up at 3:30 A.M. Imagine how you would feel if, 187 days a year, you had to get up at 3:30 A.M. You'd be miserable, you'd be depressed — you'd act like a teenager."

With such compelling evidence, it makes one wonder how children in middle and high schools have been able to function well at all in school — at least during the early morning hours. It also calls to mind how an earlier start time could have helped millions of students who haven't performed well, faced physical problems, or dropped out because they have had to wake up far earlier than they should have.

As author Daniel H. Pink states in his latest book, *When*, this is a remediable problem. "Starts matter," he writes. "We can't always control them. But this is one area where we can and therefore we must."

Veteran educators know that, each year, communities throughout the country spend millions on costly new initiatives — technology, curriculum, new buildings, to name a few — many of which have marginal positive impact on student learning.

If school superintendents and boards of education were to examine the research behind secondary school start times, it is impossible to disagree: Outdated schedules are failing many students. We can no longer be complacent. As schools look for an answer to boost student attendance, performance, and engagement, making a change in start times for secondary students is an obvious solution.

Now, which districts will read the research and have the common sense — and the courage — to make the change? ∎   15

---

 activity **Getting Started**

What is one change that you would like to propose at your school? Write briefly about how the change would improve the learning environment at your school.

Rhetorical Situation

To fully understand an argument, you first have to understand a few key concepts.

- **Speaker.** The term *speaker* can refer to a writer, artist, filmmaker, advertiser — any person or organization presenting an argument. Who is making the argument? What are their qualifications, interests, and biases? Why should we listen to them on this subject?

- **Audience.** Who is the audience for the argument? Are they likely to agree or disagree with the speaker? What background knowledge do they probably have about the subject?

- **Context.** What events or circumstances prompted the speaker to make the argument in the first place? What do readers need to know to fully understand the argument?

These three elements come together to create what is called the **rhetorical situation**, which might feel familiar to you. In Chapter 3, we worked with how these elements affect the choices you make as a writer: the words you use, the tone you take, and the types of information you include. The rhetorical situation for Polochanin's article could be summarized as follows.

- **Speaker.** From the biographical note, we know that David Polochanin teaches in the Glastonbury Public School system in Connecticut and writes articles for the *Boston Globe*, *Education Week*, and other publications. Because of his teaching experience, readers can view him as an expert on this issue, though they should also be on the lookout for any signs of bias (p. 103).

- **Audience.** This piece was originally published in *Education Week*. According to its "About Us" page, *Education Week* is "a resource for K-12 education news and information" for over a million readers "[f]rom teachers to principals to district leaders across the country." Therefore, we can assume that Polochanin's audience is made up primarily of educators who are knowledgeable about the topic and are probably looking for information, resources, and guidance.

- **Context.** While the issue of when school ought to begin has been debated for a long time, it appears that this article was written in response to California Governor Jerry Brown's veto of legislation in 2018 that would have required districts to begin school no earlier than 8:30. As readers, we bring our own context to pieces we read as well. For example, in this case, relevant context might include what we learned from later school start times due to remote learning during the COVID-19 pandemic.

Looking at the rhetorical situation in this way helps us understand the full context of the argument, which can then allow us to analyze each strategy that the writer or speaker uses to create a persuasive argument.

Rhetorical Situation

Think back on the change you would like to see at your school that you wrote about in the previous activity. Consider the rhetorical situation of your own argument by writing a sentence or two in response to these questions:

- **Speaker.** What background or expertise do you have on this topic that might make your argument worth reading or listening to?

- **Audience.** Who is the likely audience — principal, teachers, school board, parents, fellow students? What do you know about them and their knowledge of or preconceptions about your topic?

- **Context.** What local or national events have inspired you to propose this idea now? What background information do your readers need to understand the argument?

Claim and Counterargument

In Chapter 3, we discussed topic sentences — sentences that state the main idea of the paragraphs in which they appear. A **claim** is like the topic sentence of the entire argument: it states the main idea of the argument, meaning the position the author is taking on the issue. Just as we pointed out that a topic sentence is usually near the beginning of a paragraph (but not necessarily), a claim is often near the beginning of an argument (but, again, not always).

So, what is Polochanin's claim? From the title, you can determine that he thinks schools should start later in the day to accommodate adolescents' natural biological rhythms. Some claims in an argument are explicitly stated, as they are in this one, but sometimes they are implied. The best way to identify the claim is to ask yourself, *What position is the author taking on an issue — or what change is the author calling for?*

In addition to thinking about the claim, we need to consider key objections to or concerns about that claim — what we call **counterarguments**. A sound academic argument should anticipate the opposition and consider all sides of an issue. Polochanin identifies several reasons why some people might object to delaying school start time, including that such a change might require "a shift in family schedules, potential budget adjustments to accommodate more buses, challenges with after-school sports and activities, and the prospect of having students complete their homework later at night than they already do." Polochanin does not try to dismiss or vilify those who disagree with him. He tries to carefully win them over by providing more data and rationales.

The technique that Polochanin uses here is called **concede and refute**. He concedes — or admits that there are legitimate reasons why some would think differently — but then he points out what they may have missed. Consider the following example:

> Schools and their communities have been so accustomed to the current schedule that many are resistant to change. It's much easier to do what has always been done. However, when you consider the negative impact of an early school day on adolescents and pre-adolescents, the facts can no longer be ignored. Thirteen- to 18-year-olds require 8 to 10 hours of sleep daily, according to the American Academy of Sleep Medicine.

When you concede, you acknowledge the merits of the counterargument. When you refute, you uncover the weakness of the counterargument to support your own claim. If applied carefully, the concede and refute technique can be a powerful tool for changing minds.

Claim and Counterarguments

1. Working individually, with a partner, or in a small group, choose one of the following claims and discuss what a potential counterargument might be. How might you use the concede and refute technique to address that counterargument?

   - Social media has made friendships more difficult.
   - Violence in video games and movies causes violent behavior in real life.
   - Solar energy is the best solution to global warming.
   - Everyone should have access to free health care.

2. Thinking back to the audience for your argument about a change that you would like to see in your school, what is your overall claim, and what counterarguments might your audience have to your proposal and why?

Evidence

Evidence is the heart of a good argument. Stating a claim isn't enough. An effective argument uses evidence to persuade readers to share the writer's opinion. Weak or insufficient evidence will be unconvincing. Different types of evidence can be used for different effects and purposes to support a position.

Type of Evidence	General Purpose
Details and examples	To make an abstract idea concrete, or a general point more specific
Expert opinion	To show that others support the ideas in your argument
Data and statistics	To quantify the problem or solution with specific figures
Personal experience and anecdotes	To show personal connection with or knowledge of the topic

These types of evidence often overlap. A piece of data can come from research, a personal experience can serve as an example, or an expert opinion can add detail. Let's look at a few examples of how Polochanin develops his argument using evidence.

Details and examples	"Even with the California setback, the movement to push back school start times is gaining momentum nationally. From Saco, Maine, to Seattle, many districts have already successfully pushed back the start times of high schools and middle schools — and with largely positive results."
Expert opinion	"According to the American Academy of Pediatrics, adolescents who do not get the required amount of sleep are at risk for a host of serious physical problems, including obesity and diabetes; safety concerns, including drowsy driving; issues related to mental health, including increased anxiety, depression, and decreased motivation"
Data and statistics	"In 2014, a three-year, 9,000-student study from researchers at the University of Minnesota found that students whose high schools changed their schedules to start at 8:30 A.M. or later improved their performance in English, math, science, social studies, and standardized tests."
Personal experience and anecdotes	"Anyone who has taught middle and high school, or has a child in this age range, can attest to this. (Forehead on the dining room table during breakfast, anyone?) School start times forcing teens to wake up before 6 A.M. clearly do not align with teens' sleep needs."

Some people might suggest that only expert opinion and facts or data should be used as evidence, but personal experience and anecdotes can also be effective evidence. Just keep in mind that personal experience and anecdotes are rarely effective if they are the *only* evidence you offer. It's too easy for someone to raise doubts by saying that's just one example or one viewpoint. Including different types of evidence is the best way to strengthen an argument.

activity   Evidence

Thinking about the argument you have been developing about a change in your school, what might you include for each of the following types of evidence?

- Concrete details and examples
- Expert opinion
- Data and statistics
- Personal experience and anecdotes

Rhetorical Appeals

The most fundamental idea in rhetoric is that the speaker should say things that the audience will find appealing because it makes sense, stirs the emotions, or gives the speaker credibility with the audience.

The Greek philosopher Aristotle defined these three means of persuasion in any effective argument as ethos, logos, and pathos.

- **Ethos:** the appeal to the character and credibility of the speaker or writer, usually emphasizing the shared values between the author and audience
- **Logos:** the appeal to logic and reason
- **Pathos:** the appeal to emotions

These three concepts constitute what we call functional rhetoric: the rhetoric of everyday life. Once you begin to look for these appeals, you will see them all around you, in advertisements, documentaries, social media posts, and even in your own conversations.

Appeals inform every part of an argument — how it is structured, what language is used, and what evidence is chosen. If you think back to the discussion of evidence in the previous section, you would probably see that while sharing personal experiences and anecdotes are powerful ways to add ethos and pathos to an argument, examples, expert opinion, data, and hard evidence of that sort are effective at appealing to logos.

If we examine these appeals in Polochanin's argument, we can make the following observations:

- **Ethos.** It is clear that Polochanin is knowledgeable with some first-hand experience with this issue as a teacher. As readers, we tend to trust people who are experts, and he works hard to establish this trust. Additionally, notice how often he uses the pronoun *we* throughout his piece. This creates a sense of shared values and perspectives between him and the reader, essentially saying, "we're in this together, so let's fix it together."
- **Logos.** Polochanin includes results from research studies that show how standardized test scores and other key indicators improve with a later school start time. He also includes references to expert organizations, authors, and legislators. With many knowledgeable people seemingly in agreement about this issue, it would be difficult to not accept his central claim.
- **Pathos.** While Polochanin makes the majority of his argument through logos, he does not ignore the emotional side to the issue. For example, he refers to the dangerous results of an earlier start, citing "issues related to mental health, including increased anxiety, depression, and decreased motivation; and a decrease in school performance, such as cognitive impairment, problems with attention and memory, lower academic achievement, poor attendance, and higher dropout rate." He also uses a quotation to challenge his adult readers to imagine what it would feel like to wake up at 3:30 in the morning, which is what it feels like for teenagers to get up for an early start at school.

activity Rhetorical Appeals

1. How would you appeal to logos, pathos, and ethos in one of the following situations:

   - Your friends are vaping, and you want to persuade them to stop.

   - Your parent or guardian added restrictions and rules for a semester because your grades slipped. At midterm, your grades are better, and you want at least some of these restrictions relaxed.

   - Relatives or family friends invited you to visit, but getting to where they live involves travel (by train, bus, or plane). You want to travel alone, but your parent or guardian says you're too young.

2. Think about the argument you have been working with about a reform needed at your school and consider the types of evidence you identified above. Briefly describe how you might appeal to ethos, logos, and pathos.

Style

While evidence is one way to build rhetorical appeals, so is the style of the language. A descriptive passage might appeal to emotion, a reasonable tone to logic, and an authoritative and knowledgeable tone to ethos. The language choices an author makes to deliver an argument can help appeal to readers' interests, values, and concerns. Style in argument writing is very similar to style in other genres. The difference is that the purpose is to persuade. Here are some elements of style that you might encounter:

Diction: word choice

Syntax: word order / sentence structure

Imagery: literal or figurative language that appeals to the senses

Figurative language: language that is not intended to be taken literally. This includes **simile**, **metaphor**, **allusion**, **hyperbole**, and **personification**.

Let's look at a specific passage from the end of Polochanin's argument to examine his style:

> Veteran educators know that, each year, communities throughout the country spend millions on costly new initiatives — technology, curriculum, new buildings, to name a few — many of which have marginal positive impact on student learning.
>
> If school superintendents and boards of education were to examine the research behind secondary school start times, it is impossible to disagree: Outdated schedules are failing many students. We can no longer be complacent. As schools look for an answer to boost student attendance, performance, and engagement, making a change in start times for secondary students is an obvious solution.
>
> Now, which districts will read the research and have the common sense — and the courage — to make the change?

Notice how much of Polochanin's diction — "veteran educators," "marginal positive impact," "impossible to disagree," "obvious solution," "common sense" — creates a sense of authority and conviction of the correctness of his position. Look, too, at the second paragraph, which is made up of three sentences. The first and last are long sentences, but right in the middle he writes a very short one: "We can no longer be complacent." If you remember from your work with sentences in Chapter 3, short sentences like this create emphasis and cause the reader to slow down. Polochanin also ends his piece by questioning the courage of school boards and districts and challenging them to do the right thing. While Polochanin doesn't employ much figurative language or imagery in his piece, he does allude to the "Dark Ages," and he describes a student with "forehead on the dining room table during breakfast" to capture just how old-fashioned the current policies are and how sleepy most teenagers are at the beginning of school.

Style

Up to this point, you've been thinking about a possible reform you'd suggest for your school. Try writing just a few sentences of a body paragraph and experiment with your language choices. What diction, syntax, figurative language, or imagery might be persuasive to your audience? (To review any of these elements, see pp. 47–50 in Chapter 2.)

Visual Arguments

So far in this workshop, we've discussed how writers and speakers build and support their arguments through evidence, appeals, and language choices. It's essential to recognize that many of these essential elements apply to visual arguments. Argumentative images surround us — advertisements, videos, billboards, memes, charts, and diagrams. They present a point of view and try to persuade us in some way.

As you may have seen in Chapter 2, reading visual texts is similar to reading other types of texts, though some additional terminology applies. Consider the following terms, which are defined and described on page 56 of Chapter 2: color and lighting, framing and focus, layout and design, and fonts and symbols.

The visual arguments that follow focus on a school-reform initiative recommending that school districts replace the typically months-long summer break with a series of shorter breaks throughout the school year.

Notice the color and design choices made by the creators of these pie charts: the orange pops out, emphasizing just how long the breaks are in each calendar to draw clear contrasts between them. The charts appeal to logos in that each of the sections in blue are so evenly proportioned in the "Balanced" calendar — about forty-five days of almost continuous learning — compared to the various and erratic days of learning in the "Traditional" calendar. Even the diction of the words *balanced* and *traditional* helps to make the creators' case that the reform is the better choice.

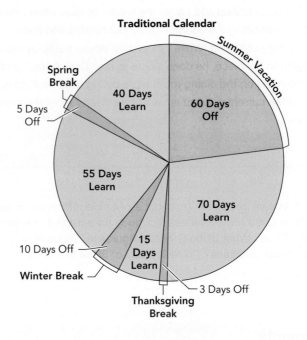

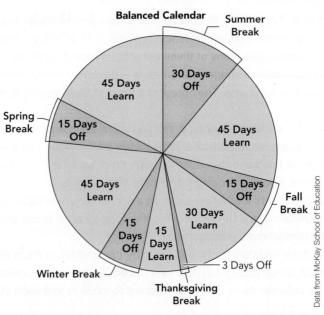

Data from McKay School of Education

Here is another visual text promoting this reform:

KIDS WHO READ BEAT
SUMMER SLIDE

Studies show that access to books during the summer prevents a drastic loss in reading skill – especially for kids in need.

Students from low-income households with access to books

Students from high-income households with access to books

Students from low-income households without access to books

READING
TEST SCORES

+24.15

+15.51

-9.77

End of School Year   June   July   Aug.   Beginning of School Year

First Book

SOURCES: 1. Change in scores between end-of-year and following year testing as shown by the California Aptitude Test. (Slates, S. L., Alexander, K. L., Entwisle, D. R., & Olson, L. S. (2012). Countercating summer slide: Social capital resources within socioeconomically disadvantaged families. Journal of Education for Students Placed at Risk, 17(3), 165.)

First Book

This image uses each of the three main rhetorical appeals:

- **Logos.** The reading scores and the achievement gap statistic provide data.
- **Pathos.** We are expected to feel sympathy for those disadvantaged students who do not have access to books or school during the summer and fall further and further behind.
- **Ethos.** Schools have an ethical responsibility to educate all of their students equally. The authors of this visual have taken the time to summarize the research for us.

This proposal for a "balanced" calendar is not without its opponents, and one writer concerned with the issue used the image on page 400 as a way to dramatize the potential drawbacks of the reform.

Look carefully at this image. The child's bare arms and the greenery in the background give the impression of summertime. Notice that the child's face is not shown; instead the viewer's eye is drawn to the hands, which look more like claws as the child appears to be trying to escape. The fence fills the frame of the image, encompassing the child entirely. Based on these details, the photograph in this context seems intended to express the idea that school in the summer is like a prison that makes children miserable. Images and visuals have the power to persuade and we have to read them as critically as we do any other arguments.

CribbVisuals/Getty Images

activity

Visual Arguments

Thinking about the reform at your school that you are proposing, describe a visual you could locate or create that might help you persuade your audience. How might you use color and lighting, framing and focus, layout and design, and fonts and symbols to help you?

REFLECTING ON Academic Vocabulary   **Essential Elements of an Argument**

Working with a partner or small group, discuss the terms in this section and that you previewed on page 388 and clarify your understanding of each. Then, share what you learned about reading and writing arguments. What did you find helpful, relevant, unnecessary, redundant, and so on?

culminating activity

Working with Argument

Throughout this chapter, you will focus on both analyzing other people's arguments and writing your own. Choose one of the options below and demonstrate your current knowledge of and skill with arguments.

1. Throughout this workshop, you have been writing about a change needed at your school. Use that work to develop an argument that includes a claim, evidence, and appeals. Address at least one counterargument and give thought to your stylistic choices.

2. Locate an editorial about an educational issue on the website of your local paper or a credible national newspaper. Write a brief analysis of the author's use of claim, evidence, appeals, counterargument, and style.

Big Words and Little Action

Greta Thunberg

When she was 15 years old, Swedish activist Greta Thunberg (b. 2003) skipped school to stand outside of the Swedish Parliament in August 2018 to call out global leaders for not addressing the seriousness of climate change. She is the youngest *Time* magazine Person of the Year, she has appeared on the *Forbes* list of the World's 100 Most Powerful Women (2019), and she has received three consecutive nominations for the Nobel Peace Prize (2019–2021). She wrote this letter, published in *Vogue*, to celebrate Earth Day 2021.

Sean Gallup/Getty Images

On Earth Day 2021, April 22nd, at the Leaders' Climate Summit led by United States president Joe Biden, countries will present their new climate commitments, including net-zero by 2050. They will call these hypothetical targets ambitious. However, when you compare the overall current best-available science to these insufficient, so-called "climate targets," you can clearly see that there's a gap — there are decades missing where drastic action must be taken.

Of course, we welcome all efforts to safeguard future and present living conditions. And these targets could be a great start if it wasn't for the tiny fact that they are full of gaps and loopholes. Such as leaving out emissions[1] from imported goods, international aviation and shipping, as well as the burning of biomass, manipulating baseline data, excluding most feedback loops and tipping points,[2] ignoring the crucial global aspect of equity and historic emissions, and making these targets completely reliant on fantasy or barely existing carbon-capturing technologies. But I don't have time to go into all that now.

The point is that we can keep using creative carbon accounting and cheat in order to pretend that these targets are in line with what is needed. But we must not forget that while we can fool others and even ourselves, we cannot fool nature and physics. The emissions are still there, whether we choose to count them or not.

[1] Harvey, Fiona. "Half UK's true carbon footprint created abroad, research finds." *The Guardian*, Apr. 2019. https://www.theguardian.com/environment/2020/apr/16/britain-climate-efforts-undermined-failure-imports-carbon

[2] Climate Reality Project. "How Feedback Loops Are Making the Climate Crisis Worse." *Climaterealityproject.org*, Jan. 2020. https://www.climaterealityproject.org/blog/how-feedback-loops-are-making-climate-crisis-worse

MLGXYZ/Getty Images

This is a photograph of wildfires near Lake Elsinore, California in 2018.
Describe the effects of framing and lighting in the image. How might Thunberg use this image to help her make a point about climate change?

Still, as it is now, the people in power get away with it since the gap of awareness is so immense. And this is the heart of the problem. If you call these pledges and commitments "bold" or "ambitious," then you clearly haven't fully understood the emergency we are in.

I've met with many world leaders and even they admit that their targets are not in line with their commitments. And that's natural. They are only doing what they consider to be politically possible. Their job is to fulfill the wishes of voters, and if voters are not demanding real climate action, then of course no real changes will happen. And thankfully, this is how democracy works. Public opinion is what runs the free world. If we want change then we must spread awareness and make the seemingly impossible become possible.

We understand that the world is complex, that many are trying their best and that what is needed isn't easy. And, of course, these very insufficient targets are better than nothing. But we cannot be satisfied with something just because it's better than nothing. We have to go further than that. We must believe that we can do this, because we can. When we humans come together and decide to fulfill something, we can achieve almost anything.

When leaders now present these pledges, they admit that they surrender on the 1.5 degrees Celsius target. They are surrendering on their promises and on our futures. I don't know about you, but I sure am not ready to give up. Not in a million years. We will keep fighting for a safe future. Every fraction of a degree matters and will *always* matter.

You may call us naive for believing change is possible, and that's fine. But at least we're not so naive that we believe that things will be solved by countries and companies making vague, distant, insufficient targets without any real pressure from the media and the general public.

The gap between what needs to be done and what we are actually doing is widening by the minute. The gap between the urgency needed and the current level of awareness and attention is becoming more and more absurd. And the gap between our so-called climate targets and the overall, current best-available science should no longer be possible to ignore.

These gaps of action, awareness, and time are the biggest elephant that has ever found itself inside any room. Until we can address this gap, no real change is possible. And no solutions will be found.

Our emperors are naked — let's call them out. And please, mind the gap.[3] ■

———
[3] —Eds. "Mind the gap" is an audiovisual warning to subway passengers to watch their step while crossing from the platform to the train. It is most commonly used in England.

Understanding and Interpreting

1. In the first paragraph, Thunberg states her purpose for writing. Restate this purpose in your own words.

2. What are the "gaps" that Thunberg identifies in paragraph 2? What is the importance of addressing those gaps at the beginning of her argument?

3. Why does Thunberg say that we should not consider the world leaders' commitments to be "bold" or "ambitious" (par. 4)?

4. What counterarguments does Thunberg raise in her argument, and to what extent does she successfully address them?

5. In paragraph 5, Thunberg says that "this is how democracy works. Public opinion is what runs the free world." What point is she making about democracy, and how does it support her argument?

6. Summarize the errors countries and leaders are making, according to Thunberg, and explain how pointing out these errors supports her purpose.

Analyzing Language, Style, and Structure

7. **Vocabulary in Context.** In paragraph 7, Thunberg writes that world leaders will "present these pledges." What does the word *pledge* mean in this context and how is that usage similar to or different from other usages, such as pledging allegiance to the flag?

8. Why might Thunberg have decided to start her argument by calling the new climate proposals "insufficient"?

9. In paragraph 2, Thunberg includes multiple examples of gaps and loopholes, but then says she doesn't "have time to go into all that now"? Does that phrase help or hinder her argument? Why?

10. Notice the variety of pronouns that Thunberg uses in her piece: *they, our, you, I, we.* Choose two of these pronouns and explain why she might have used them the way that she does.

11. Look closely at paragraph 6. What word might best describe Thunberg's tone? How does her diction reveal her attitude toward humans taking action?

12. An idiom is an expression or phrase that has meaning beyond the individual words and often requires cultural knowledge to understand. In paragraph 10, Thunberg writes that the gaps she mentions are the "elephant" in the room. What does this phrase mean and why is it useful to her argument?

13. In the last paragraph, Thunberg uses an allusion: "Our emperors are naked — let's call them out." If necessary, do a quick search on the children's story "The Emperor's New Clothes" and explain the significance of Thunberg's use of the allusion. What is the connection between the children's story and what she addresses in her letter? How does including this reference impact her message?

Topics for Composing

14. **Analysis.** Restate Thunberg's central claim in this piece. Then, choose one of the specific points that Thunberg makes to prove her overall claim and analyze how she supports that point with evidence and appeals. To what extent is that support effective?

15. **Argument.** Thunberg says, "We must believe that we can do this, because we can. When we humans come together and decide to fulfill something, we can achieve almost anything" (par. 6). Do you think she is right in this case? Why or why not? You can conduct additional research, or you can refer to your own experiences and reasoning.

16. **Argument.** One possible solution Thunberg proposes is to address the gap in public awareness of the threat of climate change. What are the pros and cons of this solution? Do you think it would be effective? Why or why not? You will likely need to conduct additional research to support your position.

17. **Connections.** Thunberg makes the following statement in her essay: "But we cannot be satisfied with something just because it's better than nothing" (par. 6). In general, do you think this is true? Describe a personal experience that supports your response. (Your experience does not need to be related to climate change.)

18. **Speaking and Listening.** Prepare for and hold a class or small group discussion about the possible steps that individuals can take to address the global issues of climate change. Be sure to listen actively to each other and try to identify points of consensus.

19. **Research.** Conduct research on the most recent actions that countries are taking to address climate change. What are some similarities and differences in the specific steps some countries are taking to address climate change? Where is progress being made?

20. **Research.** One possible solution to lowering greenhouse gas emissions includes the development of carbon-capturing technologies. Conduct research on these technological developments and the progress they have made in reducing carbon emissions.

21. **Multimodal.** Create an infographic representation of an important aspect affecting climate change, such as the current global emissions by country or by source. Be sure that your infographic includes both images and words to communicate your message clearly. Share your findings in a presentation to your peers.

Abolish the police? No. Reform policing? Absolutely

Los Angeles Times Editorial Board

The *Los Angeles Times* is a daily newspaper that has been published in Los Angeles, California, since 1881. It has the fifth-largest newspaper circulation in the United States. The Editorial Board consists of editorial writers who speak collectively to express the newspaper's opinion on current issues related to politics, governance, academia, and business.

KEY CONTEXT   In this editorial published in the *Los Angeles Times* (May, 2021), the Editorial Board expresses its viewpoint on potential approaches to policing problems in America. This conversation occurred in the wake of events that gained national attention, including the murder of George Floyd, an unarmed Black man, by a police officer in 2020.

As talks continue in the Senate over the George Floyd Justice in Policing Act of 2021, a comprehensive bill to improve and monitor police behavior, the main bone of contention is how best to hold police officers accountable for misconduct, such as the excessive force that injures and sometimes kills so many Americans, a disproportionate number of them Black men. In the background is a continuing debate that was magnified last year by the sometimes violent anti-police and anti-racism protests following Floyd's murder — and especially by the reelection campaign of President Trump, many of whose backers argued that there was little about police conduct that needed to be altered, particularly not while violent crime was rising precipitously in major American cities.

But there is another debate, another fracture, that is at least as important as the mostly left-right one that divides police reformers from backers of the status quo. On this second front, reformers quietly defend their plans for better officer training, discipline, oversight and accountability against a vocal generation of protesters and activists who argue that the idea of reforming the police is a liberal fantasy.

To support their case they point to decades of procedural and legislative changes that have left us with police who are still too quick to shoot and still too apt to harass or dehumanize members of Black, Latino and impoverished communities whom they are sworn to protect and serve.

In fact, much of the "defund the police" movement directly opposes traditional police reforms, which require larger, not smaller, budgets in order to invest in technologies like body cameras, procedural changes like oversight commissions and programs like the Los Angeles Police Department's Community Safety Partnership, which embeds police officers in public housing projects and troubled neighborhoods to build trust between officers and residents. That's money, say defunders and abolitionists, that should be spent not on police but on healthcare, schools and jobs.

That position was expressed on the street last summer and, in L.A., in City Council, Police Commission and other agencies' public hearings on city budgets and police conduct. Donna Harati, director of legal service for Homeboy Industries, offered a common sentiment in a statement to a Police Commission task force last summer.

5

Americans' Views on Policing and Police Funding

	Protecting people from crime	Using the right amount of force for each situation	Treating racial and ethnic groups equally	Holding officers accountable when misconduct occurs

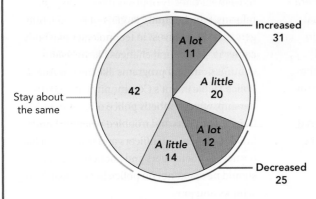

	Sept '16	June '20	Sept '16	June '20	Sept '16	June '20	Sept '16	June '20
NET	62	58	45	35	47	34	44	31
Excellent	16	15	10	8	11	9	12	9
Good	46	43	35	27	36	25	32	22
Only fair	27	26	32	28	26	26	26	27
Poor	10	15	22	36	27	39	30	42
NET	37	41	54	64	53	65	56	69

Note: No answer responses not shown.
Source: Survey of U.S. adults conducted June 16–22, 2020.
PEW RESEARCH CENTER

Americans' Views on Policing and Police Funding

- Increased 31
  - A lot 11
  - A little 20
- Decreased 25
  - A little 14
  - A lot 12
- Stay about the same 42

Note: No answer responses not shown.
Source: Survey of U.S. adults conducted June 16–22, 2020.
PEW RESEARCH CENTER

Look at these two charts created from data based on PEW Research Center surveys conducted in 2020.

Based on data in the top chart, how have people's attitudes toward policing changed over time? What may have contributed to those changes? What conclusions can you draw about the results in the bottom chart? How would the authors of this article use these results to support their position?

"Majority of Public Favors Giving Civilians the Power to Sue Police Officers for Misconduct". Pew Research Center, Washington, D.C. July 9, 2020, https://www.pewresearch.org/politics/2020/07/09/majority-of-public-favors-giving-civilians-the-power-to-suepolice-officers-for-misconduct/

"The only answer to stopping the harm and violence police cause communities is to stop the contact between police and communities," Harati said. "This requires shrinking the size and scope of policing and increasing meaningful investments in communities. We need to police people less and invest in communities more."

Numerous other speakers offered similar sentiment but were considerably less civil, their comments dripping with anger and ridicule toward police and politicians and ending with a sign-off of, "And by the way, f—you."

Many critics call for outright abolition of police, and the stance is attractive when police are seen in the historical context of enforcers of a racist status quo created by white society to keep freed Black Americans and other people of color in their place. It's not an altogether accurate view of history, but not wholly inaccurate, either. If police are framed as successors to slave-catching patrols, then police abolition takes on the aura of basic morality, and "reform" is tinged with the distasteful notions of gradualism that made racial segregation a fixture in the laws of many states for more than a century after emancipation.

But American policing, if indeed partially a successor to slave patrols, is also the descendant of the British model of professional, concierge-like problem-solvers who work in concert with residents to prevent small offenses or disputes from getting out of hand. The LAPD, heirs to both models, was once known to beat homeless "vagrants" in order to drive them out of town and — at the same time — to obligingly arrange housing for new residents.

Abolish police and the vacuum will be filled — by private security officers hired by corporations that answer to investors instead of voters, by self-appointed armed and angry vigilantes, by gangs collecting "taxes" on businesses and residents in return for protection. Professional policing is the nation's pride, separating the U.S. from countries patrolled by private forces. And it is the nation's shame — its dark id — inflicting heartless, needless death because our gun-loving society is over-armed, and because police enforce and respond to patterns of race, class and wealth to which we still cling, unwittingly or otherwise. 10

So we must reform. We must advocate for the George Floyd Justice in Policing Act. We must improve accountability, require (and pay for) bodycams, update training, mold police culture to further embrace the concierge model and let go of the occupier ethic. We must divert police away from jobs unsuited to them, like serving the homeless or mentally ill in crisis, and fund professionals better suited to those tasks. It's less bracing than "abolition" and less catchy than "defund." But we're in it for the long haul, to save lives and build a better, more just and freer society. ■

Understanding and Interpreting

1. According to the Editorial Board, what is the additional "fracture" mentioned in paragraph 2?

2. What reforms does the Board feel should be put in place? How does it say reform should be approached?

3. Looking again at paragraphs 6 through 8, what counterarguments does the Board raise? How does the Board use the counterarguments from defunders and abolitionists to further its own assertions?

4. In paragraphs 8 and 9, the Board briefly describes historical models of policing. Summarize these models and explain how they help the Board to make its argument.

5. According to the Board, how can the policing problems be remedied? Use evidence from the text to support your response.

Analyzing Language, Style, and Structure

6. **Vocabulary in Context.** In paragraph 8, the Board writes about "gradualism that made racial segregation a fixture." What does the word *gradual* mean and how does the addition of the suffix *-ism* affect its meaning in this context?

7. How do the comments by Donna Harati and the other speakers at the public hearings in paragraphs 6 and 7 differ from the Board's opinion as presented in paragraph 11? What purpose do these comments serve in the Board's argument?

8. Describe the cause and effect relationship proposed in paragraph 10. Why does the Board feel this an important point to highlight?

9. In paragraph 10, the Board describes professional policing as both the nation's "pride" and its "shame." How can something be both of these things? What is the Board hoping readers will conclude from the use of these two labels for policing?

10. Reread paragraph 10 and examine the Board's diction. What are the most descriptive and emotionally charged words and phrases in this paragraph? What tone is the Board trying to create in this paragraph and what specific words and phrases help create that tone?

11. In the last paragraph, the Board uses repetition ("we must") to introduce solutions. What is the effect of this rhetorical strategy in the conclusion?

Topics for Composing

12. **Analysis.** From the title alone, we quickly recognize the Board's overall claim. What main points does it make to prove that claim? What evidence does it use to support that claim?

13. **Analysis.** Write a response in which you analyze the Board's approach to balancing its argument with counterarguments. Is its approach effective? Why, or why not? Use examples from the text to support your analysis.

14. **Argument.** In paragraph 10, the Board claims that completely abolishing the police means replacing them with private corporate officers. Write an argument in which you agree or disagree with the idea that professional policing in the United States is more effective than policing in countries that are "patrolled by private forces." Be sure to discuss the differences between the two approaches and the potential pros and cons of each.

15. **Argument.** Write a response in which you argue for a position about a specific police reform. Conduct research if necessary and provide evidence to support your position.

16. **Connections.** Have you or a close friend or family member had a personal experience with policing? If so, describe the experience and explain how it relates to a point about needed police reforms made by the Editorial Board.

17. **Speaking and Listening.** Prepare for and hold a class or small group discussion in which you agree or disagree with defunders' and abolitionists' stances on uses for budget money. Do you agree or disagree with the claim that money should not be spent on traditional reform methods outlined in paragraph 4, but rather on "healthcare, schools and jobs" (par. 4)? Provide reasons for your thinking.

18. **Research.** Interview one or more local police officers or resource officers assigned to your school about the current state of policing in your community. What challenges do they currently face? How do they handle communication with the community? What reforms would they like to see implemented? Or, interview one or more people who have interacted with the police in either a positive or negative way. Based on their experiences, what changes in policing might they suggest?

19. Research. Conduct research on the George Floyd Justice in Policing Act of 2021. What law enforcement practices and policies does this bill address? What ultimately happened with the bill? Research what other legislation has been proposed to address police reform in your community, your state, or nationwide. Create a presentation to share your findings.

The Case for LGBT-Inclusive Education

Cirri Nottage

Cirri Nottage is a writer, educator, and consultant who works in the greater Atlanta area in Georgia. She currently operates her company, Nottage Consulting, and serves as the lead organizer for Fair Count, a nonpartisan nonprofit that worked on providing fair and accurate data for the 2020 Census. Her article below appeared as an op-ed piece for NBC News in 2016.

Cirri Nottage

The alarming rate of bullying, homelessness, HIV and suicide among LGBT youth should be an outrage: Nearly a fifth of students[1] are physically assaulted because they are LGBT; among homeless children, 25 to 50 percent are LGBT; the CDC reports[2] among youth aged 13 to 24 diagnosed with HIV in 2014, 80 percent were gay and bisexual males; and gay teens are also eight times more likely to report having attempted suicide.

Instead, the outrage swirls around who gets to use whose bathroom. Sparked by North Carolina's "bathroom bill", the legal battle over transgender rights recently escalated to include over a dozen states suing the federal government in response to the Obama administration's transgender bathroom policy. What if all the time, energy and taxpayer money spent on litigation were invested toward providing comprehensive LGBT inclusive health education for all children?

The Guttmacher Institute's analysis of state laws and policies on sex and HIV education reveals disparities that are equally alarming and illustrates how most children are not learning about sexuality.

While nine states require public school teachers to recognize common expressions of human sexuality in sexual education classes, including LGBT relationships, most states eschew such a requirement. In fact, four states demonstrate an open hostility toward teachers even mentioning any sexual relationship other than heterosexual relationships. According to South Carolina's Comprehensive Health Education Act, for example, "alternative lifestyles from heterosexual relationships" may only be discussed "in the context of instruction concerning sexually transmitted diseases."

If these gross deficiencies aren't startling enough, when you consider how bias and inter-sectionality (a theory of how social identities and related systems of discrimination overlap) further complicate learning environments, it becomes less surprising that our public schools are failing our children.

5

[1] PFLAG New York City. "Statistics You Should Know about Gay & Transgender Students." *Pflagnyc.org.* https://www.pflagnyc.org/safeschools/statistics
[2] Centers for Disease Control and Prevention. "HIV and Youth." *CDC.gov.* https://www.cdc.gov/hiv/group/age/youth/index.html

What point is this editorial cartoon making about those who support so-called "bathroom bills"? How would Nottage likely respond to the cartoon?

Curricula that ignore science, are medically inaccurate and/or fail to affirm diversity, multiple identities and normal childhood development are unethical. Students' learning is further impeded by climates that are often violent, racist, sexist, homophobic and transphobic.

Without support, many LGBT youth leave home and school when staying is no longer tolerable; tragically, many take their own lives when they believe they will never be accepted for who they are and how they express themselves.

According to Daniela Liget, a 42-year veteran school counselor, developing romantic inclinations for someone of the same sex is part of normal, healthy childhood development. "It

would be incredibly irresponsible when talking about the emotional, social changes of puberty with 10-year-olds not to say 'some of you will find that you are romantically interested in somebody of the same sex, some of you will find that you are romantically interested in somebody of the opposite sex'. . . . It's a fact of development."

Karen Rayne, PhD, an expert in sexual education, agrees. "Heteronormativity harms young people because it puts them into an identity box, molding them to our assumptions, often before they have even begun to understand their identities." Her book, *Breaking the Hush Factor: Ten Rules for Talking with Teenagers about Sex*, is a primer for adults interacting with young people grappling with their emerging understanding of identity and sexuality.

However, activist, author and ally Sam Killermann cautions against talking "facts" when discussing gender identity. Killermann publishes curriculum and activities to help educators create safe zones for LGBT students. "What we're learning is how much we don't know and that's incredibly powerful. What we do know is most kids have a good understanding of what their gender identity is by about age two or three. So when kids are saying their gender identity is different from what they are assigned at birth and people dismiss them saying, 'You're only six you can't possibly know that,' that actually goes against the science."

Rayne says, "We have to watch for such moments when we (inevitably) make assumptions about young people. We have to apologize for being dismissive and then leave space for the young people to tell us who they are, when they are ready. . . . They are looking for someone to listen to them."

The GLSEN 2013 National School Climate Survey[3] measures how schools support LGBT students. Not surprisingly the survey reveals schools with supportive educators, Gay-Straight Alliances (GSAs), anti-bullying / harassment policies and comprehensive LGBT-inclusive curricula have healthier school climates and better learning outcomes for LGBT students.

Educators say one of the main benefits of LGBT-inclusive curricula are the diverse narratives that get shared. Students see themselves reflected in stories where they usually don't appear and hear narratives that might sound

like their own. In turn, students normalize that diversity in their own lives by learning to speak up and speak out for other narratives as allies.

Learning how to use different language is part of the process, enlisting allies is another. Such massive social change requires a bottom-up grass roots movement of everyone who sees the damage done by heteronormativity. Killermann believes questioning our own assumptions and asking questions about identities we don't understand is also essential.

Rayne added, "Moving beyond the set of assumptions that heteronormativity imposes is sometimes as easy as a shift in language (from boyfriend to partner or sweetheart, for example), and sometimes invites us, the adults in the young people's lives, into a deep dialogical interaction with ourselves, with our friends, partners, and colleagues, and with the culture at large."

This cultural conversation is happening now. The attorney general's strong statement and the Obama administration's directive on transgender bathroom policy, sends a clear message that legislating identity and discriminating against transgender students because others are uncomfortable is unlawful and not who we are as a nation.

Supporting LGBT youth, improving their health and educational outcomes, and ending the stigma and violence requires cultural perceptions of sexual orientation and gender identity to evolve beyond heteronormativity. Meeting this requirement means funding education and mandating robust LGBT-inclusive curricula and culturally responsive pedagogies focused on expanding our knowledge and understanding of the diverse learning needs of every child. As this turbulent election season reminds us, our experiment in democracy depends on an educated citizenry. Our children are our future. ■

[3] Kosciew, Joseph G, et al. "The 2013 National School Climate Survey." Gay, Lesbian & Straight Education Network, 2014. https://www.glsen.org/sites/default/files/2020-03/GLSEN-2013-National-School-Climate-Survey-Full-Report.pdf

Understanding and Interpreting

1. Reread the first paragraph, noting the specific statistics Nottage includes. What appeal is at work here, and what is the effect of including this data at the beginning of the article?

2. What are some of the ways that Nottage says LGBT-inclusive curricula can make a difference?

3. Paraphrase what Nottage describes as the theory of "intersectionality" where "social identities and related systems of discrimination overlap" (par. 5). How does her reference to this theory further support her argument for LGBT support in the classroom?

4. In your own words, describe the solutions Nottage suggests in her last paragraph.

5. Look back through the article for quotations from Dr. Rayne. Summarize the points Dr. Rayne makes and explain how Nottage uses Dr. Rayne's points to support her own argument.

Analyzing Language, Style, and Structure

6. **Vocabulary in Context.** In paragraph 5, Nottage writes that there are "gross deficiencies." What does the term *gross* mean in this context?

7. How would you describe Nottage's tone in paragraph 5? What language choices does she use to support her attitude toward current learning environments?

8. Throughout her piece, Nottage intentionally uses inclusive language intended to dispel what she identifies as heteronormativity in our schools. Identify examples of her language choices and explain how they support her purpose.

9. Structurally, where does Nottage address opposing views in her argument? Does her placement hinder or help her argument? Explain.

Topics for Composing

10. **Analysis.** What is Nottage's central claim? How does she balance various types of evidence to support her claim?

11. **Analysis.** Nottage incorporates a variety of appeals (ethos, pathos, logos) in her argument. Select one appeal and use evidence from the text to analyze its effectiveness in advancing her argument.

12. **Argument.** According to Nottage, one solution for LGBT inclusivity is "funding education and mandating robust LGBT-inclusive curricula and culturally responsive pedagogies focused on expanding our knowledge and understanding of the diverse learning needs of every child" (par. 17). Write a response in which you argue whether this approach is suitable or overly complex or simplistic. What else, if anything, can, or should, be done?

13. **Connections.** Describe experiences you or your friends have had with heteronormativity at your school. In what ways are those experiences similar to or different from what Nottage describes?

14. **Speaking and Listening.** Review your school's anti-bullying and harassment policies. Hold a discussion with your peers about how well the policies are implemented and followed at your school. What are the strengths about your school's policies, or in what ways can the policies be strengthened? What part do you play in shaping or implementing these policies?

15. **Research.** Conduct research on current legislation pertaining to the LGBTQ+ rights in your state or community. What action is currently being taken to support or oppress the LGBTQ+ community? How might Nottage react to that legislation?

argument / section two

This Empty World

Nick Brandt

Nick Brandt (b. 1964) is a British photographer whose work mainly focuses on the disappearing natural world. For years, he has photographed the changing African continent. These images are taken from a collection he released in 2019 called *This Empty World*.

Nick Brandt

KEY CONTEXT   The photo essay *This Empty World* was published with the following description of the artistic process that Brandt used to create his images:

> Each image is a combination of two moments in time, captured weeks apart, almost all from the exact same locked-off camera position.
>
> Initially, a partial set is built and lit. Sometimes, such as with a dead forest, it is actually the complete set. Weeks, even months follow, whilst the animals that inhabit the region become comfortable enough to enter the frame. Once the animals are captured on camera, the full sets — bridge and highway construction sites, a petrol station, a bus station, and more — are built by the art department team. In all but a few of the photos, the camera remains fixed in place throughout.
>
> A second sequence is then photographed with full set and a large cast of people drawn from local communities and beyond.
>
> The final large-scale prints are a composite of the two elements.
>
> (Note: The images were all photographed on local Maasai community land, without protected reserve status, close to Amboseli National Park in Kenya. After the sets were removed and all their elements recycled with almost zero waste, no evidence of the shoot now remains in the landscape.)

1.

2.

3.

4.

5.

(continued)

6.

Understanding and Interpreting

1. Look closely at images 1 and 2 ("Bus Station with Elephant in Dust" and "River Bed with Hyenas"). Describe the animals in each image and explain how the colors and the framing of the scenes helps Brandt to communicate an idea about the conflict between animals and the modern world.

2. Images 3 and 4 ("Bridge Construction with Giraffe & Worker" and "Charcoal Burning with Giraffe & Worker") both include giraffes. How are the giraffes and the people posed in similar and different ways in the two images? What are possible intended effects of the poses and background choices?

3. Look at image 6 ("Highway Construction with Elephants, Workers & Fence"). What message might Brandt be trying to communicate in this picture, especially through the use of the fencing?

4. After looking through the images, reread the description of the two-shot process that Brandt used for this project and summarize how this process applies to one of the images. In other words, describe how Brandt created that particular image and how his method supports his stated mission to advocate for the natural world.

5. "Juxtaposition" refers to the intentional placement of two things near each other for the purpose of illustrating contrast. Where are the clearest examples of juxtaposition in these images and how does Brandt create the contrasts?

6. How would you describe the animals in these images? How are they represented by their settings?

Analyzing Language, Style, and Structure

7. Look back at Brandt's images specifically for his use of color and lighting. Some images have a bluish tint, some have very low lighting, while others include points of bright, stark, artificial light. What are some possible effects of Brandt's lighting and color choices on the viewer's understanding of the subject and Brandt's message?

8. "Framing" refers to what a photographer chooses to include in the frame, what to leave out, and the angle from which the viewer appears to see the image. Select one of Brandt's images and explain how his framing choices lead to a specific effect on the viewer.

9. What is the overall tone of this collection, and what does Brandt do to create that tone? How is this tone related to his purpose?

10. If you were to view these images as part of the complete photo essay online (https://www.thisemptyworld.com/), you would be able to zoom in. How would that dynamic way of viewing these images be different from the static presentation in this textbook? In other words, how would the ability to zoom and scan change how you experience individual images and the photo essay as a whole?

Topics for Composing

11. **Analysis.** The full photo essay is made up of more images than have been included here. If you consider the images provided here as a representative group, what is Brandt suggesting about the effects that humans have on the natural world? Cite specific elements of the images to support your response.

12. **Argument.** Write an argument in which you state a problem identified in Brandt's photo essay and then propose a solution. Feel free to conduct outside research to support your argument.

13. **Connections.** While you likely have not experienced wildlife in quite the same way as Brandt presents the animals in his photo essay, you may have seen wild animals in a zoo or other human-made environment. Describe a specific time you have encountered a wild (not domesticated) animal in an artificial or unusual environment. What are your emotional and rational reactions to seeing the animal in this way? How are those reactions similar to or different from your reaction to Brandt's images?

14. **Speaking and Listening.** Select one image from this collection (or one from the full collection available online) and write and deliver a short presentation that examines Brandt's use of color, lighting, framing, and other visual elements. (See p. 56 for more information on interpreting visual texts.)

15. **Research.** What is the current condition of one of the species of animals depicted in Brandt's images? Conduct research to understand how the animals are being affected by human encroachment. Are they endangered or subjected to poaching, for example?

16. **Creative Writing.** Write captions, speech bubbles, or thought bubbles for two or three of the photographs that imagine what the humans in the images might say or what the animals might be thinking if they were actually in each other's presence in real time.

17. **Multimodal.** Create a project that uses images in juxtaposition to explore a topic that is meaningful to you. While you are probably not able to create the kinds of images that Brandt was able to for his project, you can use collage or photo apps to duplicate aspects of his two-shot approach. What would you hope to communicate to your audience?

On Being a Refugee, an American —and a Human Being

Viet Thanh Nguyen

San Francisco Chronicle/ Hearst Newspapers via Getty Images/Getty Images

Viet Thanh Nguyen was born in Vietnam in 1971 and immigrated to the United States with his family when he was four years old at the end of what the United States refers to as the Vietnam War. He is the author of the Pulitzer Prize–winning novel *The Sympathizer* (2015) and its sequel *The Committed* (2021). He is also the editor of the collection of essays, *The Displaced: Refugee Writers on Refugee Lives* (2018). This piece was published in the *Financial Times* in 2017.

The United States became actively involved in the Southeast Asian country of Vietnam in the mid-1960s with the stated purpose of stopping the spread of Communism. At the war's peak, the United States had over 500,000 soldiers fighting to support the government in South Vietnam in Saigon, against the North Vietnamese government that was supported by Communist China and the Soviet Union. By the time the United States withdrew all its forces in 1975, over 50,000 Americans had died, and some estimates state that nearly 2 million Vietnamese soldiers and civilians had died as a result of the conflict. After the war, thousands of people from Vietnam as well as nearby Cambodia and Laos fled, often in small boats (hence, they are sometimes referred to as "boat people"), to places such as Malaysia, Indonesia, and Hong Kong, where they applied for permission to resettle in the United States, Canada, and other Western countries. Hundreds of thousands of refugees from the war eventually settled in the United States, and Nguyen's family was part of this group of refugees.

I am a refugee, an American, and a human being, which is important to proclaim, as there are many who think these identities cannot be reconciled. In March 1975, as Saigon was about to fall, or on the brink of liberation, depending on your point of view, my humanity was temporarily put into question as I became a refugee.

My family lived in Ban Me Thuot, famous for its coffee and for being the first town overrun by communist invasion. My father was in Saigon on business and my mother had no way to contact him. She took my 10-year-old brother and 4-year-old me and we walked 184 km to the nearest port in Nha Trang (I admit to possibly being carried). At least it was downhill. At least I was too young, unlike my brother, to remember the dead paratroopers hanging from the trees. I am grateful not to remember the terror and the chaos that must have been involved in finding a boat. We made it to Saigon and reunited with my father, and, a month later, when the communists arrived, repeated the mad scramble for our lives. That summer we arrived in America.

I came to understand that in the United States, land of the fabled American dream, it is un-American to be a refugee. The refugee embodies fear, failure, and flight. Americans of all kinds believe that it is impossible for an American to become a refugee, although it is possible for refugees to become Americans and in that way be elevated one step closer to heaven.

To become a refugee means that one's country has imploded, taking with it all the things that protect our humanity: a functional government, a mostly non-murderous police force, a reliable drinking water and food supply, an efficient sewage system (do not underestimate how important a sewage system is to your humanity; refugees know that their subhuman status as the waste of nations is confirmed by having to live in their own waste).

I was luckier than many refugees, but I still remain scarred by my experience. After I arrived in the refugee camp set up at Fort Indiantown Gap, Pennsylvania, at four years old, I was taken away from my parents and sent to live with a white sponsor family. The theory, I think, was that my parents would have an easier time of working if they didn't have to worry about me. Or maybe there was no sponsor willing to take all of us. Regardless, being taken away from my family was simply another sign of how my life was no longer in my hands, or those of my parents. My life was in the hands of strangers, and I was fortunate that they were kind, even if to this day I still remember howling as I was taken from my parents.

Like the homeless, refugees are living embodiments of a disturbing possibility: that human privileges are quite fragile, that one's home, family, and nation are one catastrophe away from being destroyed. As the refugees cluster in camps — as they dare to make a claim on the limited real estate of our conscience — we deny we can be like them and many of us do everything we can to avoid our obligations to them.

The better angels of our nature have always told us that morality means opening our doors, helping the helpless, sharing our material wealth. The reasons we come up with to deny doing such things are rationalisations. We have wealth to share with refugees, but we would rather spend it on other things. We are capable of living with foreigners and strangers, but they make us uncomfortable, and we do not want to be uncomfortable. We fear that strangers will kill us, so we keep them out.

Our fate as refugees is controlled by the strategies of the men who command the bombers. In my case, the US dropped more bombs on Vietnam, Laos, and Cambodia during the Vietnam war than it did all of Europe during the second world war. This played a role in creating refugees, and because of American guilt and anticommunist feeling, the US government took in 150,000 Vietnamese refugees in 1975. It authorised the admission of several hundred thousand more, and other Southeast Asian refugees, in the subsequent decade. What the US did exceeded what Southeast Asian countries did, which was to deny entry to the "boat people" or contain them in camps until they could find a host country like the United States. Accepting these refugees was proof that the US was paying its debt to its South Vietnamese allies, and the refugees became reminders that life under communism was horrible. We were expected to be grateful for our rescue from such a life, and many of us were and are thankful.

"But I was also one of those unfortunate cases who could not help but wonder whether my need for American charity was due to my having first been the recipient of American aid," or so I wrote in my novel *The Sympathizer*. I am a bad refugee, you see, who can't help but see that my good fortune is a stroke of bureaucratic luck and the racial politics of the United States, where Asians are considered model minorities.

Peter Kuper/CartoonStock

What message does this cartoon convey by obscuring words in the poem on the base of the Statue of Liberty? In what ways does this message relate to what Nguyen experienced when he first arrived in America?

If I was Haitian in the 1970s and 1980s, I would not have been admitted as a refugee, because I was black and poor. If I was Central American today, I would not be admitted as a refugee, even though the US has destabilised the region in the past through supporting dictatorial regimes and creating the conditions for the drug economy and drug wars. I am a bad refugee because I insist on seeing the historical reasons that create refugees and the historical reasons for denying refugee status to certain populations.

Central Americans are categorised instead by the United States as immigrants, which suspends questions over the influence of American policy on their countries of origin. The immigrant is that foreigner who has proceeded through the proper channels. The immigrant is

10

the one who wants to come, unlike the refugee, who is forced to come. The immigrant, as contrasted to the refugee, is awesome. The immigrant, in turn, makes America awesome. Or great. I forget the right word. In any case, here are the famous words on the Statue of Liberty:

> Give me your tired, your poor,
> Your huddled masses yearning to breathe free,
> The wretched refuse of your teeming shore.
> Send these, the homeless, tempest-tost to me,
> I lift my lamp beside the golden door!

Except that this has not always been true. The current xenophobia in American society that is directed against refugees and their cousins, undocumented immigrants, and even against legal immigrants, has deep roots. Inasmuch as America has been built by immigrants and is welcoming to foreigners, it has also been built on genocide, slavery, and colonialism.

These two aspects of America are contradictory but both are true at the same time, as they are true of the other liberal democracies of the west. So it is that in the US, where 51 percent of billion-dollar start-ups were founded by immigrants, and all of the 2016 Nobel Prize winners are immigrants, the country has periodically turned on its immigrants. Beginning in 1882, the United States banned Chinese immigrants. The excuse was that the Chinese were an economic, moral, sexual, and hygienic threat to white Americans. In retrospect, these reasons seem ridiculous, particularly given how well Chinese Americans have integrated into American society. These reasons should make us aware of how laughable contemporary fears about Muslims are — these fears are as irrational as the racism directed against the Chinese. Various other legal acts effectively ended non-white immigration to the country by 1924, and while the door would slowly creak open with the repeal of the Chinese Exclusion Act in 1943 (when 105 Chinese were permitted to enter annually), the United States would not embrace open immigration until 1965's Immigration Act.

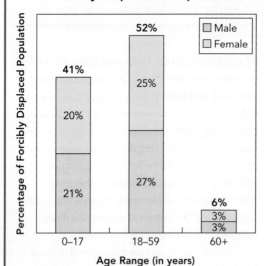

Forcibly Displaced People, 2020

Disclaimer: figures do not add up to 100 percent due to rounding.
Data from UNHCR Global Trends 2020.

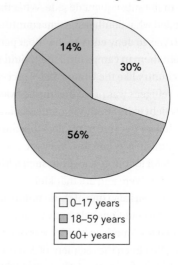

World Population by Age, 2019

Data from United Nations, Department of Economic and Social Affairs, Population Division (2019).

What conclusions can you draw about the populations of those who have been displaced? How might Nguyen use this data in his own argument?

The contemporary US has been defined by that act, with large numbers of Asian and Latino immigrants coming in and reshaping what America is (and for the better; without immigration from non-white countries, American food would be as terrible as that of pre-immigration England). But the prejudice remains. It emerges in the feeling against undocumented immigrants. Those who oppose them say we should give preference to documented immigrants, but I suspect that once the undocumented have been kicked out, these rational people will start speaking about how there are too many immigrants in general.

In truth, my own family is an example of the model minority that could be used to rebut such an argument. My parents became respectable merchants. My brother went to Harvard seven years after arriving in the States with no English. I won the Pulitzer Prize. We could be put on a poster touting how refugees make America great. And we do. But it shouldn't take this kind of success to be welcomed. Even if refugees, undocumented immigrants, and legal immigrants are not all potential billionaires, that is no reason to exclude them. Even if their fate is to be the high-school dropout and the fast-food cashier, so what? That makes them about as human as the average American, and we are not about to deport the average American (are we?).

The average American, or European, who feels that refugees or immigrants threaten their jobs does not recognise that the real culprits for their economic plight are the corporate interests and individuals that want to take the profits and are perfectly happy to see the struggling pitted against each other. The economic interests of the unwanted and the fearful middle class are aligned — but so many can't see that because of how much they fear the different, the refugee, the immigrant. In its most naked form, this is racism. In a more polite form, it takes the shape of defending one's culture, where one would rather remain economically poor but ethnically pure. This fear is a powerful force, and I admit to being afraid of it.

Then I think of my parents, who were younger than me when they lost nearly everything and became refugees. I can't help but remember how, after we settled in San Jose, California, and my parents opened a Vietnamese grocery store in the rundown downtown, a neighbouring store put a sign up in its window: "Another American driven out of business by the Vietnamese." But my parents did not give in to fear, even though they must have been afraid. And I think of my son, nearly the age I was when I became a refugee, and while I do not want him to be afraid, I know he will be. What is important is that he have the strength to overcome his fear. And the way to overcome fear is to demand the America that should be, and can be, the America that dreams the best version of itself. ■

Understanding and Interpreting

1. What does Nguyen mean when he writes, "my humanity was temporarily put into question as I became a refugee" (par. 1)?

2. Nguyen claims that it is "un-American to be a refugee" (par. 3). He then explains what he means by this in the rest of the paragraph. Summarize his main point.

3. Even though he says he was more fortunate than most refugees, Nguyen says his experience scarred him. Identify the events that seemed to contribute most to this emotional scarring.

4. In your own words, restate the "disturbing possibility" (par. 6) that refugees represent, according to Nguyen.

5. What rationalizations do people offer for not doing more to help refugees, according to Nguyen (par. 7)? Does he think these are valid reasons?

6. Why does Nguyen consider himself to be a "bad refugee" (par. 9)? Does he really think of himself that way? How do you know?

7. In paragraph 10, Nguyen tries to make a distinction between the words *refugee* and *immigrant*. What are the differences, and why is this distinction important to Nguyen's argument?

8. Nguyen writes in paragraph 11 that Americans hold "contradictory" attitudes toward immigrants. Summarize what he says in the rest of the paragraph to support that idea. How successful is he at proving his point?

9. In paragraph 13, Nguyen describes the success that his family has had in America. Why does he include this information? How does it support his position about America and refugees?

10. Reread paragraph 14 and explain why immigrants or refugees and those who oppose them should support each other. What, according to Nguyen, gets in the way of this cooperation?

Analyzing Language, Style, and Structure

11. **Vocabulary in Context.** In the first paragraph, Nguyen writes "Saigon was about to fall." What does the word *fall* mean in this context and how is that meaning similar to other uses of the word?

12. **Vocabulary in Context.** In paragraph 10, Nguyen writes that xenophobia, prejudice against people from countries other than one's own, is "directed against refugees and their cousins, undocumented immigrants." What does the word *cousins* mean in this context?

13. Reread paragraph 2, in which Nguyen describes his family's escape from Vietnam. What diction and imagery does he use to communicate the terror he felt throughout this journey?

14. In paragraph 3, Nguyen characterizes the United States as the "land of the fabled American Dream." What effect does the word *fabled* have in this sentence? What does this word choice reveal about Nguyen's attitude toward America?

15. Reread paragraph 4 and identify the tone Nguyen uses. Then, explain how his diction and use of parentheses reveal his tone in this section.

16. Nguyen writes that refugees "dare to make a claim on the limited real estate of our conscience" (par. 6). What does his word choice in this phrase reveal about his attitude toward Americans?

17. In paragraph 10, Nguyen uses the word *awesome* twice and the word *great*. How would you describe these word choices? What do they reveal about his tone?

18. In the middle of his piece, Nguyen decides to quote the inscription from the base of the Statue of Liberty. How does including it at this point in his piece help him to make his argument about the treatment of immigrants and refugees in the United States?

19. What is the effect of Nguyen's use of the word *laughable* to describe contemporary fears about Muslims (par. 11)?

20. Explain how we know that Nguyen is likely being sarcastic when he uses the word *rational* to describe people who speak out against those who are undocumented.

Topics for Composing

21. **Analysis.** While much of this piece reads like a narrative about Nguyen's own immigration story, it is also an argument that puts forward this claim: "As the refugees cluster in camps — as they dare to make a claim on the limited real estate of our conscience — we deny we can be like them and many of us do everything we can to avoid our obligations to them" (par. 6). How does Nguyen use logic, evidence, other elements of argument, and his own experiences to prove this claim?

22. **Argument.** Is Nguyen right about how America treats immigrants, undocumented immigrants, or refugees? Feel free to conduct additional research, including interviews, to help you to support your argument.

23. **Connections.** What are your or your family's experiences with relocation to or within the United States? For example, do you or your family have direct experience as immigrants or refugees, as members of a community experiencing an influx of immigrants or refugees, or as descendants of slavery or forced relocation? How are your and your family's experiences similar to and different from what Nguyen describes?

24. **Connections.** Only the conclusion of Emma Lazarus's poem "The New Colossus" is inscribed on the base of the Statue of Liberty. Locate and read the full poem. Write a brief analysis of the theme and tone of the poem and write an explanation about how the speaker of the poem might agree or disagree with Nguyen's perspective on immigrants and refugees. (Refer to Chapter 8 if you need support with analyzing poetry.)

25. **Speaking and Listening.** Conduct an interview with a family member, friend, teacher, or someone with first-hand experience with immigration or being a refugee. Prepare five or six questions ahead of time and listen closely to their responses. Explain how their experiences were similar to or different from those that Nguyen describes.

26. **Research.** Nguyen refers to the myth of the "Model Minority," which is the misperception that Asian-Americans are universally successful. Research this concept and explain how it can be damaging. How does knowing more about the myth of the "Model Minority" add to your understanding of Nguyen's argument?

27. **Research.** Conduct research to learn more about the Vietnamese "boat people" refugees in the 1970s and 1980s. Explain how this context helps you understand more about the events recounted in this piece.

28. **Research.** Conduct research on a contemporary refugee crisis. In the example you choose, explore what is driving people to leave their homes and what is being done to support them. How is the case you're examining similar to or different from what Nguyen experienced?

Hiroshima Speech

Ethan Miller/Getty Images

Barack Obama

Barack Obama (b. 1961) served as the 44th president of the United States. He also served as both Illinois state senator and U.S. senator. Prior to that he taught constitutional law at the University of Chicago. President Obama was awarded the 2009 Nobel Peace Prize and is the first African American to serve as president of the United States. He published the first volume of his memoir *A Promised Land* in 2020. In 2021, he started a podcast with musician Bruce Springsteen called *Renegades: Born in the USA*.

KEY CONTEXT In 2016, President Obama became the first sitting American president to visit Hiroshima, Japan, the site of the first atomic bomb ever used in combat. The United States dropped atomic bombs on Hiroshima and Nagasaki on August 6 and 9, 1945, killing over 100,000 people, essentially ending World War II. While no nuclear weapons have been used in combat since that time, many countries have developed the technology, and many people have been working to ban nuclear weapons altogether. Some people in the United States did not want the president to make the following speech, fearing he might apologize on behalf of the United States for dropping the atomic bomb. At the same time, there were others in the United States and in other countries who were hoping for and expecting an apology.

Seventy-one years ago, on a bright cloudless morning, death fell from the sky and the world was changed. A flash of light and a wall of fire destroyed a city and demonstrated that mankind possessed the means to destroy itself.

Why do we come to this place, to Hiroshima? We come to ponder a terrible force unleashed in a not-so-distant past. We come to mourn the dead, including over 100,000 Japanese men, women and children, thousands of Koreans, a dozen Americans held prisoner.

Their souls speak to us. They ask us to look inward, to take stock of who we are and what we might become.

It is not the fact of war that sets Hiroshima apart. Artifacts tell us that violent conflict appeared with the very first man. Our early ancestors having learned to make blades from flint and spears from wood used these tools not just for hunting but against their own kind. On every continent, the history of civilization is filled with war, whether driven by scarcity of grain or hunger for gold, compelled by nationalist fervor or religious zeal. Empires have risen and fallen.

Peoples have been subjugated and liberated. And at each juncture, innocents have suffered, a countless toll, their names forgotten by time.

The world war that reached its brutal end in Hiroshima and Nagasaki was fought among the wealthiest and most powerful of nations. Their civilizations had given the world great cities and magnificent art. Their thinkers had advanced ideas of justice and harmony and truth. And yet the war grew out of the same base instinct for domination or conquest that had caused conflicts among the simplest tribes, an old pattern amplified by new capabilities and without new constraints.

In the span of a few years, some 60 million people would die. Men, women, children, no different than us. Shot, beaten, marched, bombed, jailed, starved, gassed to death. There are many sites around the world that chronicle this war, memorials that tell stories of courage and heroism, graves and empty camps that echo of unspeakable depravity.

Yet in the image of a mushroom cloud that rose into these skies, we are most starkly reminded

Spaarnestad Photo/Bridgeman Images

This is a photograph of the aftermath of the bomb in Hiroshima.
What words or phrases from Obama's speech capture the destruction shown in this image?

of humanity's core contradiction. How the very spark that marks us as a species, our thoughts, our imagination, our language, our toolmaking, our ability to set ourselves apart from nature and bend it to our will—those very things also give us the capacity for unmatched destruction.

How often does material advancement or social innovation blind us to this truth? How easily we learn to justify violence in the name of some higher cause.

Every great religion promises a pathway to love and peace and righteousness, and yet no religion has been spared from believers who have claimed their faith as a license to kill.

Nations arise telling a story that binds 10 people together in sacrifice and cooperation, allowing for remarkable feats. But those same stories have so often been used to oppress and dehumanize those who are different.

Science allows us to communicate across the seas and fly above the clouds, to cure disease and understand the cosmos, but those same discoveries can be turned into ever more efficient killing machines.

The wars of the modern age teach us this truth. Hiroshima teaches this truth.

Technological progress without an equivalent progress in human institutions can doom us. The scientific revolution that led to the splitting of an atom requires a moral revolution as well.

That is why we come to this place. We stand here in the middle of this city and force ourselves to imagine the moment the bomb fell. We force ourselves to feel the dread of children confused by what they see. We listen to a silent cry. We remember all the innocents killed across the arc of that terrible war and the wars that came before and the wars that would follow.

Mere words cannot give voice to such suffering. But we have a shared responsibility to look directly into the eye of history and ask what we must do differently to curb such suffering again.

Some day, the voices of the *hibakusha*[1] will no 15 longer be with us to bear witness. But the memory of the morning of August 6, 1945, must never fade. That memory allows us to fight complacency. It fuels our moral imagination. It allows us to change.

And since that fateful day, we have made choices that give us hope. The United States

---

[1] A Japanese term that translates literally as "bomb-affected-people," it is used to identify the survivors of the nuclear bomb attacks. —Eds.

Sean Pavone/Alamy

This image is from the Hiroshima Peace Memorial Park, which is intended "as a historical witness that conveys the tragedy of suffering the first atomic bomb in human history and as a symbol that vows to faithfully seek the abolition of nuclear weapons and everlasting world peace."

How does the memorial communicate this intent? Identify a line from Obama's speech that would make an appropriate caption for this picture.

and Japan have forged not only an alliance but a friendship that has won far more for our people than we could ever claim through war. The nations of Europe built a union that replaced battlefields with bonds of commerce and democracy. Oppressed people and nations won liberation. An international community established institutions and treaties that work to avoid war and aspire to restrict and roll back and ultimately eliminate the existence of nuclear weapons.

Still, every act of aggression between nations, every act of terror and corruption and cruelty and oppression that we see around the world shows our work is never done. We may not be able to eliminate man's capacity to do evil, so nations and the alliances that we form must possess the means to defend ourselves. But among those nations like my own that hold nuclear stockpiles, we must have the courage to escape the logic of fear and pursue a world without them.

We may not realize this goal in my lifetime, but persistent effort can roll back the possibility of catastrophe. We can chart a course that leads to the destruction of these stockpiles. We can stop the spread to new nations and secure deadly materials from fanatics.

And yet that is not enough. For we see around the world today how even the crudest rifles and barrel bombs can serve up violence on a terrible scale. We must change our mind-set about war itself. To prevent conflict through diplomacy and strive to end conflicts after they've begun. To see our growing interdependence as a cause for peaceful cooperation and not violent competition. To define our nations not by our capacity to destroy but by what we build. And perhaps, above all, we must reimagine our connection to one another as members of one human race.

For this, too, is what makes our species unique. 20 We're not bound by genetic code to repeat the mistakes of the past. We can learn. We can choose. We can tell our children a different story, one that describes a common humanity, one that makes war less likely and cruelty less easily accepted.

We see these stories in the *hibakusha*. The woman who forgave a pilot who flew the plane

Explain the message communicated in this editorial cartoon, especially by examining how the two figures, President Obama and Uncle Sam, a common stand-in for the United States, are portrayed. In what ways does Obama's speech address the message of the cartoon?

that dropped the atomic bomb because she recognized that what she really hated was war itself. The man who sought out families of Americans killed here because he believed their loss was equal to his own.

My own nation's story began with simple words: All men are created equal and endowed by our creator with certain unalienable rights including life, liberty and the pursuit of happiness. Realizing that ideal has never been easy, even within our own borders, even among our own citizens. But staying true to that story is worth the effort. It is an ideal to be strived for, an ideal that extends across continents and across oceans. The irreducible worth of every person, the insistence that every life is precious, the radical and necessary notion that we are part of a single human family—that is the story that we all must tell.

That is why we come to Hiroshima. So that we might think of people we love. The first smile from our children in the morning. The gentle touch from a spouse over the kitchen table. The comforting embrace of a parent. We can think of those things and know that those same precious moments took place here, 71 years ago.

Those who died, they are like us. Ordinary people understand this, I think. They do not want more war. They would rather that the wonders of science be focused on improving life and not eliminating it. When the choices made by nations, when the choices made by leaders, reflect this simple wisdom, then the lesson of Hiroshima is done.

The world was forever changed here, but today the children of this city will go through their day in peace. What a precious thing that is. It is worth protecting, and then extending to every child. That is a future we can choose, a future in which Hiroshima and Nagasaki are known not as the dawn of atomic warfare but as the start of our own moral awakening. ∎

25

Understanding and Interpreting

1. After vividly describing the bombing of Hiroshima, Obama in paragraph 2 poses and answers the question, "Why do we come to this place, to Hiroshima?" How does this strategy help Obama frame the occasion for his speech? What does that also reveal about his purpose at the beginning of his speech?

2. According to Obama, "It is not the fact of war that sets Hiroshima apart" (par. 4). What does he mean by this? How does he support this claim? What, if any, assumptions does he make about war in this section?

3. What is Obama referring to when he writes, "In the span of a few years, some 60 million people would die. Men, women, children no different than us, shot, beaten, marched, bombed, jailed, starved, gassed to death" (par. 6)? Why is this context so important to his audience both in Japan and back home in the United States?

4. In paragraph 7, what does Obama call "humanity's core contradiction"? How does this phrase relate to the main point of this argument?

5. In paragraph 13, Obama states, "We listen to a silent cry." What does this mean?

6. After briefly stating reasons for hope, Obama pivots to the claim that every nation must possess the ability to defend itself, suggesting that "We may not be able to eliminate man's capacity to do evil, so nations and the alliances that we form must possess the means to defend ourselves" (par. 17). How does this address the counterarguments of those who feel the use of nuclear weapons may be justified?

Analyzing Language, Style, and Structure

7. **Vocabulary in Context.** The final word of the speech is *awakening*. What is the meaning of the word in this context? How is it similar to and different from other uses of the word? How does the word in this context help readers understand the purpose of Obama's visit and remarks?

8. Obama opens his speech with vivid imagery: "On a bright, cloudless morning, death fell from the sky and the world was changed." Notice how the images are starkly contrasting. What tone does this description establish?

9. In paragraph 1, Obama states that the dropping of the bomb "demonstrated that mankind possessed the means to destroy itself." Why does President Obama choose to say "mankind" here instead of referring to any specific country or nation involved in the bombing? How does this choice reveal his attitude toward the bombing?

10. Obama is speaking for the people of the United States directly to a Japanese audience. Identify language that seems especially supportive of U.S. policy and language that is sympathetic to the people of Japan. Does he meet the needs of both nations effectively, or would you expect this speech to be more widely accepted by one nation than the other? Why?

11. How does Obama's use of the phrase "ever more efficient killing machines" (par. 11) serve his argument?

12. In paragraph 13, Obama circles back to the opening of his speech with these lines: "That is why we come to this place. We stand here, in the middle of this city, and force ourselves to imagine the moment the bomb fell." Explain why Obama chooses to use this structure in his argument.

13. In paragraph 14, Obama writes, "we have a shared responsibility to look directly into the eye of history and ask what we must do differently to curb such suffering again." Here he personifies history. In what way is this stylistic choice effective? What does it suggest about the perspective of people who look into the eyes of history?

14. In paragraph 16, Obama shifts the focus from the challenges and casualties of war to the topic of hope: "And since that fateful day, we have made choices that give us hope." How and why has the tone changed?

15. Obama makes an allusion to the Declaration of Independence in paragraph 22, saying, "All men are created equal, and endowed all by our Creator with certain unalienable rights, including life, liberty and the pursuit of happiness." How does he use this allusion to develop his argument?

16. As the argument comes to a close, Obama again tries to answer the question of why "we" have come to Hiroshima. This time he presents a different series of images: "The first smile from our children in the morning. The gentle touch from a spouse over the kitchen table. The comforting embrace of a parent. We can think of those things and know that those same precious moments took place here, 71 years ago" (par. 23). What do these images suggest? What do these images have in common? How are these images different from, but related to, the images in paragraph 1?

Topics for Composing

17. **Analysis.** What is Obama suggesting about the nature of war and peace? Write a response in which you analyze the rhetorical choices that Obama makes in supporting his conclusion about war and peace.

18. **Argument.** In paragraph 16, Obama states, "And since that fateful day, we have made choices that give us hope." How does he support the claim that we have made better choices since Hiroshima? Do you agree or disagree with his interpretation that we, as a world, have learned from our mistakes at Hiroshima?

19. **Argument.** Prior to visiting Hiroshima to deliver this speech, Obama announced that he was not going to Japan to offer an apology. You may be wondering, why wouldn't he apologize? Take a moment to consider the significance of an apology from a head of state and make a list of possible ramifications for offering and not offering an apology. When you are done, write an argument for or against the leader of a country offering an apology to another nation or group of people. Be sure to address the counterarguments that you anticipated in your list.

20. **Argument.** Which will advance further and faster, the moral or technological imagination of humankind? You can base your response on this speech or on your own observations and reasoning, or you can conduct research for more information.

21. **Connections.** Obama says, "Nations arise telling a story that binds people together in sacrifice and cooperation, allowing for remarkable feats. But those same stories have so often been used to oppress and dehumanize those who are different" (par. 10). Can you think of a situation in which someone (you, a friend or relative, a stranger) was dehumanized or oppressed? Explain the circumstance and then identify people who filled the following roles in the circumstance: perpetrator, ally, bystander, and victim.

22. **Connections.** Read "Hiroshima" from the August 31, 1946, issue of the *New Yorker* to learn "how six survivors experienced the atomic bomb and its aftermath." How do these accounts shape your understanding of Obama's speech at Hiroshima?

23. **Speaking and Listening.** Videos of Obama delivering this speech are widely available online. After you have read the speech, listen to and watch him deliver it. How would you describe his delivery? Emotional? Dispassionate? How does watching him add to or change your understanding of the text of the speech?

24. **Research.** Why did the United States bomb Hiroshima? Find multiple sources to develop your answer. Carefully consider the bias of each source and try to find sources from multiple perspectives. When you are done researching, explain why you think there are so many different opinions regarding the justification of the bombing.

25. **Research.** While reading this speech, you may have noticed statements that diplomatically address one group or another. Obama knows that many Americans will be angered by an apology for an act that they feel saved more lives than it took, while many Japanese citizens will see anything short of an apology as unacceptable. Do a quick web search to learn more about how different groups reacted to his speech. How was it received in Japan, the United States, and other countries, such as China? Look for both positive and negative responses and summarize your findings by contrasting at least three responses to his speech.

26. **Multimodal.** Locate images from Hiroshima or Nagasaki before, during, or after the attacks and arrange them with lines from Obama's speech as captions. What effects do these images with the captions create for your viewer?

Is It Immoral to Watch the Super Bowl?

Steve Almond

Photo by Sheryl Lanzel

Steve Almond (b. 1966) is a *New York Times* best-selling author of nonfiction and short stories. He is a regular contributor to the *New York Times Magazine*, the *Rumpus*, and the *Boston Globe*. He is the author of *Against Football: One Fan's Reluctant Manifesto*, which looks at the moral and ethical issues in what is often thought of as America's favorite game. He has worked as a sports reporter and a play-by-play announcer, and he taught creative writing at Boston College. This piece appeared in the *New York Times Magazine* in 2014.

In the summer of 1978, during a preseason game, a wide receiver for the New England Patriots named Darryl Stingley lunged for a pass just out of his reach. Before he could regain his balance, he was hit by Jack Tatum, an Oakland Raiders defensive back. It was clear at once that Stingley was, in gridiron parlance, "shaken up on the play." Team doctors rushed to his side.

I was 11, a devout Raiders fan. I knew I was supposed to feel bad for Stingley, and I did in some minor, dutiful way. Mostly I was proud of Tatum, of the destructive capacities central to his mystique. The whole point of being Jack Tatum — a.k.a. the Assassin — was to level wide receivers in this manner.

The problem was that Stingley wasn't moving. The doctors kept tapping at his knees with reflex hammers. The longer Stingley lay on the chalked grass, the more ashamed I grew. Because I knew, even then, that part of my attraction to football was the thrill of such violent transactions.

What I remember most of all is the thought that dogged me in the days afterward, as it became clear that a star player had been rendered quadriplegic on national television: Surely the game of football would now be outlawed.

Obviously that never happened. Instead, Stingley wound up taking a desk job with the Patriots and being honored in the manner of a war hero. Tatum continued to terrorize opposing players. The N.F.L. juggernaut rolled on, solidifying its place atop America's Athletic Industrial Complex. And I kept right on watching, often devoting entire Sunday afternoons to football in my bachelor years.

Recently, though, medical research has confirmed that football can cause catastrophic brain injury — not as a rare and unintended consequence, but as a routine byproduct of how the game is played. That puts us fans in a morally queasy position. We not only tolerate this brutality. We sponsor it, just by watching at home. We're the reason the N.F.L. will earn $5 billion in television revenue alone next year, three times as much as its runner-up, Major League Baseball.

Never is this sponsorship more overt than next Sunday, for the Super Bowl has become an event of such magnitude that it ranks as a secular holiday at this point, as much a celebration of the sport's ability to draw multimillion-dollar

What tone does artist George Hicks convey about football in this painting called "Will He Do It?" How does Hicks establish that tone? How might Almond respond to the image? Why?

Bridgeman Images

ads as the contest itself. More than 100 million people will watch the game. Most of my friends will be parked in front of their TVs. For the first time in 35 years, I won't be among them.

Just so we're clear on this: I still love football. I love the grace and the poise of the athletes. I love the tension between the ornate structure of the game and its improvisatory chaos, and I love the way great players find opportunity, even a mystical kind of order, in the midst of that chaos.

The problem is that I can no longer indulge these pleasures without feeling complicit. It was easier years ago, when injuries like Stingley's could be filed away as freakish accidents. TV coverage was relatively primitive, the players hidden under helmets and pads, obscured by fuzzy reception, more superheroes than men. Today we see the cruelty of the game in high definition. Slow-motion replays show us the precise angle of a grotesquely twisted ankle and a quarterback's contorted face at the exact moment he is concussed.

The sport's incredible popularity has turned players into national celebrities and has made their mental and physical deterioration front-page news. In 2012, the former All-Pro linebacker Junior Seau killed himself. The autopsy confirmed that he had chronic traumatic encephalopathy, or C.T.E., the cause of the dementia that is increasingly prevalent among former players. A whole new crop of retired stars, including Tony Dorsett and Brett Favre, are just beginning to report symptoms like memory loss and depression.

There are two basic rationalizations for fans like myself. The first is that the N.F.L. is working hard to make the game safer, which is flimsy at best. The league spent years denying that the game was causing neurological damage. Now that the medical evidence is incontrovertible, it has sought to reduce high-speed collisions, fining defenders for helmet-to-helmet hits and other flagrantly violent play. Its most significant response has been to offer $765 million to settle a class-action lawsuit brought by more than 4,500 former players, but a judge recently blocked the settlement. It simply wasn't enough money.

The second argument is that players choose to incur the game's risks and are lavishly compensated for doing so. This is technically true. N.F.L. players are members of an elite fraternity that knowingly places self-sacrifice, valor and machismo above ethical or medical common sense. But most start out as kids with limited options. They may love football for its inherent virtues. But they also quickly come to see the game as a path to glory and riches. These rewards aren't inherent. They arise from a culture of fandom that views players as valuable only so long as they can perform.

10

431

WARNING

Keep your head up. Do not butt, ram, spear or strike an opponent with any part of this helmet or faceguard. This is a violation of football rules and may cause you to suffer severe brain or neck injury, including paralysis or death and possible injury to your opponent. Contact in football may result in **Concussion/Brain Injury** which no helmet can prevent. Symptoms include: loss of consciousness or memory, dizziness, headache, nausea or confusion. If you have symptoms, immediately stop and report them to your coach, trainer, and parents. Do not return to a game or contact until all symptoms are gone and you receive medical clearance. Ignoring this warning may lead to another and more serious or fatal brain injury.

NO HELMET SYSTEM CAN PROTECT YOU FROM SERIOUS BRAIN AND/OR NECK INJURIES INCLUDING PARALYSIS OR DEATH. TO AVOID THESE RISKS, DO NOT ENGAGE IN THE SPORT OF FOOTBALL.

Stefan M. Duma

In 2013, Schutt Sports began putting this warning label on football helmets sold in the United States. Robert Erb, Schutt's chief executive, says, "It's an ethical, moral and legal issue. People need to know these things."

Do you think that warning labels like this have any effect, or are they a way to keep the company from being sued? Would Almond likely agree with the need for warning labels? Would it be enough for him to begin watching football again?

But if I'm completely honest about my misgivings, it's not just that the N.F.L. is a negligent employer. It's how our worship of the game has blinded us to its pathologies.

Pro sports are, by definition, monetized arenas for hypermasculinity. Football is nowhere near as overtly vicious as, say, boxing. But it is the one sport that most faithfully recreates our childhood fantasies of war as a winnable contest.

Over the past 12 years, as Americans have sought a distraction from the moral incoherence of the wars in Afghanistan and Iraq, the game has served as a loyal and satisfying proxy. It has become an acceptable way of experiencing our savage impulses, the cultural lodestar when it comes to consuming violence. What differentiates it from the glut of bloody films and video games we devour is our awareness that the violence in football, and the toll of that violence, is real.

The struggle playing out in living rooms across the country is that of a civilian leisure class that has created, for its own entertainment, a caste of warriors too big and strong and fast to play a child's game without grievously injuring one another.

The very rules that govern our perceptions of them might well be applied to soldiers: Those who exhibit impulsive savagery on the field are heroes. Those who do so off the field are reviled monsters.

The civilian and the fan participate in the same basic transaction. We offload the mortal burdens of combat, mostly to young men from the underclass, whom we send off to battle with cheers and largely ignore when they wind up wounded.

No single episode speaks to this twisted dynamic more pointedly than the death of Pat Tillman, an idealistic N.F.L. star who enlisted in the Army after the Sept. 11 attacks. In 2004, Tillman was killed by friendly fire in a bungled ambush in Afghanistan. His superiors orchestrated an elaborate cover-up that included burning his uniform and recast the circumstances of his death as a heroic charge into enemy territory.

But suppose Tillman had survived, returned to play in the N.F.L. and wound up with brain damage at age 50. Would we see him as a victim of friendly fire? Would we acknowledge our role in his demise? Or would we construct our own personal cover-ups?

15

The N.F.L. and the bloated media cult that feeds off it rely on fans not to connect the dots between our consumption of football and brain-damaged human beings. But to an even larger extent, we rely on one another.

The N.F.L. and the bloated media cult that feeds off it rely on fans not to connect the dots between our consumption of football and brain-damaged human beings. But to an even larger extent, we rely on one another.

I had a number of difficult conversations with friends in the course of writing this, none more so than with my neighbor Sean. He stood in my kitchen listening to all of my self-righteous bullet points. When I was done, he looked at me and said, in a quiet, imploring voice, "Please don't take this away from me."

I knew exactly what he meant — or thought I did. For the past five years, he and I have sought refuge from our grinding family duties by sneaking out to watch games together. I assumed he was referring to this camaraderie.

But Sean's fandom is far more elemental than mine. He grew up in rural West Virginia, hard-core football country. He was a natural from early on, a kid with the size, speed and agility to play at least college ball. When I asked him why he quit, he told me this story:

When he was about 11, his team played a rival with the best running back in the league. It was Sean's role, as the star of the defense, to make sure the kid didn't break through the line. On one play, Sean met the running back just as he was about to burst through a gap. The running back lowered his head, in the same instinctual way Darryl Stingley had, and their helmets collided at full speed. The kid fell and lay motionless.

The boy's coaches, and later his parents, ran onto the field. Smelling salts wouldn't revive him. Eventually, an ambulance appeared. Sean was convinced that he'd killed the boy. He began to cry. But what Sean remembers most vividly was the way, right after the tackle, his teammates kept slapping his helmet, as if he'd just done the most heroic thing ever, which, in a purely football sense, he had. He also recalls trying to walk away from his teammates, because he didn't want them to see that he was crying. Even three decades later, recounting this episode shook Sean up.

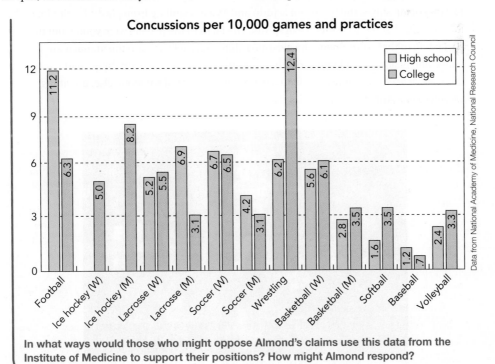

Concussions per 10,000 games and practices

Data from National Academy of Medicine, National Research Council

Legend: High school, College

- Football: 11.2 (High school), 6.3 (College)
- Ice hockey (W): 5.0 (College)
- Ice hockey (M): 8.2 (High school), 5.2 / 5.5
- Lacrosse (W): 6.9
- Lacrosse (M): 3.1, 6.7, 6.5
- Soccer (W): 4.2, 3.1
- Soccer (M):
- Wrestling: 12.4, 6.2
- Basketball (W): 5.6, 6.1
- Basketball (M): 2.8, 3.5
- Softball: 1.6, 3.5
- Baseball: 1.2, .7
- Volleyball: 2.4, 3.3

In what ways would those who might oppose Almond's claims use this data from the Institute of Medicine to support their positions? How might Almond respond?

433

The running back was not paralyzed. That's not the point of the story. It was the tremendous anguish Sean felt over his power to harm another boy. Having walked away from football — despite his passion for the game and his obvious gifts — Sean hardly needed to hear a lecture about the evils of being a fan. I felt like (and probably am) a moralizing jerk.

Don't we turn to football precisely to escape such ethical complexities, to experience the joy of watching bodies at play, to pretend, however

briefly, that life is just a fearless game? After all, I, too, recognize the desperate ardor that Frederick Exley captures in his novel "A Fan's Notes": "Whatever it was, I gave myself up to the Giants utterly. The recompense I gained was the feeling of being alive."

Still, I can't help thinking about something else Sean told me, which was how, in the hours and days after he delivered his big hit, he kept asking the same question of his coaches: "I didn't do anything wrong, did I?" ■

extending beyond the text

The passages below are from the 1990 nonfiction book *Friday Night Lights* by H. G. Bissinger, who followed a high school football team from Odessa, Texas, as they pursued the state championship. The first excerpt describes the locker room before a game against their rival school; the second focuses on the crowd when the team comes onto the field. The book was adapted into a film and then later into a television series that ran for five seasons. The image is from the television series.

> Every sound in the dressing room in the final minutes seemed amplified a thousand times — the jagged, repeated rips of athletic tape, the clip of cleats on the concrete floor like that of tap shoes, the tumble of aspirin and Tylenol spilling from plastic bottles like the shaking of bones to ward off evil spirits. The faces of the players were young, but the perfection of their equipment, the gleaming shoes and helmets and the immaculate pants and jerseys, the solemn ritual that was attached to almost everything, made them seem like boys going off to fight a war for the benefit of someone else, unwitting sacrifices to a strange and powerful god.

The stillness was ruptured by a thousand different sounds smashing into each other in wonderful chaos — deep-throated yells, violent exhortations, giddy screams, hoarse whoops. The people in the stands lost all sight of who they were and what they were supposed to be like, all dignity and restraint thrown aside because of these high school boys in front of them, their boys, their heroes, upon whom they rested all their vicarious thrills, all their dreams. No connection in all of sports was more intimate than this one, the one between town and high school.

What tone does Bissinger convey toward the players and the game of football? What specific words and phrases establish that tone? How does Bissinger's tone compare to that conveyed by the image from the television series? How is Bissinger's attitude toward football similar to and different from Almond's?

Understanding and Interpreting

1. In the opening five paragraphs, Almond recounts a memorable personal experience. What conflicting attitudes toward football — both playing and watching — does he raise in this introductory section? How does this discussion of conflicting attitudes help him build and support his argument?

2. According to Almond, what are some of the lasting impacts of football on the players, and why does he include these?

3. Almond states that he loves football and goes so far as to list the pleasures of watching the game. However, he follows that vivid description with this statement: "The problem is that I can no longer indulge these pleasures without feeling complicit" (par. 9). What reasons does Almond give for this statement?

4. In paragraph 11, Almond writes, "There are two basic rationalizations for fans like myself." Rationalizations defend controversial feelings or behaviors by making them seem rational. This is a defense mechanism that allows an individual to avoid uncomfortable truths. What are the two rationalizations Almond identifies, and what purpose do they serve in his argument?

5. What does Almond mean when he describes the belief that players participate in the game willingly and are "lavishly compensated for doing so" as being only "technically true" (par. 12)?

6. Almond writes that we "offload the mortal burdens of combat, mostly to young men from the underclass" (par. 17). What does he mean by this? What connection does this have to his central argument about watching football?

7. According to Almond, why does his neighbor Sean react so defensively to his arguments against watching football? What purpose does Sean's story play in Almond's argument?

8. In paragraph 16, Almond draws an analogy between the rules of war and football: "The very rules that govern our perceptions of [professional football players] might well be applied to soldiers: Those who exhibit impulsive savagery on the field are heroes. Those who do so off the field are reviled monsters." How does he support this assertion?

9. Throughout the article, Almond identifies a number of stakeholders in the N.F.L. Who are they and how do they profit from it? What does bringing in a range of interests add to his argument?

Analyzing Language, Style, and Structure

10. Vocabulary in Context. Near the end of the article, Almond worries that he is being a "moralizing jerk" (par. 26). What does the term *moralizing* mean in this context? Is he sincere in this concern, or is this an ironic statement? Point to evidence from the text to support your conclusions about his tone and purpose in using this phrase.

11. Vocabulary in Context. In paragraph 23, Almond writes, "But Sean's fandom is far more elemental than mine." *Elemental* is a term more often used in a science context. What is its meaning here and how is that meaning related to its scientific meaning?

12. What does the expression "shaken up on the play" mean, and how does Almond use it to make a point about how we watch football? What does referring to the phrase as "gridiron parlance" suggest about the audience Almond believes will read his essay?

13. How does Almond establish his ethos at various places throughout this piece? How does this assist him in making his case?

14. When Almond describes how high-definition television affects our perception (par. 9), he uses vivid, descriptive language. What is the effect of doing so? Is he betraying a bias, or is he successfully making his point — or both?

15. Throughout the essay, Almond makes self-critical statements, including referring to himself as a "moralizing jerk." What other examples do you find? Explain how such references undermine his ethos or add to his credibility.

16. How does paragraph 8 signal a shift in the argument? In what ways are the language and ideas a change from what preceded paragraph 8 and an introduction to what follows?

17. Throughout the essay, Almond uses personal anecdotes that call on his own experiences and recount those of other football fans and players. What role do these experiences play in building his argument?

18. Does Almond emphasize pathos or logos more in his argument? What does that emphasis suggest about who his intended audience is?

19. The inclusion of the story of football star and military volunteer Pat Tillman may seem off topic from Almond's main argument about watching or not watching football. How does Almond use this story to help support his claim?

Topics for Composing

20. Analysis. It becomes clear pretty quickly that Almond's answer to the question in the title is "yes," but what is Almond's central claim against watching football? What points does he make to support that claim?

21. Analysis. Write a response explaining how Almond builds his case against football. Analyze the strategies Almond uses to achieve his purpose. Use direct evidence from the essay to support your analysis and avoid including your own personal feelings about the topic.

22. Argument. Almond claims that watching football puts fans "in a morally queasy position. We not only tolerate this brutality. We sponsor it, just by watching at home" (par. 6). Do you agree or disagree that even watching a game puts you in "a morally queasy position"? Explain.

23. Argument. Almond remarks that "Pro sports are, by definition, monetized arenas for hypermasculinity" (par. 14). Do you agree or disagree with Almond's claim, even though there are plenty of female pro sports? Explain your response and provide examples from your own experience to support your claims.

24. **Connections.** Almond wants his readers to recognize and consider the ethics of watching the Super Bowl and supporting the N.F.L. He traces these misgivings about his values back to an experience he had at the age of eleven. Write about a time that you recognized and considered the ethics of an activity or experience in your life. Describe the activity or experience and the ethical implications. What did you need to know? What principles guided you? Did you or someone else discover an ethical responsibility to change behavior?

25. **Speaking and Listening.** Hold a class or small group discussion on the question posed in Almond's title, "Is It Immoral to Watch the Super Bowl?" Be sure to listen actively to each other during the discussion and try to find areas of consensus.

26. **Research.** When framing the ethical question of this article, Almond points to recent research that "has confirmed that football can cause catastrophic brain injury — not as a rare and unintended consequence, but as a routine byproduct of how the game is played" (par. 6). Research the long-term health risks of playing football and compare them to those of playing a different sport.

27. **Research.** Almond's friend Sean pleads, "Don't take this away from me." What would need to happen to save football for fans like Sean? Research the safety issues in football and explain the changes that could make the game safer and make supporting it no longer "morally queasy."

28. **Exposition.** Almond uses the term *ethical* several times in his piece, such as when he asks, "Don't we turn to football precisely to escape such ethical complexities, to experience the joy of watching bodies at play, to pretend, however briefly, that life is just a fearless game?" Write a piece that defines the word *ethical*. Use examples from the article to assist with the definition, along with experiences from your own life.

conversation

Is fandom a positive or negative force in our lives?

There are probably many things that you might consider yourself to be a "fan" of: a sports team, a TV show, a book series, a musician, a social media influencer, and so on. Being a fan of something generally gives us pleasure because engaging with the content can be entertaining, funny, exciting, and so on. Fandom also provides the opportunity for building community when people can come together to discuss some-times obscure or specialized knowledge about the topic with each other. And yet, there also can be a darker side of fandom. For example, there are numerous incidents of fans at sporting events throwing bottles, spitting, and cursing at players. In 2018, Kelly Marie Tran, an actor in the Star War series, effectively abandoned her Instagram account after fans of the series launched deeply racist and misogynistic online attacks against her.

If you read the Central Text in this chapter, "Is It Immoral to Watch the Super Bowl?," you saw just how much writer Steve Almond has wrestled with being a fan of football. He enjoys the speed, athleticism, and community of the sport, but he raises serious questions about the moral implications of watching something that can cause significant brain and bodily injuries.

This Conversation is an opportunity to explore this issue from multiple perspectives by examining texts and considering the question — ***Overall, is fandom a positive or negative force in our lives?***

 activity ## Starting the Conversation

1. Meet with a partner and discuss the following questions:

   a. What is one thing that you are a fan of? A specific sports team? A Musician? A YouTuber or TikToker? A movie or book series?

   b. How did you become a fan of that thing? Family? Geography? Friends? Online suggestions?

   c. About how much time do you spend being a fan of that thing? For example, how many hours do you spend watching football, streaming a favorite show, and so on?

   d. For you, are there any drawbacks to being a fan of it?

2. Create a table like the one below that will help you keep track of important information related to the ideas of being a fan, especially your own responses to the ideas you encounter in the texts you read.

Text Title / Author	Why Is Fandom Positive or Negative?	Best Evidence	Your Response

---

Source A

Olmsted, Larry. *Sports Fans are Happier People*, 2021.

No one has studied the psychological ramifications of sports fandom more than Dr. Daniel L. Wann, a psychology professor at Murray State University in Kentucky. The modern pioneer in the field, Wann has authored or coauthored close to two hundred significant journal articles and book chapters, several books, and more than one hundred papers presented at conferences globally. His first academic paper specifically on sports spectators was published in 1989, and he jokes that when he began studying sports fans as a doctoral candidate at the University of Kansas, so little had been done in this field that not only did he not have a road map for research, but that "there was no road": Wann had to create a new kind of questionnaire to identify fans and measure their level of fandom for his studies, and his Sports Spectator Identification Scale, or SSIS (now revised and expanded), is today the gold standard for researchers worldwide. "I can remember thinking, not only is there not a scale to improve upon, there's not anyone writing about this to give us ideas for what the scale should be in the first place."

In his three-plus decades of research, he's undertaken countless studies of men and women, young and old, fans of very different professional and amateur sports all around the world. The bottom line? For those who "identify with a sports team," as he defines a fan, he has found no less than twenty-four specific mental health benefits. Some of the biggest pluses that Wann and now other researchers have found include higher self-esteem; fewer bouts of depression; less alienation; lower levels of loneliness; higher levels of extroversion; higher levels of satisfaction with their social lives; more friends; higher levels of trust in others; more vigor and less fatigue; less anger; less confusion; less tension; greater frequency of experiencing positive emotions; and more conscientiousness. These sound very similar to Dr. Nichols's general happiness markers.

In 2019 Wann presented a university psychology colloquium called "The ABCs of Sport Fandom: What We Know and Where We Should Go," and explained it this way:

What we call the ABCs of psychology are affect, behavior, and cognition, or how we feel, what we do, and how we think. Sport fandom — the fact that we follow teams and sports and players — really does impact our emotional state; it really does impact what we *do,* what we think, how we perceive

the world. The big picture is that one thing fandom does is it helps to meet basic psychological needs, things like the need to belong, to feel a sense of connection to those around us. If you're in Murray, Kentucky, and you're a Racers basketball fan, it's hard to feel lonely. It's hard to feel alienated.

But it can also provide a sense of distinctiveness that can allow people to feel unique. Our ultimate goal in life is to fit in, while standing out. We want to fit *in,* but we don't want to be exactly like everyone else. *So,* you can be a sports fan that follows the local team and fits in, but you can also be a fan of a team [or sport] that maybe not a whole lot of people in that part of the country follow, so you can fit in but be different, unique, and distinct as well. People can use sports to meet these very powerful psychological needs.

A feeling of belonging leads to other mental health benefits, as the *New York Times* put it, "Sports fans suffer fewer bouts of depression and alienation than do people who are uninterested in sports."

Most of sports' psychological pluses accrue in two interrelated areas: belonging and self-esteem. The advantages of being part of a community of sports fans supporting a particular team are very real, as Dr. Wann described, "The benefits of social support are not limited to one's psychology but, rather, also predict both physical health and longevity of life." ■

Questions

1. How can being a sports fan address the ABCs of psychology, according to Dr. Wann, as quoted by Olmsted?
2. How can being a fan make us feel both part of a community and unique as individuals?
3. While Olmsted does not offer any counterarguments to his position about the benefits of being a fan, what are some possible objections?

4. **Comparison.** How is the argument Olmsted makes about being a fan similar to and different from what Almond writes about in "Is It Immoral to Watch the Super Bowl?"

5. **Informing Your Argument.** Return to the table that you created on page 438. Fill in the columns about whether Olmsted might consider fandom to be a positive or negative force in our lives, the best evidence he offers to clarify and support his ideas, and your response to what Olmsted is suggesting.

Source B

Trendacosta, Katharine. "When Fandom Is the Problem." *Gizmodo*, 27 June 2019.

"Fandom" — the participatory community that grows out of a piece of media — has come to dominate pop culture. Fandom is not simply being a fan of something. Fandom is performing being a fan by creating transformative works, collecting knowledge, cosplaying, attending conventions, and, ever-increasingly, being vocal online. Some of this has been really great for people seeking communities they can't find in real life, empowering them to be part of something that means a lot to them. And some of it has empowered only the worst elements of fan culture.

The interplay between fandom and creators of media can cause a dangerous downward spiral. The bad behavior of one enables the bad behavior of the other, until everyone else just leaves them both for dead. All of it is given a super charge by the ability to use the internet to amplify opinions and target them very specifically. So while this can allow fans to point out flaws that should be fixed, it can also lead to a dangerous amount of vitriol being directed at people who make and act in media. . . .

This year, in response to trolls preemptively leaving negative feedback for *Captain Marvel* — trying to tank the movie's audience rating before it came out — Rotten Tomatoes decided to disable comments for movies until they are released. As a further bulwark against this kind of abuse, the site later also decided to restrict the scores from non-professional reviews — the ones from regular people that comment on Rotten Tomatoes — that make up the average audience score to only those who could prove they had actually purchased a ticket to the movie. These new hoops that Rotten Tomatoes has put in place are an important check on the tactics of trolls and is a spotlight on how gross and entitled their behavior is.

The kind of trolling and harassment that follows movies like *Captain Marvel*, along with bitter infighting among vocal or "big name fans," is what turns a fandom toxic. At this point, "toxic" is almost a term of art, but it is truly the right word to describe fans so invested in a particular property that they act out to "save" or "defend" it, tainting the whole thing for everyone else. . . .

Fandom drama takes over social media after a new trailer or episode. It starts as GIFs of particularly great moments, then becomes a dissection of screenshots, and then criticisms — some legitimate and some not — start to show up. People start yelling at each other, generating post after post, tweet after tweet. All of which helps marketing, as it keeps the movie trending. In turn, trailers are becoming designed for this kind of dissection, which is why they often include Easter eggs for fans or shots that will never be in the movie. This is why you see "official" hashtags on Twitter with custom emojis. All the better to make fandom part of the official brand. . . .

There's a point at which a toxic fandom — or at least one where a very vocal minority is toxic — ruins the thing that created it. Toxic is the exact right term because it pollutes the very ground from which it grows. More than one person has mentioned *Rick and Morty* to me as a show they can't enjoy or admit they enjoy, and not because of the problems with the creators, but because of the problems with the *fans*; *Star Wars* is both a cultural juggernaut and an inexhaustible source of "the Discourse"; and a certain segment of DC fans has made it truly miserable to like, much less dislike, one of those movies. . . .

Fandom — which is much more diverse than Hollywood in general — does often have some expertise to offer. They pick up on things that seem obviously bad, like whitewashing, that mostly white Hollywood executives don't. But it is time to recognize that a toxic fandom doesn't just ruin something for the people in fandom, it can ruin the whole thing. It's time to stop catering to this particularly loud minority and it's especially time not to let "what fans want" be the sword and shield for bad decisions. ∎

Questions

1. How does Trendacosta define "fandom"? Why is it important that she defines it at the beginning of her argument?

2. What lessons does Trendacosta want her reader to draw from the online reaction to the Captain Marvel movie?

3. According to Trendacosta, how can fandom destroy the very thing it has created?

4. **Comparison.** How is the argument Trendacosta makes about being a fan similar to and different from what Almond writes about in "Is It Immoral to Watch the Super Bowl?"

5. **Informing Your Argument.** Return to the table that you created on page 438. Fill in the columns about whether Trendacosta might consider fandom to be a positive or negative force in our lives, the best evidence she offers to clarify and support her ideas, and your response to what Trendacosta is suggesting.

Source C

Oliver, David. "'Stan' culture needs to stop — or at least radically change. Here's why."
   USA Today, 7 Sept. 2021.

Swifties. Barbs. Army. Lambs.
These names correspond to celebrity fandoms. Swifties subsist on all things Taylor Swift. Barbs say "bottoms up" to anything Nicki Minaj. Army go full-on militant for BTS, and Lambs live by Mariah Carey.

Members of these groups may also be referred to as "stans" — ultrafans that will go to any length to prove their devotion to the celebrities of their choosing. But such culture can lead to everything from "addictive

tendencies" to "stalking behavior," according to research — and experts say such volatility should be reevaluated.

"It's important to not hold celebrities to impossible standards because these are fallible humans with inevitable flaws and shortcomings, just like the rest of us," says Shana Redmond, a professor of English and comparative literature at Columbia University. "What we see on social media is a small slice of who they are — we can't substitute that glamour for the whole. . . ."

"Today's use of 'stan' is slightly less sinister than the (original) Stan[1]," says Kadian Pow, a lecturer in sociology and Black studies at Birmingham City University in England. "Today's usage is more along the lines of unreasonable obsession, but not necessarily crazed stalker. . . ."

"We as human beings are 'hardwired' from birth to be attracted to familiar faces and voices. So, what happens when an individual watches constantly the faces and voices of attractive celebrities on a daily basis?" [psychology professor Gayle] Stever says. "One theory is that attachment forms that is much like the attachment one might form to any familiar person, such as a friend or family member."

Some level of celebrity worship, then, is inevitable. But that doesn't mean it will always reach the "stan" level.

Stan culture is flawed because people are flawed. How can you expect someone who is talented at singing, for example, to be great at everything? . . .

"I really, really admire my urologist because he was able to get kidney stones out of my body," says [Robert Thompson, founding director of the Bleier Center for Television and Popular Culture at the Newhouse School of Public Communications Syracuse University]. "I do not also, therefore, think my urologist is completely free and perfect in every other way." While "stan" does imply unwavering support that doesn't mean such affection is indestructible.

"If the object of adoration does the wrong thing, that iteration can very quickly shift to hostility," says David Schmid, associate professor of English at the University at Buffalo. Some fans stood by R. Kelly and Michael Jackson after sexual abuse allegations surfaced, for example. But other fans were crushed.

Such let downs aren't unexpected.

"When (figures) show themselves to be something other than what you imagine, disappointment is expected," Redmond says. "And it can happen often as we're constantly inundated with new media meant to hook us and make us fall for someone."

Schmid says some celebrities don't get involved more directly with their fans in an effort to not bite the hand that feeds them.

We've always demanded a lot from celebrities — for them to be absolutely unlike us but also relatable — a confounding contradiction.

"A celebrity cannot possibly satisfy both of those requirements at the same time," Schmid says.

Still, celebrities could do more to rein their fans in. For example, anyone who talks negatively about Taylor Swift can expect to get skewered by her Swifties.

"We talk a lot about the power that the stans have. But we're not talking enough about the power that the celebrities have over those stans," Schmid says. "And I think that needs to be more front-and-center going forward."

Such "dragging" can be "destructive," says Pow. "To keep the image unsullied, they have to target those who malign that image," Pow adds. ∎

---

[1]"Stan" comes from the Eminem song of the same name, about a dangerous super-fan of the rapper. It is also a combination of the words "stalker" and "fan." —Eds.

Questions

1. Professor Shana Redmond, quoted in this article, argues that we should not hold celebrities to unreasonable standards. Explain her reasoning.

2. What point does the author, David Oliver, make about stan culture by referencing R. Kelly and Michael Jackson?

3. How does David Schmid suggest that celebrities could improve stan culture?

4. **Comparison.** How is Oliver's argument about being a fan similar to and different from what Almond writes about in "Is It Immoral to Watch the Super Bowl?"

5. **Informing Your Argument.** Return to the table that you created on page 438. Fill in the columns about whether Oliver might consider fandom to be a positive or negative force in our lives, the best evidence he offers to clarify and support his ideas, and your response to what Oliver is suggesting.

Source D

Tran, Kelly Marie. kellymarietran. *Instagram*, 2022.

KEY CONTEXT   As stated in the introduction to this Conversation, Kelly Marie Tran, an actor in the *Star Wars* series, stopped posting on Instagram in 2018 after fans of the series launched deeply racist and misogynistic online attacks against her. This is a screenshot of Tran's Instagram page, four years after the incident.

Questions

1. As a successful working actor, Tran has many photographs that she could have selected for her profile. What do you think she is communicating by her choice of this image?

2. What do the text ("Afraid, but doing it anyway.") and the emoji reveal about Tran and her feelings about the incident?

3. Can an actor or a celebrity have and build a career without being on social media? Why or why not? How might Tran's choice to remain off Instagram affect her relationship with her fans?

4. **Comparison.** Based only on this image of Tran's Instagram profile, how do you think her attitude toward fans and fandom is similar to and different from what Almond writes about in "Is It Immoral to Watch the Super Bowl?"

5. **Informing Your Argument.** Return to the table that you created on page 438. Based only on this screenshot, fill in the columns about whether Tran might consider fandom to be a positive or negative force in our lives, the best evidence she offers to clarify and support her ideas, and your response to what Tran is suggesting.

Entering the Conversation

Throughout this section, you have read a variety of texts that deal with being a fan. Now it's time to enter the conversation by responding to the prompt you've been thinking about — *Overall, is fandom a positive or negative force in our lives?* Follow the steps below to write your argument.

1. | **Building on the Conversation.** Locate one additional text on this topic that you think adds an interesting perspective to this Conversation. This text can be of any type: an argument, a narrative, a poem, a painting, or a film clip, for example. Before you decide to add this text to the Conversation, be sure that it is a credible and relevant source; use the skills you practiced in Chapter 4 to evaluate the text (p. 99). Read and annotate the text carefully, making connections to other texts in the Conversation and "Is It Immoral to Watch the Super Bowl?" (p. 430).

2. | **Making a Claim.** Look back through the table you created and your notes on the texts in the conversation and write a statement that reflects your overall position about whether fandom is a positive or negative force in our lives. This statement will be your thesis or claim that you will try to prove in the rest of your argument.

3. | **Organizing the Ideas.** The texts in this Conversation offer a number of explanations, critiques, and celebrations of fandom. Review the chart you have been keeping throughout this Conversation and identify the texts and quotations that either support or challenge the claim that you wrote in the earlier step.

4. | **Writing the Argument.** Now that you have a claim that reflects your informed stance, it is time to write your argument. Be sure that your writing stays focused on *your position on the issue*. Refer to at least two Conversation texts, which could include the additional text you found to support your position. Review Chapter 4 (p. 119) to remind yourself of how to use sources in your own writing and refer to the Writing an Argument Workshop in this chapter (p. 466) for additional support.

5. | **Presenting the Argument (Optional).** Once you have written your argument, you might want to present it to the class or a small group. Review how to write and deliver a presentation in Chapter 3 (p. 90) and Chapter 7 (p. 479).

Let's Kill All the Mosquitoes

Daniel Engber

Daniel Engber

Daniel Engber's science and culture writing has been published widely, appearing in *Popular Science*, *Wired*, *New York Times Magazine*, the *Atlantic*, and many other publications. In 2012, Engber won the National Academies of Science Communication Award. This piece was published on the website *Slate* in 2016.

KEY CONTEXT An epidemic of Zika fever, spread mostly by the bite of an infected mosquito, began in Brazil in 2015 and affected other countries in the Americas through 2016. According to the Centers for Disease Control, as of 2022, there is no vaccine to prevent Zika infection or medication to treat it. Though contracting the virus is rarely fatal, symptoms can include a fever, rash, headaches, and birth defects.

"The level of alarm is extremely high,"[1] said the head of the World Health Organization on Thursday, describing the spread of Zika virus around the world. As well it should be: The disease, which seems likely to be causing birth defects, could affect millions of people in several dozen countries. And the virus may be on its way into the U.S. As of Friday morning, no fewer than five New York residents[2] have been diagnosed as Zika positive.

But New Yorkers, like everyone else in the United States, can take solace in two simple facts. The first is that Zika virus can't easily be transmitted from one person to another. The second is that the bugs that carry the disease — in particular, two species of mosquito, *Aedes aegypti* and *Aedes albopictus* — are not very active in the winter, and do not pose a major risk in communities with ample screens and air conditioning. According to the commissioner of New York's Department of Health, "There is virtually no risk of acquiring Zika virus in New York State at this time."[3] Other experts, too, have told Americans that there isn't cause to panic.[4]

So what's this hotness in my face, this shortening of breath? It's not panic, I assure you. It's more like rage. I'm angry at this Zika epidemic, starting with the ratty little flavivirions[5] that are doing so much harm. But to rail against the virus doesn't make much sense. It has no animal

[1] Tavernise, Sabrina. "Zika Virus 'Spreading Explosively' in Americas, W.H.O. Says." *New York Times*, January 28, 2016.

[2] Fredericks, Bob. "Zika Virus Is Here in New York." *New York Post*, January 28, 2016.

[3] Slattery, Dennis. "Three People in New York — Including One in Queens — Test Positive for Zika Virus Linked to Severe Birth Defects in Newborns." *New York Daily News*, January 23, 2016.

[4] Vergano, Dan. "Americans: Don't Panic over Zika Just Yet." *BuzzFeed News*, January 26, 2016.

[5] "Flavivirus." *Wikipedia*. https://en.wikipedia.org/wiki/Flavivirus.

intentions; it isn't even quite a full-fledged living thing.[6] My wrath is focused on a different target — not the virus but the vector. I hold a special reservoir of bile for the flying hypodermic needles[7] that harbor this pathogen, the flies that shuttle it from one country to another, spreading bioterror in their wake. I'm mad at the mosquitoes, and it's time to give 'em hell.

Who would stand against me? Events of recent years — outbreaks of dengue and chikungunya, the continued devastation of malaria — have not done much to burnish the mosquito's already-suspect brand. Indeed, these sweat-sniffing, bloodsucking parasites might reasonably be counted among the greatest fiends in human history.

Consider the statistics: Mosquito-borne diseases kill hundreds of thousands of people every year. Malaria alone claims the lives of 6 million people per decade,[8] mostly small children. The economic costs are similarly staggering, likely in the tens of billions of dollars every year. When researchers totaled up the losses caused by a single mosquito-related illness (dengue fever) in a single mosquito-ridden country (Brazil), it came out to $1.35 billion[9] annually, not including the $1 billion that must be spent to control the spread of dengue-infected flies.

You might've thought that news about the Zika outbreak would have convinced humanity to crush the mosquito. But all we keep hearing are proposals to take the battle to the virus, not its host. We're told that scientists must work hard to find a new vaccine,[10] as if that would be the best solution to the problem. The hunt for a Zika cure could take a decade[11] — and in the meantime we're left to wait and watch swarms of evil on the wing,[12] mating in midair,[13] and landing on our shores.[14] An enemy has made its way to the nation's borders. Now is not the time for soft[15] responses.

It's time to kill all the mosquitoes. It's time for mass mosquito-cide.

It's true that we already try to keep the critters in control. We spray their breeding sites with pesticides. When the bugs are in their larval stage, we try to poison them with bacteria. If they make it to the pupal stage,[16] we can suffocate them in a film of oil. But each of these modes of warfare leaves room for activism and dissent. The chemicals may drift into areas where humans live, or else they do their job too broadly and too well, killing species that we actually like. Public health officials have their own technocratic way of describing all this collateral destruction, worrying over problems such as "adulticide drift"[17] and "nontarget insect mortality."[18]

So they hedge their bets and do their best to strike a balance between mosquito death and ecosystem health. They use what's called "Integrated Mosquito Management,"[19] a euphemism for doing lots of little things at once: keeping track of where

5

---

[6] Milliken, Grennan. "Are Viruses Alive? New Evidence Says Yes." *Popular Science*, September 25, 2015.

[7] Casey, Constance. "A Hypodermic Needle with Wings." Slate.com, August 26, 2010.

[8] WHO. "Vector-Borne Diseases Fact Sheet." Feb 2016.

[9] Pepin, Kim M., et al. "Cost-effectiveness of Novel System of Mosquito Surveillance and Control." *Brazil Emerg Infect Dis.*, vol. 19, no. 4 (2013), pp. 542–50. doi: 10.3201/eid1904.120117 PMCID: PMC3647717.

[10] Barnato, Katy. "Zika Epidemic on US Doorstep Spurs Vaccine Hunt." *CNBC.com*, January 28, 2016.

[11] Cook, James. "Inside High-Security Laboratory Developing a Zika Vaccine." *BBC News*, January 27, 2016.

[12] Cornell University. Mosquito Flight video. *Cornell.edu*, March 9, 2009.

[13] Borrell, Brendan. "Mosquitoes Mate in Perfect Harmony." *Nature*, December 31, 2009.

[14] Cohen, Elizabeth. "Halting the Spread of Zika into the United States." *CNN*, February 1, 2016.

[15] Chumley, Cheryl. "Trump Likens NFL to America as 'Weak.'" *World Net Daily*, January 11, 2016.

[16] American Mosquito Control Association. "Life Cycle." *Mosquito. org.* 2014.

[17] Hennessey, Michael K., et al. "Mosquito (Diptera: Culicidae) Adulticide Drift into Wildlife Refuges of the Florida Keys." *Environmental Entomology*, vol. 21, no. 4 (August 1992), pp. 714–21. doi: 10.1093/ee/21.4.714.

[18] Kwan, J. A., et al. "Mortality of Nontarget Arthropods from an Aerial Application of Pyrethrins." *Journal of the American Mosquito Control Association*, vol. 25, no. 2 (June 2009), pp. 218–20.

[19] Florida Coordinating Council on Mosquito Control. *Florida Mosquito Control White Paper: Florida Mosquito Control: The State of the Mission as Defined by Mosquito Controllers, Regulators, and Environmental Managers*, Chapter 9 (Mosquito Control Benefits and Risks). University of Florida. 2009.

mosquitoes breed, spraying them with chemicals, fixing broken drains and picking up discarded tires, eliminating swamps. It's all quite responsible and safe. One might even brand it ecologically correct.

But the recent spread of arboviruses has me convinced that we can't win this fight with our repellent-coated hands tied behind our backs. Enough of the politeness: The ugly situation on the ground does not call for Integrated Mosquito

10

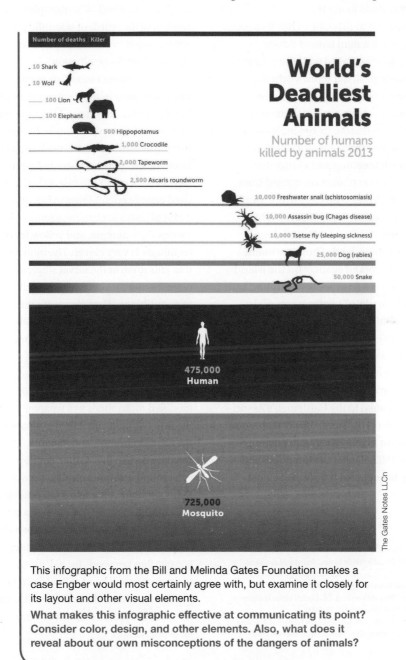

This infographic from the Bill and Melinda Gates Foundation makes a case Engber would most certainly agree with, but examine it closely for its layout and other visual elements.

What makes this infographic effective at communicating its point? Consider color, design, and other elements. Also, what does it reveal about our own misconceptions of the dangers of animals?

447

Management; it demands a program of Total Mosquito Destruction. And here's the thing: For the first time in human history, that dream could be realized. We have a better way to kill mosquitoes — a nuclear option — but up until this point we've been too afraid to use it.

The approach I'm thinking of has its origins in the 1930s, when a man named Edward F. Knipling had an idea. Faced with the problem of a deadly cattle pest, the screwworm fly, the U.S. Department of Agriculture researcher thought to turn the bugs against themselves. By breeding and releasing sterile males into the wild, he figured that he might interfere with screwworm breeding and shrink their numbers. "The general reaction ranged from skepticism to ridicule,"[20] he later wrote. But in 1953, Knipling used an Army X-ray machine to sterilize some flies[21] and released them on Florida's Sanibel Island. The experiment worked. Then it worked again,[22] on the island of Curaçao. Within a few months, Knipling had exterminated the island's native screwworm population — a full-blown screwworm massacre. By 1959, the fly was gone from all Southeastern states. Not long after that, it had disappeared from the U.S. as a whole.

Knipling won the World Food Prize for his work and was named to the Cattlemen's Association Hall of Fame. His "sterile insect technique" appealed not just to ranchers but to environmentalists. In 1962, Rachel Carson published *Silent Spring*, her epochal broadside against

the chemical industry. In the final chapter of that book, called "The Other Road," Carson singles out some "new, imaginative, and creative approaches to the problem of sharing our earth with other creatures." Chief among those was Knipling's method — "a triumphant demonstration of the worth of scientific creativity," she wrote, "aided by thorough basic research, persistence, and determination."

So why haven't scientists tried to use the same approach in the fight against mosquitoes? Actually, they have. The problem was that mosquitoes proved too fragile for the X-rays: Instead of turning sterile, the bugs just died. But in recent years, the sterile insect technique has been revived. One researcher, Luke Alphey, used genetic engineering to design a sterile strain of *Aedes aegypti* mosquito — the kind that carries Zika, dengue, and yellow fever. Alphey's technique is very clever: The bugs hold a gene that kills them at the larval stage, unless they're reared in the presence of tetracycline, a common antibiotic. That means it's possible to breed large numbers of the flies in the lab, but when they're released into the world, they cannot reproduce.

In 2002, Alphey founded Oxitec, which would become the first company to deploy genetically modified mosquitoes as a weapon. Since 2010, the firm has performed field evaluations in Brazil, the Cayman Islands, and Panama. The treatment works like this: Oxitec employees drive a van around mosquito-ridden areas at five or 10 miles per hour. A bladeless fan propels genetically modified males out through a plastic tube, and then the bugs seek and interbreed with wild females. (At a test site in Brazil, Oxitec released 800,000 flies per week, for half a year.) According to the company's head of field operations, Andy McKemey, each of these field evaluations has resulted in at least a 90 percent decrease in the local population.

[20] Knipling, E. F. "Possibilities of Insect Control or Eradication Through the Use of Sexually Sterile Males." *Journal of Economic Entomology*, vol. 48 (1955), pp. 459–62. Entomology Research Branch, Agricultural Research Service, USDA.

[21] Nagourney, Eric. "Edward Knipling, 90, Enemy of the Dangerous Screwworm." *New York Times*, March 27, 2000.

[22] Knipling, Edward B. "The Life and Vision of Edward F. Knipling Concerning the Eradication of the Screwworm". Speech. 2002.

Officials in the U.S. would like to test the Oxitec approach. An incipient attempt in the Florida Keys, however, has run afoul of some locals,[23] who worry over being guinea pigs in a Frankenfly experiment. Oxitec counters that its technique is both highly targeted (only one species of mosquito is affected) and self-limiting (if you stop releasing the GM mosquitoes, they quickly disappear from the ecosystem).

Both sides of this debate seem wrong-headed. The risks posed by Oxitec's mosquitoes are likely very modest, and in any case they must be weighed against the risks of spraying tons of poison. Then again, the alleged "benefits" of

15 Oxitec's approach — its specificity and its brief course of action — come off as yet another example of mosquito-friendly overcaution. When the field evaluations end, McKemey told me, the mosquitoes start "bouncing back" within six months. They may have been suppressed for a time, but they were not wiped out.

Why not use the tools of biomedicine to launch a final, fatal blow? In 2007, Caltech's Bruce Hay came up with a far more potent weapon: the gene driver. His approach would seed the local population of mosquitoes with lab-grown ones that contain a clever set of "selfish" genes, which tend to spread themselves and kill competitors. A technique like this could, in theory, overturn a wild population within a handful of generations, replacing every single

23 Palmer, Lisa. "Genetically Modified Mosquito Sparks a Controversy in Florida." *Yale Environment 360*, June 4, 2015.

ERNESTO BENAVIDES/Getty Images

A specialist fumigates the Nueva Esperanza graveyard in the outskirts of Lima on January 15, 2016.

What tone toward fumigation does this photograph appear to take? What choices does the photographer make to help to create this tone? What are the dangers of fumigation to control the mosquito population, versus the dangers of the methods described by Engber? Which method do you think is better in terms of risk and reward?

native organism with one from the genetically modified strain. And that GM strain could also be engineered to have resistance to the malaria parasite, or the Zika virus, or any other pathogen that a given species of mosquito spreads. Or it could be engineered to have a special vulnerability. Then the engineered mosquitoes would die off all at once, in response to some external signal — a rise in temperature, perhaps, as winter turns to spring.

Another research group's version of the gene-drive method, still in development, has even more dastardly potential. It's a reverse *Children of Men*[24] approach:[25] The engineered mosquitoes carry a set of genes that shred the X chromosomes in sperm. They can reproduce, but all their offspring will be male. "It's a very exciting idea," Hay told me. "In every generation, it's males creating males. Eventually the population runs out of females, and you're done."

These gene-drive techniques are so potent — so vast in their destructive potential — that it has been very hard for scientists to test them, even in large outdoor field enclosures.[26] The concern is that a selfish gene will not just rampage through a local population but will spread to other areas, in the same way that GM

Greg Allen/NPR

These are protest signs at a hearing in Florida to put in place some of Engber's suggestions to combat mosquitoes.

What messages are the signs intended to communicate? To what extent does Engber successfully refute the counterclaims raised in these signs?

crops have escaped into the wild.[27] A poorly run experiment could decimate global populations, or even make them disappear. Instead of killing off some *Aedes aegypti* mosquitoes in the Florida Keys, you'd have killed them off around the world.

And that would be . . . not so bad?   20

Let's imagine, for a second, that we could totally eliminate a species of mosquito — or even all 3,500 species that flit about on Earth. Would the global ecosystem shatter?

The honest answer is that no one really knows for sure. There's little evidence, though, that mosquitoes form a crucial link in any food chain, or that their niche could not be filled by something else. When science journalist Janet Fang spun out this thought experiment for *Nature* in 2010, she concluded that "life would

[24] In the 2006 film *Children of Men*, humanity is facing extinction due to widespread infertility. A secretive group of scientists called the "Human Project" is dedicated to curing this infertility. —Eds.

[25] Galizi, Roberto, et al. "A Synthetic Sex Ratio Distortion System for the Control of the Human Malaria Mosquito." *Nature Communications*, June 10, 2014, Article number: 3977 (2014). doi: 10.1038/ncomms4977.

[26] Facchinelli, Luca, et al. "Field Cage Studies and Progressive Evaluation of Genetically-Engineered Mosquitoes." *PLoS Neglected Tropical Diseases*, Roberto Barrera, Editor, vol. 7, no. 1 (2013), e2001. Published online, January 17, 2013. doi: 10.1371/journal. pntd.0002001 PMCID: PMC3547837.

[27] Gilbert, Natasha. "GM Crop Escapes into the American Wild." *Nature*, August 6, 2010.

continue as before — or even better."[28] I arrived at the same answer when I looked into the same question for a piece published three years later. "There's no food chain that we know of where mosquitoes are an inevitable link in a crucial process," one mosquito-control expert told me.

We've wiped out lots of species in the past, of course, through our blithe indifference to the natural world. It's tragic that we have no more passenger pigeons, or Tasmanian tigers, or quaggas.[29] But the sky has not (yet) fallen. Ecotragedies should be weighed against their benefits — and the benefits of mosquito-cide would be enormous. Whatever its unintended consequences (and there are always unintended consequences), the elimination of mosquitoes would save billions of human lives and trillions of dollars, in the decades to come. It would end untold suffering among the world's poorest people.

What argument is this cartoon making about mosquitoes?

And that's just the most extreme scenario. The gene-driver methods only work on individual species, anyway, so let's imagine that we could wipe out just a handful of mosquito breeds — the most unpleasant ones. What if we could press a button to destroy an invasive, deadly species like *Aedes aegypti*? What about the awful *Anopheles* mosquitoes, which transmit malaria and seem to have evolved as human parasites?[30] If we got rid of these disgusting critters, wouldn't everyone be better off? No one bit their nails when we cleared the world of polio and rinderpest.[31] Should mosquitoes get special treatment just because they're insects?

"I think you may be an outlier," Bruce Hay told me when I shared my thoughts on mosquito management. "I don't believe people are willing to take that step, even in principle." He's no fan of *Aedes* or *Anopheles*, he says, "but you can break the cycle of infection through reasonable public health measures."

Bah humbug. I put the same idea to Luke Alphey, the founder of Oxitec. "I am enough of an ecologist to be queasy about the idea of eliminating a species," he said. Besides, these gene-driver approaches are still a long way off. "They're really only lab models." But what if we went after one of those species of *Anopheles* that thrive in human settings and seem to live to spread disease? "This would not be an unreasonable thing to consider," he said at last, once I had badgered him sufficiently. Now, all we need to do is translate that not-unreasonable consideration into mosquito-destroying action.

[28] Fang, Janet. "Ecology: A World Without Mosquitoes." *Nature*, vol. 466 (2010), pp. 432–34. Published online, July 21, 2010. doi: 10.1038/466432a.

[29] A species of zebra that went extinct in the nineteenth century. —Eds.

[30] White, Bradley J., et al. "Evolution of *Anopheles gambiae* in Relation to Humans and Malaria." *Annual Review of Ecology, Evolution, and Systematics*, vol. 42 (December 2011), pp. 111–32.

[31] "Rinderpest." *Wikipedia*. https://en.wikipedia.org/wiki/Rinderpest.

extending beyond the text

Engber wrote his piece in 2016 when Zika was first beginning to spread, and its dangers were not completely known. Read this excerpt from a story that aired on National Public Radio in December, 2021, regarding results of an ongoing research study of children exposed to Zika.

5 years later, researchers assess how children exposed to Zika are developing

Selena Simmons-Duffin

A few years before COVID-19 became the current public health emergency of international concern, the Zika virus swept through Latin America. Dramatic photos of babies born with small heads [microcephaly] filled newspapers. Scientists didn't understand why it was happening or how common it was — or what prenatal Zika exposure might mean for these children as they grew older. According to the Centers for Disease Control and Prevention, 1,000 babies were born to women in the U.S. who had Zika during their pregnancies in 2016.

Now that some years have passed, more is becoming clear about Zika and its impact on children. Researchers have been assessing groups of these children as they get older and comparing them to children with no exposure to Zika.

About a year after the emergency was declared, researchers found that in the U.S., about 94% of babies born to women infected with Zika appeared to be normal at birth with no signs of microcephaly.

Then last year, Dr. Sarah Mulkey, a child neurologist in the Prenatal Pediatrics Institute at Children's National, published a study that found even among these babies that appeared normal at birth, there did seem to be some developmental differences.

"A baby doesn't have to do a lot of things — they have to eat and make lots of diapers for their parents and all that," Mulkey explains. "It's not until they get older and they're starting to get to school age that we can really assess more and more very important areas of development: Are they learning how to speak normally — learning their vocabulary? Can they run and jump and clear off the ground? Can they balance? These are things we can assess once they get older."

In late September, a few weeks before his fifth birthday, Yariel went to see Dr. Mulkey, as he has many times before. During his assessment, he strung beads and showed off his vocabulary and threw beanbags and walked along a line of yellow tape. Yariel remembers putting coins through a slot. "The coins — I was doing faster," he says. He also remembers eating pizza and getting a gift card. ■

Based on what you have read here, does Engber's solution seem appropriate? Why or why not?

Understanding and Interpreting

1. Why is the "level of alarm . . . extremely high" (par. 1)? How does this statement help us understand the rhetorical situation for this argument?

2. How do the topics shift from paragraph 1 to paragraph 3? How has the tone toward mosquitoes changed? What words or phrases signal this change in tone?

3. In paragraph 4, Engber begins to address opposition to his proposed solution. How does Engber feel about the counterarguments? How do you know?

4. Engber points out that most people aren't exploring the elimination of mosquitos. Where are they taking the battle instead? How does Engber feel about this? How does he use this to support his argument?

5. List the steps that authorities are already taking to confront the mosquito crisis, according to Engber. In what way does including these steps help Engber's argument?

6. This argument examines many potential responses to the Zika epidemic. For each plan, briefly summarize the method and identify language that reveals Engber's attitude regarding the potential of the plan:

   a. "Integrated mosquito management" (par. 9)

   b. "Total mosquito destruction" (par. 10)

   c. "The sterile insect technique" (par. 13)

   d. "Reverse *Children of Men* approach" (par. 17)

   e. "The gene-driver" (par. 23)

7. What appeals does Engber use to support the claim that "Ecotragedies should be weighed against their benefits — and the benefits of mosquito-cide would be enormous" (par. 23)? Does Engber successfully support this claim?

8. Overall, is Engber more optimistic or pessimistic about the chance that we will take what he calls "mosquito-destroying action" (par. 26)? Support your conclusions with evidence from the text.

Analyzing Language, Style, and Structure

9. **Vocabulary in Context.** In paragraph 8, Engber uses the phrase "collateral destruction" to describe the effects of the mosquito. What are some meanings of the word *collateral*, and which definition applies here? What is the meaning of the phrase in this context?

10. **Vocabulary in Context.** In paragraph 17, Engber uses the phrase "'selfish' genes" to describe the behavior of a lab-produced mosquito. How is the use of the word *selfish* in this context similar to or different from other uses? What effect is created through this use of the word in this context?

11. How does Engber create interest in the article with the title and the opening sentence?

12. In paragraph 2, what details identify Engber's target audience?

13. What does Engber mean by the phrase "special reservoir of bile" (par. 3)? How does this impact his ethos? Does his language choice make him more or less engaging in this essay? Explain.

14. In paragraph 3, Engber expresses a lot of anger. Identify sentences and phrases that appeal to pathos. Are these justified or overly emotional? Do you think these loaded words help or hurt his argument? Explain.

15. Engber uses many striking phrases in this article, many of them pertaining to the description of the mosquito. Find two to three such phrases and explain their impact on his argument by exploring connotations.

16. After making an emotional appeal for the elimination of mosquitos, Engber makes an appeal to logos in paragraph 5. Do these statistics justify his highly charged emotional response? Which of these appeals is most effective? Would one of these appeals be more or less effective without the other? Explain how the combination of appeals impacts the audience.

17. Engber writes, "An enemy has made its way to the nation's borders. Now is not the time for soft responses" (par. 6). What is the likely effect of his diction here on his audience?

18. What is the impact of the phrase "mass mosquito-cide" (par. 7)? How does this phrase add to or detract from Engber's argument?

19. Given the context, what does the phrase "ecologically correct" (par. 9) imply? How does this phrase help us understand Engber's attitude toward the subject? Does it make his argument more or less effective?

20. Why does Engber tell the story of the screwworm fly (par. 11)? How does it build on the argument presented?

21. Why does Engber make a reference to Rachel Carson's *Silent Spring* in paragraph 12? How is it intended to advance his line of reasoning?

22. In paragraph 17, why does Engber propose a course of action as a question? How does this affect his argument?

23. Given the writer's purpose and audience, how does the phrase "even more dastardly potential" (par. 18) take on unique meanings?

Topics for Composing

24. **Analysis.** Write a response in which you explore the role of humor in Engber's argument. Identify instances of humor and explain how they add to or detract from his argument.

25. **Analysis.** How effectively does Engber support his argument that we should kill all of the mosquitoes? In the end, did you find his argument convincing? Explain.

26. **Argument.** Should we be genetically modifying organisms like Engber suggests? Are there some organisms that you would be okay with modifying, but others you wouldn't? Explain. You may need to conduct additional research to support your position.

27. **Connections.** How often do you kill bugs? When you kill bugs, do you ever feel guilt? Is it immoral to kill bugs, and how is it different from killing other animals? How does Engber likely play on this difference between killing bugs and other animals to help make his case against mosquitos?

28. **Connections.** This essay was originally published online, and as such, it makes extensive use of hyperlinked references, which have been cited here as footnotes. Investigate a few of these sources and argue whether they effectively support Engber's argument. In general, do you think hyperlinked sources online are an effective form of evidence? How often do you follow these kinds of embedded links when you are reading something online? Would you prefer to have the evidence appear within the body of article? Explain your response.

29. **Speaking and Listening.** With a partner, flip a coin: one of you takes Engber's position that we should kill all mosquitos, and the other takes the position that we should not. Take a few minutes to prepare a pro/con list and have a debate on Engber's proposal. After you have debated the issue, try to reach consensus on how to deal with the dangers that mosquitoes pose to humans.

30. **Research.** The occasion for this article is the Zika epidemic. However, the article does not go into great detail about Zika. Research the virus, its impact, and what the response was at the time. At the end of your research, draw your own conclusions about the seriousness of the Zika epidemic — or other mosquito-borne illnesses — and whether or not it warrants the total elimination of a species.

31. **Creative Writing.** Write a piece from the perspective of a mosquito that responds to Engber's suggestions. Try your hand at mimicking some of Engber's style and tone.

32. **Multimodal.** Make a visual representation of the argument either for or against eliminating mosquitos. Use found or created images as well as phrases from Engber's piece to support your position.

AHA Statement on Confederate Monuments

American Historical Association Staff

The American Historical Association was founded in 1884 and incorporated by Congress in 1889. According to its website, the AHA is an organization "advocating for history education, the professional work of historians, and the critical role of historical thinking in public life." The Association publishes academic journals, holds professional conferences, and issues policy statements like the one below.

KEY CONTEXT   Periodic incidents and protests in the United States reflect deep-seated tensions regarding the nation's long history of racism. In August 2017, members of several white-supremacist groups organized a rally they called "Unite the Right" in Charlottesville, Virginia, to protest the proposed removal of a statue of General Robert E. Lee, who led the forces of the Confederacy in the United States Civil War (1861–1865). In May 2020, George Floyd, an African American man, was handcuffed and killed on a public street by Minneapolis police officer Derek Chauvin, and protests for racial justice broke out across the United States. Protesters often targeted and sometimes toppled Confederate monuments because they felt such monuments celebrate those who fought to uphold slavery and white supremacy. Many cities and towns throughout the country began reevaluating monuments, Confederate monuments in particular, and the principles of honoring the past in general.

The American Historical Association welcomes the emerging national debate about Confederate monuments. Much of this public statuary was erected without such conversations, and without any public decision-making process. Across the country, communities face decisions about the disposition of monuments and memorials, and commemoration through naming of public spaces and buildings. These decisions require not only attention to historical facts, including the circumstances under which monuments were built and spaces named, but also an understanding of what history is and why it matters to public culture.

President Donald Trump was correct in his tweet of August 16: "You can't change history, but you can learn from it." That is a good beginning, because to learn from history, one must first learn what actually happened in the past. Debates over removal of monuments should consider chronology and other evidence that provide context for why an individual or event has been commemorated. Knowledge of such facts enables debate that learns "from history."

Equally important is awareness of what we mean by "history." History comprises both facts and interpretations of those facts. To remove a monument, or to change the name of a school or street, is not to erase history, but rather to alter or call attention to a previous interpretation of history. A monument is not history itself; a monument commemorates an aspect of history, representing a moment in the past when a public or private decision defined who would be honored in a community's public spaces.

Understanding the specific historical context of Confederate monuments in America is imperative to informed public debate. Historians who specialize in this period have done careful and nuanced research to understand and explain this context. Drawing on their expertise enables us to assess the original intentions of those who erected the monuments, and how the monuments have functioned as symbols over time. The bulk of the monument building took place not in the immediate aftermath of the Civil War but from the close of the 19th century into the second decade of the 20th. Commemorating not just the Confederacy but also the "Redemption" of the South after Reconstruction, this enterprise was part and parcel of the initiation of legally mandated segregation and widespread disenfranchisement across the South. Memorials to the Confederacy were intended, in part, to obscure the terrorism required to overthrow Reconstruction, and to intimidate African Americans politically and isolate them from the mainstream of public life. A reprise of

commemoration during the mid-20th century coincided with the Civil Rights Movement and included a wave of renaming and the popularization of the Confederate flag as a political symbol. Events in Charlottesville and elsewhere indicate that these symbols of white supremacy are still being invoked for similar purposes.

To remove such monuments is neither to "change" history nor "erase" it. What changes with such removals is what American communities decide is worthy of civic honor. Historians and others will continue to disagree about the meanings and implications of events and the appropriate commemoration of those events. The AHA encourages such discussions in publications, in other venues of scholarship and teaching, and more broadly in public culture; historical scholarship itself is a conversation rooted in evidence and disciplinary standards. We urge communities faced with decisions about monuments to draw on the expertise of historians both for understanding the facts and chronology underlying such monuments and for deriving interpretive conclusions based on evidence. Indeed, any governmental unit, at any level, may request from the AHA a historian to provide consultation. We expect to be able to fill any such request.

To remove a monument, or to change the name of a school or street, is not to erase history.

We also encourage communities to remember that all memorials remain artifacts of their time and place. They should be preserved, just like any other historical document, whether in a museum or some other appropriate venue. Prior to removal they should be photographed and measured in their original contexts. These documents should accompany the memorials as part of the historical record. Americans can also learn from other countries' approaches to these difficult issues, such as Coronation Park in Delhi, India, and Memento Park in Budapest, Hungary.

These are photographs of a statue of Confederate General Robert E. Lee that until 2021 stood on Monument Avenue in Richmond. The first image is how the statue looked before the Black Lives Matter protests referred to in this article. The second shows it with graffiti and a projection of George Floyd on its base.

What does the second image communicate to the viewer, and would the authors of this article likely approve of what was done to the statue? Why or why not?

Bruce Yuanyue Bi/Getty Images

Tasos Katopodis/Getty Images

Decisions to remove memorials to Confederate generals and officials who have no other major historical accomplishment does not necessarily create a slippery slope toward removing the nation's founders, former presidents, or other historical figures whose flaws have received substantial publicity in recent years. George Washington owned enslaved people, but the Washington Monument exists because of his contributions to the building of a nation. There is no logical equivalence between the builders and protectors of a nation — however imperfect — and the men who sought to sunder that nation in the

457

name of slavery. There will be, and should be, debate about other people and events honored in our civic spaces. And precedents do matter. But so does historical specificity, and in this case the invocation of flawed analogies should not derail legitimate policy conversation.

Nearly all monuments to the Confederacy and its leaders were erected without anything resembling a democratic process. Regardless of their representation in the actual population in any given constituency, African Americans had no voice and no opportunity to raise questions about the purposes or likely impact of the honor accorded to the builders of the Confederate States of America. The American Historical Association recommends that it's time to reconsider these decisions. ■

extending beyond the text

The issue of public monuments is one that many countries and cultures have wrestled with throughout history. Read this excerpt from the introduction to *Monuments and Memory, Made and Unmade*, a collection of essays edited by Robert S. Nelson and Margaret Olin, which examines the common purposes of public monuments and what happens to the society that created them when the monuments are taken down and replaced.

from Monuments and Memory, Made and Unmade

Robert S. Nelson and Margaret Olin, eds.

More than most works of art or architecture, not to mention ordinary objects, monuments enjoy multiple social roles. As things, they share their status with other objects; the term monumentality suggests qualities of inertness, opacity, permanence, remoteness, distance, preciosity, and grandeur. Yet monuments are prized precisely because they are not merely cold, hard, and permanent. They are also living, vital, immediate, and accessible, at least to some parts of society. Because a monument can achieve a powerful symbolic agency, to damage it, much less to obliterate it, constitutes a personal and communal violation with serious consequences. While the destruction of mere things is commonplace in our takeout and throwaway world, attacking a monument threatens a society's sense of self and its past.

This potential to redirect cultural memory tempts some people to destroy or appropriate what has been built, protected, or restored with great care. The phenomenon is universal, and includes Aztec temples in Mexico after Cortez, Christian churches in Constantinople after the Ottoman conquest, or, in recent memory, mosques in Bosnia and statues of Lenin in the Soviet Union. Yet while physical destruction and social disruption have undeniable personal and economic costs, they can also inspire the creation of monuments, as well as their study and preservation. The period after the French Revolution, for example, saw the formulation of concepts crucial to the notion of the historical monument and its preservation. Because social turmoil breaks continuity with tradition and the immediate past, new monuments can represent an uncontested version of the past. ∎

Summarize how public monuments are different from other works of art, according to Nelson and Olin. What happens, according to them, when monuments are destroyed and replaced? To what extent do you think that the members of the AHA would agree or disagree with Nelson and Olin? How does the discussion in this excerpt relate to the debate over Confederate Monuments?

Understanding and Interpreting

1. Reread paragraph 2 and explain what the AHA says we need to know in order to learn "from history."

2. In paragraph 3, the AHA makes its case that changing a name or removing a statue does not "erase history." What does this do instead, according to the AHA?

3. When were most of the Confederate statues and monuments erected in the United States (par. 4) and why does this information matter to our understanding of the debate about the statues' possible removal?

4. Explain what the AHA means by this statement in paragraph 5: "To remove such monuments is neither to 'change' history nor 'erase' it. What changes with such removals is what American communities decide is worthy of civic honor."

5. How does the AHA establish its ethos? What, according to the AHA, qualifies it to weigh in on this topic?

6. The AHA doesn't appear to support the destruction of the Confederate monuments. What does it suggest cities and towns do with them?

7. In paragraph 8 the AHA addresses the "slippery slope" argument that removing the Confederate monuments will lead to the removal of other statues, including those of the Founding Fathers like George Washington. Summarize this position and explain the AHA's response to it.

8. Reread the last paragraph and identify one of the main objections the AHA has to the erecting of Confederate monuments. Although it doesn't specifically say, what might the AHA recommend for future monuments? What evidence leads you to this conclusion?

Analyzing Language, Style, and Structure

9. **Vocabulary in Context.** In the first sentence of the piece, the AHA states that it "welcomes the emerging debate." What does the word *welcome* mean in this context? How is that meaning similar to other uses of the word?

10. In paragraph 2, the AHA writes that, in order to learn from history, "one must first learn what actually happened." Why is the word *actually* so important to understanding the meaning of the sentence?

11. The AHA uses the word *terrorism* to describe the actions of those in the South who tried to prevent African Americans from voting during the era of Reconstruction. What is the effect of this word choice?

12. The AHA tries to strike a tone of authority and objectivity in this piece. What words or phrases help create this tone? To what extent does it succeed in achieving this tone, and why is this the appropriate tone for the piece or not?

Topics for Composing

13. Analysis. For the most part, the AHA's argument focuses on addressing counterarguments that some people have put forward for keeping the Confederate monuments. What are the main counterarguments the AHA raises and to what extent is it successful at refuting those objections?

14. Argument. What should communities do with statues and monuments that honor the Confederacy? Why? Or, what recommendations would you make for erecting future public monuments?

15. Connections. Identify a place or building you encounter regularly that's named for a historical figure: a street, your school, your town or state, for example. What do you know about that historical figure? Should that person continue to be honored today? If you could rename the place or building, what would you suggest? Why?

16. Speaking and Listening. With a partner or small group, hold a discussion about renaming your school. What factors should you consider in keeping the current name or choosing a new one? Try to reach consensus around a single name, if possible.

17. Research. The city of New Orleans engaged in a years-long process of evaluating the future of its Confederate monuments, and in 2021, Chicago began developing a public memorial to honor the Burge Torture Victims of police abuse. The AHA mentions the Coronation Park in Delhi, India, and Memento Park in Budapest, Hungary, as model approaches to the difficult issues surrounding memorials. Choose one of these of these places, or another that you know, research the monument(s), and explain how those involved — community members, civic leaders, artists — approached the process.

18. Creative Writing. The AHA piece is a policy statement, likely written and revised by a committee of historians, designed to project the organization's authority and objectivity in the debate. Imagine that you are someone from the AHA tasked with writing the first draft and you feel very strongly about this issue. Choose a paragraph from the AHA statement here in which you revise the objective tone to one filled with emotional details and vivid imagery and figurative language. The overall position should remain the same, but the style will change to reflect the emotional tone.

19. Multimodal. Sketch out a design for a public memorial for a historical figure or event that is meaningful to you and your local community. What words or phrases could be included in your memorial to help make it relevant and understood by the community?

20. Exposition. Write a definition of "history" based on your reading of this piece and your experience with the subject in school.

Advice to Youth

Mark Twain

Samuel Langhorne Clemens (1835–1910) was a riverboat pilot, journalist, lecturer, entrepreneur, inventor, and author who wrote under the pen name of Mark Twain. His works include two novels widely considered American classics: *The Adventures of Tom Sawyer* (1876) and *Adventures of Huckleberry Finn* (1884). He is generally recognized as the "greatest American humorist of his age."

KEY CONTEXT   The following speech was given at the Saturday Morning Club, a club for young women in Boston, on April 15, 1882. Unlike the sewing clubs and debutante balls offered to wealthy young women at the time, the Saturday Morning Club focused on intellectual and imaginative pursuits. Records reveal that many prominent individuals, including Samuel Clemens, gave talks at the club. The record also shows that Clemens was well received and invited to speak more than once.

Being told I would be expected to talk here, I inquired what sort of talk I ought to make. They said it should be something suitable to youth — something didactic, instructive, or something in the nature of good advice. Very well; I have a few things in my mind which I have often longed to say for the instruction of the young; for it is in one's tender early years that such things will best take root and be most enduring and most valuable. First, then, I will say to you my young friends — and I say it beseechingly, urgently —

Always obey your parents, when they are present. This is the best policy in the long run, because if you don't, they will make you. Most parents think they know better than you do, and you can generally make more by humoring that superstition than you can by acting on your own better judgment.

Be respectful to your superiors, if you have any, also to strangers, and sometimes to others. If a person offend you, and you are in doubt as to whether it was intentional or not, do not resort to extreme measures; simply watch your chance and hit him with a brick. That will

be sufficient. If you shall find that he had not intended any offense, come out frankly and confess yourself in the wrong when you struck him; acknowledge it like a man and say you didn't mean to. Yes, always avoid violence; in this age of charity and kindliness, the time has gone by for such things. Leave dynamite to the low and unrefined.

Go to bed early, get up early — this is wise. Some authorities say get up with the sun; some say get up with one thing, others with another. But a lark is really the best thing to get up with. It gives you a splendid reputation with everybody to know that you get up with the lark; and if you get the right kind of lark, and work at him right, you can easily train him to get up at half past nine, every time — it's no trick at all.

Now as to the matter of lying. You want to 5 be very careful about lying; otherwise you are nearly sure to get caught. Once caught, you can never again be in the eyes to the good and the pure, what you were before. Many a young person has injured himself permanently through a single clumsy and ill finished lie, the result of carelessness born of incomplete training.

This is one of a series of paintings by Thomas Cole called *The Voyage of Life* that depicts life from childhood to old age. This one is called *Youth*.

How is the process of growing up represented in this image? How is it similar to or different from how Twain represents growing up in this piece?

Thomas Cole American, 1801–1848 The Voyage of Life: Youth, 1842 oil on canvas overall: 134.3 x 194.9 cm (52 7/8 x 76 3/4 in.) framed: 162.6 x 224.5 x 17.7 cm (64 x 88 3/8 x 6 15/16 in.) Ailsa Mellon Bruce Fund 1971.16.2. National Gallery of Art.

Some authorities hold that the young ought not to lie at all. That of course, is putting it rather stronger than necessary; still while I cannot go quite so far as that, I do maintain, and I believe I am right, that the young ought to be temperate in the use of this great art until practice and experience shall give them that confidence, elegance, and precision which alone can make the accomplishment graceful and profitable. Patience, diligence, painstaking attention to detail — these are requirements; these in time, will make the student perfect; upon these only, may he rely as the sure foundation for future eminence. Think what tedious years of study, thought, practice, experience, went to the equipment of that peerless old master who was able to impose upon the whole world the lofty and sounding maxim that "Truth is mighty and will prevail" — the most majestic compound fracture of fact which any of woman born has yet achieved. For the history of our race, and each individual's experience, are sewn thick with evidences that a truth is not hard to kill, and that a lie well told is immortal. There is in Boston a monument of the man who discovered anesthesia; many people are aware, in these latter days, that that man didn't discover it at all, but stole the discovery from another man. Is this truth mighty, and will it prevail? Ah no, my hearers, the monument is made of hardy material, but the lie it tells will outlast it a million years. An awkward, feeble, leaky lie is a thing which you ought to make it your unceasing study to avoid; such a lie as that has no more real permanence than an average truth. Why, you might as well tell the truth at once and be done with it. A feeble, stupid, preposterous lie will not live two years — except it be a slander upon somebody. It is indestructible, then of course, but that is no merit of yours. A final word: begin your practice of this gracious and beautiful art early — begin now. If I had begun earlier, I could have learned how.

Never handle firearms carelessly. The sorrow and suffering that have been caused through the innocent but heedless handling of firearms by the young! Only four days ago, right in the next farm house to the one where I am spending the summer, a grandmother, old and gray and sweet, one of the loveliest spirits in the land, was sitting at her work, when her young grandson crept in and got down an old, battered, rusty gun which had not been touched for many years and was supposed not to be loaded, and pointed it at her, laughing and threatening to shoot. In her fright she ran screaming and pleading toward the door on the other side of the room; but as she passed him he placed the gun almost against her very breast and pulled the trigger! He had supposed it was not loaded. And he was right — it wasn't. So there wasn't any harm done. It is the only case of that kind I ever heard of. Therefore, just the same, don't you meddle with old unloaded firearms; they are the most deadly and unerring things that have ever been created by man. You don't have to take any pains at all with them; you don't have to have a rest, you don't have to have any sights on the gun, you don't have to take aim, even. No, you just pick out a relative and bang away, and you are sure to get him.

A youth who can't hit a cathedral at thirty yards with a Gatling gun in three quarters of an hour, can take up an old empty musket and bag his grandmother every time, at a hundred. Think

what Waterloo[1] would have been if one of the armies had been boys armed with old muskets supposed not to be loaded, and the other army had been composed of their female relations. The very thought of it makes one shudder.

There are many sorts of books; but good ones are the sort for the young to read. Remember that. They are a great, an inestimable, and unspeakable means of improvement. Therefore be careful in your selection, my young friends; be very careful; confine yourselves exclusively to Robertson's *Sermons*, Baxter's *Saints' Rest, The Innocents Abroad*, and works of that kind.

But I have said enough. I hope you will treasure up the instructions which I have given you, and make them a guide to your feet and a light to your understanding. Build your character thoughtfully and painstakingly upon these precepts, and by and by, when you have got it built, you will be surprised and gratified to see how nicely and sharply it resembles everybody else's. ■

---

[1] The Battle of Waterloo was an 1815 battle where French leader Napoleon Bonaparte was finally defeated by the British and Prussians after conquering much of western Europe. —Eds.

extending beyond the text

Read the following sayings by Benjamin Franklin from the mid-1700s.

from Poor Richard's Almanac

Benjamin Franklin

- Fish and Visitors stink after three days.
- How few there are who have courage enough to own their Faults, or resolution enough to mend them!
- A country man between two lawyers, is like a fish between two cats.
- Who has deceiv'd thee so oft as thy self?
- There are no ugly loves, nor handsome prisons.
- Eat few Suppers, and you'll need few Medicines.

(continued)

- To err is human, to repent divine; to persist devilish.
- Well done is better than well said.
- Keep Conscience clear, Then never fear.
- If you would have guests merry with cheer, be so yourself, or so at least appear.
- The use of money is all the advantage there is in having money.
- He that goes far to marry, will either deceive or be deceived.
- Experience keeps a dear school, yet Fools will learn in no other.

Choose one or two and explain how the advice is similar to or different from that offered by Mark Twain, especially in terms of the intended humor.

Understanding and Interpreting

1. What does the first paragraph communicate about Twain's level of interest in and preparedness for the speech he is delivering? What does this reveal about his attitude toward his task?

2. According to Twain, why should the young obey their parents (par. 2)?

3. Oftentimes Twain intentionally contradicts himself. Find an example of a contradiction in his speech and explain how it would be understood by his audience as intentional humor.

4. How important is it to Twain that young people respect their superiors? How do you know?

5. Twain remarks, "in this age of charity and kindliness, the time has gone by for such things. Leave dynamite to the low and unrefined" (par. 3). Describe the tone that Twain uses here. How does Twain's tone help us understand his message?

6. How does Twain feel about lying? What is his advice? How serious is he about the advice he gives? How do you know?

7. Twain suggests to his audience: "Confine yourselves exclusively to Robertson's *Sermons*, Baxter's *Saints' Rest*, *The Innocents Abroad*, and works of that kind" (par. 8). Is this sincere advice from Twain or not? How do you know?

8. In his conclusion, Twain writes, "Build your character thoughtfully and painstakingly upon these precepts, and by and by, when you have got it built, you will be surprised and gratified to see how nicely and sharply it resembles everybody else's." What does he mean, and how does it cast new light on all of the advice that preceded it?

9. What are some changes that Twain would like to see in the society of his time? How do you know?

Analyzing Language, Style, and Structure

10. **Vocabulary in Context.** In paragraph 2, Twain uses the word *humoring*. What does the word mean in this context? How is the meaning similar to or different from the word *humor*?

11. **Vocabulary in Context.** In paragraph 4, Twain states that "a lark is really the best thing to get up with." How does Twain play on the meaning of the word *lark*? Explain the multiple meanings implied here.

12. Twain uses the word *eminence* in paragraph 5. How does his use of this word contribute to the humor?

13. Locate a section in which Twain intentionally mocks adults. How does his diction create this humor, and how does the humor help him make his point about adults?

14. Twain introduces his first point with some rhetorical flourishes: "First, then, I will say to you my young friends — and I say it beseechingly, urgently — " Why does he use the words *beseechingly, urgently*? How do these words convey his attitude toward the subject?

15. Twain develops humor through irony — using language that appears on the surface to mean the opposite of what he intends to say — and hyperbole, or exaggeration. Find examples of statements that are surprising or exaggerated. Explain how these rhetorical strategies help Twain make his point.

16. How does Twain use contrasts to make his point in this long sentence: "Think what tedious years of study, thought, practice, experience, went to the equipment of that peerless old master who was able to impose upon the whole world the lofty and sounding maxim that 'Truth is mighty and will prevail' — the most majestic compound fracture of fact which any of woman born has yet achieved" (par. 5)? Identify the elements contrasted and explain how these elements connect to the purpose of the speech.

17. This speech was written for an audience of young women. Where in the speech does Twain seem especially aware of the gender and age of his audience? How does he alter his language to communicate something to this specific audience?

Topics for Composing

18. **Analysis.** Write a response in which you explain how Twain uses humor to satirize social norms. Identify two or three social norms that he satirizes and explain how he uses diction and other language choices to criticize the norm.

19. **Argument.** A satire aims for humor. Sometimes, a satire also offers constructive social criticism. Is Twain trying to do both, or was this speech merely for the sake of entertainment? Explain.

20. **Connections.** Twain's speech calls into question the authority of elders. To what extent can elders give you useful advice that will help you live your life? Provide examples from your own experience to argue why we should or should not listen to our elders.

21. **Speaking and Listening.** Choose a section of about a paragraph in length from this piece that you think is at least somewhat funny. Read it aloud to a partner or small group, emphasizing the humor through your voice, inflection, facial expressions, and gestures. Afterward, discuss how performing the passage helped to communicate the humor of the written text.

22. **Research.** "Advice to Youth" is a classic example of Juvenalian satire written by someone considered to be a master of the form. Research the history of satire and read at least one more work of satire. Use what you learned to explain how "Advice to Youth" fits the classic definition of satire.

23. **Creative Writing.** Make a list of your own pet peeves and choose one to focus on. Identify a group that is guilty — or potentially guilty — of this behavior. Write a satirical speech to this audience in which you celebrate the behavior ironically. Exaggerate the annoying behavior and treat it with undeserved enthusiasm in an effort to show how foolish it is.

24. **Exposition.** Twain explains various rules throughout his piece. Choose one of these rules and rewrite it and any supporting points in plain language, without the humor. Then, write a brief explanation of the differences between your version and Twain's.

Writing an Argument

We discussed various elements of argument in the Skill Workshop at the beginning of this chapter — rhetorical situation, claims, evidence, appeals, and style — and you probably have had an opportunity to apply your understanding of these elements to various arguments in this chapter. Now it's time to put this knowledge to work by writing your own argument.

Step 1. Your Topic

Arguments you write can take many different forms. If you're running for an elected position, you might deliver a persuasive speech, an argument for why you're the best candidate. If you are applying for an internship or a part-time job, you might have to write a letter or email to pitch your qualifications. You could post a short argument on social media to get signatures on a petition calling for some action you want to promote.

Notice how each of the scenarios above involves a topic that you are passionate about and have an interest in. Sometimes in school you will be assigned a specific topic to argue — "Identify the most important factor that led to the outbreak of World War I" — and sometimes you'll be given wide latitude to choose your own topic.

So, your first task in this workshop will be to select a topic that you are passionate about. While professional writers are often assigned their topics by their editors in the same way you are sometimes assigned a prompt by your teachers, the writers and speakers of the arguments in this chapter likely chose their topics because they have an interest in and strong opinions about them. Here are some of the texts in this chapter grouped into categories:

Politics	Health and Science	Ethics
"Abolish the Police?"	"Big Words and Little Action" "Let's Kill All the Mosquitos"	"Is It Immoral to Watch the Super Bowl?" "On Being a Refugee"
Education	**Pop Culture**	**History**
"The Case for LGBT-Inclusive Education"	"When Fandom Is the Problem"	"Hiroshima Speech"

 Topic

1. Brainstorm a list of issues that interest you in some of the categories listed in the table above. Consider other categories not included such as gender, sports, money, and so on.

2. Choose one of the issues from your brainstorming and write a brief explanation about why you care about the topic. Why is it an important one to you, your family, your community, the country, or the world?

Step 2. Your Claim

One way to think about the word *claim* is to think about ownership. Just as a prospector stakes a claim to a piece of land where there might be gold to mine, in an argument, you're staking a claim to your position: this is your view on this issue.

What is absolutely essential is that your claim has to be **debatable** — something that reasonable people might disagree about. Avoid a claim that is either obviously right, obviously wrong, or simply a matter of personal preference. In all of those cases, you'll find that there is not enough complexity or debate for building an argument.

If your claim is something obviously wrong, like "the world is flat," you'll find no credible evidence that will convince your audience. If your claim is obviously correct, like "the earth revolves around the sun," you'll find lots of evidence to support your claim; but why would your audience bother to read your argument when they already know that the claim is true? While it's possible to prove something subjective, like "I believe vanilla is a more sophisticated flavor than chocolate," what is not debatable for a reader is a claim of personal preference, such as: "I like the taste of vanilla better than chocolate." Reasonable people might disagree about which flavor is more sophisticated, but there is no evidence in the world that can prove or disprove someone's personal tastes.

In "Is It Immoral to Watch the Super Bowl?" Steve Almond explains his decision to stop watching this major sports event. He states his claim and then explains it:

> [M]edical research has confirmed that football can cause catastrophic brain injury — not as a rare and unintended consequence, but as a routine byproduct of how the game is played. That puts us fans in a morally queasy position. We not only tolerate this brutality. We sponsor it, just by watching at home. We're the reason the N.F.L. will earn $5 billion in television revenue alone next year.

His position is that football fans who ignore the damaging effects of the sport are morally responsible for the injuries sustained by the players. That claim launches him into further exploration and development of his viewpoint.

The claim of an argument is the position the writer takes, and it articulates the purpose of the rest of the argument. It's clear from Almond's claim that his purpose is to provoke his readers into questioning their own justifications for watching such a violent sport.

Claim

Think about the topic you identified in the previous activity: what is your purpose? What are you hoping that your reader will do, believe, or consider differently after reading your argument?

1. Write a claim for your argument on the topic you have chosen. State your position, but try to avoid phrases like "I think" or "I believe," since that's obvious if you're writing the claim.

2. Meet with a partner and discuss whether the claim you have made is, in fact, debatable. Are there multiple sides and perspectives? Would reasonable people disagree on the issue based on credible facts and evidence? Conduct brief research on your topic to see if there are multiple perspectives on the issue.

Step 3. Your Audience

We've discussed how important it is for writers or speakers to use language that appeals to their audiences. As you plan your argument, you will want to determine who your audience is, what their concerns and values are, and, maybe most importantly, why they might think differently about the issue than you do. Remember, your argument is intended to lead your readers to some kind of action or new thinking about your topic, so you need to think of your audience as at least somewhat skeptical of your proposals. Keep your audience in mind as you plan the points you want to cover, the possible objections they might have, the evidence you want to present, and the tone you want to use.

Let's return to Almond's argument about the Super Bowl. Since this is one of the biggest sporting events in the world, Almond knows that many of his readers are probably avid sports fans who get together with friends and family to watch the Super Bowl. They're likely to resist the argument that it's wrong to watch their team. After all, it's sports, football is a national pastime, and getting together for the game is for many a tradition with family and friends. Throughout the piece, he anticipates their objections to his proposal that we stop watching football: the National Football League is trying hard to make the game safer through better equipment, medical training, and penalties for illegal hits, and N.F.L. players are extraordinarily well paid for the risks that they take. Almond knows these objections of his football-savvy audience ahead of time, which allows him to pitch his arguments accordingly.

He does not rail against his audience in a condescending, demeaning tone, but rather, he is conciliatory because he is one of them: "Just so we're clear on this: I still love football. I love the grace and the poise of the athletes. I love the tension between the ornate structure of the game and its improvisatory chaos." The powerful emotional argument is softened a bit by this tone.

As you probably realize by this point, understanding and appealing to your audience is a primary consideration as you plan your argument. It informs all of your decisions.

 activity

Audience

Who is the likely audience for your argument? What do you know about their possible objections to your claim? (If you have trouble identifying any objections, perhaps your topic isn't as debatable as it should be, or you might need to conduct some additional research on those who think differently.) What sort of tone will you try to take with your audience? Aggressive? Encouraging? Humorous? Calm? Why?

Step 4. Identifying and Organizing Your Points

Once you have arrived at your claim and given some initial thoughts to your audience's concerns and possible objections, it's time to figure out how to support your claim. If you think back to Chapter 2 on writing, you might remember that a well-developed paragraph begins with a topic sentence, which is then followed by a point you want to make, a piece of evidence supporting that point, and then an explanation of how that evidence proves the point.

Arguments follow a similar structure. An argument begins with a claim, but to prove that claim, a writer has to make a series of points, including addressing the possible objections of the reader. For each point, the writer needs to provide evidence, which we will explore in the next step.

Think back to the Skill Workshop at the start of this chapter and consider the claim that David Polochanin is trying to prove as identified in the title of his piece: "We already know school starts too early." He identifies several key points that he wants to prove that will lead his readers to agree with his overall claim:

1. A later start leads to better attendance.
2. A later start increases academic performance.
3. Some districts don't want to change. (counterargument)
4. Starting school too early can cause mental and physical health problems for students.

Each one of these separate points needs to be proven and supported in the way that you have been learning to construct paragraphs. As you think about your argument and how you want to structure it, break down your claim into the points you want to make in order to prove it and the likely counterarguments that might be raised. Then, lead and finish with your most powerful points. Lead with a strong point to get your readers' attention, and finish with a strong point, because the last thing they read is the thing they're most likely to remember.

Identifying and Organizing Your Points

activity

Thinking about your overall claim and your audience's concerns and possible objections, what are three to five points you will likely need to make in order to convince your readers? Rank your points from strongest to weakest. Identify the order in which you might want to organize your piece. You'll have an opportunity to dig deeper into your specific evidence and ways to address the counterarguments later in this workshop.

Step 5. Your Supporting Evidence

Once you have a topic, a claim, and you have begun thinking of points to make to persuade your audience (including counterarguments that you need to address), it's time to start proving your argument with evidence. As you have likely read elsewhere in this book, evidence comes in many different forms, and a good argument does not rely on just a single type.

Be sure to also provide evidence for every point you make. It's not enough to simply say that something is true. A point that isn't proven with evidence is called an unsupported **assertion**, and it's a very common weakness in arguments. Always try to ask yourself about every point you make, "How do I know this?" or "What would help me convince someone that I am right about my position?"

The table below includes examples of the four main types of evidence that you may have seen earlier in the Skill Workshop (p. 388) and that should be part of an argumentative essay. In this case, imagine that the claim we are trying to prove is that in-person instruction is more effective than remote, online learning:

Type of Evidence	Example
Research and expert opinions	An article written by a school board member who visited in-person schools and interviewed students in remote learning situations
Data and statistics	Assessment scores that show a steep decline in students' skills during remote learning
Personal experience and anecdotes	Interviews with students and teachers who describe the difficulty of getting questions answered and work completed during remote learning
Details and examples	The number of students who participated in online versus in-person instruction last year

A successful argument will not rely solely on, say, personal anecdotes because your audience might think that the argument applies only to you, the writer. Conversely, an argument that is made up only of data and statistics might feel cold and impersonal and less engaging to readers. Writers of effective arguments include a variety of types of evidence and choose evidence that will be convincing to their audience.

Even if you are already somewhat informed about your topic, this an opportunity to dig deeper. Good arguments are ones that have considered the issue from multiple perspectives, especially from the point of view of people who likely will disagree with you. It's important to carefully and critically evaluate the credibility of your sources. Look back at Chapter 4 (pp. 99–106) for more information on locating and evaluating sources.

Once you have collected your evidence, you will have to explain how that evidence helps to prove the point or overall claim. It works in the same way as the paragraph structure presented in Chapter 3 (p. 85) and Chapter 4 (p. 119). Look at how Greta Thunberg in "Big Words and Little Action" (pp. 401–403) uses evidence to support her assertion that the carbon emissions targets set by countries are not enough to slow climate change:

> Of course, we welcome all efforts to safeguard future and present living conditions. And these targets could be a great start if it wasn't for the tiny fact that they are full of gaps and loopholes. Such as leaving out emissions from imported goods, international aviation and shipping, as well as the burning of biomass, manipulating baseline data, excluding most feedback loops and tipping points, ignoring the crucial global aspect of equity and historic emissions, and making these targets completely reliant on fantasy or barely existing carbon-capturing technologies.

Supporting Evidence

1. Create a table similar to the one on page 394 to begin identifying the evidence you will use to support your claim. Try to have at least two examples for each type of evidence. Feel free to conduct research as needed, including interviews of family or friends who can provide you with personal experiences and anecdotes. Be sure to look back at Chapter 4 to help you evaluate the credibility of sources, as well as how to integrate and cite them properly to avoid plagiarism.

2. Choose one of the points you identified in the activity above (p. 469) and write a paragraph that uses some of the evidence you identified to support your claim. Show the paragraph to a partner to receive feedback on how well you have supported your point.

Step 6. Your Rhetorical Appeals

As you probably have seen throughout this chapter, there are three main types of rhetorical appeals writers use as they build their arguments.

- **Ethos:** appeals to character, credibility, and shared values
- **Logos:** appeals to logic
- **Pathos:** appeals to emotion

As you build your argument, it's important that you work to develop all three of these appeals.

Appealing to Ethos

The purpose of ethos is to convince your audience that you have credibility to speak on the topic, and that you share their values and concerns. As a student, you might not have academic or professional credentials to call upon, but you are in a unique position to comment on the world around you. You are a student — you have first-hand experience with learning and the education system. You are a resident of a town or city, a state, and a country, and you have the standing to address matters important to those communities. You are a member of a generation that is going to inherit the world (and its problems). You are a person with skills and interests. The fact is, with the right angle, you are qualified to discuss almost any topic, but it's important to recognize the limits of your experience and expertise and use evidence to fill in those gaps. You also build ethos through the way you use language. A strong, clear, reasonable tone will convince your readers that you are worth paying attention to.

In "On Being a Refugee, an American — and a Human Being," author Viet Thanh Nguyen establishes his own ethos as someone credible to talk about this issue of the treatment of refugees because of his own first-hand experience:

> Then I think of my parents, who were younger than me when they lost nearly everything and became refugees. I can't help but remember how, after we settled in San Jose, California, and my parents opened a Vietnamese grocery store in the rundown downtown, a neighbouring store put a sign up in its window: "Another American driven out of business by the Vietnamese." But my parents did not give in to fear, even though they must have been afraid.

Appealing to Logos

An argument that includes only appeals to ethos probably won't convince your most skeptical readers. Logos is the core of your argument, because it is what you appeal to when you prove your points. The success of your appeal to logos depends on the research you put into your argument in order to find compelling and relevant facts, eye-opening statistics, and credible research (which is also a good way to build your ethos). You took the time and put in the effort to really understand the issue, showing your reader that you are a well-informed, reasonable person.

One way that writers make these appeals is through the evidence they select. Whether you are providing testimony from an expert in the field, citing statistical information, or presenting facts from current events or history, you're using logos. Notice how David Polochanin uses logos to support his point that schools should start later in the day:

> Scores rise, too, when schools align their schedules with adolescent biological clocks. In 2014, a three-year, 9,000-student study from researchers at the University of Minnesota found that students whose high schools changed their schedules to start at 8:30 A.M. or later improved their performance in English, math, science, social studies, and standardized tests.

Appealing to Pathos

The purpose of pathos is to stir the emotions, to grab the reader's attention. This is by far the most powerful of the appeals, but it's a double-edged sword. Pathos is often used to manipulate and is frequently abused. It's what fuels sensationalist advertisements, over-the-top rants, and misleading propaganda. It's the appeal most likely to draw your readers in, but also the most likely to turn your readers away, if you overuse it. Appealing to pathos with your language can be an opportunity to let your writing shine, to really give it some feeling, but use it sparingly. Pathos is a great way to begin your argument (maybe with a personal story to grab your reader's attention), or to end your piece (like an anecdote about how your topic affects real people). Think back on the incident that Nguyen recounts about his parents in the discussion of ethos at the top of this page; it not only establishes his informed perspective, it also engages his readers emotionally while communicating what refugees face.

Look at how Barack Obama uses emotionally charged language in his speech commemorating the dropping of an atomic bomb on Hiroshima, Japan:

> That is why we come to this place. We stand here, in the middle of this city, and force ourselves to imagine the moment the bomb fell. We force ourselves to feel the dread of children confused by what they see. We listen to a silent cry. We remember all the innocents killed across the arc of that terrible war, and the wars that came before, and the wars that would follow.

When it comes to pathos, it's not just what you say, but *how* you say it. Diction, syntax, figurative language, and imagery are powerful tools for you to use in your writing to appeal to pathos.

Rhetorical Appeals

Give some thought to how you will appeal to your audience, based on what you know about your readers. Think about your strategy for using each type of appeal, and then respond to the questions below in a sentence or two describing your strategy.

1. Ethos: why are you a credible authority on this topic, and how will you establish shared values in your argument?

2. Logos: what evidence from the chart you created above will likely appeal to the logical side of your audience?

3. Pathos: what types of evidence will you use from your chart that might appeal to your readers' emotions? Try writing a sentence or two on your topic that employs diction intended to create an emotional response in your reader.

Step 7. Counterarguments

When you first identified your audience, you also began thinking about counterarguments — the ideas of those who think differently. It is important that you not only raise counterarguments but also address them in a respectful way. Notice how Steve Almond raises a counterargument that some people offer for why it is okay to watch football despite the injuries it causes the players:

> The second argument [in support of football] is that players choose to incur the game's risks and are lavishly compensated for doing so. This is technically true. N.F.L. players are members of an elite fraternity that knowingly places self-sacrifice, valor and machismo above ethical or medical common sense. But most start out as kids with limited options. They may love football for its inherent virtues. But they also quickly come to see the game as a path to glory and riches. These rewards aren't inherent. They arise from a culture of fandom that views players as valuable only so long as they can perform.

473

Look how he smoothly presents the idea that the players choose this and are well paid for it, which is what many people who love watching football will claim. Other sentence frames that work well to introduce the other side are as follows:

Some will say that _____ is not true because _____.

Opponents of _____ will argue _____.

While it is true that _____, my concern is _____.

While it is important to include the counterarguments, just including them isn't enough. You need to seriously consider them. That is why you begin by conceding some part of the counterargument, to show that you are a reasonable person who has carefully considered all sides, but then ultimately find a way to refute some aspect of the counterargument. Notice how Almond refutes that point about players choosing to play first by agreeing with it "technically" and then shifting to explaining how most players "start out as kids with limited options." When you concede and refute, you might use sentence starters like these:

Yes, _____, but _____.

While there is some truth to this, it is important to keep in mind that _____.

It's a good point, but it fails to take into account _____.

It's never to your advantage to simply ignore views that run counter to yours. You risk losing your audience and being dismissed by those who think differently because you have not fully investigated or accurately presented the issue. By incorporating the counterargument into your own argument, you're on the offensive and thus in a stronger position to persuade your audience.

 activity

Counterarguments

Try drafting a paragraph that raises and refutes a counterargument to your claim using one or more of the sentence frames above if they are useful. If you have trouble doing either part of this, be sure to conduct additional research on your topic.

Step 8. Your Introduction

In general, an effective introduction begins with a "hook" intended to entice your audience. If the topic or your position is likely one the audience will not like or will disagree with or be skeptical about, use your introduction to ease them into thinking about it — and at least considering it from your perspective.

Let's look at the way some of the authors in this chapter hook their readers.

Personal Anecdote

> I am a refugee, an American, and a human being, which is important to proclaim, as there are many who think these identities cannot be reconciled. In March 1975, as Saigon was about to fall, or on the brink of liberation, depending on your point of view, my humanity was temporarily put into question as I became a refugee.

— Viet Thanh Nguyen, *On Being a Refugee, an American — and a Human Being*

Dramatic Facts

> The alarming rate of bullying, homelessness, HIV and suicide among LGBT youth should be an outrage: Nearly a fifth of students are physically assaulted because they are LGBT; among homeless children, 25 to 50 percent are LGBT; the CDC reports among youth aged 13 to 24 diagnosed with HIV in 2014, 80 percent were gay and bisexual males; and gay teens are also eight times more likely to report having attempted suicide.

— Cirri Nottage, *The Case for LGBT-Inclusive Education*

There are other approaches, but these are strong ways to open an argument because they connect to an audience by appealing to pathos. If you want someone to listen, you need to get their attention.

Once you have your reader's attention, your introduction needs to provide some context for your argument as well as a statement of your claim. Look at the beginning of the speech that President Barack Obama delivered in Hiroshima, Japan:

> Seventy-one years ago, on a bright cloudless morning, death fell from the sky and the world was changed. A flash of light and a wall of fire destroyed a city and demonstrated that mankind possessed the means to destroy itself.

} *Hook*

> Why do we come to this place, to Hiroshima? We come to ponder a terrible force unleashed in a not-so-distant past. We come to mourn the dead, including over 100,000 Japanese men, women and children, thousands of Koreans, a dozen Americans held prisoner.

} *Context*

> Their souls speak to us. They ask us to look inward, to take stock of who we are and what we might become.

} *Claim*

Notice how he includes an engaging hook, but then he provides some context for why he is speaking now, and then his claim: we need "to take stock of who we are and what we might become."

Introduction

Draft an introduction for the argument you've been working on using a personal anecdote, dramatic facts, or other approach to engage your readers. Be sure to provide enough context for them to understand your claim.

Step 9. Your Conclusion

Many writers struggle with the conclusion. At its worst, the final paragraph ends with a limp repetition of what's already been said. When you're writing your conclusion, ask yourself, "So what?" This is your closing argument to the "jury" of your readers or listeners. You've presented a position (yours) on an issue of some importance, you've included evidence to support it, you've tried to present that evidence with an effective style — but so what?

As with an introduction, there are many strategies to writing an effective conclusion. Let's explore how several of the authors in this chapter did it.

A Challenging Question

Now, which districts will read the research and have the common sense — and the courage — to make the change?

— David Polochanin, *We Already Know School Starts Too Early. It's Time to Do Something About It.*

Extension

We must divert police away from jobs unsuited to them, like serving the homeless or mentally ill in crisis, and fund professionals better suited to those tasks. It's less bracing than "abolition" and less catchy than "defund." But we're in it for the long haul, to save lives and build a better, more just and freer society.

— *Los Angeles Times* Editorial Board, *Abolish the police? No. Reform policing? Absolutely*

Emotional Plea

And the way to overcome fear is to demand the America that should be, and can be, the America that dreams the best version of itself.

— Viet Thanh Nguyen, *On Being a Refugee, an American — and a Human Being*

Some arguments have such an urgency about them that ending with an emotional appeal can be an effective way to urge the audience to action. If your purpose is to get people to change their behavior, for instance, an emotional appeal might work.

Conclusion

Try sketching out a conclusion to your argument, using one or more of the approaches demonstrated above. Be sure to answer the question "So what?" Give your reader a reason why your argument and position truly matters.

Step 10. Finalizing Your Argument

By this point, you have all the pieces you need for your argument: a claim, possible counterclaims, evidence, appeals, an introduction, and a conclusion. This section will help you pull all of the pieces together into a full argument.

Drafting

As you draft your final piece, be sure to consider the following details:

1. Putting your strongest evidence first.
2. Using transitions between ideas and paragraphs to help your reader move through your argument easily. Some common transitional words and phrases for argument writing are *most important, additionally, however, therefore, on the other hand*, and so on.
3. Addressing the counterclaim somewhere in the middle of your essay, sandwiched between your evidence. Using some of the transitional words and phrases to concede and refute as described earlier in this workshop (p. 474).
4. Maintaining the most appropriate and effective tone for your audience and your purpose.

Revising

Revising gives you a good opportunity to think again about your argument's purpose and audience. In most cases, your audience will be your teacher or an evaluator (in the case of a standardized test). In both situations, that means using a somewhat formal tone, but your writing can still be engaging for you and your audience. Reread your argument for the following:

- **Look back at your claim.** Since you wrote your claim early on in the workshop, does it still relate to your argument? See Revision Workshop 1: Effective Thesis and Essay Structure in the back of the book if you need more assistance.
- **Look back at your use of evidence.** Is there a variety of types of evidence? See Revision Workshop 4: Appropriate Evidence and Support in the back of the book for help with this aspect of your argument.

- **Revisit the main counterarguments for your position.** Have you refuted them successfully? Is your treatment of counterarguments fair and ethical? Review the Skill Workshop (p. 388) if you have trouble identifying and refuting counterarguments.
- **Look back at your body paragraphs.** Have you balanced evidence with your own commentary about how that evidence supports your claim? See Revision Workshop 3: Balanced Evidence and Commentary in the back of the book if you need more help with this part of your essay.
- **Evaluate your organizational structure.** Is it clear enough for the reader to follow? Are there other approaches to the organization that might be more effective? See Revision Workshop 5: Effective Transitions or Revision Workshop 2: Effective Topic Sentences and Unified Paragraphs in the back of the book if you think that your reader may have trouble following your essay.
- **Revisit your introduction.** Does it hook the reader and provide context to understand the claim? Does your conclusion include an appeal to pathos and a call to action? If not, consider looking at Revision Workshop 8: Effective Introductions and Conclusions in the back of the book.
- **Take another look at your language choices.** Are they appropriate for your purpose and audience and as effective as they could be? See Revision Workshop 6: Effective Syntax or Revision Workshop 7: Effective Diction in the back of the book to further develop your style and voice.

Editing

Remember, editing is the very last thing you'll do. You and your teacher know better than anyone the types of spelling, grammar, and convention errors you need to focus on in your writing development. Be sure to refer to one or more of the Grammar Workshops in the back of the book if you encounter an issue and aren't sure how to overcome it.

public speaking extension

Argument Writing

You have spent this workshop crafting an argument that puts forward and supports a claim for your readers. What if you want to share that same piece through a presentation to a live audience? What do you need to add, change, or delete to make the argument clear and engaging for listeners? Great public speakers often seem comfortable because they are knowledgeable about their topics. After working through Writing Workshop 1, convincing readers of your position, you are well informed on your topic and can transfer that knowledge to a live audience. As you work through this process, refer to the elements of a presentation in Chapter 3 (p. 90) and use the steps that follow to turn your written argument into an oral presentation.

Content

- **Your hook.** Reread the beginning paragraph of your argument. Would this introduction capture the listener's attention? Read it aloud to yourself a few times. Does it sound dramatic or interesting? Does it communicate to your listeners the importance of the issue you are going to discuss? If it feels too long when you read it aloud, cut it down, so that it is only two or three sentences.

- **Your claim.** You will want to be very clear about your position on the issue. You may want to break your thesis into two sentences to ensure that your listeners can easily grasp your claim and the main reason for your position.

- **Your reasons and evidence.** While your argumentative essay may have included multiple reasons for your claim, for a short presentation, you might want to focus on only the strongest reason to support your claim. Include evidence that is clear and focused; an appeal to logos might be most effective.

- **Your counterclaim.** Even for a short presentation, you need to address the opposition. Be prepared for those listeners who will think to themselves, "Yes, but what about . . . ?" When you raise the main objection that people might have to your position, be sure to also refute the objection.

- **Your closing.** For an oral presentation, probably the strongest way to end your speech is with a call to action that you can deliver directly to your audience. It will be compelling and immediate for them. If you chose this method in your written conclusion, it is likely appropriate here; if you chose a different method, however, you might want to consider revising to use this approach.

Delivery

A presentation of an argument will take on a mostly formal tone, but you can smile, gesture, or laugh at appropriate times to connect with your audience. Because you may be presenting information that might be unfamiliar to your listeners, you will want to move slowly and clearly through your evidence, maybe adding transitions, such as "first, second . . . ," "finally," or "most important." You can use your fingers to count off evidence or a gesture to show the importance of an idea or particular piece of evidence.

Visuals

Make sure that any visuals you include are relevant, appropriate, and work to focus attention on your words and delivery (rather than distract your audience). Possible visuals for a presentation of an argument might include charts or data to appeal to logos, or a compelling photograph to appeal to pathos. Be sure to take a moment to explain any visuals and how they connect to your position. If you are changing visuals during your presentation, be sure to allow a little time for the audience to react, especially with detailed visuals that might take time to process.

Writing an Analysis of Argument

In this workshop, you will not be writing your own argument; instead you will be writing an analysis of someone else's argument. Analyzing an argument — that is, taking it apart in order to understand how it works — serves two purposes. First, such analysis puts us in a better position to determine whether an argument is effective. We get to ask ourselves whether the author has achieved a specific purpose by persuading a particular audience of a claim. If so, how? If not, why not? Second, by analyzing arguments that other people have made, we learn some strategies to employ in our own arguments.

You may already have explored part of the second purpose in the previous Writing Workshop by trying out different elements of argument in order to craft your own. The choices you made in terms of evidence, appeals, and language determined the effect you might have on your audience.

When we analyze someone else's argument, we think critically about the choices they make. Often, we ask what "rhetorical strategies" the writer uses to achieve a purpose. What effect do the writer's choices have on the intended audience? Think about the definition of "strategy": a plan of action or policy designed to achieve a major or overall aim. Anyone crafting an argument has a strategy, or it's not a very good argument. In this workshop, we're going to analyze the rhetorical strategies writers and speakers use. This practice is called "rhetorical analysis."

A writing prompt for a rhetorical analysis like this might read as follows:

In a well-developed essay, discuss how the author uses rhetorical strategies such as evidence, diction, syntax, and rhetorical appeals to achieve a specific purpose.

To model a response to this prompt, we're going to focus on the Central Text in this chapter, "Is It Immoral to Watch the Super Bowl?" by Steve Almond. Because it is fairly lengthy and because you may not have read it earlier in this chapter, we'll examine only a few paragraphs of his argument in this workshop.

Before you start your analysis, you should think about what the prompt asks you to do. In this case, the prompt boils down to this: "discuss how the author uses rhetorical strategies to achieve a specific purpose." Unpacking that instruction reveals several questions to answer when analyzing Almond's piece:

1. What is Almond's main purpose?
2. What rhetorical strategies does he use?
3. How do these strategies help achieve his purpose?

Please note that this prompt does NOT ask us to write about whether we agree or disagree with the author's claim. In the example we are modeling, we might disagree with Steve Almond's position against watching football, but the purpose of a rhetorical analysis essay is to focus on the author's strategies and to leave our own feelings about the topic out of our essay. This may be difficult to do at first, but the steps in this workshop will help maintain focus on analysis rather than opinion.

 activity

Getting Started

While we model rhetorical analysis steps with the Almond piece about the Super Bowl, you will be working with another text of your choosing. Skim back through the texts that you read in this chapter or other argumentative texts that you have encountered and find one that you feel that you understand and that includes rhetorical strategies you could analyze. With a partner, discuss each other's selections and why you chose them. If, after that conversation, you feel comfortable with the text you've selected, apply the prompt on page 481 to that text. If at any time the text you selected doesn't quite work for your analysis, you can always come back to this activity to locate another text.

Step 1. Reading and Making Observations

For this kind of rhetorical analysis, you'll probably need to read the piece at least twice, the first time for understanding, looking for an overall impression that might include the main idea, the purpose, and who the speaker is. When you read a second time, then, you're ready to focus on the style: the choices of language and structure that the writer employs. The annotated passage below is a sample of this annotation process in action.

> Just so we're clear on this: I still love football. I love the grace and the poise of the athletes. I love the tension between the ornate structure of the game and its improvisatory chaos, and I love the way great players find opportunity, even a mystical kind of order, in the midst of that chaos.
>
> *establishes his ethos as a fan*
>
> The problem is that I can no longer indulge these pleasures without feeling complicit. It was easier years ago, when injuries like Stingley's could be filed away as freakish accidents. TV coverage was relatively primitive, the players hidden under helmets and pads, obscured by fuzzy reception, more superheroes than men. Today we see the cruelty of the game in high definition. Slow-motion replays show us the precise angle of [a grotesquely twisted ankle and a quarterback's contorted face at the exact moment he is concussed.]
>
> *powerful and vivid diction*

The sport's incredible popularity has turned players into national celebrities and has made their mental and physical deterioration front-page news. In 2012, the former All-Pro linebacker Junior Seau killed himself. The autopsy confirmed that he had chronic traumatic encephalopathy, or C.T.E., the cause of the dementia that is increasingly prevalent among former players. A whole new crop of retired stars, including Tony Dorsett and Brett Favre, are just beginning to report symptoms like memory loss and depression.

specific evidence of injuries to football stars

There are two basic rationalizations for fans like myself. [The first is that the N.F.L. is working hard to make the game safer, which is flimsy at best.] The league spent years denying that the game was causing neurological damage. Now that the medical evidence is incontrovertible, it has sought to reduce high-speed collisions, fining defenders for helmet-to-helmet hits and other flagrantly violent play. Its most significant response has been to offer $765 million to settle a class-action lawsuit brought by more than 4,500 former players, but a judge recently blocked the settlement. It simply wasn't enough money.

addressing a counterargument

refuting that counterargument

The second argument is that players choose to incur the game's risks and are lavishly compensated for doing so. This is technically true. N.F.L. players are members of an elite fraternity that knowingly places self-sacrifice, valor and machismo above ethical or medical common sense. But most start out as kids with limited options. They may love football for its inherent virtues. But they also quickly come to see the game as a path to glory and riches. These rewards aren't inherent. They arise from a culture of fandom that views players as valuable only so long as they can perform.

addressing a second counterargument

refuting that counterargument

But if I'm completely honest about my misgivings, it's not just that the N.F.L. is a negligent employer. It's how our worship of the game has blinded us to its pathologies. Pro sports are, by definition, monetized arenas for hypermasculinity. Football is nowhere near as overtly vicious as, say, boxing. But it is the one sport that most faithfully recreates our childhood fantasies of war as a winnable contest.

vivid diction

Reading and Making Observations

Look back at the argument you selected for your own analysis in the earlier activity and prepare to reread it two more times.

1. On your first rereading, identify the writer's purpose, key evidence used, and possible audiences for the argument.

2. On your second rereading, annotate the text by asking questions and noting examples of style: diction, syntax, figurative language, and structural choices.

Step 2. Finding a Focus

The Almond excerpt is rich with possibilities — too many to include all of them in a brief analysis. As you look over the observations from a second reading, what really jumps out is the role Almond assumes.

- Almond establishes his ethos as a football fan.
- He reflects on the rationalizations he and others have used.
- He uses vivid language to describe the harm football can cause.

We are starting to classify our observations as rhetorical strategies — and linking them to meaning and purpose. We're noticing the effect of his rhetorical choices, such as the way Almond appeals to his readers by focusing on himself as a fan who is probably just like the reader, and his use of powerful, vivid details to appeal to the readers' emotions.

 Finding a Focus

Return to the argument you selected, especially the annotations you made during the second reading. Consider the following:

- What do you notice about the author at this point in your analysis?
- What is the author's central purpose?
- Who is the likely audience of the argument?
- Where are the rhetorical strategies the author uses?
- How do those strategies lead to achieving the author's purpose?

Step 3. Creating a Thesis Statement

When you're writing a rhetorical analysis, your thesis statement should connect directly with your purpose. In this case, the prompt defines your purpose: discuss the rhetorical strategies Almond uses to achieve his purpose. Your thesis should take into account both of these elements. Consider the following:

WEAK THESIS

In "Is It Immoral to Watch the Super Bowl?" Steve Almond questions whether he should continue to watch football because of the damage it does to the players.

The statement is accurate: Almond does question the morality of watching football. But all this thesis does is summarize the main point without identifying Almond's purpose or indicating the rhetorical strategies he uses to achieve it.

WEAK THESIS

In "Is It Immoral to Watch the Super Bowl?" Steve Almond calls upon his own experience as a longtime football fan.

Again, this is also an accurate statement because Almond does indeed establish his ethos — his credibility — with stories about being a football fan. So, this thesis reflects a rhetorical strategy but fails to tie those to the writer's purpose.

WORKING THESIS

Drawing on his experience as a football fan, Steve Almond raises and refutes key rationalizations of football fandom and stirs emotions as he argues that football fans perpetuate and excuse the sport's violence despite the obvious injury being done.

Let's consider the content of the thesis by itself first. Does this working thesis address the writer's purpose? Yes: "football fans perpetuate and excuse the sport's violence." Does it identify rhetorical strategies that Almond uses to achieve his purpose? Yes again: he uses his own experiences, addresses the counterarguments, and stirs emotions.

Thesis

Using the argument that you selected and looked closely at in the previous activities, write a working thesis for your rhetorical analysis. Remember that your thesis should clearly identify the writer's purpose *and* the rhetorical strategies the writer uses to achieve that purpose. This working thesis is your guide as you develop your essay, though you should continue to revise, add to, or streamline it as you write.

Step 4. Proving Your Point

Now that we have a working thesis to focus our analysis, the next step is to provide evidence to support it. With rhetorical analysis, support comes from the text itself with your commentary on it. That commentary is where you'll support your thesis by tying the rhetorical strategies to the author's likely purpose for using them.

To emphasize the link between purpose and strategies, you might want to use a graphic organizer to gather evidence and explain its connection to the argument's purpose and your thesis. Here's one approach:

Rhetorical Strategy	Textual Evidence	Commentary
Establishing ethos as a fan	"Just so we're clear on this: I still love football. I love the grace and the poise of the athletes. I love the tension between the ornate structure of the game and its improvisatory chaos, and I love the way great players find opportunity, even a mystical kind of order, in the midst of that chaos."	It is likely that many of Almond's readers who are fans have heard a lot about the dangers of football, but probably not from writers who really love the game like they do. Almond creates a connection between himself and the readers in a shared love of the game.
Raising counterarguments	"[The N.F.L.] has sought to reduce high-speed collisions, fining defenders for helmet-to-helmet hits and other flagrantly violent play." "[P]layers choose to incur the game's risks and are lavishly compensated for doing so."	These are two of the most likely arguments that people who continue to watch football make; if Almond didn't raise them, his readers would have them in the backs of their minds
Stirring emotions	"Slow-motion replays show us the precise angle of a grotesquely twisted ankle and a quarterback's contorted face at the exact moment he is concussed." "[I]t is the one sport that most faithfully recreates our childhood fantasies of war as a winnable contest."	These are details intended to appeal to the readers' emotions and specifically make us recognize that we are complicit in perpetuating the violence on screen.

 activity ## Finding Support

Return to the argument you have been working with in the previous activities and gather evidence to support your working thesis. Consider using a graphic organizer like the one above to help you identify and organize your examples. If you are unable to identify at least four or five passages from the text that support your thesis, you might want to consider a new thesis that you can prove, or maybe select a different argument.

Presenting Evidence

The next step is moving from notes, which are a kind of outline, to the actual writing of paragraphs. Although the way you explain your analysis varies depending upon what kind of text you're analyzing and what your focus is, developmental paragraphs all have a focus or topic sentence, textual evidence, and commentary. Remember the model in Chapter 3 on pages 85–86: we discussed how to make a point, back it up with evidence, and then comment on how the evidence proves the point. Following is a paragraph that employs this model to explain Almond's ethos.

Topic sentence states the strategy used and its purpose. Should be derived from the working thesis. — In order to speak with authority about the negative impact of continuing to watch football despite our awareness of the dangers to the players, Almond establishes his credibility as a fan. He opens his argument by recalling a time when — *Textual evidence* he was 11 and saw a player, Darryl Stingley, get hit on TV so violently that he became a paraplegic. He tells this story with a sense of mixed emotions: excitement of the hit itself mixed with a sense of shame. These are the mixed emotions that Almond hopes will resonate with his audience. A few paragraphs later, he says, "I still love football. I love the grace — *Additional textual evidence* and the poise of the athletes. I love the tension between the ornate structure of the game and its improvisatory chaos."

Explanation/commentary tying the strategy to his original purpose — By citing both his personal involvement and enjoyment of the sport, Almond emphasizes to his readers that his concerns about football are coming from someone who is as deeply conflicted about it as they are.

The annotations above illustrate the alternation of textual evidence and explanation. Remember that simply providing textual evidence is not likely to be persuasive. Because you can't guarantee that a reader will see that evidence as you do, your explanation gives you the chance to tell your audience why this evidence is important. Do not summarize in great detail the argument you're analyzing; assume your reader has some level of familiarity with the text. Although some summary may be necessary for establishing context, summary is not the same as analysis.

Presenting Evidence

Using the model above as a guide, write a body paragraph for your own working thesis, which states your point about one rhetorical strategy the author uses, incorporates at least two pieces of textual evidence, and explains how your evidence supports your point.

Step 5. Expanding to an Essay

Once you've made notes about purpose, rhetorical strategies, and their effects, using a graphic organizer or some other method, you're likely to have enough material for a full essay. So far, we've discussed your thesis and how to support it in a paragraph with textual evidence and explanation. You'll need at least one or two more paragraphs — along with an introduction and conclusion. Let's consider some effective ways to open and close a rhetorical analysis.

Introductory Paragraph

For most essays, the point of the introductory paragraph is to engage readers and generate interest in the topic. A standard introduction has three parts:

1. An opening hook
2. A connection to the piece being analyzed
3. A thesis statement that indicates the focus of your analysis

An analysis of "Is It Immoral to Watch the Super Bowl?" raises questions about the ethical and moral complicity of being a football fan. This an interesting topic that you probably have an opinion about, but when you write a rhetorical analysis, you're not being asked your view of the topic; you're analyzing how someone else develops an argument on the subject. That makes your introduction a little trickier because you want to let the reader know that your purpose is to analyze this text, not comment on the viewpoint being expressed.

Normally, the hook draws your readers in, maybe provokes them, gives them something to think about. Even if you're writing under time constraints and for your teacher as your primary reader, an effective opening previews what you intend to discuss, analyze, or prove.

With a question	Is there really anything wrong with being a fan of football? The fans aren't the ones hurting the players, right?
With a fact or statistic	Injuries have been steadily increasing in the N.F.L., reaching 801 injuries in the 2020 season, with no sign of a slowdown.
With a statement	Everyone knows that football is a dangerous and violent sport.
With a story or anecdote	I played football when I was younger, and I remember one game when someone on the other team broke their leg. It happened so quickly, and the kid was screaming in pain. I wish I could say that I quit that day, but I didn't.

Regardless of what your hook is, it has to lead to the argument you're analyzing. That connection has to be clear and straightforward. A good rule of thumb is to include a brief summary of the main idea of the text, its title, and the full name of the author.

Hook ——————— [Injuries have been steadily increasing in the N.F.L., reaching 801 injuries in the 2020 season, with no sign of a slowdown.] [And ——— *Connection* Steve Almond, a longtime fan, has finally had enough, as he says in his editorial "Is It Immoral to Watch the Super Bowl?"]

Thesis ——————— [Drawing on his experience as a football fan, Almond raises and refutes key rationalizations of football fandom and stirs emotions as he argues that football fans perpetuate and excuse the sport's violence despite the obvious injury being done.]

Introduction

activity

Following the model above, write a draft of your introductory paragraph. Think about the way you want to hook the reader and how you want to lead into your thesis statement with a connecting statement that includes the author and title.

Concluding Paragraph

So what? That's the question you should ask yourself as you finish your analysis. The worst approach you can take is to end with something like "I would like to conclude by saying what I've just said in new words." Instead of repeating what you've already written, you want to emphasize the importance of your key points in a way that brings closure to your readers — and maybe even leaves them thinking.

Your introduction can work with your conclusion to frame your essay. So, for instance, if you began with a personal story, an anecdote, you might return to it. Or you might return to the question you used as a hook. Notice how the following concluding paragraph uses the hook to answer the "So what?" question.

As injuries continue to pile up and the TV ratings for the N.F.L. continue to rise, we have to wonder if Almond's piece will make any difference. While Almond creates a persuasive piece, effectively establishing his ethos, using vivid language, and skillfully countering the main arguments people use to keep watching football, his writing appears to have inspired little, if any, action. It was written in 2014 and few significant changes to safety protocols have been put in place by the N.F.L. and the Super Bowl has been held every year since. Perhaps Almond's goal is not to reform the whole sport of football, but rather to raise just enough ethical doubt in his reader that, perhaps, just one more fan might choose to turn off the television on Super Bowl Sunday as he has done.

Conclusion

Write a concluding paragraph for your essay. Remember to tie it back to your thesis and the points in your body paragraphs. Avoid simply repeating what you have already stated.

Step 6. Finalizing the Essay

Now that you have a complete draft of your essay, you can move on to the final phase of the writing process: revising and editing. These two acts are sometimes thought of as being the same, but they're not. Revision is when you look back at large-scale elements of your essay, such as how well you support your claim, what kinds of evidence you use, how effective your word choices are, and to what extent you have led your reader easily through your essay. Editing, on the other hand, focuses on fine-tuning the language, grammar, punctuation, spelling, and other conventions. Editing is usually the very last thing you do before you finalize your piece, looking carefully for any errors that you tend to make. The following are suggestions for you to consider as you finalize your essay.

Revising

Revising gives you a good opportunity to think again about your essay's purpose and audience. In most cases, your audience will be your teacher or an external evaluator in the case of a standardized test. In both situations, that means using a somewhat formal tone, but your writing can still be engaging for you and your audience.

Reread your essay for the following:

- **Look back at your thesis.** Since you wrote this early on in the workshop, does it still relate to the analysis you ended up writing? If you need more assistance with this, be sure to look at Revision Workshop 1: Effective Thesis and Essay Structure in the back of the book.

- **Look back at your focus.** Is it still at the center of your analysis? Have you focused on analyzing the author's choices and not expressing your own opinions on the topic? If you need more assistance with this, be sure to look at Revision Workshop 2: Effective Topic Sentences and Unified Paragraphs in the back of the book.

- **Look back at your body paragraphs.** Have you balanced the evidence with your own explanation about how that evidence supports your thesis? If you need more assistance with this, be sure to look at Revision Workshop 4: Appropriate Evidence and Support in the back of the book.

- **Revisit the essay prompt.** Does your essay draw a clear connection between the rhetorical choices and the point the author is trying to make? Have you analyzed the author's use of evidence, appeals, or stylistic choices? Be sure to look back at the Skill Workshop (p. 388) at the beginning of this chapter if you need more practice with this.
- **Take another look at your introduction and conclusion.** Does your introduction grab the reader's attention and effectively preview your topic? Does your conclusion wrap up in a way that highlights your focus? Review Revision Workshop 8: Effective Introductions and Conclusions in the back of the book if you need additional support with these parts of your essay.

Editing

Remember, editing is the very last thing you'll do before finalizing your essay. You and your teacher know better than anyone the types of spelling, grammar, and convention errors you need to focus on in your writing development. Be sure to refer to one or more of the Grammar Workshops in the back of the book if you encounter an issue and aren't sure how to overcome it.

Poetry

O f all the types of texts found in this book, you might think that poetry is the one you are least likely to encounter in your day-to-day life. If so, you might wonder why schools even teach it. As Robert Polito, poet and former president of the Poetry Foundation, explains, "If you can read a poem, you can read a film, read a painting, read a political speech. . . . Through reading poems, you really can learn how to think." The U.S. Poet Laureate Juan Felipe Herrera thinks that poetry helps us "notice things that are almost impossible to take into account if we do not stop our rush through our precious life."

Poetry is where we turn when common language just won't do. It is the language of love, of ceremony, of significance. Weddings, inaugurations, graduations, and funerals all call for poetry. It elevates us beyond the everyday. Because of its widespread and prominent role in our lives, poetry is an essential type of text for you to learn how to read, understand, and even write.

Contents

Essential Elements of Poetry

In this workshop, you will develop your poetry analysis skills by examining the features that are fundamental to understanding how poetry is crafted and what it means. In the extension at the end (p. 507), you will also have the chance to write your own poems as a way to better understand how poetry works.

PREVIEWING Academic Vocabulary   **Essential Elements of Poetry**

In this section, you will encounter the following terms as you think about how to analyze a poem. Working individually or with a partner or small group, consider what you already know about the meaning of each term.

1. Speaker
2. Style and Tone
   Diction
   Syntax
   Figurative language
   Imagery

3. Theme
   Symbol
4. Shifts
5. Sound
6. Form

Let's begin our exploration of the tools that poets use to craft their poems by reading one of the most famous poems of all time, "Stopping by Woods on a Snowy Evening," by Robert Frost. Using this piece as a model, we will walk through each of the significant features of a work of poetry.

Stopping by Woods on a Snowy Evening

Robert Frost

Robert Frost (1874–1963) is probably the most well-known American poet. His work has won four Pulitzer Prizes, and he received the Congressional Gold Medal. Some of his most famous poems are "The Road Not Taken," "Fire and Ice," "Mending Wall," and "Acquainted with the Night." Like this poem, much of Frost's work takes place in rural settings and communicates its ideas in simple language. According to Frost, "A poem begins in delight and ends in wisdom."

Whose woods these are I think I know.
His house is in the village though;
He will not see me stopping here
To watch his woods fill up with snow.

My little horse must think it queer   5
To stop without a farmhouse near
Between the woods and frozen lake
The darkest evening of the year.

He gives his harness bells a shake
To ask if there is some mistake.   10
The only other sound's the sweep
Of easy wind and downy flake.

The woods are lovely, dark and deep,
But I have promises to keep,
And miles to go before I sleep,   15
And miles to go before I sleep. ■

Getting Started

Think of a song you like that is sung from a first-person perspective, meaning that the singer uses the word *I* just as the speaker does in Frost's poem. Obtain a copy of the lyrics so that you can annotate them. Share the song with a classmate and discuss why you like it, focusing mostly on the lyrics rather than the music.

Speaker

Arguably the most important element in any poem is the **speaker**, which is what we call the narrator of a poem. Why is the speaker important? The speaker is the source of the language, and more than any other genre, poetry is about language. Getting to the heart of the poem, really understanding it, is usually about understanding the attitude of the speaker toward the subject, which is the definition of tone that you likely encountered in an earlier chapter. So, the speaker is important because the attitude of the speaker toward the subject sets the tone for the poem, and tone is important because it informs what language is used in the poem.

When reading poetry, there is a tendency to equate the "speaker" with the "poet," especially when the poem includes the word *I*. But we have to be careful here. Sometimes the speaker is the poet, but more often the speaker is just a **persona** that the poet has adopted, a character the poet is playing. *Persona* is a Greek word meaning "mask," so in this context, it is a mask that the author puts on for the sake of presenting a particular idea in poetic form. Another poem by the same author that uses

495

the word *I* might have an entirely different speaker — the author might wear a different mask there. Even if the poem contains some biographical elements (for instance, Frost has said that he once stopped by some woods on a snowy evening), a speaker can convey attitudes or beliefs that the poet doesn't fully share. We also use the term *speaker* even when there is no discernable *I* narrator. The safest bet is to assume that the speaker does not represent the author; instead, the speaker is the voice of the persona adopted by the author.

Let's examine the speaker in "Stopping by Woods on a Snowy Evening." We know that the speaker is passing unseen and alone with a horse on the darkest night of the year through woods owned by someone who lives in town. The speaker decides to stop to look at the woods filling with snow. The horse's bells shake and the speaker, who finds the woods "lovely," has "promises to keep" and "miles to go before I sleep." The poem ends, however, with the speaker still in the woods, not actually leaving yet. Through careful examination, we can probably conclude that the speaker is caught between the peace and serenity of the natural world and the duties and responsibilities of life beyond the woods. This inner conflict of the speaker — and the poet's presentation of it — is the key to understanding the poem, which we'll continue examining below.

activity ## Speaker

Return to the lyrics of the song you selected. Describe what is literally happening in the song, focusing on the speaker or the persona (not the singer). What do you know about the speaker from the song? What are the speaker's interests, background, and attitude toward the topic of the song? How would you describe the persona the speaker uses? Be sure to address instances of the word *I* in the song.

Style and Tone

While the previous section dealt mostly with trying to identify the persona or speaker of a poem, this section will focus on the style choices the poet makes through that persona to create a specific tone. **Tone** is defined as the speaker's attitude toward the subject. Once we know the speaker's attitude, we'll be on our way to developing an interpretation of the poem's theme, which we will address in the next section. You are likely familiar with the elements of style, but here we will look at those elements specifically in the context of poetry.

- **Diction:** word choice
- **Syntax:** sentence structure
- **Figurative language:** words or phrases that are not meant to be taken literally
- **Imagery:** descriptions and details that appeal to our senses

When poets choose which elements of diction, syntax, imagery, and figurative language to use, they keep in mind what effect those choices create for their readers.

Diction

One of the key differences between poetry and prose is the premium that poets put on their word choice, which is also called **diction**. This certainly applies to "Stopping by Woods on a Snowy Evening," which contains only 108 words. If Frost is trying to communicate feelings of serenity and peace, words and phrases like *frozen lake*, *sweep of easy wind*, and *downy flake* certainly help him do so.

> "In poetry, every word matters."
> — William Butler Yeats

You can also think about the overall level of formality in the diction of a poem, rather than focusing on individual words. For instance, is the language generally formal or informal? Slang or elevated? Sometimes poetry uses a mix of formalities.

In the case of Frost, we could say that he uses common, everyday words throughout, with most of the words containing just one syllable. This diction characterizes the speaker as a common person and gives the poem a comforting familiarity and effortless power.

Syntax

Unlike most prose writing, poetry does not need to follow typical conventions of punctuation, grammar, or sentence structure. When you think about **syntax**, the structure of sentences, in the context of poetry, you need to think less in terms of right and wrong, or correct and incorrect, and more in terms of the effect. For instance, how does the syntax influence how the poem is supposed to be read?

Notice the unusual word order of the first two lines in Frost's poem:

> Whose woods these are I think I know.
> His house is in the village though;

If Frost had wanted a more typical sentence structure, he could have used this word order: *I think I know whose woods these are / Though his house is in the village.*

Part of the effect of Frost's word order choice is to make the ends of each line rhyme (we'll discuss rhyme a bit later). The strangeness of the word order of that first line creates a pleasing rhythm, but also a sense of uncertainty or unease from the very start. And notice that the last line of the second stanza, "The darkest evening of the year," is not smoothly connected to the other parts of the sentence, resulting in a somewhat jarring stop.

A syntactical choice called **enjambment** occurs when a line ends but the sentence and the idea must continue on to the next line to complete the meaning. Frost does this repeatedly in this poem, such as in these lines:

> He will not see me stopping here
> To watch his woods fill up with snow.

Enjambment in this poem allows Frost to connect the ideas in each line and create a rhythm that flows easily.

Figurative language

Figurative language refers to words or phrases that are not meant to be taken literally. As described in Chapter 2, the most common types of figurative language are

- **Simile:** a comparison between unlike things using *like* or *as*
- **Metaphor:** a direct comparison between unlike things, without the words *like* or *as*
- **Hyperbole:** a deliberate exaggeration or overstatement
- **Personification:** giving human qualities to nonhuman things, including objects, animals, aspects of nature, and so on
- **Allusion:** a reference to something well known — a piece of literature, art, a historical event, and so on

One of the dangers of examining a poem for its figurative language is that it can turn into a hunt to see who can find the most metaphors or allusions. What's the point in that? It is never enough to simply identify the elements. Instead, we need to focus on how the poet uses language to create a particular effect.

The fact that Frost's poem does not use much figurative language makes each example of figurative language more powerful. There is hyperbole in the line "watch his woods fill up with snow"; the woods are not truly filling up, but the hyperbole communicates how totally immersed the speaker feels in the setting. There is also personification of the speaker's horse, which "must think it queer" and gives its bells a shake "To ask if there is some mistake." Giving the horse human qualities illustrates just how alone and apart from other humans the speaker is at this point.

Imagery

Perhaps this poem's most dominant stylistic element is **imagery**, descriptions and details that appeal to the senses. In so many places, Frost directly appeals to the reader's senses, especially the sight of the "frozen lake," the "deep and dark" woods filling with snow, and the sounds of the horse's bells and "easy wind and downy flake." The imagery is what creates the immersive environment that captivates the speaker.

Combining stylistic elements

Let's look at a couple of lines to see how Frost combines poetic elements of style to convey a specific tone. We'll start by considering the speaker's use of figurative language:

> My little horse must think it queer
> To stop without a farmhouse near
> Between the woods and frozen lake
> The darkest evening of the year.

Here the speaker uses figurative language, personification of the horse, to convey embarrassment at stopping in the woods, concluding that the "horse must think it queer." Next, let's consider diction. The word choice of *queer* — which, at the time of Frost's writing, meant different or unusual — reinforces that the speaker finds this solitary behavior, taking a sentimental moment of reflection in the middle of nowhere, a bit out of the ordinary. That sentiment is reinforced by some of Frost's unusual syntactical choices, such as "stop without a farmhouse near." Including the imagery of the "frozen lake" and "darkest evening" emphasizes the speaker's sense of isolation, creating a somber tone.

> "All good poetry is the spontaneous overflow of powerful feelings."
> — William Wordsworth

Style and Tone

Return to the lyrics of one of your favorite songs. What stylistic elements — diction, syntax, figurative language, and imagery — are most apparent in the song? What tone do these elements help to create in the song? How do they create that tone?

Theme

In the previous section, we discussed how a poem is crafted to communicate tone, but now it's time to determine what a poem is *about*, the **theme**. It is the theme that gives the poem its significance — the insight the poem offers us into ourselves or the world around us. Poetry, by its very nature, is often abstract, intentionally written to avoid neat interpretation, which can be frustrating at times if you're hoping to get "the right answer." Poetry often implies meaning, rather than directly stating it. Therefore, we have to pay close attention to the author's use of **symbols** — settings, objects, or events that carry more than a just a literal meaning.

So, what can we read as symbols in "Stopping by Woods on a Snowy Evening" to help us identify the poem's significance? Thinking about the discussion of the speaker above, we should be asking ourselves, *Why does the speaker stop? And why does the speaker feel the need to leave?* The speaker is certainly transfixed

> "It is difficult / to get the news from poems / yet men die miserably every day / for lack / of what is found there."
> — William Carlos Williams

by the woods, calling them "lovely, dark and deep." But the speaker cannot stay in the woods, citing promises to keep and miles to go before getting home.

So symbolically, the woods could represent a desire, a longing for something that is new and quiet and peaceful. But life — represented in the "promises" — demands that the speaker return to reality and leave the woods behind. It is interesting that we do not see the speaker actually leave the woods to head back to reality. The speaker remains caught between desire and responsibilities.

Another line that could be read symbolically is the repeated line at the end: "But I have promises to keep / And miles to go before I sleep, / And miles to go before I sleep." The repetition of that phrase makes us stop and think. Certainly, it emphasizes how far the speaker has yet to go, but perhaps the speaker is not just talking about travel, and perhaps not just talking about sleep. If the repetition of the final line signals that it has symbolic importance, it could mean that the "miles to go before I sleep" refers not to this this journey, but to life. Restating this literally, it might read, "years to go before my final rest." If we follow that symbolic reading through, then the dark woods might be death. But the speaker's not going into them quite yet.

So, after considering the symbols that Frost uses, it could be that a theme of this poem is that it is important to stop and appreciate beautiful things in life, like a new snow in the woods, because life can be long and tiring — full of "promises to keep" to work or family.

Now, this is just one possible interpretation of the poem. A Google search of "theme in 'Stopping by Woods . . .'" would generate thousands of entries and probably just as many interpretations. As we said, poetry thrives in the abstract and on the multiplicity of interpretations, but this does not mean that every interpretation is a valid one. An effective interpretation of the significance of the poem should be grounded specifically in evidence from the text.

activity Interpretation of Theme

Return to the lyrics of the song you've been working with. Write a few sentences about the significance of the song — the possible themes. Are parts of the song intended to be read symbolically? What ideas about ourselves or the world around us is the song trying to communicate? Be sure to have evidence from the song in mind to support your interpretation.

Shifts

As you start looking for theme — the ideas behind a poem — you will begin to notice key moments in a poem. Often, a **shift** in setting, point of view, rhyme scheme, language choice, tone, or other elements signals these moments.

Once you start looking carefully for these kinds of shifts, you'll be surprised at just how many poems and songs have them. When we talked about theme, we mentioned that the repetition in the last stanza was intended to grab our attention to point out something significant. As you will examine a little later in this workshop, there was also a shift in its rhyme scheme at that same place in the poem. In addition, the last stanza shifts in topic, from the physical description of the sights and sounds of the woods, to the last three lines in which the speaker returns to thinking about life and responsibilities, "promises to keep." As if that weren't enough, these lines *also* shift in tone, from peacefulness to weariness. So, to sum up, the last stanza signals a shift in the poem by changing the rhyme, topic, and tone, and by introducing repetition.

Identifying shifts in poetry helps us identify significance by asking ourselves, *Why did the poet create this shift?* The shift at the end of the poem is the turning point for the speaker: can the speaker pull away from the solitude and quietness of the woods to return to real life? The shifts in rhyme, topic, and tone all contribute to our understanding of the importance of this question that Frost raises, and only somewhat answers.

Shifts

Return to the lyrics of the song you're working with. Look for shifts, specifically changes in setting or tone, or even how the singer delivers a line. What do you notice about that moment of shift? Why does it happen? Does it point toward a theme or message of the song?

Sound

Another aspect of poetry that distinguishes it from prose is the importance of **sound** — both the sounds the words create and the rhythms created by how the words are arranged and punctuated. Poets, like musicians, often use sound just because it is pleasing to the ear, but they can also use it as a way to reinforce meaning. Frost himself referred to some of his poems as "talk songs" because of the emphasis he placed on the sound qualities of his work. Just as with the figurative language elements discussed earlier, it would be a mistake to try to hunt for all of the sound devices found in a poem. Instead, stay attuned to how a poem sounds to see how sound might help you to draw or refine an appropriate interpretation of the poem's tone or theme.

Rhyme

Probably the most recognizable aspect of a poem's sound is rhyme. **Rhyme** is the repetition of similar vowel sounds, or vowel and consonant combinations. There are many types of rhymes, but these are the types you're most likely to come across:

- **End rhyme:** rhyme at the end of two or more lines of poetry
- **Internal rhyme:** rhyme within a line of poetry
- **Slant rhyme/near rhyme:** rhyme in which the sounds are similar but not exactly the same, such as rhyming "park" and "cart"

Rhyme creates pleasing repetitive patterns. It creates a sense of harmony among the words in a poem — a unifying feeling. It's no surprise that many of the stories and songs parents use to soothe young children are nursery rhymes: "Hickory, dickory, dock. / The mouse ran up the clock." In addition to the sound created, rhymes can also connect words to each other that otherwise might not seem related, adding emphasis.

The pattern or rhyme within a poem is called the **rhyme scheme**. Some rhyme schemes are very strict and complex. Other poems have no distinct rhyme scheme. It usually depends on whether a poet chooses to work in a traditional form, which we will discuss a bit later. The point of rhyme scheme is often emphasis. Look again at the first stanza of "Stopping by Woods on a Snowy Evening" and notice how the rhymes at the ends of lines 1, 2, and 4 help unify the sounds around the word *snow*:

> Whose woods these are I think I know.
> His house is in the village though;
> He will not see me stopping here
> To watch his woods fill up with snow.

Rhythm

While not all poems contain rhyme, most poems have some element of rhythm. When you are listening to your favorite song and you find yourself tapping along with the beat, you are mimicking in some ways the rhythm of the song. In poetry, we call the beat of a poem the **meter**, which refers to the pattern of stressed and unstressed syllables. Like rhyme, rhythm is often pleasing to the ear, as we anticipate the pattern and allow ourselves to be swept up into the work. Notice that every line in "Stopping by Woods on a Snowy Evening" has exactly eight syllables:

> He gives his harness bells a shake
> To ask if there is some mistake.
> The only other sound's the sweep
> Of easy wind and downy flake.

When you read these lines aloud, you can really hear the poem's rhythm with its alternating pattern of stressed and unstressed syllables; the following syllables in the first line, for instance, receive slightly more stress:

> He **GIVES** his **HAR**ness **BELLS** a **SHAKE**

Like in this poem, rhythm can give a very musical, sing-song, almost hypnotic quality to a poem.

Additional Elements of Sound

When reading poetry, you will also likely encounter the following additional sound devices:

- **Alliteration** most often refers to the repetition of consonant sounds in a sequence of words, usually at the beginning of a word or stressed syllable, such as "<u>d</u>escending <u>d</u>ew <u>d</u>rops" or "<u>l</u>uscious <u>l</u>emons." Alliteration is based on the sounds of letters rather than the spelling of words; for example, "<u>k</u>een" and "<u>c</u>ar" alliterate, but "car" and "cite" do not.
- **Assonance** refers specifically to the repetition of internal vowel sounds in nearby words that do not end the same; for example, "asl<u>ee</u>p under a tr<u>ee</u>," or "<u>ea</u>ch <u>e</u>v<u>e</u>ning."
- **Dissonance** refers to deliberate use of inharmonious words, phrases, or syllables to create harsh-sounding effects. From Ted Hughes's "Wind": "The wind flung a magpie away and a black-Back gull bent like an iron bar slowly."
- **Onomatopoeia** refers to the use of a word that imitates or resembles the sound it is meant to convey. *Buzz, rattle, bang,* and *sizzle* are all examples of onomatopoeia.

In "Stopping by Woods on a Snowy Evening," Frost makes extensive use of sound elements, alliteration in particular. Read the following lines out loud, listening for an "s" sound:

> He gives his harness bells a shake
> To ask if there is some mistake.
> The only other sound's the sweep
> Of easy wind and downy flake.

Remember, this poem has only 108 words, so all of these "s" sounds are not by accident. Like all good poets, Frost chooses his words for both meaning and sound. If you recall one of the interpretations put forward above, the woods represent something new and compelling for the speaker; the alliteration of the "s" sound creates a lulling, calming feeling adding to the hypnotic quality of the setting that draws the speaker in.

Sound

Return to the lyrics of the song you've been working with. For this part, it might be helpful to listen to it performed. What sound elements are most apparent in the song? How are rhyme and rhythm used? Do you notice any shifts of sound in the song? How do these sounds help to communicate the theme?

Form

Another element that we look at in poetry is the **form**, or structure, that the poet uses, usually in terms of the rhythm and rhyme scheme. Some poems use a very strict and formulaic structure, while others employ a looser structure or no structure.

A key term in understanding form is **stanza**, which refers to groups of lines separated from others, similar to paragraphs in prose. Frost uses a type of stanza in this poem called a **quatrain**. This term is based on the word *quad*, which is derived from the Latin word for four. As you can see, each stanza is exactly four lines. Another common type of stanza, which Frost doesn't use in this poem, is a **couplet**, which includes two lines.

You've read "Stopping by Woods on a Snowy Evening" enough times to recognize that there is definitely a structure in place. In the previous section, we discussed how the poem uses eight syllables for each line, but now let's look a little more closely at the rhyme scheme by using letters to designate the patterns of the rhymes in the poem.

Whose woods these are I think I know. **A**
His house is in the village though; **A**
He will not see me stopping here **B**
To watch his woods fill up with snow. **A**

My little horse must think it queer **B**
To stop without a farmhouse near **B**
Between the woods and frozen lake **C**
The darkest evening of the year. **B**

He gives his harness bells a shake **C**
To ask if there is some mistake. **C**
The only other sound's the sweep **D**
Of easy wind and downy flake. **C**

The woods are lovely, dark and deep, **D**
But I have promises to keep, **D**
And miles to go before I sleep, **D**
And miles to go before I sleep. **D**

Notice the rhyme pattern: the first three stanzas start with rhymed pairs, continue with an unrhymed line, and then return to the rhyme of the first two lines. Looking even more closely, notice that the unrhymed line in each stanza becomes the main rhyme for the stanza that follows. The pattern established in the first three stanzas, however, changes in the last one, in which all of four of the lines rhyme. In the previous section on shifts, we identified that stanza as a major shift in the poem. Deviating from the rhyme scheme is yet another way that Frost signals that shift.

Like many songs, some poems contain a **refrain**, which is a line that repeats at times within the work. The last lines of this poem constitute a refrain, drawing additional importance through repetition.

So, why does form matter? A strict structure like this one can bring unity to a work, allowing those rhymed lines to move us easily, inevitably, from stanza to stanza. In particular, we really notice form when it shifts, as it does in this poem, as a signal to the reader of importance as the speaker contemplates the woods, contrasting with the responsibilities still ahead.

There are a number of different poetic forms, some of which you will see in the poems in this chapter. The following are some of the most common forms:

- **Free verse** refers to lines that closely follow the natural rhythms of speech, not adhering to any specific rhyming or meter pattern.
- **Haiku** is a Japanese verse form of three unrhymed lines in five, seven, and five syllables. Its goal is to create a single, memorable image for the reader.
- **Sonnet** refers to a poem of fourteen lines using a wide range of formal rhyme schemes, in English typically having ten syllables per line. Many sonnet forms end with a couplet, a pair of successive rhyming lines, usually of the same length.
- **Villanelle** is a form consisting of five three-line stanzas and a final quatrain, with the first and third lines of the first stanza repeating alternately in the following stanzas.

Rather than simply identifying a poem's form, the important questions to consider when examining a poem for its form are

- Is there a structure in place?
- How strictly does the poet follow that structure?
- Where and why might the poet deviate from that structure?
- Where do repetitions occur? Why?
- How might a change in form signal a shift that can guide us to the meaning of the poem?

Form

Return to the lyrics of the song you've been working with. Songs often use categories like verse, chorus, and bridge to describe the form. What do you notice about the song's form, structure, and/or repetitions? Is there a strict or loose form in place? Do you notice any shifts of form in the song? How do these elements help the songwriter communicate the theme?

Literary Elements and Theme

Throughout this Workshop, you have been thinking about the key literary elements of poetry — style, sound, form, shifts, and tone — as a way to help you understand the tools poets use to create their work. But as we've said before, just identifying these elements is not the point. The point is to think about *how* the poet uses those tools to create a text and communicate ideas.

Look at this summary of how the various elements help Robert Frost convey one theme of "Stopping by Woods on a Snowy Evening" — that we are often caught between our desires and our responsibilities.

"Stopping by Woods on a Snowy Evening"

Poetic Element	Contribution to Theme
Speaker	An explanation of this theme requires us to examine how the speaker is sensitive to and deeply aware of the surrounding natural beauty. The speaker is caught, mesmerized by the falling snow, but pulled by the need to leave.
Shift	The shifts in tone and rhyme scheme in the last stanza emphasize the importance of the moment in which the speaker feels the pull of the need to leave with "miles to go."
Imagery	The details and description of the snowy woods are intended to communicate the speaker's desire to stay; the woods are dark and deep. They represent what the speaker could have but cannot keep.
Sound	The alliteration and the rhymes create a sense of calmness and peacefulness as the speaker watches and feels drawn in by the woods.

REFLECTING ON Academic Vocabulary   **The Essential Elements of Poetry**

Working with a partner or small group, discuss the terms in this section and that you previewed on page 494 and clarify your understanding of each. Then, share what you learned about reading and analyzing poetry. What did you find helpful, relevant, unnecessary, redundant, and so on?

culminating activity

Examining Elements of Poetry

Return to the lyrics of the song you have been analyzing throughout this workshop. Draw an interpretation of a possible theme of the song. Then complete a table for the song like the one above, in which you explain how two or more of the following elements of the song contribute to the tone and theme: speaker, style, shift, and/or sound.

creative writing extension

Writing Poetry

In this extension, you'll have a chance to experiment with some of the key elements of poetry you explored in the Skill Workshop to deepen your understanding and appreciation of poetry.

Getting Started

Try out two or three of the prompts below as a guide to help you tap into your own creativity and ideas. The goal here is NOT necessarily to have a draft of a poem but just to experiment with writing poetry.

1. The following are the opening lines from a poem called "Where I'm From," in which poet George Ella Lyon lists the features that describe the speaker's home. Write your own "Where I'm From," using the beginning of this poem as a guide:

   > I am from clothespins,
   > from Clorox and carbon-tetrachloride.
   > I am from the dirt under the back porch.

2. Found poems are created when you collect words from other sources and arrange them differently to create an entirely new meaning. Choose any text from this book that is not a poem and select ten to twenty words or phrases that strike you for whatever reason. Arrange and rearrange these words, and add new ones, to create a poem of your own structure.

3. Nature is a great source for poetry. Choose a tree in your neighborhood or near your school and describe it with as much detail as possible, including any sound the tree might create. Sketch out a few lines of a poem to explain why this tree matters to you or your neighborhood.

4. Think about a person you know well: a friend, a parent, grandparent, or yourself, for example. Write a poem that describes that person, including important actions and personality, to someone who has not met the person.

5. Look through the various images found in this book or look around the classroom. Write a poem that describes the setting or the perspective of a person in the image or in your classroom.

6. Choose a poem in this chapter or the lyrics of a song you like. Rewrite the piece changing at least three words in every line.

7. Try making an erasure poem by taking a text and blacking out certain words or phrases with a marker.

Speaker

Like the narrator of a short story, the speaker in a poem is not the writer, but rather the persona the writer has adopted for the poem. A poet gives careful thought to how the speaker presents the message to the reader.

Speaker

1. Write a few lines of a poem from the perspective of an inanimate object that you see or use every day, like your phone, a pen, a car, a coffee cup, a stop sign, and so on. Use the word *I* as if you were the object.

2. Now, rewrite those same lines from the perspective of a human interacting with that object. Use the word *I* as if you were the person interacting with the object.

3. Last, rewrite those lines without using the word *I*.

See the Skill Workshop discussion of speaker on pages 495–496 for more help, if needed.

Diction

When you write poetry, you'll find that choosing the right word makes all the difference in creating the right effect. Because of its compact nature, poetry puts a premium on precision, and your reader is more attuned to the connotations of the words you choose.

Diction

This activity is intended to generate a long list of words that you might draw from throughout the rest of this extension. See the Skill Workshop discussion of diction on page 497 for more help, if needed.

Step 1. Try to answer as many of the questions below as possible, though don't worry if you cannot think of something for some of them; plan on sharing with your classmates to get a list of fifty to sixty different words. Keep adding to this list.

1. What are words that you tend to use *only* with close friends or family members?

2. What are words that adults you know say regularly?

3. What are words that you use only in specialized situations (on the soccer field, in a place of worship, at a grandparent's house, etc.)?

4. List as many nouns (people, places, things) as you can see wherever you are right now.

5. List as many nouns (people, places, things) as you can that name things you know about but have never seen in person.

6. What are words that you really like, but hardly ever use?

7. What are words that you do not like, for whatever reason?

8. Skim through the poems in this chapter, and list words that strike you.

9. List words that identify emotions, but do not include *happy, sad,* or *angry*.

10. List some of your favorite interjections: *Oh! lol! No way!*

11. List some interesting abstract nouns (an idea, quality, or state rather than a concrete object) that mean something to you, such as *freedom*, *justice*, *power*.

12. List verbs that communicate some kind of physical movement you engage in.

13. List verbs that communicate some kind of physical movement you rarely engage in.

Step 2. Select twenty to twenty-five of the words that you listed and arrange them into a poem, adding words if you need to. Now, revise it by cutting the total number of words in the poem by about half. What changes as you cut? What is gained and what is lost?

Syntax

One of the main features that distinguishes writing poetry from writing prose is that you are not constrained in the same way by grammar and mechanics. When you write poetry, the rules of grammar apply when they suit your purpose. For example, if you need readers to pause in certain places, then use commas or dashes.

As a poet, you also have to decide when to break a line and when to group things into stanzas. These are not grammatical choices per se, but line breaks and stanza breaks work like a type of punctuation. They define what goes together and what should be separated. The key is to understand your own reasoning for where these breaks appear. Here are some common purposes for line breaks:

- To create a specific rhythm
- To create a specific end rhyme
- To contain and separate small ideas
- To create a specific visual pattern
- To create tension and suspense

Syntax

Read the following excerpt from a poem that was written without line breaks or much punctuation. Then, rewrite a small part of the poem by creating new syntax for it. Add line breaks, stanzas, commas, periods, or any kind of punctuation where you want. Try to create some kind of effect through your syntactical choices. See the Skill Workshop discussion of syntax on page 497 for more help, if needed.

(continued)

this beginning may have always meant this end

Camille T. Dungy

coming from a place where we meandered mornings and met quail, scrub jay, mockingbird, i knew coyote, like everyone else, i knew cactus, knew tumbleweed, lichen on the rocks and pill bugs beneath, rattlers sometimes, the soft smell of sage and the ferment of cactus pear. coming from this place, from a place where grass might grow greener on the hillside in winter than in any yard, where, the whole rest of the year, everything i loved, chaparral pea, bottle brush tree, jacaranda, mariposa, pinyon and desert oak, the kumquat in the back garden and wisteria vining the porch, the dry grass whispering long after the last rains, raccoons in and out of the hills, trash hurled by the hottest wind, the dry grass tall now and golden, lawn chairs, eucalyptus, everything, in a place we knew, every thing, we knew, little and large and mine and ours, except horror, all of it, everything could flame up that quickly, could flare and be gone. ■

Figurative Language

Some poets tend to use a lot of figurative language — similes, metaphors, personification, and so on — while others use it rarely. That said, figurative language can help you to express powerful, vivid, interesting ideas concisely.

(activity) **Figurative Language**

This activity will be an opportunity to play around with a published poem by adding more figurative language. See the Skill Workshop discussion of figurative language on page 498 for more help, if needed.

Step 1. With a partner, read aloud and discuss the last two stanzas of the poem "Annabelle Lee" by Edgar Allan Poe, in which the speaker expresses his overwhelming sadness at the death of his bride, Annabel Lee:

But our love it was stronger by far than the love
  Of those who were older than we —
  Of many far wiser than we —
And neither the angels in Heaven above
  Nor the demons down under the sea
Can ever dissever my soul from the soul
  Of the beautiful Annabel Lee;

For the moon never beams, without bringing me dreams
  Of the beautiful Annabel Lee;
And the stars never rise, but I feel the bright eyes
  Of the beautiful Annabel Lee;
And so, all the night-tide, I lie down by the side
  Of my darling — my darling — my life and my bride,
  In her sepulchre[1] there by the sea —
  In her tomb by the sounding sea.

[1]—Eds. A tomb or grave.

Step 2. Both partners need their own a copy of the excerpt of the poem. You will take turns rewriting one line of the poem by adding one of the following types of figurative language and pass it to your partner, and so continue back and forth in this manner for five rounds:

1. Rewrite a line to add a simile.

2. Change that simile in #1 to a metaphor.

3. Rewrite a line to include personification.

4. Change that personification of #3 to hyperbole.

5. Rewrite a line to add an allusion to something that a modern reader would likely know.

Step 3. Discuss how your additions of figurative language affected the poem and its message.

Imagery

Writing poetry is about communicating an experience, feeling, or perspective in an interesting and concise way. One of the most important techniques that you will use to achieve this is imagery, which refers to the ways that language captures the senses: sight, sound, taste, touch, and smell.

Imagery

Look closely at this digital art photograph called *Bird Kingdom 5, 2018* by Johan Lilja. Write two or three lines of poetry that describe the scene, trying to recreate the image for someone who has not seen it by considering all of the senses. See the Skill Workshop discussion of imagery on page 498 for more help, if needed.

activity

Bird Kingdom 5, 2018 (digital photo art)/Lilja, Johan/Johan Lilja/Private Collection/Bridgeman Images

Sound

Your poems require such careful word choice because the words that you select often are chosen for their sounds, in addition to their meaning. Sound in poetry is created through rhyme and rhythm, created by the patterns of syllables and sentence variety.

Sound

Read the following poem and rewrite a few lines by doing the following:

- Rhyme three or four words, either at the end or in the middle of the line.
- Use a purposeful number of syllables to create a consistent rhythm.
- Add two or more of the other sound devices listed on page 503.

See the Skill Workshop discussion of sound on pages 501–503 for more help, if needed.

Who Has Seen the Wind?

Christina Rossetti

Who has seen the wind?
Neither I nor you.
But when the leaves hang trembling,
The wind is passing through.

Who has seen the wind?
Neither you nor I.
But when the trees bow down their heads,
The wind is passing by.

Presentation of a Poem (optional)

Throughout this Creative Writing Extension, you drafted lines of several poems, some original and some revisions of lines from other poems. Since poetry is often written to be delivered out loud (some performance or "slam" poets even feel that how the poem is delivered is integral to the poem's meaning), you may be asked to recite one of your pieces to a partner, small group, or the class. If you are presenting, you might want to begin with sharing a brief overview of your poetic lines with your audience, including the purpose or what inspired you to write them. While some performance poets read their writing from a notebook or piece of paper, many more prefer to have it memorized so that they can deliver it with as much emotion, eye contact, facial expression, and body language as possible. You would want to give careful thought to which words and phrases you would emphasize through volume, pitch, or gestures. Your goal would be to communicate the tone and meaning of your writing, which you can do by revealing your own emotions during the presentation.

Final Reflection

Throughout these activities, you have been mostly playing around with the various poetic elements rather than working on a single, polished piece, but you likely have learned a lot about how and why poems are constructed for particular effect. Write an explanation of what writing poetry has taught you about reading poetry. What have you begun to notice that you might not have otherwise?

what can a poem do?

Darius V. Daughtry

Darius V. Daughtry is a poet, playwright, director, and educator. He is also the founding director of the Art Prevails Project, a community-based organization fostering the arts in South Florida. His first poetry collection, *And the Walls Came Tumbling* (2019), explores the effects of race, class, and gender on society.

Photo by Eduardo Schneider

a poem cannot save a life
cannot Luke Cage your skin
fend off a dark alley attack
cannot make you less woman
or less poor   5
or less Black
and
thus
treated equally

a poem cannot stop a bullet   10
stop a bomb
stop terror on your doorstep
your step
even with poem in hand
could be your last   15
a blast would turn the paper poem is written on into dust
particles
      simile up in smoke
metaphors
      just molecules forgotten   20

a poem cannot turn back time's hand
erase mistakes made
or cut, copy, paste memories
a poem cannot delete history's horrors

but a poem can love   25
        like hold you and scold you at the same time
a poem can rip away the untruths that have cocooned us
a poem can make you butterfly
        not fly
                you already fly   30
but a poem can make you float
no need to watch your step

quiet as kept
a poem can introduce you to yourself
help you discover those hidden   35
        forbidden parts
a poem be like a mirror sometimes
help you see the crust in your eyes
and the plank

on second thought   40
a poem can save a life
like wise words granddaddy whispered
like the layer of truth just below the scriptures

a poem cannot stop a bullet
but can swallow the hate and spit back   45
        a sonnet
that sonic booms
a room till
quotes
float like balloons   50
goblins and goons
soon just nod their heads
snap their fingers
to what's written and said

isn't it ironic   55

they say the pen is mightier than the sword
but there were few writers on my block
mostly fighters on my block
dropouts that pulled all-nighters on my block

they'd blue and red light us on my block   60
then indict us on my block
what if there were more writers on my block

on your block
in every barrio and borough
conclave and commonwealth   65
courtroom and capitol hill
what if they all spilled ink
on pages
allowed the innerworkings of their hearts
to scribble a poem or two   70

I wonder where we'd be if the masses knew
just what a poem could do. ■

Understanding and Interpreting

1. Reread the first three stanzas. What is in common among all of the things Daughtry says a poem cannot do? What tone does the speaker establish regarding these at the beginning of his poem?

2. What might "history's horrors" (l. 24) refer to? How does this phrase help illustrate other ideas the speaker raises in this poem?

3. Explain what Daughtry means when he writes in stanza 5, "a poem can introduce you to yourself / help you discover those hidden / forbidden parts" (ll. 34–36).

4. Up until line 57 in stanza 9, the speaker has not used *I*, *me*, or *my* to designate an individual person; but in this stanza the speaker ends each line after the first with "my block." What can you interpret about the speaker from this use of *my*? You should re-examine earlier portions of the poem to help you support your interpretation.

5. Irony is the use of words that mean the opposite of the intended meaning, oftentimes for humor. What is the speaker referring to when he says, "isn't it ironic" (l. 55)?

Analyzing Language, Style, and Structure

6. **Vocabulary in Context.** In the second-to-last line of the poem, Daughtry writes, "I wonder where we'd be if the masses knew." What is the meaning of the word *masses* in this context?

7. In line 2, Daughtry uses an allusion to "Luke Cage." Feel free to conduct quick research if you are unfamiliar with the name. What does this allusion communicate? What does the allusion reveal about at least part of the intended audience for this poem?

8. Even though poets regularly use poetic elements in their work, they rarely name those elements as Daughtry does in lines 18–20: "simile up in smoke / metaphors / just molecules forgotten." What is the possible effect of using these terms within the poem?

9. Notice that the first shift in this poem occurs in stanza 4 (l. 25), when the speaker begins to talk about what a poem can do. What other shifts do you notice in the poem? What signals those shifts, and how do they help communicate the poem's themes?

10. Reread stanza 9 (ll. 56–62), looking for diction, syntax, and poetic elements, especially rhyme. Make an interpretation of the effect of a particular language choice in this stanza and how it helps Daughtry communicate an idea about being a writer.

11. In stanza 10 (ll. 63–70), Daughtry uses a number of different words to describe places where people gather. What does this list accomplish, and how does it connect with references to "my block" in the previous stanza?

12. Structurally, Daughtry begins with what a poem cannot do and then moves to what it can do. What are possible effects of his choice of structure?

Topics for Composing

13. **Analysis.** Answer the question that Daughtry asks rhetorically in the last two lines of the poem, "I wonder where we'd be if the masses knew / just what a poem could do." According to Daughtry in this poem, what might happen if this were true? Support your analysis with evidence from the poem.

14. **Argument.** Daughtry wonders in line 56 whether "the pen is mightier than the sword." Is it? Write an argument in which you agree or disagree with this common phrase. Use evidence from the poem and your own experience to support your position.

15. **Connections.** What are your personal feelings about writing and reading poetry? When have you felt that "a poem can introduce you to yourself" or "be like a mirror"?

16. **Speaking and Listening.** This poem is clearly intended to be read aloud. Choose two stanzas and read it aloud to yourself enough times to either memorize it or be very familiar with it. Try to add pauses, emphasis, gestures, and movement to help communicate the poem's message. Present it to a partner or small group and receive feedback on your delivery.

17. **Research.** Daughtry explores the idea that "the pen is mightier than the sword." Conduct research on someone who has brought about significant social or historical change by using words instead of weapons.

18. **Creative Writing.** Write your own poem modeled on this one in which you have at least one stanza that states your own view of what a poem cannot do and then at least one stanza about what it can do.

19. **Multimodal.** Starting at line 57, the speaker describes "my block" with vivid imagery. Create a presentation using words, pictures, and sounds that capture your block, apartment complex, or neighborhood. How is your presentation of your block similar to and different from what Daughtry describes?

The Raven

Edgar Allan Poe

Edgar Allan Poe (1809–1849) was an American author who wrote poetry, literary criticism, and short stories, including many well-known ones that focus on murder, death, torture, and crime, such as "The Fall of the House of Usher," "The Black Cat," "The Pit and the Pendulum," and "The Tell-tale Heart." His work as a poet also takes on dark topics and themes. For example, in "Annabelle Lee," a man becomes obsessed after the death of his love; and in this poem, "The Raven," a similarly depressed figure has difficulty moving on after the death of his "lost Lenore." The poem was first published in 1845.

Once upon a midnight dreary, while I pondered, weak and weary,
Over many a quaint and curious volume of forgotten lore —
   While I nodded, nearly napping, suddenly there came a tapping,
   As of some one gently rapping, rapping at my chamber door.
"'Tis some visitor," I muttered, "tapping at my chamber door —   5
   Only this and nothing more."

Ah, distinctly I remember it was in the bleak December;
And each separate dying ember wrought its ghost upon the floor.
   Eagerly I wished the morrow; — vainly I had sought to borrow
   From my books surcease of sorrow — sorrow for the lost Lenore —   10
For the rare and radiant maiden whom the angels name Lenore —
   Nameless *here* for evermore.

And the silken, sad, uncertain rustling of each purple curtain
Thrilled me — filled me with fantastic terrors never felt before;
   So that now, to still the beating of my heart, I stood repeating   15
   "'Tis some visitor entreating entrance at my chamber door —
Some late visitor entreating entrance at my chamber door; —
   This it is and nothing more."

Presently my soul grew stronger; hesitating then no longer,
"Sir," said I, "or Madam, truly your forgiveness I implore;   20
   But the fact is I was napping, and so gently you came rapping,
   And so faintly you came tapping, tapping at my chamber door,
That I scarce was sure I heard you" — here I opened wide the door; —
   Darkness there and nothing more.

Deep into that darkness peering, long I stood there wondering, fearing,   25
Doubting, dreaming dreams no mortal ever dared to dream before;
   But the silence was unbroken, and the stillness gave no token,
   And the only word there spoken was the whispered word, "Lenore?"
This I whispered, and an echo murmured back the word, "Lenore!" —
    Merely this and nothing more.   30

Back into the chamber turning, all my soul within me burning,
Soon again I heard a tapping somewhat louder than before.
   "Surely," said I, "surely that is something at my window lattice;
   Let me see, then, what thereat is, and this mystery explore —
Let my heart be still a moment and this mystery explore; —   35
    'Tis the wind and nothing more!"

Open here I flung the shutter, when, with many a flirt and flutter,
In there stepped a stately Raven of the saintly days of yore;
   Not the least obeisance made he; not a minute stopped or stayed he;
   But, with mien of lord or lady, perched above my chamber door —   40
Perched upon a bust of Pallas[1] just above my chamber door —
    Perched, and sat, and nothing more.

Then this ebony bird beguiling my sad fancy into smiling,
By the grave and stern decorum of the countenance it wore,
   "Though thy crest be shorn and shaven, thou," I said, "art sure no craven,   45
   Ghastly grim and ancient Raven wandering from the Nightly shore —
Tell me what thy lordly name is on the Night's Plutonian[2] shore!"
    Quoth the Raven "Nevermore."

Much I marvelled this ungainly fowl to hear discourse so plainly,
Though its answer little meaning — little relevancy bore;   50
   For we cannot help agreeing that no living human being
   Ever yet was blessed with seeing bird above his chamber door —
Bird or beast upon the sculptured bust above his chamber door,
    With such name as "Nevermore."

But the Raven, sitting lonely on the placid bust, spoke only   55
That one word, as if his soul in that one word he did outpour.
   Nothing farther then he uttered — not a feather then he fluttered —
   Till I scarcely more than muttered "Other friends have flown before —
On the morrow *he* will leave me, as my Hopes have flown before."
    Then the bird said "Nevermore."   60

---

[1] A name for the Greek goddess Athena. The origin of the epithet is murky, but comes from the word meaning "maiden." —Eds.
[2] A reference to the Greek god of the underworld, called either Pluto or Hades. In Greek mythology, the river Styx is the border between the land of the living and the land of the dead; thus the reference here to the "Plutonian shore." —Eds.

Startled at the stillness broken by reply so aptly spoken,
"Doubtless," said I, "what it utters is its only stock and store
   Caught from some unhappy master whom unmerciful Disaster
   Followed fast and followed faster till his songs one burden bore —
Till the dirges of his Hope that melancholy burden bore   65
      Of 'Never — nevermore'."

But the Raven still beguiling all my fancy into smiling,
Straight I wheeled a cushioned seat in front of bird, and bust and door;
   Then, upon the velvet sinking, I betook myself to linking
   Fancy unto fancy, thinking what this ominous bird of yore —   70
What this grim, ungainly, ghastly, gaunt, and ominous bird of yore
      Meant in croaking "Nevermore."

This I sat engaged in guessing, but no syllable expressing
To the fowl whose fiery eyes now burned into my bosom's core;
   This and more I sat divining, with my head at ease reclining   75
   On the cushion's velvet lining that the lamp-light gloated o'er,
But whose velvet-violet lining with the lamp-light gloating o'er,
      She shall press, ah, nevermore!

Then, methought, the air grew denser, perfumed from an unseen censer
Swung by Seraphim whose foot-falls tinkled on the tufted floor.   80
   "Wretch," I cried, "thy God hath lent thee — by these angels he hath sent thee
   Respite — respite and nepenthe[3] from thy memories of Lenore;
Quaff, oh quaff this kind nepenthe and forget this lost Lenore!"
      Quoth the Raven "Nevermore."

"Prophet!" said I, "thing of evil! — prophet still, if bird or devil! —   85
Whether Tempter sent, or whether tempest tossed thee here ashore,
   Desolate yet all undaunted, on this desert land enchanted —
   On this home by Horror haunted — tell me truly, I implore —
Is there — *is* there balm in Gilead?[4] — tell me — tell me, I implore!"
      Quoth the Raven "Nevermore."   90

"Prophet!" said I, "thing of evil! — prophet still, if bird or devil!
By that Heaven that bends above us — by that God we both adore —
   Tell this soul with sorrow laden if, within the distant Aidenn,[5]
   It shall clasp a sainted maiden whom the angels name Lenore —
Clasp a rare and radiant maiden whom the angels name Lenore."   95
      Quoth the Raven "Nevermore."

---

[3] In Greek mythology, a medicine that treats sorrow. —Eds.

[4] A Biblical reference to Jeremiah, 8.19–22, in which the Lord condemns the land of Judah to death. The Lord says: "Why have they aroused my anger with their images, / with their worthless foreign idols?" and Jeremiah laments: "Since my people are crushed, I am crushed; / I mourn, and horror grips me. / Is there no balm in Gilead? / Is there no physician there? / Why then is there no healing / for the wound of my people?" —Eds.

[5] An alternate spelling for Eden, the Biblical paradise in the book of Genesis. —Eds.

519

"Be that word our sign of parting, bird or fiend!" I shrieked, upstarting —
"Get thee back into the tempest and the Night's Plutonian shore!
   Leave no black plume as a token of that lie thy soul hath spoken!
   Leave my loneliness unbroken! — quit the bust above my door!   100
Take thy beak from out my heart, and take thy form from off my door!"
     Quoth the Raven "Nevermore."

   And the Raven, never flitting, still is sitting, *still* is sitting
On the pallid bust of Pallas just above my chamber door;
   And his eyes have all the seeming of a demon's that is dreaming,   105
   And the lamp-light o'er him streaming throws his shadow on the floor;
And my soul from out that shadow that lies floating on the floor
     Shall be lifted — nevermore! ■

extending beyond the text

These images are from Gustave Doré's 1883 illustration of "The Raven."

Gustave Doré

Gustave Doré

Try to match the lines from the poem that might connect to each image. What specific lines from the poem lead you to this conclusion, and how are the images similar to or different from what you had imagined?

Understanding and Interpreting

1. To be sure that you have a clear understanding of the plot of this poem, give just a brief summary in response to the following:

   a. What is the speaker doing in the first stanza?

   b. Why is the speaker so depressed, as revealed in the second stanza?

   c. What does the speaker see when he opens the door the first time in stanza 5 (ll. 25–30), and, in your own words, what does he say out loud?

   d. What does the Raven do and say in stanzas 7–8 (ll. 37–48)?

   e. What does the speaker think about the Raven in stanzas 9–12 (ll. 49–72)?

   f. In your own words, what is the speaker asking of the Raven in stanza 16 (ll. 91–96)?

   g. Where are the Raven and the speaker at the end of the poem?

2. Why is the speaker so willing to think that it is Lenore at his chamber door?

3. While the bird is likely literally in the room with the speaker, the image of the Raven is not meant to be read literally by the audience. What does it symbolize in this poem? How do you know?

4. What is the relationship between the speaker and the Raven? How does this relationship help convey meaning?

Analyzing Language, Style, and Structure

5. **Vocabulary in Context.** Line 67 reads, "But the Raven still beguiling all my fancy into smiling." What is the meaning of the word *fancy* in this use, and how is it different from other uses of the word?

6. What is the mood or atmosphere that Poe establishes in stanzas 3–5 (ll. 13–30), and how do his diction and imagery help create it?

7. Poe uses personification to characterize the Raven in stanzas 7–10 (ll. 37–60), beyond having it speak. Identify two or more examples of personification and explain the impression the Raven has on the speaker.

8. Reread lines 71–72 and explain how the diction helps to create the speaker's tone: "What this grim, ungainly, ghastly, gaunt, and ominous bird of yore / Meant in croaking 'Nevermore'."

9. How does Poe use imagery and repetition to show the speaker's further descent into depression and madness in stanzas 13–16 (ll. 73–96)?

10. Poe uses a number of allusions with religious and mythological connections. Identify one or more of his allusions and explain how it contributes to the tone of the speaker toward Lenore, the Raven, or the speaker's own grief.

11. This poem is famous for its sound elements, particularly rhythm and internal rhyme. Look back closely at the poem and identify places where Poe uses rhyme or meter to connect words and phrases for a particular effect.

12. Where do significant shifts occur in this poem? Consider changes in tone and syntax. What effect do these shifts have?

Topics for Composing

13. **Analysis.** Write a response in which you analyze the role of the Raven's repeated response "Nevermore" in conveying a theme of the poem. Be sure to comment on the role this repetition plays.

14. **Argument.** The final line of the poem is, "And my soul from out that shadow that lies floating on the floor / Shall be lifted — nevermore!" In other words, the speaker concludes that because of his grief, he will never be happy again. Is this true in real life, or does grief fade over time for most people? Write your argument based on your own experiences or those of people you know, or conduct research on what experts have written about this topic.

15. **Connections.** Describe a time when you or someone you know felt loss or grief similar to what Poe describes this poem. What were some of the causes? If those feelings changed over time, describe how they changed.

16. **Speaking and Listening.** This is one of the most famous poems of all time, in part because of its rhyme, sound, and meter. With a partner, choose one stanza that really stood out for you both. Take turns reading that stanza aloud to each other several times each, emphasizing the rhymes and rhythm. Then, discuss how reading the poem aloud changes or enhances your feelings about or interpretations of the piece.

17. **Research.** The raven is a very popular figure in mythology and folklore. Research depictions of ravens in such stories and compare them to the raven in this poem. Alternatively, research the influence that this poem has had since its publication, especially on raven imagery in popular culture.

18. **Creative Writing.** Choose an animal to personify in a manner similar to the personification of the raven in this poem. Write a few lines of poetry or prose that express how that animal conveys a particular emotion.

19. **Multimodal.** Create a multimodal illustration of the poem's ideas of grief and loss, but with a different character, setting, and plot than those of the poem. Yours should not be about a lonely man and a raven, but it should include lines from the poem and found or created images to represent your new setting and plot.

Space Monkey

David Alpaugh

David Alpaugh (b. 1941) is a poet and teacher from California, whose writing has been published in literary journals and in three collections of his work. This poem is an example of a visual poem. Originally published in *Rattle* in 2008, it was part of an issue dedicated to multimedia poetry, which included poem-paintings, collages, comic poems, found poems, landscape haiku, and even poems written on Venetian blinds. According to Alpaugh, visual poems provide the "poem's words with a third dimension that commands the eye and affords the complex pleasure of a triple-read."

Dan Robertson

523

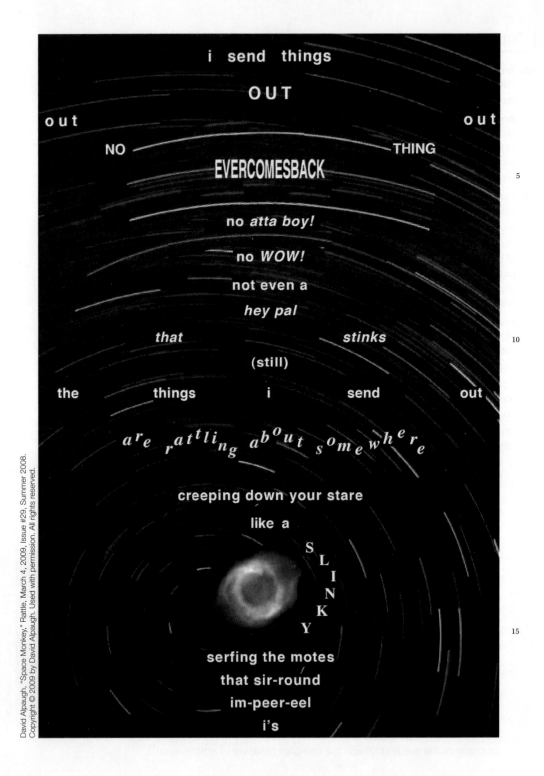

Understanding and Interpreting

1. The entire poem is less than fifty words. Paraphrase the poem in twenty-five to fifty words of your own, maintaining the "I," but otherwise using none of Alpaugh's unfamiliar or misspelled words.

2. Describe what you know or think you know about the speaker of this poem. What emotions does the speaker express? What evidence from the text supports your conclusions?

3. What might the "things" be that the speaker is "sending" out, and what do you do you think happens to those "things"?

4. Line 11, "(still)," signals a shift in subject and tone. Explain what is different in the second part of the poem, and how does Alpaugh's choice of parentheses help communicate this shift?

5. To the left of the word *slinky* is an image of a nebula, a body of interstellar clouds from across the galaxy. What might the nebula symbolize in this poem?

Analyzing Language, Style, and Structure

6. **Vocabulary in Context.** In line 14, Alpaugh writes "creeping down your stare." The word *stare* is a homophone, a word that sounds the same as another but uses different spelling and carries a different meaning. What are the multiple meanings of this word and what meaning or meanings might Alpaugh intend here?

7. Alpaugh uses fonts and upper- and lower-case letters creatively. Choose one or two examples and explain how these choices might help illustrate a point Alpaugh is making about communication.

8. Lines 13 and 15 are structurally different from the other lines in the poem. What effect was Alpaugh likely going for with these choices?

9. Spelling becomes more creative, less correct as the poem progresses. What might Alpaugh be suggesting through his spelling choices?

10. This poem has a visual component. How might Alpaugh's use of color, white lines, and the image of the nebula help to communicate a particular tone?

Topics for Composing

11. **Analysis.** Overall, what is Alpaugh suggesting about interpersonal communication? How does he use poetic and visual elements to present these ideas?

12. **Argument.** To what extent is getting feedback or a response to writing essential to communication? Use your own examples and reasoning to support your position.

13. **Connections.** How do you feel when you send a text to a friend who doesn't text back, or when you post something on social media and don't receive any response? Which words or images from this poem capture these feelings you have experienced?

14. **Speaking and Listening.** How would you read this poem aloud to account for the changes in font and style? Share your version out loud with a partner and compare how you each read it.

15. **Research.** Though not as widely published as other forms of poetry, visual poems, also called "concrete poems" have a long history, dating back thousands of years. Conduct research on the history of this form of poetry, identify some of its most significant practitioners, and explain how it has developed over time, especially with advancements in technology.

16. **Creative Writing.** Copy all of the words from Alpaugh's poem onto a separate piece of paper or into a document. Rearrange the order and structure, adding or deleting no more than eight to ten words to create a new poem.

17. **Multimodal.** Make your own visual poem, using techniques you see in Alpaugh's poem. You can write your own words and find images, or you can locate a poem or song lyrics that you like and create the images yourself. Try to connect the images and words, experimenting with colors and fonts in a way that communicates your ideas.

We Real Cool

Gwendolyn Brooks

Born in Topeka, Kansas, and raised in Chicago, Gwendolyn Brooks (1917–2000) authored over twenty books of poetry, including her breakout work, *A Street in Bronzeville* (1945), and *Annie Allen* (1949), for which she became the first African American author to receive the Pulitzer Prize. In 1968, she was named the poet laureate of Illinois, and from 1985 to 1986, she served as consultant in poetry to the Library of Congress — the first African American woman to hold this position. She is one of the most highly regarded and influential poets of the twentieth century. "We Real Cool" is from her third collection of poetry, *The Bean Eaters* (1960).

Everett Collection Inc/Alamy

THE POOL PLAYERS.
SEVEN AT THE GOLDEN SHOVEL.

We real cool. We
Left school. We

Lurk late. We
Strike straight. We

Sing sin. We   5
Thin gin. We

Jazz June. We
Die soon. ∎

extending beyond the text

Below is a painting by renowned American artist Jacob Lawrence called "Pool Parlor" (1942). This piece was one of the first by an artist of color to be added to the collection at the Metropolitan Museum of Art in New York City.

© 2022 The Jacob and Gwendolyn Knight Lawrence Foundation, Seattle/Artists Rights Society (ARS), New York. Image © The Metropolitan Museum of Art. Image source: Art Resource, NY

In what ways does this painting capture some aspects of the tone of "We Real Cool"? What specific lines from the poem are best represented in the painting? You may want to conduct additional research on Lawrence and examine his "Migration" series of paintings to learn more about his importance to art history.

Understanding and Interpreting

1. What can you infer about the speakers of the poem? What are the "we" like? What do they think about themselves? How do you know?

2. What is the reader expected to conclude about the final sentence? How does this statement illustrate a shift from all of the previous sentences?

3. Look back at the epigraph of the poem: "The Pool Players. Seven at the Golden Shovel." What information does it reveal and how does this help the reader better understand the speakers' situation?

Analyzing Language, Style, and Structure

4. Vocabulary in Context. In line 7, *jazz* is used as a verb. What does that word likely mean when it is used in this way? What is its effect within the poem?

5. Reread the poem and notice that each sentence has exactly three syllables. What effect is created through this pattern of very short sentences?

6. Brooks uses enjambment on the end of every line, starting a new sentence at the end of the line with the word *We*. What effect does this choice create?

7. Look closely at the rhymes and other sound devices in this poem. How do these help Brooks achieve a particular attitude toward the speakers?

8. Some of the sentences in the poem create concrete images of the speakers' actions, but some are more abstract. Identify examples of each type and explain how these two types of sentences work together or in conflict with each other.

Topics for Composing

9. Analysis. What attitude toward life do the speakers present? How do you know? How is their attitude similar to or different from the author's? What evidence from the poem gives you this impression?

10. Argument. Are the speakers in the poem to be pitied or celebrated? What evidence from the poem supports your position?

11. Connections. With which "We" statement do you most or least identify? Explain the connection between that statement in the poem and an event or feeling you've experienced.

12. Speaking and Listening. In an interview from 1970, Brooks offers stage directions for how "We Real Cool" should be read aloud:

> First of all, let me tell you how that's supposed to be said, because there's a reason why I set it out as I did. . . . The "We" — you're supposed to stop after the "We" and think about their validity, and of course there's no way for you to tell whether it should be said softly or not, I suppose, but I say it rather softly because I want to represent their basic uncertainty, which they don't bother to question every day, of course.

Work with a partner and read the poem several times following her directions. How do the poet's instructions on how to read it contribute to your experience and understanding of the poem?

13. Research. Gwendolyn Brooks is a significant figure in American literature and culture. She was the first Black author to win the Pulitzer Prize, the first Black woman poetry consultant to the Library of Congress, and a key figure in the Civil Rights Movement. Conduct research into her life, focusing specifically on how Brooks used her poetry and her fame to advance the fight for social justice causes.

14. Creative Writing. Rewrite the lines from this poem with a setting that is familiar to you: your school, the basketball court, your neighborhood, and so on. Retain the first sentence and try to keep the same three-syllable pattern, but change the words to reflect the new setting.

I Woke Up—Smiling

Ha Jin

Born in Liaoning Province, China, Ha Jin (b. 1956) grew up during
the Cultural Revolution, a time of violence and persecution intended
to purge capitalism and traditional Chinese culture and to create a
pure Communist society. He volunteered to serve in the People's
Liberation Army from age 14 to 19 and studied in the United States
to complete a PhD at Brandeis University. After the massacre of
student democracy protestors in Tiananmen Square in 1989, Jin
decided to remain in the United States and write solely in English.
Jin has published several books of poetry and short fiction as well
as six novels, one of which, *Waiting* (1999), won the National Book Award.

Ulf Andersen/Getty Images

I was told that I was a sad man.
Sadness is a fatal disease in this place
where happiness is a key to success.
If you are sad, you are doomed to fail —
you can't please your boss,   5
your long face won't attract customers,
a few sighs are enough
to let your friends down.

Yesterday afternoon I met Pham,
a Vietnamese man who was once a general.   10
He came to this country
after nine years' imprisonment.
Now he works hard as a custodian
and always avoids
meeting his former soldiers here,   15
because every one of them
is doing better than he is.
"Sadness," he told me,
"is a luxury for me.
I have no time for it.   20
If I feel sad
I won't be able to support my family."

His words filled me with shame,
although I learned long ago
a busy bee feels no sorrow.   25
He made me realize I'm still a fortunate one
and ought to be happy and grateful

for having food in my stomach
and books to read.

I returned home humming a cheerful tune.　　　30
My wife smiled wondering
why I had suddenly become lighthearted.
My son followed me, laughing and frolicking,
while I was capering on the floor.

Last night　　　35
I went to a party in my dream.
Voices and laughter were drifting in a large hall
that was full of paintings and calligraphy.
Strolling with ease
I ran into the handwriting of yours　　　40
hung in the air
piece by piece waving like wings.
Dumbfounded, I turned
and saw you sitting on a chair,
motionless, the same lean detached face,　　　45
only your blue clothes had grown darker.
Something snapped in my chest
and my tears flowed.
What's the use of promising?
I have promised, a hundred times,　　　50
but never returned. Wherever we go
our cause is the same:
to make a living and raise children.
If a poem arises, it's merely
an accidental blessing.　　　55

For several hours my heart ached,
but I woke up — smiling. ■

Understanding and Interpreting

1. What do we learn about the speaker from the first stanza? How does the speaker define "success" at the beginning of the poem?

2. Summarize the second stanza, focusing on what the speaker learns from Pham.

3. What does Pham, the former general, mean when he says that sadness "is a luxury for me"?

4. How does the speaker's meeting with Pham affect him, especially in stanzas 3 and 4?

5. Stanza 5 signifies a shift. Describe any differences in the setting, tone, topic or other feature in this section of the poem.

6. In stanza 5, the speaker addresses "you." Reread the stanza and draw an interpretation about who "you" might be. What evidence from the text supports your interpretation?

7. Reread lines 54–55 ("If a poem arises, it's merely / an accidental blessing"). What does a "poem" symbolize?

8. Based on what you know from reading the whole piece, what do you think "this place" in the second line of the poem refers to?

9. Why does the speaker wake up smiling at the end of the poem? What does he learn in his dream that makes this happen?

Analyzing Language, Style, and Structure

10. **Vocabulary in Context.** In line 49, the speaker asks, "What's the use of promising?" What is the meaning of the word *promising* in this context, and what is another use of the word that might also be relevant here?

11. The beginning of stanza 5 includes a sentence with unusual syntax. A more common sentence structure might have been, "Last night, I dreamed I went to a party." What is the effect of Jin's syntactical choices here?

12. This poem does not include much figurative language, but in lines 40–42, Jin writes, "I ran into the handwriting of yours / hung in the air / piece by piece waving like wings." What is the effect of this imagery and simile?

13. In line 51, Jin switches from "I" to "we" and "our." What is the likely intended effect of this change of pronouns at this point in the poem?

14. This poem consists of six stanzas. What is the topic of each stanza, and why did Jin likely construct his poem in this way? How does the last stanza connect with the first?

Topics for Composing

15. **Analysis.** What is Jin suggesting about success and "our cause" (l. 52) in this poem? What evidence from the text supports your interpretation of this theme?

16. **Argument.** Reread the first stanza. To what degree is it true what the speaker says — that if you're sad, you shouldn't show it for the reasons stated in that stanza? Does the rest of the poem support that position? Does real life support that position? Use evidence from the poem and your own experiences to support your response.

17. **Argument.** In stanza 3, Jin writes, "a busy bee feels no sorrow." What does this statement mean, and is it true? Write an argument about whether you agree with this statement, using your own experiences and those of others you know to support your position.

18. **Connections.** Everyone experiences sadness one time or another. What are some of the causes of your own sadness, and what helps you to put your sadness in context as the speaker of this poem learns to do?

19. **Speaking and Listening.** Hold a class or small group discussion on what defines "success" in everyday life. After hearing various perspectives, try to reach consensus on two or three characteristics of success. Be prepared to explain how those characteristics make your definition similar to or different from "success" as it is defined in the poem.

20. **Creative Writing.** Rewrite stanza 4 — in poetry form — from the perspective of the speaker's wife or son. Focus on what is revealed by the change of speaker.

21. **Multimodal.** Reread stanza 5, in which the speaker recounts his dream. Locate or create a series of images that depict the dream or an interpretation of the dream and label the images with words from the poem.

Harold's Chicken Shack #86

Nate Marshall

Mercedes Zapata

Nate Marshall (b. 1989) is from the South Side of Chicago, the setting of this poem. A spoken-word poet, he was a star of the award-winning full-length documentary *Louder Than a Bomb* (2010), and he is the coeditor of the poetry collection *The BreakBeat Poets: New American Poetry in the Age of Hip-Hop* (2015). The winner of numerous poetry awards, his work has appeared in *Poetry Magazine*, *Indiana Review*, *The New Republic*, and elsewhere. This poem is from his book *Wild Hundreds* (2015).

KEY CONTEXT The title and the epigraph of the poem refer to a restaurant chain of over thirty locations called Harold's Chicken Shack, which originated on the South Side of Chicago. In the process of trying to make it a national chain, the daughter of the original owner is trying to expand the chain and create more consistent quality among the restaurants. She said in an interview, "We're trying to eliminate the shack. I want to set a standard."

> *we're trying to eliminate the shack.*
> —*Kristen Pierce, Harold's CEO & daughter of founder Harold Pierce*

when i went to summer camp the white kids had a tendency
to shorten names of important institutions. make Northwestern
University into *NU*. international relations into *IR*. everybody
started calling me *Nate*. before this i imagined myself

Nathaniel A. maybe even *N. Armstead* to big up my granddad.   5
i wrote my whole name on everything. eventually i started
unintentionally introducing myself as *Nate*. it never occurred
to me that they could escape the knowing of my name's
real length. as a shorty

most the kids in my neighborhood couldn't say my name.　　10
Mick-daniel, Nick-thaniel, MacDonnel shot across the courts
like wild heaves toward the basket. the subconscious visual
of a chicken shack seems a poor fit for national expansion.

Harold's Chicken is easier, sounds like Columbus's flag stuck
into a cup of cole slaw. shack sounds too much like home　　15
of poor people, like haven for weary
　　　　　　　　　　like building our own. ■

extending beyond the text

In an article for *Rumpus* magazine, Marshall talks with fellow poet José Olivarez. They discuss the difficulty they sometimes face as people of color in America.

OLIVAREZ: So let me ask you where do you go to see representations of yourself? Where is your mirror in the world?

MARSHALL: I think I go back home. I go to hoods around Chicago where I can see folks who look like me and hear people who sound like me. I think that also just extends to black communities everywhere. When I think about who I am I think it's tied up in race AND class. In a lot of ways I just feel more comfortable in spaces populated by poor and working folks who know something of what it is to grind in similar ways to how I came up. I think I often feel a kind of dysphoria because I'm not necessarily in the same class now as where I was as a kid and I don't totally know how I feel about that. How about you? What shapes your mirror self and where do you go to find it?

OLIVAREZ: Man. I remember when you and I were just starting to become friends we were talking on the phone and you said something that stuck with me. You said something like I like talking to you because I can switch back and forth between academic talk and hip-hop in speech. Something like that. And I think I feel most comfortable around people like that. Where I can be very serious and academic and then turn around and be the silly dude from Calumet City that I am. I think I find mirrors in Mexican grocery stores. In Lechoneras in the Bronx where I can hear people talk like my mom and dad and sometimes they play Vicente Fernandez, but I think the places where I can most fully be myself and feel most seen are among my chosen family of artists and friends that encourage me to be my full self at all times.

How do you see what they describe playing out in "Harold's Chicken Shack #86," or in any of the other poems in this chapter? When do you feel like your "full self," or where is "your mirror in the world"?

Understanding and Interpreting

1. Who shortens the speaker's name, and how does he feel about it in the first stanza?

2. Reread stanzas two and three. What had the speaker envisioned about his own name and the identity it gave him?

3. What does the following line reveal about the speaker: "it never occurred / to me that they could escape the knowing of my name's / real length" (ll. 7–9)?

4. Explain what the speaker means when he says that the original name is a "poor fit for national expansion" (l. 13).

5. How does the second part of the poem — lines 12–17 — relate to the personal stories of the first part? Specifically consider the issues of race and social class.

6. Considering the epigraph (the quotation from Harold's CEO Kristen Pierce), the last stanza, and what we learn about the shortening of the speaker's name and "important institutions," what connection can you draw between the name of the speaker and what happens to the name of Harold's Chicken Shack? Why does the connection matter to him?

Analyzing Language, Style, and Structure

7. **Vocabulary in Context.** In line 16, Marshall refers to Harold's Chicken as a "haven for weary." What are the different meanings of the word *haven*? How does the connotation of the word add to its effect in this context?

8. The speaker uses casual language but takes the subject seriously. How would you describe the tone in this poem — the speaker's attitude toward the subject? Explain how specific diction and syntactical choices help Marshall achieve this tone.

9. The speaker describes the attempts at pronouncing his name as being "like wild heaves toward the basket" (l. 12). What does this simile convey about the speaker's attitude toward those who don't use his name?

10. Halfway through line 12, there is a significant shift not only in topic, but also in tone. What stylistic elements contribute to this new tone?

11. How do the allusion to "Columbus's flag" and the final simile in the poem about the word *shack* in lines 15–17 help make a larger point about race and social class in America?

Topics for Composing

12. **Analysis.** What does the phrase "eliminate the shack" in the epigraph really mean, according to the speaker? Explain your response using evidence from the poem.

13. **Argument.** Prior to the 1950s and the rise of the McDonald's franchise, most restaurants were individually owned and operated, offering unique menus and experiences. Today, you can go into most chain restaurants and experience nearly the same food, service, and décor. Do you think this development in food service is overall more positive or negative? Why? To what extent might the speaker of the poem agree or disagree with your position? Why?

14. **Connection.** How do you feel about your name? What significance does it have for you? Has anyone ever deliberately mispronounced your name or given you a nickname without your permission? Describe the circumstances and your feelings about them.

15. **Speaking and Listening.** Meet with a small group and discuss restaurants or businesses that have significance for you. What draws you to those particular places, and how might you feel if they were to change significantly? Try to reach consensus about the factors that make a restaurant or business meaningful to you.

16. **Research.** This poem could also be seen as an examination of gentrification — a process by which longtime residents of lower-income communities, disproportionately those of color, are pushed out by rising real estate prices when middle- and upper-class people move in. Conduct research on gentrification in Chicago, the setting of this poem, or in your own city, town, or state. What factors led to the gentrification and what were the results for the neighborhood and its residents?

17. **Creative Writing.** Think about a location that has had meaning in your life for a long time. It could be a restaurant or summer camp, as in this poem, or it could be your elementary school, a park you know well, or a friend's house. Write two stanzas of a poem. The first should describe the location as you remember it when you were young, and the second should describe it as you see it today. Try to draw contrasts or connections between the two perspectives through your imagery, tone, or other poetic elements.

Kindness

Naomi Shihab Nye

A poet, novelist, editor, and political activist, Naomi Shihab Nye was born in 1952 in St. Louis, Missouri. The daughter of a Palestinian father and an American mother, she grew up in Jerusalem and San Antonio, Texas. These cultural experiences have influenced her poetry, for which she has won many awards and fellowships. Nye, who has been a visiting writer all over the world, describes herself as a "wandering poet." The poem "Kindness" is from her collection *Words under the Words: Selected Poems* (1980).

Roberto Ricciuti/Getty Images

Before you know what kindness really is
you must lose things,
feel the future dissolve in a moment
like salt in a weakened broth.
What you held in your hand,   5
what you counted and carefully saved,
all this must go so you know
how desolate the landscape can be
between the regions of kindness.
How you ride and ride   10
thinking the bus will never stop,
the passengers eating maize and chicken
will stare out the window forever.

Before you learn the tender gravity of kindness
you must travel where the Indian in a white poncho   15
lies dead by the side of the road.
You must see how this could be you,
how he too was someone
who journeyed through the night with plans
and the simple breath that kept him alive.   20

Before you know kindness as the deepest thing inside,
you must know sorrow as the other deepest thing.
You must wake up with sorrow.
You must speak to it till your voice
catches the thread of all sorrows   25
and you see the size of the cloth.
Then it is only kindness that makes sense anymore,
only kindness that ties your shoes
and sends you out into the day to gaze at bread,
only kindness that raises its head   30
from the crowd of the world to say
It is I you have been looking for,
and then goes with you everywhere
like a shadow or a friend. ■

extending beyond the text

Look closely at the painting below from the mid-seventeenth century called *The Seven Acts of Mercy*.

The Seven Acts of Mercy (oil on card)/Teniers, David the Younger (1610-90)/Louvre, Paris, France/Bridgeman Images

What acts of kindness are depicted in this image? What is the overall tone of the painting, and how does the artist create this tone? Identify one line from the poem that would fit well as a caption for this painting and one that would not. Explain your choices.

Understanding and Interpreting

1. Each stanza begins with something "you" have to experience or understand before you can know what kindness is. Paraphrase each of these experiences.

2. Explain what the speaker suggests we should learn from the "Indian in a white poncho" (ll. 15–16).

3. In the last stanza, the speaker concludes by saying after all the sad experiences, "it is only kindness that makes sense anymore" (l. 27). How does the speaker come to this conclusion from the evidence provided earlier?

4. Overall, according to this poem, what do you need in order to understand kindness? How would you explain the theme of the poem?

Analyzing Language, Style, and Structure

5. **Vocabulary in Context.** Carefully examine the phrase in line 14: "the tender gravity of kindness." What is the meaning of *gravity* in this context, and how is it modified by the word *tender*? Then, explain how these two words together relate to "kindness."

6. In lines 3–4, Nye writes that to feel loss, you must "feel the future dissolve in a moment / like salt in a weakened broth." Explain what this simile is intended to communicate.

7. What is the effect of the repetition at the beginning of each stanza?

8. Reread lines 7–13, in which the speaker compares the idea of loss to travel. Analyze this metaphor and explain how it relates to what the speaker is suggesting about kindness.

9. In the last stanza, Nye personifies kindness in different ways. Analyze the examples below and explain how each example builds on another, helping her communicate a theme:

   a. "ties your shoes" (l. 28)

   b. "sends you out into the day to gaze at bread" (l. 29)

   c. "raises its head . . . to say / It is I you have been looking for" (ll. 30–32)

   d. "goes with you everywhere / like a shadow or a friend" (ll. 33–34)

10. Like most complex poems, this one has multiple tones. Explain one dominant tone you identify from Nye's diction and imagery or explain a significant shift in tone that is signaled by a change in diction, syntax, or other poetic element.

Topics for Composing

11. **Analysis.** In a well-supported response using examples taken directly from the text, explain how the speaker's strong use of imagery helps to convey a theme of this poem.

12. **Argument.** On the surface, kindness seems like such a basic concept: be nice to each other. Why does Nye make it seem so much more complex? Do you agree that people have to know the things she describes to really show, receive, appreciate, and understand kindness?

13. **Connection.** Write about a time when you have experienced loss and sorrow similar to that which the speaker describes in the first part of the poem, or something like the kindness that the speaker describes at the end.

14. **Speaking and Listening.** Meet with a partner or a small group and share experiences you have had with kindness, either that you provided or received. As you listen closely to each other, what do you identify as common causes or results of the acts of kindness you experienced?

15. **Research.** Find a news story about someone who experienced an act of kindness following a loss or tragedy. Write about whether the person in the news story would likely agree — or not — with how the speaker of the poem thinks about kindness.

16. **Creative Writing.** Write your own poem that begins the same way with a different topic: "Before you know what _____ really is, you must _____."

17. **Multimodal.** Locate images from the news or other sources that you feel exemplify "kindness." Include words and phrases from the poem as captions.

18. **Exposition.** Write a definition of the word *kindness*. Use examples from your own life experiences — as well as any from the poem that resonate with you — to explain and support your definition.

Sonnet 18: Shall I compare thee to a summer's day?

William Shakespeare

Oli Scarff/Getty Images

William Shakespeare (1564–1616) was an English poet, actor, and playwright. He is considered the greatest writer in the English language and the world's most famous playwright. He is credited with 38 plays, 154 sonnets, and two long narrative poems. Little is known of his life aside from the fact that he married Anne Hathaway when he was eighteen, worked as an actor-playwright in London, and retired in 1613. His sonnets are often grouped by scholars into categories based on the figure he is addressing: The Fair Youth, the Dark Lady, and the Rival Poet. This one is from the first grouping, Fair Youth, which includes poems that tend to focus on love and the challenge of relationships.

KEY CONTEXT   To be able to successfully analyze a sonnet, you need to understand its form. Traditionally, an English sonnet is a fourteen-line poem with a strict rhyme scheme (*abab cdcd efef gg*). Most English sonnets, like those Shakespeare wrote, have ten syllables in each line, written in iambic pentameter, a pattern of alternating stressed and unstressed syllables. Additionally, a sonnet is often divided into subparts: a group of four lines is called a "quatrain" and the last two lines are called a "couplet." An English sonnet consists of three quatrains and a couplet.

As you read Shakespeare's work, you'll notice that while it is written in English, some of the words are now archaic and not in frequent use today, though many of them are straightforward:

- *thee* and *thou* mean "you"
- *hath* means "has"
- *thy* means "your"

Shakespeare also sometimes invented words to fit in rhythm or rhyme schemes, and some words in this sonnet are spelled unusually or have suffixes attached to them, as in *owest*, *wander'st*, and *growest*. You can read these just as they would be without the *-est* suffixes.

Shall I compare thee to a summer's day?
Thou art more lovely and more temperate:
Rough winds do shake the darling buds of May,
And summer's lease hath all too short a date:
Sometime too hot the eye of heaven shines,   5
And often is his gold complexion dimm'd;
And every fair from fair sometime declines,
By chance or nature's changing course untrimm'd;
But thy eternal summer shall not fade
Nor lose possession of that fair thou owest;   10
Nor shall Death brag thou wander'st in his shade,
When in eternal lines to time thou growest:
So long as men can breathe or eyes can see,
So long lives this, and this gives life to thee. ∎

extending beyond the text

Below is a painting called "The Soul of the Rose" by John William Waterhouse. The piece is said to be inspired by the poem "Come to the Garden, Maud," by Alfred Lord Tennyson, which includes the following lines:

> And the soul of the rose went into my blood,
>   As the music clash'd in the hall;
>
> . . .
>
> But the rose was awake all night for your sake,
>   Knowing your promise to me;
> The lilies and roses were all awake,
>   They sigh'd for the dawn and thee.

The Soul of the Rose, 1908 (oil on canvas)/Waterhouse, John William (1849-1917)/Private Collection/Bridgeman Images

In what ways does the painting reflect the tone or imagery of the excerpt from the Tennyson poem? How does the painting relate to the tone or theme of the Shakespeare sonnet?

Understanding and Interpreting

1. The poem starts with a simple question: how are "you" similar to or different from a day in summer? How does line 2 begin to answer that question?

2. Lines 3–6 describe things that can be wrong with a day in summer. Summarize the speaker's objections in each of the lines.

3. In lines 7–8, the speaker identifies the most significant problem with a summer day. What is it, in your own words?

4. The beginning of the third quatrain (l. 9) signifies a shift — signaled by the word *But* — as the speaker switches attention from summer to "you." What does the speaker say is the main difference between "you" and the day in summer the speaker describes in the previous sections?

5. What does the phrase "When in eternal lines to time thou growest" (l. 12) refer to, and what is its significance to the meaning of the poem?

6. The final two lines — the couplet — provide a type of solution to the "problem" raised in lines 7–8. What does the speaker think will happen in the future? What words or phrases from the poem support your interpretation?

7. What can you infer about the speaker's attitude toward the speaker's own poetry? What evidence from the text supports your response?

Analyzing Language, Style, and Structure

8. **Vocabulary in Context.** The following are words that you probably know from other contexts. Describe familiar meanings of these words and explain their meanings in the context of this piece:

   a. *temperate* (l. 2)

   b. *lease* (l. 4)

   c. *complexion* (l. 6)

   d. *possession* (l. 10)

9. How does the structure of this sonnet help the reader understand its meaning? In other words, how do the messages in each quatrain and the couplet work together to create the argument the speaker is making?

10. What is the "eye of heaven" (l. 5) and how does this metaphor help draw a connection between the summer's day and "you"?

11. One purpose for rhyming is to connect words and ideas that would not necessarily seem related. Identify a pair of rhymes from this sonnet, and explain what ideas are connected.

12. One reason why this is one of Shakespeare's most popular sonnets is because of its complexity and its use of extended metaphors — comparisons that appear throughout a poem, not just in a single line. Choose one or more of the following topics and explain how Shakespeare uses the extended metaphor at various places in the poem to communicate a possible theme:

   a. Light/dark

   b. Life/death

   c. Youth/immortality

Topics for Composing

13. **Analysis.** What is the speaker of this sonnet suggesting about how love is affected by beauty, life, and language?

14. **Argument.** Is the speaker's argument about love and beauty true? The speaker claims that both are eternal because they appear in the poem and thus survive death. Write a response in which you agree or disagree with this claim and the evidence the speaker provides.

15. **Connections.** The speaker is hoping that his poetry will lead to eternal fame. While you may not have such large ambitions, what do you hope that you become known for? Why?

16. **Speaking and Listening.** Shakespeare intended his poetry, like his plays, to be heard, not just read. Choose one of the quatrains in this poem and read it several times aloud to a partner; perhaps even try to memorize it. Discuss how speaking the words aloud helps with understanding meaning, including any archaic or otherwise unusual language.

17. **Research.** Shakespeare has over 150 sonnets credited to him. This sonnet is considered to be a part of his Fair Youth series, but another group (sonnets 127–154) is often referred to as the Dark Lady series. Read two or more sonnets in that series and conduct research on who the mysterious subject — the Dark Lady — might be.

18. **Creative Writing.** Try writing your own sonnet, using the same format that Shakespeare uses in this piece (see the Key Context on p. 538 for details about the form). Or, instead of starting from scratch, try deleting one word from each line in Sonnet 18 and replacing it with one of your own, keeping the syllables and rhymes the same. Then try replacing two or more words in each line, and so on, until most of the words in the poem are your own.

19. **Multimodal.** A diorama is a three-dimensional model depicting a scene. Create a diorama with found or created images or objects to illustrate a line or two from this poem. The words from the poem should also appear somewhere in the representation.

Turning the Ship for Home and Then the Telling

Pippa Little

Pippa Little was born in Tanzania and grew up in Scotland. She is a poet, reviewer, translator, and editor whose work has been published in British literary journals and in the collections *Time Begins to Hurt* (2021), *Twist* (2017), and *Overwintering* (2012). This poem originally appeared in *Ghost Fishing: An Eco-Justice Poetry Anthology* (2018).

Pippa Little

The captain's sun-sizzled, wears a cap with "Die Trying"
stuck at an angle, fists the lumpish red of lobsters.
He's sailing the Algetia back from the Eastern Garbage Patch,
an unmapped country he can't board,
for it jiggles and scrambles and discards itself   5
like knitting twirling off the needles,

but at its deep clotted heart it pulls in close,
clamps whales and crabs alike in nets and knots
and chokes — not only the lines, the ropes, the spars
but all the plastic tops and jagged fragments   10
whale-swallowed, a whole ocean's innards
spiked orange, fluorescent pink, green, blue —
pulled and sucked by the sea into a whorl
that grows, accrues, accumulates
hour after hour in daylight and dark,   15
where he is powerless except in witness
his mourning the world takes for crazy. ∎

extending beyond the text

Look closely at the photo collage below called *You Eat What They Eat* by Christine So.

Christine So

What message does So communicate about the environment through her choices of objects, colors, and other visual elements? In what ways does her message relate to what Little suggests in her poem?

Understanding and Interpreting

1. While most of this poem is a detailed description of the Eastern Garbage Patch, it also tells a story. Paraphrase lines 1–3 and 16–17 to recount the action of the poem.

2. What key details does the speaker use to describe the ship's captain, and what do these details illustrate about him?

3. Many poems have speakers who clearly identify themselves with words like *I, me, my,* or *we.* The speaker in this poem does not, but that does not mean that there is no speaker. What interpretation can you draw about the speaker of this poem: who might the speaker be, what does the speaker care about, what does the speaker seem to know or not know, and so on? Identify evidence from the poem to support your interpretation.

4. What does the speaker mean by describing the captain as "powerless except in witness" (l. 16)?

5. How does the speaker expect the world will respond to what the captain sees? Why do you think the speaker believes this?

Analyzing Language, Style, and Structure

6. **Vocabulary in Context.** In line 4, Little writes that the patch is a country the captain "can't board." What does *board* mean in this context?

7. Reread lines 1–2, 5–8, and 14–16 aloud to yourself, specifically listening for the sounds that Little creates with her diction. What are the sounds, and what are possible intended effects of those sounds?

8. What does the simile in line 6 — "like knitting twirling off the needles" — communicate about the garbage patch?

9. Reread lines 7–9. What is the effect of Little's use of personification here — rather than straightforward description — to characterize the garbage patch?

10. In line 11, the speaker claims that the patch contains "a whole ocean's innards." What does this use of hyperbole communicate to the reader?

11. Reread lines 13–15 aloud to yourself. What do you notice about her use of verbs and the rhythm her diction and syntax create here near the end of the poem?

12. Look at the unusual syntax of the final line. In prose, the line would be something like, "The world takes his mourning for crazy." What is the effect of Little's syntactical choices in this last line of her poem?

Topics for Composing

13. **Analysis.** Write an explanation of how the title of this poem, "Turning the Ship for Home and Then the Telling," relates to a possible theme Little is presenting.

14. **Argument.** What are the most likely solutions to an environmental problem like the Eastern Garbage Patch? Conduct research to identify the support you need to make your argument. Based on your findings and your understanding of the poem, how might the speaker react to the proposed solutions?

15. **Argument.** We have known about the impact of human activity on the environment for a long time now, but we tend to either dismiss those warnings as "crazy," as in this poem, or we deliberately ignore them. Why is this? What is it about human nature that can make us unwilling to recognize dangers that we don't personally witness?

16. **Connections.** What is something that you have used and discarded that might have ended up in our oceans? What steps can you personally take to help keep oceanic garbage patches from growing larger?

17. **Speaking and Listening.** Meet with a group and discuss seemingly insurmountable challenges like climate change, gun violence, or political polarization. In what ways do you find yourself feeling like the captain of the ship who is only a "witness" to the problem? How do you try to make even a small difference with difficult issues? How do you avoid becoming cynical about the future? Try to develop a list of strategies and approaches that work for your group.

18. **Research.** Conduct research on the Great Pacific Garbage Patch. Present your findings on what has caused it and what its future is expected to be like.

19. **Multimodal.** Create or locate images of an environmental challenge to our oceans and other bodies of water (for example, the Great Pacific Garbage Patch). Add captions to the images of your own creation, modeling them on the words and phrases Little uses in this poem, especially in lines 5–12.

20. **Exposition.** Explain why garbage from all over the world tends to accumulate in certain places. You will likely need to conduct research on ocean currents, chemical properties of the trash, and other factors.

Because I could not stop for Death

Emily Dickinson

Born into a prominent family in Amherst, Massachusetts, Emily Dickinson (1830–1886) was famously shy and reclusive. While Dickinson wrote more than seventeen hundred poems, only ten were published during her lifetime. Today, she is widely recognized as one of the most original voices in American literature, and this poem — typical of her style and themes — is one of her most well known. Her life has been fictionalized in the Apple TV show *Dickinson*.

Todd-Bingham picture collection, 1837-1966 (inclusive). Manuscripts & Archives, Yale University

Because I could not stop for Death —
He kindly stopped for me —
The Carriage held but just Ourselves —
And Immortality.

We slowly drove — He knew no haste   5
And I had put away
My labor and my leisure too,
For His Civility —

We passed the School, where Children strove
At Recess — in the Ring —   10
We passed the Fields of Gazing Grain —
We passed the Setting Sun —

Or rather — He passed us —
The Dews drew quivering and chill —

For only Gossamer,[1] my Gown —   15
My Tippet[2] — only Tulle[3] —

We paused before a House that seemed
A Swelling of the Ground —
The Roof was scarcely visible —
The Cornice[4] — in the Ground —   20

Since then — 'tis Centuries — and yet
Feels shorter than the Day
I first surmised the Horses' Heads
Were toward Eternity — ■

---

[1]Very light, delicate. Specifically, resembling a spider's cobweb. —Eds.
[2]A long woman's scarf. —Eds.
[3]Thin, light netting used on clothing. —Eds.
[4]A horizontal ornamentation or molding found in architecture. —Eds.

extending beyond the text

This is an image from the TV show *Dickinson*, a fictionalized account of Emily Dickinson's life. The episode from which this image is taken is called "Because I could not stop for Death."

What is the effect of the color choices in this image, and how would you describe the relationship between the two figures in the scene? What lines in the poem may have inspired the show's creators to depict the scene in this way?

Understanding and Interpreting

1. Before you dive into the interpretation, think about what is literally happening in the poem. Write a one-sentence summary of the actions of the speaker and of Death in each stanza.

2. How does the speaker seem to react to meeting and riding with Death? What specific words or phrases lead you to this conclusion?

3. Identify the references to time. How much time passes, looking especially at the last stanza? What do you notice about how time is presented in this poem?

4. Metonymy refers to the use of a symbol to stand in for something closely related. For example, if someone were to write "The Crown," we might interpret it as a reference to royal power or authority. Locate examples of metonymy in this poem and explain how you might interpret them.

Analyzing Language, Style, and Structure

5. **Vocabulary in Context.** You likely know what the word *passed* means, but what dual meaning is intended in the lines of this poem?

6. One of the dominant poetic elements here is the personification of Death. How is he characterized, and what is the likely intended effect that characterization?

7. Reread stanzas 3 and 5, looking specifically at the imagery of the settings. What words and phrases describe and draw contrast between these two settings? What is achieved by contrasting them?

8. Examine stanza 4 closely, beginning with "The Dews." How does Dickinson use diction to create a particular feeling or atmosphere in this stanza? Knowing what is happening in this poem, what makes this stanza so important?

9. This poem follows a strict syllable rhythm pattern. Identify the pattern and explain where and why that pattern changes.

Topics for Composing

10. **Analysis.** What does this poem suggest about how we should view life and death? Be sure to use specific examples from the text to support your interpretation.

11. **Argument.** Is the speaker glamorizing death, or is the speaker being realistic about it? Write an argument supporting one of those interpretations or one of your own.

12. **Connections.** Many creative works take on death as a subject. Choose another text — a movie, a song, a poem, a piece of artwork, for example — that focuses on death and draw a connection between the discussions of death in that piece and in this poem.

13. **Connections.** In addition to her poetry, Dickinson wrote many letters. In one to a friend, she asked,

> Does not Eternity appear dreadful to you . . . I often get thinking of it and it seems so dark to me that I almost wish there was no Eternity. To think that we must forever live and never cease to be. It seems as if Death which all so dread because it launches us upon an unknown world would be a relief to so endless a state of existence.

How has this poem captured — or not captured — the ideas of her letter? Locate additional letters online that Dickinson wrote and explain any other connections between them and this poem.

14. **Speaking and Listening.** One of the most effective ways to understand Dickinson's unusual approach to grammar, especially her use of dashes and capitalization, is to read her poems aloud. Meet with a partner or small group and take turns reading sections of the poem to each other, recognizing that the dashes could be signals for a longer pause and the capitalizations for emphasis. After you have read and heard the poem a few times, what conclusions can you draw about how her syntax helps to communicate meaning?

15. **Research.** Although Dickinson wrote over a thousand poems, only a very small number of them were ever published during her lifetime. Those published before her death were often edited to conform to standardized rules of capitalization and punctuation. Research her life with a focus on the publication history of her work. What can you learn about why she published so few during her lifetime and what happened to her work afterward?

16. **Creative Writing.** Write an update of the poem for today. What would a ride with Death be like? What would you say and see along the way?

17. **Multimodal.** This poem is filled with striking images. Choose one or two to illustrate with created or found images and label each with lines from the poem.

Let America Be America Again

Langston Hughes

Langston Hughes (1902–1967) grew up in the African American community of Joplin, Missouri. He spent a year at Columbia University and became involved with the Harlem Renaissance but was shocked by the racial prejudice at the university and left, traveling through West Africa and Europe. He wrote verse, prose, and drama as well as musicals and opera, and he is remembered for his celebration of the uniqueness of African American culture. "Let America Be America Again" was originally published in 1936 in *Esquire* magazine.

Corbis Historical/Getty Images

KEY CONTEXT This poem was written in 1935, during the American Great Depression, a time of widespread unemployment caused in part by a massive stock market crash in 1929. This was also a time of significant racial injustice, still decades before Dr. Martin Luther King Jr. led the civil rights movement. King's "I Have a Dream" speech includes the line from this poem, "America never was America to me."

Let America be America again.
Let it be the dream it used to be.
Let it be the pioneer on the plain
Seeking a home where he himself is free.

(America never was America to me.)   5

Let America be the dream the dreamers
    dreamed —
Let it be that great strong land of love
Where never kings connive nor tyrants scheme
That any man be crushed by one above.

(It never was America to me.)   10

O, let my land be a land where Liberty
Is crowned with no false patriotic wreath,
But opportunity is real, and life is free,
Equality is in the air we breathe.

(There's never been equality for me,   15
Nor freedom in this "homeland of the free.")

Say, who are you that mumbles in the dark?
And who are you that draws your veil across the
    stars?

I am the poor white, fooled and pushed apart,
I am the Negro bearing slavery's scars.   20
I am the red man driven from the land,
I am the immigrant clutching the hope I seek —
And finding only the same old stupid plan
Of dog eat dog, of mighty crush the weak.

I am the young man, full of strength and hope,   25
Tangled in that ancient endless chain
Of profit, power, gain, of grab the land!
Of grab the gold! Of grab the ways of
    satisfying need!
Of work the men! Of take the pay!
Of owning everything for one's own greed!   30

I am the farmer, bondsman to the soil.
I am the worker sold to the machine.

I am the Negro, servant to you all.
I am the people, humble, hungry, mean —
Hungry yet today despite the dream.   35
Beaten yet today — O, Pioneers!
I am the man who never got ahead,
The poorest worker bartered through the years.

Yet I'm the one who dreamt our basic dream
In the Old World while still a serf of kings,   40
Who dreamt a dream so strong, so brave, so true,
That even yet its mighty daring sings
In every brick and stone, in every furrow turned
That's made America the land it has become.
O, I'm the man who sailed those early seas   45
In search of what I meant to be my home —
For I'm the one who left dark Ireland's shore,
And Poland's plain, and England's grassy lea,
And torn from Black Africa's strand I came
To build a "homeland of the free."   50

The free?

Who said the free? Not me?
Surely not me? The millions on relief today?
The millions shot down when we strike?
The millions who have nothing for our pay?   55
For all the dreams we've dreamed
And all the songs we've sung
And all the hopes we've held
And all the flags we've hung,
The millions who have nothing for our pay —   60
Except the dream that's almost dead today.

O, let America be America again —
The land that never has been yet —
And yet must be — the land where *every* man is free.
The land that's mine — the poor man's, Indian's,   65
    Negro's, ME —
Who made America,
Whose sweat and blood, whose faith and pain,
Whose hand at the foundry, whose plow in the
    rain,
Must bring back our mighty dream again.

Sure, call me any ugly name you choose —   70
The steel of freedom does not stain.
From those who live like leeches on the people's
    lives,
We must take back our land again,
America!

O, yes,   75
I say it plain,
America never was America to me,
And yet I swear this oath —
America will be!

Out of the rack and ruin of our gangster death,   80
The rape and rot of graft, and stealth, and lies,
We, the people, must redeem
The land, the mines, the plants, the rivers.
The mountains and the endless plain —
All, all the stretch of these great green states —   85
And make America again! ■

extending beyond the text

The following photographs are part of a collection in the Library of Congress that documents different aspects of life during the Great Depression, when this poem was originally published.

Library of Congress, Prints & Photographs Division, FSA/OWI Collection [LC-USF33- 009202-M3]

Library of Congress, Prints & Photographs Division, Reproduction number LC-USF34-055397-D (b&w film neg.)

Library of Congress, Prints & Photographs Division, Reproduction number LC-DIG-ppmsca-12888 (digital file from print made by the Library) LC-USF331-030577-M2 (b&w film copy neg. from print) LC-USZ62-115416 (b&w film copy neg. from print made by the Library)

Based on the figures, framing, and lighting in these images, how would you describe the tone of each of these photographs? Taken as a whole, what might these images be suggesting about life in the United States during the Great Depression? What lines from Hughes's poem would serve as appropriate captions for each photograph?

Understanding and Interpreting

1. The speaker first refers to him- or herself in line 5, and then several times soon thereafter in a series of parenthetical asides. Who is the speaker, and how do you know? How do the speaker's parenthetical statements respond to or contradict other statements in the poem?

2. In lines 17–18, the speaker addresses "you" who "draws your veil across the stars." What does this metaphor mean in the context of the poem?

3. According to the speaker, who "made" America? And how did they "make" it? Point to specific textual examples to support your response.

4. Reread lines 19–38, which are divided into three stanzas. Summarize who the speaker claims to be in each stanza, and explain how the contrast between the topics in the stanzas helps Hughes to make a point about America.

5. Explain the following lines in terms of what Hughes is suggesting about America:

   a. "O, let my land be a land where Liberty / Is crowned with no false patriotic wreath" (ll. 11–12)

   b. "Tangled in that ancient endless chain / Of profit, power, gain, of grab the land!" (ll. 26–27)

   c. "In search of what I meant to be my home" (l. 46)

   d. "The steel of freedom does not stain" (l. 71)

6. Even though it is a poem, this piece is also clearly an argument. What does Hughes identify as the problem, and what does he argue is the solution?

7. Ultimately, is the speaker optimistic or pessimistic about the future of America? What evidence from the poem leads you to this conclusion?

Analyzing Language, Style, and Structure

8. **Vocabulary in Context.** In line 80, the word *rack* is used in an unconventional way. Define the meaning of the word in this context and describe how this use of the word adds to Hughes's point.

9. There are several shifts in topic, structure, and tone in this poem. Explain the shifts in the following lines and their effects:

   a. Lines 17–18

   b. Line 51

   c. Line 70

10. The word *let* is used in the title and throughout the poem. What are the implications of the word *let*, rather than, say *make*, and how do they relate to the central message of the poem?

11. So much of this poem is about power: who has it, who doesn't, and why. Look carefully back through the piece and identify two or more phrases that directly address the idea of power. Explain how the language choices communicate a particular tone toward the idea of power.

12. What is achieved by putting some lines in parentheses? Why are some lines in italics? And why are some lines their own stanzas?

13. Reread lines 56–61. What point is Hughes emphasizing here? Why?

14. Forms of the word *dream* are used thirteen times. Look back through the poem to identify three or four uses of the word. What can you conclude about what Hughes might feel about the American Dream based on his use of the word?

15. Look for any rhyming patterns that Hughes employs. When does he rhyme, when does he not, and what effect is created by the presence or absence of rhyme?

16. Hughes uses exclamation points, dashes, parentheses, and question marks to give readers a sense of how his poem should sound. Analyze at least one section in which he uses punctuation for specific effect.

17. What is the effect of the imagery of the last stanza? How does it help make the case for Hughes's point about America?

18. Trace and explain how Hughes structures his poem to examine America's past, present, and future.

Topics for Composing

19. **Analysis.** According to the speaker of the poem, does the dream of America accurately reflect the freedom and opportunity the United States offers? Or is that dream just an ideal that we strive for but perhaps never reach? What evidence from the text, specifically language choices, leads you to this conclusion?

20. **Argument.** Is this poem, written in 1935, out of date or still relevant? Why? Use evidence from the poem, as well as your own experiences or additional research to support your position.

21. **Connections.** What does "America" mean to you? What lines from the poem most accurately reflect your experiences with or attitudes toward America?

22. **Speaking and Listening.** Meet with a small group and share your family's history in America. Prior to the discussion, you may want to ask parents, relatives, friends, and so on to add to your own knowledge. Afterward, reflect on similarities and differences among your group's families' experiences.

23. **Research.** Hughes lists multiple historical examples of people coming to the United States or exploiting its resources. Choose one of his references, research its background, and evaluate the accuracy of his representation.

24. **Research.** Langston Hughes is a towering figure in American literature and culture, widely influential among writers and artists, especially those associated with what became known as the Harlem Renaissance of the 1920s and 30s. Conduct research into Hughes's life, focusing specifically on his innovative poetic style and his influence on others. Be sure to research this specific poem's influence as well.

25. **Creative Writing.** Write your own poem that communicates your feelings toward the United States and the American Dream. Try to play around with multiple perspectives and time periods as Hughes does in his piece.

26. **Multimodal.** Combining found images or your own artwork with words or phrases from this poem, create a piece that presents your view of the United States. Show it to several people and write down their responses to your piece. Did they interpret it the way that you had intended? Why or why not?

conversation

How do we find common ground?

You need only to glance at a headline on most news sites to know that as a country, the United States is more divided than united these days. We seem to disagree regularly and loudly about politics, the environment, religion, community health, and just about everything else. Sometimes these disagreements can lead to lost friendships and split families or even to large-scale political violence.

But it doesn't need to be this way. If you read the Central Text in this chapter, "Let America Be American Again," you saw that despite the long history of discrimination and exploitation in this country, the speaker in Langston Hughes's poem expresses optimism about the future of America if we can recognize more of our similarities than our differences. And Hughes is not alone in thinking about ways to bring us together and find "common ground."

This Conversation of texts will present you with a number of different ways that people are trying to bridge the gaps among us. At the end of the Conversation, you'll have an opportunity to enter the dialogue by adding your viewpoint to those of these authors in response to the following question — ***What are the most effective or least effective means for identifying common ground among people who have different perspectives?***

Starting the Conversation

1. Meet with a partner and discuss the following questions:
   a. What are some large disagreements that you see happening in the country today?
   b. How are these disagreements affecting you, your friends, your family, and your community?
   c. What sometimes gets in the way of finding common ground with someone you disagree with about a contentious topic?
2. Create a table like the one below that will help you keep track of important information related to the ideas of finding common ground, especially your own responses to the ideas you encounter in the texts you read.

Text Title/Author	Steps the Author Might Suggest for Finding Common Ground	Best Evidence	Your Response

Source A

Tognotti, Chris. "Finding Common Ground in Political Conversations." *Bustle*,
17 Feb. 2017.

It feels like it's getting harder and harder to find areas of shared, consensus agreement when it comes to American politics, or hey, even geopolitics. Polarization has for the past several years been at sky-high levels within the United States. . . . And yet, when you're actually talking with someone, you might find it important to find some unity somewhere, however small. In that spirit, here are [a few] ways to find common political ground regardless of your party affiliation. . . .

1. Don't Get Heated or Start Slinging Accusations

It doesn't matter how undeniably, completely right you are about an issue, and increasingly, it doesn't even matter what the facts might be. When people start political conversations nowadays, they're usually firmly dug-in to one side or another — almost everyone has done this at some point in their lives, it's just that it all seems more sympathetic and righteous when you agree with the issue at hand.

Making absolutely no judgment about the rightness or wrongness of your position, it's important to take every opportunity to tamp down the heat if you're hoping for an illuminating conversation with someone you strongly disagree with. As hard as it often is, sometimes politeness and restraint matter, even if you find the person's views intensely objectionable in many respects.

2. Ask Them about Their Views and Motivations, Rather Than Assuming

You might disagree with somebody on policy or ideology, but if you start assuming and asserting what the source of the disagreement is — insisting somebody only supports a so-called religious freedom law because they're homophobic, for example — the conversation is going to get iced much faster than if you give someone room to explain themselves in their own words.

Again, this doesn't mean you can't listen and assess that your initial conclusions were on-point, nor does it mean that someone shouldn't be called anti-LGBTQ if they support a policy with profound anti-LGBTQ implications. But for the purpose of actually talking to someone, putting them on immediate defense will be the end of anything insightful. . . .

3. Speak Earnestly about Your Fears and Concerns

If you can manage to be both respectful and unassuming, but also very direct, earnest, and beseeching of someone else's basic understanding about your fears and concerns, you might just get to a point where someone will feel a sense of sympathy or empathy with you, if not necessarily your perspective or cause.

This is basically a prerequisite for having a conversation across hard ideological lines that has any hope of changing someone else's perspective, however, so it's something to shoot for if you feel safe being open with someone.

4. Instead of Bracing for Argument, Just Listen for a While

If you're starting a conversation with somebody you just know you're going to have huge disagreements with, it's incredibly easy, even without realizing it, to slide into argument mode. You know, the certain mixture of body language, verbal tone, and internal simmering that makes it clear to the other person that they're now in a confrontation. And when confronted, people are more likely to meet force with force, to rise to the challenge and aim for a decisive rebuke.

And this may feel satisfying or give you a charge, but if you're looking for common ground, even with someone you deeply disagree with, it's unbelievably useful to consciously stay out of argument mode, and stay in listening mode instead. Rather than prepping your next response in your head while the other person talks, just listen. . . .

5. Don't Sugarcoat Your Differences, but Don't Burn Everything to the Ground Either

You might be surprised how well two people with widely conflicting worldviews can get along, so long as those views are out in the open, respectfully argued, and neither of them cross boundaries that are simply too reprehensible for the other (that last part is a big sticking point,

obviously). But broadly, if you're willing to engage in good faith with another person who's willing to do the same — trying this with someone determined to argue in bad faith won't work, and is likely not worth your time — you might find a mutual, if grudging, respect between the two of you.

There are obviously a lot of ways to approach the search for some shared values or common ground, and these are but a handful. And it's worth noting that you'll often run across people in your life who simply don't merit the trouble — you only need to spend a few minutes scrolling through various people's Twitter mentions to get some pretty vivid examples. But if you've become fatigued at all by the constant warring and jousting, and you want to try to chat with someone politically opposed to you in a more open way, these should be strong tips to start from. ∎

Questions

1. According to Tognotti, why is it important to "tamp down the heat" of an argument? What does this strategy accomplish?

2. What role, according to Tognotti, does listening play in finding common ground?

3. Does Tognotti believe that we should mostly keep our opinions to ourselves to avoid conflict? Explain the author's position.

4. **Comparison.** How is the argument Tognotti makes about finding common ground similar to and different from what Hughes writes about in "Let America Be America Again"? Is Tognotti as optimistic about healing America as Hughes is?

5. **Informing Your Argument.** Return to the table that you created on page 553. Fill in the columns about the steps that Tognotti might suggest to find common ground, the best evidence he offers to clarify and support his ideas, and your response to what Tognotti is suggesting.

Source B

Morrison, Leigh. "Common Ground Does Not Spell Compromise." *The Inclusion Solution*, 10 Jan. 2019.

Several weeks ago, I stumbled across Tayari Jones' essay "There's Nothing Virtuous About Finding Common Ground," published in

TIME Magazine. The title immediately caught my attention for several reasons, not the least of which being that, at The Winters Group, we identify "establishing common ground" as an essential component of successful conversations across differences. I have also found in my personal interactions around equity and inclusion that arriving at a shared understanding of foundational ideas is necessary to push the conversation forward. In light of this, I was curious and initially skeptical about Jones' critique. . . .

In essence, my initial skepticism to Jones' message amounts to semantics; while these terms are often used interchangeably, it seems that it is less "common ground" and more "compromise" that Jones takes issue with in the context of current sociopolitical rhetoric. While operating without compromise is rarely a feasible tactic in politics, the fact remains that, in developing policy in response to moral violations, it may not be appropriate to "meet in the middle."

Next, the question becomes: if we are not willing to compromise, how can we approach the moral side of the spectrum in our understanding and, more broadly, our policies? *This* is where common ground enters the equation.

To agree upon what is moral, we must start by affirming the humanity of all parties involved. This may seem self-evident, and yet, it's rarely a practice that is intentionally built into most of our daily lives. As Jones observes, "Many people understand politics as merely a matter of rhetoric and ideas. Some people will experience wars only in news snippets." I am just as guilty as the next person of often casually scrolling through news sources reading numbers of casualties as statistics rather than lives — because it's emotionally easier (and in some ways, accurate) to conclude "this doesn't affect me."

In order to achieve empathy — a first step toward common moral understanding of a

situation — we must be, in some way, able to put ourselves in someone else's place. As Jones remarks in her essay, she identified with schoolchildren killed in South Africa — and by extension, was deeply emotionally invested in this injustice — by virtue of being a schoolchild valuing her own safety and that of her peers. She notes that, despite her differences from those schoolchildren, "my empathy with them was complete." At times, we find this empathy built into our understandings by virtue of our shared identity or experience with another person or group, as Jones found. But too often, . . . as a result of systems of oppression we all function within, and privileges we hold, we are initially unable to view someone else's plight with empathy because we are too far removed from it.

How do we move beyond this stumbling block? Where shared understanding is not built in naturally for us, we must find it. And that requires starting with a shred of commonality, however small. "We all want safety for ourselves and our families," is one place we often begin in our sessions when identifying common ground. Once we have established initial commonality that humanizes others, we have the potential to develop empathy, become more curious, and invest in learning about their experiences.

Practicing empathy requires the intention to do so and a continued commitment. Our privileges can make it easy not to practice it (ex. as referred to above, reading the news and keeping emotional distance from the events). Which means practicing empathy may require external prompting or reminders to oneself [to] cultivate it for our cultural others. This is part of "the work," and an important practice to strive for and remain committed to. ∎

5

Questions

1. According to Morrison, what is the difference between "compromise" and "common ground"?

2. What does Morrison mean when she writes that "we must start by affirming the humanity of all parties involved"? How is this step crucial to finding common ground?

3. Why is practicing empathy so important in discussions across differences, according to Morrison?

4. **Comparison.** What similarities do you notice about finding common ground between Morrison's essay and what Hughes writes about in "Let America Be America Again"?

5. **Informing Your Argument.** Return to the table that you created on page 553. Fill in the columns about the steps that Morrison might suggest for finding common ground, the best evidence she offers to clarify and support her ideas, and your response to what Morrison is suggesting.

Source C

Spellings, Margaret, and John Bridgeland. "You're being fed lies: How Americans can find truth in the age of misinformation." *USA Today*, 9 Dec. 2021.

The past several years have seen a massive, sometimes malicious, assault on our sense of shared reality. The combination of social media and conspiracy theories has increased the reach and velocity of destructive lies. As a result, both the physical and political health of our country have been placed at risk. . . .

On America's civic health, the tribalization of information is a serious threat to democracy. Many Americans live in ideological bubbles where their main sources of information gain profit by feeding fear and anger. . . .

A new Public Agenda/USA TODAY Hidden Common Ground report found that half of Americans say partisan divisiveness has made it harder to solve problems in their communities, and a rising number of Americans are concerned that we no longer know how to disagree constructively as a nation.

Americans have always had strong disagreements about policy, an assumption of our constitutional order. Leaders and experts have proposed very different paths up the mountain. But now it seems they are climbing entirely different mountains of news and truth.

It both undermines the possibility of productive agreement and makes productive disagreement more difficult. Democratic discourse becomes nearly impossible when people no longer inhabit the same reality.

Any American with a smartphone has access to an almost infinite supply of information. But smartphones are not equipped with editors to sort reliable from dodgy information, persuasion from manipulation, and the urgent from the absurd. This requires every consumer to be their own editor — a skill not broadly taught in America.

This seems true for young people. A 2016 survey by the Stanford History Education group found less than one-third of Advanced Placement students could identify a biased Tweet as slanted. Nearly all students failed to complete basic tasks like evaluating the source of a video, distinguishing between news stories and advertisements, and assessing the credibility of a website. . . .

When the flow of misinformation is hard to stop, it is the filter that matters most — young minds with critical skills to determine truth from falsehood. Our nation is failing to foster

5

critical thinking, media literacy and an ability to understand other perspectives. Just as young people should be taught coding, they must be taught the decoding of news and information as a prerequisite of informed citizenship. . . .

The demand for modern civic education needs to come from parents, school leaders and state officials. It is time for concerned parents to engage at school board meetings with a positive, nonpartisan agenda of critical thinking and responsible citizenship. This is the ultimate answer to irrationality and bitterness in our common life.

There is also a legitimate federal role. The federal government should not dictate a common curriculum, which would invite disastrous political discord, but can provide resources for school districts to choose a curriculum of their own.

The Civics Secures Democracy Act[1] — itself a model of civic cooperation with

bipartisan sponsorship from both houses of Congress — would establish the priority of civic education in American education and devote $1 billion each year for schools to afford quality resources.

One example would be material from the News Literacy Project, a nonprofit dedicated to making students smart, active consumers of news and information. These programs teach the importance of accurate and vetted information and strengthen students' mental immune system against deception.

This type of education is important for students themselves. What parent wants his or her child to be gullible and easily led? What's more, informed citizens can engage in informed discourse, which is the basis of self-government, and make rational choices on everything from public debt to public health.

Young people need to be instructed in the values of democracy — equality, freedom and mutual respect. But they also need to be instructed in the methods of democracy — critical thinking and respect for truth. This is the way to reestablish our common bonds in a shared reality. ∎

10

[1]This was a bill introduced in Congress in 2021 to "establish or strengthen academic programs to promote American political thought and history; the history, achievements, and impact of American representative democracy and constitutional democracies globally; and the means of participation in political and civic life." —Eds.

Questions

1. What do the authors mean when they write that we live in "ideological bubbles," and what problems can this cause?

2. How do the authors define "media literacy"? Why do they feel it is such an important skill, especially for young people?

3. According to the authors, why is finding common ground essential to democracy?

4. **Comparison.** How is the argument Spellings and Bridgeland make about finding common ground similar to and different from what Hughes writes about in "Let America Be America Again"?

5. **Informing Your Argument.** Return to the table that you created on page 553. Fill in the columns about the steps that Spellings and Bridgeland might suggest for finding common ground, the best evidence they offer to clarify and support their ideas, and your response to what they are suggesting.

Source D
PEW Research Center. "Partisan Antipathy: More Intense, More Personal."
pewresearch.org, 10 Oct. 2019.

Democrats' And Republicans' Views of Each Other

% of Republicans who say Democrats are more ____ than other Americans

			About the same
Closed-minded	64	Open-minded 12	24
Unpatriotic	63	Patriotic 2	33
Immoral	55	Moral 4	41
Lazy	46	Hard-working 3	51
Unintelligent	36	Intelligent 2	62

% of Democrats who say Republicans are more ____ than other Americans

			About the same
Closed-minded	75	Open-minded 3	20
Immoral	47	Moral 5	46
Unintelligent	38	Intelligent 4	57
Unpatriotic	23	Patriotic 19	57
Lazy	20	Hard-working 6	73

Notes: Partisans do not include leaners. No answer responses not shown.
Source: Survey of U.S. adults conducted Sept. 3-15, 2019.

PEW RESEARCH CENTER

"Partisan Antipathy: More Intense, More Personal" Pew Research Center, Washington, D.C. October 10, 2019, https://www.pewresearch.org/politics/2019/10/10/partisan-antipathy-more-intense-more-personal/

Areas of Disagreement Between Democrats and Republicans

On important issues facing the country, most Republican voters and Democratic voters ... (%)

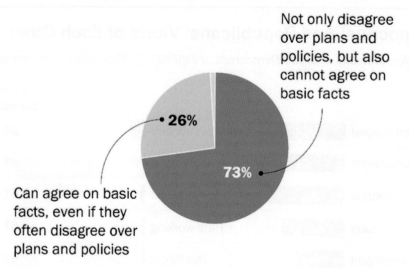

Not only disagree over plans and policies, but also cannot agree on basic facts

73%

26%

Can agree on basic facts, even if they often disagree over plans and policies

Source: Survey of U.S. adults conducted Sept. 3-15, 2019.

PEW RESEARCH CENTER

"Partisan Antipathy: More Intense, More Personal" Pew Research Center, Washington, D.C. October 10, 2019, https://www.pewresearch.org/politics/2019/10/10/partisan-antipathy-more-intense-more-personal/

Questions

1. Based on the data in the first graph, write a statement about how some percentage of Republicans view Democrats, and a statement about how some percentage of Democrats view Republicans.

2. Write a headline and the first sentence or two of a news story that might accompany these graphs.

3. Despite the obvious differences these charts show, what are some areas of agreement between Democrats and Republicans?

4. How does the design of the charts help illustrate the challenges we face in finding common ground?

5. **Informing Your Argument.** How do these charts relate to the prompt you have been thinking about — ***What are the most effective or least effective means for identifying common ground among people who have different perspectives?***

Entering the Conversation

Throughout this Conversation, you have read a variety of texts that deal with ways of finding common ground among those who have differences of opinion. Now it's time to enter the conversation by responding to the prompt you've been thinking about — **What are the most effective or least effective means for identifying common ground among people who have different perspectives?** Follow these steps to write your argument:

1. | **Building on the Conversation.** Locate one additional text on this topic that you think adds an interesting perspective to this Conversation. This text can be of any type: an argument, a narrative, a poem, a painting, or a film clip. Before you decide on adding this text to the Conversation, be sure that it is a credible and relevant source, which you can determine by evaluating it with the skills you practiced in Chapter 4 (p. 99). Read and annotate the text carefully, making connections to other texts in the Conversation and "Let America Be America Again" (p. 548).

2. | **Making a Claim.** Look back through the table you created and your notes on the texts in the conversation and write a statement that reflects your overall position about the most or least effective ways of finding common ground. This statement will be your thesis or claim that you will try to prove in the rest of your argument.

3. | **Organizing the Ideas.** The texts in this Conversation offer a number of suggestions for finding common ground. Review the table you have been keeping throughout this Conversation and identify the texts and quotations that either directly support or oppose the claim that you wrote in the earlier step.

4. | **Writing the Argument.** Now that you have a claim that reflects your informed stance, it is time to write your argument. Be sure that your writing stays focused on your position on the issue, and refer to at least two Conversation texts, which could include the additional text you found to support your position. Review Chapter 4 (p. 119) to remind yourself of how to use sources in your own writing and refer to the Writing an Argument Workshop in Chapter 7 (p. 466) for additional help with constructing and supporting your argument.

5. | **Presenting the Argument (Optional).** Once you have written your argument, you might want to present it to the class or a small group. Review how to write and deliver a presentation in Chapter 3 (p. 90) and Chapter 7 (p. 479).

Ego-Tripping (there may be a reason why)

Nikki Giovanni

One of the most widely read American poets, Yolanda Cornelia "Nikki" Giovanni (b. 1943) was born in Cincinnati, Ohio, graduated from Fisk University, and went on to graduate school at the University of Pennsylvania. She has written more than a dozen volumes of poetry, three collections of essays, and many children's books. Among her many awards and honors are three NAACP Image Awards, the Langston Hughes Medal for poetry, and the Rosa L. Parks Woman of Courage Award. She has said that she wrote "Ego-Tripping" "to give something to girls . . . I wanted the young women to know that we too are wonderful, everything that happened we did it. That poem came from a lot of love." This poem was first published in *Ego-Tripping and Other Poems for Young People* in 1973.

I was born in the congo
I walked to the fertile crescent and built
    the sphinx[1]
I designed a pyramid so tough that a star
    that only glows every one hundred years falls   5
    into the center giving divine perfect light
I am bad

I sat on the throne
    drinking nectar with allah
I got hot and sent an ice age to europe   10
    to cool my thirst
My oldest daughter is nefertiti[2]
    the tears from my birth pains
    created the nile
I am a beautiful woman   15

---

[1] A mythological creature that has a woman's head and a lion's body. —Eds.
[2] A powerful Egyptian queen in the fourteenth century B.C. —Eds.

I gazed on the forest and burned
    out the sahara desert
    with a packet of goat's meat
    and a change of clothes
I crossed it in two hours   20
I am a gazelle so swift
    so swift you can't catch me

    For a birthday present when he was three
I gave my son hannibal[3] an elephant
    He gave me rome for mother's day   25
My strength flows ever on

My son noah[4] built new/ark and
I stood proudly at the helm
    as we sailed on a soft summer day
I turned myself into myself and was   30
    jesus
    men intone my loving name

    All praises All praises
I am the one who would save

I sowed diamonds in my back yard   35
My bowels deliver uranium
    the filings from my fingernails are
    semi-precious jewels
    On a trip north
I caught a cold and blew   40
My nose giving oil to the arab world
I am so hip even my errors are correct
I sailed west to reach east and had to round off
    the earth as I went
    The hair from my head thinned and gold was   45
    laid across three continents

I am so perfect so divine so ethereal so surreal
I cannot be comprehended
    except by my permission

I mean . . . I . . . can fly   50
    like a bird in the sky . . . ■

---

[3] Military leader of Carthage who famously marched into battle against Rome on war elephants during the Second Punic War. —Eds.
[4] A biblical figure who was ordered by God to build a boat (ark) and fill it with one male and female of every species in order to survive the Great Flood. —Eds.

563

Understanding and Interpreting

1. In each stanza the speaker takes on a new persona or role. Identify or describe each new persona and explain how it is similar to other personas the speaker takes on in other stanzas.

2. What is the "fertile crescent" that the speaker refers to in line 2? You may need to conduct brief research. What is the significance of starting the poem in this way?

3. Draw an interpretation about why the speaker adopts different personas throughout the poem.

4. Explain the line: "I am so hip even my errors are correct" (l. 42).

5. Explain a possible meaning for these lines: "I cannot be comprehended / except by my permission" (ll. 48–49).

6. The final two stanzas are a shift from the historical and geographical focus of the previous stanzas. What is the speaker like here, and how does that characterization connect to the personas of the previous stanzas?

Analyzing Language, Style, and Structure

7. **Vocabulary in Context.** In line 47, the speaker says, "I am so perfect so divine so ethereal so surreal." What is the meaning of the words *ethereal* and *surreal* in this context? How can those words be used in different contexts for different purposes?

8. There are a number of allusions to people and places in this poem. What is in common among the allusions, and what effect do they create?

9. What connection is created through Giovanni's syntactical choices at the ends of each of the first two stanzas?

10. Giovanni regularly mixes 1970s slang with more elevated diction. What is the result of this mixing?

11. What can you speculate about her choice of spelling of "new/ark" in line 27?

12. Hyperbole is a chief poetic device at work in this poem. Locate and explain two or more examples of exaggeration that assist Giovanni in making her point.

13. Describe the tone that the speaker takes toward herself. What stylistic choices create this tone, and how does this tone help Giovanni communicate a theme?

14. The final two lines include the poem's most simplistic simile, its only end rhyme, and the only place Giovanni uses punctuation (ellipses). What effect is created through these stylistic choices?

Topics for Composing

15. **Analysis.** Identify the geographical and historical progression that the speaker traces in the poem and write an analysis of how these different locations and time periods help Giovanni illustrate a theme of the poem.

16. **Argument.** Being on an "ego trip" is usually thought of as being a bad thing, but Giovanni does not appear to agree in this poem. Write an argument in support of or disagreement with Giovanni's interpretation and support your response with evidence from the text and from your own experiences.

17. **Connections.** What personal qualities do you possess that you might celebrate in a way that's similar to the speaker's celebration of self in this poem?

18. **Speaking and Listening.** Because this is one of Giovanni's most famous poems, videos of her and others reading "Ego-Tripping" are widely available online. Listen to or watch one of Giovanni's readings and one or two others and compare them. In what ways are they similar and different? Support your response with specific details.

19. **Research.** Choose two of the many allusions that Giovanni uses, research their backgrounds, and explain their specific meaning to the poem.

20. **Creative Writing.** Write a few lines of poetry modeled on Giovanni's poem that reflect your or your family's cultural and historical background. Mimic her tone or express a different outlook toward your own history.

21. **Multimodal.** All of Giovanni's allusions are historical. Create a collage of found or created images of contemporary figures, musicians, actors, politicians, or others that might update some of the allusions, while keeping the meaning roughly the same. Add lines from the poem as captions for your images.

22. **Exposition.** Write your own definition of the phrase "ego trip" and compare it to what Giovanni presents here.

from *Whereas*

Layli Long Soldier

Layli Long Soldier is a writer, artist, and dual citizen of both the Oglala Lakota Nation and the United States of America. She is the author of the chapbook *Chromosomory* (2010) and the full-length collection, *Whereas* (2017), from which this excerpt was taken and which won the National Books Critics Circle Award and was a finalist for the National Book Award.

Chris Felver/Premium Archive/Getty Images

KEY CONTEXT In 2009, the U.S. Congress passed and President Obama signed a resolution intended to acknowledge and apologize for mistreatment of Native Peoples by the Federal Government. It was, however, signed without any public ceremony, reading, or announcement, and no Native Americans were present. Long Soldier read the resolution months later and said she was struck by some language choices that minimize the violence done to Native Americans. The resolution reads in part as follows:

> To acknowledge a long history of official depredations and ill-conceived policies by the Federal Government regarding Indian tribes and offer an apology to all Native Peoples on behalf of the United States.
>
> Whereas for millennia, Native Peoples have honored, protected, and stewarded this land we cherish;
>
> Whereas the arrival of Europeans in North America opened a new chapter in the history of Native Peoples;

Whereas while establishment of permanent European settlements in North America did stir conflict with nearby Indian tribes, peaceful and mutually beneficial interactions also took place;

Whereas Native Peoples and non-Native settlers engaged in numerous armed conflicts in which unfortunately, both took innocent lives, including those of women and children;

Whereas Native Peoples are endowed by their Creator with certain unalienable rights, and among those are life, liberty, and the pursuit of happiness: Now, therefore, be it

Resolved by the Senate and House of Representatives of the United States of America in Congress assembled,

SECTION 1. RESOLUTION OF APOLOGY TO NATIVE PEOPLES OF THE UNITED STATES.

(a) ACKNOWLEDGMENT AND APOLOGY.

The United States, acting through Congress —

(1) recognizes the special legal and political relationship Indian tribes have with the United States and the solemn covenant with the land we share;

(2) commends and honors Native Peoples for the thousands of years that they have stewarded and protected this land;

(3) recognizes that there have been years of official depredations, ill-conceived policies, and the breaking of covenants by the Federal Government regarding Indian tribes;

(4) apologizes on behalf of the people of the United States to all Native Peoples for the many instances of violence, maltreatment, and neglect inflicted on Native Peoples by citizens of the United States;

(b) DISCLAIMER. — Nothing in this Joint Resolution —

(1) authorizes or supports any claim against the United States; or

(2) serves as a settlement of any claim against the United States.

According to her publisher's website, Long Soldier wrote her collection *Whereas* as a way to confront "the coercive language of the United States government in its responses, treaties, and apologies to Native American peoples and tribes, and reflects that language in its officiousness and duplicity back on its perpetrators." She oftentimes uses, repurposes, erases, and mimics the specific language from the resolution in this collection.

What follows are four poems from *Whereas* that manipulate the language of the four numbered parts of Section 1. Resolution of Apology above. For example, the first poem below, labeled (1), refers directly to this sentence from the Resolution of Apology: "(1) recognizes the special legal and political relationship Indian tribes have with the United States and the solemn covenant with the land we share." The same correlation exists for the poems labeled (2), (3), and (4).

(1)

I recognize

the special legal and
political   relationship
Indian tribes have with
the United States and

the solemn

covenant with the land
we share.

(2)

I

commend   this land

and   this   land

honor   this   land

Native   this   land

Peoples   this land

for   this   land

the   this   land

thousands   this   land

of   this   land

years   this   land

that   this land

they   this   land

have   this   land

stewarded   this   land

and   this   land

protected   this land   this land   this land   this land   this land   this land   this

                                                       this

(3)

I

recognize

that [1]

official [2]

ill- [3]

breaking of [4]

the [5]

Indian [6]

---

*1. there have been years of   2. depredations,   3. conceived policies, and the
4. covenants by   5. Federal Government regarding   6. tribes*

(4) I have thought carefully about certain terms in English, the language in which the Apology is written. Likewise, since the Apology is issued to Native people, I have considered Native languages. For months, I dwelled on the word "apologizes." As you may already know, in many Native languages, there is no word for "apologize." The same goes for "sorry." This doesn't mean that in Native communities where the word "apologize" is not spoken, there aren't definite actions for admitting and amending wrongdoing. Thus, I wonder how, without the word, this text translates as a gesture —

The United States, acting
through Congress —
▉▉▉▉ on behalf of the
people of the United States to
all Native Peoples for the
many instances of violence,
maltreatment, and neglect
inflicted on Native Peoples
by citizens of the United
States;

extending beyond the text

Below is an image by Wendy Red Star, a member of the Apsáalooke (Crow) tribe, called *Fall* from her *Four Seasons* series. Working in various artistic mediums, Red Star creates art that upends stereotypical and often stoic representations of Native Americans, like those frequently seen in history books and popular culture.

Fall, from the series Four Seasons, 2006 (chromogenic print/Red Star, Wendy (b.1981)/San Francisco Museum of Modern Art/San Francisco Museum of Modern Art (SFMOMA), CA, USA/Bridgeman Images

Looking at this image, what might Red Star be suggesting about stereotypical representations and how do her choices about what to include in her image communicate that message? In what ways does Red Star's work resemble Long Soldier's visual approach in her poetry?

Understanding and Interpreting

1. How did you read poem (2)? Across? Down? Diagonally? How does the way that you read this piece affect its meaning? What is a possible effect of including the square in the middle of the poem?

2. If you read poem (3) by reading the footnotes where they are marked, you will have the exact sentence of item 3 in the original Resolution of Apology. Now, reread the top part of the poem without the footnotes. What might Long Solider be trying to communicate with just those words? Now, read just the footnotes themselves in order. What might Long Solider be trying to communicate with just those words? What are similarities and differences between the top and bottom parts of this poem?

3. Poem (4) is the first one of this group that contains words that are not taken directly from a corresponding item in the original Resolution of Apology — in this case, item 4. In the first part of the poem, paraphrase what the speaker says about apologies in many Native American communities.

Analyzing Language, Style, and Structure

4. **Vocabulary in Context.** The first line of poem (1) states, "I recognize." What does the word *recognize* mean in this context, and how is it similar to or different from other uses of the word?

5. At the beginning of poems (1), (2), and (3), Long Soldier uses language from the original Resolution of Apology, but replaces the subject "United States" with the subject "I." How does that replacement affect the meaning of the text?

6. In poem (1), Long Soldier bolds four words that are not bolded in the original Resolution of Apology. What effect is created by bolding and separating these words from the rest of the text?

7. How does the repetition in poem (2) help Long Solider illustrate a theme of the poem? How do the structure and design of this poem also contribute to that theme?

8. What effect is created through Long Solider's use of footnotes in poem (3)? How does the structural choice here help her tone and purpose?

9. Reread the second part of poem (4) and explain the differences in meaning between this and the original with the removal of the word *apologizes*. What is Long Soldier hoping to communicate by removing this word?

Topics for Composing

10. **Analysis.** Throughout these four poems, what is Long Solider suggesting about the U.S. government's apology to Native peoples? What evidence from the texts supports your interpretation?

11. **Analysis.** Conduct a close reading of the excerpt from the Resolution of Apology on pages 565–566, looking specifically at the way the language is carefully constructed to admit some wrongdoing on the part of the United States, but also blaming Native Americans in some measure. Write an analysis of the word choice or sentence structure of the Resolution of Apology that tries to equalize actions on both sides.

12. **Argument.** "Reparations" refers to the making of amends, by offering money or other compensation to those who have been wronged. In addition to an apology, should the U.S. government provide reparations to Native American populations for the harms done to their ancestors? Conduct research and refer to the poems to support your response.

13. **Connections.** How do you characterize an effective apology? Describe a time when you have been on the receiving end of an apology and explain what made it effective or ineffective.

14. **Speaking and Listening.** Hold a class or small group discussion on the following questions: Should the U.S. government have apologized to Native Americans in this way? How could or should it have been handled differently? Is an apology enough? Try to reach consensus.

15. **Research.** Locate and read the full Resolution of Apology online. Identify one statement that refers to information that you would like to learn more about, such as "Whereas the Federal Government violated many of the treaties ratified by Congress and other diplomatic agreements with Indian tribes." In this case, you might conduct research on which treaties were violated and what the effects were.

16. **Research.** On September 21, Canada celebrates a National Day of Truth and Reconciliation, which commemorates the legacy of the Canadian Indian residential school system. Conduct research on this occasion and the way that Canada has apologized to its indigenous populations. Compare Canada's response to that of the United States.

17. **Creative Writing.** Locate an official document that has meaning to you like the apology that Long Soldier identifies. Manipulate the language of the document, using erasure and other structural modifications to create new text.

18. **Exposition.** Write a definition of an effective apology. Compare it to an ineffective apology. Which best describes the apology made by the United States to Native Americans, based on what you read in the Key Context and in the poems?

Ode on a Grecian Urn

John Keats

John Keats was born in London in 1795. After the death of his parents, he was taken out of school and apprenticed to a surgeon and apothecary, which is an older term for pharmacist. He became a licensed apothecary but almost immediately abandoned medicine for poetry. Keats is considered one of the major poets of the Romantic movement, though his work was not well received while he was alive. When he died at age twenty-five from tuberculosis, he had been writing poetry seriously for only about six years and publishing for only four. "Ode on a Grecian Urn" was published in 1820 and is considered one of the greatest odes in the English language.

KEY CONTEXT And "ode" is typically a short poem that celebrates a person, place, event, or idea. The speaker of this ode is directly addressing the figures painted on the side of a carved marble urn from ancient Greece that depicts scenes from mythology.

Thou still unravish'd bride of quietness,
    Thou foster-child of silence and slow time,
Sylvan[1] historian, who canst thus express
    A flowery tale more sweetly than our rhyme:
What leaf-fring'd legend haunts about thy shape   5
    Of deities or mortals, or of both,
        In Tempe or the dales of Arcady?[2]
    What men or gods are these? What maidens loth?[3]

---

[1] An adjective meaning "relating to forests." —Eds.
[2] Both Tempe and Arcady (also spelled Arcadia) are regions of Greece known for their natural beauty. Arcadia has come to mean any idyllic peaceful rural setting. —Eds.
[3] A variant spelling of *loathe*, meaning unwilling or reluctant. —Eds.

What mad pursuit? What struggle to escape?
       What pipes and timbrels? What wild ecstasy?   10

Heard melodies are sweet, but those unheard
       Are sweeter; therefore, ye soft pipes, play on;
Not to the sensual ear, but, more endear'd,
       Pipe to the spirit ditties of no tone:
Fair youth, beneath the trees, thou canst not leave   15
       Thy song, nor ever can those trees be bare;
         Bold Lover, never, never canst thou kiss,
Though winning near the goal yet, do not grieve;
       She cannot fade, though thou hast not thy bliss,
         For ever wilt thou love, and she be fair!   20

Ah, happy, happy boughs! that cannot shed
       Your leaves, nor ever bid the Spring adieu;
And, happy melodist, unwearied,
       For ever piping songs for ever new;
More happy love! more happy, happy love!   25
       For ever warm and still to be enjoy'd,
         For ever panting, and for ever young;
All breathing human passion far above,
       That leaves a heart high-sorrowful and cloy'd,
         A burning forehead, and a parching tongue.   30

Who are these coming to the sacrifice?
       To what green altar, O mysterious priest,
Lead'st thou that heifer lowing at the skies,
       And all her silken flanks with garlands drest?
What little town by river or sea shore,   35
       Or mountain-built with peaceful citadel,
         Is emptied of this folk, this pious morn?
And, little town, thy streets for evermore
       Will silent be; and not a soul to tell
         Why thou art desolate, can e'er return.   40

O Attic[4] shape! Fair attitude! with brede
       Of marble men and maidens overwrought,
With forest branches and the trodden weed;
       Thou, silent form, dost tease us out of thought

---

[4]Attica is a specific region of ancient Greece. In this instance, Keats is referring to the shape common to Greek urns. —Eds.

As doth eternity: Cold Pastoral![5]   45
    When old age shall this generation waste,
        Thou shalt remain, in midst of other woe
Than ours, a friend to man, to whom thou say'st,
     "Beauty is truth, truth beauty, — that is all
        Ye know on earth, and all ye need to know." ■   50

___

[5]The term *pastoral* refers to a work of art or literature that portrays an idealized version of rural life. —Eds.

extending beyond the text

These are still images from a film called *Bright Star*, about the relationship between Keats and Fanny Brawne, whom he had hoped to marry but couldn't because of his financial situation and his increasingly poor health.

How do these images from the film capture a feeling similar to that conveyed through "Ode on a Grecian Urn"? Consider elements such as lighting, framing, and color.

Understanding and Interpreting

1. Summarize what the speaker sees on the side of the urn in the first stanza. How does the speaker describe and feel about the woman on the urn?

2. Explain the meaning of lines 11–12: "Heard melodies are sweet, but those unheard / Are sweeter; therefore, ye soft pipes, play on." What do these lines tell you about the speaker?

3. In lines 15–20, the speaker describes a different portion of the scene on the urn. How is this scene similar to and different from the scene in the first stanza?

4. Explain the meaning of lines 19–20: "She cannot fade, though thou hast not thy bliss, / For ever wilt thou love, and she be fair!" What does this reveal about the speaker's attitude toward life and love?

5. The speaker moves on to two different scenes on the urn in stanzas 3 and 4. Summarize those scenes and contrast them with the other scenes.

6. How do lines 26–27 ("For ever warm and still to be enjoy'd, / For ever panting, and for ever young") help us understand what the speaker seems to be most afraid of?

7. The urn has been captivating the speaker throughout the poem, but that seems to change in the last stanza. What seems to trigger a return to the real world outside of the urn, and what does the speaker seem to take away from the time spent looking at the urn?

8. Paraphrase the last two lines of the poem, and explain whether you think the speaker believes that declaration to be true or not. Is the art the speaker has been looking at helpful in the real world?

Analyzing Language, Style, and Structure

9. **Vocabulary in Context.** In line 46, Keats writes, "When old age shall this generation waste." What does the word *waste* mean in this context? How is it similar to or different from other uses of the word?

10. What is the effect of the series of questions at the end of the first stanza? What do they reveal about the emotions of the speaker?

11. At various points in the poem Keats uses the word *maidens*, as in line 42: "Of marble men and maidens overwrought." What does the word mean in the context and the time period of the poem? What does the pairing of *men* and *maidens* tell us about the speaker's attitude toward women?

12. In the third stanza, the speaker describes all of the aspects of the image on the urn that seem perfect. What stylistic choices does Keats make to communicate the speaker's attitude?

13. Based on the language choices of the first three stanzas, what are we expected to conclude is *not* perfect in the real world outside of the picture of the urn?

14. This poem contains many paradoxes, in which the figures on the urn are full of life but ultimately frozen in the positions in which they were created. Identify and explain language choices Keats makes to present these paradoxes.

15. Reread the fourth stanza carefully, looking closely at the imagery and syntax as the speaker describes the town. How do these stylistic choices convey a particular attitude toward its inhabitants?

16. How does the phrase "Cold Pastoral!" (l. 45) signal a shift in this poem? What is its effect?

17. The form of this poem is strict. There are five stanzas of ten lines, each containing ten syllables. But look closely at the rhyming structure and determine its pattern. How does the rhyme connect ideas within and across the stanzas?

Topics for Composing

18. Analysis. Overall, what theme is Keats suggesting about life, love, and art in this poem? Support your response with evidence from the text.

19. Argument. Keats essentially makes the argument that anticipation is better than the actual experience. Is this true? Support your argument with your own reasoning and evidence from the poem.

20. Connections. If you could freeze a moment in time from your life and display it on something like the urn in this poem, what would that moment be and why? On what object would you choose to display that moment? Why?

21. Research. Keats died young, at only twenty-five years old, of tuberculosis, from which he was already suffering when he published this poem. Research the English Romantic poets and their attitudes toward death and love. To what extent is this poem representative of the Romantic period or not?

22. Creative Writing. Choose a piece of artwork that you find interesting and describe it in detail, as Keats does with the urn, focusing on the figures in the piece and your personal connections to them. Imagine the figures to be alive like Keats does and try to gather some kind of meaning or message from them. Your response can be in poetry or prose.

23. Multimodal. Look back carefully at the poem and draw or locate images that would appear on the urn that the speaker refers to. Label each image with words from the poem that inspired it.

from Song of Myself

Walt Whitman

Walt Whitman (1818–1892) was born on Long Island, New York, and for a time worked as a schoolteacher before becoming a printer, editor, and writer for the *Brooklyn Eagle* newspaper. He published his masterpiece, *Leaves of Grass*, of which "Song of Myself" was a part, in 1855, but he continued to add to and revise it until his death. While today he is considered one of the greatest American poets, during his lifetime his work was scorned by some critics and sometimes censored because of its frank sexual references.

NARA/Science Source

KEY CONTEXT The full poem is divided into 52 sections and contains over 1,300 lines. We have included only the first three sections and the very last section of the poem in this excerpt.

1

I celebrate myself, and sing myself,
And what I assume you shall assume,
For every atom belonging to me as good belongs to you.

I loafe and invite my soul,
I lean and loafe at my ease observing a spear of summer grass.   5

My tongue, every atom of my blood, form'd from this soil, this air,
Born here of parents born here from parents the same, and their parents the same,
I, now thirty-seven years old in perfect health begin,
Hoping to cease not till death.

Creeds and schools in abeyance, 10
Retiring back a while sufficed at what they are, but never forgotten,
I harbor for good or bad, I permit to speak at every hazard,
Nature without check with original energy.

2

Houses and rooms are full of perfumes, the shelves are crowded with perfumes,
I breathe the fragrance myself and know it and like it, 15
The distillation would intoxicate me also, but I shall not let it.

The atmosphere is not a perfume, it has no taste of the distillation, it is odorless,
It is for my mouth forever, I am in love with it,
I will go to the bank by the wood and become undisguised and naked,
I am mad for it to be in contact with me. 20

The smoke of my own breath,
Echoes, ripples, buzz'd whispers, love-root, silk-thread, crotch and vine,
My respiration and inspiration, the beating of my heart, the passing of blood and air through
        my lungs,
The sniff of green leaves and dry leaves, and of the shore and dark-color'd sea-rocks, and of
        hay in the barn,
The sound of the belch'd words of my voice loos'd to the eddies of the wind, 25
A few light kisses, a few embraces, a reaching around of arms,
The play of shine and shade on the trees as the supple boughs wag,
The delight alone or in the rush of the streets, or along the fields and hill-sides,
The feeling of health, the full-noon trill, the song of me rising from bed and meeting the sun.

Have you reckon'd a thousand acres much? have you reckon'd the earth much? 30
Have you practis'd so long to learn to read?
Have you felt so proud to get at the meaning of poems?

Stop this day and night with me and you shall possess the origin of all poems,
You shall possess the good of the earth and sun, (there are millions of suns left,)
You shall no longer take things at second or third hand, nor look through the eyes of the dead, 35
        nor feed on the spectres in books,
You shall not look through my eyes either, nor take things from me,
You shall listen to all sides and filter them from your self.

3

I have heard what the talkers were talking, the talk of the beginning and the end,
But I do not talk of the beginning or the end.

There was never any more inception than there is now,   40
Nor any more youth or age than there is now,
And will never be any more perfection than there is now,
Nor any more heaven or hell than there is now.

Urge and urge and urge,
Always the procreant[1] urge of the world.   45

Out of the dimness opposite equals advance, always substance and increase, always sex,
Always a knit of identity, always distinction, always a breed of life.

To elaborate is no avail, learn'd and unlearn'd feel that it is so.

Sure as the most certain sure, plumb in the uprights, well entretied, braced in the beams,
Stout as a horse, affectionate, haughty, electrical,   50
I and this mystery here we stand.

Allen Crawford/Tin House Books

Allen Crawford/Tin House Books

These are pages from *Whitman Illuminated* by Allan Crawford that include text from "Song of Myself" and images. The one on the left comes from Section 1 that you read, while the one on the right is from a section that was not included in this excerpt.

How does Crawford capture the essence of the language of the first section, and how can you interpret Crawford's illustration for the section not included here?

---

[1]Producing offspring, or children. —Eds.

Clear and sweet is my soul, and clear and sweet is all that is not my soul.

Lack one lacks both, and the unseen is proved by the seen,
Till that becomes unseen and receives proof in its turn.

Showing the best and dividing it from the worst age vexes age,   55
Knowing the perfect fitness and equanimity of things, while they discuss I am silent, and go
       bathe and admire myself.

Welcome is every organ and attribute of me, and of any man hearty and clean,
Not an inch nor a particle of an inch is vile, and none shall be less familiar than the rest.

I am satisfied — I see, dance, laugh, sing;
As the hugging and loving bed-fellow sleeps at my side through the night, and withdraws at   60
       the peep of the day with stealthy tread,
Leaving me baskets cover'd with white towels swelling the house with their plenty,
Shall I postpone my acceptation and realization and scream at my eyes,
That they turn from gazing after and down the road,
And forthwith cipher and show me to a cent,
Exactly the value of one and exactly the value of two, and which is ahead?   65

52
The spotted hawk swoops by and accuses me, he complains of my gab and my loitering.

I too am not a bit tamed, I too am untranslatable,
I sound my barbaric yawp over the roofs of the world.

The last scud[2] of day holds back for me,
It flings my likeness after the rest and true as any on the shadow'd wilds,   70
It coaxes me to the vapor and the dusk.

I depart as air, I shake my white locks at the runaway sun,
I effuse my flesh in eddies, and drift it in lacy jags.

I bequeath myself to the dirt to grow from the grass I love,
If you want me again look for me under your boot-soles.   75

You will hardly know who I am or what I mean,
But I shall be good health to you nevertheless,
And filter and fibre your blood.

Failing to fetch me at first keep encouraged,
Missing me one place search another,   80
I stop somewhere waiting for you. ■

———
[2]A low, rain-heavy cloud. —Eds.

extending beyond the text

The following is a transcript of a scene from the movie *Dead Poet's Society*, in which a new English teacher, Mr. Keating, at a private boarding school in the 1950s, asks a student to read aloud from an introduction to a textbook of poetry.

from **Dead Poets Society**

Tom Schulman (writer), Peter Weir (director)

NEIL: "Understanding Poetry," by Dr. J. Evans Pritchard, Ph.D. To fully understand poetry, we must first be fluent with its meter, rhyme and figures of speech, then ask two questions: (1) How artfully has the objective of the poem been rendered; and (2) How important is that objective? Question 1 rates the poem's perfection; question 2  rates its importance. And once these questions have been answered, determining the poem's greatness becomes a relatively simple matter. If the poem's score for perfection is plotted on the horizontal of a graph and its importance is plotted on the vertical, then calculating the total area of the poem yields the measure of its greatness. A sonnet by Byron might score high on the vertical but only average on the horizontal. A Shakespearean sonnet, on the other hand, would score high both horizontally and vertically, yielding a massive total area, thereby revealing the poem to be truly great. As you proceed through the poetry in this book, practice this rating method. As your ability to evaluate poems in this matter grows, so will your enjoyment and understanding of poetry.

KEATING: Excrement. That's what I think of Mr. J. Evans Pritchard. We're not laying pipe. We're talking about poetry. How can you describe poetry like American Bandstand? "Oh, I like Byron. I give him a 42, but I can't dance to it." Now, I want you to rip out that page. Go on. Rip out the entire page. You heard me. Rip it out. Rip it out! Go on. Rip it out! . . .
Keep ripping, gentlemen! This is a battle. A war. And the casualties could be your hearts and souls. Thank you, Mr. Dalton. Armies of academics going forward, measuring poetry. No! We'll not have that here. No more Mr. J. Evans Pritchard. Now, my class, you will learn to think for yourselves again. You will learn to savor words and language. No matter what anybody tells you, words and ideas can change the world.

What point is Keating making about the ideas of J. Evans Pritchard? What does he offer instead? Do you agree or disagree with Keating? Explain your response. Why might Whitman likely agree or not?

Understanding and Interpreting

1. What immediate connection does the speaker draw between "I" and "you" in the first section?

2. Explain what the line "Creeds and schools in abeyance" (l. 10) communicates about the perspective of the speaker.

3. How do you interpret the speaker's attitude toward life and the world in the first section?

4. What is the significance of the multiple settings described in these lines: "The delight alone or in the rush of the streets, or along the fields and hill-sides, / The feeling of health, the full-noon trill, the song of me rising from bed and meeting the sun" (ll. 28–29)?

5. What is achieved by the use of the direct questions of "you" in lines 30–32?

6. Summarize what the speaker says will happen after stopping "this day and night with me" in lines 33–37.

7. In line 52, the speaker says, "Clear and sweet is my soul, and clear and sweet is all that is not my soul." Look back through the poem and locate other places where the speaker says something similar — where two things that might seem to be opposites are presented as equals. What conclusions can you draw about the speaker from these lines?

8. Lines 53–56 discuss how we should know and learn things. What is the speaker's suggestion about this?

9. In the last section of the poem, the speaker says, "I too am not a bit tamed, I too am untranslatable, / I sound my barbaric yawp over the roofs of the world" (ll. 67–68). Paraphrase these lines and explain what they reveal about the speaker.

10. Near the end of the poem, the speaker says, "I bequeath myself to the dirt to grow from the grass I love" (l. 74). Is this attitude toward life and death similar to or different from the attitude expressed in the first section of the poem? Explain.

Analyzing Language, Style, and Structure

11. **Vocabulary in Context.** In line 49, the speaker uses the word *plumb*. What is the meaning of the word in this context? How might you use this word in a different context?

12. **Vocabulary in Context.** What is the meaning of *spectres*, and how is it used in line 35? How is this word used differently in other contexts?

13. Explain how Whitman uses language in the first section to convey the speaker's ease with the world.

14. Examine the first two stanzas in Section 2. The first takes place indoors and the second is outdoors. Explain how the diction helps Whitman contrast the two settings.

15. Explain how Whitman uses imagery in lines 21–29 to communicate the connection between the speaker and nature.

16. From the beginning of the poem, the speaker seems to be alone, but in line 26, the speaker says, "A few light kisses, a few embraces, a reaching around of arms." Is this line supposed to be taken literally or figuratively? How do you know?

17. Even though this poem is usually categorized as "free verse," meaning that it does not use a consistent meter or rhyme structure, Whitman clearly relies on rhythm and pattern at various times in his poem. See, for example, lines 40–45, with the repeated word *now* building and culminating to the repeated word *urge*. Locate and explain another section in which he repeats certain phrases or uses punctuation to create a particular rhythm, rhyme, or structure.

18. At the beginning of section 52, the final part of a poem that is over 1300 lines in length, the speaker says, "The spotted hawk swoops by and accuses me, he complains of my gab and my loitering." What is the light joke here, and what is the effect of using personification to communicate it?

19. How do the imagery and diction in the last section of the poem communicate Whitman's tone toward life and nature?

Topics for Composing

20. **Analysis.** Identify one line from the excerpt of this poem that you think most effectively communicates a primary theme of the piece. Explain how this one line presents that theme most effectively.

21. **Argument.** Whitman appears to mock the very idea of the poetry analysis you have been doing in this chapter, asking "Have you felt so proud to get at the meaning of poems?" Describe Whitman's view of how poetry should be experienced. Then, using evidence from the poem and your own experiences, argue for the best approach to experiencing and understanding poetry.

22. **Connection.** Choose any line from the poem that strikes you for whatever reason. Write about how that line relates to your own life, family, experiences, feelings, or make some other personal connection.

23. **Research.** Published in 1882, the poem was criticized by some and even subjected to legal actions for its frank depictions of sexuality. Research the reactions at the time of publication and the laws that governed obscenity and censorship in the United States at the time, and explain why parts of this poem might have been subjected to scrutiny under those laws.

24. **Creative Writing.** Try your hand at writing in free verse about a topic you know well. Don't worry at first about rhyme, structure, or meter. Then, rewrite a portion of your free verse by changing some words or phrases to generate a rhyme or a rhythmic pattern. What is different in effect between these two pieces?

25. **Multimodal.** Select a line from the poem and locate or create an image that would pair well with the line. Share your image and line with others and consider whether it had the effect you had intended.

Writing an Analysis of Poetry

When we analyze poetry, we try to understand it better by looking at how writers use poetic elements such as diction, syntax, figurative language, sound, and form to deliver an idea — a theme. Poets make many choices as they are writing: *Should I rhyme these words? Does a simile help communicate my idea? Who should the speaker of my poem be, and why?* Being a writer is all about *choices*, right down to carefully choosing individual words to bring a poem to life, and in an analysis, your goal is to explain to the reader *why* the writer made certain choices. Answering the "why?" is key.

Since you have probably read at least a few poems from this chapter by this point, you know that poets take special care with the words they use, and that requires us to conduct a careful and close reading to be able to interpret a poem's meaning.

We'll practice some analysis using a portion of the Central Text in this chapter, "Let America Be America Again" (pp. 548–549), by Langston Hughes. A writing prompt for an analysis of this poem might read as follows:

> *Read this poem carefully and, in a well-developed essay, explain the speaker's attitude toward the subject. You should focus on how the author uses poetic elements, such as imagery, figurative language, diction, syntax, form, or sound to communicate this tone.*

Before we even get to the text, we need to break down the prompt and think about what it is asking us to do; in this case, we need to do two things:

- consider the speaker's attitude toward the subject, the tone
- consider which poetic elements help Hughes to reveal this tone

Once we have figured out what the prompt is asking us to do, we have a focus for our reading.

 activity · **Getting Started**

Return to a poem in this chapter that you found interesting or choose a poem you've read for another class or on your own that has a clearly identifiable speaker. Write a brief response about why the poem interests you and what you think you know about the speaker. After you are done, discuss with a partner whether the poem seems like one you would like to analyze for tone and style.

Step 1. Reading and Making Observations

As with any text, the first thing you should do is read it for understanding, to be able to summarize what is literally happening in the poem, free from any analysis of poetic elements or symbols, interpretation, or meaning. As you read, think too about the feelings the poem raises for you. On your second reading, read for style. Begin noticing the specific poetic elements identified in the prompt, asking questions about unknown allusions or other places of confusion or ambiguity.

We have annotated the poem below as a sample of what reading for style might look like. Since the Central Text of the chapter, "Let America Be America Again," is pretty long, we'll practice some analysis using just a section from it.

Let America be America again.

Repetition of "let" —— Let it be the dream it used to be.

Let it be the pioneer on the plain

Seeking a home where he himself is free.

(America never was America to me.) —— *Why is this in parentheses? This is the first time we have an "I" identified.*

Let America be the dream the dreamers dreamed —— *Three different uses of the same word*

Let it be that great strong land of love

Where never kings connive nor tyrants scheme —— *Is there a rhyming pattern? "scheme" and "dreamed" kind of rhyme, but "love" and "above" definitely rhyme.*

That any man be crushed by one above.

The speaker identifies him- or herself only in parentheses. Are these like an aside or a response to what was in the previous stanza? —— (It never was America to me.)

O, let my land be a land where Liberty —— *Capitalized "Liberty." Is this a reference to the Statue of Liberty? It has a crown.*

Is crowned with no false patriotic wreath,

But opportunity is real, and life is free,

Equality is in the air we breathe.

(There's never been equality for me,

Who is the "you"? Are the words in parentheses the "mumbles in the dark"? Is this a response to the previous lines? —— Nor freedom in this "homeland of the free.") —— *Third time with the parentheses. Definitely a response to the speaker.*

Say, who are you that mumbles in the dark?

And who are you that draws your veil across the stars?

I am the poor white, fooled and pushed apart,

I am the Negro bearing slavery's scars.

I am the red man driven from the land,

I am the immigrant clutching the hope I seek—

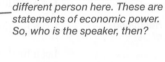

There is a connection among all of the different people here. It's not race, but maybe economic power?

And finding only the same old stupid plan

This is the longest stanza so far.

Of dog eat dog, of mighty crush the weak.

I am the young man, full of strength and hope,

Tangled in that ancient endless chain

Of profit, power, gain, of grab the land! ————

The speaker identifies as a different person here. These are statements of economic power. So, who is the speaker, then?

Of grab the gold! Of grab the ways of satisfying need!

Of work the men! Of take the pay!

activity Reading and Making Observations

Return to the poem that you located in the previous activity, read it twice — first for understanding, and then closely for style — and make notes in the manner above:

1. What is literally happening in the poem? Perhaps write stanza-by-stanza summaries.

2. Annotate the poem by asking questions and noting examples of figurative language, syntax, sound devices, and other poetic elements.

Step 2. Finding a Focus

As with any good poem, there are many different things we could focus on in "Let America Be America Again," but it's clear from the annotations above that thinking about who this speaker actually is and why Hughes created the speaker in this manner is a significant tool to help us understand the work as a whole. Here are some initial thoughts about the speaker:

- At first, we hear from the "I" speaker only in parentheses. Each parenthetical aside seems to respond directly to some of the ideas in the stanza immediately preceding it.

- There is an interesting shift in the seventh stanza with the inclusion of "you." Who is the "you" here? Is it whoever spoke the lines in parentheses? Is it the reader?

- Additional shifts happen when the "I" speaker identifies with a wide range of people from a variety of ethnic and economic backgrounds in the last two stanzas.

We're not quite sure yet exactly what our point will be about the speaker in the poem, but we have identified some of the key elements that will help us tackle the interpretation, and that is enough for right now.

Finding a Focus

Return to the poem that you selected for your analysis, looking carefully at the annotations you made during the third reading. Consider the following:

- What are some common patterns or trends that you have seen at this point?
- What are you noticing about the speaker at this point in your analysis?
- Where are the significant shifts in tone, setting, or form?
- How does the poet use figurative language, imagery, sound, or form to create meaning?

If you have trouble locating a focus, perhaps you will want to select a different poem.

Step 3. Creating a Thesis Statement

Whether you're writing a thesis sentence for a full essay or just a topic sentence for an analytical paragraph, the recipe remains the same. You want to introduce the idea you are looking to explore and take an interpretive stance on the idea you have about the poem. Don't just tell readers what your essay is going to be about; tell them what your position is on that topic. Having a strong thesis clarifies your thinking and sets up a strong argument for your analysis. As we've seen throughout this chapter, poetry is complex and multifaceted. Ten people could read the same poem and come up with ten different ways to analyze it; therefore, your thesis should be unique to you and your ideas about the poem. For the topic we've been exploring, we might write a thesis sentence like this:

WEAK THESIS

In "Let America Be America Again," the speaker talks about America and its history of discrimination.

This thesis mostly summarizes the poem. It doesn't take an interpretive stance on the poem and doesn't address many of the questions we asked as we took notes on the passage. One way to gauge whether you have a strong thesis is to see if anyone could reasonably disagree with it. This one clearly does not meet that requirement. Here's another possibility:

WEAK THESIS

The speaker of "Let America Be America Again," takes on many different personas throughout the poem to show different perspectives of the American Dream.

This one is better because it takes an interpretative stance about the speaker, but it addresses only the first part of the prompt; there is no mention of the poetic elements and how they convey the speaker's attitude toward the subject. Here's one that might be a little closer to what we want from a thesis:

WORKING THESIS

By adopting conflicting personas and using rhyme and allusion, the speaker of "Let America Be America Again" reveals a tone of optimism, rather than despair, about the country.

This thesis states the topic, but it also takes a stand on why Hughes created his speaker the way he did. It is, of course, not the only possible thesis. Someone else writing about the poem might focus solely on the voice of the speaker in the parentheses or might find more of a despairing tone in some of the poet's diction in describing and commenting on the American Dream. These differences help identify our statement as an effective thesis; reasonable people can take a different view of the poem than the one we've expressed.

 Thesis

Return to the poem that you selected and, after looking closely at the Activity on page 585, write a working thesis that takes an interpretive stance on the speaker of that poem. Remember that your thesis should introduce the idea you want to explore and take a position on that idea, while addressing one or two key poetic elements. A strong thesis is unique to the poem you are analyzing, and reasonable people could disagree with the position you take.

Step 4. Proving Your Point

Now that we have a focus for our analysis with our thesis, the next step is to prove that our interpretation is valid. Some people might suggest that poetry is so subjective that readers can draw any conclusions they want; and while, yes, poetry by its very nature allows for multiple interpretations, an analysis has to be a valid reading of the text itself. While you can never prove a point about literature with quite the same decisiveness as you can in, say, math or science, you can make your case by drawing evidence directly from the text and combining that with your own commentary.

Based on our working thesis, what exactly do we need to prove? Let's look back at our thesis:

WORKING THESIS

By adopting conflicting personas and using rhyme and allusion, the speaker of "Let America Be America Again" reveals a tone of optimism, rather than despair, about the country.

There are two basic points in this thesis that need to be proven:

POINT 1   The speaker of "Let America Be America Again" takes on different personas with conflicting views of the American Dream.

POINT 2   These conflicting personas and the use of rhymes and allusions result in an optimistic tone toward America.

Is this true? Are there really multiple personas? Are they actually in conflict with each other? Is the tone actually optimistic? Because there are no automatic answers to any of these questions, you know you're in the place of analysis. Easy answers don't require essays to explain them. In order to address these questions, we need to go back to the text.

Gathering Evidence

One of the benefits of working with a poem is that because of its length, you can easily read, reread, and re-reread it many times looking for evidence. However you choose to gather the evidence — and there are lots of ways, including the graphic organizer on the next page — the most important part is that you are considering at this point how evidence from the poem might support your thesis; be sure that you can explain it in terms of your working thesis. Also, leave yourself open to adjusting your thesis or your interpretation of the poem based on this step. Maybe through this process, you will arrive at a new insight or approach; don't be too fixed in your perspective at this point.

One way to make sure you are connecting your quotation to your thesis is with a table like this. It will help make the connection clear and enable you to think through the purpose of each quotation and how it connects to your larger point.

Working Thesis: By adopting conflicting personas and using rhyme and allusion, the speaker of "Let America Be America Again" reveals a tone of optimism, rather than despair, about the country.

Quotation	How the Quotation Supports My Point
Lines 14–16: Equality is in the air we breathe. (There's never been equality for me, Nor freedom in this "homeland of the free.")	The speaker uses "we" in the first part of the quotation and then contradicts the statement in the very next line by saying it actually isn't true. This proves the various personas the speaker takes on are in conflict with each other.

Finding Support

activity

Go back to the poem you have chosen and gather evidence to support your working thesis. Whether you use note cards, take notes in a document, or fill in a graphic organizer is up to you. This activity is a good opportunity to try out a system and see how it works. If you are unable to identify at least four or five pieces of evidence from the text that support your thesis, you might want to consider a new thesis that you can prove, or maybe select a different poem.

Presenting Evidence

When you present your ideas, there are specific parts that you will need to include. You must make your point, frame your quotations, and explain how the two are connected.

In Chapter 3 about writing, you may have read about how to use evidence by making the point, backing up the point with evidence, and then commenting on how the evidence proves the point. If we begin to incorporate our point, evidence, and explanations in a paragraph, it might look something like this:

Point ———— [Hughes creates various personas of the speaker that are often in conflict with one another.] For example, the speaker states, "Let it be the pioneer on the plain / Seeking a home where he himself is free," followed immediately by "(America never was America to me.)" Again, a few lines later, the speaker states, "But opportunity is real, and life is free, / *Evidence* Equality is in the air we breathe," followed immediately by this contrasting view of freedom: "(There's never been equality for me / Nor freedom in this 'homeland of the free.')". [So in this poem, rather than offering one perspective on America, the speaker presents at least two often contradictory perspectives on the meaning of America.] ———— *Explanation/ commentary*

What we have created here is a short but focused analytical paragraph. If we find more quotations to support our points, we can continue to build the paragraph by continuing with this structure, as long as we stay on the same topic, like this:

Point ———— [Hughes creates various personas of the speaker that are often in conflict with one another.] For example, the speaker states, "Let it be the pioneer on the plain / Seeking a home where he himself is free," *Evidence* followed immediately by "(America never was America to me.)" Again, a few lines later, the speaker states, "But opportunity is real, and life is free, / Equality is in the air we breathe," followed immediately by this contrasting view of freedom: "There's never been equality for me / Nor freedom in this 'homeland of the free.')". *Evidence*

[So in this poem, rather than offering one perspective on America, the speaker presents at least two often contradictory perspectives on the meaning of America.] *Explanation/ commentary*

[This— *Additional, related point* continues throughout the poem and even broadens beyond the two contradictory perspectives at the beginning.] The speaker takes on additional personas, saying:

Additional evidence

I am the poor white, fooled and pushed apart.

I am the Negro bearing slavery's scars.

I am the red man driven from the land.

I am the immigrant clutching the hope I seek

Interestingly, even though the speaker stands in for many different people here, it's clear that all four of them are more united in their similarities than in their differences, which allows for Hughes to strike an optimistic tone despite the contrasting perspectives of America that he presents. *Explanation/ commentary*

With evidence and explanations that connect the evidence to our point presented like this, we have a good draft of an analytical paragraph. The second point of our working thesis is focused on how rhyming and allusions contribute to an optimistic tone toward America. If we were to follow the same steps as the body paragraph above, we would have a second body paragraph or more that uses supporting evidence to prove this point. Depending on how you structured your thesis, you may or may not have a second point to argue.

Body Paragraphs

activity

Using the model above as a guide, write a body paragraph or two for your own working thesis that states your point, incorporates at least two pieces of textual evidence, and explains how your evidence supports your point. This last part — the analysis or commentary — is the most important part of your paragraph; be sure to keep your interpretation front and center.

Step 5. Expanding to an Essay

Throughout this workshop, you've been developing most of the pieces you need for an analytical essay on a poem. We have a thesis and a couple of body paragraphs. If we add another body paragraph or two, an introduction, and a conclusion, we'll have all the remaining pieces for an essay.

Introductory Paragraph

The point of the introductory paragraph is to engage your reader and create interest in the topic. A standard introduction has three parts:

1. An opening hook
2. A connection to the piece being analyzed
3. A thesis statement

The hook is about drawing readers in and getting them thinking about the kinds of ideas or issues that are at play in your analysis. This is a great place to just raise questions or identify issues. No one is expecting you to have the answers to these questions or solutions to these problems.

For an essay on "Let America Be America Again," we might want to raise ideas about the American Dream, or about inequality and racism. Even though the poem was written in the 1930s, we could contextualize it with a contemporary issue to help our audience relate to and understand the poem.

Many writers will tell you that the first sentence is the hardest to write. Here are a few classic ways to begin your introductory paragraph:

With a question	Is the American Dream a reality or is it always just a dream?
With a definition	Writer James Truslow Adams coined the term *American Dream* in 1931, calling it "that dream of a land in which life should be better and richer and fuller for everyone, with opportunity for each according to ability or achievement."
With a statement	While the Declaration of Independence says that "all men are created equal," America has rarely lived up to that ideal, enslaving African Americans and long denying voting rights to minorities, women, and other marginalized groups.
With a story or anecdote	My great-grandmother used to tell us the story of the first time she saw America as a young girl. The boat that brought her to this country pulled into New York harbor, and all of the passengers crowded on the deck to look up at the Statue of Liberty. Her first thought? Disappointment. She had imagined it much bigger and made of solid gold.

Once we have a hook, it's time to show our readers how the ideas we've brought up apply to the poem we are about to analyze. This transition doesn't have to be fancy. It's usually a simple connecting statement that includes a bit of summary of the poem and includes the author and title.

> While the Declaration of Independence says that "all men are created equal," America has rarely lived up to that ideal, enslaving African-Americans and long denying voting rights to minorities, women, and other marginalized groups. — **Hook**
>
> Langston Hughes examines this discrepancy between America's promise and its reality in his poem "Let America Be America Again," published in 1936. — **Connection to the piece**
>
> By adopting conflicting personas and using rhyme and allusion, the speaker of "Let America Be America Again" reveals a tone of optimism, rather than despair, about the country. — **Thesis**

Introduction

activity

Following the model above, write a draft of your introductory paragraph. Think about the way you want to hook the reader and how you want to lead into your thesis statement with a connecting statement that includes the author and title.

Concluding Paragraph

As with any essay you write, a solid conclusion will bring your paper full circle by restating in new words your thesis and the main points you analyzed in each of the body paragraphs. It should bring completeness and closure to the reader with the satisfaction that your assertion is a sound one.

Notice how the draft of the concluding paragraph below for the model text ties back to the thesis and a synthesis of the ideas in the body paragraphs.

> Hughes's classic poem is ultimately a yearning for an America that has never quite existed. He gives voice to those who have been excluded from the American Dream in the past. He points out the many ways that injustice has chipped away at the American Dream. And yet, Hughes's tone is hopeful, the speaker of his poem expressing belief that someday the dream of America will come true.

activity Conclusion

Write a concluding paragraph for your essay. Remember to tie it back to your thesis, the points in your body paragraphs, and avoid simply repeating what you have already stated.

Bringing It All Together

If you take all of the pieces you've written and put them together, you should have a short analytical essay. Remember that all of these steps are just here to help you get started. Once you feel more in control of what it means to make an interpretation, prove a point, and comment on evidence, you can start to bend these rules to suit your purposes. Writing is not about formulas or templates. It's about communicating ideas.

Step 6. Finalizing the Essay

Now that you have a complete draft of your essay, you can move on to the final phase of the writing process: revising and editing. These two acts are sometimes thought of as being the same, but they're not. Revision is when you look back at large-scale structural elements of your essay, such as how well you support your claim, what kinds of evidence you use, how effective your word choices are, and to what extent you have led your reader easily through your essay. Editing, on the other hand, focuses on fine-tuning the language, grammar, punctuation, spelling, and other conventions. Editing is usually the very last thing you do before you finalize your piece, looking carefully for any errors that you tend to make. The following are suggestions for you to consider as you finalize your essay.

Revising

Revising gives you a good opportunity to think again about your essay's purpose and audience. In most cases, your audience will be your teacher or an external evaluator in the case of a standardized test. In both situations, that means using a somewhat formal tone, but your writing can still be engaging for you and your audience.

Reread your essay for the following:

- **Look back at your thesis.** Since you wrote this early on in the workshop, does it still relate to the analysis you ended up writing? If you need more assistance with thesis statements, be sure to look at Revision Workshop 1: Effective Thesis and Essay Structure in the back of the book.

- **Look back at your focus.** Is it still at the center of your analysis? Make sure that ideas and evidence in your paragraphs connect back to the focus. If you need more assistance, be sure to look at Revision Workshop 2: Effective Topic Sentences and Unified Paragraphs in the back of the book.

- **Revisit your body paragraphs.** Have you balanced the evidence with your own commentary about how that evidence supports your thesis? If you need more assistance with this, be sure to look at Revision Workshop 4: Appropriate Evidence and Support in the back of the book.

- **Look back at your analysis.** Does it draw a clear connection between the speaker's tone and the poem's stylistic elements? Be sure to revisit the Skill Workshop at the beginning of this chapter if you need more practice with this.

- **Check your introduction and conclusion.** Does your introduction grab the reader's attention and effectively preview your topic? Does your conclusion wrap up in a way that highlights your focus? Review Revision Workshop 8: Effective Introductions and Conclusions in the back of the book if you need additional support with these parts of your essay.

Editing

Editing is the very last thing you'll do before finalizing your essay. You and your teacher know better than anyone the types of spelling, grammar, and convention errors you need to focus on in your writing development. Below is a short checklist of things to keep in mind. Be sure to refer to one or more of the Grammar Workshops in the back of the book if you encounter an issue and aren't sure how to overcome it.

- Check your writing for the use of present tense verbs. Literature *lives*, so the analysis should discuss how the author *uses* (rather than *used*) poetic elements, and that the speaker *is* (rather than *was*) portrayed in a certain way.

- Make sure you've written in third person point of view and avoid the use of pronouns like *I* and *you*.

- If the verb tense or pronoun is not in the correct form, change it in the sentence and use brackets [ ] to indicate the change.

public speaking extension

Oral Interpretation of a Poem

You have spent this workshop crafting an analysis of a poem that puts forward a focused thesis on a topic, but in this extension activity, you will have the opportunity to deliver your poem orally to your class or a small group. You will not be presenting the analysis of the poem that you wrote in this workshop; instead you will deliver a performance of the poem that communicates your interpretation of the poem's tone and meaning to your audience.

Preparing Your Script

Since the bulk of your presentation will be the reading of your chosen poem, you will need to spend time considering how you will deliver the words and phrases of the poem so that your audience will understand your interpretation. And because this will be like a performance, you will want to print a clean copy of your poem that you can mark as a script with the following elements:

1. **Tone**. Based on your analysis of the poem, you should be able to identify its tone or tones. At the top of your script, write the tone(s) you will be trying share with your audience and write as many synonyms for the tone as you can. For "Let America Be America Again," we identified the tone as "optimistic," so we might also write at the top, "hopeful, confident, cheerful, idealistic," for example. Everything you will do in the performance of your poem will be to try to communicate these feelings to your audience.

2. **Emphasis**. Underline words or phrases in your poem that you will emphasize in your delivery. *How* you say a word adds meaning beyond the word's denotation and connotation. Think about the differences in meaning of the following sentences depending on which word is emphasized:

   a. I <u>really</u> thought I knew her.

   b. I really <u>thought</u> I knew her.

   c. I really thought <u>I</u> knew her.

   d. I really thought I knew <u>her</u>.

   Mark the places in your poem where the emphasis of certain words or phrases might help to communicate meaning. Think especially about what you can reveal about the speaker's identity, interests, concerns, feelings, and so on.

3. **Punctuation**. Paying close attention to syntax will help you to share the poem in the way that the author intended. Circle all the punctuation on your script, so that you will remember to

   a. Take a short pause at every comma

   b. Take a slightly longer pause at a dash or a semicolon

   c. Come to a full stop when you get to a period (or at the end of a stanza)

d. Speak louder when you see an exclamation point

e. Raise the pitch of your voice at the end if you see a question mark

4. **Sound**. Your poem may or may not have a clear rhyming pattern, but look carefully at your script and highlight any words that rhyme. Doing so will remind you to emphasize those words to help your listeners understand the poet's intent of connecting those words or creating that pattern. You will also want to highlight any examples of alliteration or assonance to be able to slightly exaggerate those words to communicate the intended sound.

Practicing Your Delivery

Just as actors rehearse their lines before going onstage or the cameras start filming, you will want to practice reading your poem aloud many times before you deliver it to your audience. Because your goal is to communicate the poem's meaning and tone only through your delivery, emphasizing key words, adjusting your volume, and using appropriate and effective gestures and facial expressions will be crucial. Continue to adjust the notes on your script to reflect changes as you practice. Try to either memorize the poem or know it well enough that you can make eye contact with your audience at times that would be effective. Practice with a partner or film yourself so that you can review and adjust your delivery as needed.

Delivering Your Presentation

Now that you have a script that you have practiced reading and you are comfortable with your recitation, it's time to deliver your presentation, which includes the following three parts:

1. **Introduction**. State the author and title of the poem and include no more than a sentence or two about any context that might be essential for your audience to know in order to understand your poem. For "Let America Be America Again," we might state that it was published during the Great Depression, a time of widespread unemployment and poverty in America.

2. **Recitation**. After your introduction, take a pause and then begin delivering your poem with all the emphasis, pauses, and sound elements that will help you to communicate the author's tone and the poem's meaning.

3. **Closing**. Make eye contact with your audience and say "thank you."

Visuals (optional)

Normally, you will not have any visuals with this type of presentation since you do not want anything to distract from your performance of the poem. If you decide to add visuals, such as a painting or photograph that connects with the tone of the poem, make sure it is relevant, appropriate, and works to enhance your words and delivery. The image should be able to stand on its own without any explanation, since that is not part of the presentation.

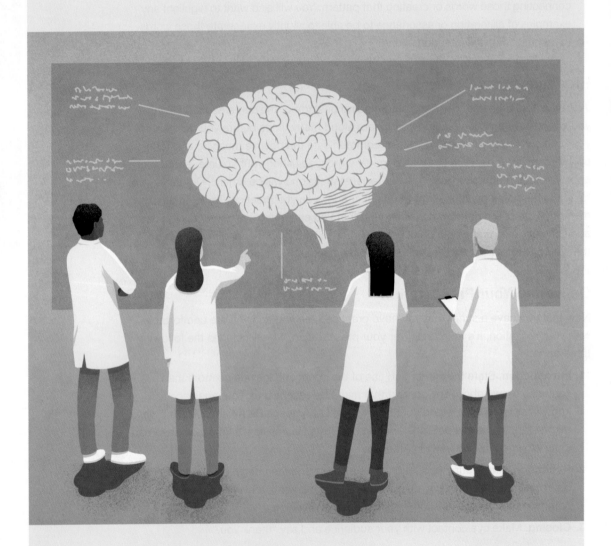

Exposition

Exposition and expository writing might be the most boring names ever given to writing that can actually be quite interesting. Expository writing is how we explore ideas and explain things. It's how we answer questions and try to understand the world. What if we wanted to explore the best movie snacks? Or explain how games draw us in and keep us playing? What if we wanted to explain what the planet would look like if humans were suddenly wiped from the face of the earth? You'll find pieces on all of these topics in this chapter, because explaining whatever we find interesting is what exposition is all about.

What exposition *is not* is just a compilation of facts and data or a summary of a topic. While it may include these things, expository writing seeks to explain a concept or topic in a clear, compelling way that engages the reader.

In this chapter, you will have the opportunity to read and analyze a variety of expository texts and learn how to explain things clearly. This chapter will help you think not only about the content of the texts and how the authors structurally organize information to achieve their purposes, but also how you can incorporate these methods into your own writing.

Contents

Essential Elements of Exposition

The primary goal of expository texts is to *explain*. When we explain something to someone, we break the topic down into parts so that our audience can understand it better. Just as fiction writing has specific elements that authors use to engage an audience (e.g., conflict, character, setting), expository texts have elements and features that authors incorporate to share their ideas with readers. In this workshop, we'll look at some of the tools writers use to explain things — the essential elements of exposition.

PREVIEWING Academic Vocabulary   **Essential Elements of Exposition**

In this section, you will encounter the following terms as you think about how to analyze expository writing. Working individually or with a partner or small group, consider what you already know about the meaning of each term.

1. Exposition
2. Main idea
3. Purpose and audience
4. Evidence

5. Explanation and commentary
6. Style and tone

7. Expository strategies
   Description
   Compare/contrast
   Cause/effect
   Problem/solution

Let's begin by reading a piece by Stephen King called "Stephen King's Guide to Movie Snacks." In this expository text, King explains his approach to the snacking part of the movie-going experience.

Stephen King's Guide to Movie Snacks

Stephen King

Stephen King (b. 1947) is best known as the author of popular horror stories such as *Carrie* (1973), *The Shining* (1977), *The Stand* (1978), and *It* (1986). In all, he has published more than sixty novels and 200 short stories. Much of his work has been adapted for both film and television, including *The Stand*, *Castle Rock*, and *The Outsider*. His memoir *On Writing* is a classic look at the craft of writing. This piece appeared in *Entertainment Weekly* in 2008.

Jim Spellman/Getty Images

The Bard of Horror takes a gastronomical tour of the movie-theater concession stand — all hail the cholesterol-lowering properties of diet soda

For a magazine that prides itself on the many aspects of the movie business it covers, *EW* hasn't had much to say over the years concerning the important subject of snacks. Oh, an occasional piece about how much they cost, but few words on their culinary wonderfulness. This needs correcting, because, while some people eat snacks while they are at the movies, there are some who go to the movies so they can eat snacks. That would be me. So let me impart a few lessons years of snacking have taught me.

First, support your theater. Buy at the snack bar and damn the expense. You could probably sneak your own food in, but if you're caught, you'll be thrown out. As for bringing healthier snacks from home: Did you really hire a babysitter and drive six miles so you could sneak cucumber slices half-drowned in buttermilk ranch out of a slimy plastic bag? Is that what you call living it up?

If you want to get healthy, there are places for that: They're called "health clubs." And I find there's something giddy about tossing down $4.50 for a box of Gummi Bears or a bag of chocolate raisins. It makes me feel like a high roller, especially when the matinee ticket itself only costs 50 cents more.

I always start my order with the ritual drink — Diet Pepsi if possible, Coke Zero as a fallback, Diet Coke the court of last resort. A big diet cola sops up the calories and cholesterol contained in movie snack food just like a big old sponge soaks up water. This is a proven fact. One expert (me) believes a medium diet cola drink can lower your cholesterol by 20 points and absorb as much as one thousand empty calories. And if you say that's total crap, I would just point out I don't call it a ritual drink for nothing. Sometimes I add a strawberry smoothie with lots of whipped cream, but I'm always sure to take enough sips of my ritual drink to absolve me of those calories, too.

With my calorie-absorbent drink in hand, 5 I can then safely order a large popcorn with extra butter. Of course it isn't really butter, it's some sort of mystery substance squeezed from the sweat glands of small animals, but I have developed such a taste for it over my years of filmgoing that the real stuff tastes wrong, somehow.

If the counter guy puts on the glandular butter substitute himself, I watch carefully to make sure he greases the middle of the bag as well as the top layer. If it's self-serve (at the beginning I didn't like this option, but now I do), I proceed to hammer on that red button until I have what I call a "heavy bag." You know you have a heavy bag when the bottom starts to sag and ooze large drops of a yellow puslike substance before you even get into the theater. And don't forget the salt. Popcorn salt is a little strong for my taste (and it looks like powdered urine); I prefer plain table salt. Half a shaker is about right.

With a "heavy bag," caution is a must. Don't put it on your lap; when the movie's over and the lights come up, people will think you wet your pants. Courtesy is also a must. Don't put it on the seat beside you, or the next person is going to sit on a seat that oozes. Not cool, bro.

My candy of choice is Junior Mints. And while I don't bring bootleg food into the movies, I do bring bootleg toothpicks. Then, as I relax in my seat, I take a toothpick and poke five or six Junior Mints onto it. It ends the dreaded Chocolate Hand, and it's also kind of fun to eat candy off a stick. I call them Mint-Kebabs.

And although it's a matter of personal choice, I myself don't eat movie meat (go on, snicker, I can take it). My motto is "Never buy a hot dog that's been waiting in a foil Baggie under a heat lamp." For all you know, that stray dog could have been there since *Revenge of the Sith*.[1] Nachos are good, but only if you get the reserve swimming pool of cheese sauce, because one is never enough.

Now that I think of it, the same could be said 10 of snacks. But remember: Start with the ritual drink. After that, you're on your own. ∎

---

[1] *Revenge of the Sith* (2005) is the sixth film in the Star Wars franchise created by George Lucas. —Eds.

activity · Getting Started

Freewrite for a few minutes about a hobby or something you enjoy doing for entertainment, such as playing videogames or sports, listening to music, completing puzzles, experimenting with robotics, or reading. What do you like about this activity? What is special or interesting about this activity? For example, you might freewrite about your favorite music and explain why you enjoy listening to or performing it.

Main Idea

Now that we've read King's article, the first question we should ask is, "What is he talking about?" We know the topic is a humorous guide for selecting movie snacks, but what point does King want his readers to understand about movie snacks? The answers to these questions would lead us to the main idea of the text. The **main idea** in expository texts is the most important point that writers make about their topics. It can also be referred to as the thesis statement, though in expository writing, it is not necessarily a debatable idea. For more information on main idea, you may want to review the Reading for Understanding section of Chapter 2 on page 31.

Titles of expository texts often can give us important clues about the author's main idea. From the title of this piece, we can conclude that King will offer information about different snack options and which ones he recommends. As is sometimes the case with expository texts, however, King does not state his main idea directly; we get at the main idea only through reading carefully and trying to account for all of the details and examples. After reading his piece, therefore, we could summarize his main idea as something like "snacking at the movies is an experience unto itself, and certain rules should be observed to ensure a comfortable, courteous, and quality snacking experience." This main idea is an attempt to distill all of the ideas he raises into a single statement. You might write a differently worded main idea, but this one captures much of what he explains throughout the rest of his piece. King emphasizes that snacks should be bought at the theater and prepared and handled a certain way, and he describes which snacks he selects and the reasons for his choices.

If we decided to focus on music in the Getting Started activity, a possible main idea might be something like this: "the key to an effective playlist for running is matching the length of the workout with the length of the list and the variety and pace of the songs."

Main Idea

Using the topic you wrote about in the Getting Started activity, narrow your focus down to one aspect—your main idea—that you could write a "guide" about, along the lines of King's focus on the snacks part of the movie-going experience. Try to write your main idea in a single sentence.

Purpose and Audience

You likely remember the concepts of purpose and audience from other chapters in this book. The **purpose** is what the speaker or writer is trying to accomplish. The **audience** is whom the speaker or writer is addressing. In the case of exposition, the purpose is to explain the main idea in a way that the audience will find understandable, interesting, entertaining, or useful. King's purpose is to explain the rules that should be observed to ensure a comfortable, courteous, and quality snacking experience while at the movies. Once the purpose is established, the next important questions are, *Who is King's audience for his piece? How does his audience affect what he writes?*

King is known for his thriller and horror stories, but this is a far lighter subject. He wrote this piece for *Entertainment Weekly*, a publication that focuses on the latest movie, TV, music, and video game releases, so his audience is probably interested in and knowledgeable about popular culture. They would likely understand the reference when he describes an old hot dog that "could have been there since *Revenge of the Sith*," a movie that was three years old even at the time he wrote this. Also, he assumes that his audience can choose to go out to a movie theater rather than rent something at home and has money to spend on the snacks there. He provides other clues about his intended audience when he asks, "Did you really hire a babysitter?" and suggests that "there's something giddy about tossing down $4.50 for a box of Gummi Bears." Clearly, he is not writing for teenagers or even young adults, but for older people with some disposable income. If he were writing for teenagers, he might have had to change his movie references and spend more time explaining the value of going out to a movie theater.

Let's apply this thinking to the playlist example that we began developing earlier. First, what is our purpose? Thinking back to our main idea, our goal is to explain how the length of the playlist, the pace of the songs, and variety can make an effective collection of music for running. Let's imagine that we are writing for a science magazine geared toward the general public, and our audience is made up of adults who love science and classic rock. And while our audience may know music in general and love to run, they may not know specifics about how to select music with the right tempo for running. And because we can make some assumptions about their age and music tastes, we can include references to classic rock musicians that they might already know. Knowing your audience will affect what you include, or not, in your piece.

activity Purpose and Audience

In the previous activities, you wrote about something you enjoy doing, selected one aspect of that activity to focus on, and identified a main idea. Since your purpose is to explain that idea, now you need to think about who your audience could be for that piece. Is there a particular age range for your audience? Gender identity? Socio-economic level? What does your audience already know about your topic, or what do you want to them to learn? Write a few sentences about what you know about your intended audience for your expository piece and briefly describe how that knowledge might affect how you explain your main idea.

Evidence and Examples

Providing evidence is key to supporting your purpose for writing — the explanation of your main idea. One of the primary ways a writer explains something is by including examples. Examples help us understand what is being discussed by going from general to specific, making broad or abstract ideas clear and concrete. For instance, if King were to simply say, "Eat movie snacks," that broad statement would raise a lot of questions. Why should I eat movie snacks? All snacks, or just a select few? King answers some of these questions by using specific examples:

> I always start my order with the ritual drink — Diet Pepsi if possible, Coke Zero as a fallback, Diet Coke the court of last resort. A big diet cola sops up the calories and cholesterol contained in movie snack food just like a big old sponge soaks up water.

The most common types of examples follow. If you already worked through Chapter 7, they will look familiar because they are the same types of information that would serve as evidence in an argument. In expository writing, however, we are developing an explanation, not proving a point, so their use here is slightly different.

Types of Examples	Why a Writer Might Use Them
Details and specifics	To provide concrete information
Research and expert opinion	To show what experts think about the topic
Data and statistics	To give a quantitative example
Personal experience and anecdotes	To show personal connection with or knowledge of the topic

Throughout his article, King explains his main idea by including examples that draw on his own anecdotal experiences with buying snacks at the movie theater. While most articles use real facts and data, King maintains his humor by offering made-up statistics when explaining that diet colas soak up unhealthy snack calories and lower cholesterol "by 20 points," a fact provided by the only mentioned "expert" — himself. He also includes details about which specific snacks he likes and specific examples regarding how he likes to eat them. He includes Diet Pepsi as his "ritual drink" and Junior Mints as his "candy of choice." He also mentions snacks he wouldn't eat, like the "movie meat" hot dogs or the nachos, unless they have the "reserve swimming pool" of extra cheese. He provides examples of snacks he likes and snacks he doesn't. You may or may not agree with his examples, and you might even be thinking about additional ones that could complement or replace the ones he uses, but the purpose is clear: to explain his main idea with specific examples.

Evidence and Examples

Return to the previous activity and review what you have written so far about your hobby or interest. Generate a list of examples you might use to help explain your main idea more clearly to your audience. What specific examples could you include to help your readers understand your main idea? Try to include one of each of the different kinds of examples identified in the table on page 602.

Explanation

When including evidence or examples in their writing, authors follow up with **explanation** — also referred to as **commentary** — that provides more insight into how or why the evidence and examples support their main idea.

To help his audience better understand what he likes most about his movie snacks, King examines what makes them his favorites. These explanations allow King to illustrate his main idea: how to have a comfortable, courteous, and quality snacking experience at the movies. On the point of quality, he explains the "benefits" of diet colas over regular colas and offers commentary on the consistency of movie theater popcorn butter — the "mystery substance squeezed from the sweat glands of small animals" and "glandular butter substitute" — which, according to King, is better tasting than real butter. King addresses comfort and courtesy when he examines the consequences of having a "heavy bag" of imitation butter popcorn, warning readers to not place it in their laps or leave it on the seat next to them. Even his take on how to eat Junior Mints as "Mint-Kebabs" to avoid the "dreaded Chocolate Hand" backs up his idea that a specific approach to movie snacks provides clear benefits.

Let's apply this thinking to our main idea about creating effective playlists for running. For support, we could include evidence from a research study showing that songs at 120–125 beats per minute (BPM), typical of most classic rock music, are ideal for sustained exercise. Our commentary on this evidence could include an explanation of how this tempo is ideal for steady running and that the pace can be increased for a faster workout, depending on the runner's desired intensity.

activity

Explanation

Return to your Evidence/Example list from the previous activity. Select one type of evidence or example you included and write a few sentences that explain to your audience the relationship between your evidence or example and your main idea.

Style and Tone

As writers consider the best way to effectively explain something to their audience, they must make choices about how best to present the information. That means not only using examples and explanations that help support their main idea, but also using a writing style appropriate for the intended audience and purpose. In Chapter 3 (p. 67), we explain that **tone** is the author's attitude toward the subject, which is revealed through a writer's language and style choices. Tone is the same for expository writing as it is for fiction, poetry, or argument writing — it's how writers express their feelings toward the subject and encourage their audience to care about it. Exposition still incorporates the following elements of style:

Diction: word choice

Syntax: word order and sentence structure

Figurative language: language that is not intended to be taken literally; includes simile, metaphor, allusion, hyperbole, and personification

Imagery: literal or figurative language that appeals to the senses

Let's look at how King uses elements of style to help create his tone, which is clearly intended to be humorous and informal. Sure, he could have just said, "You should buy movie snacks at the theater," and then proceeded to explain in a dry and uninteresting way what choices he recommends. But he doesn't do that. Instead, he uses diction and imagery, like "greases," "glandular butter substitute," and "yellow puslike substance" (par. 6), to describe the liquid theater butter he prefers on his popcorn to create a "heavy bag." While these words would normally disgust a consumer, they provide humorous descriptions that emphasize his preference for unhealthy options.

King's use of figurative language also enables his audience to better understand the "culinary wonderfulness" of movie snacks. He emphasizes feeling "like a high roller" when paying expensive prices for Gummi Bears or chocolate raisins, and how a diet cola "sops up the calories and cholesterol . . . like a big old sponge soaks up water." His use of exaggeration when "hammer[ing] on that red button" to release more imitation butter in his popcorn bag adds to the comical effect of his message.

Additionally, King varies his syntax, or sentence structure, to give his writing an informal feel. Look at how he varies his sentence structure in paragraph 7:

> With a "heavy bag," caution is a must. Don't put it on your lap; when the movie's over and the lights come up, people will think you wet your pants. Courtesy is also a must. Don't put it on the seat beside you, or the next person is going to sit on a seat that oozes. Not cool, bro.

These are just a few of the style choices that King makes to engage his audience, develop his humorous and informal tone, and connect with his pop-culture-knowledgeable, movie-watching readers.

Let's consider style and tone in our music playlist example. If our piece were to be published in a magazine that presents scientific research to the general public, we likely would strive for a formal and scientific style and tone, including technical terminology and longer sentences to explain our main idea to our audience.

Style and Tone

Think about the topic that you have been writing about throughout this workshop.

Step 1. What is the tone that you might employ in your piece about your chosen topic? See page 67 for a list of common tone words.

Step 2. Write a sentence or two that includes one or more stylistic choices described above that might help you to communicate that tone.

Expository Strategies

There are many ways to explain things, but a handful of common tools can help writers achieve their purpose as they develop their explanations. These strategies are sometimes called **methods of development**, but we're going to call them simply **expository strategies**, because they are strategies that writers can use to create expository texts. The following are the most common:

- **Description:** to make something vivid and concrete
- **Comparison and contrast:** to highlight similarities and differences
- **Cause and effect:** to show causal relationships
- **Problem and solution:** to highlight an issue and a possible solution or solutions

Although these different strategies are sometimes introduced as stand-alone ways of organizing an essay, the reality is that authors, like King, will often draw on multiple strategies, using whatever tool is most effective, to explain the main idea and achieve the writer's purpose. The patterns do not drive the writing; the purpose drives the writing.

Description

Descriptive writing includes sensory imagery and details to explain how something looks, feels, tastes, sounds, and so on. Descriptive writing explains what it's like to experience things, and it makes something abstract seem concrete and vivid.

King's article is full of such language, and we can see how his descriptive language helps us understand his humorous take on his point. Consider, for example, the two descriptions that follow. In the first, King describes snacks from home; in the second, snacks from the theater.

> Did you really hire a babysitter and drive six miles so you could sneak cucumber slices half-drowned in buttermilk ranch out of a slimy plastic bag?

> And I find there's something giddy about tossing down $4.50 for a box of Gummi Bears or a bag of chocolate raisins. It makes me feel like a high roller.

With these two descriptions, King illustrates and supports his preference for movie theater snacks in an entertaining way.

Compare and Contrast

To help readers understand a topic more clearly, authors will draw comparisons or show contrast with something else. In other words, they compare and contrast. A Venn diagram (named for the philosopher who invented it, John Venn), consisting of two overlapping circles, can be a useful tool for applying this strategy. There are several different ways to use it. For our purposes in this workshop, we will place shared characteristics in the area where the two circles overlap, and place differences in the outside circles. In the case of our main idea about creating a playlist for running, we might choose to draw a comparison between classic rock and classical music, two types of music that people in our intended audience might enjoy. A Venn diagram for this comparison might look like this:

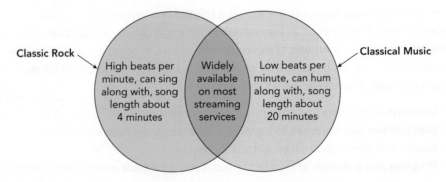

Both classic rock and classical music are widely available on streaming services and would be easy to put into our playlist. However, when we compare beats per minute and track length for these two types of music, we can make the case that classic rock might be a better choice than classical music for our running playlist. By using this strategy, we turn a matter of personal opinion (classic rock is better for running than classical music) into a recommendation based on clear reasoning and identifiable rules.

An effective comparison or contrast should explain why the similarity or difference is important or interesting. King doesn't just say he likes fake movie butter on his popcorn. We get further clarification when King explains that imitation butter is superior to real butter, which "tastes wrong somehow." He also comically compares popcorn salt to real salt, emphasizing that he doesn't prefer the "too strong" popcorn salt over the "half a shaker" of real salt. The point is that King compares and contrasts different aspects of movie snacks so that he can explain how to have a quality snacking experience.

Cause and Effect

Explaining causes and effects is how we figure out why things happen and for what reason, or how we predict what will happen if we do something. In history class, you explore the causes and effects of social, political, and economic events. In chemistry class, you conduct experiments to examine the causes and effects of different chemical reactions.

Let's look at how King incorporates this technique in his writing. He uses cause and effect when explaining that a diet cola is a healthy option: when you drink diet cola (cause) it "sops up the calories and cholesterol contained in movie snack food" (effect). He uses cause and effect again when describing how he gets a "heavy bag" of buttered popcorn (effect) by "greasing the middle" if the counter guy flavors it (cause), or by "hammer[ing] on that red button" if King does it himself (cause). While this example shows how several causes can lead to a single effect, the structure can also work in the opposite direction to highlight a cause that produces one or more effects. For example, King says that selecting a diet cola (cause) results in calorie absorption and cholesterol reduction (effects).

Problem and Solution

Sometimes, writers will present a problem and then explain one or more possible solutions to that problem. This strategy gives writers a chance to not only help readers understand the problem in detail, but to understand how it might be addressed. Some essays are written entirely in this format, while other times, writers may employ this strategy in a few sentences or a single paragraph. King employs this approach throughout, such as when he suggests that if you don't want to look like you have wet pants after the movie (problem), don't put the popcorn in your lap (solution).

Expository Strategies

Throughout this section, we have examined the various expository strategies that King uses in his piece and are common in exposition. Thinking about your own topic, which of these strategies might make the most sense for your audience, purpose, and tone? Why?

Additional Elements of Exposition

In addition to the elements explained above, you may also encounter the elements of expository writing listed below. Just as you may not see all of what we have talked about so far in a single text, the following may show up only occasionally, sometimes in surprising ways. Keep in mind that these are tools that authors use to ensure the information they share has the greatest impact on their audience.

- **Headings and subheadings.** One way authors arrange their information in order to explain something clearly is by using headings and subheadings. That is, they organize information into smaller chunks of related content.
- **Specialized vocabulary.** Expository writing often includes specialized vocabulary that refers to things or concepts specific to the topic or discipline. These terms may be unfamiliar to you, but they are usually explained by the writer.
- **Graphics and illustrations.** These are visual supports like cartoons, tables, charts, and infographics, which aid or extend comprehension of the content. Graphics and illustrations usually include a caption or other information to explain what the picture is about.

REFLECTING ON Academic Vocabulary   Essential Elements of Exposition

Look back at the list of terms that you previewed on page 598. Now that you have read about them and practiced with these terms, what has changed about your understanding of expository texts? Which of the skills that you practiced in this section do you feel confident using? Which ones do you think you need to develop further? How do you know?

culminating activity

Writing an Exposition

Write a short expository piece about the hobby or activity that you've been considering throughout this workshop. Choose one of the expository strategies — description, compare/contrast, cause/effect, or problem/solution — that you think will serve your topic best, and keep your audience and purpose in mind.

from Trashed

Derf Backderf

John (Derf) Backderf (b. 1959) is a well-known writer-artist whose collection of original works is part of the Billy Ireland Cartoon Museum at Ohio State University. His comic strip, *The City*, appeared in over 140 publications in its twenty-plus years in syndication. Among his many awards, Backderf won the Robert F. Kennedy Journalism Award for cartooning in 2006. His graphic novels include *Punk Rock & Trailer Parks* (2010), *My Friend Dahmer* (2012), and *Trashed* (2015). *Trashed* is a graphic novel based on Backderf's own experiences as a sanitation worker.

KEY CONTEXT Backderf's semi-autobiographical graphic novel follows a crew of sanitation workers as they collect garbage. He takes readers along the garbage route, from curbside pickup to landfill dumps, and provides a glimpse into the history of humanity's relationship with the garbage generated by everyday life. This excerpt focuses on that history and the staggering amount of trash we toss daily in our "throwaway" society, as captured in this photo of a California garbage collection facility.

L V T E T I A · V R B S · P A R I S I O R V M

In the 1400s, **THE PILES** OF STINKING GARBAGE OUTSIDE THE WALLS OF PARIS WERE SO HIGH, CITY DEFENSES WERE COMPROMISED.

FINALLY, AFTER 4,000-PLUS YEARS OF LIVING KNEE-DEEP IN THEIR OWN FILTH, OUR ANCESTORS DECIDED THERE **MUST** BE A BETTER WAY.

IT WAS THE ENGLISH WHO DEVELOPED EUROPE'S FIRST HIGHLY EFFICIENT METHOD OF TRASH COLLECTION AND RECYCLING.

BY THE 1800s, A LEGION OF **'DUST MEN'** COLLECTED ALL REFUSE IN LONDON. EVERYTHING WAS SORTED IN HUGE YARDS ON THE OUTSKIRTS OF THE CITY.

NEARLY **100 PERCENT** OF LONDON'S WASTE WAS REUSED OR RECYCLED. IT'S THE SAME PRINCIPLE WE STILL EMPLOY.

BENJAMIN FRANKLIN WAS AMERICA'S SANITATION PIONEER. HE FORMED THE FIRST STREET-CLEANING FORCE IN PHILADELPHIA IN 1792.

PHILADELPHIA'S TRASH WAS HAULED OUT OF THE CITY BY SLAVES, WHO DUMPED IT INTO THE DELAWARE RIVER DOWNSTREAM.

In pre-civil war America, the common solution to garbage on city streets **was pigs.** New York City had **so many** free-roaming hogs that **Charles Dickens** in "American Notes" begged city fathers to rid the metropolis of the "ugly brutes."

Trash collection as a function of government didn't become commonplace until the 1880s.

CITY OF CLEVELAND

By 1900, cities decided that **burning trash** was the best method of disposal. But the municipal **incinerators** were poorly designed and difficult to maintain.

Most were scrapped by 1920.

After World War II, landfills were the near-universal destination for the nation's trash. Often communities would "reclaim" wetlands. Dumps were largely unregulated. Not until 1979 did the E.P.A. issue rules on how landfills were built and operated.

From 1960 on, household waste in the U.S. increased dramatically, as **conspicuous consumption** and **built-in obsolescence** became the norm. We became a **throwaway society.**

How much garbage do we produce? With the trash **Americans** generate, the E.P.A. estimates that in **just 18 months,** we could form a bumper-to-bumper line of full garbage trucks that would stretch all the way to **the moon!** **Europeans** aren't much better, and **Canadians** generate more garbage per capita than anyone on earth!

BUT...THE E.P.A.'S FIGURE OF **2.89 POUNDS OF TRASH DAILY** IS **WAY** LOW. AN INDEPENDENT BIANNUAL STUDY BY **COLUMBIA UNIVERSITY** FINDS OUR ANNUAL GARBAGE TOTAL **ISN'T** 254 MILLION TONS... IT'S **389 MILLION TONS!** AND WE RECYCLE ONLY **29 PERCENT**, NOT THE 34.3 PERCENT THE E.P.A. CLAIMS.

THE TRUTH? EACH OF US MAKES **5.06 POUNDS OF GARBAGE** A DAY. NO BIG DEAL, RIGHT? THAT **DOESN'T** SEEM LIKE MUCH...

...**EVEN IF** THIS GUY MAKES ALMOST **TWICE** AS MUCH TRASH AS THE E.P.A. ESTIMATES HE DOES. THAT'S STILL JUST ONE **5-POUND BAG.**

AH, BUT THAT ONE BAG QUICKLY TURNS INTO ABOUT **35 POUNDS OF TRASH A WEEK.**

HMMM.

AND ROUGHLY **150 POUNDS A MONTH.**

AND **1,847 POUNDS A YEAR!**

365 SMALL BAGS MAKE **QUITE** A PILE, NO?

YIKES!

Understanding and Interpreting

1. In what way does panel 3 on page 610 emphasize the problems created by tossing garbage into the street?

2. Explain the connection Backderf makes on page 611 between the "dust men" and recycling.

3. In panel 5 on page 612, Backderf uses the terms *conspicuous consumption* and *built-in obsolescence*. Explain what these terms mean. What ideas about society in the 1960s do these terms help Backderf convey?

4. What do we find out about how garbage was collected and removed or recycled throughout history in different countries? What point is Backderf making by pointing out this information?

5. What is Backderf's overall main idea in this excerpt? Provide evidence from the text to support your response.

6. Throughout the selection, Backderf incorporates facts and statistics. How do these facts and statistics further support his main idea and purpose?

Analyzing Language, Style, and Structure

7. **Vocabulary in Context.** In the very first panel of this selection (p. 610), Backderf uses the term *headache* to describe trash disposal. What does this term mean in this context?

8. **Vocabulary in Context.** In panel 3 on page 611, Backderf says that Benjamin Franklin formed the first "street-cleaning force." What does *force* mean in this context?

9. What do you notice about the difference visually between the panels that address "A Brief History of Garbage" and the last five panels of the piece? What effect is Backderf creating through this contrast?

10. Graphic novels require that an author convey action in a small amount of space. How does Backderf's use of examples and descriptions both effectively and succinctly convey his message?

11. In panel 1 on page 611, Backderf states that "after 4,000-plus years of living knee-deep in their own filth, our ancestors decided there must be a better way." What tone do the visuals and language in this panel convey?

12. Backderf sets certain words in boldface. What effect do these choices create?

13. In the first two panels on page 613, the figure in the panel directly addresses the audience. What is the effect of this shift in point of view?

14. How does the visual in the last panel on page 613 support the text in the previous panels? Does the final image on page 614 contradict his statement in the first panel of the essay? Explain.

15. What do you notice about the size of the last panel relative to the size of the other panels in the story? How do the panel sizes allow Backderf to create emphasis and direct the readers' attention?

Topics for Composing

16. **Analysis.** Analyze how Backderf's use of color, framing, or other visual elements conveys his tone. How do his choices emphasize a point he is making about trash?

17. **Argument.** What impact has the development of garbage collection, recycling, and removal systems had on societal behavior? Are we making our lives better or worse? Provide evidence from the text, your own experiences, or other sources to support your position.

18. **Connections.** Take a moment to reflect on how much trash you throw out each day. Write a response about ways in which you might curb the amount of trash you discard.

19. **Speaking and Listening.** Backderf refers to the "built-in obsolescence" of consumption and to Americans as a "throwaway society" in panel 5 on page 612. With a partner or small group, generate a list of consumer products that are designed with "built-in obsolescence" and that Backderf would consider part of "throwaway society." Discuss reasons why these products might have been designed not to last. Be prepared to share your list with the whole class and to listen to their ideas.

20. **Research.** Research the ideas that Backderf brings up about consumerism, consumption, and waste. How serious are the problems he identifies? Are there any solutions? If so, what are the benefits and drawbacks of potential solutions?

21. **Multimodal.** Create a presentation that demonstrates the amount of trash created by your home, school, or community. In your presentation, include graphs, tables, pictures, video, or audio that would inform your audience of your findings in an engaging way.

from A Theory of Fun for Game Design

Raph Koster

Raph Koster (b. 1971) is a well-known figure in the gaming industry, having been the lead designer and director in numerous wide-release games such as *Ultima Online: The Second Age* and *Star Wars Galaxies*. He has professional credits not only for game programming but also in art, soundtrack music, and writing. The focus of many of his speeches — the relationship between fun and learning — is the subject of this excerpt from his illustrated book *A Theory of Fun for Game Design* (2013).

Informa PLC

Prologue

My grandfather wanted to know whether I felt proud of what I do. It seemed a reasonable question: there he was, aging and soon to pass away, though at the time I didn't know that; a man who had spent his life as a fire chief, raising six children. One of them followed in his footsteps, became a fire chief himself, and now sells bathtub linings. There's a special education teacher, an architect, a carpenter. Good, solid, wholesome professions for good, solid, wholesome people. And there I was — making games rather than contributing to society.

I told him that I felt I did contribute. Games aren't just a diversion; they're something valuable and important. And my evidence was right in front of me — my kids, playing tic-tac-toe[1] on the floor.

Watching my kids play and learn through playing had been a revelation for me. Even though my profession was making games, I often felt lost in the complexities of making large modern entertainment products rather than understanding why games are fun and what fun is.

---

[1] *Tic-tac-toe:* Also known as noughts and crosses. Tic-tac-toe, and its cousins go-moku (a game where the board is variously 13 × 13 or 15 × 15 and you have to get five in a row) and *Qubic* (a 4 × 4 × 4 cube) are all amenable to mathematical analysis. Tic-tac-toe in particular is fairly trivial, since there are only 125,168 possible games, and the vast majority of the possibility space collapses the moment you regard the board as having rotational symmetry. If both players employ the optimal strategy, the game will always end in a draw.

My kids were leading me, without my quite knowing it, toward a theory of fun. And so I told my grandfather, "Yes, this is something worthwhile. I connect people, and I teach people." But as I said it, I didn't really have any evidence to offer.

What Games Are

What is fun?

5

If you dig into the origins of the word, you'll find that it comes either from *"fonne,"* which is "fool" in Middle English, or from *"Jonn,"* which means "pleasure" in Gaelic. Either way, fun is defined as "a source of enjoyment." This can happen via physical stimuli, aesthetic appreciation, or direct chemical manipulation.

Fun is all about our brains feeling good — the release of endorphins[2] into our system. . . .

One of the releases of chemicals triggering good feelings is at that moment of triumph when we learn something or master a task. This almost always causes us to break out into a smile.[3] After all, it is important to the

survival of the species that we learn — therefore our bodies reward us for it with moments of pleasure. There are many ways we find fun in games, and I will talk about the others. But learning is the one I believe to be the most important.

Fun from games arises out of mastery. It arises out of comprehension. It is the act of solving puzzles that makes games fun.

In other words, with games, learning is the drug.[4]

10

I'm not kidding when I say we're on drugs when we're having fun! Endorphins are an opiate. The "chill down the spine" effect is often explained as the release of endorphins into the spinal fluid. Pleasure is not the only thing that gives us this effect, of course — adrenaline rushes caused by fear provide a similar sensation.

Boredom is the opposite of learning. When a game stops teaching us, we feel bored. Boredom is the brain casting about for new information. It is the feeling you get when there

My kids are learning tic-tac-toe these days.

Raph Koster, A Theory of Fun for Game Design. ©2005 by Raph Koster. Paraglyph Press, Inc.

---

[2]*Endorphins:* "Endorphin" is abbreviated from "endogenous morphine."

[3]*Break out in a smile:* There's good evidence that the smile can cause us to be happy and not just the other way around. For more reading on emotions, we recommend the work of Paul Ekman.

---

[4]*Learning is the drug:* "Fun is the emotional response to learning." (Chris Crawford, March 2004). Also, Biederman and Vessel's research shows that curiosity itself is inherently pleasurable.

but you'll only play it
until you master the pattern.

are no new visible patterns to absorb. When a book is dull and fails to lead you on to the next chapter, it is failing to exhibit a captivating pattern. When you feel a piece of music is repetitive or derivative, it grows boring because it presents no cognitive challenge. And of course, it could arise when a pattern is present but "going over our heads."

We shouldn't underestimate the brain's desire to learn. If you put a person in a sensory deprivation chamber, he or she will get very unhappy very quickly. The brain craves stimuli. At all times, the brain is casting about trying to learn something, trying to integrate information into its worldview. It is insatiable in that way.

This *doesn't* mean it necessarily craves new *experiences* — mostly, it just craves new *data*. New data is all it needs to flesh out a pattern. A new experience might force a whole new system

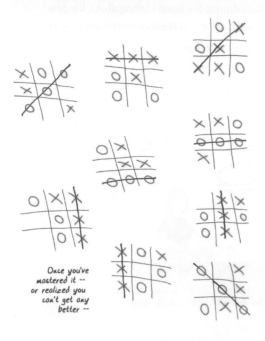

Once you've
mastered it --
or realized you
can't get any
better --

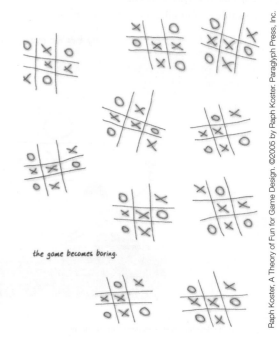

the game becomes boring.

on the brain, and often the brain doesn't *like* that. It's disruptive. The brain doesn't like to do more work than it has to. That's why we have the term "sensory overload,"[5] as an opposite to "sensory deprivation."

Games grow boring when they fail to unfold new niceties in the puzzles they present. But they have to navigate between the Scylla and Charybdis[6] of deprivation and overload, of excessive order and excessive chaos, of silence and noise.

This means that it's easy for the player to get bored before the end of the game. After all, people are *really* good at pattern-matching and dismissing noise and silence that doesn't fit the pattern they have in mind.

Here are some ways in which boredom might strike, killing the pleasurable learning experience that games are supposed to provide:

- The player might grok[7] how the game works from just the first five minutes, and then the game will be dismissed as trivial, just as an adult dismisses tic-tac-toe. This doesn't mean the player actually solved the game; she may have just arrived at a good-enough strategy or heuristic[8] that lets her get by. "Too easy," might be the remark the player makes.
- The player might grok that there's a ton of depth to the possible permutations in a game, but conclude that these permutations are below their level of interest — sort of

like saying, "Yeah, there's a ton of depth in baseball, but memorizing the RBI stats[9] for the past 20 years is not all that useful to me."

- The player might fail to see any patterns whatsoever, and nothing is more boring than noise. "This is too hard."
- The game might unveil new variations in the pattern too slowly, in which case the game may be dismissed as trivial too early, even though it does have depth. "The difficulty ramps too slowly."
- The game might also unveil the variations too quickly, which then leads to players losing control of the pattern and giving up because it looks like noise again. "This got too hard too fast," they'll say.
- The player might master everything in the pattern. He has exhausted the fun, consumed it all. "I beat it."

Basically, all games are edutainment.

15

---

[5]*Sensory overload:* The input capacity of the conscious mind is only around 16 bits a second. Sensory overload can be thought of as the difference between the amount of *information* and the amount of *meaning*. You can have a large stack of information — such as a book typed by monkeys — that is very low in meaning. When the amount of information is too high and we fail to extract meaning from it, we say we're in overload.

[6]*Scylla and Charybdis:* In Greek myth, these two monsters sat on opposite sides of a narrow strait. Sailors wishing to pass inevitably ran too close to one or the other.

[7]*Grok:* to fully understand; a term that first appeared in Robert A. Heinlein's 1961 science fiction novel, *Stranger in a Strange Land*, and was adopted by the computer programmer culture. —Eds.

[8]*Heuristic:* A structure to help simplify problem-solving, often informed by previous experience. —Eds.

---

[9]*RBI:* "Runs batted in" in baseball. This statistic is tracked per player and is incremented by one each time a run is scored as a result of the player's turn at bat, no matter who actually scores the run, provided it wasn't the result of an opponent error or the cause of a forced double play.

Any of these will result in the player stating that she is bored. In reality, some of these are boredom+frustration, and some are boredom+triumph, and so on. If your goal is to keep things fun (read as "keep the player learning"), boredom is always the signal to let you know you have failed.

The definition of a good game is therefore "one that teaches everything it has to offer before the player stops playing."

That's what games are, in the end. Teach- 20 ers. Fun is just another word for learning.[10]

---

[10]*Fun is another word for learning:* The theoretician of play Brian Sutton Smith called this just one of the "rhetorics of play." He identified several more in his book *The Ambiguity of Play*, including using games of chance to determine your fate, or using games to determine the fate of nations. We tend to regard almost all of the rhetorics he identifies as differing sources of learning and practice, and the balance (such as the two just mentioned) as more like alternative uses of games.

Games teach you how aspects of reality work, how to understand yourself, how to understand the actions of others, and how to imagine.

One wonders, then, why learning is so damn boring to so many people. It's almost certainly because the method of transmission is wrong. We praise good teachers by saying that they "make learning fun." Games are very good teachers . . . of something. The question is, what do they teach?

Either way, I have an answer for my late grandfather, and it looks like what I do fits right alongside the upstanding professions of my various aunts and uncles. Fireman, carpenter, and . . . teacher. ■

extending beyond the text

In her groundbreaking 2011 book *Reality Is Broken*, scholar Jane McGonigal argues that we need to harness the motivational aspects of video games in order to make the world a better place. She mentions that by 2011 players had invested nearly 50 billion hours (5.93 million years) into playing *World of Warcraft*. In this excerpt, she considers what motivates players to play for so long.

from Reality Is Broken

Jane McGonigal

What accounts for *World of Warcraft*'s unprecedented success? More than anything else, it's the feeling of "blissful productivity" that the game provokes. Blissful productivity is the sense of being deeply immersed in work that produces immediate and obvious results. The clearer the results, and the faster we achieve them, the more blissfully productive we feel. And no game gives us a better sense of getting work done than *WoW*.

Your primary job in *World of Warcraft* is self-improvement — a kind of work nearly all of us find naturally compelling. You have an *avatar*, and your job is to make that avatar better, stronger, and richer in as many different ways as possible: more experience, more abilities, stronger armor, more skills, more talent, and a bigger reputation.

Each of these improvable traits is displayed in your avatar profile, alongside a point value. You improve yourself by earning more points, which requires managing a constant work flow of quests, battles, and professional training. The more points you earn, the higher your level, and the higher your level, the more challenging work you unlock. This process is called "leveling up." The more challenging the work, the more motivated you are to do it, and the more points you earn . . . It's a *virtuous circle* of productivity. As Edward Castronova, who is a leading researcher of virtual worlds, puts it, "There is zero unemployment in *World of Warcraft*." The *WoW* work flow is famously designed so that there is always something to do, always different ways to improve your avatar. ■

What is McGonigal suggesting about motivation within the game and its application to the world outside of the game? Compare her theory of motivation to Koster's theory. On what points might McGonigal and Koster agree or disagree?

Understanding and Interpreting

1. Koster explains the likely origins of the word *fun*. How does he define the word *fun*?

2. What role does mastery of a game play in having fun, according to Koster?

3. How does Koster define boredom? What does he say the brain needs?

4. How do the images on pages 618 and 619 help illustrate Koster's definition of boredom?

5. According to Koster, what are the different effects of "sensory overload" and "sensory deprivation" on fun?

6. How does Koster find balance among fun, games, and learning? What commonalities does he suggest they have?

7. What is Koster's main idea about this topic? What does he want his readers to learn?

Analyzing Language, Style, and Structure

8. **Vocabulary in Context.** In paragraph 13, Koster mentions that the brain is "casting about trying to learn something." What does he mean by the word *casting* in this context?

9. Note the use of personal pronouns in the text and the inclusion of personal anecdotes as examples. How do these elements help Koster connect with his audience and explain his main idea?

10. Why might Koster have included the ages of his children in the image on page 617? What point about the tic-tac-toe game might he be emphasizing in this picture?

11. Koster compares his line of work with his relatives' jobs. Why does he make this comparison? How does it assist in communicating his main idea?

12. Koster states in paragraph 13 that "[i]f you put a person in a sensory deprivation chamber, he or she will get very unhappy very quickly" because "[t]he brain craves stimuli. At all times, the brain is casting about trying to learn something." How does pointing out this cause-and-effect relationship help him explain the connection between games and fun?

13. What is the intended effect of the allusion to Scylla and Charybdis in paragraph 15? How does the allusion connect to the ideas that follow it?

14. What is the effect in paragraph 17 of using a bulleted list to communicate the ways in which boredom might strike? How might this information have been received differently if Koster had presented it in paragraph form?

Topics for Composing

15. **Analysis.** Examine Koster's use of cause-and-effect as an expository strategy in this excerpt. How does using this strategy assist him in communicating his main idea?

16. **Argument.** In paragraph 10, Koster states that "with games, learning is the drug." Write an argument in which you agree with, disagree with, or qualify this statement. Provide examples from your own and others' experiences learning inside and outside of school, as well as additional research and evidence to support your reasoning.

17. **Connections.** Describe the activities you participate in or games you play to have fun. How do your examples of fun complement or contradict Koster's definition of fun?

18. **Speaking and Listening.** With a partner or small group, select a game that you can play together. It can be a board game, a game on your phone, a game on the computer, or some other game of your choosing, as long as it can be collaborative. As you play, discuss and evaluate the experience for elements of "fun" as described in Koster's article.

19. **Research.** Research ways in which gaming is transforming learning in other fields such as business, engineering, and medicine. In an essay or presentation, share your findings on how gaming has made strides to improve performance in these areas.

20. **Multimodal.** Create a plan for your own educational game. Your description should use images and text to explain the subject of the game, how players would engage with it, and what experiences the game would offer players. The game you describe might be a 3-D board game, online game, or app for a handheld device. You might need to conduct some research about games that are already on the market in your same field of interest. What would your game offer that these do not? Share your game design or prototype with an audience to get feedback.

How Native American Is Native American Enough?

Tommy Orange

Tommy Orange is an American writer and novelist born and raised in Oakland, California. He is an enrolled member of the Cheyenne and Arapaho Tribes of Oklahoma. His involvement in mental health outreach and storytelling projects with urban Native American communities influences much of his writing. His debut novel, *There There* (2018), is a collection of stories told from indigenous perspectives on urban life. It won the PEN/ Hemingway Award, the National Book Critics Circle John Leonard Prize, the Center for Fiction First Novel Prize, the American Book Award, and it was a finalist for the 2019 Pulitzer Prize. This piece, "How Native American Is Native American Enough," appeared on the *Buzzfeed* news website in 2018.

I'm not trying to be more Native than I am. Less white than I am. I'm trying to be honest about what I have to include. More often than not I've introduced myself as half Native. I know what people want to know as soon as I say that I'm Native: How much? I watch them wait to see what I'll say about it. They don't want to have to ask, and they know I don't want to have to say it.

They're testing me that way, so when the quiet between us becomes too much for me, I mumble out the side of my mouth: *From my dad's side.* The other half of me is apparent. My skin is light and I have freckles. I'm brown around the summer months and whiter in the winter. But I look like my dad if you saw me next to him. We have the same head and body. Same barrel chest, same nose. I reference my dad when I bring up being Native because I'm always doing it, qualifying my quantity. My amount. Where it comes from. And it's never enough. Too many claim great-grandparents. People are tired of hearing about great-grandparents, and great-great-grandparents even more so. It's too much math. Do I think we shouldn't include smaller fractions in the definition of what it means to be Native? I don't know. What I do know is that if I don't include the amount that I am, people assume less. So if asked whether or not I'm Native, I say yeah, and then, maybe sadly, maybe with assertion, maybe both, I say: half.

Those with less than half lose more than half the battle at the outset. One Native grandparent equals one-quarter blood quantum.[1] Should someone with this amount not be allowed to identify as Native, if their grandmother raised them? If they didn't even know that grandparent? What about great-great-grandparents? That's an eighth — if there's only one. What equations make sense to keep doing? How come math isn't taught with stakes? There are Natives enrolled in tribes with less than a 30 second's worth of Native blood in them — as in, less than 30 seconds after hearing about that kind of low-percentage ancestry, you'll probably have dismissed them as faking. You. Everyone.

There are full-blooded Native people raised by white families in white communities who don't know a thing about what it means to be Native or how to live in such a way as to be identified as such.

Walking between worlds is an old Native half-breed trope. I've never felt that I've walked in two worlds. The half-world feels more like being pulled apart and told to speak in singular terms — to pick a side. Actively identifying as a Native person if you have a valid claim is important work — an act against systematically designed erasure.

A half is not a number. Mathematically speaking, it doesn't count as a number. I never did well in math, but I understand fractions better now. When I was talking to my dad recently he said, "The way I got it worked out, it's like this, you're 3/64 short of being half Cheyenne."

That's about 4% less than half. According to a poll conducted by the Atlantic, 4% of Americans believe lizard people control politics. So I'm that amount of crazy Americans short of being half Native American.

But I'm not half, technically. I can't, for example, technically call myself biracial. I'd have to include 1/32 Sioux* blood and 1/64 German blood. I know this because my dad knows this. Growing up they called him *Vehoe.* It means white man. It also means spider, and references a mythological trickster figure. He told me I'm less than half. He didn't mean it in any way. My dad's an engineer. Exact math matters to him. As it does to all of us who have to figure out the kind of math involved in the equation: Enough Blood times Not Enough Blood equals eligibility or ineligibility for tribal enrollment and therefore citizenship in a sovereign nation.

But I am half Native — Cheyenne — from my dad. This half of me is a cutting fraction, which cuts if I rub up against it too firmly, if I slide my finger along its edge. Halving is the beginning

5

[1] *Blood quantum*: The term used to describe the amount of ancestral Native American blood a person possesses. —Eds.

*Most Lakota people I've met don't like to be called Sioux because it's the given white name, but when I asked my dad if we're Lakota or Dakota or Nakota, he just said, "The way my grandma told it to me, we're Sioux." There was an *And that's that* feel to the way he said it.

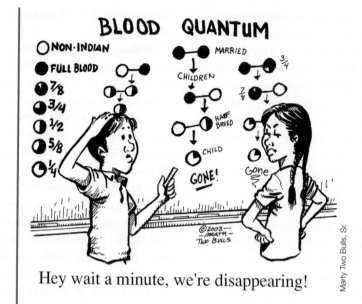

BLOOD QUANTUM

- ○ NON-INDIAN
- ● FULL BLOOD
- ◕ 7/8
- ◕ 3/4
- ◑ 1/2
- ◑ 5/8
- ◔ 1/4

MARRIED

CHILDREN

3/4

7/8

HALF BREED

CHILD

GONE!

Gone

Hey wait a minute, we're disappearing!

Marty Two Bulls, Sr.

Look at this cartoon by Oglala Lakota artist Marty Two Bulls, Sr. **What point is the cartoon making about a focus on blood quantum? How does it support or contradict the points that Orange makes in his article?**

of erasure. I'm doing it here again. Qualifying myself. Worried about what you will think of me.

I had a son in 2011. He'd be a quarter. The last in my line to be able to call himself Cheyenne, officially. He would have been. But he is an eighth Cheyenne. An eighth nothing.

We are very clear with our son at home. He knows he's Native. But what that will mean for him in 20 years, I don't know. And what it will mean for his children?

There is something you'd never know about if you weren't Native or had a close Native relation or friend. It's called the CDIB. Certificate of Degree of Indian Blood. This is a real, actual, official piece of paper with a record writ in fraction how much "Indian blood" I have. An official document about an amount of blood in my body. Which is a metaphor. But it isn't. It's real. We don't have enough blood to keep going

for our people. It stops. Ends. My son won't have a CDIB.

As it is, I am an enrolled member of the Cheyenne and Arapaho Tribes of Oklahoma. On my Certificate of Degree of Indian Blood it says I am one-quarter Cheyenne. One-fourth. The one indicates a person who did not die. Who was not killed. Whose blood has since thinned, and is more than probably on the way down that sloping line. To the stopping point.

My blood is not enough because my dad's dad never accepted him as a son. So he is half nothing, resulting in my quarter nothingness. This is how I became biracial and bi-nihilist. My son cannot be enrolled in our tribe as a result of being an eighth nothing, as a result of not having the proper documents to prove he has the required amount of blood in his body. It has to be funny that after spilling all that blood, our blood, our government, which first imposed

10

624

this blood law — that we keep such close track of it — make sure we don't lose its quantity, or quality, or, what are we talking about again? If my skin is white, that's because that's what my mom is. And if it isn't brown, it isn't because of what my dad isn't. I'm not half of two things or made up of fractions. I am made up of whole things, things that are things unto themselves. ■

Understanding and Interpreting

1. In paragraph 1, why does Orange hesitate when telling people that he has Native American ancestry? Why might he feel this way, based on what you learned from this piece?

2. What challenge does Orange establish in paragraphs 1 and 2 about people asking if he's Native American?

3. According to Orange in paragraph 4, what is the "important work" and why is it important?

4. What does Orange emphasize as the reason for knowing the exact math of his "blood quantum" in paragraph 7?

5. What is the Certificate of Degree of Indian Blood? Why is it important to Orange's main idea?

6. What concern does Orange seem to have for his son? What evidence from the text supports your response?

7. In your own words, state the main idea of Orange's article. What is he explaining to his readers?

Analyzing Language, Style, and Structure

8. **Vocabulary in Context.** In paragraph 2, Orange asks why "math isn't taught with stakes." What might he mean by the word *stakes* in this context? How does this term add to your understanding of his question about the use of math in his article?

9. How does Orange address his audience in the first paragraph? What assumptions, if any, does he make about his readers? How do you know, based on what he includes or does not include?

10. In paragraph 2, Orange includes a series of rhetorical questions. What is the intended effect of this stylistic choice? How does it help him to communicate a part of his main idea?

11. Reread paragraph 2 for Orange's use of syntax. What is the effect of his sentence structure choices, especially regarding the last three sentences?

12. How would you describe Orange's tone in paragraph 6? What evidence supports your observation? Why is this tone appropriate for his main idea?

13. Explain the metaphor in paragraph 8, in which Orange describes his Cheyenne half from his dad as "a cutting fraction." What does he mean, and what does this statement reveal about his attitude toward this kind of quantification of heritage?

14. Identify moments in which Orange uses cause-and-effect relationships. How does establishing these relationships help him to communicate his main idea?

15. Reread paragraphs 9–11. How does Orange's diction indicate his tone toward the topic of his son's blood quantum? Provide evidence from the text to support your observations.

16. In his concluding paragraph, what does Orange mean by becoming "biracial and bi–nihilist"? How do his language choices here reflect his attitude toward tracking his Native American heritage?

Topics for Composing

17. **Analysis.** Orange refers to fractions and math regularly in this piece. He is not using them solely to explain the concept of blood quantum, but rather to express his attitude toward it. Analyze how he uses mathematical terminology to establish his tone and to communicate his main idea. Support your response with evidence from the text.

18. **Argument.** Write a response in which you argue whether or not Orange answers the question he poses in the title, "How Native American Is Native American Enough?" Be sure to include evidence and examples to support your reasoning.

19. **Connections.** In what ways have you felt like you had to quantify, qualify, or otherwise explain who you are? The explanation could be related to your ancestry, as in Orange's experience, or your status as a diligent student, a strong singer, or a good athlete, for example. Write about a time when you felt compelled to explain to others why you identify yourself as having certain qualities or belonging to a certain group. In what ways was your experience similar to or different from what Orange describes?

20. **Speaking and Listening.** On your own, prepare for a discussion of the point Orange makes about "erasure" in his article. Then, with a group, try to come to consensus on the following questions: Is Orange's discussion of erasure unique to him or to Native Americans? If not, where else do you see erasure in our society, and how does Orange's writing help you understand its significance? Try to come to consensus about the definition and effects of this type of erasure.

21. **Research.** In paragraphs 11 and 12, Orange mentions that he has a Certificate of Degree of Indian Blood (CDIB) and is "an enrolled member of the Cheyenne and Arapaho Tribes of Oklahoma." Research who issues the Certificate of Degree of Indian Blood and how it is obtained. What differences are there for different tribes in obtaining membership?

22. **Research.** As of 2020, there were 574 federally recognized tribes across 34 states. Research a federally recognized tribe near you to learn more about the history of the tribe and describe the current status of its members and its land.

exposition / section two

from Earth without People

Alan Weisman

Alan Weisman (b. 1947) is an award-winning journalist and *New York Times* best seller who is well known for writing about humanity's influence on the environment. This article appeared in *Discover* magazine in 2005. It later became part of his book *The World without Us* (2007), which was named the top nonfiction book of 2007 by *Time* and *Entertainment Weekly* and was turned into a documentary on the History Channel, titled *Life after People*.

Tania/A3/contrasto/Redux

What would happen to our planet if the mighty hand of humanity simply disappeared?

Given the mounting toll of fouled oceans, overheated air, missing topsoil, and mass extinctions, we might sometimes wonder what our planet would be like if humans suddenly disappeared. Would Superfund sites revert to Gardens of Eden? Would the seas again fill with fish? Would our concrete cities crumble to dust from the force of tree roots, water, and weeds? How long would it take for our traces to vanish? And if we could answer such questions, would we be more in awe of the changes we have wrought, or of nature's resilience?

A good place to start searching for answers is in Korea, in the 155-mile-long, 2.5-mile-wide mountainous Demilitarized Zone, or DMZ, set up by the armistice ending the Korean War. Aside from rare military patrols or desperate souls fleeing North Korea, humans have barely set foot in the strip since 1953. Before that, for 5,000 years, the area was populated by rice farmers who carved the land into paddies. Today those paddies have become barely discernible, transformed into pockets of marsh, and the new occupants of these lands arrive as dazzling white squadrons of red-crowned cranes that glide over the bulrushes in perfect formation, touching down so lightly that they detonate no land mines. Next to whooping cranes, they are the rarest such birds on Earth. They winter in the DMZ alongside the endangered white-naped cranes, revered in Asia as sacred portents of peace.

If peace is ever declared, suburban Seoul, which has rolled ever northward in recent decades, is poised to invade such tantalizing real estate. On the other side, the North Koreans are building an industrial megapark. This has spurred an international coalition of scientists

627

called the DMZ Forum to try to consecrate the area for a peace park and nature preserve. Imagine it as "a Korean Gettysburg and Yosemite rolled together," says Harvard University biologist Edward O. Wilson, who believes that tourism revenues could trump those from agriculture or development.

If people were no longer present anywhere on Earth, a worldwide shakeout would follow. From zebra mussels to fire ants to crops to kudzu, exotics would battle with natives. In time, says Wilson, all human attempts to improve on nature, such as our painstakingly bred horses, would revert to their origins. If horses survived at all, they would devolve back to Przewalski's horse, the only true wild horse, still found in the Mongolian steppes. "The plants, crops, and animal species man has wrought by his own hand would be wiped out in a century or two," Wilson says. In a few thousand years, "the world would mostly look as it did before humanity came along—like a wilderness."

As serenely natural as the DMZ now is, it would be far different if people throughout Korea suddenly disappeared. The habitat would not revert to a truly natural state until the dams that now divert rivers to slake the needs of Seoul's more than 20 million inhabitants failed—a century or two after the humans had gone. But in the meantime, says Wilson, many creatures would flourish. Otters, Asiatic black bears, musk deer, and the nearly vanquished Amur leopard would spread into slopes reforested with young daimyo oak and bird cherry. The few Siberian tigers that still prowl the North Korean–Chinese borderlands would multiply and fan across Asia's temperate zones. "The wild carnivores would make short work of livestock," he says. "Few domestic animals would remain after a couple of hundred years. Dogs would go feral, but they wouldn't last long: They'd never be able to compete."

The new wilderness would consume cities, much as the jungle of northern Guatemala consumed the Mayan pyramids and megalopolises of overlapping city-states. From A.D. 800 to 900, a combination of drought and internecine warfare over dwindling farmland brought 2,000 years of civilization crashing down. Within 10 centuries, the jungle swallowed all.

Mayan communities alternated urban living with fields sheltered by forests, in contrast with

5

John Henshall/Alamy

This photo is of the Demilitarized Zone, or DMZ, located on the border of South Korea and North Korea. Despite its existence as a "neutral" zone between North and South Korea, the tense political relations between the two countries pose a direct contrast to its serenity.

To what extent does this image reflect Weisman's theories about what would happen if humans were to disappear?

today's paved cities, which are more like man-made deserts. However, it wouldn't take long for nature to undo even the likes of a New York City. Jameel Ahmad, civil engineering department chair at Cooper Union College in New York City, says repeated freezing and thawing common in months like March and November would split cement within a decade, allowing water to seep in. As it, too, froze and expanded, cracks would widen. Soon, weeds such as mustard and goosegrass would invade. With nobody to trample seedlings, New York's prolific exotic, the Chinese ailanthus tree, would take over. Within five years, says Dennis Stevenson, senior curator at the New York Botanical Garden, ailanthus roots would heave up sidewalks and split sewers.

That would exacerbate a problem that already plagues New York — rising groundwater. There's little soil to absorb it or vegetation to transpire it, and buildings block the sunlight that could evaporate it. With the power off, pumps that keep subways from flooding would be stilled. As water sluiced away soil beneath pavement, streets would crater.

Eric Sanderson of the Bronx Zoo Wildlife Conservation Society heads the Manhattan Project, a virtual re-creation of pre-1609 Manhattan. He says there were 30 to 40 streams in Manhattan when the Dutch first arrived. If New Yorkers disappeared, sewers would clog, some natural watercourses would reappear, and others would form. Within 20 years, the water-soaked steel columns that support the street above the East Side's subway tunnels would corrode and buckle, turning Lexington Avenue into a river.

New York's architecture isn't as flammable   10
as San Francisco's clapboard Victorians, but within 200 years, says Steven Clemants, vice president of the Brooklyn Botanic Garden, tons of leaf litter would overflow gutters as pioneer weeds gave way to colonizing native oaks and maples in city parks. A dry lightning strike, igniting decades of uncut, knee-high Central Park grass, would spread flames through town.

As lightning rods rusted away, roof fires would leap among buildings into paneled offices filled with paper. Meanwhile, native Virginia creeper and poison ivy would claw at walls covered with lichens, which thrive in the absence of air pollution. Wherever foundations failed and buildings tumbled, lime from crushed concrete

Julia Solis

This image is of the inside of an abandoned building in Detroit, Michigan.

Describe which elements of the image have succumbed to nature and which elements are still intact. How does the image confirm Weisman's predictions about the decomposition of man-made buildings under the encroachment of nature?

would raise soil pH, inviting buckthorn and birch. Black locust and autumn olive trees would fix nitrogen, allowing more goldenrods, sunflowers, and white snakeroot to move in along with apple trees, their seeds expelled by proliferating birds. Sweet carrots would quickly devolve to their wild form, unpalatable Queen Anne's lace, while broccoli, cabbage, brussels sprouts, and cauliflower would regress to the same unrecognizable broccoli ancestor.

Unless an earthquake strikes New York first, bridges spared yearly applications of road salt would last a few hundred years before their stays and bolts gave way (last to fall would be Hell Gate Arch, built for railroads and easily good for another thousand years). Coyotes would invade Central Park, and deer, bears, and finally wolves would follow. Ruins would echo the love song of frogs breeding in streams stocked with alewives, herring, and mussels dropped by seagulls. Missing, however, would be all fauna that have adapted to humans. The invincible cockroach, an insect that originated in the hot climes of Africa, would succumb in unheated buildings. Without garbage, rats would starve or serve as lunch for peregrine falcons and red-tailed hawks. Pigeons would genetically revert back to the rock doves from which they sprang.

It's unclear how long animals would suffer from the urban legacy of concentrated heavy metals. Over many centuries, plants would take these up, recycle, redeposit, and gradually dilute them. The time bombs left in petroleum tanks, chemical plants, power plants, and dry-cleaning plants might poison the earth beneath them for eons. One intriguing example is the former Rocky Mountain Arsenal next to Denver International Airport. There a chemical weapons plant produced mustard and nerve gas, incendiary bombs, napalm, and after World War II, pesticides. In 1984 it was considered by the arsenal commander to be the most contaminated spot in the United States. Today it is a national

wildlife refuge, home to bald eagles that feast on its prodigious prairie dog population.

However, it took more than $130 million and a lot of man-hours to drain and seal the arsenal's lake, in which ducks once died minutes after landing and the aluminum bottoms of boats sent to fetch their carcasses rotted within a month. In a world with no one left to bury the bad stuff, decaying chemical containers would slowly expose their lethal contents. Places like the Indian Point nuclear power plant, 35 miles north of Times Square, would dump radioactivity into the Hudson long after the lights went out.

Old stone buildings in Manhattan, such as Grand Central Station or the Metropolitan Museum of Art, would outlast every modern glass box, especially with no more acid rain to pock their marble. Still, at some point thousands of years hence, the last stone walls — perhaps chunks of St. Paul's Chapel on Wall Street, built in 1766 from Manhattan's own hard schist — would fall. Three times in the past 100,000 years, glaciers have scraped New York clean, and they'll do so again. The mature hardwood forest would be mowed down. On Staten Island, Fresh Kills's four giant mounds of trash would be flattened, their vast accumulation of stubborn PVC plastic and glass ground to powder. After the ice receded, an unnatural concentration of reddish metal — remnants of wiring and plumbing — would remain buried in layers. The next toolmaker to arrive or evolve might discover it and use it, but there would be nothing to indicate who had put it there.

Before humans appeared, an oriole could fly from the Mississippi to the Atlantic and never alight on anything other than a treetop. Unbroken forest blanketed Europe from the Urals to the English Channel. The last remaining fragment of that primeval European wilderness — half a million acres of woods straddling the border between Poland and Belarus, called the

15

Andrew Lichtenstein/Getty Images

In the time since Weisman wrote this article, the Fresh Kills landfill has been turned into a large park. This image shows children playing there.

How would you describe the scene in the photo? Is there anything in the photo that would indicate that this was once a landfill? What would Weisman say would happen to this landfill-turned-park once humans have disappeared?

Bialowieza Forest — provides another glimpse of how the world would look if we were gone. There, relic groves of huge ash and linden trees rise 138 feet above an understory of hornbeams, ferns, swamp alders, massive birches, and crockery-size fungi. Norway spruces, shaggy as Methuselah, stand even taller. Five-century-old oaks grow so immense that great spotted woodpeckers stuff whole spruce cones in their three-inch-deep bark furrows. The woods carry pygmy owl whistles, nutcracker croaks, and wolf howls. Fragrance wafts from eons of mulch.

High privilege accounts for such unbroken antiquity. During the 14th century, a Lithuanian duke declared it a royal hunting preserve. For centuries it stayed that way. Eventually, the forest was subsumed by Russia and in 1888 became the private domain of the czars. Occupying Germans took lumber and slaughtered game during World War I, but a pristine core was left intact, which in 1921 became a Polish national

park. Timber pillaging resumed briefly under the Soviets, but when the Nazis invaded, nature fanatic Hermann Göring decreed the entire preserve off limits. Then, following World War II, a reportedly drunken Josef Stalin agreed one evening in Warsaw to let Poland retain two-fifths of the forest.

To realize that all of Europe once looked like this is startling. Most unexpected of all is the sight of native bison. Just 600 remain in the wild, on both sides of an impassable iron curtain erected by the Soviets in 1980 along the border to thwart escapees to Poland's renegade Solidarity movement. Although wolves dig under it, and roe deer are believed to leap over it, the herd of the largest of Europe's mammals remains divided, and thus its gene pool. Belarus, which has not removed its statues of Lenin, has no specific plans to dismantle the fence. Unless it does, the bison may suffer genetic degradation, leaving them vulnerable to a disease that would wipe them out.

If the bison herd withers, they would join all the other extinct megafauna that even our total disappearance could never bring back. In a glass case in his laboratory, paleoecologist Paul S. Martin at the University of Arizona keeps a lump of dried dung he found in a Grand Canyon cave, left by a sloth weighing 200 pounds. That would have made it the smallest of several North American ground sloth species present when humans first appeared on this continent. The largest was as big as an elephant and lumbered around by the thousands in the woodlands and deserts of today's United States. What we call pristine today, Martin says, is a poor reflection of what would be here if *Homo sapiens* had never evolved.

"America would have three times as many 20 species of animals over 1,000 pounds as Africa does today," he says. An amazing megafaunal menagerie roamed the region: Giant armadillos resembling armor-plated autos; bears twice the size of grizzlies; the hoofed, herbivorous toxodon, big as a rhinoceros; and saber-toothed tigers. A dozen species of horses were here, as well as the camel-like litoptern, giant beavers, giant peccaries, woolly rhinos, mammoths, and mastodons. Climate change and imported disease may have killed them, but most paleontologists accept the theory Martin advocates: "When people got out of Africa and Asia and reached other parts of the world, all hell broke loose." He is convinced that people were responsible for the mass extinctions because they commenced with human arrival everywhere: first, in Australia 60,000 years ago, then mainland America 13,000 years ago, followed by the Caribbean islands 6,000 years ago, and Madagascar 2,000 years ago.

Yet one place on Earth did manage to elude the intercontinental holocaust: the oceans. Dolphins and whales escaped for the simple reason that prehistoric people could not hunt enough giant marine mammals to have a major impact on the population. "At least a dozen species in the ocean Columbus sailed were bigger than his biggest ship," says marine paleoecologist Jeremy Jackson of the Smithsonian Tropical Research Institute in Panama. "Not only mammals — the sea off Cuba was so thick with 1,000-pound green turtles that his boats practically ran aground on them." This was a world where ships collided with schools of whales and where sharks were so abundant they would swim up rivers to prey on cattle. Reefs swarmed with 800-pound goliath grouper, not just today's puny aquarium species. Cod could be fished from the sea in baskets. Oysters filtered all the water in Chesapeake Bay every five days. The planet's shores teemed with millions of manatees, seals, and walrus.

Within the past century, however, humans have flattened the coral reefs on the continental shelves and scraped the sea grass beds bare; a dead zone bigger than New Jersey grows at the mouth of the Mississippi; all the world's cod fisheries have collapsed. What Pleistocene humans did in 1,500 years to terrestrial life, modern man has done in mere decades to the oceans — "almost," Jackson says. Despite mechanized overharvesting, satellite fish tracking, and prolonged butchery of sea mammals, the ocean is still bigger than we are. "It's not like the land," he says. "The great majority of sea species are badly depleted, but they still exist. If people actually went away, most could recover."

Even if global warming or ultraviolet radiation bleaches the Great Barrier Reef to death, Jackson says, "it's only 7,000 years old. New reefs have had to form before. It's not like the world is a constant place." Without people, most excess industrial carbon dioxide would dissipate within 200 years, cooling the atmosphere. With no further chlorine and bromine leaking skyward, within decades the ozone layer would replenish, and ultraviolet damage would subside. Eventually, heavy metals and toxins would flush through the system; a few intractable PCBs might take a millennium.

During that same span, every dam on Earth would silt up and spill over. Rivers would again carry nutrients seaward, where most life would be, as it was long before vertebrates crawled onto the shore. Eventually, that would happen again. The world would start over.

The Wilds of New York

If humans were to vanish from New York, how soon would nature take over? Scientists predict that within . . . 25

10 years: Sidewalks crack and weeds invade. Hawks and falcons flourish, as do feral cats and dogs. The rat population, deprived of human garbage, crashes. Cockroaches, which thrive in warm buildings, disappear. Cultivated carrots, cabbages, broccoli, and brussels sprouts revert to their wild ancestors.

20 years: Water-soaked steel columns supporting subway tunnels corrode and buckle. Bears and wolves invade Central Park.

50 years: Concrete chunks tumble from buildings, whose steel foundations begin to crumble. Indian Point nuclear reactors leak radioactivity into the Hudson River.

100 years: Oaks and maples re-cover the land.

300 years: Most bridges collapse. 30

1,000 years: Hell Gate Bridge, built to bring the railroad across the East River, finally falls.

10,000 years: Indian Point nuclear reactors continue to leak radioactivity into the Hudson River.

20,000 years: Glaciers move relentlessly across the island of Manhattan and its environs, scraping the landscape clean. ■

extending beyond the text

Some scientists believe that we are currently in the midst of the Sixth Mass Extinction crisis that the Earth has faced, with the first five taking place during prehistory, such as when the dinosaurs suddenly died out. Research documenting the current event was published in 2021 in the journal *Biological Reviews*, and was referenced in the *University of Hawai'i News*:

> "Drastically increased rates of species extinctions and declining abundances of many animal and plant populations are well documented," [says Robert Cowie, who] estimated that since the year 1500, Earth could already have lost between 7.5% and 13% of the two million known species — a staggering 150,000 to 260,000 species.

Since most of these species are not mammals, but small invertebrates like slugs, much of this extinction has gone unnoticed.

What additional information would you want to investigate to determine for yourself that we are in the middle of a mass extinction event? How would the results of the research included here support or contradict what Weisman is suggesting in his piece?

Understanding and Interpreting

1. Why does Weisman begin to "start searching for answers" in Korea? What importance does the Demilitarized Zone (DMZ) have?

2. Reread paragraphs 4 and 5. What are some ways Weisman predicts that animals would respond to the absence of humanity?

3. In paragraph 6, Weisman claims, "The new wilderness would consume cities" and he spends the next several paragraphs explaining that statement. Summarize the effects he describes and identify two or three of his most detailed descriptions of the effects on cities.

4. What examples does Weisman offer to support the idea that the disappearance of humans might have profound effects on plants or animals that have adapted to human existence? What purpose might these examples serve?

5. What does Weisman mean when he writes, "High privilege accounts for such unbroken antiquity" (par. 17)? What details does he include in the rest of that paragraph to explain that statement?

6. Reread paragraphs 21–24. What does Weisman say helped oceanic animals "elude the intercontinental holocaust" in the past? What does he say will be the fate of oceanic life without humans? What conclusion does he draw as a result of that predicted fate?

7. Weisman includes a timeline of scientific predictions for New York at the end of his article. What purpose does including the timeline serve?

8. Most of what Weisman says would happen to Earth without humans are hypothesized future situations or effects. What lends credibility to these imagined consequences? How does he support his ideas about what might happen? What specific facts and information does he include?

Analyzing Language, Style, and Structure

9. **Vocabulary in Context.** In paragraph 17, Weisman writes that the Bialowieza Forest, located between Poland and Belarus, is the result of "high privilege." What does Weisman mean by *privilege* in this context?

10. Reread the rhetorical questions in the opening paragraph. What is the effect of beginning the piece with these questions?

11. How does Weisman incorporate cause-and-effect relationships in paragraphs 6 and 7 to substantiate his observations about an Earth without people? How does this expository strategy assist him in communicating his main idea?

12. In paragraph 7, how does Weisman's language (diction and imagery) help to illustrate his main idea?

13. In paragraph 13, Weisman refers to the "urban legacy of concentrated heavy metals." What connotative association does the word *legacy* have in the way it is used here?

14. Analyze Weisman's use of verbs in paragraphs 21–24. How does his use of vivid verbs in these paragraphs reveal his tone toward the subject?

15. In paragraph 16, Weisman compares the Norway spruce trees to the biblical character Methuselah. Why might Weisman mention Methuselah in this simile? Conduct some research to help you with your response.

16. Look at how Weisman fluctuates between what might happen in the future with jumps to historical events and observations on present conditions. How does balancing the three affect the reader's understanding of the main idea?

Topics for Composing

17. **Analysis.** How would you describe the tone that Weisman takes toward the future of the Earth? Pessimistic? Hopeful? Foreboding? Joyful? Analyze how his diction and syntax create this tone and how this tone contributes to his main idea.

18. **Argument.** You've probably heard the saying, "You don't know what you have until it's gone." The premise of Weisman's book is that we don't know the impact we're having until people are removed from the equation — that our world is threatened if we don't change our behavior or disappear completely. Write an argument in which you contend that Weisman has or has not effectively called for change. Remember to provide evidence from the text to support your response.

19. **Connections.** Weisman's depiction of a world without people is not unlike the settings of some dystopian books, movies, or video games that you've likely encountered. Write a piece in which you reflect on similarities and differences between the world Weisman describes and the world depicted in a text you're familiar with.

20. **Research.** Investigate a specific example of humanity's impact on the environment, either positive or negative. If positive, how do we sustain the impact? If negative, what solutions are being proposed?

21. **Creative Writing.** Write a short story about what the world would be like without a particular *something*: without trees, animals, fast food, books, money, or even gravity. Try to illustrate what might happen without this particular something. Or, write a short story in which you imagine that you are one of only a few people left in the world that Weisman describes. Try to describe your surroundings and what would you do for survival.

from Quiet: The Power of Introverts in a World That Can't Stop Talking

Susan Cain

Susan Cain (b. 1968) is a former corporate lawyer turned author and speaker who shares with audiences the value and power of introverts. Her top-selling book, *Quiet: The Power of Introverts in a World That Can't Stop Talking* (2012), from which this excerpt was taken, won multiple awards, was the subject of a *Time* magazine cover story, and has been translated into over 30 different languages.

Kimberly White/Getty Images Entertainment/ Getty Images

Montgomery, Alabama. December 1, 1955. Early evening. A public bus pulls to a stop and a sensibly dressed woman in her forties gets on. She carries herself erectly, despite having spent the day bent over an ironing board in a dingy basement tailor shop at the Montgomery Fair department store. Her feet are swollen, her shoulders ache. She sits in the first row of the Colored section and watches quietly as the bus fills with riders. Until the driver orders her to give her seat to a white passenger.

The woman utters a single word that ignites one of the most important civil rights protests of the twentieth century, one word that helps America find its better self.

The word is "No."

The driver threatens to have her arrested.

"You may do that," says Rosa Parks.   5

A police officer arrives. He asks Parks why she won't move.

"Why do you all push us around?" she answers simply.

"I don't know," he says. "But the law is the law, and you're under arrest."

On the afternoon of her trial and conviction for disorderly conduct, the Montgomery Improvement Association holds a rally for Parks at the Holt Street Baptist Church, in the poorest section of town. Five thousand gather to support Parks's lonely act of courage. They squeeze inside the church until its pews can hold no more. The rest wait patiently outside, listening through loudspeakers. The Reverend Martin Luther King Jr. addresses the crowd. "There comes a time that people get tired of being trampled over by the iron feet of oppression," he tells them. "There comes a time when people get tired of being pushed out of the glittering sunlight of life's July and left standing amidst the piercing chill of an Alpine November."

He praises Parks's bravery and hugs her. She 10 stands silently, her mere presence enough to galvanize the crowd. The association launches a citywide bus boycott that lasts 381 days. The people trudge miles to work. They carpool with strangers. They change the course of American history.

I had always imagined Rosa Parks as a stately woman with a bold temperament, someone who could easily stand up to a busload of glowering passengers. But when she died in 2005 at the age of ninety-two, the flood of obituaries recalled her as soft-spoken, sweet, and small in stature. They said she was "timid and shy" but had "the courage of a lion." They were full of phrases like "radical humility" and "quiet fortitude." What does it mean to be quiet *and* have fortitude? these descriptions asked implicitly. How could you be shy *and* courageous?

These are pictures of two of the most significant leaders of the Civil Rights Movement of the 1950s and 60s. On the left, Rosa Parks sits in the front of a bus in Montgomery, Alabama, after the Supreme Court ruled segregation illegal on the city bus system. She was arrested on December 1, 1955, for refusing to give up her seat in the front of a bus in Montgomery, which set off a successful boycott of the city buses. In the photo on the right, Martin Luther King Jr. waves to the crowd of more than 200,000 people gathered on the Mall during the March on Washington in 1963, after delivering his "I Have a Dream" speech.

What aspects of these images give you clues to Parks's introverted tendencies and King's extroverted ones? How might these scenes look different if their personality traits were reversed?

Parks herself seemed aware of this paradox, calling her autobiography *Quiet Strength* — a title that challenges us to question our assumptions. Why *shouldn't* quiet be strong? And what else can quiet do that we don't give it credit for?

Our lives are shaped as profoundly by personality as by gender or race. And the single most important aspect of personality — the "north and south of temperament," as one scientist puts it — is where we fall on the introvert-extrovert spectrum. Our place on this continuum influences our choice of friends and mates, and how we make conversation, resolve differences, and show love. It affects the careers we choose and whether or not we succeed at them. It governs how likely we are to exercise, commit adultery, function well without sleep, learn from our mistakes, place big bets in the stock market, delay gratification, be a good leader, and ask "what if."[1] It's reflected in our brain pathways, neurotransmitters, and remote corners of our nervous systems. Today introversion and extroversion are two of the most exhaustively researched subjects in personality psychology, arousing the curiosity of hundreds of scientists.

These researchers have made exciting discoveries aided by the latest technology, but they're part of a long and storied tradition. Poets and philosophers have been thinking about introverts and extroverts since the dawn of recorded time. Both personality types appear in the Bible and in the writings of Greek and Roman physicians, and some evolutionary psychologists say that the history of these types reaches back even farther than that: the animal kingdom also boasts "introverts" and "extroverts," as we'll see, from fruit flies to pumpkinseed fish to rhesus monkeys. As with other complementary pairings — masculinity and femininity, East and West, liberal and conservative — humanity would be unrecognizable, and vastly diminished, without both personality styles.

Take the partnership of Rosa Parks and Martin Luther King Jr.: a formidable orator refusing to give up his seat on a segregated bus wouldn't have had the same effect as a modest woman who'd clearly prefer to keep silent but for the exigencies of the situation. And Parks didn't have the stuff to thrill a crowd if she'd tried to stand up and announce that she had a dream. But with King's help, she didn't have to.

Yet today we make room for a remarkably narrow range of personality styles. We're told that to be great is to be bold, to be happy is to be sociable. We see ourselves as a nation of extroverts — which means that we've lost sight of who we really are. Depending on which study you consult, one third to one half of Americans are introverts — in other words, *one out of every two or three people you know*. (Given that the United States is among the most extroverted of nations, the number must be at least as high in other parts of the world.) If you're not an introvert yourself, you are surely raising, managing, married to, or coupled with one.

If these statistics surprise you, that's probably because so many people pretend to be extroverts. Closet introverts pass undetected on playgrounds, in high school locker rooms, and in the corridors of corporate America. Some fool even themselves, until some life event — a layoff, an empty nest, an inheritance that frees them to spend time as they like — jolts them into taking stock of their true natures. You have only to raise the subject of this book with your friends and acquaintances to find that the most unlikely people consider themselves introverts.

It makes sense that so many introverts hide even from themselves. We live with a value system that I call the Extrovert Ideal — the omnipresent belief that the ideal self is gregarious, alpha, and comfortable in the spotlight. The

15

---

[1] Answer key: exercise: extroverts; commit adultery: extroverts; function well without sleep: introverts; learn from our mistakes: introverts; place big bets: extroverts; delay gratification: introverts; be a good leader: in some cases introverts, in other cases extroverts, depending on the type of leadership called for; ask "what if": introverts.

EXTROVERTS MAY RULE THE WORLD...

BUT INTROVERTS CREATE WORLDS!

Maureen Marzi Wilson/Introvert Doodles

Does this image provide too simplistic a view of extroverts and introverts, or does it accurately depict Cain's main point?

archetypal extrovert prefers action to contemplation, risk-taking to heed-taking, certainty to doubt. He favors quick decisions, even at the risk of being wrong. She works well in teams and socializes in groups. We like to think that we value individuality, but all too often we admire one *type* of individual — the kind who's comfortable "putting himself out there." Sure, we allow technologically gifted loners who launch companies in garages to have any personality they please, but they are the exceptions, not the rule, and our tolerance extends mainly to those who get fabulously wealthy or hold the promise of doing so.

Introversion — along with its cousins sensitivity, seriousness, and shyness — is now a second-class personality trait, somewhere between a disappointment and a pathology. Introverts living under the Extrovert Ideal are like women in a man's world, discounted because of a trait that goes to the core of who they are. Extroversion is an enormously

appealing personality style, but we've turned it into an oppressive standard to which most of us feel we must conform.

The Extrovert Ideal has been documented in many studies, though this research has never been grouped under a single name. Talkative people, for example, are rated as smarter, better-looking, more interesting, and more desirable as friends. Velocity of speech counts as well as volume: we rank fast talkers as more competent and likable than slow ones. The same dynamics apply in groups, where research shows that the voluble are considered smarter than the reticent — even though there's zero correlation between the gift of gab and good ideas. Even the word *introvert* is stigmatized — one informal study, by psychologist Laurie Helgoe, found that introverts described their own physical appearance in vivid language ("green-blue eyes," "exotic," "high cheekbones"), but when asked to describe generic introverts they drew a bland

20

and distasteful picture ("ungainly," "neutral colors," "skin problems").

But we make a grave mistake to embrace the Extrovert Ideal so unthinkingly. Some of our greatest ideas, art, and inventions — from the theory of evolution to van Gogh's sunflowers to the personal computer — came from quiet and cerebral people who knew how to tune in to their inner worlds and the treasures to be found there. Without introverts, the world would be devoid of

> the theory of gravity
> the theory of relativity
> W. B. Yeats's "The Second Coming"
> Chopin's nocturnes
> Proust's *In Search of Lost Time*
> Peter Pan
> Orwell's *Nineteen Eighty-Four* and *Animal Farm*
> The Cat in the Hat
> Charlie Brown
> *Schindler's List, E. T.,* and *Close Encounters of the Third Kind*
> Google
> Harry Potter[2]

When I started writing this book, the first thing I wanted to find out was precisely how researchers define introversion and extroversion. I knew that in 1921 the influential psychologist Carl Jung had published a bombshell of a book, *Psychological Types,* popularizing the terms *introvert* and *extrovert* as the central building blocks of personality. Introverts are drawn to the inner world of thought and feeling, said Jung, extroverts to the external life of people and activities. Introverts focus on the meaning they make of the events swirling around them; extroverts plunge into the events themselves. Introverts

recharge their batteries by being alone; extroverts need to recharge when they don't socialize enough. If you've ever taken a Myers-Briggs personality test, which is based on Jung's thinking and used by the majority of universities and Fortune 100 companies, then you may already be familiar with these ideas.

But what do contemporary researchers have to say? I soon discovered that there is no all-purpose definition of introversion or extroversion; these are not unitary categories, like "curly-haired" or "sixteen-year-old," in which everyone can agree on who qualifies for inclusion. For example, adherents of the Big Five school of personality psychology (which argues that human personality can be boiled down to five primary traits) define introversion not in terms of a rich inner life but as a lack of qualities such as assertiveness and sociability. There are almost as many definitions of *introvert* and *extrovert* as there are personality psychologists, who spend a great deal of time arguing over which meaning is most accurate. Some think that Jung's ideas are outdated; others swear that he's the only one who got it right.

Still, today's psychologists tend to agree on several important points: for example, that introverts and extroverts differ in the level of outside stimulation that they need to function well. Introverts feel "just right" with less stimulation, as when they sip wine with a close friend, solve a crossword puzzle, or read a book. Extroverts enjoy the extra bang that comes from activities like meeting new people, skiing slippery slopes, and cranking up the stereo. "Other people are very arousing," says the personality psychologist David Winter, explaining why your typical introvert would rather spend her vacation reading on the beach than partying on a cruise ship. "They arouse threat, fear, flight, and love. A hundred people are very stimulating compared to a hundred books or a hundred grains of sand."

---

[2]Sir Isaac Newton, Albert Einstein, W. B. Yeats, Frederic Chopin, Marcel Proust, J. M. Barrie, George Orwell, Theodor Geisel (Dr. Seuss), Charles Schulz, Steven Spielberg, Larry Page, J. K. Rowling.

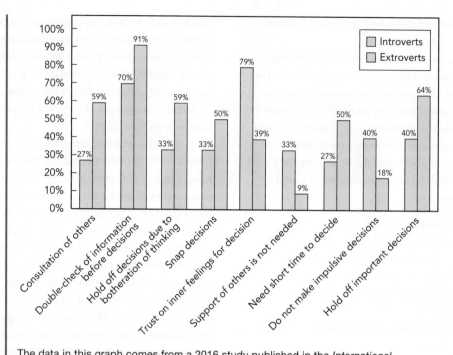

The data in this graph comes from a 2016 study published in the *International Journal of Research in Medical Sciences*. The study examined the influence of extroversion and introversion on decision-making and the connections to personality characteristics.

What conclusions can you draw from this data about the connections between personality characteristics and extroversion/introversion? Taking into account your own level of extroversion or introversion, where does your own decision-making fall on this graph? How would Cain likely use this graph in her piece to communicate her main idea?

Many psychologists would also agree that introverts and extroverts work differently. Extroverts tend to tackle assignments quickly. They make fast (sometimes rash) decisions, and are comfortable multitasking and risk-taking. They enjoy "the thrill of the chase" for rewards like money and status.

Introverts often work more slowly and deliberately. They like to focus on one task at a time and can have mighty powers of concentration. They're relatively immune to the lures of wealth and fame.

25 Our personalities also shape our social styles. Extroverts are the people who will add life to your dinner party and laugh generously at your jokes. They tend to be assertive, dominant, and in great need of company. Extroverts think out loud and on their feet; they prefer talking to listening, rarely find themselves at a loss for words, and occasionally blurt out things they never meant to say. They're comfortable with conflict, but not with solitude.

Introverts, in contrast, may have strong social skills and enjoy parties and business meetings, but after a while wish they were home in their pajamas. They prefer to devote their social energies to close friends, colleagues, and family. They listen more than they talk, think before they speak, and often feel as if they express themselves better in writing than in conversation. They tend to dislike conflict. Many have a horror of small talk, but enjoy deep discussions.

A few things introverts are not: The word *introvert* is not a synonym for hermit or misanthrope. Introverts *can* be these things, but most are perfectly friendly. One of the most humane phrases in the English language — "Only connect!" — was written by the distinctly introverted E. M. Forster in a novel exploring the question of how to achieve "human love at its height."

Nor are introverts necessarily shy. Shyness 30 is the fear of social disapproval or humiliation, while introversion is a preference for environments that are not overstimulating. Shyness is inherently painful; introversion is not. One reason that people confuse the two concepts is that they sometimes overlap (though psychologists debate to what degree). Some psychologists map the two tendencies on vertical and horizontal axes, with the introvert-extrovert spectrum on the horizontal axis, and the anxious-stable spectrum on the vertical. With this model, you end up with four quadrants of personality types: calm extroverts, anxious (or impulsive) extroverts, calm introverts, and anxious introverts. In other words, you can be a shy extrovert, like Barbra Streisand, who has a larger-than-life personality and paralyzing stage fright; or a non-shy introvert, like Bill Gates, who by all accounts keeps to himself but is unfazed by the opinions of others.

You can also, of course, be both shy *and* an introvert: T. S. Eliot was a famously private soul who wrote in "The Waste Land" that he could "show you fear in a handful of dust." Many shy

people turn inward, partly as a refuge from the socializing that causes them such anxiety. And many introverts are shy, partly as a result of receiving the message that there's something wrong with their preference for reflection, and partly because their physiologies, as we'll see, compel them to withdraw from high-stimulation environments.

But for all their differences, shyness and introversion have in common something profound. The mental state of a shy extrovert sitting quietly in a business meeting may be very different from that of a calm introvert — the shy person is afraid to speak up, while the introvert is simply overstimulated — but to the outside world, the two appear to be the same. This can give both types insight into how our reverence for alpha status blinds us to things that are good and smart and wise. For very different reasons, shy and introverted people might choose to spend their days in behind-the-scenes pursuits like inventing, or researching, or holding the hands of the gravely ill — or in leadership positions they execute with quiet competence. These are not alpha roles, but the people who play them are role models all the same.

If you're still not sure where you fall on the introvert-extrovert spectrum, you can assess yourself here. Answer each question "true" or "false," choosing the answer that applies to you more often than not.[3]

1. ___ I prefer one-on-one conversations to group activities.
2. ___ I often prefer to express myself in writing.
3. ___ I enjoy solitude.
4. ___ I seem to care less than my peers about wealth, fame, and status.

---

[3]This is an informal quiz, not a scientifically validated personality test. The questions were formulated based on characteristics of introversion often accepted by contemporary researchers.

5. ___ I dislike small talk, but I enjoy talking in depth about topics that matter to me.

6. ___ People tell me that I'm a good listener.

7. ___ I'm not a big risk-taker.

8. ___ I enjoy work that allows me to "dive in" with few interruptions.

9. ___ I like to celebrate birthdays on a small scale, with only one or two close friends or family members.

10. ___ People describe me as "soft-spoken" or "mellow."

11. ___ I prefer not to show or discuss my work with others until it's finished.

12. ___ I dislike conflict.

13. ___ I do my best work on my own.

14. ___ I tend to think before I speak.

15. ___ I feel drained after being out and about, even if I've enjoyed myself.

16. ___ I often let calls go through to voice mail.

17. ___ If I had to choose, I'd prefer a weekend with absolutely nothing to do to one with too many things scheduled.

18. ___ I don't enjoy multitasking.

19. ___ I can concentrate easily.

20. ___ In classroom situations, I prefer lectures to seminars.

The more often you answered "true," the more introverted you probably are. If you found yourself with a roughly equal number of "true" and "false" answers, then you may be an ambivert — yes, there really is such a word.

But even if you answered every single question as an introvert or extrovert, that doesn't mean that your behavior is predictable across all circumstances. We can't say that

every introvert is a bookworm or every extrovert wears lampshades at parties any more than we can say that every woman is a natural consensus-builder and every man loves contact sports. As Jung felicitously put it, "There is no such thing as a pure extrovert or a pure introvert. Such a man would be in the lunatic asylum."

This is partly because we are all gloriously complex individuals, but also because there are so many different *kinds* of introverts and extroverts. Introversion and extroversion interact with our other personality traits and personal histories, producing wildly different kinds of people. So if you're an artistic American guy whose father wished you'd try out for the football team like your rough-and-tumble brothers, you'll be a very different kind of introvert from, say, a Finnish businesswoman whose parents were lighthouse keepers. (Finland is a famously introverted nation. Finnish joke: How can you tell if a Finn likes you? He's staring at your shoes instead of his own.)

Many introverts are also "highly sensitive," which sounds poetic, but is actually a technical term in psychology. If you are a sensitive sort, then you're more apt than the average person to feel pleasantly overwhelmed by Beethoven's "Moonlight Sonata" or a well-turned phrase or an act of extraordinary kindness. You may be quicker than others to feel sickened by violence and ugliness, and you likely have a very strong conscience. When you were a child you were probably called "shy," and to this day feel nervous when you're being evaluated, for example when giving a speech or on a first date. Later we'll examine why this seemingly unrelated collection of attributes tends to belong to the same person and why this person is often introverted. (No one knows exactly how many introverts are highly sensitive, but we know that 70 percent of sensitives are introverts, and the

35

other 30 percent tend to report needing a lot of "down time.")

All of this complexity means that not everything you read in *Quiet* will apply to you, even if you consider yourself a true-blue introvert.

For one thing, we'll spend some time talking about shyness and sensitivity, while you might have neither of these traits. That's OK. Take what applies to you, and use the rest to improve your relationships with others. ∎

Understanding and Interpreting

1. What effect does Rosa Parks's story have at the beginning of Cain's excerpt? What point does Parks's story emphasize?

2. Cain asks in paragraph 12, "And what else can quiet do that we don't give it credit for?" What evidence does Cain include to answer this question later in the text?

3. How does Cain define what she calls the *Extrovert Ideal* in paragraph 18?

4. Which characteristics outlined in paragraphs 18–20 does Cain associate with extroverted and introverted personalities?

5. What point does Cain establish about the definition of introverts in paragraph 23? How does knowing what "researchers have to say" relate to that definition?

6. What important points does Cain outline from paragraph 24 to paragraph 27? How do these points assist her in communicating her main idea?

7. What does Cain say that introverts *are not* in paragraph 29? Why is this definition essential to Cain's main idea?

8. Why does Cain emphasize the differences and commonalities between shy people and introverts in paragraphs 30–32?

9. Who might be her intended audience? How do you know? What does she include in her piece to appeal to that audience?

Analyzing Language, Style, and Structure

10. **Vocabulary in Context.** In paragraph 17, Cain mentions "closet introverts." What does she mean by the word *closet* in this context?

11. What is the effect of introducing the topic with a historical narrative, from paragraph 1 to paragraph 12?

12. What point does Cain make in paragraph 14 by including a brief history of inquiry into personality types? How does the example in paragraph 15 further support that point?

13. In paragraph 21, Cain includes a list of influential scientific and literary creations that wouldn't exist without introverts. What effect is created by leaving out most of the names of these introverts and instead focusing on what they created?

14. How do the cause-and-effect relationships Cain outlines in paragraphs 27 and 28 clarify the definitions of introverts and extroverts and assist her in explaining her main idea?

15. What is the purpose for including the personality inventory at the end of the selection? What does Cain hope the reader takes away?

Topics for Composing

16. **Analysis.** Throughout the excerpt, Cain incorporates many examples to emphasize the characteristics of extroverts and introverts. Write an analysis about the effectiveness of the examples that Cain includes and how they further clarify the main idea for her audience.

17. **Argument.** Argue whether or not understanding the personality traits of another person will help improve our relationship with that person. How important is it to understand someone else's personality?

18. **Argument.** Does Cain seem to value one personality type over the other in her piece? Write an argument explaining why you do or do not think so, using evidence from the text to support your position.

19. **Connections.** Take the personality quiz that Cain provides on pages 641–642. Do your results identify you as an introvert, an extrovert, or an ambivert? Do you agree with the results? Why or why not?

20. **Speaking and Listening.** Partner with someone in your class who is a self-described opposite of your personality. For example, if you're a self-described introvert, pair with someone who identifies as an extrovert. Once you've found a partner, discuss the challenges that introverts and extroverts feel they face in school, based on your experiences. Reflect with each other on how the conversation went. Do your behaviors reflect those mentioned in Cain's text? Did anything about your conversation with the other person surprise you? Explain why or why not.

21. **Research.** In her piece, Cain briefly mentions the term *ambivert*, which is used to describe someone who is equal parts introvert and extrovert. Conduct research on this concept and explain how common this personality type is and what benefits and challenges ambiverts might face, compared to others.

22. **Multimodal.** In paragraph 30, Cain explains that some psychologists represent the personality spectrum as quadrants on *x-y* axes. Conduct a study or survey in your classroom or across your school to find out where most students or faculty lie on the spectrum. Present your findings in a graph or a chart with ideas from Cain's piece to help explain your findings.

Peculiar Benefits

Roxane Gay

Roxane Gay (b. 1974) is an American writer and professor of English whose books include *Bad Feminist* (2014), *Difficult Women* (2017), and her memoir, *Hunger: A Memoir of (My) Body* (2017). In addition to her books, Gay is involved in numerous film and television projects and is the author of *Black Panther: World of Wakanda* (2017) for Marvel. She is also a contributing opinion writer for the *New York Times* and an essay editor for *The Rumpus*, in which "Peculiar Benefits" (2012) appeared.

When I was young, my parents took our family to Haiti during the summers. For them, it was a homecoming. For my brothers and me it was an adventure, sometimes, a chore, and always a necessary education on privilege and the grace of an American passport. Until visiting Haiti, I had no idea what poverty really was or the difference between relative and absolute poverty. To see poverty so plainly and pervasively left a mark on me.

To this day, I remember my first visit, and how at every intersection, men and women, shiny with sweat, would mob our car, their skinny arms stretched out, hoping for a few gourdes or American dollars. I saw the sprawling slums, the shanties housing entire families, the trash piled in the streets, and then, the gorgeous beach, and the young men in uniforms who brought us Coca Cola in glass bottles and made us hats and boats out of palm fronds. It was hard for a child who grew up on cul-de-sacs to begin to grasp the contrast between such inescapable poverty alongside almost repulsive luxury and then, the United States, a mere eight hundred miles away, with its gleaming cities rising out of the landscape, and the well-maintained inter-states stretching across the country, the running water and the electricity. It wasn't until many, many years later that I realized my education on privilege began long before I could appreciate it in any meaningful way.

Privilege is a right or immunity granted as a peculiar benefit, advantage, or favor. There is racial privilege, gender (and identity) privilege, heterosexual privilege, economic privilege, able-bodied privilege, educational privilege, religious privilege and the list goes on and on. At some point, you have to surrender to the kinds of privilege you hold because everyone has something someone else doesn't.

The problem is, we talk about privilege with such alarming frequency and in such empty ways, we have diluted the word's meaning. When people wield the word *privilege* it tends to fall on deaf ears because we hear that word so damn much the word has become white noise.

One of the hardest things I've ever had to do is accept and acknowledge my privilege. This is something I am still working on. I'm a woman, a person of color, and the child of immigrants but I also grew up middle class and then upper middle class. My parents raised my siblings and me in a strict but loving environment. They were and are happily married so I didn't have to deal with divorce or crappy intramarital dynamics. I attended elite schools. My master's and doc-toral degrees were funded. I got a tenure track position my first time out. My bills are paid. I have the time and resources for frivolity. I am reasonably well published. I have an agent so I have every reason to believe my novel will find a home. My life has been far from perfect but I have a whole lot of privilege. It's somewhat embarrassing for me to accept just how much privilege I have.

What point is this editorial cartoon making about privilege? Based on what you have read, would Gay believe that this cartoon would be helpful or not in explaining the concept of "privilege"? Why?

Clay Bennett/Cartoonist Group

It's also really difficult for me to accept my privilege when I consider the ways in which I lack privilege or the ways in which my privilege hasn't magically rescued me from a world of hurt. On my more difficult days, I'm not sure what's more of a pain in my ass — being black or being a woman. I'm happy to be both of these things, but the world keeps intervening. There are all kinds of infuriating reminders of my place in the world — random people questioning me in the parking lot at work as if it is unfathomable that I'm a faculty member, whispers of Affirmative Action when I achieve a career milestone I've busted my ass for, the persistence of lawmakers trying to legislate the female body, street harassment, strangers wanting to touch my hair, you know how it is.

The ways in which I do not have privilege are significant, but I am lucky and successful. Any number of factors related to privilege have contributed to these circumstances. What I remind myself of, regularly, is this: the acknowledgment of my privilege is not a denial of the ways I have been and am marginalized, the ways I have suffered.

We tend to believe that accusations of privilege imply we have it easy and because life is hard for nearly everyone, we resent hearing that. Of course we do. Look at white men when they are accused of having privilege. They tend to be immediately defensive (and, at times, understandably so). They say, "It's not my fault I am a white man." They say, "I'm working class," or "I'm [insert other condition that discounts their privilege]," instead of simply accepting that, in this regard, yes, they benefit from certain privileges others do not. To have privilege in one or more areas does not mean you are wholly privileged. To acknowledge privilege is not a denial of the ways you are marginalized, the ways you have suffered. Surrendering to the acceptance

of privilege is difficult but it is really all that is expected.

At times we forget that accepting privilege is not a game. John Scalzi recently wrote about privilege without invoking the word privilege by using the difficulty levels of video games as a metaphor. His framework works well but his metaphor is only a starting point in understanding privilege and its effects. More than one commenter said something like, "I own my privilege, now what?" as if there is some unknown territory beyond the acknowledgment of privilege.

You don't necessarily have to do anything once you acknowledge your privilege. You don't have to apologize for it. You don't need to diminish your privilege or your accomplishments because of that privilege. You need to understand the extent of your privilege, the consequences of your privilege, and remain aware that people who are different from you move through and experience the world in ways you might never know anything about. They might endure situations you can never know anything about. You could, however, use that privilege for the greater good — to try to level the playing field for everyone, to work for social justice, to bring attention to how those without certain privileges are disenfranchised. While you don't have to do anything with your privilege, perhaps it should be an imperative of privilege to share the benefits of that privilege rather than hoard your good fortune. We've seen what the hoarding of privilege has done and the results are shameful.

When we talk about privilege, some people start to play a very pointless and dangerous game where they try to mix and match various demographic characteristics to determine who wins at the Game of Privilege. Who would win in a privilege battle between a wealthy black woman and a wealthy white man? Who would win a privilege battle between a queer white man and a queer Asian woman? Who would win in a privilege battle between a working class white man and a wealthy, differently abled, Mexican woman? We can play this game all day. We will never find a winner. Playing the Game of Privilege is mental masturbation — it only feels good to the players.

Privilege is relative and contextual. Few people in this world, and particularly in the United States, have no privilege at all. Among those of us who participate in intellectual communities, privilege runs rampant. We have disposable time and the ability to access the Internet regularly. We have the freedom to express our opinions without the threat of retaliation. We have smart phones and iProducts and desktops and laptops. If you are reading this essay, you have some kind of privilege. It may be hard to hear that, I know, but if you cannot recognize your privilege, you have a lot of work to do; get started.

President Barack Obama enjoys a great deal of privilege. He is wealthy, educated, young, and extraordinarily successful. He is in what appears to be a loving marriage. He has two healthy children. He is the president of the United States and, arguably, the most powerful man in the world. Even as he enjoys such immense privilege, Obama knows what all successful people of color know. All the wealth and power in the world won't shield you from racial epithets, assumptions about how you've achieved your success, and resentment from people who feel that the trappings of privilege are their rightful due.

Given that even very privileged people can be marginalized, how do we measure privilege? What is the correct hierarchy? We can't measure privilege. We shouldn't even try. Our energies would be better directed to what truly matters.

Too many people have become self-appointed privilege police, patrolling the halls of discourse, ready to remind people of their privilege, whether those people have denied that privilege or not. In online discourse, in particular, the specter of privilege is always looming darkly. When someone writes from their experience, there is often someone else, at the ready, pointing a trembling finger, accusing that writer of having various kinds of privilege. How dare someone speak to a personal experience without accounting for every possible configuration of privilege or the lack thereof? We lose sight of this but we would live in a world of silence if the only people who were allowed to write or speak from experience or about difference were those absolutely without privilege.

When people wield accusations of privilege, more often than not, they want to be heard and seen. Their need is acute, if not desperate, and that need rises out of the many historical and ongoing attempts to silence and render invisible marginalized groups. Must we satisfy our need to be heard and seen at the expense of not allowing anyone else to be heard and seen? Does privilege automatically negate any merits of what a privilege holder has to say?

We need to get to a place where we discuss privilege by way of observation and acknowledgment rather than accusation. We need to be able to argue beyond the threat of privilege. We need to stop playing Privilege or Oppression Olympics because we'll never get anywhere until we find more effective ways of talking through difference. We should be able to say this is my truth and have that truth stand without a hundred clamoring voices shouting, giving the impression that multiple truths cannot coexist. At some point, doesn't privilege become beside the point? ∎

15

extending beyond the text

Read John Scalzi's comparison of the concept of privilege to the difficulty settings on a video game, which Gay mentions in her piece.

from Straight White Male: The Lowest Difficulty Setting There Is

John Scalzi

I've been thinking of a way to explain to straight white men how life works for them, without invoking the dreaded word "privilege," to which they react like vampires being fed a garlic tart at high noon. It's not that the word "privilege" is incorrect, it's that it's not *their* word. When confronted with "privilege," they fiddle with the word itself, and haul out the dictionaries and find every possible way to talk about the word but not any of the things the word signifies.

So, the challenge: how to get across the ideas bound up in the word "privilege," in a way that your average straight white man will *get*, without freaking out about it?

Being a white guy who likes women, here's how I would do it:

Dudes. Imagine life here in the US — or indeed, pretty much anywhere in the Western world — is a massive role playing game, like World of Warcraft except appallingly mundane, where most quests involve the acquisition of money, cell phones and donuts, although not always at the same time. Let's call it The Real World. You have installed The Real World on your computer and are about to start playing, but first you go to the settings tab to bind your keys, fiddle with your defaults, and choose the difficulty setting for the game. Got it?

Okay: In the role playing game known as The Real World, "Straight White Male" is   5
the lowest difficulty setting there is.

This means that the default behaviors for almost all the non-player characters in the game are easier on you than they would be otherwise. The default barriers for completions of quests are lower. Your leveling-up thresholds come more quickly. You automatically gain entry to some parts of the map that others have to work for. The game is easier to play, automatically, and when you need help, by default it's easier to get.

Now, once you've selected the "Straight White Male" difficulty setting, you *still* have to create a character, and how many points you get to start — and how they are apportioned — will make a difference. Initially the computer will tell you how many points you get and how they are divided up. If you start with 25 points, and your dump stat is wealth, well, then you may be kind of screwed. If you start with 250 points and your dump stat is charisma, well, then you're probably fine. Be aware the computer makes it difficult to start with more than 30 points; people on higher difficulty settings generally start with even fewer than that. . . .

You can lose playing on the lowest difficulty setting. The lowest difficulty setting is still the easiest setting to win on. The player who plays on the "Gay Minority Female" setting? *Hardcore.*

And maybe at this point you say, hey, I like a challenge, I want to change my difficulty setting! Well, here's the thing: In The Real World, you don't unlock any rewards or receive any benefit for playing on higher difficulty settings. The game is just *harder*, and potentially a lot less fun. And you say, okay, but what if I want to replay the game later on a higher difficulty setting, just to see what it's like? Well, here's the *other* thing about The Real World: You only get to play it once. So why make it more difficult than it has to be? Your goal is to *win* the game, not make it difficult.

Oh, and one other thing. Remember when I said that you could choose your difficulty setting in The Real World? Well, I lied. In fact, the computer chooses the difficulty setting for you. You don't get a choice; you just get what gets given to you at the start of the game, and then you have to deal with it.

So that's "Straight White Male" for you in The Real World (and also, in the real world): The lowest difficulty setting there is. All things being equal, and even when they are not, if the computer — or life — assigns you the "Straight White Male" difficulty setting, then brother, you've caught a break. ■

10

Summarize Scalzi's extended metaphor comparing the idea of privilege to the difficulty settings in a video game. Do you think his explanation would be useful to his target audience? Why or why not? Gay says that Scalzi's framework is "only a starting point in understanding privilege and its effects." Based on your reading of Gay's piece, what does Scalzi not include that she thinks is essential?

Understanding and Interpreting

1. Summarize what Gay learns from her family visits to Haiti, which she describes in paragraphs 1 and 2.

2. Reread paragraphs 3 and 4. Paraphrase Gay's definition of the word *privilege* and state her likely purpose for writing this piece.

3. Even though Gay says that she is "a woman, a person of color, and the child of immigrants," she also says that she is privileged (par. 5). In what ways is she privileged?

4. In paragraph 6, Gay says that her privilege hasn't "rescued [her] from a world of hurt." Summarize the ways that "the world keeps intervening."

5. Why, according to Gay, do some white men react defensively to the idea of privilege? What does she say about their defensiveness?

6. Although Gay writes that we do not necessarily need to do anything once we've identified our privilege, what does she suggest that we could do in paragraph 10?

7. Gay writes that we cannot and should not "measure privilege" (pars. 14–15). Why?

8. What point is Gay making about the drawbacks of people wielding accusations of privilege, especially in online dialogues (pars. 16–17)?

9. Summarize Gay's hope for the future as described in the last paragraph of her piece.

Analyzing Language, Style, and Structure

10. **Vocabulary in Context.** In her opening paragraph, Gay describes "the difference between relative and absolute poverty" in Haiti. What does the word *relative* mean in this context, and how is it different from other uses of the word?

11. Analyze the contrasting imagery that Gay uses to describe Haiti in paragraph 2.

12. What are possible effects of Gay's choice to begin with a personal anecdote of her family's trips to Haiti? How does that choice help her build her piece?

13. Why do you think it was important for Gay to identify her own privilege near the beginning of her piece (pars. 5–6)?

14. Reread paragraph 11 in which Gay describes the "Game of Privilege." What is her tone in this section, and how does she use diction and syntax to communicate her attitude toward this "Game"?

15. How does the mention of President Obama (par. 13) help to communicate a part of Gay's main idea?

16. Reread paragraphs 15–17 looking at Gay's use of rhetorical questions, which are questions asked to make a point, rather than get an answer. Identify one example and explain the point Gay is trying to make through this syntactical choice.

Topics for Composing

17. **Analysis.** What is the main idea that Gay hopes to communicate about "privilege" in this piece? Analyze how she uses description, compare and contrast, cause-and-effect, or other expository strategies to explain her main idea.

18. **Argument.** Write an argument in which you agree or disagree with Gay's definition of privilege. Use your own or other people's experiences to support your position.

19. **Connections.** Evaluate your own degree of privilege using the points that Gay raises here. What, if anything, do you think that you could or should do with your privilege? Why?

20. **Speaking and Listening.** In paragraph 15, Gay describes how accusations regarding privilege can hamper meaningful conversation, especially online. With a small group or the whole class, discuss whether your personal experiences, online or in person, support Gay's conclusions.

21. **Research.** What gaps in privilege exist within the United States? Research how differences in economic, educational, or other status can cause "people who are different from you [to] move through and experience the world in ways you might never know anything about" (par. 10). How do these factors affect the group's access to or experience with privilege as it is defined by Gay — "a right or immunity granted as a peculiar benefit, advantage, or favor"?

22. **Multimodal.** In paragraph 2, Gay describes the contrast between the beach and the sprawling slums in Haiti. Locate or create contrasting images that illustrate a particular aspect of privilege. Using Gay's text or writing of your own, create captions for the images that clarify the contrasts.

How One Stupid Tweet Blew Up Justine Sacco's Life

Jon Ronson

Jon Ronson (b. 1967) is an award-winning Welsh journalist, author, filmmaker, and radio announcer. His most well-known books include *Them: Adventures with Extremists* (2001), *The Men Who Stare at Goats* (2004) , and *So You've Been Publicly Shamed* (2015), which explores high-profile public shamings, including that of Justine Sacco. This article appeared in the *New York Times Magazine* in 2015.

As she made the long journey from New York to South Africa, to visit family during the holidays in 2013, Justine Sacco, 30 years old and the senior director of corporate communications at IAC, began tweeting acerbic little jokes about the indignities of travel. There was one about a fellow passenger on the flight from John F. Kennedy International Airport:

"'Weird German Dude: You're in First Class. It's 2014. Get some deodorant.' — Inner monologue as I inhale BO. Thank God for pharmaceuticals."

Then, during her layover at Heathrow:

"Chilly — cucumber sandwiches — bad teeth. Back in London!"

And on Dec. 20, before the final leg of her trip to Cape Town: 5

"Going to Africa. Hope I don't get AIDS. Just kidding. I'm white!"

She chuckled to herself as she pressed send on this last one, then wandered around Heathrow's international terminal for half an hour, sporadically checking her phone. No one replied, which didn't surprise her. She had only 170 Twitter followers.

Sacco boarded the plane. It was an 11-hour flight, so she slept. When the plane landed in Cape Town and was taxiing on the runway, she turned on her phone. Right away, she got a text from someone she hadn't spoken to since high school: "I'm so sorry to see what's happening." Sacco looked at it, baffled.

Then another text: "You need to call me immediately." It was from her best friend, Hannah. Then her phone exploded with more texts and alerts. And then it rang. It was Hannah. "You're the No. 1 worldwide trend on Twitter right now," she said.

Sacco's Twitter feed had become a horror 10 show. "In light of @JustineSacco disgusting racist tweet, I'm donating to @care today" and "How did @JustineSacco get a PR job?! Her level of racist ignorance belongs on Fox News. #AIDS can affect anyone!" and "I'm an IAC employee and I don't want @JustineSacco doing any communications on our behalf ever again. Ever." And then one from her employer, IAC, the corporate owner of The Daily Beast, OKCupid and Vimeo: "This is an outrageous, offensive comment. Employee in question currently unreachable on an intl flight." The anger soon turned to excitement: "All I want for Christmas is to see @JustineSacco's face when her plane lands and she checks her inbox/voicemail" and "Oh man, @JustineSacco is going to have the most painful phone-turning-on moment ever when her

Justine Sacco
@JustineSacco

Going to Africa. Hope I don't get AIDS. Just kidding. I'm white!

◄ Reply ↻ Retweet ★ Favorite ••• More

2,678
RETWEETS

1,206
FAVORITES

10:19 AM - 20 Dec 13 ♀ from Hillingdon, London

Despite being deleted, Justine Sacco's tweet is still easily found online.
How do you interpret her text? Although short, what about the text supports your interpretation? What are the positives and negatives of the Internet's ability to store information indefinitely?

plane lands" and "We are about to watch this @JustineSacco bitch get fired. In REAL time. Before she even KNOWS she's getting fired."

The furor over Sacco's tweet had become not just an ideological crusade against her perceived bigotry but also a form of idle entertainment. Her complete ignorance of her predicament for those 11 hours lent the episode both dramatic irony and a pleasing narrative arc. As Sacco's flight traversed the length of Africa, a hashtag began to trend worldwide: #HasJustineLandedYet. "Seriously. I just want to go home to go to bed, but everyone at the bar is SO into #HasJustineLandedYet. Can't look away. Can't leave" and "Right, is there no one in Cape Town going to the airport to tweet her arrival? Come on, Twitter! I'd like pictures #HasJustineLandedYet."

A Twitter user did indeed go to the airport to tweet her arrival. He took her photograph and posted it online. "Yup," he wrote, "@JustineSacco HAS in fact landed at Cape Town International. She's decided to wear sunnies as a disguise."

By the time Sacco had touched down, tens of thousands of angry tweets had been sent in response to her joke. Hannah, meanwhile, frantically deleted her friend's tweet and her account — Sacco didn't want to look — but it was far too late. "Sorry @JustineSacco," wrote one Twitter user, "your tweet lives on forever."

In the early days of Twitter, I was a keen shamer. When newspaper columnists made racist or homophobic statements, I joined the pile-on. Sometimes I led it. The journalist A. A. Gill once wrote a column about shooting a baboon on safari in Tanzania: "I'm told they can be tricky to shoot. They run up trees, hang on for grim life. They die hard, baboons. But not this one. A soft-nosed .357 blew his lungs out." Gill did the deed because he "wanted to get a sense of what it might be like to kill someone, a stranger."

I was among the first people to alert social media. (This was because Gill always gave my television documentaries bad reviews, so I tended to keep a vigilant eye on things he could be got

15

Zac
@ZacSpeaks

Follow

Yup. @JustineSacco HAS in fact landed at Cape Town international. She's decided to wear sunnies as a disguise.

RETWEETS 1,105   LIKES 413

9:29 PM - 20 Dec 2013

78   1.1K   413

Describe Sacco's body language in this photo. Does posting Sacco's location and picture at the airport go too far? What are the repercussions for both Sacco and the author of the tweet?

for.) Within minutes, it was everywhere. Amid the hundreds of congratulatory messages I received, one stuck out: "Were you a bully at school?"

Still, in those early days, the collective fury felt righteous, powerful and effective. It felt as if hierarchies were being dismantled, as if justice were being democratized. As time passed, though, I watched these shame campaigns multiply, to the point that they targeted not just powerful institutions and public figures but really anyone perceived to have done something offensive. I also began to marvel at the disconnect between the severity of the crime and the gleeful savagery of the punishment. It almost

felt as if shamings were now happening for their own sake, as if they were following a script.

Eventually I started to wonder about the recipients of our shamings, the real humans who were the virtual targets of these campaigns. So for the past two years, I've been interviewing individuals like Justine Sacco: everyday people pilloried brutally, most often for posting some poorly considered joke on social media. Whenever possible, I have met them in person, to truly grasp the emotional toll at the other end of our screens. The people I met were mostly unemployed, fired for their transgressions, and they seemed broken somehow — deeply confused and traumatized.

One person I met was Lindsey Stone, a 32-year-old Massachusetts woman who posed for a photograph while mocking a sign at Arlington National Cemetery's Tomb of the Unknowns. Stone had stood next to the sign, which asks for "Silence and Respect," pretending to scream and flip the bird. She and her co-worker Jamie, who posted the picture on Facebook, had a running joke about disobeying signs — smoking in front of No Smoking signs, for example — and documenting it. But shorn of this context, her picture appeared to be a joke not about a sign but about the war dead. Worse, Jamie didn't realize that her mobile uploads were visible to the public.

Four weeks later, Stone and Jamie were out celebrating Jamie's birthday when their phones started vibrating repeatedly. Someone had found the photo and brought it to the attention of hordes of online strangers. Soon there was a wildly popular "Fire Lindsey Stone" Facebook page. The next morning, there were news cameras outside her home; when she showed up to her job, at a program for developmentally disabled adults, she was told to hand over her keys. ("After they fire her, maybe she needs to sign up as a client," read one of the thousands of Facebook messages denouncing her. "Woman needs help.") She barely left home for the year

central text / Jon Ronson

653

that followed, racked by PTSD, depression and insomnia. "I didn't want to be seen by anyone," she told me last March at her home in Plymouth, Mass. "I didn't want people looking at me."

Instead, Stone spent her days online, watch- 20 ing others just like her get turned upon. In particular she felt for "that girl at Halloween who dressed as a Boston Marathon victim. I felt so terrible for her." She meant Alicia Ann Lynch, 22, who posted a photo of herself in her Halloween costume on Twitter. Lynch wore a running outfit and had smeared her face, arms and legs with fake blood. After an actual victim of the Boston Marathon bombing tweeted at her, "You should be ashamed, my mother lost both her legs and I almost died," people unearthed Lynch's personal information and sent her and her friends threatening messages. Lynch was reportedly let go from her job as well.

I met a man who, in early 2013, had been sitting at a conference for tech developers in Santa Clara, Calif., when a stupid joke popped into his head. It was about the attachments for computers and mobile devices that are commonly called dongles. He murmured the joke to his friend sitting next to him, he told me. "It was so bad, I don't remember the exact words," he said. "Something about a fictitious piece of hardware that has a really big dongle, a ridiculous dongle. . . . It wasn't even conversation-level volume."

Moments later, he half-noticed when a woman one row in front of them stood up, turned around and took a photograph. He thought she was taking a crowd shot, so he looked straight ahead, trying to avoid ruining her picture. It's a little painful to look at the photograph now, knowing what was coming.

The woman had, in fact, overheard the joke. She considered it to be emblematic of the gender imbalance that plagues the tech industry and the toxic, male-dominated corporate culture that arises from it. She tweeted the picture to her 9,209 followers with the caption: "Not

cool. Jokes about . . . 'big' dongles right behind me." Ten minutes later, he and his friend were taken into a quiet room at the conference and asked to explain themselves. A day later, his boss called him into his office, and he was fired.

"I packed up all my stuff in a box," he told me. (Like Stone and Sacco, he had never before talked on the record about what happened to him. He spoke on the condition of anonymity to avoid further damaging his career.) "I went outside to call my wife. I'm not one to shed tears, but" — he paused — "when I got in the car with my wife I just. . . . I've got three kids. Getting fired was terrifying."

The woman who took the photograph, Adria 25 Richards, soon felt the wrath of the crowd herself. The man responsible for the dongle joke had posted about losing his job on Hacker News, an online forum popular with developers. This led to a backlash from the other end of the political spectrum. So-called men's rights activists and anonymous trolls bombarded Richards with death threats on Twitter and Facebook. Someone tweeted Richards's home address along with a photograph of a beheaded woman with duct tape over her mouth. Fearing for her life, she left her home, sleeping on friends' couches for the remainder of the year.

Next, her employer's website went down. Someone had launched a DDoS attack, which overwhelms a site's servers with repeated requests. SendGrid, her employer, was told the attacks would stop if Richards was fired. That same day she was publicly let go.

"I cried a lot during this time, journaled and escaped by watching movies," she later said to me in an email. "SendGrid threw me under the bus. I felt betrayed. I felt abandoned. I felt ashamed. I felt rejected. I felt alone."

Late one afternoon last year, I met Justine Sacco in New York, at a restaurant in Chelsea called Cookshop. Dressed in rather chic business attire, Sacco ordered a glass of white wine. Just three weeks had passed since her trip to Africa, and she was still a person of interest to the media. Websites had already ransacked her Twitter feed for more horrors. [. . .] A New York Post photographer had been following her to the gym.

"Only an insane person would think that white people don't get AIDS," she told me. It was about the first thing she said to me when we sat down.

Sacco had been three hours or so into her flight when retweets of her joke began to overwhelm my Twitter feed. I could understand why some people found it offensive. Read literally, she said that white people don't get AIDS, but it seems doubtful many interpreted it that way. More likely it was her apparently gleeful flaunting of her privilege that angered people. But after thinking about her tweet for a few seconds more, I began to suspect that it wasn't racist but a reflexive critique of white privilege — on our tendency to naïvely imagine ourselves immune from life's horrors. Sacco, like Stone, had been yanked violently out of the context of her small social circle. Right?

"To me it was so insane of a comment for anyone to make," she said. "I thought there was no way that anyone could possibly think it was literal." (She would later write me an email to elaborate on this point. "Unfortunately, I am not a character on 'South Park' or a comedian, so I had no business commenting on the epidemic in such a politically incorrect manner on a public platform," she wrote. "To put it simply, I wasn't trying to raise awareness of AIDS or piss off the world or ruin my life. Living in America puts us in a bit of a bubble when it comes to what is going on in the third world. I was making fun of that bubble.")

I would be the only person she spoke to on the record about what happened to her, she said. It was just too harrowing — and "as a publicist," inadvisable — but she felt it was necessary, to show how "crazy" her situation was, how her punishment simply didn't fit the crime.

"I cried out my body weight in the first 24 hours," she told me. "It was incredibly traumatic. You don't sleep. You wake up in the middle of the night forgetting where you are." She released an apology statement and cut short her vacation. Workers were threatening to strike at the hotels she had booked if she showed up. She was told no one could guarantee her safety. . . .

"All of a sudden you don't know what you're supposed to do," she said. "If I don't start making steps to reclaim my identity and remind myself of who I am on a daily basis, then I might lose myself."

The restaurant's manager approached our table. She sat down next to Sacco, fixed her with a look and said something in such a low volume I couldn't hear it, only Sacco's reply: "Oh, you think I'm going to be grateful for this?"

We agreed to meet again, but not for several months. She was determined to prove that she could turn her life around. "I can't just sit at home and watch movies every day and cry and feel sorry for myself," she said. "I'm going to come back."

After she left, Sacco later told me, she got only as far as the lobby of her office building before she broke down crying.

A few days after meeting Sacco, I took a trip up to the Massachusetts Archives in Boston. I wanted to learn about the last era of American history when public shaming was a common form of punishment, so I was seeking out court transcripts from the 18th and early 19th centuries. I had assumed that the demise of public punishments was caused by the migration from villages to cities. Shame became ineffectual, I thought, because a person in the stocks could just lose himself or herself in the anonymous crowd as soon as the chastisement was over. Modernity had diminished shame's power to shame — or so I assumed.

I took my seat at a microfilm reader and began to scroll slowly through the archives. For the first hundred years, as far as I could tell, all that happened in America was that various people named Nathaniel had purchased land near rivers. I scrolled faster, finally reaching an account of an early Colonial-era shaming.

On July 15, 1742, a woman named Abigail Gilpin, her husband at sea, had been found "naked in bed with one John Russell." They were both to be "whipped at the public whipping post 20 stripes each." Abigail was appealing the ruling, but it wasn't the whipping itself she wished to avoid. She was begging the judge to let her be whipped early, before the town awoke. "If your honor pleases," she wrote, "take some pity on me for my dear children who cannot help their unfortunate mother's failings." 40

There was no record as to whether the judge consented to her plea, but I found a number of clips that offered clues as to why she might have requested private punishment. In a sermon, the Rev. Nathan Strong, of Hartford, Conn., entreated his flock to be less exuberant at executions. "Go not to that place of horror with elevated spirits and gay hearts, for death is there! Justice and judgment are there!" Some papers published scathing reviews when public punishments were deemed too lenient by the crowd: "Suppressed remarks . . . were expressed by large numbers," reported Delaware's Wilmington Daily Commercial of a disappointing 1873 whipping. "Many were heard to say that the punishment was a farce. . . . Drunken fights and rows followed in rapid succession."

The movement against public shaming had gained momentum in 1787, when Benjamin Rush, a physician in Philadelphia and a signer of the Declaration of Independence, wrote a paper calling for its demise — the stocks, the pillory, the whipping post, the lot. "Ignominy is universally acknowledged to be a worse punishment than death," he wrote. "It would seem strange that ignominy should ever have been adopted as a milder punishment than death, did we not know that the human mind seldom arrives at

truth upon any subject till it has first reached the extremity of error."

The pillory and whippings were abolished at the federal level in 1839, although Delaware kept the pillory until 1905 and whippings until 1972. An 1867 editorial in The Times excoriated the state for its obstinacy. "If [the convicted person] had previously existing in his bosom a spark of self-respect this exposure to public shame utterly extinguishes it. . . . The boy of 18 who is whipped at New Castle for larceny is in nine cases out of 10 ruined. With his self-respect destroyed and the taunt and sneer of public disgrace branded upon his forehead, he feels himself lost and abandoned by his fellows."

At the archives, I found no evidence that punitive shaming fell out of fashion as a result of newfound anonymity. But I did find plenty of people from centuries past bemoaning the outsize cruelty of the practice, warning that well-meaning people, in a crowd, often take punishment too far.

It's possible that Sacco's fate would have been different had an anonymous tip not led a writer named Sam Biddle to the offending tweet. Biddle was then the editor of Valleywag, Gawker Media's tech-industry blog. He retweeted it to his 15,000 followers and eventually posted it on Valleywag, accompanied by the headline, "And Now, a Funny Holiday Joke From IAC's P.R. Boss." 45

In January 2014, I received an email from Biddle, explaining his reasoning. "The fact that she was a P.R. chief made it delicious," he wrote. "It's satisfying to be able to say, 'O.K., let's make a racist tweet by a senior IAC employee count this time.' And it did. I'd do it again." Biddle said he was surprised to see how quickly her life was upended, however. "I never wake up and hope I [get someone fired] that day — and certainly never hope to ruin anyone's life." Still, he ended his email by saying that he had a feeling she'd be "fine eventually, if not already."

He added: "Everyone's attention span is so short. They'll be mad about something new today."

What aspects in this image emphasize public demonstrations of punishment? What are the similarities and differences between public shamings in the past and now?

INTERFOTO/Alamy

Four months after we first met, Justine Sacco made good on her promise. We met for lunch at a French bistro downtown. I told her what Biddle had said — about how she was probably fine now. I was sure he wasn't being deliberately glib, but like everyone who participates in mass online destruction, uninterested in learning that it comes with a cost.

"Well, I'm not fine yet," Sacco said to me. "I had a great career, and I loved my job, and it was taken away from me, and there was a lot of glory in that. Everybody else was very happy about that."

Sacco pushed her food around on her plate, 50 and let me in on one of the hidden costs of her experience. "I'm single; so it's not like I can date, because we Google everyone we might date," she said. "That's been taken away from me too." She was down, but I did notice one positive change in her. When I first met her, she talked about the shame she had brought on her family. But she no longer felt that way. Instead, she said, she just felt personally humiliated.

Biddle was almost right about one thing: Sacco did get a job offer right away. But it was an odd one, from the owner of a Florida yachting company. "He said: 'I saw what happened to you. I'm fully on your side,'" she told me. Sacco knew nothing about yachts, and she questioned his motives. ("Was he a crazy person who thinks

white people can't get AIDS?") Eventually she turned him down.

After that, she left New York, going as far away as she could, to Addis Ababa, Ethiopia. She flew there alone and got a volunteer job doing P.R. for an NGO working to reduce maternal-mortality rates. "It was fantastic," she said. She was on her own, and she was working. If she was going to be made to suffer for a joke, she figured she should get something out of it. "I never would have lived in Addis Ababa for a month otherwise," she told me. She was struck by how different life was there. Rural areas had only intermittent power and no running water or Internet. Even the capital, she said, had few street names or house addresses.

Addis Ababa was great for a month, but she knew going in that she would not be there long. She was a New York City person. Sacco is nervy and sassy and sort of debonair. And so she returned to work at Hot or Not, which had been a popular site for rating strangers' looks on the pre-social Internet and was reinventing itself as a dating app.

But despite her near invisibility on social media, she was still ridiculed and demonized across the Internet. Biddle wrote a Valleywag post after she returned to the work force: "Sacco, who apparently spent the last month hiding in

657

Ethiopia after infuriating our species with an idiotic AIDS joke, is now a 'marketing and promotion' director at Hot or Not."

"How perfect!" he wrote. "Two lousy has-beens, gunning for a comeback together." 55

Sacco felt this couldn't go on, so six weeks after our lunch, she invited Biddle out for a dinner and drinks. Afterward, she sent me an email. "I think he has some real guilt about the issue," she wrote. "Not that he's retracted anything." (Months later, Biddle would find himself at the wrong end of the Internet shame machine for tweeting a joke of his own: "Bring Back Bullying." On the one-year anniversary of the Sacco episode, he published a public apology to her on Gawker.)

Recently, I wrote to Sacco to tell her I was putting her story in The Times, and I asked her to meet me one final time to update me on her life. Her response was speedy. "No way." She explained that she had a new job in communications, though she wouldn't say where. She said, "Anything that puts the spotlight on me is a negative."

It was a profound reversal for Sacco. When I first met her, she was desperate to tell the tens of thousands of people who tore her apart how they had wronged her and to repair what remained of her public persona. But perhaps she had now come to understand that her shaming wasn't really about her at all. Social media is so perfectly designed to manipulate our desire for approval, and that is what led to her undoing. Her tormentors were instantly congratulated as they took Sacco down, bit by bit, and so they continued to do so. Their motivation was much the same as Sacco's own — a bid for the attention of strangers — as she milled about Heathrow, hoping to amuse people she couldn't see. ■

extending beyond the text

Although he doesn't use the term, what Ronson describes is an example of what has since become known as "cancel culture," in which a person or a company may be ostracized, usually online, for a real or perceived action or remark, ranging in severity from insensitive to criminal. It has also become a politically charged term with both Republicans and Democrats accusing each other's supporters of trying to "cancel" the other's. While some people believe that "cancelling" can hold the powerful accountable, others see it as an infringement on First Amendment rights to free speech. In the following excerpt, writer and lawyer Dan Kovalik makes what he calls the progressive case against "cancel culture."

from Cancel This Book: The Progressive Case Against Cancel Culture

Dan Kovalik

The tension arises . . . because, though the individual has the right to free expression, such expression may infringe on others' rights, and particularly on others' rights to be included and to participate equally in the institution or forum in which the speech is being made. It is this right of participation that, [Columbia University professor john a. powell] argues, should be protected in resolving this tension:

> There is reason to believe or construct a notion of harm that is similar in both contexts and that is not so broad that it destroys free speech or equality. Not all harms are to be avoided, but only a limited class of harms. I have identified the central harm that is to be avoided as the harm to participation and membership and, as a corollary, the harm to communicative self-respect and autonomy. There

are other harms, such as offense, that will not rise to this level. I have argued that the harm which undermines, distorts, or destroys the ability to participate in critical institutions and locations is of the first order and should be cognizable in and regulated by our jurisprudence. . . . Free speech and equality should be promoted by this approach, in part, because they support, and are necessary for participation. When there is a sharp conflict between free speech and equality, I would try to resolve the tension in a way that protects the right of participation.

In short, speech that offends, but does not interfere with another's right of participation, should not be banned or otherwise suppressed. Rather, such speech, as I took from Professor powell's class, should be met with speech; with argument and dialogue, as a means to advance both free speech and hopefully equality, as well. Such dialogue is especially important, and especially possible, when the speaker is at least well-intentioned, though possibly ill-informed or mistaken about proper semantics. Professor powell, who comes from a place of deep compassion, argues that such people should be treated with understanding and empathy, rather than with judgment and derision. ■

Summarize Kovalik's objections to "cancel culture" and explain whether Ronson would agree, based on what you read. Would Justine Sacco agree with Kovalik? Why or why not?

Understanding and Interpreting

1. Reread the opening section of the piece and summarize Sacco's actions before she boarded the plane to South Africa. What is the likely effect of Ronson starting his piece with this information about Sacco?

2. Describe the initial responses to Sacco's tweet in paragraph 10–13. How do these responses shape your views of Sacco? Of those who responded? Why might Ronson have included these tweeted responses?

3. In paragraphs 14 and 15, how does Ronson describe his own involvement with online shaming? What might be his motivation for including that description?

4. Reread paragraphs 17–27. What commonalities does Ronson discover by interviewing those who have been "pilloried brutally" on social media? Why might exposing these commonalties be important for readers to understand his main idea?

5. Like others he interviews, Ronson seeks out Sacco to better understand how she was affected by the situation. How is Sacco's conversation with Ronson in paragraphs 29–34 intended to shape readers' perceptions of her character?

6. Ronson includes examples from the history of public shaming. Which of these examples has the most or least relevance to Sacco's situation? How do these examples add to the reader's understanding and interpretation of the article?

7. Reread paragraphs 45–47. What do we learn from these paragraphs about how Sacco's tweet went viral and the reasoning that Sam Biddle offers for his decision to retweet it? How does Biddle's inclusion in the article add to Ronson's purpose?

8. Identify places in which Ronson shares both the "crime" and the resulting public responses, many of which call for punishment. What conclusions does Ronson expect for the reader to draw from these examples?

9. What is Ronson's main idea in this article? What ideas does he want readers to take away from Sacco's experience?

Analyzing Language, Style, and Structure

10. **Vocabulary in Context.** In paragraph 11, Ronson writes that Sacco's ignorance of what was unfolding online "lent the episode both dramatic irony and a pleasing narrative arc." Explain what the word *arc* means as it is used in this context.

11. How do the three tweets mentioned at the beginning of the article serve as an effective hook to draw the reader in?

12. What is the importance of including others' experiences along with Sacco's? How does weaving in others' experiences create an effective structural technique?

13. Reread paragraph 16. Describe the tone that Ronson's use of language and syntax creates, and explain how this tone helps him to communicate his main idea. Use examples from the text to support your observation.

14. Explain how the incorporation of narrative elements strengthens Ronson's main idea.

15. Discuss the effect of including the actual comments tweeted by commentators. How does including these influence the reader's perception of the events?

16. In paragraph 16, Ronson describes the "gleeful savagery" of Internet shamings. How does this particular word combination effectively convey one aspect of Ronson's main idea?

17. Ronson very much makes himself a part of the article. Explain whether writing in first person is an effective way to engage his readers and communicate his main idea.

18. How does Ronson use details and imagery of his second meeting with Sacco (pars. 48–50) to characterize her? Does his use of language portray her in a positive or negative light? What evidence supports your response?

Topics for Composing

19. **Analysis.** Identify Ronson's tone in this piece, offering specific examples of style that illustrate that tone. Then analyze how Ronson's tone is appropriate or not for communicating his main idea.

20. **Argument.** Argue whether you feel that our society should pass laws against public shaming on social media. If you favor such laws, what changes would you expect to see in how people behave online toward each other? If you are not in favor of such laws, what other guidelines might there be, and who would be responsible for creating and enforcing them? Use evidence from the text and your own experiences and reasoning to support your viewpoint.

21. **Argument.** Most of the examples Ronson discusses in his piece involve women as the targets of shaming. What role, if any, does gender play in determining who is shamed online? Use this article, your own experience, and additional research to support your position.

22. **Argument.** Do you agree or disagree with Ronson's points about social media and motivation in the last paragraph? Explain your response.

> Social media is so perfectly designed to manipulate our desire for approval, and that is what led to [Sacco's] undoing. Her tormentors were instantly congratulated as they took Sacco down, bit by bit, and so they continued to do so. Their motivation was much the same as Sacco's own — a bid for the attention of strangers — as she milled about Heathrow, hoping to amuse people she couldn't see.

23. **Connections.** Reread your own social media posts or those of a friend. How would you characterize the tone of those posts? Would you be embarrassed if someone you respected read them? What might happen if those posts were given to a journalist? How would people define you or your friend by those posts? Would it be a fair judgment? Why or why not?

24. **Speaking and Listening.** *Schadenfreude* is a term that means "pleasure from the misfortune of others." Ronson explains in paragraph 10 that "The anger soon turned to excitement" and later in paragraph 11 that "Sacco's tweet had become not just an ideological crusade against her perceived bigotry but also a form of idle entertainment." Engage in a discussion about why we might revel in someone else's mistakes. What dangers might there be in delighting in someone else's humiliation?

25. **Research.** Research the cyberbullying laws for your state or the guidelines from your school. How are these rules and guidelines defined? Explore the gray areas and what, if anything, is being done to update or refine those laws or guidelines.

26. **Research.** Although Sacco's experience happened in 2013, social media continues to come under fire. According to documents revealed in 2021 by whistleblower Frances Haugen, Facebook has created an algorithm that targets users with content that they'll most likely engage with, potentially exposing users to toxic content and fueling polarization. Conduct research into how the algorithm works, and what, if anything, Facebook and other social media companies do to encourage engagement.

27. **Research.** Sam Biddle, the person who initially retweeted Sacco's joke, told Ronson that Sacco will be fine because, "Everyone's attention span is so short." Is this true? Conduct research on Sacco today, years after the event, or on any of the others Ronson mentions in his piece, such as Alicia Ann Lynch, Adria Richards, or Lindsey Stone, to find out if the initial event they were shamed for still affects them today.

28. **Exposition.** In paragraph 31, Ronson includes an email from Sacco in which she notes, "Unfortunately, I am not a character on 'South Park' or a comedian, so I had no business commenting on [AIDS] in such a politically incorrect manner on a public platform." Write an explanation about the differences between a comedian who makes controversial jokes onstage or in performance and noncelebrities, like Justine Sacco, who do so.

conversation

Is online activism effective?

In 2019, a volunteer organization, Crisis Relief Singapore, began a public relations campaign called "Liking Isn't Helping," in which the ads showed real images of people suffering the effects of floods, earthquakes, and war superimposed with people giving a "thumbs up" sign around them, implying that simply clicking "like" on Facebook doesn't really address the problems of the world. Now that social media is an organizing force in our lives, people have begun questioning our ability to create meaningful change via the Internet. Some have used the term *slacktivism* (a combination of *slacker* and *activism*) to describe those who engage with causes only by retweeting, sharing hashtags, or signing online petitions rather than participating in marches and protests, writing to politicians, or providing other forms of offline, in-person support. And yet many successful online campaigns have raised awareness and money for important causes, such as the 2014 ALS Ice Bucket challenge that raised over $115 million for research to cure the deadly disease. But what makes a successful online campaign, and do our activities on social media really matter in the world? These are the questions that you'll explore in this conversation. At the end, you'll have an opportunity to enter the discussion by adding your viewpoint to those of these authors in response to the following question — *To what extent can we influence social, cultural, or political change online?*

661

activity Starting the Conversation

Take a moment to write informally about your initial thinking on this topic before you explore it further by reading additional texts.

1. Jot down some political or cultural issues that you are passionate about and changes that you'd like to see in the world. Select one that you feel most strongly about.

2. With a partner or small group, discuss how you engage or would like to engage with others about your identified issue both online and offline.

3. Create a table like the one below to help you keep track of ideas related to how we can or cannot influence social, cultural, or political change online. Include your own responses to the ideas you encounter in the texts you read.

Text Title/Author	Thoughts about Influencing Social, Cultural, or Political Change with Online Posts	Best Evidence	Your Reaction

Source A

Mullally, Siobhan. "The Realities of Slacktivism." *Alternatives Journal*, 18 Jan. 2021.

As a borderline millennial/Gen Z individual, I am quite versed in the world of social media, having been introduced to Facebook, Twitter, and Instagram from as early as 10 years old. Back then, I mainly used social media to follow my favourite boy bands and have meaningless conversations ("hey" "what's up" "nothing much" "same") with my friends whom I had seen at school earlier that day. But once I got older, as I developed into a young environmentalist and social justice advocate, social media became a vital tool and the main conduit for which activism took place. Now, more than ever, I find myself completely immersed in the realm of social media where using hashtags and sharing posts are key forms of activism, no matter the cause.

Social media activism is a form of advocacy that can include protesting, campaigning, or raising awareness through the use of social media platforms. By using hashtags, online movements can rapidly spread through the world of media, and gain momentum and attention by "trending," which means becoming one of the top concerns on social media at a given time. But social media activism can often come across as lazy and fake when it is not followed by genuine action, so critics coined a new term for this online facade: "slacktivism." How do we differentiate between genuine activism on social media platforms and slacktivism?

A trend I see amongst my fellow young people on social media is that we each have an "image" that we've created of ourselves on our profiles.

We are concerned with our aesthetic—what our online presence says about us—and those things are driven by what we post and share on social media. That even applies to people who don't post anything at all. The silence, unwillingness, or lack of interest in sharing and posting content still upholds a certain image.

What we share and post contributes to and upholds our online reputations by showing what we care about; however, it is all too often that I see people sharing posts that contribute to their identity as an activist, yet it seems that no real action or growth have followed. And isn't change the main goal of activism? Raising awareness only goes so far before the sharing and posting needs to turn into demonstrating and changing.

I'll be honest with you, I am completely guilty of slacktivism myself. I have shared plenty of posts on Instagram, adding my own comments encouraging or challenging people to "wake up" to those issues because I support the cause and want to share it, yet sometimes that's as far as my activism goes. Sometimes I even find myself doing the opposite of what I have shared and advocated for online. I'm sure there have been times when I've shared a bunch of posts about the importance of buying local, seasonal produce, and then gone to the store and bought a bag of oranges from Spain. Or perhaps there was

a post about a crisis in a developing country that had been circulating through my social media feed and I shared it without actually doing any of the work, like signing the petitions, donating, or educating myself further on the issue at hand. . . .

So, can the progress of movements actually be stalled if people are just sharing the content but no one is taking action or actively trying to change? This is how the rise of social media activism can be counterproductive to genuine activism. The act of retweeting a post on Twitter may allow people to feel as though they have done their part and satisfied their "activist duty," even when no action or transformation has really taken . . . Maybe my social media activity gave me a sense of fulfillment that allowed me to mentally check off the "activism" box in my mind, giving me more space to make less sustainable choices, given that I had "already done my good for the day."

We have been living in an online world for a while now, and the global pandemic has only accelerated the extent of online life. As young activists, it may seem harder than ever to do anything beyond the online work. But even during the pandemic, we can take part in both social media activism and activism in our offline lives as well. Online activism needs to be followed by real action that supports those ideas. ■

Questions

1. How does Mullally define social media activism? Why is slacktivism a concern for her?

2. In paragraph 2, Mullally asks, "How do we differentiate between genuine activism on social media platforms and slacktivism?" What is one example that she provides to answer her question?

3. How are activism and having an online presence related, according to Mullally? Do you agree or disagree? Why?

4. **Comparison.** Explain whether those who criticized Justine Sacco were engaging in social activism or slacktivism. How do you know? Why might Ronson likely agree or disagree with Mullally's conclusions?

5. **Informing Your Argument.** Return to the table that you created on page 662. Fill in the columns about how Mullally might think about influencing social, cultural, or political change with online posts, the best evidence she offers to clarify and support her ideas, and your response to what Mullally is suggesting.

Source B

Lloyd, Justine. "What is 'Slacktivism' and Can It Change the World?" *The Lighthouse*, 26 Nov. 2020.

There has been much talk about "slacktivism," aka "clicktivism," armchair activism, or hashtag activism, the implication being that hearting an endangered koala, commenting, or posting a pithy quote might *feel* that you have contributed, but have you, really?

Debate is ongoing about whether online activism is eroding traditional forms of protest, and right now, we have a kind of hybrid model between physical protest and online protest.

Talk about "slacktivism" actually dismisses the value of small provocations. Activism is often called a ladder of participation — supporting a cause by writing a comment online is actually a first step. Later you might sign a petition, write to a politician, be part of a coordinated letter-writing campaign that feeds into an inquiry, a bill before parliament, a royal commission.

Around any technology there is, first, a moral panic, where people see (and blame) the technology itself as causing a change, rather than seeing the longer-term changes surrounding the technology.

But we have now moved on from the moral panic stage and are taking a more mature position where really skilled and highly knowledgeable activists are looking at social media very carefully and being very strategic about how it is used. [5]

The positive part of social media is that it's not a top-down model of media, everyone can have a say, a voice, and that's really exciting. Social movements are starting to get their heads around the possibilities. . . .

A movement is made up of multiple actions and multiple people and organisations, and each person's small part in it is really important.

Change builds over time and often it takes a change of government, ideology or political approach for it to arrive at its moment. . . .

At university, I am teaching a generation who are digital natives, who only know an online study and work environment. For six months of this year they couldn't go to physically see their friends; high school students couldn't even go to school. Being online is a way of life.

Some of the students in my unit, "Activism and Social Change," have done fantastic research on the #FridaysForFuture school strikes that evolved globally from Greta Thunberg's 2018 protest against climate change inaction. . . . [10]

Destroy the Joint is an interesting example of going from online activism to the economic jugular. What has evolved into a movement for gender equality and civil discourse in Australia started as a hashtag, Twitter and Facebook page that arose from the opinion of broadcaster Alan Jones that "women are destroying the joint."

The movement triggered a sponsor boycott reported to have cost his radio network some $2 million. Again, advertisers were forced to consider whether media outlets that were misogynistic and abusive were the right fit for them.

The sharing to social media of the death of George Floyd by police in Minneapolis in May highlighted tragic and visible evidence of issues that the Black Lives Matter movement had been protesting about since 2013. This was citizen media intervention, images taken by an onlooker with a camera and then shared to social media with the hashtag #POLICEBRUTALITY, fuelling a worldwide movement. . . .

This transparency around power hasn't been possible before. People speaking back and to each other, documenting and recording keeps a check on power, and that's incredibly important. ∎

Questions

1. How does Lloyd rate slacktivism's importance on the "ladder of participation"?

2. Lloyd says that "highly knowledgeable activists are looking at social media very carefully and being very strategic about how it is used," but then follows with "everyone can have a say, a voice, and that's really exciting" (pars. 5–6). According to Lloyd, does there appear to be a difference between the "knowledgeable activist" and "everyone having a voice"?

3. What conclusions does Lloyd draw about the uses of power at the end of her piece?

4. **Comparison.** Lloyd primarily focuses on activism as a change agent for good. Does Lloyd's approach apply to what happened to Sacco? How could Lloyd address what happened to Sacco with the students in her "Activism and Social Change" class?

5. **Informing Your Argument.** Return to the table that you created on page 662. Fill in the columns about how Lloyd might think about influencing social, cultural, or political change with online posts, the best evidence she offers to clarify and support her ideas, and your response to what Lloyd is suggesting.

Source C

Nixon, Mishma. "Social Media Activism Can Work, but We Don't Need to Shame People Into It." *Teen Vogue*, 2 Mar. 2021.

Every time I open Twitter, I am hit with a barrage of information about a new international crisis or incident. Sometimes these are big events that take over the whole feed, no matter what niche community you are part of. But most of the time, global events don't receive the same attention as something like the Capitol riot in Washington, DC.[1]

This dynamic can be frustrating. We can talk for ages about American exceptionalism and how global and Western media has a singular focus on the U.S., as if the rest of the world doesn't matter enough. Trust me, as a citizen of Sri Lanka — a third world country that is plagued by corruption, discrimination, and violent censorship — who attends college in Iowa, I understand that frustration completely. What I don't understand is the expectation that ordinary civilians, especially but not limited to Americans, will become passionate activists in response to every global event. . . .

It's not that social media activism isn't useful, and it can't always be discounted as performative. In a 2020 paper in the journal *Science*, University of North Carolina, Chapel Hill professors Deen Freelon, Alice Marwick, and Daniel Kreiss wrote that while one objection to digital activism is that it can't "substitute for more impactful actions such as voting or offline protest," it isn't without its own merit. They cited research that showed social media activism is a complement for offline engagement and that "sharing information about politics on social media predicted offline political activities such as attending political meetings, contacting public officials, and donating money to campaigns."

[1] On January 6, 2021, thousands of supporters of President Donald Trump entered the U.S. Capitol illegally in an attempt to disrupt the certification of the election that he lost. Five people died during or shortly after the attack and hundreds were injured. —Eds.

Still, this does not mean that everyone needs to be a social media activist. Activists do lifelong work; they train, organize, and constantly face the consequences of their efforts. What good is your activism if you are shoehorned into it? Why do we want every influencer, member of our respective fandoms, and random mutuals to be calling out every instance of injustice in the world? . . .

To understand and develop an informed opinion about the depth of a crisis in a country, you need to have a grasp of the political, historical, and cultural context of the situation and the place, which is no easy feat. Not to mention, the information you find may be skewed, censored, and altered by various political parties. . . .

Does this mean you shouldn't care about or discuss global issues? It's not my intention to tell you that you have to stay silent in situations like this, especially if you have the platform and

knowledge to make real change. My point is, we shouldn't expect everyone to take up the baton on every single issue. Time and time again, I see some teen influencer posting some half-hearted, obligatory message about a global event they don't really seem to care about. All this leaves us with is people posting out of a sense of moral superiority, a culture of shame and guilt, with a complete disregard for the reality that not everyone is cut out to be an activist.

5

It can be more valuable to devote yourself to a few issues you care most about — educate yourself, invest time and energy, learn from others in the movement — rather than dabbling in every world crisis. As we've seen during the pandemic, as mutual aid networks sprang up to provide groceries and support to neighbors, helping the people in your community is often where you can really make a difference. ∎

Questions

1. What does Nixon mean when she suggests that not everyone should be an activist?
2. Nixon identifies barriers to developing an opinion about a crisis. What are those barriers? How, according to Nixon, do these barriers limit a person's ability to understand the depth of a crisis?
3. What does Nixon propose as a solution to the need to respond to "every global event"? Do you agree with her solution? Why, or why not?
4. **Comparison.** Nixon writes that in order to "understand and develop an informed opinion about the depth of a crisis in a country, you need to have a grasp of the political, historical, and cultural context of the situation and the place." Do you believe that Ronson would agree with this? Why, or why not?
5. **Informing Your Argument.** Return to the table that you created on page 662. Fill in the columns about how Nixon might think about influencing social, cultural, or political change with online posts, the best evidence she offers to clarify and support her ideas, and your response to what Nixon is suggesting.

Source D

Martz, John. "Beyond Slacktivism." *The Nib*, 27 Jul. 2017.

Questions

1. What is Martz suggesting about each of the figures in the cartoons? How are they examples of slacktivism?

2. What similarities do you notice about the way Martz has drawn the people in each image? What is significant about their portrayal as it relates to the cartoonist's ideas about activism?

3. Look at Martz's names for the people in the cartoons. How do the names support the corresponding image and the author's humorous tone toward "activists"?

4. **Comparison.** Explain which of these images best represents those who attacked Sacco online.

5. **Informing Your Argument.** Return to the table that you created on page 662. Fill in the columns about how Martz might think about influencing social, cultural, or political change with online posts, the best evidence he offers to clarify and support his ideas, and your response to what Martz is suggesting.

Entering the Conversation

Throughout this section, you have read a variety of texts that deal with online activism. Now it's time to enter the conversation by responding to the prompt you've been thinking about — *To what extent can we influence social, cultural, or political change online?* Follow the steps below to write your argument.

1. | Building on the Conversation. Locate one additional text on this topic that you think adds an interesting perspective to this Conversation. This text can be of any type: an argument, a narrative, a poem, a painting, or a film clip, for example. Before you decide to add this text to the Conversation, be sure that it is a credible and relevant source; use the skills you practiced in Chapter 4 to evaluate the text (p. 99). Read and annotate the text carefully, making connections to other texts in the Conversation and "How One Stupid Tweet Blew Up Justine Sacco's Life" (p. 651).

2. | Making a Claim. Look back through the table you created and your notes on the texts in the conversation and write a statement that reflects your overall position about the effectiveness of online activism. This statement will be your thesis or claim that you will try to prove in the rest of your argument.

3. | Organizing the Ideas. The texts in this Conversation offer a number of explanations, critiques, and celebrations of online activism. Review the table you have been keeping throughout this Conversation and identify the texts and quotations that either support or challenge the claim that you wrote in the earlier step.

4. | Writing the Argument. Now that you have a claim that reflects your informed stance, it is time to write your argument. Be sure that your writing stays focused on your position on the issue. Refer to at least two Conversation texts, which could include the additional text you found to support your position. Review Chapter 4 (p. 119) to remind yourself of how to use sources in your own writing and refer to the Writing an Argument Workshop in Chapter 7 (p. 466) for additional support.

5. | Presenting the Argument (Optional). Once you have written your argument, you might want to present it to the class or a small group. Review how to write and deliver a presentation in Chapter 3 (p. 90) and Chapter 7 (p. 479).

from Men Explain Things to Me

Rebecca Solnit

Rebecca Solnit (b. 1961) is an environmentalist, activist, historian, essayist, and journalist who has written seventeen books, including *Men Explain Things to Me* (2014), a collection of essays including the one below of the same name, originally published in 2008. Although she never actually uses the term, this piece is credited with popularizing the term *mansplaining*.

David Levenson/Getty Images

I still don't know why Sallie and I bothered to go to that party in the forest slope above Aspen. The people were all older than us and dull in a distinguished way, old enough that we, at forty–ish, passed as the occasion's young ladies. The house was great — if you like Ralph Lauren-style chalets — a rugged luxury cabin at 9,000 feet complete with elk antlers, lots of kilims, and a wood-burning stove. We were preparing to leave, when our host said, "No, stay a little longer so I can talk to you." He was an imposing man who'd made a lot of money.

He kept us waiting while the other guests drifted out into the summer night, and then sat us down at his authentically grainy wood table and said to me, "So? I hear you've written a couple of books."

I replied, "Several, actually."

He said, in the way you encourage your friend's seven-year-old to describe flute practice, "And what are they about?"

They were actually about quite a few dif-ferent things, the six or seven out by then, but I began to speak only of the most recent on that summer day in 2003, *River of Shadows: Ead-weard Muybridge and the Technological Wild West*, my book on the annihilation of time and space and the industrialization of everyday life.

He cut me off soon after I mentioned Muybridge. "And have you heard about the *very important* Muybridge book that came out this year?"

So caught up was I in my assigned role as ingénue that I was perfectly willing to entertain the possibility that another book on the same subject had come out simultaneously and I'd somehow missed it. He was already telling me about the very important book — with that smug look I know so well in a man holding forth, eyes fixed on the fuzzy far horizon of his own authority.

Here, let me just say that my life is well-sprinkled with lovely men, with a long succession of editors who have, since I was young, listened and encouraged and published me, with my infinitely generous younger brother,

5

with splendid friends of whom it could be said — like the Clerk in *The Canterbury Tales* I still remember from Mr. Pelen's class on Chaucer — "gladly would he learn and gladly teach." Still, there are these other men, too. So, Mr. Very Important was going on smugly about this book I should have known when Sallie interrupted him to say, "That's her book." Or tried to interrupt him anyway.

But he just continued on his way. She had to say, "That's her book" three or four times before he finally took it in. And then, as if in a nineteenth-century novel, he went ashen. That I was indeed the author of the very important book it turned out he hadn't read, just read about in the *New York Times Book Review* a few months earlier, so confused the neat categories into which his world was sorted that he was stunned speechless — for a moment, before he began holding forth again. Being women, we were politely out of earshot before we started laughing, and we've never really stopped.

I like incidents of that sort, when forces that are usually so sneaky and hard to point out slither out of the grass and are as obvious as, say, an anaconda that's eaten a cow or an elephant turd on the carpet.

When *River of Shadows* came out, some pedant wrote a snarky letter to the *New York Times* explaining that, though Muybridge had made improvements in camera technology, he had not made any breakthroughs in photographic chemistry. The guy had no idea what he was talking about. Both Philip Prodger, in his wonderful book on Muybridge, and I had actually researched the subject and made it clear that Muybridge had done something obscure but powerful to the wet-plate technology of the time to speed it up amazingly, but letters to the editor don't get fact-checked. And perhaps because the book was about the virile subjects of cinema and technology, the Men Who Knew came out of the woodwork.

A British academic wrote in to the *London Review of Books* with all kinds of nitpicking corrections and complaints, all of them from outer space. He carped, for example, that to aggrandize Muybridge's standing I left out technological predecessors like Henry R. Heyl. He'd apparently not read the book all the way to page 202 or checked the index, since Heyl was there (though his contribution was just not very significant). Surely one of these men has died of embarrassment, but not nearly publicly enough.

10

In a now-infamous instance of mansplaining, Kanye West explains why Beyoncé should have won the 2009 MTV award for best music video, instead of Taylor Swift.

Even if you knew nothing of the incident, how do their body language and facial expressions illustrate a "mansplaining" event?

Christopher Polk/Getty Images

The Slippery Slope of Silencings

Yes, guys like this pick on other men's books too, and people of both genders pop up at events to hold forth on irrelevant things and conspiracy theories, but the out-and-out confrontational confidence of the totally ignorant is, in my experience, gendered. Men explain things to me, and other women, whether or not they know what they're talking about. Some men.

Every woman knows what I'm talking about. It's the presumption that makes it hard, at times, for any woman in any field; that keeps women from speaking up and from being heard when they dare; that crushes young women into silence by indicating, the way harassment on the street does, that this is not their world. It trains us in self-doubt and self-limitation just as it exercises men's unsupported overconfidence.

I wouldn't be surprised if part of the trajec- 15
tory of American politics since 2001 was shaped by, say, the inability to hear Coleen Rowley, the FBI woman who issued those early warnings about al-Qaeda, and it was certainly shaped by a Bush administration to which you couldn't tell anything, including that Iraq had no links to al-Qaeda and no WMDs, or that the war was not going to be a "cakewalk." (Even male experts couldn't penetrate the fortress of their smugness.)

Arrogance might have had something to do with the war, but this syndrome is a war that nearly every woman faces every day, a war within herself too, a belief in her superfluity, an invitation to silence, one from which a fairly nice career as a writer (with a lot of research and facts correctly deployed) has not entirely freed me. After all, there was a moment there when I was willing to let Mr. Important and his overweening confidence bowl over my more shaky certainty.

Jessica Meir ✔
@Astro_Jessica   ✔ Follow

My first venture >63,000', the space equivalent zone, where water spontaneously boils! Luckily I'm suited!
9:05 PM · 8 Sep 2016 · California, USA

↩   ⟲ 301   ♥ 1,187

                                   ⚙ ≗ Follow

@Astro_Jessica Wouldn't say it's spontaneous. The pressure in the room got below the vapor pressure of the water at room temp. Simple thermo

In this Twitter exchange, astronaut Jessica Meir is told by a person with no scientific credentials why water boils at low pressures.

Describe the tone of the man's explanations. What evidence supports your observation? Do you believe the nature of social media encourages exchanges like this? Imagine Solnit came across this exchange, and write a tweet from her perspective, based on what you have read here. Explain your response.

Don't forget that I've had a lot more confirmation of my right to think and speak than most women, and I've learned that a certain amount of self-doubt is a good tool for correcting, understanding, listening, and progressing — though too much is paralyzing and total self-confidence produces arrogant idiots, like the ones who have governed us since 2001. There's a happy medium between these poles to which the genders have been pushed, a warm equatorial belt of give and take where we should all meet.

More extreme versions of our situation exist in, for example, those Middle Eastern countries where women's testimony has no legal standing; so that a woman can't testify that she was raped without a male witness to counter the male rapist. Which there rarely is.

Credibility is a basic survival tool. When I was very young and just beginning to get what feminism was about and why it was necessary, I had a boyfriend whose uncle was a nuclear physicist. One Christmas, he was telling — as though it were a light and amusing subject — how a neighbor's wife in his suburban bomb-making community had come running out of her house naked in the middle of the night screaming that her husband was trying to kill her. How, I asked, did you know that he wasn't trying to kill her? He explained, patiently, that they were respectable middle-class people. Therefore, her-husband-trying-to-kill-her was simply not a credible explanation for her fleeing the house yelling that her husband was trying to kill her. That she was crazy, on the other hand. . . .

Even getting a restraining order — a fairly new legal tool — requires acquiring the credibility to convince the courts that some guy is a menace and then getting the cops to enforce it. Restraining orders often don't work anyway. Violence is one way to silence people, to deny their voice and their credibility, to assert your right to control over their right to exist. About three women a day are murdered by spouses or ex-spouses in this country. It's one of the main causes of death in pregnant women in the U.S. At the heart of the struggle of feminism to give rape, date rape, marital rape, domestic violence, and workplace sexual harassment legal standing as crimes has been the necessity of making women credible and audible.

I tend to believe that women acquired the status of human beings when these kinds of acts started to be taken seriously, when the big things that stop us and kill us were addressed legally from the mid-1970s on; well after, that is, my birth. And for anyone about to argue that workplace sexual intimidation isn't a life or death issue, remember that Marine Lance Corporal Maria Lauterbach, age 20, was apparently killed by her higher-ranking colleague last winter while she was waiting to testify that he raped her. The burned remains of her pregnant body were found in the fire pit in his backyard in December.

Being told that, categorically, he knows what he's talking about and she doesn't, however minor a part of any given conversation, perpetuates the ugliness of this world and holds back its light. After my book *Wanderlust* came out in 2000, I found myself better able to resist being bullied out of my own perceptions and interpretations. On two occasions around that time, I objected to the behavior of a man, only to be told that the incidents hadn't happened at all as I said, that I was subjective, delusional, overwrought, dishonest — in a nutshell, female.

Most of my life, I would have doubted myself and backed down. Having public standing as a writer of history helped me stand my ground, but few women get that boost, and billions of women must be out there on this six-billion-person planet being told that they are not reliable witnesses to their own lives, that the truth is not their property, now or ever. This goes way beyond Men Explaining Things, but it's part of the same archipelago of arrogance.

Men explain things to me, still. And no man has ever apologized for explaining, wrongly, things that I know and they don't. Not yet, but according to the actuarial tables, I may have another forty-something years to live, more or less, so it could happen. Though I'm not holding my breath. ■

20

Understanding and Interpreting

1. How does the man respond when he learns that the book he's raving about is actually Solnit's (par. 9)? Why does she "like incidents of that sort"?

2. In paragraph 8, Solnit mentions men who do not fit the "mansplaining" mold. How does this help illustrate a larger point she is making?

3. In paragraph 14, Solnit writes, "Every woman knows what I'm talking about." Summarize what she says in the rest of the paragraph that every woman knows.

4. How does Solnit respond to criticism of her work? What do her responses say about her as a person?

5. Explain what Solnit means when she writes, "Credibility is a basic survival tool" (par. 19).

6. In paragraphs 19, 20, and 21, Solnit provides examples of women's experiences with violence. At first glance, these might seem off topic, but explain how these examples relate to and support her main idea.

7. Does Solnit depict men as unwitting or as intentionally demeaning? What evidence from the text supports your response?

8. After reading the piece through to the end, reread the opening section again. How does that conversation Solnit has with the man help reinforce the main idea of the text?

Analyzing Language, Style, and Structure

9. **Vocabulary in Context.** In paragraph 23, Solnit refers to an "archipelago of arrogance" to describe a set of behaviors that she's observed. What is an *archipelago*, and what is its meaning in this context?

10. Even though she does not explicitly use the term, how does Solnit denotatively and connotatively define the concept of *mansplaining*?

11. How would you describe Solnit's style of writing? How would the article's impact have been different if she had written in a different style — a list or strictly memoir, for example, or without the use of her first-person perspective?

12. What is the effect of capitalizing "Mr. Very Important" in paragraph 8 and the "Men Who Knew" in paragraph 11?

13. Analyze Solnit's tone toward the following:

    a. men in general

    b. the U.S. government

    c. women's situations in other countries

14. Reread the final paragraph of this piece. Is Solnit optimistic or pessimistic about the chances of improving the issues she describes? What specific diction and syntax help her to communicate that perspective?

Topics for Composing

15. **Analysis.** Ultimately, what does Solnit believe causes "mansplaining" and what are its effects? Analyze the reasoning and evidence Solnit uses, drawing your support directly from the text.

16. **Argument.** Are the effects of "mansplaining" that Solnit identifies as bad as she suggests? Write an argument that supports or contradicts Solnit's premise. Use examples from your own or others' experiences or conduct research to illustrate your position.

17. **Connections.** Although she doesn't use the term, Solnit's experiences could also be referred to as "microaggressions," which are statements, actions, or incidents regarded as indirect, subtle, or unintentional discrimination against members of a marginalized group. Describe a time when you or someone you know experienced a microaggression. What was the outcome of the incident?

18. **Speaking and Listening.** Watch a favorite movie or episode of a TV show and track examples of "mansplaining" in them. In a small group or as a class, discuss whether Solnit's observations hold up in other media outlets. Share your findings, observations, and conclusions and listen closely to others' perspectives.

19. **Research.** The movie *Hidden Figures* is about the team of black female scientists who helped send Americans into space; they went unrecognized for their mathematical and scientific contributions for over fifty years. Research other ways in which women have lent their talents and expertise to professional fields but had to wait, or in some cases may still be waiting, to receive credit for their contributions.

20. **Research.** This essay came out over a decade ago, and since then "mansplaining" has become a common phrase and topic for others to discuss. Look into what research has been done on this topic, and report whether it supports, challenges, or qualifies Solnit's claims about the damage that can stem from this attitude toward women.

21. **Multimodal.** Create or locate images online of men and women in conversation that might represent the ideas of "mansplaining," such as the image of Kanye West on page 670. Write captions for the images of the spoken and unspoken dialogue that illustrate one or more of the points Solnit makes in her piece.

Information Overload Helps Fake News Spread, and Social Media Knows It

Filippo Menczer and Thomas Hills

Filippo Menczer is a professor of Informatics and Computer Science at Indiana University. Thomas Hills is a professor of psychology and director at the University of Warwick in England. This piece was originally published in 2020 in *Scientific American*.

KEY CONTEXT Beginning in 2019, the virus known as COVID-19 led to significant upheavals in much of society. Early in the pandemic, many businesses were forced to close to slow the transmission and many companies, states, and localities passed mask requirements and, eventually, vaccine mandates. These measures were opposed by some people, many of whom received their information about the virus from social media, which at times included misinformation.

Consider Andy, who is worried about contracting COVID-19. Unable to read all the articles he sees on it, he relies on trusted friends for tips. When one opines on Facebook that pandemic fears are overblown, Andy dismisses the idea at first. But then the hotel where he works closes its doors, and with his job at risk, Andy starts wondering how serious the threat from the new virus really is. No one he knows has died, after all. A colleague posts an article about the COVID "scare" having been created by Big Pharma in collusion with corrupt politicians, which jibes with Andy's distrust of government. His Web search quickly takes him to articles claiming that COVID-19 is no worse than the flu. Andy joins an online group of people who have been or fear being laid off and soon finds himself asking, like many of them, "What pandemic?" When he learns that several of his new friends are planning to attend a rally demanding an end to lockdowns, he decides to join them. Almost no one at the massive protest, including him, wears a mask. When his sister asks about the rally, Andy shares the conviction that has now become part of his identity: COVID is a hoax.

This example illustrates a minefield of cognitive biases. We prefer information from people we trust, our in-group. We pay attention to and are more likely to share information about risks — for Andy, the risk of losing his job. We search for and remember things that fit well with what we already know and understand. These biases are products of our evolutionary past, and for tens of thousands of years, they served us well. People who behaved in accordance with them — for example, by staying away from the overgrown pond bank where someone said there was a viper — were more likely to survive than those who did not.

Modern technologies are amplifying these biases in harmful ways, however. Search engines direct Andy to sites that inflame his suspicions, and social media connects him with like-minded people, feeding his fears. Making matters worse, bots — automated social media accounts that impersonate humans — enable misguided or malevolent actors to take advantage of his vulnerabilities.

Compounding the problem is the proliferation of online information. Viewing and producing blogs, videos, tweets and other units of information called memes has become so cheap and easy that the information marketplace is inundated. Unable to process all this material, we let our cognitive biases decide what we should pay attention to. These mental shortcuts influence which information we search for, comprehend, remember and repeat to a harmful extent.

The need to understand these cognitive vulnerabilities and how algorithms use or manipulate them has become urgent. At the University of Warwick in England and at Indiana University Bloomington's Observatory on Social Media (OSoMe, pronounced "awesome"), our teams are using cognitive experiments, simulations, data mining and artificial intelligence to comprehend the cognitive vulnerabilities of social media users. Insights from psychological studies on the evolution of information conducted at Warwick inform the computer models developed at Indiana, and vice versa. We are also developing analytical and machine-learning aids to fight social media manipulation. Some of these tools are already being used by journalists, civil-society organizations and individuals to detect inauthentic actors, map the spread of false narratives and foster news literacy. [5]

Information Overload

The glut of information has generated intense competition for people's attention. As Nobel Prize–winning economist and psychologist Herbert A. Simon noted, "What information consumes is rather obvious: it consumes the attention of its recipients." One of the first consequences of the so-called attention economy is the loss of high-quality information. The OSoMe team demonstrated this result with a set of simple simulations. It represented users of social media such as Andy, called agents, as nodes in a network of online acquaintances. At each time step in the simulation, an agent may either create a meme or reshare one that he or she sees in a news feed. To mimic limited attention, agents are allowed to view only a certain number of items near the top of their news feeds.

Running this simulation over many time steps, Lilian Weng of OSoMe found that as agents' attention became increasingly limited, the propagation of memes came to reflect the power-law distribution of actual social media: the probability that a meme would be shared a given number of times was roughly an inverse power of that number. For example, the likelihood of a meme being shared three times was approximately nine times less than that of its being shared once.

This winner-take-all popularity pattern of memes, in which most are barely noticed while a few spread widely, could not be explained by some of them being more catchy or somehow more valuable: the memes in this simulated world had no intrinsic quality. Virality resulted purely from the statistical consequences of information proliferation in a social network of agents with limited attention. Even when agents preferentially shared memes of higher quality, researcher Xiaoyan Qiu, then at OSoMe, observed little improvement in the overall quality of those shared the most. Our models revealed that even when we want to see and share high–quality information, our inability to view everything in our news feeds inevitably leads us to share things that are partly or completely untrue.

Cognitive biases greatly worsen the problem. In a set of groundbreaking studies in 1932, psychologist Frederic Bartlett told volunteers a Native American legend about a young man who hears war cries and, pursuing them, enters a dreamlike battle that eventually leads to his real death. Bartlett asked the volunteers, who were non-Native, to recall the rather confusing story at increasing intervals, from minutes to years later. He found that as time passed, the rememberers tended to distort the tale's culturally unfamiliar parts such that they were either lost to memory or transformed into more familiar things. We now know that our minds do this all the time: they adjust our understanding of new information so that it fits in with what we already know. One consequence of this so-called confirmation bias is that people often seek out, recall and understand information that best confirms what they already believe.

This tendency is extremely difficult to correct. Experiments consistently show that even when people encounter balanced information containing views from differing perspectives, they tend to find supporting evidence for what they already believe. And when people with divergent beliefs about emotionally charged issues such as climate change are shown the same information on these topics, they become even more committed to their original positions.

Making matters worse, search engines and social media platforms provide personalized recommendations based on the vast amounts of data they have about users' past preferences. They prioritize information in our feeds that we are most likely to agree with — no matter how fringe — and shield us from information that might change our minds. This makes us easy targets for polarization. Nir Grinberg and his co-workers at Northeastern University recently showed that conservatives in the U.S. are more receptive to misinformation. But our own analysis of consumption of low-quality information on Twitter shows that the vulnerability applies to both sides of the political spectrum, and no one can fully avoid it. Even our ability to detect online manipulation is affected by our political bias, though not symmetrically: Republican users are more likely to mistake bots promoting conservative ideas for humans, whereas Democrats are more likely to mistake conservative human users for bots.

10

What point does this cartoon make about human nature and information? Why would the authors of this article likely agree or disagree with it?

Pat Byrnes/CartoonStock

Social Herding

In New York City in August 2019, people began running away from what sounded like gunshots. Others followed, some shouting, "Shooter!" Only later did they learn that the blasts came from a backfiring motorcycle. In such a situation, it may pay to run first and ask questions later. In the absence of clear signals, our brains use information about the crowd to infer appropriate actions, similar to the behavior of schooling fish and flocking birds.

Such social conformity is pervasive. In a fascinating 2006 study involving 14,000 Web-based volunteers, Matthew Salganik, then at Columbia University, and his colleagues found that when people can see what music others are downloading, they end up downloading similar songs. Moreover, when people were isolated into "social" groups, in which they could see the preferences of others in their circle but had no information about outsiders, the choices

of individual groups rapidly diverged. But the preferences of "nonsocial" groups, where no one knew about others' choices, stayed relatively stable. In other words, social groups create a pressure toward conformity so powerful that it can overcome individual preferences, and by amplifying random early differences, it can cause segregated groups to diverge to extremes.

Social media follows a similar dynamic. We confuse popularity with quality and end up copying the behavior we observe. Experiments on Twitter by Bjarke Mønsted and his colleagues at the Technical University of Denmark and the University of Southern California indicate that information is transmitted via "complex contagion": when we are repeatedly exposed to an idea, typically from many sources, we are more likely to adopt and reshare it. This social bias is further amplified by what psychologists call the "mere exposure" effect: when people are repeatedly exposed to the same stimuli, such as certain faces, they grow to like those stimuli more than those they have encountered less often.

Such biases translate into an irresistible urge to pay attention to information that is going viral — if everybody else is talking about it, it must be important. In addition to showing us items that conform with our views, social media platforms such as Facebook, Twitter, YouTube and Instagram place popular content at the top of our screens and show us how many people have liked and shared something. Few of us realize that these cues do not provide independent assessments of quality.

In fact, programmers who design the algorithms for ranking memes on social media assume that the "wisdom of crowds" will quickly identify high-quality items; they use popularity as a proxy for quality. Our analysis of vast amounts of anonymous data about clicks shows that all platforms — social media, search engines and news sites — preferentially serve up information from a narrow subset of popular sources.

15

677

To understand why, we modeled how they combine signals for quality and popularity in their rankings. In this model, agents with limited attention — those who see only a given number of items at the top of their news feeds — are also more likely to click on memes ranked higher by the platform. Each item has intrinsic quality, as well as a level of popularity determined by how many times it has been clicked on. Another variable tracks the extent to which the ranking relies on popularity rather than quality. Simulations of this model reveal that such algorithmic bias typically suppresses the quality of memes even in the absence of human bias. Even when we want to share the best information, the algorithms end up misleading us.

Echo Chambers

Most of us do not believe we follow the herd. But our confirmation bias leads us to follow others who are like us, a dynamic that is sometimes referred to as homophily — a tendency for like-minded people to connect with one another. Social media amplifies homophily by allowing users to alter their social network structures through following, unfriending, and so on. The result is that people become segregated into large, dense and increasingly misinformed communities commonly described as echo chambers.

At OSoMe, we explored the emergence of online echo chambers through another simulation, EchoDemo. In this model, each agent has a

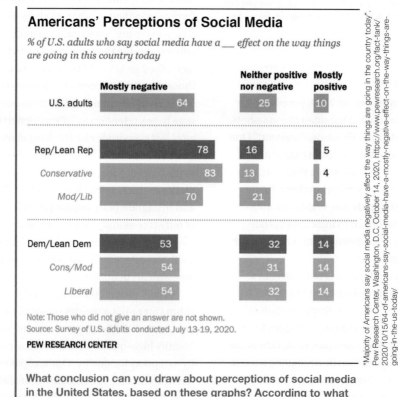

Americans' Perceptions of Social Media

% of U.S. adults who say social media have a ___ effect on the way things are going in this country today

	Mostly negative	Neither positive nor negative	Mostly positive
U.S. adults	64	25	10
Rep/Lean Rep	78	16	5
Conservative	83	13	4
Mod/Lib	70	21	8
Dem/Lean Dem	53	32	14
Cons/Mod	54	31	14
Liberal	54	32	14

Note: Those who did not give an answer are not shown.
Source: Survey of U.S. adults conducted July 13-19, 2020.

PEW RESEARCH CENTER

What conclusion can you draw about perceptions of social media in the United States, based on these graphs? According to what you have read, would the authors of this article be surprised by these findings? Why or why not?

political opinion represented by a number ranging from −1 (say, liberal) to +1 (conservative). These inclinations are reflected in agents' posts. Agents are also influenced by the opinions they see in their news feeds, and they can unfollow users with dissimilar opinions. Starting with random initial networks and opinions, we found that the combination of social influence and unfollowing greatly accelerates the formation of polarized and segregated communities.

Indeed, the political echo chambers on Twitter are so extreme that individual users' political leanings can be predicted with high accuracy: you have the same opinions as the majority of your connections. This chambered structure efficiently spreads information within a community while insulating that community from other groups. In 2014 our research group was targeted by a disinformation campaign claiming that we were part of a politically motivated effort to suppress free speech. This false charge spread virally mostly in the conservative echo chamber, whereas debunking articles by fact-checkers were found mainly in the liberal community. Sadly, such segregation of fake news items from their fact-check reports is the norm.

Social media can also increase our negativity. In a recent laboratory study, Robert Jagiello, also at Warwick, found that socially shared information not only bolsters our biases but also becomes more resilient to correction. He investigated how information is passed from person to person in a so-called social diffusion chain. In the experiment, the first person in the chain read a set of articles about either nuclear power or food additives. The articles were designed to be balanced, containing as much positive information (for example, about less carbon pollution or longer-lasting food) as negative information (such as risk of meltdown or possible harm to health).

The first person in the social diffusion chain told the next person about the articles, the second told the third, and so on. We observed an overall increase in the amount of negative information as it passed along the chain — known as the social amplification of risk. Moreover, work by Danielle J. Navarro and her colleagues at the University of New South Wales in Australia found that information in social diffusion chains is most susceptible to distortion by individuals with the most extreme biases.

Even worse, social diffusion also makes negative information more "sticky." When Jagiello subsequently exposed people in the social diffusion chains to the original, balanced information — that is, the news that the first person in the chain had seen — the balanced information did little to reduce individuals' negative attitudes. The information that had passed through people not only had become more negative but also was more resistant to updating.

A 2015 study by OSoMe researchers Emilio Ferrara and Zeyao Yang analyzed empirical data about such "emotional contagion" on Twitter and found that people overexposed to negative content tend to then share negative posts, whereas those overexposed to positive content tend to share more positive posts. Because negative content spreads faster than positive content, it is easy to manipulate emotions by creating narratives that trigger negative responses such as fear and anxiety. Ferrara, now at the University of Southern California, and his colleagues at the Bruno Kessler Foundation in Italy have shown that during Spain's 2017 referendum on Catalan independence, social bots were leveraged to retweet violent and inflammatory narratives, increasing their exposure and exacerbating social conflict.

Rise of the Bots

Information quality is further impaired by social bots, which can exploit all our cognitive loopholes. Bots are easy to create. Social media

20

25

platforms provide so-called application programming interfaces that make it fairly trivial for a single actor to set up and control thousands of bots. But amplifying a message, even with just a few early upvotes by bots on social media platforms such as Reddit, can have a huge impact on the subsequent popularity of a post.

At OSoMe, we have developed machine-learning algorithms to detect social bots. One of these, Botometer, is a public tool that extracts 1,200 features from a given Twitter account to characterize its profile, friends, social network structure, temporal activity patterns, language and other features. The program compares these characteristics with those of tens of thousands of previously identified bots to give the Twitter account a score for its likely use of automation.

In 2017 we estimated that up to 15 percent of active Twitter accounts were bots — and that they had played a key role in the spread of misinformation during the 2016 U.S. election period. Within seconds of a fake news article being posted — such as one claiming the Clinton campaign was involved in occult rituals — it would be tweeted by many bots, and humans, beguiled by the apparent popularity of the content, would retweet it.

Bots also influence us by pretending to represent people from our in-group. A bot only has to follow, like and retweet someone in an online community to quickly infiltrate it. OSoMe researcher Xiaodan Lou developed another model in which some of the agents are bots that infiltrate a social network and share deceptively engaging low-quality content — think of click-bait. One parameter in the model describes the probability that an authentic agent will follow bots — which, for the purposes of this model, we define as agents that generate memes of zero quality and retweet only one another. Our simulations show that these bots can effectively suppress the entire ecosystem's information quality by infiltrating only a small fraction of the network. Bots can also accelerate the formation

of echo chambers by suggesting other inauthentic accounts to be followed, a technique known as creating "follow trains."

Some manipulators play both sides of a divide through separate fake news sites and bots, driving political polarization or monetization by ads. At OSoMe, we recently uncovered a network of inauthentic accounts on Twitter that were all coordinated by the same entity. Some pretended to be pro-Trump supporters of the Make America Great Again campaign, whereas others posed as Trump "resisters"; all asked for political donations. Such operations amplify content that preys on confirmation biases and accelerate the formation of polarized echo chambers.

Curbing Online Manipulation

Understanding our cognitive biases and how algorithms and bots exploit them allows us to better guard against manipulation. OSoMe has produced a number of tools to help people understand their own vulnerabilities, as well as the weaknesses of social media platforms. One is a mobile app called Fakey that helps users learn how to spot misinformation. The game simulates a social media news feed, showing actual articles from low- and high-credibility sources. Users must decide what they can or should not share and what to fact-check. Analysis of data from Fakey confirms the prevalence of online social herding: users are more likely to share low-credibility articles when they believe that many other people have shared them.

Another program available to the public, called Hoaxy, shows how any extant meme spreads through Twitter. In this visualization, nodes represent actual Twitter accounts, and links depict how retweets, quotes, mentions and replies propagate the meme from account to account. Each node has a color representing its score from Botometer, which allows users to see the scale at which bots amplify misinformation. These tools have been used by investigative journalists to uncover the roots of

30

misinformation campaigns, such as one pushing the "pizzagate" conspiracy in the U.S. They also helped to detect bot-driven voter-suppression efforts during the 2018 U.S. midterm election. Manipulation is getting harder to spot, however, as machine-learning algorithms become better at emulating human behavior.

Apart from spreading fake news, misinformation campaigns can also divert attention from other, more serious problems. To combat such manipulation, we have recently developed a software tool called BotSlayer. It extracts hashtags, links, accounts and other features that co-occur in tweets about topics a user wishes to study. For each entity, BotSlayer tracks the tweets, the accounts posting them and their bot scores to flag entities that are trending and probably being amplified by bots or coordinated accounts. The goal is to enable reporters, civil-society organizations and political candidates to spot and track inauthentic influence campaigns in real time.

These programmatic tools are important aids, but institutional changes are also necessary to curb the proliferation of fake news. Education can help, although it is unlikely to encompass all the topics on which people are misled. Some governments and social media platforms are also trying to clamp down on online manipulation and fake news. But who decides what is fake or manipulative and what is not? Information can come with warning labels such as the ones Facebook and Twitter have started providing, but can the people who apply those labels be trusted? The risk that such measures could deliberately or inadvertently suppress free speech, which is vital for robust democracies, is real. The dominance of social media platforms with global reach and close ties with governments further complicates the possibilities.

One of the best ideas may be to make it more difficult to create and share low-quality information. This could involve adding friction by forcing people to pay to share or receive information. Payment could be in the form of time, mental work such as puzzles, or microscopic fees for subscriptions or usage. Automated posting should be treated like advertising. Some platforms are already using friction in the form of CAPTCHAs and phone confirmation to access accounts. Twitter has placed limits on automated posting. These efforts could be expanded to gradually shift online sharing incentives toward information that is valuable to consumers.

Free communication is not free. By decreasing the cost of information, we have decreased its value and invited its adulteration. To restore the health of our information ecosystem, we must understand the vulnerabilities of our overwhelmed minds and how the economics of information can be leveraged to protect us from being misled. ∎ 35

Understanding and Interpreting

1. The authors first discuss "cognitive biases" in paragraph 2. How do the authors define them and why are they important to understand for this topic?

2. The authors discuss "cognitive vulnerabilities" beginning in paragraph 5. How do they define them?

3. The authors quote psychologist Hebert A. Simon, who writes, "What information consumes is rather obvious: it consumes the attention of its recipients." Explain what this means and how it relates to what the authors call "the attention economy" (par. 6).

4. Summarize the findings of the experiment of sharing the meme in paragraphs 6–8 or the experiment about the Native American legend (par. 9). What conclusion is the reader expected to draw from the experiment?

5. According to the authors, how do social media and search engines make the challenges of cognitive biases even worse (par. 11)?

6. What role does "social conformity" play in the sharing of information online, especially through social media?

7. According to the authors, why do some things go viral? What is problematic about this type of popularity?

8. What do the authors mean by "echo chambers" and what negative effects do the authors associate with them?

9. Summarize the results of Robert Jagiello's experiments on the social diffusion chain (pars. 21–23), and explain why it can be so dangerous.

10. What are "bots" and what role do they play in how information is shared? To what extent are bots a negative or positive force in the online environment, according to the authors?

11. The authors conclude their piece by offering possible solutions. Explain how the authors think the following might address the concerns they raise:

   a. Apps such as Fakey, Hoaxy, and BotSlayer

   b. Making people pay to share information

Analyzing Language, Style, and Structure

12. **Vocabulary in Context.** In paragraph 3, the authors describe "misguided or malevolent actors." What does the word *actors* mean in this context and how is it different from other uses of the word?

13. Much of this piece refers to scientific experiments and data. What is the effect of starting the piece with the story of Andy?

14. In paragraph 3, the authors suggest that the search engines that Andy uses "inflame his suspicions." What is the effect of the word *inflame* in this context?

15. How do the authors establish their ethos at the beginning of the piece, particularly in paragraph 5?

16. In paragraph 28, the authors use the word *infiltrate* to describe the actions of a bot. What is the connotation of this word and why might the authors have chosen it? What are other similar emotionally charged words that stand out to you in a piece that predominately takes on a neutral, academic tone?

17. The authors regularly personify the process of how information is shared, as in paragraph 28: "bots can effectively suppress the entire ecosystem's information quality." Why might the authors choose to use personification, and what are other similar uses that you have identified in this piece?

Topics for Composing

18. **Analysis.** Analyze this piece for its use of appeals. How do the authors balance logos with pathos and ethos? Refer to specific examples and diction from the piece to support your analysis.

19. **Argument.** What are the best possible ways to improve the information ecosystem and limit the impact of misinformation? Use this piece, your own experiences, and additional research to support your position.

20. **Connections.** Describe your own information ecosystem. Where do you get your information? How, why, and with whom do you share information online? How similar are your experiences to those described by the authors of this piece?

21. **Speaking and Listening.** In a small group, try to replicate the social diffusion chain experiment described in paragraphs 21–23. Start by locating a balanced news article about a controversial topic. You will want to look at a mainstream news source with a reputation for being objective. One member of the group verbally shares a summary of the article with another group member individually who then verbally shares the summary with another member, and so on for at least three to four rounds. No one should write anything down; you are sharing the information verbally only. Afterward, everyone in the group should read the initial article and explain how the information stayed balanced or became distorted.

22. **Research.** In 2017, the authors "estimated that up to 15 percent of active Twitter accounts were bots." Conduct research to determine whether that percentage has changed and what, if anything, social media companies have done to crack down on the prevalence of bots on the Internet.

23. **Research.** In 2021, a whistleblower named Frances Haugen released information that revealed some of Facebook's internal practices. In particular, Haugen revealed that Facebook can manipulate its own algorithm to encourage wider sharing of the most extreme posts. Conduct research on the details that Haugen revealed and what, if anything, Facebook has done to address this issue.

24. **Creative Writing.** Try writing a "fake news" article or a meme that might attract a lot of views based on the ideas presented in this piece.

On the Decay of Friendship

Samuel Johnson

Despite a life of hardship and health issues, Samuel Johnson (1737–1784) was one of the most prolific writers of his time. Known as the author of *A Dictionary of the English Language* (1755), which took eight years to complete, he also wrote critical reviews, poems, and essays that often explored moral and religious topics. This essay was published in a periodical paper called *The Wisdom of the Rambler, Adventurer, and Idler* in 1758.

After Sir Joshua Reynolds/Art Images/Getty Images

Life has no pleasure higher or nobler than that of friendship. It is painful to consider that this sublime enjoyment may be impaired or destroyed by innumerable causes, and that there is no human possession of which the duration is less certain.

Many have talked in very exalted language, of the perpetuity of friendship, of invincible constancy, and unalienable kindness; and some examples have been seen of men who have continued faithful to their earliest choice, and whose affection has predominated over changes of fortune, and contrariety of opinion.

But these instances are memorable, because they are rare. The friendship which is to be practiced or expected by common mortals, must take its rise from mutual pleasure, and must end when the power ceases of delighting each other.

Many accidents therefore may happen by which the ardor of kindness will be abated, without criminal baseness or contemptible inconstancy on either part. To give pleasure is not always in our power; and little does he know himself who believes that he can be always able to receive it.

Those who would gladly pass their days together may be separated by the different course of their affairs; and friendship, like love, is destroyed by long absence, though it may be increased by short intermissions.

What we have missed long enough to want it, we value more when it is regained; but that which has been lost till it is forgotten, will be found at last with little gladness, and with still less if a substitute has supplied the place. A man deprived of the companion to whom he used to open his bosom, and with whom he shared the hours of leisure and merriment, feels the day at first hanging heavy on him; his difficulties oppress, and his doubts distract him; he sees time come and go without his wonted gratification, and all is sadness within, and solitude about him. But this uneasiness never lasts long; necessity produces expedients, new

amusements are discovered, and new conversation is admitted.

No expectation is more frequently disappointed, than that which naturally arises in the mind from the prospect of meeting an old friend after long separation. We expect the attraction to be revived, and the coalition to be renewed; no man considers how much alteration time has made in himself, and very few inquire what effect it has had upon others. The first hour convinces them that the pleasure which they have formerly enjoyed, is forever at an end; different scenes have made different impressions; the opinions of both are changed; and that similitude of manners and sentiment is lost which confirmed them both in the approbation of themselves.

Friendship is often destroyed by opposition of interest, not only by the ponderous and visible interest which the desire of wealth and greatness forms and maintains, but by a thousand secret and slight competitions, scarcely known to the mind upon which they operate. There is scarcely any man without some favorite trifle which he values above greater attainments, some desire of petty praise which he cannot patiently suffer

What point is the cartoon trying to make about friendship? What creates the intended humor? How might Samuel Johnson respond to the idea of a friendship contract? Respond using evidence directly from the text.

to be frustrated. This minute ambition is sometimes crossed before it is known, and sometimes defeated by wanton petulance; but such attacks are seldom made without the loss of friendship; for whoever has once found the vulnerable part will always be feared, and the resentment will burn on in secret, of which shame hinders the discovery.

This, however, is a slow malignity, which a wise man will obviate as inconsistent with quiet, and a good man will repress as contrary to virtue; but human happiness is sometimes violated by some more sudden strokes.

A dispute begun in jest upon a subject which a moment before was on both parts regarded with careless indifference, is continued by the desire of conquest, till vanity kindles into rage, and opposition rankles into enmity. Against this hasty mischief, I know not what security can be obtained; men will be sometimes surprised into quarrels; and though they might both haste into reconciliation, as soon as their tumult had subsided, yet two minds will seldom be found together, which can at once subdue their discontent, or immediately enjoy the sweets of peace without remembering the wounds of the conflict.

Friendship has other enemies. Suspicion is always hardening the cautious, and disgust repelling the delicate. Very slender differences will sometimes part those whom long reciprocation of civility or beneficence has united. *Lonelove* and *Ranger*[1] retired into the country to enjoy the company of each other, and returned in six weeks, cold and petulant; *Ranger*'s pleasure was to walk in the fields, and *Lonelove*'s to sit in a bower; each had complied with the other in his turn, and each was angry that compliance had been exacted.

The most fatal disease of friendship is gradual decay, or dislike hourly increased by causes too slender for complaint, and too numerous for removal. Those who are angry may be reconciled; those who have been injured may receive a recompense: but when the desire of pleasing and willingness to be pleased is silently diminished, the renovation of friendship is hopeless; as, when the vital powers sink into languor, there is no longer any use of the physician. ∎

---

[1]*Lonelove* and *Ranger*: two characters created by Johnson to demonstrate how good friends can be broken apart by slight personality differences. —Eds.

Understanding and Interpreting

1. Reread paragraphs 1–3 and summarize in two to three sentences what Johnson is saying about friendship's importance and role in our lives.

2. In paragraphs 5 through 7, Johnson explains how long absences can affect friendship. What does he say changes after a long absence, and how can this lead to a loss of friendship?

3. In paragraphs 8 and 9, explain what Johnson means by the "slow malignity" and the "sudden strokes" of a decaying friendship?

4. Summarize what Johnson means in paragraph 8 when he writes: "for whoever has once found the vulnerable part will always be feared, and the resentment will burn on in secret, of which shame hinders the discovery." How does being vulnerable affect friendship, according to Johnson?

5. What are the main causes for the decay of friendship, according to Johnson? What does he suggest about the role of power in a friendship?

Analyzing Language, Style, and Structure

6. **Vocabulary in Context.** Johnson explains that a long absence from friends results in the loss of "manners and sentiment" (par. 7). What does the word *manners* mean in this context?

7. At the end of this essay, Johnson makes a connection between declining health and decaying friendship, saying that "when the vital powers sink into languor, there is no longer any use of the physician." Explain how this figurative language helps to illustrate a point he is making about friendship.

8. How does Johnson structure the progression of his ideas in the essay? How does this structure assist him in making his points about friendship clear to the reader?

9. Reread the Lonelove and Ranger story in paragraph 11. Why might each have expressed anger and how does this example help Johnson to make a point about friendship?

10. Describe the overall tone of the essay. How do Johnson's diction and details about friendship reveal his attitude toward the idea of friendship?

Topics for Composing

11. **Analysis.** Analyze how Johnson employs the cause-and-effect expository strategy to explain the decay of friendship. Point to specific examples from the text to support your analysis.

12. **Argument.** Are the causes of friendship decay that Johnson identifies relevant in today's world? Why or why not? Use your own experiences and those of people you know to support your position.

13. **Connections.** Johnson explains that friendship is dependent upon several factors and is fragile. Describe a friendship that you have lost or maintained that faced one or more of the challenges that Johnson identifies. What reasons outlined by Johnson were responsible for the strengthening or decaying of the friendship?

14. **Speaking and Listening.** Conduct interviews with at least five people of varying ages and experiences about what has led to the continuation or loss of a friendship. Share your findings with a small group and try to come to a consensus on which two or three factors are essential to maintaining a friendship.

15. **Research.** Do the experts agree with Johnson? Look into current research about what creates and destroys friendships, especially over time, and compare the current findings to what Johnson contends.

16. **Creative Writing.** Write a short story, poem, or song lyrics that present a friendship in some state of "decay," along the lines of what Johnson describes.

17. **Multimodal.** Make a collage of found or created images of friendships that are in one or more of the stages that Johnson identifies. Locate a song that reflects the tone of your collage and use it as the soundtrack for a multimodal presentation about friendship.

18. **Exposition.** Take a more positive spin on Johnson's topic. Explain what causes people to become friends and what makes friendships endure.

Writing Exposition

Now that you've had the opportunity to read and discuss multiple expository texts, it's time to practice your own expository writing skills. In this workshop, you will continue to experiment with the elements of exposition by writing an original expository piece on a topic of your choice.

Step 1. Your Topic

As mentioned in the introduction to this chapter, authors typically write about topics that they are interested in. Alan Weisman describes what the world would be like if humans suddenly disappeared. Tommy Orange questions society's evaluation of Native American bloodlines. Roxane Gay shares her perspective on privilege and new ways to talk about it. The point is that these topics are all very different from each other; what they share is that the authors choose to explain something they find interesting or worth caring about in the world around them.

The first step for writing your expository text is to observe the world around you and select a topic that you find interesting or care about. You can start by thinking about the variety of topics presented in this chapter. If one of them was interesting to you, use it as a springboard for writing about your own observations and ideas on the same topic. You could even continue on the topic you started in the Skill Workshop at the beginning of this chapter. Or, select a new topic of interest to you that you would like to explore.

Once you have a topic, it's important to narrow your focus to make it a manageable project. If you think back to the Skill Workshop of this chapter, Stephen King doesn't just write about movies in general or snacks in general. He narrows his focus to deliver a humorous guide about which snacks to enjoy at the movies and why and how to go about enjoying them.

Getting Started

An exposition can start with something you know, or with something you don't know but would like to explore and explain. Almost anything can be an interesting exposition topic, if you dig into it. To help you think of some topics for your exposition, create a table like the one below, filling in as many entries as you can. When you have finished brainstorming, select one topic that you would like to try writing about in this workshop.

(continued)

writing workshop

activity

1. Things That You Enjoy or That Interest You	A Question You Have about This Topic or an Aspect You Want to Explore
video games	I wonder how the stories in video games are written?
2. Things That You Would Like to Know More About	A Question You Have about This Topic or an Aspect You Want to Explore
ants	I've heard ants have interesting social structures, but I don't know any details. What are some of the things they do to work together as a social organization?

If creating your own version of the table above did not lead you to a possible topic, consider writing a brief response to one or more of the following prompts to help you generate a topic for your exposition piece. Don't worry if you don't already know much about the topic. If your writing is mostly questions you would like to find answers to, that's a good place to start.

1. Describe the positive or negative effects of one of the following: cell phones in school, video games, or social media.

2. Define one of the following concepts: perseverance, friendship, forgiveness, or leadership.

3. Explain the important qualities of one of the following for someone who is unfamiliar with the topic: your favorite sport, sports team, athlete, movie, or type of music; or your town, neighborhood, or school.

4. Compare one of the following pairs: middle and high school, virtual and in-person school, or dogs and cats as pets.

Step 2. Gathering Information

Even writers who are knowledgeable about their topics likely still need to gather more information before they are comfortable writing about them. For instance, even though Tommy Orange has personal experience with tribal membership, he had to conduct additional research into the specifics of blood quantum histories and policies in order to write "How Native American Is Native American Enough?" Susan Cain, who is clearly knowledgeable about personality types, consulted a number of experts when writing *Quiet: The Power of Introverts in a World that Won't Stop Talking*. They both likely took time to ensure that the sources they consulted were credible, as described in Chapter 4 (p. 99). This doesn't mean that writers gather information only through formal research. They might gain insights by talking with friends and family members, or by reading books or watching movies.

Gathering Information

In the activity above, you identified a topic that you might be interested in writing about. Now it's time to gather some additional information. Depending on your topic, you might need to conduct research about dates, times, important people, and so on. While you do not necessarily need to collect information in any particular way, you will want to make sure that you are keeping track of the sources and where you located them.

Step 3. Your Main Idea (Thesis)

Once you have a topic you want to explore and you have gathered some information about that topic, it's important to clarify the main idea of your exposition. Because expository texts tend to be focused on explaining something rather than arguing, we often use the term *main idea* to refer to the point the author explains in an expository text. However, *thesis* is the most common term for the central point in academic writing — the writing you do in school — so we will apply that term to the main idea in your expository writing for this workshop.

It's very likely that you won't be able to state your main idea or thesis until you have looked at your topic in detail, uncovering as much information as you can, which you did in the step above. Once you do feel like you know enough about your topic, you will be able to identify your main idea. Narrowing from a broad topic to a main idea will also make your piece easier to write and allow you to go into more depth. Notice how some of the authors in this chapter narrowed their focus into a main idea:

- Tommy Orange takes the idea of Native American heritage and focuses his writing on the use of "blood quantum," or the amount of ancestral Native American heritage a person can claim, to question the practice of quantifying Native American status.
- Raph Koster narrows his focus on gameplay to explaining the connection among teaching, learning, and having fun while playing games.
- Rebecca Solnit narrows her ideas about female identities and voices to the specific effects that "mansplaining" has on them.

These writers could talk in general terms about Native American ancestry, gameplay, and female voices, but narrowing the focus to one particular main idea — a thesis — helps to convey the author's message about that topic. For more information on main idea, you may want to review the Skill Workshop in this chapter and the Reading for Understanding section of Chapter 2 on page 31.

Main Idea (Thesis)

Once you have a narrowed topic and have conducted research in order to explore it further, write down two to three key points that you want to explain to your audience and express them in a single sentence. This statement is what we'll refer to as your thesis for the rest of the workshop.

Step 4. Your Purpose and Audience

We've already discussed in the Skill Workshop at the beginning of this chapter that the purpose of an expository text is to explain your main idea. It's essential that you can identify your intended audience so that you know what you should include in or exclude from your writing. In Chapter 3 (pp. 68–69), we emphasized how Martin Luther King Jr.'s language changed when his audience and purpose changed. He understood the difference between delivering a speech in front of civil rights marchers to inspire them and speaking more casually to a television audience to entertain them.

Let's look at this panel from Derf Backderf's graphic novel, *Trashed* (pp. 610–614), in which his purpose is to explain how much trash Americans throw out in an 18-month period. What can we assume about his audience? It's clear that his audience is made up of Americans because he says "we" and he compares Americans' garbage to that of Europeans and Canadians. He is also likely appealing to people who might be interested in changing their trash-producing activities by including the image of the trucks that stretch to the moon. The point is this: effective expository writers understand that what you say, and how you say it, depend upon whom you're addressing.

Purpose and Audience

Now that you have drafted a thesis statement, your purpose is to explain that point to an audience. Think specifically about your audience. Why would they want this information? What will you need to keep in mind about them as you write? How familiar are they with your topic? Write a few ideas down about what your audience might already know about your topic and what information you will need to include or might want to exclude.

Step 5. Your Evidence and Examples

As you learned in the Skill Workshop (pp. 598–608), evidence and examples are the heart and soul of any explanation. They take an idea from vague to specific, from abstract to concrete. Without examples, why would anyone believe that your explanation is correct? To refresh your memory, these are the most common kinds of evidence and examples:

- Details and specifics
- Research and expert opinion
- Data and statistics
- Personal experience and anecdotes

With this in mind, let's think about how Rebecca Solnit uses examples in her piece *Men Explain Things to Me*. She begins with a shocking personal anecdote:

> He kept us waiting while the other guests drifted out into the summer night, and then sat us down at his authentically grainy wood table and said to me, "So? I hear you've written a couple of books."
>
> I replied, "Several, actually."
>
> He said, in the way you encourage your friend's seven-year-old to describe flute practice, "And what are they about?"
>
> They were actually about quite a few different things, the six or seven out by then, but I began to speak only of the most recent on that summer day in 2003, *River of Shadows: Eadweard Muybridge and the Technological Wild West*, my book on the annihilation of time and space and the industrialization of everyday life.
>
> He cut me off soon after I mentioned Muybridge. "And have you heard about the *very important* Muybridge book that came out this year?"
>
> . . . So, Mr. Very Important was going on smugly about this book I should have known when Sallie interrupted him to say, "That's her book." Or tried to interrupt him anyway.
>
> But he just continued on his way. She had to say, "That's her book" three or four times before he finally took it in.

691

This powerful anecdote is one of the most memorable things about Solnit's piece. It's a classic example of putting your best example right up front. But Solnit doesn't stop there. What makes Solnit's exposition effective is that she goes on to incorporate other specific examples. For instance, she reiterates the thorough research she conducted on Muybridge and Heyl's contributions to camera technologies to address her critics, and she includes the newspaper story involving Marine Lance Corporal Maria Lauterbach to emphasize that her experience is not unique. So, Solnit uses a variety of types of examples and evidence to communicate her main idea.

How many examples should you use in your piece? A basic rule of thumb could be this: one is okay, two would be better, three might be needed, if your audience is likely to be reluctant to trust your explanation. And it is just as important to vary your types of evidence, as Solnit does above, by supporting a personal anecdote with related research, for example.

Evidence and Examples

Return to your notes about the kind of information you need to include in your writing, and jot down some key examples and evidence that would further support the development of your topic and help your audience understand it better. Try for a variety of different types as Solnit does in the examples above. Identify your strongest entries.

Step 6. Your Commentary

It's not enough to present examples to your readers, but then never explain how they relate to your main idea or why they are significant for understanding your topic. Look at how Raph Koster provides commentary, or explanation, for the connection between stimuli and the brain's ability to learn:

> We shouldn't underestimate the brain's desire to learn. If you put a person in a sensory deprivation chamber, he or she will get very unhappy very quickly. The brain craves stimuli. At all times, the brain is casting about trying to learn something, trying to integrate information into its worldview. It is insatiable in that way.
>
> This *doesn't* mean it necessarily craves new *experiences* — mostly, it just craves new *data*. New data is all it needs to flesh out a pattern. A new experience might force a whole new system on the brain, and often the brain doesn't *like* that. It's disruptive.
>
> The brain doesn't like to do more work than it has to. That's why we have the term "sensory overload," as an opposite to "sensory deprivation."
>
> Games grow boring when they fail to unfold new niceties in the puzzles they present. But they have to navigate between the Scylla and Charybdis of deprivation and overload, of excessive order and excessive chaos, of silence and noise.

Koster doesn't just say, "The brain likes to learn." He proceeds to explain under what conditions the brain tends to learn and analyzes how the brain responds to types of stimuli — the brain distinguishes between new data and new experiences. Providing these explanations helps to clarify for his audience that understanding how the brain responds to data and experiences is necessary for understanding how games play a role in fun and learning.

Explanation

Return to the examples or evidence in the previous activity that you identified as your strongest. Write a paragraph or two that explains the examples or evidence you located in your research, modeled on the paragraphs by Koster above. Be sure that your explanations return to your thesis.

Step 7. Your Style and Tone

At this point, you've done a lot of thinking and writing about your topic using evidence and examples and further explaining them for your audience. Now you're going to focus on your language and style to create the most appropriate tone for your audience. This doesn't mean using flowery or over-the-top language, but it should mean letting your voice come through.

One of the more interesting examples of language and style in this chapter is Samuel Johnson's exploration of what causes friendships to end in his essay, "On the Decay of Friendship." Take a look at how Johnson's language and style create a somber tone when describing the end of friendships:

> The most fatal disease of friendship is gradual decay, or dislike hourly increased by causes too slender for complaint, and too numerous for removal. Those who are angry may be reconciled; those who have been injured may receive a recompense: but when the desire of pleasing and willingness to be pleased is silently diminished, the renovation of friendship is hopeless; as, when the vital powers sink into languor, there is no longer any use of the physician.

Since his purpose in this piece was to explain the pain of a friendship ending, phrases like "fatal disease," "gradual decay," and "silently diminished" all create that subdued and joyless tone appropriate and effective for the subject.

As you think about your subject, consider what tone works best for your purpose and audience. Will you take a mournful approach, as Johnson does, or will you follow the humor of Stephen King's "Guide to Movie Snacks," the withering sarcasm of Rebecca Solnit's "Men Explain Things to Me," or the contemplation of Alan Weisman's "Earth without People"? Ensure that the words and language you select emphasize a voice appropriate for your audience and purpose.

activity Language and Style

Go back through the exercises you've completed so far in the preceding activities. What tone are you trying for, and why is this tone appropriate for your audience? Review common tone words in Chapter 3 (p. 67). Read some of what you have already written and determine if your tone is appropriate and effective. Add to or revise a few sentences about your topic emphasizing your choice of words to exhibit your voice. What do you want to say to your audience? What is the best way to say it? What words and details will you incorporate to strengthen your voice when talking about this topic?

Step 8. Your Expository Strategies

Throughout this chapter, you have been exposed to how authors incorporate different expository strategies: description, comparison and contrast, cause and effect, and problem and solution. The key to using these strategies is to use them only when they serve your purpose of explaining the main idea to their audience. The trick is to consider your thesis and audience, and to choose your strategies accordingly.

For instance, imagine your purpose is to explain how the stories for video games are written. To approach that question, you might compare it to how a novel is written. Or you might look carefully at how the writing of the story depends on other elements of the game-making process, in which case you would use cause and effect. As you can see, the strategy you use doesn't depend on your topic, but on the main idea you want to convey.

We mentioned before that authors often blend structural elements of expository writing. For example, Stephen King blends analysis, cause and effect, and descriptions in his "Guide to Movie Snacks." And while Alan Weisman's "Earth without People" is primarily set up as a cause-and-effect piece, he also incorporates description. Now that it's your turn to write an exposition, you'll need to stay flexible, too. Select what you need to suit your purpose, and don't feel limited to one strategy or another. Now let's look at some of the tools at your disposal.

Description

Description is the colorful part of exposition. It can stir emotion or add punch to your explanation. It's a very common way to begin a piece and hook your readers. A word of advice: a little often goes a long way.

Let's look at how Alan Weisman uses details as he describes how Nature takes over in man's absence in this excerpt from "Earth without People":

> Meanwhile, native Virginia creeper and poison ivy would claw at walls covered with lichens, which thrive in the absence of air pollution. Wherever foundations failed and buildings tumbled, lime from crushed concrete would raise soil pH, inviting buckthorn and birch. Black locust and autumn olive trees would fix nitrogen, allowing goldenrods, sunflowers, and white snakeroot to move in along with the apple trees, their seeds expelled by proliferating birds.

Like all of these strategies, description isn't for adding impressive flowery language. It's for helping you present your main idea and achieve your purpose. In Weisman's case, this descriptive passage helps explain how exactly plants begin to take back the earth, once humans leave. His descriptive language paints a picture for readers to help them better visualize the process he is explaining.

Comparison and Contrast

Comparison and contrast is one of the most common and most powerful forms of exposition. If we want to understand the world, we need to do so in context. How are fascism and communism similar or different? How successful is Amazon in comparison to other major companies? How hard is it to build a bridge versus building a tunnel? Comparing and contrasting things gives us perspective.

Susan Cain uses comparison and contrast to help understand the difference between introverts and extroverts:

> Still, today's psychologists tend to agree on several important points: for example, that introverts and extroverts differ in the level of outside stimulation that they need to function well. Introverts feel "just right" with less stimulation, as when they sip wine with a close friend, solve a crossword puzzle, or read a book. Extroverts enjoy the extra bang that comes from activities like meeting new people, skiing slippery slopes, and cranking up the stereo.

Here, we can see the differences in how introverts and extroverts respond to levels of stimulation.

Cause and Effect

Cause and effect is the best tool we have to answer the hardest question in the world, *Why?* When we ask why, we're looking for the cause, and how that cause resulted in an effect. Keep in mind that this strategy can go both ways: you can start with a cause and look at its effect, or start with an effect and look for the cause. But keep in mind that there is rarely just one cause, or just one effect. Investigating the complexity of causes and effects is what makes an exposition interesting.

Filippo Menczer and Thomas Hills write about the impact that algorithm manipulators have on exploiting our cognitive biases. They want others to know the role technology plays in influencing our beliefs and straining our attention spans. Consider this passage, for example:

> Compounding the problem is the proliferation of online information. Viewing and producing blogs, videos, tweets and other units of information called memes has become so cheap and easy that the information marketplace is inundated. Unable to process all this material, we let our cognitive biases decide what we should pay attention to. These mental shortcuts influence which information we search for, comprehend, remember and repeat to harmful extent.

In this paragraph, Menczer and Hills conclude that we filter out and gravitate toward information controlled by our cognitive biases (effect) because there is just too much information for us to consume (cause).

Problem and Solution

Another strategy to use in expository writing is to present a problem, or issue, and then provide one or more possible solutions. Some writers structure their entire essay this way, while others may just use it as a part of their essay.

Roxane Gay provides the following solution to the problem with how we acknowledge and address privilege:

> You don't necessarily *have* to do anything once you acknowledge your privilege. You don't have to apologize for it. You don't need to diminish your privilege or your accomplishments because of that privilege. You need to understand the extent of your privilege, the consequences of your privilege, and remain aware that people who are different from you move through and experience the world in ways you might never know anything about. They might endure situations you can never know anything about. You could, however, use that privilege for the greater good — to try to level the playing field for everyone, to work for social justice, to bring attention to how those without certain privileges are disenfranchised. While you don't have to do anything with your privilege, perhaps it should be an imperative of privilege to share the benefits of that privilege rather than hoard your good fortune. We've seen what the hoarding of privilege has done and the results are shameful.

Gay's proposals include not only understanding "the extent of your privilege, the consequences of your privilege" and the awareness that others' experiences are different, but also recognizing that we could "share the benefits of that privilege rather than hoard your good fortune."

Expository Strategies

Think about your topic, thesis, examples, and explanation you've written so far. What strategies do you think might be useful in writing your exposition? Do your examples and explanations seem to fit any of the expository strategies listed? Once you have identified your strategies, sketch out how you might use them, perhaps drafting an outline of possible structures for your piece based on your chosen strategies.

Step 9. Expanding to an Essay

By this point, you have come a long way in writing your expository essay. You have all of the pieces of your exposition: topic, main idea, examples, and expository strategies. It's time to put all of these pieces together and begin to draft your full exposition. As you do, be sure to consider such important details as these:

- **Use effective transitions.** Transitions between ideas and paragraphs are essential to help your reader move through your explanation easily. Some common transitional words and phrases for expository writing are *most important*, *additionally*, *however*, *therefore*, *on the other hand*, and so on.
- **Maintain an appropriate tone.** Think back on what you identified about your intended audience and be sure that your diction is appropriate for your readers. Have you considered how formal or informal you want your piece to be, or how you want your reader to feel about your topic?

The key parts that are missing from your essay are the introduction and the conclusion, which we'll discuss next.

Introductory Paragraph

Expository texts may be explanations, but that does not mean they need to be dry and boring. The point of the introductory paragraph is to engage your reader and create interest in the topic. One way to do that is to engage your audience right from the beginning so that they'll want to read on.

Sometimes your hook comes after you've already written quite a bit about your topic. If you can't think of a way to engage your audience before writing your piece, then wait until afterward to see if completing the text gives you a better idea of which opener would be the best one to introduce the topic to your audience.

There are several ways to hook your audience:

- **Start with a striking description.** Rebecca Solnit lures her audience's attention with vivid imagery and descriptive details in her opening lines in "Men Explain Things to Me" (p. 669).

  > I still don't know why Sallie and I bothered to go to that party in the forest slope above Aspen. The people were all older than us and dull in a distinguished way, old enough that we, at forty-ish, passed as the occasion's young ladies. The house was great — if you like Ralph Lauren-style chalets — a rugged luxury cabin at 9,000 feet complete with elk antlers, lots of kilims, and a wood-burning stove.

- **Start with an anecdote or narrative.** Like others in this chapter, Filippo Menczer and Thomas Hills open their article "Information Overload Helps Fake News Spread, and Social Media Knows It" (p. 674) with an anecdote.

  > Consider Andy, who is worried about contracting COVID-19. Unable to read all the articles he sees on it, he relies on trusted friends for tips. When one opines on Facebook that pandemic fears are overblown, Andy dismisses the idea at first. But then the hotel where he works closes its doors, and with his job at risk, Andy starts wondering how serious the threat from the new virus really is. No one he knows has died, after all. A colleague posts an article about the COVID "scare" having been created by Big Pharma in collusion with corrupt politicians, which jibes with Andy's distrust of government. His Web search quickly takes him to articles claiming that COVID-19 is no worse than the flu. Andy joins an online group of people who have been or fear being laid off and soon finds himself asking, like many of them, "What pandemic?"

- **Start with a provocative question.** In his opening paragraph to "Earth without People" (p. 627), Alan Weisman ponders several questions about what the world would be like if humans vanished without warning.

  > Given the mounting toll of fouled oceans, overheated air, missing topsoil, and mass extinctions, we might sometimes wonder what our planet would be like if humans suddenly disappeared. Would Superfund sites revert to Gardens of Eden? Would the seas again fill with fish? Would our concrete cities crumble to dust from the force of tree roots, water, and weeds? How long would it take for our traces to vanish? And if we could answer such questions, would we be more in awe of the changes we have wrought, or of nature's resilience?

- **Start with an interesting fact or observation.** Derf Backderf opens his graphic novel *Trashed* (p. 610) in the first panel with this observation:

  > Trash disposal has been a headache since man first began living in settlements. And there is evidence that ancient man generated even more garbage on a daily basis than modern man!

Introductory Paragraph

Try writing a hook for your expository piece by using one or more of the methods described above: an interesting description, an anecdote or personal narrative, a question, or an observation or fact. Be sure to include your thesis at the end of your introductory paragraph to set up the rest of the essay.

Concluding Paragraph

As with any essay you write, a solid conclusion will bring your paper full circle by restating (not repeating) your thesis and the main points you analyzed in each of the body paragraphs. It should bring completeness and closure to the reader with the satisfaction that you've fully explained your topic to them so that they understand it better.

Look at how Jon Ronson concludes his article about Justin Sacco's Twitter experience:

> It was a profound reversal for Sacco. When I first met her, she was desperate to tell the tens of thousands of people who tore her apart how they had wronged her and to repair what remained of her public persona. But perhaps she had now come to understand that her shaming wasn't really about her at all. Social media is so perfectly designed to manipulate our desire for approval, and that is what led to her undoing. Her tormentors were instantly congratulated as they took Sacco down, bit by bit, and so they continued to do so. Their motivation was much the same as Sacco's own — a bid for the attention of strangers — as she milled about Heathrow, hoping to amuse people she couldn't see.

After all Sacco had been through with being publicly shamed on social media, Ronson concludes that the experience likely had more to do with the general public's insatiable appetite for tormenting someone they didn't even know, and society's encouragement of such behavior.

Concluding Paragraph

Write a concluding paragraph for your essay. Remember to tie it back to your thesis, the ideas you presented in your body paragraphs and avoid simply repeating what you have already stated.

Bringing It All Together

If you take all of the pieces you've written in this workshop and put them together — your introduction and thesis, your evidence and examples with explanations and analysis related to your main idea, and your conclusion — you should have a short expository essay.

Remember that all of these guiding activities are one way to help you improve your expository writing. Once you feel more in control of how to write expository essays, you can start to bend these rules to suit your purposes. Writing is not about formulas or templates. It's about communicating ideas.

Step 10. Finalizing Your Essay

Now that you have a complete draft of your essay, you can move on to the final phase of the writing process: revising and editing. These two acts are sometimes thought of as being the same, but they're not. Revision is when you look back at large-scale structural elements of your essay, such as how well you support your claim, what kinds of evidence you use, how effective your word choices are, and to what extent you have led your reader easily through your essay. Editing, on the other hand, focuses on fine-tuning the language, grammar, punctuation, spelling, and other conventions. Editing is usually the very last thing you do before you finalize your piece, looking carefully for any errors that you tend to make. The following are suggestions for you to consider as you finalize your essay:

Revising

Revising gives you a good opportunity to think again about your essay's purpose and audience. In most cases, your audience will be your teacher or an external evaluator in the case of a standardized test. In both situations, that means using a somewhat formal tone, but your writing can still be engaging for you and your audience. Reread your essay for the following:

- **Look back at your thesis.** Since you wrote this early on in the workshop, does it still relate to the essay you ended up writing? If you need more assistance with this, be sure to look at Revision Workshop 1: Effective Thesis and Essay Structure in the back of the book.
- **Look back at your focus.** Is it still at the center of your expository essay, or are you rambling on about other ideas without tying them back to the focus? If you need more assistance with this, be sure to look at Revision Workshop 2: Effective Topic Sentences and Unified Paragraphs in the back of the book.
- **Revisit your body paragraphs.** Have you balanced the evidence and examples with your own commentary about how they support your thesis? Have you clearly explained your topic to your audience? If you need more assistance with this, be sure to look at Revision Workshop 4: Appropriate Evidence and Support in the back of the book.

- **Check your introduction and conclusion.** Does your introduction grab the reader's attention and effectively preview your topic? Does your conclusion wrap up in a way that highlights your focus? Review Revision Workshop 8: Effective Introductions and Conclusions in the back of the book if you need additional support with these parts of your essay.

Editing

Remember, editing is the very last thing you'll do before finalizing your essay. You and your teacher know better than anyone the types of spelling, grammar, and convention errors you need to focus on in your writing development. Be sure to refer to one or more of the Grammar Workshops in the back of the book if you encounter an issue and aren't sure how to overcome it.

Exposition

You have spent this workshop crafting an expository essay that explains and analyzes a topic for readers, but what if you wanted to share that same piece through a presentation to a live audience? What would you need to add, change, or delete to make the essay sound engaging? Think about great public speakers you may have seen. They often seem comfortable because they are knowledgeable about their topics, and because you have just spent this workshop trying to explain a topic to readers, you should easily be able to transfer this knowledge to a live audience. As you work through this process, refer to the elements of a presentation in Chapter 3 (p. 90), and use these steps to turn your written expository essay into an oral presentation.

Content

- **Your hook.** Reread the beginning paragraph of your expository essay. Would the hook you wrote for someone who reads your essay capture the listener's attention? Read it aloud to yourself a few times. Does it sound dramatic or interesting? Does it communicate to your listeners the topic you are going to discuss? If it feels too long when you read it aloud, cut it down, so that it is only two or three sentences.
- **Your thesis.** You will want to be very clear about the specific idea you want your audience to understand about your topic. You may want to break your thesis up into two sentences to ensure that your listeners know what specific points about your topic you will be explaining.
- **Your evidence and examples.** While your expository essay may have included plenty of evidence and examples for your topic, for a short presentation you might want to focus only on the strongest ones. Include evidence and examples that are clear and focused and would be most likely to help your audience understand your topic.
- **Your analysis and explanation.** When presenting to a live audience, you may need to shorten some of the explanations you give in your essay. Decide what information is necessary for your audience to hear and rewrite your sentences to include the most important information for the presentation.
- **Your closing.** Look back at how you ended your expository essay, and highlight the strongest sentence or two that communicate to your audience the thesis and what you want them to learn most about your topic — the takeaway. Rewrite it so that it will be engaging for a live audience.

Delivery

Like other speeches you deliver in school, a presentation of an expository essay will take on a mostly formal tone, but that does not mean that you cannot smile, gesture, or laugh at appropriate times. Because the information you present might be unfamiliar to your listeners, you will want to move slowly and clearly through your explanations, maybe using transitions that seamlessly carry your ideas from one to the next. You can use hand movements to emphasize points or show the importance of particular examples or evidence.

Visuals

As with visuals for any presentation, you need to make sure that anything you include is relevant, appropriate, and works to enhance, not detract, from your words and delivery. Possible visuals for an expository presentation might include charts, data, or a compelling photograph to visually support your explanations. Be sure to take time to explain your visuals and demonstrate their relevance to your thesis. If you are changing visuals during your presentation, be sure to allow a little time for the audience to react, especially if the visual is something that they might need more time to process.

Drama

> All the world's a stage,
>
> And all the men and women merely players;
>
> They have their exits and their entrances,
>
> And one man in his time plays many parts
>
> — William Shakespeare, *As You Like It*

Perhaps one of Shakespeare's most quoted passages, his idea — that drama is life, and life is drama — continues to ring true. Humans have played their parts in drama from the earliest Greek classics to the contemporary productions enjoyed today. At its core, drama is life lived in front of an audience. Plays show, rather than tell, what takes place. The stage is where characters are confronted with conflict and grapple with relationships in real time with a live audience. The audience experiences the actions and emotions along with the performers. It is what makes drama thrilling and unique — different from reading a book, more intimate than watching a movie. Much like life, drama can be a tragedy or a comedy, or a bit of both. It can be a short one-act play, a full-length drama, or even a musical.

In this chapter, you will have the opportunity to read and analyze dramatic texts and experiment with elements of drama through your own writing. Activities in this chapter will help you think not only about the tools playwrights use to move their audiences, but how you can incorporate those methods into your own writing.

Contents

Essential Elements of Drama

Many of the elements of drama are shared with fiction and narrative. After all, these genres are all telling stories — whether real or not. Drama has conflict, plot, character, setting, and theme, to name a few elements, but drama also has elements that are specific to its genre and that set it apart from fiction and narrative. Perhaps the biggest difference is that drama takes place on a stage, not just on the page, and that changes everything.

PREVIEWING Academic Vocabulary   **Essential Elements of Drama**

In this section, you will encounter the following terms as you think about how to analyze drama. Working individually or with a partner or small group, consider what you already know about the meaning of each term.

1. Cast of Characters/ Dramatis Personae
2. Stage directions
3. Costumes
4. Dialogue
5. Monologue
6. Soliloquy
7. Blocking
8. Act
9. Scene
10. Conflict
11. Staging
12. Set
13. Props
14. Lighting
15. Tragedy
16. Comedy

Let's take a closer look at these essential elements of drama in action using a section from Jonathan Rand's play *Check Please* as our model and walking through each of the significant features of a work of drama.

from Check Please

Jonathan Rand

Jonathan Rand (b. 1980) is a popular American playwright whose works have been widely performed in the United States and throughout the world. A graduate of the University of Pennsylvania, Rand has written twenty-two plays, four of which were Heideman Award finalists. His play excerpted here, *Check Please*, is often produced in North American high schools. It depicts a series of dates in a restaurant, where GUY and GIRL find themselves confronted with a variety of strange people and awkward interactions.

Jonathan Rand

KEY CONTEXT In the script to this play, Rand provides the following production notes and stage directions, which contain some additional information about lighting and staging the play.

I originally wrote this play with the intention of having the same two actors play the roles of GIRL and GUY, and having thirteen different actors play the rest of the roles. Another fun option would be to cast the play using four total actors, with all 12 characters split between two quick-change artists. The other option (which I least prefer) would be to cast every scene with a different pair of actors. While this would be a great opportunity to get heaps of people involved in the production, it does cheapen the conclusion of the play.

Every scene is a pairing of male vs. female. I wrote it this way simply because I only have first-hand experience with heterosexual dating. Should your production group wish to mix and match the characters' genders, I absolutely approve of it. . . .

I envision the stage setup as two small dinner tables at opposite sides of the stage, with GUY and GIRL facing away from each other. I also imagine there would never be a need for a full blackout — just a quick lighting switch at the end of each scene to move from GIRL's table to GUY's table, and so on. If full blackouts make more sense to your production, then by all means, blackout away.

Cast of Characters

GIRL
GUY

LOUIS
MELANIE
KEN
MARY
MARK

Setting

A restaurant

Time

Now

Scene 1

LOUIS Hi.
GIRL Hi there.
LOUIS It's great to meet you.
GIRL You, too.
LOUIS So how long have you lived in the city? 5
GIRL Oh, eighteen months? I think? It doesn't feel like it's been that long.
LOUIS I've been here three years. It's a great city.
GIRL Oh, definitely. What do you like most about it? 10
LOUIS What do you like most about living here?

[*Pause, as* GIRL *is only slightly noticeably confused.*]

GIRL Well . . . I love walking my dog in the park. Especially on a pretty day.
LOUIS Yeah? Is that the truth? I love to ride my bike around the city — when the traffic is light 15 of course.

[*He chuckles.*]

GIRL Same here.
LOUIS Oh and also — and this may just be me — but I have this thing for walking my dog in the park on a pretty day. 20
GIRL No, I like that, too. I said so earlier.
LOUIS So do you like watching TV?

GIRL No.

LOUIS Me, too! I love it!

[*Pause.*]

GIRL [*Curious:*] Are you listening to me at all? 25

LOUIS Sometimes I like to curl up with a bag of popcorn and just chow down while I watch *Home Improvement*. Do you like *Home Improvement*?

GIRL You really aren't listening to me. 30

LOUIS Me, too! That's a riot. Tim Allen just cracks — me — up.

GIRL This is ridiculous . . .

[*Throughout the below monologue,* GIRL *gradually tries out different tactics to see how self-centered and non-reactive* LOUIS *truly is. She tries saying things to him like "pardon me" and "hi"; she tries whistling at him a little; she even tries touching his nose with her index finger or a spoon for a few seconds. No matter what she does,* LOUIS *just keeps on trucking, as if she wasn't there.*]

LOUIS I mean, his comedy is just choice. It's like his comic timing was a gift from the gods, you 35 know? You know what I'm talking about? Man . . . I'm just blown away every time I see the show, or one of his movies. Did you see *The Santa Clause*? Ah! If you haven't, go and rent it *right away*. That is one funny guy. He 40 reminds me of me, actually. We have the same sense of humor. My old roommate, Bill? He says I'm the funniest guy he's ever met. Hey — he's entitled to his opinion, right? Anyway, I've got my personality flaws. 45 Sometimes I'm too funny. People don't realize it when I'm being serious!! Do you believe that?! But jeez, enough about me. I'm talkin' like a motormouth here! Tell me about you.

GIRL Or we could just end the date right now, 50 since you're the biggest tool I've ever met.

[*A slightly long pause; we assume he is going to break.*]

LOUIS I'm a Capricorn myself.

[*Scene.*]

Scene 2

[*This next scene will work best if* MELANIE *is truly sweet, innocent, and adorable when she's focused on the date.*]

GUY Hi.

MELANIE Hi.

GUY It's so great to finally meet you.

MELANIE Same here!

GUY So . . . What do you — 5

MELANIE Wait, before you — Sorry. [*Meekly:*] This is so rude, but the Bears game is on right now? You don't mind if I check the score . . .

GUY Oh sure. Totally.

MELANIE [*As she pulls out her cell phone to check her web-browser:*] Thanks. I know this is such 10 an awful thing to do on a first date, but it's late in the fourth quarter, and it's do-or-die if we wanna make the playoffs.

GUY It's no problem at all. Really.

MELANIE Thanks. [*As she checks:*] I love the 15 Bears. They're really strong this season. [*Sees score; reacts a little.*] Okay, I'm done. [*Cheerily:*] That wasn't so bad, was it?

GUY What's the score?

MELANIE Packers by seven. 20

GUY Uh-oh.

MELANIE Nah, it's no big deal. It's just a game, right? So c'mon — enough about football. Let's hear about "Mister Mystery." Harriet's told me tons about you. 25

GUY Man . . . The pressure's on now.

[*They laugh together, genuinely.* MELANIE's *laugh then fades directly into her next line, which is suddenly serious.*]

MELANIE I'm just gonna check on the game one more time.

[*She digs into her purse.*]

GUY [*Smiling:*] No worries.

MELANIE Is it all right with you if I put on this 30 little earpiece thingy? It won't be distracting, I promise.

GUY Sure.

MELANIE [*As she puts the earpiece in her ear:*] I'm making the worst first impression, aren't I? 35

GUY Not at all.

MELANIE It's just because it's for the playoffs. I'm usually pretty normal.

GUY It's really no —

MELANIE [*Throws her hands up:*] Ah! 40

GUY What?

MELANIE Oh. Nothing. The line only gives A-Train this huge running lane, but he fumbles after two yards. The ball rolled out of bounds, so we're cool, but come on — it's for 45 the playoffs. You don't just drop the ball like that, you know? Now you're third and long, and the whole season is riding on one play.

GUY That's —

MELANIE WHAT?! 50

GUY What?

MELANIE PASS THE BALL!!

GUY What's wrong?

MELANIE Miller! He doesn't pass it. The man refuses to pass the ball this season. It's third 55 and long — Who hands it off on third and long? Is he suddenly AFRAID OF HIS RECEIVERS?!

[*GUY looks around subtly at the other patrons.*]

Oh my God, I'm sorry. I'm being loud, aren't I.

GUY [*Trying hard to be convincing:*] No . . .

MELANIE Oh, I am. I'm so sorry. Look, how about 60 this: I'll make it up to you. After dinner I'll buy you dessert at this tiny little bistro on 11th that nobody knows about. It's gotta be one of my absolute favorite places to go. It's so precious. I think you'll just — PASS THE BALL!! Jesus, 65 people! This is FOOTBALL, not FREEZE TAG. It's FOURTH DOWN — pass the FRIGGING BALL!

GUY Listen — we could go to a bar or something if you want — watch the game on TV. 70

MELANIE Oh please, no. I wouldn't do you that to you. The game's basically over. [*She takes a deep breath, and is now very calm.*] Okay. I'm done. I got a little carried away there, didn't I? Let's order. 75

[*They peruse for a moment, as if nothing has happened.*]

GUY Oh. [*Indicating the menu:*] Harriet said we should definitely try the —

[MELANIE *suddenly lets out a bloodcurdling shriek and rips the menu in half. Beat.*]

GUY Or, we could order something else. [*Beat.*] Your menu tore a little.

MELANIE [*Downtrodden:*] They lost . . . 80

GUY Oh. Oh, I'm sorry.

MELANIE [*Starting to tear up:*] They lost. They just blew the playoffs.

GUY Well, I —

[MELANIE *breaks down, bawling.* GUY *thinks for a moment, then takes out a handkerchief and offers it to* MELANIE. *She uses it to blow her nose.*]

GUY I'm so sorry. Can I do anything to help? 85

MELANIE [*Still weepy:*] The Bears suck . . .

GUY Aww, no. They don't suck.

MELANIE They do . . . They suck.

GUY They're probably just having a bad season —

[MELANIE *grabs his collar, pulls him extremely close, and speaks in a horrifying, monstrous, deep voice.*]

MELANIE THE BEARS SUCK. 90

GUY [*Very weakly:*] The Bears suck.

[*Scene.*]

Scene 3

GIRL Hi.

KEN Hello.

[*He kisses her hand, lingering there a second too long.*]

GIRL It's great to meet you.

KEN The pleasure . . . is all mine.

GIRL So . . . where are you from? I can't place the 5 accent.

KEN I was raised in the mountains of Guam . . . and was born . . . on the shore of New Jersey.

[*Beat.*]

GIRL Do you want to order some appetizers?

KEN Anything . . . which will ensure happiness 10 for your beautiful lips.

[*He looks at menu, unaware of her subtle look of disbelief. She finally looks down at her menu.*]

GIRL Ooh! The shrimp cocktail looks good.

KEN Shrimp . . . A creature of the ocean. The ocean . . . which is not nearly as lovely as the ocean of your eyes. 15

[*Pause.*]

GIRL Listen, can I ask you sort of a . . . barbed question?

KEN Anything which your heart desires will be —

GIRL Yeah yeah. So — are you going to be doing this for the rest of dinner? 20

KEN Whatever do you mean?

GIRL All of this . . . sketchy, provocative garbage?

[*Pause.*]

KEN Yes.

[*Scene.*] [. . .]

Scene 4

GUY Hi.

MARY Hi.

GUY It's so great to finally meet you.

MARY Same here! Listen: I was wondering if you were free next Friday. 5

GUY Ah, I think so. Why?

MARY Well, if dinner goes well tonight, I wanted to go ahead and line up a second date.

GUY Oh. Okay, sure.

MARY See, 'cause here's the thing: My parents are 10 having a housewarming party at their new place on August 2nd, and if you and I hit it off tonight and end up seriously dating, that party would be the perfect opportunity for you to meet my parents. So naturally I'd like to 15 squeeze in several healthy-sized dates before then. If we don't, my parents might be a little bit skeptical of our relationship, which could in turn be disastrous for our future, when you eventually pop the question. Not only would 20 it make my whole family uncertain and uncomfortable during the ceremony, but it would also most likely carry over during our sixteen-day honeymoon in St. Martin. Even more importantly, it would be just awful if you had to deal with skeptical in-laws during the 25 years down the road, and all because of a little thing like not setting aside fourteen healthy-sized dates before the housewarming party. Think about how a family conflict like that could upset Jocelyn. 30

GUY Jocelyn?

MARY Our little darling. Middle child. Bryan first; then Jocelyn, and of course, little Madison.

[*Pause.*]

GUY Wow . . . 35

MARY What? What is it? You don't like the name Madison?

GUY What? No. I mean, yes. No, that's a great name.

MARY Something's on your mind. Honey, you can tell me. You're talking to your little sugar 40 pumpkin, remember? Tell me.

GUY Well, it's just — You just seem to have our whole relationship figured out — and we just met thirty seconds ago. [*Chuckling a little:*] I mean, you've got everything pinned down 45 but the wedding dress.

MARY Does that make you uncomfortable?

[*Beat.*]

[*As she withdraws several boxes:*] Because if it does, we can pick it out now.

[*Scene.*] [. . .]

> **KEY CONTEXT** Note that the excerpt included here jumps from Scene 4 to Scene 13. The scenes not included here focus on additional, increasingly odd dates of Girl and Guy. This next scene is the final one in the play.

Scene 13

[*Lights up to* MARK *in his burlap sack. He is reading the menu. Long pause.*]

GIRL Why don't you just give up.

MARK If you've got a bone to pick with me, why don't you just come out and say it?

GIRL You're wearing a burlap sack.

[*Pause.*]

MARK That's your opinion. 5

[*Pause.* GIRL *stands and takes her jacket.*]

GIRL I need to go powder my nose.

[*Beat.*]

MARK Nice jacket.

GIRL You, too.

[GIRL *exits toward* GUY's *table. The lights on* GIRL's *table remain up as lights come up on* GUY's *table. . . .* GIRL *and* GUY *bump into each other.*]

GIRL Oh, sorry.

GUY No. My fault. 10

[*A short moment of instant chemistry. Then* GUY *shakes it off, as does* GIRL.]

GUY Well, goodnight.

GIRL Goodnight. 5

[*They start to go their separate ways.*]

GUY Wait a second. [*Pause.*] This may sound like a really random question, but . . . do you like football? 15

GIRL A little. [*Beat.*] Do you own any burlap?

Getting Started

Choose a television show that you know well in which the majority of action takes place in a single location, as in the images below from *The Wonder Years* and *The Big Bang Theory*. TV sitcoms, such as *The Office*, *Friends*, and *black-ish*, frequently use this approach. With a classmate, discuss what the show is about and what makes that show one of your favorites.

Erika Doss/© ABC/Getty Images

(continued)

711

NG Images/Alamy

Characters

Unlike fiction, which typically introduces characters as they enter the story, a dramatic text reveals the names of all the characters up front in the **Cast of Characters**, which is sometimes written in Latin as **Dramatis Personae**. There are a few ways that playwrights can list characters, but you will find that most list them either in order of importance or in order of appearance.

In *Check Please*, Guy and Girl are listed first and a space sets off those names from the names of the minor characters that follow. By placing them first, Rand establishes that Guy and Girl play a more significant role in the action than the other characters do. The remaining characters are listed in order of appearance, which gives the audience a sense of chronological sequencing as each new character is introduced.

Types of Characters

As in other types of storytelling, plays will usually have a protagonist, antagonist, and supporting or minor characters. The **protagonist** is the main character who drives the action of the story. The **antagonist** is a character who opposes the actions of the protagonist, either intentionally or unintentionally. The **supporting** or **minor characters** may add more depth to the story or further complicate the conflict for the protagonist. One common type of supporting character is the **foil**. The purpose of the foil is to contrast with a main character in order to highlight an aspect or trait. And just like a novel or short story, drama can have more than one of these types of characters. In the case of *Check Please*, the protagonists are Girl and Guy, and all of their dates could be considered supporting or minor characters, or maybe even foils, since their odd behaviors illustrate just how normal Guy and Girl are. But they might be viewed as antagonists because they are keeping Guy and Girl from finding each other.

While it is rare, plays may have a **narrator**, which can be a person on stage who is not part of the action, a character who steps outside of the action to provide narration, or simply a voice from off stage. In some plays, including Shakespeare's *Romeo and Juliet* in this chapter, the Chorus fulfills the role of the narrator, providing commentary on the action and filling in plot details.

Characterization

Characterization in drama falls into the same categories that you might remember from other genres — direct and indirect characterization — but how authors approach those things in drama can be a bit different.

Direct Characterization

As you may have seen in Chapter 6, authors of fiction sometimes use direct characterization to describe their characters, such as in this example: "He was a tall man who was angry all the time." Playwrights also use direct characterization. Although Rand does not do so in *Check Please*, sometimes playwrights list the age, gender, and other general character traits at the very beginning in the Cast of Characters, as in this example from a play called *Boxcar — El Vagon* by Sylvia Gonzalez S.:

> **ROBERTO.** Border patrol officer, 30s, Chicano/Hispanic; Understands Spanish. Job is weighing on him.

Another way to achieve direct characterization in drama is through **stage directions**, the playwright's instructions to the actors on how to interact with the set, props, and each other (e.g., *they draw their swords and fight*), or how to deliver their lines (e.g., *angrily, in disbelief*).

For instance, in Scene 2 of *Check Please*, Rand provides this direct characterization of the character Melanie:

> [*This next scene will work best if* MELANIE *is truly sweet, innocent, and adorable when she's focused on the date.*]

Direct Characterization

Return to the TV show that you selected earlier and write a Cast of Characters or Dramatis Personae that might appear with an episode. Identify each of the characters as protagonists, antoagonists, supporting characters, foils, and so on with a brief statement that describes each character like the example from *Boxcar — El Vagon* above. Last, write a stage direction or two for one of the characters that might directly reveal some aspect of that character.

Indirect Characterization

More common than direct characterization in drama, **indirect characterization** occurs through what the character says, as well as the character's appearance, gestures, movements, and body language. This often can come in the form of **blocking**, a type of stage direction that tells the actors where to go and how to move (e.g., *exit stage left, sneaks casually toward the knife*), as well as other stage directions. In Scene 2 of *Check Please*, for instance, Rand includes these stage directions: "[MELANIE *suddenly lets out a bloodcurdling shriek and rips the menu in half. Beat.*]" Rand does not say directly that Melanie is too obsessed with sports, but the stage directions communicate that characterization clearly.

Another tool that playwrights have at their disposal for indirect characterization are **costume** choices, including directions about clothes and other items the actors should wear or carry. Though these decisions are often left to the director of the play, playwrights sometimes provide specific descriptions, such as Rand's choice to have Mark appear dressed in a burlap sack in Scene 13 or to have Melanie wear her earpiece to hear the game in Scene 2.

Characters in drama are primarily developed through the things they say, especially through **dialogue**, which is when characters speak to each other. The heavy reliance on developing characters indirectly through dialogue is one of the things that makes drama unique as a genre. It puts an emphasis on showing the audience, rather than simply telling them, what the characters are like. Put simply, audiences need to read into the dialogue to draw conclusions about characters' beliefs and motivations.

In *Check Please*, Rand does most of his character development indirectly, through dialogue. If we look specifically at any of the characters, we can determine some of their traits based on the conversations they have and their responses to the behaviors of the other characters. For example, look at these lines in Scene 1:

> LOUIS So do you like watching TV?
> GIRL No.
> LOUIS Me, too! I love it!
>
>   [*Pause.*]
>
> GIRL [*Curious:*] Are you listening to me at all?
> LOUIS Sometimes I like to curl up with a bag of popcorn and just
>   chow down while I watch *Home Improvement*. Do you like *Home
>   Improvement?*
> GIRL You really aren't listening to me.
> LOUIS Me, too! That's a riot. Tim Allen just cracks — me — up.

Through this dialogue, we get a clear picture of the self-absorbed character Louis, who never listens. We also get a sense of who Girl is in comparison to Louis — the only normal person in a sea of oddballs. She begins as just "*curious*" about Louis's behavior, but quickly quits pretending to play along. Her patience has run out. Sometimes playwrights will give additional stage directions about how the specific lines should be spoken, such as "angrily" or "whispers." Rand also uses a stage direction at times called a "beat," which signals a slight pause in the action, as in Scene 2: "Or, we could order something else. [*Beat.*] Your menu tore a little." Oftentimes this stage direction helps to create tension and conflict between characters.

Occasionally, characters give a speech, either to themselves, to the audience, or to another character, which is called a **monologue**. This type of speech is often introspective, revealing much about what the character is thinking and feeling. A type of monologue in which the character is in conversation with him- or herself is called a **soliloquy**. These are common in Shakespearean drama, and they give us insights into the characters' inner conflicts and motivations.

Indirect Characterization

Return to the TV show that you wrote about earlier and think about one or two of the main characters. What does the audience learn about the characters through their costumes, what they say (either in dialogue or a monologue), and gestures, movements, or facial expressions that they make?

Plot and Structure

You are likely familiar with the plot pyramid that is often used to describe the rise and fall of action in a story.

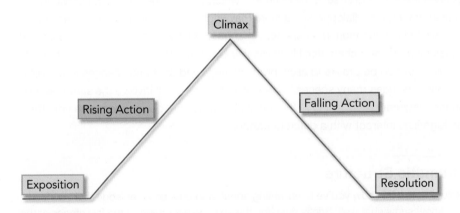

- **Exposition** provides background information about the characters, settings, or major ideas.
- The **rising action** includes the major conflicts that the characters face.
- The **climax** is where the tension of the conflict is greatest.
- The **falling action** includes the events immediately after the climax.
- The **resolution** includes the events that wrap up the story.

Playwrights often divide their plays into sections called acts and scenes. How many acts and scenes playwrights decide to use varies according to their purpose

715

and the sort of story they want to tell. Whether it is fiction, drama, or a television show, at its core a story is about **conflict**: what characters want or desire and why they do or do not get it. Conflict is the heart of drama. It drives the characters, the action, and the plot throughout the scenes and acts and keeps the audience engaged. As in fiction, conflict in drama can come from an external force (an antagonist, perhaps), or from an internal struggle (a moral dilemma, for instance), or both.

Acts

In a full-length play lasting more than an hour, an **act** in a play denotes a major division in the structure of the plot. While it is common for plays, including Shakespeare's, to have five acts, the number varies. Complex eight-act plays were popular in the Renaissance, and four-act plays were popular in the nineteenth century. Today, most plays are either one act or three acts. With all of these options, playwrights are free to choose the number of acts that best suits the action, flow, and themes of the story. *Check Please* is an example of a one-act play, in which the entirety of the action takes place in one location — the restaurant — and the plot has only a few conflicts. Structuring the act with multiple scenes that toggle between the different dates that Guy and Girl encounter and the conflicts that arise as a result of their interactions keeps the setting simple so that the focus is on the characters' personalities.

Scenes

Scenes are the smaller sections of an act, which feature brief situations between characters through dialogue and action. Playwrights can move from one scene to the next when time, location, or characters change. In that way, scenes are useful for further developing plot and character. However, if we look at it from the production standpoint, scenes can also be breaks to allow prop, scenery, and costume changes to take place.

Rand includes many scenes in his one-act play that all involve the same setting (in the restaurant, happening in the present), but he changes scenes each time the protagonists interact with a different partner.

 Dramatic Structure

Return to the TV show you've been writing about, and choose an episode that you feel you know somewhat well. Briefly describe the episode according to the five stages of the plot pyramid discussed earlier (p. 715). Can you identify specific scenes within an act?

Setting

The **setting** is the time period, location, and environment of the play. It may change as the scenes change. The **staging** is how the director chooses to portray that setting on stage, including the design of the set, the lighting, and the props. The **set** includes all of the scenery, furniture, and other structures that make up the setting onstage. **Props**, short for *properties*, are all of the items actors interact with in the play.

In the case of *Check Please*, the setting occurs in one location — the restaurant — but the author provides more specific stage directions in the production notes:

> I envision the stage setup as two small dinner tables at opposite sides of the stage, with GUY and GIRL facing away from each other. I also imagine there would never be a need for a full blackout — just a quick lighting switch at the end of each scene to move from GIRL's table to GUY's table, and so on. If full blackouts make more sense to your production, then by all means, blackout away.

A small number of props are identified in *Check Please*, but they are crucial, such as the menu that Melanie shreds when her team loses the game. The focus, though, is primarily on the interactions and conversations, so only a few props and staging ideas are presented. Rand also incorporates **lighting** as a dramatic element. As the scenes change, he suggests that the lights on one couple be dimmed, or blacked out, as the lights on the other are illuminated. Staging the action this way represents the transitions between scenes.

Regardless of whether the setting is a matter of stage directions or staging, all of these decisions as to how the production should look are deliberate choices to build a convincing backdrop and create emotion. It's also important to remember that, sometimes, how the props are used and where they are placed can have significant, even symbolic, meaning.

Setting

Return to the television show you've been thinking about and describe the most common set of the show and any props that are usually present. What do the set, props, or lighting reveal about the setting, characters, or conflicts?

Tragedy and Comedy

Plays traditionally fall into two basic categories — tragedies and comedies — although writers can also blend these two traditional forms into what are called tragicomedies.

A **tragedy** is a drama portraying events that are "terrible and pitiful," according to Aristotle. In many cases, they tell the story of the downfall of a great figure — the **tragic hero**. That downfall is caused by the hero's **tragic flaw** (often pride — which, in the context of tragedy, is called by the Greek term *hubris*). The result of watching the tragic hero's downfall is usually a **catharsis** for the audience, meaning a purging of and release from feelings of pity or fear.

You likely have seen many comedies on television and in the movies, but the official definition of a comedy is just a little different from what you are probably used to. A **comedy** is the mirror image of a tragedy. Comedies follow heroes as they rise, rather than fall. Comedies usually have **comic heroes** who are simple or common people, with an **endearing trait**, who experience some sort of success, whether it is finding love or achieving greatness. Though comedies can be funny and make the audience laugh, they don't necessarily do so; the literary term *comedy* specifically refers to a drama with a happy, rather than a tragic ending. Movies classified as "romantic comedies" fit this definition: characters usually face conflicts around such issues as race, gender, or socioeconomic differences, but their stories always end happily. While there are serious and dramatic elements to the play, *Check Please* is written as a comedy that centers on the humorous interactions that Guy and Girl have with other characters, and because ultimately it ends happily with Guy and Girl finding each other, it fits the literary definition of a comedy.

activity Tragedy and Comedy

Return to the television show you've been think about. How do you classify it? Is it a comedy? A tragedy? Does it have elements of both? Explain.

Theme

Theme refers to an idea in a text that comments on life or the world. It's not the subject of a play, but it's something that the writer wants to communicate about that topic. For example, a playwright's topic might be "family," but a possible theme is "family gets you through the hard times." One thing to keep in mind is that there is hardly ever just one theme. A play might address several minor themes in addition to a major theme. Themes in drama are usually developed through the action and dialogue of the characters, but they can also be developed or reinterpreted through choices in casting, staging, lighting, and costuming.

In *Check Please*, one possible theme is "however odd the path is to finding your match in this world, each step along the way brings you closer to the person you are destined to be with." It was important for Guy and Girl to meet people who didn't suit them, so that they could learn what they like and don't like. Ultimately, if they hadn't endured all of those awful dates, they never would have bumped into each other by accident in that restaurant, nor made such an immediate connection over things as silly as whether they like football or own burlap.

Look at this summary of how the various elements help the playwright convey one possible theme of *Check Please*: how love will find a way despite or because of the struggles to get there.

Dramatic Element	Example	How Does This Element Contribute to a Possible Theme?
Protagonist	Guy and Girl are the two protagonists.	The audience sees them separately suffering through a series of bad dates until the very last scene.
Antagonist/ supporting characters	Even though all the bad dates could be considered supporting characters, they are also antagonists opposing Guy's and Girl's hopes of finding love.	The antagonists represent the struggle to find genuine connection with other people.

Dramatic Element	Example	How Does This Element Contribute to a Possible Theme?
Setting	All of the action takes place in one restaurant with Guy and Girl back-to-back.	Guy and Girl are so close to finding each other throughout the play, just at different tables.
Props/costumes	Melanie wears an earpiece and tears a menu; Mark dresses in a burlap sack.	Guy wants a connection that Melanie cannot provide and Mark's odd choice in clothing pushes Girl away.
Lighting	From Rand's staging notes: "a quick lighting switch at the end of each scene to move from GIRL's table to GUY's table"	The lighting emphasizes Guy's and Girl's similarities as they suffer through their bad dates.
Tragic flaw/ endearing trait	The endearing trait for Guy and Girl is probably persistence.	If Guy and Girl did not have persistence, they would not have been able to get through all of those bad dates to eventually find each other.

Theme

Think back to the television episode you have been working with. Describe a possible theme developed in that show.

Additional Elements of Drama

In addition to the elements explained above, you will also encounter many of the dramatic elements listed below. Each element serves a purpose and impacts how the audience responds to the action on the stage.

Dramatic Irony

Dramatic irony occurs when the audience knows something that the characters on stage do not. Primarily, the audience has information that a character is not privy to. For example, we find dramatic irony in the closing scene of *Check Please* when Guy and Girl finally meet each other and inquire about objects of interest that they encountered earlier with other dates, in this case football and burlap. Neither Guy nor Girl would have an understanding of each other's question:

[*A short moment of instant chemistry. Then* GUY *shakes it off, as does* GIRL.]

GUY Well, goodnight.
GIRL Goodnight.

　[*They start to go their separate ways.*]

GUY Wait a second. [*Pause.*] This may sound like a really random question, but . . . do you like football?
GIRL A little. [*Beat.*] Do you own any burlap?

Symbol

A **symbol** is something literal that stands for or represents something else. In drama, symbolism can be achieved through the characters, a prop on the stage, the lighting, or even colors and costuming. The earpiece that Melanie puts in, for instance, becomes a symbol of her inability to focus on what's right in front of her.

As you read your way through this chapter, look to see how the authors use these elements of dramatic writing. You may not find them all in every text, but knowing what to look for will help you in your analyses and comprehension.

REFLECTING ON Academic Vocabulary   **Essential Elements of Drama**

Look back at the list of terms that you previewed on page 706. Now that you have read about them and practiced with these terms, what has changed about your understanding of dramatic texts? Which of the skills that you practiced in this section do you feel confident using? Which ones do you think you need to develop further? How do you know?

---

culminating activity

Analyzing Dramatic Elements

Look back at the dramatic elements vocabulary list on page 706, and create a table for the television show you have been working with in the activities throughout this workshop, similar to the sample for *Check Please* on page 718. Include a column that gives examples of three or four dramatic elements in the television show, and a column in which you explain how the dramatic elements contribute to a possible theme of that show (which you identified in the activity on p. 719). Feel free to use the graphic organizer below, or create your own method for identifying and explaining your ideas.

Dramatic Element (e.g., Protagonist, Setting, Props, Costumes)	Example from the Show	How Does This Element Contribute to a Possible Theme of the Show?

creative writing extension

Drama

If the goal of this chapter is for you to better understand drama as a genre, one of the best ways to do this is to understand how it works from the inside out. In the Skill Workshop, you applied your understanding of the elements of drama to a television show with which you were already familiar. In the following activities, you'll be able to try out some of those elements you learned about in the Skill Workshop as if you are a playwright yourself.

Getting Started

Look over the images below from stage productions of three different operas and write down your initial feelings about them. Share and compare your thoughts with a partner. One of these images will become the basis for the activities that follow.

Jack Vartoogian/Getty Images/Getty Images

George Karger/Getty Images

Jack Vartoogian/Getty Images/Getty Images

Characters

The Cast of Characters is a list of the main and supporting characters with names and sometimes brief descriptions. It generally appears at the very beginning of the play and lets the audience know who is who.

Characters

Imagine that one of the images you examined above is a scene from a play you are writing. Create a list of characters for your play with a brief description of who they are, what they are like, or any other important information necessary for your audience to know up front. Your list may include more figures than are shown in the image you've chosen. Identify some of your characters as protagonist, antagonist, foil, and supporting. See the Skill Workshop discussion of characters on page 712 for more help, if needed.

Conflict

Drama, perhaps more than any other genre, puts the conflicts and tensions between the characters front and center. Everything else — dialogue, characterization, even setting — helps heighten the conflicts between the characters.

Conflict

Return to your Cast of Characters and write a description of a conflict your protagonist might face. Think about how you might present the conflict in your scene and jot down some initial notes about how you see the conflict being presented. See the Skill Workshop discussion of conflict on page 716 for more help, if needed.

Dialogue

Unlike fiction, which often uses a wide range of characterization elements, including physical descriptions and internal thoughts, the primary method that playwrights have to develop their characters is through what they say onstage. What traits about your characters will you need to establish through what is said and through the interactions with others?

Punctuating Dialogue

Dialogue in drama writing follows a specific format. Most important is that playwrights change lines whenever a new character speaks, and the names of those speaking are indicated in bold or capital letters. Notice, too, that the dialogue in a play is not set in quotation marks, as it would be in fiction.

Playwrights use punctuation to emphasize the dialogue between characters. Look at Rand's use of ellipses to incorporate pauses in Ken's dialogue. Notice how the pauses further emphasize Ken's overly dramatic character.

> **GIRL** It's great to meet you.
>
> **KEN** The pleasure . . . is all mine.
>
> **GIRL** So . . . where are you from? I can't place the accent.
>
> **KEN** I was raised in the mountains of Guam . . . and was born . . . on the shore of New Jersey.
>
> [*Beat.*]
>
> **GIRL** Do you want to order some appetizers?

Dialogue

Return to your Cast of Characters. What are some characteristics that two characters possess? Kind, generous, frustrated, quick-tempered, shallow, arrogant, courageous? Write out a brief dialogue exchange between two of the characters that tries to illustrate one or more of their character traits, keeping in mind the effects punctuation might also provide. Remember, you can use only dialogue to accomplish this, so choose your characters' words carefully and use appropriate punctuation to help you to write effective dialogue. Review page 714 in the Skill Workshop if you need more assistance with this.

Stage Directions

In addition to dialogue, stage directions are ways for the playwright to communicate emotions and motivations to the actors. For instance, a pause (sometimes referred to in a script as a "beat") can emphasize suspense or build mood. Likewise, indicating that an actor should lean in closely to another when speaking can create intensity.

Stage Directions

Return to the dialogue you wrote for the previous activity. Add some stage directions that help reveal the emotions at work in the scene. You could include gestures, movement, pauses, sound effects, and so on. The stage directions can also include the way that a character says the dialogue, such as "shouts," "whispers," "sarcastically," and so on. You can also include details of the characters' costumes if it helps describe them. Review page 714 in the Skill Workshop if you need more assistance with this.

Setting

There are two primary ways to establish setting in drama. There is the setting of the play's story — the time and place in which it occurs — and then there is the setting onstage. That may include the physical arrangement of furniture on the stage, props used by the actors, costuming, or the lighting and sound effects that are incorporated into the performance.

Setting

Describe the set of a play version of one of the images you examined on page 721. As you describe your set, keep these key questions in mind:

- What feeling or mood do you want to create through the setting of this scene?
- What makes that setting interesting and believable for the audience?

Consider sketching a picture of the stage and remember that the stage limits the extent to which you can establish setting. You may wish to review elements of setting in the Skill Workshop on page 716.

Plot and Structure

At this point in this extension, you have described a protagonist, one or more conflicts, and the set of your adaptation of one or more of the images on page 721. Now it's time to start thinking a little bit more about the story you can tell, based on the image. Your plot should draw on and connect the elements of the plot diagram on page 715. Distilling your idea down to the basics like this is a good way to get a handle on the story.

Plot and Structure

Sketch out a plot diagram (see p. 715) for events that can stem from the image. Be sure to consider how the conflicts you've identified in the earlier activity (p. 722) can form the rising action leading to the climax. Don't worry if you cannot fill in all of the gaps. Try to have a rough idea of your resolution in mind — whether or not your protagonist overcomes obstacles, for example — as you sketch your diagram. See the Skill Workshop discussion of plot on page 715 for more help, if needed.

Final Reflection

Whether you put all of these pieces of your script together into a complete, developed scene from a play or not, you likely have learned a lot about how and why elements of drama are used to create particular effects. What has the experience of being a playwright taught you about the elements of drama? What have you begun to notice that you might not have otherwise?

Prologue to The Tragedy of Romeo and Juliet

William Shakespeare

Oli Scarff/Getty Images

William Shakespeare (1564–1616) was an English poet, actor, and playwright who is considered one of the greatest writers in the English language and the world's most famous playwright. He is credited with 38 plays, 154 sonnets, and two long narrative poems. Little is known of his life aside from the fact that he married Anne Hathaway when he was eighteen, worked as an actor-playwright in London, and retired in 1613. There is some speculation among scholars and historians that he might not be the author of all of the plays that bear his name. Regardless, the plays credited to him are among the most widely produced around the world, including the comedies *Much Ado about Nothing* and *Twelfth Night*, the historical plays *Richard III* and *Henry V*, and especially the tragedies *Hamlet, Othello, Macbeth, Julius Caesar*, and *Romeo and Juliet*.

KEY CONTEXT   Shakespearean Language. One of the most striking features of Shakespeare's plays for contemporary audiences is his language; it can often sound very old-fashioned to us today. Even though, technically, he was writing in what is called Early Modern English, there are many words he uses regularly that we just don't use anymore. Many of them are straightforward, though, such as the following:

- *thee* and *thou* mean "you"
- *hath* means "has"
- *thy* means "your"
- *doth* means "does"
- *wherefore* means "why"

Shakespeare also created thousands of words himself to fit in rhythm or rhyme scheme, including such common words today as *torture, gossip, tranquil, zany*, and *champion*. Words created for *Romeo and Juliet* include *uncomfortable, alligator* from the Spanish word for "lizard," as well as the phrases "star-crossed lovers" and "wild goose chase." Sometimes Shakespeare created new words by attaching prefixes and suffixes to common words in unique ways, as in *owest, wander'st,* and *growest*. You can read these just as they would be without the *–est* suffixes.

As you read the Prologue to *Romeo and Juliet* in this section, and *Romeo and Juliet* in Section 2, it's also important to keep in mind that people in Elizabethan times didn't walk around the streets of

London speaking in verse like the characters in this play. They may have used some of the same vocabulary, but Shakespeare constructs the language in the play in order to make it artful, not to realistically capture the speech of his time. Reading the language can certainly be challenging, but with practice, time, and use of the notes throughout the play, you will begin to see patterns and gain more familiarity and comfort with the Shakespearean language of *Romeo and Juliet*.

The Use of Sonnets. Three times in *Romeo and Juliet*, you will see that Shakespeare includes a sonnet, including the Prologue here. English sonnets, also called Shakespearean sonnets, have some distinct features:

- A strict rhyme scheme of abab cdcd efef gg.
- That rhyme scheme creates a structure of three "quatrains" (a group of four lines) and a concluding "couplet" (a two-line pair).
- Each line includes ten syllables.
- Those ten syllables are written in iambic pentameter, meaning five sets of alternating stressed and unstressed syllables (called *iambs*).

The Prologue. This is the opening scene in *Romeo and Juliet*, and it acts as an introduction to the play, summarizing the main action and even spoiling the ending. Onstage, the prologue is often delivered by a single performer, acting as a sort of a narrator; when adapted into film, it is often delivered as a voice-over narration. Below are three versions of the Prologue: the original written by Shakespeare and the first few pages of two graphic novel adaptations. On page 730, you might also consider several images from a 1996 film adaptation of the Prologue.

THE PROLOGUE

[*Enter Chorus.*]

CHORUS:
    Two households, both alike in dignity,°
        In fair Verona, where we lay our scene,
    From ancient grudge° break to new mutiny,
        Where civil blood makes civil hands unclean.°
    From forth the fatal loins of these two foes   5
        A pair of star-crossed° lovers take their life;
    Whose misadventured° piteous overthrows
        Doth with their death bury their parents' strife.
    The fearful passage of their death-marked° love,
        And the continuance of their parents' rage   10
    Which, but their children's end, naught could remove,
        Is now the two hours' traffic° of our stage;
    The which if you with patient ears attend,
    What here shall miss,° our toil shall strive to mend.°

                               [*Exit.*]

The Prologue. 1. dignity: social status. **3. ancient grudge:** longstanding feud **4. civil blood . . . unclean:** i.e., the blood of citizens soils the hands of fellow citizens. **6. star-crossed:** thwarted by the influence of a malignant star. **7. misadventured:** unlucky, unfortunate. **9. death-marked:** not only "foredoomed" but "with death as their objective." **12. two hours' traffic:** the conventional time designated for a performance. **14. miss:** prove inadequate in the performance. **14. mend:** improve (in the future).

Prologue to Romeo and Juliet: The Graphic Novel

John McDonald

John McDonald created the script for this graphic adaptation of *Romeo and Juliet*. As script writer, he divided the play into over 600 comic book panels, each describing the images that graphic artists would create to accompany the dialogue and stage directions. What follows are panels created according to those descriptions for the Prologue.

Prologue to Romeo and Juliet

Gareth Hinds

Gareth Hinds is the author and illustrator of several graphic novels and picture books based on classic literature and mythology, such as short stories by Edgar Allen Poe, *The Odyssey*, *Macbeth*, and this adaption of *Romeo and Juliet*.

extending beyond the text

In 1996, director Baz Luhrmann adapted *Romeo and Juliet*, updating it to a contemporary setting. The film, staring Leonardo Dicaprio and Claire Danes, focuses on rival gangs. In Luhrmann's adaptation, the Prologue is delivered in its entirety by a television newscaster as the camera gets closer to the TV screen. Then portions of the Prologue are read aloud by a different actor as a voiceover while corresponding images flash quickly across the screen. Look at some of these images below, for example.

What specific visual choices does the director make in this adaptation that update the Prologue in an effective way for contemporary audiences? Based on these images, what, if anything, is lost or gained in this film adaptation of the Prologue?

Understanding and Interpreting

1. What important information about the characters does the audience learn from the Prologue? What do we learn about the relationship between the two families?

2. Based on the information conveyed through the Prologue, restate the plot of *Romeo and Juliet* in your own words.

3. What does "star-crossed lovers" mean? How does this phrase help to set the tone of the play?

4. What point is made by telling the audience how the play ends ("lovers take their life") at the very beginning of the play? How might this information influence the audience's understanding of and reaction to the rest of the play?

5. What do we know about the Chorus that delivers the Prologue, especially from the use of the pronouns *we* and *our*? What does the Chorus represent and what is the Chorus asking of the audience?

6. In the original Prologue the only setting description is "In fair Verona, where we lay our scene." Describe the setting in the McDonald graphic novel version of the Prologue. What additional information do readers of the graphic novel Prologue receive regarding Verona and the setting in general?

7. Describe the setting of the Hinds graphic novel version. In what ways is it similar to and different from the original and the McDonald version?

Analyzing Language, Style, and Structure

8. **Vocabulary in Context.** In line 4 (p. 726), the Chorus uses the word *civil* twice. What does this word mean in this context? What other meanings of *civil* have you encountered?

9. **Vocabulary in Context.** In line 12 (p. 726), the Chorus uses the word *traffic*. How is the use of the word in this context similar to or different from modern or more familiar uses?

10. Reread the Prologue and count the number of words or phrases that refer to death or violence. What effect is achieved through these language choices? Where are words of violence mixed with those that refer to love? What is the effect of these juxtapositions?

11. An oxymoron is a figure of speech in which two ideas that seem contradictory appear in the same phrase, such as "less is more." Explain why "death-marked love" in line 9 (p. 726) is an oxymoron. What is its effect?

12. Look closely at the second frame of the McDonald graphic novel adaptation. Describe the image in the background and explain the effect of that image in conjunction with the words being spoken.

13. Unlike the McDonald graphic novel adaptation, the Hinds version does not include any people; the Chorus operates more like a voiceover in a film. What effect is created through this choice? How is the tone created similar to or different from that of the original text or the McDonald version?

Topics for Composing

14. **Analysis.** What kinds of themes do you anticipate might be addressed in the play, based solely on the Prologue? Include specific lines or visuals to support your interpretation.

15. **Analysis.** The Prologue is written in the form of a sonnet, the structure of which you can review in the Key Context above. Explain how the structure of the sonnet, specifically its rhymes and the final couplet, creates a particular tone at beginning of the play.

16. **Argument.** Some have argued that Shakespeare plays should be performed rather than read because that was his original intent and because his plays were not widely available in print during his lifetime. Based on the three versions of the Prologue included here, why do you think this is true or not?

17. **Connections.** Think of a movie, book, or television show that gives away at least part of the ending at the very beginning, like Shakespeare, Hinds, and McDonald do here in the Prologue. What similarities or differences do you see in how that text handles the reveal, compared to these versions of the Prologue?

18. **Connections.** Think about a long-standing conflict you're familiar with. What fueled it initially, and why did it keep going? Why do people seem to have so much trouble resolving long conflicts like this one? What kinds of concerns seem resistant to compromise?

19. **Speaking and Listening.** Shakespeare did not include any stage directions for how the Prologue should be delivered to an audience. Working with a partner or small group, rehearse and present your performance of the Prologue to the rest of your class. Consider choices in voice, gestures, movements, and other elements of staging that will help convey your interpretation of the Prologue.

20. **Research.** Conduct research on the use of a Chorus in drama, especially in the ancient Greek dramas. What was the purpose and function of a traditional Chorus? Shakespeare did not use a Chorus in many of his plays, but why might he have chosen to do so for this play, based only on what you know from the Prologue?

21. **Creative Writing.** Rewrite the Prologue in your own words as a modern-day story introduction in prose, as a free verse poem, as lyrics to a song, or as a thread of social media posts. While the information should remain the same, your tone might change as a result of your choices.

22. **Multimodal.** Create your own graphic novel adaptation of the Prologue, but change the setting from Verona to a time and place of your choice. Be sure the full text of the Prologue is included and give some careful thought for how to align the text and the images in your adaptation.

The Tragedy of Romeo and Juliet

William Shakespeare

KEY CONTEXT   **Theater in Shakespeare's Time.** Shakespeare wrote and performed many of his plays, including *Romeo and Juliet*, during the Elizabethan Era, named for Queen Elizabeth I of England, whose forty-five-year reign (1558–1603) was one of the country's most stable and prosperous time periods. Queen Elizabeth loved and supported the arts, especially the theater, and during her time, large audiences would go to see plays in London by Shakespeare, Christopher Marlowe, Ben Jonson, and others.

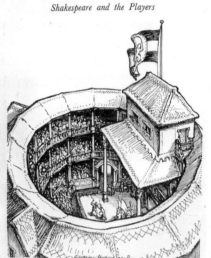

Shakespeare and the Players

Bridgeman Images

Going to the theater was one of the most popular leisure activities during Shakespeare's time, and most of the theaters, including the Globe (pictured right) where most of Shakespeare's plays were performed, were large, open-air spaces where people could pay a penny to stand in front of the stage (these audience members were called "the groundlings") or pay more for seats in the balconies that ringed the stage. The stages, sets, and costumes were much simpler than what we expect from theater today, so the writing had to communicate the details of setting and tone. Additionally, at the time, women were not allowed to perform onstage, so female characters were often portrayed by young boys; older female characters, like the Nurse in *Romeo and Juliet*, were probably played by adult men. Many of Shakespeare's plays subtly poke fun at the gender roles, especially when we remember that all of the female characters would have been played by men.

Time Period and Setting of *Romeo and Juliet*. While Shakespeare wrote and performed this play in the late 1500s in England, during the Elizabethan Era, the play itself is set during medieval times, probably during the 1300s in Verona, Italy, and was supposedly based, at least in part, on a true story of two lovers from rival families. Like many significant cities at the time, Verona was its own city-state, ruled by a prince and protected by walls on all sides. Verona would have been the center of all political, economic, social, and religious power for everyone nearby at the time. At right is a photo of Verona, parts of which remain unchanged from medieval times.

Factions in *Romeo and Juliet*. *Romeo and Juliet* is largely about two warring factions in Verona, the Montagues and the Capulets. Remembering who belongs to which faction can often be confusing, so we have sorted the characters in *Romeo and Juliet* into three categories: the Montagues, the Capulets, and those who are not directly affiliated with either family.

altrendo travel/Getty Images

A view of Verona, Italy.

Montague	Capulet	Unaffiliated
Romeo Montague	Juliet Capulet	Escalus — Prince of Verona
Montague — Romeo's father	Capulet — Juliet's father	Paris — young nobleman who wants to marry Juliet
Lady Montague — Romeo's mother	Lady Capulet — Juliet's mother	Friar Laurence
Benvolio — nephew to Montague, and cousin to Romeo	Tybalt — nephew to Lady Capulet	Friar John
	Nurse — attendant to Juliet	An Apothecary
Mercutio — kinsman to the Prince, and friend to Romeo, though not related to him	Sampson and Gregory — servants to Capulet	Citizens of Verona
		The Chorus
		Musicians
Balthasar — servant to Romeo	Peter — servant to Juliet's nurse	Page (to Paris)
Abraham — servant to Montague	Rosaline — Romeo's love interest at the beginning of the play, and Capulet's niece	

Dramatis Personae

CHORUS

ESCALUS, *Prince of Verona*

MERCUTIO, *the Prince's kinsman and Romeo's friend*

PARIS, *a young count and kinsman of the Prince*

PAGE *to Count Paris*

MONTAGUE

MONTAGUE'S WIFE

ROMEO, *son of the Montagues*

BENVOLIO, *Montague's nephew and Romeo's friend*

ABRAHAM, *a servant of the Montague household*

BALTHASAR, *a servant of the Montague household attending Romeo*

CAPULET

CAPULET'S WIFE

JULIET, *daughter of the Capulets*

NURSE

TYBALT, *nephew of Capulet's Wife*

PETRUCHIO, *Capulet's kinsman*

SECOND CAPULET, *an old man, Capulet's kinsman*

PETER, *a servant of the Capulet household attending the Nurse*

SAMSON,
GREGORY,
ANTHONY,
POTPAN,
CLOWN *or* SERVANT,
Other SERVANTS,
   servants of the Capulet household

FRIAR LAURENCE,
FRIAR JOHN,
   Franciscan friars

APOTHECARY
Three MUSICIANS (*Simon Catling, Hugh Rebeck, and James Soundpost*)
Three WATCHMEN
Citizens, Maskers, Torchbearers, Guards, Servants, and Attendants
SCENE: *Verona; Mantua*

ACT 1

Scene 1

[*Enter Samson and Gregory, with swords and bucklers,° of the house of Capulet.*]

SAMSON Gregory, on my word, we'll not carry coals.°

GREGORY No, for then we should be colliers.°

SAMSON I mean, an° we be in choler, we'll draw.°

GREGORY Ay, while you live, draw your neck out of collar. 5

SAMSON I strike quickly, being moved.

GREGORY But thou art not quickly moved to strike.

SAMSON A dog of the house of Montague moves me. 10

GREGORY To move is to stir, and to be valiant is to stand.° Therefore, if thou art moved, thou runn'st away.

SAMSON A dog of that house shall move me to stand. I will take the wall° of any man or maid 15 of Montagues.

GREGORY That shows thee a weak slave, for the weakest goes to the wall.°

SAMSON 'Tis true, and therefore women, being the weaker vessels, are ever thrust to the wall. 20 Therefore I will push Montague's men from the wall and thrust his maids to the wall.

GREGORY The quarrel is between our masters and us their men.°

SAMSON 'Tis all one. I will show myself a tyrant: 25 when I have fought with the men, I will be civil with the maids—I will cut off their heads.

GREGORY The heads of the maids?

SAMSON Ay, the heads of the maids, or their maiden heads. Take it in what sense thou 30 wilt.

GREGORY They must take it in sense that feel it.

SAMSON Me they shall feel while I am able to stand, and 'tis known I am a pretty piece of flesh. 35

GREGORY 'Tis well thou art not fish;° if thou hadst, thou hadst been Poor John.° Draw thy tool. Here comes of the house of Montagues.

[*Enter two other servingmen Abraham and another.*]

SAMSON My naked weapon is out. Quarrel. I will back thee. 40

GREGORY How, turn thy back and run?

SAMSON Fear me not.°

GREGORY No, marry.° I fear thee!

SAMSON Let us take the law of our sides. Let them begin. 45

GREGORY I will frown as I pass by, and let them take it as they list.°

Act 1, Scene 1. 0. sd *bucklers:* small shields. 1–2. carry coals: submit passively to indignity or insult. 3. colliers: (1) coal carriers, (2) term of abuse (from the dirtiness of the trade and the reputation of colliers for cheating). 4. an: if. 4. in choler, we'll draw: draw (our swords) in anger (with play, in 4, on "draw . . . collar" = slip out of the hangman's noose). 11–12. moved . . . stand: to react emotionally, to take a firm and courageous position under threat of attack. 15. take the wall: assert social position or physical superiority. 18. weakest . . . wall: In a fight the weakest were driven up against the wall. 23–24. quarrel . . . men: i.e., we have no quarrel with women. 36. fish: with play on "woman" or "prostitute" (slang). 37. poor-John: cheap, popularly associated with women ("weaker vessels," "fish"). 42. Fear me not: i.e., don't worry about my support (backing). Gregory (35) pretends to take the words literally: "Don't be afraid of me." 43. marry: indeed. 47. list: wish, please.

SAMSON Nay, as they dare. I will bite my thumb° at them, which is disgrace to them if they bear it.

[*Samson makes taunting gestures.*]

ABRAHAM Do you bite your thumb at us, sir? 50

SAMSON I do bite my thumb, sir.

ABRAHAM Do you bite your thumb at us, sir?

SAMSON [*Aside to Gregory*] Is the law of our side if I say ay?

GREGORY [*Aside to Samson*] No. 55

SAMSON [*To Abraham*] No, sir, I do not bite my thumb at you, sir, but I bite my thumb, sir.

GREGORY Do you quarrel, sir?

ABRAHAM Quarrel, sir? No, sir.

SAMSON But if you do, sir, I am for you. I serve as 60 good a man as you.

ABRAHAM No better.

SAMSON Well, sir.

[*Enter Benvolio.*]

GREGORY [*To Samson*] Say "better." Here comes one° of my master's kinsmen. 65

SAMSON [*To Abraham*] Yes, better, sir.

ABRAHAM You lie.

SAMSON Draw, if you be men. Gregory, remember thy washing° blow.

[*They fight.*]

BENVOLIO Part, fools! 70

Put up your swords. You know not what you do.

[*Enter Tybalt with sword drawn.*]

TYBALT What, art thou drawn among these heartless hinds?°

Turn thee, Benvolio, Look upon thy death.

BENVOLIO I do but keep the peace. Put up thy sword,

Or manage° it to part these men with me. 75

TYBALT What, drawn and talk of peace? I hate the word

As I hate hell, all Montagues, and thee.

Have at thee,° coward! [*They fight.*]

[*Enter three or four Citizens with clubs or partisans.*]

CITIZENS Clubs, bills, and partisans!° Strike! Beat them down!

Down with the Capulets ! Down with the 80 Montagues!

[*Enter old Capulet in his gown, and his Wife.*]

CAPULET What noise is this? Give me my long sword,° ho!

CAPULET'S WIFE A crutch, a crutch! Why call you for a sword?

CAPULET My sword, I say! Old Montague is come

And flourishes his blade in spite of° me. 85

[*Enter old Montague and his Wife.*]

MONTAGUE Thou villain Capulet! — Hold me not; let me go.

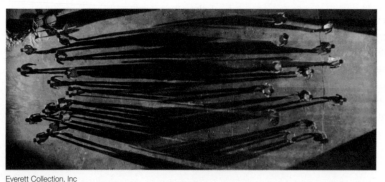

This is an image of rival gangs facing off in the 2021 film *West Side Story*, a musical that adapts portions of *Romeo and Juliet*.

How has the director used lighting and framing to illustrate the danger of the conflict?

Everett Collection, Inc

---

48. bite my thumb at: a provocative, probably obscene gesture. **65. one:** i.e., Tybalt, who is seen approaching. **69. washing:** slashing with great force. **72. heartless hinds:** cowardly menials. **75. manage:** handle, wield. **78. Have at thee:** a common formula, warning of immediate attack. **79. Clubs, bills, and partisans:** weapons. **82. long sword:** an old-fashioned, heavy, often two-handed sword. **85. in spite of:** out of spite for.

These images show Tybalt's first appearances in a 1996 film adaptation of *Romeo and Juliet* (top) and a 2019 stage ballet version (bottom).

What lines from Scene 1 might have inspired the actors' portrayals? How are these two versions similar and different?

MONTAGUE'S WIFE Thou shalt not stir one foot to
    seek a foe.

[*Enter Prince Escalus, with his train.*]

PRINCE Rebellious subjects, enemies to peace,
    Profaners of this neighbor-stainèd steel° —   90
    Will they not hear? What, ho! You men, you
      beasts,
    That quench the fire of your pernicious rage
With purple fountains issuing from your veins,
On pain of torture,° from those bloody hands
Throw your mistempered° weapons to the   95
    ground
And hear the sentence of your movèd prince.
Three civil brawls, bred of an airy° word,
By thee, old Capulet, and Montague,
Have thrice disturbed the quiet of our streets
And made Verona's ancient citizens   100

---

90. Profaners . . . steel: those who desecrate the purity of steel with the blood of neighbors.   **94. On pain of torture:** i.e., failure to obey will be punished by torture.   **95. mistempered:** (1) figuratively, tempered (= made hard and resilient) in hot blood instead of icy water; (2) ill-tempered, angry.   **97. airy:** empty, vain.

737

Cast by their grave-beseeming ornaments°
To wield old partisans, in hands as old,
Cankered with peace, to part your cankered°
    hate.
If ever you disturb our streets again
Your lives shall pay the forfeit of the peace.   105
For this time all the rest depart away.
You, Capulet, shall go along with me,
And, Montague, come you this afternoon,
To know our farther pleasure in this case,
To old Freetown, our common judgment-   110
    place.
Once more, on pain of death, all men depart.

[*Exeunt all but Montague, Montague's Wife,
and Benvolio.*]

MONTAGUE Who set this ancient quarrel new
    abroach?
Speak, nephew, were you by when it began?
BENVOLIO Here were the servants of your
    adversary,
And yours, close fighting ere I did approach.   115
I drew to part them. In the instant came
The fiery Tybalt with his sword prepared,°
Which, as he breathed defiance to my ears,
He swung about his head and cut the winds
Who, nothing hurt withal,° hissed him in   120
    scorn.
While we were interchanging thrusts and blows,
Came more and more, and fought on part and
    part°
Till the Prince came, who parted either part.°
MONTAGUE'S WIFE O, where is Romeo? Saw you
    him today?
Right glad I am he was not at this fray.   125
BENVOLIO Madam, an hour before the
    worshiped sun
Peered forth the golden window of the east,
A troubled mind drave° me to walk abroad,°
Where, underneath the grove of sycamore°
That westward rooteth from this city's side,   130

So early walking did I see your son.
Towards him I made, but he was ware° of me
And stole into the covert° of the wood.
I, measuring his affections by my own,
Which then most sought where most might   135
    not be found,
Being one too many by my weary self,
Pursued my humor, not pursuing his,
And gladly shunned who gladly fled from me.
MONTAGUE Many a morning hath he there
    been seen,
With tears augmenting the fresh morning's dew,   140
Adding to clouds more clouds with his deep
    sighs;
But all so soon as the all-cheering sun
Should in the farthest east begin to draw
The shady curtains from Aurora's° bed,
Away from light steals home my heavy son   145
And private in his chamber pens himself,
Shuts up his windows,° locks fair daylight out,
And makes himself an artificial night.
Black° and portentous must this humor° prove
Unless good counsel may the cause remove.   150
BENVOLIO My noble uncle, do you know the
    cause?
MONTAGUE I neither know it nor can learn of him.
BENVOLIO Have you importuned him by any
    means?
MONTAGUE Both by myself and many other
    friends.
But he, his own affections' counsellor,°   155
Is to himself—I will not say how true,
But to himself so secret and so close,
So far from sounding° and discovery,°
As is the bud bit with an envious worm
Ere he can spread his sweet leaves to the air   160
Or dedicate his beauty to the sun.
Could we but learn from whence his sorrows
    grow,
We would as willingly give cure as know.

[*Enter Romeo.*]

---

101. **grave beseeming ornaments**: accessories proper to the dignity of age. Lady Capulet has sarcastically suggested a "crutch" (72). 103. **Cankered . . . cankered**: rusted, corroded (from disuse) . . . malignant, diseased. 117. **prepared**: already drawn. 120. **nothing hurt withal**: not a bit injured thereby. 122. **on part and part**: on one side and the other. 123. **either part**: both parties. 128. **drive**: drove. 128. **abroad**: from home. 129. **sycamore**: a tree associated with dejected lovers. 132. **ware**: aware. 133. **covert**: shelter, hiding place. 144. **Aurora**: goddess of the dawn. 147. **windows**: shutters. 149. **Black**: malignant, baneful. 149. **humour**: inclination, mood. 155. **his own affections' counsellor**: the (only) confidant of his own feelings. 158. **sounding**: investigation by cautious or indirect questioning. 158. **discovery**: laying open to view, exposure.

BENVOLIO See where he comes. So please you, step aside.

I'll know his grievance or be much denied. 165

MONTAGUE I would thou wert so happy by thy stay
To hear true shrift. Come, madam, let's away.

[*Exeunt Montague and his Wife.*]

BENVOLIO Good morrow, cousin.

ROMEO   Is the day so young?

BENVOLIO But new struck nine.

ROMEO   Ay me! Sad hours
seem long.

Was that my father that went hence so fast? 170

BENVOLIO It was. What sadness lengthens
Romeo's hours?

ROMEO Not having that° which, having, makes
them short.

BENVOLIO In love?

ROMEO Out— 175

BENVOLIO Of love?

ROMEO Out of her favor where I am in love.

BENVOLIO Alas, that Love, so gentle in his view,°
Should be so tyrannous and rough in proof!°

ROMEO Alas, that Love, whose view is muffled still,° 180
Should without eyes see pathways to his will!°
Where shall we dine?—O me! What fray was
here?
Yet tell me not, for I have heard it all.
Here's much to do with hate, but more with love.°
Why, then, O brawling love, O loving hate, 185
O anything of nothing first create,
O heavy lightness, serious vanity,
Misshapen chaos of well-seeming forms,
Feather of lead, bright smoke, cold fire, sick
health,
Still-waking sleep, that is not what it is! 190
This love feel I, that feel no love in this.
Dost thou not laugh?

BENVOLIO   No, coz, I rather weep.

ROMEO Good heart, at what?

BENVOLIO   At thy good heart's oppression.

ROMEO Why, such is love's transgression.°
Griefs of mine own lie heavy in my breast, 195
Which thou wilt propagate, to have it pressed
With more of thine. This love that thou hast
shown
Doth add more grief to too much of mine own.
Love is a smoke made with the fume of sighs;
Being purged, a fire sparkling in lovers' eyes; 200
Being vexed, a sea nourished with lovers' tears.
What is it else? A madness most discreet,
A choking gall,° and a preserving sweet.
Farewell, my coz.

BENVOLIO   Soft!° I will go along.
An if° you leave me so, you do me wrong. 205

ROMEO Tut, I have lost myself. I am not here.
This is not Romeo; he's some other where.

BENVOLIO Tell me in sadness,° who is that you love?

ROMEO What, shall I groan and tell thee?

BENVOLIO Groan? Why, no, but sadly tell me who. 210

ROMEO Bid a sick man in sadness make his will—
A word ill urged to one that is so ill!
In sadness, cousin, I do love a woman.

BENVOLIO I aimed so near when I supposed you
loved.

ROMEO A right good mark-man!° And she's fair 215
I love.

BENVOLIO A right fair mark, fair coz, is soonest hit.

ROMEO Well, in that hit you miss.° She'll not be hit
With Cupid's arrow. She hath Dian's wit,°
And, in strong proof° of chastity well armed,
From love's weak childish bow she lives 220
unharmed.°
She will not stay the siege of° loving terms,
Nor bide th' encounter of assailing eyes,
Nor ope her lap to saint-seducing gold.°
O, she is rich in beauty, only poor
That when she dies, with beauty dies her store. 225

BENVOLIO Then she hath sworn that she will
still° live chaste?

---

173. **that:** i.e., the reciprocation of his love.   178. **view:** appearance (i.e., the boy Cupid).   179. **rough in proof:** harsh in actual experience.
180. **whose . . . still:** whose vision is always ("still") blindfolded.   181. **Should . . . will:** should, though blindfolded, nevertheless be able to see to
impose his will (upon us as lovers).   184. **Here's . . . love:** Here's a great disturbance on account of the feud—but my unhappy love causes me
even more disturbance than that.   194. **love's transgression:** the way love oversteps its proper bounds; hence, love's sin.   203. **gall:** bitterness.
204. **Soft:** stay, stop.   205. **And if:** if.   208. **sadness:** seriousness (without witty sparring).   215. **mark-man:** marksman.   217. **hit you miss:**
i.e., your aim (or guess) is wide of the mark.   218. **Dian's wit:** Diana's wisdom (in eschewing love). Diana was the goddess of chastity.   219. **strong
proof:** impenetrable armor.   220. **From . . . uncharmed:** uncharmed from = exempt from the spell of.   221. **stay the siege of:** undergo the threat of
capture.   223. **ope . . . gold:** a reference to Danae, who was seduced by Jove in the form of a golden shower.   226. **still:** always.

739

ROMEO She hath, and in that sparing makes huge
    waste,
  For beauty starved° with her severity
  Cuts beauty off from all posterity.
  She is too fair, too wise, wisely too fair,   230
  To merit bliss by making me despair.
  She hath forsworn to love, and in that vow
  Do I live dead that live to tell it now.
BENVOLIO Be ruled by me. Forget to think of her.
ROMEO O, teach me how I should forget to think!   235
BENVOLIO By giving liberty unto thine eyes:
  Examine other beauties.

ROMEO   'Tis the way
  To call hers, exquisite, in question more.°
  These happy masks that kiss fair ladies' brows,
  Being black, puts us in mind they hide the fair. 240
  He that is strucken° blind cannot forget
  The precious treasure of his eyesight lost.
  Show me a mistress° that is passing° fair:
  What doth her beauty serve but as a note°
  Where I may read who passed that passing fair? 245
  Farewell. Thou canst not teach me to forget.
BENVOLIO I'll pay that doctrine, or else die in
  debt.   [*Exeunt.*]

---

228. starved: killed.   **238. hers . . . more:** her beauty (being exquisite) into more heightened consideration ("question") by comparison.   **241. strucken:** struck.   **243. a mistress:** i.e., any lady-love (other than Romeo's).   **243. passing:** surpassingly; surpassed.   **244. note:** explanatory marginal gloss.

extending beyond the text

Many people of Shakespeare's time believed in a concept called the "Great Chain of Being" with God at the top, followed by angelic beings, humans, animals, plants, and finally, minerals. Within these categories were further categories, as seen in this image. For instance, animals were arranged according to the food chain, and humans were arranged with kings at the top, then nobles, then peasants.

Bridgeman Images

How have you seen the Great Chain of Being at work already in *Romeo and Juliet*? Is it holding steady or breaking apart? Explain.

Scene 2

[Enter Capulet, County Paris, and the Clown a Servingman.]

CAPULET But Montague is bound° as well as I,
    In penalty alike, and 'tis not hard, I think,
    For men so old as we to keep the peace.
PARIS Of honorable reckoning° are you both,
    And pity 'tis you lived at odds so long.   5
    But now, my lord, what say you to my suit?
CAPULET But saying o'er what I have said before:
    My child is yet a stranger in the world;
    She hath not seen the change of fourteen years.°
    Let two more summers wither in their pride   10
    Ere we may think her ripe to be a bride.
PARIS Younger than she are happy mothers made.
CAPULET And too soon marred are those so early
      made.°
    The earth hath swallowed all my hopes but she;
    She's the hopeful lady of my earth.°   15
    But woo her, gentle Paris, get her heart;
    My will to her consent is but a part;
    And, she agreed,° within her scope of choice
    Lies my consent and fair according voice.°
    This night I hold an old accustomed feast,°   20
    Whereto I have invited many a guest
    Such as I love; and you among the store,
    One more, most welcome, makes my number
      more.
    At my poor house look to behold this night
    Earth-treading° stars that make dark heaven   25
      light.
    Such comfort as do lusty young men feel
    When well-appareled April on the heel
    Of limping winter treads, even such delight
    Among fresh fennel° buds shall you this night
    Inherit° at my house. Hear all, all see,   30
    And like her most whose merit most shall be;
    Which on more view of many, mine, being one,

May stand in number, though in reckoning none.
Come, go with me.

    [To the Servingman, giving a paper.]

        Go, sirrah,° trudge about
Through fair Verona; find those persons out   35
Whose names are written there, and to them say,
My house and welcome on their pleasure stay.°

    [Exit with Paris.]

SERVINGMAN Find them out whose names are
    written here! It is written that the shoemaker
    should meddle with his yard° and the tailor with   40
    his last, the fisher with his pencil, and the
    painter with his nets;° but I am sent to find those
    persons whose names are here writ, and can
    never find what names the writing person hath
    here writ. I must to the learned. —In good time!   45

[Enter Benvolio and Romeo.]

BENVOLIO Tut, man, one fire burns out another's
      burning,
    One pain is lessened by another's anguish;
    Turn giddy, and be holp° by backward turning;°
    One desperate grief cures with another's
      languish.
    Take thou some new infection to thy eye,   50
    And the rank poison of the old will die.°
ROMEO Your plantain leaf° is excellent for that.
BENVOLIO For what, I pray thee?
ROMEO   For your broken shin.
BENVOLIO Why, Romeo, art thou mad?
ROMEO Not mad, but bound more than a   55
      madman is;
    Shut up in prison, kept without my food,
    Whipped and tormented and —God-den,°
      good fellow.
SERVINGMAN God gi' god-den.° I pray, sir, can
    you read?

Act 1, Scene 2. **1. bound:** legally obligated (to keep the peace). **4. reckoning:** reputation. **9. not . . . years:** i.e., not yet fourteen years old.
13. marred . . . made: a common proverbial jingle, with play on "married" and, perhaps, "maid." **15. hopeful . . . earth:** (she is) the only
remaining hope of my life in this world (= earth). **18. And she agreed:** and once she has consented. **18–19. within . . . voice** i.e., I will accept
whomever she chooses. **20. old accustomed feast:** i.e., a feast held regularly for years past. **25. Earth-treading:** i.e., mortal. **29. fennel:**
fragrant yellow-flowered plant, believed to cleanse the stomach and preserve and clear the sight. **30. Inherit :**possess. **34. sirrah:** form of address
to an inferior. **37. on their pleasure stay:** wait on their will (to attend). **39–42. It . . . nets:** Typically the "Clown" associates each attribute with
the wrong individual. **40. yard:** measuring-rod. **46–51. Tut . . . die:** a string of moral "sentences" on the common theme that one grief or pain
drives out another grief or pain. **48. holp:** helped. **48. backward turning** turning in the reverse direction. **52. plantain leaf:** Plantain leaves
were used as poultices for something minor like a "broken" (= skinned) shin (see 53). Romeo is sarcastically referring to the stream of proverbial
wisdom Benvolio has just let loose. **57. God-den:** good evening. (Used loosely for any time between noon and night.) **58. God gi' god-den:**
God give ye good evening.

ROMEO Ay, mine own fortune in my misery.

SERVINGMAN Perhaps you have learned it   60
without book.° But, I pray, can you read
anything you see?

ROMEO Ay, if I know the letters and the language.

SERVINGMAN Ye say honestly. Rest you merry!
        [*Going.*]

ROMEO Stay, fellow, I can read.   65
        [*He reads the letter.*]

    "Signor Martino and his wife and daughters,
    County Anselme and his beauteous sisters,
    The lady widow of Vitruvio,
    Signor Placentio and his lovely nieces,
    Mercutio and his brother Valentine,   70
    Mine uncle Capulet, his wife, and daughters,
    My fair niece Rosaline, and Livia,
    Signor Valentio and his cousin Tybalt,
    Lucio and the lively Helena."

A fair assembly. Whither should they come?   75

SERVINGMAN Up.

ROMEO Whither? To supper?

SERVINGMAN To our house.

ROMEO Whose house?

SERVINGMAN My master's.   80

ROMEO Indeed, I should have asked thee that
before.

SERVINGMAN Now I'll tell you without asking.
My master is the great rich Capulet; and if
you be not of the house of Montagues,   85
pray, come and crush° a cup of wine. Rest
you merry!   [*Exit.*]

BENVOLIO At this same ancient feast of Capulet's
Sups the fair Rosaline whom thou so loves,
With all the admirèd beauties of Verona.   90
Go thither, and with unattainted° eye
Compare her face with some that I shall show,
And I will make thee think thy swan a crow.

ROMEO When the devout religion of mine eye
Maintains such falsehood, then turn tears to   95
    fires;
And these who, often drowned, could never die,°
Transparent° heretics, be burnt for liars!
One fairer than my love? The all-seeing sun

Ne'er saw her match since first the world begun.

BENVOLIO Tut, you saw her fair, none else being by,   100
Herself poised° with herself in either eye;
But in that crystal scales let there be weighed
Your lady's love against some other maid
That I will show you shining at this feast,
And she shall scant show well that now   105
    seems best.

ROMEO I'll go along, no such sight to be shown,
But to rejoice in splendor of mine own.°[*Exeunt.*]

Scene 3

[*Enter Capulet's Wife and Nurse.*]

WIFE Nurse, where's my daughter? Call her forth
to me.

NURSE Now, by my maidenhead° at twelve year old,
I bade her come. What,° lamb! What, ladybird!
God forbid. Where's this girl? What, Juliet!

[*Enter Juliet.*]

JULIET How now? Who calls?   5

NURSE Your mother.

JULIET Madam, I am here. What is your will?

WIFE This is the matter. — Nurse, give leave°
    awhile,
We must talk in secret. — Nurse, come back
    again;
I have remembered me, thou's° hear our   10
    counsel.
Thou knowest my daughter's of a pretty age.°

NURSE Faith, I can tell her age unto an hour.

WIFE She's not fourteen.

NURSE   I'll lay fourteen of my teeth —
And yet, to my teen° be it spoken, I have but
    four —
She's not fourteen. How long is it now   15
To Lammastide?°

WIFE   A fortnight and odd days.

NURSE Even or odd, of all days in the year,
Come Lammas Eve at night shall she be
    fourteen.
Susan and she — God rest all Christian souls! —

---

61. **without book:** by heart (rote learning by ear). 86. **crush:** drink. 91. **unattainted:** unprejudiced. 96. **these . . . die:** i.e., these eyes that survived death though repeatedly drowned (in tears). 97. **Transparent:** manifest (with play on "clear"); "heretics" (= renegades) and "burnt" carry on the religious imagery initiated in 94. 101. **poised:** weighed, balanced. 107. **mine own:** i.e., the expected sight of his own Rosaline. **Act 1, Scene 3.** 2. **maidenhead:** virginity; a vulgar oath suitable to the Nurse. 3. **What:** a common exclamation of impatience. 8. **give leave:** leave us. 10. **thou s':** thou shalt. 11. **pretty age:** i.e., an age at which marriage may properly be considered. 14. **teen:** grief. 16. **Lammas-tide:** August 1.

Were of an age. Well, Susan is with God; 20
She was too good for me. But, as I said,
On Lammas Eve at night shall she be fourteen,
That shall she, marry, I remember it well.
'Tis since the earthquake now eleven years,
And she was weaned — I never shall forget it — 25
Of all the days of the year, upon that day;
For I had then laid wormwood to my dug,°
Sitting in the sun under the dovehouse wall.
My lord and you were then at Mantua —
Nay, I do bear a brain!° But, as I said, 30
When it did taste the wormwood on the nipple
Of my dug and felt it bitter, pretty fool,°
To see it tetchy and fall out wi' th' dug!
"Shake,"° quoth the dovehouse. 'Twas no
    need, I trow,°
To bid me trudge!° 35
And since that time it is eleven years,
For then she could stand high-lone;° nay, by
    the rood,°
She could have run and waddled all about.
For even the day before, she broke her brow,°
And then my husband — God be with his soul! 40
'A° was a merry man — took up the child.
"Yea," quoth he, "dost thou fall upon thy face?
Thou wilt fall backward when thou hast more
    wit,
Wilt thou not, Jule?" and, by my holidam,°
The pretty wretch left crying and said "Ay." 45
To see now how a jest shall come about!°
I warrant, an I should live a thousand years,
I never should forget it. "Wilt thou not, Jule?"
    quoth he,
And, pretty fool, it stinted° and said "Ay."
WIFE Enough of this. I pray thee, hold thy peace. 50
NURSE Yes, madam. Yet I cannot choose but laugh
To think it should leave crying and say "Ay."
And yet, I warrant, it had upon its brow
A bump as big as a young cockerel's stone —
A perilous knock — and it cried bitterly. 55

"Yea," quoth my husband. "Fall'st upon thy
    face?
Thou wilt fall backward when thou comest to
    age,
Wilt thou not, Jule?" It stinted and said "Ay."
JULIET And stint thou too, I pray thee, Nurse, say I.
NURSE Peace, I have done. God mark thee to his 60
    grace!
Thou wast the prettiest babe that e'er I nursed.
An I might live to see thee married once,
I have my wish.
WIFE Marry, that "marry" is the very theme
I came to talk of. Tell me, daughter Juliet, 65
How stands your disposition to be married?
JULIET It is an honor that I dream not of.
NURSE An honor? Were not I thine only nurse,
I would say thou hadst sucked wisdom from
    thy teat.°
WIFE Well, think of marriage now. Younger than 70
    you
Here in Verona, ladies of esteem
Are made already mothers. By my count
I was your mother much upon these years°
That you are now a maid. Thus then in brief:
The valiant Paris seeks you for his love. 75
NURSE A man, young lady! Lady, such a man
As all the world — why, he's a man of wax.°
WIFE Verona's summer hath not such a flower.
NURSE Nay, he's a flower, in faith, a very flower.
WIFE What say you? Can you love the gentleman? 80
This night you shall behold him at our feast.
Read o'er the volume of young Paris' face
And find delight writ there with beauty's pen;
Examine every married lineament
And see how one another lends content,° 85
And what obscured in this fair volume lies
Find written in the margent° of his eyes.
This precious book of love, this unbound lover,
To beautify him, only lacks a cover.
The fish lives in the sea, and 'tis much pride 90
For fair without the fair within to hide.

---

27. laid . . . dug: rubbed wormwood (a plant proverbial for its bitter taste) on my nipple. This causes the milk to taste so bitter that a baby will give up breast-feeding and be "weaned" (25). **30. bear a brain:** have a good memory. **32. fool:** used as a term of endearment. **34. "Shake!":** Look lively, move! **34. trow:** think (expressing annoyance). **35. trudge:** be off. **37. high-lone:** all by herself. **37. rood:** (Christ's) cross. **39. broke her brow:** cut or bruised her forehead (from a fall). **41. 'A:** he. **44 holidam:** "holy dame" (i.e., the Virgin Mary). **46. To . . . about:** i.e., just look how something spoken in jest may become reality (referring to Juliet's projected married state). **49. stinted:** stopped (crying). **68–69. were . . . teat:** mock modesty from the Nurse. Thy teat = the teat (mine) that suckled you. **73. much upon these years:** at about the same age. **77. man of wax:** a man formed of all perfections (like an ideal wax figure). **85. one another lends content:** each part bestows satisfaction and pleasure. **87. margent:** margin. The margins of early books and manuscripts often contained glosses and commentary explaining the text.

743

This image from a 2002 a stage production of *Romeo and Juliet* shows the Nurse, Lady Capulet/Wife, and Juliet (left to right).

Based only on the facial expressions and gestures in this image, how would you describe the relationship among the three women? In what ways is the relationship shown here similar to or different from what you imagine based only on the language of the play?

Donald Cooper/Alamy

That book in many's eyes doth share the glory	Or shall we on without apology?
That in gold clasps locks in the golden story;	**BENVOLIO** The date is out of such prolixity.°
So shall you share all that he doth possess,	We'll have no Cupid hoodwinked° with a scarf,
By having him, making yourself no less. 95	Bearing a Tartar's painted bow of lath, 5
NURSE No less? Nay, bigger. Women grow by men.°	Scaring the ladies like a crow-keeper;°
WIFE Speak briefly: can you like of° Paris' love?	Nor no without-book° prologue, faintly spoke
JULIET I'll look to like, if looking liking move,	After the prompter, for our entrance;
But no more deep will I endart° mine eye	But, let them measure us by what they will,°
Than your consent gives strength to make it fly. 100	We'll measure them a measure, and be gone. 10

[*Enter Servingman.*]

SERVINGMAN Madam, the guests are come, supper served up, you called, my young lady asked for, the Nurse cursed in the pantry, and everything in extremity. I must hence to wait. I beseech you, follow straight.° 105

WIFE We follow thee. [*Exit Servingman.*] Juliet, the County stays.°

NURSE Go, girl, seek happy nights to happy days.

[*Exeunt.*]

Scene 4

[*Enter Romeo, Mercutio, Benvolio, with five or six other maskers; torchbearers.*]

ROMEO What, shall this speech be spoke for our excuse?

ROMEO Give me a torch.° I am not for this ambling.
Being but heavy, I will bear the light.

MERCUTIO Nay, gentle Romeo, we must have you dance.

ROMEO Not I, believe me. You have dancing shoes With nimble soles; I have a soul of lead 15 So stakes me to the ground I cannot move.

MERCUTIO You are a lover; borrow Cupid's wings And soar with them above a common bound

ROMEO I am too sore enpiercèd° with his shaft To soar with his light feathers, and so bound. 20 I cannot bound a pitch° above dull woe. Under love's heavy burden do I sink.°

MERCUTIO And, to sink in it, should you burden love — Too great oppression for a tender thing.

96. No...men No indeed, not smaller! Women grow larger (= swell in pregnancy) through men.   **97. like of:** be pleased with.   **99. endart:** shoot as a dart.   **105. straight:** immediately.   **107. stays:** waits.   **Act 1, Scene 4.   3. date...prolixity:** Such tedious verbiage is now out of fashion.   **4. hoodwinked:** blindfolded.   **6. crow-keeper:** scarecrow.   **7. without-book:** (supposedly) memorized.   **9. measure...will:** judge us by any standards they may choose, with double play, in 10, on "measure" = (1) traverse, tread, mete out; (2) a stately dance.   **11. torch:** As a torch-bearer, Romeo could not join in the dancing.   **19. enpiercèd:** pierced through.   **21. pitch:** height (the upper limit of a falcon's flight).   **22. sink:** give way (as under a weight).

This is an engraving of Queen Mab made in 1850.

What elements from this image are also found in Mercutio's description of Mab? How is the tone toward Mab in the speech similar to or different from the tone in the engraving?

"QUEEN MAB," BY H. FIDEY, IN THE EXHIBITION OF THE NEW SOCIETY OF PAINTERS IN WATER COLOURS—SEE NEXT PAGE.

Look and Learn/Illustrated Papers Collection/Bridgeman Images

ROMEO Is love a tender thing? It is too rough,   25
  Too rude, too boisterous, and it pricks like thorn.
MERCUTIO If love be rough with you, be rough
    with love;
  Prick love for pricking, and you beat love down.°
  Give me a case° to put my visage in.

                    [*He puts on a mask.*]

  A visor for a visor!° What care I   30
  What curious eye doth quote deformities?
  Here are the beetle brows° shall blush for me.
BENVOLIO Come knock and enter, and no
    sooner in
  But every man betake him to his legs.°
ROMEO A torch for me. Let wantons light of heart   35
  Tickle the senseless rushes with their heels,
  For I am proverbed with a grandsire phrase:°
  I'll be a candle holder and look on.
  The game was ne'er so fair, and I am done.
MERCUTIO Tut, dun's the mouse,° the constable's   40
  own word.

If thou art dun, we'll draw thee from the mire°
Of — save your reverence — love,° wherein
  thou stickets
Up to the ears. Come, we burn daylight,° ho!
ROMEO Nay, that's not so.
MERCUTIO   I mean, sir, in delay
  We waste our lights in vain, like lamps by day.   45
  Take our good meaning, for our judgment sits
  Five times in that ere once in our five wits.°
ROMEO And we mean well in going to this masque,
  But 'tis no wit to go.
MERCUTIO   Why, may one ask?
ROMEO I dreamt a dream tonight.   50
MERCUTIO   And so did I.
ROMEO Well, what was yours?
MERCUTIO   That dreamers often lie.
ROMEO In bed asleep, while they do dream
  things true.
MERCUTIO O, then, I see Queen Mab° hath been
  with you.

---

28. Prick . . . down: (1) Grieve love in return for wounding you and you will defeat it; (2) stimulate or goad love for the purpose of copulation and you will deflate it. **29. case:** mask. **30. A visor for a visor:** i.e., a mask for an ugly face. **30–32. what . . . me:** Beetle brows = overhanging eyebrows. **34. betake . . . legs:** join in the dancing. **37. proverbed . . . phrase:** furnished (and thus supported) with a proverb by an ancient ("grandsire") saying. **40. dun's the mouse:** Don't be done (dun). **41. Dun . . . mire:** proverbial, meaning "things are at a standstill" **42. Of . . . love:** or, with apology, love (with play on "sir-reverence" = dung). **43. burn daylight:** waste time. **46–47. Take . . . wits:** Accept our true meaning, for true meaning derives from the reason ("judgement"), which is five times as trustworthy as the interpretation such meaning receives through the five senses ("wits"). **53. Queen Mab:** The Celtic "Mabh" ("child" in Welsh) was the chief of the Irish fairies, but Shakespeare is the first in England to attribute the name to the fairy queen. Shakespeare, moreover, seems to play on "quean" (= jade, hussy) and on "mab" (= a slattern or loose woman) and suggests Mab's identity with an incubus or succubus in 92 (the hag = the nightmare).

She is the fairies' midwife,° and she comes
In shape no bigger than an agate-stone°   55
On the forefinger of an alderman,
Drawn with a team of little atomi°
Over men's noses as they lie asleep.
Her chariot is an empty hazelnut,
Made by the joiner squirrel or old grub,°   60
Time out o' mind the fairies' coachmakers.
Her wagon spokes made of long spinners'° legs,
The cover of the wings of grasshoppers,
Her traces of the smallest spider web,
Her collars of the moonshine's watery beams,   65
Her whip of cricket's bone, the lash of film,°
Her waggoner° a small gray-coated gnat,
Not half so big as a round little worm
Pricked from the lazy finger of a maid.°
And in this state° she gallops night by night   70
Through lovers' brains, and then they dream
    of love;
O'er courtiers' knees, that dream on curtsies
    straight;
O'er lawyers' fingers, who straight dream on fees;
O'er ladies' lips, who straight on kisses dream,
Which oft the angry Mab with blisters plagues   75
Because their breaths with sweetmeats°
    tainted are.
Sometimes she gallops o'er a courtier's nose,
And then dreams he of smelling out a suit.°
And sometimes comes she with a tithe-pig's° tail
Tickling a parson's nose as 'a lies asleep;   80
Then dreams he of another benefice.°
Sometimes she driveth o'er a soldier's neck,
And then dreams he of cutting foreign throats,
Of breaches, ambuscadoes,° Spanish blades,°
Of healths five fathom deep, and then anon   85
Drums in his ear, at which he starts and wakes,
And being thus frighted swears a prayer or two
And sleeps again. This is that very Mab
That plats the manes of horses in the night,
And bakes the elflocks in foul sluttish hairs,   90
Which once untangled much misfortune bodes.°
This is the hag,° when maids lie on their backs,
That presses them and learns° them first to bear,°
Making them women of good carriage.°
This is she —   95

ROMEO   Peace, peace, Mercutio, peace!
Thou talk'st of nothing.

MERCUTIO   True, I talk of dreams,
Which are the children of an idle brain,
Begot of nothing but vain fantasy,
Which is as thin of substance as the air,
And more inconstant than the wind, who woos 100
Even now the frozen bosom of the north,
And being angered, puffs away from thence,
Turning his side° to the dew-dropping south.

BENVOLIO This wind you talk of blows us from
    ourselves.
Supper is done, and we shall come too late.   105

ROMEO I fear, too early; for my mind misgives
Some consequence yet hanging in the stars
Shall bitterly begin his fearful date
With this night's revels, and expire the term
Of a despisèd life closed in my breast   110
By some vile forfeit of untimely death.
But He that hath the steerage of my course
Direct my suit! On, lusty gentleman.

BENVOLIO Strike, drum.

[*They march about the stage, and retire to one
side.*]

Scene 5

[*Servingmen come forth with napkins.*]

FIRST SERVINGMAN Where's Potpan, that he
    helps not to take away? He shift a trencher?°
    He scrape a trencher?

54. **fairies' midwife:** i.e., the person among the fairies whose department it was to deliver the fancies of sleeping men of their dreams, those "children of an idle brain." 55. **agate-stone:** refers to the tiny figures carved in agate and set in seal rings. 57. **little atomi:** creatures small as atoms. 60. **joiner squirrel . . . grub:** The sharp-toothed squirrel, like a "joiner" (= furniture maker), and the mature ("old") grub (= larva of an insect, especially the beetle) bore holes in nuts. 62. **spinners':** spiders' or daddy-longlegs'. 66. **film:** membrane, either animal or vegetable (?); gossamer (?). 67. **waggoner:** driver of a chariot. "Waggon" was used as a poetic equivalent of "chariot," which also explains the use of "waggon-spokes" (62). 68–69. **worm . . . maid:** It was supposed that when maids were idle, worms (ticks or mites) bred in their fingers. 70. **state:** pomp, dignity. 76. **sweetmeats:** candied fruit or confectionery. 78. **smelling out a suit:** discovering (by his sagacity) someone with a petition to further at court from whom he may collect a fee for his influence. 79. **tithe-pig's:** a pig due as tithe (a tenth part of one's income) to the church, which often ended up on the parson's table. 81. **another benefice:** The holding of two or more church livings was still common long after Elizabethan times. 84. **breaches, ambuscadoes:** breaking down of fortifications, ambushes. 84. **Spanish blades:** The best swords were made from Toledo steel. 90–91. **bakes . . . bodes:** Elves, who naturally hated "sluts and sluttery," were believed to cake ("bake") or mat the dirty hair of slovens, who, it was proposed, would suffer further torment at their hands if the locks were untangled. 92. **the hag:** Shakespeare here identifies Mab with the nightmare, which induced evil, particularly sexual, dreams. 93. **learns:** teaches. 93. **bear:** (1) the weight of a man, (2) children. 94. **carriage:** (1) deportment, (2) burden. 103. **Turning his side:** reversing his direction. **Act 1, Scene 5.** 2. **trencher:** wooden plate.

SECOND SERVINGMAN When good manners shall
lie all in one or two men's hands, and they   5
unwashed too, 'tis a foul thing.

FIRST SERVINGMAN Away with the joint stools,
remove the court cupboard,° look to the plate.°
Good thou, save me a piece of marchpane,° and,
as thou loves me, let the porter let in Susan   10
Grindstone and Nell. [*Exit Second Servingman.*]
Anthony and Potpan!

[*Enter two more Servingmen.*]

THIRD SERVINGMAN Ay, boy, ready.

FIRST SERVINGMAN You are looked for and called
for, asked for and sought for, in the great   15
chamber.

FOURTH SERVINGMAN We cannot be here and
there too. Cheerly, boys! Be brisk awhile,
and the longer liver take all.   [*Exeunt.*]

[*Enter Capulet and family and all the guests
and gentlewomen to the maskers.*]

CAPULET [*To the maskers*]
Welcome, gentleman! Ladies that have their toes   20
Unplagued with corns will walk a bout° with you.
Ah, my mistresses, which of you all
Will now deny to dance? She that makes dainty,°
She, I'll swear, hath corns. Am I come near ye°
now?
Welcome, gentlemen! I have seen the day   25

That I have worn a visor and could tell
A whispering tale in a fair lady's ear
Such as would please. 'Tis gone, 'tis gone, 'tis
gone.
You are welcome, gentlemen! Come,
musicians, play.

[*Music plays, and they dance.*]

A hall,° a hall! Give room! And foot it, girls.   30
[*To Servingmen.*] More light, you knaves,° and
turn the tables up,
And quench the fire; the room is grown too hot.
[*To his cousin.*] Ah, sirrah, this unlooked-for
sport comes well.
Nay, sit, nay, sit, good cousin Capulet,
For you and I are past our dancing days.   35
How long is 't now since last yourself and I
Were in a mask?

SECOND CAPULET By 'r Lady, thirty years.

CAPULET What, man? 'Tis not so much, 'tis not
so much;
'Tis since the nuptial° of Lucentio,
Come Pentecost as quickly as it will,   40
Some five-and-twenty years, and then we
masked.

SECOND CAPULET 'Tis more, 'tis more. His son is
elder, sir;
His son is thirty.

This is a publicity image for a 1954 film version of *Romeo and Juliet*. It appears to depict a scene from the Capulet ball in Act 1.

Make an inference about which characters are which based on costumes, facial expressions, and body language.

Moviestore collection Ltd/Alamy

---

8. court-cupboard: sideboard.   **8. plate:** silverware (flagons, salts, dishes, etc.).   **9. marchpane:** marzipan.   **21. walk a bout:** dance a round.   **23. makes dainty:** seems loath or hesitant.   **24. come near ye:** hit the target (by zeroing in on a sensitive point).   **30. A hall:** Clear the floor (for dancing). **31. knaves:** fellows (used of servants, without abusive intent).   **39. nuptial:** wedding.

CAPULET   Will you tell me that?
His son was but a ward° two years ago.
ROMEO [*To a Servingman*]
What lady's that which doth enrich the hand   45
Of yonder knight?
SERVINGMAN   I know not, sir.
ROMEO O, she doth teach the torches to burn
    bright!
It seems she hangs upon the cheek of night
As a rich jewel in an Ethiop's ear —
Beauty too rich for use, for earth too dear!°   50
So shows a snowy dove trooping with crows
As yonder lady o'er her fellows shows.
The measure done, I'll watch her place of stand,
And, touching hers, make blessed my rude
    hand.
Did my heart love till now? Forswear it,° sight! 55
For I ne'er saw true beauty till this night.
TYBALT This, by his voice, should be a Montague.
Fetch me my rapier, boy. What dares the slave
Come hither, covered with an antic face,
To fleer and scorn at our solemnity?°   60
Now, by the stock and honor of my kin,
To strike him dead I hold it not a sin.
CAPULET Why, how now, kinsman? Wherefore
    storm you so?
TYBALT Uncle, this is a Montague, our foe,
A villain that is hither come in spite°   65
To scorn at our solemnity this night.
CAPULET Young Romeo is it?
TYBALT   'Tis he, that villain Romeo.
CAPULET Content thee, gentle coz, let him alone.
'A bears him like a portly gentleman,°
And, to say truth, Verona brags of him   70
To be a virtuous and well governed youth.
I would not for the wealth of all this town
Here in my house do him disparagement.
Therefore be patient; take no note of him.

It is my will, the which if thou respect,   75
Show a fair presence and put off these frowns,
An ill-beseeming semblance° for a feast.
TYBALT It fits when such a villain is a guest.
I'll not endure him.
CAPULET   He shall be endured.
What, goodman boy?° I say he shall. Go to!   80
Am I the master here, or you? Go to.
You'll not endure him! God shall mend my soul,
You'll make a mutiny among my guests!
You will set cock-a-hoop!° You'll be the man!°
TYBALT Why, uncle, 'tis a shame.   85
CAPULET   Go to, go to,
You are a saucy boy. Is 't so, indeed?
This trick may chance to scathe you. I know
    what.°
You must contrary me!° Marry, 'tis time. —
Well said, my hearts! — You are a princox,° go.
Be quiet, or — More light, more light! — For   90
    shame!
I'll make you quiet, what! — Cheerly, my hearts!
TYBALT Patience perforce with willful choler
    meeting
Makes my flesh tremble in their different greeting.
I will withdraw. But this intrusion shall,
Now seeming sweet, convert to bitterest gall.   95
[*Exit.*]
ROMEO [*To Juliet*]
If I profane with my unworthiest hand
This holy shrine,° the gentle sin is this:°
My lips, two blushing pilgrims,° ready stand
To smooth that rough touch with a tender kiss.
JULIET Good pilgrim,° you do wrong your hand   100
    too much,
Which mannerly devotion shows in this;
For saints have hands that pilgrims' hands do
    touch,
And palm to palm is holy palmers' kiss.

---

44. ward: i.e., not of age; under the control of a guardian.   **50. Beauty . . . dear:** beauty that is too precious to be used in merely physical terms (with play on "use" = increase, interest) and too valuable [with play on "dear" = of (too) high price] for this world.   **55. Forswear it:** break your former oath (of love to Rosaline).   **60. fleer . . . solemnity:** jeer . . . festive celebration.   **65. in spite:** out of malice or grudge.   **69. bears . . . gentleman:** carries himself like a dignified gentleman.   **77. semblance:** facial appearance or expression.   **80. goodman boy:** a double insult: a yeoman (not a gentleman) and a youngster, but here applied to a "saucy" (86) young man.   **84. set cock-a-hoop:** cast off all restraint, become reckless.
84. You'll be the man: i.e., you'll play the big hero, will you.   **87. This trick . . . what:** This behavior may injure your financial expectations, and I have the power to see that it does.   **88. contrary me:** oppose my will.   **89. princox:** pert, conceited youth.   **97. holy shrine:** i.e., Juliet's hand (a part for the whole "saint").   **97. gentle sin is this:** i.e., compared with the "rough touch" (99) of my hand, this sin (= the kiss proposed in 98–99) is a gentle amends.   **98. lips, two blushing pilgrims:** i.e., "pilgrims" because worshipping at the "shrine" (97), "blushing" because red.
100. Good pilgrim: Juliet's "Good pilgrim" arises naturally enough out of the "shrine"/ "pilgrims" allusion in 97–98.

These images depict the moments when Romeo and Juliet first meet. The top image is from the 1996 film version of *Romeo and Juliet* and the bottom is from a 2019 staged ballet version.

How do the costume choices, gestures, movement, and facial expressions communicate some aspects of their characters when they meet for the first time? In what ways are these depictions similar and different?

Robbie Jack / Getty Images

ROMEO Have not saints lips, and holy palmers
    too?
JULIET Ay, pilgrim, lips that they must use in   105
    prayer.
ROMEO O, then, dear saint, let lips do what hands
    do.
    They pray; grant thou, lest faith turn to
    despair.°
JULIET Saints do not move,° though grant for
    prayers' sake.
ROMEO Then move not, while my prayer's effect
    I take.   [*He kisses her.*]
    Thus from my lips, by thine, my sin is purged.   110

JULIET Then have my lips the sin that they have
    took?
ROMEO Sin from my lips? O trespass sweetly
    urged!°
    Give me my sin again.   [*He kisses her.*]
JULIET   You kiss by th' book.°
NURSE [*Approaching*]
    Madam, your mother craves a word with you.
                   [*Juliet retires.*]
ROMEO What° is her mother?   115
NURSE   Marry, bachelor,°
    Her mother is the lady of the house,
    And a good lady, and a wise and virtuous.

---

107. They . . . despair: Lips pray, and you should grant their prayers for fear that sound belief ("faith") may turn to hopeless unbelief ("despair").
108. move: take the initiative.   **112. urged:** argued.   **113. by th' book:** like an expert.   **115. What:** who.   **115. bachelor:** young gentleman.

I nursed her daughter that you talked withal.°
I tell you, he that can lay hold of her
Shall have the chinks.°   120
ROMEO   Is she a Capulet?
O dear account!° My life is my foe's debt.°
BENVOLIO [*Approaching*]
Away, begone! The sport is at the best.°
ROMEO Ay, so I fear; the more is my unrest.

[*The maskers prepare to leave.*]

CAPULET Nay, gentlemen, prepare not to be gone.
We have a trifling foolish banquet° towards.°   125

[*One whispers in his ear.*]

Is it e'en so? Why, then, I thank you all.
I thank you, honest gentlemen. Good night.
More torches here! Come on then, let's to bed.
[*To his cousin.*] Ah, sirrah, by my fay, it waxes late.
I'll to my rest.   [*All proceed to leave*   130
                              but Juliet and the Nurse.]
JULIET Come hither, Nurse. What is yond
gentleman?
NURSE The son and heir of old Tiberio.
JULIET What's he that now is going out of door?

NURSE Marry, that, I think, be young Petruchio.
JULIET What's he that follows here, that would   135
not dance?
NURSE I know not.
JULIET Go ask his name. [*The Nurse goes.*] If he
be marrièd,
My grave is like to be my wedding bed.
NURSE [*Returning*]
His name is Romeo, and a Montague,
The only son of your great enemy.   140
JULIET My only love sprung from my only hate!
Too early seen unknown, and known too late!
Prodigious° birth of love it is to me
That I must love a loathèd enemy.
NURSE What's tis? What's tis?   145
JULIET   A rhyme I learned even now
Of one I danced withal.°

[*One calls within "Juliet."*]

NURSE   Anon,° anon!
Come, let's away. The strangers all are gone.

[*Exeunt*]

---

118. withal: with.   **120. the chinks:** plenty of coin (slang).   **121. dear account:** costly reckoning.   **121. my life . . . debt:** I owe my life (in loving Juliet) as a debt to my foe.   **122. sport . . . best:** i.e., the proper moment to leave.   **125. banquet:** dessert (fruit, wine, sweets).   **125. towards:** just ready.   **143. Prodigious:** ominous, monstrous (half love, half hate; compare 137).   **145–46. A rhyme . . . withal:** Juliet is being evasive; she hasn't danced with Romeo.   **147. Anon:** coming presently.

extending beyond the text

Based on the text of *Romeo and Juliet*, we are expected to believe that the star-crossed lovers fall in love at first sight. Read the excerpt below, from a collection called *Explain That*, edited by Felcitiy Lewis, on the science behind instant attraction.

from What Is Love at First Sight?
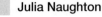
Julia Naughton

What is love at first sight?

One hundred milliseconds — that's precisely how long it takes to evaluate a potential [mate]. And if, after that split second, you deem that person to be attractive, emotions will begin to kick in as well as some animal-like instincts.

Anthropologist Helen Fisher explored the process of communicating our attraction to another person [through gazing] in her book *Anatomy of Love*, first published in 1992. "The gaze is probably the most striking human courting ploy," Fisher writes. In cultures where eye contact between the sexes is permitted, "men and women often stare intently at potential mates for about two to three seconds during which their pupils may dilate — a sign of extreme interest. Then the starer drops his or her eyelids and looks away."

So what is it that makes our pupils dilate? What is it that triggers a snap judgement that could lead to a romantic connection? . . . The medial prefrontal cortex, near the front of the brain, is responsible for such judgements. Researchers in Dublin discovered that one particular area of this region — the rostromedial prefrontal cortex, a segment located lower in the brain — goes one step further in evaluating physical attractiveness by asking, "Is this person a good match for me?" This is the same brain region known to be important in social decisions, particularly how similar someone is to you, the study's authors explained. Essentially, we are evaluating someone's attractiveness in those initial milliseconds while also determining their compatibility. ■

Everett Collection, Inc

Using only the text from the play and this excerpt, explain whether Romeo and Juliet experienced love at first sight. To what extent do you believe this exists outside of a science laboratory and fiction?

Understanding and Interpreting

1. In Act 1, Scene 1, the play begins with two servants of the Capulets who encounter two other servants of the Montagues. Trace the social status of the characters as we meet them in the rest of the scene and draw an interpretation of why Shakespeare may have introduced his characters in this order.

2. An interesting way to examine characters in *Romeo and Juliet* is to consider the first few lines a major character speaks on stage. Look back at Benvolio's and Tybalt's first few lines (Act 1, Scene 1, ll. 70–78). What is immediately established about both of the characters from these lines?

3. What do we learn about Capulet, Montague, and their wives when we meet them briefly at the end of the brawl (Act 1, Scene 1, ll. 82–88)?

4. Shakespeare, in general, does not provide many stage directions, but we can likely envision particular gestures, movements, or other actions of one character based on what another

character says in response. Look closely at the fight scene and draw an interpretation about the conflict. Then, identify an action or two we would probably see onstage based on the characters' dialogue and explain why you envision it the way that you do. What costumes or props might you envision based on your interpretation of the scene?

5. What has so upset the Prince, the main authority in Verona, in Act 1, Scene 1, lines 89–111? How does he threaten Capulet and Montague?

6. Explain the significance of Romeo saying, "I have lost myself. I am not here. / This is not Romeo; he's some other where" (Act 1, Scene 1, ll. 206–207).

7. In Act 1, Scene 1, lines 217–225, Romeo explains that the object of his desire (Rosaline, we learn later) has decided to never marry. Explain how his reaction to her decision illustrates what he thinks of love and beauty. How does Benvolio's advice to him support his perspective on what it means to love?

8. Explain what we learn about Juliet in the exchange between Capulet and Paris, who wants to marry Capulet's daughter, Juliet (Act 1, Scene 2, ll. 6–33). What does Capulet suggest about Juliet's own role in deciding whom and if she will marry?

9. "Fate" refers to the forces that control the outcome of events, regardless of individual choices a person might make. By Act 1, Scene 2, in what ways has fate already played a role in how the story of *Romeo and Juliet* will unfold?

10. What do Juliet's first lines (Act 1, Scene 3, ll. 5 and 7) of the play suggest about her character?

11. What do you conclude about the Nurse's character in Act 1, Scene 3? Is she foolish? Wise? Thoughtful? Supportive? What lines from the scene give you this impression?

12. Explain what the following lines say about Juliet's current interest in love, marriage, and family duty:

    a. "It is an honor that I dream not of" (Act 1, Scene 3, l. 67).

    b. "I'll look to like, if looking liking move,

    But no more deep will I endart mine eye

    Than your consent gives strength enough to make it fly" (Act 1, Scene 3, ll. 98–100).

13. Based on Scene 2 with Romeo and Scene 3 with Juliet, what similarities and differences between them can you identify? Consider character traits, but also their families and the settings we have seen them in so far.

14. Compare and contrast Romeo's attitude toward love with Mercutio's by examining how they view Cupid differently in Act 1, Scene 4, ll. 11–29. What lines from each character support your response?

15. Mercutio says in Scene 4 that dreams are "the children of an idle brain, / begot of nothing but vain fantasy" (Act 1, Scene 4, ll. 97–98). Based on how Romeo responds, do you think he agrees with Mercutio? How is his response foreshadowing?

16. How does Romeo react when he sees Juliet for the first time (Act 1, Scene 5, ll. 47–56), and what does this say about Romeo, especially considering what he had already said to Benvolio earlier in Act 1?

17. What assumptions does Tybalt make about Romeo when he sees him at their party, uninvited, in Act 1, Scene 5? What does Capulet's response suggest about his thoughts on Romeo and the feud?

18. Look back at the dialogue between Juliet and Romeo (Act 1, Scene 5, ll. 96–113) when they speak to each other for the first time. How is Romeo aggressively pursuing Juliet, and how does she try to slow down his pursuit?

19. What are some possible interpretations of Juliet's line, "You kiss by th' book" (Act 1, Scene 5, l. 113)?

20. We know from Act 1, Scene 5, lines 45–56, that Romeo saw Juliet, but there is no corresponding dialogue that suggests that she saw him, though it seems likely since she does not immediately pull away from him when he grasps her hand in line 96. Make an interpretive statement about a characteristic of Juliet (bold, shy, curious, etc.) and then describe directions, including gestures, movements, costumes, and props, that might make sense for a director of this scene to include to show Juliet's character.

21. Reread Juliet's dialogue with the Nurse in Act 1, Scene 5, lines 131–147. What do Juliet's questions reveal about her character that we have not seen of her so far in the play?

22. Compare each character's responses when Romeo and Juliet learn their families are enemies (Act 1, Scene 5, ll. 121–147).

Analyzing Language, Style, and Structure

23. **Vocabulary in Context.** In Act 1, Scene 4, line 9, Benvolio uses the word *measure*. What does the word mean in this context? How is that meaning similar to or different from other uses of the word that you have encountered?

24. **Vocabulary in Context.** In Act 1, Scene 4, line 45, Mercutio says "We waste our lights in vain." What does the word *vain* mean in this context? What are other meanings of the word?

25. Puns are jokes based on words that sound alike but have different meanings. Sampson and Gregory engage in a number of puns in the opening scene before they meet the Montagues (Act 1, Scene 1, ll. 1–69). Identify as many puns as you can find in their exchange and explain the intended humor of the wordplay.

26. Shakespeare often makes distinctions among characters in the ways that they speak. What do you notice about the differences in the language used by the Montague servants, Abraham and Samson (Act 1, Scene 1, ll. 39–63), and the Prince (Act 1, Scene 1, ll. 89–111) in the opening scene of the play?

27. Reread Romeo's dialogue with Benvolio about his family's feud with the Capulets (Act 1, Scene 2, ll. 88–107). How do his language choices reveal his attitude toward the fight?

28. Of Rosaline, Romeo says in Scene 2, "The all-seeing sun / Ne'er saw her match since first the world begun" (Act 1, Scene 2, ll. 98–99). What does this personification and hyperbole reveal about Romeo?

29. Examine Juliet's mother's extended metaphor describing Paris, the man who wants to marry Juliet (Act 1, Scene 3, ll. 82–95). What are the meaning and purpose of this comparison?

30. When Romeo and Juliet speak to each other for the first time (Act 1, Scene 5, ll. 96–109), the dialogue is in the form of a sonnet. How does the sonnet structure lead to important words being connected through rhyme? What is the significance of the structure of the final rhyming couplet? This is one of three sonnets in the play. What is the effect of Shakespeare's choice to use a sonnet here?

31. Explain the analogy between lips and pilgrims that is started by Romeo and continued by Juliet (Act 1, Scene 5, ll. 98–105).

Topics for Composing

32. **Analysis.** Complete a close reading of what is often referred to as the "Queen Mab Speech" by Mercutio in Act 1, Scene 4, lines 54–71, by considering the following:

   a. Summarize what Mercutio literally describes about Queen Mab: what she looks like, the clothes she wears, and a few of the dreams that she causes as "she gallops . . . through lovers' brains" (Act 1, Scene 4, ll. 54–69).

b. Reread closely, looking for figurative language in this speech, identifying specifically the references to sex and violence.

c. Finally, explain what you believe is the purpose of the speech. What is the effect of Shakespeare's choice to have Mercutio deliver this speech at this point in the play?

33. Analysis. Not surprisingly, there has been a lot of talk about love in this first act. At this point in the play, what message do Romeo's actions and dialogue convey about love? Write a response explaining your observations using evidence from the text to support your ideas.

34. Analysis. In a play that is considered a tragedy, there are a number of moments of intentional humor. Identify two or more places where Shakespeare inserts humor into the play and explain its function within the story so far.

35. Argument. Write a response in which you argue whether or not Romeo's love for Juliet is genuine at this point in the play. Why or why not? Use examples from the text to support your answer.

36. Connections. When have you felt like Romeo as described by his parents in Scene 1, lines 125–149? What was the cause, and what was successful in cheering you up? Write a response in which you share your experience.

37. Speaking and Listening. In Scene 5, lines 57–95, Tybalt and Capulet react differently to Romeo's presence at the ball — Tybalt wants to confront Romeo and Capulet wants to leave him alone because he's doing no harm. With a small group, discuss your ideas about their reactions in relation to the current feud between the two families. Try to reach consensus regarding which characters seem to be the biggest perpetrators of the ongoing feud. Support your group's decision with evidence from the text.

38. Research. Locate and read portions of Arthur Brooke's 1562 poem titled "The Tragical Historye of Romeus and Juliet," which was a significant source for Shakespeare's play. Explain the similarities and differences you notice between the two texts so far.

39. Creative Writing. Write a film script adaptation of Act 1, Scene 5, in which Romeo and Juliet first meet, set in a different time period and place. Consider how the different setting and time period might influence the characters' behaviors, language, and interactions in your adaptation.

ACT 2

[*Enter Chorus.*]

CHORUS:

> Now old desire doth in his deathbed lie,
>   And young affection gapes° to be his heir;
> That fair° for which love groaned for and would die,
>   With tender Juliet matched, is now not fair.
> Now Romeo is beloved and loves again°,   5
>   Alike bewitchèd by the charm of looks;
> But to his foe supposed° he must complain°,
>   And she steal love's sweet bait from fearful hooks.
> Being held a foe, he may not have access
>   To breathe such vows as lovers use° to swear;   10
> And she as much in love, her means much less
>   To meet her new-belovèd anywhere.
> But passion lends them power, time means, to meet,
>   Tempering extremities° with extreme sweet.

[*Exit.*]

---

2. **gapes:** waits open-mouthed (to swallow his inheritance).   3. **That fair:** that fair lady (Rosaline).   5. **again:** in return.   7. **foe supposed:** i.e., Juliet (because a Capulet).   7. **complain:** lament (as a lover).   10. **use:** are accustomed.   14. **Temp'ring extremities:** allaying desperate difficulties.

Scene 1

[*Enter Romeo alone.*]

ROMEO Can I go forward when my heart is here?
Turn back, dull earth,° and find thy centre° out.

[*Romeo retires.*]

[*Enter Benvolio with Mercutio.*]

BENVOLIO Romeo! My cousin Romeo! Romeo!
MERCUTIO   He is wise;
And, on my life, hath stolen him home to bed.
BENVOLIO He ran this way and leapt this orchard   5
wall.
Call, good Mercutio.
MERCUTIO   Nay, I'll conjure° too.
Romeo! Humours!° Madman! Passion! Lover!
Appear thou in the likeness of a sigh.
Speak but one rhyme, and I am satisfied;
Cry but "Ay me!" Pronounce but "love" and   10
"dove."
Speak to my gossip Venus° one fair word,
One nickname for her purblind° son and heir,
Young Abraham Cupid,° he that shot so trim°
When King Cophetua loved the beggar maid. —
He heareth not, he stirreth not, he moveth not;   15
The ape is dead,° and I must conjure him. —
I conjure thee by Rosaline's bright eyes,
By her high forehead and her scarlet lip,
By her fine foot, straight leg, and quivering
thigh,
And the demesnes° that there adjacent lie,   20
That in thy likeness thou appear to us!
BENVOLIO An if he hear thee, thou wilt anger him.
MERCUTIO This cannot anger him. 'Twould
anger him
To raise a spirit in his mistress' circle
Of some strange nature, letting it there stand   25
Till she had laid it and conjured it down;
That were some spite. My invocation
Is fair and honest; in his mistress' name
I conjure only but to raise up him.
BENVOLIO Come, he hath hid himself among   30
these trees
To be consorted° with the humorous° night.
Blind is his love, and best befits the dark.
MERCUTIO If love be blind, love cannot hit the
mark.
Now will he sit under a medlar tree
And wish his mistress were that kind of fruit   35
As maids call medlars when they laugh
alone.
O, Romeo, that she were, O, that she were
An open-arse, and thou a poppering pear!
Romeo, good night. I'll to my truckle-bed;°
This field-bed° is too cold for me to sleep.   40
Come, shall we go?
BENVOLIO   Go, then, for 'tis in vain
To seek him here that means not to be found.

[*Exit with Mercutio.*]

Scene 2

ROMEO [*Coming forward*]
He° jests at scars that never felt a wound.
[*A light appears above, as at Juliet's window.*]
But soft, what light through yonder window
breaks?
It is the east, and Juliet is the sun.
Arise, fair sun, and kill the envious moon,
Who is already sick and pale with grief   5
That thou her maid° art far more fair than she.
Be not her maid, since she is envious;
Her vestal livery° is but sick and green°
And none but fools do wear it. Cast it off.

[*Juliet is visible at her window.*]

It is my lady, O, it is my love!   10
O, that she knew she were!

Act 2, Scene 1.   **2. dull earth:** figuratively, Romeo's body.   **2. centre:** soul (= heart = Juliet).   **6. conjure:** raise him, with my magic words (see next line), like a spirit (since he is no longer visible).   **7. Humours:** whimsies, caprices (fancies proper to a lover).   **11. gossip Venus:** familiar acquaintance; Venus, the goddess of love.   **12. purblind:** totally blind.   **13. Abraham Cupid:** i.e., rogue Cupid (from the cant term "Abraham man," a beggar who cheated the public by pretending madness).   **13. trim:** neatly, accurately.   **16. ape is dead:** i.e., like a performing monkey playing dead.   **20. demesnes:** park lands, for use or pleasure; probably used with a bawdy quibble.   **31. consorted:** associated.   **31. humorous:** damp [with reference to "night" as suitable for the melancholy ("humorous") lover].   **39. truckle-bed:** low bed running on castors, usually pushed under a high or "standing" bed when not in use.   **40. field-bed** bed upon the ground.   Act 2, Scene 2.   **1. He:** i.e., Mercutio, not Benvolio.   **6. her maid:** i.e., a votary of Diana, goddess of the moon and patroness of virgins.   **8. vestal livery:** virgin garb.   **8. sick and green:** referring to the so-called green-sickness, a kind of anemia.

She speaks, yet she says nothing.° What of
    that?
Her eye discourses; I will answer it.
I am too bold. 'Tis not to me she speaks.
Two of the fairest stars° in all the heaven,   15
Having some business, do entreat her eyes
To twinkle in their spheres till they return.
What if her eyes were there, they in her head?
The brightness of her cheek would shame
    those stars
As daylight doth a lamp; her eyes in heaven   20
Would through the airy region° stream° so
    bright
That birds would sing and think it were not
    night.
See how she leans her cheek upon her hand!
O, that I were a glove upon that hand,
That I might touch that cheek!   25

JULIET   Ay me!
ROMEO   She speaks!
O, speak again, bright angel, for thou art
As glorious to this night, being o'er my head,
As is a wingèd messenger° of heaven
Unto the white-upturnèd° wondering eyes
Of mortals that fall back° to gaze on him   30
When he bestrides the lazy puffing clouds
And sails upon the bosom of the air.

JULIET O Romeo, Romeo, wherefore art thou
    Romeo?
Deny thy father and refuse thy name!
Or, if thou wilt not, be but sworn my love,   35
And I'll no longer be a Capulet.

ROMEO [*Aside*]
Shall I hear more, or shall I speak at this?

JULIET 'Tis but thy name that is my enemy;
Thou art thyself, though° not a Montague.
What's Montague? It is nor hand, nor foot,   40
Nor arm, nor face, nor any other part
Belonging to a man. O, be some other name!
What's in a name? That which we call a rose
By any other word° would smell as sweet;
So Romeo would, were he not Romeo called,   45

Retain that dear perfection which he owes°
Without that title. Romeo, doff ° thy name,
And for° thy name, which is no part of thee,
Take all myself.

ROMEO   I take thee at thy word!
Call me but love, and I'll be new baptized;   50
Henceforth I never will be Romeo.

JULIET What man art thou that, thus bescreened°
    in night,
So stumblest on my counsel?°

ROMEO   By a name
I know not how to tell thee who I am.
My name, dear saint, is hateful to myself,   55
Because it is an enemy to thee;
Had I it written, I would tear the word.

JULIET My ears have not yet drunk a hundred
    words
Of thy tongue's uttering, yet I know the sound:
Art thou not Romeo and a Montague?   60

ROMEO Neither, fair maid, if either thee dislike.°

JULIET How camest thou hither, tell me, and
    wherefore?
The orchard walls are high and hard to climb,
And the place death, considering who thou art,
If any of my kinsmen find thee here.   65

ROMEO With love's light wings did I o'erperch°
    these walls,
For stony limits cannot hold love out,
And what love can do, that dares love attempt;
Therefore thy kinsmen are no stop to me.

JULIET If they do see thee, they will murder thee.   70

ROMEO Alack, there lies more peril in thine eyes
Than twenty of their swords. Look thou but
    sweet,
And I am proof° against their enmity.

JULIET I would not for the world they saw thee
    here.

ROMEO I have night's cloak to hide me from their   75
    eyes;
And but° thou love me, let them find me here.
My life were better ended by their hate
Than death proroguèd, wanting of° thy love.

---

12. **speaks . . . nothing:** i.e., I can only see her lips move, not hear what she says.   15. **stars:** i.e., planets.   21. **airy region:** the sky or upper limit of the air; the heavens.   21. **stream:** emit continuous beams of light.   28. **wingèd messenger:** i.e., angel.   29. **white-upturnèd:** (eyes) showing the whites in looking up.   30. **fall back:** i.e., tilt their heads back in "wond'ring."   39. **though:** even if.   44. **word:** appellation.   46. **owes:** owns, possesses.   47. **doff:** cast aside.   48. **for:** in return for.   52. **bescreened:** concealed, hidden.   53. **counsel:** private deliberation.   61. **dislike:** displease.   66. **o'erperch:** fly over.   73. **proof:** invulnerable (as if in armor).   76. **but:** unless.   78. **proroguèd, wanting of:** deferred, lacking.

JULIET By whose direction foundst thou out this place?

ROMEO By love, that first did prompt me to 80
inquire.

He lent me counsel, and I lent him eyes.
I am no pilot; yet, wert thou as far
As that vast° shore washed with the farthest sea,
I should adventure° for such merchandise.

JULIET Thou knowest the mask of night is on my 85
face,

Else would a maiden blush bepaint° my cheek
For that which thou hast heard me speak
tonight.
Fain° would I dwell on form° — fain, fain deny
What I have spoke; but farewell compliment!°
Dost thou love me? I know thou wilt say "Ay," 90
And I will take thy word. Yet if thou swear'st
Thou mayst prove false. At lovers' perjuries,
They say, Jove laughs. O gentle Romeo,
If thou dost love, pronounce it faithfully.
Or if thou thinkest I am too quickly won, 95
I'll frown and be perverse and say thee nay,
So thou wilt woo, but else° not for the world.
In truth, fair Montague, I am too fond,°
And therefore thou mayst think my havior light.
But trust me, gentleman, I'll prove more true 100
Than those that have more coying to be
strange.°
I should have been more strange, I must confess,
But that thou overheardst, ere I was ware,
My true-love° passion. Therefore pardon me,
And not impute this yielding to light° love, 105
Which° the dark night hath so discoverèd.

ROMEO Lady, by yonder blessèd moon I vow,
That tips with silver all these fruit-tree tops —

JULIET O, swear not by the moon, th' inconstant
moon,
That monthly changes in her circled orb,° 110
Lest that thy love prove likewise variable.

ROMEO What shall I swear by?

JULIET   Do not swear at all
Or, if thou wilt, swear by thy gracious self,°
Which is the god of my idolatry,
And I'll believe thee. 115

ROMEO   If my heart's dear love —

JULIET Well, do not swear. Although I joy in thee,
I have no joy of this contract° tonight.
It is too rash, too unadvised, too sudden,
Too like the lightning, which doth cease to be
Ere one can say "It lightens." Sweet, good 120
night!
This bud of love, by summer's ripening breath,
May prove a beauteous flower when next we
meet.
Good night, good night! As sweet repose and rest
Come to thy heart as that within my breast!

ROMEO O, wilt thou leave me so unsatisfied? 125

JULIET What satisfaction canst thou have tonight?

ROMEO Th' exchange of thy love's faithful vow for
mine.

JULIET I gave thee mine before thou didst request it;
And yet I would it were to give again.

ROMEO Wouldst thou withdraw it? For what 130
purpose, love?

JULIET But to be frank° and give it thee again.
And yet I wish but for the thing I have.°
My bounty is as boundless as the sea,
My love as deep; the more I give to thee,
The more I have, for both are infinite. 135

[The Nurse calls within.]

I hear some noise within; dear love, adieu! —
Anon,° good Nurse! — Sweet Montague, be true.
Stay but a little, I will come again.

[Exit, above.]

ROMEO O blessèd, blessèd night! I am afeard,
Being in night, all this is but a dream, 140
Too flattering-sweet to be substantial.°

[Enter Juliet, above.]

---

83. **vast:** far-stretching. 84. **adventure:** venture, as a merchant adventurer in pursuit of riches. 86. **bepaint:** i.e., (would be seen to) color.
88. **Fain:** gladly. 88. **dwell on form:** observe decorum. 89. **compliment:** the hollow game of conventional civility. 97. **else:** otherwise.
98. **fond:** doting, overtender. 101. **have . . . strange:** show a greater affectation of reserve in order to appear hard to win. 104. **true-love:** faithful
love. 105. **light:** wanton, easy. 106. **Which:** referring to "yielding." 110. **circled orb:** the sphere in which the moon circles in the Ptolemaic
astronomy. 113. **gracious self:** yourself, full of all graces. 117. **contract:** mutual agreement; accented on the second syllable. 131. **frank:** (1)
bounteous, (2) freely outspoken. 132. **yet . . . have:** I only wish, however, for what I still possess (i.e., her inexhaustible love for Romeo).
137. **Anon:** presently, very soon. 141. **substantial:** real, solid (as opposed to the stuff of dreams).

JULIET Three words, dear Romeo, and good
    night indeed.
    If that thy bent of° love be honorable,
    Thy purpose marriage, send me word
      tomorrow,
    By one that I'll procure to come to thee,   145
    Where and what time thou wilt perform the
      rite;
    And all my fortunes at thy foot I'll lay
    And follow thee my lord throughout the
      world.
NURSE [*Within*] Madam!
JULIET I come, anon. — But if thou meanest not 150
    well,
    I do beseech thee —
NURSE [*Within*]   Madam!
JULIET   By and by° I come—
    To cease thy strife° and leave me to my grief.
    Tomorrow will I send.
ROMEO So thrive my soul —
JULIET   A thousand times
    good night!

                    [*Exit, above.*]

ROMEO A thousand times the worse, to want thy 155
    light.
    Love goes toward love as schoolboys from
      their books,
    But love from love, toward school with heavy
      looks.   [*He starts to leave.*]

    [*Enter Juliet above again.*]

JULIET Hist! Romeo, hist! O, for a falconer's voice,
    To lure° this tassel-gentle° back again!
    Bondage is hoarse° and may not speak aloud, 160
    Else would I tear the cave where Echo lies°
    And make her airy tongue more hoarse than
      mine
    With repetition of "My Romeo!"
ROMEO It is my soul that calls upon my name.

How silver-sweet sound lovers' tongues by 165
    night,
    Like softest music to attending ears!
JULIET Romeo!
ROMEO   My niësse?°
JULIET   What o'clock tomorrow
    Shall I send to thee?
ROMEO   By the hour of nine.
JULIET I will not fail. 'Tis twenty years till then. —
    I have forgot why I did call thee back. 170
ROMEO Let me stand here till thou remember it.
JULIET I shall forget, to have thee still° stand
    there,
    Remembering how I love thy company.
ROMEO And I'll still stay, to have thee still
    forget,
    Forgetting any other home but this. 175
JULIET 'Tis almost morning. I would have thee
    gone —
    And yet no farther than a wanton's° bird,
    That lets it hop a little from his hand,
    Like a poor prisoner in his twisted gyves,°
    And with a silken thread plucks it back again, 180
    So loving-jealous° of his° liberty.
ROMEO I would I were thy bird.
JULIET   Sweet so would I.
    Yet I should kill thee with much cherishing.°
ROMEO Good night, good night! Parting is such
    sweet sorrow
    That I shall say good night till it be morrow. 185

                    [*Exit, above.*]

ROMEO Sleep dwell upon thine eyes, peace in thy
    breast!
    Would I were sleep and peace, so sweet to
    rest!
    Hence will I to my ghostly sire's° close cell,
    His help to crave, and my dear hap° to tell.

                    Exit.

---

143. bent of: inclination to.   **151. By and by:** immediately.   **152. strife:** striving, endeavor.   **158–59. Hist . . . lure:** A falconer called a hawk to the lure (an apparatus constructed of a bunch of feathers baited with raw flesh, to which was attached a long cord or thong).   **159. tassel-gentle:** tercel-gentle, a male hawk, appropriate to a prince (Romeo).   **160. Bondage is hoarse:** One in confinement, as Juliet is under her father, must call softly (as if hoarse).   **161. cave where Echo lies:** Punished by Juno, Echo could repeat only the tag ends of what she heard others say; repulsed by Narcissus, with whom she had fallen in love, she dwelt in caves.   **167. niësse:** a young, unfledged hawk.   **172. to . . . still:** in order to . . . ever.   **177. wanton's:** spoiled, pampered child's.   **179. in his twisted gyves:** (1) entwined in his fetters (transposed adjective), (2) in his intertwined fetters.   **181. loving-jealous:** lovingly mistrustful.   **181. his:** its.   **183. kill . . . cherishing:** smother with too much love.   **188. ghostly sire's:** spiritual father's.   **189. dear hap:** good fortune.

extending beyond the text

Act 2, Scene 2 of *Romeo and Juliet* is perhaps the most famous scene in theater history. It is often referred to as "the balcony scene," and the setting of Juliet on her balcony with Romeo below might be the first image that springs to mind when we think of *Romeo and Juliet*. But, as Lois Leveen points out in the *Atlantic* article "*Romeo and Juliet* Has No Balcony," there is no balcony in the play: "The word 'balcony' never appears in Shakespeare's play. In fact, Shakespeare didn't know what a balcony was [because] there was no balcony in all of Shakespeare's England." She goes on to point out that "audiences may care less about the original text than about adaptations and revisions that appeal to the sensibilities of the current era." Below are images from three stage and screen depictions of "the balcony scene."

What does the "balcony" seem to symbolize in the play, especially in the power differences and the relationship between Romeo and Juliet? Looking closely at the three depictions of "the balcony scene" above, which version is most closely informed by the text? What does the balcony seem to symbolize in each? Which interpretation of the scene do you find most interesting, and why? What would the effect be if a director chose not to have a balcony at all?

Scene 3

[Enter Friar Laurence alone, with a basket.]

FRIAR LAURENCE The gray-eyed morn smiles on
    the frowning night,
Check'ring the eastern clouds with streaks of
    light,
And fleckled° darkness like a drunkard reels
From forth day's path and Titan's fiery
    wheels.°
Now, ere the sun advance° his burning eye,   5
The day to cheer and night's dank dew to dry,
I must up-fill this osier cage° of ours°
With baleful° weeds and precious-juicèd
    flowers.°
The earth that's nature's mother is her tomb;
What is her burying grave, that is her womb; 10
And from her womb children of divers kind
We sucking on her natural bosom find,
Many for many virtues excellent,
None but for some, and yet all different.
O, mickle° is the powerful grace that lies 15
In plants, herbs, stones, and their true
    qualities.
For naught so vile that on the earth doth live
But to the earth some special good doth give;
Nor aught so good but, strained from that fair
    use,
Revolts from true birth,° stumbling on abuse.° 20
Virtue itself turns vice, being misapplied,
And vice sometime's by action dignified.°

[Enter Romeo.]

Within the infant rind of this weak flower
Poison hath residence and medicine power:°
For this, being smelt, with that part° cheers 25
    each part;
Being tasted, stays all senses with the heart.
Two such opposèd kings encamp them still

In man as well as herbs — grace and rude will;
And where the worser is predominant,
Full soon the canker° death eats up that plant. 30
ROMEO Good morrow, Father.
FRIAR LAURENCE   Benedicite!°
What early tongue so sweet saluteth me?
Young son, it argues a distempered head
So soon to bid good morrow to thy bed.
Care keeps his watch in every old man's eye, 35
And where care lodges sleep will never lie;
But where unbruisèd youth with unstuffed
    brain
Doth couch his limbs, there golden sleep doth
    reign.
Therefore thy earliness doth me assure
Thou art uproused with some distemp'rature; 40
Or if not so, then here I hit it right:
Our Romeo hath not been in bed tonight.
ROMEO That last is true. The sweeter rest was
    mine.
FRIAR LAURENCE God pardon sin! Wast thou with
    Rosaline?
ROMEO With Rosaline, my ghostly father? No. 45
I have forgot that name, and that name's woe.
FRIAR LAURENCE That's my good son. But where
    hast thou been, then?
ROMEO I'll tell thee ere thou ask it me again.
I have been feasting with mine enemy,
Where on a sudden one hath wounded me 50
That's by me wounded. Both our remedies
Within thy help and holy physic° lies.
I bear no hatred, blessèd man, for, lo,
My intercession likewise steads° my foe.°
FRIAR LAURENCE Be plain, good son, and 55
    homely° in thy drift.
Riddling° confession finds but riddling shrift.°
ROMEO Then plainly know my heart's dear love
    is set

Act 2, Scene 3. **3. fleckled:** dappled. **4. Titan's fiery wheels:** the burning wheels of the chariot of the sun god, the Titan Helios. **5. advance:** raise, lift up. **7. osier cage:** basket made of willow twigs. **7 ours:** i.e., not his, but the common property of his order, the Franciscans. **8. baleful:** full of active evil, poisonous. **8. precious-juicèd flowers:** i.e., flowers (as opposed to "weeds") that contain rare healing essences. **15. mickle:** great. **20. true birth:** i.e., its proper nature. **20. stumbling on abuse:** falling into perversion. **22. And vice . . . dignified:** i.e., a quality that is in itself a fault may, under certain circumstances, result in a good action. **24. medicine power:** i.e., healing hath power. **25. that part:** i.e., its scent. **30. canker:** canker worm (which devours the bud secretly from within). **31. Benedicite!** Bless you! **52. holy physic:** spiritual remedy (through marriage). **54. intercession likewise steads:** petition also benefits. **54. foe:** i.e., Juliet (as a Capulet). **55. homely:** direct. **56. Riddling:** ambiguous, enigmatic. **56. shrift:** absolution.

This is a scene from a 1968 film version of *Romeo and Juliet* with Romeo and Friar Laurence.

What effect are the actors creating in this scene through their facial expressions and gestures? What lines from Act 2, Scene 3 might the actors have been speaking when this image was taken? Why?

Ronald Grant Archive/Alamy

On the fair daughter of rich Capulet.
As mine on hers, so hers is set on mine,
And all combined, save what thou must   60
   combine
By holy marriage. When and where and how
We met, we wooed, and made exchange of vow
I'll tell thee as we pass;° but this I pray,
That thou consent to marry us today.

FRIAR LAURENCE Holy Saint Francis, what a   65
   change is here!
Is Rosaline, that thou didst love so dear,
So soon forsaken? Young men's love then lies
Not truly in their hearts, but in their eyes.
Jesu Maria, what a deal of brine°
Hath washed thy sallow° cheeks for Rosaline!   70
How much salt water thrown away in waste
To season love, that of it doth not taste!°
The sun not yet thy sighs from heaven clears,
Thy old groans yet ringing in mine ancient
   ears.
Lo, here upon thy cheek the stain doth sit   75
Of an old tear that is not washed off yet.
If e'er thou wast thyself° and these woes thine,
Thou and these woes were all for Rosaline.

And art thou changed? Pronounce this
   sentence° then:
Women may fall,° when there's no strength in   80
   men.

ROMEO Thou chidst me oft for loving Rosaline.

FRIAR LAURENCE For doting, not for loving, pupil
   mine.

ROMEO And badst me bury love.

FRIAR LAURENCE   Not in a grave
   To lay one in, another out to have.

ROMEO I pray thee, chide not. She whom I love   85
   now
Doth grace for grace and love for love allow.
The other did not so.

FRIAR LAURENCE   O, she knew well
Thy love did read by rote, that could not spell.°
But come, young waverer, come, go with me.
In one respect° I'll thy assistant be;   90
For this alliance may so happy prove
To turn your households' rancor to pure love.

ROMEO O, let us hence! I stand on° sudden haste.

FRIAR LAURENCE Wisely and slow. They stumble
   that run fast.

[Exeunt.]

---

63. pass: go along. **69. brine:** i.e., salt tears, the "season" (72) or preservative of love. **70. sallow:** sickly yellow. **72. that . . . taste:** that (despite all the seasoning of tears) your love ("it") now appears insipid (without flavor). **77. wast thyself:** i.e., sincere, without pretense. **79. sentence:** moral maxim, aphorism. **80. may fall:** may be excused for falling. **88. Thy . . . spell:** i.e., the expression of your love was a schoolboy exercise of memory (rote learning) by one who couldn't read ("spell") and thus understand what he was mouthing. **90. In one respect:** for a special reason. **93. stand on:** insist on (as a necessity).

Scene 4

[*Enter Benvolio and Mercutio.*]

MERCUTIO Where the devil should° this Romeo
    be?
  Came he not home tonight?°

BENVOLIO Not to his father's. I spoke with his
    man.

MERCUTIO Why, that same pale hardhearted
    wench, that Rosaline,
  Torments him so that he will sure run mad.   5

BENVOLIO Tybalt, the kinsman to old Capulet,
  Hath sent a letter to his father's house.

MERCUTIO A challenge, on my life.

BENVOLIO Romeo will answer it.°

MERCUTIO Any man that can write may answer a 10
    letter.

BENVOLIO Nay, he will answer the letter's master,
    how° he dares, being dared.

MERCUTIO Alas poor Romeo! He is already dead,
    stabbed with a white wench's black eye, run   15
  through the ear with a love song, the very pin°
  of his heart cleft with the blind bow-boy's
  butt-shaft.° And is he a man to encounter Tybalt?

BENVOLIO Why, what is Tybalt?

MERCUTIO More than Prince of Cats.° O, he's the 20
  courageous captain of compliments.° He
  fights as you sing prick-song,° keeps time,
  distance, and proportion;° he rests his minim
  rests, one, two, and the third in your bosom.
  The very butcher of a silk button,° a duellist, a 25
  duellist, a gentleman of the very first house,°

of the first and second cause. Ah, the
immortal° *passado*! The *punto reverso*! The
hay!

BENVOLIO The what?   30

MERCUTIO The pox of such antic, lisping,
  affecting phantasimes,° these new tuners of
  accent!° "By Jesu, a very good blade! A new tall
  man! A very good whore!" Why, is not this a
  lamentable thing, grandsire, that we should   35
  be thus afflicted with these strange flies, these
  fashion-mongers, these pardon-me's,° who
  stand so much on the new form that they
  cannot sit at ease on the old bench? O, their
  bones, their bones!   40

[*Enter Romeo.*]

BENVOLIO Here comes Romeo, here comes
    Romeo.

MERCUTIO Without his roe,° like a dried herring.
  O flesh, flesh, how art thou fishified!° Now is
  he for° the numbers that Petrarch flowed in.
  Laura to° his lady was but a kitchen   45
  wench — marry, she had a better love to
  berhyme her — Dido a dowdy, Cleopatra a
  gypsy, Helen and Hero hildings° and harlots,
  Thisbe a gray eye or so, but not to the purpose.°
  Signor Romeo, *bonjour*! There's a French   50
  salutation to your French slop.° You gave us
  the counterfeit° fairly last night.

ROMEO Good morrow to you both. What
  counterfeit did I give you?

MERCUTIO The slip, sir, the slip. Can you not   55
  conceive?

Act 2, Scene 4. **1. should:** can. **2. tonight:** last night. **9. answer it:** accept the challenge. **13. how:** as, or to what extent. **16. very pin:** the center of the center. A "pin" was the black peg affixed to the center of the archer's target. **18. butt-shaft:** an unbarbed arrow used in shooting at the butts. **20. Prince of Cats:** Tybert is the name of the cat in *The History of Reynard the Fox*. **21. captain of compliments:** complete master of all the laws of ceremony. **22. as you sing prick-song:** very precisely, as one sings from written or printed music. **22–23. time . . . proportion:** (1) (in dueling) the minimum proper bodily movement and footwork, due "distance" from the opponent, and rhythm; (2) (in music) tempo, properly observed intervals, and correct relation between parts. **25. butcher . . . button:** It was a trick in dueling to show your mastery by "pinking" your opponent's buttons. **26. very first house:** best dueling school, with heraldic play on "of the noblest birth." **28. immortal:** (1) famous, (2) fatal. **32. affecting phantasimes:** affected gallants. **32–33. new tuners of accent:** those whose English is vitiated with new-fangled foreign words and affected pronunciations. **37. pardon-me's:** Frenchified gallants. **42. Without his roe:** (1) minus his manhood, thin and emasculated by love; (2) without his dear **43. fishified:** turned cold-blooded **44. for:** in favor of. **45–49. Laura . . . purpose:** Except for Laura, to whom Petrarch addressed his two series of sonnets, the women named are classical figures (real or fictional) celebrated for their beauty, none of whom is comparable to Rosaline as Romeo, according to Mercutio, supposedly envisions her. Mercutio never learns of Romeo's love for Juliet. **45. to:** in comparison with. **48. hildings:** good-for-nothings. **51. to your French slop:** to match your loose-fitting, short breeches. Not having gone home, Romeo is still in his masking costume and dancing pumps. **52. gave us the counterfeit:** deceived, played a trick on us.

ROMEO Pardon, good Mercutio, my business was great, and in such a case as mine a man may strain courtesy.

MERCUTIO That's as much as to say, such a case as yours constrains a man to bow in the hams.   60

ROMEO Meaning, to curtsy.

MERCUTIO Thou hast most kindly hit it.

ROMEO A most courteous exposition.

MERCUTIO Nay, I am the very pink of courtesy.   65

ROMEO Pink for flower.

MERCUTIO Right.

ROMEO Why then is my pump° well flowered.

MERCUTIO Sure wit,° follow me this jest now till thou hast worn out thy pump, that when the   70 single° sole of it is worn, the jest may remain, after the wearing, solely singular.°

ROMEO O single-soled jest, solely singular for the singleness!°

MERCUTIO Come between us,° good Benvolio.   75 My wits faint.

ROMEO Switch and spurs,° switch and spurs! Or I'll cry a match.°

MERCUTIO Nay, if our wits run the wild-goose chase, I am done, for thou hast more of the   80 wild goose in one of thy wits than, I am sure, I have in my whole five.° Was I with you there for the goose?°

ROMEO Thou wast never with me for anything when thou wast not there for the goose.°   85

MERCUTIO I will bite thee by the ear° for that jest.

ROMEO Nay, good goose, bite not.°

MERCUTIO Thy wit is a very bitter sweeting;° it is a most sharp sauce.°

ROMEO And is it not, then, well served in to a   90 sweet goose?

MERCUTIO O, here's a wit of cheverel,° that stretches from an inch narrow to an ell° broad!

ROMEO I stretch it out for that word "broad,"   95 which, added to the goose, proves thee far and wide a broad° goose.

MERCUTIO Why, is not this better now than groaning for love? Now art thou sociable, now art thou Romeo; now art thou what   100 thou art, by art° as well as by nature. For this driveling love is like a great natural° that runs lolling° up and down to hide his bauble° in a hole.

BENVOLIO Stop there, stop there.   105

MERCUTIO Thou desirest me to stop in my tale against the hair.

BENVOLIO Thou wouldst else have made thy tale large.

MERCUTIO O, thou art deceived; I would have   110 made it short, for I was come to the whole depth of my tale and meant indeed to occupy the argument no longer.

ROMEO Here's a goodly gear!

[*Enter Nurse and her man Peter.*]

A sail, a sail!   115

MERCUTIO Two, two: a shirt and a smock.°

NURSE Peter!

PETER Anon!

NURSE My fan, Peter.

---

68. pump: light shoe (suitable for dancing).   **69. Sure wit!** Oh, clever fellow!   **71. single:** slight, thin.   **72. solely singular:** uniquely alone. **73–74. single-soled . . . singleness:** trivial, threadbare jest, remarkable ("singular") only for being one of a kind.   **75. Come between us:** i.e., as a second in a duel.   **77. Swits and spurs:** (ride all out with) switch and spurs — i.e., keep the game going as hard as you can.   **78. cry a match:** claim the victory.   **79–83. Nay . . . goose:** goose = (1) a bird proverbial for its stupidity; hence (2) a simpleton or nitwit (65); (3) a prostitute (68). **82. whole five:** i.e., five wits, either (1) the five senses or (2) the general mental faculties.   **85. for the goose:** (1) as a foolish fellow, (2) in search of a prostitute.   **86. bite . . . ear:** a sign of fondness, but Mercutio is annoyed.   **87. Nay . . . not:** Be a "good" goose and don't bite (spoken ironically, with the suggestion that your opponent is inferior).   **88. bitter sweeting:** kind of apple.   **89. sharp sauce:** (1) "biting" riposte, (2) tart relish. **92. cheverel:** soft kid leather, unusually stretchable.   **93. ell:** forty-five inches. Romeo's wit is properly only "an inch" — i.e., very small. **97. broad:** obvious [with probable play on "broad" = indecent.   **101. by art:** by application of acquired skill, as opposed to "by nature." **102. natural:** idiot, fool.   **103. lolling:** sticking out his tongue.   **103. bauble:** (1) fool's short stick decorated with a fool's head and sometimes with a bladder for striking offenders.   **116. shirt and a smock:** man and a woman.

MERCUTIO Good Peter, to hide her face, for her 120
fan's the fairer face.

NURSE God gi' good morrow, gentlemen.

MERCUTIO God gi' good e'en, fair
gentlewoman.

NURSE Is it good e'en? 125

MERCUTIO 'Tis no less, I tell ye, for the bawdy
hand of the dial is now upon the prick of
noon.°

NURSE Out upon you! What a man are you?

ROMEO One, gentlewoman, that God hath made 130
for himself to mar.

NURSE By my troth,° it is well said. "For himself
to mar," quoth 'a?° Gentlemen, can any of
you tell me where I may find the young
Romeo? 135

ROMEO I can tell you; but young Romeo will be
older when you have found him than he was
when you sought him. I am the youngest of
that name, for fault of a worse.°

NURSE You say well. 140

MERCUTIO Yea, is the worst well? Very well took,°
i' faith, wisely, wisely.

NURSE If you be he, sir, I desire some confidence°
with you.

BENVOLIO She will indite° him to some supper. 145

MERCUTIO A bawd,° a bawd, a bawd! So ho!

ROMEO What hast thou found?

MERCUTIO No hare, sir, unless a hare, sir, in a
lenten pie, that is something stale and hoar
ere it be spent.°   [He sings.] 150

> An old hare hoar,
> And an old hare hoar,
> Is very good meat in Lent.
> But a hare that is hoar
> Is too much for a score,° 155
> When it hoars° ere it be spent.

Romeo, will you come to your father's? We'll
to dinner° thither.

ROMEO I will follow you.

MERCUTIO Farewell, ancient lady. Farewell, 160
[Singing] "Lady, lady, lady."°

[Exeunt Mercutio and Benvolio.]

NURSE I pray you, sir, what saucy merchant° was
this that was so full of his ropery?°

ROMEO A gentleman, Nurse, that loves to hear
himself talk, and will speak more in a minute 165
than he will stand to in a month.

NURSE An 'a speak anything against me, I'll take
him down,° an 'a were lustier than he is, and
twenty such Jacks;° and if I cannot, I'll find
those that shall. Scurvy knave! I am none of 170
his flirt-gills.° I am none of his skains-mates.°
[To Peter.] And thou must stand by, too, and
suffer every knave to use me at his pleasure!°

PETER I saw no man use you at his pleasure. If I
had, my weapon should quickly have been 175
out; I warrant you, I dare draw as soon as
another man, if I see occasion in a good
quarrel, and the law on my side.

NURSE Now, afore God, I am so vexed that every
part about me quivers. Scurvy knave! Pray 180
you, sir, a word; and as I told you, my young
lady bid me inquire you out. What she bid me
say, I will keep to myself. But first let me tell
ye, if ye should lead her in a fool's paradise,°
as they say, it were a very gross kind of 185
behavior, as they say. For the gentlewoman is
young; and therefore if you should deal
double with her, truly it were an ill thing to be
offered to any gentlewoman, and very weak
dealing. 190

ROMEO Nurse, commend me° to thy lady and
mistress. I protest° unto thee —

---

128. prick of noon: the point on the dial marking twelve o'clock. 132. troth: faith (variant of "truth"). 133. quoth 'a: literally, "said he," but here as often a sarcastic interjection meaning "indeed." 139. for fault of a worse: for lack of a worse (bearer of that name). 141. took: understood, interpreted. 143. confidence: conference. 145. indite: Benvolio means "invite," but is mimicking the Nurse's supposed malapropism. 146. bawd: (1) procurer, gobetween; (2) hare (in North-Midland dialect). 150. spent: used up. 155. too much for a score not worth marking up on the reckoning ("score"). 156. hoars: (1) turns moldy, (2) whores. 158. dinner: In Elizabethan times dinner was eaten about midday. 161. "lady, lady": Mercutio ironically applies a refrain-tag to the Nurse from a ballad, "The Constancy of Susanna". 162. merchant: fellow. 163. ropery: knavery. 167–68. take him down: humble him. 169. Jacks: ill-mannered fellows, knaves. 171. flirt-gills: loose women. 171. skains-mates unexplained, but perhaps cutthroat companions. 173. use me at his pleasure: treat me as he pleased. 184. lead . . . paradise: i.e., seduce her. 191. commend me: convey my best wishes. 192. protest: solemnly undertake or vow.

NURSE Good heart, and i' faith I will tell her as
    much. Lord, Lord, she will be a joyful
    woman.   195

ROMEO What wilt thou tell her, Nurse? Thou dost
    not mark me.°

NURSE I will tell her, sir, that you do protest,
    which, as I take it, is a gentlemanlike offer.

ROMEO Bid her devise   200
    Some means to come to shrift° this afternoon,
    And there she shall at Friar Laurence' cell
    Be shrived° and married. Here is for thy pains.

[He offers money.]

NURSE No, truly, sir, not a penny.

ROMEO Go to, I say you shall.   205

NURSE This afternoon, sir? Well, she shall be
    there.

ROMEO And stay, good Nurse, behind the abbey
    wall.
    Within this hour my man shall be with thee
    And bring thee cords made like a tackled stair,°
    Which to the high topgallant of my joy   210
    Must be my convoy in the secret night.
    Farewell. Be trusty, and I'll quit° thy pains.
    Farewell. Commend me to thy mistress.

[Romeo starts to leave.]

NURSE Now God in heaven bless thee! Hark you,
    sir.

ROMEO What sayst thou, my dear Nurse?   215

NURSE Is your man secret?° Did you ne'er hear
    say,
    "Two may keep counsel, putting one away"?

ROMEO I warrant thee, my man's as true as steel.

NURSE Well, sir, my mistress is the sweetest
    lady — Lord, Lord! When 'twas a little prating 220
    thing — O, there is a nobleman in town, one
    Paris, that would fain lay knife aboard;°
    but she, good soul, had as lieve° see a toad, a
    very toad, as see him. I anger her sometimes
    and tell her that Paris is the properer° man,   225
    but I'll warrant you, when I say so, she looks

as pale as any clout° in the versal° world.
    Doth not rosemary° and Romeo begin both
    with a letter?

ROMEO Ay, Nurse, what of that? Both with an R. 230

NURSE Ah, mocker! That's the dog's name;
    R is for the — No; I know it begins with
    some other letter; and she hath the
    prettiest sententious° of it, of you and
    rosemary, that it would do you good to   235
    hear it.

ROMEO Commend me to thy lady.

NURSE Ay, a thousand times. *[Exit Romeo.]* Peter!

PETER Anon!

NURSE Before, and apace.°   *[Exeunt.]* 240

Scene 5

[Enter Juliet.]

JULIET The clock struck nine when I did send the
    Nurse;
    In half an hour she promised to return.
    Perchance she cannot meet him. That's not so.
    O, she is lame!° Love's heralds should be
        thoughts,
    Which ten times faster glide than the sun's   5
        beams
    Driving back shadows over louring hills.
    Therefore do nimble-pinioned° doves draw
        Love,
    And therefore hath the wind-swift Cupid
        wings.
    Now is the sun upon the highmost hill°
    Of this day's journey, and from nine till twelve 10
    Is three long hours, yet she is not come.
    Had she affections and warm youthful blood,
    She would be as swift in motion as a ball;
    My words would bandy° her to my sweet love,
    And his to me.   15
    But old folks, many feign as they were dead° —
    Unwieldy, slow, heavy, and pale as lead.

[Enter Nurse and Peter.]

---

197. **mark me:** pay attention to what I am saying.   201. **shrift:** confession.   203. **shrived:** given absolution after confession.   209. **tackled stair:** rope ladder.   212. **quit:** reward.   216. **secret:** to be trusted with a secret.   222. **lay knife aboard:** assert his claim.   223. **lieve:** lief, willingly.   225. **properer:** handsomer.   227. **clout:** washed-out rag.   227. **versal:** universal (vulgarism), whole.   228. **rosemary:** herb associated with weddings, but also with funerals.   234. **sententious:** probably a malapropism for "sentences" = witty or moral sayings.   240. **apace:** quickly. **Act 2, Scene 5. 4. lame:** slow, infirm (from age).   7. **nimble-pinioned:** swift-winged.   9. **highmost hill:** i.e., the meridian.   14. **bandy:** strike (as a ball) to and fro.   16. **old . . . dead:** some old people like to take advantage of their age by pretending to be immobile ("dead").

O God, she comes! — O honey Nurse, what
    news?
Hast thou met with him? Send thy man away.
NURSE Peter, stay at the gate.   20

                        [Exit Peter.]

JULIET Now, good sweet Nurse — O Lord, why
    lookest thou sad?
Though news be sad, yet tell them merrily;
If good, thou shamest the music of sweet news
By playing it to me with so sour a face.
NURSE I am aweary. Give me leave awhile.   25
    Fie, how my bones ache! What a jaunce° have
    I had!
JULIET I would thou hadst my bones, and I thy
    news.
    Nay, come, I pray thee, speak. Good, good
    Nurse, speak.
NURSE Jesu, what haste! Can you not stay
    awhile?°
    Do you not see that I am out of breath?   30
JULIET How art thou out of breath, when thou
    hast breath

To say to me that thou art out of breath?
The excuse that thou dost make in° this delay
Is longer than the tale thou dost excuse.
Is thy news good or bad? Answer to that;   35
Say either, and I'll stay the circumstance.°
Let me be satisfied; is 't good or bad?
NURSE Well, you have made a simple° choice. You
    know not how to choose a man. Romeo? No,
    not he. Though his face be better than any   40
    man's, yet his leg excels all men's; and for a
    hand, and a foot, and a body, though they be
    not to be talked on,° yet they are past compare.
    He is not the flower° of courtesy, but, I'll warrant
    him, as gentle as a lamb. Go thy ways, wench.   45
    Serve God.° What, have you dined at home?
JULIET No, no; but all this did I know before.
    What says he of our marriage? What of that?
NURSE Lord, how my head aches! What a head
    have I!
    It beats° as it would fall in twenty pieces.   50
    My back o' t'other° side — ah, my back, my
    back!
    Beshrew your heart for sending me about

Simon Dack Archive/Alamy

This is an image from a 2008 stage production
of *Romeo and Juliet* with Juliet, left, and the
Nurse.

**How would you describe the relationship
between these two characters, based on
this image? What lines from the text can you
identify from this scene that might illustrate
this relationship?**

---

26. jaunce: literally, *"a prance"* — i.e., a tiring jolting journey.   **29. stay awhile:** wait a moment.   **33. in:** in regard to.   **36. stay the circumstance:**
wait for the details.   **38. simple:** foolish, silly (like a simpleton).   **43. be . . . on:** are not worth talking about.   **44. flower:** height.   **45–46. Go . . .
God:** We've had enough of this, girl, behave yourself.   **50. beats:** throbs.   **51. a't'other:** on the other.

To catch my death with jauncing up and
    down!

JULIET I' faith, I am sorry that thou art not well.
    Sweet, sweet, sweet Nurse, tell me, what says   55
    my love?

NURSE Your love says, like an honest°
    gentleman,
    And a courteous, and a kind, and a
    handsome,
    And, I warrant, a virtuous — Where is your
    mother?

JULIET Where is my mother? Why, she is
    within,
    Where should she be? How oddly thou   60
    repliest!
    "Your love says, like an honest gentleman,
    'Where is your mother?'"

NURSE   O God's Lady° dear!
    Are you so hot?° Marry, come up,° I trow.
    Is this the poultice for my aching bones?
    Henceforward do your messages yourself.   65

JULIET Here's such a coil!° Come, what says
    Romeo?

NURSE Have you got leave to go to shrift today?

JULIET I have.

NURSE Then hie you hence to Friar Laurence'
    cell;
    There stays a husband to make you a wife.   70
    Now comes the wanton° blood up in your
    cheeks;
    They'll be in scarlet straight at any news.°
    Hie you to church. I must another way,
    To fetch a ladder, by the which your love
    Must climb a bird's nest soon when it is dark.   75
    I am the drudge, and toil in your delight,
    But you shall bear the burden° soon at night.
    Go. I'll to dinner. Hie you to the cell.

JULIET Hie to high fortune! Honest Nurse,
    farewell.   [*Exeunt separately.*]

Scene 6

[*Enter Friar Laurence and Romeo.*]

FRIAR LAURENCE So smile the heavens upon this
    holy act
    That after-hours with sorrow chide us not!

ROMEO Amen, amen! But come what sorrow
    can,
    It cannot countervail the exchange of joy
    That one short minute gives me in her   5
    sight.
    Do thou but close° our hands with holy
    words,
    Then love-devouring death do what he dare;
    It is enough I may but call her mine.

FRIAR LAURENCE These violent delights have
    violent ends
    And in their triumph die, like fire and   10
    powder,
    Which as they kiss consume. The sweetest
    honey
    Is loathsome in his own deliciousness,
    And in the taste confounds° the appetite.
    Therefore love moderately. Long love doth so;
    Too swift arrives as tardy as too slow.   15

[*Enter Juliet.*]

    Here comes the lady. O, so light a foot
    Will ne'er wear out the everlasting flint.
    A lover may bestride the gossamer
    That idles in the wanton° summer air,
    And yet not fall; so light is vanity.°   20

JULIET Good even to my ghostly confessor.

FRIAR LAURENCE Romeo shall thank thee,
    daughter, for us both.

JULIET As much to him, else is his thanks too
    much.

ROMEO Ah, Juliet, if the measure° of thy joy
    Be heaped° like mine, and that° thy skill be   25
    more

---

56. **honest:** honorable, trustworthy; compare 78.   62. **God's Lady:** i.e., the Virgin Mary.   63. **hot:** overeager (with undertone of "lustful"). 63. **Marry come up:** Behave yourself.   66. **coil:** disturbance, fuss.   71. **wanton:** undisciplined, rebellious.   72. **They'll . . . news:** any sudden news always makes your cheeks scarlet in a second.   77. **bear the burden:** carry (1) the responsibility, (2) the weight of your lover.   **Act 2, Scene 6.**   6. **close:** join (in marriage).   13. **taste confounds:** the tasting ruins or destroys.   19. **wanton:** sportive, playful.   20. **vanity:** the insubstantiality of earthly happiness.   24. **measure:** quantity, amount.   25. **heaped:** i.e., his joy overflows the "measure."   25. **and that:** and if.

While Shakespeare does not include the scene in which Romeo and Juliet actually get married, most film and stage versions and many paintings have depicted it.

Look at the various depictions of the scene and compare the interpretations they convey about Romeo and Juliet's love for each other.

Lebrecht Music and Arts Photo Library/Alamy

768

To blazon° it, then sweeten with thy breath
This neighbor air, and let rich music's
    tongue°
Unfold the imagined° happiness that both
Receive in either° by this dear encounter.
JULIET Conceit,° more rich in matter° than in   30
    words,
    Brags of his substance, not of ornament.°

They are but beggars that can count their worth.
But my true love is grown to such excess
I cannot sum up sum of half my wealth.
FRIAR LAURENCE Come, come with me, and we will   35
    make short work;
For, by your leaves, you shall not stay alone
Till Holy Church incorporate two in one.

[Exeunt.]

---

26. blazon: celebrate, portray.   **27. rich music's tongue:** i.e., the harmony of Juliet's words.   **28. imagined:** inner, but unexpressed.
29. in either: in each other.   **30. Conceit:** understanding (the "imagined" idea).   **30. matter:** substance (the true "inner" content as opposed to
the "outer" expression = words).   **31. Brags . . . ornament:** takes just pride in its truth, not in dressing itself in mere words (i.e., strong, true feeling
does not need words).

Understanding and Interpreting

1. Reread lines 1–6 of the Chorus in Act 2, and explain what we are expected to conclude about Romeo and how he loves.

2. What challenges do Romeo and Juliet face going forward, according to the Chorus at the beginning of Act 2, and what will assist them?

3. After Romeo runs and hides from his friends in Act 2, Scene 1, Mercutio teases him. Summarize two or more of the jokes that Mercutio makes at Romeo's expense, and explain how the jokes reveal Mercutio's feelings about love.

4. In one of the most well-known lines in literature, Juliet says "Romeo, Romeo, wherefore art thou Romeo?" (Act 2, Scene 2, l. 33). What does Juliet mean here? Summarize the remainder of her speech in lines 33–49, explaining her perspective on his name.

5. In Act 1, Romeo says of himself, "I am not here / This is not Romeo" (Act 1, Scene 1, ll. 206–207) and here in Act 2, he says "I never will be Romeo" (Act 2, Scene 2, l. 51). What do these lines reveal about Romeo and his own sense of self and connection to family?

6. Look carefully at Act 2, Scene 2, lines 62–124 and identify evidence that illustrates Juliet's reasonable cautiousness and Romeo's recklessness and optimism.

7. Explain what Romeo means when he says, "My life were better ended by their hate / Than death proroguèd, wanting of thy love" (ll. 77–78). What does this illustrate about his character?

8. Reread Juliet's speech from Act 2, Scene 2, lines 85–106, when she asks him, "Dost thou love me?" What do these lines reveal about her character and ways in which she is different from or similar to Romeo?

9. At several points in Act 2, Scene 2, Juliet is very clear about what she expects from Romeo. What is it, and does she get what she hopes for?

10. Act 2, Scene 2 is Romeo and Juliet's most extended conversation in the entire play. What aspects of their relationship and attitudes toward love are revealed in this scene? What lines illustrate this?

11. Act 2, Scene 3 begins with a lengthy soliloquy by Friar Laurence about plants and nature. Based on the events of the play so far, what interpretation can you make about the purpose of the soliloquy here?

12. In Act 2, Scene 3, how does Friar Laurence react when he learns that Romeo is now in love with Juliet, not Rosaline? What does this suggest both about Friar Laurence and Romeo?

13. What is Friar Laurence suggesting about love in the following lines from Act 2, Scene 3:

    a. "Young men's love then lies / Not truly in their hearts, but in their eyes" (ll. 67–68).

    b. "Women may fall, when there's no strength in men" (l. 80).

    c. "O, she knew well / Thy love did read by rote, that could not spell" (ll. 87–88).

14. What important plot development do we learn from Benvolio about Tybalt at the beginning of Act 2, Scene 4? What do Mercutio and Benvolio think Romeo will do?

15. What is Romeo like with his friends in Act 2, Scene 4? How does his behavior with them differ from his behavior with Juliet?

16. Look at what Mercutio says to Romeo in Act 2, Scene 4, lines 99–101, "now art thou Romeo." What does he mean by this, and how should we interpret the line in light of similar ways that Romeo has described himself in the play so far?

17. What is the relationship like between Juliet and the Nurse? What textual evidence from the play supports your interpretation of their relationship?

18. Just before they are married at the end of Act 2, Romeo and Juliet once again express their love for each other in Scene 6, lines 24–34. Summarize what each says and explain the similarities and differences in their ideas about love.

19. How does Friar Laurence seem to feel about their wedding? Why does he decide to perform the ceremony? What evidence from the text supports your conclusion?

Analyzing Language, Style, and Structure

20. **Vocabulary in Context.** In the beginning of Act 2, the Chorus uses the word *complain* in line 7. What does *complain* mean in this context? In what ways is this usage different from and similar to modern usage?

21. **Vocabulary in Context.** In Act 2, Scene 2, line 101, Juliet uses the word *strange* to describe how she thinks she ought to have been with Romeo. What does *strange* mean in this context? In what ways is this usage different from and similar to modern usage?

22. Compare the tone of the sonnet presented by the Chorus at the beginning of Act 2 with the first sonnet in the Prologue (p. 726). What is the attitude of the Chorus in both sonnets toward Romeo and Juliet, and what specific word choice and figurative language illustrate the tone? This is the third and final sonnet in *Romeo and Juliet*. Draw an interpretation about why Shakespeare may have placed the final sonnet at this point in the plot.

23. Outside Juliet's window, Romeo says that "Juliet is the sun" (Act 2, Scene 2, l. 3). Explain this metaphor, as well as his later reference to the moon, symbolized by the Roman goddess Diana, the protector of virgins (Act 2, Scene 2, l. 4).

24. In Act 2, Scene 2, lines 107–108, Romeo offers to swear his love by the moon. Explain why Juliet finds his analogy insufficient and what this suggests about her.

25. In Act 2, Scene 2, lines 133–135, Juliet compares her love to the sea. Explain the meaning of her simile.

26. Explain Romeo's use of a simile comparing himself to a schoolboy in Act 2, Scene 2, lines 156–157.

27. Reread Act 2, Scene 2, lines 164–166, and examine Shakespeare's use of alliteration here. What sounds are created, and for what effect?

28. In Act 2, Scene 2, lines 158–183, there are many allusions to birds. Identify and explain the meaning of at least two references in this section.

29. At the end of Act 2, Scene 2, Juliet says, "Parting is such sweet sorrow" (l. 184). What is achieved by putting the words *sweet* and *sorrow* together like this? How can parting be both?

30. Mercutio engages in more wordplay at the beginning of Act 2, Scene 4. Choose one or more of his language choices and explain the intended humor.

31. Notice how much of the dialogue in Act 2, Scene 4 is written in prose, not in verse. What are possible reasons for and effects of this choice?

32. Identify the language choices in Juliet's lines in Act 2, Scene 5, lines 47–79 that illustrate her anxiety about Romeo.

33. In Act 2, Scene 6, lines 9–13, Friar Laurence offers two analogies about love. Examine these analogies and explain how they support his advice to "love moderately."

Topics for Composing

34. **Analysis.** Do Romeo and Juliet share the same view of love? Write a response explaining your observations. Be sure to support your response with examples from the text.

35. **Analysis.** How would you characterize Juliet so far in this play? Where does she get to go, and with whom does she interact? Compare and contrast her situation with that of Romeo, and write an explanation of how their respective situations might affect the choices they make.

36. **Analysis.** How does Shakespeare's use of language make the case that Romeo and Juliet are truly in love? Refer to specific lines in the text to support your answer.

37. **Argument.** So much of the outcome of the play rests on the decision that Friar Laurence makes in Act 2, Scene 3, to marry Romeo and Juliet. Based on what he knows about Romeo, is this a wise decision on Friar Laurence's part? Write a response in which you argue whether or not Friar Laurence makes the right decision.

38. **Connections.** Is Juliet right when she states, "What's in a name? That which we call a rose / by any other word would smell as sweet"? In other words, do names themselves not matter at all? Write a response in which you support or reject this idea, based your own experiences or those of family or friends.

39. **Speaking and Listening.** With a partner, try to come to a consensus on a list of characteristics that define a healthy relationship. Then, discuss the development of relationships in the play so far — between adults and children, friends and family. Select one or two relationships and explain whether they exhibit the same characteristics that you and your partner listed.

40. **Research.** Juliet is thirteen at the time of her marriage at the end of this act. Research whether this was typical in the 1300s in Italy, or even in Shakespeare's time in the 1600s. What about today? What are the laws about child brides in the United States and around the world? How many girls Juliet's age get married in our time?

41. **Research.** You probably encounter references to *Romeo and Juliet* frequently in popular culture. Locate a contemporary allusion to the play in a movie, song, television show, story, or other text. Explain the allusion and how its use provides commentary on the play and on the text in which the allusion is made.

42. **Creative Writing.** Rewrite a couple of exchanges between Romeo and Juliet during the balcony scene (Act 2, Scene 2, lines 1–189) in contemporary English, using allusions and metaphors more recognizable to a modern audience. What is gained and lost in your translation?

ACT 3

Scene 1

[*Enter Mercutio, Benvolio, and men.*]

BENVOLIO I pray thee, good Mercutio, let's retire.
   The day is hot, the Capels° are abroad,
   And if we meet we shall not scape a brawl,
   For now, these hot days, is the mad blood
      stirring.

MERCUTIO Thou art like one of these fellows that   5
   when he enters the confines of a tavern, claps
   me° his sword upon the table and says, "God
   send me no need of thee!" and by the operation°
   of the second cup draws him on the drawer,°
   when indeed there is no need.   10

BENVOLIO Am I like such a fellow?

MERCUTIO Come, come, thou art as hot a Jack in
   thy mood° as any in Italy, and as soon moved
   to be moody, and as soon moody to be
   moved.°   15

BENVOLIO And what to?

MERCUTIO Nay, an there were two° such, we
   should have none shortly, for one would kill
   the other. Thou! Why, thou wilt quarrel with a
   man that hath a hair more or a hair less in his   20
   beard than thou hast. Thou wilt quarrel with a
   man for cracking nuts, having no other reason
   but because thou hast hazel eyes. What eye
   but such an eye would spy out such a quarrel?
   Thy head is as full of quarrels as an egg is full   25
   of meat,° and yet thy head hath been beaten
   as addle as an egg for° quarreling. Thou hast
   quarreled with a man for coughing in the
   street, because he hath wakened thy dog that
   hath lain asleep in the sun. Didst thou not fall   30
   out with a tailor for wearing his new doublet°
   before Easter? With another, for tying his new
   shoes with old ribbon? And yet thou wilt
   tutor me from° quarreling!

BENVOLIO An I were so apt° to quarrel as thou   35
   art, any man should buy the fee simple of my
   life for an hour and a quarter.

MERCUTIO The fee simple! O simple!°

[*Enter Tybalt, Petruchio, and others.*]

BENVOLIO By my head, here come the Capulets .

MERCUTIO By my heel, I care not.   40

TYBALT [*To his companions*]
   Follow me close, for I will speak to them. —
   Gentlemen, good e'en. A word with one of you.

MERCUTIO And but one word with one of us?
   Couple it with something: make it a word and
   a blow.   45

TYBALT You shall find me apt enough to that, sir,
   an you will give me occasion.

MERCUTIO Could you not take some occasion°
   without giving?

TYBALT Mercutio, thou consortest with Romeo.   50

MERCUTIO "Consort"? ° What, dost thou make us
   minstrels? An thou make minstrels of us,
   look to hear nothing but discords. Here's my
   fiddlestick;° here's that shall make you dance.
   Zounds, "consort"!   55

BENVOLIO We talk here in the public haunt of men.
   Either withdraw unto some private place,
   Or reason coldly of your grievances,
   Or else depart; here all eyes gaze on us.

MERCUTIO Men's eyes were made to look, and let   60
   them gaze.
I will not budge for no man's pleasure, I.

[*Enter Romeo.*]

TYBALT Well, peace be with you, sir. Here comes
   my man.

MERCUTIO But I'll be hanged, sir, if he wear your
   livery.°

Act 3, Scene 1.   **2. Capels:** Capulets   **6–7. claps me:** places (noisily).   **8. operation:** effect, influence.   **9. drawer:** tapster.   **13. mood:** anger, quarrelsome humor.   **14–15. as soon moved . . . moved:** as quickly provoked to be angry and as quickly angry for being provoked.   **17. two:** Mercutio plays on Benvolio's "to" in 16.   **26. meat:** edible substance (yolk and white).   **27. addle . . . for:** as muddled and worthless as a bad egg as a result of; compare "addle-pated."   **31. his new doublet:** i.e., the new jacket he has just created.   **34. tutor me from:** warn me against (as a tutor might warn his pupil).   **35. apt:** prone.   **38. simple:** weak-minded, stupid.   **48. occasion:** excuse.   **51. Consort?** an insult to a gentleman.   **54. fiddlestick:** i.e., rapier.   **63. wear your livery:** Tybalt's "livery" (= uniform or heraldic badge).

This image from a 2019 ballet stage version shows Tybalt confronting Romeo.

How do the costumes, props, and body language communicate the tension between these characters and their perspectives on the encounter?

Marry, go before to field,° he'll be your follower;
Your worship in that sense may call him "man." 65

TYBALT Romeo, the love I bear thee can afford
No better term than this: thou art a villain.°

ROMEO Tybalt, the reason that I have to love thee
Doth much excuse the appertaining° rage
To such a greeting. Villain am I none. 70
Therefore, farewell. I see thou knowest me not.

TYBALT Boy,° this shall not excuse the injuries
That thou hast done me. Therefore turn and
draw.

ROMEO I do protest I never injured thee,
But love thee better than thou canst devise 75
Till thou shalt know the reason of my love.
And so, good Capulet—which name I tender°
As dearly as mine own—be satisfied.

MERCUTIO O calm, dishonorable, vile submission!
Alla stoccata° carries it away. [*He draws.*] 80
Tybalt, you rat-catcher,° will you walk?

TYBALT What wouldst thou have with me?

MERCUTIO Good king of cats, nothing but one
of your nine lives, that I mean to make bold
withal, and, as you shall use me hereafter, 85
dry-beat° the rest of the eight. Will you pluck

your sword out of his pilcher° by the ears?
Make haste, lest mine be about your ears
ere it be out.

TYBALT I am for you. [*He draws.*] 90

ROMEO Gentle Mercutio, put thy rapier up.

MERCUTIO Come, sir, your *passado*. [*They fight.*]

ROMEO Draw, Benvolio, beat down their
weapons.
Gentlemen, for shame, forbear this outrage!
Tybalt, Mercutio, the Prince expressly hath 95
Forbid this bandying° in Verona streets.
Hold, Tybalt! Good Mercutio!

[*Tybalt under Romeo's arm stabs Mercutio.*]

[*Away Tybalt with his followers.*]

MERCUTIO I am hurt.
A plague o' both your houses! I am sped.°
Is he gone, and hath nothing?

BENVOLIO What art thou hurt?

MERCUTIO Ay, ay, a scratch, a scratch; marry, 'tis 100
enough.
Where is my page? Go, villain,° fetch a surgeon.

[*Exit Page.*]

---

64. go before to field: lead the way to the place of combat (i.e., set an example).   **67. villain:** a very serious insult demanding reprisal, carrying not only the sense of "depraved scoundrel" but undertones of "low-born fellow."   **69. appertaining:** appropriate (to a member of the Capulet family).   **72. Boy:** a term of contempt.   **77. tender:** value, hold in regard.   **80. "Alla stoccata":** literally "at the thrust," an Italian fencing term of the kind Mercutio despises; here used as a nickname for Tybalt.   **81. rat-catcher** i.e., "King of Cats."   **86. dry-beat:** to beat without drawing blood, but vaguely used to mean "beat hard."   **87. pilcher:** contemptuous term for "scabbard."   **96. bandying:** contention, strife.   **98. sped:** dispatched, done for.   **101. villain:** fellow.

ROMEO Courage, man, the hurt cannot be much.

MERCUTIO No, 'tis not so deep as a well, nor so
wide as a church door, but 'tis enough, 'twill
serve. Ask for me tomorrow, and you shall   105
find me a grave° man. I am peppered, I
warrant, for this world.° A plague o' both your
houses! Zounds, a dog, a rat, a mouse, a cat, to
scratch a man to death! A braggart, a rogue, a
villain, that fights by the book of arithmetic!°   110
Why the devil came you between us? I was
hurt under your arm.

ROMEO I thought all for the best.

MERCUTIO Help me into some house, Benvolio,
Or I shall faint. A plague o' both your houses!   115
They have made worm's meat of me. I have it,
And soundly too. Your houses!

[Exit supported by Benvolio.]

ROMEO This gentleman, the Prince's near ally,°
My very° friend, hath got this mortal hurt
In my behalf; my reputation stained   120
With Tybalt's slander° — Tybalt, that an hour
Hath been my cousin! O sweet Juliet,
Thy beauty hath made me effeminate,
And in my temper softened valor's steel!°

[Enter Benvolio.]

BENVOLIO O Romeo, Romeo, brave Mercutio is   125
dead!
That gallant spirit hath aspired° the clouds,
Which too untimely here did scorn the
earth.

ROMEO This day's black fate on more days doth
depend;°
This but begins the woe others must end.

[Enter Tybalt.]

BENVOLIO Here comes the furious Tybalt back   130
again.

ROMEO Alive in triumph, and Mercutio slain!
Away to heaven, respective lenity,°
And fire-eyed fury be my conduct now!
Now, Tybalt, take the "villain" back again
That late thou gavest me, for Mercutio's   135
soul
Is but a little way above our heads,
Staying° for thine to keep him company.
Either thou or I, or both, must go with him.

TYBALT Thou, wretched boy, that didst consort°
him here,
Shalt with him hence.   140

ROMEO   This shall determine that.

[They fight. Tybalt falls.]

This scene from a 1996 film version shows
Mercutio's death.

**Explain how the costumes, props,
facial expressions, and other elements
of drama contribute to this scene's
emotional power.**

C20TH FOX / Alamy

---

106. grave: i.e., dead (and buried).   **106–107. peppered . . . world:** dead, I swear, so far as this life is concerned.   **110. fights . . . arithmetic:**
fences precisely, by the numbers (i.e., a textbook fencer).   **118. ally:** relative.   **119. very:** true.   **121. slander:** i.e., the insults heaped on Romeo
which he had failed to answer, as the terms of honor dictated, by dueling.   **124. in . . . steel** weakened the (manly) steel-like courage of my natural
disposition.   **126. aspired:** mounted up to.   **128. day's . . . depend** the malignant consequence ("black fate") of today's events hangs on the future.
132. respective lenity: considerate mildness.   **137. Staying:** waiting.   **139. consort:** associate with.

BENVOLIO Romeo, away, begone!

    The citizens are up,° and Tybalt slain.

    Stand not amazed.° The Prince will doom thee

      death

    If thou art taken. Hence, begone, away!

ROMEO O, I am fortune's fool!   145

BENVOLIO   Why dost thou stay?

                      [Exit Romeo.]

    [Enter Citizens.]

FIRST CITIZEN Which way ran he that killed

    Mercutio?

    Tybalt, that murderer, which way ran he?

BENVOLIO There lies that Tybalt.

FIRST CITIZEN   Up, sir, go with me.

    I charge thee in the Prince's name, obey.

    [Enter Prince (attended), old Montague,

    Capulet, their Wives, and all.]

PRINCE Where are the vile beginners of this fray? 150

BENVOLIO O noble Prince, I can discover all

    The unlucky manage° of this fatal brawl.

    There lies the man, slain by young Romeo,

    That slew thy kinsman, brave Mercutio.

CAPULET'S WIFE Tybalt, my cousin! O my   155

    brother's child!

    O Prince! O cousin! Husband! O, the blood is

      spilled

    Of my dear kinsman! Prince, as thou art true,

    For blood of ours shed blood of Montague.

    O cousin, cousin!

PRINCE Benvolio, who began this bloody fray?   160

BENVOLIO Tybalt, here slain, whom Romeo's

    hand did slay.

    Romeo, that spoke him fair, bid him bethink°

    How nice° the quarrel was, and urged withal

    Your high displeasure. All this — utterèd

    With gentle breath, calm look, knees humbly 165

      bowed —

    Could not take truce° with the unruly spleen°

    Of Tybalt deaf to peace, but that he tilts

    With piercing steel at bold Mercutio's breast,

    Who, all as hot, turns deadly point to point,

Bridgeman Images

Shakespeare's audience at the time of his writing believed strongly in the role that fate played in their lives. This painting shows the Roman goddess Fortuna with her "wheel of fortune."

Explain how this image helps you better understand Romeo's line "I am Fortune's fool." In what ways does this image present a positive or negative view of fate?

And, with a martial scorn, with one hand   170

    beats

Cold death aside and with the other sends

It back to Tybalt, whose dexterity

Retorts it.° Romeo he cries aloud,

"Hold, friends! Friends, part!" and swifter than

    his tongue

His agile arm° beats down their fatal points,   175

---

142. up: aroused.   **143. amazed:** filled with consternation.   **152. manage:** conduct.   **162. bethink:** consider.   **163. nice:** insignificant, trifling.   **166. take truce:** make peace.   **166. unruly spleen:** ungoverned fiery temper.   **173. Retorts it:** returns the thrust.   **175. arm:** i.e., sword.

And twixt them rushes; underneath whose
    arm
An envious° thrust from Tybalt hit the life
Of stout° Mercutio, and then Tybalt fled;
But by and by comes back to Romeo,
Who had but newly entertained° revenge,   180
And to 't they go like lightning, for, ere I
Could draw to part them was stout Tybalt slain,
And, as he fell, did Romeo turn and fly.
This is the truth, or let Benvolio die.
CAPULET'S WIFE He is a kinsman to the   185
    Montague.
Affection makes him false; he speaks not true.
Some twenty of them fought in this black
    strife,
And all those twenty could but kill one life.
I beg for justice, which thou, Prince, must
    give.
Romeo slew Tybalt; Romeo must not live.   190
PRINCE Romeo slew him, he slew Mercutio.
Who now the price of his dear blood doth
    owe?

MONTAGUE Not Romeo, Prince, he was
    Mercutio's friend;
His fault concludes but° what the law should
    end,
The life of Tybalt.   195
PRINCE   And for that offense
Immediately we do exile him hence.
I have an interest in your heart's proceeding;°
My blood° for your rude brawls doth lie
    a-bleeding;
But I'll amerce° you with so strong a fine
That you shall all repent the loss of mine.   200
I will be deaf to pleading and excuses;
Nor tears nor prayers shall purchase out°
    abuses.
Therefore use none. Let Romeo hence in
    haste,
Else, when he is found, that hour is his last.
Bear hence this body and attend our will.   205
Mercy but murders, pardoning those that kill.°

    [Exeunt, some carrying Tybalt's body.]

---

177. envious: malicious.   **178. stout:** strong, brave.   **180. entertained:** allowed the thought of.   **194. concludes but:** only finishes.
197. interest . . . proceeding: personal concern in the reaction dictated by your feelings.   **198. My blood:** i.e., Mercutio, the Prince's kinsman.
199. amerce: punish, penalize.   **202. purchase out:** buy out, make amends for.   **206. Mercy . . . kill:** Mercy only leads to further murders by
pardoning murderers.

extending beyond the text

After killing Tybalt in Act 3, Romeo says, "I am fortune's fool." He believes that his actions and future are controlled by fate, not his own choices. Read the discussion of fate below from a book by Hannah Critchlow, the Science Outreach Fellow at Magdalene College, University of Cambridge.

from The Science of Fate: The New Science of Who We Are—And How to Shape our Best Future

Hannah Critchlow

Since the dawn of humanity our species has been trying to figure out what, or who, is calling the shots. The question of whether we can determine our life's course or should accept that it is largely beyond our control is well up there on our list of thorny conundrums to resolve. Are we fully conscious agents possessed of free will or closer to pre-programmed machines, running on deep drives of which we may not even be aware? At different times and in different places human beings have answered this question in many ways. We've asserted that we're animated by a divinely bestowed soul, or inspired by the quasi-godlike powers of our own mind, or powered by the neurochemistry zapping round our brains. Whatever the flavour of the answer, the problem of whether or not we can steer our own way arises directly out of being an animal in which consciousness is so well developed that it enables us to ponder consciousness itself.

Over the past two decades there has been an explosion of study of this previously inaccessible realm, driven by massive technological advance. That study — the discipline of neuroscience — is illuminating the question of whether we are in control of our outcomes or destined at birth to follow a particular path by (sometimes literally) shining a light into the brain's deepest regions. It turns out that there is still some power in the old idea of fate, though not in the sense the Ancient Greeks understood it, as an external force. In its twenty-first-century incarnation, our fate is buried within our physical selves, in the hard-wiring of our brains and our genetic inheritance. A straightforward (if devastating) example of biology as fate would be carrying the genetic mutation for Huntington's disease, where individuals carrying a single genetic change will eventually develop problems with coordination, reasoning, flexibility in thinking, decision making and, in some cases, psychosis. A more complex manifestation is the highly nuanced way that we as individuals are predisposed to certain behaviours rather than others. ■

Summarize how Critchlow defines the concept of fate in its pre-twenty-first century iteration. How does she apply this concept to what we know, based on neuroscience? What are possible connections between her ideas and the ways that characters in this play think about fate?

Scene 2

[*Enter Juliet alone.*]

JULIET Gallop apace, you fiery-footed steeds,
   Towards Phoebus' lodging!° Such a wagoner
   As Phaëthon would whip you to the west
   And bring in cloudy night immediately.
   Spread thy close curtain, love-performing   5
      night,
   That runaways' eyes may wink,° and Romeo
   Leap to these arms, untalked of and unseen.
   Lovers can see to do their amorous rites
   By their own beauties; or, if love be blind,
   It best agrees with night. Come, civil° night,   10
   Thou sober-suited matron all in black,
   And learn° me how to lose a winning match
   Played for a pair of stainless maidenhoods.
   Hood my unmanned blood, bating° in my
      cheeks,
   With thy black mantle till strange love grow   15
      bold,
   Think true love acted simple modesty.

Act 3, Scene 2.   **2. lodging:** i.e., the west, below the horizon.   **6. That . . . wink:** so that the eyes of (1) the horses of the sun or (2) vagrant night wanderers may (1) close in sleep or (2) pretend to see nothing.   **10. civil:** grave, sober.   **12. learn:** teach.   **14. Hood . . . unmanned . . . bating:** cover, blindfold . . . untamed (i.e., not trained by a man, with play on "husbandless") . . . fluttering (to break loose); all terms from falconry.

Come, night. Come, Romeo. Come, thou day
   in night;
For thou wilt lie upon the wings of night
Whiter than new snow upon a raven's back.
Come, gentle night, come, loving, black-   20
   browed night,
Give me my Romeo, and when I shall die
Take him and cut him out in little stars,
And he will make the face of heaven so fine
That all the world will be in love with night
And pay no worship to the garish sun.°   25
O, I have bought the mansion of a love
But not possessed it, and though I am sold,
Not yet enjoyed. So tedious is this day
As in the night before some festival
To an impatient child that hath new robes   30
And may not wear them. O, here comes my
   nurse,

[*Enter Nurse, with cords.*]

And she brings news, and every tongue that
   speaks
But Romeo's name speaks heavenly eloquence.
Now, Nurse, what news? What hast thou
   there? The cords
That Romeo bid thee fetch?   35
NURSE   Ay, ay, the cords.
                            [*She throws them down.*]
JULIET Ay me, what news? Why dost thou wring
   thy hands?
NURSE Ah, weraday!° He's dead, he's dead, he's
   dead!
We are undone, lady, we are undone!
Alack the day, he's gone, he's killed, he's dead!
JULIET Can heaven be so envious?°   40
NURSE   Romeo can,
Though heaven cannot. O Romeo, Romeo!
Whoever would have thought it? Romeo!
JULIET What devil art thou, that dost torment me
   thus?
This torture° should be roared in dismal hell.

Hath Romeo slain himself? Say thou but "Ay,"   45
And that bare vowel "I" shall poison more
Than the death-darting eye of cockatrice.°
I am not I, if there be such an "Ay,"
Or those eyes° shut, that makes thee answer "Ay."
If he be slain, say "Ay," or if not, "No."   50
Brief sounds determine of my weal or woe.
NURSE I saw the wound. I saw it with mine eyes —
God save the mark!° — here on his manly
   breast.
A piteous corpse, a bloody piteous corpse;
Pale, pale as ashes, all bedaubed in blood,   55
All in gore-blood. I swoonèd at the sight.
JULIET O, break, my heart! Poor bankrupt, break
   at once!
To prison, eyes; ne'er look on liberty!
Vile earth,° to earth resign;° end motion° here,
And thou and Romeo press one heavy bier!   60
NURSE O Tybalt, Tybalt, the best friend I had!
O courteous Tybalt! Honest gentleman!
That ever I should live to see thee dead!
JULIET What storm is this that blows so contrary?°
Is Romeo slaughtered, and is Tybalt dead?   65
My dearest cousin, and my dearer lord?
Then, dreadful trumpet,° sound the general
   doom!
For who is living, if those two are gone?
NURSE Tybalt is gone, and Romeo banishèd;
Romeo that killed him, he is banishèd.   70
JULIET O God! Did Romeo's hand shed Tybalt's
   blood?
NURSE It did, it did. Alas the day it did!
JULIET O serpent heart, hid with a flowering face!
Did ever dragon keep° so fair a cave?
Beautiful tyrant! Fiend angelical!   75
Dove-feathered raven! Wolvish-ravening lamb!
Despisèd substance of divinest show!
Just opposite to what thou justly° seem'st,
A damnèd saint, an honorable villain!
O nature, what hadst thou to do in hell   80
When thou didst bower° the spirit of a fiend

21–25. Give . . . sun: i.e., let me have Romeo to myself as long as I am alive, and when I die then I will share him with the whole world as a source of light that will put the sun to shame.   **37. weraday:** alas (variant of "well-a-day").   **40. envious:** malicious.   **44. torture:** i.e., the Nurse's manner of telling her news.   **47. death-darting . . . cockatrice:** a fabled creature with the body of a serpent and the head of a cock (often called "basilisk"), which could kill with a glance.   **49. those eyes:** i.e., Romeo's eyes.   **53. God save the mark!:** Exclamation, used as apology when something horrible (as here), disgusting, indecent, or profane has been mentioned.   **59. Vile earth:** i.e., her body.   **59. resign:** surrender.   **59. motion:** physical movement — i.e., the property of life.   **64. so contrary:** i.e., from Romeo's death to Tybalt's.   **67. trumpet:** i.e., the last trump, which would announce the Last Judgment ("general doom").   **74. keep:** inhabit (as the guardian).   **78. Just . . . justly:** exact . . . exactly.   **81. bower:** lodge (as in an arbor).

In mortal paradise of such sweet flesh?
Was ever book containing such vile matter
So fairly bound? O, that deceit should dwell
In such a gorgeous palace!   85

NURSE   There's no trust,
No faith, no honesty in men; all perjured,
All forsworn, all naught,° all dissemblers.
Ah, where's my man? Give me some aqua-
     vitae.°
These griefs, these woes, these sorrows make
     me old.
Shame come to Romeo!   90

JULIET   Blistered be thy tongue
For such a wish! He was not born to shame.
Upon his brow shame is ashamed to sit;
For 'tis a throne where honor may be crowned
Sole monarch of the universal earth.
O, what a beast was I to chide at him!   95

NURSE Will you speak well of him that killed your
     cousin?

JULIET Shall I speak ill of him that is my
     husband?
Ah, poor my lord, what tongue shall smooth
     thy name
When I, thy three-hours wife, have mangled it?
But wherefore, villain, didst thou kill my   100
     cousin?
That villain cousin would have killed my
     husband.
Back, foolish tears, back to your native spring!
Your tributary drops° belong to woe,
Which you, mistaking,° offer up to joy.
My husband lives, that Tybalt would have   105
     slain,°
And Tybalt's dead, that would have slain my
     husband.
All this is comfort. Wherefore weep I then?
Some word there was, worser than Tybalt's
     death,
That murdered me. I would forget it fain,
But O, it presses to my memory   110

Like damnèd guilty deeds to sinners' minds:
"Tybalt is dead, and Romeo — banishèd."
That "banishèd," that one word "banishèd,"
Hath slain ten thousand Tybalts. Tybalt's death
Was woe enough, if it had ended there;   115
Or, if sour woe delights in fellowship
And needly will be ranked with other griefs,°
Why followed not, when she said "Tybalt's dead,"
"Thy father," or "thy mother," nay, or both,
Which modern lamentation might have   120
     moved?
But with a rear-ward° following Tybalt's death,
"Romeo is banishèd" — to speak that word
Is father, mother, Tybalt, Romeo, Juliet,
All slain, all dead. "Romeo is banishèd!"
There is no end, no limit, measure, bound,   125
In that word's death; no words can that woe
     sound.°
Where is my father and my mother, Nurse?

NURSE Weeping and wailing over Tybalt's corpse.
Will you go to them? I will bring you thither.

JULIET Wash they his wounds with tears? Mine   130
     shall be spent,
When theirs are dry, for Romeo's banishment.
Take up those cords. Poor ropes, you are
     beguiled,
Both you and I, for Romeo is exiled.
He made you for a highway to my bed;
But I, a maid, die maiden-widowèd.   135
Come, cords, come, Nurse. I'll to my wedding
     bed,
And death, not Romeo, take my maidenhead!

NURSE [*Taking up the cords*]
Hie to your chamber. I'll find Romeo
To comfort you. I wot° well where he is.
Hark ye, your Romeo will be here at night.   140
I'll to him. He is hid at Laurence' cell.

JULIET O, find him! Give this ring to my true
     knight,   [*Giving a ring*]
And bid him come to take his last farewell.

                              [*Exeunt separately.*]

---

87. naught: wicked, vicious.   **88. aqua-vitae:** strong drink (e.g., brandy).   **103. tributary drops:** tears paid as tribute.   **104. mistaking:** i.e., her tears wrongly take what is a glad occasion (Romeo's survival) for a sad one.   **105. that . . . slain:** that Tybalt wished to slay.   **117. needly . . . griefs:** Juliet is saying, here and in what follows, that if "sour woe" demands company, why couldn't Tybalt's death have been "ranked" with something comparable, news of her parents' death (a lesser woe), rather than with the fact of Romeo's banishment (a greater woe).   **121. rear-ward:** rearguard (suggesting a surprise attack from behind).   **126. sound:** (1) give adequate expression to, (2) plumb the depth of.   **139. wot:** know.

Scene 3

[*Enter Friar Laurence.*]

FRIAR LAURENCE Romeo, come forth; come
        forth, thou fearful man.
    Affliction is enamored of thy parts,°
    And thou art wedded to calamity.

[*Enter Romeo.*]

ROMEO Father, what news? What is the Prince's
        doom?
    What sorrow craves acquaintance at my hand   5
    That I yet know not?
FRIAR LAURENCE   Too familiar
    Is my dear son with such sour company.
    I bring thee tidings of the Prince's doom.
ROMEO What less than doomsday° is the Prince's
        doom?
FRIAR LAURENCE A gentler judgment vanished°   10
        from his lips:
    Not body's death, but body's banishment.
ROMEO Ha, banishment? Be merciful, say
        "death";
    For exile hath more terror in his look,
    Much more than death. Do not say
        "banishment."
FRIAR LAURENCE Here from Verona art thou   15
        banishèd.
    Be patient,° for the world is broad and wide.
ROMEO There is no world without° Verona walls
    But purgatory, torture, hell itself.
    Hence "banishèd" is banished from the
        world,
    And world's exile is death. Then "banishèd"   20
    Is death mistermed.° Calling death
        "banishèd,"
    Thou cutt'st my head off with a golden ax
    And smilest upon the stroke that murders me.
FRIAR LAURENCE O deadly sin! O rude
        unthankfulness!
    Thy fault our law calls death, but the kind   25
        Prince,

Taking thy part, hath rushed aside° the law
And turned that black word "death" to
        "banishment."
This is dear mercy, and thou seest it not.
ROMEO 'Tis torture, and not mercy. Heaven is
        here
    Where Juliet lives, and every cat and dog   30
    And little mouse, every unworthy thing,
    Live here in heaven and may look on her,
    But Romeo may not. More validity,°
    More honorable state, more courtship lives
    In carrion flies than Romeo. They may seize   35
    On the white wonder of dear Juliet's hand
    And steal immortal blessing from her lips,
    Who even in pure and vestal° modesty
    Still blush, as thinking their own kisses sin;
    But Romeo may not, he is banishèd.   40
    Flies may do this, but I from this must fly.
    They are free men, but I am banishèd.
    And sayest thou yet that exile is not death?
    Hadst thou no poison mixed, no sharp-ground
        knife,
    No sudden mean of death, though ne'er so   45
        mean,°
    But "banishèd" to kill me? "Banishèd"?
    O Friar, the damnèd use that word in hell;
    Howling attends it. How hast thou the heart,
    Being a divine, a ghostly° confessor,
    A sin absolver, and my friend professed,   50
    To mangle me with that word "banishèd"?
FRIAR LAURENCE Thou fond° mad man, hear me
        a little speak.
ROMEO O, thou wilt speak again of banishment.
FRIAR LAURENCE I'll give thee armor to keep off
        that word,
    Adversity's sweet milk,° philosophy,   55
    To comfort thee, though thou art banishèd.
ROMEO Yet "banishèd"? Hang up philosophy!
    Unless philosophy can make a Juliet,
    Displant° a town, reverse a prince's doom,
    It helps not, it prevails not. Talk no more.   60

Act 3, Scene 3. **2. parts:** qualities, endowments. **9. doomsday:** the final judgment (i.e., death). **10. vanished:** (1) breathed out like so much air, (2) issued without possibility of recall. **16. Be patient:** Compose yourself. **17. without:** outside the bounds of. **21. mistermed:** called by the wrong name (i.e., a name that pretends to mercy, a euphemism). **26. rushed aside:** forced out of place. **33. validity:** true worth. **38. vestal:** maidenly, virgin. **45. mean . . . mean:** method, instrument . . . low, base. **49. ghostly:** spiritual. **52. fond:** foolish. **55. Adversity's sweet milk:** a palliative against adversity. **59. Displant:** uproot (i.e., move Verona from one place to another).

This image shows the walls of a French city dating back to the 13th Century, around the time in which *Romeo and Juliet* is set.

Based on this picture, the Key Context on pages 733–734, and what you know about Romeo, why might he think being banished from the city of Verona is even worse than death?

FRIAR LAURENCE O, then I see that madmen have
   no ears.

ROMEO How should they, when that wise men
   have no eyes?

FRIAR LAURENCE Let me dispute with thee of thy
   estate.°

ROMEO Thou canst not speak of that thou dost
   not feel.

Wert thou as young as I, Juliet thy love,   65

An hour but married, Tybalt murderèd,

Doting° like me and like me banishèd,

Then mightst thou speak, then mightst thou
   tear thy hair,

And fall upon the ground, as I do now,

Taking the measure of an unmade grave.   70

   [He falls upon the ground.]

[Knock, within]

FRIAR LAURENCE Arise. One knocks. Good
   Romeo, hide thyself.

ROMEO Not I, unless the breath of heartsick
   groans,

Mistlike, infold me from the search of eyes.

   [Knock.]

FRIAR LAURENCE Hark, how they knock! — Who's
   there? — Romeo, arise.

Thou wilt be taken. — Stay awhile! —   75
   Stand up.

   [Knock.]

Run to my study. — By and by!° — God's will,

What simpleness° is this? — I come, I come!

   [Knock.]

Who knocks so hard? Whence come you?
   What's your will?   *[Going to the door.]*

NURSE *[Within]*

Let me come in, and you shall know my
   errand.

I come from Lady Juliet.   80

---

63. dispute . . . estate: discuss your present situation.   **67. Doting:** deranged (by love), lovesick.   **76. By and by!:** In a moment!
77. simpleness: foolish behavior.

FRIAR LAURENCE   Welcome then

[*He opens the door.*]

[*Enter Nurse.*]

NURSE O holy Friar, O, tell me, holy Friar,
    Where's my lady's lord, where's Romeo?
FRIAR LAURENCE There on the ground, with his
    own tears made drunk.
NURSE O, he is even in my mistress' case,
    Just in her case! O woeful sympathy!°   85
    Piteous predicament! Even so lies she,
    Blubbering and weeping, weeping and
        blubbering. —
    Stand up, stand up! Stand, an you be a man.
    For Juliet's sake, for her sake, rise and stand!
    Why should you fall into so deep an O?°   90
ROMEO Nurse!   [*He rises.*]
NURSE Ah, sir, ah, sir! Death's the end of all.
ROMEO Spakest thou of Juliet? How is it with her?
    Doth not she think me an old° murderer,
    Now I have stained the childhood of our joy   95
    With blood removed but little from her own?
    Where is she? And how doth she? And what
        says
    My concealed lady° to our cancelled° love?
NURSE O, she says nothing, sir, but weeps and
        weeps,
    And now falls on her bed, and then starts up,   100
    And "Tybalt" calls, and then on Romeo cries,°
    And then down falls again.
ROMEO   As if that name
    Shot from the deadly level° of a gun,
    Did murder her, as that name's cursèd hand
    Murdered her kinsman. O, tell me, Friar, tell   105
        me,
    In what vile part of this anatomy
    Doth my name lodge? Tell me, that I may sack

The hateful mansion.

[*He draws a weapon, but is restrained.*]

FRIAR LAURENCE   Hold thy desperate hand
    Art thou a man? Thy form cries out thou art;
    Thy tears are womanish, thy wild acts denote   110
    The unreasonable fury of a beast.
    Unseemly woman in a seeming man,
    And ill-beseeming beast in seeming both!°
    Thou hast amazed me. By my holy order,
    I thought thy disposition better tempered.°   115
    Hast thou slain Tybalt? Wilt thou slay thyself,
    And slay thy lady, that in thy life lives,
    By doing damnèd hate upon thyself?
    Why railest thou on thy birth, the heaven, and
        earth,
    Since birth, and heaven, and earth,° all three   120
        do meet
    In thee at once, which thou at once wouldst
        lose?°
    Fie, fie, thou shamest thy shape, thy love,
        thy wit,°
    Which, like a usurer, abound'st in all,
    And usest none in that true use indeed
    Which should bedeck thy shape, thy love,   125
        thy wit.°
    Thy noble shape is but a form of wax,
    Digressing from the valor of a man;
    Thy dear love sworn but hollow perjury,
    Killing that love which thou hast vowed to
        cherish;
    Thy wit, that ornament to shape and love,   130
    Misshapen° in the conduct° of them both,
    Like powder in a skilless soldier's flask°
    Is set afire by thine own ignorance,
    And thou dismembered with thine own
        defense.°

---

85. woeful sympathy: mutual sharing of grief.   **90. deep an O:** profound groan.   **94. old:** accustomed.   **98. concealed lady:** secret wife.
98. cancelled: rendered void, nullified (legal term).   **101. cries:** exclaims against.   **103. level:** aim.   **112–13. Unseemly . . . both:** Romeo, in
outward appearance ("seeming") a man, is behaving in a manner improper ("Unseemly") even to a woman, and in this mixture ("seeming both") is
a kind of *lusus naturae*, unnatural ("ill-beseeming") even among beasts.   **115. tempered:** balanced.   **120. birth, and heaven, and earth:** i.e.,
nativity and parentage, spiritual part (soul), and physical body.   **121. lose:** i.e., by suicide (105–08) Romeo would damn his soul.   **122. thy shape,
thy love, thy wit:** your form as a man (made in the image of God), your sworn faith to Juliet and your reason or intellect.   **123–25. Which . . . wit:**
Romeo is misusing his natural wealth (shape, love, wit), like a usurer, making it breed unnaturally instead of putting it to natural productive and
beneficial use ("true use").   **131. Misshapen:** wrongly directed (with play on "shape").   **131. conduct:** guidance.   **132. flask:** powder horn.
133–34. Is . . . defence: i.e., your reason ("wit"), which should be your defense (like a soldier's powder), turned to passion ("set afire") through your
misuse of it ("ignorance"), has become the means to destroy you ("thou dismembered").

What, rouse thee, man! Thy Juliet is alive,	135
For whose dear sake thou wast but lately
	dead;°
There art thou happy. Tybalt would° kill thee,
But thou slewest Tybalt; there art thou happy.
The law that threatened death becomes thy
	friend
And turns it to exile; there art thou happy.	140
A pack of blessings light upon thy back,
Happiness courts thee in her best array,
But like a mishavèd and sullen wench
Thou pouts upon thy fortune and thy love.
Take heed, take heed, for such die miserable.	145
Go, get thee to thy love, as was decreed;°
Ascend her chamber; hence and comfort her.
But look thou stay not till the watch be set,°
For then thou canst not pass to Mantua,
Where thou shalt live till we can find a time	150
To blaze° your marriage, reconcile your friends,
Beg pardon of the Prince, and call thee back
With twenty hundred thousand times more joy
Than thou went'st forth in lamentation.
Go before, Nurse. Commend me to thy lady,	155
And bid her hasten all the house to bed,
Which heavy sorrow makes them apt unto.
Romeo is coming.
NURSE O Lord, I could have stayed here all the
	night
To hear good counsel. O, what learning is! —	160
My lord, I'll tell my lady you will come.
ROMEO Do so, and bid my sweet prepare to chide.°
NURSE [*Giving a ring*]
Here, sir, a ring she bid me give you, sir.
Hie you, make haste, for it grows very late.

[*Exit.*]

ROMEO How well my comfort is revived by this!	165
FRIAR LAURENCE Go hence. Good night. And
	here stands all your state:
Either be gone before the watch be set,
Or by the break of day disguised from hence.

Sojourn in Mantua. I'll find out your man,°
And he shall signify from time to time	170
Every good hap to you that chances here.
Give me thy hand. 'Tis late. Farewell, good night.
ROMEO But that a joy past joy calls out on me,
It were a grief so brief° to part with thee.
Farewell.	[*Exeunt separately.*]	175

Scene 4

[*Enter old Capulet, his Wife, and Paris.*]

CAPULET Things have fallen out, sir, so unluckily
That we have had no time to move° our
	daughter.
Look you, she loved her kinsman Tybalt dearly,
And so did I. Well, we were born to die.
'Tis very late. She'll not come down tonight.	5
I promise you, but for your company
I would have been abed an hour ago.
PARIS These times of woe afford no times to woo.
Madam, good night. Commend me to your
	daughter.
WIFE I will, and know her mind early tomorrow.	10
Tonight she's mewed up to her heaviness.°
CAPULET Sir Paris, I will make a desperate
	tender°
Of my child's love. I think she will be ruled
In all respects by me; nay, more, I doubt it not.
Wife, go you to her ere you go to bed.	15
Acquaint her here of my son Paris' love,
And bid her, mark you me, on Wednesday next —
But soft,° what day is this?
PARIS	Monday, my lord.
CAPULET Monday! Ha, ha!° Well, Wednesday is
	too soon;
O' Thursday let it be. O' Thursday, tell her,	20
She shall be married to this noble earl.
Will you be ready? Do you like this haste?
We'll keep no great ado — a friend or two;
For hark you, Tybalt being slain so late,
It may be thought we held him carelessly,	25

---

136. wast but lately dead: i.e., just now tried to kill thyself. **137. would:** wished. **146. decreed:** determined. **148. watch be set:** With the posting of the guard, the city gates would be closed. **151. blaze:** make known, proclaim. **162. chide:** i.e., reprimand him for Tybalt's death. **169. find out your man:** i.e., keep in touch with your personal servant (Balthasar). **174. brief:** hastily. **Act 3, Scene 4. 2. move:** propose the matter to. **11. mewed . . . heaviness:** shut up (literally, caged like a moulting hawk) with her sorrow. **12. desperate tender:** bold offer (implying some risk). **18. soft:** wait a moment. **19. ha, ha!:** i.e., the humming sound one makes while considering something; not laughter.

Being our kinsman, if we revel much.
Therefore we'll have some half a dozen friends,
And there an end. But what say you to
    Thursday?

PARIS My lord, I would that Thursday were
    tomorrow.

CAPULET Well, get you gone. O' Thursday be it,   30
    then.
    [*To his Wife.*] Go you to Juliet ere you go to bed;
    Prepare her, wife, against° this wedding day. —
    Farewell, my lord. — Light to my chamber, ho! —
    Afore me,° it is so very late
    That we may call it early by and by.°   35
    Good night.

                               [*Exeunt.*]

Scene 5

[*Enter Romeo and Juliet aloft at the window.*]

JULIET Wilt thou be gone? It is not yet near day.
It was the nightingale, and not the lark,
That pierced the fearful° hollow of thine ear;
Nightly she sings on yond pomegranate tree.
Believe me, love, it was the nightingale.   5

ROMEO It was the lark, the herald of the morn,
No nightingale. Look, love, what envious streaks
Do lace the severing° clouds in yonder east.
Night's candles° are burnt out, and jocund° day
Stands tiptoe on the misty mountain tops.   10
I must be gone and live, or stay and die.

JULIET Yond light is not daylight, I know it, I.
It is some meteor that the sun exhaled°
To be to thee this night a torchbearer
And light thee on thy way to Mantua.   15
Therefore stay yet. Thou need'st not to be
    gone.

ROMEO Let me be ta'en; let me be put to death.
I am content, so thou wilt have it so.
I'll say yon gray is not the morning's eye;
'Tis but the pale reflex of Cynthia's brow.°   20
Nor that is not the lark whose notes do beat

The vaulty heaven so high above our heads.
I have more care to stay than will to go.
Come, death, and welcome! Juliet wills it so.
How is 't, my soul? Let's talk. It is not day.   25

JULIET It is, it is. Hie hence, begone, away!
It is the lark that sings so out of tune,
Straining harsh discords and unpleasing sharps.
Some say the lark makes sweet division;
This doth not so, for she divideth us.   30
Some say the lark and loathèd toad changed
    eyes;
O, now I would they had changed voices too,
Since arm from arm that voice doth us affray,°
Hunting thee hence with hunt's-up° to the day.
O, now begone! More light and light it grows.   35

ROMEO More light and light, more dark and dark
    our woes!

[*Enter Nurse hastily.*]

NURSE Madam!

JULIET Nurse?

NURSE Your lady mother is coming to your
    chamber.
The day is broke; be wary, look about.   [*Exit.*] 40

JULIET Then window, let day in, and let life out.

ROMEO Farewell, farewell! One kiss, and I'll
    descend.

[*They kiss. He climbs down from the window.*]

JULIET Art thou gone so? Love, lord, ay, husband,
    friend!°
I must hear from thee every day in the hour,
For in a minute there are many days.°   45
O, by this count° I shall be much in years°
Ere I again behold my Romeo!

ROMEO [*From below her window*] Farewell!
I will omit no opportunity
That may convey my greetings, love, to thee.   50

JULIET O, think'st thou we shall ever meet
    again?

ROMEO I doubt it not, and all these woes shall serve
For sweet discourses in our times to come.

---

32. against: in anticipation of.   **34. Afore me:** a mild oath.   **35. by and by:** immediately.   **Act 3, Scene 5. 3. fearful:** timorous (because afraid to hear).   **8. severing:** Streaks of light are parting (1) the clouds, (2) the lovers.   **9. Night's candles:** stars.   **9. jocund:** sprightly, cheerful.   **13. meteor . . . exhaled:** Meteors were believed to be formed by vapors drawn up from the earth by the sun and then ignited.   **20. reflex of Cynthia's brow:** reflection of the moon's (i.e., Cynthia's) face.   **33. affray:** startle (making us separate).   **34. hunt's-up:** a morning song serenading the bride the day after the wedding.   **43. friend:** lover.   **44–45. day . . . days:** i.e., because each minute seems like many days.   **46. count:** method of computation.   **46. much in years:** aged.

These paintings depict the scene when Romeo leaves Juliet for what will be the last time they see each other alive.

What are the similarities and differences in tone among the images? What lines from the play might have inspired the artists to depict the scene in these ways?

JULIET O God, I have an ill-divining° soul!
Methinks I see thee, now thou art so low,   55
As one dead in the bottom of a tomb.
Either my eyesight fails or thou lookest pale.
ROMEO And trust me, love, in my eye so do you.
Dry sorrow drinks our blood.° Adieu, adieu!

[*Exit.*]

JULIET O Fortune, Fortune! All men call thee   60
fickle.
If thou art fickle, what dost thou with him
That is renowned for faith? Be fickle, Fortune.
For then, I hope, thou wilt not keep him long,
But send him back.

[*Enter Mother (Capulet's Wife).*]

WIFE   Ho, daughter, are you up?
JULIET Who is 't that calls? It is my lady   65
mother.
Is she not down so late, or up so early?
What unaccustomed cause procures her
hither? [*She goeth down from the window.*]
WIFE Why, how now, Juliet?
JULIET   Madam I am not well
WIFE Evermore weeping for your cousin's death?
What, wilt thou wash him from his grave with   70
tears?
An if thou couldst, thou couldst not make him
live;
Therefore, have done. Some grief shows much
of love,
But much of grief shows still some want of wit.
JULIET Yet let me weep for such a feeling loss.
WIFE So shall you feel the loss, but not the   75
friend
Which you weep for.
JULIET   Feeling so the loss,
I cannot choose but ever weep the friend.
WIFE Well, girl, thou weep'st not so much for his
death
As that the villain lives which slaughtered him.

JULIET What villain, madam?   80
WIFE   That same villain Romeo
JULIET [*Aside*]
Villain and he be many miles asunder. —
God pardon him! I do, with all my heart;
And yet no man like he doth grieve my heart.
WIFE That is because the traitor murderer lives.
JULIET Ay, madam, from the reach of these my   85
hands.
Would none but I might venge my cousin's
death!
WIFE We will have vengeance for it, fear thou not.
Then weep no more. I'll send to one in
Mantua,
Where that same banished runagate° doth
live,
Shall give him such an unaccustomed dram°   90
That he shall soon keep Tybalt company.°
And then, I hope, thou wilt be satisfied.
JULIET Indeed, I never shall be satisfied
With Romeo till I behold him — dead —
Is my poor heart so for a kinsman vexed.   95
Madam, if you could find out but a man
To bear a poison, I would temper° it,
That Romeo should, upon receipt thereof,
Soon sleep in quiet. O, how my heart abhors
To hear him named, and cannot come to   100
him
To wreak the love° I bore my cousin
Upon his body that hath slaughtered him!
WIFE Find thou the means, and I'll find such a
man.
But now I'll tell thee joyful tidings, girl.
JULIET And joy comes well in such a needy time.°   105
What are they, beseech your ladyship?
WIFE Well, well, thou hast a careful° father, child,
One who, to put thee from thy heaviness,
Hath sorted out° a sudden° day of joy
That thou expects not, nor I looked not for.   110
JULIET Madam, in happy time, what day is that?

---

54. ill-divining: intuitively anticipating evil. **59. Dry . . . blood:** It was believed that each sigh took a drop of blood from the heart and hence shortened life. **89. runagate** fugitive, renegade. **90. unaccustomed dram:** unusual draught (of poisoned liquor). **91. company:** i.e., in death. **97. temper:** mix, compound. **101. wreak the love:** (1) avenge the love (for Tybalt), (2) bestow the love (on Romeo). **105. needy time:** time that stands in need of (joy). **107. careful:** solicitous (for your good). **109. sorted out:** selected, appointed. **109. sudden:** speedy, coming quickly.

WIFE Marry, my child, early next Thursday morn,
The gallant, young, and noble gentleman,
The County Paris, at Saint Peter's Church
Shall happily make thee there a joyful bride. 115

JULIET Now, by Saint Peter's Church, and Peter too,
He shall not make me there a joyful bride!
I wonder at this haste, that I must wed
Ere he that should be husband comes to woo.
I pray you, tell my lord and father, madam, 120
I will not marry yet, and when I do I swear
It shall be Romeo, whom you know I hate,
Rather than Paris. These are news indeed!

WIFE Here comes your father. Tell him so yourself,
And see how he will take it at your hands. 125

[*Enter Capulet and Nurse.*]

CAPULET When the sun sets, the earth doth drizzle dew,°
But for the sunset of my brother's son
It rains downright.°
How now, a conduit,° girl? What, still in tears?
Evermore showering? In one little body 130
Thou counterfeits a bark, a sea, a wind;
For still thy eyes, which I may call the sea,
Do ebb and flow with tears; the bark thy body is,
Sailing in this salt flood; the winds, thy sighs,
Who, raging with thy tears, and they with them, 135
Without a sudden calm,° will overset
Thy tempest-tossèd body. — How now, wife?
Have you delivered to her our decree?

WIFE Ay, sir, but she will none, she gives you thanks.°
I would the fool were married to her grave! 140

CAPULET Soft, take me with you,° take me with you, wife.
How? Will she none? Doth she not give us thanks?
Is she not proud? Doth she not count her blest,

This is a photograph of a marble sculpture by Auguste Rodin of Romeo and Juliet.

How does his sculpture capture some aspect of their love?

Bogdanova, Tamara/SuperStock

Unworthy as she is, that we have wrought°
So worthy a gentleman to be her bride? 145

JULIET Not proud you have, but thankful that you have.
Proud can I never be of what I hate,
But thankful even for hate that is meant love.

CAPULET How, how, how, how, chopt-logic?°
What is this?
"Proud," and "I thank you," and "I thank you 150
not,"

---

126. earth doth drizzle dew: earth sheds fine spray-like drops. Shakespeare imagines the earth weeping at the death of the sun (= sunset).
128. It rains downright: i.e., there is an absolute flood (of tears from Juliet). **129. conduit:** fountain. Conduits were often made in the form of human figures. **136. Without a sudden calm:** unless you quickly cease weeping and sighing and calm down. **139. will . . . thanks:** refuses the "decree," thank you very much (i.e., Juliet answers sarcastically). **141. take . . . you:** let me understand you. **144. wrought:** persuaded.
149. chopt-logic: (1) sophistical argument, (2) one who argues sophistically.

This is Capulet, Juliet's father, in the 1996 film adaptation at the moment when he orders Juliet to marry Paris.

How do the actor's gestures and facial expresssions, as well as the costumes and staging help to communicate Capulet's state of mind in this scene?

Moviestore Collection Ltd/Alamy

And yet "not proud"? Mistress minion,° you,
Thank me no thankings, nor proud me no
    prouds,
But fettle° your fine joints 'gainst Thursday
    next
To go with Paris to Saint Peter's Church,
Or I will drag thee on a hurdle° thither.   155
Out, you greensickness carrion!° Out, you
    baggage!°
You tallow-face!
WIFE [*To Capulet*] Fie, fie! What, are you mad?
JULIET [*Kneeling*]
    Good father, I beseech you on my knees,
    Hear me with patience but to speak a word.
CAPULET Hang thee, young baggage, disobedient 160
    wretch!
I tell thee what: get thee to church o' Thursday
Or never after look me in the face.
Speak not, reply not, do not answer me!
My fingers itch. Wife, we scarce thought us blest
That God had lent us but this only child;   165
But now I see this one is one too much,
And that we have a curse in having her.
Out on her, hilding!
NURSE   God in heaven bless her!
You are to blame, my lord, to rate° her so.

CAPULET And why, my Lady Wisdom? Hold   170
    your tongue,
Good Prudence. Smatter° with your gossips, go.
NURSE I speak no treason.
CAPULET   O, God-i-goden!°
NURSE May not one speak?
CAPULET   Peace you mumbling fool!
Utter your gravity° o'er a gossip's bowl,
For here we need it not.   175
WIFE   You are too hot.
CAPULET God's bread,° it makes me mad!
Day, night, hour, tide, time, work, play,
Alone, in company, still my care hath been
To have her matched. And having now
    provided
A gentleman of noble parentage,   180
Of fair demesnes,° youthful, and nobly
    ligned,°
Stuffed, as they say, with honorable parts,°
Proportioned as one's thought would wish a
    man—
And then to have a wretched puling fool,°
A whining mammet, in her fortune's tender,° 185
To answer, "I'll not wed, I cannot love,
I am too young; I pray you, pardon me."

---

151. Mistress minion: madam spoiled darling. **153. fettle:** make ready, prepare (a stable term carried on in "fine joints"). **155. hurdle:** flat frame on which traitors were drawn through the streets to execution. **156. green-sickness carrion:** someone as pale as a corpse. **156. baggage:** good-for-nothing. **169. rate:** berate. **171. smatter:** prate, chatter. **172. God-i-goden:** exclamation of annoyance. **174. gravity:** wise advice (ironic). **176. God's bread:** an oath by the body (= "bread") of God. **181. demesnes:** estates (by inheritance). **181. nobly ligned:** descended, by line, from noble forebears. **182. parts:** qualities. **184. puling fool:** crying, whining child. **185. in her fortune's tender:** at the moment when fortune offers you a gift ("tender").

But, an you will not wed, I'll pardon you.
Graze where you will, you shall not house with
   me.
Look to 't, think on 't. I do not use to jest.   190
Thursday is near. Lay hand on heart; advise.°
An you be mine, I'll give you to my friend;
An you be not, hang, beg, starve, die in the
   streets,
For, by my soul, I'll ne'er acknowledge thee,
Nor what is mine shall never do thee good.   195
Trust to 't, bethink you. I'll not be forsworn.

                  [*Exit.*]

JULIET Is there no pity sitting in the clouds
   That sees into the bottom of my grief?
   O sweet my Mother, cast me not away!
   Delay this marriage for a month, a week;   200
   Or if you do not, make the bridal bed
   In that dim monument where Tybalt lies.
WIFE Talk not to me, for I'll not speak a word.
   Do as thou wilt, for I have done with thee.

                  [*Exit.*]

JULIET O God! — O Nurse, how shall this be   205
   prevented?
   My husband is on earth, my faith in heaven.
   How shall that faith return again to earth,
   Unless that husband send it me from heaven
   By leaving earth? Comfort me, counsel me.
   Alack, alack, that heaven should practice   210
   strategems
   Upon so soft° a subject as myself!
   What sayst thou? Hast thou not a word of joy?
   Some comfort, Nurse.
NURSE   Faith, here it is.
   Romeo is banished, and all the world to nothing°
   That he dares ne'er come back to challenge   215
   you,°
   Or if he do, it needs must be by stealth.
   Then, since the case so stands as now it doth,
   I think it best you married with the County.
   O, he's a lovely gentleman!
   Romeo's a dishclout to° him. An eagle, madam,   220
   Hath not so green,° so quick,° so fair an eye
   As Paris hath. Beshrew my very heart,

Andrew_Howe/E+/Getty Images

This engraving captures the scene when Juliet
refuses her father's order to marry Paris.

**How does the artist depict Juliet and the
other characters, and how does the artist
illustrate the conflict between them?**

   I think you are happy in this second match,
   For it excels your first; or if it did not,
   Your first is dead — or 'twere as good he were   225
   As living° here and you no use of him.
JULIET Speak'st thou from thy heart?
NURSE And from my soul too. Else beshrew them
   both.
JULIET Amen!
NURSE What?   230
JULIET Well, thou hast comforted me marvelous
   much.
   Go in, and tell my lady I am gone,
   Having displeased my father, to Laurence' cell
   To make confession and to be absolved.
NURSE Marry, I will; and this is wisely done.   235

                  [*Exit.*]

---

191. Lay . . . advise: consider deeply, take counsel (within yourself).   **211. soft:** (1) gentle, tenderhearted; (2) weak, impressionable.   **214. all . . .
nothing:** all odds against none.   **215. challenge you:** claim you as his.   **220. dishclout to:** dishrag by comparison with.   **221. green:** Green eyes
were considered especially admirable and rare.   **221. quick:** lively, keen. Eagles were known for the extraordinary keenness of their sight.
226. living: i.e., you living.

JULIET Ancient damnation! O most wicked fiend!
  Is it more sin to wish me thus forsworn,
  Or to dispraise my lord with that same tongue
  Which she hath praised him with above
    compare
  So many thousand times? Go, counselor,   240

Thou and my bosom henceforth shall be
    twain.°
I'll to the Friar to know his remedy.
If all else fail, myself have power to die.

[*Exit.*]

---

241. twain: separated, estranged.

extending beyond the text

Most scholars believe that Shakespeare wrote this play between 1594 and 1596, and that the play reflects the views of that time regarding marriage. And yet in 1690, less than 100 years later, British philosopher John Locke presented some fairly radical ideas about marriage. Read the following excerpt from his writing on the subject.

from Second Treatise of Civil Government

John Locke

Conjugal society is made by a voluntary compact between man and woman, . . . leaves the wife in the full and free possession of what by contract is her peculiar right, and gives the husband no more power over her life than she has over his; the power of the husband being so far from that of an absolute monarch, that the wife has in many cases a liberty to separate from him, where natural right, or their contract allows it; whether that contract be made by themselves in the state of nature, or by the customs or laws of the country they live in; and the children upon such separation fall to the father or mother's lot, as such contract does determine. ■

Summarize Locke's view on the ideal relationship between marriage partners. To what extent do you believe that it reflects or contradicts the views of the characters in *Romeo and Juliet*?

Understanding and Interpreting

1. In the exchange between Mercutio, Tybalt, and Benvolio before Romeo arrives (Act 3, Scene 1), each of the three men displays his character traits clearly. Explain how each behaves in lines 35–61, and identify a line that clearly illustrates his character.

2. Mercutio's death in Act 3, Scene 1 begins a series of events that culminates in the deaths of Romeo and Juliet. How does the line "a plague o' both your houses" signal a significant turning point in the play?

3. After Mercutio's death, Romeo says, "My reputation stained / with Tybalt's slander . . . / O sweet Juliet, thy beauty hath made me effeminate, / And in my temper soften valor's steel" (Act 3, Scene 1, ll. 120–124). Explain what Romeo means by this, and explain how this illustrates a change in Romeo's character from what we have seen so far.

4. What does Romeo mean when he says, "O, I am fortune's fool" (Act 3, Scene 1, l. 145)?

5. Why does the Prince likely make the decision to spare Romeo, according to the text in Act 3, Scene 1? How do Capulet's wife and Montague attempt to influence the Prince's decision?

6. Explain how Juliet is feeling at the beginning of Act 3, Scene 2 before the arrival of the Nurse. What evidence from the text helps you draw this interpretation?

7. It takes the Nurse a long time to actually tell Juliet clearly what happened with Tybalt and Romeo in Act 3, Scene 2, leading to a lot of confusion. Why does she do this? Write an interpretative statement about the Nurse's character and describe a few acting choices that the two actors could make onstage to help communicate their emotions and the confusion of this scene.

8. The Nurse says, "Tybalt, the best friend I had! O courteous . . . honest gentleman!" (Act 3, Scene 2, ll. 61–62). How does her impression of Tybalt compare to other people's characterization of him and from what we have seen in the play? In what ways should Tybalt be seen as a "gentleman"?

9. While Juliet's first reaction in Act 3, Scene 2 is to be angry at Romeo for killing Tybalt, her anger does not last long. What causes her to change her feelings, and what does this illustrate about her character?

10. What is Romeo's reaction to hearing he has been banished from Verona in Act 3, Scene 3? What reasons does he offer for his reaction to the news?

11. Summarize a few of the reasons that Friar Laurence gives to persuade Romeo not to kill himself (Act 3, Scene 3, ll. 108–154).

12. The last time that we saw Capulet talk to Paris about Juliet, he made it clear that Juliet would have to consent to the marriage. What has changed here in Act 3, Scene 4? What may have led to this change in Capulet's course of action?

13. At the beginning of Act 3, Scene 5, Juliet thinks the birdsong she hears is that of a nightingale, but Romeo knows it's the lark. Soon after, however, Juliet realizes her mistake and acknowledges it is the lark, the sign of morning when Romeo needs to leave, which Romeo then denies. Look back at how each of them responds to the birdsong and explain what their reactions reveal about their characters.

14. Explain what Juliet means when she says, "Then window, let day in, and let life out" (Act 3, Scene 5, l. 41).

15. In Act 3, Scene 5, who is more optimistic about their future, Romeo or Juliet? How do you know? Explain whether or not the attitudes they convey here are consistent with their attitudes in previous scenes.

16. In Act 3, Scene 5, lines 60–64, Juliet addresses Fortune directly. Explain what she is asking of Fortune.

17. Reread what Juliet's mother says in Act 3, Scene 5, lines 87–92. Explain what she is planning and how it might influence Juliet's actions later in this scene.

18. In Act 3, Scene 5, Capulet seems like an entirely different character in comparison to his earlier appearances in this play. What has changed, and what might be causing his anger? What can you infer about Juliet's mother from her actions, inactions, and dialogue in this scene?

19. Once her parents leave, Juliet turns to the Nurse and asks for "a word of joy . . . some comfort" (Act 3, Scene 5, ll. 212–213). What advice does she receive from the Nurse, and why might the Nurse say this?

20. Act 3, Scene 5, lines 236–243 represent a significant change for Juliet. Explain what these lines signify for her at this point in the play and how they represent a change in character.

Analyzing Language, Style, and Structure

21. **Vocabulary in Context.** In Act 3, Scene 1, lines 50–55, Mercutio and Tybalt use the word *consort* in multiple ways. What is implied in its use here, and what are other uses of the word?

22. **Vocabulary in Context.** In Act 3, Scene 4, line 25, Capulet says he doesn't want people saying of Tybalt that they "held him carelessly." How is *carelessly* used in this context, and how is the word used differently today?

23. **Vocabulary in Context.** Several times in Act 3, Scene 5, both Juliet and Capulet use the word *proud*. What is the meaning of the word in this context, and what are other meanings of the word?

24. Without Romeo around to tease at the beginning of Act 3, Scene 1, Mercutio turns his wit on Benvolio. Identify and summarize one or more jokes that he makes at Benvolio's expense. Based on what you know about Benvolio, are Mercutio's jokes about him accurate or not?

25. When Tybalt confronts Romeo in Act 3, Scene 1, it is a moment of dramatic irony, since the reader/viewer knows things about the situation that some of the characters do not. Identify what causes the dramatic irony and explain how the characters, especially Mercutio, Tybalt, and Romeo, react differently based on the knowledge they have at the time.

26. Shakespeare provides little in the way of stage directions for the fight scene in Act 3, Scene 1, stating simply "They fight" (l. 92). Based on the dialogue and the reactions of characters, write an interpretative statement about a possible tone of the fight, then describe some of the acting choices you might suggest in the first fight between Mercutio and Tybalt to communicate that tone. Does the tone change during the second fight between Tybalt and Romeo? What staging choices would you include for the second fight? What textual evidence from the play leads you to your choices?

27. Mercutio has been a joker through much of the play so far, and his speech in Act 3, Scene 1 before dying is no exception, so much so that his imminent death is not taken seriously by Romeo and Benvolio at first. Reread lines 103–112 and explain the puns he is making about his own death.

28. After Tybalt's death in Act 3, Scene 1, the Prince conducts a sort of trial to determine responsibility, with Benvolio offering the majority of the testimony. Although Capulet's wife says of Benvolio, "He is a kinsman to the Montague / Affection makes him false; he speaks not true" (Act 3, Scene 1, ll. 185–186), reread Benvolio's testimony in lines 161–184 and analyze his diction choices and use of evidence to determine whether his affiliation with the Montagues has, in fact, skewed his testimony.

29. Act 3, Scene 2 begins with another instance of dramatic irony, in which the audience is aware of the events that Juliet is not. What is a possible intended effect that the placement of this scene has on the audience?

30. In her speech in Act 3, Scene 2, lines 1–31, Juliet directly calls the night, but she describes the night in many different ways. Closely examine different words or phrases she uses to characterize the night, and explain what these choices reveal about her tone in this scene.

31. Beginning with "O serpent heart, hid with flowering face!" (Act 3, Scene 2, l. 73) through line 85, Juliet describes Romeo once she learns he killed Tybalt. What do you notice about the juxtaposition of words she uses for Romeo? How does her word choice reflect her tone toward Romeo at this point in the play?

32. Explain the metaphor that Romeo uses when he says, "I have stained the childhood of our joy / With blood removed but little from her own" (Act 3, Scene 3, ll. 95–96).

33. In Act 3, Scene 4, Capulet is trying to speedily set a wedding date for Juliet and Paris, without seeming hasty or inappropriately uncaring regarding the recent death of Tybalt. How does Capulet's language in this scene reflect these tensions?

34. Throughout Act 3, Scene 5, Romeo and Juliet debate whether the birdsong they hear is that of a nightingale or a lark. Reread descriptions of both birds and explain how their tone toward each bird is reflected in their language choices.

35. Juliet is extremely clever and a quick thinker, especially in Act 3, Scene 5 when she has to speak to her mother about Tybalt's death without lying to her as she talks about Romeo. Closely examine the dialogue in that exchange (Act 3, Scene 5, ll. 74–102), and explain how carefully Juliet chooses her words in order to create multiple meanings.

36. Look back carefully at the language that Juliet's parents use toward her after she says she will not marry Paris (Act 3, Scene 5, ll. 149–204). How does the diction reflect a specific tone they have toward her?

Topics for Composing

37. **Analysis.** Romeo says, "O, I am fortune's fool" (Act 3, Scene 1, l. 145) after killing Tybalt. Identify and explain the role that fate has played in Romeo's and Juliet's lives so far. To what extent do they seem to be controlled by forces larger than themselves?

38. **Analysis.** A "foil" in literature is a character whose traits reveal or amplify significant traits of another character, usually through contrast. Explain how Mercutio is a foil for Romeo.

39. **Analysis.** Act 3, Scene 5 is the last time Romeo and Juliet see each other alive. With this knowledge, reread the scene and write a response highlighting any foreshadowing of this fact in Shakespeare's language choices.

40. **Argument.** Was the Prince's judgment to banish rather than execute Romeo a fair one based on the time period and conditions as described in the play? In a contemporary courtroom, what might have happened to Romeo? Why? Write a response in which you make a claim and support your argument with evidence from the play.

41. **Connections.** Juliet has a significant fight with her parents about their expectations for her. Write about a time when your expectations for yourself differed from someone else's ideas about the direction your life should take. What was the nature of the disagreement? And what was the outcome?

42. **Research.** Banishment from the city of Verona seems like a big deal in the play, so much so that Romeo considers it barely better than death. Research what cities such as Verona were like in Italy during the Middle Ages, and explain why banishment might have seemed like such a terrible punishment.

43. **Creative Writing.** Rewrite Benvolio's speech about the events of the fight as if it were told from the point of view of a Capulet. Analyze what changed and why.

44. **Multimodal.** Events move very quickly in this play. Create a timeline or a calendar that shows when and about what time the significant events in the play occur.

ACT 4

Scene 1

[*Enter Friar Laurence and County Paris.*]

FRIAR LAURENCE On Thursday, sir? The time is
 very short.

PARIS My father Capulet will have it so,
 And I am nothing slow° to slack his haste.

FRIAR LAURENCE You say you do not know the
 lady's mind?
 Uneven is the course.° I like it not.   5

PARIS Immoderately she weeps for Tybalt's
 death,
 And therefore have I little talked of love,
 For Venus smiles not in a house of tears.
 Now, sir, her father counts it dangerous
 That she do give her sorrow so much sway,   10
 And in his wisdom hastes our marriage
 To stop the inundation of her tears,
 Which, too much minded by herself alone,°
 May be put from her by society.°
 Now do you know the reason of this haste.   15

FRIAR LAURENCE [*Aside*]
 I would I knew not why it should be slowed. —
 Look, sir, here comes the lady toward my cell.

 [*Enter Juliet.*]

PARIS Happily met, my lady and my wife!

JULIET That may be, sir, when I may be a wife.

PARIS That "may be" must be, love, on Thursday   20
 next.

JULIET What must be shall be.

FRIAR LAURENCE   That's a certain text

PARIS Come you to make confession to this father?

JULIET To answer that, I should confess to you.

PARIS Do not deny to him that you love me.

JULIET I will confess to you that I love him.   25

PARIS So will ye, I am sure, that you love me.

JULIET If I do so, it will be of more price,°
 Being spoke behind your back, than to your face.

PARIS Poor soul, thy face is much abused with
 tears.

JULIET The tears have got small victory by that,   30
 For it was bad enough before their spite.

PARIS Thou wrong'st it more than tears with that
 report.

JULIET That is no slander, sir, which is a truth;
 And what I spake, I spake it to my face.°

PARIS Thy face is mine, and thou hast slandered it. 35

JULIET It may be so, for it is not mine own. —
 Are you at leisure, holy Father, now,
 Or shall I come to you at evening Mass?

FRIAR LAURENCE My leisure serves me, pensive°
 daughter, now.
 My lord, we must entreat the time alone.   40

PARIS God shield° I should disturb devotion!
 Juliet, on Thursday early will I rouse ye.
 Till then, adieu, and keep this holy kiss. [*Exit.*]

JULIET O, shut the door! And when thou hast
 done so,
 Come weep with me — past hope, past cure,   45
 past help!

FRIAR LAURENCE Ah, Juliet, I already know thy
 grief;
 It strains me past the compass of my wits.°
 I hear thou must, and nothing may prorogue° it,
 On Thursday next be married to this county.

JULIET Tell me not, Friar, that thou hearest of this, 50
 Unless thou tell me how I may prevent it.
 If in thy wisdom thou canst give no help,
 Do thou but call my resolution wise
 And with this knife° I'll help it° presently.°

 [*She shows a knife.*]

 God joined my heart and Romeo's, thou our   55
 hands;
 And ere this hand, by thee to Romeo's sealed,°

Act 4, Scene 1.   **3. nothing slow:** in no way reluctant.   **5. Uneven is the course:** The manner of proceeding is inequitable (i.e., one-sided).
13. too . . . alone: too mind-consuming when she is without company.   **14. society:** companionship.   **27. more price:** greater worth.
34. to my face: (1) openly, (2) about my face.   **39 pensive:** sad, mournful.   **41. shield:** forbid.   **47. strains . . . wits:** forces me beyond the limits
of my power to think clearly.   **48. prorogue:** postpone, delay.   **54. knife:** Elizabethan ladies sometimes wore small household knives at their
girdles.   **54. it:** i.e., the intolerable situation, not her "resolution" (53).   **54. presently:** immediately.   **56. sealed:** contracted.

Shall be the label to another deed,
Or my true heart with treacherous revolt
Turn to another, this shall slay them both.
Therefore, out of thy long-experienced time,° 60
Give me some present counsel, or, behold,
Twixt my extremes° and me this bloody knife
Shall play the umpire, arbitrating that
Which the commission° of thy years and art°
Could to no issue of true honor bring. 65
Be not so long° to speak; I long to die
If what thou speak'st speak not of remedy.

FRIAR LAURENCE Hold, daughter. I do spy a kind
    of hope,
Which craves as desperate an execution
As that is desperate which we would prevent. 70
If, rather than to marry County Paris,
Thou hast the strength of will to slay thyself,
Then is it likely thou wilt undertake
A thing like death to chide away this shame,
That cop'st° with Death himself to scape 75
    from it;
And if thou darest, I'll give thee remedy.

JULIET O, bid me leap, rather than marry Paris,
From off the battlements of any tower,
Or walk in thievish ways, or bid me lurk
Where serpents are; chain me with roaring 80
    bears,
Or hide me nightly in a charnel-house,°
O'ercovered quite with dead men's rattling
    bones,
With reeky° shanks and yellow chopless°
    skulls;
Or bid me go into a new-made grave
And hide me with a dead man in his tomb — 85
Things that, to hear them told, have made me
    tremble —
And I will do it without fear or doubt,
To live an unstained wife to my sweet love.

FRIAR LAURENCE Hold, then. Go home, be
    merry, give consent
To marry Paris. Wednesday is tomorrow. 90

This is a photograph of a ballet version of *Romeo and Juliet*, specifically the scene in which Friar Laurence offers Juliet the potion.

Explain what the costumes, props, and acting choices illustrate about the characters and their conflicts.

Danilo Moroni/Alamy

Tomorrow night look that thou lie alone;
Let not the Nurse lie with thee in thy chamber.
Take thou this vial, being then in bed,

[*Showing her a vial*]

And this distilling liquor drink thou off,
When presently through all thy veins shall run 95
A cold and drowsy humor;° for no pulse
Shall keep his native progress, but surcease;°
No warmth, no breath shall testify thou livest;
The roses in thy lips and cheeks shall fade
To wanny° ashes, thy eyes' windows fall° 100
Like death when he shuts up the day of life;
Each part, deprived of supple government,°

---

60. long-experienced time: i.e., the wisdom of age. **62. extremes:** desperate straits. **64. commission:** authority, warrant. **64. art:** skill derived from experience and knowledge. **66. long:** slow ("long" here chosen for the following quibble on "long to die"). **75. cop'st:** (art willing) to deal or encounter. **81. charnel-house:** a small building attached to a church containing the bones of those whose graves have been dug up to make way for new burials. **83. reeky:** emitting a strong and disagreeable fume or smell, used adjectivally. **83. chopless:** lacking the lower jaw. **96. A cold and drowsy humour:** a fluid ("humour") inducing cold and drowsiness. **97. his . . . surcease:** its natural movement, but cease. **100. wanny:** pale. **100. eyes' windows fall:** eyelids close. **102. supple government:** control of muscular movement.

This is an image from a 2013 film version of *Romeo and Juliet*.

If you knew nothing of the action of the play, what might you infer about the characters and the conflict depicted in this scene? What lines from Act 4, Scene 1 do you think are being delivered at the moment shown in this image?

Moviestore Collection Ltd/Alamy

Shall, stiff and stark° and cold, appear like death.
And in this borrowed likeness of shrunk death
Thou shalt continue two-and-forty hours,   105
And then awake as from a pleasant sleep.
Now, when the bridegroom in the morning comes
To rouse thee from thy bed,° there art thou dead.
Then, as the manner of our country is,
In thy best robes uncovered on the bier   110
Thou shalt be borne to that same ancient vault
Where all the kindred of the Capulets lie.
In the meantime, against° thou shalt awake,
Shall Romeo by my letters know our drift,°
And hither shall he come; and he and I   115
Will watch thy waking, and that very night
Shall Romeo bear thee hence to Mantua.
And this shall free thee from this present shame,
If no inconstant toy nor womanish fear
Abate thy valor in the acting it.   120

JULIET [*Taking the vial*]
Give me, give me! O, tell not me of fear!

FRIAR LAURENCE Hold, get you gone. Be strong and prosperous
In this resolve. I'll send a friar with speed
To Mantua, with my letters to thy lord.

JULIET Love give me strength, and strength shall   125
help afford.
Farewell, dear Father!   [*Exeunt separately.*]

Scene 2

[*Enter Father Capulet, Mother* (*Capulet's Wife*), *Nurse, and Servingmen, two or three.*]

CAPULET So many guests invite as here are writ.

[*Exit one or two Servingmen.*]

Sirrah, go hire me twenty cunning cooks.

SERVINGMAN You shall have none ill, sir, for I'll try if they can lick their fingers.

CAPULET How canst thou try them so?   5

SERVINGMAN Marry, sir, 'tis an ill cook that cannot lick his own fingers; therefore he that cannot lick his fingers goes not with me.

CAPULET Go, begone.   [*Exit Servingman.*] 10
We shall be much unfurnished for this time.°
What, is my daughter gone to Friar Laurence?

NURSE Ay, forsooth.

CAPULET Well, he may chance to do some good on her.
A peevish self-willed harlotry° it is.   15

[*Enter Juliet.*]

NURSE See where she comes from shrift with merry look.

CAPULET How now, my headstrong, where have you been gadding?

---

103. stark: rigid; essentially "stiff."   **107–108. bridegroom . . . bed:** It was customary for the bridegroom to serenade the bride early in the morning on the wedding day.   **113. against:** in anticipation of the time when.   **114. drift:** purpose.   **Act 4, Scene 2.**   **11. this time:** i.e., the wedding festivities (then planned for Thursday).   **15. harlotry:** silly girl.

JULIET Where I have learned me to repent the sin
  Of disobedient opposition
  To you and your behests, and am enjoined   20
  By holy Laurence to fall prostrate here,

                [Kneeling]

  To beg your pardon. Pardon, I beseech you!
  Henceforward I am ever ruled by you.
CAPULET Send for the County! Go tell him of this.
  I'll have this knot knit up tomorrow morning.° 25
JULIET I met the youthful lord at Laurence' cell
  And gave him what becomèd love I might,
  Not stepping o'er the bounds of modesty.
CAPULET Why, I am glad on 't. This is well.
  Stand up.   *[Juliet rises.]*
  This is as 't should be. Let me see the County; 30
  Ay, marry, go, I say, and fetch him hither.
  Now, afore God, this reverend holy friar,
  All our whole city is much bound to him.
JULIET Nurse, will you go with me into my closet
  To help me sort such needful ornaments   35
  As you think fit to furnish me tomorrow?
WIFE No, not till Thursday. There is time enough.
CAPULET Go, Nurse, go with her. We'll to church
  tomorrow.   *[Exeunt Juliet and Nurse.]*
WIFE We shall be short in our provision.
  'Tis now near night.   40
CAPULET   Tush, I will stir about,
  And all things shall be well, I warrant thee, wife.
  Go thou to Juliet, help to deck up her.
  I'll not to bed tonight. Let me alone.
  I'll play the huswife for this once. — What ho! —
  They are all forth. Well, I will walk myself 45
  To County Paris, to prepare up him
  Against tomorrow. My heart is wondrous light,
  Since this same wayward girl is so reclaimed.

                [Exeunt.]

Scene 3

[Enter Juliet and Nurse.]

JULIET Ay, those attires are best. But, gentle
  Nurse,
  I pray thee, leave me to myself tonight;

For I have need of many orisons
To move the heavens to smile upon my state,
Which, well thou knowest, is cross° and full of 5
  sin.

[Enter Mother (Capulet's Wife).]

WIFE What, are you busy, ho? Need you my help?
JULIET No, madam, we have culled° such
  necessaries
As are behoveful° for our state° tomorrow.
So please you, let me now be left alone,
And let the Nurse this night sit up with you,   10
For I am sure you have your hands full all
In this so sudden business.
WIFE   Good night.
Get thee to bed and rest, for thou hast need.

    [Exeunt Capulet's Wife and Nurse.]

JULIET Farewell! God knows when we shall meet
  again.
I have a faint cold° fear thrills° through my   15
  veins
That almost freezes up the heat of life.
I'll call them back again to comfort me.
Nurse! — What should she do here?
My dismal° scene I needs must act alone.
Come, vial.   *[She takes out the vial.]* 20
What if this mixture do not work at all?
Shall I be married then tomorrow morning?
No, no, this shall forbid it. Lie thou there.

[She lays down a dagger.]

What if it be a poison which the Friar
Subtly° hath ministered to have me dead,   25
Lest in this marriage he should be dishonored
Because he married me before to Romeo?
I fear it is; and yet methinks it should not,
For he hath still been tried° a holy man.
How if, when I am laid into the tomb,   30
I wake before the time that Romeo
Come to redeem me? There's a fearful point!
Shall I not then be stifled in the vault,
To whose foul mouth no healthsome air
  breathes in,

---

25. tomorrow morning: Capulet changes the marriage day to Wednesday, a sudden change that will have fatal consequences.   **Act 4, Scene 3.**
5. cross: contrary to my desire, unfavorable.   **7. culled:** picked out.   **8. behoveful:** needful, fitting.   **8. state:** social degree.   **15. faint cold:** causing faintness and coldness.   **15. thrills:** pierces, shivers.   **19. dismal:** (1) fatal, (2) full of dread, (3) miserable.   **25. Subtly:** cunningly, craftily.   **29. tried:** tested, proved.

And there die strangled ere my Romeo comes?   35
Or, if I live, is it not very like,
The horrible conceit of° death and night,
Together with the terror of the place —
As in a vault, an ancient receptacle,
Where for this many hundred years the bones   40
Of all my buried ancestors are packed;
Where bloody Tybalt, yet but green in earth,°
Lies festering in his shroud; where, as they say,
At some hours in the night spirits resort —
Alack, alack, is it not like that I,   45
So early waking, what with loathsome smells,
And shrieks like mandrakes'° torn out of the
   earth,

That living mortals, hearing them, run mad —
O, if I wake, shall I not be distraught,
Environèd° with all these hideous fears,   50
And madly play with my forefathers' joints,
And pluck the mangled Tybalt from his shroud,
And in this rage, with some great kinsman's bone
As with a club dash out my desperate brains?
O, look! Methinks I see my cousin's ghost   55
Seeking out Romeo, that did spit his body
Upon a rapier's point. Stay, Tybalt, stay!
Romeo, Romeo, Romeo! Here's drink — I drink
   to thee.

[*She drinks and falls upon her bed, within the
curtains.*]

Donald Cooper/Alamy

Donald Cooper/Alamy

BHE FILMS/DINO DE LAURENTIIS CINEMATOGRAFICA/VERONA
PROD/Ronald Grant Archive/Alamy

Here are three different depictions of the moment
at which Juliet decides to take the potion that Friar
Laurence gave her.

**How do the set, costume, and acting choices
illustrate Juliet's mindset at this particular time?
In what ways are these three depictions similar
and different?**

---

37. conceit of: conception induced by the thought of.   **42. green in earth:** freshly buried.   **47. mandrakes':** The mandrake plant (mandragola)
was believed to be generated from the droppings of dead bodies at the gallows' foot, to resemble a man because of its bifurcated foot, and to shriek as
it was pulled out of the earth. To hear the mandrake's shriek was supposed to cause either death or madness.   **50. Environèd:** surrounded.

Scene 4

[*Enter Lady of the House (Capulet's Wife) and Nurse.*]

WIFE Hold, take these keys, and fetch more
    spices, Nurse.

NURSE They call for dates and quinces in the
    pastry.°

[*Enter old Capulet.*]

CAPULET Come, stir, stir, stir! The second cock°
    hath crowed.
    The curfew bell° hath rung; 'tis three o'clock.
    Look to the baked meats, good Angelica.   5
    Spare not for cost.

NURSE   Go, you cot-quean,° go,
    Get you to bed. Faith, you'll be sick tomorrow
    For this night's watching.°

CAPULET No, not a whit. What, I have watched
    ere now
    All night for lesser cause, and ne'er been sick.   10

WIFE Ay, you have been a mouse-hunt° in your
    time,
    But I will watch you from such watching now.

[*Exeunt Lady and Nurse.*]

CAPULET A jealous hood, a jealous hood!

[*Enter three or four Servingmen with spits and logs, and baskets.*]

    Now, fellow, what is there?

FIRST SERVINGMAN Things for the cook, sir, but I   15
    know not what.

CAPULET Make haste, make haste. [*Exit First
    Servingman.*] Sirrah, fetch drier logs.
    Call Peter. He will show thee where they are.

SECOND SERVINGMAN I have a head, sir, that will
    find out logs
    And never trouble Peter for the matter.

CAPULET Mass,° and well said. A merry   20
    whoreson, ha!

Thou shalt be loggerhead.° [*Exit Servingman.*]
    Good faith, 'tis day.
The County will be here with music straight,°
For so he said he would. I hear him near.

[*Play music within.*]

Nurse! Wife! What ho! What, Nurse, I say!
Enter Nurse.

Go waken Juliet, go and trim her up.   25
I'll go and chat with Paris. Hie, make haste,
Make haste. The bridegroom he is come
    already.
Make haste, I say.

[*Exit Capulet.*]

Scene 5

[*The Nurse goes to the bed.*]

NURSE Mistress! What, mistress! Juliet! Fast,°
    I warrant her, she.
Why, lamb, why, lady! Fie, you slugabed!
Why, love, I say! Madam! Sweetheart! Why,
    bride!
What, not a word? You take your pennyworths°
    now.
Sleep for a week; for the next night, I warrant,   5
The County Paris hath set up his rest
That you shall rest but little. God forgive me,
Marry, and amen! How sound is she asleep!
I needs must wake her. Madam, madam,
    madam!
Ay, let the County take you in your bed;   10
He'll fright you up, i' faith. Will it not be?

[*She opens the bedcurtains.*]

What, dressed, and in your clothes, and down
    again?
I must needs wake you. Lady, lady, lady!
Alas, alas! Help, help! My lady's dead!

Act 4, Scene 4. **2. pastry:** room where pie paste was prepared. **3. second cock:** The conventional times of cockcrowing were (1) midnight, (2) three a.m., and (3) an hour before dawn. **4. curfew bell:** Strictly, curfew (French *couvre feu*) was rung at eight in the evening, but the term was loosely used for other ringings. **6. cot-quean:** used of a man who usurped the place of housewife. **8. watching:** loss of sleep. **11. mouse-hunt:** literally, a weasel, but here a woman-chaser. "Mouse" was an amorous term of endearment for a woman. **20. Mass:** i.e., by the mass. **21. loggerhead:** that his head has a natural affinity to a block of wood. **22. straight:** immediately. **Act 4, Scene 5.** **1. Fast:** fast asleep. **4. pennyworths:** i.e., what little you can get.

O, weraday, that ever I was born!   15
Some aqua vitae, ho! My lord! My lady!

[*Enter Capulet's Wife.*]

WIFE What noise is here?
NURSE   O lamentable day!
WIFE What is the matter?
NURSE   Look look O heavy day
WIFE O me, O me! My child, my only life!
Revive, look up, or I will die with thee!   20
Help, help! Call help.

[*Enter Father Capulet.*]

CAPULET For shame, bring Juliet forth. Her lord
is come.
NURSE She's dead, deceased. She's dead, alack
the day!
WIFE Alack the day, she's dead, she's dead, she's
dead!
CAPULET Ha! Let me see her. Out,° alas! She's   25
cold.
Her blood is settled, and her joints are stiff;
Life and these lips have long been separated.
Death lies on her like an untimely frost
Upon the sweetest flower of all the field.
NURSE O lamentable day!   30
WIFE   O woeful time!
CAPULET Death, that hath ta'en her hence to
make me wail,
Ties up my tongue and will not let me speak.

[*Enter Friar Laurence and the County Paris,
with Musicians.*]

FRIAR LAURENCE Come, is the bride ready to go
to church?
CAPULET Ready to go, but never to return.
O son, the night before thy wedding day   35
Hath Death lain with thy wife. There she lies,
Flower as she was, deflowered by him.
Death is my son-in-law, Death is my heir;
My daughter he hath wedded. I will die
And leave him all; life, living, all is Death's.   40

PARIS Have I thought long° to see this morning's
face,
And doth it give me such a sight as this?
WIFE Accurst, unhappy, wretched, hateful day!
Most miserable hour that e'er time saw
In lasting labor of his pilgrimage!   45
But one, poor one, one poor and loving child,
But one thing to rejoice and solace in,
And cruel Death hath catched° it from my
sight!
NURSE O woe! O woeful, woeful, woeful day!
Most lamentable day, most woeful day   50
That ever, ever I did yet behold!
O day, O day, O day! O hateful day!
Never was seen so black a day as this.
O woeful day, O woeful day!
PARIS Beguiled, divorcèd, wrongèd, spited, slain!   55
Most detestable Death, by thee beguiled,
By cruel, cruel thee quite overthrown!
O love! O life! Not life, but love in death!°
CAPULET Despised, distressèd, hated, martyred,
killed!
Uncomfortable time, why cam'st thou now   60
To murder, murder our solemnity?°
O child! O child! My soul, and not my child!
Dead art thou! Alack, my child is dead,
And with my child my joys are burièd.
FRIAR LAURENCE Peace, ho, for shame!   65
Confusion's cure° lives not
In these confusions. Heaven and yourself
Had part in this fair maid; now heaven hath
all,
And all the better is it for the maid.
Your part in her you could not keep from
death,
But heaven keeps his part in eternal life.   70
The most you sought was her promotion,°
For 'twas your heaven she should be advanced;°
And weep ye now, seeing she is advanced
Above the clouds, as high as heaven itself?
O, in this love° you love your child so ill   75

---

25. Out: an exclamation of lament.   **41. thought long:** been impatient.   **48. catched:** snatched.   **58. O love . . . death:** not "my life," as I have so often called you, but still in death my loved one.   **61. solemnity:** festive (marriage) rites.   **65. Confusion's cure:** the remedy for this state of frenzied disorder.   **71. promotion:** material advancement.   **72. advanced:** promoted (raised socially through an advantageous marriage).   **75. in this love:** in your concern for her mere earthly welfare (as compared with the love of heaven).

That you run mad, seeing that she is well.
She's not well married that lives married long,°
But she's best married that dies married young.
Dry up your tears, and stick your rosemary
On this fair corpse, and, as the custom is,   80
And in her best array, bear her to church;
For though fond nature bids us all lament,
Yet nature's tears are reason's merriment.°

CAPULET All things that we ordainèd festival
Turn from their office° to black funeral: 85
Our instruments to melancholy bells,
Our wedding cheer° to a sad burial feast,
Our solemn hymns to sullen dirges change,
Our bridal flowers serve for a buried corpse,
And all things change them to the contrary.   90

FRIAR LAURENCE Sir, go you in, and, madam, go
with him,
And go, Sir Paris. Everyone prepare
To follow this fair corpse unto her grave.
The heavens do lour upon you for some ill;°
Move° them no more by crossing their high will. 95

[*Exeunt.*] [*Nurse and Musicians remain.*]

FIRST MUSICIAN Faith, we may put up our pipes
and be gone.

NURSE Honest good fellows, ah, put up, put up!
For well you know this is a pitiful case.   [*Exit.*]

FIRST MUSICIAN Ay, by my troth, the case may be
amended.

[*Enter Peter.*]

PETER Musicians, O, musicians, "Heart's ease."   100
"Heart's ease." O, an you will have me live,
play "Heart's ease."

FIRST MUSICIAN Why, "Heart's ease"?

PETER O, musicians, because my heart itself plays
"My heart is full." O, play me some merry   105
dump° to comfort me.

FIRST MUSICIAN Not a dump we! 'Tis no time to
play now.

PETER You will not, then?

FIRST MUSICIAN No.   110

PETER I will then give it you soundly.°

FIRST MUSICIAN What will you give us?

PETER No money, on my faith, but the gleek;° I
will give you the minstrel.°

FIRST MUSICIAN Then will I give you the   115
serving-creature.°

PETER Then will I lay the serving-creature's
dagger on your pate. I will carry no crotchets.°
I'll re you, I'll fa° you. Do you note me?

FIRST MUSICIAN An you re us and fa us, you note us. 120

SECOND MUSICIAN Pray you, put up your dagger
and put out your wit.

PETER Then have at you with my wit! I will
dry-beat you with an iron wit, and put up my
iron dagger. Answer me like men: 125
"When griping griefs the heart doth wound,
And doleful dumps the mind oppress,
Then music with her silver sound" —
Why "silver sound"? Why "music with her silver
sound"? What say you, Simon Catling?°   130

FIRST MUSICIAN Marry, sir, because silver hath a
sweet sound.

PETER Prates°! What say you, Hugh Rebeck?°

SECOND MUSICIAN I say "silver sound" because
musicians sound° for silver.   135

PETER Prates too! What say you, James
Soundpost?

THIRD MUSICIAN Faith, I know not what to say.

PETER O, I cry you mercy you are the singer. I will
say for you. It is "music with her silver sound" 140
because musicians have no gold for sounding:
"Then music with her silver sound
With speedy help doth lend redress."   [*Exit.*]

FIRST MUSICIAN What a pestilent knave is this same!

SECOND MUSICIAN Hang him, Jack! Come, we'll in 145
here, tarry for the mourners, and stay dinner.

[*Exeunt.*]

---

77. not . . . long: i.e., a long marriage is not necessarily a good marriage.   **82–83. For . . . merriment:** For though human nature, which is weak ("fond") in judgment, prompts us all to lament, yet reason bids us rejoice — for death is to me advantage.   **85. office:** function.   **87. cheer:** fare, viands.   **94. ill:** sin (committed by you).   **95. Move:** provoke.   **105–106. merry dump:** an oxymoron, "dump" meaning a mournful song. **111. soundly:** thoroughly.   **113. gleek** scoffing rebuke.   **114. give you the minstrel:** i.e., describe you as a worthless fellow.   **116. serving-creature:** a riposte "in kind" ("creature" for "man" being intentionally derogatory).   **118. carry no crotchets:** (1) put up with no whims or airs, (2) take no part in singing quarter-notes or such frivolities.   **119. re . . . fa** notes of the scale used figuratively as verbs meaning "to give you a beating."   **130. Catling:** a small lute (or fiddle) string made out of catgut.   **133. Prates:** (He) talks but says nothing.   **133. Rebeck:** an early, three-stringed form of fiddle.   **135. sound:** i.e., play or sing.

extending beyond the text

At this point in your reading, you might have developed strong feelings — either positive or negative — about why schools continue to teach Shakespeare over four hundred years after his death. Read the following excerpt in which the author, Ken Ludwig, addresses the question of why teach Shakespeare.

from How to Teach Your Children Shakespeare

Ken Ludwig

The answer to the . . . question [Why Shakespeare?] is that Shakespeare isn't just one of the many great authors in the English language; Shakespeare is, indisputably, one of the two great bedrocks of Western civilization in English. (The other is the King James translation of the Bible.) Not only do Shakespeare's plays themselves contain the finest writing of the past 450 years, but most of the best novels, plays, poetry, and films in the English language produced since Shakespeare's death in 1616 — from Jane Austen to Charles Dickens, from *Ulysses* to *The Godfather* — are heavily influenced by Shakespeare's stories, characters, language, and themes. As Falstaff says in *Henry IV, Part 2*: "I am not only witty in myself, but the cause that wit is in other men." Shakespeare is not only creative in himself — he is the cause of creation in other writers.

For many of us, Shakespeare has become a kind of Bible for the modern world, bringing us together intellectually the way religious services have traditionally done. For more than five thousand years, Moses, Jesus, and the other towering figures of the Old and New Testaments were the archetypes of our consciousness. In modern society, Hamlet and Macbeth, Juliet and Ophelia, have been added to their number. To know some Shakespeare gives you a head start in life.

Also, Shakespeare's powers as a writer simply exceed those of every other writer in the history of the English language. Here is an excerpt from the diary of the distinguished English novelist and essayist Virginia Woolf, who speaks here for every writer I know:

> I read Shakespeare *directly* after I have finished writing, when my mind is agape and red and hot. Then it is astonishing. I never yet knew how amazing his stretch and speed and word-coining power is, until I felt it utterly outpace and outrace my own, seeming to start equal and then I see him draw ahead and do things I could not in my wildest tumult and utmost press of mind imagine. [T]he words drop so fast one can't pick them up. . . . Why then should anyone else attempt to write. This is not "writing" at all. Indeed, I could say that Shakespeare surpasses literature altogether, if I knew what I meant. ■

Summarize why Ludwig thinks we should continue to read Shakespeare? What does Virginia Woolf add to the position? To what extent do you agree or disagree with either of them?

Understanding and Interpreting

1. Though many people have talked about Paris to Juliet, Act 4, Scene 1 is the first time we see him interact with Juliet. What are your impressions of him from what he says to Friar Laurence and to Juliet in this scene?

2. Summarize the main details of Friar Laurence's plan to keep Juliet from marrying Paris in Scene 1. What is his overall objective, and what are some potential pitfalls?

3. Describe Juliet's behavior with her father on her return from Friar Laurence's in Act 4, Scene 2. How have Capulet's views of her changed since the previous time they were together in Act 3?

4. At the beginning of Act 4, Scene 3, Juliet dismisses the Nurse and tells her mother she needs no help. We know that she wants to be alone to drink the potion from Friar Laurence, but why else might her being alone be significant in this scene?

5. What are Juliet's fears as she prepares to take the potion (Act 4, Scene 3, ll. 15–58)? How does she convince herself to go through with it? What does her decision suggest about her character?

6. Examine the reactions of the following characters to Juliet's faked death, in Act 4, Scene 4, focusing specifically on what they are grieving most for and how they communicate that grief:

    a. Capulet

    b. Capulet's Wife

    c. Nurse

    d. Paris

7. Explain how Friar Laurence comforts Juliet's parents in Act 4, Scene 5, especially considering that he knows she's not dead.

Analyzing Language, Style, and Structure

8. **Vocabulary in Context.** In Act 4, Scene 2, line 33, Capulet says of Friar Laurence that "our whole city is much bound to him." What does the word *bound* mean in this context? What are other possible meanings of this word that could be considered foreshadowing?

9. As she had to do with her mother in Act 3, Juliet has to be careful when speaking to Paris in Act 4, Scene 1 to avoid offending him or revealing too much. Analyze her word choice. How does she use her words skillfully to achieve this effect?

10. Look back through Act 4, Scene 1 and identify references that Juliet makes to death as she talks to Friar Laurence. What do her language choices reveal about her at this point in the play?

11. Examine the figurative language Shakespeare employs in Juliet's monologue in Act 4, Scene 3 to describe the tomb where she is supposed to awaken. How does the language reflect the shift in tone that the play has taken?

12. Though often cut in productions of *Romeo and Juliet* because it is not essential to the plot, what is the likely purpose of Act 4, Scene 4 with Juliet's father and the servingmen?

13. Reread lines 34–40 in Act 4, Scene 5, in which Capulet informs Paris and Friar Laurence of Juliet's "death." Analyze the use of personification and the extended metaphor of Death.

14. The end of Act 4, Scene 5 with Peter and the musicians is another moment that is often cut in productions of the play. Read the dialogue and make an inference or two about why Shakespeare includes this part.

Topics for Composing

15. **Analysis.** Write an analysis of Juliet's character in Act 4, explaining how and why she has changed from earlier in the play. Use evidence from the text to support your ideas.

16. **Analysis.** Romeo does not appear in this act at all. Analyze the effect of his absence on Juliet and the tone of the play. Support your response with evidence from the text.

17. **Argument.** Reread Juliet's soliloquy in Act 4, Scene 3, lines 14–58. Write a response in which you argue whether or not Juliet exhibits maturity or selfishness in this scene. Support your assertions using evidence from the text.

18. **Speaking and Listening.** Make a list of each main character in Act 4 and write a brief explanation of how each responds to Juliet's death. Then, in a small group, compare your observations and discuss how individual characters' responses tell us more about those characters at this point in the story. Do some characters seem to change significantly in response to Juliet's death? If so, which ones? Use evidence from the text to support your observations. Try to reach consensus with your group.

19. **Connections.** Juliet faces an almost impossible choice when she is told to marry Paris, even though she is already married to Romeo. When have you faced a situation in which you felt there were no good choices? Describe the situation you found yourself in and how you handled it.

20. **Research.** Capulet threatens to disown Juliet if she does not marry Paris. Research the legal rights that women might have had during the Middle Ages. Were women's rights at the time of the play's action different than they were during the time of Shakespeare's writing? What about today? Create a presentation in which you share your observations and explanations.

21. **Research.** Though the play is generally thought to be set in the fourteenth century, its cultural conventions are more likely reflective of Shakespeare's own time. Research either wedding or funeral traditions of Elizabethan England. Which aspects of tradition does Shakespeare include for Juliet's wedding or her funeral? Which does he exclude?

22. **Creative Writing.** Write a speech for Friar Laurence in which he proposes a different plan to Juliet that might have had a higher chance of success. Be sure to keep the same time period constraints in place.

ACT 5

Scene 1

[*Enter Romeo.*]

ROMEO If I may trust the flattering truth of sleep,
My dreams presage some joyful news at hand.
My bosom's lord sits lightly in his throne,
And all this day an unaccustomed spirit
Lifts me above the ground° with cheerful   5
    thoughts.
I dreamt my lady came and found me dead —

Strange dream that gives a dead man leave to
    think! —
And breathed such life with kisses in my lips
That I revived and was an emperor.
Ah me, how sweet is love itself possessed   10
When but love's shadows° are so rich in joy!

[*Enter Romeo's man (Balthasar, booted).*]

News from Verona! How now, Balthasar,

Act 5, Scene 1.   5. Lifts . . . ground: i.e., he is figuratively walking on air.   **11. love's shadows:** i.e., dreams.

Dost thou not bring me letters from the Friar?
How doth my lady?° Is my father well?
How fares my Juliet? That I ask again,   15
For nothing can be ill if she be well.

BALTHASAR Then she is well, and nothing can
    be ill.
Her body sleeps in Capels' monument,
And her immortal part with angels lives.
I saw her laid low in her kindred's vault   20
And presently took post to tell it to you.
O, pardon me for bringing these ill news,
Since you did leave it for my office,° sir.

ROMEO Is it e'en so? Then I defy you, stars!
Thou knowest my lodging. Get me ink and   25
    paper,
And hire post-horses.° I will hence tonight.

BALTHASAR I do beseech you, sir, have patience.
Your looks are pale and wild, and do import
Some misadventure.

ROMEO   Tush, thou art deceived.
Leave me, and do the thing I bid thee do.   30
Hast thou no letters to me from the Friar?

BALTHASAR No, my good lord.

ROMEO   No matter. Get thee gone,
And hire those horses. I'll be with thee
    straight.   [*Exit Balthasar.*]
Well, Juliet, I will lie with° thee tonight.
Let's see for means.° O mischief, thou art swift 35
To enter in the thoughts of desperate men!
I do remember an apothecary—
And hereabouts 'a dwells—which late I noted
In tattered weeds,° with overwhelming°
    brows,
Culling of simples.° Meager were his looks;   40
Sharp misery had worn him to the bones;
And in his needy shop a tortoise hung,
An alligator stuffed, and other skins
Of ill-shaped fishes; and about his shelves
A beggarly account° of empty boxes,   45

Green earthen pots, bladders, and musty
    seeds,
Remnants of packthread,° and old cakes of
    roses
Were thinly scattered to make up a show.
Noting this penury, to myself I said,
"An if a man did need a poison now,   50
Whose sale is present death° in Mantua,
Here lives a caitiff° wretch would sell it him."
O, this same thought did but forerun my
    need,
And this same needy man must sell it me.
As I remember, this should be the house.   55
Being holiday, the beggar's shop is shut.
What, ho! Apothecary!   [*Enter Apothecary.*]

APOTHECARY   Who calls so loud?

ROMEO Come hither, man. I see that thou art
    poor.
Hold, there is forty ducats.° [*He shows gold.*]
    Let me have
A dram° of poison, such soon-speeding gear°   60
As will disperse itself through all the veins
That the life-weary taker may fall dead,
And that the trunk° may be discharged of
    breath
As violently as hasty powder fired
Doth hurry from the fatal cannon's womb.   65

APOTHECARY Such mortal drugs I have, but
    Mantua's law
Is death to any he that utters° them.

ROMEO Art thou so bare and full of
    wretchedness,
And fearest to die? Famine is in thy cheeks,
Need and oppression° starveth° in thy eyes,   70
Contempt and beggary hangs° upon thy back.
The world is not thy friend, nor the world's
    law;
The world affords no law to make thee rich.
Then be not poor, but break it,° and take this.

14. **lady:** Juliet, not his mother.   23. **for my office:** as my duty.   26. **post-horses:** horses kept at an inn for hire by travelers or post riders.
34. **lie with:** i.e., (1) in death, (2) as a lover.   35. **see for means:** consider how to accomplish it.   39. **weeds:** garments.   39. **overwhelming:**
overhanging.   40. **Culling of simples:** gathering medicinal herbs.   45. **beggarly account:** poor store or number.   47. **Remnants of**
packthread bits of stout twine for tying up bundles.   51. **Whose . . . death:** the sale of which carries the punishment of immediate death
(to the seller).   52. **caitiff:** miserable, pitiable.   59. **forty ducats:** The ducat was a small gold coin then worth about ten shillings; forty ducats
was then a substantial sum.   60. **dram:** draught or drink (literally, half a fluid ounce).   60. **soon-speeding gear:** quick-working stuff.
63. **trunk:** body.   67. **utters:** sells.   70. **Need and oppression:** oppressive poverty.   70. **starveth:** are hungry.   71. **hangs:** i.e., as in tatters.
74. **it:** i.e., the law.

APOTHECARY My poverty but not my will consents. 75
ROMEO I pay thy poverty and not thy will.
APOTHECARY Put this in any liquid thing you will
  And drink it off, and if you had the strength
  Of twenty men it would dispatch you straight.

[He gives poison, and takes the gold.]

ROMEO There is thy gold — worse poison to 80
    men's souls,
  Doing more murder in this loathsome world
  Than these poor compounds that thou mayst
    not sell.
  I sell thee poison; thou hast sold me none.
  Farewell. Buy food, and get thyself in flesh. —
  Come, cordial° and not poison, go with me 85
  To Juliet's grave, for there must I use thee.

[Exeunt separately.]

Scene 2

[Enter Friar John to Friar Laurence.]

FRIAR JOHN Holy Franciscan friar! Brother, ho!

[Enter Friar Laurence.]

FRIAR LAURENCE This same should be the voice
    of Friar John.
  Welcome from Mantua! What says Romeo?
  Or if his mind be writ, give me his letter.
FRIAR JOHN Going to find a barefoot brother out — 5
  One of our order — to associate me°
  Here in this city visiting the sick,
  And finding him, the searchers of the town,°
  Suspecting that we both were in a house
  Where the infectious pestilence did reign, 10
  Sealed up the doors and would not let us
    forth,
  So that my speed° to Mantua there was stayed.
FRIAR LAURENCE Who bare my letter, then, to
    Romeo?
FRIAR JOHN I could not send it — here it is again —

Nor get a messenger to bring it thee, 15
  So fearful were they of infection.

[He gives a letter.]

FRIAR LAURENCE Unhappy fortune! By my
    brotherhood,
  The letter was not nice° but full of charge,°
  Of dear import,° and the neglecting it°
  May do much danger. Friar John, go hence. 20
  Get me an iron crow° and bring it straight
    unto my cell.
FRIAR JOHN Brother, I'll go and bring it thee.

[Exit.]

FRIAR LAURENCE Now must I to the monument
    alone.
  Within this three hours will fair Juliet wake.
  She will beshrew° me much that Romeo 25
  Hath had no notice of these accidents;
  But I will write again to Mantua,
  And keep her at my cell till Romeo come —
  Poor living corpse, closed in a dead man's
    tomb!

[Exit.]

Scene 3

[Enter Paris, and his Page bearing flowers, perfumed water, and a torch.]

PARIS Give me thy torch, boy. Hence, and stand
    aloof.°
  Yet put it out, for I would not be seen.
  Under yond yew trees lay thee all along,
  Holding thy ear close to the hollow ground.
  So shall no foot upon the churchyard tread, 5
  Being loose, unfirm, with digging up of graves,
  But thou shalt hear it. Whistle then to me
  As signal that thou hearest something approach.
  Give me those flowers. Do as I bid thee. Go.
PAGE *[Aside]*

---

85. cordial medicine that invigorates the heart.   **Act 5, Scene 2.   6. associate me:** act as my companion.   **8. searchers of the town:** health officers, whose duty it was to view dead bodies and report on the cause of death.   **12. my speed:** successful performance (of my journey).
18. nice: unimportant, trivial.   **18. charge** weighty matter.   **19. dear import:** important consequence.   **19. neglecting it:** failure to deliver its contents.   **21. crow** crowbar.   **25. beshrew** reprove, blame.   **Act 5, Scene 3.   1. stand aloof:** withdraw to a distance.

I am almost afraid to stand alone   10
Here in the churchyard, yet I will adventure.

> [*He retires.*]

PARIS [*Strewing flowers and perfumed water*]
Sweet flower, with flowers thy bridal bed I
   strew —
O woe! Thy canopy° is dust and stones —
Which with sweet water nightly I will dew,
Or wanting° that, with tears distilled by°   15
   moans.
The obsequies that I for thee will keep
Nightly shall be to strew thy grave and weep.

> [*Whistle Boy.*]

The boy gives warning something doth
   approach.
What cursèd foot wanders this way tonight,
To cross° my obsequies and true love's rite?   20
What, with a torch? Muffle me, night, awhile.

> [*He retires.*]

[*Enter Romeo and Balthasar, with a torch, a
mattock,° and a crowbar.*]

ROMEO Give me that mattock and the wrenching
   iron.   [*He takes the tools.*]
Hold, take this letter. Early in the morning
See thou deliver it to my lord and father.

> [*He gives a letter and takes a torch.*]

Give me the light. Upon thy life I charge thee,   25
Whate'er thou hearest or seest, stand all aloof
And do not interrupt me in my course.°
Why I descend into this bed of death
Is partly to behold my lady's face,
But chiefly to take thence from her dead finger 30
A precious ring — a ring that I must use
In dear employment.° Therefore hence,
   begone.
But if thou, jealous,° dost return to pry

In what I farther shall intend to do,
By heaven, I will tear thee joint by joint   35
And strew this hungry churchyard with thy
   limbs.
The time and my intents are savage-wild,
More fierce and more inexorable far
Than empty tigers or the roaring sea.
BALTHASAR I will be gone, sir, and not trouble ye. 40
ROMEO So shalt thou show me friendship. Take
   thou that.   [*He gives him money.*]
Live, and be prosperous; and farewell, good
   fellow.
BALTHASAR [*Aside*]
For all this same, I'll hide me hereabout.
His looks I fear, and his intents I doubt.

> [*He retires.*]

ROMEO Thou detestable maw, thou womb of   45
   death,
Gorged with the dearest morsel of the earth,
Thus I enforce thy rotten jaws to open,
And in despite° I'll cram thee with more food.

> [*He begins to open the tomb.*]

PARIS This is that banished haughty Montague
That murdered my love's cousin, with which   50
   grief
It is supposèd the fair creature died,
And here is come to do some villainous
   shame°
To the dead bodies. I will apprehend him.

> [*He comes forward.*]

Stop thy unhallowed toil, vile Montague!
Can vengeance be pursued further than death? 55
Condemnèd villain, I do apprehend thee.
Obey and go with me, for thou must die.
ROMEO I must indeed, and therefore came I hither.
Good gentle youth, tempt not a desperate
   man.

---

13. **thy canopy:** i.e., of thy bed. 15. **wanting:** lacking. 15. **distilled by:** extracted out of. 20. **cross:** thwart, interfere with. 21. sd *mattock:*
a kind of pick-axe. 27. **course:** intended proceeding. 32. **dear employment:** important business. 33. **jealous:** suspicious. 48. **in despite:** to
spite thee — by making thee eat when thou art already gorged with food. 52. **do some villainous shame:** dismember the bodies (in revenge).

Fly hence and leave me. Think upon these gone; 60
Let them affright thee. I beseech thee, youth,
Put not another sin upon my head
By urging me to fury. O, begone!
By heaven, I love thee better than myself,
For I come hither armed against myself. 65
Stay not, begone. Live, and hereafter say
A madman's mercy bid thee run away.

PARIS I do defy thy conjuration,°
And apprehend thee for a felon here.

ROMEO Wilt thou provoke me? Then have at 70
    thee, boy!   [*They fight.*]

PAGE O Lord, they fight! I will go call the watch.

                           [*Exit.*]

PARIS O, I am slain! [*He falls.*] If thou be merciful,
    Open the tomb, lay me with Juliet.   [*He dies.*]

ROMEO In faith, I will. Let me peruse this face.
    Mercutio's kinsman, noble County Paris! 75
    What said my man when my betossèd soul
    Did not attend him as we rode? I think
    He told me Paris should have married Juliet.
    Said he not so? Or did I dream it so?
    Or am I mad, hearing him talk of Juliet, 80
    To think it was so? O, give me thy hand,
    One writ with me in sour misfortune's book.

I'll bury thee in a triumphant grave.

            [*He opens the tomb.*]

A grave? O, no! A lantern, slaughtered youth,
For here lies Juliet, and her beauty makes 85
This vault a feasting presence full of light.
Death, lie thou there, by a dead man interred.

          [*He lays Paris in the tomb.*]

How oft when men are at the point of death
Have they been merry, which their keepers°
    call
A lightening before death! O, how may I 90
Call this a lightening? O my love, my wife!
Death, that hath sucked the honey of thy
    breath,
Hath had no power yet upon thy beauty.
Thou art not conquered; beauty's ensign yet
Is crimson in thy lips and in thy cheeks, 95
And death's pale flag is not advancèd there.
Tybalt, liest thou there in thy bloody sheet?
O, what more favor can I do to thee
Than with that hand that cut thy youth in
    twain
To sunder his that was thine enemy? 100
Forgive me, cousin! Ah, dear Juliet,

These are images from two different versions of the same moment from the play when Romeo enters the tomb to see Juliet.

What is similar and different in the ways the directors set the mood of the scene?

---

68. conjuration: admonition, solemn entreaty.   **89. keepers:** (1) sick-nurses, (2) jailors.

Why art thou yet so fair? Shall I believe
That unsubstantial Death is amorous,
And that the lean abhorrèd monster keeps
Thee here in dark to be his paramour?   105
For fear of that I still will stay with thee
And never from this palace of dim night
Depart again. Here, here will I remain
With worms that are thy chambermaids. O,
       here
Will I set up my everlasting rest°   110
And shake the yoke of inauspicious stars
From this world-wearied flesh. Eyes, look your
       last!
Arms, take your last embrace! And, lips, O you
The doors of breath, seal with a righteous kiss
A dateless bargain to engrossing death!   115

                    [*He kisses Juliet.*]

Come, bitter conduct,° come, unsavory guide,
Thou desperate pilot, now at once run on
The dashing rocks thy seasick weary bark!°
Here's to my love. [*He drinks.*] O true
       apothecary!
Thy drugs are quick.° Thus with a kiss I die.   120

                    [*He dies.*]

[*Enter (at the other end of the churchyard)*
Friar Laurence with lantern, crow, and spade.]

FRIAR LAURENCE Saint Francis be my speed!°
       How oft tonight
Have my old feet stumbled at graves!° Who's
       there?
BALTHASAR Here's one, a friend, and one that
       knows you well.
FRIAR LAURENCE Bliss be upon you. Tell me,
       good my friend,
What torch is yond that vainly lends his light   125
To grubs and eyeless skulls? As I discern,
It burneth in the Capels' monument.
BALTHASAR It doth so, holy sir, and there's my
       master,
One that you love.

FRIAR LAURENCE   Who is it?
BALTHASAR   Romeo.
FRIAR LAURENCE How long hath he been there?   130
BALTHASAR   Full
       half an hour.
FRIAR LAURENCE Go with me to the vault.
BALTHASAR   I dare not, sir.
My master knows not but I am gone hence,
And fearfully did menace me with death
If I did stay to look on his intents.
FRIAR LAURENCE Stay, then, I'll go alone. Fear   135
       comes upon me.
O, much I fear some ill unthrifty° thing.
BALTHASAR As I did sleep under this yew tree here
I dreamt my master and another fought,
And that my master slew him.
FRIAR LAURENCE [*Advancing to the tomb*]
                    Romeo!
Alack, alack, what blood is this which stains   140
The stony entrance of this sepulcher?
What mean these masterless and gory swords
To lie° discolored° by this place of peace?

                    [*He enters the tomb.*]

Romeo! O, pale! Who else? What, Paris too?
And steeped in blood? Ah, what an unkind° hour   145
Is guilty of this lamentable chance!
The lady stirs.

                    [*Juliet wakes.*]

JULIET O comfortable Friar, where is my lord?
I do remember well where I should be,
And there I am. Where is my Romeo?   150

                    [*A noise within.*]

FRIAR LAURENCE I hear some noise. Lady, come
       from that nest
Of death, contagion, and unnatural sleep.
A greater power than we can contradict
Hath thwarted our intents. Come, come away.
Thy husband in thy bosom there lies dead,   155
And Paris, too. Come, I'll dispose of thee
Among a sisterhood of holy nuns.

---

110. set . . . rest: make a final desperate commitment of myself.   **116. conduct:** i.e., the poison.   **118. seasick weary bark:** small ship worn out by the buffeting of the sea.   **120. quick:** fast-acting (with play on "quick" = life-giving).   **121. speed:** aid.   **122. stumbled at graves:** considered a bad omen.   **136. unthrifty:** unfortunate.   **143. To lie:** i.e., lying.   **143. discoloured:** unnaturally stained (with blood).   **145. unkind:** unnatural, injurious (with suggestion of bad astrological influence).

United Archives GmbH/Alamy

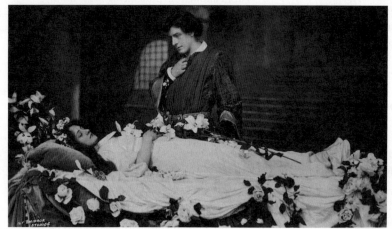

Lebrecht Music & Arts/Alamy

These are images of Juliet in her tomb from two different film versions.

How does the use of costumes, set design, and props communicate a similar or different mood for the scene?

Stay not to question, for the watch is coming.
Come, go, good Juliet. [*A noise again.*] I dare
no longer stay.　　　[*Exit Friar Laurence.*]
JULIET　Go, get thee hence, for I will not away.　160
What's here? A cup,° closed in my true love's
hand?
Poison, I see, hath been his timeless° end.
O churl, drunk all, and left no friendly drop
To help me after? I will kiss thy lips;
Haply some poison yet doth hang on them,　165
To make me die with a restorative.

[*She kisses him.*]

Thy lips are warm.

[*Enter Paris's Boy and Watch (at the other end of the churchyard).*]

FIRST WATCH　Lead, boy. Which way?
JULIET　Yea, noise? Then I'll be brief. O happy
dagger!　　　[*She takes Romeo's dagger.*]
This is thy sheath. There rust, and let me die.　170

[*She stabs herself and falls.*]

---

161. cup: i.e., presumably, the vial containing the poison.　**162. timeless:** untimely.

PAGE This is the place, there where the torch
 doth burn.
FIRST WATCH The ground is bloody. Search
 about the churchyard.
 Go, some of you, whoe'er you find attach.

        [*Exeunt some.*]

Pitiful sight! Here lies the County slain,
And Juliet bleeding, warm, and newly dead, 175
Who here hath lain this two days burièd.
Go tell the Prince. Run to the Capulets.
Raise up the Montagues. Some others search.

        [*Exeunt others.*]

We see the ground whereon these woes do lie,
But the true ground of all these piteous woes 180
We cannot without circumstance° descry.

[*Enter some of the Watch, with Romeo's man
Balthasar.*]

SECOND WATCH Here's Romeo's man. We found
 him in the churchyard.
FIRST WATCH Hold him in safety° till the Prince
 come hither.

[*Enter Friar Laurence, and another Watchman
with tools.*]

THIRD WATCH Here is a friar, that trembles, sighs,
 and weeps.
 We took this mattock and this spade from him 185
 As he was coming from this churchyard's side.
FIRST WATCH A great suspicion. Stay the Friar too.

[*Enter the Prince and attendants.*]

PRINCE What misadventure is so early up
 That calls our person from our morning rest?

[*Enter Capels (Capulet and his Wife).*]

CAPULET What should it be that is so shrieked 190
 abroad?
CAPULET'S WIFE O, the people in the street cry
 "Romeo,"
 Some "Juliet," and some "Paris," and all run
 With open outcry toward our monument.
PRINCE What fear is this which startles in our ears?

FIRST WATCH Sovereign, here lies the County 195
 Paris slain,
 And Romeo dead, and Juliet, dead before,
 Warm and new killed.
PRINCE Search, seek, and know how this foul
 murder comes.
FIRST WATCH Here is a friar, and slaughtered
 Romeo's man,
 With instruments upon them fit to open 200
 These dead men's tombs.
CAPULET O heavens! O wife, look how our
 daughter bleeds!
 This dagger hath mistane,° for lo, his house
 Is empty on the back of Montague,
 And it mis-sheathèd in my daughter's bosom! 205
CAPULET'S WIFE O me! This sight of death is as a
 bell
 That warns my old age to a sepulcher.

Enter Montague.

PRINCE Come, Montague, for thou art early up
 To see thy son and heir now early down.
MONTAGUE Alas, my liege, my wife is dead 210
 tonight;
 Grief of my son's exile hath stopped her
 breath.
 What further woe conspires against mine age?
PRINCE Look, and thou shalt see.
MONTAGUE [*Seeing Romeo's body*]
 O thou untaught! What manners is in this,
 To press before thy father to a grave? 215
PRINCE Seal up the mouth of outrage for a while,
 Till we can clear these ambiguities
 And know their spring,° their head, their true
 descent;
 And then will I be general° of your woes
 And lead you even to death. Meantime 220
 forbear,
 And let mischance be slave to patience.
 Bring forth the parties of suspicion.
FRIAR LAURENCE I am the greatest,° able to do least,
 Yet most suspected, as the time and place
 Doth make against me, of this direful murder; 225

---

181. circumstance: detailed information. **183. in safety:** under guard. **203. mistane:** mistaken its proper habitation ("house"). **218. spring:** source. **219. general:** leader in your pursuit of justice. **223. greatest:** (1) principal suspect, (2) highest in social rank (?).

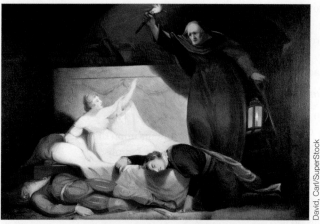

David, Carl/SuperStock

Here are two different interpretations of the scene when Friar Laurence discovers the bodies in the tomb.

What feelings are created in each, and how do the artists create these feelings through their choices?

Artokoloro/Alamy

And here I stand, both to impeach and purge°
Myself condemnèd and myself excused.

PRINCE Then say at once what thou dost know in
   this.

FRIAR LAURENCE I will be brief, for my short date
   of breath°
Is not so long as is a tedious tale.   230
Romeo, there dead, was husband to that Juliet,
And she, there dead, that Romeo's faithful wife.
I married them, and their stol'n marriage day

Was Tybalt's doomsday, whose untimely
   death
Banished the new-made bridegroom from   235
   this city,
For whom, and not for Tybalt, Juliet pined.
You, to remove that siege° of grief from her,
Betrothed and would have married her
   perforce°
To County Paris. Then comes she to me,
And with wild looks bid me devise some means 240

---

226. impeach and purge: accuse (as guilty) and exonerate (as innocent).   **229. my short date of breath:** the brief time (of life) left me in which
to speak.   **237. siege:** assault.   **238. perforce:** by compulsion.

To rid her from this second marriage,
Or in my cell there would she kill herself.
Then gave I her — so tutored by my art —
A sleeping potion, which so took effect
As I intended, for it wrought on her   245
The form° of death. Meantime I writ to Romeo
That he should hither come as this dire night
To help to take her from her borrowed grave,
Being the time the potion's force should cease.
But he which bore my letter, Friar John,   250
Was stayed by accident, and yesternight
Returned my letter back. Then all alone
At the prefixèd hour of her waking
Came I to take her from her kindred's vault,
Meaning to keep her closely at my cell   255
Till I conveniently could send to Romeo.
But when I came, some minute ere the time
Of her awakening, here untimely lay
The noble Paris and true° Romeo dead.
She wakes, and I entreated her come forth   260
And bear this work of heaven with patience.
But then a noise did scare me from the tomb,
And she, too desperate, would not go with me,
But, as it seems, did violence on herself.
All this I know, and to the marriage   265
Her nurse is privy; and if aught in this
Miscarried by my fault, let my old life
Be sacrificed some hour before his time
Unto the rigor of severest law.

PRINCE We still have known thee for a holy man.   270
     Where's Romeo's man? What can he say to this?

BALTHASAR I brought my master news of Juliet's
     death,
     And then in post he came from Mantua
     To this same place, to this same monument.
     This letter he early bid me give his father,   275

                    [Showing a letter]

     And threatened me with death, going in the
     vault,
     If I departed not and left him there.

PRINCE [Taking the letter]
     Give me the letter. I will look on it.

Where is the County's page, that raised the
     watch?
Sirrah, what made your master in this place?   280

PAGE He came with flowers to strew his lady's
     grave,
     And bid me stand aloof, and so I did.
     Anon comes one with light to ope the tomb,
     And by and by° my master drew on him,
     And then I ran away to call the watch.   285

PRINCE This letter doth make good the Friar's
     words,
     Their course of love, the tidings of her death;
     And here he writes that he did buy a poison
     Of a poor 'pothecary, and therewithal
     Came to this vault to die, and lie with Juliet.   290
     Where be these enemies? Capulet, Montague,
     See what a scourge is laid upon your hate,
     That heaven finds means to kill your joys° with
     love.
     And I, for winking at° your discords, too
     Have lost a brace° of kinsmen. All are   295
     punished.

CAPULET O brother Montague, give me thy hand.
     This is my daughter's jointure,° for no more
     Can I demand.

MONTAGUE   But I can give thee more,
     For I will raise° her statue° in pure gold,
     That while Verona by that name is known   300
     There shall no figure at such rate be set°
     As that of true and faithful Juliet.

CAPULET As rich shall Romeo's by his lady's lie;
     Poor sacrifices of° our enmity!

PRINCE A glooming peace° this morning with it   305
     brings;
     The sun, for sorrow, will not show his head.
     Go hence to have more talk of these sad
     things.
     Some shall be pardoned, and some punishèd;
     For never was a story of more woe
     Than this of Juliet and her Romeo.   310

                              [Exeunt.]

                    FINIS

---

246. form: outward appearance.   **259. true:** faithful to his love (in death).   **284. by and by:** immediately, at once.   **293. kill your joys:**
(1) turn your happiness to sorrow, (2) kill your children.   **294. winking at:** closing my eyes to.   **295. brace:** pair (Mercutio and Paris).
297. This my daughter's jointure: The handclasp of friendship (ending the feud) is Juliet's jointure (= marriage settlement made by the
bridegroom's father).   **299. raise:** cause to be set up.   **299. statue:** i.e., recumbent effigy on a tomb.   **301. at such rate set:** be held in such
esteem.   **304. Poor sacrifices of:** (1) pitiful victims of, (2) inadequate atonement for.   **305. glooming peace:** peace overshadowed by clouds.

extending beyond the text

In the Prologue, we learn that Romeo and Juliet will "take their life," but does this play have to be a tragedy? The First Folio version, published shortly after Shakespeare's death, does not actually include the deterministic Prologue. Read the following analysis of the role of the Prologue and the ending of the play by Emma Smith, professor of Shakespeare Studies at Oxford University.

from **This Is Shakespeare**

Emma Smith

So far I've suggested that the play was always already tragic. But there's an alternative reading. Perhaps that tumbling hectic pace overshoots comedy and brings *Romeo and Juliet* to its tragic conclusion. The play misses a comic redemption by a matter of minutes. It's entirely appropriate to the play's characteristic impatience that it ends with Romeo killing himself just that bit too quickly to realize that Juliet is not actually dead. Perhaps this is a play that becomes, rather than is, tragic. A Restoration adaptation performed it on alternate nights with a happy ending. Young people, programmed towards romantic love and sexual reproduction, really belong in a comedy. Disapproving parents also have a role as archetypal blocking figures in comedy, a genre that tends to see the young win out over their elders' blinkered prejudices. . . .

If, after all, this is a play that could have turned out differently—if only the friar's messenger had not been quarantined by the plague, if only Juliet had woken seconds earlier—then perhaps the presence of the Prologue does something different. If this is a tragedy morphing out of a comic matrix, as Susan Snyder would put it, perhaps the purpose of the Chorus is more pointedly pre-emptive. It might look as if this could all turn out well, but you've already heard that it won't. Don't get your hopes up. These comic-looking elements are actually all foreclosed in a tragic narrative. Even if the play itself looks evitable rather than inevitable, the Prologue makes clear that there's only one way it can end. ■

Explain why *Romeo and Juliet* comes close to being a comedy rather than a tragedy, according to Smith. To what extent do you agree or disagree? What else would need to change in this play for it to become a comedy?

Understanding and Interpreting

1. Act 5 begins with Romeo recounting another dream. How does Romeo interpret the meaning of his dream?

2. What does Romeo mean when he says, "I defy you, stars!" (Act 5, Scene 1, l. 24), and how is this different from other times he has addressed the power of fate over him and his life?

3. In line 18 of Act 5, Scene 1, Romeo learns of Juliet's "death," and by line 28, based on Balthazar's observation that he looks "pale and wild," Romeo has already decided on suicide. What does the pace of his decision-making suggest about Romeo at this point in the play?

4. Why is so much made of the Apothecary's poverty in Act 5, Scene 1? How is he in contrast to Romeo?

5. Explain how fate has intervened upon the plot yet again in Act 5, Scene 2.

6. Examine Romeo's mental state as evidenced in the speech right before he fights with Paris (Act 5, Scene 3, ll. 58–67).

7. Does Romeo want to fight Paris? Why does he? Shakespeare tells us "They fight" and "[Paris] dies" (Act 5, Scene 3, ll. 70–73), not how they fight or how he dies. If you were the director of a stage or film version of this scene, what gestures, movements, and facial expressions would you want to each of the actors to use to communicate a particular interpretation of Romeo and of Paris? What textual evidence supports your interpretation?

8. What choices does Friar Laurence make when he arrives at the tomb that lead to Juliet's death in Act 5, Scene 3? What does this reveal about his character? How might an actor portraying Friar Laurence in this scene behave based on this interpretation of his character? Why?

9. What follows Juliet's death in Act 5, Scene 3, lines 148–170 is mostly exposition allowing the rest of the characters to learn what happened. How do Romeo's and Juliet's parents react to the news?

10. Is Friar Laurence's account of the story (Act 5, Scene 3, ll. 229–269) accurate and complete? To what extent does he claim or avoid responsibility for his own part in the tragedy?

11. What does the Prince mean when he says to Capulet and Montague, "See what a scourge is laid upon your hate. / That heaven finds means to kill your joys with love" (Act 5, Scene 3, ll. 292–293)?

12. Is the feud settled at the end of the play? What evidence supports your interpretation?

13. Summarize what the Prince says in the final lines, and explain why it is significant that he has the last speech of the play.

Analyzing Language, Style, and Structure

14. **Vocabulary in Context.** In Act 5, Scene 2, line 18, Friar Laurence says that "[t]he letter was not nice but full of charge." What is the meaning of the word *charge* as it is used in this context? How is that usage similar to or different from current meanings of the word?

15. Many times throughout the play, Shakespeare creates dramatic irony, meaning that the audience has information the characters do not. How does dramatic irony play out most tragically in Act 5, Scene 1, and what is the effect of this on the audience?

16. Reread Romeo's description of the poison he is seeking from the Apothecary in Act 5, Scene 1, lines 60–65. Explain how his choice of figurative language reflects his state of mind.

17. Before Romeo begins opening Juliet's tomb, Romeo warns Balthazar not to tell anyone what he is doing. Look at his language directed to his servant (Act 5, Scene 3, ll. 32–39). What does this dialogue reveal about how Romeo has changed over the course of the play?

18. Explain the extended metaphor that Romeo uses to describe the tomb (Act 5, Scene 3, ll. 45–48).

19. Looking at Juliet for the last time, Romeo wonders, "why art thou yet so fair?" Analyze the personification he uses to answer his own question (Act 5, Scene 3, ll. 102–112), and explain how it helps him make his own decision to kill himself.

20. Reread the last lines spoken by the Prince (Act 5, Scene 3, ll. 305–310). How do the figurative language and sound elements create an effective closing to the play?

Topics for Composing

21. **Analysis.** Write a thematic analysis that makes a claim about what the play might be suggesting regarding one of the topics below. Be sure to use evidence from the text to support your interpretation.

    a. Love

    b. Loyalty

    c. Fate

    d. Youth

    e. Power

22. **Analysis.** Even though it has a large number of humorous moments, especially from Mercutio and the Nurse, the full title of this play is *The Tragedy of Romeo and Juliet*. Look back at the definition of "tragedy" in the Skill Workshop (p. 717) and write an analysis of how this play fits that classic definition. How are the protagonists examples of tragic heroes or not?

23. **Analysis.** There have been multiple film versions of *Romeo and Juliet*. Watch the death scene from Act 5 from at least two versions and analyze the effects created by the different choices made by each director. Which one is most similar in tone to the original text?

24. **Argument.** Write an argument about who is most responsible for the deaths of Romeo and Juliet. Consider the following: fate, Friar Laurence, Romeo, Juliet, the families, the Prince, Tybalt, Mercutio.

25. **Argument.** Were Romeo and Juliet truly in love? Explain your argument with evidence from the text, as well as your own examples and reasoning.

26. **Speaking and Listening.** With a partner, take turns reading aloud the Prince's final words to the two families (Act 5, Scene 3, lines 305–310) with different tones — one condemning, the other with compassion. Which do you find to be a more powerful interpretation of the Prince's closing remarks? Why?

27. **Connections.** How might *Romeo and Juliet* have been different if the characters were living today with access to modern technology, including phones and social media? Would they fall in love the same way? What different conflicts might they face? How might the ending be different?

28. **Research.** Conduct research to discover what a performance of *Romeo and Juliet* might have been like during Shakespeare's lifetime. What were the stage and the seating areas like? How much would it have cost, and who would have probably been in the audience? Was it a popular play?

29. **Creative Writing.** Write a different ending in which Friar Laurence's plan succeeds. What happens to Romeo and Juliet? What happens to the feud in Verona?

30. **Multimodal.** There are many references to *Romeo and Juliet* in popular music. Locate a song that includes an allusion to the play and create a multimodal presentation focused on exploring that allusion. Include found or created images to represent the aspect of the play or characters that are referenced and what the allusion means in the context of the song. Is the allusion an effective or an accurate one? Why or why not?

conversation

How do we make decisions?

"Trust your gut" is a common phrase that means that your initial instinct is the right one — that deep down, your "gut" reaction to decision-making is better than carefully weighing a choice you need to make. But is that always the case? When faced with opportunities or challenges, we oftentimes have to make decisions very quickly, almost instantaneously; other times we have the luxury of being able to think through those decisions more methodically and rationally. Does one approach lead to a better outcome? Does it depend on the situation?

Various characters make decisions throughout *Romeo and Juliet*, some with deadly consequences. Some of these decisions are based on rational thought, others driven by gut reactions. How do we know the difference, and is one method inherently better than the other? How might *Romeo and Juliet* have ended differently if the young couple had thought through their circumstances and relationship, rather than acting on feelings alone? Friar Laurence, rather than following his gut feeling, thinks through how he might end the fued between families, and yet his actions still lead to catastrophe.

The texts in this Conversation explore the connection between actions and decisions — impulse and reasoning — and offer a variety of viewpoints on the subject. After reading them, you will have an opportunity to enter the conversation by sharing your own viewpoint in response to the following question — ***Do we make better decisions with our "gut" or with our rational brain?***

Starting the Conversation

Take a moment to write informally about your initial thinking on this topic before you explore it further by reading additional texts.

1. Jot down a brief list of recent decisions you had to make and how you made those decisions — by trusting your gut or by thinking through them rationally. Looking at your list, indicate which method seems to dominate. Then, think about the results of those decisions you made and whether or not they ended up being the right ones.

2. With a partner or small group, discuss your decision-making process and the results of those decisions.

3. Create a table like the one below to help you keep track of ideas about decision-making as you read the texts in this Conversation. Add your own responses to the ideas you encounter in the texts you read.

Title/Author	Do We Make Better Decisions with Our "Gut" or with Our Rational Brain?	Best Evidence	Your Response

Source A

Gladwell, Malcolm. *Blink: The Power of Thinking without Thinking*. 1 Jan. 2005.

The Internal Computer

The part of our brain that leaps to conclusions. . . is called the adaptive unconscious, and the study of this kind of decision making is one of the most important new fields in psychology. The adaptive unconscious is not to be confused with the unconscious described by Sigmund Freud, which was a dark and murky place filled with desires and memories and fantasies that were too disturbing for us to think about consciously. This new notion of the adaptive unconscious is thought of, instead, as a kind of giant computer that quickly and quietly processes a lot of the data we need in order to keep functioning as human beings. When you walk out into the street and suddenly realize that a truck is bearing down on you, do you have time to think through all your options? Of course not. The only way that human beings could ever have survived as a species for as long as we have is that we've developed another kind of decision-making apparatus that's capable of making very quick judgments based on very little information. As the psychologist Timothy D. Wilson writes in his book *Strangers to Ourselves*:

> The mind operates most efficiently by relegating a good deal of high-level, sophisticated thinking to the unconscious, just as a modern jetliner is able to fly on automatic pilot with little or no input from the human, "conscious" pilot. The adaptive unconscious does an excellent job of sizing up the world, warning people of danger, setting goals, and initiating action in a sophisticated and efficient manner.

Wilson says that we toggle back and forth between our conscious and unconscious modes of thinking, depending on the situation. A decision to invite a coworker over for dinner is conscious. You think it over. You decide it will be fun. You ask him or her. The spontaneous decision to argue with that same coworker is made unconsciously — by a different part of the brain and motivated by a different part of your personality.

Whenever we meet someone for the first time, whenever we interview someone for a job, whenever we react to a new idea, whenever we're faced with making a decision quickly and under stress, we use that second part of our brain. How long, for example, did it take you, when you were in college, to decide how good a teacher your professor was? A class? Two classes? A semester? The psychologist Nalini Ambady once gave students three ten-second videotapes of a teacher — with the sound turned off — and found they had no difficulty at all coming up with a rating of the teacher's effectiveness. Then Ambady cut the clips back to five seconds, and the ratings were the same. They were remarkably consistent even when she showed the students just two seconds of videotape. Then Ambady compared those snap judgments of teacher effectiveness with evaluations of those same professors made by their students after a full semester of classes, and she found that they were also essentially the same. A person watching a silent two-second video clip of a teacher he or she has never met will reach conclusions about how good that teacher is that are very similar to those of a student who has sat in the teacher's class for an entire semester. That's the power of our adaptive unconscious. ■

Questions

1. What, according to Gladwell, is the difference between the "adaptive unconscious" and the "unconscious"? Why is it important to make this distinction?

2. According to Gladwell, what role does information have in our decision-making process?

3. Why does Gladwell include the results of Ambady's experiment using short video clips to judge teacher effectiveness? How does that study relate to Gladwell's main point?

4. **Comparison.** Psychologist Timothy D. Wilson, whom Gladwell quotes, states that "[t]he adaptive conscious does an excellent job of sizing up the world, warning people of danger, setting goals, and initiating action in a sophisticated and efficient manner." Does his explanation of the adaptive conscious apply to any of the characters in *Romeo and Juliet*? If so, to whom, and how does this explanation support the decisions they make?

5. **Informing Your Argument.** Return to the table you created on page 817. Fill in the columns with information about how Gladwell seems to regard the roles of gut instinct and rational thinking in decision-making. Provide evidence he offers to clarify and support his ideas, and your response to what Gladwell suggests.

Source B

Pearl, Robert. "The Science of Regrettable Decisions." *Vox*, 23 Jul. 2019.

As *Full House* actress Lori Loughlin and her husband await their next court date, they stand accused of paying a $500,000 bribe to get their daughters into the University of Southern California as crew team recruits.[1] Their defense is said to rest on the belief that they were making a perfectly legal donation to the university and its athletic teams (their children never rowed a competitive race in their lives).

Legal strategies and moral considerations aside, this strange behavior has left many observers wondering, "What were they thinking?" Surely, Loughlin and her family must have considered someone at the university would audit the admissions records or realize the coach's high-profile recruits had never rowed a boat.

We may never know exactly what Loughlin and her family were thinking. But as a physician

who has studied how perception alters behavior, I believe that to understand what compelled them to do something so foolish, a more relevant question would be, "What were they perceiving?"

Understanding the science of regrettable decisions

Several years ago, I joined forces with my colleague George York, a respected neurologist affiliated with the University of California Davis, to understand why smart people make foolish choices in politics, sports, relationships, and everyday life. . . .

We compared the scientific findings with an endless array of news stories and firsthand accounts of real people doing remarkably irrational things: We examined the court testimony of a cop who, despite graduating top five in his academy, mistook his gun for a Taser and killed an innocent man. We dug through the career wreckage of a once-rising politician who,

5

---

[1]Since the article's publication, Loughlin and her spouse were convicted. Both served brief prison sentences. —Eds.

despite knowing the risks, used his work phone to send sexually explicit messages. And we found dozens of studies confirming that doctors, the people we trust to keep us safe from disease, fail to wash their hands one out of every three times they enter a hospital room, a mistake that kills thousands of patients each year.

When we read about famous people ruining their lives or hear about normal people becoming famous for public follies, we shake our heads in wonder. We tell ourselves we'd never do anything like that.

But science tells us that we would, far more often than we'd like to believe.

What alters our perceptions

In the scientific literature, George and I noticed an interesting pattern: Under the right circumstances, a subconscious neurobiological sequence in our brains causes us to perceive the world around us in ways that contradict objective reality, distorting what we see and hear. This powerful shift in perception is unrelated to our intelligence, morals, or past behaviors. In fact, we don't even know it's happening, nor can we control it.

George and I named this phenomenon "brainshift" and found that it happens in two distinct situations: those involving high anxiety and those associated with major reward.

Under these conditions, all of us would do   10
something just as regrettable as the headline-grabbing stories above, contrary to what we tell ourselves. Phrased differently, we don't consciously decide to act a fool. Rather, once our perception is distorted, we act in ways that seem reasonable to us but foolish to observers. . . .

When reward opportunities put us in life-threatening situations

To demonstrate the mind-altering effects of a dangerous situation, we turn to a 2010 episode of NBC's *Dateline* called "What Were You Thinking?"

Host Chris Hansen sets the scene: "We rented this room on the fourth floor of an old building and hired these temp workers who were told they'd be doing clerical work for the day."

The workers don't know it, but everyone in the room is a *Dateline* staffer who knows what's about to happen. As smoke begins to fill the room, the staffers pretend nothing's wrong. The smoke is harmless, of course, but the temp workers don't know that. It would appear the building's on fire and yet 90 percent of applicants remain seated, even after the room has completely filled with smoke. When asked why they ignored the threat, the subjects reported that they didn't see the situation as dangerous.

We can't assign this illogical behavior to "groupthink" or "peer pressure," or any explanation other than altered perception. When our safety is in jeopardy, we don't decide to die with others just to fit in. Parents like to ask children whether they'd jump off a bridge if their friends did. They know the answer is no.

Based on the available neurobiological   15
data, the most logical conclusion is that these temp workers, seeking the reward of a full-time position, experienced a subconscious shift in perception that led them to behave in ways they probably regretted once the show was aired. . . .

Can we protect ourselves from this?

Based on our research, the first big step toward avoiding the dangerous consequences of brainshift is to be aware that we are all vulnerable, regardless of our ethics, social status, or IQ.

Next, we must be cognizant of situations that stoke our fears and desires: Those involving money, sex, and fame/recognition are good places to start. Before making decisions, we should ask a trusted friend or even an outsider for an opinion.

When situations allow, consult an independent expert. If an investment opportunity seems too good to be true, try talking yourself out of it. If your counterargument seems rational, listen.

Finally, and particularly in the context of reward, write down the answer to these questions:

1. What's the worst thing that could happen?
2. How would I feel if that outcome occurred?

Had Lori Loughlin and her husband asked these questions — with the reward of a USC acceptance letter on the line — they might not be facing potential jail time. ■ 20

Questions

1. According to Pearl, what is the difference between asking "what were they thinking" and "what were they perceiving"? What role does perception play in our decision-making process?

2. How does Pearl define "brainshift"? Under what circumstances does brainshift occur? What examples in the text illustrate brainshift?

3. What solutions does Pearl propose for avoiding the dangerous consequences of brainshift? Do his solutions seem logical? Why, or why not?

4. **Comparison.** Pearl says that "[u]nder the right circumstances, a subconscious neurobiological sequence in our brains causes us to perceive the world around us in ways that contradict objective reality, distorting what we see and hear." To which characters in *Romeo and Juliet* does this apply? In what ways?

5. **Informing Your Argument.** Return to the table you created on page 817. Fill in the columns with information about how Pearl seems to regard the roles of gut instinct and rational thinking in decision-making. Provide evidence he offers to clarify and support his ideas, and your response to what Pearl suggests.

Source C

Morse, Gardiner. "Decisions and Desire." *Harvard Business Review*, Jan. 2006.

When we make decisions, we're not always in charge. We can be too impulsive or too deliberate for our own good; one moment we hotheadedly let our emotions get the better of us, and the next we're paralyzed by uncertainty. Then we'll pull a brilliant decision out of thin air — and wonder how we did it. Though we may have no idea how decision making happens, neuroscientists peering into our brains are beginning to get the picture. What they're finding may not be what you want to hear, but it's worth your while to listen.

The closer scientists look, the clearer it becomes how much we're like animals. We have dog brains, basically, with a human cortex stuck on top, a veneer of civilization. This cortex is an evolutionarily recent invention that plans, deliberates, and decides. But not a second goes by that our ancient dog brains aren't conferring with our modern cortexes to influence their choices — for better and for worse — and without us even knowing it.

Using scanning devices that measure the brain's activity, scientists can glimpse how the different parts of our brain, ancient and modern, collaborate and compete when we make decisions. Science is not going to produce anytime soon a formula for good decision making or for manipulating people's decisions (the hype surrounding "neuromarketing" notwithstanding). But the more we understand

821

how we make decisions, the better we can manage them. . . .

Most of us are taught from early on that sound decisions come from a cool head, as the neurologist Antonio Damasio noted in his 1994 book *Descartes' Error*. The last thing one would want would be the intrusion of emotions in the methodical process of decision making. The high–reason view, Damasio writes, assumes that "formal logic will, by itself, get us to the best available solution for any problem. . . . To obtain the best results, emotions must be kept out." Damasio's research demolished that notion. Building on the work of many thinkers in the field . . . , Damasio showed that patients with damage to the part of the prefrontal cortex that processes emotions (or, in a way, "listens" to them) often struggle with making even routine decisions.

Neuroscience research . . . teaches us that our emotional brains needn't always operate beneath our radar. Richard Peterson, a psychiatrist who applies behavioral economics theory in his investment consulting business, advises clients to cultivate emotional self-awareness, notice their moods as they happen, and reflect on how their moods may influence their decisions. In particular, he advises people to pay close attention to feelings of excitement (a heightened expression of reward seeking) and fear (an intense expression of loss aversion) and ask, when such a feeling arises, "What causes this? Where did these feelings come from? What is the context in which I'm having these feelings?" By consciously monitoring moods and the related decisions, Peterson says, people can become more savvy users of their gut feelings. ■

Questions

1. What does Morse say scientists have discovered about our competing animal and human brains?

2. What part does Morse seem to suggest that emotion plays in the decision-making process? What evidence in the text supports your reasoning?

3. According to Morse, how do advances in neuroscience affect our understanding of how we make decisions?

4. **Comparison.** Antonio Damasio, author of the book *Descartes' Error*, demonstrated the connection between emotions and decision-making by noting that "patients with damage to the part of the prefrontal cortex that processes emotions . . . often struggle with making even routine decisions." How does his idea — that emotions are needed for decision-making — apply, or not, to *Romeo and Juliet*?

5. **Informing Your Argument.** Return to the table you created on page 817. Fill in the columns with information about how Morse seems to regard the roles of gut instinct and rational thinking in decision-making. Provide evidence he offers to clarify and support his ideas, and your response to what Morse suggests.

Source D

Docter, Pete. *Inside Out*, 2015.

KEY CONTEXT This is a publicity image from the animated Pixar film *Inside Out*, directed and co-written by Pete Docter. The film follows five personified emotions — Sadness, Joy, Anger, Disgust, and Fear (left to right) — inside the mind of a young girl named Riley as she struggles with adjusting to a new home.

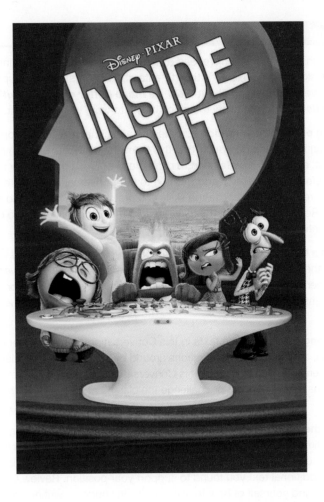

Questions

1. How do the colors, facial expressions, and gestures of the figures in the image convey the particular emotion that each character represents?

2. In your experience, how do conflicts among those five emotions lead to effective or poor decision-making?

3. All of these five emotions represent the "gut" explored in this conversation. Imagine that there was a sixth character that might represent reason or rational thought. What colors, facial expressions, and gestures might that character exhibit in the image above?

4. **Comparison.** Choose one or two main characters from *Romeo and Juliet* and think about specific decisions they make. Which of the five emotions in the image above are most at work? Do those emotions lead to a good or a bad decision? Would the outcomes change if the characters acted on other emotions instead? If so, which emotions?

5. **Informing Your Argument.** Return to the table you created on page 817. Based on this image, add your thoughts regarding what this film might suggest about the roles of gut instinct and rational thinking in decision-making, the best evidence it offers to clarify and support related ideas, and your response to what the image suggests.

Entering the Conversation

Throughout this section, you have read a variety of texts that deal with instinctive and rational decision-making. Now it's time to enter the Conversation by responding to the prompt you've been thinking about — ***Do we make better decisions with our "gut" or with our rational brain?*** Follow the steps below to write your argument.

1. | Building on the Conversation. Locate one additional text on this topic that you think adds an interesting perspective to this Conversation. This text can be of any type: an argument, a graphic or data chart, a narrative, a poem, a painting, or a film clip, for example. Before you decide to add this text to the Conversation, be sure that it is a credible and relevant source; use the skills you practiced in Chapter 4 to evaluate the text (p. 99). Read and annotate the text carefully, making connections to other texts in the Conversation and *Romeo and Juliet*.

2. | Making a Claim. Look back through the table you created and your notes on the texts in the Conversation and write a statement that reflects your overall position about whether we make better decisions with our "gut" or with our rational brain. This statement will be your thesis or claim that you will try to prove in the rest of your argument.

3. | Organizing the Ideas. The texts in this Conversation offer a number of explanations, critiques, and observations around decision-making. Review the table you have been keeping throughout this Conversation and identify the texts and quotations that either support or challenge the claim that you wrote in the previous step.

4. | Writing the Argument. Now that you have a claim that reflects your informed stance, it is time to write your argument. Be sure that your writing stays focused on your position on the issue. Refer to at least two Conversation texts, which could include the additional text you found to support your position. Review Chapter 4 (p. 119) to remind yourself of how to use sources in your own writing and refer to the Writing an Argument Workshop in Chapter 7 (p. 466) for additional support.

5. | Presenting the Argument (Optional). Once you have written your argument, you might want to present it to the class or a small group. Review how to write and deliver a presentation in Chapter 3 (p. 90) and Chapter 7 (p. 479).

B. T. Ryback ■ *from* A Roz by Any Other Name, *825*

from A Roz by Any Other Name

B. T. Ryback

Brett (B. T.) Ryback is an actor, composer, and playwright whose credits include the retelling of Shakespeare's *Macbeth* titled *Weird*, and the musicals *Passing Through* and *Joe Schmoe Saves the World*, and others. In addition to his extensive work in theater and acting, he also works as a composer and lyricist on a variety of projects in the Kidswrites program and the Next Actor's Summer Theatre for young people in Milwaukee, Wisconsin.

Brett Ryback

KEY CONTEXT   As you will see in the excerpts included here, *A Roz by Any Other Name* is a playful exploration of the character Rosalind, Romeo's former love interest in *Romeo and Juliet*, who is mentioned in Shakespeare's play but has no lines. Rosalind, the niece of Capulet, is the reason why Romeo attends the Capulet ball in the first place, where he ultimately meets and falls in love with Juliet. Note that in Shakespeare's original text, she is called "Rosaline," but here she is "Rosalind," or "Roz" to her friends.

Cast of Characters
ROSALIND, *a very beautiful young woman who gets what she wants*
VERA, *her best friend*
CORDONNA, *her no-nonsense nurse*
STEFANO, *a young, simpleminded poet*

Time
The early 1600s

Place
Rosalind's bedroom chamber, Verona, Italy
*Note: It is the playwright's intention that this play not be done with any dialect. Though the actors must weave naturally in and out of heightened language, the characters should at all times maintain a modern sensibility.

[*The curtain rises on a bedroom chamber. There is an archway at left, which acts as a door to the room. The door is framed by various lit candles, which offer the only source of light in the room. In the back of the room are two glass doors that open onto a balcony, beneath which we can see a few trees or shrubs. There is a moment of silence before it is shattered by* ROSALIND *bursting into the room. She is dressed in a princess costume complete with tiara.*]

ROSALIND [*Screaming.*] That Mule! That stubborn, stupid . . . *bloodsucking* Mule! I have never been so humiliated in all my life!
VERA [*Rushing in after* ROSALIND.] Roz, stop, please . . .   5
ROSALIND I just — I mean, who does he think he is? Who does he think I am?
VERA Sit down, you'll feel better.
ROSALIND I have been sitting all night, Vera! I don't think I'll ever need to sit again after   10
tonight. Waiting for that stupid, stubborn —

825

VERA Blood-sucking?

ROSALIND Blood-sucking Mule! A cloth! A cloth for my head!

[VERA *brings her a cloth.* ROSALIND *dabs herself furiously.*]

I'm sweating, Vera. Look at me sweat. I never sweat. I hate sweating. 15

VERA We rushed home so quickly.

ROSALIND [*Still dabbing.*] Oh, no, this isn't "rush sweat." This is *anger* sweat.

VERA Careful you don't dab yourself to death. 20

ROSALIND [*She stops with a cry.*] Oh! And he never asked for one dance. After all I did for him, all the time we shared, he acted like I wasn't even there.

VERA You broke his heart. 25

ROSALIND He deserves it after tonight!

VERA Rosalind, hush, you don't want to wake anyone up. I'll get the tea and then we can talk. You'll feel better, I promise.

[VERA *exits back down the steps.*]

ROSALIND The nerve he has! Did he think no one 30 would see? Did he think *I* wouldn't see? I sat there all night waiting for him to ask me to dance. I ought to tell his parents. Ha! His mother would die right on the spot if I marched up to her and said, "Lady Montague, 35 do you know who I saw your Romeo locking lips with all night long? That's right, *m'lady, Juliet Capulet!* CAPULET!" Ha! Oh, she would die on the spot.

[VERA *enters with a tray, two cups and a teakettle.*]

I've got it! I'll report Romeo to his parents and 40 suggest that Lord Montague demand a pound of Juliet's flesh in restitution for this embarrassment.

VERA [*Rather uninterested.*] What a brilliant idea, Roz. Forgive me if I don't move fast enough. 45

ROSALIND Ten pounds! And they can take it off her behind!

VERA Pound for pound I'd say it's the worst idea I've ever heard.

[ROSALIND *fumes.*]

I swear, the situations I find myself in with you. 50 How do you handle all this . . . excitement?

ROSALIND I'd hardly call this exciting. Insulting is more like it.

VERA Oh, come, Roz, he wasn't breaking any rules.

ROSALIND How dare you take his side! Am I not 55 your best-sworn friend? After all we've been through together, you join with him in scorning me! 'Tis not friendly — 'tis not maidenly! What allegiance do you owe that Mule?

VERA I'm only trying to help you think rationally. 60 You have always been a challenge, Roz, but I care enough to fight you *because* I am your best-sworn friend. Here, try some tea.

[ROSALIND *reluctantly does.*]

ROSALIND Chamomile. Thank you.

[*A beat.*]

Ugh! Those stupid Montague boys. Put six of 65 them together and you still don't get half a brain.

VERA Was all of this so surprising? *You* found *him*, Roz. That day we were all at the beach. You, me, and Giovanni. You saw this wretched-looking, scrawny little thing walking along the 70 sand and you turned to me with that look. Poor Gianni was so oblivious. So you waited for him to go into the water, and then you walked up to that stick of a boy and said something typically Rosalind — 75

ROSALIND He was using a piece of driftwood and I think I said, "You must be a painter or a poet. You handle your stick so well."

VERA [*Laughing.*] I don't know where you come up with those. 80

ROSALIND Practice.

VERA And you came back over to me and looked at me and said, "A Montague. Not bad." Poor Gianni never figured out what happened.

ROSALIND It wasn't Romeo that happened, Vera. 85 You needn't tear a dead leaf from a tree; the right gust of wind will do the job on its own.

VERA And Rosalind had her wind. [*A beat.*] He was very handsome and strong, but oh, how that boy cried. Like a poet he cried. 90

ROSALIND You sound just like him.

VERA I said he cried is all. You forget, Roz, that the best friend must often serve two masters.

ROSALIND Well, rest assured you won't need to be holding Romeo's hand. He found some whore 95 to do it for you. I just . . . I don't understand. A Capulet! I mean, it's one thing to see manure on the street, but to actually pick it up and take it home with you?
But then what can one expect from a Mule? 100 But honestly, a Capulet! To go from a Constantini to a Capulet. Even alphabetically it's backwards.

VERA The Capulets aren't as undistinguished as they once were. Why do you think there has been a resurrection in the fights between the 105 two houses? You should consider it a blessing to be out of that mess.

ROSALIND [*Blood rising.*] A blessing! Is gold blessed to have been exchanged for silver? I couldn't be more humiliated if he ran 110 off with a Putori, the trashiest family in Verona!

VERA Maybe he saw something more in her.

ROSALIND More than what? Than me?

VERA It isn't impossible.

ROSALIND I dare you to continue that thought. 115

VERA Believe it or not, Rosalind, there are other women in the world besides you. A little competition never hurt anyone.

ROSALIND I don't recall Helen of Troy having any competition! 120

VERA And I don't recall Helen of Troy losing any men!

ROSALIND Well, thank you, Vera, for the wonderful history lesson!

[*This last outburst is the loudest. We hear a door slam, and heavy feet, exasperatingly making their way up the stairs.*]

VERA I told you, you would wake someone up! 125

ROSALIND Not that wretched woman, please!

[*Appearing at the door is* CORDONNA. *She has just been woken up and is obviously not pleased about it.*]

CORDONNA Rosalind Constantini, if you don't shut your godforsaken mouth, I'll have the smith drive a nail through your lips that'll have you sipping soup through a straw for the 130 rest of your life.

ROSALIND Well, it'd be nice to find that *some* of the help does work around here.

CORDONNA [*Shaking her head.*] Ungrateful brat.

ROSALIND [*Meeting her.*] Vicious horse. 135

CORDONNA [*Mildly.*] Evening, Vera. I can only imagine what this one has roped you in to doing here at all hours of the night.

VERA We just returned from a costume party, ma'am. 140

CORDONNA Oh, dear, you can call me Cordonna.

ROSALIND She also answers to "Dinner is served."

CORDONNA You know, I'd say you were raised by wolves if it wasn't such an insult to wolves.

ROSALIND Given *your* family history, I'd say I was 145 raised by wolves, too.

CORDONNA Putori trash!

ROSALIND Careful, Vera, I think she's going to rear.

CORDONNA And what are you supposed to be? A prostitute? 150

ROSALIND I'm a princess.

CORDONNA [*She laughs.*] Yeah. And I'm the Pope. What are you two doing making all that noise up here?

VERA Rosalind had bitter luck tonight. 155

CORDONNA No one's replaced poor Romeo?

VERA Someone's replaced poor Rosalind.

[ROSALIND *turns, shocked at what* VERA *just said.*]

CORDONNA My, my, my, how the mighty do fall. So who was it?

ROSALIND I don't believe this has anything to do 160 with my *laundry*, so perhaps you should keep your little hooves out!

CORDONNA Give her another day. She'll find someone new to build up, lead on, and then dump like yesterday's bread. 165

ROSALIND [*Breaking slightly.*] Cordonna, please.

CORDONNA [*She considers.*] Well, if you do happen to find some tears in there, be sure to let them out quietly. Some of us sleep at night. Good night, Vera. 170

This image is from a 2013 film version of *Romeo and Juliet*, in which Rosaline and Romeo's cousin Benvolio watch Romeo meet Juliet.

What might the Rosaline character of *A Roz by Any Other Name* have to say to Benvolio in this situation? Why?

VERA Good night, Cordonna.

[CORDONNA *exits.*]

ROSALIND That is exactly what I'm afraid of. The minute people find out that Rosalind Constantini has been trumped by a Capulet, I'm ruined. My reputation, my dignity, my 175 pride — all gone. I must do something to get Romeo back. I need a plan . . .

VERA [*Becoming excited.*] Like what?

ROSALIND I'm not sure. But whatever it is, it must be brilliantly clever. 180

VERA What if you simply apologized and asked to have him back?

ROSALIND Too easy. He'd never fall for it. I've got it! Perhaps I will dress as a boy, befriend Romeo, and then convince him to take back 185 his true love, the lustrous Rosalind!

[VERA *laughs.*]

I'm serious!

VERA You dress as a boy? That is for some other Rosalind. Get some rest, Roz.

[VERA *goes to open the large glass doors. As she does, we see* STEFANO *appear at ground level. Unbeknownst, he has been waiting, anxiously for these very doors to open. Excitedly, he hides just below the balcony.*]

The night air will calm you. Sunrise must be 190 only a few hours away.

[*At this moment, in an effort to get their attention,* STEFANO *hoots like an owl.*]

STEFANO Who!

ROSALIND [*Walking out to the balcony.*] Vera, it cannot nearly be sunrise soon. The night-owl still sings. 195

[STEFANO *hoots again.*]

STEFANO Who!

ROSALIND I wonder what he's doing now.

VERA Who?

ROSALIND Romeo! [*She sighs.*] Oh, Romeo. Wherefore art thou such a stupid idiot? 200

STEFANO Who?

ROSALIND What do you mean "who"? I just told you.

VERA I didn't say anything.

ROSALIND Um, yes, you did, I just heard you. I said "Romeo, Oh, Romeo, wherefore art thou 205 such a moron," and you said, "Who?" just like that stupid night-owl.

[*A beat. She sees* STEFANO, *gasps, and rushes back into the room.*]

There's someone outside my window!

VERA [*Teasing.*] Who?

ROSALIND Oh, would you stop already! There's a 210
man prowling outside my window! Just below
the balcony. He was staring at me all wide-
eyed. He must be insane! Of course! Romeo
has sent an insane murderer to slay me while I
sleep! Oh, I am undone! 215

VERA Stop. He cannot get to us in here.

ROSALIND Right. Because no one's ever *climbed*
the balcony before!

[STEFANO, *confused at what has taken place,*
hoots again.]

STEFANO Who!

VERA He calls. 220

ROSALIND Summoning some devil no doubt!
Romeo seeks to destroy me with witchcraft.

[*She steps defiantly toward the window.*]

How now, spirit! Speak your purposes or else
retreat to the depths from whence you came.

STEFANO [*Timidly.*] Please, m'lady, I mean no 225
malintent.

ROSALIND What's that? I couldn't hear you over
the growl of my two hungry Rottweilers. Who
sent you?

STEFANO I come of my own accord, I swear! 230

VERA He sounds harmless.

ROSALIND No man is harmless around a woman.
He's always poised to draw his weapon.

[VERA *sneaks forward onto the balcony to take*
a look.]

VERA I recognize him. He was at the party!

ROSALIND Was he? 235

VERA What's your name, scoundrel?

STEFANO Stefano, your grace.

ROSALIND [*Aside.*] Stefano Capulet? Can that be
right?

VERA State your purpose. 240

STEFANO I have followed your graces from the
masquerade, where I first laid eyes on such
beauty.

ROSALIND [*To* VERA] Followed our graces?
Chased our skirts is more likely. 245

STEFANO Your companion was in such an upset
state, that it didn't seem appropriate to
approach you at the time. When I saw you run
into the house, I thought for sure I had lost
you, until the light from yonder window 250
broke upon the dew-kissed grass, betraying
your secret counsel, leading me to the fair
maiden of the house!

ROSALIND [*To* VERA] A likely story! Romeo must
have put him up to this. 255

VERA Sir, as the light doth betray our counsel, so
doth the wind betray your words, mis-
delivering your compliments to the wrong
ears. I am not the maiden of this house.

STEFANO Not you, miss. Your friend. The lustrous 260
Rosalind.

[*At this,* ROSALIND's *ears perk up. She inches*
forward.]

ROSALIND Who was it, again, that did catch your
eye?

STEFANO Rosalind was her name. Or so I was
told. But if it is not, then lend me some 265
parchment that I may write it down and tear it
to bits, so that the name never resounds on my
lips again.

ROSALIND No need for the parchment. My name
is Rosalind. 270

STEFANO Can it truly be that I am beholding such
beauty in my presence? That on yonder
balcony, becrouched and hidden, lies the true
object of my eyes' fancy?

VERA He's awful. 275

ROSALIND Shh. Let him finish.

STEFANO Oh, happy night that has brought me
through forest, meadow, and a few really wet
areas that I'm not too sure about to your
window's edge. 280

[STEFANO *pauses for a beat, and then lets out*
a shout of joy.]

VERA What was that?

ROSALIND Excitement, I think.

VERA Or a war cry. We should probably step
away from the window.

ROSALIND Nonsense. He's harmless. . . . 285

> **KEY CONTEXT** In lines not included in the
> excerpt, Rosalind plans to try to make Romeo
> jealous by befriending Stefano. When Stefano
> enters her chambers, Rosalind convinces him
> to write her a poem so that it could be read
> aloud to Romeo as part of her plan.

ROSALIND A poem! I will inspire you to write a
poem right now.

STEFANO Now?

ROSALIND I don't see why not.

VERA Inspiration cannot be forced, Roz.

ROSALIND It can when you're a muse, *Ver!* 290

VERA I don't think you should.

ROSALIND Vera, may I talk to you in private for a
moment? It will only take a moment, Stefano,
I promise.

[*The two huddle together away from* STEFANO.]

What are you doing?

VERA Did you listen to his story, Roz? This boy likes 295
you a lot! He is very sensitive and very fragile.

ROSALIND I know. It's almost too perfect! He'll
write a poem about me and then I'll get him to
read it aloud to Romeo and Juliet. It's bound
to get Romeo's blood boiling! 300

VERA Rosalind, you're not listening! He doesn't
deserve this.

ROSALIND And I didn't deserve what Romeo did
to me! We don't always get what we want,
Vera. Now play along or leave!

[*Before* VERA *can speak,* ROSALIND *turns
back to* STEFANO, *who has been attempting to
write his first lines.*]

STEFANO I think I have something. 305

ROSALIND Already! There must be a record for
how quickly a muse has inspired her subject's
thoughts.

VERA I do believe Rosalind holds many records
for speed.

ROSALIND Let's hear it!

STEFANO It's a sonnet. 310

[*He clears his throat.*]

Tell me, Love, by what name art thou known?
Art thou called Aurora by the dawn?
For blinding bright your beauty now is shown.
A camel and a squid will never spawn.

[*He looks up at them.*]

I'm still working on that line. 315

[*Back to the poem.*]

By midday you are called Eurus's child,
Who blows about me warmly as the breeze,

And shields me from getting much too mild . . .

[*A beat.*]

What rhymes with "breeze"?

ROSALIND Oh. Um . . . trees. 320

VERA Stees.

ROSALIND Bees. Freeze.

VERA Prees.

ROSALIND Squeeze.

VERA Crees. Drees. 325

ROSALIND [*To* VERA] Crees? Drees? Those aren't
words.

VERA Sorry.

STEFANO I've got it!
Who blows about me warmly as the breeze,
And shields me from getting much too mild, 330
By feeding me a large amount of cheese.

ROSALIND We'll iron that one out in the rewrites.
Let's keep plowing ahead. How about:
At night have you some other Roman name?
Are you known as Luna or Selini? 335

[*She thinks.*]

Are you known as Luna or Selini . . .

[*They all think a moment. Finally,* STEFANO
turns to ROSALIND.]

STEFANO My muse! Of course!
At night have you some other Roman name?
Are you known as Luna or Selini?
In faith, I shall put all of them to shame, 340
And call thee the beautiful Rosalind Constantini.

[ROSALIND *is slightly taken back, but does her
best not to show it.*]

ROSALIND We are but two lines away, and I have
just the pairing.
And still the name above means nothing yet.
Till coupled with Stefano Capulet.

STEFANO Well done, my grace! 345

ROSALIND I have inspired a true work of art! And
our names are so entwined in the writing they
will be but married in the ear of anyone who
beholds them! You must be very proud.

STEFANO Yes! 350

ROSALIND You must read this to everyone you
know. Your father, your mother, brothers,
sisters, cousins . . . yes, especially your cousins.

STEFANO Indeed, I shall. Who is Stefano Capulet?

[ROSALIND *stops cold.*]

ROSALIND I beg your pardon? 355

STEFANO The fellow in the poem I just wrote, who has the same first name as I, but not the same last name . . . who is he?

ROSALIND Why don't be silly! It's *your* name.

STEFANO Oh! It's *my* name! I get it. 360

ROSALIND Yes!

STEFANO It's like a pen name.

ROSALIND Let me get this straight. Your name is —

STEFANO Stefano.

ROSALIND But not Stefano *Capulet*? 365

STEFANO That's correct.

VERA What *is* your full name?

STEFANO Of course. It's Stefano Giovanni Francesco Putori.

ROSALIND Putori. Stefano Putori.

STEFANO That's right. 370

ROSALIND So you're not cousins with Juliet Capulet.

STEFANO Uh-uh.

ROSALIND You're not even *related* to the Capulets, are you?

STEFANO Uh-uh. Who are they?

VERA The party. Tonight. It was the Capulets' party. How did you get in? 375

ROSALIND You weren't even wearing a costume!

STEFANO Well, my father was given an open invitation. He's a mason. He must have done business with them. 380

ROSALIND Oh, my. I'm afraid I've made a terrible mistake. I thought . . . You aren't . . .

STEFANO I hope I didn't lead you astray at all, my grace. It would shame me greatly to know that I have done wrong by you. 385

ROSALIND Yes, well, perhaps you should have thought of that before you chose not to reveal your whole identity to me. This changes everything.

[STEFANO *is obviously crushed.*]

STEFANO Please . . . I beg your forgiveness . . . I . . . please . . . 390

VERA [*Gently.*] Stefano, would you be so kind as to bring us some tea? The fire should still be on.

[*Helplessly,* STEFANO *exits.*]

You ought to be ashamed of yourself.

ROSALIND Me!? You were the one who said he was a Capulet in the first place. 395

The ABC series, *Still Star-Crossed* (2016) was another retelling of Rosalind's story. In this series, the Prince forces the betrothal of Rosalind to Benvolio after the deaths of Romeo and Juliet in order to end the feud between the two families.

How might the Rosalind that Ryback portrays respond to a betrothal to Benvolio, based on what you know of his character in *Romeo and Juliet*?

831

VERA I never said that. I said I recognized him from the party, but like always you invented something else in your head. You built him up to be something he wasn't, and when you finally realized that he's not, you dumped him 400 just like everyone else.

ROSALIND How dare you accuse me of such shallowness? How was I to know who he was?

VERA You never stopped to think about him in the first place! If you had listened to me before — 405

ROSALIND Me, me, me! That's all you care about. What good has listening to you ever done?

VERA Perhaps you should try and find out.

ROSALIND You're supposed to support me.

VERA You can't treat people like this, Rosalind. It 410 isn't right. People aren't puppets that you can use at your disposal. I say this as your friend.

ROSALIND What would you know about friendship? You have been against me all night. You think I'm out to break every heart I can. If I had *known* 415 that Stefano was some stupid country bumpkin from a trashy family, if I had *known* he couldn't help me get Romeo back, I never would have invited him up here in the first place!

VERA Just because you wear a stupid princess 420 costume, you think you can boss everyone around, don't you! I ought to tear it to shreds!

[VERA *goes after* ROSALIND'*s dress. ROSALIND *turns to run away and the two stop abruptly to see* STEFANO *standing at the door silently. He has heard enough.*]

STEFANO [*Quietly.*] It's a costume?

ROSALIND . . . the party . . .

[ROSALIND *looks as though she is about to say more.*]

STEFANO No, no. I can see myself out. There 425 is no need for wasted words. You gave me something so wonderful, I should have known that it did not belong to me.

[*He is about to turn to go, but stops to take one last look at the room.*]

This place really looked so beautiful from the outside.

[STEFANO *exits.* ROSALIND *and* VERA *are left looking at each other. There is a moment of silence. Then.*]

ROSALIND This is all your fault! 430

VERA My fault!?

ROSALIND You had to go and open your stupid mouth! You are such an ignorant pig!

VERA You're just upset that for the second time tonight someone has left you because they 435 found out what kind of a monster you really are!

[*At this* ROSALIND *winds up and slaps* VERA *directly across the face. After a moment of shock for the both of them,* VERA *turns slowly towards* ROSALIND.]

All these years I pitied the wrong people.

[VERA *quietly grabs her things and walks to the door.*]

No man to bore you, no friend to get in the way: Rosalind Constantini finally has what she 440 wants. She's alone.

[VERA *exits.* ROSALIND *is indignant at first. She takes her tiara from her head and snaps it. She turns quickly and throws it at the door. She takes* STEFANO'*s poem and starts tearing it to shreds. As she does, she is suddenly overcome with tears and collapses on the ground, weeping. A few moments later,* CORDONNA *appears at the door.*]

CORDONNA It's going to be all right.

[ROSALIND *turns, surprised. She tries to hide her tears.*]

ROSALIND I'm fine. Please leave.

[CORDONNA *ignores her and walks closer.*]

CORDONNA You sit atop mountains and every now and then you're bound to fall down a little. 445

ROSALIND I said, I don't need your . . .

[*She cries.*]

CORDONNA Fine, fine. I'll go.

ROSALIND No. Wait! I'm sorry! Oh, God, I'm so sorry!

[CORDONNA *rushes to hold* ROSALIND.]

CORDONNA Hush, child. It's not that bad. You're going to be all right. 450

ROSALIND He was right. I'm so hideous inside. All I ever wanted was what I couldn't have. And now all I want is something I don't deserve.

CORDONNA Now, now, there's only one thing anyone your age truly deserves and that's a second chance. What you decide to do with it is what makes you worthy of anything else. 455

ROSALIND But Vera is right. I'm alone.

CORDONNA As long as Rosalind Constantini keeps waking up her battered nurse in the middle of the night, she'll never be alone. 460

[ROSALIND *laughs.* CORDONNA *smiles and then picks up a piece of the torn poem from the floor.*]

What's this? Look, here is writ "the beautiful Ros'lind Constantini."

ROSALIND Such a name I do not deserve.

CORDONNA And yet someone believed that you did.

ROSALIND A poor, naive boy who knew nothing of who I am. 465

[ROSALIND *considers this.*]

He knew nothing about me, and even so he wrote such pretty poetry. Oh, hateful hands, to tear such loving words! Injurious wasps, to feed on such sweet honey, and kill the bees that yield it with your stings! How can I mend this, Cordonna? 470

CORDONNA I think we have some paste in the cupboard.

ROSALIND I had something beautiful and I tore it up. I will never learn.

VERA You will if you just try.

[ROSALIND *and* CORDONNA *turn to find* VERA *standing in the doorway.*]

ROSALIND You've come back! 475

VERA Yes, I've come back.

ROSALIND I can't imagine why you would.

VERA [*A beat.*] Neither can I.

ROSALIND You were right to leave. I'm sorry. I was . . . I was wrong. I don't know why I keep making the same mistakes. 480

VERA It happens. A lot. To you.

ROSALIND I know.

VERA But I stood by you, Roz.

ROSALIND I know.

VERA Every single time. 485

ROSALIND I know, I know!

VERA For years I envied you. You were beautiful, you were popular, you had anything you asked for, and I hated you for it. But tonight I realized — you aren't perfect at all. You're just Rosalind. And that's what makes me your friend. 490

ROSALIND Truly?

VERA Truly. But I am not going to watch you hurt those boys any longer. Or yourself! 495

ROSALIND I suppose I don't know my own strength.

VERA Perhaps you might keep an eye on your weaknesses, too.

ROSALIND I will try, Vera. I promise.

[*The girls hug.*]

I hope you'll forgive me. 500

VERA I came back, didn't I? That seems a good enough start to me.

ROSALIND Me too. But quickly, now, we must grab our things.

VERA Why? Where are we going?

ROSALIND I have to get him back!

VERA Wait, Rosalind, no! What are you doing? You have to stop! You have to LET ROMEO GO! 505

ROSALIND Romeo? No, silly! Stefano Putori! A poet needs his muse.

[VERA *smiles at her.*]

VERA And Rosalind needs her poet.

ROSALIND Come on! The night is young!

VERA You go. I will hear about it when you return. I've had enough excitement for a while. 510

ROSALIND Are you sure?

VERA Completely.

[ROSALIND *smiles and runs out of the room.* CORDONNA *follows her to the door and turns to* VERA.]

CORDONNA You are a good friend. 515

VERA And you, a good nurse.

CORDONNA Perhaps between the two of us she'll become some sort of decent person.

VERA [*She laughs.*] The night is young!

[VERA *follows* CORDONNA *to the door, stopping to blow out the few candles as they exit. The stage goes dark as . . .*]

[*The curtain falls.*]

Understanding and Interpreting

1. Throughout the play, Ryback shares insight into Rosalind's current and past relationships. What do we learn about Rosalind's experiences with relationships through her conversation with Vera? What evidence can you find to support your observations?

2. A foil is a character that contrasts with a main character to highlight an aspect or trait. How does Vera serve as a foil to Rosalind?

3. What do lines 94–102 reveal about Rosalind's attitude toward a societal class system? In what way does her view interfere with her relationships?

4. How would you describe the relationship Rosalind has with Cordonna for most of the play? What influences might be responsible for Rosalind's treatment of Cordonna?

5. How is the relationship between Rosalind and Cordonna in this play similar to or different from the relationship between Juliet and the Nurse in *Romeo and Juliet*?

6. What is your impression of Stefano based on his dialogue in lines 246–253? What does this first impression say about his character? How does your impression of him change as the play progresses?

7. What commentary about poetry, the characters, or even Shakespeare might Ryback be making when he presents the moment in which Stefano composes his sonnet (lines 310–345)?

8. In a dramatic twist, Rosalind finds out that Stefano is not a Capulet after all and that her advances are for nothing. Likewise, Stefano finds out that Rosalind is not a true princess. How were they misled? How does this turn of events change the course of action for both characters?

9. In both this play and *Romeo and Juliet*, there is confusion with identities. Reread Act 1, Scene 5, lines 116–146 of *Romeo and Juliet* when the lovers discover their families are enemies, and lines 363–429 of *A Roz by Any Other Name* when Stefano and Roz realize that they have mistaken each other's identities. How does the confusion with names complicate the plot in both plays? Compare the events that occur in both plays after reality is revealed. How does Rosalind's discovery that Stefano is not a Capulet compare to Romeo's discovery that Juliet is?

10. How does the friendship between Rosalind and Vera and the relationship between Rosalind and Cordonna change in the course of the play? How does Ryback define friendship through the plot, action, and characters in his play?

11. A dynamic character is one who experiences a significant change over the course of a story. Explain the changes that Rosalind goes through and how they make her a dynamic character.

Analyzing Language, Style, and Structure

12. **Vocabulary in Context.** In line 74, Vera relates the story of Rosalind's first meeting with Romeo, describing him as a "stick of a boy." What is the meaning of the word *stick* as it's used in this context?

13. **Vocabulary in Context.** In line 148, Rosalind says to Vera to be careful because Cordonna is "going to rear." What does the word *rear* mean in this context?

14. Because Ryback's play is one scene and one act, he must establish character very quickly. How does the dialogue in the opening lines characterize Rosalind and Vera early on?

15. What does Rosalind's description of Romeo in lines 1–14 say about her true feelings for him? What do these lines reveal about Rosalind at this point?

16. An allusion is a reference to something with historical, cultural, or literary significance. In lines 120–121, Rosalind and Vera mention Helen of Troy. How is this allusion important in further defining Rosalind's personality?

17. In the production notes, Ryback states, "Though the actors must weave naturally in and out of heightened language, the characters should at all times maintain a modern sensibility." What is the purpose and effect of blending modern sensibilities and heightened language in this play?

18. Stefano explains that he knew he'd found Rosalind's room when the "light from yonder window broke" (l. 250), which parallels the moment that Romeo remarks, "But soft, what light through yonder window breaks" (Act 1, Scene 5, l. 2) when he finds Juliet's window. What is Ryback suggesting by including this allusion to the language of *Romeo and Juliet*?

19. Stage directions can offer insight into the characters in a play. Find two or three examples of how Ryback uses stage directions to help characterize Rosalind.

20. Puns are jokes based on words that sound alike but have different meanings. Identify a few places where Ryback uses puns and explain how they add humor to the play.

21. When Stefano first enters the scene (ll. 235–280), how does his dialogue differ from that of Rosalind and Vera? What purpose might Ryback have for making such distinctions in language?

22. Look at Ryback's use of punctuation during the moments after Rosalind realizes that Stefano is not a Capulet in lines 363–392. How does his use of punctuation accentuate the action and dialogue in this section?

23. How has Rosalind's language changed at the end of the play in lines 464–481? How does the change in her language reflect a change in her character?

Topics for Composing

24. **Analysis.** In contrast to the five-act tragedy of *Romeo and Juliet*, Ryback's play is a one-act comedy. Write an analysis of Ryback's comedic approach to dramatic elements such as character, action, and dialogue. How does he employ them, and what makes them effective in this comedic twist on the Shakespearean drama?

25. **Analysis.** Ryback's desire to play with Shakespearean language inspired him to write this play. Analyze the language Ryback uses in *A Roz by Any Other Name*, and discuss how embracing and digressing from Shakespearean language affects the audience's understanding of a major theme of the play.

26. **Argument.** Who, or what, is responsible for the change in Rosalind's character? Write an argument in which you make an assertion and support your claim with evidence from the text.

27. **Connections.** One of Ryback's motivations for writing is to highlight minor characters in Shakespeare's works — characters that don't have a lot of stage time, but that Ryback thinks would have interesting backstories. Research plays, movies, or television shows that have also explored a minor character's backstory and explain how the character was portrayed.

28. **Connections.** Describe how you define the value of friendship. Based on your definition, would you have forgiven Rosalind as Vera and Cordonna do? Have you been in a situation in which your friendship with another was tested? What was the outcome?

29. **Speaking and Listening.** With a partner, perform a few lines from the play that embody Ryback's humorous tone. As you and your partner perform the scene, pay attention to how you emphasize the language choices Ryback makes with your voice and body language.

30. **Creative Writing.** Write another scene for Ryback's play in which Rosalind reunites with Stefano and confesses her love to him. What will she say to him? How will he react?

31. **Exposition.** Write a response in which you explain how friendships can help people improve themselves. In what ways do friendships in Ryback's play operate according to your explanation?

Analysis of Drama

Analyzing dramatic text is very similar to analyzing fiction and poetry. Playwrights use many of the same elements you see in fiction and poetry: language, setting, imagery, theme, character, and conflict. In drama, the reader must also take into consideration additional elements such as staging and props, costuming, stage directions, and lighting and sound effects. The ways in which these elements are used can have a profound effect on character, conflict, and plot.

In the Skill Workshop on page 706, you looked at how Jonathan Rand uses elements of drama to achieve a purpose or effect in his play *Check Please*. If you worked through the Creative Writing Extension on page 721, you practiced with dramatic elements by creating a scene, or scenes, for your own drama. You were asked to create characters, develop plot, incorporate action, construct dialogue, outline staging, describe setting, and consider how they all work together to create a dramatic story. Being a playwright is about making these choices.

As you analyze dramatic texts, you will explain why playwrights make the choices they do and how those affect the reader's or audience's overall understanding of the play. We'll practice some analysis using a portion of the Central Text in this chapter, Shakespeare's *Romeo and Juliet*. A typical writing prompt for an analysis of drama might read as follows:

Analyze how the playwright uses elements of drama — such as dialogue, setting, and stage directions — to develop the characters and reveal a theme of the play.

Before we write a response to a prompt of this sort, we need to break it down to understand what it is asking us to do. In this case, we need to do two things:

1. Identify elements the playwright uses.
2. Explain how those elements of drama develop the characters and relate to a theme of the play.

This prompt suggests three specific dramatic elements that you might consider in your analysis — dialogue, setting, and stage directions. However, when writing your own analysis, you might want to focus on only one or two dramatic elements. You are not required to use all three suggestions. What is more important is that you show how the elements you choose develop character and reveal a theme. Once we have figured out what the prompt is asking us to do, we have a focus for our reading.

Getting Started

activity

For our sample analysis, we will focus on the fight scene with Mercutio, Tybalt, and Romeo in Act 3. Find a different passage from *Romeo and Juliet* that you would like to analyze that is 50–100 lines long. Aim for an important or revealing moment with strong dramatic elements (dialogue, setting, and/or stage directions). You might decide not to focus on all three dramatic elements in your essay, but your excerpt should provide enough information for a thorough analysis of at least one. Write briefly about why you selected the passage and what interests you most about it. Then talk with a partner about whether the passage seems to be one you could analyze for characterization and theme.

Step 1. Reading and Making Observations

As with any text, the first thing you should do is read it for understanding, to be able to summarize what is literally happening in the play, free from any analysis of dramatic elements, symbols, interpretation, or meaning. In the case of our model excerpt, we might say something like this: In these lines from Act 3, Scene 1, the tension between the rival families escalates into a duel that changes the course of the plot and the fates of the characters. Here, Tybalt challenges Romeo to a fight, but it is Mercutio who ends up fighting. As a result, Mercutio, who is not a member of either family, is fatally stabbed.

On our second reading, we will examine the specific elements of drama identified in the prompt, asking questions about unknown allusions or other places of confusion or ambiguity. Our notes below are just samples of this process in action.

BENVOLIO By my head, here come the Capulets.
MERCUTIO By my heel, I care not.

Benvolio is cautious, Mercutio is rash.

TYBALT [*To his companions*]
 Follow me close, for I will speak to them. —
 Gentlemen, good e'en. A word with one of you.
MERCUTIO And but one word with one of us?
 Couple it with something: make it a word and a blow.

Mercutio is first to bring up violence.

TYBALT You shall find me apt enough to that, sir,
 an you will give me occasion.
MERCUTIO Could you not take some occasion without giving?
TYBALT Mercutio, thou consortest with Romeo.
MERCUTIO "Consort"? What, dost thou make us minstrels?
 An thou make minstrels of us, look to hear
 nothing but discords. Here's my fiddlestick; here's
 that shall make you dance. Zounds, "consort"!

Mercutio is joking/mocking. He doesn't take the danger seriously.

BENVOLIO We talk here in the public haunt of men.
 Either withdraw unto some private place,
 Or reason coldly of your grievances,
 Or else depart; here all eyes gaze on us.

Setting is important here: fighting in public vs. in private. Benvolio is again trying to keep the peace.

MERCUTIO Men's eyes were made to look, and let them gaze.
I will not budge for no man's pleasure, I. ——————

Mercutio is not part of this feud, but he's making the situation worse. This encounter is doomed to tragedy because of him.

[*Enter Romeo*]

TYBALT Well, peace be with you, sir. Here comes my man.
MERCUTIO But I'll be hanged, sir, if he wear your livery.
Marry, go before to field, he'll be your follower;
Your worship in that sense may call him "man."
TYBALT Romeo, the love I bear thee can afford
No better term than this: thou art a villain.
ROMEO Tybalt, the reason that I have to love thee
Doth much excuse the appertaining rage
To such a greeting. Villain am I none.
Therefore, farewell. I see thou knowest me not.

Romeo mentions love, reminding us that he just married Juliet, and this is happening at his happiest moment. A cruel twist of Fate.

Romeo tries to leave, but Mercutio and Tybalt are too aggressive to let him.

TYBALT Boy, this shall not excuse the injuries
That thou hast done me. Therefore turn and draw.

Continues to challenge Romeo.

ROMEO I do protest I never injured thee,
But love thee better than thou canst devise
Till thou shalt know the reason of my love.
And so, good Capulet — which name I tender
As dearly as my own — be satisfied.

Again, Romeo tries to deescalate the situation.

MERCUTIO O calm, dishonorable, vile submission!
Alla stoccata carries it away. [*He draws*] —— *Brief, aggressive stage direction.*
Tybalt, you ratcatcher, will you walk?
TYBALT What wouldst thou have with me?
MERCUTIO Good king of cats, nothing but one of your
nine lives, that I mean to make bold withal, and, as
you shall use me hereafter, dry-beat the rest of the
eight. Will you pluck your sword out of his pilcher by
the ears? Make haste, lest mine be about your ears ere
it be out.

Mercutio says he wants Tybalt's "nine lives," a threat to kill him.

TYBALT I am for you. [*He draws.*]
ROMEO Gentle Mercutio, put thy rapier up. —— *Still tries to resolve the conflict.*
MERCUTIO Come, sir, your *passado*. [*They fight*]
ROMEO Draw, Benvolio, beat down their weapons.
Gentlemen, for shame, forbear this outrage!
Tybalt, Mercutio, the Prince expressly hath
Forbid this bandying in Verona streets.
Hold, Tybalt! Good Mercutio!

Trying to calm the situation, Romeo only makes it worse by getting Benvolio involved.

Setting: Verona's streets are to be kept safe, but instead they have become the battleground.

The dialogue here continues to characterize Romeo as the mediator. He keeps pleading with them to stop.

[*Tybalt under Romeo's arm stabs Mercutio.*
Away Tybalt (with his followers).]

Stage directions — confusing: did Tybalt miss Romeo in the fray, or was he intentionally aiming at Mercutio? Bad luck?

MERCUTIO I am hurt.
A plague o' both your houses! I am sped.
Is he gone, and hath nothing?
BENVOLIO What, art thou hurt?
MERCUTIO Ay, ay, a scratch, a scratch; marry, 'tis enough.
Where is my page? Go, villain, fetch a surgeon.

He is angry that he is a victim of a feud that he was not, until now, directly involved in, but the incident was largely his fault.

[*Exit Page*]

ROMEO Courage, man, the hurt cannot be much.

MERCUTIO No, 'tis not so deep as a well, nor so wide as a church-door; but 'tis enough, 'twill serve. Ask for me tomorrow, and you shall find me a grave man. I am peppered, I warrant, for this world. A plague o' both your houses! Zounds, a dog, a rat, a mouse, a cat, to scratch a man to death! A braggart, a rogue, a villain, that fights by the book of arithmetic! Why the devil came you between us? I was hurt under your arm.

Despite his injury, he continues to use puns.

A parallel: Romeo comes between two warring parties and a loved one dies.

A key line. Romeo with good intentions, but doomed by ill Fate.

ROMEO I thought all for the best.

MERCUTIO Help me into some house, Benvolio,
Or I shall faint. A plague o' both your houses!
They have made worm's meat of me. I have it,
And soundly too. Your houses!

[Exit supported by Benvolio]

Reading and Making Observations

Return to the excerpt from *Romeo and Juliet* that you have selected for your analysis. Keep in mind that it should be about the same length as the passage above and should be an important or revealing moment with strong dramatic elements (dialogue, setting, and/or stage directions). Remember that even if you decide not to focus on all three dramatic elements in your essay, your excerpt should provide enough information for a thorough analysis of at least one.

Read your chosen excerpt at least twice:

1. First read for understanding. What is happening?

2. Then read for meaning. Annotate the excerpt by asking questions, noting important ideas, and identifying the key elements of drama used by the playwright to develop the characters and reveal a theme.

Step 2. Finding a Focus

How do we begin to pull together our annotations to find a focus for our analysis? Since our analysis will discuss Shakespeare's use of dramatic elements, like dialogue, setting, and stage directions to develop the characters and reveal a theme in the play, we could begin by summarizing some key points that we noted in our model excerpt:

- There is a direct contrast between the inflammatory language used by Mercutio and Tybalt and the pleading language used by Benvolio and Romeo.
- This incident happens after Romeo's marriage to Juliet. Romeo and Juliet are "star–crossed" lovers, doomed by Fate, and Fate seems to have a hand in this incident as well.
- The personalities of Mercutio and Tybalt are perfectly paired for conflict.
- Mercutio is also irritated with Romeo's "vile submission" to Tybalt. In a cruel twist of fate, Romeo's unwillingness to fight drives Mercutio's decision to fight.

839

- Shakespeare's short, violent stage directions highlight the aggression, and sometimes confusion, of the scene.
- Mercutio suffers the ultimate price as the victim caught between the two feuding families, a point he makes when he invokes "a plague o' both [their] houses" because "they have made worm's meat of [him]."
- The scene takes place in the public streets of Verona. Despite being warned about fighting in the streets and hearing both Benvolio's and Romeo's pleas for peace, Mercutio and Tybalt continue the conflict.

As we review these observations, it becomes evident that the dialogue is used to contrast the hot-headed Mercutio and Tybalt with the peacekeepers Romeo and Benvolio, further developing these characters. It's also clear that Fate is at work in this scene, setting up events in such a way that all of Romeo's attempts to keep the peace and intervene only make the situation worse. These ideas will be the focus of our analysis.

activity · Finding a Focus

So far, you have been given an example of what it looks like to annotate a passage for dramatic elements in relation to character and theme, and you've practiced with an excerpt of your choosing. Now it's time to review your completed annotations on your selected excerpt and begin to develop a focus for your analysis. Remember to review your annotations for how the playwright uses dramatic elements to develop character and reveal a theme of the play. If you struggle with finding a focus for the excerpt you selected, try finding another one and follow the same steps as our *Romeo and Juliet* model above.

Step 3. Creating a Thesis Statement

When creating your thesis statement, remember that it should incorporate the *what* as well as the *how*. Our analysis will look not only at *what* Shakespeare does (Shakespeare uses elements of drama to develop his characters and themes), but *how* he does this (Shakespeare uses dialogue to show how the characters' personalities inflame the situation). You're essentially taking a position on an idea that you will then set out to prove using evidence from the text.

For the topic we've been exploring, we might write a thesis sentence like this:

WEAK THESIS

In this excerpt from *Romeo and Juliet*, I will analyze Shakespeare's use of dramatic elements.

What's insufficient about this thesis statement is that it doesn't discuss the *how*, and doesn't give our analysis a focus. Let's try to narrow the focus a bit more.

WEAK THESIS

In this analysis, I will discuss how Shakespeare uses setting, dialogue, and stage directions to develop the characters and reveal a theme of the play.

Better, but not quite right just yet. Upon closer inspection, this thesis simply restates the prompt on page 836. What else do we need to do? We have to word the thesis in such a way that it connects to the ideas we want to express in our analysis. How does language specifically emphasize the characters' personalities and intensify the conflict? We need to make a claim.

WORKING THESIS

Shakespeare uses dialogue, setting, and stage directions to reveal how the characters Mercutio and Tybalt are embodiments of the ill fate haunting the star–crossed lover, Romeo.

This thesis addresses not only the *what* (the specific elements used), but *how* Shakespeare uses them (the elements help develop the characters of Mercutio and Tybalt in order to create conflict and further the theme of Romeo being an ill-fated, star-crossed lover).

There are other thesis statements that we could create for this excerpt. Our focus is on fate, but someone could also analyze Mercutio's motivations, compare and contrast Mercutio and Tybalt's behavior with that of Romeo and Benvolio, or analyze how dramatic irony plays a central part in the scene. For the rest of this workshop, we'll use the working thesis above as our starting point.

Creating a Thesis

activity

Using the passage that you selected and annotated in the previous activities, write a working thesis that takes into account how Shakespeare uses dramatic elements to emphasize character and reveal a theme from the play. Remember that your thesis should introduce the idea you want to explore and take an interpretive stance on that idea.

Step 4. Proving Your Point

Now that we have a focus for our analysis, the next step is to prove that our interpretation is valid. While responses to literature are somewhat subjective, that doesn't mean we can interpret literature any way we want. The interpretation has to be based on a valid reading of the text itself. The way we prove that in academic writing is by drawing evidence directly from the text and combining that with our own commentary.

Based on our working thesis, what exactly do we need to prove? Here again is the working thesis for our sample analysis:

WORKING THESIS

Shakespeare uses dialogue, setting, and stage directions to reveal how the characters Mercutio and Tybalt are embodiments of the ill fate haunting the star-crossed lover, Romeo.

In our analysis, we'll need to prove two points:

POINT 1   Mercutio and Tybalt are embodiments of the ill fate haunting Romeo.

POINT 2   Shakespeare reveals the significance of their characters through dialogue, setting, and stage directions.

In order to address these points, we will need to go back to the text for evidence.

Gathering and Organizing Evidence

There are many ways to gather and organize your evidence. You can group similar ideas together or even color-code evidence that is related. Some writers like to use graphic organizers or draft a brief outline of their ideas with possible supporting evidence.

Whichever system you use is up to you. Keep in mind as you gather and organize your information that quotations alone are not enough to prove your point. It is your job as the writer to point out *how* each quotation proves the point you're making. Using a table like the one below will not only help you organize your evidence but also help you think about how the quotations you select connect to your larger point.

Working Thesis: Shakespeare uses dialogue, setting, and stage directions to reveal how the characters Mercutio and Tybalt are embodiments of the ill fate haunting the star-crossed lover, Romeo.

Focus	Quotation	How the Quotation Supports the Point
Dialogue	"**Tybalt** Gentlemen, good e'en. A word with one of you. **Mercutio** And but one word with one of us? Couple it with something: make it a word and a blow."	Mercutio brings up violence, even when Tybalt appears to be polite. This exchange makes violence almost inevitable.
Dialogue	"**Mercutio** O calm, dishonorable, vile submission!"	Mercutio is arguing that Romeo's calmness and submission are dishonorable. Even though this isn't his feud, he is driving the conflict with Tybalt and is ultimately the victim of it.

activity   Gathering Evidence

Return to your working thesis and start gathering evidence to support the specific points you need to prove. Remember that whether you outline, categorize, color-code, or fill in a graphic organizer is up to you. Try any of these methods to see which system works best.

Presenting Evidence

To present and support your ideas, you will need to make your point, frame your quotations, and then explain how the two are connected. In the writing chapter of this book, on pages 85–86, we talked about how to make a point, support it with evidence, and then comment on how the evidence proves the point. If we were to create a draft of a paragraph examining the way in which one element, dialogue, reveals how Mercutio and Tybalt are embodiments of the ill fate haunting Romeo, we might come up with something like this:

> In the fight scene in the streets of Verona, Shakespeare shows through the dialogue that Mercutio and Tybalt are characters at odds—one teasing, the other temperamental. } *The point*
>
> They are a volatile mix. The fight scene begins with Tybalt asking to have "a word" and Mercutio immediately offering to "make it a word and a blow." Up to this point, Mercutio } *Evidence*
>
> has not been directly involved in the conflict. He is not a Montague or a Capulet. And yet, he escalates the feud and initiates violence with the Capulets without knowing that Romeo has recently wedded into the family. } *Explanation*

The draft we just created is a good start on a short but focused analytical paragraph. If we find more quotations to support our points, we build on the paragraph by continuing with this structure, as long as we stay on the same topic, like this:

> In the fight scene in the streets of Verona, Shakespeare shows through the dialogue that Mercutio and Tybalt are characters at odds—one teasing, the other temperamental. } *The point*
>
> They are a volatile mix. The fight scene begins with Tybalt asking to have "a word" and Mercutio immediately offering to "make it a word and a blow." Up to this point, Mercutio } *Evidence*
>
> has not been directly involved in the conflict. He is not a Montague or a Capulet. And yet, he escalates the feud and initiates violence with the Capulets without knowing that } *Explanation*
>
> Romeo has recently wedded into the family. As the fight ends and Mercutio is stabbed, he blames Romeo and the feud between the two houses for what has happened to him. } *Another point*
>
> Mercutio says "Why the devil came you between us?" and Romeo replies "I thought all for the best." } *More evidence*
>
> Even though Mercutio begins the fight, it is Romeo coming between Mercutio and Tybalt that causes Mercutio's death, just as Romeo coming between the two warring houses causes Juliet's death. Despite Romeo's best intentions, his ill fate leads to the chaos and death around him, as shown by the conflict between Mercutio and Tybalt. } *Another explanation*

843

The evidence and commentary given above, along with the connections to our points, have given us a credible draft of an analytical paragraph.

To continue to build our analytical essay we could look at the other elements of drama identified in our working thesis — setting and stage directions — to show how Shakespeare uses them to create this ill-fated encounter.

Writing a Body Paragraph

Using the model analytical paragraph above as a guide, write a body paragraph for your own working thesis that states your point, incorporates at least two pieces of textual evidence, and explains how your evidence supports your point. If your working thesis leads to a second point to argue, you can repeat the steps in another body paragraph.

Step 5. Expanding to an Essay

Whether you realize it or not, we've come a long way in writing an analytical essay. We have a thesis, and we even have a solid body paragraph or two. If we add an introduction and a conclusion, we'll probably have a solid draft analysis of this passage. If we were asked to write about the entire play, our paper would get longer, as we would have more to say about how Shakespeare develops the characters and theme through dramatic elements.

The key parts missing from our essay at this point are the introduction and conclusion. Let's work on those.

Introductory Paragraph

The point of the introductory paragraph is to engage your reader and create interest in the topic. A standard introduction has three parts:

1. An opening hook
2. A connection to the piece being analyzed
3. A thesis statement

The hook is about drawing readers in and getting them to think about the kinds of ideas or issues that are at play in your analysis. This is a great place to just raise questions or identify issues. No one is expecting you to actually have the answers to these questions, or solutions to these problems; they are intended only to hook your reader's interest.

Many writers will tell you that the first sentence is the hardest to write. Here are a few classic ways to begin your introductory paragraph:

With a question	Does fate drive our behavior, or does it only seem like it in retrospect?
With a statement	Some people believe that everything happens for a reason and they say we should not fight our destiny.
With a story or anecdote	We have all been caught in the middle of an argument at one point in our lives.

Once we have a hook, it's time to show our readers how the ideas we've brought up apply to the reading we are about to analyze. This transition doesn't have to be fancy. It's usually a simple connecting statement that includes a bit of summary.

[Does fate drive our behavior, or does it only seem like it in retrospect?] In *Romeo and Juliet*, Shakespeare tells us a story of "star-crossed" lovers whose lives are subject to the whims of fate, which operates through various characters in the play. [Shakespeare uses dialogue, setting, and stage directions to reveal how the characters Mercutio and Tybalt are embodiments of the ill fate haunting the star-crossed lover, Romeo.]

— *The hook*

The connection to the piece

Thesis statement

Introduction

activity

Following the model, write a draft of your introductory paragraph. Think about how you want to hook the reader and lead into your thesis statement.

Concluding Paragraph

As with any essay you write, a solid conclusion will bring your paper full circle by restating (not repeating) your thesis and the main points you analyzed in each of the body paragraphs. It should bring completeness and closure to the reader with the satisfaction that your assertion is a sound one.

Notice how the draft below of the concluding paragraph for the model text ties back to the thesis and provides a synthesis of the ideas in the body paragraphs.

The circumstances surrounding the skirmish between Tybalt and Romeo that lead to Mercutio's death and change the course of the plot can be attributed to one idea: fate. Shakespeare uses dialogue in this passage to not only bring the characters to life, but to demonstrate how those personalities spur the conflict and deliver Romeo's ill-fate. From Mercutio's taunts and insults, to Tybalt's cold aggression and Romeo's innocent interference, Shakespeare creates a tragic scene in which, yet again, a loved one dies because of fate's vendetta against Romeo.

activity — Conclusion

Write a concluding paragraph for your essay. Remember to tie it back to your thesis, the points in your body paragraphs, and avoid simply repeating what you have already stated.

Bringing It All Together

If you take all of the pieces you've written and put them together, you have a solid draft of a short analytical essay. Remember that all of the steps in this workshop are here just to help you get started. Once you feel more in control of what it means to make an interpretation, prove a point, and comment on textual evidence, you can start to bend these rules to suit your purposes. Writing is not about formulas or templates. It's about communicating ideas.

Step 6. Finalizing the Essay

Now that you have a complete draft of your essay, you can move on to the final phase of the writing process: revising and editing. These two acts are sometimes thought of as being the same, but they're not. Revision is when you look back at large-scale structural elements of your essay, such as how well you support your claim, what kinds of evidence you use, how effective your word choices are, and to what extent you have led your reader easily through your essay. Editing, on the other hand, focuses on fine-tuning the language, grammar, punctuation, spelling, and other conventions. Editing is usually the very last thing you do before you finalize your piece, looking carefully for any errors that you tend to make. The following are suggestions for you to consider as you finalize your essay.

Revising

Revising gives you a good opportunity to think again about your essay's purpose and audience. In most cases, your audience will be your teacher or an external evaluator in the case of a standardized test. In both situations, that means using a somewhat formal tone, but your writing can still be engaging for you and your audience. Reread your essay for the following:

- **Look back at your thesis.** Since you wrote this early on in the workshop, does it still relate to the analysis you ended up writing? If you need more assistance with this, be sure to look at Revision Workshop 1: Effective Thesis and Essay Structure in the back of the book.

- **Check your focus.** Is it still at the center of your analysis? Make sure that ideas and evidence in your paragraphs connect back to the focus. If you need more assistance with this, be sure to look at Revision Workshop 2: Effective Topic Sentences and Unified Paragraphs in the back of the book.
- **Revisit your body paragraphs.** Have you balanced the evidence with your own commentary about how that evidence supports your thesis? If you need more assistance with this, be sure to look at Revision Workshop 4: Appropriate Evidence and Support in the back of the book.
- **Look back at your argument.** Does your essay draw a clear connection between the elements of drama and the development of character and a possible theme of the play? Return to the Skill Workshop (p. 706) at the beginning of this chapter if you need more practice with this.
- **Check your introduction and conclusion.** Does your introduction grab the reader's attention and effectively preview your topic? Does your conclusion wrap up in a way that highlights your focus? Review Revision Workshop 8: Effective Introductions and Conclusions in the back of the book if you need additional support with these parts of your essay.

Editing

Remember, editing is the very last thing you'll do before finalizing your essay. You and your teacher know better than anyone the types of spelling, grammar, and convention errors you need to focus on in your writing development. Below is a short checklist of things to keep in mind. Be sure to refer to one or more of the Grammar Workshops in the back of the book if you encounter an issue and aren't sure how to overcome it.

- Check your writing for the use of present tense verbs. Literature *lives*, so the analysis should discuss how the playwright *uses* (rather than *used*) dramatic elements, and that the characters *are* (rather than *were*) portrayed in a certain way.
- Make sure you've written in third person point of view and avoid the use of pronouns like *I* and *you*.
- If the verb tense or pronoun is not in the correct form, change it in the sentence and use brackets [ ] to indicate the change. *Example*: Tybalt tells Mercutio that "[Mercutio] will give [him] occasion" to speak (Act 3, Scene 1, line 47). Using brackets to replace the words *you* and *me* from the original quotation with [*Mercutio*] and [*him*] in the integrated quotation keeps the surrounding sentence grammatical and easy for readers to understand.

public speaking extension

Performance of a Scene

Throughout this workshop, you have been analyzing a scene from *Romeo and Juliet*. For this extension activity, rather than presenting your analysis, you will work collaboratively with a small group to rehearse and perform a scene from the play. Since members of your group may have chosen to analyze different scenes for their essays, your first step should be to decide on which one you would like to perform based on the number of people in your group and which scene you think you can perform most effectively. Depending on the size of your group, you might want to have one member be a director of the scene instead of an actor to allow for someone to provide feedback during rehearsals, cue up music or lighting, and support other details of the production.

Preparing for Your Performance

Before you begin rehearsing, your group should read through the scene several times and discuss various interpretations of characters, conflicts, and possible theme. Once your group has settled on what you want to communicate about the scene to an audience, you will produce a "staging notebook" for your scene that will include the following:

- An annotated copy of your scene that will act as your script for your performance. Actors will have copies of the script with their own lines highlighted and notes on how the lines will be performed. Mark words for emphasis and include markings for gestures, movements, and facial expressions when your character is speaking as well as when you have no lines.
- A description of the set design, which will include everything that the audience will see in your scene, such as furniture, structures, props, and so on.
- A description of other theatrical elements, including sound effects, lighting, music, and costumes.

Rehearsing Your Scene

As you practice your performance, discuss the following as a group:

- How do the actors emphasize key lines, and how does that help to communicate an interpretation of the scene? Are the gestures and movements effective at capturing elements of the characters?

- How can you use theatrical elements, such as set design, sound, music, and lighting, to help to create the mood of the scene and assist in communicating your interpretation?
- What are the most appropriate — and available — props and costumes that will help you to communicate your interpretation?
- If you made any changes to the original script, what is added to or absent from the scene in your interpretation? In other words, where have you diverted from the original and why?
- How do the conflicting motives of the characters in this scene advance the plot of the drama? How are you making these conflicts clear in your performance?

Presenting Your Scene

Keep the following in mind as you perform your scene:

1. Face the audience when you are speaking.
2. Speak loudly enough so that the people the furthest away from you can hear.
3. Make eye contact with the actor who is speaking to you.
4. Use gestures, movement, and facial expressions that are effective and appropriate for your character.

Reflecting on Your Performance

With your group or on your own, reflect on your group's performance. To what extent were you able to present Shakespeare's words effectively? What would you change about your performance and why? What else would you have done with this performance if you had unlimited time and budget?

Mythology

Long before the invention of the printing press or the Internet, early humans passed down stories orally from generation to generation. Some of these stories became part of religious practices, some became epic tales still told today, and most were forgotten to time and history. These stories belong to a broad genre called "mythology."

There is a reason why people sometimes say that ambitious, massive, or significant things are "of mythic proportions." Myths are stories of creation, life and death, good and evil, humans and nature, and natural phenomena like earthquakes and volcanoes. Their characters are gods, heroes, and heroines. Myths seek a truth about life's biggest questions. Yes, today we know scientifically that earthquakes are caused by shifting tectonic plates; but the stories of, say, Namazu, the Japanese Earthshaker god depicted as a giant catfish, can remind us of the need for balance between the natural and human worlds. This chapter will explore why myths still matter to us today, and how elements of mythology continue to influence contemporary texts and cultures.

Contents

Essential Elements of Mythology

Mythology is not intended to be read literally. While myths may share elements from many other genres, like fiction and poetry, what makes those elements mythic — a mythic character, a mythic plot, a mythic setting — is how those elements operate on the symbolic level.

Myths are traditional stories of deep importance to a culture that relate early history, the actions of deities, or explanations of natural or social phenomena. Stories with mythic elements have been passed down orally from generation to generation, but contemporary writers and filmmakers also tap into this kind of storytelling in comic books and superhero films, for example. Many texts take on the elements of mythology but might not fit a strict definition of a "myth." These include the following:

- **Fables.** Stories, usually very short, that feature animals with human characteristics and which often put forward a lesson or a moral. "The Tortoise and the Hare" is one of the most widely known fables.
- **Fairy tales.** Stories that feature magical creatures and lands, often with princesses, princes, and other royalty. These usually take the form of children's stories. "Cinderella" is one of the most recognizable fairy tales.
- **Legends.** Stories from the past that might have at one point been based in reality but cannot be authenticated. The legend of King Arthur is one of the most famous.
- **Tall tales.** Stories like legends, but relying on broad exaggerations, often for humorous effect. The tale of Paul Bunyan and his blue ox, Babe, might be one of the most widely shared tall tales.

This is not intended to suggest that all such stories are myths, but rather that all of these types of texts have mythic elements that require us to read symbolically.

PREVIEWING Academic Vocabulary   **Essential Elements of Mythology**

In this section, you will encounter the following terms as you think about how to analyze mythology. Working individually or with a partner or small group, consider what you already know about the meaning of each term.

1. Theme
2. Mythic archetypes
3. Archetypal plots
   Hero's journey
   Trickster tales
4. Archetypal characters
5. Archetypal settings

Let's begin our study of mythic texts by reading a Greek myth about the changing of the seasons: *The Myth of Demeter and Persephone.*

from The Myth of Demeter and Persephone

Padraic Colum

Padraic Colum (1881–1972) was an Irish poet, dramatist, and collector of folklore. He is most famous for his adaptations of the myths of ancient Greece and Rome, which earned him three Newbery Medals for contributions to literature for young people.

KEY CONTEXT   Demeter was the Greek goddess of agriculture and was the sister and a wife of Zeus, the king of the Greek gods. In this myth, Persephone, the child of Demeter and Zeus, is kidnapped by Hades, the god of the Underworld. Hermes, the messenger god, plays a role in securing her release.

Everett Collection Inc/Alamy

Once when Demeter was going through the world, giving men grain to be sown in their fields, she heard a cry that came to her from across high mountains and that mounted up to her from the sea. Demeter's heart shook when she heard that cry, for she knew that it came to her from her daughter, from her only child, young Persephone. . . .

Persephone had been playing with the nymphs who are the daughters of Ocean — Phæno, Ianthe, Melita, Ianeira, Acaste — in the lovely fields of Enna. They went to gather flowers — irises and crocuses, lilies, narcissus, hyacinths and rose-blooms — that grow in those fields. As they went, gathering flowers in their baskets, they had sight of Pergus, the pool that the white swans come to sing in.

Beside a deep chasm that had been made in the earth a wonder flower was growing — in color it was like the crocus, but it sent forth a perfume that was like the perfume of a hundred flowers. And Persephone thought as she went toward it that having gathered that flower she would have something much more wonderful than her companions had.

She did not know that Hades, the lord of the Underworld, had caused that flower to grow there so that she might be drawn by it to the chasm that he had made.

As Persephone stooped to pluck the wonder flower, Hades, in his chariot of iron, dashed up through the chasm, and grasping the maiden by the waist, set her beside him.   5

The maiden cried out, first because her flowers had been spilled, and then because she was being reft away. She cried out to her mother, and her cry went over high mountains and sounded up from the sea. The daughters of Ocean, affrighted, fled and sank down into the depths of the sea.

In his great chariot of iron that was drawn by black steeds Hades rushed down through the chasm he had made. Into the Underworld he went, and he dashed across the River Styx, and he brought his chariot up beside his throne. And on his dark throne he seated Persephone, the fainting daughter of Demeter.

No more did the Goddess Demeter give grain to men; no more did she bless their fields: weeds grew where grain had been growing, and men feared that in a while they would famish for lack of bread.

She wandered through the world, her thought all upon her child, Persephone, who had been taken from her. Once she sat by a well by a wayside, thinking upon the child that she might not come to and who might not come to her.

She saw four maidens come near; their grace 10 and their youth reminded her of her child. They stepped lightly along, carrying bronze pitchers in their hands, for they were coming to the Well of the Maiden beside which Demeter sat.

The maidens thought when they looked upon her that the goddess was some ancient woman who had a sorrow in her heart. Seeing that she was so noble and so sorrowful looking, the maidens, as they drew the clear water into their pitchers, spoke kindly to her.

"Why do you stay away from the town, old mother?" one of the maidens said. "Why do you not come to the houses? We think that you look as if you were shelterless and alone, and we should like to tell you that there are many houses in the town where you would be welcomed."

Demeter's heart went out to the maidens, because they looked so young and fair and simple and spoke out of such kind hearts. She said to them: "Where can I go, dear children? My people are far away, and there are none in all the world who would care to be near me."

Said one of the maidens: "There are princes in the land who would welcome you in their houses if you would consent to nurse one of their young children. But why do I speak of other princes beside Celeus, our father? In his house you would indeed have a welcome. But lately a baby has been born to our mother, Metaneira, and she would greatly rejoice to have one as wise as you mind little Demophoön."

All the time that she watched them and 15 listened to their voices Demeter felt that the grace and youth of the maidens made them like Persephone. She thought that it would ease her heart to be in the house where these maidens were. . . .

But still she kept away from the assemblies of the gods. Zeus sent a messenger to her, Iris with the golden wings, bidding her to Olympus. Demeter would not join the Olympians. Then,

one after the other, the gods and goddesses of Olympus came to her; none were able to make her cease from grieving for Persephone, or to go again into the company of the immortal gods.

And so it came about that Zeus was compelled to send a messenger down to the Underworld to bring Persephone back to the mother who grieved so much for the loss of her. Hermes was the messenger whom Zeus sent. Through the darkened places of the earth Hermes went, and he came to that dark throne where the lord Hades sat, with Persephone beside him. Then Hermes spoke to the lord of the Underworld, saying that Zeus commanded that Persephone should come forth from the Underworld that her mother might look upon her.

Then Persephone, hearing the words of Zeus uttered the only cry that had left her lips since she had sent out that cry that had reached her mother's heart. And Hades, hearing the command of Zeus that might not be denied, bowed his dark, majestic head.

She might go to the Upperworld and rest herself in the arms of her mother, he said. And then he cried out: "Ah, Persephone, strive to feel kindliness in your heart toward me who carried you off by violence and against your will. I can give to you one of the great kingdoms that the Olympians rule over. And I, who am brother to Zeus, am no unfitting husband for you, Demeter's child."

So Hades, the dark lord of the Underworld 20 said, and he made ready the iron chariot with its deathless horses that Persephone might go up from his kingdom.

Beside the single tree in his domain Hades stayed the chariot. A single fruit grew on that tree, a bright pomegranate fruit. Persephone stood up in the chariot and plucked the fruit from the tree. Then did Hades prevail upon her to divide the fruit, and, having divided it, Persephone ate seven of the pomegranate seeds.

It was Hermes who took the whip and the reins of the chariot. He drove on, and neither the sea nor the water-courses, nor the glens nor the mountain peaks stayed the deathless horses of Hades, and soon the chariot was brought near to where Demeter awaited the coming of her daughter.

And when, from a hilltop, Demeter saw the chariot approaching, she flew like a wild bird to clasp her child. Persephone, when she saw her mother's dear eyes, sprang out of the chariot and fell upon her neck and embraced her. Long and long Demeter held her dear child in her arms, gazing, gazing upon her. Suddenly her mind misgave her. With a great fear at her heart she cried out: "Dearest, has any food passed your lips in all the time you have been in the Underworld?"

She had not tasted food in all the time she was there, Persephone said. And then, suddenly, she remembered the pomegranate that Hades had asked her to divide. When she told that she had eaten seven seeds from it Demeter wept, and her tears fell upon Persephone's face.

"Ah, my dearest," she cried, "if you had not eaten the pomegranate seeds you could have stayed with me, and always we should have been together. But now that you have eaten food in it, the Underworld has a claim upon you. You may not stay always with me here. Again you will have to go back and dwell in the dark places under the earth and sit upon Hades' throne. But not always you will be there. When the flowers bloom upon the earth you shall come up from the realm of darkness, and in great joy we shall go through the world together, Demeter and Persephone."

And so it has been since Persephone came back to her mother after having eaten of the pomegranate seeds. For two seasons of the year she stays with Demeter, and for one season she stays in the Underworld with her dark lord. While she is with her mother there is springtime upon the earth. Demeter blesses the furrows, her heart being glad because her daughter is with her once more. The furrows become heavy with grain, and soon the whole wide earth has grain and fruit, leaves and flowers. When the furrows are reaped, when the grain has been gathered, when the dark season comes, Persephone goes from her mother, and going down into the dark places, she sits beside her mighty lord Hades and upon his throne. Not sorrowful is she there; she sits with head unbowed, for she knows herself to be a mighty queen. She has joy, too, knowing of the seasons when she may walk with Demeter, her mother, on the wide places of the earth, through fields of flowers and fruit and ripening grain. ■

25

Getting Started

Think about a myth, fable, legend, tall tale, or fairy tale that you know well. It could be from a novel, movie, or television show. What is the myth about? With a classmate, discuss what makes that myth one of your favorites.

Theme

When reading mythology, we must always read it for its meaning. Mythology is not meant to be taken literally. It tells stories intended to convey deeper meaning, to deliver symbolic messages about the world. So, while we should read literally in order to understand the plot, setting, and characters of the myth, it is okay to move quickly to reading for meaning, because conveying a thematic message is the primary purpose of this genre.

What can be challenging for a modern reader is to understand what a myth meant for its original audience, while also thinking about what it means for us now. For instance, this myth of Demeter and Persephone may have originally been told to explain the changing of the seasons. But now that we know that it is the tilt of the earth and distance from the sun that causes the seasons, we can — and should — interpret the meaning of this story differently. So, what are we left with that we can analyze for theme? What is the significance of this myth to us today?

One way to look at this myth from a modern perspective is by thinking of the relationship between Demeter and Persephone as representing parent–child relationships as a whole. Inevitably, children grow up and leave home, and this significant change is bound to cause some level of loss and confusion on both sides. Eventually, however, a new relationship between Demeter and Persephone is formed. It is no longer exclusively just the two of them, but Demeter has to adjust to sharing her daughter as Persephone moves on to the next phase of her life, as the new Queen of the Underworld.

As with any complex literary text, myths can have multiple interpretations, and this is just one. For instance, look at these two artistic depictions of the Persephone and Demeter myth. While the one on the left focuses on the horror of Persephone's abduction, the second emphasizes Demeter's grief at the loss of her daughter.

PAINTING/Alamy

We might also read the story as a warning of the threats that exist in the world. Demeter and Persephone are living in a blissful eternal spring until Hades, representing death and the unknown, abducts Persephone. Knowledge of evil in the world changes us, leaving behind the innocence of childhood and changing forever the way we view the world. Persephone — and Demeter — can never fully return to the way they were before. Or, maybe the story represents the grief we feel at the death of our loved ones, and the story offers us a way to take solace in the rebirth that perhaps comes after, though in a much different form. The point of analyzing the seemingly simple story of Demeter and Persephone is to illustrate that mythology, when read for theme — not just plot or character — still connects with modern audiences. It is the deeper, symbolic meanings of the myth that matter.

Theme

Think back on the myth that you identified in the earlier activity. What is its relevance to today's world? What theme(s) could you draw from the story in the way we did with the myth of Demeter and Persephone?

Mythic Archetypes

In the section above, we proposed that myths still matter because we continue to find meaning in them today, but we didn't explain why myths work this way. Carl Jung, an influential psychiatrist from the early twentieth century, believed that our minds have an unconscious part, filled with ideas and thoughts of which we are unaware. Additionally, he suggested the existence of a "collective unconscious," which we share with all humans, deeply embedded in our minds stretching back across time. In this theory, mythology is what one scholar called the "representations of the contents of the deepest recesses of the human psyche: the world of the archetypes."

In the study of mythology, the term *archetype* refers to patterns of plot, setting, and character that reoccur regularly, with the creators oftentimes not fully aware that they are repeating long-established patterns. Jung wrote that "the collective unconscious . . . appears to consist of mythological motifs or primordial images, for which reason the myths of all nations are its real exponents. In fact, the whole of mythology could be taken as a sort of projection of the collective unconscious." Researchers, including anthropologists and archeologists, have found some evidence of Jung's theories, noting the similarities of stories and symbols of ancient cultures that had little contact with each other. This is why many contemporary films, stories, and even video games share many of the same archetypes that appear in myths from thousands of years ago: they are the patterns that define humanity, regardless of culture, race, and country of origin.

Joseph Campbell, a scholar who spent his life studying mythology from around the world, described myths as "music we dance to, even when we cannot name the tune." Below, we break the archetypes down into three main categories present in the literary texts you have encountered throughout this book: plot, characters, and settings.

Archetypal Plots

While there are a number of archetypal plots in mythology and other mythic texts, the two most common are the hero's journey and trickster tales. Both of these types of stories have been widely adopted in modern storytelling, as you'll start to realize once you begin looking for them.

The Hero's Journey. Mythologist Joseph Campbell defined the hero's journey in his influential book *The Hero with a Thousand Faces*. In it, he mapped many myths onto a single plot structure, which he called the "monomyth" of the world, because it shows up in so many different countries and cultures. The hero's journey often includes a series of specific stages, but the most significant ones are as follows:

- **Stage 1: The Call to Adventure.** Heroes are presented with and reluctantly accept challenges that take them away from home. It means leaving the safety and security of the known world and crossing into a new and dangerous world, which heroes usually do only after meeting with mentors who assists them in crossing the threshold to the unfamiliar. In the first *Matrix* film, Neo, the protagonist, receives a literal phone call to adventure — a message encouraging him to follow the white rabbit to Morpheus, who gives him a choice, as seen this image:

- **Stage 2: The Road of Trials.** This is when heroes endure tests of strength, resourcefulness, and endurance. Heroes survive by relying on their own character traits but also often with the assistance of a supernatural guide, a magician, a god, a fairy godmother, and so on. After surviving the trials, archetypal heroes are symbolically reborn in some way — physically, emotionally, or spiritually. Usually, heroes at some point gain a significant reward — for instance, a magic sword or a lightsaber.
- **Stage 3: The Return.** After surviving the trials, heroes return home, changed in many ways: older, more mature, more thoughtful. Heroes use this new wisdom or the reward to restore order to the land, defeat enemies, or bring new ideas and peace. One example is the final scene of *Encanto*, in which Mirabel leads her family to the home that she has helped them to restore by bravely seeking the truth.

Let's return to the Demeter and Persephone myth to see how the aspects of this archetypal plot are represented:

- **Stage 1:** Like many heroes who are reluctant to answer the call to adventure, Persephone has little choice when she leaves the comfort and safety of her home and crosses into a far stranger and more dangerous place. While he does not seem so at the time, Hades becomes a type of mentor initiating her into the Underworld.
- **Stage 2:** Persephone endures many trials on her journey, including separation from her mother, cold, and hunger. She receives magical assistance from the gods, specifically Hermes, who negotiates her release.
- **Stage 3:** Most importantly, Persephone returns home, but she is significantly changed, now married and the Queen of the Underworld, her mother's equal in many ways. Her return brings springtime back to the world, but with the cost of knowing that it cannot last.

You may be familiar with this diagram that represents the traditional plot structure:

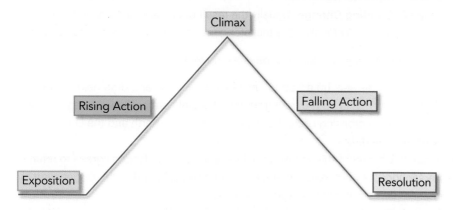

One of the reasons why this plot structure is found in so many stories is that it fits the pattern of the hero's journey archetype. The exposition often establishes the hero within the context of the known world of Stage 1. The rising action includes many of the conflicts faced in Stage 2: Road of Trials, most specifically the most difficult challenge in the climax, sometimes called "the innermost cave." The falling action and the resolution often include a return home, as described in Stage 3 of the journey. It may be surprising as you start to notice how many stories you know fall into this archetypal pattern, perhaps proving Jung correct in his theories of a collective unconscious that writers tap into as they write their stories.

Trickster Tales. Cultures from all over the world have trickster tales, including, most notably, African stories of the spider Anansi, African American folk tales of Br'er Rabbit, and Native American coyote myths. Loki, of Norse mythology, is probably the most well-known trickster character today, thanks to the character's prominence in the Marvel Cinematic Universe. The archetypal plot of a trickster tale shares some of the aspects of the hero's journey, in that tricksters often travel to an unfamiliar world and return home with something that is beneficial to the gods or others, though mostly beneficial to themselves. The main difference is that tricksters' journeys are of their own making; their often-selfish desires cause them to take on the adventure in the first place. The outcome is also rarely something that they originally intended. We can generally break down a trickster tale into the following three stages:

- **Stage 1: Crossing the Boundary.** Whether it is breaking a social taboo, moving between heaven and earth, gods and mortals, or man and animals, the first step of any trickster tale is a transgression of social norms. Often the boundary that is crossed is represented by the trickster taking something that rightfully belongs to someone else or initiating a contest or wager that it doesn't appear the trickster can win.
- **Stage 2: Resolving the Conflict.** By crossing the boundary, the trickster has created some sort of conflict, which must be resolved. This might be a contest that the trickster has to win, or a wrong that must be righted. The trickster often finds a clever way of achieving victory.
- **Stage 3: Creating Change.** Usually the result of crossing the boundary and resolving the conflict is that the trickster generates progress or creates change.

In the Persephone myth, Hades operates as the trickster.

- **Stage 1.** Hades sets up a trap to ensnare Persephone and drag her into the Underworld. This is both a transgression of social norms — kidnapping the child of a god — and a crossing of the boundary between the earth and the Underworld, the living and the dead.
- **Stage 2.** Ultimately, this conflict must be resolved, and Hades agrees to return Persephone, but not before he tricks her into being bound to the Underworld by encouraging her to eat pomegranate seeds.
- **Stage 3.** The change that is created is that the world now has seasons. Without Hades's transgression, that change would not have been created.

activity · Archetypal Plots

Think about a movie, book, or story that you know well that you think employs either the "hero's journey" or the "trickster tale" archetype, maybe the one you thought about earlier or a different one. In what ways does your text fit with the plot archetype? Explain how the three stages of the archetype are represented.

Archetypal Characters

Just as the plots of many films and stories reflect the hero's journey archetype, so do many characters reflect archetypes that show up in different myths, fables, films, novels, and fairy tales. In Chapter 6, you may have read about the primary types of characters in a story:

- The **protagonist** is the most prominent character in a story, whose actions or inactions often drive the story. In mythology, this is usually the hero or the trickster, as described in the archetypal plots above. T'Challa, for example, is the protagonist of the *Black Panther* film.

PictureLux / Alamy

- The **antagonist** is the character who opposes the actions of the protagonist, either intentionally or unintentionally. This is not always a villain, but a character who makes it difficult for the hero to complete the journey. There is often more than one antagonist in a myth.
- Other characters, called **supporting or minor characters**, may appear in myths to add more depth to the story or to cause additional conflicts for the protagonist to face. One common type of supporting character is the **foil**. The purpose of the foil is to provide contrast with the protagonist in order to highlight an aspect or trait. In the *Harry Potter* series, for instance, a foil to Harry could be Hermione, whose analytical approach to problem solving contrasts with Harry's action-oriented approach.

As we mentioned at the beginning of this workshop, the goal for reading a myth is to be able to analyze it for its theme rather than for its literal meaning, and this is also true when looking specifically at characters and characterization in mythology. The following are descriptions of archetypal characters that often show up in mythology — some are antagonists to the hero, and some are foils or other supporting characters — and because they are archetypes, many will probably seem familiar to you from other stories and films. The important part is to always think about the symbolic meaning of these characters: what do they represent to the hero and the hero's journey?

- The **Mentor** is a guide and teacher who provides valuable information, instruction, or weapons to the hero and encourages the hero to start on the journey. Oftentimes, the mentor dies or leaves the hero, requiring the hero to complete the journey independently. Examples include Dumbledore (*Harry Potter*), Gandalf the Grey (*Lord of the Rings*), and Obi-wan (*Star Wars*).

- The **Shadow** is often the chief antagonist that the hero must defeat or tame before the hero can complete the journey. The name "the Shadow" implies that this character is in some way a reflection of the hero, sharing traits and characteristics with the hero, but in a more sinister form. Examples include Ares (*Wonder Woman*), The Joker (*Batman*), and Thanos (various Marvel films).

- An **Absent Parent** is an archetypal character found in mythology and other stories. Many heroes are orphans — Cinderella, Harry Potter, and Anne Shirley from *Anne of Green Gables* — and sometimes the hero is reunited with a parent at some point in the journey.

- A **Monster** or **Dragon** is often one of the antagonists the hero faces on the journey and represents evil, or a wilderness that the hero civilizes. Hercules kills the multiheaded Hydra, Shang-Chi has to defeat the Dweller-in-Darkness, and Little Red Riding Hood faces a wolf pretending to be her grandmother.

- The **Companion** is a character, sometimes animal or magical, who assists the hero on the journey and who often provides friendship and support as needed. Sometimes this character is included for humorous effect, and oftentimes companions let heroes show their true selves. Examples include Timon and Pumbaa in *The Lion King*, Grogu in *The Mandalorian*, and Katy in *Shang-Chi*.

- The **Tempter/Temptress** is a character who tries to use money, fame, sex, or other temptations to prevent the hero from completing the journey. While sometimes the Tempter/Temptress might also be the Shadow (Darth Vader, for example), tempting the hero for evil reasons, sometimes the Tempter/Temptress is unaware of harming the hero.

- The **Damsel in Distress** is a common archetype of a character — often a woman, but not always — who needs to be rescued by the hero. This archetype can be seen in its most basic form in fairy tales like Sleeping Beauty, Snow White, and Rapunzel. This type of character is often found in action or horror movies, although today it is often seen as an outdated and stereotyped role. The *Shrek* films play off these stereotypes, as in this scene from *Shrek the Third*, in which the princesses unite to fight back.

RGR Collection/Alamy

- The **Trickster** is usually the protagonist in a trickster story but can also be a supporting character in a hero's journey tale. As we discussed on page 859, the trickster intentionally breaks the rules of the gods, society, and nature. Examples of the trickster archetype are cartoon characters Bart Simpson and Bugs Bunny, Hermes from Greek mythology, and Loki from Norse mythology and the *Avenger* films and the television show *Loki*.

This description of character archetypes is extensive, and the short Myth of Persephone includes just a few of them. In the Archetypal Plot section, we looked at Persephone as a hero who crossed into a new land and returned having significantly changed. But what if we were to view her mother Demeter as the hero? In this case, her daughter could be seen as the damsel in distress who was able to be freed only because Demeter refused to allow the fields to grow crops. Hades could certainly be seen as a Shadow character — he is dark where Demeter is light; he represents death, while she brings forth life. As Demeter grieves, she experiences the temptation offered by the maidens she encounters who offer her the opportunity to nurse a child, though Demeter resists the desire to let go of Persephone. Demeter is also given magical assistance through Hermes and Zeus, who help return her daughter to the living world. Hades should also be viewed as a type of trickster character since it was his plan to arrange for Persephone to eat the seven pomegranate seeds, guaranteeing her return to the Underworld.

Archetypal Characters

Think about the story, film, or book that you considered earlier — or a new one — and identify as many of the archetypal characters from the descriptions above as you can. Compare yours with those of your classmates and discuss why there are similar characters across various stories.

Archetypal Settings

If some of the archetypal plots and characters described above felt familiar to you, the settings found in mythology probably will as well. Settings in myths are used like in any other text. The setting of the myth is the world of the story. This includes the physical setting as well as the culture and time period. The setting sets the mood, and it sets the ground rules. Is this a time and place where magic rules? Can trees and animals talk? Mythology often takes place in a time before history, and the settings are often more important for their symbolic meaning than anything else. Archetypal settings are often locations along a hero's journey. The following are some common archetypal settings:

- **Threshold.** This place symbolizes the movement between the known and the unknown worlds and is the last place heroes see before fully committing to the journey. It usually includes a number of strange details that are disorienting to the hero. Platform 9¾ and Diagon Alley in *Harry Potter* act as threshold settings.

- **Wilderness or Forest.** Many myths are set in a time before civilization had fully settled all areas of the natural world, so the wilderness and forests can symbolize the unknown world, where the laws of nature rule instead of the laws of mankind. The wilderness is often a place where heroes might have little power or control. Katniss in the *Hunger Games* has to survive not only the other contestants trying to kill her, but also the wind, rain, and other natural elements of the game environment.

- **Garden.** A place where humanity lives in harmony with nature, the garden symbolizes innocence and security. Sometimes the garden can be ruined or poisoned, and often heroes have to leave it behind on the journey. Examples might include Rivendell and the Shire in the *Lord of the Rings*, Wakanda in *The Black Panther*, or Themyscira in *Wonder Woman*.

- **Wasteland.** In many ways, the wasteland is the opposite of the garden. It symbolizes loneliness and despair, the place where there is no growth, and heroes have to pass through it on their journeys; the setting itself can be a trial to be overcome. Look for instance at these two settings that appear in *The Lord of the Rings* film series: the first is clearly an idealized garden archetype, while the second is a location used in the film to represent a desolate wasteland.

Travel Pix/Alamy

Mike Robinson/Alamy

- **Maze or Labyrinth.** Many heroes face a setting that represents a puzzling dilemma or a great uncertainty represented by a maze or confusing and disorientating space, such as the maze at the end of *Harry Potter and the Goblet of Fire*.
- **Underworld/Innermost Cave.** Many heroes travel to dark settings from which they must emerge, symbolically conquering death. Sometimes this is a trip to an actual Underworld, or it could be a dark, confining space such as a cave, den, dungeon, or lair. Joseph Campbell called this stage the "innermost cave" to emphasize that this descent can have a psychological or spiritual component — despair, hopelessness, a loss of faith — what he calls "the dark night of the soul." Oftentimes this is well into the hero's journey. The title character of the film *Moana*, for example, goes into a literal cave, deep in the ocean, full of monsters, to retrieve Maui's magical fishhook from Tamatoa, the giant crab monster.
- **Castle.** This is a place of safety that sometimes holds the treasure heroes seek or the damsel who needs rescuing. It may represent home or some other powerful place. Asgard, home of Thor and Loki in the Marvel Cinematic Universe, is an example.

We see a number of these archetypal settings in the myth of Persephone and Demeter. The place where they live before she is abducted is a Garden, perfect and abundant in flowers and crops, which then becomes a wasteland in Demeter's depression, as she searches desperately for her daughter. Obviously, Persephone travels to and returns from the Underworld, symbolically dying and being reborn. In many tellings of the story, Persephone crosses the river Styx as a threshold to get to the Underworld, and she enters a maze-like path as she descends. Each of these are settings in and of themselves, but the real value comes in examining them for their symbolic meaning and how each represents a different aspect of the hero's journey or trickster tale.

Archetypal Settings

Return to the story, film, or book that you thought about earlier — or consider a new one — and identify as many of the archetypal settings from the list above as you can. What do these settings represent in the story? How do they reflect different aspects of the main character's journey?

Archetypes and Culture

Carl Jung and others identified archetypes that are present in stories from around the world and used them as evidence of the "collective unconscious," but it is essential to note that the presence of patterns in many stories does not mean that a single culture or historical perspective has produced these patterns. Even though there are plenty of similarities in stories across cultures, many components are unique to particular times and cultures. So, a study of archetypes is not intended to homogenize a culture's stories and their mythologies, but rather to ponder what connects all of humanity.

Many elements of the Persephone myth are specific to the time and place of its origin — ancient Greece. For instance, the myth presents a time and place in which agriculture was the dominant industry; it represents the afterlife as a dark Underworld; it includes a sky god, Zeus, who rules all; and it even includes references to the pomegranate seeds, a fruit plentiful in the Mediterranean since ancient times. So, even with all of the archetypes present in the myth that might make it seem similar to so many other stories, it contains unique historical and cultural elements as well.

activity · Archetypes and Culture

Return to one of the myths, movies, or stories that you have been thinking about in this workshop. What cultural elements found in the story are likely unique to the time, place, and people who developed the story?

REFLECTING ON Academic Vocabulary **Essential Elements of Mythology**

Look back at the list of terms that you previewed on page 852. Now that you have read about them and practiced with these terms, what has changed about your understanding of mythology? Which of the skills that you practiced in this section do you feel confident using? Which ones do you think you need to develop further? How do you know?

culminating activity

Analyzing Mythic Archetypes

Read the following piece called "Dazhbog and Lada," retold by Pyotr Simonov from a myth passed down in Russian and other Slavic Eastern European cultures. Identify as many of the character, setting, and plot archetypes described in this workshop as you can. Then, write a brief analysis about how we could interpret this myth symbolically. Additionally, if you wish, you can compare it to the story of Demeter and Persephone, with which it shares many aspects.

Dazhbog and Lada

Pyotr Simonov

The sea god, Tsar Mora, had nine beautiful daughters who lived in grottoes in the blue-green depths of the sea. His favourite child of all was Lada. She was fair of face and her tresses were long and golden. Every day she would row on the sea and out to the ocean in a golden boat with silver oars. The great whales and dancing porpoises kept her company and listened in wonder to the mysterious, captivating songs that welled up from the depths of her soul.

One day, Dazhbog the sun god was crossing the heavens in his gleaming chariot drawn by twelve fire-breathing horses with golden manes. As he passed, he leaned out to gaze upon the lovely siren whose sad notes had reached his ears. Lada looked up and playfully splashed some water at him, and immediately the sun god fell deeply in love with her. He descended on a sunbeam to the seashore and called for Tsar Mora, imploring him to allow his daughter to join him in the Golden Palace of the East. The sea god became angry: "Give up my precious daughter — Lada? It's unthinkable!" He ordered his giant sea horses to thrash and trample upon Dazhbog until he fell senseless under their feet.

But Dazhbog's father, the divine tsar of the sky, Savrog the all-powerful god, heard the cries of his child, and caused a black cloud to blot out the rays of the sun. In the darkness, Dazhbog was able to escape from the power of Tsar Mora, but he resolved to win Lada despite her father's opposition to the marriage.

Together with his faithful brother, Svarozhich the fire god, who knew the weaknesses of women, Dazhbog devised a plan. Along the seashore they spread out a collection of glamorous dresses and a pair of wonderful green slippers. Then they hid behind a nearby oak tree. The young goddess saw these lovely things from her boat, and they so took her fancy that she rowed quickly to the shore to admire and to take them. As her boat touched the sand Svarozhich leaped out, snatched her away, and carried her to his brother. When he learned of this, Tsar Mora raged with fury. He raised up mighty storms whose waves smashed angrily against the cliffs. But Lada was never to return to her watery home. She married Dazhbog and because of her radiant beauty she was given charge of the spring, the season of light, life and growth. In due time she bore Dazhbog a son, who was named Iarilo.

Joseph Bruchac ■ *from* Native American Stories, *868*

from Native American Stories

Joseph Bruchac

© Chris Felver/Bridgeman Images

Joseph Bruchac (b. 1942), a citizen of the Nulhegan Abenaki tribe, is a writer and professional storyteller of the traditional legends of the Adirondacks and the Native peoples of the Northeastern Woodlands. He writes poetry, novels, and short stories and is a respected collector of Native American myths and stories.

KEY CONTEXT   The three stories included here are from Bruchac's collection *Native American Stories* and focus on different heroes from three distinct cultures in different parts of what is now the United States:

1. Gluscabi: from the Abenaki of the Northeast Woodlands
2. Fisher: from the Anishinaabe of the Great Lakes Region
3. The Hero Twins: from the Zuni of the American Southwest

As you read the following stories, you will identify many commonalities among them, yet their cultural roots are also, in many ways, distinct. Keep in mind what Bruchac writes in *Our Stories Remember*:

> There really is no such thing as *The* American Indian or *The* Native American. Seeing all Indians as being alike is as foolish as not being able to see them at all. . . . Native America is made up of many cultures, hundreds of them. There is not just one history of the American Indian but countless histories. Moreover, those histories are not static, but growing and changing, adding new layers of growth each year just as living trees do. There are so many stories, as many as the leaves on those trees. . . . Storytelling among the more than three hundred living Indian nations of the United States has not ended. New stories and new storytellers are born every day.

Gluscabi and the Wind Eagle

Long ago, Gluscabi lived with his grandmother, Woodchuck, in a small lodge beside the big water.

One day Gluscabi was walking around when he looked out and saw some ducks in the bay.

"I think it is time to go hunt some ducks," he said. So he took his bow and arrows and got into his canoe. He began to paddle out into the bay and as he paddled he sang:

Ki yo wah ji neh

yo ho hey ho

Ki yo wah ji neh

Ki yo wah ji neh.

But a wind came up and it turned his canoe and blew him back to shore. Once again Gluscabi began to paddle out and this time he sang his song a little harder:

KI YO WAH JI NEH

YO HO HEY HO

KI YO WAH JI NEH

KI YO WAH JI NEH.

But again the wind came and blew him back   5
to shore.

Four times he tried to paddle out into the bay and four times he failed. He was not happy. He went back to the lodge of his grandmother and walked right in, even though there was a stick leaning across the door, which meant that the person inside was doing some work and did not want to be disturbed.

"Grandmother," Gluscabi said, "What makes the wind blow?"

Grandmother Woodchuck looked up from her work. "Gluscabi," she said, "Why do you want to know?"

Then Gluscabi answered her just as every child in the world does when they are asked such a question.

"Because," he said.   10

Grandmother Woodchuck looked at him. "Ah, Gluscabi," she said. "Whenever you ask such questions I feel there is going to be trouble. And perhaps I should not tell you. But I know that you are so stubborn you will never stop asking until I answer you. So I shall tell you. Far from here, on top of the tallest mountain, a great bird stands. This bird is named Wuchowsen, and when he flaps his wings he makes the wind blow."

"Eh-hey, Grandmother," said Gluscabi, "I see. Now how would one find that place where the Wind Eagle stands?"

Again Grandmother Woodchuck looked at Gluscabi. "Ah, Gluscabi," she said, "Once again

I feel that perhaps I should not tell you. But I know that you are very stubborn and would never stop asking. So, I shall tell you. If you walk always facing the wind you will come to the place where Wuchowsen stands."

"Thank you, Grandmother," said Gluscabi. He stepped out of the lodge and faced into the wind and began to walk.

He walked across the fields and through   15
the woods and the wind blew hard. He walked through the valleys and into the hills and the wind blew harder still. He came to the foothills and began to climb and the wind still blew harder. Now the foothills were becoming mountains and the wind was very strong. Soon there were no longer any trees and the wind was very, very strong. The wind was so strong that it blew off Gluscabi's moccasins. But he was very stubborn and he kept on walking, leaning into the wind. Now the wind was so strong that it blew off his shirt, but he kept on walking. Now the wind was so strong that it blew off all his clothes and he was naked, but he still kept walking. Now the wind was so strong that it blew off his hair, but Gluscabi still kept walking, facing into the wind. The wind was so strong that it blew off his eyebrows, but still he continued to walk. Now the wind was so strong that he could hardly stand. He had to pull himself along by grabbing hold of the boulders. But there, on the peak ahead of him, he could see a great bird slowly flapping its wings. It was Wuchowsen, the Wind Eagle.

Gluscabi took a deep breath. "GRAND-FATHER!" he shouted. The Wind Eagle stopped flapping his wings and looked around. "Who calls me Grandfather?" he said.

Gluscabi stood up. "It's me, Grandfather. I just came up here to tell you that you do a very good job making the wind blow."

The Wind Eagle puffed out his chest with pride. "You mean like this?" he said and flapped his wings even harder. The wind which he made was so strong that it lifted Gluscabi right off his feet, and he would have been blown right off the mountain had he not reached out and grabbed a boulder again.

"GRANDFATHER!!!" Gluscabi shouted again.

The Wind Eagle stopped flapping his wings. 20 "Yesss?" he said.

Gluscabi stood up and came closer to Wuchowsen. "You do a very good job of making the wind blow, Grandfather. This is so. But it seems to me that you could do an even better job if you were on that peak over there."

The Wind Eagle looked toward the other peak. "That may be so," he said, "but how would I get from here to there?"

Gluscabi smiled. "Grandfather," he said, "I will carry you. Wait here." Then Gluscabi ran back down the mountain until he came to a big

basswood tree. He stripped off the outer bark and from the inner bark he braided a strong carrying strap which he took back up the mountain to the Wind Eagle. "Here, Grandfather," he said. "let me wrap this around you so I can lift you more easily." Then he wrapped the carrying strap so tightly around Wuchowsen that his wings were pulled in to his sides and he could hardly breathe. "Now, Grandfather," Gluscabi said, picking the Wind Eagle up, "I will take you to a better place." He began to walk toward the other peak, but as he walked he came to a place where there was a large crevice, and as he stepped over it he let go of the carrying strap and the Wind Eagle slid down into the crevice, upside down, and was stuck.

"Now," Gluscabi said, "It is time to hunt some ducks."

This painting is called *Thunder Butte* by Lance Smith, a citizen of Cherokee Nation.

While this image depicts a buffalo rather than an eagle, how is the imagery in this painting similar to what is described in this story? How does the painting capture mythical elements?

He walked back down the mountain and there was no wind at all. He walked till he came to the treeline and still no wind blew. He walked down to the foothills and down to the hills and the valleys and still there was no wind. He walked through the forests and through the fields, and the wind did not blow at all. He walked and walked until he came back to the lodge by the water, and by now all his hair had grown back. He put on some fine new clothing and a new pair of moccasins and took his bow and arrows and went down to the bay and climbed into his boat to hunt ducks. He paddled out into the water and sang his canoeing song:

Ki yo wah ji neh

yo ho hey ho

Ki yo wah ji neh

Ki yo wah ji neh.

But the air was very hot and still and he began to sweat. The air was so still and hot that it was hard to breathe. Soon the water began to grow dirty and smell bad and there was so much foam on the water he could hardly paddle. He was not pleased at all and he returned to the shore and went straight to his grandmother's lodge and walked in.

"Grandmother," he said, "What is wrong? The air is hot and still and it is making me sweat and it is hard to breathe. The water is dirty and covered with foam. I cannot hunt ducks at all like this."

Grandmother Woodchuck looked up at Gluscabi. "Gluscabi," she said, "what have you done now?"

And Gluscabi answered just as every child in the world answers when asked that question, "Oh, nothing," he said.

"Gluscabi," said Grandmother Woodchuck again, "Tell me what you have done."

Then Gluscabi told her about going to visit the Wind Eagle and what he had done to stop the wind.

25

"Oh, Gluscabi," said Grandmother Woodchuck, "will you never learn? Tabaldak, The Owner, set the Wind Eagle on that mountain to make the wind because we need the wind. The wind keeps the air cool and clean. The wind brings the clouds which gives us rain to wash the Earth. The wind moves the waters and keeps them fresh and sweet. Without the wind, life will not be good for us, for our children or our children's children."

Gluscabi nodded his head. "Kaamoji, Grandmother," he said. "I understand."

Then he went outside. He faced in the direction from which the wind had once come and began to walk. He walked through the fields and

Robert Bird/Alamy

This is a picture of a 40-foot statue outside of a museum in Nova Scotia, Canada. It depicts Glooscap, an Abenaki word meaning "man from nothing" and is an alternative spelling for Gluscabi.

How does this statue depict Glooscap and how is this depiction similar to or different from how the same figure is represented in the story?

30

through the forests and the wind did not blow and he felt very hot. He walked through the valleys and up the hills and there was no wind and it was hard for him to breathe. He came to the foothills and began to climb and he was very hot and sweaty indeed. At last he came to the mountain where the Wind Eagle once stood and he went and looked down into the crevice. There was Wuchowsen, the Wind Eagle, wedged upside down.

"Uncle?" Gluscabi called. 35

The Wind Eagle looked up as best he could. "Who calls me Uncle?" he said.

"It is Gluscabi, Uncle. I'm up here. But what are you doing down there?"

"Oh, Gluscabi," said the Wind Eagle, "a very ugly naked man with no hair told me that he would take me to the other peak so that I could do a better job of making the wind blow. He tied my wings and picked me up, but as he stepped over this crevice he dropped me in and I am stuck. And I am not comfortable here at all."

"Ah, Grandfather . . . er, Uncle, I will get you out."

Then Gluscabi climbed down into the crev- 40 ice. He pulled the Wind Eagle free and placed him back on his mountain and untied his wings.

"Uncle," Gluscabi said, "It is good that the wind should blow sometimes and other times it is good that it should be still."

The Wind Eagle looked at Gluscabi and then nodded his head. "Grandson," he said, "I hear what you say."

So it is that sometimes there is wind and sometimes it is still to this very day. And so the story goes. ■

How Fisher Went to the Skyland: The Origin of the Big Dipper

Fisher was a great hunter.

He was not big, but he was known for his determination and was regarded as one

with great power. Fisher's son wanted to be a great hunter also. One day the son went out to try to catch something. It was not easy, for the snow was very deep and it was very cold everywhere. In those days it was always winter on the Earth and there was no such thing as warm weather. The son hunted a long time with no luck. Finally, though, he saw a squirrel. As quietly as he could he sneaked up and then pounced, catching the squirrel between his paws. Before he could kill it, though, the squirrel spoke to him.

"Grandson," said the squirrel, "don't kill me. I can give you some good advice."

"Speak then," said the young fisher.

"I see that you are shivering from the cold. 5 If you do what I tell you, we may all enjoy warm weather. Then it will be easy for all of us to find food and not starve as we are doing now."

"Tell me what to do, Grandfather," the young fisher said, letting the squirrel go.

The squirrel climbed quickly up onto a high branch and then spoke again. "Go home and say nothing. Just sit down in your lodge and begin to weep. Your mother will ask you what is wrong, but you must not answer her. If she tries to comfort you or give you food, you must refuse it. When your father comes home, he will ask you why you are weeping. Then you can speak. Tell him the winds are too cold and the snow is too deep. Tell him that he must bring warm weather to the Earth."

So the young fisher went home. He sat in the corner of the lodge and cried. His mother asked what was wrong, but he did not answer. She offered him food, but he pushed it away. When his father returned and saw his only son weeping, he went to his side.

"What is wrong, son?" Fisher said. Then the young fisher said what the squirrel had told him to say.

"I am weeping because the wind is too cold 10 and the snow is too deep. We are all starving because of the winter. I want you to use your powers to bring the warm weather."

"The thing you are asking of me is hard to do." said Fisher, "but you are right. I will do all I can to grant your wish."

Then Fisher had a great feast. He invited all of his friends and told them what he planned to do.

"I am going to go to the place where the skyland is closest to the Earth," he said. "There in the skyland the people have all the warm weather. I intend to go there to bring some of that warm weather back. Then the snow will go away and we will have plenty to eat."

All of Fisher's friends were pleased and offered to go with him. So when Fisher set out, he took the strongest of his friends along. Those friends were Otter, Lynx and Wolverine.

The four of them traveled for a long time through the snow. They went toward the mountains, higher and higher each day. Fisher had with him a pack filled with dried venison and they slept at night buried under the snow. At last, after many, many days, they came to the highest mountain and climbed to its top. Then Fisher took a pipe and tobacco out of his pouch.

"We must offer our smoke to the Four Directions," Fisher said. The four of them smoked and sent their prayers to Gitchee Manitou[1], asking for success. The sky was very close above them, but they had to find some way to break through into the land above. "We must jump up," said Fisher. "Who will go first?"

"I will try," said Otter. He leaped up and struck the sky but did not break through. Instead he fell back and slid on his belly all the way to the bottom of the mountain. To this day all otters slide like that in the snow.

"Now it is my turn," said Lynx. He jumped too, striking hard against the sky and falling back unconscious. Fisher tried then, but even he did not have enough power.

"Now it is your turn," said Fisher to Wolverine. "You are the strongest of us all."

Wolverine leaped. He struck hard against the sky and fell back, but he did not give up. He leaped again and again until he had made a crack in the sky. Once more he leaped and finally broke through. Fisher jumped through the hole in the sky after him.

The skyland was a beautiful place. It was warm and sunny, and there were plants and flowers of all kinds growing. They could hear the singing of birds all around them, but they could see no people. They went farther and found many long lodges. When they looked inside, they found that there were cages in the lodges. Each cage held a different bird.

"These will make for fine hunting," Fisher said. "Let us set them free."

Quickly Wolverine and Fisher chewed through the rawhide that bound the cages together and freed the birds. The birds all flew down through the hole in the sky. So there are many kinds of birds in the world today.

Wolverine and Fisher now began to make the hole in the skyland bigger. The warmth of the skyland began to fall through the hole and the land below began to grow warmer. The snow began to melt and the grass and plants beneath the snow began to turn green.

But the sky people came out when they saw what was happening. They ran toward Wolverine and Fisher, shouting loudly.

"Thieves," they shouted. "Stop taking our warm weather!"

Wolverine jumped back through the hole to escape, but Fisher kept making the hole bigger. He knew that if he didn't make it big enough, the sky people would quickly close the hole again and it would be winter again in the land below. He chewed the hole larger and larger. Finally, just when the sky people were very close, he stopped.

The hole was big enough for enough warm weather for half of the year to escape through,

[1]Gitchee Manitou: The Great Spirit of the Algonquian tribes —Eds.

This is an abstract painting called *Power of the West* by Robert Orduno.

What might the artist be suggesting through the use of color and imagery? What connections can you draw between the painting and the story?

Robert Orduno

but it was not big enough for enough warm weather to last all the time. That is why the winter still comes back every year. Fisher knew that the sky people might try to close the hole in the sky. He had to take their attention away from it and so he taunted them.

"I am Fisher, the great hunter," he said. "You cannot catch me." Then he ran to the tallest tree in the skyland. All the sky people ran after him. Just as they were about to grab him, he leaped up into the tree and climbed to the highest branches, where no one could follow.

At first the sky people did not know what to do. Then they began to shoot arrows at him. But Fisher wasn't hurt, for he had a special power. There was only one place on his tail where an arrow could kill him. Finally, though, the sky

30

people guessed where his magic was and shot at that place. An arrow struck the fatal spot. Fisher turned over on his back and began to fall.

But Fisher never struck the Earth. Gitchee Manitou took pity on him because he had kept his promise and done something to help all the people. Gitchee Manitou placed Fisher high up in the sky among the stars.

If you look up into the sky, you can still see him, even though some people call that pattern of stars The Big Dipper. Every year he crosses the sky. When the arrow strikes him, he rolls over onto his back in the winter sky. But when the winter is almost ended, he faithfully turns to his feet and starts out once more on his long journey to bring the warm weather back to the Earth. ■

This is a picture of a quilt called, "Sky Woman's Gift," created by Faye Lone, a member of the Tonawanda Seneca Nation.

What do you see in the image that makes that title appropriate, and how does it resemble the Skyland of this story?

Faye Lone, Tonawanda Seneca, Hawk Clan. SKY WOMAN'S GIFT, National Museum of the American Indian, Smithsonian Institution (25/9606)

The Hero Twins and the Swallower of Clouds

To the American Indian people of the dry Southwest, few things are more important than rain.

The people speak of different kinds of rain: the male rain, which strikes hard on the Earth and washes away; the female rain, which falls gently and steadily, soaking the soil. Many stories are told of the rain, and songs relate to the coming of the rain. One of the corn-grinding songs of the Zuni people praises the mountains, from which the clouds come:

Clouds come rising out of my beautiful
      mountain.
Up in the sky, the rain makers are sitting.
One after another rain clouds are coming.
Over there the flowers are coming.
Here the young corn is growing.

The clouds are powerful and benevolent, connected to the kachinas, those helping spirits of the ancestors. So when the Zuni tell the story of the giant, Swallower of Clouds, they tell of a very terrible monster indeed.

When the world was young, they say, a giant lived in the cliffs above Cañon de Chelly. The food he lived on was human beings, and he caught the clouds and squeezed them into his mouth for drink. The people called him Swallower of Clouds, and the bravest of the men tried to destroy him. However, anyone who went out to kill the giant was never seen again. Before long, because he was swallowing all the clouds, snow stopped falling to the north. Because he was swallowing all the clouds, the rain no longer came from the west. Because he was swallowing all the clouds, the mist above the mountains to the east disappeared. Because he was swallowing all the clouds, the springs to the south dried up. The crops dried up and died. The people were suffering and some began to die.

The Hero Twins saw what was happening. 5

"We will go and kill Swallower of Clouds," they said. Then started on their way to the cliffs where he lived. But as they were following the path to the cliffs, they saw a spider web next to the trail.

"Grandmother Spider," they said, greeting the maker of webs, "Are you well?"

"I am well, Grandchildren," said the spider. "Where are you going?"

"We are going to kill the giant, Swallower of Clouds," they said.

"That is good," Grandmother Spider said, "but 10 first let me warn you. The giant has a trick. He stretches himself out on top of the cliffs. He pretends to be sleeping and then tells whoever comes to pass under his legs, which are arched over the trail. As soon as someone passes under, though, he grabs them and throws them over the cliff."

"Grandmother," said the Hero Twins, "what should we do?"

"Let me go ahead of you," said Grandmother Spider. "Wait for a while and then follow." Then

This is a photograph of ancient Zuni Indian ruins in New Mexico, the general area in which this story takes place.

What do you notice about the landscape and the clouds that make this an effective visualization of the setting of this story?

Mark Andrews/Alamy

Grandmother Spider set out. She did not go far before she came to the giant. He was stretched out on top of the cliff with his legs over the trail. He was as huge as a hill and his legs were bigger than tree trunks. He pretended to sleep, for he had heard the Hero Twins were coming to fight him. Grandmother Spider, though, was so small the giant did not see her. She climbed up a rock behind him and then let herself down on his forehead with a strand of silk. While he kept his eyes closed, pretending to sleep, she wove her web across his eyes so that he could not open them up.

Now the Hero Twins, having waited for a while, started on their way. When they came close to the place where Swallower of Clouds lay, they began to sing a war song.

"Who is that?" said Swallower of Clouds as the Hero Twins came closer, "I am old and tired, too old and tired to move out of the way. Just pass under my legs."

But when the Hero Twins came close to the giant, they split up. One ran to the right and one ran to the left. The giant tried to open his eyes to see what they were doing, but he was blinded by the spider web.

"Where are you, Little Ones?" he said, striking at them and missing. "Just pass under my legs."

Swallower of Clouds struck again at the Hero Twins, but he could not see them and he missed. Then the Twins leaped up and struck him with their clubs. One struck him in the head. The other struck him in the stomach. They killed Swallower of Clouds with their clubs. Then they threw him over the same cliffs where he had thrown all the people he had killed. Now the clouds were able to pass again through the mountains. The snow returned to the north. The rain came again from the west. The mists formed once more above the mountains to the east. The springs to the south flowed once more. Again the crops of the people grew and the people were well and happy.

It is said that when the giant fell, he struck so hard that his feet drove into the Earth. He still stands there to this day with his blood dried red all along his great stiff body. Though some call that great stone by other names, the Zunis know it is the Swallower of Clouds. When they see it they are thankful for the deed of the Hero Twins and the life-giving rain. ■

15

Michael J. Caduto and Joseph Bruchac, "Gluscabi and the Wind Eagle," "How Fisher Went to the Skyland: The Origin of the Big Dipper," and "The Hero Twins and the Swallower of Clouds" from *Native American Stories* told by Joseph Bruchac from *Keeper of the Earth*. Copyright © 1991 by Joseph Bruchac.

extending beyond the text

In an article for the *Washington Post* in 2021, reporter Dana Hedgpeth, a member of the Haliwa-Saponi tribe in North Carolina, notes that "People react with surprise or disbelief when we tell someone that we're from a tribe that is Indigenous to the United States. Many people assume all American Indians are dead . . . . For many of us, the message to the rest of society is simple: 'We're still here.'" Writer Tommy Orange, a citizen of the Cheyenne and Arapaho Tribes of Oklahoma, who grew up in Oakland, California, also explores this idea in his novel *There, There*. Read this excerpt from the novel in which Orange challenges common stereotypes of Native Americans in popular culture, including old Westerns.

> Urban Indians were the generation born in the city. We've been moving for a long time, but the land moves with you like memory. An Urban Indian belongs to the city, and cities belong to the earth. Everything here is formed in relation to every other living and nonliving thing from the earth. All our relations. The process that brings anything to its current form — chemical, synthetic, technological, or otherwise — doesn't make the product not a product of the living earth. Buildings, freeways, cars — are these not of the earth? Were they shipped in from Mars, the moon? Is it because they're processed, manufactured, or that we handle them? Are we so different? Were we at one time not something else entirely, *Homo sapiens*, single-celled organisms, space dust, unidentifiable pre-bang quantum theory? Cities form in the same way as galaxies. Urban Indians feel at home walking in the shadow of a downtown building. We came to know the downtown Oakland skyline better than we did any sacred mountain range, the redwoods in the Oakland hills better than any other deep wild forest. We know the sound of the freeway better than we do rivers, the howl of distant trains better than wolf howls, we know the smell of gas and freshly wet concrete and burned rubber better than we do the smell of cedar or even fry bread — which isn't traditional, like reservations aren't traditional, but nothing is original, everything comes from something that came before, which was once nothing. Everything is new and doomed. We ride buses, trains, and cars across, over and under concrete plains. Being Indian has never been about returning to the land. The land is everywhere or nowhere. ■

Summarize the qualities that define the "Urban Indian," according to Orange. Even though this is set in contemporary America, what is in common between what Orange describes here and the hero myths you read in this section?

877

Understanding and Interpreting

1. Briefly summarize the three stages (Call to Adventure, Road of Trials, and Return) of the hero's journey (p. 858) of the three stories included here. To what extent are all the stages represented in all three stories? What similarities and differences do you notice in the way the hero's journey is presented in each story?

2. In what ways is Gluscabi as much a trickster figure as a hero? How is he different as a character from the heroes in the other two stories?

3. Identify at least two characters, other than the hero, from two different stories that represent the same archetype — shadow or companion, for example. (Review the character archetypes on p. 861, if needed.) Explain how the characters act in archetypal ways and how they support or oppose the heroes on their journeys.

4. Look back carefully at the three stories and identify at least one setting that appears to be an archetype. Explain how that setting fits the definition on page 863.

5. In the Skill Workshop, you read that Carl Jung and others identified archetypes as evidence of the "collective unconscious," and that even though there can be similarities across cultures, there are unique cultural aspects to all stories. Skim back through the three stories and note any elements of setting, language, or other details that make the three stories unique to their geographic and cultural origins. As similar as each of these stories might be, what makes them distinct from each other?

Analyzing Language, Style, and Structure

6. **Vocabulary in Context.** At the end of the Hero Twins story, when the giant fell "he struck so hard that his feet drove into the Earth." What does the word *drove* mean in this context and how is it similar to or different from other uses of the word?

7. All of these stories sound like fables or fairy tales in that they take place outside of time, or before history began. Identify language choices that Bruchac uses to create this feeling.

8. In the story of Gluscabi, the plot follows a pattern of repeated actions. Identify this pattern and explain the effect that this might create for someone listening to, rather than reading, this story.

9. In the story of Fisher, how does Bruchac use imagery to contrast the world of the skyland (par. 22) and the rest of the world?

10. Reread paragraph 4 of the story of the Hero Twins. What effect is created through the repetition of the word *because*, and how does that repetition give the story a mythical feel?

11. Reread the second-to-last paragraph in the story of the Hero Twins. What do you notice about the sentence structure and what feelings do those choices create for the reader?

Topics for Composing

12. **Analysis.** In the Skill Workshop, you learned that while a lot of mythology, including these three stories, works to explain natural phenomena that we can now explain through science, we can still read mythology symbolically by asking, "What is the significance of this myth to us today?" Choose one of the stories in this collection and explain possible themes for a modern audience, using evidence from the story to support your interpretation.

13. **Analysis.** The characters in each of these stories make decisions, sometimes multiple decisions. Write an analysis about how the characters investigate their options and what ultimately motivates them to act in one way or another. You should refer to at least two of the stories in your analysis.

14. **Argument.** Laguna Pueblo author Leslie Marmon Silko writes in her book *Ceremony*, "I will tell you something about stories, . . . They aren't just entertainment. Don't be fooled. They are all we have, you see. All we have to fight off illness and death. You don't have anything if you don't have stories." Can myths help people understand and deal with real-world situations, decisions, or problems? Why or why not? Write an argument about whether or not mythology is more than "just entertainment," as Silko suggests. You can draw on your own experiences reading mythology or watching television shows or movies with mythic elements to support your response.

15. **Connections.** In addition to being hero stories, these three also seek to explain how things like the wind, the stars, and certain rock formations came about. What are some creation stories you know that explain natural elements or phenomena? How are those stories similar to and different from these? You may know some of these stories already or you may need to conduct research into some myths that have these purposes.

16. **Speaking and Listening.** Like most mythology, these stories were passed down orally from generation to generation before being written down. Working with a partner or a small group, choose a short section (three or four paragraphs) from one of the stories in the collection, reread it several times, and then take turns retelling the story aloud to each other. The goal is not to memorize the section and recount it exactly as written, but rather to see how the story changes as people tell and retell it.

17. **Research.** Conduct research into the Abenaki, Anishinaabe, or Zuni, the cultures that produced these stories. What can you learn about their precolonial history, their experiences with European explorers and settlers, and their interactions with the United States government and current tribal status?

18. **Creative Writing.** Rewrite one of these stories with a contemporary setting and characters. Try to update while keeping some of the archetypes represented in the original.

19. **Multimodal.** Create or locate illustrations for a portion of one of these stories, using some of the words and phrases from the text as captions for your illustrations. Write a brief "artist's statement" about what you were hoping to achieve with your illustrations.

central text   Homer ▪ *from* The Odyssey, *880*

conversation / What defines a hero? *917*

from **The Odyssey**

Homer

Translated by Robert Fitzgerald

classicpaintings/Alamy

Homer is the name given to the author of the major ancient Greek epics, including *The Iliad* and *The Odyssey*. There is considerable debate around whether Homer was, in fact, a real person or was simply a shorthand name for the whole tradition of oral storytelling that codified these stories in about the seventh century B.C.

KEY CONTEXT   *The Odyssey* tells the story of Odysseus as he tries to return home to Ithaka to rejoin his wife, Penélopê, and his son, Telémakhos. Odysseus left his home to fight alongside other Greeks in the Trojan War against the city of Troy. The story of the Trojan War is recounted in *The Iliad*, in which Odysseus is a minor character who came up with the idea of hiding Greek soldiers in a wooden horse that was presented as a gift to the Trojans. This Trojan Horse was brought inside the city gates and led to the Greeks' victory in the ten-year war. After leaving Troy to return home, Odysseus and his crew face many challenges — from humans, gods, and creatures — and visit unfamiliar places, including the Underworld.

     Meanwhile, back home at Ithaka, most assume that Odysseus has died at sea, and suitors have arrived to propose marriage to Odysseus's wife, Penélopê, and take over his estate. His son, Telémakhos, is still too young to defend or take over the household. After a ten-year journey, Odysseus finally makes it to Ithaka to find his land overrun with the suitors eating and drinking his house into ruin.

     The Odyssey in its entirety is made up of twenty-four Books, or sections, but we have included only a portion of it here. We have grouped the excerpts into three sets in the following manner:

- Section 1: excerpts from Books 1, 2, and 5
- Section 2: excerpts from Books 9 and 12
- Section 3: excerpts from Books 16, 21, 22, and 23

The following are other important elements to help you understand *The Odyssey*:

Epic Simile/Metaphor

Like other similes and metaphors, epic similes and metaphors compare two unlike things, but they are exaggerated to grander proportions to emphasize the heroic nature of the character or event. For example, "all the sea was like a cauldron / seething over intense fire" (Book 12, ll. 89–90).

Homeric Epithets

These are repeated terms or phrases that describe the nature of gods, mortals, or objects. They are designed not only to help the speaker remember the oral poem but also to add pattern and familiarity for the audience, who would be listening to the poem rather than reading it. Examples include "rosy-fingered Dawn" and "grey-eyed goddess Athena."

Xenia

A concept that was important in ancient Greek culture, *xenia*, or "guest friendship," means showing hospitality to strangers who visit your home and showing respect to your host. This is a concept that is illustrated throughout the myth, with some characters displaying good *xenia* and others not.

Key Characters

Mortals

- **Odysseus:** The hero of the story. He endures many troubles and hardships in his struggle to save his life and return home to his family.
- **Telémakhos:** The son of Odysseus. Throughout the story, he grows into a mature and capable young man.
- **Penélopê:** The wife of Odysseus and mother to Telémakhos. She is mourning her husband and is being forced to choose a suitor to marry.
- **Antínoös:** The lead suitor of Penélopê.
- **Eurýmakhos:** A main suitor of Penélopê.
- **Eumaios:** A swineherd in Ithaka who is loyal to Odysseus.
- **Eurýkleia:** A faithful servant in the house of Odysseus in Ithaka.
- **Laërtês:** The father of Odysseus.

Gods

- **Athena:** The goddess of wisdom. She is a major supporter of Odysseus and helps him return home and regain what is his.
- **Zeus:** The ruler of the gods, who allows Athena to help Odysseus return home.
- **Poseidon:** The god of the sea. He bears a grudge against Odysseus for blinding Polyphêmos, his son.
- **Kalýpso:** A minor goddess who lives on the island of Ogýgia. She holds Odysseus prisoner for many years. She is the daughter of Atlas, and her island is where we first meet Odysseus.
- **Kirkê:** A minor goddess or witch who lives on the island of Aiaia. She turns some of Odysseus's men into pigs, but she eventually befriends Odysseus and helps him on his journey.

Monsters

- **Polyphêmos:** A Cyclops. He is the one-eyed son of Poseidon and is blinded by Odysseus.
- **Seirênês:** A group of creatures who enchant sailors with their singing in order to lure them into sailing into the rocky shore of their island. Today, we tend to refer to them as "the Sirens."
- **Kharybdis:** A sea monster that swallows and spits out large amounts of water.
- **Skylla:** A sea monster with six necks and twelve flapping feet.

BOOK 1 A Goddess Intervenes

Sing in me, Muse, and through me tell the
    story
of that man skilled in all ways of contending,
the wanderer, harried for years on end,
after he plundered the stronghold
on the proud height of Troy.
                              He saw the townlands and 5
learned the minds of many distant men,
and weathered many bitter nights and days
in his deep heart at sea, while he fought only
to save his life, to bring his shipmates home.
But not by will nor valor could he save them, 10
for their own recklessness destroyed them all —
children and fools, they killed and feasted on
the cattle of Lord Hêlios, the Sun,
and he who moves all day through heaven
took from their eyes the dawn of their return. 15

Of these adventures, Muse, daughter of Zeus,
tell us in our time, lift the great song again.
Begin when all the rest who left behind them
headlong death in battle or at sea
had long ago returned, while he alone still
    hungered 20
for home and wife. Her ladyship Kalypso
clung to him in her sea-hollowed caves —
a nymph, immortal and most beautiful,
who craved him for her own.
                              And when long years and seasons
wheling brought around that point of time 25
ordained for him to make his passage
    homeward,
trials and dangers, even so, attended him
even in Ithaka, near those he loved.
Yet all the gods had pitied Lord Odysseus,
all but Poseidon, raging cold and rough 30

extending beyond the text

In 2018, Emily Wilson released the first published translation of *The Odyssey* by a woman. Look at the opening lines of her translation below and compare it to the version above.

from The Odyssey

trans. Emily Wilson

Tell me about a complicated man.
Muse, tell me how he wandered and was lost
when he had wrecked the holy town of Troy,
and where he went, and who he met, the pain
he suffered in the storms at sea, and how
he worked to save his life and bring his men
back home. He failed to keep them safe; poor fools,
they ate the Sun God's cattle, and the god
kept them from home. Now goddess, child of Zeus,
tell the old story for our modern times.
Find the beginning.

What similarities and differences did you notice between the two versions? How do these two versions illustrate the idea that translation involves interpretation?

against the brave king till he came ashore
at last on his own land.
                      But now that god
had gone far off among the sunburnt races,
most remote of men, at earth's two verges,
in sunset lands and lands of the rising sun,   35
to be regaled by smoke of thighbones burning,
haunches of rams and bulls, a hundred fold.
He lingered delighted at the banquet side.

In the bright hall of Zeus upon Olympos
the other gods were all at home, and Zeus,   40
the father of gods and men, made conversation.
For he had meditated on Aigísthos, dead
by the hand of Agamémnon's son, Orestês,
and spoke his thought aloud before them all:
"My word, how mortals take the gods to task!   45
All their afflictions come from us, we hear.
And what of their own failings? Greed and folly
double the suffering in the lot of man.
See how Aigísthos, for his double portion,
stole Agamémnon's wife and killed the soldier   50
on his homecoming day. And yet Aigísthos
knew that his own doom lay in this. [. . .]
Now he has paid the reckoning in full."

The grey-eyed goddess Athena replied to Zeus:
"O Majesty, O Father of us all,   55
that man is in the dust indeed, and justly.
So perish all who do what he had done.
But my own heart is broken for Odysseus,
the master mind of war, so long a castaway
upon an island in the running sea;   60
a wooded island, in the sea's middle,
and there's a goddess in the place, the daughter
of one whose baleful mind knows all the deeps
of the blue sea — Atlas, who holds the columns
that bear from land the great thrust of the sky.   65
His daughter will not let Odysseus go,
poor mournful man; she keeps on coaxing him
with her beguiling talk, to turn his mind
from Ithaka. But such desire is in him
merely to see the hearthsmoke leaping upward   70
from his own island, that he longs to die.
Are you not moved by this, Lord of Olympos?

Had you no pleasure from Odysseus' offerings
beside the Argive ships, on Troy's wide
    seaboard?
O Zeus, what do you hold against him now?"   75

To this the summoner of cloud replied:
"My child, what strange remarks you let escape
    you.
Could I forget that kingly man, Odysseus?
There is no mortal half so wise; no mortal
gave so much to the lords of open sky.   80
Only the god who laps the land in water,
Poseidon, bears the fighter an old grudge
since he poked out the eye of Polyphêmos,
brawniest of the Kyklopês. Who bore
that giant lout? Thoösa, daughter of Phorkys,   85
an offshore sea lord: for this nymph had lain
with Lord Poseidon in her hollow caves.
Naturally, the god, after the blinding —
mind you, he does not kill the man;
he only buffets him away from home.   90
But come now, we are all at leisure here,
let us take up this matter of his return,
that he may sail. Poseidon must relent
for being quarrelsome will get him nowhere,
one god, flouting the will of all the gods."   95

The grey-eyed goddess Athena answered him:
"O Majesty, O Father of us all,
if it now please the blissful gods
that wise Odysseus reach his home again,
let the Wayfinder, Hermês, cross the sea   100
to the island of Ogýgia; let him tell
our fixed intent to the nymph with pretty braids,
and let the steadfast man depart for home.
For my part, I shall visit Ithaka
to put more courage in the son, and rouse him   105
to call an assembly of the islanders,
Akhaian gentlemen with flowing hair.
He must warn off that wolf pack of the suitors
who prey upon his flocks and dusky cattle.
I'll send him to the mainland then, to Sparta   110
by the sand beach of Pylos; let him find
news of his dear father where he may
and win his own renown about the world."

BOOK 2 A Hero's Son Awakens

When primal Dawn spread on the eastern sky
her fingers of pink light, Odysseus' true son
stood up, drew on his tunic and his mantle,
slung on a sword-belt and a new-edged sword,
tied his smooth feet into good rawhide sandals,   5
and left his room, a god's brilliance upon him.
He found the criers with clarion voices and told
      them
to muster the unshorn Akhaians in full
      assembly.
The call sang out, and the men came streaming
      in;
and when they filled the assembly ground, he
      entered,   10
spear in hand, with two quick hounds at heel;
Athena lavished on him a sunlit grace
that held the eye of the multitude. Old men
made way for him as he took his father's
      chair. [. . .]

["]My distinguished father is lost,   15
who ruled among you once, mild as a father,
and there is now this greater evil still:
my home and all I have are being ruined.
Mother wanted no suitors, but like a pack
they came — sons of the best men here among
      them —   20
lads with no stomach for an introduction
to Ikários, her father across the sea;
he would require a wedding gift, and give her
to someone who found favor in her eyes.
No; these men spend their days around our
      house   25
killing our beeves and sheep and fatted goats,
carousing, soaking up our good dark wine,
not caring what they do. They squander
      everything.
We have no strong Odysseus to defend us,
and as to putting up a fight ourselves —   30
we'd only show our incompetence in arms.
Expel them, yes, if I only had the power;
the whole thing's out of hand, insufferable.
My house is being plundered: is this courtesy?

Where is your indignation? Where is your
      shame?   35
Think of the talk in the islands all around us,
and fear the wrath of the gods,
or they may turn, and send you some devilry.
Friends, by Olympian Zeus and holy Justice
that holds men in assembly and sets them free,   40
make an end of this! Let me lament in peace
my private loss. Or did my father, Odysseus,
ever do injury to the armed Akhaians?
Is this your way of taking it out on me,
giving free rein to these young men?   45
I might as well — might better — see my treasure
and livestock taken over by you all;
then, if you fed on them, I'd have some remedy,
and when we met, in public, in the town,
I'd press my claim; you might make restitution.   50
This way you hurt me when my hands are
      tied." [. . .]

                              A wave of sympathy
ran through the crowd, all hushed; and no one
      there
had the audacity to answer harshly
except Antínoös, who said:
                              "What high and mighty   55
talk, Telémakhos! No holding you!
You want to shame us, and humiliate us,
but you should know the suitors are not to
      blame —
it is your own dear, incomparably cunning
      mother.
For three years now — and it will soon be four —   60
she has been breaking the hearts of the
      Akhaians,
holding out hope to all, and sending promises
to each man privately — but thinking other wise.

Here is an instance of her trickery:
she had her great loom standing in the hall   65
and the fine warp of some vast fabric on it;
we were attending her, and she said to us:
'Young men, my suitors, now my lord is dead,

This painting by Max Klinger (1895) depicts Penélopê with her shroud, waiting for the return of Odysseus.

Examine the facial expressions, color, and other elements and write a statement about the painter's attitude toward Penélopê and her situation.

The Stapleton Collection/Bridgeman Images

let me finish my weaving before I marry,
or else my thread will have been spun in vain. 70
It is a shroud I weave for Lord Laërtês,
when cold death comes to lay him on his bier.
The country wives would hold me in dishonor
if he, with all his fortune, lay unshrouded.'
We have men's hearts; she touched them; we
    agreed. 75
So every day she wove on the great loom —
but every night by torchlight she unwove it;
and so for three years she deceived the
    Akhaians.
But when the seasons brought the fourth
    around,
one of her maids, who knew the secret, told us; 80
we found her unraveling the splendid shroud.
She had to finish then, although she hated it.

Now here is the suitors' answer —
you and all the Akhaians, mark it well:
dismiss your mother from the house, or make her
    marry 85
the man her father names and she prefers.
Does she intend to keep us dangling forever?
She may rely too long on Athena's gifts —
talent in handicraft and a clever mind;
so cunning — history cannot show the like 90
among the ringleted ladies of Akhaia,
Mykênê with her coronet, Alkmênê, Tyro.

Wits like Penélopê's never were before,
but this time — well, she made poor use of them.
For here are suitors eating up your property 95
as long as she holds out — a plan some god
put in her mind. She makes a name for herself,
but you can feel the loss it means for you.
Our own affairs can wait; we'll never go anywhere
    else,
until she takes an Akhaian to her liking." [. . .] 100

Clear-headed Telémakhos replied to this:
"Eurýmakhos, and noble suitors all,
I am finished with appeals and argument.
The gods know, and the Akhaians know, these
    things.
But give me a fast ship and a crew of twenty 105
who will see me through a voyage, out and
    back.
I'll go to sandy Pylos, then to Sparta,
for news of Father since he sailed from Troy —
some traveller's tale, perhaps, or rumored fame
issued from Zeus himself into the world. 110
If he's alive, and beating his way home,
I might hold out for another weary year;
but if they tell me that he's dead and gone,
then I can come back to my own dear country
and raise a mound for him, and burn his gear, 115
with all the funeral honors that befit him,
and give my mother to another husband." [. . .]

extending beyond the text

Read the following poem by Dorothy Parker written from the point of view of Penelope. The "he" in the poem refers to Odysseus.

Penelope

Dorothy Parker

In the pathway of the sun,
  In the footsteps of the breeze,
Where the world and the sky are one,
  He shall ride the silver seas.
  He shall cut the glittering wave.
I shall sit at home, and rock;
Rise, to heed a neighbor's knock;
Brew my tea, and snip my thread;
Bleach the linen for my bed.
  They will call him brave.

What is Penelope's attitude toward Odysseus in this poem, and how can we interpret the final line? How is this depiction of Penelope similar to or different from what you have read so far in *The Odyssey*?

BOOK 5 Sweet Nymph and Open Sea

KEY CONTEXT Books 1–4 of *The Odyssey* are often called "The Telemachy" because they focus on the travels of Telémakhos looking for information on his missing father with the help of the disguised Athena. In the section of Books 2, 3, and 4 not included here, Telémakhos visits King Nestor of Pylos and King Meneláos and Queen Helen of Sparta, and he learns new customs and the role of hospitality, *xenia*, and that his father was last seen imprisoned on Kalypso's island. Meanwhile, back in Ithaka, the suitors are planning on ambushing Telémakhos's ship on his return and killing him.

Book 5 begins with Hermês delivering the order from Zeus that Kalypso must release Odysseus. Though she fights the order at first, suggesting that the gods are jealous of her and Odysseus, she eventually relents and tells Odysseus that she will release him.

>   The sweet days of his life time
> were running out in anguish over his exile,
> for long ago the nymph had ceased to please.
> Though he fought shy of her and her desire,
> he lay with her each night, for she compelled him. 5
> But when day came he sat on the rocky shore
> and broke his own heart groaning, with eyes wet
> scanning the bare horizon of the sea.
> Now she stood near him in her beauty, saying:
>
> "O forlorn man, be still. 10
> Here you need grieve no more; you need not feel
> your life consumed here; I have pondered it,
> and I shall help you go.
> Come and cut down high timber for a raft
> or flatboat; make her broad-beamed, and
>   decked over, 15
> so you can ride her on the misty sea.
> Stores I shall put aboard for you — bread, water,

and ruby-colored wine, to stay your hunger —
give you a seacloak and a following wind
to help you homeward without harm —
    provided   20
the gods who rule wide heaven wish it so.
Stronger than I they are, in mind and power."

For all he had endured, Odysseus shuddered.
But when he spoke, his words went to the mark:
"After these years, a helping hand? O goddess,   25
what guile is hidden here?
A raft, you say, to cross the Western Ocean,
rough water, and unknown? Seaworthy ships
that glory in god's wind will never cross it.
I take no raft you grudge me out to sea.   30
Or yield me first a great oath, if I do,
to work no more enchantment to my harm."

At this the beautiful nymph Kalypso smiled
and answered sweetly, laying her hand upon
    him:
"What a dog you are! And not for nothing
    learned,   35
having the wit to ask this thing of me!
My witness then be earth and sky
and dripping Styx that I swear by —
the gay gods cannot swear more seriously —
I have no further spells to work against you.
But what I shall devise, and what I tell you,   40
will be the same as if your need were mine.

Fairness is all I think of. There are hearts
made of cold iron — but my heart is kind." [. . .]

"Son of Laërtês, versatile Odysseus,   45
after these years with me, you still desire
your old home? Even so, I wish you well.
If you could see it all, before you go —
all the adversity you face at sea —
you would stay here, and guard this house, and be 50
immortal — though you wanted her forever,
that bride for whom you pine each day.
Can I be less desirable than she is?
Less interesting? Less beautiful? Can mortals
compare with goddesses in grace and form?"   55

To this the strategist Odysseus answered:
"My lady goddess, here is no cause for anger.
My quiet Penélopê — how well I know —
would seem a shade before your majesty,
death and old age being unknown to you,   60
while she must die. Yet, it is true, each day
I long for home, long for the sight of home.
If any god has marked me out again
for shipwreck, my tough heart can undergo it.
What hardship have I not long since endured   65
at sea, in battle! Let the trial come."

Now as he spoke the sun set, dusk drew on,
and they retired, this pair, to the inner cave
to revel and rest softly, side by side.

This painting by Luca Giordano depicts Odysseus and Kalypso.

What details of setting and characters seem to be similar to and different from the text of this section of *The Odyssey*?

© Dario Grimaldi/Bridgeman Images

Understanding and Interpreting

Book 1

1. *The Odyssey* starts off by asking for the Muse to "sing in me." What does this mean, and what does this reveal about the storyteller of this myth?

2. Look back through the excerpt from Book 1 and explain what we learn about Odysseus from what Athena and Zeus say about him. What plot do they retell, and what do they think of him?

3. Explain the Greek gods' feelings about mortals as described in Book 1.

4. In Book 1, we get a look at the inner workings and decision-making of the Greek gods. Explain how they operate and support your response with a line or two from the text.

5. Beginning with "O Majesty, O Father of us all" (l. 55), identify the two significant actions that Athena and Hermês will undertake. Why is each of these actions important?

Book 2

6. How is Telémakhos characterized in the first fourteen lines of Book 2? How do the Ithakans respond to him initially?

7. What arguments does Telémakhos present against the actions of the suitors? How does Antínoös, the lead suitor, respond to Telémakhos (ll. 55–100)?

8. What do we learn about Penélopê, Telémakhos's mother, from the story that Antínoös tells about her "trickery" (ll. 64–82)? What does this reveal about her character?

9. What can we infer from Book 2 about the roles of women in the culture of the time of *The Odyssey*? What evidence supports your inference?

Book 5

10. The first time we hear Odysseus speak is his reply to Kalypso when she offers to help him leave (ll. 25–32). What does his reply suggest about him?

11. Make an interpretative statement about Kalypso's attitude toward Odysseus from her actions and her words in this section. Does she love Odysseus or not? How do you know?

12. What archetypal characters (p. 861) do Athena, Kalypso, and Hermês represent in this section of *The Odyssey*?

13. In what ways is Kalypso's island an archetypal setting (p. 863)? What does it represent to Odysseus's journey?

14. In line 56, Odysseus is referred to by the epithet "the strategist." In what ways does his reply to Kalypso's questions illustrate this epithet? (See Key Context for a definition and examples of epithets, p. 881.)

15. Even though Odysseus has been on his journey for some time when we first meet him in Book 5, in what ways is his departure here like stage 1 of the hero's journey (p. 860)?

Analyzing Language, Style, and Structure

Book 1

16. **Vocabulary in Context.** In the second line of the myth, Homer describes Odysseus as a "man skilled in all ways of contending." What does the word *contending* mean in this context?

17. What does it suggest that this myth starts not with Odysseus, but with the gods?

18. In lines 55–75, how does Athena use specific language choices to convince her father that Odysseus should be allowed to go home?

19. In Book 1, we see a number of epithets (p. 881) that describe the gods and Odysseus. Choose one or two and explain what essence of the character each epithet reveals.

20. What does the metaphor of the "wolf pack" achieve in lines 108–9.

Book 2

21. Vocabulary in Context. In lines 52–55, the speaker says that "no one there had the audacity to answer harshly except Antínoös." What does the word *audacity* mean in this context, and how is that meaning different from other uses of the word?

22. Reread Telémakhos's speech, beginning with "My distinguished father is lost" (ll. 15–51), and analyze the language choices he uses here to persuade his audience about the suitors.

23. Book 2 is called "A Hero's Son Awakens." What specific language choices in this book give the reader the impression of Telémakhos's metaphorical awakening?

Book 5

24. Vocabulary in Context. When Kalypso finally decides to release Odysseus, he says to her, "yield me first a great oath, if I do, to work no more enchantment to my harm" (ll. 31–32). What does the word *yield* mean in this context? How is it similar to or different from other uses you know?

25. How is Odysseus described when we first meet him in Book 5 on Kalypso's island? Explain what those language choices reveal about him.

26. Reread Odysseus's final two lines in Book 5 (ll. 65–66) and explain what his diction and syntax reveal about his feelings at this point in the myth.

Topics for Composing

27. Analysis. Based only on what you have read in these first books, how are father and son similar and different? What archetypal aspects of the hero's journey are found in each of their stories?

28. Analysis. A concept that was important in ancient Greek culture was *xenia*, or "guest friendship," which means showing hospitality to strangers who visit your home and showing respect to your host. Where have you seen this idea play out so far in *The Odyssey*? Who has shown good or poor guest friendship?

29. Analysis. *The Odyssey* is the story of Odysseus's voyage home, and yet we do not even meet him until Book 5. What is the effect of starting the story with Telémakhos and the homeland instead of with Odysseus?

30. Argument. To what extent are the rules governing the suitors' behavior clear? Do they have a legal right to do what they are doing? Are Telémakhos's and Penélopê's actions wrong?

31. Connections. Describe a time when you may have felt a little out of your depth like Telémakhos does in Book 2. What actions (or inactions) did you take to try to gain control of the situation?

32. Connections. Books 1–4 of *The Odyssey* are sometimes called "The Telemachy" because they focus mostly on Telémakhos and his trip to Pylos and Sparta (referred to at the end of the excerpt in Book 2) to gather news about his father Odysseus. Read the rest of the Telemachy and identify the components of the hero's journey archetype that are present.

33. Speaking and Listening. Select an excerpt from *The Odyssey* of five to ten lines and try to commit it to memory. Practice reading it aloud to yourself multiple times. Recite your section to a partner or small group, and afterward discuss how the language and the rhythm intentionally create patterns to support oral storytelling.

34. **Research.** Do some research to identify what is known — and unknown — about the poet Homer, to whom *The Odyssey* is credited. Or, conduct research on the performances of *The Odyssey* that were shared by poets of the ancient world. How did they memorize all of the content? How and when did they perform, and for what audiences?

35. **Creative Writing.** In the excerpts included here, Penélopê does not speak. The suitor Antínoös accuses her of fraud with the tapestry, but Telémakhos, not she, responds to him. Write a short piece, in poetry form if you wish, about what Penélopê might have said in that situation, or what she might have said to herself back in her room.

36. **Multimodal.** Choose a scene from the sections of *The Odyssey* that you found compelling. Adapt that scene into graphic form, including thought and speech bubbles. Use created or found images for the setting and background.

BOOK 9 New Coasts and Poseidon's Son

KEY CONTEXT The raft that Odysseus uses to leave Kalypso's island is nearly sunk by Poseidon, god of the seas, for reasons mentioned in Book 1, and which will be made clear here in Book 9. Eventually, Odysseus washes up on the shore of the Phaeacians, who care for him. In return for their hospitality, Odysseus tells them the story of his adventures from the time that he left Troy to when he arrived on Kalypso's island. Unlike other portions, Books 9–12 of *The Odyssey* are told in the first-person, as Odysseus recounts his journey to his hosts, starting when he still had his full crew after leaving Troy.

["]Nine days I drifted on the teeming sea
before dangerous high winds. Upon the tenth
we came to the coastline of the Lotos Eaters,
who live upon that flower. We landed there
to take on water. All ships' companies   5
mustered alongside for the mid-day meal.
Then I sent out two picked men and a runner
to learn what race of men that land sustained.
They fell in, soon enough, with Lotos Eaters,
who showed no will to do us harm, only   10
offering the sweet Lotos to our friends —
but those who ate this honeyed plant, the Lotos,
never cared to report, nor to return:
they longed to stay forever, browsing on
the native bloom, forgetful of their homeland.   15
I drove them, all three wailing, to the ships,
tied them down under their rowing benches,
and called the rest: 'All hands aboard;
come, clear the beach and no one taste
the Lotos, or you lose your hope of home.'   20
Filing in to their places by the rowlocks
my oarsmen dipped their long oars in the surf,
and we moved out again on our sea faring.

In the next land we found were Kyklopês,
giants, louts, without a law to bless them.   25

In ignorance leaving the fruitage of the earth in
     mystery
to the immortal gods, they neither plow
nor sow by hand, nor till the ground, though
     grain —
wild wheat and barley — grows untended, and
wine-grapes, in clusters, ripen in heaven's rain.   30
Kyklopês have no muster and no meeting,
no consultation or old tribal ways,
but each one dwells in his own mountain cave
dealing out rough justice to wife and child,
indifferent to what the others do.

                              Well, then: 35
across the wide bay from the mainland
there lies a desert island, not far out,
but still not close inshore. Wild goats in
     hundreds
breed there; and no human being comes
upon the isle to startle them — no hunter   40
of all who ever tracked with hounds through
     forests
or had rough going over mountain trails.
The isle, unplanted and untilled, a wilderness,
pastures goats alone. And this is why:
good ships like ours with cheekpaint at the
     bows   45

are far beyond the Kyklopês. No shipwright
toils among them, shaping and building up
symmetrical trim hulls to cross the sea
and visit all the seaboard towns, as men do
who go and come in commerce over water.   50
This isle — seagoing folk would have annexed it
and built their homesteads on it: all good land,
fertile for every crop in season: lush
well-watered meads along the shore, vines in
        profusion,
prairie, clear for the plow, where grain would
        grow   55
chin high by harvest time, and rich sub-soil.
The island cove is landlocked, so you need
no hawsers out astern, bow-stones or mooring:
run in and ride there till the day your crews
chafe to be under sail, and a fair wind blows.   60
You'll find good water flowing from a cavern
through dusky poplars into the upper bay.
Here we made harbor. Some god guided us
that night, for we could barely see our bows
in the dense fog around us, and no moonlight   65
filtered through the overcast. No look-out,
nobody saw the island dead ahead,
nor even the great landward rolling billow
that took us in: we found ourselves in shallows,
keels grazing shore: so furled our sails   70
and disembarked where the low ripples broke.
There on the beach we lay, and slept till
        morning.

When Dawn spread out her finger tips of rose
we turned out marvelling, to tour the isle,
while Zeus's shy nymph daughters flushed wild
        goats   75
down from the heights — a breakfast for my men.
We ran to fetch our hunting bows and
        long-shanked
lances from the ships, and in three companies
we took our shots. Heaven gave us game
        a-plenty:
for every one of twelve ships in my squadron   80
nine goats fell to be shared; my lot was ten.
So there all day, until the sun went down,
we made our feast on meat galore, and wine —
wine from the ship, for our supply held out,
so many jars were filled at Ísmaros   85

from stores of the Kikonês that we plundered.
We gazed, too, at Kyklopês Land, so near,
we saw their smoke, heard bleating from their
        flocks.
But after sundown, in the gathering dusk,
we slept again above the wash of ripples.   90

When the young Dawn with finger tips of rose
came in the east, I called my men together
and made a speech to them:
                        'Old shipmates, friends,
the rest of you stand by; I'll make the crossing
in my own ship, with my own company,   95
and find out what the mainland natives are —
for they may be wild savages, and lawless,
or hospitable and god fearing men.'

At this I went aboard, and gave the word
to cast off by the stern. My oarsmen followed,   100
filing in to their benches by the rowlocks,
and all in line dipped oars in the grey sea.

As we rowed on, and nearer to the mainland,
at one end of the bay, we saw a cavern
yawning above the water, screened with laurel,   105
and many rams and goats about the place
earthfast between tall trunks of pine and rugged
towering oak trees.
                    A prodigious man
slept in this cave alone, and took his flocks
to graze afield — remote from all companions,   110
knowing none but savage ways, a brute
so huge, he seemed no man at all of those
who eat good wheaten bread; but he seemed
        rather
a shaggy mountain reared in solitude.
We beached there, and I told the crew   115
to stand by and keep watch over the ship;
as for myself I took my twelve best fighters
and went ahead. I had a goatskin full
of that sweet liquor that Euanthês' son,
Maron, had given me. He kept Apollo's   120
holy grove at Ísmaros; for kindness
we showed him there, and showed his wife and
        child,
he gave me seven shining golden talents
perfectly formed, a solid silver winebowl,

How does this painting by Nicolas Poussin (1649) depict the land of the Kyklopês? What type of archetypal setting does this painting depict?

Photo © Fine Art Images/Bridgeman Images

and then this liquor — twelve two-handled jars   125
of brandy, pure and fiery. Not a slave
in Maron's household knew this drink; only
he, his wife and the storeroom mistress knew;
and they would put one cupful — ruby-colored,
honey-smooth — in twenty more of water,   130
but still the sweet scent hovered like a fume
over the winebowl. No man turned away
when cups of this came round.

                 A wineskin full
I brought along, and victuals in a bag,
for in my bones I knew some towering brute   135
would be upon us soon — all outward power,
a wild man, ignorant of civility.

We climbed, then, briskly to the cave. But
   Kyklops
had gone afield, to pasture his fat sheep,
so we looked round at everything inside: 140
a drying rack that sagged with cheeses, pens
crowded with lambs and kids, each in its class:
firstlings apart from middlings, and the 'dewdrops,'
or newborn lambkins, penned apart from both.
And vessels full of whey were brimming there —   145
bowls of earthenware and pails for milking.

My men came pressing round me, pleading:
                        'Why not
take these cheeses, get them stowed, come back,
throw open all the pens, and make a run for it?
We'll drive the kids and lambs aboard. We say   150
put out again on good salt water!'
                       Ah,
how sound that was! Yet I refused. I wished
to see the caveman, what he had to offer —
no pretty sight, it turned out, for my friends.
We lit a fire, burnt an offering,   155
and took some cheese to eat; then sat in silence
around the embers, waiting. When he came
he had a load of dry boughs on his shoulder
to stoke his fire at suppertime. He dumped it
with a great crash into that hollow cave,   160
and we all scattered fast to the far wall.
Then over the broad cavern floor he ushered
the ewes he meant to milk. He left his rams
and he-goats in the yard outside, and swung
high overhead a slab of solid rock   165
to close the cave. Two dozen four-wheeled
   wagons,
with heaving wagon teams, could not have stirred
the tonnage of that rock from where he
   wedged it

over the doorsill. Next he took his seat
and milked his bleating ewes. A practiced job   170
he made of it, giving each ewe her suckling;
thickened his milk, then, into curds and whey,
sieved out the curds to drip in withy baskets,
and poured the whey to stand in bowls
cooling until he drank it for his supper.   175
When all these chores were done, he poked the fire,
heaping on brushwood. In the glare he saw us.

'Strangers,' he said, 'who are you? And where from?
What brings you here by sea ways — a fair traffic?
Or are you wandering rogues, who cast your lives   180
like dice, and ravage other folk by sea?'

We felt a pressure on our hearts, in dread
of that deep rumble and that mighty man.
But all the same I spoke up in reply:

'We are from Troy, Akhaians, blown off course   185
by shifting gales on the Great South Sea;
homeward bound, but taking routes and ways
uncommon; so the will of Zeus would have it.
We served under Agamémnon, son of Atreus —
the whole world knows what city   190
he laid waste, what armies he destroyed.
It was our luck to come here; here we stand,
beholden for your help, or any gifts
you give — as custom is to honor strangers.
We would entreat you, great Sir, have a care   195
for the gods' courtesy; Zeus will avenge
the unoffending guest.'

                    He answered this
from his brute chest, unmoved:
                              'You are a ninny,
or else you come from the other end of nowhere,
telling me, mind the gods! We Kyklopês   200
care not a whistle for your thundering Zeus
or all the gods in bliss; we have more force by far.
I would not let you go for fear of Zeus —
you or your friends — unless I had a whim to.
Tell me, where was it, now, you left your ship —   205
around the point, or down the shore, I wonder?'

He thought he'd find out, but I saw through this,
and answered with a ready lie:
                              'My ship?

Poseidon Lord, who sets the earth a-tremble,
broke it up on the rocks at your land's end.   210
A wind from seaward served him, drove us there.
We are survivors, these good men and I.'

Neither reply nor pity came from him,
but in one stride he clutched at my companions
and caught two in his hands like squirming
    puppies   215
to beat their brains out, spattering the floor.
Then he dismembered them and made his meal,
gaping and crunching like a mountain lion —
everything: innards, flesh, and marrow bones.
We cried aloud, lifting our hands to Zeus,   220
powerless, looking on at this, appalled;
but Kyklops went on filling up his belly
with manflesh and great gulps of whey,
then lay down like a mast among his sheep.
My heart beat high now at the chance of action,   225
and drawing the sharp sword from my hip I went
along his flank to stab him where the midriff
holds the liver. I had touched the spot
when sudden fear stayed me: if I killed him
we perished there as well, for we could never   230
move his ponderous door way slab aside.
So we were left to groan and wait for morning.

When the young Dawn with finger tips of rose
lit up the world, the Kyklops built a fire
and milked his handsome ewes, all in due order,   235
putting the sucklings to the mothers. Then,
his chores being all dispatched, he caught
another brace of men to make his breakfast,
and whisked away his great door slab
to let his sheep go through — but he, behind,   240
reset the stone as one would cap a quiver.
There was a din of whistling as the Kyklops
rounded his flock to higher ground, then stillness.
And now I pondered how to hurt him worst,
if but Athena granted what I prayed for.   245
Here are the means I thought would serve my turn:
a club, or staff, lay there along the fold —
an olive tree, felled green and left to season
for Kyklops' hand. And it was like a mast
a lugger of twenty oars, broad in the beam —   250
a deep-sea-going craft — might carry:
so long, so big around, it seemed. Now I
chopped out a six foot section of this pole

893

Bridgeman Images

How does this depiction of *The Kyklops* by painter Odilon Redon (1914) differ from the print text of *The Odyssey*? What elements of the painting help create this depiction?

and set it down before my men, who scraped it;
and when they had it smooth, I hewed again   255
to make a stake with pointed end. I held this
in the fire's heart and turned it, toughening it,
then hid it, well back in the cavern, under
one of the dung piles in profusion there.
Now came the time to toss for it: who ventured   260
along with me? whose hand could bear to thrust
and grind that spike in Kyklops' eye, when mild
sleep had mastered him? As luck would have it,
the men I would have chosen won the toss —
four strong men, and I made five as captain.   265

At evening came the shepherd with his flock,
his woolly flock. The rams as well, this time,
entered the cave: by some sheep-herding whim —
or a god's bidding — none were left outside.
He hefted his great boulder into place   270
and sat him down to milk the bleating ewes
in proper order, put the lambs to suck,
and swiftly ran through all his evening chores.
Then he caught two more men and feasted on
    them.
My moment was at hand, and I went forward   275

holding an ivy bowl of my dark drink,
looking up, saying:
                              'Kyklops, try some wine.
Here's liquor to wash down your scraps of men.
Taste it, and see the kind of drink we carried
under our planks. I meant it for an offering   280
if you would help us home. But you are mad,
unbearable, a bloody monster! After this,
will any other traveller come to see you?'

He seized and drained the bowl, and it went down
so fiery and smooth he called for more: 285
'Give me another, thank you kindly. Tell me,
how are you called? I'll make a gift will please you.
Even Kyklopês know the wine-grapes grow
out of grassland and loam in heaven's rain,
but here's a bit of nectar and ambrosia!'   290

Three bowls I brought him, and he poured them
    down.
I saw the fuddle and flush come over him,
then I sang out in cordial tones:
                                       'Kyklops,
you ask my honorable name? Remember
the gift you promised me, and I shall tell you.   295
My name is Nohbdy: mother, father, and friends,
everyone calls me Nohbdy.'

                              And he said:
'Nohbdy's my meat, then, after I eat his friends.
Others come first. There's a noble gift, now.'

Even as he spoke, he reeled and tumbled
    backward,   300
his great head lolling to one side; and sleep
took him like any creature. Drunk, hiccuping,
he dribbled streams of liquor and bits of men.

Now, by the gods, I drove my big hand spike
deep in the embers, charring it again,   305
and cheered my men along with battle talk
to keep their courage up: no quitting now.
The pike of olive, green though it had been,
reddened and glowed as if about to catch.
I drew it from the coals and my four fellows   310
gave me a hand, lugging it near the Kyklops
as more than natural force nerved them; straight
forward they sprinted, lifted it, and rammed it
deep in his crater eye, and I leaned on it

Is Odysseus portrayed heroically in this painting by Pellegrino Tibaldi (1549)? Is the Kyklops presented in the same way here as in the print text? Explain by referring to visual elements of the painting and the print text.

Alfredo Dagli Orti/Art Resource, NY

turning it as a shipwright turns a drill   315
in planking, having men below to swing
the two-handled strap that spins it in the groove.
So with our brand we bored that great eye socket
while blood ran out around the red hot bar.
Eyelid and lash were seared; the pierced ball   320
hissed broiling, and the roots popped.
                       In a smithy
one sees a white-hot axehead or an adze
plunged and wrung in a cold tub, screeching
    steam —
the way they make soft iron hale and hard —:
just so that eyeball hissed around the spike.   325
The Kyklops bellowed and the rock roared round
    him,
and we fell back in fear. Clawing his face
he tugged the bloody spike out of his eye,
threw it away, and his wild hands went groping;
then he set up a howl for Kyklopês   330
who lived in caves on windy peaks nearby.
Some heard him; and they came by divers ways
to clump around outside and call:

                      'What ails you,
Polyphêmos? Why do you cry so sore
in the starry night? You will not let us sleep.   335
Sure no man's driving off your flock? No man
has tricked you, ruined you?'

                  Out of the cave
the mammoth Polyphêmos roared in answer:
'Nohbdy, Nohbdy's tricked me, Nohbdy's ruined
    me!'

To this rough shout they made a sage reply: 340
'Ah well, if nobody has played you foul
there in your lonely bed, we are no use in pain
given by great Zeus. Let it be your father,
Poseidon Lord, to whom you pray.'

                  So saying
they trailed away. And I was filled with laughter   345
to see how like a charm the name deceived
    them.
Now Kyklops, wheezing as the pain came on him,
fumbled to wrench away the great doorstone
and squatted in the breach with arms thrown wide
for any silly beast or man who bolted —   350
hoping somehow I might be such a fool.
But I kept thinking how to win the game:
death sat there huge; how could we slip away?
I drew on all my wits, and ran through tactics,
reasoning as a man will for dear life,   355
until a trick came — and it pleased me well.
The Kyklops' rams were handsome, fat, with heavy
fleeces, a dark violet.

                Three abreast
I tied them silently together, twining
cords of willow from the ogre's bed;   360
then slung a man under each middle one
to ride there safely, shielded left and right.
So three sheep could convey each man. I took
the woolliest ram, the choicest of the flock,
and hung myself under his kinky belly,   365
pulled up tight, with fingers twisted deep
in sheepskin ringlets for an iron grip.
So, breathing hard, we waited until morning.

895

When Dawn spread out her finger tips of rose
the rams began to stir, moving for pasture, 370
and peals of bleating echoed round the pens
where dams with udders full called for a milking.
Blinded, and sick with pain from his head wound,
the master stroked each ram, then let it pass,
but my men riding on the pectoral fleece 375
the giant's blind hands blundering never found.
Last of them all my ram, the leader, came,
weighted by wool and me with my meditations.
The Kyklops patted him, and then he said:
'Sweet cousin ram, why lag behind the rest 380
in the night cave? You never linger so,
but graze before them all, and go afar
to crop sweet grass, and take your stately way
leading along the streams, until at evening
you run to be the first one in the fold. 385
Why, now, so far behind? Can you be grieving
over your Master's eye? That carrion rogue
and his accurst companions burnt it out
when he had conquered all my wits with wine.
Nohbdy will not get out alive, I swear. 390
Oh, had you brain and voice to tell
where he may be now, dodging all my fury!
Bashed by this hand and bashed on this rock wall
his brains would strew the floor, and I should have
rest from the outrage Nohbdy worked upon me.' 395

He sent us into the open, then. Close by,
I dropped and rolled clear of the ram's belly,
going this way and that to untie the men.
With many glances back, we rounded up
his fat, stiff-legged sheep to take aboard, 400
and drove them down to where the good ship lay.
We saw, as we came near, our fellows' faces
shining; then we saw them turn to grief
tallying those who had not fled from death.
I hushed them, jerking head and eyebrows up, 405
and in a low voice told them: 'Load this herd;
move fast, and put the ship's head toward the
     breakers.'
They all pitched in at loading, then embarked
and struck their oars into the sea. Far out,
as far off shore as shouted words would carry, 410
I sent a few back to the adversary:

'O Kyklops! Would you feast on my companions?
Puny, am I, in a Caveman's hands?
How do you like the beating that we gave you,
you damned cannibal? Eater of guests 415
under your roof! Zeus and the gods have paid you!'

The blind thing in his doubled fury broke
a hilltop in his hands and heaved it after us.
Ahead of our black prow it struck and sank
whelmed in a spuming geyser, a giant wave 420
that washed the ship stern foremost back to shore.
I got the longest boathook out and stood
fending us off, with furious nods to all
to put their backs into a racing stroke —
row, row, or perish. So the long oars bent 425
kicking the foam sternward, making head
until we drew away, and twice as far.
Now when I cupped my hands I heard the crew
in low voices protesting:

                    'Godsake, Captain!
Why bait the beast again? Let him alone!' 430
'That tidal wave he made on the first throw
all but beached us.'

                    'All but stove us in!'
'Give him our bearing with your trumpeting,
he'll get the range and lob a boulder.'

                              'Aye
He'll smash our timbers and our heads together!' 435

I would not heed them in my glorying spirit,
but let my anger flare and yelled:
                    'Kyklops,
if ever mortal man inquire
how you were put to shame and blinded, tell him
Odysseus, raider of cities, took your eye: 440
Laërtês' son, whose home's on Ithaka!'[. . .]

At this he stretched his hands out in his darkness
toward the sky of stars, and prayed Poseidon:
'O hear me, lord, blue girdler of the islands,
if I am thine indeed, and thou art father: 445
grant that Odysseus, raider of cities, never
see his home: Laërtês' son, I mean,
who kept his hall on Ithaka. Should destiny
intend that he shall see his roof again
among his family in his father land, 450
far be that day, and dark the years between.
Let him lose all companions, and return
under strange sail to bitter days at home.'[. . .]

At first glance, this painting by Alexandre Decamps (1855) seems to be a pretty literal recounting of the Kyklops hurling boulders at the escaping Greeks.

Closely examine the painting for its details of setting and characterization to draw an interpretation about what the painting might be suggesting about this encounter between the monster and the Greeks. How is this depiction similar to or different from the portrayal in *The Odyssey*?

© Peter Willi/Bridgeman Images

Now all day long until the sun went down
we made our feast on mutton and sweet wine, 455
till after sunset in the gathering dark
we went to sleep above the wash of ripples.

When the young Dawn with finger tips of rose
touched the world, I roused the men, gave orders
to man the ships, cast off the mooring lines; 460
and filing in to sit beside the rowlocks
oarsmen in line dipped oars in the grey sea.
So we moved out, sad in the vast offing,
having our precious lives, but not our
    friends.["]

extending beyond the text

Read the following poem by Nikki Giovanni, in which she compares a tropical storm to the Cyclops.

The Cyclops in the Ocean

Nikki Giovanni

Moving slowly . . . against time . . . patiently majestic . . . The Cyclops . . . in the ocean . . . meets no Ulysses . . .

Through the night . . . he sighs . . . throbbing against the shore . . . declaring . . . for the adventure . . .

A wall of gray . . . gathered by a slow touch . . . slash and slither . . . through the waiting screens . . . separating into nodules . . . making my panes . . . accept the touch . . .

Not content . . . to watch my frightened gaze . . . he clamors beneath the sash . . . dancing to my sill . . .

Certain to die . . . when the sun . . . returns . . .

What is the speaker's attitude toward the Cyclops that never met Ulysses, which is the Roman name for Odysseus? How does the speaker create this tone? How is the Cyclops in the poem similar to or different from how that figure is portrayed in *The Odyssey*?

897

BOOK 12   Sea Perils and Defeat

KEY CONTEXT In Book 10, Odysseus and his men stop at the island of the witch Kirkê, who drugs his men and turns them into pigs. With the intervention of Hermês, who tells Odysseus how to counteract the drug, he is able to defeat her. She becomes a lover and ally, returning his men to human form. She gives Odysseus directions to get to the Underworld in Book 11 and suggestions on how to defeat other obstacles at the beginning of Book 12.

["]'Dear friends,
more than one man, or two, should know those
    things
Kirkê foresaw for us and shared with me,
so let me tell her forecast: then we die
with our eyes open, if we are going to die,   5
or know what death we baffle if we can.
Seirênês weaving a haunting song over the sea
we are to shun, she said, and their green shore
all sweet with clover; yet she urged that I
alone should listen to their song. Therefore   10
you are to tie me up, tight as a splint,
erect along the mast, lashed to the mast,
and if I shout and beg to be untied,
take more turns of the rope to muffle me.'

I rather dwelt on this part of the forecast,   15
while our good ship made time, bound outward
    down
the wind for the strange island of Seirênês.
Then all at once the wind fell, and a calm
came over all the sea, as though some power
lulled the swell.
            The crew were on their feet   20
briskly, to furl the sail, and stow it; then,
each in place, they poised the smooth oar blades
and sent the white foam scudding by. I carved
a massive cake of beeswax into bits
and rolled them in my hands until they
    softened —   25
no long task, for a burning heat came down
from Hêlios, lord of high noon. Going forward
I carried wax along the line, and laid it
thick on their ears. They tied me up, then, plumb
amidships, back to the mast, lashed to the mast,   30
and took themselves again to rowing. Soon,
as we came smartly within hailing distance,
the two Seirênês, noting our fast ship
off their point, made ready, and they sang [. . .]

The lovely voices in ardor appealing over the
    water   35
made me crave to listen, and I tried to say
'Untie me!' to the crew, jerking my brows;
but they bent steady to the oars. Then Perimêdês
got to his feet, he and Eurýlokhos,
and passed more line about, to hold me still.   40
So all rowed on, until the Seirênês
dropped under the sea rim, and their singing
dwindled away.

            My faithful company
rested on their oars now, peeling off
the wax that I had laid thick on their ears;   45
then set me free.
            But scarcely had that island
faded in blue air than I saw smoke
and white water, with sound of waves in
    tumult —
a sound the men heard, and it terrified them.
Oars flew from their hands; the blades went
    knocking   50
wild alongside till the ship lost way,
with no oarblades to drive her through the
    water.

Well, I walked up and down from bow to stern,
trying to put heart into them, standing over
every oarsman, saying gently,
            'Friends,   55
have we never been in danger before this?
More fearsome, is it now, than when the
    Kyklops
penned us in his cave? What power he had!
Did I not keep my nerve, and use my wits
to find a way out for us?
            Now I say   60
by hook or crook this peril too shall be
something that we remember.

Walt Disney/courtesy Everett Collection

Leeds Museums and Galleries, UK/Bridgeman Images

National Gallery of Victoria, Melbourne/Bridgeman Images

Here are three different portrayals of the Sirens.

What similarities and differences do you notice among the three portrayals? What interpretations can you draw about the ways that the viewer should feel about the Sirens in each?

Heads up, lads!
We must obey the orders as I give them.
Get the oarshafts in your hands, and lay back
hard on your benches; hit these breaking seas.   65
Zeus help us pull away before we founder.
You at the tiller, listen, and take in
all that I say — the rudders are your duty;
keep her out of the combers and the smoke;
steer for that headland; watch the drift, or we   70
fetch up in the smother, and you drown us.'

That was all, and it brought them round to action.
But as I sent them on toward Skylla, I
told them nothing, as they could do nothing.
They would have dropped their oars again, in panic,   75
to roll for cover under the decking. Kirkê's
bidding against arms had slipped my mind,
so I tied on my cuirass and took up
two heavy spears, then made my way along
to the foredeck — thinking to see her first from
     there,   80

the monster of the grey rock, harboring
torment for my friends. I strained my eyes
upon that cliffside veiled in cloud, but nowhere
could I catch sight of her.

And all this time,
in travail, sobbing, gaining on the current,   85
we rowed into the strait — Skylla to port
and on our starboard beam Kharybdis, dire
gorge of the salt sea tide. By heaven! when she
vomited, all the sea was like a cauldron
seething over intense fire, when the mixture   90
suddenly heaves and rises.

The shot spume
soared to the landside heights, and fell like rain.

But when she swallowed the sea water down
we saw the funnel of the maelstrom, heard
the rock bellowing all around, and dark   95
sand raged on the bottom far below.
My men all blanched against the gloom, our
     eyes

899

were fixed upon that yawning mouth in fear
of being devoured.
                          Then Skylla made her strike,
whisking six of my best men from the ship.   100
I happened to glance aft at ship and oarsmen
and caught sight of their arms and legs,
     dangling
high overhead. Voices came down to me
in anguish, calling my name for the last time.

A man surfcasting on a point of rock   105
for bass or mackerel, whipping his long rod
to drop the sinker and the bait far out,

will hook a fish and rip it from the surface
to dangle wriggling through the air:
                              so these
were borne aloft in spasms toward the cliff.   110

She ate them as they shrieked there, in her den,
in the dire grapple, reaching still for me —
and deathly pity ran me through
at that sight — far the worst I ever suffered,
questing the passes of the strange sea.
                              We rowed on. 115
The Rocks were now behind; Kharybdis, too,
and Skylla dropped astern.["]

extending beyond the text

Read the following excerpt from a poem depicting the sirens.

from The Sirens

James Russell Lowell

Look how the gray old Ocean
From the depth of his heart rejoices,
Heaving with a gentle motion,
When he hears our restful voices;
List how he sings in an undertone,
Chiming with our melody;
And all sweet sounds of earth and air
Melt into one low voice alone,
That murmurs over the weary sea,
And seems to sing from everywhere,—
"Here mayst thou harbor peacefully,
Here mayst thou rest from the aching oar;
     Turn thy curvëd prow ashore,
And in our green isle rest forevermore!
          Forevermore!"
And Echo half wakes in the wooded hill,
     And, to her heart so calm and deep,
     Murmurs over in her sleep,
Doubtfully pausing and murmuring still,
          "Evermore!"

Thus, on Life's weary sea,
Heareth the marinere
Voices sweet, from far and near,
Ever singing low and clear,
Ever singing longingly.

. . .

The waters gurgle longingly,
As if they fain would seek the shore,
To be at rest from the ceaseless roar,
To be at rest forevermore,—
    Forevermore.
Thus, on Life's gloomy sea,
Heareth the marinere
Voices sweet, from far and near,
Ever singing in his ear,
"Here is rest and peace for thee!" ∎

The speaker of the poem represents the sirens singing to a sailor passing by. How do the sirens try to convince the sailor to come to them? How is the portrayal of the sirens in this poem similar to or different from their depiction in *The Odyssey*?

Understanding and Interpreting

Book 9

1. Summarize what happens to Odysseus's men with the Lotus Eaters (ll. 1–23). Explain what archetype the Lotus Eaters represent.

2. Skim back through the section where Odysseus and his men first see the land of the Kyklopês (ll. 24–72). Why does Odysseus define the land as "uncivilized," and explain how it compares to more familiar places where he and his men have lived or visited.

3. Odysseus and his men could have left the land of the Kyklopês after one night. What rationale does Odysseus offer for exploring the island instead? What does this suggest about his character?

4. Once inside the cave, Odysseus and his men again had the chance to leave before encountering the Kyklops. What do his men suggest in lines 147–51, and why does Odysseus refuse?

5. What are the differences between the expectations that Odysseus and the Kyklops — named Polyphêmos, we later learn — have about the role of hospitality as seen in their first dialogue exchange (ll. 178–212)?

6. Odysseus is a quick thinker who is willing to lie when he feels it is necessary. Identify the most significant places that demonstrate his mental agility in escaping the Kyklops in Book 9.

7. What kind of leader is Odysseus based on some of his actions in Book 9? Identify strengths and weaknesses with evidence from the text.

8. Why might Odysseus feel it necessary to shout at the Kyklops, calling him an "Eater of guests" (l. 415) and even continuing after being warned by his crew? What do these actions reveal about Odysseus?

9. Explain how the Kyklops represents an archetypal character in this story.

10. Odysseus and his men could have been spared the wrath of Poseidon — Polyphêmos's father — if he hadn't told the Kyklops his name (ll. 437–41). What factors may have led Odysseus to do this?

Book 12

11. Prior to this section of Book 12, Kirkê gives Odysseus a much fuller prediction of the conflicts and challenges Odysseus and his men will face than what he eventually shares with his men. Locate moments in Book 12 in which Odysseus acknowledges he is not giving his men the complete picture of their situation, and explain what these moments reveal about his character.

12. Odysseus alone is the one who listens to the song of the Seirênês (ll. 35–43). Why does he do this, and how does this action fit with the characteristics he has demonstrated so far in this myth?

13. Once they are free of the Seirênês, Odysseus and his men begin heading to Skylla and Kharybdis. Reread the speech he delivers to his men (ll. 55–71) and explain how he motivates them. What does this say about his leadership style?

14. What archetypal settings have you seen in this section (Books 9 and 12)? How can these settings be analyzed symbolically to explain some part of the hero's journey?

15. What effect do the deaths of his men seem to have on Odysseus in this section? Why does he call it the "worst I ever suffered" (l. 114)?

16. This section represents a significant part of the Road of Trials stage of the hero's journey archetype. What aspects of Odysseus's character have been revealed through the ways that he has survived these challenges?

Analyzing Language, Style, and Structure

Book 9

17. **Vocabulary in Context.** In Book 9, line 237, Odysseus says of the Kyklops: "his chores being all dispatched." What does the word *dispatched* mean in this context? What other uses of the word have you encountered?

18. Starting with Book 9 and continuing for the next several books of *The Odyssey*, Odysseus himself is the narrator. How does this shift in point of view affect how we might view Odysseus?

19. Examine how the diction choices in lines 108–14, in which Odysseus describes the first Kyklops he sees, reveal his attitude toward the creature.

20. A number of moments in Book 9 foreshadow the disaster that befalls Odysseus and his crew. Locate one example and explain how it acts as foreshadowing.

21. Epic similes and metaphors are used to emphasize the grand size and scope of people, places, and things in *The Odyssey*. Locate and explain the effect of specific examples of these in Book 9.

22. Reread the section in which Polyphêmos first eats two of Odysseus's men (ll. 213–19). How are the language choices intended to horrify the listener or reader?

23. One of the epithets that Odysseus uses for himself is "Odysseus, raider of cities" (l. 440). What does this suggest about how Odysseus views himself?

Book 12

24. **Vocabulary in Context.** In line 35, Odysseus describes the Seirênês as "the lovely voices in ardor." What does the word *ardor* mean in this context?

25. There are several examples of epic similes and metaphors in this section, especially in the initial descriptions of Skylla and Kharybdis beginning with lines 84–91. Identify and explain the effect of one or more of the comparisons.

26. Reread the metaphor comparing the actions of Skylla to those of a man surfcasting in lines 105–10. What is achieved through this metaphor?

Topics for Composing

27. **Analysis.** In what ways has Odysseus's story to this point portrayed the hero's journey archetype? Which archetypal characters and settings are present and what do they represent?

28. **Analysis.** As you may have read earlier, *xenia* refers to the concept of guest-friendship in ancient Greek culture. What further evidence about the role and importance of *xenia* have you seen in Book 9? Who has shown good or poor *xenia*? What is the importance of *xenia* in this myth?

29. **Argument.** Is Odysseus an effective leader? What qualities make him one, or not?

30. **Connections.** Based on this myth, the saying "siren's song" has come to mean an alluring but deceptive utterance or appeal, *especially* one that lures the listener to unfortunate or destructive ends. What are possible siren songs in your life, and what are your reactions to them?

31. **Connections.** The phrase "between a rock and a hard place" applies to the moment in which Odysseus steers between two difficult paths — Skylla and Kharybdis — neither of which is a good option. Describe a situation in which you found yourself between a rock and a hard place. How did you manage to steer between them, or not?

32. **Connections.** Read more of *The Odyssey* than what is included here, specifically the books that focus on Kirkê, a witch whom Odysseus defeats then befriends, and those that focus on Odysseus's trip to the Underworld. How do these sections add to or change your understanding of Odysseus? How do the archetypal characters and settings in these other sections add to your understanding of the hero's journey of Odysseus?

33. **Speaking and Listening.** Meet with a partner or a small group and discuss modern, real-life examples of the Lotus Eaters described at the beginning of Book 9. Come to consensus on one that you think is the best example.

34. **Research.** Archeological finds have led some people to conclude that elements of *The Odyssey* might, in fact, be true. Research some of the most credible sources to consider the likelihood of the truth of *The Odyssey*.

35. **Creative Writing.** This excerpt does not include the song that the Seirênês sing as Odysseus and his men pass by. Write some lines of a song that might have the effect that Odysseus says made him "crave to listen."

36. **Multimodal.** Many passages in Books 9 and 12 are highly descriptive, especially those regarding the Kyklopês or Skylla and Kharybdis. Create a page or two of your own graphic novel adaptation of a particularly visual scene, using the words from the original text as dialogue, captions, or thought bubbles.

BOOK 16   Father and Son

KEY CONTEXT   After Odysseus has told his story to the Phaeacians, they help him return home. When he lands on the shores of Ithaka, he meets Athena, who disguises him as an old beggar. He soon meets up with his loyal swineherd, Eumaios, who takes him in. Meanwhile, Athena has protected Telémakhos's ship, returning from his journey to find his father, from the suitors' attack and directs Telémakhos to the swineherd's house.

But there were two men in the mountain hut—
Odysseus and the swineherd. At first light
blowing their fire up, they cooked their breakfast
and sent their lads out, driving herds to root
in the tall timber.
             When Telémakhos came,   5
the wolvish troop of watchdogs only fawned on
    him
as he advanced. Odysseus heard them go
and heard the light crunch of a man's footfall—
at which he turned quickly to say:
               "Eumaios,
here is one of your crew come back, or maybe   10
another friend: the dogs are out there snuffling
belly down; not one has even growled.
I can hear footsteps—"

             But before he finished
his tall son stood at the door.
              The swineherd
rose in surprise, letting a bowl and jug   15
tumble from his fingers. Going forward,
he kissed the young man's head, his shining eyes
and both hands, while his own tears brimmed
    and fell.
Think of a man whose dear and only son,
born to him in exile, reared with labor,   20
has lived ten years abroad and now returns:
how would that man embrace his son! Just so
the herdsman clapped his arms around
    Telémakhos
and covered him with kisses—for he knew
the lad had got away from death. [. . .]   25

Odysseus moved aside, yielding his couch,
but from across the room Telémakhos checked
    him:
"Friend, sit down; we'll find another chair
in our own hut. Here is the man to make one! [. . .]

                  "Oh, Uncle,   30
what's your friend's home port? How did he come?
Who were the sailors brought him here to
    Ithaka?
I doubt if he came walking on the sea."

And you replied, Eumaios—O my swineherd—
"Son, the truth about him is soon told.   35
His home land, and a broad land, too, is Krete,
but he has knocked about the world, he says,
for years, as the Powers wove his life. Just now

Prismatic Pictures/Bridgeman Images

This painting by Newell Wyeth (1929) depicts the minor character Eumaios.

How do the colors, setting, and other aspects portray him as one whom Odysseus could trust?

he broke away from a shipload of Thesprotians
to reach my hut. I place him in your hands.　　40
Act as you will. He wishes your protection."

The young man said:
　　　　　　　"Eumaios, my protection!
The notion cuts me to the heart. How can I
receive your friend at home? I am not old enough
or trained in arms. Could I defend myself　　45
if someone picked a fight with me? [. . .]

　　　　　　　　　　　　Impossible
to let him stay in hall, among the suitors.
They are drunk, drunk on impudence, they might
injure my guest — and how could I bear that?　　50
How could a single man take on those odds?
Not even a hero could.
　　　　　　　The suitors are too strong."
At this the noble and enduring man, Odysseus,
addressed his son:
　　　　　　　"Kind prince, it may be fitting

for me to speak a word. All that you say　　55
gives me an inward wound as I sit listening.
I mean this wanton game they play, these fellows,
riding roughshod over you in your own house,
admirable as you are. But tell me,
are you resigned to being bled? The townsmen,　　60
stirred up against you, are they, by some oracle?
Your brothers — can you say your brothers fail you?
A man should feel his kin, at least, behind him
in any clash, when a real fight is coming.
If my heart were as young as yours, if I were　　65
son to Odysseus, or the man himself,
I'd rather have my head cut from my shoulders
by some slashing adversary, if I
brought no hurt upon that crew!["] [. . .]

The swineherd, roused, reached out to get his
　　sandals,　　70
tied them on, and took the road.

　　　　　　　　　　　Who else
beheld this but Athena? From the air
she walked, taking the form of a tall woman, [. . .]
"Son of Laërtês and the gods of old,
Odysseus, master of land ways and sea ways,　　75
dissemble to your son no longer now.
The time has come: tell him how you together
will bring doom on the suitors in the town.
I shall not be far distant then, for I
myself desire battle."

　　　　　　　　　Saying no more,　　80
she tipped her golden wand upon the man,
making his cloak pure white, and the knit tunic
fresh around him. Lithe and young she made him,
ruddy with sun, his jawline clean, the beard
no longer grey upon his chin. And she　　85
withdrew when she had done.
　　　　　　　　　Then Lord Odysseus
reappeared — and his son was thunderstruck.
Fear in his eyes, he looked down and away
as though it were a god, and whispered:

　　　　　　　　　　　"Stranger,
you are no longer what you were just now!　　90
Your cloak is new; even your skin! You are
one of the gods who rule the sweep of heaven!

**How does the artist of this image of the
reunion between Odysseus and Telémakhos
capture the traits of each character?**

Be kind to us, we'll make you fair oblation
and gifts of hammered gold. Have mercy on us!"

The noble and enduring man replied: 95
"No god. Why take me for a god? No, no.
I am that father whom your boyhood lacked
and suffered pain for lack of. I am he."

Held back too long, the tears ran down his cheeks
as he embraced his son. [. . .]   100

                              "I came
to this wild place, directed by Athena,
so that we might lay plans to kill our enemies.["] [. . .]

   "O Father, all my life your fame
as a fighting man has echoed in my ears —   105
your skills with weapons and the tricks of
      war —
but what you speak of is a staggering thing,
beyond imagining, for me. How can two men
do battle with a houseful in their prime?
For I must tell you this is no affair   110
of ten or even twice ten men, but scores,

throngs of them. [. . .]
If we go in against all these
I fear we pay in salt blood for your vengeance.
You must think hard if you would conjure up   115
the fighting strength to take us through."

                                        Odysseus
who had endured the long war and the sea
answered:
                    "I'll tell you now.
Suppose Athena's arm is over us, and Zeus
her father's, must I rack my brains for more?"   120

Clearheaded Telémakhos looked hard and said:
"Those two are great defenders, no one doubts it,
but throned in the serene clouds overhead;
other affairs of men and gods they have
to rule over."

               And the hero answered: 125
"Before long they will stand to right and left
      of us
in combat, in the shouting, when the test comes —
our nerve against the suitors' in my hall.["]

BOOK 21   The Test of the Bow

KEY CONTEXT   Still disguised as a beggar, Odysseus is treated poorly by the suitors, but kindly by Penélopê, to whom Odysseus does not reveal himself. He does, however, tell her that her husband is alive and is soon returning. Planning his revenge, Odysseus has solicited the help from a few of his loyal house staff, and Penélopê has set up a challenge for the suitors to meet in order to win her hand in marriage.

                    "My lords, hear me:
suitors indeed, you commandeered this house
to feast and drink in, day and night, my
      husband
being long gone, long out of mind. You found
no justification for yourselves — none   5
except your lust to marry me. Stand up, then:
we now declare a contest for that prize.
Here is my lord Odysseus' hunting bow.
Bend and string it if you can. Who sends an arrow
through iron axe-helve sockets, twelve in line?   10
I join my life with his, and leave this place, my home,
my rich and beautiful bridal house, forever
to be remembered, though I dream it only." [. . .]

                              So one by one
the young men warmed and greased the bow for   15
      bending,
but not a man could string it. They were
      whipped.
Antínoös held off; so did Eurýmakhos,
suitors in chief, by far the ablest there. [. . .]

Eurýmakhos had now picked up the bow.
He turned it round, and turned it round   20
before the licking flame to warm it up,
but could not, even so, put stress upon it
to jam the loop over the tip
                    though his heart groaned to bursting.

This painting by John Robertson (1900) shows Penélopê addressing the suitors.

How does the artist communicate the power Penélopê holds at this moment?

"Go on, take him the bow! Do you obey this
    pack?[. . .]"

              Eumaios picked up
bow and quiver, making for the door,   45
and there he placed them in Odysseus' hands.
    [. . .]

                And Odysseus took his time,
turning the bow, tapping it, every inch,
for borings that termites might have made
while the master of the weapon was abroad.   50
The suitors were now watching him, and some
jested among themselves:
                  "A bow lover!"
"Dealer in old bows!"
                "Maybe he has one like it
at home!"
       "Or has an itch to make one for himself."
"See how he handles it, the sly old buzzard!"   55
And one disdainful suitor added this:
"May his fortune grow an inch for every inch he
    bends it!"

Then he said grimly:
                "Curse this day.   25
What gloom I feel, not for myself alone,
and not only because we lose that bride.
Women are not lacking in Akhaia,
in other towns, or on Ithaka. No, the worst
is humiliation — to be shown up for children   30
measured against Odysseus — we who cannot
even hitch the string over his bow.
What shame to be repeated of us, after us!" [. . .]

The swineherd had the horned bow in his hands
moving toward Odysseus, when the crowd   35
in the banquet hall broke into an ugly din,
shouts rising from the flushed young men:
                    "Ho! Where
do you think you are taking that, you smutty
    slave?" [. . .]

He faltered, all at once put down the bow, and
    stood
in panic, buffeted by waves of cries,   40
hearing Telémakhos from another quarter
shout:

But the man skilled in all ways of contending,
satisfied by the great bow's look and heft,
like a musician, like a harper, when   60
with quiet hand upon his instrument
he draws between his thumb and forefinger
a sweet new string upon a peg: so effortlessly
Odysseus in one motion strung the bow.
Then slid his right hand down the cord and   65
    plucked it,
so the taut gut vibrating hummed and sang
a swallow's note.
             In the hushed hall it smote the suitors
and all their faces changed. Then Zeus
    thundered
overhead, one loud crack for a sign.
And Odysseus laughed within him that the son   70
of crooked-minded Kronos had flung that omen
    down.
He picked one ready arrow from his table
where it lay bare: the rest were waiting still
in the quiver for the young men's turn to come.
He nocked it, let it rest across the handgrip,   75
and drew the string and grooved butt of the arrow,
aiming from where he sat upon the stool.

907

Now flashed
arrow from twanging bow clean as a whistle
through every socket ring, and grazed not one,
to thud with heavy brazen head beyond. 80
                                    Then quietly
Odysseus said:
                    "Telémakhos, the stranger
you welcomed in your hall has not disgraced
    you.
I did not miss, neither did I take all day
stringing the bow. My hand and eye are sound, 85

not so contemptible as the young men say.
The hour has come to cook their lordships'
    mutton —
supper by daylight. Other amusements later,
with song and harping that adorn a feast."

He dropped his eyes and nodded, and the prince 90
Telémakhos, true son of King Odysseus,
belted his sword on, clapped hand to his spear,
and with a clink and glitter of keen bronze
stood by his chair, in the forefront near his father.

BOOK 22   Death in the Great Hall

Now shrugging off his rags the wiliest fighter of
    the islands
leapt and stood on the broad door sill, his own
    bow in his hand.
He poured out at his feet a rain of arrows from
    the quiver
and spoke to the crowd:
    "So much for that. Your clean-cut game is over.
Now watch me hit a target that no man has hit
    before,
if I can make this shot. Help me, Apollo."   5

He drew to his fist the cruel head of an arrow for
    Antínoös
just as the young man leaned to lift his beautiful
    drinking cup,
embossed, two-handled, golden: the cup was in
    his fingers:
the wine was even at his lips: and did he dream
    of death?   10
How could he? In that revelry amid his throng of
    friends
who would imagine a single foe — though a
    strong foe indeed —
could dare to bring death's pain on him and
    darkness on his eyes?
Odysseus' arrow hit him under the chin
and punched up to the feathers through his throat. 15

Backward and down he went, letting the winecup
    fall
from his shocked hand. Like pipes his nostrils
    jetted
crimson runnels, a river of mortal red,

and one last kick upset his table
knocking the bread and meat to soak in dusty blood. 20
Now as they craned to see their champion where
    he lay
the suitors jostled in uproar down the hall,
everyone on his feet. Wildly they turned and
    scanned
the walls in the long room for arms; but not a
    shield,
not a good ashen spear was there for a man to
    take and throw.   25
All they could do was yell in outrage at
    Odysseus:
"Foul! to shoot at a man! That was your last shot!"
"Your own throat will be slit for this!"
                        "Our finest lad is down!
You killed the best on Ithaka."
                        "Buzzards will tear your eyes out!"

For they imagined as they wished — that it was a
    wild shot,   30
an unintended killing — fools, not to
    comprehend
they were already in the grip of death.
But glaring under his brows Odysseus answered:
"You yellow dogs, you thought I'd never make it
home from the land of Troy. You took my house
    to plunder,   35
twisted my maids to serve your beds. You dared
bid for my wife while I was still alive.
Contempt was all you had for the gods who rule
    wide heaven,
contempt for what men say of you hereafter.
Your last hour has come. You die in blood." [. . .]   40

This painting by Nicolas André Monsiau (1791) depicts the killing of the suitors, and Odysseus ordering the maids to clean up after the killing.

How is the viewer of this painting expected to feel about the killings? What visual elements create these feelings? How do the emotions created by this painting compare to the emotions created by the text of this scene?

In blood and dust
he saw that crowd all fallen, many and many slain.

Think of a catch that fishermen haul in to a
    halfmoon bay
in a fine-meshed net from the white-caps of the sea:
how all are poured out on the sand, in throes for 45
    the salt sea,
twitching their cold lives away in Hêlios' fiery air:
so lay the suitors heaped on one another.

Odysseus at length said to his son:
"Go tell old Nurse I'll have a word with her.
What's to be done now weighs on my mind." [. . .] 50

Said the great soldier then:
            "Rejoice
inwardly. No crowing aloud, old woman.
To glory over slain men is no piety.
Destiny and the gods' will vanquished these,
and their own hardness. They respected no one, 55
good or bad, who came their way.
For this, and folly, a bad end befell them.
Your part is now to tell me of the women,
those who dishonored me, and the innocent."

His own old nurse Eurýkleia said:
            "I will, then. 60

Child, you know you'll have the truth from me.
Fifty all told they are, your female slaves,
trained by your lady and myself in service,
wool carding and the rest of it, and taught
to be submissive. Twelve went bad, 65
flouting me, flouting Penélopê, too.
Telémakhos being barely grown, his mother
would never let him rule the serving women —
but you must let me go to her lighted rooms
and tell her. Some god sent her a drift of sleep." 70

But in reply the great tactician said:
"Not yet. Do not awake her. Tell those women
who were the suitors' harlots to come here."

She went back on this mission through his hall.
Then he called Telémakhos to his side 75
and the two herdsmen. Sharply Odysseus said:
"These dead must be disposed of first of all.
Direct the women. Tables and chairs will be
scrubbed with sponges, rinsed and rinsed again.
When our great room is fresh and put in order, 80
take them outside, these women,
between the roundhouse and the palisade,
and hack them with your swordblades till you cut
the life out of them, and every thought of sweet
Aphroditê under the rutting suitors, 85
when they lay down in secret."

909

As he spoke
here came the women in a bunch, all wailing,
soft tears on their cheeks. They fell to work
to lug the corpses out into the courtyard
under the gateway, propping one   90
against another as Odysseus ordered,
for he himself stood over them. In fear
these women bore the cold weight of the dead.
The next thing was to scrub off chairs and tables
and rinse them down. Telémakhos and the
    herdsman   95
scraped the packed earth floor with hoes,
but made the women carry out all blood and mire.
When the great room was cleaned up once again,
at swordpoint they forced them out, between
the roundhouse and the palisade, pell-mell   100
to huddle in that dead end without exit.

Telémakhos, who knew his mind, said curtly:
"I would not give the clean death of a beast
to trulls who made a mockery of my mother
and of me too — you sluts, who lay with suitors." 105

He tied one end of a hawser to a pillar
and passed the other about the roundhouse
    top,
taking the slack up, so that no one's toes
could touch the ground. They would be hung
    like doves
or larks in springes triggered in a thicket,   110
where the birds think to rest — a cruel nesting.
So now in turn each woman thrust her head
into a noose and swung, yanked high in air,
to perish there most piteously.
Their feet danced for a little, but not long. [. . .] 115

BOOK 23   The Trunk of the Olive Tree

She turned then to descend the stair,
her heart in tumult. Had she better keep her
    distance
and question him, her husband? Should she run
up to him, take his hands, kiss him now?
Crossing the door sill she sat down at once   5
in firelight, against the nearest wall,
across the room from the lord Odysseus.
                                        There
leaning against a pillar, sat the man
and never lifted up his eyes, but only waited
for what his wife would say when she had seen him. 10
And she, for a long time, sat deathly still
in wonderment — for sometimes as she gazed
she found him — yes, clearly — like her husband,
but sometimes blood and rags were all she saw.
Telémakhos' voice came to her ears:

                            "Mother,   15
cruel mother, do you feel nothing,
drawing yourself apart this way from Father?
Will you not sit with him and talk and question him?
What other woman could remain so cold?
Who shuns her lord, and he come back to her   20
from wars and wandering, after twenty years?
Your heart is hard as flint and never changes!"

Penélopê answered:
                        "I am stunned, child.

I cannot speak to him. I cannot question him.
I cannot keep my eyes upon his face.   25
If really he is Odysseus, truly home,
beyond all doubt we two shall know each other
better than you or anyone. There are
secret signs we know, we two."

                        A smile
came now to the lips of the patient hero, Odysseus, 30
who turned to Telémakhos and said:
"Peace: let your mother test me at her leisure. [. . .]"

                                Penélopê
spoke to Odysseus now. She said:
                        "Strange man,
if man you are . . . This is no pride on my part   35
nor scorn for you — not even wonder, merely.
I know so well how you — how he — appeared
boarding the ship for Troy. But all the same . . .

Make up his bed for him, Eurýkleia.
Place it outside the bedchamber my lord   40
built with his own hands. Pile the big bed
with fleeces, rugs, and sheets of purest linen."

With this she tried him to the breaking point,
and he turned on her in a flash raging:
"Woman, by heaven you've stung me now!   45
Who dared to move my bed?

No builder had the skill for that — unless
a god came down to turn the trick. No mortal
in his best days could budge it with a crowbar.
There is our pact and pledge, our secret sign,   50
built into that bed — my handiwork
and no one else's!
           An old trunk of olive
grew like a pillar on the building plot,
and I laid out our bedroom round that tree,   55
lined up the stone walls, built the walls and roof,
gave it a door way and smooth-fitting doors.
Then I lopped off the silvery leaves and branches,
hewed and shaped that stump from the roots up
into a bedpost, drilled it, let it serve   60
as model for the rest. I planed them all,
inlaid them all with silver, gold and ivory,
and stretched a bed between — a pliant web
of oxhide thongs dyed crimson.
                There's our sign!
I know no more. Could someone else's hand   65
have sawn that trunk and dragged the frame away?"

Their secret! as she heard it told, her knees
grew tremulous and weak, her heart failed her.
With eyes brimming tears she ran to him,
throwing her arms around his neck, and kissed
    him,   70
murmuring:
          "Do not rage at me, Odysseus!
No one ever matched your caution! Think
what difficulty the gods gave: they denied us
life together in our prime and flowering years,
kept us from crossing into age together.   75

Forgive me, don't be angry. I could not
welcome you with love on sight! I armed myself
long ago against the frauds of men,
impostors who might come — and all those many
whose underhanded ways bring evil on! [. . .]   80
But here and now, what sign could be so clear
as this of our own bed?
No other man has ever laid eyes on it —
only my own slave, Aktoris, that my father
sent with me as a gift — she kept our door.   85
You make my stiff heart know that I am yours."

Now from his breast into his eyes the ache
of longing mounted, and he wept at last,
his dear wife, clear and faithful, in his arms, [. . .]
              So they came   90
into that bed so steadfast, loved of old,
opening glad arms to one another.
Telémakhos by now had hushed the dancing,
hushed the women. In the darkened hall
he and the cowherd and the swineherd slept.   95

The royal pair mingled in love again
and afterward lay revelling in stories:
hers of the siege her beauty stood at home
from arrogant suitors, crowding on her sight,
and how they fed their courtship on his cattle,   100
oxen and fat sheep, and drank up rivers
of wine out of the vats.
             Odysseus told
of what hard blows he had dealt out to others
and of what blows he had taken — all that story.
She could not close her eyes till all was told. ∎   105

This painting depicts the scene when Penélopê and Odysseus are reunited.

What elements did the artist Jacob Jordaens include to illustrate the tension of the moment?

classicpaintings/Alamy

extending beyond the text

Read the following excerpt from the end of *The Penelopiad*, a novella by Margaret Atwood that retells some events from *The Odyssey*. The text is narrated by Penelope, speaking from the Underworld long after her death. In the first section of *The Penelopiad*, Penelope says of Odysseus, "He was always so plausible. Many people have believed that his version of events was the true one, give or take a few murders, a few beautiful seductresses, a few one-eyed monsters. Even I believed him, from time to time." Throughout the novella, Atwood includes songs sung by a chorus of Penelope's maids whom Odysseus ordered to be killed. In this section, Atwood envisions what a courtroom trial would be like for Odysseus, charged with the murders of the suitors and of the maids.

from **The Penelopiad**

Margaret Atwood

ATTORNEY FOR THE DEFENCE Your Honour, permit me to speak to the innocence of my client, Odysseus, a legendary hero of high repute, who stands before you accused of multiple murders. Was he or was he not justified in slaughtering, by means of arrows and spears — we do not dispute the slaughters themselves, or the weapons in question — upwards of a hundred and twenty well-born young men, give or take a dozen, who, I must emphasise, had been eating up his food without his permission, annoying his wife, and plotting to murder his son and usurp his throne? It has been alleged by my respected colleague that Odysseus was not so justified, since murdering these young men was a gross overreaction to the fact of their having played the gourmand a little too freely in his palace. . . .

   And let us consider the odds. A hundred and twenty, give or take a dozen, to one, or — stretching a point — to four, because Odysseus did have accomplices, as my colleague has termed them; that is, he had one barely grown relative and two servants untrained in warfare — what was to prevent these young men from pretending to enter into a settlement with Odysseus, then leaping upon him one dark night when his guard was down and doing him to death? It is our contention that, by seizing the only opportunity Fate was likely to afford him, our generally esteemed client Odysseus was merely acting in self-defence. We therefore ask that you dismiss this case.

JUDGE I am inclined to agree.

ATTORNEY FOR THE DEFENCE Thank you, Your Honour.

JUDGE What's that commotion in the back? Order! Ladies, stop making a spectacle of yourselves! Adjust your clothing! Take those ropes off your necks! Sit down!

THE MAIDS You've forgotten about us! What about our case? You can't let him off! He hanged us in cold blood! Twelve of us! Twelve young girls! For nothing!

JUDGE [*to Attorney for the Defence*] This is a new charge. Strictly speaking, it ought to be dealt with in a separate trial; but as the two matters appear to be intimately connected, I am prepared to hear arguments now. What do you have to say for your client?

ATTORNEY FOR THE DEFENCE He was acting within his rights, Your Honour. These were his slaves.

JUDGE Nonetheless he must have had some reason. Even slaves ought not to be killed at whim. What had these girls done that they deserved hanging?

ATTORNEY FOR THE DEFENCE They'd had sex without permission.

JUDGE Hmm. I see. With whom did they have the sex?

ATTORNEY FOR THE DEFENCE With my client's enemies, Your Honour. The very ones who had designs on his wife, not to mention his life.

[*Chuckles at his witticism.*]

JUDGE I take it these were the youngest maids.

ATTORNEY FOR THE DEFENCE Well, naturally. They were the best-looking and the most beddable, certainly. For the most part.

[*The Maids laugh bitterly.*]

JUDGE [*leafing through book:* **THE ODYSSEY**] It's written here, in this book — a book we must needs consult, as it is the main authority on the subject — although it has pronounced unethical tendencies and contains far too much sex and violence, in my opinion — it says right here — let me see — in Book 22, that the maids were raped. The Suitors raped them. Nobody stopped them from doing so. Also, the maids are described as having been hauled around by the Suitors for their foul and/or disgusting purposes. Your client knew all that; he is quoted as having said these things himself. Therefore, the maids were overpowered, and they were also completely unprotected. Is that correct?

ATTORNEY FOR THE DEFENCE I wasn't there, Your Honour. All of this took place some three or four thousand years before my time.

JUDGE I can see the problem. Call the witness Penelope.

PENELOPE I was asleep, Your Honour. I was often asleep. I can only tell you what they said afterwards.

JUDGE What who said?

PENELOPE The maids, your Honour.

JUDGE They said they'd been raped?

PENELOPE Well, yes, Your Honour. In effect.

JUDGE And did you believe them?

PENELOPE Yes, Your Honour. That is, I tended to believe them.

JUDGE I understand they were frequently impertinent.

PENELOPE Yes, Your Honour, but . . .

JUDGE But you did not punish them, and they continued to work as your maids?

PENELOPE I knew them well, Your Honour. I was fond of them. I'd brought some of them up, you could say. They were like the daughters I never had. [*Starts to weep.*] I felt so sorry for them! But most maids got raped, sooner or later; a deplorable but common feature of palace life. It wasn't the fact of their being raped that told against them, in the mind of Odysseus. It's that they were raped without permission.

JUDGE [*chuckles*] Excuse me, Madam, but isn't that what rape is? Without permission?

ATTORNEY FOR THE DEFENCE Without permission of their master, Your Honour.

(*continued*)

JUDGE Oh. I see. But their master wasn't present. So, in effect, these maids were forced to sleep with the Suitors because if they'd resisted they would have been raped anyway, and much more unpleasantly?

ATTORNEY FOR THE DEFENCE I don't see what bearing that has on the case.

JUDGE Neither did your client, evidently. [*Chuckles.*] However, your client's times were not our times. Standards of behaviour were different then. It would be unfortunate if this regrettable but minor incident were allowed to stand as a blot on an otherwise exceedingly distinguished career. Also I do not wish to be guilty of an anachronism. Therefore I must dismiss the case. ■

1. What is the main argument and evidence put forward to justify the killing of the suitors by the defense attorney for Odysseus? Why do you agree or disagree with those explanations?

2. Why does the judge ultimately dismiss the case against Odysseus for killing the maids? Explain why this a just ruling or not.

3. This excerpt from *The Penelopiad* asks us to view an ancient text through modern ideas of justice and gender roles. Should we? Or should we view it only within the time period of its creation? Why?

Understanding and Interpreting

Book 16

1. Who did Odysseus originally think Telémakhos was when he first saw him and why (ll. 9–13)?

2. How does Telémakhos feel about the current situation with the suitors (ll. 42–52)? What does this assessment reveal about him?

3. How does Odysseus, still in disguise, respond to Telémakhos about the suitors? What is he intending to communicate, especially through the questions he asks Telémakhos in lines 59–62?

4. What does this section of Book 16 of *The Odyssey* reveal about the role of the gods' influence on the affairs of humans?

Book 21

5. According to Eurýmakhos, what is the purpose of the test that is set out for the suitors (ll. 25–33)?

6. How has Telémakhos changed since Book 2? What evidence from this section best illustrates those changes?

7. When Odysseus strings the bow, there is thunder, and he laughs. What does his decision to laugh at this moment say about Odysseus?

8. After Odysseus successfully shoots the arrow through the socket rings, what does Telémakhos do, and what does this say about his character at this point in the myth (ll. 89–93)?

Book 22

9. At the beginning of Book 22, Odysseus speaks as himself to the suitors for the first time and immediately begins to act. What do the dialogue and actions suggest about Odysseus?

10. After the death of Antínoös, Odysseus again addresses the suitors in lines 34–40. What do these lines reveal about Odysseus's motivations for killing the suitors?

11. Certainly one of the most horrific acts of *The Odyssey* is the killing of the maids who supported the suitors. In earlier sections it is made clear that they were raped by the suitors, and Penélopê is not consulted before they are killed. What does this act reveal about Odysseus, Telémakhos, and the time period and culture of *The Odyssey*?

Book 23

12. Describe and explain Penélopê's initial thoughts when she first sees Odysseus as himself (ll. 1–14).

13. Why is Telémakhos upset with Penélopê at the beginning of this book? What does her response to him suggest about her?

14. Summarize the test that Penélopê sets out for Odysseus and explain how he passes it. In what ways is this also a test for Penélopê?

15. When she finally throws her arms around Odysseus, what reasons does she offer for her initial reluctance (ll. 71–86)?

Analyzing Language, Style, and Structure

Book 16

16. **Vocabulary in Context.** In line 23, just before Odysseus reveals his identity to his son, "the herdsman clapped his arms around Telémakhos." What does the word *clapped* mean here?

17. In line 19, the speaker seems to directly address the audience, saying, "Think of a man whose dear and only son . . ." What effect is created by this direct address, and why might it be effective at this point in the myth?

18. Throughout *The Odyssey*, the speaker includes epithets (p. 881) for the characters. What are some of the epithets used for Odysseus and Telémakhos in this section, and how do they reflect significant character traits?

19. Examine the diction that describes Odysseus's transformation back to himself (ll. 80–86) and explains Telémakhos's reaction to seeing him in this way.

Book 21

20. **Vocabulary in Context.** In lines 87–88, just as Odysseus strings the bow, he tells the suitors, "Other amusements later, with song and harping that adorn a feast." What does *harping* mean in this context, and how is that usage different from other usages you know?

21. Reread Penélopê's speech to the suitors at the beginning of Book 21. What is her tone toward the suitors, and how do her diction choices help to communicate that tone?

22. Explain the irony of the suitor's teasing of the disguised Odysseus in line 57: "May his fortune grow for every inch he bends it!"

23. Reread lines 58–67, in which Odysseus is bending the bow and the speaker compares him to a musician. Explain the components of that epic simile and its effect, especially in terms of the plot and setting of the scene.

Book 22

24. **Vocabulary in Context.** In line 70, Homer writes of Penélopê, "Some god sent her a drift of sleep." What does *drift* mean in this context?

25. The speaker goes into great detail with the death of Antínoös in lines 7–20. Reread the moments before his death and immediately afterward to examine the effect of the diction and syntax choices in this scene.

26. In lines 43–47, the speaker uses an epic metaphor to compare the fallen suitors to a fisherman's catch. Explain how this comparison illustrates the speaker's attitude toward Odysseus and the suitors.

915

27. Reread the section of the deaths of the maids (ll. 98–115). Examining the details and the similes used, what can you interpret about the speaker's feelings toward their deaths? What textual evidence supports your interpretation?

Book 23

28. Vocabulary in Context. When Penélopê and Odysseus are reunited, she says to him, "they denied us life together in our prime and flowering years." What does the word *prime* mean in this context?

29. Look back through Book 23 and explain how the speaker's diction creates the conflict that Penélopê faces when she is unsure about Odysseus's identity.

30. Examine Telémakhos's diction choices to describe Penélopê in lines 15–22. How do these choices help reveal his attitude toward her?

31. What effect is created through the repetition of the forms of the word *story* in the final section of the book? Why is the idea of stories so significant in this myth?

Topics for Composing

32. Analysis. The final stage of the hero's journey is a return home, a changed person. Based on what you have read in *The Odyssey*, how has Odysseus changed on his return? What does "home" symbolize for Odysseus?

33. Analysis. Reread lines 98–115 in Book 22 that describe the killing of the maids. Clearly, a modern audience will find this act horrifying, but what about the speaker? What do the language choices in these lines reveal about the speaker's attitude toward their deaths? Focus on Homer's use of figurative language and imagery in conveying that tone.

34. Analysis. When reading myths, we anticipate reading for theme, the meaning of the work beyond the literal action that occurs. What themes can we draw from *The Odyssey* about topics such as family, loyalty, justice, adventure, hospitality, and others?

35. Argument. Did Odysseus have to kill all of the suitors? Did the suitors have a legitimate claim to the throne and Penélopê? Does the punishment fit their crimes? Support your position with evidence from the text.

36. Connections. As you saw in the Skill Workshop (p. 852), a key part of the Hero's Journey is the Return Home, like Odysseus's return to Ithaka. Think about movies, television shows, video games, or other stories that include a character returning home at the end. Explain how that homecoming is similar to or different from the one in *The Odyssey* and how well it fits the archetype.

37. Connections. Read more of *The Odyssey* than what is included here, specifically the books that focus on Penélopê. How do these sections add to or change your understanding of her, Telémakhos, and Odysseus?

38. Speaking and Listening. Meet with a small group and make a list of heroes from mythology or other stories, including film and television. Discuss the qualities in common among those heroes and Odysseus and arrive at a common definition of a hero based on *The Odyssey* and the other texts you discussed.

39. Creative Writing. Write a scene in which Odysseus begins another hero's journey. What would be the "call to adventure," where would he go, and why?

40. Multimodal. Create a two- or three-dimensional map of Odysseus's hero's journey, labeling his various stops with key lines from the text that illustrate the importance of that location to his development as a character. What did he learn or gain at each stop?

conversation

What defines a hero?

What do we mean when we say a person is a hero? The term can be applied to a player who makes the winning shot in a basketball game, the main character of an action film, a soldier who saves a fellow soldier, someone who survives cancer, or a president or public figure who achieved political success or social change. These are all different circumstances and different types of people who have been labeled "heroes."

Recently, we seem to be obsessed with heroes, specifically fictional superheroes. On the list of the top-grossing films or popular television shows of the 2020s, you will see television shows and movies featuring Spiderman, Batman, Wonder Woman, Black Panther, and Shang-Chi. We can add to this list films featuring other types of heroes like Katniss Everdeen, Harry Potter, and the protagonists of the various *Star Wars* films and TV shows. We want to watch characters being heroic, but what qualities unify these fictional heroes? And how do these qualities relate to the fact that according to a 2014 Harris poll, 32 percent of adults identify a family member of theirs as a "hero"? Can you be a hero without having a cape, a secret identity, or a magic wand?

Perhaps all of this just means that the word itself has lost its meaning, or maybe that our culture today cannot agree on the qualities of a hero. In this Conversation, you will have an opportunity to read a variety of texts and then share your own viewpoint in response to the following question — ***What defines a hero?***

Starting the Conversation

Take a moment to make notes about your initial thinking on this topic before you explore it further by reading additional texts.

1. Who are some real or fictional people whom you consider to be heroes?
2. With a partner or small group, share your list of heroes and see if there are any commonalities. Is there a common definition of a hero among those in your group?
3. Create a table like the one below to help you keep track of ideas related to how to define a hero, and your own responses to the ideas you encounter in the texts you read:

Title/Author	What Defines a Hero?	Best Evidence	Your Response

Source A

Weeks, Linton. "Heroic Acts to Protect the Word Hero." National Public Radio, 2011.

Has the word "hero" been so overused that it's losing its meaning? These three recent examples show how people are employing the term. You decide if the usage is appropriate.

On CBS News, Melissa Castellanos tells viewers that "the Super Senior who bravely fought off jewel thieves with her handbag has been unmasked. She's [a] 71-year-old grand-mother . . . and she's being called a hero by her community."

On NBC's *Today Show*, Ann Curry says: "An elderly Memphis woman ordered a Domino's [pizza] every day for the past three years. But when her calls suddenly stopped, her regular delivery driver became concerned and took action, and now that delivery driver is being hailed a hero for saving that elderly woman's life."

According to CNN, Philadelphia Eagles quarterback Michael Vick, who spent time in prison for animal abuse, "is being honored as a hero next month at a black-tie event in Norfolk, Va., for his 'resilience in overcoming obstacles' and becoming 'a true example of life success for all to emulate,' according to event organizers." Are these people heroes?

More Than a Role Model

Though they may be exceptional people, they might not fit the definition of hero as determined by the Pittsburgh-based Carnegie Hero Fund Commission.[1] "Since our establishment in 1904," says Executive Director Walter F. Rutkowski, "the commission has always applied a narrow definition — or more appropriately, a classic definition — to 'hero': someone who voluntarily leaves a point of safety to assume life risk to save or attempt to save the life of another."

Other people who use the word "hero" may do so in different contexts, Rutkowski says, "but since we do not have exclusive rights to the word, it is counterproductive to cringe on hearing same. We know, and would prefer to see, that 'role model' or 'positive role model' is the more appropriate term for use in many of these contexts."

People do broaden the definition — and the list. Former Secretary of Education William Bennett, in his 1997 work *The Children's Book of Heroes*, includes exemplary figures, such as Abraham Lincoln, Jackie Robinson and Mother Teresa.

Retired shop teacher Don Jones, who maintains the USA Hero website,[2] defines hero as "someone who acts to help another with no thought for herself or himself or someone who is admired for achievements or noble qualities." His roster includes poet Emily Dickinson, and actors Morgan Freeman and Jodie Foster.

Today we sometimes toss the word "hero" around without thinking much about it. We use it to name TV shows. We speak of a Hollywood celebrity as our childhood hero. Alan M. Webber, a founding editor of *Fast Company* magazine, offers a reason that we use the term so freely.

"I suspect that if the American public's nerves weren't quite so badly frayed by all the

5

10

[1]"Home — Carnegie Hero Fund Commission." *Carnegie Hero Fund Commission*, Carnegie Hero Fund Commission, www.carnegiehero.org/.

[2]Jones, Donald. "American Heroes Who Inspire the World." *American Hero Biographies | USA Hero Essay Research Links*, USA Hero/Don Jones, January 13, 2017, www.usa-hero.com/.

over–attention to bad behavior, if we weren't all addicted to a culture of celebrity and extreme amplification of every news story, in other words, if the whole country were only a little bit more sane," Webber writes on *The Washington Post* website, "then we'd have a more modulated reaction to most events, the good, the bad and the ugly. And we'd reserve the word 'hero' . . . for actions and circumstances that actually merit their application."

So maybe we need a new word for that narrow definition of heroism. Truehero, perhaps. Or epichero.

"Threshold of Heroism"

U.S. Army Gen. Norman Schwarzkopf once said that "it doesn't take a hero to order men into battle. It takes a hero to be one of those men who goes into battle."

And the German writer Johann Wolfgang von Goethe said: "The hero draws inspiration from the virtue of his ancestors."

Our ancestral heroes first appeared in the oral storytelling tradition. They were superhumans, almost gods, and the actions they took were mostly in the best interest of humankind. The dictionary traces the word's meaning from "a being of godlike prowess and beneficence" to "a warrior-chieftain of special strength, courage or ability" during the Homeric period of ancient Greece.

By the *Encyclopaedia Britannica* of 1911, the word had come to be applied "generally to all who were distinguished from their fellows by superior moral, physical or intellectual qualities." [15]

Around that time, Pittsburgh steel magnate Andrew Carnegie set aside $5 million to recognize ordinary folks who perform extraordinary feats of heroism. In the ensuing years his Carnegie Hero Fund Commission has granted more than 9,400 awards — and nearly $33 million — to people who have risked their lives to save others.

The extraordinary exploits include pulling someone from a burning building, standing between someone and an attacking animal, rescuing a drowning swimmer, thwarting an assault on a citizen and other facing-death-to-save-a-life acts. About a fifth of the awards have been granted posthumously.

The 21-member commission is constantly receiving nominations for the next round of heroes. Another batch — of up to 23 heroes — is scheduled to be recognized on April 7.

What makes Rutkowski cringe is when "victims" are viewed as heroes, "such as when a threat is put upon a person who then combats it to save him/herself and while doing so saves others," he says.

As an example, Rutkowski points to US Airways Capt. Chesley Sullenberger, of Hudson River–landing fame. In a recent edition of the commission's newsletter, the group's president, Mark Laskow, wrote an essay about Sullenberger. In the article, Laskow quotes an interviewer from the Smithsonian Institution who asks Sullenberger, "What is your definition of a hero?" [20]

Sullenberger replies: "My wife actually looked it up in the dictionary. We decided between ourselves that it describes someone who chooses to put himself at risk to save another."

He continues: "That didn't quite fit my situation, which was thrust upon me suddenly. Certainly, my crew and I were up to the task. But I'm not sure it quite crosses the threshold of heroism. I think the idea of a hero is important. But sometimes in our culture we overuse the word, and by overusing it we diminish it."

When the engines stopped on US Airways Flight 1549 in January 2009, Laskow writes, "Capt. Sullenberger was not in a place of safety. On the contrary, he was in the same peril as the passengers whose lives he saved with his piloting skill. He did not have the opportunity to make a moral choice to take on the risk — it 'was thrust upon' him. I have no doubt that if he did have such a choice, he would not have hesitated to place himself in danger to save his passengers. That just wasn't the actual situation in which he found himself."

In addition to possessing fine piloting and philosophical skills, Laskow writes, Sullenberger "is admirably modest and self-aware. In the midst of continuing, well-earned acclaim for his cool competency, he took the measure of his act and demurred from the title 'hero.'"

And, in a broader sense of the word, that could be called heroic. ■ 25

Questions

1. Linton Weeks begins his article with quotations about three people who were called "heroes." What do these three have in common? In what ways are they different?

2. In paragraph 5, the Carnegie Foundation offers a definition of "hero." Explain how the three examples identified earlier would or would not fit its definition.

3. In paragraph 19, Weeks writes that the head of the Carnegie Foundation cringes when victims are viewed as heroes. What is the difference between a hero and a victim, and how does the story of Captain Sullenberger illustrate these differences?

4. **Comparison.** According to what is included here, would the Carnegie Foundation likely have granted Odysseus their award? Why or why not? Would a different character from *The Odyssey* win the award?

5. **Informing Your Argument.** Return to the table that you created on page 917. Fill in the columns about how Weeks defines a hero, the best evidence he offers to clarify and support his ideas, and your response to what Weeks is suggesting.

Source B

Hackney, Suzette. "Simone Biles is a role model for prioritizing her own mental health over an Olympic medal." *USA Today*, 2021.

U.S. Olympic gymnast Simone Biles, adorned with bedazzled goats on her leotard, struts into competition with the pressure of living up to the GOAT acronym: the greatest of all time.

Biles proved to be just that when she decided to withdraw from the team competition Tuesday [during the Tokyo Olympics in 2021].

The most decorated gymnast in World Championships history, Biles is a hero and role model — not because she pushed through her pain for another medal but because she quit to take care of herself.

"I have to do what's right for me and focus on my mental health and not jeopardize my health and well-being," Biles said. "That's why I decided to take a step back."

Part of being great is recognizing when you 5 can't be great. Biles has shown the world what true strength looks like.

Mental, physical health linked

She's helping young people realize that it's OK to take care of themselves. She's teaching them to prioritize their bodies because mental health and physical health are inextricably linked.

Biles has been open about her depression after being sexually abused by team doctor Larry Nassar. She has overcome so much in her young life. Yet those now criticizing her actions exemplify the harsh reality of how stigmatizing issues of mental health are, particularly in the world of athletics.

I applaud Biles and Naomi Osaka, who withdrew from both the French Open and Wimbledon, for prioritizing their mental health over others' physical expectations of them. These athletes aren't superhuman; they're human. We can sit on our couches, snacking on potato chips, judging and demanding to be entertained. But the vast majority of us have never excelled to the level of an elite athlete.

While we can accept a tweaked ankle or hamstring injury, we refuse to acknowledge how difficult it can be to focus mentally and emotionally and still compete at the highest level. And often these athletes rely upon their families and friends to keep them grounded. But the stands are empty this year. They can't look into the audience for support. They can't see a parent's proud face sending a message that everything will be OK.

"I'm kind of nervous I might freak out over that," Biles has said of missing her parents. "I don't feel set and comfortable until I find where they are in the crowd."

Biles was honest about the stress she was feeling at the Summer Games. After the preliminary rounds, she shared some thoughts on Instagram offering clues that she was struggling.

"It wasn't an easy day or my best but I got through it," she wrote. "I truly do feel like I have the weight of the world on my shoulders at times. I know I brush it off and make it seem like pressure doesn't affect me but damn sometimes it's hard hahaha! The Olympics is no joke!"

Nothing is funny about pressure

She's right. Nothing is funny about the immense pressure she must have felt to be perfect. Imagine how difficult it was to make the decision to step aside with the world — literally — watching. She deserves credit for showcasing such courage.

Athletes are finally starting to put their own well-being before sport. Biles is helping usher in a culture where they don't have to sacrifice their health for medals, championship trophies and our entertainment.

Biles remains the GOAT of U.S. women's gymnastics. She remains an inspiration for all the young girls watching and dreaming of becoming an elite athlete. She's setting an example of self-love and preservation for them — and it's one that should not be ignored. ■

Questions

1. According to Hackney, why should we applaud Biles's decision to withdraw from the team event?
2. How do most people tend to view the mental health of athletes, and how does that view compare with attitudes toward mental health in general, according to Hackney?
3. Why should Biles be considered a hero or a role model, according to Hackney?
4. **Comparison.** Describe how, according to Hackney, Biles provides inspiration and to whom. Is there a figure in *The Odyssey* who could be regarded as "inspiring"? In what ways are their forms of inspiration similar and different?
5. **Informing Your Argument.** Return to the table that you created on page 917. Fill in the columns about how Hackney defines a hero, the best evidence she offers to clarify and support her ideas, and your response to what Hackney is suggesting.

Ewing, Eve. "You Are a Threat to Them." *New York Times*, 23 April, 2021.

KEY CONTEXT   Eve Ewing is a writer of *Ironheart*, the story of a Black teen girl from Chicago named Riri Williams who becomes one of Marvel's superheroes. Ewing was targeted online in 2017 by those who were upset at diverse images of superheroes in comics.

As a Black woman with an established public internet presence, I was used to harassment. I had some tried-and-true strategies: block, mute, ignore and go do something else with your day.

But there was something fundamental that I didn't understand, and it bugged me. Of all the things I had said and done in public, of all my commentary about policing and politics and education and media, nothing had attracted a firestorm like the one prompted by the mere rumor that I might be writing Ironheart.

Why this? Pretend stories about a girl who flies around the city and shoots energy beams out of her armored super suit — this was the thing that made them so angry?

Writing for Marvel seemed to me to be about the least political thing I had ever done. To me, this was about fun. It was the stuff of youthful miracles, a shiny new bike and unlimited arcade tokens rolled into one.

More than anything, I was concerned with the essentials of writing something decent. Riri had an origin story furnished by the writer Brian Michael Bendis and the artist Mike Deodato. She was a teen genius who had tragically lost loved ones to gun violence and was now attending M.I.T.

My job, as I saw it, was to puzzle out the deeper elements of who she is with and without her armor. What fears and desires motivate her? What are her quirks and flaws? Who are the people in her life who love her?

I knew I had to figure out how Riri might see things as someone who grew up in a hyper-policed community, including her thoughts on 5 who gets labeled a criminal. . . .

The not-so-hidden secret of superhero stories is that readers want to understand who the person is when they're not suited up.

Once you figure that out, then you can get to the titanic battles over the future of the universe. But for me, this was all in good fun.

Don't get me wrong—I knew that what I was doing was historic. At the time I was hired, I was the fifth Black woman writer in Marvel's nearly 80-year history. Still, why Riri and I were so divisive, I didn't get.

I mused aloud about this to Ta-Nehisi Coates, who himself had been targeted for his writing on Captain America.

"If you do this," he told me, "you will face the most racism and sexism you've ever dealt with in your life. And you will also have the most fun you've ever had writing anything."

I told him I was all in on the fun part but I was confused by the racism and sexism part. Why were people so angry?

"No, Eve," he said. "Don't you see? They're right."

I didn't see.

"They're right. About you. About us. About these characters," he said. "You are a threat to them. . . . "

Superheroes reflect our shared cultural mythologies: what it means to be good, to be courageous, to face unbeatable odds. In recent years, "representation matters" has become a refrain acknowledging how vital it is that children see possibilities for themselves in media.

But superheroes represent something beyond that. It's not only that if little Black girls see Ironheart being brave, they will understand that they can do the same because they look like her. It's that superheroes serve as a shared cultural mirror, paragons of what bravery even is.

For example, in one of my favorite panels from the series . . . I wanted to show the unbridled joy Black kids from Chicago would feel if they got to meet Ironheart and experience flying for the first time. It's important to me to push against the adultification of Black children, and show them being silly and having fun. This is also a full-circle moment because, early in the story arc, Ironheart catches the boy in green committing a petty crime, but instead of punishing him, she wants to help him.

If kids who are scared and alone call out in their heart of hearts for protection and the face they see in their mind's eye is a Black teen girl from the South Side of Chicago, or a Muslim Pakistani-American nerd from Jersey City (Kamala Khan, a.k.a. Ms. Marvel), or an undocumented Mexican-American kid from Arizona who can fly (Joaquín Torres, also known as Falcon)—if those faces become cultural stand-ins for the ideals we strive for in our society, in the ways that Superman, Batman and Captain America have been for generations . . . man, if I was a white supremacist, that would make me mad, too. ∎

Questions

1. What does Ewing suggest caused the backlash to her further developing the story of a Black teen superhero?
2. What does writer Ta-Nehisi Coates mean when he tells Ewing, "They're right. About you. About us. About these characters. . . . You are a threat to them"?
3. Based on what you read in the article, in what ways does Ewing present Riri as similar to other superheroes, and in what ways is Riri different?
4. **Comparison.** How are the traits that Ewing says define her hero, Ironheart, similar to or different from the characteristics displayed by Odysseus? Include evidence from both pieces to illustrate the comparisons.
5. **Informing Your Argument.** Return to the table that you created on page 917. Fill in the columns about how Ewing defines a hero, the best evidence she offers to clarify and support her ideas, and your response to what Ewing is suggesting.

Source D

Lee, Ang (director). *Billy Lynn's Long Halftime Walk*. 2016.

KEY CONTEXT   Below is a publicity still from a fiction film about a solider who returns from war in Iraq to find himself celebrated as a hero during halftime of a football game on Thanksgiving Day.

Questions

1. Describe the set design and costumes in this scene. How are they intended to create feelings of heroism and patriotism?

2. Describe the facial expression of the actor, Joe Allwyn, who plays the soldier Billy Lynn. What might Allwyn be trying to communicate to the audience?

3. Most of the plot of the film takes place in harrowing flashbacks to Billy's time in Iraq. How would you imagine violent scenes of war would contrast with this image, and what point might director Ang Lee be suggesting about heroes through this contrast?

4. **Comparison.** How is the way that Billy is celebrated in this image similar to or different from how Odysseus is treated on his return? Include evidence from both pieces to illustrate the comparisons.

5. **Informing Your Argument.** Return to the table that you created on page 917. Fill in the columns about how director Ang Lee defines a hero in this image, the best evidence he offers to clarify and support his ideas, and your response to what Lee is suggesting in this image.

Entering the Conversation

Throughout this Conversation, you have read a variety of texts about heroism. Now it's time to enter the conversation by responding to the prompt you've been thinking about — *What defines a hero?* Follow these steps to write your argument:

1. | Building on the Conversation. Locate one additional text on this topic that you think adds an interesting perspective to this Conversation. This text can be of any type — an argument, a narrative, a poem, a painting, or a film clip, for example. Before you decide to add this text to the Conversation, be sure that it is a credible and relevant source, which you can determine by evaluating it with the skills you practiced in Chapter 4 (p. 99). Read and annotate the text carefully, making connections to other texts in the Conversation and *The Odyssey*.

2. | Making a Claim. Look back through the table you created and your notes on the texts in the conversation and write a statement that reflects your overall position about what defines a hero. This statement will be your thesis or claim that you will try to prove in the rest of your argument.

3. | Organizing the Ideas. The texts in this Conversation offer a number of definitions of a hero. Review the table you have been keeping throughout this Conversation and identify the texts and quotations that either directly support or oppose the claim that you wrote in the earlier step.

4. | Writing the Argument. Now that you have a claim that reflects your informed stance, it is time to write your argument. Be sure that your writing stays focused on your position on the issue, and refer to at least two Conversation texts, which could include the additional text you found to support your position. Review Chapter 4 (p. 119) to remind yourself of how to use sources in your own writing, and refer to the Writing an Argument Workshop in Chapter 7 (p. 466) for additional support in how to construct and support your argument.

5. | Presenting the Argument (Optional). Once you have written your argument, you might want to present it to the class or a small group. Review how to write and deliver a presentation in Chapter 3 (p. 90) and Chapter 7 (p. 479).

KEY CONTEXT FOR ANANSI STORIES The three texts in this section focus on Anansi, a trickster archetype often represented as a spider, with roots in precolonial West African culture, that also appears in Jamaican and African American folktales brought to the Americas through the slave trade. Like other myths, Anansi stories have symbolic meaning beyond their seemingly straightforward plots and characters. As a trickster character, Anansi is used to breaking boundaries and challenging the rules of society and is often depicted as a keeper of knowledge and stories. According to Emily Zobel Marshall, Anansi stories have come to represent the "struggles of black slaves. Like Anansi, the slaves worked at overturning the structured hierarchy of their environment, developing coded strategies of survival and resistance." Telling an Anansi story became both a hope for freedom and an act of rebellion.

The three stories in this section are intended to show the progression of Anansi from Africa to the Americas. The first one is a retelling of a folktale from Nigeria, the second is an excerpt from a graphic novel that depicts Anansi on a slave ship leaving Africa, and the final one is a story of Anansi in Jamaica, written in dialect intended to reflect the speech of that island's residents. Because Anansi is part of an oral tradition passed from generation to generation, his name is spelled many ways, including Ananse and Anancy; you will see variations of his name in these stories.

Spider and the Crows

Translated by Dianne Stewart, Edited by Nelson Mandela

This piece is from *Favorite African Folktales*, a collection edited by Nelson Mandela (1918–2013). Mandela was a South African revolutionary and politician who served as the first democratically elected president of South Africa from 1994 to 1999. He was awarded the Nobel Peace Prize in 1993. In the foreword to the collection, Mandela quotes the Ashanti storytellers' traditional conclusion of their tales: "This is my story which I have related, if it be sweet or if it be not sweet, take some elsewhere and let it come back to me." This particular story was translated by Dianne Stewart, an author, journalist, and creative writing teacher in South Africa.

The spider plays a dramatic role in many African stories. He is often exceptionally resourceful — as is evident in this Nigerian folktale. In the stories of the Ashanti he is known as Kwaku Anansi.

Long ago there was a great famine in a certain land and no one had anything to eat; no one, that is, except the crows. Every day they flew a great distance to pick figs from a tree that stood in the middle of a wide river. Then they brought the fruit home to eat.

When Spider heard about this, he immediately thought of an ingenious plan. He smeared his hindquarters with beeswax, took a potsherd and went to the crows on the pretext of borrowing a burning coal.

The crows were busy eating when he arrived and all around them on the ground lay figs.

"Morning, dear friends," said Spider, sitting down carefully on one of the delicious figs. "Could you give me a burning coal?"

Taking the burning coal, Spider thanked the crows and walked away with the fig firmly attached to his sticky hindquarters.

The crows did not suspect anything because the cunning thief, pretending to be courteous, walked backward as he left them.

At home, Spider extinguished the burning coal and quickly went back to the crows to ask for more fire. This time Spider chose the largest and ripest fig and, after some time, walked away cheekily with his spoils.

And then he did it a third time. But now the birds were beginning to get suspicious. "Why do you keep coming to get a burning coal from us?" they asked.

"By the time I get home, the coal is burned out. This happens every time," answered Spider.

"You are lying!" said the oldest crow. "I'm sure you put it out so that you have an excuse to return here again. You are just after our food, you sly creature!"

Spider began to cry bitterly. "Oh, no! That's not true! The coal burned itself out. Oh! Ever since my parents died, life has been difficult for me. When they were still alive my parents assured me that if ever I needed anything I should ask their friends, the crows. Yes, that's just what they said. And now, look how you treat me," he sobbed.

"Oh, stop crying now!" said the oldest crow, picking up a fig. "Take this and go home. If you come back again tomorrow morning at daybreak, we'll take you to the fig tree."

"Thank you kindly, dear friends," said Spider and ran home as fast as his legs could carry him.

That night, just as the crows were dozing off, Spider took a bundle of straw and made a large fire near the birds' nest.

"It's morning! It's morning!" called Spider as the flames rose high in the sky. "Just look how red the sun has made the eastern sky."

But the oldest crow answered, "No, Spider, you made a fire. Wait until you hear the cock crow."

Spider crept into the henhouse and disturbed the fowls until the hens began to cackle and the large cock crowed.

"Wake up! It's morning!" he called out.

"Trickster! You have woken the fowls, Spider!" answered the oldest crow. "Come, let us rather wait until we hear the first call to prayer."

"Allah is great! Allah is great!" called Spider from behind a bush.

But the oldest crow said, "No, I recognize that voice. It's you who called, Spider. Go home and stay there! I'll call you when the sun rises."

All Spider could do was wait. He went home and fell asleep.

Eventually, when it began to get light, the crows woke him and each crow gave him a feather.

With his borrowed feathers, Spider flew with the crows to the fig tree in the middle of the wide river. But every time one of the crows wanted to pick a fig he shrieked, "No, you can't! I saw it first! It's mine!"

And then he would take the fig and put it in his bag. Things continued in this way until there was no fruit left on the tree. Spider picked all the figs for himself and the crows got none.

"Now I know that you really are a trickster!" said the oldest crow. Angrily, the crows snatched back the feathers that they had lent him and flew away, leaving him alone.

And there Spider stayed, all alone in the fig tree, completely surrounded by water. And for the first time in his life, he didn't know what to do.

Later when darkness descended, he began to cry.

"If I don't want to stay here in the tree for the rest of my life, I'll just have to jump into the air like the crows," Spider said to himself at last. 30

He took a deep breath and . . . plop! He fell into the water right among the crocodiles!

"And what do we have here?" asked an old crocodile. "Can we eat it?"

"Don't be ridiculous!" Spider answered quickly and he began to sob. "I'm one of you. Don't you know that everyone has been searching for me for years? I ran away in the days of your grandfathers, when I was very small. And no one has ever found me. You are the first of my family members I've met."

Spider cried so hard that the tears splashed on the ground. The crocodiles themselves cried crocodile tears. "You poor thing!" they cried, sniffing loudly. "Don't worry, you can stay here with us, in the hole on the bank where we lay our eggs."

But one of the crocodiles was suspicious and examined Spider very carefully. "We must first make sure that he really is one of us," he thought. 35

"Come, let's give the stranger a little mud soup," he said quietly to another crocodile. "If he drinks it, then we'll know he speaks the truth. If he doesn't want it, we'll know that he tells lies and he is definitely not one of us."

And so it was done.

When Spider saw the gourd of mud soup, he pretended that he was very excited. "Where did you find this delicious recipe of my grandmother's?" he asked, pretending to drink the soup. But he quietly dug a hole with his back feet and made a tiny hole in the bottom of the gourd with his front feet.

"That was delicious!" he declared, putting the gourd behind him while the concoction oozed into the ground.

"Well, he's definitely one of us," the crocodiles said to each other when they saw the empty gourd. So they allowed Spider to sleep 40

Joseph Laurro

This is a painting by Joseph Laurro called *Anansi the Spiderman*.

What visual elements in this painting capture some aspect of Anansi's character as depicted in this myth?

in the hole together with a group of small crocodiles and a hundred and one crocodile eggs.

Before Spider crept in, he said, "Remember now, children, if you hear a plop in the night, don't be afraid. It will just be me burping as a result of your mother's delicious mud soup."

When all the crocodiles were asleep, Spider took an egg and threw it into the fire.

Plop! The egg burst open.

"That's the strange grandfather-uncle of ours burping," said the little crocodiles to each other.

And the large crocodiles who overheard them said. "Quiet, children, one mustn't speak about family like that!" 45

But Spider said, "Leave them alone. They are my grandchildren. They can say what they like."

So he baked the eggs in the fire, one after the other, and ate every single one. All through the night the crocodiles heard plop every now and then. And every time someone said, "It's just our strange grandfather-uncle who is burping."

By morning, there was only one egg left.

When the adult crocodiles asked the young ones to turn the eggs, Spider said quickly, "Don't worry, I've done it already."

Then the crocodiles suggested that the eggs 50 be counted.

"I'll bring them out one at a time for you," said Spider.

He brought the egg out of the hole, put it in front of the crocodiles, and the crocodiles made a mark on it.

Spider disappeared into the hole again, licked off the mark, and brought it back. Again the crocodiles marked the egg.

And so he carried the same egg back and forth.

"Two . . . three . . . four . . ." the crocodiles 55 counted the eggs until they reached one hundred and one.

"All of our eggs are still there," they said every day, entirely satisfied.

"I'm so glad I have found my blood relatives again," said Spider one day. "But I want to go

and fetch my wife and children, so that we can all be together."

"Go and do so," said the crocodiles. "But come back quickly so that you can play with us again and help us count the eggs."

"Of course," said Spider, the trickster. "It's a great game, isn't it? If you help me to cross the river, I'll come back very soon."

The crocodiles put him in a canoe, and two 60 of them rowed him away.

But one of the pair, who thought further than his long snout, did not trust the situation. When they were in the middle of the river, he turned around and said, "Wait a minute. I'm coming back now. I just want to go and check the eggs."

And thus the crocodiles discovered the one marked egg.

"Such a trickster!" they screamed. "Bring him back immediately! He is not one of us!" they shouted across the river.

But the crocodile who was rowing the canoe was a bit deaf.

"Listen!" Spider said to the rower. "They say 65 you must hurry. It's nearly high tide," and he spurred the crocodile on until he was safely on the other side. And so he got clean away. ■

from How Anansi Came to the Americas

Michael Auld

Michael Auld was born in Jamaica, West Indies, and moved to the United States at nineteen years old. His ANANSESEM comic strip about Anansi the Spider-man was published in newspapers throughout the Caribbean. This is an excerpt from his graphic novel *How Anansi Came to the Americas*, published in 2017.

KEY CONTEXT Before this excerpt, Anansi was doing what he usually does: trying to escape from a situation he created. In this case, he ate a pig that was killed by Osebo, the tiger, and to get away from him, Anansi hid in the bag carried by a captive who was being led to a slave ship for transportation to the Americas. On hearing the humans in chains, Anansi wakes up on the ship at the beginning of this section and begins praying to Nyame, the sky god of the Akan people of the Ashanti Region of present-day Ghana.

Michael Auld, excerpt from How Anansi Came to the Americas from *Africa: A Folkloric Graphic Novel About the Famous Spider-man*. Copyright © 2017 by Michael Auld. Used with permission. AnansiStories live on the Internet at anansistories.com. (Credit covers art on pp. 930–945.)

SOON... HIS EYES BECAME MORE ACCUSTOMED TO THE DARKNESS WHICH SURROUNDED HIM

ANANSI COULD BARELY MAKE OUT THE SHAPES OF PEOPLE CHAINED TO EACH OTHER

ALTHOUGH ANANSI COULD NOT SEE WELL IN THE DARKNESS...

...HE COULD SMELL THE ODORS OF SWEAT AND DECAY

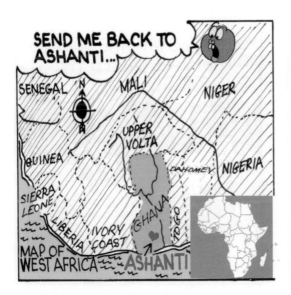

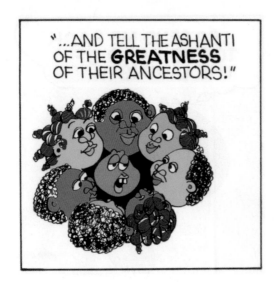

AT NIGHT ANANSI WOULD COMFORT THE SLAVES WITH TALES OF LIFE OF LAUGHTER AND OF TEARS.

ANANSI NOT ONLY BECAME THE COMFORTER OF THE ASHANTI SLAVE...

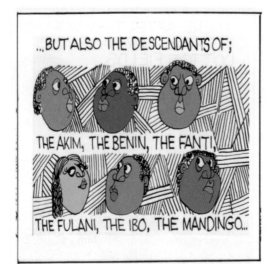

...BUT ALSO THE DESCENDANTS OF;

THE AKIM, THE BENIN, THE FANTI,

THE FULANI, THE IBO, THE MANDINGO...

...THE YORUBA, AND ALL THE TRIBES BROUGHT TO THE NEW WORLD!

ONE DAY IN THE DISTANT FUTURE THE SLAVES OF THE LAND WERE TO EVENTUALLY BECOME THE **MASTERS** OF THE LAND!

ANANSI REMEMBERED HIS DUTY TO NYAME AND EVEN TO THIS DAY ANANSI STORIES ARE STILL TOLD BY ANANSI'S PEOPLE.

THIS IS WHY NYAME GAVE ANANSI A LONG LIFE.

PROVERB: "*THE LONGEST LIVER SEES THE MOST.*"

Anancy an Common-Sense

Louise Bennett

Poet and storyteller Louise Bennett (1919–2006) was one of Jamaica's most popular literary and cultural figures, often writing, as she does in this story, in dialect that faithfully represents the unique Jamaican vernacular. This story is from a collection of stories called *Anancy and Miss Lou* (1979), in the introduction to which Bennett strongly suggests that her stories be read aloud to fully appreciate the language.

Once upon a time Anancy tink to himself seh dat if him coulda collect up all de common-sense ina de worl an keep it fi himself, den him boun to get plenty money an plenty powah, for everybody would haffi come to him wid dem worries an him woulda charge dem very dear wen him advise dem.

Anancy start fi collect up an collect up all de common-sense him coulda fine an put dem ina one big-big calabash. Wen him search an search an couldn't fine no more common-sense Anancy decide fi hide him calabash full a common-sense pon de top of a high-high tree which part nobody else coulda reach it.

So Anancy tie a rope roun de neck a de calabash an tie de two end a de rope togedda, an tie de rope roun him neck so dat de calabash wasa res pon him belly. Anancy start fi climb up de high-high tree, which part him was gwine hide de calabash, but him couldn't climb too good nor too fas for de calabash wasa get in him way everytime him try fi climb. Anancy try an try so till all of a sudden him hear a voice buss out a laugh backa him, an wen him look him see a lickle bwoy a stan up a de tree root an a laugh an halla seh: "Wat a foo-fool man! If yuh want to climb de tree front ways, why yuh don't put de calabash behine yuh?"

945

Well sah, Anancy soh bex fi hear dat big piece a common-sense come outa de mout a such a lickle bit a bwoy afta him did tink dat him did collect all de common-sense in de worl, dat Anancy grab off de calabash from roun him neck an fling it dung a de tree root, an de calabash bruck up in minces an de common-sense dem scatter out ina de breeze all ovah de worl an everybody get a lickle bit a common-sense. Is Anancy meck it.

Jack Mandora, me noh choose none. ■   5

Understanding and Interpreting

1. The dialect in "Anancy an Common-Sense" can make comprehension a little more challenging than usual. Write a four- or five-sentence summary of the plot of the story.

2. Briefly summarize the three stages (Boundary Crossing, Resolution Conflict, and Creating Change) of the trickster's archetype (p. 860) of the three stories included here, noting that not every stage will be fully represented. What similarities and differences do you notice in the way the archetype is presented in each story?

3. Identify at least two archetypal characters (p. 861) that appear in more than one of the stories, not including the trickster. Explain how those characters act in archetypal ways and how they support or oppose the tricksters on their journeys.

4. Look back carefully at the three stories and identify at least one setting that appears to be an archetype. Explain how that setting fits the definition on page 863.

5. Why did the sky god in *How Anansi Came to the Americas* want Anansi to go to the Americas, and what did Anansi accomplish there?

6. Many folktales have a lesson that is supposed to be learned when listening to the story. What is the intended lesson of "Anancy an Common-Sense"?

7. In the Skill Workshop, we explained that Carl Jung and others identified archetypes as evidence of the "collective unconscious." Even though there can be similarities across cultures, there are unique cultural aspects to all stories. Skim back through the three stories and note any elements of setting, language, or other details that make the three stories unique to their geographic and cultural origins. As similar as each of these stories might be, what makes them distinct from each other?

Analyzing Language, Style, and Structure

8. **Vocabulary in Context.** In "Spider and the Crows," the author uses the word *pretext* in paragraph 3. Think about the context, as well as the root *text* and the prefix *pre*. What does this word mean?

9. The story "Spider and the Crows" uses variations of the phrase "He is not one of us" at several points in the story. What is the effect of this repetition?

10. The graphic novel *How Anansi Came to the Americas* employs many different visual styles, colors, and fonts. Choose two particularly effective panels in which Auld uses contrasting styles and explain their differences and their intended effects.

11. The last line of "Anancy an Common-Sense" is a typical ending of Anansi stories from Jamaica, "Jack Mandora, me noh choose none," which means essentially, "I have told it the way I received it and no blame should be attributed to the listener, storyteller, or writer." What is the effect of ending the story with this phrase? How is the reader or listener expected to react?

Topics for Composing

12. **Analysis.** In the Key Context on page 926, you read about the possible symbolic meanings of Anansi. Using these stories as evidence, explain what Anansi represents through the trickster archetype.

13. **Argument.** Are tricksters heroes? Using the Anansi stories and any other trickster tales you are familiar with, write an argument explaining and supporting your position.

14. **Connections.** Anansi is one of many trickster characters in mythology, movies, television, and videogames. Choose another trickster that you know — Bugs Bunny, Bart Simpson, Loki, the Joker, Captain Jack Sparrow, Tyrion Lannister are a few examples — and compare that one to Anansi from the stories in this chapter. To what extent do they each fit the trickster archetype?

15. **Speaking and Listening.** While popular culture features an increasing number of female heroes, including Wonder Woman, Black Widow, Furiosa, Ripley, and Buffy, we do not see many female tricksters. With a partner or in small groups, discuss the implications of gender on the idea of trickster tales and try to come to some consensus about why the trickster archetype seems largely confined to male figures.

16. **Research.** Conduct research on the historical and cultural impact of the Anansi character beyond what was included in the Key Context on page 926. Why is Anansi such an important figure whose stories show up in so many different cultures?

17. **Creative Writing.** Write your own trickster tale set in the present day. Be sure that your character includes elements of the trickster archetype and includes some of the boundary crossing that is typical of the character.

18. **Multimodal.** Using *Anansi Comes to the Americas* as a guide, create a few pages of a graphic adaptation of one of the other trickster tales in this collection, using some text from the original as captions or thought or speech bubbles.

Writing an Analysis of Mythology

As you may have seen in previous chapters, analysis is the process of taking something apart in order to understand it better. When we analyze mythology, we're looking at how the myth presents particular archetypes and how these archetypes illustrate themes of the myth that continue to hold meaning for us today.

Since you have probably read some myths from this chapter by this point, you know that analyzing them requires you to think about the uses of various archetypes in order to determine the myth's possible meanings. If you need to review the most common plot, character, and setting archetypes, be sure to look back at the Skill Workshop in this chapter (p. 852). As you saw throughout this chapter, there are a number of topics to analyze when writing about mythology, including character and setting archetypes, as well as trickster stories, like those about Anansi. For our purposes in this workshop, we'll focus on the most common archetype in mythology: the hero's journey.

A writing prompt for an analysis of a myth might read as follows:

In a well-developed essay, explain how the hero's journey archetype and other significant character and setting archetypes found in a myth help readers understand possible themes of that text.

So, the objective of this analytical task is to do three things:

1. Identify how the myth fits some aspects of the hero's journey archetype.
2. Recognize the most significant character and setting archetypes.
3. Explain how these archetypes lead the reader to possible themes of the myth.

For the purposes of this workshop, we will be modeling an analysis of *The Odyssey*, identifying and tracing the most significant archetypes found in the myth.

Getting Started

Look back through the myths in this chapter or consider texts that you have read, including fables, fairy tales, legends, or even films you've seen that include mythic elements. For the purposes of this workshop, be sure to select a text that includes at least some elements of the hero's journey and has some identifiable setting and character archetypes to be able to respond to a prompt similar to the one above.

Step 1. Identifying Archetypes

As with any myth, there are many different things you could focus on in *The Odyssey*, but some of the most significant archetypes are identified below. Here is how *The Odyssey* fits into the structure of the hero's journey archetype:

Stage 1: Call to Adventure	Stage 2: Road of Trials	Stage 3: Return
Before departing for the Trojan War, Odysseus is reluctant to leave his home in Ithaka and, in fact, pretends to be crazy to avoid leaving. Eventually, however, he journeys to distant Troy. (See Key Context, p. 880.)	Most of *The Odyssey* is a long road of trials that Odysseus survives, such as the Kyklops, the Seirênês, and Skylla and Charybdis. Along the way, he receives aid from many of the gods.	Odysseus returns home, reuniting first with his son and then with his wife. He kills the suitors who were tormenting his family, and he restores the order of his house.

Here are some of the most significant character archetypes found in *The Odyssey*, specifically identified by how they help or hinder Odysseus on his journey:

Character Archetype	Character	How Does the Character Relate to Odysseus's Journey?
Mentor	Athena	She asks Zeus to order Kalypso to release him; she assists him during the battle with the suitors.
Shadow	Antínoös	The chief suitor prevents Odysseus from easily reclaiming his home in Ithaka; he hopes to marry Penélopê and replace Odysseus as king.
Absent Parent	Odysseus	He is away from his son for twenty years; Telémakhos has to learn from others.
Monster/Dragon	Kyklops	He is a cannibal and the opposite of civilization, as represented by Odysseus. Odysseus uses his cunning, strength, and leadership to defeat the Kyklops.
Companion	Telémakhos	In the last part of *The Odyssey*, Telémakhos accompanies and supports Odysseus in the final battle.
Tempter/ Temptress	Kirkê, Seirênês, Kalypso	Many figures try to prevent — intentionally or not — Odysseus from returning home. They each promise Odysseus different things to end his journey: immortality, love, fame.
Damsel in Distress	Penélopê	While Penélopê exerts what power she has through her intelligence and cunning, she is trapped by suitors and the authority of her son and her husband. She is not freed until Odysseus kills the suitors.
Trickster	Odysseus	Tricksters are boundary crossers, and Odysseus goes to many places where no Greeks had traveled before. He is also clever, always coming up with new and deceptive ways to get what he wants. Sometimes his arrogance, like with the Kyklops, causes him even more trouble.

The following are some of the most significant setting archetypes found in *The Odyssey* and how they relate to Odysseus's journey.

Setting Archetype	Setting	How Does It Relate to Odysseus and His Journey?
Threshold	Troy	Just after the war ends, Odysseus is with all of the other Greeks in a familiar country they had lived in for the past ten years. This is the last familiar place he will see until he arrives home ten years later.
Wilderness/ Forest	Kyklopês island	Their island is untended and wild. It is a place of conflict for Odysseus.
Garden	Kalypso's island; The Swineherd's hut	Both of these settings are refuges for Odysseus on his journey, connected to the natural world.
Wasteland	The Sea	While not seen much in the excerpts from *The Odyssey* included here, Odysseus spends a lot of his time on the empty, unforgiving sea, far away from the known world.
Maze/ Labyrinth	Underworld	While not included in these excerpts from *The Odyssey*, Odysseus and his men journey to the Land of the Dead where they see the "shades" of people they know, only after winding their way through the mysterious path of the Underworld.
Castle	Ithaka	His palace in Ithaka is the place of power for Odysseus and he needs to conquer it to finally be home.

Identifying Archetypes

Complete tables like the ones above for the mythic text you have selected. *The Odyssey* is a long piece and therefore has many archetypes; you may not have half as many as are included above, but if you are not able to identify at least some aspects of the hero's journey and at least a few archetypal characters or settings, you may want to select a different text with more readily identifiable archetypes.

Step 2. Analyzing the Archetypes

So far in this workshop, we have identified archetypes found in *The Odyssey* and your own selected mythic text. That is the first part of the prompt, and now it's time to move on to the second part of the prompt, in which we analyze how knowing the symbolic meaning of these archetypes can assist us in making a claim about possible themes of the myth. Since *The Odyssey* is a very long text, let's focus on the archetypes found in just one stage of the hero's journey (Odysseus's return to Ithaka) and see how the archetypes help us understand the myth's relevance to us today. For your own text, which is likely much shorter, you might want to examine the archetypes from more than one stage of the journey.

Archetype	Symbolic Meaning	Possible Thematic Connections
Hero's Journey Stage 3: The Return	The hero returns from the unknown world back to a familiar place, but the hero is much changed.	Odysseus's return is a culmination of his long struggle, and his reward is reclaiming his home, his son, and his wife. Home is something worth fighting and killing for.
Shadow	This is the hero's opposite and the dark side of the hero that must be overcome.	Odysseus overcomes the Shadow when he kills Antínoös, the strongest and boldest of the suitors. Like Odysseus, he was arrogant and a leader; but Odysseus has learned caution on his journey that he uses to triumph over Antínoös and the others. Violence is needed when rational thought and discussion are not successful.
Damsel in Distress	The damsel represents purity and provides the hero with additional motivation on the journey.	Penélopê, clearly, is the damsel who needs rescuing. She has almost no real authority even in her own home until Odysseus frees her from the suitors. Power is determined, in this context, by gender and social custom of the time.
Garden	The garden is an unspoiled place symbolizing peace and harmony.	Before moving to his palace in Ithaka, Odysseus spends time with the swineherd in his rural hut, surrounded by nature and animals. It is a place of calm before the storm of the battle for his castle. It is in this place that Odysseus is finally reunited with his son, which signifies the importance of the father-son relationship in an unstable and uncaring world.
Castle	The castle symbolizes where the treasure is held that the hero must attain in order to complete the journey. It is a place of power and strength for the hero.	The castle is Odysseus's palace in Ithaka, and it has been overrun by people hostile to him and his family. His final battle is to regain the castle, and before he can take the final treasure — home at last with his wife and son — he orders a thorough cleaning of the Great Hall to get rid of the blood and the symbolic power the suitors had over him. Home is, again, worth fighting for.

Analyzing the Archetypes

Return to the tables you made earlier that identified the various archetypes present and begin to do what we did above: explain how the symbolic meaning of the archetype might connect to possible themes of the myth. Don't feel as if you need to push too hard to get to a unifying theme at this point; just closely examine the archetypes and their meanings. If you have trouble explaining at least two or three archetypes, perhaps you will want to select a different myth or a different excerpt.

Step 3. Finding a Focus and Creating a Thesis Statement

For a thesis for an essay on this prompt, you will want to introduce the idea you are looking to explore and take an interpretive stance on the idea you have about the myth. These stories are passed down through generations, passed between and within cultures, and changed repeatedly. Mythology is complex and multifaceted; therefore, your thesis should be unique to you and your ideas about the myth. Looking back at the table we created in Step 2, it's clear that a lot of the archetypes we found in the last part of *The Odyssey* focus on the importance of home, so let's try to include that in the thesis we construct.

For the topic we've been exploring, we might write a thesis sentence like this:

WEAK THESIS

In the last part of *The Odyssey*, there are many archetypes about home.

This thesis identifies only one aspects of the hero's journey. It doesn't take an interpretive stance on the myth and doesn't address the symbolic meaning of the archetypes.

WEAK THESIS

The final part of the hero's journey is called the Return Home, and *The Odyssey* fits this because Odysseus has to fight the suitors when he returns to Ithaka.

This thesis reads more like a summary of the end of the myth. One way to gauge whether you have a strong thesis is to see if it seems unique to your own reading of the myth. This one clearly does not meet that criterion.

Here's one that might be a little closer to what we want from a thesis:

WORKING THESIS

Through the character and setting archetypes of the final stage of the hero's journey in *The Odyssey*, we can understand the importance of fighting for home and the values that home represents.

activity **Thesis**

Using the myth that you selected, and after looking closely at the tables you created above, write a working thesis that *takes an interpretive stance* on the archetypes of that myth. Remember that your thesis should introduce the idea you want to explore and take a position on that idea. A strong thesis is unique to the myth you are analyzing, and reasonable people could disagree with the position you take.

Step 4. Proving Your Point

Once you have a thesis for your essay, you need to prove it by referring to specific examples from the myth and an explanation of the archetypes.

Gathering Evidence

There are many methods, including the graphic organizer below, for gathering the supporting evidence you need to prove your thesis. Be sure to leave yourself open to changing your thesis or your interpretation of the myth based on this step. Maybe, through this process, you will arrive at a new insight or approach; don't be too fixed in your perspective at this point.

One way to make sure you are connecting your quotations to your thesis is with a table like this. It will help make the relationship clear and enable you to think through the purpose of each quotation and how it connects to your larger point.

Working Thesis: Through the character and setting archetypes of the final stage of the hero's journey in *The Odyssey*, we can understand the importance of fighting for home and the values it represents.

Quotation	How the Quotation Supports the Point
"He drew to his fist the cruel head of an arrow for Antínoös just as the young man leaned to lift his beautiful drinking cup, embossed, two-handled, golden: the cup was in his fingers: the wine was even at his lips: and did he dream of death? How could he? In that revelry amid his throng of friends who would imagine a single foe—though a strong foe indeed— could dare to bring death's pain on him and darkness on his eyes? Odysseus' arrow hit him under the chin and punched up to the feathers through his throat."	The killing of the archetypal Shadow, Antínoös, the one who tries to be just like Odysseus, begins the culmination of Odysseus's journey to fully returning home. The violence of the act is vividly described and illustrates the lengths to which Odysseus will go to reclaim what is most important to him, his home and family, tormented for years by Antínoös and other suitors. Only through the death of the Shadow does Odysseus earn his full reward.

Finding Support

Go back to the myth you have chosen and gather evidence to support your working thesis. Remember that whether you use note cards, take notes in a document, or fill in a graphic organizer is up to you. This activity is a good opportunity to try out a system and see how it works. If you are unable to identify at least four or five passages from the text that support your thesis, you might want to consider a new thesis that you can prove or maybe select a different myth.

Presenting Evidence

When you present your ideas, you must make your point, frame your quotations, and explain how the two are connected.

In Chapter 3 about writing, you may have read about how to use evidence by making the point, backing up the point with evidence, and then commenting on how the evidence proves the point. If we begin to incorporate our point, evidence, and explanations in a paragraph, it might look something like this:

> The final stage of the Hero's Journey is the return to home, but in a departure from the usual joyful homecoming, Odysseus's homecoming leads him to the main conflict of his story. Odysseus returns to find the suitors attempting to take his place—eat his food, live in his home, and marry his wife. They are the embodiment of the Shadow archetype, the dark reflection of the hero. At the beginning of *The Odyssey*, the leader of the suitors, Antínoös, declares, "For here are suitors eating up your property . . . Our own affairs can wait; we'll never go anywhere else, until [Penélopê] takes an Akhaian to her liking." As the main antagonist in this part of the myth, Antínoös is the final obstacle to the completion of Odysseus's homecoming, and he wants to take Odysseus's place as king and husband. Fittingly, the hero has to triumph over the Shadow, which Odysseus does with the first arrow of the battle that "hit [Antínoös] under the chin / and punched up to the feathers through his throat." Only with the support of his Companion and his willingness to commit violence against the Shadow is Odysseus able to regain his rightful place at home.

What we have created here is a short but focused analytical paragraph. If we were to follow the same steps as the body paragraph above for another main point, we would have a second body paragraph that uses supporting evidence to prove this point, probably focusing on the role that the setting archetypes play in conveying theme. Depending on how you structured your thesis, you may or may not have more points to argue.

activity / Proving Your Point

Using the model above as a guide, write a body paragraph or two for your own working thesis that states your point, incorporates at least two pieces of textual evidence, and explains how your evidence supports your point. This last part — the explanation and commentary — is the most important part of your paragraph; be sure to keep your interpretation front and center.

Step 5. Expanding to an Essay

Throughout this workshop, you've been developing most of the pieces you need for an analytical essay about a myth. We have a thesis and a body paragraph. If we add another body paragraph or two, an introduction, and a conclusion, we have all the remaining pieces for an essay.

Introductory Paragraph

The point of the introductory paragraph is to engage your reader and create interest in the topic. A standard introduction has three parts:

1. An opening hook
2. A connection to the piece being analyzed
3. A thesis statement

The hook is about drawing in readers and getting them thinking about the kinds of ideas or issues that are at play in your analysis. This is a great place to just raise questions or identify issues. Many writers will tell you that the first sentence is the hardest to write. Here are a few classic ways to begin your introductory paragraph:

With a question	What is worth fighting for? For what goal or purpose would you be willing to commit acts of violence? What are your own limits?
With a definition	From the dictionary, *home* means a "place where one lives," but "home" often carries more symbolic meaning. Home usually also refers to the feelings associated with that place—good, bad, and in between.
With a statement	The hero's journey is an archetype that is found within stories from around the world, and even though there are many differences among these types of stories, one commonality is that the hero usually returns to a home that is changed and in danger.

Once we have a hook, it's time to show our readers how the ideas we've brought up apply to the myth we are about to analyze. This transition doesn't have to be fancy. It's usually a simple connecting statement that includes a bit of summary along with the author and title.

What is worth fighting for? For what goal or purpose would you be willing to —————— *The hook*
commit acts of violence? What are your own limits? In the ancient Greek myth
The Odyssey, the hero Odysseus goes to great lengths, including committing — *Connection to the piece*
significant acts of violence, to return to and reclaim his home after a ten-year
journey. Through the character and setting archetypes of the final stage of the
hero's journey in *The Odyssey*, we can understand importance of fighting for — *Thesis*
home and the values it represents.

Introduction

Following the model above, write a draft of your introductory paragraph. Think about the way you want to hook the reader and how you want to lead into your thesis statement with a connecting statement that includes the author and title.

Concluding Paragraph

As with any essay you write, a solid conclusion will bring your paper full circle by restating in new words your thesis and the main points you analyzed in each of the body paragraphs. It should bring completeness and closure to the reader with the satisfaction that your assertion is a sound one. Notice how this draft of the concluding paragraph does just that.

> Home matters. Home for Odysseus represents the love for his wife and son, but also his authority as king, all of which he was without during his long journey in *The Odyssey*. His home represents the Castle archetype, which had to be cleared of opposition, specifically the Shadow archetype of Antínoös and the threat to Odysseus's power that he represents. The brutal and graphic killings of the suitors and the maids demonstrate the lengths to which Odysseus is willing to go to regain his power and authority after a long journey home.

Conclusion

Write a concluding paragraph for your essay. Remember to tie it back to your thesis and the points in your body paragraphs, and to avoid simply repeating what you have already stated.

Bringing It All Together

If you take all of the pieces you've written and put them together, you have a solid draft of a short analytical essay. Remember that everything you've done in this workshop is to help you get started. Once you feel more in control of what it means to make an interpretation, prove a point, and comment on evidence, you can start to bend these rules to suit your purposes. Writing is not about formulas or templates. It's about communicating ideas.

Step 6. Finalizing the Essay

Now that you have a complete draft of your essay, you can move on to the final phase of the writing process: revising and editing. These two acts are sometimes thought of as being the same, but they're not. Revision is when you look back at large-scale structural elements of your essay, such as how well you support your claim, what kinds of evidence you use, how effective your word choices are, and to what extent you have led your reader easily through your essay. Editing, on the other hand, focuses on fine-tuning the language, grammar, punctuation, spelling, and other conventions. Editing is usually the very last thing you do before you finalize your piece, looking carefully for any errors that you tend to make. The following are suggestions for you to consider as you finalize your essay.

Revising

Revising gives you a good opportunity to think again about your essay's purpose and audience. In most cases, your audience will be your teacher or an external evaluator in the case of a standardized test. In both situations, that means using a somewhat formal tone, but your writing can still be engaging for you and your audience.

Reread your essay for the following:

- **Revisit your thesis.** Since you wrote this early on in the workshop, does it still relate to the analysis you ended up writing? If you need more assistance with this, be sure to look at Revision Workshop 1: Effective Thesis and Essay Structure in the back of the book.
- **Check your focus.** Is it still at the center of your analysis? Make sure that ideas and evidence in your paragraphs connect back to the focus. If you need more assistance with this, be sure to look at Revision Workshop 2: Effective Topic Sentences and Unified Paragraphs in the back of the book.
- **Look back at your body paragraphs.** Have you balanced the evidence with your own commentary about how that evidence supports your thesis? If you need more assistance with this, be sure to look at Revision Workshop 4: Appropriate Evidence and Support in the back of the book.
- **Make sure you've addressed the prompt.** Does your essay analyze the archetypes and connect them to possible themes? Be sure to look back at the Skill Workshop (p. 852) at the beginning of this chapter if you need more practice with this.
- **Look back at your introduction and conclusion.** Does your introduction grab the reader's attention and effectively preview your topic? Does your conclusion wrap up in a way that highlights your focus? Review Revision Workshop 8: Effective Introductions and Conclusions in the back of the book if you need additional support with these parts of your essay.

- **Check your explanations of archetypes.** Do not assume that your reader has the same understanding of the symbolic meanings for the archetypes, so be sure to take a little bit of time in your analysis to explain what you mean by, say, the Call to Adventure.
- **Revisit your use of examples.** Do not merely summarize the plot or events in the myth. Although some summary may be necessary for establishing context, summary is not analysis. Focus on the significance of the archetypes.

Editing

Remember, editing is the very last thing you'll do before finalizing your essay. You and your teacher know better than anyone the types of spelling, grammar, and convention errors you need to focus on in your writing development. Below is a short checklist of things to keep in mind. Be sure to refer to one or more of the Grammar Workshops in the back of the book if you encounter an issue and aren't sure how to overcome it.

- Write using present tense verbs. Even though it is often very old, mythology still *lives*, so your analysis should discuss how the myth *illustrates*, *reveals*, or *presents* themes in a certain way.
- Use third person point of view and avoid the use of pronouns like *I* and *you* when you are analyzing the myths, though exceptions could be made for introductions and conclusions.

Analysis of Mythology

You have spent this workshop crafting an analysis of a myth that presents a focused thesis with support and commentary. What if you wanted to share that same piece through a presentation to a live audience? What would you need to add, change, or delete to make your essay sound engaging? As you work through this process, refer to the elements of a presentation in Chapter 3 (p. 90), and use these steps to turn your written analysis into an oral presentation.

Content

- **Your introduction.** Reread the beginning paragraph of your written analysis. Would this capture the listener's attention? Read it aloud to yourself a few times. Does it sound dramatic or engaging? Remember that you chose to work with a particular myth because it interested you. Does your introduction convey that interest? Does it communicate to your listeners the particular aspects of the myth you are going to discuss? If it feels too long when you read it aloud, cut it down, so that it is only two or three sentences.
- **Your main idea.** You will want to be very clear about what you are analyzing. You may want to break your thesis up into two sentences to ensure that your listeners know each element that will be included in the presentation.
- **Your supporting evidence.** While your analytical essay may have included multiple points that you address, for a short presentation you might want to focus only on the strongest element that you analyzed. Include evidence that is clear, focused, and supports the importance of the element you selected.
- **Your closing.** Look back at how you ended your written analysis and highlight the strongest sentence or two that communicate to your audience the ideas you've presented and the overall meaning of the myth. For a live audience, it may be especially important to give them a question or comment to inspire further thought about the ideas you have presented.

Delivery

Like other speeches you deliver in school, a presentation of an analysis of a myth will take on a mostly formal tone, but you can smile, gesture, or laugh at appropriate times. Because you may be presenting information that might be unfamiliar to your listeners, you will want to move slowly and clearly through your points, maybe using transitions, such as "first, second . . . ," "finally," or "most important." You can use your fingers to count off evidence or a gesture to show the importance of a particular piece of evidence.

Visuals

As with visuals for any presentation, you need to make sure that anything you include is relevant, appropriate, and works to enhance your words and delivery. Possible visuals for a presentation of an analysis of a myth might include a passage from the text that you want to discuss in detail or bullet points related to your main idea. If you display artwork, movie posters, or other images to represent the character, setting, or plot archetypes, include commentary to explain how those visuals relate to your analysis. If you are changing visuals during your presentation, be sure to allow a little time for the audience to react, especially if the new visual is something that they might need more time to process.

Revision Workshops

Young adult novelist Robert Cormier said, "The beautiful part of writing is that you don't have to get it right the first time, unlike, say [brain surgery]. You can always do it better, find the exact word, the apt phrase, the leaping simile." Revision is an essential, but often over-looked, step in the writing process. It is the time when you look back at large-scale structural elements of your essay, such as how well you support your claim, what kinds of evidence you use, how effective your word choices are, and to what extent you have led your reader easily through your essay. The idea behind the Revision Workshops that follow is that every piece you write offers something you can work on. The key to becoming a stronger writer is to begin to identify for yourself those areas of improvement. The activities in these work-shops ask you to return to a piece that you are currently writing or have recently finished so that the work you do in these workshops is immediately relevant to your needs.

Effective Thesis and Essay Structure

When you write an essay, you are generally trying to convey a point or multiple points. You might be creating an argument, telling a story, or providing insight into literature you have read. Regardless of your reason for the essay, you must provide a structure that helps the reader follow your point(s) easily. In general, essays should include an introduction (containing your thesis), body paragraph(s), and a conclusion.

In this workshop, we will ask you to take a close look at how effective your thesis statement is and how well it aligns with the topic sentences of your body paragraphs. While we will be modeling this process through a literary analysis essay, we will also point out how it might be applied to an argumentative essay.

Crafting a Thesis

Your thesis statement is a sentence that presents your claim or the main point of your essay. It needs to provide a strong foundation so that your ideas are clear and focused. Consider the foundation of a building: if it is weak, the building may crumble. A weak thesis will lead to an essay that crumbles under scrutiny. To start thinking about crafting an effective thesis, let's consider the following prompt:

Stories often feature characters who undergo personal change or development. Identify a story in which a major or minor character changes in a significant way. Explain how that character develops, what causes those changes, and how the author uses characterization to reveal a theme.

In general, prompts ask a question or give you something to consider. Your job is to answer the prompt thoroughly and effectively. Look closely at the prompt to understand what you need to do to address it. Does it have more than one part? If so, it is important to respond to all parts of the prompt. In this case, the prompt asks you to consider three things: *(1) how the character develops, (2) what causes those changes,* and *(3) how the author uses characterization to reveal a theme.*

Let's determine how we might answer the prompt using Amy Tan's story, "Two Kinds" (p. 331). What will our thesis statement be? In the story, we know that Jing-mei struggles under her mother's pressure to turn her into a prodigy. Let's look at the following statements in response to how Jing-mei changes and how those changes help Tan to express a specific theme.

WEAK THESIS

In this section of "Two Kinds," Jing-mei rebels against her mother.

This thesis states what happens, but it doesn't address why or how a theme is revealed. It doesn't take an interpretive stance on the story, and it doesn't directly address all the parts of the prompt.

WEAK THESIS

The motivations behind Jing-mei's rebellion against becoming a prodigy in "Two Kinds" are complex and drive her to create her own definition of a prodigy.

This thesis is a little closer, but not quite there because it doesn't clearly tell us why she rebels. What are the motivations? Why does she have these motivations?

WORKING THESIS

Tired of failing to be the sort of prodigy her mother would like her to be, Jing-mei creates her own definition of a prodigy, unleashing the strong, willful girl within herself.

This thesis states what happens, but also takes a stand on why: Jing-mei is pushed to change by her mother's behavior. It also addresses why she changes in the way that she does: she doesn't feel in control of her identity, so she takes control. Now we have a roadmap to use while writing the essay.

If you are currently working on an argument rather than a literary analysis, the elements of a thesis are roughly the same. Your thesis should clearly state the claim that you are hoping to prove, as well as the main points you are planning to explore. Imagine that someone is writing an argument about police reform in the United States.

WEAK THESIS

I think that we need more police reform to address recent shootings of unarmed citizens.

This thesis states only the writer's position on the issue; it does not provide a roadmap for the argument. Providing specifics about the meaning of "reform" would help establish a roadmap.

WORKING THESIS

Because tragic confrontations between the police and the public often stem from a lack of oversight and training, cities and towns across the country should require all officers to wear body cameras, train officers in alternative response techniques, and invest in social services to help address calls related to mental health and other noncriminal emergencies.

In this thesis, we not only get the writer's claim but also the main areas of focus that the essay will address.

ACTIVITY **Check Your Thesis**

Take a look at the thesis statement in the essay you are currently revising. Does your prompt have more than one question? Does your thesis answer all components of the question? Does it take a position on the issue? Does it suggest how your essay might be structured? Show your thesis to a classmate to receive feedback.

Revising Topic Sentences

Now that you have settled on a thesis, you are ready to build support for your idea. The purpose of body paragraphs is to provide evidence and details in support of your thesis. In order to stay on track and fully support your thesis, it can be helpful to include brainstorming in your pre-writing process. What evidence and ideas in the text support your claim? You may not end up using everything you brainstormed. However, you will have a range of evidence to choose from.

After you have done a close reading of the literature you are analyzing and have gathered your notes, or have researched the topic of your argumentative essay, you are ready to support your thesis statement. But how are you going to organize all of that evidence? How are you going to structure your essay? That's where topic sentences come in. The topic sentences of your body paragraphs are claims that define the points you'd like to make in your essay. Your reasons and evidence then support those claims.

Let's return to our essay on Tan's "Two Kinds" to see how we might organize our body paragraphs. Again, here is our working thesis:

WORKING THESIS

Tired of failing to be the sort of prodigy her mother would like her to be, Jing-mei creates her own definition of a prodigy, unleashing the strong, willful girl within herself.

The topic sentences of your paragraphs should be statements that support the thesis. While no specific number of body paragraphs is required, you should certainly be able to come up with at least two or three topic sentences that dig into your thesis in more detail and expand on its claims. For instance, here are some of the claims (though certainly not all of them) that can be made about our working thesis:

- Jing-mei demonstrates fatigue from the constant pressures to become the prodigy her mother desires. (Supports the first part of the prompt.)

- Jing-mei realizes that her own definition of a prodigy can differ from her mother's. (Supports the second part of the prompt.)
- Tan demonstrates Jing-mei's transformation from trying to become the prodigy her mother wants to establishing her own identity. (Supports the third part of the prompt.)

These clear areas of focus suggested by the thesis can lead to a clear essay structure when made into topic sentences.

Here are a few possible topic sentences for this essay:

- While some may read Jing-mei's resistance to her mother's training as rebellion, it seems more like fatigue from a lifetime of frustrating exercises and pressure.
- At one point in the story, Jing-mei realizes that her own definition of a prodigy can help her push back on her mother's expectations.
- Jing-mei's new-found identity as a willful, powerful girl gives her the strength to exert more control over her life.

Notice that these topic sentences relate directly back to the thesis statement. Make sure your topic sentences are not just summary statements from the story. A topic sentence *must* be an arguable claim.

If you are currently working on an argumentative essay, the process remains the same for aligning your topic sentences with your thesis. Again, here is the working thesis for the argument in favor of police reform:

WORKING THESIS

Because tragic confrontations between the police and the public often stem from a lack of oversight and training, cities and towns across the country should require all officers to wear body cameras, train officers in alternative response techniques, and invest in social services to help address calls related to mental health and other noncriminal emergencies.

The topic sentences that could be derived from this thesis might look like this:

- The use of body cameras would help both police and citizens during incidents because they can provide a visual record of events.
- Alternative response techniques are beneficial for police officers to know because they offer an alternative method to deadly force.
- Instead of cuts to social programs, communities should invest in better social services to help those in need.

Notice how each of these topic sentences takes a portion of the thesis to examine, but each one is also a claim in itself.

ACTIVITY Check Your Topic Sentences

Choose a topic sentence from a body paragraph in an essay that you are currently working on. Meet with a partner and explain how that topic sentence is derived from your thesis. Ask your partner whether or not the topic sentence makes an arguable claim and relates directly to your thesis.

---

culminating activity

culminating activity

Effective Thesis and Essay Structure

Return to the essay that you have been working on and highlight the thesis statement. Then, highlight each of your topic sentences in a different color. Check that each topic sentence makes an arguable claim and that each is related directly to the thesis statement. If not, be sure to revise accordingly.

workshop 2

Effective Topic Sentences and Unified Paragraphs

As we build support for an argument or analysis, we think about various points that support our position. We want our topic sentences to lead our readers along our line of reasoning. Unified paragraphs that focus on proving the claim in the topic sentence help make our writing clear and convincing.

In this workshop, you will evaluate and revise your topic sentences and check that your paragraphs are unified. We will be working with an analysis of Amy Tan's short story, "Two Kinds" (p. 331), as we look at samples of effective and ineffective topic sentences and examine unity in the body paragraphs. Whether you are working on an analysis or argument essay, at the end of this workshop, you will be able to apply a critical eye to your own writing and revise your paper to make it stronger and more effective.

Examining Topic Sentences

An effective topic sentence accomplishes two goals. First, it introduces a claim that makes a point that is useful for proving your overall thesis. Second, it leads your reader to an understanding of what a body paragraph will be about. As you plan your writing, think about which claims you need to make to prove your thesis and convince your reader that your argument or interpretation is valid.

Identifying your main claims is a key early step in building your essay. These reasons why you believe your position is valid will become your topic sentences. Ideally, your reader should be able to read from topic sentence to topic sentence to follow your line of reasoning and see the argument at a glance. Topic sentences can appear anywhere within your paragraph, especially as you become more comfortable with writing analytical or argumentative essays. For now, though, let's keep it straightforward and make each topic sentence the first sentence in each paragraph.

One error that many students make with topic sentences is writing a sentence that summarizes or provides simple facts, rather than writing a topic sentence as a claim. Let's look at some examples. These are sample topic sentences for an essay on the development of Jing-mei's character in "Two Kinds." Jing-mei is resistant to her mother's expectation that she become a child prodigy.

WEAK TOPIC SENTENCE
Jing-mei struggles to complete the tests her mother gives her.

This sentence is not a claim because it is not arguable. It simply states a fact. It would not make an effective topic sentence.

WEAK TOPIC SENTENCE

Jing-mei struggles with the tests her mother gives her because she constantly fails them.

This statement would make a slightly better topic sentence because it asserts that Jing-mei's failures with the tests are the reason why she struggles. However, it is not specific enough to lead to a strong interpretive paragraph that will make a convincing point in the paper.

EFFECTIVE TOPIC SENTENCE

While some may read Jing-mei's resistance to her mother's training as a rebellion, it seems more like fatigue from a lifetime of frustrating exercises and pressure.

This is the best of the three sentences. It presents a strong claim about the *effect* of her mother's testing and pressure on Jing-mei.

If you are writing an argument rather than a literary analysis, the elements of an effective topic sentence remain the same. As an example, imagine that you are writing an argument about the need for expanded electives at your school. The following are examples of topic sentences about one part of that argument: the connection to future careers.

WEAK TOPIC SENTENCE

School is boring to me because it doesn't have anything to do with what I want to do later in life.

This is just a personal opinion, rather than a claim. While some students might agree with this statement, it doesn't take a position that can be argued.

EFFECTIVE TOPIC SENTENCE

For students to be engaged in their schoolwork, they need to be able to make connections to the real world and to future career opportunities.

This is a stronger topic sentence because it is a claim: there are people who might think differently about the causes of student engagement. Also, it is focused on the idea of careers.

ACTIVITY Examining Your Topic Sentences

1. Write your thesis statement from the piece you are currently revising.

2. Select a topic sentence from one paragraph in your essay.

3. Evaluate the topic sentence as either weak or effective, and explain why. These questions may help you to examine your topic sentence:

   • Is the topic sentence a claim—an arguable statement that must be supported?
   • Does the topic sentence simply summarize?
   • Does the topic sentence help to build a convincing case for your thesis?

4. Revise the sentence as needed.

Building Paragraph Unity

What is paragraph unity? Paragraphs are unified when they focus on proving one claim. Unity begins with a strong topic sentence. From there, all of the evidence and commentary must focus on supporting that claim. You must be choosy about what goes into your paragraph, and when you are revising, you must critically evaluate every sentence in your paragraph. Ask yourself these questions:

- Does each sentence belong here?
- Does each sentence relate to and support the claim in my topic sentence?
- Is my evidence the best evidence to prove this particular claim?
- Am I using commentary to explain how this evidence proves my point?
- At the end of my paragraph, do I circle back to my overall thesis, trying to tie my paragraph to my thesis?

Commentary is the key to unity. As you might recall, any time you use a piece of evidence, you must add commentary after it to explain how it proves your point. While the purpose of a piece of evidence might be obvious to you, it's likely not obvious to your readers. You have to tell them why that evidence is important. This is the connective tissue for building your body paragraphs and for building your argument as a whole.

Let's examine some revisions to improve the following sample paragraph. This is a paragraph analyzing the development of Jing-mei's character in the story "Two Kinds." (Because different assignments, classes, and teachers have different requirements for citing sources, we have opted not to cite any sources here. For formal guidelines for documenting sources in an English class, see the MLA guidelines in the back of this book.)

ORIGINAL

While some may read Jing-mei's resistance to her mother's training as rebellion, it seems more like fatigue from a lifetime of frustrating exercises and pressure. One such training exercise involves memorizing "a page from the Bible for three minutes and [reporting] everything [she] could remember." Not able to go far, Jing-mei finally stops short, saying, ". . . that's all I remember, Ma." The sad, apologetic, and affectionate tone of ". . . that's all I remember, Ma" makes Jing-mei's response to the exercises not defiance, but defeat. She seems worn down. An angry child would not use the affectionate term "Ma." Despite Jing-mei's lack of performance, her mother does not stop with the exercises and continues to push Jing-mei's limits. At one point, Jing-mei's mother says to Jing-mei that she is "not the best" because she's "not trying." The mother does not see the effect that her relentless testing has on Jing-mei. Her desire for Jing-mei to become a prodigy is more important to her than Jing-mei's happiness. After a while, Jing-mei simply stops trying because "after seeing once again [her] mother's disappointed face, something insider [her] began to die."

Even though this paragraph begins with a strong topic sentence that makes a claim, it is not particularly unified. Notice that it is supposed to be focused on Jing-mei's fatigue from her mother's constant pressure and exercises. But, in the middle of the paragraph (with the underlined sentences), it switches its focus to the mother's pursuit of turning her daughter into a prodigy. The writer got a little off track and strayed too far from the topic sentence. This is very easy to do in a literary analysis, because there are often many pieces of evidence that you want to use. Let's look at a revision with changes from the previous paragraph underlined:

REVISION

While some may read Jing-mei's resistance to her mother's training as rebellion, it seems more like fatigue from a lifetime of frustrating exercises and pressure. One such training exercise involves memorizing "a page from the Bible for three minutes and [reporting] everything [she] could remember." Not able to go far, Jing-mei finally stops short, saying, ". . . that's all I remember, Ma." The sad, apologetic, and affectionate tone of ". . . that's all I remember, Ma" makes Jing-mei's response to the exercises not defiance, but defeat. She seems worn down. An angry child would not use the affectionate term "Ma." Later in the story, Jing-mei admits that it is not necessarily the tests, but her failure that truly upsets her. She says that "after seeing, once again, [her] mother's disappointed face, something inside [her] began to die." In a situation like this, in which the tests are arbitrary and failure results in a mother's disappointment, it is no surprise that a hurting child would crack and then change the rules of the game.

Looking at the topic sentence, there are two strong ideas presented here — that Jing-mei has grown resistant to her mother's tests, and that her resistance is caused by fatigue, not necessarily rebellion. The evidence and the commentary in this revision all focus on Jing-mei's frustration and fatigue, support the topic sentence, and connect with the thesis — that because of her mother's pressure to become a prodigy, Jing-mei discovers and asserts her own definition of what a prodigy is. The paragraph furthers the point that Jing-mei's character development is leading her to define her own measure of success.

If you are writing an argument rather than a literary analysis, the idea of paragraph unity is the same. Make sure that you examine and develop a single idea in each paragraph. Let's look at this example of a possible paragraph about the need for more electives in high school.

ORIGINAL

Students need to be able to make connections to the real world and to future career opportunities, and having the opportunity to participate in a wide variety of electives allows for time in high school to practice skills that prepare them for a career. For example, taking a cooking class would teach students important skills that they can use every day and is helpful for understanding nutrition. Another great elective for students would be a class on computer repair. Because we use computers so often in learning and life, knowing how to repair a computer would come in handy.

This paragraph begins with a clear topic sentence about the importance of offering a variety of electives as a first step to exploring careers. However, while the student writer examines the different possible electives that could be offered, there is no mention of careers. At times, the paragraph feels like a summary of the skills learned from participating in possible electives, so this paragraph lacks unity and focus on the topic sentence.

Let's look at a revision:

REVISION

For students to be engaged in their schoolwork, they need to be able to make connections to the real world and to future career opportunities. The opportunity to participate in a wide variety of electives allows students to practice skills that prepare them for a career. For example, taking a cooking class would teach students skills needed to enroll in a culinary arts program that could lead to a career in the restaurant business. In this class, students would be exposed to a variety of skills, techniques, and cuisines that would transfer to further training or an employment opportunity. Another great elective option for students would be a class on repairing computers. Computer repair technicians are in high demand because we use computers so often that there is always a need for an expert to fix them.

This revision keeps much of the same evidence, but it is far more unified, because each of the examples is explained in terms of the need for elective options to make connections to the real world and students' futures.

ACTIVITY **Building Paragraph Unity**

Look back at the essay you are revising and revise one paragraph to improve its unity. Then show your revision to a partner for feedback. Is your partner getting a clear idea of your point in the paragraph?

culminating activity

Effective Topic Sentences and Unified Paragraphs

Look back at the essay you are revising. Use these questions to help guide your revision of your body paragraphs for unity:

- Is your evidence related to your topic sentence, or is it only somewhat relevant?
- Do you get off topic or stray too far from your topic sentence? If so, would that information be more effective in a separate paragraph?
- Where can you identify commentary that refers to your thesis? Is there a smooth and clear connection between your evidence in this paragraph and your overall argument?

workshop 3

Balanced Evidence and Commentary

As you use sources to develop an essay, it's important to stay focused on your ideas. You need to support your ideas with evidence—but remember to also explain your ideas with commentary. Commentary is your voice, your own explanation of how the evidence supports your point.

Chapter 3 offers details on how to construct a paragraph with evidence and commentary (p. 85). Here we will take a deeper look into developing a balanced approach to presenting evidence and providing commentary on your topic, focusing on two key questions:

- Do you have enough commentary to keep the emphasis on your voice?
- Is your commentary insightful and related to your overall purpose?

To address these questions, we will be working with Steve Almond's opinion piece called "Is It Immoral to Watch the Super Bowl" (p. 430), which appeared in the *New York Times* in 2014. We will examine sample paragraphs using evidence and commentary in a close reading analysis of Almond's argument. If you are writing your own argument, rather than analyzing someone else's, this instruction and these examples will also apply to your writing task. After completing this workshop, you should be able to apply your observations and skills to your own writing and examine how you are developing your own ideas with a balance of evidence and commentary.

Examining Quantity of Evidence Versus Commentary

Balancing compelling evidence with insightful commentary is the goal. You don't want your paragraph to be mostly evidence or just a summary of the evidence. Nor do you want your commentary to be the entire paragraph. With the former problem, your own position won't be as prominent as it needs to be. With the latter, your paragraph won't be as convincing as it needs to be without a solid foundation of evidence to support your views. (Because different assignments, classes, and teachers have different requirements for citing sources, we have opted not to cite any sources here. For formal guidelines for documenting sources in an English class, see the MLA guidelines in the back of this book.)

Let's take a look at two examples with plenty of evidence from a source, but not enough commentary to keep the focus on our voice and ideas.

LONG QUOTATION WITH INSUFFICIENT COMMENTARY

In his article, Steve Almond contends that viewers are complicit in the injuries suffered by the athletes. He writes, "Medical research has confirmed that football can cause catastrophic brain injury — not as a rare and unintended consequence, but as a routine byproduct of how the game is played. That puts us fans in a morally queasy position. We not only tolerate this brutality. We sponsor it, just by watching at home." Almond's focus on the brain injuries helps the reader to understand his argument against watching football.

Notice how the large block of textual evidence, underlined above, leaves little room for our commentary to control the main idea in this paragraph. So, how do we fix it? One way is to use shorter quotations as evidence. Do we really need all four sentences from Almond, or would one be enough? In general, you will want to avoid large blocks of evidence like this sample. Instead, you can include one sentence, or even just phrases or words from the text in quotations as your evidence.

Let's look at another example, in which our evidence is underlined:

SHORT QUOTATIONS WITH INSUFFICIENT COMMENTARY

In his article, Steve Almond compares the brutality of football to warfare. He states that football "is the one sport that most faithfully recreates our childhood fantasies of war as a winnable contest." According to Almond, "Americans have sought a distraction from the moral incoherence of the wars in Afghanistan and Iraq." When watching football "the civilian and the fan participate in the same basic transaction. We offload the moral burdens of combat." It's clear that similar feelings come up with football and warfare.

This paragraph does not make the same mistake as the first sample; there are smaller blocks of text and just a few words from Almond in some places. But the evidence still makes up about half of the overall paragraph. In other words, our voice and argument are still overwhelmed by Almond's words and ideas. A good rule of thumb is to have about twice as much commentary as evidence, which lets your own ideas remain central.

Finally, here is a model paragraph with a nice balance of evidence and commentary:

BALANCED EVIDENCE AND COMMENTARY

In order to speak with authority about the negative impact of continuing to watch football despite our awareness of the dangers to the players, Almond establishes his credibility as a fan. He opens his argument by recalling a time when he was 11 and saw a player, Darryl Stingley, get hit on TV so violently that he became a paraplegic. He tells this story with a sense of mixed emotions: excitement of the hit itself mixed with a sense of shame, saying "part of my attraction to football was the thrill of such violent transactions." These are the mixed emotions that Almond hopes will resonate with his audience. A few paragraphs later, he says, "I still love football. I love the grace and the poise of the athletes. I love the tension between the ornate structure of the game and its improvisatory chaos." By citing both his personal involvement and enjoyment of the sport, Almond emphasizes to his readers that his concerns about football are coming from someone who is as deeply conflicted about it as they are.

This revision begins with a sentence that establishes the purpose of the paragraph. Each piece of evidence, underlined above, is followed by a sentence or two of commentary describing why the evidence is important. This paragraph balances commentary with evidence to maintain control of the intended point for the paragraph and paper as a whole. Look back at the previous paragraphs and notice how much more in balance the commentary is with the evidence in this one.

ACTIVITY Examining the Quantity of Evidence Versus Commentary

Look back at a paragraph in the essay you are currently revising and highlight all of the evidence. Assess how much evidence you have included. Is it taking up a large proportion of your paragraph? Is there perhaps not enough evidence? Is there evidence that is excessively long, and perhaps could be shortened? Finally, revise your paragraph so that it has a good mix of your voice and evidence.

Improving the Quality of Your Commentary

Just as important as making sure your voice isn't overwhelmed by the amount of evidence you provide is making sure you are writing commentary that expresses your ideas and your position rather than summarizing the evidence. Look at this sample paragraph, in which patches of summary are underlined:

SUMMARY INSTEAD OF COMMENTARY

Being a fan of a violent sport like football puts the viewer in a difficult ethical position, according to Steve Almond. When Almond was 11, he witnessed a devastating hit on a receiver, "who had been rendered quadriplegic on national television: Surely the game of football would now be outlawed." <u>Almond assumed, as a child, that football would be banned.</u> After Almond described all of the reasons to his neighbor, Sean, that he doesn't watch football anymore, Sean "looked at me and said, in a quiet, imploring voice, 'Please don't take this away from me.'" <u>Sean didn't want to stop watching football.</u>

In this example, not only is there not enough commentary, but we're merely echoing the evidence instead of making a statement that uses the evidence to further our point. Notice how we mostly restate Almond's ideas in our own words. The goal of commentary is to explain how the evidence you include supports the points you are trying to make. A good technique to help with this might be to create a graphic organizer like the following one, in which you place the evidence you think you want to include on the left and your explanation for it on the right. An example from the evidence in the paragraph above is included:

Evidence from the Source	Explanation of the Evidence
"Just so we're clear on this: I still love football. I love the grace and the poise of the athletes. I love the tension between the ornate structure of the game and its improvisatory chaos, and I love the way great players find opportunity, even a mystical kind of order, in the midst of that chaos."	It is likely that many of Almond's readers who are fans have heard a lot about the dangers of football, but probably not from writers who really love the game like they do; Almond creates a connection between himself and the readers in a shared love of the game.

If you are struggling with identifying the differences between summary and commentary, consider using some of the following words or phrases that can help lead you into explanation, rather than summary:

- This quotation proves that _____.
- The author's point illustrates _____.
- In other words, _____.
- Therefore, we can conclude that _____.

Now take a look at a revised paragraph in which the commentary, underlined, focuses on explanation rather than summary:

REVISION

Being a fan of a violent sport like football puts the viewer in a difficult ethical position, according to Steve Almond. When Almond was 11, he witnessed a devastating hit on a receiver, "who had been rendered quadriplegic on national television: Surely the game of football would now be outlawed." <u>As a child, Almond was naïve enough to think that someone in authority—doctors, politicians, team owners—would recognize that football is just too dangerous, but now, as an adult, he sees that it is the viewer, the consumer of the product, who has to make the decision to watch or not.</u> After Almond described all of the reasons to his neighbor, Sean, that he doesn't watch football anymore, Sean "looked at me and said, in a quiet, imploring voice, 'Please don't take this away from me.'" In his plea, Sean implies that once he is made aware of the dangers and the ethical implications, he cannot simply watch, free from the guilt and shame.

Not only is there more commentary than evidence in this paragraph, but the quality of the commentary is higher because it explains how that evidence supports the main point that watching football can put viewers into difficult ethical positions. With the amount and the quality of the commentary, this paragraph demonstrates that our own voice is central.

ACTIVITY Improving the Quality of Commentary

Look back at a paragraph in the essay you are currently revising and highlight all of the commentary. Then, ask a partner to assess the quality of the commentary. Does it offer analysis of the evidence, or merely summarize the evidence? Revise your paragraph to improve the commentary.

---

culminating activity

Balanced Evidence and Commentary

Return to the essay you have been revising and highlight your own commentary in one color and the evidence in another. *Your* words should appear to be a significantly larger proportion of the paragraph than the evidence you are using. *Your voice* is making this argument, and it must remain in control rather than allowing the evidence to drive your argument. Then, review your paragraphs one by one. Examine each one critically. Use this final checklist to tie together all of the skills relating to evidence and commentary that you have worked on in this workshop.

- Is your evidence mostly short, integrated words and phrases from the text you are writing about? Have you made sure that your evidence does not overwhelm your voice?
- Is your commentary clear? Does it further your point?
- Does your commentary make your voice prominent and your ideas understandable?
- Have you removed repetitive commentary that merely echoes or summarizes the evidence you have presented?

workshop 4

Appropriate Evidence and Support

Like a lawyer in the courtroom, when writing an evidence-based analysis or argument, your job is to provide evidence that supports your case. You must examine the information available, establish a position, and present evidence to support that position.

Before we really dig in, though, we must consider this question: what is evidence? You might recall from your work in Chapter 3 (p. 85) that evidence is any information used to support a topic sentence. There are many kinds of evidence, from personal experience to statistics, and each kind can serve a different purpose in your argument. In Chapter 4 (p. 103), we talked about how to assess the credibility of a piece of evidence by looking at its currency, biases, relevance to the topic, and other factors. Keep those things in mind as you look at the evidence in your writing and work through this workshop on appropriate evidence and support.

In this workshop, you will practice providing evidence to support a claim you have made by addressing the following three questions:

- Is there enough evidence?
- Is the evidence varied?
- Is the evidence relevant?

This workshop applies to writing your own argument. However, we will identify places where the activities might be relevant to analyzing a piece of literature or nonfiction.

Examining the Quantity of Evidence

The first question you should ask about your writing is, "Do I have enough evidence to prove my point?" Let's start by reading this sample paragraph from Steve Almond's essay "Is It Immoral to Watch the Super Bowl" (p. 430) that uses evidence to support a claim about the ethics of watching football. (Because different assignments, classes, and teachers have different requirements for citing sources, we have opted not to cite any sources here. For formal guidelines for documenting sources in an English class, see the MLA guidelines in the back of this book.)

> ORIGINAL
>
> Football is too violent and those who watch and support the N.F.L. are complicit in the injuries of the players. Steve Almond, a long-time football fan, writes in a piece for the *New York Times* that injuries put "us fans in a morally queasy position. We not only tolerate this brutality. We sponsor it, just by watching at home. We're the reason the N.F.L. will earn $5 billion in television revenue." It's clear that the health of the players is more important than the entertainment we might get from watching the sport.

This paragraph makes a claim:

> Football is too violent and those who watch and support the N.F.L. are complicit in the injuries of the players.

It also provides some evidence for the claim:

> Injuries put "us fans in a morally queasy position. We not only tolerate this brutality. We sponsor it, just by watching at home. We're the reason the N.F.L. will earn $5 billion in television revenue."

As you may have seen in Chapter 7 (p. 393), an argument can be supported by personal experience, facts and statistics, and expert opinion. Is this paragraph alone enough to convince you that football is too violent to watch? Probably not, because we've provided information from only one source, Steve Almond. To be persuasive, you need enough evidence to prove the point you want to make. How much evidence you need depends on the complexity of your topic and the length of your assignment. You should expect to include more than one piece of evidence. Look at this revision to the example above with additional evidence (underlined):

REVISION

Football is too violent and those who watch and support the N.F.L. are complicit in the injuries of the players. Steve Almond, a long-time football fan, writes in a piece for the *New York Times* that injuries put "us fans in a morally queasy position. We not only tolerate this brutality. We sponsor it, just by watching at home. We're the reason the N.F.L. will earn $5 billion in television revenue." It is compelling that someone who has enjoyed watching football for as long as Almond has is questioning the morality of supporting the N.F.L. with our viewership. <u>Additionally, researchers at New York University have been studying the long-term effects of repeated head injuries in football concluding that "while players may currently hide their concussions in order to play, they may not be able to hide from them in the future. In a 2009 study at the University of Michigan commissioned by the N.F.L., 6 percent of retired N.F.L. players over the age of 50 had been diagnosed with Alzheimer's, dementia, or another memory-related disease."</u> So, it's not just the broken bones or sprains that we might see during the televised games, but the long-lasting effects on players that should be part of our decisions to watch or not.

Now we have a paragraph that is at least getting closer to having enough evidence with the addition of the research.

If you are writing an analysis rather than an argument, a good rule of thumb is that you should have at least two or three examples from various parts of the text that you are analyzing in each paragraph. If your analysis is focusing on a poet's use of metaphor, for example, it is important to show that the writer employs a pattern, so you will want to point out several uses of metaphor throughout the poem to prove your topic sentence.

ACTIVITY **Examining the Quantity of Your Evidence**

Choose a paragraph from the analysis or argument that you are currently revising. Identify the claim in the paragraph and then highlight the evidence used to support that claim. Show your paragraph to a partner who should tell you whether or not you have included enough evidence to support the claim you made.

Using Varied Evidence

One thing to keep in mind as you are developing the support for your argument is that you want to not only have enough evidence but also varied types of evidence. Let's imagine that we are writing a piece not about football specifically, but about being a fan of something in general. We established that Steve Almond could qualify as an "expert" on his topic because he is a long-time fan of football. However, he does not present much in the way of facts and statistics to prove his point. As a result, we might need to look at other sources to get a variety of types of evidence about the benefits and dangers of being a fan of something like football, a TV show, or a musician or actor. Take a look at some passages from Almond and a few other writers from the Conversation in Chapter 7 (pp. 437–444) about fandom:

> "Just so we're clear on this: I still love football. I love the grace and the poise of the athletes. . . . The problem is that I can no longer indulge these pleasures without feeling complicit."
>
> —Steve Almond, *Is It Immoral to Watch the Superbowl?*

> "Sport fandom — the fact that we follow teams and sports and players — really does impact our emotional state. . . . Some of the biggest pluses that [Dr. Daniel] Wann and now other researchers have found include higher self-esteem; fewer bouts of depression; less alienation; lower levels of loneliness; higher levels of extroversion; higher levels of satisfaction with their social lives; more friends; higher levels of trust in others; more vigor and less fatigue; less anger; less confusion; less tension; greater frequency of experiencing positive emotions; and more conscientiousness."
>
> —Larry Olmsted, *Sports Fans Are Happier People*

> "The interplay between fandom and creators of media can cause a dangerous downward spiral. The bad behavior of one enables the bad behavior of the other, until everyone else just leaves them both for dead. All of it is given a super charge by the ability to use the internet to amplify opinions and target them very specifically. So while this can allow fans to point out flaws that should be fixed, it can also lead to a dangerous amount of vitriol being directed at people who make and act in media."
>
> —Katherine Trendacosta, *When Fandom Is the Problem*

> " 'If the object of adoration does the wrong thing, that iteration can very quickly shift to hostility,' says David Schmid, associate professor of English at the University at Buffalo. Some fans stood by R. Kelly and Michael Jackson after sexual abuse allegations surfaced, for example. But other fans were crushed."
>
> —David Oliver, *Stan Culture Needs to Stop—Or At Least Radically Change. Here's Why.*

Now, let's sort some of this evidence into the different types that we discussed in Chapter 7 (p. 393).

Personal Experience and Anecdotes	Facts and Data/ Statistics	Scholarly Research and Expert Opinion
"Just so we're clear on this: I still love football." (Almond)	"Some of the biggest plusses Wann and now other researchers have found include higher self-esteem; fewer bouts of depression . . ." (Olmsted)	" 'If the object of adoration does the wrong thing, that iteration can very quickly shift to hostility,' says David Schmid, associate professor of English at the University at Buffalo." (Oliver)

A paragraph about fandom will be significantly improved by having more than just one voice and more than one type of evidence from the table above. A well-balanced paragraph will include all of these types of evidence when possible. (Because different assignments, classes, and teachers, have different requirements for citing a source, we have opted not to cite any sources here. For formal guidelines for documenting sources in an English class, see the MLA guidelines in the back of this book.)

This applies mostly to the writing of your own argument. In general, when you are writing a literary or rhetorical analysis, you will focus on a single text, so you probably will not have a variety of types of evidence.

ACTIVITY Using Varied Evidence

Return to the paragraph that you revised in the previous activity. Label each piece of evidence as Personal Experience, Facts and Data/Statistics, or Scholarly Research and Expert Opinion. Do you have a balance of varied types of evidence? What could you add that might provide more variety?

Using Relevant Evidence

So far in this workshop, you have tried to add *more* evidence to a paragraph and you revised it to include a *variety* of evidence. Now it's time to consider how *relevant* your evidence is to your claim. When you are writing an argument, you must avoid simply sprinkling in evidence for support. Every piece of evidence must help prove the claim, and each piece should represent a different point on the issue to move your argument forward.

Let's consider this claim about fandom:

> Fans are complicit in the injuries caused by playing a violent sport like football or the bad behaviors of the subjects of their fandom.

The additional sources we looked at on page 976 all deal with fandom in some way. But which ones help to prove the point about the complicity of fans? Just because the evidence deals with the same topic doesn't guarantee that it is relevant to the point we want to make.

Let's look the paragraph below, and ask ourselves whether the underlined evidence directly relates to the point we're making:

ORIGINAL

> Fans are complicit in the injuries caused by playing a violent sport like football or the bad behaviors of the subjects of their fandom. Steve Almond, a long-time football fan, writes in a piece for the *New York Times* that injuries put "us fans in a morally queasy position. We not only tolerate this brutality. We sponsor it, just by watching at home. We're the reason the N.F.L. will earn $5 billion in television revenue." If even someone who has enjoyed watching football for as long as Almond has questions the morality of supporting the N.F.L. with our viewership, we know we should reconsider our own fandom. Being a fan can also have positive effects: according to Larry Olmsted, "[Dr. Daniel] Wann and now other researchers have found [benefits that] include higher self-esteem [and] fewer bouts of depression." Not everything related to fandom is bad.

Some of the evidence here is relevant, but the summary of the research by Dr. Wann supports fandom rather than highlighting the dark side of fan culture. Unless we intend to present that research as a counterargument that we will address, we might want to find something that better supports our argument. We could return to the original source to see if there is a more relevant quotation to include. Alternatively, we could look for an entirely different source. Look at the following revision, in which we've replaced the evidence of Dr. Wann's research with something more relevant (underlined).

REVISION

Fans are complicit in the injuries caused by playing a violent sport like football or the bad behaviors of the subjects of their fandom. Steve Almond, a long-time football fan, writes in a piece for the *New York Times* that injuries put "us fans in a morally queasy position. We not only tolerate this brutality. We sponsor it, just by watching at home. We're the reason the N.F.L. will earn $5 billion in television revenue." If even someone who has enjoyed watching football for as long as Almond has questions the morality of supporting the N.F.L. with our viewership, we know we should reconsider our own fandom. This also applies to the actions of players off the field with numerous credible accusations of domestic abuse and sexual assaults leveled against the players. As David Schmid, associate professor of English at the University at Buffalo, writes, "If the object of adoration does the wrong thing, that iteration can very quickly shift to hostility. . . . Some fans stood by R. Kelly and Michael Jackson after sexual abuse allegations surfaced, for example. But other fans were crushed." Viewers should not be required to support the bad behavior of those involved or to deny the obvious negative outcomes of watching a violent sport like football.

Notice how the evidence is more directly related to the ideas of complicity than the previous evidence. While this example comes from an argumentative essay, you will ask yourself similar questions about relevance when you are writing a literary or rhetorical analysis essay. Sometimes with literary or rhetorical analysis we think that as long as we are including quotations from the text they should automatically be relevant, but make sure the passages from the text you are analyzing are clearly relevant to what you are hoping to prove in your thesis.

ACTIVITY Using Relevant Evidence

Return to the paragraph that you have been revising throughout this workshop and explain how each piece of your evidence is either relevant or not relevant to your claim, along the lines of what we modeled above. Revise any of the sentences that include evidence that you decide is not relevant.

culminating activity

Appropriate Evidence and Support

Throughout this workshop, you have been working with just one of your body paragraphs. Now, go ahead and look closely at the remaining paragraphs. Highlight each piece of evidence, and ask yourself the following questions:

1. Do I have enough evidence in each paragraph?
2. Do I have a variety of types of evidence in each paragraph?
3. Is each piece of evidence relevant to my claim and the topic sentence?

Receive feedback from a partner about how well you have used evidence in your essay.

workshop 5

Effective Transitions

One of the goals of any piece of writing is clarity. Writers want readers to follow their ideas and understand exactly what they're communicating. When presenting ideas, writers should connect them, creating a train of thought that readers can easily follow. If you think of an actual train, each car is connected with a hook. If one of those hooks is missing or comes undone, the train disconnects and cannot reach its destination intact. Writing is much like that train. All of your ideas need to be linked together so that readers can follow your thinking. We call these links *transitions*. They can be single words, phrases, or sentences that guide readers smoothly and clearly from one point to the next.

In this workshop, you will explore various ways to link your ideas together, creating transitions to provide clarity for your readers. Transitions are necessary in any type of writing, whether it be a single paragraph or a ten-page research paper. Since much of the writing you will be asked to do will be analysis, we will model the use of transitions in an analytical essay about *The Tragedy of Romeo and Juliet* (p. 733), a play by William Shakespeare. Note, however, that the ideas included here can apply easily to an argumentative essay or any other mode of writing. You will choose a piece you are working on to apply the techniques in the activities that follow. The goal is to include meaningful and effective transitions in your writing.

Linking Ideas by Purpose

The goal of this workshop is not to have you start sprinkling transitional words and phrases randomly into your writing. Rather, it is for you to understand when it might make sense to include them to assist your reader. In this section, we will walk you through some of the most common reasons that you might consider integrating transitional words and phrases into your essays.

Showing Support and Drawing Conclusions

Oftentimes in analytical and argumentative writing, you have to demonstrate a connection between your evidence and the way that it supports your position. Key words and phrases for this purpose include the following: *in other words, for one thing, as an illustration, for this reason, notably, including, surely, in general, for example, to emphasize, as can be seen, generally speaking, given these points, as has been noted, for the most part, after all, in fact.*

Look at these examples of how we might connect evidence to our position in an essay about Shakespeare's use of action and dialogue to characterize Mercutio and Tybalt during an ill-fated encounter in Act 3, scene 1. Transition words are underlined.

> Mercutio responds to Tybalt's request to have "a word with one of you" by telling him to "couple it with something: make it a word and a blow." In fact, it is Mercutio who taunts Tybalt even when he appears to be polite. This exchange makes violence almost inevitable.

> Notably, Mercutio is irritated with Romeo's "dishonorable, vile submission" to Tybalt. In a cruel twist of fate, Romeo's unwillingness to fight drives Mercutio's decision to fight.

Showing Cause and Effect

Similar to showing support and drawing conclusions, sometimes in your analytical or argumentative writing, you need to prove that one thing led to another. This might include an example that proves a point you are making about a piece of literature, or that a real-life event caused something else to happen as part of your argument. Key words and phrases for this purpose include the following: *as long as, for the purpose of, since, while, with this in mind, in order to, seeing that, so that, when, because of, due to, as a result, in that case, for this reason, consequently, therefore, accordingly.*

Here are some examples of how we might use transitions (underlined) in a statement of cause and effect while writing about Mercutio and Tybalt:

> Because of Tybalt's aggressive behavior toward Romeo, Mercutio feels the need to step in and defend his friend.

> As a result of his intervention, Mercutio becomes the target of Tybalt's anger.

Showing Similarity or Opposition

Sometimes in your writing you want to show how one example or piece of evidence is similar to or different from another. While this is particularly effective in argumentative writing, these types of transitions can be used for this purpose in a literary analysis essay as well. Key words and phrases for this purpose include the following: *in addition, not to mention, to say nothing of the fact, equally important, by the same token, also, moreover, of course, likewise, similarly, additionally, although this may be true, in contrast, on the other hand, on the contrary, at the same time, in spite of, even so, though, then again, but, unlike, even though, although, instead, however, nevertheless, regardless.*

Here are some examples of how we might use transitions (underlined) to show similarity or opposition:

> Although they are warned about fighting in the streets and both Romeo and Benvolio argue for peace, Mercutio and Tybalt continue the conflict.

> Even though Mercutio is neither a Capulet nor a Montague, he pays the ultimate price as the victim caught between the two feuding families.

Showing Order or Sequence

A final purpose for which you might use transitional words and phrases in your writing is to help readers understand the order or sequence of events either within the text you are analyzing or within your own writing. Key words and phrases for this purpose include the following: *at the present time, from time to time, at the same time, to begin with, as long as, first, second, third . . . , finally, after, until, then, when, once, next.*

The example below demonstrates how we might use transitions (underlined) to show the order of events:

> When Mercutio defends Romeo, he becomes a victim of the feud between the Montagues and the Capulets, though he belongs to neither family.

ACTIVITY Linking Ideas by Purpose

Choose a paragraph from a piece that you are currently working on. Look back through that paragraph and identify one or more of the following purposes that you might be trying to achieve:

- Showing support and drawing a conclusion
- Showing cause and effect
- Showing similarity or opposition
- Showing order or sequence

With those purposes in mind, look closely at the sentences within that paragraph. Do you use any transitional words or phrases to achieve those purposes? If not, add ones from the lists above that might help readers follow your ideas. If you do use some, evaluate how effective they are. Revise any that seem ineffective.

Linking Ideas for Paragraph Coherence

At the beginning of this workshop, we shared the metaphor that transitions are like the links between cars of a train. In the previous section, the transitional words and phrases were mostly about connecting a single train car to another. But what about the whole train? This section of the workshop will focus on looking beyond the sentence level to consider your paragraphs. The next section will focus on the entirety of your essay.

As you likely know from other workshops in this book and other classroom instruction, a solid body paragraph of an analytical or argumentative essay usually consists of three elements: a topic sentence, some evidence, and your commentary about that evidence. Transitions among each of these parts are a great way to build what is called *coherence* within a paragraph, meaning that the paragraph flows logically from sentence to sentence. Most of the effective transitional words and phrases that build coherence are the same as those you examined in the previous section, so it is mostly a matter of perspective. Instead of looking at just one or two sentences for your revision, you should be looking at the whole paragraph to see its flow. Read through the first paragraph that follows. Then compare its coherence with the second one, which has several transitional words and phrases underlined. (Because different assignments, classes, and teachers have different requirements for citing sources, we have opted not to cite any sources here. For formal guidelines for documenting sources in an English class, see the MLA guidelines in the back of this book.)

ORIGINAL

Shakespeare shows through dialogue that Mercutio and Tybalt are characters at odds — one teasing, the other temperamental. They are a volatile mix. The fight scene begins with Tybalt asking to have "a word" and Mercutio immediately offering to "make it a word and a blow." Mercutio has not been directly involved in the conflict. He is not a Montague or a Capulet. He escalates the feud and initiates violence with the Capulets without knowing that Romeo has recently wedded into the family. Mercutio is stabbed and blames Romeo and the feud between the two houses for what has happened to him. Mercutio says "Why the devil came you between us?" and Romeo replies "I thought all for the best." Mercutio begins the fight, but it is Romeo's interference between Mercutio and Tybalt that causes Mercutio's death.

REVISION

In the fight scene in the streets of Verona, Shakespeare shows through the dialogue that Mercutio and Tybalt are characters at odds—one teasing, the other temperamental. They are a volatile mix. The fight scene begins with Tybalt asking to have "a word" and Mercutio immediately offering to "make it a word and a blow." Up to this point, Mercutio has not been directly involved in the conflict. He is not a Montague or a Capulet. And yet, he escalates the feud and initiates violence with the Capulets without knowing that Romeo has recently wedded into the family. As the fight ends and Mercutio is stabbed, he blames Romeo and the feud between the two houses for what has happened to him. Mercutio says "Why the devil came you between us?" and Romeo replies "I thought all for the best." Even though Mercutio begins the fight, it is Romeo's interference between Mercutio and Tybalt that causes Mercutio's death.

To be clear, it is not that the revised paragraph is somehow "better" just because it has *more* transitional words and phrases. In fact, an argument could be made that it actually includes too many. The goal of looking at the paragraphs in this way, however, is to see how the revised paragraph tries to move the reader through the ideas of the paragraph as smoothly and clearly as possible.

> **ACTIVITY** Linking Ideas for Paragraph Coherence
>
> Return to a piece that you are currently working on and choose a paragraph other than the one you selected for the previous activity. Read through the paragraph two or three times, out loud if possible. Consider whether or not the paragraph flows easily and has coherence. Does your reader know when you are shifting to a new idea? Or building on a previous one? Are the examples you use clearly identified as evidence or as conclusions? Ask a partner to read it as well to check for coherence and to make any suggestions for transitional words or phrases that might make it easier to read.

Linking Ideas for Essay Coherence

Now it's time to look at the last aspect of transitions — how a piece of writing flows from paragraph to paragraph within the whole essay. Often we write essays one paragraph at a time, and we might at first forget to connect those paragraphs. A topic sentence is intended to communicate the main idea of a paragraph, but can the first sentence in a paragraph also link to the previous paragraph? And can the last sentence in a paragraph somehow connect to the first one of the next? These are the questions that we're going to consider in this section of the workshop. Instinctively, you know how this works, but you may have seen ineffective approaches. For example, the first body paragraph in an essay might begin with "First," and the second one with "Second" or "Next," and the last body paragraph with "Finally." The idea behind this approach is certainly a good one. It's effective at leading the reader through the ideas of the essay. However, the execution makes the writing sound formulaic and doesn't help readers understand the relationships among paragraphs.

The best way to approach gaining coherence in your overall essay is to focus on the ending of one paragraph and the beginning of the next and employ some of the transitional words and phrases you've been working with throughout this workshop. At the same time, you need to consider how you can connect the paragraphs with similar ideas.

Look at the following sections from a sample essay about how Shakespeare uses dialogue, setting, and stage directions to characterize Mercutio and Tybalt. The first example is the end of a body paragraph on Shakespeare's use of dialogue to emphasize character. Following that, you'll see the beginning of a paragraph on his use of setting.

ORIGINAL

As the fight ends and Mercutio is stabbed, he blames Romeo and the feud between the two houses for what has happened to him. Mercutio says "Why the devil came you between us?" and Romeo replies "I thought all for the best." Even though Mercutio begins the fight, it is Romeo's interference between Mercutio and Tybalt that causes Mercutio's death.

Shakespeare uses setting and stage directions to emphasize the conflict between Mercutio and Tybalt.

There's a topic sentence about Shakespeare's use of setting and stage directions from Act 3, scene 1 that was written as part of a separate paragraph without any thought to how it might fit in with the previous paragraph. If the essay is full of similar paragraphs without transitions between them, it will read like a series of separate, unrelated ideas.

Read the revision below that tries to connect these paragraphs both through the use of a transition and also by connecting with the idea raised at the end of the first body paragraph. The changes are underlined.

REVISION

As the fight ends and Mercutio is stabbed, he blames Romeo and the feud between the two houses for what has happened to him. Mercutio says "Why the devil came you between us?" and Romeo replies "I thought all for the best." Even though Mercutio begins the fight, it is Romeo's interference between Mercutio and Tybalt that causes Mercutio's death.

In addition to building characterization through dialogue, Shakespeare uses setting and stage directions to further emphasize the conflict between Mercutio and Tybalt.

While the topic sentence of the second paragraph remains the same, the addition of the transitional phrase makes for a smoother connection between the two ideas.

ACTIVITY Linking Ideas for Essay Coherence

Return to a piece that you are currently working on and look carefully at the ending of one paragraph and the beginning of another. What can you add to make the flow between them smoother? Can you add a transitional word or phrase? Can you connect the paragraphs through the ideas in each?

---

culminating activity

Effective Transitions

So far in this workshop, you have been working with making connections between ideas and developing coherence within and between paragraphs. Now, it's time to look carefully through your entire essay with the following questions in mind:

1. Have I linked all of my ideas based on their purposes?

2. Do all of my paragraphs have coherence and flow smoothly?

3. Do all of my paragraphs connect to those that come before and after?

Receive feedback from a partner about how well you have used transitional words and phrases in your essay.

---

workshop 6

Effective Syntax

When we are writing, we are often just hoping to communicate our ideas as quickly, efficiently, and clearly as possible. However, we should also strive to write in a way that's memorable, interesting, and varied. For that reason, we should always go back after drafting and revise for syntax — the arrangement of the words in our sentences — that can lead to more effective communication.

In this workshop, you have an opportunity to practice revising your syntax by examining your sentence beginnings, sentence variety, and sentence types. Since much of the writing you do takes the form of analytical essays, we'll model these revision techniques with a sample body paragraph of an essay about a poem called "Let America Be America Again" (p. 548) written by Langston Hughes. Choose at least one paragraph from an essay that you are currently working on to apply these techniques in the activities that follow.

Examining Syntax

The first step in thinking about how to revise your writing for its syntax is to make sure that you have a clear understanding of what's happening in each of your sentences within a paragraph. To get started, read this sample analytical paragraph about the poem "Let America Be America Again." We've numbered each sentence. (Because different assignments, classes, and teachers have different requirements for citing sources, we have opted not to cite any sources here. For formal guidelines for documenting sources in an English class, see the MLA guidelines in the back of this book.)

(1) The speaker in Langston Hughes's poem takes on various personas that are often in conflict with one another. (2) The speaker says that "equality is in the air," but then says "There's never been equality for me." (3) The speaker is conflicted about what America really is and what it should be. (4) The speaker feels this way because of the different ways that America treats its citizens. (5) The speaker eventually states that "I am the poor white . . . the Negro . . . the red man . . . the immigrant." (6) The speaker's broad identification as multiple people allows for Hughes to express how America has betrayed its promises.

This is a perfectly fine paragraph that communicates its ideas about the speaker clearly. However, take a look at this table that identifies aspects of the six sentences in the paragraph:

Sentence #	First Words (Part of Speech)	# of Words	Ending Punctuation	Internal Punctuation
1	The speaker (noun)	21	period	none
2	The speaker (noun)	18	period	none
3	The speaker (noun)	14	period	none
4	The speaker (noun)	15	period	none
5	The speaker (noun)	14	period	ellipses
6	The speaker's (noun)	18	period	none

All six of the sentences in this paragraph begin with "The speaker." While there certainly are times when you might want to repeat a particular sentence structure for a specific effect (called *parallelism*), in this case, the repetition of the exact same sentence beginning is likely to become monotonous for your reader. One of the ways to achieve more lively writing is to avoid repeated words and patterns in your sentences. By examining the paragraph this way, several weaknesses become immediately clear. Not only have we started each sentence with a noun — and often the same word — but each of the sentences is almost the same length and has the same ending punctuation. Only one sentence has internal punctuation, which means that these sentences are almost all the same type.

ACTIVITY Examining Your Syntax

Choose a paragraph from the piece that you are currently revising and fill in a table for it as we did in the preceding example.

Sentence #	First Words (Part of Speech)	# of Words	Ending Punctuation	Internal Punctuation

Then, draw some conclusions about what you notice by considering the following questions:

- Do all or most of your sentences start in a similar way? Do they usually begin with a noun?
- Are your sentences varied in length?

- Do all or most of your sentences end with periods?
- Do your sentences include any semicolons, colons, dashes, or other internal punctuation?
- Overall, how varied is your sentence structure in this paragraph? What changes might make your writing livelier and more varied and engaging?

Varying Sentence Beginnings

We noticed that the first three sentences all begin with "The speaker," which does not sound interesting to the reader. An easy way to break up this pattern would be to use a pronoun instead in sentence #2. And because the speaker is not identified by gender, we will use "he or she," although the nongendered "they" could also work.

ORIGINAL

(1) The speaker in Langston Hughes's poem takes on various personas that are often in conflict with one another. (2) The speaker says that "equality is in the air," but then says, "There's never been equality for me."

REVISION

The speaker in Langston Hughes's poem takes on various personas that are often in conflict with one another. He or she says that "equality is in the air," but then says "There's never been equality for me."

In English, sentences often begin with the subject, as in the sample paragraph. This construction, however, can be varied, so that sentence #3 could instead begin with a phrase that describes the speaker.

ORIGINAL

(1) The speaker in Langston Hughes's poem takes on various personas that are often in conflict with one another. (2) The speaker says that "equality is in the air," but then says, "There's never been equality for me." (3) The speaker is conflicted about what America really is and what it should be.

REVISION

The speaker in Langston Hughes's poem takes on various personas that are often in conflict with one another. He or she says that "equality is in the air," but then says, "There's never been equality for me." Conflicted about what America really is, the speaker hopes for what it could be.

Sometimes sentences need to be combined, to both mix things up and to draw a tight connection between two ideas. Consider the example and revision below, in which the ideas in sentences 4 and 5 are combined.

ORIGINAL

(1) The speaker in Langston Hughes's poem takes on various personas that are often in conflict with one another. (2) The speaker says that "equality is in the air," but then

says "There's never been equality for me." **(3)** The speaker is conflicted about what America really is and what it should be. **(4)** The speaker feels this way because of the different ways that America treats its citizens. **(5)** The speaker eventually states that "I am the poor white . . . the Negro . . . the red man . . . the immigrant." **(6)** The speaker's broad identification as multiple people allows for Hughes to express how America has betrayed its promises.

REVISION

The speaker in Langston Hughes's poem takes on various personas that are often in conflict with one another. He or she says that "equality is in the air," but then says, "There's never been equality for me." Conflicted about what America really is, the speaker hopes for what it could be. The speaker feels this way because of the different ways that America treats its citizens identifying that "I am the poor white . . . the Negro . . . the red man . . . the immigrant."

As you look at the revised paragraph above, you'll see that now only two sentences begin with "The speaker . . ." The point of this exercise is not to alter every sentence, but rather to become more aware of how your sentence structures can affect your readers.

> **ACTIVITY** Sentence Beginnings
>
> Look back at the paragraph that you analyzed with the table earlier and revise two or more of the sentences by varying how some of them start. Show your revision to a partner to see if your changes are more effective than your original.

Varying Sentence Lengths

All of the sentences in the original sample paragraph on page 985 were between fourteen and twenty-one words, which can feel monotonous for readers. Varying sentence lengths keeps your readers' attention and guides their understanding of your ideas. Short sentences, for example, can create a sense of urgency or punch to emphasize an idea, whereas longer sentences may feel smooth and flowing and allow you to develop complex ideas. If you are familiar with music, you might think of short sentences as being staccato, while long sentences are legato. Often, writers will use changes in sentence length or sentence types to create rhythmic effects. The most common is to follow a series of long sentences with a short one to create impact. However, the pattern can work the other way as well.

Notice the impact of this technique in the following excerpt from Jane Austen's *Pride and Prejudice*:

> Mr. Bennet was so odd a mixture of quick parts, sarcastic humor, reserve, and caprice, that the experience of three-and-twenty years had been insufficient to make his wife understand his character. Her mind was less difficult to develop. She was a woman of mean understanding, little information, and uncertain temper.

The suddenness of the short length of the second sentence, especially in contrast to the very long sentence that precedes it, emphasizes the differences between the two characters. Again, think about the effect of writing with this type of varied syntax. You are able to communicate information to your readers not only with the words you select but also with the length of the sentences in your writing.

Let's look back at the model paragraph we've been revising, and notice what happens when we add a short sentence in the middle of the paragraph during revision.

ORIGINAL

The speaker in Langston Hughes's poem takes on various personas that are often in conflict with one another. He or she says that "equality is in the air," but then says, "There's never been equality for me." Conflicted about what America really is, the speaker hopes for what it could be. The speaker feels this way because of the different ways that America treats its citizens identifying that "I am the poor white . . . the Negro . . . the red man . . . the immigrant."

REVISION

The speaker in Langston Hughes's poem takes on various personas of the speaker that are often in conflict with one another. He or she says that "equality is in the air," but then says, "There's never been equality for me." America falls short. Conflicted about what America really is, the speaker hopes for what it could be. The speaker feels this way because of the different ways that America treats its citizens identifying that "I am the poor white . . . the Negro . . . the red man . . . the immigrant."

Not only does this additional short sentence break up the pattern of roughly the same number of words in each sentence, but its shortness directs the reader to the impact of the conflicting views of America.

> **ACTIVITY** Varying Your Sentence Length
>
> Return to the piece that you are revising (and maybe to the paragraph that you created a table for earlier) to see if there are places where you can revise your sentence length to add variety or create a specific effect for your reader, as in the example above. Show your revision to a partner to see if your changes are more effective than your original.

Varying Sentence Types

As you saw in the table of the example paragraph earlier, all of the sentences ended with a period, so all are what we call *declarative* sentences. You can, however, also create syntactical variety by asking questions in your writing, which would end with a question mark. You can show emphasis by using an exclamation point (though this is not regularly used in academic, expository writing). As you may have seen in Chapter 3 on writing (pp. 75–77), all of the sentences in the sample paragraph are what we call *simple* sentences. A goal for your writing, as you become more advanced in your skills, is to try for variety in the types of sentences you construct.

- **Simple sentences** can grab the reader's attention or provide information in a direct way. If you use too many, however, your writing can come across as amateurish, choppy, or bland. A simple sentence contains one independent clause. An independent clause is a group of words that contains a subject and verb. It's called *independent* because it can stand by itself and still make sense.

- **Compound sentences** can be used to emphasize balance, to compare or contrast ideas, convey cause-effect relationships, or group similar ideas together. Compound sentences contain two independent clauses joined by a comma and a conjunction or by a semicolon alone.
- **Complex** sentences also can emphasize balance, but they contain an independent clause and one or more dependent clauses. A dependent clause is a clause that does not make sense when it stands alone.

When you are thinking about varying your sentence types, you should consider where you can ask questions or use exclamation points (if appropriate for your purpose and audience), and when you can use internal punctuation to form compound or complex sentences. In the original below, which has already been revised for sentence beginnings and length, most of the sentences are simple sentences. Look at how much livelier and more engaging the writing is when we have taken the time to vary the types of sentences we use.

ORIGINAL

(1) The speaker in Langston Hughes's poem takes on various personas that are often in conflict with one another. **(2)** The speaker says that "equality is in the air," but then says "There's never been equality for me." **(3)** The speaker is conflicted about what America really is and what it should be. **(4)** The speaker feels this way because of the different ways that America treats its citizens. **(5)** The speaker eventually states that "I am the poor white . . . the Negro . . . the red man . . . the immigrant." **(6)** The speaker's broad identification as multiple people allows for Hughes to express how America has betrayed its promises.

REVISION

The speaker in Langston Hughes's poem takes on various personas that are often in conflict with one another; he or she says that "equality is in the air," but then says, "There's never been equality for me." The speaker is conflicted about what America really is and what it should be because of the different ways that America treats its citizens. America is not the same for everyone. When the speaker broadly identifies with all Americans, stating that "I am the poor white . . . the Negro . . . the red man . . . the immigrant," this allows for Hughes to express how America has betrayed its promises.

ACTIVITY Sentence Types

Return to the piece that you are revising, or the paragraph that you created a table for earlier and identify all of the simple sentences you used. Then, revise one or more of those simple sentences into a compound or a complex sentence. Show your revision to a partner to see if your changes are more effective than your original and if you have constructed your sentences properly.

culminating activity

Effective Syntax

Return to the essay you have been revising and choose a paragraph you have not yet revised in this workshop. Then, follow these directions:

1. Fill in a table about your sentences like you did earlier on page 985.

2. Revise the paragraph by applying all three of the elements you've explored: beginnings, lengths, and type. Be sure that you are making the changes that reflect how you want to communicate your ideas; don't change just for the sake of change.

3. Show it to a partner to reflect on how the changes in sentence variety affect the reader and make your writing more engaging and lively.

workshop 7

Effective Diction

As you probably already know, *diction* refers to word choice. Choosing words appropriate to your particular type of writing and your audience is key. For example, in writing a scientific lab report, you would choose words that are accurate rather than creative. In writing a personal narrative, on the other hand, you would have more freedom to choose words that build imagery and stimulate the imagination.

There are a few basic rules that generally apply to all good writing when it comes to diction. How important it is to follow these rules, or how frequently you might be able to bend or ignore them, depends on the context for your writing, including your purpose and audience.

In this workshop, we'll demonstrate various ways of considering diction in an argument, literary analysis, or rhetorical analysis. And throughout, you will return to a piece that you are currently working on to look for places where you can revise your diction.

Considering Your Audience and Purpose

The first things you should consider when you are thinking about diction are the audience and purpose for your writing. As you are already aware, your word choice in a text message to a friend is different from your word choice in an essay for your English class. Part of the difference stems from the level of formality. When you are writing a piece for school, you are generally expected to take on a scholarly, academic voice. However, when you are writing a text to a friend, you can be more informal, likely including slang, abbreviations, and emojis, most of which would seem out of place in a rhetorical analysis essay. If you were writing a piece of fiction or a narrative for English class, your diction would probably include vivid details and description that would seem out of place in a lab report for science class. The latter writing would instead include scientific terms and measurements that are appropriate to that purpose.

In the case of an analytical or argumentative essay, your level of formality might be high, but your writing should still be interesting. Your purpose is to persuade your audience that your interpretation of a text or your position on an issue is a sound one, so you should use strong verbs and detailed descriptions whenever possible to engage and persuade your audience. Look, for instance, at the following section from a narrative by Julia Alvarez called "La Gringuita" (p. 177), in which Alvarez describes what it was like to return to the Dominican Republic to see her family:

> My parents, anxious that we not lose our tie to our native land, and no doubt thinking of future husbands for their four daughters, began sending us "home" every summer to Mami's family in the capital. And just as we had once huddled in the school playground, speaking Spanish for the comfort of it, my sisters and I now hung out together in "the D.R.," as we referred to it, kibitzing in English on the crazy world around us: the silly rules for girls, the obnoxious behavior of macho guys, the deplorable situation of the poor. My aunts and uncles tried unsuccessfully to stem this tide of our Americanization, whose main expression was, of course, our use of the English language. "Tienen que hablar en espanol," they commanded. "Ay, come on," we would say as if we had been asked to go back to baby talk as grown-ups.

In this passage, Alvarez uses highly charged and emotional words to describe the challenges of communication and the differences between the American and Dominican cultures, such as *silly*, *obnoxious*, and *deplorable*.

While you might not have the opportunity to use quite such powerfully descriptive diction when you are writing a literary or rhetorical analysis, you can still include words that make it clear that your interpretation is an accurate one. For instance, here is an introductory paragraph of an analysis of Alvarez's narrative. Note that there is a clear purpose to draw the reader into this essay through engaging diction:

> What does "home" mean? People who have moved away from where they grew up often continue to refer to that place as "home," even after years away. But can we really ever truly be at "home" if we have lost the language and the culture of our birth? In the narrative "La Gringuita," author Julia Alvarez tries to answer these questions. With emotional and descriptive language, she develops a searching and yearning tone toward the lost language and culture of her native country, the Dominican Republic.

ACTIVITY Considering Your Audience and Purpose

Look back at the piece you are currently revising. Who is your intended audience? What is your purpose? How do your audience and purpose affect your diction? Look closely at one paragraph of your piece for words or phrases that seem appropriate for your audience and purpose. Do you notice any that seem inappropriate because of their level of formality or for other reasons?

Keeping Connotation in Mind

Now that you have thought about how your word choice needs to reflect your audience and purpose, the next element to consider is the emotional impact that your diction might have on your reader. You may have already learned that the "denotation" of a word is its dictionary definition, whereas its "connotation" extends that literal meaning to include the feelings associated with that particular word.

Look, for instance, at another description that Alvarez offers about how she is treated by her family in the Dominican Republic:

> They treated me like a ten-year-old, or so I thought, monitoring phone calls, not allowing male visitors, explaining their <u>carefulness</u> by reminding me that my parents had entrusted them with <u>my person</u> and they wanted to return me in the same condition in which I had arrived. Out there in <u>the boonies, the old-world traditions</u> had been preserved full strength. But I can't help thinking that in part, Utcho and Betty treated me like a ten-year-old because I <u>talked like a ten-year-old</u> in my halting, childhood Spanish. I couldn't explain about women's liberation and the quality of mercy not being strained, in Spanish.

Although narrative and fiction writing give you more freedom with word choice, you can still be creative when making effective diction choices in more formal academic writing, such as literary or rhetorical analysis. Look, for instance, at these two paragraphs of an analysis of Alvarez's narrative; the second one includes words and phrases underlined for their diction.

ORIGINAL

Alvarez uses descriptive language to reveal a longing for home, but her tone toward the language and culture gap she feels when visiting the Dominican Republic is also conflicted. Toward the end of the narrative, she describes a date with a local boy, who cannot understand what she is trying to say about the stars they are looking at: "From this tropical perspective, the stars seemed to form different constellations in the night sky. Even the Big Dipper, which was so easy to spot in New England, seemed to be misplaced here. Tonight, it lay on its side, right above us." But she cannot get him to understand their differences.

REVISION

Alvarez uses descriptive language to reveal a longing for home, but her tone toward the language and culture gap she feels when visiting the Dominican Republic is also conflicted. Toward the end of the narrative, she <u>agonizingly</u> recounts a date with a local boy, who cannot understand what she is trying to say about the stars they are looking at: "From this tropical perspective, the stars seemed to form different constellations in the night sky. Even the Big Dipper, which was so easy to spot in New England, seemed to be misplaced here. Tonight, it lay on its side, right above us." <u>Frustrated and demoralized</u>, she cannot get him to understand their differences.

Compare the emotional qualities of the original word *describes* with "agonizingly recounts" in the revision. Both are accurate, but the new diction conveys urgency and a clear idea about how the writer is interpreting Alvarez's choices. There are many words at your disposal when writing a literary or rhetorical analysis rather than words like *says*, *includes*, or *describes* to characterize what an author might be doing in a text. Consider words like these: *argues, believes, reports, suggests, claims, advocates, supports, condemns, observes, concedes, recommends, asserts.*

> **ACTIVITY** Keeping Connotation in Mind
>
> Go back into one paragraph of the essay that you are currently revising. Look closely at your diction. Are there words that you could change so that they include more emotional associations? Or words that could make your analysis of a text clearer and livelier? Be sure to keep your audience and purpose in mind as you make any changes.

Being Concise

Stating your ideas without a lot of extra words can make your writing stronger and clearer. It's called being *concise*. Here are some examples of wordiness, along with some ways that you can trim them for conciseness:

Wordy Diction	Concise Diction
because of the fact that	since
at that point	when, then
all of a sudden	suddenly
in order to	to
has the ability to	can

Some phrases are just filler and you might want to consider cutting them altogether. Oftentimes, no meaning is lost when they are cut from your writing. They can be the writing equivalent of saying "ummm." Here are some examples related to the sample analysis we've been looking at. In each case, the underlined wordy phrase could likely be deleted without loss of meaning.

The point I'm trying to make is that Alvarez is too dismissive of her Dominican family's culture.

The fact of the matter is everyone feels a little out of place sometimes.

The thing is that Alvarez tries to communicate a sense of loneliness and frustration.

For all intents and purposes, Alvarez makes an essential point about the ways that culture and language can be so easily lost.

It is important to note that not all people feel the same way that Alvarez does.

> **ACTIVITY** Being Concise
>
> Look carefully at one paragraph of the piece you are currently revising and try to identify places where your language might be a little wordy. Revise those sentences to make the language more concise without sacrificing meaning. Show your paragraph to a partner to see if together you can identify any additional wordiness.

Effective Diction

Throughout this workshop, you have been looking closely at a single paragraph from the essay you are currently revising. Now, spend some time with the rest of your piece and examine its diction. Working with a partner, consider the following:

1. Is your diction appropriate for your audience and purpose?
2. Do you include words with the most effective connotations?
3. Have you revised words or phrases for conciseness?

workshop 8

Effective Introductions and Conclusions

Introductions and conclusions can be the hardest parts of an essay to write. It's difficult to know where to begin and how to conclude without repeating yourself. What makes things a bit easier is knowing the purpose of both of these pieces and remembering that they don't have to be perfect the first time. Draft something and then revise to strengthen it.

In this workshop, we will be modeling introductory and concluding paragraphs of an analysis essay on "How One Stupid Tweet Blew Up Justine Sacco's Life" by Jon Ronson (p. 651). We will focus specifically on how to start this essay in an engaging way and wrap it up in a satisfying manner. And even though the model here is an analysis essay, the advice is relevant to the revision of an argument essay as well.

Revising Introductions

As you likely remember from the Writing Workshops in this book, most introductions have three pieces:

a. The hook
b. The context
c. The claim (thesis)

For this Revision Workshop, we will focus on the hook and the context, because Revision Workshop 1 covers the claim or thesis in detail.

Effective Hooks

The hook is how you grab your reader's attention. It could be an interesting anecdote, a relevant quotation, a startling statistic, or an observation or question. The hook isn't just there for shock value; it has to be relevant to your thesis and your argument as a whole. The hook should be intriguing; it should make readers want to read further in your essay. Let's take a look at some examples of different types of hooks that come from various pieces in this book.

PROVOCATIVE STATEMENT

Common sense, as a general idea, seems easy to define. But when it comes to the time that middle and high school students start school in most places across the United States, the education community has been doing it wrong — with numerous, hard-to-ignore studies, sleep experts, and national organizations rightly blasting the negative impact on adolescents to begin class around 7:30 A.M.

— David Polochanin, *We Already Know School Starts Too Early.*
It's Time to Do Something About It

INTRIGUING QUOTATION

"The level of alarm is extremely high," said the head of the World Health Organization on Thursday, describing the spread of Zika virus around the world.

— Daniel Engber, *Let's Kill All the Mosquitoes*

RHETORICAL QUESTION

What would happen to our planet if the mighty hand of humanity simply disappeared?

— Alan Weisman, from *Earth without People*

INSIGHTFUL OBSERVATION

I am a refugee, an American, and a human being, which is important to proclaim, as there are many who think these identities cannot be reconciled.

— Viet Thanh Nguyen, *On Being a Refugee,*
an American — and a Human Being

STARTLING STATISTIC

The alarming rate of bullying, homelessness, HIV and suicide among LGBT youth should be an outrage: Nearly a fifth of students are physically assaulted because they are LGBT; among homeless children, 25 to 50 percent are LGBT; the CDC reports among youth aged 13 to 24 diagnosed with HIV in 2014, 80 percent were gay and bisexual males; and gay teens are also eight times more likely to report having attempted suicide.

— Cirri Nottage, *The Case for LGBT-Inclusive Education*

Now that we have a wide variety of types of hooks to choose from, let's look at a few possible hooks we might use for our rhetorical analysis of Ronson's argument, based on this thesis statement:

> In "How One Stupid Tweet Blew Up Justine Sacco's Life," Jon Ronson draws evidence from Justine Sacco's and others' online experiences to emphasize the aftermath of being publicly humiliated on social media.

WEAK HOOK

> Like many on social media, Sacco had to deal with the repercussions of her tweet.

This is a bland general statement and a little too obvious. A general statement can still be intriguing, surprising, establish common ground, or otherwise draw the reader in. This particular general point, however, does not do any of those things. Let's examine another.

WEAK HOOK

> Being publicly humiliated on social media can have long-lasting effects on all those involved.

While the instinct to begin an essay with something broad like this is not necessarily bad, the statement needs to be interesting. Very few people would object to this statement, so it is not particularly engaging. Let's try again with a hook that will grab our readers' interest and get them to think.

STRONG HOOK

Online mobs and critics can be powerful. On one hand, they can force appropriate justice and change; on the other hand, they can destroy people's lives.

When you read this hook, you immediately start asking questions. *Where does the power come from? How is it used or misused? In what ways can it destroy lives?* There are many ways to write a good hook, but if your hook gets your audience to start asking questions, that means they are curious and engaged. That's a good start.

ACTIVITY Revising Your Hook

Return to the piece you are revising. Try out two or three of the approaches listed above for a hook. Which ones do you like best? Are any of them overly broad? Are they clichés? Do they connect to the thesis? Do they get the reader to ask questions and wonder about the topic? Now, choose one that you think is most effective and add it to the piece you are working on.

Providing Context and Making a Connection

Once you have a hook, you need to build a bridge between it and your thesis or your claim, if you are writing an argument essay. Since your hook is likely to be a statement not specifically about the text that you're analyzing or the position you take on an issue, you need to provide context to show how your general statement relates to the text. In short, you need to build a connection to the text being analyzed. In addition to building a bridge, this context section generally includes the background information the reader needs to understand the thesis or claim that follows.

For instance, the example hook that we selected in the previous section refers to online shaming. So part of the work this context statement needs to do is to move us from the idea of online shaming to how Ronson emphasizes its effects on the lives of those who experienced it in "How One Stupid Tweet Blew Up Justine Sacco's Life." Let's try it:

Hook — Online mobs and critics can be powerful. On one hand, they can force appropriate justice and change; on the other hand, they can destroy people's lives. Such was the case for Justine Sacco who, like many others,

Context — became the target of online hate mobs and critics after posting a thoughtless tweet. In "How One Stupid Tweet Blew Up Justine Sacco's

Thesis — Life," Jon Ronson draws evidence from Justine Sacco's and others' online experiences to emphasize the aftermath of being publicly humiliated on social media.

If you are writing an argument rather than an analysis, the format of your introduction will be similar, but you will have to be sure that you define any key terms readers will need for understanding your ideas.

> **ACTIVITY** Context and Connection
>
> Return to the piece you are revising and analyze your introductory paragraph. Highlight the hook in one color and the thesis in another. Label the remaining sentences as context and connection. Then, ask yourself the following questions:
>
> - Are any of my sentences unlabeled? If so, do they belong in my introduction?
> - Does my context provide all the information my readers need before they begin reading my essay?
> - Is my connection smooth?
>
> Based on your responses to these questions, revise your introduction in order to strengthen it.

Writing a Conclusion

Conclusions are tricky. You need to wrap up your essay, but just summarizing your argument or analysis is, frankly, boring. You need to do more than just summarize, but what? Ideally, your conclusion should answer this question: "So what?" If you're writing a persuasive argument, this question is oftentimes easy to answer. Your conclusion might include a call to action, or you might want to leave your readers with a lasting impression that could change how they think about the issue. In some cases, a return to pathos, the emotional core of an argument, is a great ending: a story or image that tugs again at your reader's heart.

In an academic analysis, this question might be asking why your argument is important to the world. On the other hand, it could just be asking why the analysis is important for understanding the text. Your conclusion is your opportunity to present a deeper understanding of the topic, or to talk about its significance. Let's look at a conclusion for our sample Ronson essay:

> In a way, Ronson blames the social media platform itself, pointing out that even Sacco realizes that the public shaming was not just about her. By design, social media platforms continuously reward people for the number of likes and retweets they receive, further motivating them to continue the onslaught of attacks. According to Ronson, Sacco's experience had more to do with society's insatiable appetite for tormenting strangers and the social media incentives for doing so. Perhaps, however, the stories and examples Ronson shares can change how these social platforms influence behaviors and can help us to remember that at the other end of that tweet, that post, that online comment, is a real human being and that our digital entertainment should not come at a cost to others.

This conclusion makes a few different moves. The first sentence sets up the "So what?" by presenting an alternative — that it's not just the person, but the platform that is at issue. The conclusion stresses the importance of Ronson's use of stories and examples from those who have experienced online shaming. Why is it important? Because sharing these stories could change the way others behave in online environments. The conclusion ends with a call to action of sorts: let's learn from the experiences of those presented here and apply what we've learned to our own online behavior. Finally, this conclusion makes another clever move, which is that it refers back to the hook. That sort of "book-ending," as it's sometimes called, gives a satisfying sense that the analysis has come full circle. Even a conclusion of an analytical essay can be a place of some rhetorical flourish and make your reader glad to have made it to the end of your piece.

ACTIVITY Revising Your Conclusion

Return to the essay you are revising and look at your conclusion. Ask yourself the following questions:

- Does my conclusion summarize my findings?
- Does my conclusion answer the question, "So what?"
- Does my conclusion have a call to action?
- Does my conclusion demonstrate a deeper understanding of the topic?

If you answered "yes" to only the first question, return to your conclusion and try to revise it using one or two of the strategies found in this list.

---

culminating activity

Effective Introductions and Conclusions

Now that you have revised both your introduction and your conclusion, it's time to read them together to see how they fit with each other. Ideally, these two parts should work in tandem, maybe with the introduction raising a question that the conclusion answers or expands on. Or maybe they both include a quotation by the same person. Perhaps the statistics raised in both parts of the essay complement each other. Take this opportunity to bring your introduction and your conclusion together in a way that is satisfying and memorable to the reader.

Guide to Useful Terms and Concepts for Understanding Grammar

Term	Definition	Example
active voice	active voice verbs show that the subject of the sentence does the action	We made a mistake.
adjective	a word that modifies a noun or pronoun; adjectives often answer questions such as *which? how many? what kind?*	Mr. Everett scolded the two rowdy children.
adverb	a word that modifies a verb, an adjective, another adverb, or a clause; adverbs often answer the questions *where? when? how? why? to what extent? under what conditions?*	His gratingly loud voice always bothered me, but it was especially bad in the park.
antecedent	the noun, pronoun, or phrase that a pronoun refers to	The contestant who answers the most questions correctly will win the jackpot. (pronoun *who* refers to antecedent *contestant*)
clause	a group of words that includes a subject and a verb	My grandmother made a cake. (*independent clause*) You are wonderful. (*independent clause*) Because we liked the movie (*dependent clause*)
collective noun	a noun that indicates a group or collection of people or things: *team, group, committee, audience, bunch*	The team threw up its hands.
comparative	a form of an adjective or adverb used to compare two things; many adjectives form the comparative with *-er*, and many adverbs form the comparative with *more*	My brother is taller than I am. She works more quickly than Jack does.

(continued)

Guide to Useful Terms and Concepts for Understanding Grammar

compound noun	two or more nouns joined with *and*, *or*, or *nor*	Neither Juan nor his brothers took the class.
		The drummer and the bassist kept the beat.
coordinating conjunction	a word that connects words, phrases, or clauses of equal importance: *for, and, nor, but, or, yet, so*	The girl laughed, but her mother got angry.
correlative conjunction	a two-part conjunction (*either . . . or, both . . . and, neither . . . nor, not only . . . but also, just as . . . so, whether . . . or*)	Whether the guests arrive or not, the birthday party will happen tomorrow.
helping verb	a form of *be* or *have* or other verbs (*will, would, can, could, should, may, might, must*) that work along with a main verb	I am going home. You may need help. They have been friends for years. He had not started the project.
indefinite pronoun	a pronoun that does not refer to specific people or things: *everyone, someone, everything, anything, nothing, either, none, all, much*	Everyone loves tacos.
independent clause	a clause with both a subject and verb; a clause that does not include a subordinating conjunction	Both boys will arrive on time.
intransitive verb	a verb that does not take an object	Go over there and lie down.
irregular verb	a verb that does not follow a regular pattern; most irregular verbs are irregular in the past tense form and/or in the past participle form, but some common verbs (*be* and *have*) are also irregular in the present tense	We shook hands. (irregular past tense form; a regular verb would add *-d* or *-ed*) We have shaken hands. (irregular past participle form; a regular verb would add *-d* or *-ed*) I am hungry. (irregular first person present tense form; a regular verb would use the base form) He has your address. (irregular third person present tense form; a regular verb would add *-s*)
linking verb	a verb that indicates a state of being, rather than an action; linking verbs do not take objects, but are followed by subject complements that take an adjective form: *be, look, appear, seem, feel, sound, smell*	The soup smelled good. You seem angry. We feel terrible about the misunderstanding. She is correct.

Guide to Useful Terms and Concepts for Understanding Grammar

noun	a word that names a person, place, thing, or idea	The <u>children</u> sulked as their <u>father</u> fed them <u>vegetables</u>. <u>Anger</u> is bad for your <u>health</u>.
noun phrase	a phrase that functions as a noun in a sentence	<u>Imagining possibilities</u> is my job. (The phrase *imagining possibilities* acts as a noun and serves as the subject of the sentence.)
number	singular or plural verb	He <u>eats</u> pasta. (verb agrees with singular subject) They <u>eat</u> their vegetables. (verb agrees with plural subject)
object	the noun or pronoun (or noun phrase or clause) that receives the action of a transitive verb	She sent a <u>package</u>.
passive voice	passive voice verbs show that the subject of the sentence is being acted on; passive voice uses a form of the helping verb *be* plus a past participle	A mistake <u>was made</u>.
past participle form	the form of a verb, usually ending in *-ed*, used with a helping verb to form perfect tenses	They have <u>been</u> friends for years. (*have been* is a present perfect verb phrase) He had not <u>started</u> the project. (*had . . . started* is a past perfect verb phrase)
person	first person (*I, we*), second person (*you*), or third person (*he, she, it, they*) point of view	I <u>am</u> watching you. (verb agrees with first person subject) You <u>have</u> my attention. (verb agrees with second person subject) She <u>plays</u> remarkably well. (verb agrees with third person subject)
phrase	a group of words that lacks a subject, a verb, or both	without a care in the world
present participle	the form of a verb, usually ending in *-ing*, used with a helping verb to form continuous tenses	He is <u>thinking</u> of a song he used to know.
pronoun	a word that stands in for a noun, another pronoun, a noun clause, or a noun phrase: *I, me, you, he, she, it, him, her, we, us, they, them*	We were best friends until <u>she</u> moved and <u>we</u> lost touch.
relative pronoun	*who, which, that* used as the subject of a dependent clause, with the antecedent in another clause	The contestant <u>who</u> answers the most questions correctly will win the jackpot. (relative pronoun begins the dependent clause "who answers the most questions correctly")

(continued)

Guide to Useful Terms and Concepts for Understanding Grammar

subject	part of a sentence or clause that tells who or what is doing an action, occurring, or existing; an essential part of a clause or sentence	<u>My grandmother</u> made a cake. <u>You</u> are wonderful. <u>Both boys</u> will arrive on time.
subject complement	an adjective that follows a linking verb and describes the subject of a sentence	The soup smelled <u>good</u>. (*good* describes *the soup*) You seem <u>angry</u>. (*angry* describes *you*) We feel <u>terrible</u> about the misunderstanding. (*terrible* describes *we*) She is <u>correct</u>. (*correct* describes *she*)
subordinate clause (also called dependent clause)	a clause that includes a subordinating conjunction; a clause that cannot stand alone	Because we liked the movie (*Because* is a subordinating conjunction)
subordinating conjunction	a connecting word that makes a clause dependent (unable to stand alone): *after, although, because, before, if, even if, since, unless, until, when, while*	<u>After</u> you ate lunch <u>Because</u> we liked the movie <u>Until</u> the light turned green
superlative	a form of an adjective or adverb used to compare more than two things; many adjectives form the superlative with *-est,* and many adverbs form the superlative with *most*	Dan is the <u>tallest</u> person on the team. Of all the employees, Rashida writes <u>most effectively</u>.
transitive verb	a verb that takes an object	We <u>made</u> a mistake. (the verb *make* is transitive; the object, *mistake*, shows what is made)
verb	an action, state, or occurrence; an essential part of a clause or sentence	My cousin <u>made</u> a cake. You <u>are</u> wonderful. Both boys <u>will arrive</u> on time.
verbal	words that are made of verb forms but do not function as verbs	<u>Driving</u> makes me nervous. <u>To sleep</u> late was a treat.
verb tense	verb tense shows whether the verb's action or state happened or will happen in the past, present, or future; tenses include past, past perfect, present, present perfect, future, and future perfect	*past:* You <u>wanted</u> a car. *past perfect:* You <u>had wanted</u> a car for years when you finally <u>got</u> one. *present:* You <u>want</u> a car. *perfect:* You <u>have wanted</u> a car for years. *future:* You <u>will want</u> a car someday. *future perfect:* You <u>will have wanted</u> a car for years when you finally get one.

workshop 1

Active and Passive Voice

Understanding Active and Passive Voice

The voice of a verb indicates whether the subject of a sentence is acting or being acted on.

For definitions and examples of grammar concepts—key to understanding active and passive voice—see the **Guide to Grammar Terms** *table on pages 999–1002.*

Active Voice

Active voice means that the subject of the sentence is doing the action.

> The guidance counselor advised him to take challenging classes.

The subject is *guidance counselor,* the verb is *advised,* and the object is *him.* The guidance counselor is doing the advising, so the sentence is in the active voice.

Passive Voice

Passive voice means that the subject is being acted on by someone or something. A passive voice verb phrase includes a form of *be* plus a past participle.

> He was advised to take challenging classes.

The subject is *he,* and the verb is *was advised.* This sentence doesn't say who was doing the advising; if it did, it would say something like this: *The guidance counselor advised him to take challenging classes.*

Revising Inappropriate Passive Voice

Passive voice is not always wrong. However, when it is used inappropriately, it can make sentences vague. In general, you should use the active voice in academic writing, because it clearly indicates who is doing what, and because it makes the prose more immediate.

> INAPPROPRIATE PASSIVE VOICE
> The championship will be won by us.

The performer of the action should be the subject of this sentence unless the writer has a good reason to emphasize the championship and de-emphasize those who will win it.

To change passive voice to active voice, identify the doer of the action. If it is a pronoun, as in this case, change it from an object form (*me, her, us, them,* and so on) to a subject form (*I, she, we, they,* and so on). Make the doer the subject of the sentence and change the verb from the passive form (a form of *be* plus a past participle) to the active form in the same tense.

> ACTIVE VOICE
> We will win the championship.

Breaking the Rule: Uses of the Passive Voice

Note that the passive voice is useful in some circumstances, such as when you don't know who did the action or when you want to emphasize the recipient of the action rather than the doer.

> APPROPRIATE PASSIVE VOICE
> Several seniors were swindled out of their savings.

Those doing the swindling may be unknown, or the writer may want to focus attention on the seniors who were tricked — or both. The passive voice is appropriate in either case.

You may see the passive voice used in some kinds of professional writing. In journalism, for example, the passive voice emphasizes the recipient of the action, who may be more newsworthy than the doer of the action.

> APPROPRIATE PASSIVE VOICE
> John McCain was first elected to the Senate in 1986.

The writer wants to emphasize the senator rather than the voters who elected him. In addition, using the passive voice is expected or even required in much scientific and technical writing.

APPROPRIATE PASSIVE VOICE

Study participants were asked to describe what they had seen.

Although the active voice often produces more energetic writing, you can use the passive voice if it is conventional for the type of writing you are doing or if it helps you achieve appropriate emphasis or another desired effect.

ACTIVITY 1 Identifying Passive and Active Voice

In the following sentences, underline the complete subject and double-underline the verb or verb phrase. Then, identify whether the sentence is in the active voice or the passive voice.

EXAMPLE: The children were sitting listlessly under the only tree on the playground. *Active*

1. According to scientists, bird populations are declining in North America.
2. The players were discouraged by a string of defeats.
3. After the accident, recommendations were made for improving safety at the intersection.
4. Servers are expected to report their tips.
5. The guidance counselor will be conducting a workshop on college applications this afternoon.

ACTIVITY 2 Changing Passive Voice to Active Voice

In each of the following sentences, change any passive-voice constructions to active voice.

EXAMPLE: As I jogged around the lake at dawn, the attention of a stray dog was attracted by the sound of my footsteps.

REVISION: *As I jogged around the lake at dawn, the sound of my footsteps attracted the attention of a stray dog.*

1. When the pigeons were startled by a barking dog, the whole flock ascended from the parking lot with loudly flapping wings.
   REVISION: _____

2. The bridge was weakened by the rushing flood waters that came with the spring thaw.
   REVISION: _____

3. Mistakes were admitted by the police officers during the press conference, but the crowd did not think the apology went far enough.
   REVISION: _____

4. The dessert appeared after a spectacular banquet had been served by our hosts.
   REVISION: _____

5. Free tickets were being given by the promoters to anyone who had a valid student ID.
   REVISION: _____

ACTIVITY 3 Revising a Paragraph for More Effective Use of Passive and Active Voice

The following paragraph, written for a general audience, includes some inappropriate use of the passive voice. Revise the paragraph to make more effective use of active voice. Note that not all sentences require revision. Be prepared to explain why you decided to make any change.

Cats have long been seen as aloof and uninterested in human companionship. Even cat lovers may believe that cats are motivated more by a desire for food than by an interest in social interaction when they seek out human beings. But it has been suggested by several recent studies that cats do, in fact, bond with human companions. Cats domesticated themselves in prehistoric times—unlike dogs, who were intentionally domesticated by humans. Could it be that cats actually like to spend time with people, or that at least some cats like to be around some people some of the time? The answer given by scientists who study cats is a clear "yes." In one study, cats were brought to an unfamiliar place by their owners, and then the cats were left alone for a while to look around. When the owners returned, a majority of the cats acknowledged the familiar humans right away and then continued investigating the new space. It is believed that this behavior shows "secure attachment" in the same way that babies feel attached to caregivers. Other studies show that cats know their own names, even if they do not always come when they are called by humans, and that familiar humans are preferred over strangers by cats. Dog lovers may not be persuaded by such research that cats care about humans as much as dogs do. However, people who love cats will probably be happy to hear that affection for its owner can actually be felt by a cat and that the bond between human and cat can at least sometimes be mutual.

ACTIVITY 4 Revising Passive and Active Voice in Your Own Writing

Look over the most recent writing you've done to see if you have used the passive voice in any inappropriate ways. As you review, revise any inappropriate uses of passive voice you find. If you find any examples of passive voice that you believe are appropriate and serve a specific purpose, write a note explaining why you believe they do not require revision.

workshop 2

Adjectives and Adverbs

Understanding Adjectives and Adverbs

Adjectives and adverbs are both modifiers that help make your writing livelier and more specific. Adjectives modify nouns and pronouns; adverbs modify verbs, adjectives, and other adverbs.

Common problems with adjectives and adverbs happen when writers confuse adjectives and adverbs or have trouble using comparative and superlative forms appropriately.

*For definitions and examples of grammar concepts key to understanding adjectives and adverbs, see the **Guide to Grammar Terms** table on pages 999–1002.*

Revising Adjectives and Adverbs

In informal speech, many people use adjectives in place of adverbs, most often saying *real* instead of *really, good* instead of *well,* and *bad* instead of *badly.* They also use adverbs in place of adjectives, especially after linking verbs such as *feel.* In formal writing, be sure you choose the right word for the job.

To check for adjective-adverb confusion, identify the word or phrase being modified. If it is a verb, an adjective, or another adverb, make sure the modifier is an adverb.

Adjective Used When Adverb Is Needed

> The cow must have jumped real high to get over the moon.

An adjective, *high,* is being modified. The modifier should be an adverb, not the adjective *real.*

> **REVISION**
> The cow must have jumped really high to get over the moon.

If the modifier follows a linking verb such as *seem, feel,* or *be,* the modifier should be an adjective.

Adverb Used When Adjective Is Needed

> She felt badly about her angry words.

The modifier follows the linking verb *felt,* so the modifier is a subject complement, and the word being modified is the subject, *she.* The modifier should be the adjective *bad,* not the adverb *badly.*

> **REVISION**
> She felt bad about her angry words.

Using *Well* Correctly

Finally, take extra care with the word *well,* which is usually an adverb but also serves as an adjective when it means "healthy": *I am not well today.*

> **WELL AS AN ADVERB**
> They work well together.

> **WELL AS AN ADJECTIVE**
> Two weeks after the fever began, he was finally well again.

Using Comparative and Superlative Forms

When you use adjectives and adverbs to compare two or more things, you'll need to use comparative (*happier, more effectively*) and superlative (*happiest, most effectively*) forms. Comparative forms of many short adjectives add *-er,* while superlative forms typically add *-est.* Comparative forms of most adverbs use *more,* while superlative forms typically use *most.* However, many adjectives and adverbs have irregular comparative or superlative forms.

Wrong Form of Comparative or Superlative

The most common problems with comparative and superlative adjectives and adverbs include using the wrong form—using a comparative when a superlative is needed (or vice versa), and using double comparatives or superlatives.

If you aren't sure of the standard comparative or superlative form for a particular adjective or adverb, check a dictionary.

> The day at the water park was the ~~funnest time~~ *most fun* I ever had.

> The speech was poorly written, and his delivery was even ~~worser~~ *worse.*

Comparative-Superlative Confusion

If you are comparing two items, use the comparative form. If you are comparing three or more items, use the superlative.

> When my brother and I used to race, he was always ~~fastest~~ *faster.*

Two people — *my brother* and *I* — are being compared, so the comparative form is needed.

> The doctor asked some of the ~~stranger~~ *strangest* questions the patient had ever heard.

The patient has heard more than two questions in his or her lifetime, so the superlative form is needed.

Double Comparatives or Superlatives

Using double comparatives or superlatives is seen as an error in academic and formal English.

> The visiting team was ~~more~~ better prepared than the local one.
>
> Her ~~most~~ hardest task was developing self-confidence.

Breaking the Rule: Using Adjectives and Adverbs Informally

Once you understand how to use adjectives and adverbs appropriately in formal and academic writing, you may notice adjectives used in place of adverbs, double comparatives and superlatives, and other nonstandard usage in writing that aims for an informal tone — for example, in advertisements (like Apple's *"Think different"* slogan) or dialogue. Using adjectives and adverbs informally, the way many speakers do, can give your writing a casual flavor that may be appropriate in some situations.

ACTIVITY 1 Identifying Problems with Adjectives and Adverbs

In each of the following sentences, underline every adjective and double-underline every adverb. If the sentence contains an error, identify the problem. If the sentence is correct, write **Correct**.

EXAMPLE: The dog smelled <u>badly</u>, so we gave him a bath.

PROBLEM: *An adjective should follow a linking verb like "smelled," but "badly" is an adverb.*

1. She felt terribly sick and performed poor on the test.

   PROBLEM: _____

2. My mother and father argue about which of them does the most work around the house.

   PROBLEM: _____

3. The exhausted boy behaved badly in the grocery store.

   PROBLEM: _____

4. People who get a small amount of exercise are usually more healthier than people who sit all day.

   PROBLEM: _____

5. The engine was running smooth until the car began to cross the desert at the hottest time of the day.

   PROBLEM: _____

ACTIVITY 2 Revising Adjective and Adverb Errors

Correct any adjective or adverb errors in the following sentences. If the sentence is correct as written, write **Correct**. Be prepared to explain why you made each revision.

EXAMPLE: I could not have asked for a more better friend.

REVISION: *I could not have asked for a better friend.*

1. July is one of the hotter months of the year in Chicago.

   REVISION: _____

2. We were glad we had camped out overnight to get tickets to the concert because the line was real long by morning.

   REVISION: _____

3. Both teams played poorly, and the result was one of the boringest games Karina had ever seen.

   REVISION: _____

4. Suddenly, the rain stopped, and a spectacularly beautiful double rainbow appeared.

   REVISION: _____

5. The cake looked delicious, but it tasted terribly.

   REVISION: _____

ACTIVITY 3 Revising a Paragraph for Adjective and Adverb Problems

The following paragraph was written for a general audience and may include adjective and adverb problems. Revise the paragraph to correct any issues you identify.

Copenhagen, the capital of Denmark, tops many lists as the world's bestest city for riding bicycles. More bicycles than cars cross the city each day, with near 40 percent of Copenhagen residents biking regularly to work. Infrastructure in the capital city encourages biking. Copenhagen is fairly flat, so bike riders do not face any real difficult hills or other obstacles. For short trips, Copenhagen residents seem to feel badly about driving when they can bike instead. For longer trips, however, cycling to work instead of driving has not always seemed like the best option. Commuting by bike must be easy, or people will not do it. Therefore, planners have tried to ensure that biking is the most fastest way to get to work, even for those who live outside Copenhagen. Biking distances of more than three or four miles used to be difficulter than it is now. But the towns surrounding Copenhagen have built bike superhighways separated from roads to encourage cyclists to ride to the capital. These bike superhighways, with well-maintained pavement and lights, allow even long-distance riders to bike safe in Denmark. When biking is the efficientest way to travel, who needs a car?

ACTIVITY 4 Revising Adjectives and Adverbs in Your Own Writing

Look over the most recent writing you've done to see if you have used any adjectives or adverbs in nonstandard ways. As you review, revise any adjectives and adverbs you find that are likely to seem like mistakes to your readers. If you find any adjectives or adverbs that you used to create dialogue, an informal tone, or a specific effect and that seem to serve their purpose, write a note explaining why you believe they do not require revision.

workshop 3

Capitalization

Understanding Capitalization

Capitalization marks proper nouns, proper adjectives, and many words in titles of books, films, and other works, as well as the first words of sentences and lines of poetry. Following conventions for capitalization can help prevent confusion.

*For definitions and examples of grammar concepts key to understanding capitalization, see the **Guide to Grammar Terms** table on pages 999–1002.*

Proper Nouns and Proper Adjectives

A proper noun is the name of a specific person, place, or thing. Proper nouns are always capitalized, and so are the proper adjectives that are formed from proper nouns.

PROPER NOUN	PROPER ADJECTIVE
Charles Dickens	Dickensian

In some cases, a noun may be capitalized when it is part of a name, but not capitalized when it is a common noun that refers to a generic instance.

PROPER NOUN	COMMON NOUN
Cuyahoga River	a river
Psychology 101	reverse psychology
Washington Monument	a monument

Proper nouns and proper adjectives typically fall into the following categories:

NAMES, TITLES PRECEDING NAMES
Barry Jenkins
Mighty Mouse
Senator McCain

NATIONS, NATIONALITIES, LANGUAGES
Argentina
Puerto Rican
Spanish

PLACES
Rockaway Beach
Columbus, Georgia
Main Street

MONUMENTS, STRUCTURES, SHIPS, TRAINS, AIRCRAFT, SPACECRAFT
Vietnam Veterans' Memorial
Grand Central Terminal
USS *Indianapolis*
Acela
Spirit of St. Louis
Apollo 13

ORGANIZATIONS, BUSINESSES, ACADEMIC AND GOVERNMENT INSTITUTIONS, SPECIFIC COURSE NAMES
League of Women Voters
General Electric
Harvard University
Federal Bureau of Investigation
Introduction to Sociology

BRANDS
Sensodyne
Android

ERAS AND HISTORICAL EVENTS
the Jurassic period
the Civil War

1009

DAYS OF THE WEEK, MONTHS, HOLIDAYS

Tuesday

September

Thanksgiving

RELIGIONS AND RELIGIOUS TERMS

Hinduism

Holy Week

the Qur'an

Titles

Most words in titles and subtitles of creative works such as films, books, articles, and songs should be capitalized. In general, capitalize the first and last word of a title or subtitle and all important words. Typically, you will not capitalize *a, an,* or *the,* most prepositions, the word *to,* or coordinating conjunctions such as *and* and *or* unless they are the first or last word of a title or subtitle.

It's a Wonderful Life

Pride and Prejudice

"I Want to Hold Your Hand"

Revising Unnecessary Capitalization

Capitalizing words that don't need to be capitalized may be an even more common problem than failing to capitalize proper nouns. The following categories often cause problems.

Unnecessary Capitalization of Titles

Professor Mary Jackson was my history *professor* ~~Professor~~ last semester.

Don't capitalize titles or occupations such as *president* except when they directly precede a person's name (*President Biden*).

Unnecessary Capitalization of Relationship Word

My *father's* ~~Father's~~ Aunt Annie has always been my favorite relative.

Don't capitalize a family relationship word unless it is used as a substitute for a name or as part of a name.

We asked Dad to give his advice.

Unnecessary Capitalization of a Compass Direction

The path of the eclipse moves *west* ~~West~~ to *east* ~~East~~, beginning in the Pacific Northwest.

Don't capitalize compass directions (*north, south, east, west, northwest,* and so on) unless you are using them to refer to a geographical region (*Pacific Northwest*).

Unnecessary Capitalization of Seasons

What classes are you taking this *fall* ~~Fall~~?

Don't capitalize seasons (*spring, summer, fall, winter*).

Breaking the Rule: Changing Conventions for Capitalization

Some people's names and brands use unconventional capitalization. If a brand or product uses capital letters in the middle of a word, as in *iPad or FedEx,* write the name as given in company advertising or on the product itself. Capitalize a person's name following the person's own preferences: *bell hooks, Valerie van der Graaf.*

ACTIVITY 1 Identifying Capitalization Errors

In the following sentences, write *Missing* if any required capitalization is missing, *Unnecessary* if there is unnecessary capitalization, or *Correct* if the sentence includes no errors in capitalization.

EXAMPLES: Felicia and her Husband spent their Winter break at a ski lodge. *Unnecessary*

We went to grandma's house after school. *Missing*

1. When Spring comes, I want to see the Rocky Mountains.
2. During the depression, senator Huey Long of Louisiana introduced a program to limit individual wealth.
3. The committee meeting will be cancelled for the next two Tuesdays.
4. She is a Film major, but her favorite class last semester was Human Biology.
5. Harold would like to buy a new iphone next year, so he took a part-time job at Johnson's Garden Depot.

ACTIVITY 2 Revising Capitalization Errors

Revise each of the following items to correct capitalization errors.

> EXAMPLE: The Washington state department of transportation operates Ferries from Seattle to Bainbridge Island.
>
> REVISION: *The Washington State Department of Transportation operates ferries from Seattle to Bainbridge Island.*

1. My father chose Hans Christian Andersen's Fairy Tale "the Little Mermaid" as a bedtime story because he was familiar with the Disney Movie.

   REVISION: _____

2. The doctor told Mrs. Sandoval that she should get a flu shot before the New Year.

   REVISION: _____

3. She studied spanish and art history before she decided to become a Librarian.

   REVISION: _____

4. Congress unanimously chose George Washington to lead the continental army during the American revolution, but as Commander-in-Chief, he accepted no wages.

   REVISION: _____

5. The Empire state building has appeared in many films, including *King Kong* and *Sleepless In Seattle*.

   REVISION: _____

ACTIVITY 3 Revising a Paragraph for Capitalization

The following paragraph was written for a general audience and may include problems with capitalization. Revise the paragraph to correct any problems you find. Some sentences may not contain errors.

New York City has a number of statues of female figures, including Central Park's statue of Alice from *Through the looking glass*. However, of all the city's Public statues, only five feature women who actually lived. Visitors will find two of the five in Riverside Park along the Hudson river. One is a statue of Joan Of Arc, a french martyr who lived in the Fifteenth Century. The other is Eleanor Roosevelt, who was first lady of the United States throughout world war II. Bryant Park is home to a statue of Gertrude Stein, the Author of *the Autobiography of Alice B. Toklas*. The intersection of Broadway and 39th Street is known as Golda Meir square and features a bust of Meir, a woman raised in the American midwest who became Israel's first female Prime Minister in 1969. The fifth is a statue of Harriet Tubman, who escaped from slavery and helped dozens of others flee to Freedom. Fortunately, several new statues of women from History are planned. A statue featuring suffragists will include Elizabeth Cady Stanton and Susan B. Anthony, who fought for a woman's Right to Vote, and Sojourner Truth, whose speech "Ain't I a woman" noted that african american women needed the Vote as well. In addition, the "She built NYC" campaign is creating several new Monuments to pioneering women. If all goes well, New York City may soon have more statues of women to look up to.

ACTIVITY 4 Revising Capitalization in Your Own Writing

Look over the most recent writing you've done to see if you made any errors with capitalization. As you review, add any missing capital letters and change any unnecessary capital letters that you find.

---

workshop 4

Comma Splices and Run-On Sentences

Understanding Comma Splices and Run-On (Fused) Sentences

A comma splice is a sentence with two independent clauses, each one able to stand on its own, that are connected with nothing more than a comma.

COMMA SPLICE

Bad weather threatened the harvest, the storm clouds suddenly separated and revealed blue skies.

A run-on sentence, also called a fused sentence, runs two independent clauses together without any kind of punctuation or conjunction.

RUN-ON

Bad weather threatened the harvest the storm clouds suddenly separated and revealed blue skies.

"Bad weather threatened the harvest" and "the storm clouds suddenly separated and revealed blue skies" are both independent clauses that could be separate sentences. Connecting them with a comma alone results in a comma splice, and connecting them with no punctuation between them results in a run-on sentence.

Both clauses include subjects (*Bad weather* and *the storm clouds*), and both include verbs (*threatened* and the compound verb *separated and revealed*). Neither begins with a subordinating conjunction, which can turn an independent clause into a subordinate clause.

To understand and fix comma splices and run-ons, you'll need to recognize independent clauses, which must include a subject and a verb and do *not* begin with a subordinating conjunction such as *because*.

For definitions and examples of grammar concepts key to understanding comma splices and run-ons, see the **Guide to Grammar Terms** *table on pages 999–1002.*

Revising Comma Splices and Run-Ons

Comma splices and run-ons can cause problems for readers because the relationship between the two independent clauses isn't clear. When you fix an inappropriate comma splice or a run-on sentence, you have several options. Each option connects the ideas in different ways, so which method you choose is up to you and depends on what you want to communicate.

Separate the Clauses into Two Sentences

If the ideas in the two independent clauses are not closely related, you can use a period to separate the independent clauses into two complete sentences:

> Bad weather threatened the harvest. The storm clouds suddenly separated and revealed blue skies.

Join the Clauses with a Semicolon

A semicolon can separate two independent clauses in a single sentence. Revising this way suggests a closer connection between the clauses than making two separate sentences.

> Bad weather threatened the harvest; the storm clouds suddenly separated and revealed blue skies.

Adding a conjunctive adverb such as *however* after the semicolon adds more information about the relationship between the clauses.

> Bad weather threatened the harvest; however, the storm clouds suddenly separated and revealed blue skies.

Join the Clauses with a Comma and a Coordinating Conjunction

Connecting independent clauses with a comma and a coordinating conjunction (*for, and, nor, but, or, yet, so*) indicates that the two clauses are equally important and closely connected.

> Bad weather threatened the harvest, but the storm clouds suddenly separated and revealed blue skies.

Rewrite One of the Independent Clauses as a Subordinate Clause

If one of the clauses is less important, or leads to the other clause, you can make it a dependent clause by beginning with a subordinating conjunction.

> Although bad weather threatened the harvest, the storm clouds suddenly separated and revealed blue skies.

Adding the subordinating conjunction *although* to the beginning of the first clause creates a subordinate clause that can be joined to the independent clause that follows. (Notice that when you begin a sentence with a subordinate clause, you should follow it with a comma.)

> Bad weather threatened the harvest until the storm clouds suddenly separated and revealed blue skies.

Adding the subordinating conjunction *until* to the beginning of the second clause creates a subordinate clause that can be joined to the initial independent clause. This revision emphasizes the bad weather, not the blue skies that followed. (Notice that when the subordinate clause follows the independent clause, you don't usually separate the clauses with a comma — unless the subordinate clause begins with *although* or another conjunction that shows contrast.)

Breaking the Rule: Appropriate Uses of Comma Splices

Once you understand what comma splices are and how to avoid creating them by mistake, you may start to notice comma splices in writing that aims for an informal tone — for example, in advertisements and social media messages. Used intentionally, comma splices, especially those that include very short clauses, can help writing sound casually conversational.

> My sister saves, my brother splurges. I'm somewhere in between.

As with any literary technique, comma splices should be used with care. In academic and other formal writing, many readers will always see a comma splice as a mistake. For that reason, you should think about your audience before you decide to include a comma splice.

ACTIVITY 1 Identifying Comma Splices and Run-Ons

Underline every independent clause in the following examples. Identify any comma splices or run-ons. If a sentence is correct, write **Correct**.

> EXAMPLES: The squirrels in the park are fearless, one tried to steal my lunch. *Comma splice*
>
> Although they are fun to watch, people should not feed them. *Correct*

1. Vintage film posters can be expensive, but fans of old movies may be able to find moderately priced copies.

2. The chair was bright yellow, the color seemed appealing to me but revolting to my sister.

3. South of town is a reservoir where people swim in warm weather the water is cool and inviting.

4. She left her jacket in the cafeteria when she came back, it was gone.

5. Try to listen to him politely, ignore everything that he asks you to do.

ACTIVITY 2 Revising Comma Splices and Run-Ons

Rewrite each of the following items to eliminate the comma splices and run-ons. Revise each item in two different ways, using any of the methods discussed above for fixing comma splices and run-ons.

> EXAMPLE: The palm trees whipped back and forth a hurricane was coming.
>
> REVISION 1: *The palm trees whipped back and forth; a hurricane was coming.*
>
> REVISION 2: *The palm trees whipped back and forth because a hurricane was coming.*

1. In centuries past, people wore makeup to hide blemishes sometimes the makeup contained deadly ingredients, such as mercury or lead.

    REVISION 1: _____

    REVISION 2: _____

2. Every town in the county contributed a float to the annual parade, local high schools sent marching bands led by drum majors and baton twirlers.

    REVISION 1: _____

    REVISION 2: _____

3. Knowing how to cook is an important part of sticking to a budget if you have to buy prepared food, you will spend more money.

    REVISION 1: _____

    REVISION 2: _____

4. The house sat on a corner lot, when snow fell, Roberto had to shovel two sidewalks instead of one.

REVISION 1: _____

REVISION 2: _____

5. The setting sun lined up precisely between the tall buildings, a red-orange glow lit up both the sky and the faces of pedestrians.

REVISION 1: _____

REVISION 2: _____

ACTIVITY 3 Revising a Paragraph for Comma Splices and Run-Ons

The following paragraph was written for a general audience and may include comma splices and run-ons. Revise the paragraph to correct any problems you find. Some sentences may not contain errors.

Knolling is a method of arranging objects, the arrangement places items in straight lines or at right angles to each other. The term "knolling" was invented by a janitor who worked for a furniture designer in the 1980s the janitor, Andrew Kromelow, liked to arrange and photograph his tools in clean lines and rows that reminded him of the company's Knoll furniture. Curators may use knolling to depict collections in intriguing ways. Museums display items such as pencils, flyswatters, and mobile phones using knolling visitors may find the patterns more interesting than any individual object. Knolling, sometimes called "flat lay," can also be a way to look at all the small parts that make up a whole for instance, some knollers have taken photos of all the items they are taking on a trip. Other knolling experiments include lining up many similar items by color, a photo of pieces of toast arranged each slice from untoasted to burned. Recently, some larger-scale knolling has made a splash on social media, with paramedics and firefighters lying on the ground at right angles next to their vehicles and gear the images are captured by drone. Viewers may think at first that these pictures show toys and dolls, they show life-sized equipment and real human beings. Many people find something very pleasing about the orderly arrangement of everyday objects, images of knolled items that are well organized and well photographed can attract a lot of attention online. Who knows those images may also inspire others to get knolling.

ACTIVITY 4 Revising Comma Splices and Run-Ons in Your Own Writing

Look over the most recent writing you've done to see if you have created any comma splices or run-ons. As you review, revise any comma splices or run-ons you find that are likely to seem like mistakes to your readers. If you find a comma splice that you used intentionally and that seems to serve its purpose, write a note explaining why you believe it does not require revision.

workshop 5

Coordination and Subordination

Understanding Coordination and Subordination

Workshop 4 (see p. 1012) explains how to use coordination and subordination to fix run-on and comma splice errors. Coordination and subordination are not simply correctness issues, however. They are ways of joining parts of sentences to emphasize important ideas, give readers information, and vary rhythm. Knowing how to use them well can make your writing clearer and more interesting to read.

Coordination joins two ideas with a **coordinating conjunction** to show that both ideas are equally important. Subordination joins two ideas with a **subordinating conjunction** to show that one idea is less important than the other.

*For definitions and examples of grammar concepts key to understanding coordination and subordination, see the **Guide to Grammar Terms** table on pages 999–1002.*

Coordination

Coordinating conjunctions join ideas of equal importance. The coordinating conjunctions are *and, but, for, nor, or, so,* and *yet.* Coordinating conjunctions can join **words** (*Maxine and Jackson*), **phrases** (*a box of chocolates or a dozen roses*), or **independent clauses** that could stand on their own as sentences (*I sat at the desk, but I could not study*). When you use coordinating conjunctions to join clauses, place a comma before the conjunction.

The conjunction you choose tells readers something about the relationship between the clauses joined.

COORDINATION TO SHOW ADDITION

Maxine picked up the books from the library, and Jackson returned them.

COORDINATION TO SHOW CHOICE

Your mother might like a box of chocolates for her birthday, or you could give her flowers.

COORDINATION TO SHOW CONTRAST

We were tired, but we were too excited to sleep.

COORDINATION TO SHOW RESULTS

The bus was late, so we started walking to school.

Subordination

Like coordination, subordination links ideas and shows the relationships between them. However, subordination de-emphasizes one clause to indicate that the other clause is more important. The less emphatic clause, called a **dependent clause** or **subordinate clause**, is indicated by a subordinating conjunction. Dependent clauses such as *when I woke up* cannot stand on their own as sentences because their sense depends on information in another clause. When the dependent clause comes first in the sentence, you should put a comma after it; when the dependent clause follows an independent clause, no comma is used.

Some common subordinating conjunctions show how clauses are related in time (*before, after, until, while, when*), indicate cause and effect (*because*), or show that the relationship between the clauses is conditional (*if, although, unless*).

SUBORDINATION TO SHOW TIME

After Maxine brought the books home, Jackson started to read them.

SUBORDINATION TO SHOW CAUSE AND EFFECT

We started walking to school because the bus was late.

SUBORDINATION TO SHOW A CONDITIONAL RELATIONSHIP

If you give your mother flowers, you will delight her.

Relative pronouns such as *who*, *which*, and *that* can also introduce dependent clauses called **relative clauses**. Relative pronouns may refer to an antecedent in an independent clause. In such cases the relative clause usually acts as a modifier, describing the antecedent. In other cases, relative clauses can act as nouns and serve as the subject or object of an independent clause.

Relative Clause to Modify Antecedent

My sister, who prefers to keep her things tidy, hates sharing a room with me.

The relative pronoun *who* refers to the antecedent *sister*. The relative clause *who prefers to keep her things tidy* describes the sister. Subordinating the sister's preference for tidiness emphasizes the main idea, that she *hates sharing a room with me*.

Relative Clause Acting as a Noun

He said that he would wait.

The relative clause *that he would wait* acts as a noun in this sentence. It serves as the object of the verb *said*.

Simple, Compound, Complex, and Compound-Complex Sentences

A *simple sentence* consists of a single independent clause.

SIMPLE SENTENCE
A skunk walked out of the woods.

A sentence that joins two or more independent clauses with coordination is called a *compound sentence*.

COMPOUND SENTENCE
A skunk walked out of the woods, but it ignored me.

A sentence that joins two or more clauses with subordination is called a *complex sentence*.

COMPLEX SENTENCE
A skunk walked out of the woods *as I was walking my dog*.

Finally, a sentence that joins clauses with both coordination and subordination is a *compound-complex sentence.*

COMPOUND-COMPLEX SENTENCE
A skunk walked out of the woods *as I was walking my dog*, but it ignored me.

Joining Ideas with Coordination and Subordination

You can use coordination and subordination to transform short, choppy simple sentences into writing that is clearer and more interesting to read, as the following example shows.

NO COORDINATION OR SUBORDINATION
Marisol woke up. The sun was rising. She heard a strange sound outside. It was surprisingly loud. A pigeon was building a nest. Marisol thought. Baby pigeons might be fun to watch. They also might keep her awake.

REVISED
Marisol woke up as the sun was rising. She heard a strange sound outside, which was surprisingly loud. A pigeon was building a nest. Marisol thought that baby pigeons might be fun to watch, but they also might keep her awake.

The first two sentences in the revision are complex sentences that use subordination; the third remains a simple sentence; and the fourth uses both coordination and subordination to form a compound-complex sentence.

Sentences that are all roughly the same length and all follow roughly the same pattern can be boring for readers. Mixing things up with a combination of shorter and longer sentences, and using a combination of coordination and subordination to form compound, complex, and compound-complex sentences, helps to keep readers interested. Because only you can decide what you want to emphasize in your writing and what you want readers to know about the relationships among your ideas, you have many choices to make about coordination and subordination as a writer.

ACTIVITY 1 Identifying Coordination and Subordination

Underline every independent clause in the following sentences, double-underline every dependent (subordinate) clause, put parentheses around coordinating conjunctions, and put brackets around subordinating conjunctions. Then, identify the type of sentence.

> **EXAMPLE:** Everyone told me [that] I would like camping, (but) I hated the bugs, (and) I could not sleep [because] I heard noises. *Compound-complex*

1. Because her headache had lasted for three days, she asked her doctor for migraine medication.

2. Seeing ladybugs in the garden makes me happy, and they are astonishingly good at killing pests such as aphids, which makes me even happier.

3. People who drive too fast can cause accidents, but people who drive too slowly are equally dangerous.

4. We had planned to spend the day at the beach until we learned that only local residents were allowed to swim there.

5. Although the dog had never seen a Frisbee before, it turned out to be extremely good at catching one in midair, so we included it in our game.

ACTIVITY 2 Revising Sentences with Coordination and Subordination

Revise each of the following sets of simple sentences to create the type of sentence indicated.

> **EXAMPLE:** The children played in the apple orchard in the spring. Bees covered the blossoms.
>
> **COMPLEX:** *The children played in the apple orchard in the spring when bees covered the blossoms.*

1. The moving truck stopped outside the house. Movers began to carry boxes out and load them.

   COMPOUND: _____

2. The hallway was dark and uninviting. The single lightbulb had burned out.

   COMPLEX: _____

3. Maya's mother was angry with her. Maya had skipped school. Her mother refused to let her go to her friend's slumber party.

   COMPOUND-COMPLEX: _____

4. It was the middle of summer. The sun set late. My little nephew did not want to go to bed before dark.

   COMPOUND: _____

5. The neighborhood sponsored a mural by a local artist. The neighborhood had pulled together through tough times. The artist had studied abroad and returned.

   COMPLEX: _____

ACTIVITY 3 Revising a Paragraph with Coordination and Subordination

The following paragraph consists mainly of simple sentences. Revise to make the paragraph more readable using coordination and subordination.

> An event called NaNoWriMo happens every November. NaNoWriMo is short for National Novel Writing Month. You may want to write a novel. You should try it. Over the course of the month, you try to write 50,000 words. You can complete a short novel by the end of November. The daily total exceeds 1600 words. Completing 50,000 words makes you a winner. Nobody else has to see the writing. It does not have to be polished. Most participants simply try to pound out a complete first draft. They do not edit their work. They do not expect to end up with a perfect manuscript. November has just thirty days. That does not allow time for careful revision. Of course, you can continue work on your drafts after November ends. In fact, doing so is encouraged. Some books have been drafted during NaNoWriMo. They were later published. One writer even got a movie deal from a book. She wrote it during NaNoWriMo in 2006.

ACTIVITY 4 Using Coordination and Subordination in Your Own Writing

Look over the most recent writing you've done to see if you can use coordination or subordination more effectively to vary your sentences and keep readers interested.

workshop 6

Commonly Confused Words

Understanding Homophones

Many commonly confused words are homophones, words that sound the same but are spelled differently and have different meanings. If you use the wrong one, you may confuse or distract your readers.

*For definitions and examples of grammar concepts key to understanding homophones, see the **Guide to Grammar Terms** table on pages 999–1002.*

While computer spellcheckers have made a huge difference for writers, spellcheckers cannot catch homophone errors because a wrong homophone is nevertheless a correctly spelled word. Finding and correcting homophone errors requires that you learn commonly confused words so you can avoid choosing the wrong one.

Revising Commonly Confused Words

These word groups are some of the most commonly confused. If you aren't sure where to begin to avoid homophone problems, start by learning to differentiate this manageable number of homophones.

accept/except

Accept is a verb that means *receive* or *agree*. *Except* is a preposition that means *other than*.

> We accept the blame for eating all the plums except the unripe one.

advice/advise

Advice is a noun, and *advise* is a verb that means *give advice*.

> Their advice was usually helpful, but I wanted someone else to advise me on this matter.

1019

affect/effect

Generally, *affect* is used as a verb, and *effect* is used as a noun.

> Our advice had no <u>effect</u> on his behavior, but it <u>affected</u> his view of us.

it's/its

It's is a contraction meaning *it is* or *it has. Its* is a possessive pronoun meaning *belonging to it.*

> Everything in the dining room is in <u>its</u> proper place, so <u>it's</u> time to welcome the guests.

lead/led

Lead is a noun and refers to a metallic element. *Led* is the past tense of the verb *lead* (which rhymes with *seed*).

> He <u>led</u> Professor Plum to the conservatory and accused him of murder with a <u>lead</u> pipe.

loose/lose

Loose is an adjective meaning *not tight* or *unrestrained. Lose* is a verb meaning *misplace.*

> My sandal strap was <u>loose</u>, so I was afraid I might <u>lose</u> my shoe.

sight/site

A *sight* is something that is seen. A *site* is a place.

> We went to the <u>site</u> hoping to meet others interested in the cause, but there was no one in <u>sight</u>.

than/then

Than is used in making comparisons; *then* is an adverb that answers the question *When?*

> Carlos is taller <u>than</u> Marty now, but wait a few years and see what happens <u>then</u>.

their/there/they're

Their is a possessive pronoun meaning *belonging to them. There* is an adverb that answers the question *Where? They're* is a contraction that means *they are.*

> Go over <u>there</u> and take <u>their</u> phones away. <u>They're</u> disrupting the class.

to/too/two

To is a preposition meaning *toward* or part of an infinitive verb form (*to be*). *Too* means *also. Two* is a number.

> The <u>two</u> hikers were going <u>to</u> Brixton, <u>too</u>, so we gave them a ride.

weather/whether

Weather is a noun that refers to the atmospheric conditions. *Whether* is part of a correlative conjunction, *whether . . . or.*

> <u>Whether</u> the <u>weather</u> cooperates or not, the wedding will happen tomorrow.

who's/whose

Who's is a contraction meaning *who is* or *who has. Whose* is a possessive pronoun that means *belonging to whom.*

> Ahmed wants to know <u>whose</u> car we're taking and <u>who's</u> driving.

you're/your

You're is a contraction meaning *you are. Your* is a possessive pronoun that means *belonging to you.*

> <u>You're</u> the one who answered <u>your</u> phone during the meeting.

ACTIVITY 1 Identifying Homophone Errors

In the following sentences, underline any word that is incorrectly used. If the sentence contains no homophone errors, write **Correct.**

> EXAMPLE: If you eat at <u>there</u> restaurant, <u>you're</u> meal will be expensive but delicious.

1. The temperature this morning is much colder then yesterday, so remember too bundle up.

2. The coach told us to play as if we could not loose, but some of us could not accept his advise.

3. Patricia led the horse to it's stall.

4. The fishermen checked the weather forecast, wondering how their catch might be affected.

5. Anyone who's visiting the sight tomorrow must wear a hard hat.

ACTIVITY 2 Revising Homophone Errors

Revise each of the following items to correct homophone errors.

> EXAMPLE: The man who's dog dug up our yard would not except responsibility for the damage.
>
> REVISION: *The man whose dog dug up our yard would not accept responsibility for the damage.*

1. The neighbors held one of there loud parties and invited everyone accept Thomas.
   REVISION: _____

2. The site of my family waiting at the airport too meet me made me wonder weather moving away had been a good decision.
   REVISION: _____

3. A round-trip bus ticket is less expensive than two one-way tickets, but if my little brother looses it before the return journey, its not worth the cost.
   REVISION: _____

4. The pitcher through the ball wildly, and it past by the startled batter's ear.
   REVISION: _____

5. Your going to need you're wallet if you're planning to buy something to eat.
   REVISION: _____

ACTIVITY 3 Revising a Paragraph for Homophone Errors

A spellcheck found no problems with the following paragraph written for a student audience. Revise the paragraph to correct any homophone errors that you find. Some sentences may not contain errors.

You can find information online about almost any news story your interested in. However, its not always easy to tell weather what you've read is true. Their are different kinds of "fake news" and misinformation, and some are more harmful then others. Honest mistakes can be made buy anyone, including a professional journalist. Reputable news sources will publish corrections if material in they're publications turns out too be incorrect. At the other end of the spectrum is deliberate misinformation, which happens when an article is published by someone who's hole purpose is to trick you. Sometimes people create false stories for the money that advertising can bring; others want to influence people's beliefs or even make them loose faith in the idea of truth itself. If a story seems to outrageous to be true, it probably is, so the best advise is to investigate on your own. You should no that people are more likely to share information that confirms what they already believe. Never simply except that information is correct because you read it on a popular sight, because it has been shared widely, or because it tells a story you want to hear. A little research can help you find out the facts behind a story that might have lead you to believe a lie. To fight misinformation, do you're homework!

ACTIVITY 4 Revising Homophone Errors in Your Own Writing

Look over the most recent writing you've done to see if you have made any errors with homophones. As you review, correct any errors that you find.

---

workshop 7

Fragments

Understanding Fragments

A sentence fragment is a group of words that looks like a sentence but isn't a complete sentence. A sentence must include at least one independent clause, and it must have a subject and a verb. If any of those elements is missing, it's a fragment.

A fragment may happen when a writer treats a phrase or subordinate clause as if it were a complete sentence.

*For definitions and examples of grammar concepts key to understanding fragments, see the **Guide to Grammar Terms** on pages 999–1002.*

PHRASE FRAGMENT

Barking and chasing the waves. The dog ran into the ocean.

"Barking and chasing the waves" is not a complete sentence. It has no subject and no complete verb, so it is a phrase, not an independent clause.

PHRASE FRAGMENT

The dog failed to catch the foam. But did not stop trying.

"But did not stop trying" has no subject, so it is neither a complete sentence nor an independent clause. The phrase is part of a compound verb (*failed . . . but did [not] stop*).

PHRASE FRAGMENT

The dog looked for help. With a funny expression on its face.

"With a funny expression on its face" is not a complete sentence. It includes no subject and no verb, so it is a phrase, not an independent clause.

SUBORDINATE CLAUSE FRAGMENT

Another dog stared for a while and then wandered away. Because the waves seemed impossible to catch.

"Because the waves seemed impossible to catch" is not a complete sentence. Although it has a subject (*the waves*) and a verb (*seemed*), the subordinating conjunction *because* means that it is a subordinate clause, not an independent clause.

Revising Fragments

To fix a fragment, you can either join it to another sentence or rewrite the fragment to turn it into a complete sentence.

JOIN A FRAGMENT TO ANOTHER SENTENCE

Barking and chasing the waves, the dog ran into the ocean. The dog failed to catch the foam but did not stop trying. The dog looked for help with a funny expression on its face. *Another dog stared for a while, and then wandered away because the waves seemed impossible to catch.*

TURN A FRAGMENT INTO A SENTENCE

The dog ran into the ocean. It was barking and chasing the waves. The dog failed to catch the foam. However, it did not stop trying. The dog looked for help. It had a funny expression on its face. Another dog stared for a while and then wandered away. *The waves seemed impossible to catch.*

Notice that rewriting a fragment as a complete sentence may involve adding or removing words — or both.

Breaking the Rule: Appropriate Uses of Fragments

Once you understand what fragments are and how to avoid creating them by mistake, you may start to notice fragments in writing by professionals and experts. Used intentionally, fragments can be an effective way to add emphasis.

> We drove for hours, and finally we saw a motel. *Old and shabby, yes, but open.*

> The pillow exploded, and the feathers went everywhere. *On the bed. On the floor. Out the window.*

As with any literary technique, fragments should be used with care, but a good fragment can have a profound impact on your reader.

ACTIVITY 1 Identifying Fragments

Underline any fragments you find in the following examples. (Some items may not contain a fragment.)

EXAMPLE: My favorite comedy series is too unconventional. <u>For my parents.</u>

1. If more people lived downtown. The streets would not be deserted at night. The neighborhood is eerily quiet after dark.
2. Corn on the cob is my favorite summer treat. When local corn is ripe in August, I eat it every day. Not even ice cream tastes better.
3. Although zombie movies are usually horror films. Zombies can appear in any genre. Even comedy films.
4. Every afternoon, the plaza is filled with skateboarders. Practicing their jumps. While tourists record every move on their phones.
5. Because the train station needed repair, the city decided to demolish it. Inspiring a campaign to save the classic building. It was over 150 years old.
6. As Mary began the last mile of the marathon, the sun came out. A rainbow crossed the sky. Looking up, she felt she might finish after all.

ACTIVITY 2 Revising Fragments

Rewrite each of the following items to eliminate the sentence fragments. Revise each item in two different ways: (1) combine the fragment with a complete sentence, and (2) rewrite the fragment as a sentence of its own.

EXAMPLE: After the music stopped. The crowd waited patiently, hoping for another song.

REVISION 1: *After the music stopped, the crowd waited patiently, hoping for another song.*

REVISION 2: *The music stopped. The crowd waited patiently, hoping for another song.*

1. Because Roberto needed to stop for gas. He realized he would be late to work that morning.

   REVISION 1: _____

   REVISION 2: _____

2. Creepy gargoyles staring down from the top of the cathedral. The statues are also spouts that move rainwater away from the building.

   REVISION 1: _____

   REVISION 2: _____

3. The jewel thieves were athletic as well as bold. Hopping over an iron fence and scaling the museum's walls.

   REVISION 1: _____

   REVISION 2: _____

4. Annoyed by my constant questions. My sister marched into her room and slammed the door.

   REVISION 1: _____

   REVISION 2: _____

5. The players celebrated their historic victory. With the crowd's deafening cheers still ringing in their ears.

   REVISION 1: _____

   REVISION 2: _____

ACTIVITY 3 Revising a Paragraph for Fragments

The following paragraph was written for a general audience and may include fragments. Revise the paragraph to correct problems with fragments. (You may determine that some fragments are appropriate; if so, be prepared to explain why you made the choice not to revise them.)

In the late nineteenth century, the notorious Dalton Gang committed several train robberies in Oklahoma. Which made people compare the outlaws with other well-known thieves of the West. Such as Jesse and Frank James. According to contemporary sources. Bob Dalton was the mastermind of the gang, which included his brothers Grat and Emmett. Because Bob Dalton wished to outdo the James Gang. He created a plan to rob two banks in the town of Coffeyville, Kansas. On the same day in 1892. Unfortunately for the Daltons, news of their plan had leaked. In addition, the Dalton family had once lived near Coffeyville. Where Emmett had gone to school. Therefore, their faces were familiar to the townspeople. The daring daylight robbery went badly wrong for the outlaws. By the time the shooting had stopped. Bob and Grat and two other members of the gang had been killed, and Emmett, the youngest Dalton, was badly wounded. Having survived the Coffeyville robbery. Emmett served fourteen years in a Kansas penitentiary. Where he was described as a model prisoner. After his release, he and his wife went to California. Emmett later wrote a book. And made silent films about the Dalton Gang, even acting in one. Unlike his brother Bob, however. Emmett was not particularly interested in being famous. He ended up with a successful career in construction. Building houses in Hollywood.

ACTIVITY 4 Revising Fragments in Your Own Writing

Look over the most recent writing you've done to see if you have created any fragments. As you review, revise any fragments you find that are likely to seem like mistakes to your readers. If you find a fragment that you used to create a special effect and that seems to serve its purpose, write a note explaining why you believe it does not require revision.

workshop 8
Misplaced and Dangling Modifiers

Understanding Misplaced and Dangling Modifiers

Modifiers are words, phrases, or clauses that act as adjectives and adverbs, clarifying or adding shades of meaning to your writing. Modifiers need to be positioned near the words they modify. Misplaced and dangling modifiers can cause confusion or unintentionally comic effects.

*For definitions and examples of grammar concepts key to understanding misplaced and dangling modifiers, see the **Guide to Grammar Terms** table on pages 999–1002.*

Revising Misplaced and Dangling Modifiers

Misplaced Modifiers

The solution to a misplaced modifier is to revise the sentence so that readers don't have to guess at its meaning.

MISPLACED MODIFIER

Two FBI agents gave a presentation on the psychological makeup of the killer in the conference room.

In this sentence, the modifier is "in the conference room," which was intended to tell

1025

the reader where the presentation took place. Because the modifier is misplaced (placed too far from the word it modifies), it seems to be saying that the killer is *in the conference room*.

> REVISION
>
> Two FBI agents gave a presentation in the conference room on the psychological makeup of the killer.

Squinting Modifiers

If a misplaced modifier is positioned so that readers can't tell which of two words, phrases, or clauses it is supposed to modify, it is called a squinting modifier. The solution for squinting modifiers, too, is to revise the sentence so readers will understand what is being modified.

> SQUINTING MODIFIER
>
> Speaking a new language often helps students learn vocabulary words.

Should students *speak often*, or does speaking *help often*?

> POSSIBLE REVISIONS
>
> Speaking often in a new language helps students learn vocabulary words.
>
> Speaking a new language can often help students learn vocabulary words.

Moving the word *often* — and making changes to the wording of the sentence — allows the writer's meaning to be completely clear.

Dangling Modifiers

Sometimes the word or words being modified may be left out of the sentence completely. The modifier in such cases is called a dangling modifier. Although readers may be able to guess what the dangling modifier refers to, they shouldn't have to guess — and dangling modifiers can still be confusing or unintentionally comical. To correct a dangling modifier, decide what the modifier is supposed to modify. Then, revise the sentence to include that missing element, either by making it the subject of the main clause or by revising the dangling modifier as a clause that includes the missing word or words.

> DANGLING MODIFIER
>
> Spot used to chase my sister as a puppy.

The phrase *as a puppy* seems to modify the noun *sister*, who is not a dog.

> POSSIBLE REVISION
>
> As a puppy, Spot used to chase my sister.

The modifier is probably supposed to modify *Spot,* so moving *As a puppy* right before *Spot* eliminates the dangling modifier.

ACTIVITY 1 Identifying Misplaced and Dangling Modifiers

In each of the following sentences, underline the modifier. If it is misplaced, squinting, or dangling, identify the problem. If the sentence is correct, write **Correct.**

> EXAMPLE: Cackling and flapping, the henhouse erupted in a loud commotion. *Dangling*

1. Efficient and well-managed, the diner served a remarkable number of hungry local residents every morning.
2. Writing a summary quickly taught the students to look for main ideas.
3. Denying that the graffiti was mine, four cans of spray paint in my locker seemed to provide proof of guilt.
4. Two witnesses pointed out the suspect who had stolen the prize poodle in the police lineup.
5. Making a terrible screeching noise, Aunt Lucille noticed that the car's brakes were faulty.

ACTIVITY 2 Revising Misplaced and Dangling Modifiers

Correct misplaced, squinting, and dangling modifiers in the following sentences by revising each sentence in two different ways.

> **EXAMPLE:** After leaving an envelope hidden in the hollow tree, the secret of the neighborhood's most mysterious house was revealed.
>
> **REVISION 1:** *After the old man left an envelope hidden in the hollow tree, the secret of the neighborhood's most mysterious house was revealed.*
>
> **REVISION 2:** *After leaving an envelope hidden in the hollow tree, the old man revealed the secret of the neighborhood's most mysterious house.*

1. Covered in cat hair, guests avoided the sofa in the lobby of the quaint little inn.

   REVISION 1: _____

   REVISION 2: _____

2. The radio announcer proclaimed a great military victory over a crackling speaker.

   REVISION 1: _____

   REVISION 2: _____

3. Laughing often makes people feel more optimistic.

   REVISION 1: _____

   REVISION 2: _____

4. Carrying a bushel of rutabagas home from the farmer's market, an unexpected dinner was sure to follow.

   REVISION 1: _____

   REVISION 2: _____

ACTIVITY 3 Revising a Paragraph for Misplaced and Dangling Modifiers

The following paragraph may include dangling and misplaced modifiers. Revise the paragraph to correct any issues you identify.

Advertising often makes a difference in the success of a product. Clever and memorable, products with great ads attract customers. Consider the billboards for Burma-Shave, a brand of shaving cream that dotted U.S. highways from 1927–1963. Americans' fondness for driving slowly resulted in the spread of billboard advertising. With a series of six or seven red billboards, each featuring one line of a comic rhyming poem, motorists waited for the punch line on the next-to-last billboard. The final sign always revealed the product name, "Burma-Shave." Increasingly famous, people driving along the highway loved the clever campaign. Proudly announcing, "If you/Don't know/Whose signs/These are/You can't have/Driven very far," motorists enjoyed being in on the joke. However, the days were numbered of Burma-Shave's success. Although showing no signs of being tired of the billboards, highways improved and cars went much faster. At fifty or sixty miles per hour, the distance needed between the billboards became too great. The Burma-Shave brand disappeared. Now in the Smithsonian Museum's collection, however, people will probably remember the Burma-Shave ad campaign better than they remember most modern billboard advertising.

ACTIVITY 4 **Revising Misplaced and Dangling Modifiers in Your Own Writing**
Look over the most recent writing you've done to see if you have used any misplaced or dangling modifiers that might confuse readers. If you find any, revise them.

workshop 9
Parallelism

Understanding Parallelism

Parallelism, or parallel structure, uses repeated grammatical forms to show relationships between similar parts of sentences. Parallel structure is commonly found in lists and comparisons. However, you can use parallelism for many other purposes, including highlighting logical relationships, improving sentence clarity, creating rhythm, and adding emphasis.

*For definitions and examples of grammar concepts key to understanding parallelism, see the **Guide to Grammar Terms** table on pages 999–1002.*

Revising for Parallelism

When you join two or more items in a list or series with a coordinating conjunction such as *and*, make sure that all the items in the list are parallel to one another.

Lack of Parallelism in a List

A great leader should know how to plan, how to inspire, and should take responsibility for mistakes.

The items in the list are *how to plan, how to inspire,* and *should take responsibility for*

mistakes. The first two have parallel structures, but the third does not.

PARALLEL

A great leader should know how to plan, inspire, and take responsibility for mistakes.

Lack of Parallelism with a Coordinating Conjunction

Is there anyone here able to drive me downtown or who can lend me a bicycle?

The phrases joined with the coordinating conjunction *or — able to drive me downtown* and *who can lend me a bicycle* — are not parallel.

PARALLEL

Is there anyone here who can drive me downtown or lend me a bicycle?

In this revision, both phrases work with *who can,* so the parts are parallel.

When you use a two-part correlative conjunction such as *either . . . or,* be sure to use parallel structures with each part of the conjunction.

Lack of Parallelism with a Correlative Conjunction

He wanted not only to learn French, but also an introduction to French culture.

The phrase after *not only* begins with an infinitive, *to learn*. The phrase after *but also* begins with a noun phrase, *an introduction,* so the structures after each part of the conjunction are not parallel.

PARALLEL

He wanted not only to learn French, but also to get an introduction to French culture.

If you make a comparison, be careful to use parallel structure for the items you are comparing.

Lack of Parallelism in a Comparison

Asking forgiveness is often easier than to get permission.

The items being compared are *asking forgiveness* and *to get permission.* The structures are not parallel.

PARALLEL

Asking forgiveness is often easier than getting permission.

ACTIVITY 1 Identifying Problems with Parallelism

In the following sentences, underline items that need to have parallel structures. If the structures are parallel, write ***Correct***. If they are not parallel, write ***Incorrect***.

EXAMPLES: The soccer players in the park are wearing team jerseys from Argentina, from Brazil, and one player appears to support France. *Incorrect*

Either you give me my money back or I report you to the Better Business Bureau. *Correct*

1. We could not assemble the bicycle kit because it had a missing seat, broken spokes, and someone wrote terrible instructions.

2. The actors were prepared not only to say their lines but also gave a thrilling performance.

3. You have a good chance of getting the job thanks to your polished résumé, flexible schedule, and retail experience.

4. Cooking for friends is more relaxing and less expensive than to go out for dinner.

5. After a week of trying out for the soccer team, Harry wanted to snack, sleep, and he planned to catch up on movies over the weekend.

ACTIVITY 2 Revising Problems with Parallelism

Rewrite each of the following items to eliminate any problems with parallelism.

EXAMPLE: Civilians who fly an American flag must either take it down at dusk or they should illuminate it.

REVISION: *Civilians who fly an American flag must either take it down at dusk or illuminate it.*

1. Keeping succulent plants alive is easy if you follow simple guidelines: water them very rarely, provide indirect light, and the soil should be well drained.

REVISION: _____

2. Before last weekend's hiking trip, we stocked up on high-energy snacks, reviewed the trail maps carefully, and we forgot to fill the car's gas tank.

REVISION: _____

3. She could either keep working on the essay past midnight or she could get up before dawn to finish it.

   REVISION: _____

4. Singing in the chorus, building sets with the stage crew, and costume design are good ways to participate in the drama club.

   REVISION: _____

5. Construction meant that pedestrians had to walk across a busy intersection, up an unpaved path, and go along a muddy ditch to get back to the sidewalk.

   REVISION: _____

ACTIVITY 3 Revising a Paragraph for Problems with Parallelism

The following paragraph includes problems with parallelism. Revise any errors that you find. Some sentences may be correct as written.

Anyone who has ever wished either to reduce clutter or who does not want to take care of a large home might be interested in tiny house living. To be officially "tiny," a house must have an area of less than 400 square feet. Most tiny homes are not only small but also offer a lot of efficiency. Residents of tiny homes typically sleep in a loft space, own furniture that serves more than one purpose, and for entertaining, they go elsewhere. People who are attracted to life in tiny houses may be interested in living simply or to go off the grid. Living simply can be possible in a tiny house because it is usually less expensive to maintain one than the upkeep of an ordinary house. Nevertheless, much depends on whether the house is on a foundation or on wheels, whether or not the homeowner also owns the land, and on local regulations that the homeowner may have to comply with. As some tiny house residents have noted, living in a very small space is easier in a community than when the resident is isolated. In that case, a good way to test living in a tiny space in a vibrant community may be to live in an urban apartment.

ACTIVITY 4 Revising Problems with Parallelism in Your Own Writing

Look over the most recent writing you've done to see if you have made any errors with parallel structures. As you review, revise any parallelism problems you find.

Pronoun-Antecedent Agreement

Understanding Pronoun-Antecedent Agreement

When you use a pronoun such as *it, them,* or *which,* the pronoun refers to another word — a noun, noun phrase, or another pronoun — called the antecedent. Pronouns have to agree with the antecedent in number and gender.

Pronoun-antecedent agreement problems usually come up in just a few situations, when the antecedent is one of the following:

- A compound joined with *and, or,* or *nor*
- A collective noun
- An indefinite pronoun
- A singular noun without an identified gender

Revising Pronoun-Antecedent Agreement

To fix pronoun-antecedent agreement problems, identify the pronoun and its antecedent, and then revise the pronoun, the antecedent, or the whole sentence to eliminate the agreement error.

*For definitions and examples of grammar concepts key to understanding pronoun-antecedent agreement problems, see the **Guide to Grammar Terms** table on pages 999–1002.*

Compound Antecedents

One common type of pronoun-antecedent agreement error involves compound antecedents joined with *and, or,* or *nor.* If a compound antecedent uses *and,* you should use a plural pronoun.

Agreement Error with Compound Antecedent

Both Mr. Devere and his son used his knowledge of sports to find a career.

The compound antecedent *Mr. Devere and his son* refers to two people, not one, so it requires a plural pronoun.

REVISION

Both Mr. Devere and his son used their knowledge of sports to find a career.

If the compound antecedent uses *or* or *nor,* you should make sure that the pronoun agrees with the closer part of the compound antecedent.

Agreement Error with Compound Antecedent

Either Anita or the boys spend her afternoon at the museum daily.

The parts of the compound antecedent are joined with *or,* so the pronoun should agree with the closer antecedent, *boys,* not with *Anita.*

REVISION

Either Anita or the boys spend their afternoon at the museum daily.

Note: If the revised sentence sounds strange, try switching the parts of the compound antecedent to see if the sentence improves. If changing the order doesn't help, try revising the sentence.

Collective Noun Antecedents

Another trouble spot for pronoun-antecedent agreement involves antecedents that are collective nouns, which are usually singular unless the members of the group are acting as individuals.

Agreement Error with Collective Noun Antecedent

The crowd roars their approval.

The verb *roars* suggests that the collective noun *crowd* is acting as one unit, so a singular pronoun is needed.

REVISION

The crowd roars its approval.

Antecedents with Indefinite Pronouns

Traditionally, indefinite pronouns such as *everyone, anyone,* or *none* have been considered singular antecedents, even when they seem to include more than one person. If you use a plural pronoun with a singular indefinite pronoun antecedent, many readers will consider it an error.

Agreement Error with Indefinite Pronoun Antecedent

Does anyone have a credit card with them?

Using the plural pronoun *them* with the grammatically singular *anyone* is sometimes seen as a pronoun-antecedent agreement error.

POSSIBLE REVISION

Does anyone have a credit card with him or her?

This revision is very formal, and some readers may find it awkward.

POSSIBLE REVISION

Does anyone have a credit card?

In this case, omitting the pronoun is a good revision strategy.

Avoiding Sexism

Singular nouns that refer to a category of person (*student, gymnast, physicist*) can also cause problems. Decades ago, using a singular masculine pronoun with such antecedents was considered appropriate, but many readers today find it sexist and awkward to use *he* and *him to* refer to a person who does not identify as male. Because some readers also don't consider a plural pronoun such as *they* appropriate for singular antecedents, you will have to think carefully about revising such sentences.

Agreement Issue with Singular Pronoun Antecedent

A student driver must recognize that their car can be dangerous.

Many readers — but not all — will see a pronoun-antecedent agreement error between the antecedent *driver* and the pronoun *their*. (See the "Breaking the Rule" section that follows for more information.)

SEXIST REVISION

A student driver must recognize that his car can be dangerous.

Any student driver who does not identify as male is excluded in this revision.

POSSIBLE REVISION

Student drivers must recognize that their cars can be dangerous.

This revision makes the generic *driver* plural, so the pronoun *their* agrees.

POSSIBLE REVISION

A student driver must recognize that a car can be dangerous.

In this revision, the problematic pronoun is eliminated.

Breaking the Rule: Changing Standards for Pronoun-Antecedent Agreement

Once you understand what pronoun-antecedent agreement is and how to avoid agreement problems, you may start to notice the "singular *they*" appearing in journalistic writing and other edited texts. The use of *they* to refer to grammatically singular indefinite pronouns such as *everyone* has often been called an error in formal writing (for example, in sentences such as *Everyone must receive their immunizations*), even though it is commonly used in speech as a way to avoid the sexist use of *he* or the awkward and formal *he or she.* In recent years, however, many publications and writers have begun to accept *they* as agreeing with a singular antecedent to avoid inappropriately gendered references.

The winner of the speaking contest will have their choice of several prizes.

Be aware that some readers may not know that the restriction against the "singular *they*" is changing. You may still want to avoid the "singular *they*" if your audience won't realize that you have made an informed decision to use it.

The winner of the speaking contest can choose among several prizes.

The winner of the speaking contest will have a choice of several prizes.

ACTIVITY 1 Identifying Problems with Pronoun-Antecedent Agreement

In each sentence, underline the pronoun and double-underline the antecedent to which the pronoun refers. If there is a pronoun-antecedent agreement error or related issue in the sentence, briefly explain the problem. If there is no problem, write **None.**

> EXAMPLE: <u>Everyone</u> waiting for an interview should leave <u>his</u> résumé at the desk.
>
> PROBLEM: *The pronoun is sexist; it does not agree in gender with the antecedent "everyone."*

1. Either the Santana sisters or Marcus should give their speech at the beginning of the ceremony.

   PROBLEM: _____

2. Can someone let me borrow his or her phone?

   PROBLEM: _____

3. The waiting crowd waved its hands and shouted wildly when the singer entered the hotel lobby.

   PROBLEM: _____

4. A soldier should obey his commanding officer at all times.

   PROBLEM: _____

5. Give the documents to Ms. D'Souza and the attaché when they arrive.

   PROBLEM: _____

ACTIVITY 2 Revising Pronoun-Antecedent Agreement Errors

Underline the pronoun and double-underline the antecedent in each of the following items. Then, rewrite each sentence in at least two different ways to correct problems with pronoun-antecedent agreement. Be ready to explain your choices.

> EXAMPLE: The <u>cat</u> and the <u>rabbits</u> ate <u>its</u> food in separate rooms.
>
> REVISION 1: *The cat and the rabbits ate their food in separate rooms.*
>
> REVISION 2: *The cat and the rabbits ate in separate rooms.*

1. A writer can create his own schedule, but flexibility is sometimes a mixed blessing.

   REVISION 1: _____

   REVISION 2: _____

1033

2. Everyone should try to resolve their interpersonal problems through direct, open communication.

   REVISION 1: _____

   REVISION 2: _____

3. Either cooking an elaborate meal or grabbing fast food can have their pros and cons.

   REVISION 1: _____

   REVISION 2: _____

4. The parliament has met their obligation to consider the law fairly.

   REVISION 1: _____

   REVISION 2: _____

ACTIVITY 3 Revising a Paragraph for Pronoun-Antecedent Agreement Errors

The following paragraph, written for a general audience, includes pronoun-antecedent agreement errors and other related problems. Revise the paragraph to correct any problems you find. Some sentences may not contain any errors, and some sentences may contain pronouns that would disturb only some readers. If you decide not to change a sentence, be ready to explain why.

Curling is a sport in which a team use their brooms to scrub an ice rink in order to make a big round rock slide smoothly to a target spot. But in addition to rocks and brooms, an unusual thing about curling is the fact that everyone who curls is supposed to be on their best behavior. The Curling Code of Ethics says that neither insults nor intimidation has their place in the sport. There are no referees to blow the whistle on a player who tries to hide their mistakes. Instead, someone who commits a foul by touching (or "burning") the curling stone is expected to say so, even if he knows that nobody else saw the foul. Both winners and losers are expected to show good sportsmanship and treat their opponents to a drink after the game ends. Curling may look odd, but anyone who treats honorable behavior as their sport's highest goal must be on the right track.

ACTIVITY 4 Revising Pronoun-Antecedent Agreement Problems in Your Own Writing

Look over the most recent writing you've done to see if you have any problems with pronoun-antecedent agreement. As you review, revise any mismatched pronouns and antecedents that are likely to confuse your readers. If you find anything that some readers might consider a pronoun-antecedent error but that you prefer not to change, make a note of your decision.

Pronoun Reference

Understanding Pronoun Reference

When you use a pronoun such as *it, them,* or *which,* the pronoun refers to another word — a noun, noun phrase, or another pronoun — called the antecedent. Pronoun reference problems occur when readers can't tell which word or words serve as the antecedent of a particular pronoun or can't identify any antecedent.

*For definitions and examples of grammar concepts key to understanding pronoun reference, see the **Guide to Grammar Terms** table on pages 999–1002.*

Revising Pronoun Reference

To identify and fix problems with pronoun reference, identify the pronoun and then find its antecedent. If the antecedent is ambiguous, vague, missing, or otherwise unclear, rewrite the sentence to clarify the meaning.

Sometimes, the pronoun could refer to more than one antecedent.

Ambiguous Antecedent

Office policy bans personal phone calls, which many employees dislike.

Do many employees dislike the policy or the personal calls? The antecedent of *which* is unclear.

REVISION

Office policy bans personal phone calls, a rule that many employees dislike.

The revision clarifies that the pronoun *that* refers to the office policy against personal calls.

CLEAR REVISION

Office policy bans personal phone calls because many employees dislike them.

The revision leaves no doubt that the pronoun *them* refers to the phone calls.

At other times, the pronoun — usually *that, which,* or *it* — is so vague that readers can't tell exactly what part of a clause or phrase serves as the pronoun's antecedent.

Vague Antecedent

The bookshelves were filled to overflowing with paperbacks, hardcovers, and reference books, which contributed to the mess in the room.

Does *which* refer to a particular kind of book, to all the books, to the bookshelves, or to something else? The antecedent of *which* is vague.

CLEAR REVISION

The bookshelves were filled to overflowing with paperbacks, hardcovers, and reference books, a chaotic jumble that contributed to the mess in the room.

In this revision, the pronoun *that* refers specifically to the phrase *a chaotic jumble,* which restates the appearance of the shelves described in the independent clause.

Another problem occurs when a writer uses a pronoun such as *it, you,* or *they* without any real antecedent. This kind of usage is common in conversation, but inappropriate in formal writing.

Missing Antecedent

On this website, they suggest that the end of the world is coming.

Who are *they*? Here, the pronoun seems to refer to unknown people.

CLEAR REVISION

This website suggests that the end of the world is coming.

Removing the mystery pronoun *they* eliminates the confusion.

Finally, be aware that some readers object to using a possessive as an antecedent in formal writing.

Possessive Antecedent

Joanna's review showed how much she had loved the book.

Although readers can infer that *she* refers to Joanna, the sentence does not contain a noun that can be the antecedent of *she*. The possessive form *Joanna's* acts as an adjective rather than as a noun. Some readers will find such sentences ungrammatical.

CLEAR REVISION

Her review showed how much Joanna had loved the book.

The antecedent of *her* is now a noun, *Joanna*.

ACTIVITY 1 Identifying Problems with Pronoun Reference

In each sentence, underline the pronoun. If the sentence contains a pronoun reference problem, describe the problem. If there is no problem, write **None.**

EXAMPLE: Sonia told Maria that <u>she</u> should take a vacation.

PROBLEM: *The pronoun "she" could refer to either Sonia or Maria.*

1. Ed's sister announced that he had bought the winning lottery ticket.

   PROBLEM: _____

2. They said on the radio that the storm will bypass this area.

   PROBLEM: _____

3. The twelve-story building had an elevator until it was condemned.

   PROBLEM: _____

4. The students played cards until midnight and watched a couple of horror movies afterward, which may not have been a good idea the night before the physics final.

   PROBLEM: _____

5. Three-year-old Sara put pretzels on a plate for her imaginary friend Sheela.

   PROBLEM: _____

ACTIVITY 2 Revising Pronoun Reference Problems

Rewrite the following items to correct any problems with pronoun reference. If a sentence contains no error, write **Correct.**

EXAMPLE: Donna called Olivia to say that her dog had escaped.

REVISION: *Donna found that her dog had escaped, so she called Olivia.*

1. My brother's car is towed to the garage almost weekly, but he insists the car has many good years left.

   REVISION: _____

2. Neville whispered to Mr. Middlebury that he needed to leave the party immediately.

   REVISION: _____

3. During the kite-flying competition, enthusiastic kite handlers and onlookers cheered swooping and diving kites of all shapes and hues, which led to amazing photographs.

   REVISION: _____

4. Valerie enjoys traditional French cooking because she loves butter and cream, but her sister tells her that too much fat is unhealthy.

   REVISION: _____

5. The anchorwoman told every actress who came to the set that she needed a new contract.

   REVISION: _____

ACTIVITY 3 Revising a Paragraph for Pronoun Reference Problems

The following paragraph, written for a general audience, may include unclear or missing antecedents or other pronoun reference problems. Revise the paragraph to correct any problems you find. Some sentences may not contain any errors.

Tom Blake's name may not be famous everywhere, but he is widely known in the world of surfing. They claim on Wikipedia that Blake was "one of the most influential surfers in history" because of his revolutionary design changes to the traditional surfboard. Blake was born in Milwaukee, Wisconsin, in 1902. He grew up near Lake Superior and first heard of surfing from an educational film in high school, which may have influenced his later choices. In Detroit in 1920, Blake met Duke Kahanamoku, who had helped to popularize surfing around the world. Blake believed he had invited him to visit his native Hawaii. In the 1920s, Blake and Kahanamoku became friends, and he both learned to surf and also studied antique surfboards in a Honolulu museum. Blake's innovations included hollowing out and reinforcing the surfboards of the era, which were too heavy for many people to carry. But according to modern-day board designers, Blake's greatest contribution to surfing involved adding a fin to the traditional board's flat bottom so it could be maneuvered in the water. Previously, a surfer had to dip one foot in the water to turn, and that made performance surfing difficult. In inventing lightweight finned boards, Blake made surfing a more accessible sport.

ACTIVITY 4 Revising Pronoun Reference Problems in Your Own Writing

Look over the most recent writing you've done to see if you have any problems with pronoun reference. As you review, revise any unclear or missing antecedents you find that are likely to confuse your readers.

workshop 12

Shifts in Pronoun Person and Number

Understanding Inappropriate Shifts in Pronoun Person and Number

In writing, a shift in person is a change in pronoun, such as from the second person *you* to the third person *someone,* that happens in the middle of a sentence or paragraph. A shift in number moves between singular and plural subjects. Shifting between person and/or number without a good reason may confuse readers.

*For definitions and examples of grammar concepts key to understanding inappropriate shifts in pronoun person and number, see the **Guide to Grammar Terms** table on pages 999–1002.*

Revising Shifts in Pronoun Person and Number

Shifts in person and/or number can make sense to readers when different people are the subjects of clauses in a sentence.

Intentional Shifts in Person and Number

> I had a problem with my car, so my friends loaned me theirs.

The first-person singular subject of the first clause, *I,* and the third-person plural subject of the second clause, *my friends,* are different people, so shifts in both person and number are appropriate.

When shifts in person and/or number happen without a change in the people being referred to, such shifts can cause confusion.

Unintentional Shift in Person and/or Number

> Anyone can find a job if you are willing to work hard.

The third person subject, *Anyone,* of the main clause and the second person subject, *you,* of the subordinate clause seem to refer to the same

people, so this shift in perspective is confusing. By shifting to *you,* the writer may be aiming to avoid the choice between the awkward singular *he or she* and the traditionally plural *they* with the grammatically singular antecedent *anyone,* but the shift is not a good solution.

You have options for revising shifts in person.

REVISION
> You can find a job if you are willing to work hard.

If the writer is talking directly to readers, *you* is appropriate. Another option is to rearrange the sentence.

REVISION
> Anyone who is willing to work hard can find a job.

Here, the writer avoids having to choose between *he or she* and *they* with the antecedent *anyone.* (See Workshop 10 on Pronoun-Antecedent Agreement for more information.)

Breaking the Rule: Changing Standards for Shifts in Number

You may have noticed the "singular *they*" in journalistic writing and other edited texts. The use of *they* to refer to grammatically singular indefinite pronouns such as *everyone* has often been called an error in formal writing (for example, in sentences such as *Everyone must receive their immunizations*), even though it is commonly used in speech as a way to avoid the sexist use of *he* or the awkward and formal *he or she.* In recent years, many publications and writers have begun to accept *they* as agreeing with a singular antecedent when the gender of the antecedent is not known.

> The winner of the speaking contest will have their choice of several prizes.

Be aware that some readers may not know that the restriction against the "singular *they*" is changing. You may still want to avoid the "singular *they*" if your audience won't realize that you have made an informed decision to use it.

The winner of the speaking contest can choose among several prizes.

The winner of the speaking contest will have a choice of several prizes.

ACTIVITY 1 Identifying Inappropriate Shifts in Person and Number

Determine whether each of the following sentences contains an inappropriate shift in person or number. If the sentence contains an inappropriate shift, explain the problem. If the sentence is correct as written, write **None.**

EXAMPLE: We followed the recipe, but you could tell the results were going to be disastrous.

PROBLEM: *Inappropriate shift from first-person "We" to second-person "you"*

1. A person may be absolutely certain that there are no monsters under the bed, but I still have to check.

   PROBLEM: _____

2. Everyone already knows too much about our family history in this town.

   PROBLEM: _____

3. Finding the discipline to practice a difficult new skill is not easy, but anyone can learn new skills if you practice them hard enough.

   PROBLEM: _____

4. When I start feeling restless during the long introduction, you get worried that the comedian will have trouble winning over the crowd.

   PROBLEM: _____

5. Most of us on the student newspaper have their specialties, which include feature writing, opinion writing, and photography.

   PROBLEM: _____

ACTIVITY 2 Revising Inappropriate Shifts in Person and Number

Revise each of the following sentences in two different ways to correct any inappropriate shifts in person and number.

EXAMPLE: A vegetarian may have to explain to family members why you stopped eating meat.

REVISION 1: *Vegetarians may have to explain to family members why they stopped eating meat.*

REVISION 2: *A vegetarian may have to explain to family members the decision not to eat meat.*

1. One does not need to understand how and why dough rises if they want to bake bread.

   REVISION 1: _____

   REVISION 2: _____

2. For someone to be accepted to West Point, you have to demonstrate leadership skills and excellent academic qualifications.

   REVISION 1: _____

   REVISION 2: _____

3. As the child of immigrant parents, you felt like a cultural interpreter.

   REVISION 1: _____

   REVISION 2: _____

4. We were willing to wait overnight in the ticket line, but you weren't allowed to put chairs or sleeping bags on the sidewalk.

   REVISION 1: _____

   REVISION 2: _____

ACTIVITY 3 Editing a Paragraph for Inappropriate Shifts in Person and Number

Edit the following paragraph, written for a student audience, to revise any inappropriate shifts in person and number. If you decide that some shifts are acceptable, be ready to explain your reasoning.

Anyone who has studied a foreign language knows that you can rarely translate idioms literally. Those who create word-for-word translations will find that his or her results may sound comical—and may be very difficult to understand. For instance, most of us would not think twice about using an English expression like "It's raining cats and dogs" if you needed to indicate heavy rain. But if someone translates the literal words into another language, a listener may think they are trying to be confusing. A Portuguese-English phrase book published in 1855 by a man who spoke no English used a Portuguese-French phrase book and a French-English dictionary to create famously terrible translations. Even for readers who spoke no Portuguese, one was likely to find the English phrases mystifying and hilarious. Humorist Mark Twain said that the book was "perfect." People might agree that many expressions from the book, like "to craunch the marmoset," have a certain flair, even if you have no idea what they mean.

ACTIVITY 4 Revising Inappropriate Shifts in Your Own Writing

Look over the most recent writing you've done to see if you have created any inappropriate shifts in person and number. Revise any shifts you find that are likely to seem like mistakes to your readers. If some shifts seem acceptable to you, be ready to explain why you decided not to revise them.

workshop 13

Shifts in Verb Tense

Understanding Shifts in Verb Tense

In writing, a shift in verb tense is a change from one verb tense to another that happens in the middle of a paragraph or even in the middle of a sentence. At times, you will have a good reason to change tenses — but making such shifts without a good reason may confuse readers.

For definitions and examples of grammar concepts key to understanding inappropriate shifts in verb tense, see the **Guide to Grammar Terms** *table on pages 999–1002.*

Revising Inappropriate Shifts in Verb Tense

Shifts make sense to readers when the events being described in a sentence or paragraph happen at different times and require different tenses.

Intentional Shift

> The castle burned down and fell into the swamp, but we will rebuild it.

The past tense verbs *burned* and *fell* make sense because the castle's destruction happened in the past. The future tense *will rebuild* makes sense because the rebuilding has not happened yet.

> When the events of the sentence or paragraph happen at the same time, a tense shift is unnecessary and distracting.

Unintentional Shift

> The castle stood on the edge of the swamp for years, and then it suddenly catches fire.

The shift from the past tense verb *stood* to the present tense verb *catches* is unnecessary and does not make sense in the sentence.

> **REVISION**
>
> The castle stood on the edge of the swamp for years, and then it suddenly caught fire.

If you're writing about literature, use the present tense to describe the actions of characters or to analyze what the writer does. You can think of literature as always happening right now, since readers can experience the work at any time.

Using the Present Tense to Write about Literature

> Some of Jane Austen's best-loved heroines ~~were~~ *are* poor but plucky girls who unexpectedly end up with rich husbands.

Notice, however, that when you discuss the work's publication or anything about the work or the author that is tied to a particular time, the past tense is appropriate.

> Austen herself ~~does~~ *did* not earn much from her novels during her lifetime.

The phrase *during her lifetime* places the information in this sentence in the past, so the past tense *did* is correct.

ACTIVITY 1 Identifying Inappropriate Shifts in Verb Tense

In each of the following sentences, underline all the verbs and verb phrases. If the sentence contains an inappropriate shift in tense, write *Shift*; if it is correct as written, write *Correct*.

> **EXAMPLES:** Every August, the Perseid meteor shower fills the sky with light, so astronomers hope the weather will be clear. *Correct*
>
> Startled, we leaped from our sleeping bags, and then we race away from the terrifying sound as fast as we can move. *Shift*

1. If you worked nearby, you would be able to spend less time traveling to the job.

2. As the morning sun's rays broke over the horizon, the vampire races toward home.

3. My dog Pickles escapes the yard and roams the neighborhood, but the little boy next door found him and brought him home.

4. When movie versions of Shakespeare's *Hamlet* are made, the actor who plays Hamlet was often forty years old, even though the play's hero was a college student.

5. The witness answered the defense attorney's questions without hesitation, but suddenly, during the cross-examination, he freezes.

ACTIVITY 2 Revising Inappropriate Shifts in Verb Tense

Revise each of the following sentences to correct any inappropriate shifts in verb tense. If the sentence is correct as written, write **Correct**.

> *open*
> **EXAMPLE:** Kittens' eyes ~~opened~~ a few days after birth, and they start exploring their surroundings in three to four weeks.

1. A rainy gust from the storm blew the screen door open, and the children and their babysitter spend the next half hour moving several very startled tiny tree frogs back outdoors.

   REVISION: _____

2. Most of the chocolate in Vivian's bag of Halloween candy had disappeared, but when she accused her sister of eating it, their mother admitted responsibility.

   REVISION: _____

3. Marjane Satrapi's graphic novel *Persepolis* explored the author's rebellious youth when she was growing up in Iran in the 1980s.

   REVISION: _____

4. According to psychological research, unskilled people often greatly overestimate their own abilities, a cognitive bias that was called the Dunning-Kruger effect.

   REVISION: _____

5. The teenagers in town followed a long tradition of driving up and down Main Street on Saturday nights because there are few other entertainment options.

   REVISION: _____

ACTIVITY 3 Editing a Paragraph for Inappropriate Shifts in Verb Tense

Edit the following paragraph to revise any inappropriate shifts in verb tense.

Is advertising as a profession doomed? This may seem like a strange question in an era when ads appeared everywhere. However, research suggests that the field of advertising had changed. Advertisers today have to contend with a constantly growing and changing number of platforms, from print to television to digital, and each required different kinds of advertising. For example, social media ads often appeared in the corner of a screen for just a few seconds, while television ads last thirty seconds or longer and aim to attract a viewer's full attention. Perhaps an even bigger problem for advertisers today, however, was that more people than ever before dislike ads so much that they are sometimes willing to pay more to avoid them. If social media users could pay a small fee never again to see ads about weird tricks to lose abdominal fat, will they do it?

┌───
ACTIVITY 4 Revising Inappropriate Shifts in Verb Tense in Your Own Writing

Look over the most recent writing you've done to see if you have created any inappropriate shifts in verb tense. As you review, revise any shifts you find that are likely to seem like mistakes to your readers.
└───

workshop 14
Subject-Verb Agreement

Understanding Subject-Verb Agreement

The subject and verb(s) in a sentence have to agree in person and number.

Subject-verb agreement errors happen most often when a writer loses track of the subject of the sentence. Misidentifying the subject happens most often in just a few tricky situations:

- When words come between the subject and verb
- When the subject follows the verb
- When the sentence has a compound subject
- When the subject is a collective noun
- When the subject is an indefinite pronoun
- When the subject is *who, which,* or *that*
- When the subject is singular but ends in *–s*

For definitions and examples of grammar concepts key to understanding subject-verb agreement, see the **Guide to Grammar Terms** *table on pages 999–1002.*

Revising Subject-Verb Agreement

Taking the time to identify the simple subject that the verb needs to agree with will help you fix — and avoid — subject-verb agreement errors.

Words between Subject and Verb

> *make*
> The flowers along the side of the road ~~makes~~ the long drive more cheerful.

Although the verb *makes* is closer to the singular noun *road*, it does not agree with the plural subject *flowers*. Look for prepositional phrases and other words that may come between the

subject and verb, and be careful not to mistake any of them for the sentence's subject.

Subject Follows Verb

> *are*
> There ~~is~~ too many people here today.

The verb *is* does not agree with the plural subject that follows it, *people.* The word *there* is not a noun and is not the subject of this (or any) sentence.

Compound Subject

> *run*
> My two dogs and my cat ~~runs~~ into the kitchen, hoping to be fed.

The verb *runs* does not agree with the compound subject, *My two dogs and my cat,* which is plural because the two subjects *My two dogs* and *my cat* are connected with *and*.

> *have*
> Either my cat or my two dogs ~~has~~ broken the screen door.

The verb *has* does not agree with the simple subject *dogs,* which is plural. When the two subjects are connected with *or,* the verb agrees with the closer subject. If making the verb agree with the closer subject results in a sentence that sounds strange, try switching the parts of the compound subject (and, again, making the verb agree with the closer subject) to see if the sentence sounds better that way: *Either my two dogs or my cat has broken the screen door.*

Collective Noun Subject

> *votes*
> The committee ~~vote~~ on how to spend the bake-sale money.

1043

The verb *vote* does not agree with the collective noun *committee,* which is usually singular unless the members are acting as individuals.

Indefinite Pronoun Subject

> Of the two candidates, neither ~~have~~ *has* earned our support.

The verb *have* does not agree with the indefinite pronoun *neither,* which is singular. Most indefinite pronouns take singular verb forms; a few (*both, few, many, several*) take plural verb forms; and a few others (*all, any, enough, more, most, none, some*) can be either singular or plural, depending on the context.

Who, Which, or That as Subject

> Air conditioning does not cause colds that ~~comes~~ *come* in the summer.

The verb *comes* does not agree with the plural noun *colds,* which is the antecedent of the relative pronoun *that. Who, which,* and *that* may refer either to singular or plural antecedents, so you will need to identify the specific antecedent to choose a verb that agrees with any relative pronoun.

Singular Subject That Ends in –s

> The news ~~continue~~ *continues* to be depressing.

The verb *continue* does not agree with the subject *news,* which is singular.

ACTIVITY 1 Identifying Subject-Verb Agreement Errors

Underline the simple subject or subjects of every clause in the following examples, and double-underline the verbs. Put any dependent clause in parentheses. Finally, mark any sentence that contains a subject-verb agreement error with **SV**; if the sentence is correct, write **C**.

> **EXAMPLES:** In the sparrow's nest <u>was</u> two cowbird <u>eggs</u>. *SV*
>
> The baby <u>birds</u> (that <u>hatch</u> from those eggs) <u>will be</u> much bigger than sparrows. *C*

1. A bag of marbles were given to each child at the birthday party.
2. There was no fingerprints anywhere on the museum cases that the jewel thieves had opened.
3. Neither of the specials that the waiter described sound good to me.
4. He and everyone who works at the school is planning ways to raise funds for the choir tour.
5. The bundle of letters, which was kept in a box in the writer's attic, is a discovery that has thrilled scholars.

ACTIVITY 2 Revising Subject-Verb Agreement Errors

Rewrite the following items to correct any subject-verb agreement errors. If a sentence contains no error, write **Correct**.

> **EXAMPLE:** Bat populations in many parts of the country has been affected by a deadly disease called white-nose syndrome.
>
> **REVISION:** *Bat populations in many parts of the country have been affected by a deadly disease called white-nose syndrome.*

1. Everyone in these hills have a story to tell about the way life used to be.

   REVISION: _____

2. Was the rooster and the cat squabbling in the yard this morning?

   REVISION: _____

3. The first joke does not even make Miss Stanton smile, but the final series of anecdotes causes her to laugh so hard that tears come to her eyes.

   REVISION: _____

4. At the county courthouse is clerks waiting impatiently for the judge to arrive.

   REVISION: _____

5. There is a couple of methods that may help you get rid of hiccups, but nothing is certain to work.

   REVISION: _____

ACTIVITY 3 Revising a Paragraph for Subject-Verb Agreement

The following paragraph, written for a general audience, may include subject-verb agreement errors. Revise the paragraph to correct any problems you find. Some sentences may not contain any errors.

In the early 1930s, making a living by farming in some parts of the Great Plains were first difficult and then impossible. Native prairie grasses with deep roots that had once held the soil in place was uprooted over time so that farmers could plant food crops such as wheat. Then the rain stopped falling. In the resulting "Dust Bowl" conditions, strong winds picked up the dry soil and blew it around in "black blizzards" that was unstoppable and made the land barren. As a result, there was soon few surviving farms in the hardest-hit counties in the Texas and Oklahoma panhandles. Many families lost everything and was forced to move away from their farms. However, in the Dust Bowl region nowadays is many farms and ranches. Is a repeat of the 1930s conditions possible? According to scientists, the biggest problem for farmers remain a severe drought. Dry topsoil is simply more likely to blow away. But irrigation systems are in place in the region now that was unknown in the Dust Bowl era. In addition, the crops planted on an Oklahoma farm today has the ability to thrive on less water. Finally, thanks to the volunteers of the Depression-era Civilian Conservation Corps, who planted millions of trees in the 1930s, the Great Plains are now more resistant to the forces of soil erosion and destructive, unstoppable winds.

ACTIVITY 4 Revising Subject-Verb Agreement Errors In Your Own Writing

Look over the most recent writing you've done to see if you have made any subject-verb agreement errors. If you find any, revise them.

workshop 15

Verb Form and Tense

Understanding Verb Form and Tense

No sentence is complete without a verb, so understanding how verbs work is essential.

For definitions and examples of grammar concepts key to understanding verb forms and verb tenses, see the Guide to Grammar Terms table on pages 999–1002.

Verbs give readers a lot of information about what happened and when it happened. Forming verbs and verb phrases effectively is essential for making your writing credible and clear.

Revising Verb Forms

Most verbs have five different forms — the base form, the past tense form, the past participle form, the present participle form, and the third person singular or *-s* form.

base	describe	have	go
past tense	described	had	went
past participle	described	had	gone
present participle	describing	having	going

An important exception is the verb *be,* which uses two present tense forms (*am* and *are*) instead of the base form *be,* which uses *is* as a third person singular form instead of a regular *-s* form, and which uses two past tense forms (*was* and *were*).

Most verbs, such as *describe* in the preceding table, are regular, which means that the past tense and the past participle are the same and are formed by adding *-d* or *-ed* to the base form. However, several dozen verbs are irregular, including *have, go,* and other very common verbs such as *eat, drink, sleep, see,* and *think.* The only way to be sure of the forms of an irregular verb is to look them up and learn the ones you don't already know.

The most common problems with verb forms occur with the past tense and past participle

forms of irregular verbs. Using spoken and other nonstandard verb forms in formal writing can be very distracting for readers.

Choose Appropriate Past Tense Forms

NONSTANDARD

He swum as fast as he could, but he did not win the race.

STANDARD

He swam as fast as he could, but he did not win the race.

The standard past tense form of *swim* is *swam,* not *swum.*

Choose Appropriate Past Participle Forms

NONSTANDARD

The pizza finally arrived after the guests had went home.

STANDARD

The pizza finally arrived after the guests had gone home.

The standard past participle form of *go* is *gone,* not *went.*

Revising Verb Tenses

A verb's tense indicates the timing of an action or state of existence.

Simple Tenses

The three *simple tenses* describe actions and states in the present, past, and future.

simple past	I *spoke*, he *danced*
simple present	I *speak*, he *dances*
simple future	I *will speak*, he *will dance*

The simple past uses the past tense form of the verb; the simple present usually uses the base form or the *-s* form of the verb; and the simple future uses the helping verb *will* and the base form of the verb. The simple present tense can indicate an action that happens regularly ("Class ends at 11:10") as well as a one-time action in the present; the simple present is also used for writing about literature, movies, and art ("Scout and Jem find Boo Radley intriguing").

Perfect Tenses

The three *perfect tenses* describe actions or events that last for some time. To form a perfect tense, you need a verb phrase that includes a form of the helping verb *have* and the past participle of the main verb.

past perfect	she *had eaten*, we *had walked*
present perfect	she *has eaten*, we *have walked*
future perfect	she *will have eaten*, we *will have walked*

Progressive Forms

The three *progressive* forms indicate ongoing actions or conditions in the past, present, or future. To indicate a progressive action, you need a verb phrase that includes a form of the helping verb *be* and the present participle of the main verb.

past progressive	I *was watching*, they *were waiting*
present progressive	I *am watching*, they *are waiting*

future progressive	I *will be watching*, they *will be waiting*

Perfect Progressive Forms

Perfect progressive forms combine progressive forms with a perfect tense to show actions or conditions that are ongoing and that last for some time.

past perfect progressive	I *had been watching*, they *had been waiting*
present perfect progressive	I *have been watching*, they *have been waiting*
future perfect progressive	I *will have been watching*, they *will have been waiting*

Breaking the Rule: Appropriate Uses of Nonstandard Forms

You may sometimes want to use nonstandard verbs forms in informal writing or in dialogue that reports the way someone speaks. Used intentionally, nonstandard forms can show off a writer's ability to use multiple dialects or languages effectively, a skill that is sometimes called *code-switching.* As with any literary technique, nonstandard forms should be used in appropriate contexts. Be sure the reader will know that you are using the nonstandard form intentionally.

ACTIVITY 1 Identifying Nonstandard Verb Forms

In the following examples, underline the complete verb in every clause. Double-underline any verb forms that are nonstandard. Some sentences may not include any nonstandard forms.

EXAMPLE: My mother <u>was</u> angry that we <u>had <u>drank</u></u> all the milk.

1. After the cattle had went to the watering hole, they stood calmly under the elm trees.

2. Her father asked why she had not wrote her aunt to thank her for the gift.

3. He throwed dozens of wild pitches, but the manager let him stay in the game.

4. The cat lay in the sun until the day grew warm, and then it went under a chair.

5. Before the car alarm started to go off, a garbage truck had drove down the street, and the workers had tossed each empty metal can back to the curb with a loud clang.

ACTIVITY 2 Revising Verbs

Revise each of the following items to correct any verb forms that are not standard. Some sentences may not require any correction.

EXAMPLE: As I set the envelopes on the table, I seen a car coming up the driveway.

REVISION: *As I set the envelopes on the table, I saw a car coming up the driveway.*

1. We thought we had overcame our nervousness before leaving for the party, but the moment we walked in the door, our anxiety returned.

   REVISION: _____

2. Marie has rode competitively in equestrian events since she was nine years old.

   REVISION: _____

3. The film suggested that if aliens had taken over the planet, few humans would have been able to tell the difference.

   REVISION: _____

4. Sergio lay the tablecloth on the table and then sat the china dishes carefully on it.

   REVISION: _____

5. Before Mark announced that he needed more volunteers, Fauzia had rose to say that she wanted to participate.

   REVISION: _____

ACTIVITY 3 Revising Verbs in a Paragraph

The following paragraph, written for a general audience, includes verb form errors. Revise the paragraph to correct those errors. Some sentences may not contain any incorrect verb forms.

Many people enjoy crafting because they can create heirlooms and gifts out of items they have maked. Craft projects take time and effort, and a lot of crafters who have began with good intentions end up never finishing a project. Sometimes these people carry the project with them through life. Shannon Downey, who enjoys embroidery, has boughten unfinished sewing projects at estate sales and finished them for crafters who have past away. When she came across an unfinished quilt with hexagonal pieces representing all fifty states, she knowed she had to complete it. The quilter, Rita Smith, had died at 99. The hexagons had state birds and flowers drew on them, but only two had been stitched. Downey asked crafters from her Instagram feed to volunteer to help. Her request had took off. More than a thousand people had soon wrote to Downey offering to embroider a hexagon for the #RitasQuilt project. Downey embroiders, but she does not quilt, so she founded thirty quilters prepared to stitch the embroidered pieces together. "Humans are amazing. Community can be built anywhere," she wrote in an Instagram post. Many people following #RitasQuilt have spoke up to say that the project proves that "social media can be used for good."

ACTIVITY 4 Revising Verb Form Problems in Your Own Writing

Look over the most recent writing you've done to see if you've used any inappropriate verb forms. As you review, revise any nonstandard forms you find that are likely to seem like mistakes to your readers. If you find a nonstandard form that you used to create a special effect and that seems to serve its purpose, be ready to explain why it does not require revision.

APPENDIX
Speaking and Listening

part 1
Steps to Creating a Speech

1. Audience Analysis

Audience analysis is researching and thinking critically about your audience to make your message relevant to them. Research could include asking your audience questions, handing out questionnaires, or examining demographic characteristics like age, gender, and cultural background. Understanding that every audience is motivated differently is the first step toward shaping your message.

2. Topic Selection

To select a speech topic, first brainstorm a list of your own interests and then ask yourself which might pique the curiosity of your audience as well as fit the occasion of the speech. Current events or controversies can make ideal topics because audiences are likely to be aware of and care about them.

3. Speech Purpose

Every speech has one of three general speech purposes: to *inform* an audience about something, to *persuade* an audience to adopt a position, or to *commemorate an occasion* such as a graduation, a wedding, or a funeral.

Every speech also has a specific purpose. The specific purpose of an informative speech is whatever the speaker wants to teach the audience (e.g., trying to educate others about online scams). In a persuasive speech, it's the action the speaker wants the audience to take (e.g., trying to convince coworkers to recycle). In an occasional speech, it's what the speaker wants the audience to feel about the occasion (e.g., trying to make classmates feel proud of their achievements at a graduation ceremony).

4. Thesis Statement

While your general and specific speech purposes reflect your own goals as a speaker, your thesis statement is a single sentence that communicates to your audience the main idea of your speech. For example:

GENERAL PURPOSE
To persuade.

SPECIFIC PURPOSE
To persuade the audience to vote.

THESIS STATEMENT
Audience members should vote because voting not only fulfills the duty of every citizen in a democracy but also bonds voters to their communities and gives those communities a voice in how government is run.

5. Developing Main Points

Support your thesis with two or three main points. In an informative speech, main points are concepts you want your audience to understand. In a persuasive speech, your main points are more specific claims to support your overall argument. In a speech to commemorate an occasion, your main points are stories and arguments that illustrate the occasion's significance.

6. Supporting Materials

Supporting materials are facts, rationales, anecdotes, or other forms of evidence that support your thesis and its main points. These materials can be drawn from personal experience or outside research. The more specific and well-researched your supporting materials are, the more credible your message will be.

7. Major Speech Parts

An introduction opens a speech and tells the audience who the speaker is and what the speech is about. An effective introduction usually begins with a quotation, anecdote, or example that grabs the audience's attention and contains a thesis that illustrates the topic's relevance to the audience.

The body of a speech contains each main point and its supporting materials. The main points in an effective body are organized logically, so that the audience can follow and appreciate the speech. Each main point should be developed using convincing supporting materials.

A speech conclusion reiterates the main points and connects them to the thesis. An effective conclusion often leaves the audience with an image, story, or idea to ponder and, depending on the speech topic, may also urge the audience to take action.

8. Outlining

Audiences are more receptive to a message with a clear organizational pattern. Creating a speech outline helps you organize the main points, examples, and other supporting materials in your speech.

    I. Main Point 1
      A. Specific Claim X
         i. Supporting Evidence
      B. Specific Claim Y
         ii. Supporting Evidence

Working outlines elucidate main points in complete sentences. Speaking outlines, on the other hand, use simple phrases or keywords, often printed on a sheet of paper or index cards that you can use for reference when delivering your speech.

9. Presentation Aids

Presentation aids are visual and audio supplements (e.g., props, diagrams, recordings) designed to help your audience grasp your points. A presentation aid can be as elaborate as a multimedia slide show or as simple as a quotation on a whiteboard. For more on the effective use of presentation aids, see Part 5.

10. Practicing Speeches

Practice is the key to delivering a successful speech. Every rehearsal enhances your delivery—how you express your ideas through spoken words, gestures, and visual aids. The more familiar you are with your message, the more comfortable you will be in front of an audience. One rule of thumb is to rehearse a speech at least six times before giving it.

part 2

Informative Speeches

Informative speeches impart knowledge, raise awareness, or deepen an audience's understanding of a phenomenon. An informative speech might analyze a controversy, report on an event, or demonstrate a procedure.

11. Making It Matter

An informative speech isn't just a dumping ground for data. You must get the people in your audience invested in your topic so that they will retain the information you give them in your speech.

11a. Apply Audience Analysis
Analyze your audience to learn its level of familiarity with and interest in your topic, then adjust your

thesis accordingly. It's difficult for the members of an audience to retain pertinent information when they are overwhelmed by facts, figures, or descriptions.

11b. Facilitate Active Listening
Even interested audiences will need help processing a large amount of new information. The following will help you keep your audience engaged:

- Opening with an introduction that previews the thesis and its main points
- Using transition phrases (e.g., "First of all . . ."; "The next reason why . . ."; "We've just spoken about X. Now we'll examine Y . . .") to clearly delineate separate ideas

- Using internal previews to tell the audience what main points are coming up
- Using internal summaries to remind your audience of the main points that have just been discussed
- Using repetition, parallelism, rhetorical questions, and other rhetorical devices to reinforce your main points
- Selecting an organizational pattern that highlights the relationships among your main points

12. Informative Speech Topics

Informative speech topics can include people, things, events, phenomena, processes, ideas, and/or issues. Often the topic of a speech fits more than one of those categories. For example, a speech informing an audience about a scientific phenomenon might also inform that audience about the people who first discovered it and provide an overview of an issue to which it connects. The following table shows examples of different types of informative speech topics.

Topics	Examples
People Examines individuals' and groups' effect on society	• Steve Jobs, cofounder of Apple • Kathryn Bigelow, film director • Alcoholics Anonymous, a substance–abuse support group • Someone the speaker knows personally
Things or phenomena Examines characteristics of subjects that are not human	• The history of ballet • The rise of the use of drones in warfare • The reintroduction of wolves into the American West
Events Examines past and present events	• The Peloponnesian War • The 2008 financial crisis • The Civil Rights Act of 1964
Processes Examines, and often explains, how something works	• How bees make honey • How orcas communicate • How to throw a fastball
Ideas Examines opinions, theories, and/or beliefs	• Workplace ethics • Online privacy • String theory
Issues Examines controversies to raise awareness of clashing viewpoints (rather than to take a position)	• Impact of American anti-drug laws • Standardized testing in schools • Diplomatic relations between the United States and China

13. Communicating Information

To communicate information effectively in a speech, you must define, describe, demonstrate, and/or explain it. When preparing an informative speech, choose which strategy, or combination of strategies, best fits your topic.

13a. Define

Defining your topic is vital, particularly when it is complex (e.g., "What is a supermassive black hole?") or new to the audience. There are several ways to define concepts:

OPERATIONAL DEFINITION

The speaker describes what something does: *A plant is a life form that processes sunlight, water, and carbon dioxide into sugar.*

DEFINITION BY NEGATION

The speaker describes what something is not: *Happiness is the absence of fear.*

DEFINITION BY EXAMPLE

The speaker lists multiple examples of a concept: *Citrus fruits include oranges, lemons, limes, grapefruits, and tangerines.*

DEFINITION BY SYNONYM

The speaker lists alternative words and phrases that represent the concept: *A narrative is a story or a series of events.*

DEFINITION BY WORD ORIGIN

The speaker shows the root origin of a term: *Poltergeist derives from the German* poltern, *which means "create a disturbance," and* Geist, *which means "ghost."*

13b. Describe

To describe a concept, provide details that allow each of your audience members to paint a mental picture of it. This is particularly effective when your description contains important information or emotional content. For instance, a speaker informing an audience about health care in the United States might describe the sights and sounds of a typical emergency room.

13c. Demonstrate

When a process or concept is particularly complex, use speaking strategies that ensure your audience fully understands the topic at hand. Demonstration is an effective strategy in informative speeches about how something works or how to perform a task. Speakers can either physically demonstrate a topic (as on a cooking show) or merely walk the audience through it verbally.

13d. Explain

Speakers can explain a concept by showing its causes, illustrating its relationships to other topics, and offering an interpretation and analysis of the topic. Explanation is a solid strategy to lead with when the subject of your informative speech is unfamiliar to your audience.

14. Reducing Confusion

Information can prove difficult to digest when it relates to a complex topic (e.g., *prosody* in poetry), a highly abstract process (e.g., *accounting standards* in business), or an idea that challenges conventional thinking (such as *low-fat foods may not actually be healthier*). You can help your audience absorb and retain complex information using the following strategies:

- Comparing unfamiliar concepts to familiar ones using analogies. For example, a speaker might explain antibodies and illnesses by likening them to a local militia and an invading force.
- Correcting erroneous assumptions the audience may hold about the topic. For example, Twizzlers are advertised as a low-fat food, but they contain a lot of sugar and are devoid of nutritional value.

15. Organizing Information

A well-organized speech makes it easy for the audience to follow along. Informative speeches can be organized according to topic, chronology, space, cause and effect, and narrative patterns. For example, you can organize a speech about Joe Biden's presidency topically by arranging your points according to the controversies and policies of his term in office. The same speech organized chronologically could address events in order from his election to his successor's election. To organize that speech causally, you might frame each of Biden's policy achievements as a reaction to preceding political, social, and/or economic crises. You may also use the problem-solution pattern (see Section 22a) in informative speeches, though it's more common in persuasive speeches.

part 3

Persuasive Speeches

Persuasive speeches aim to influence the beliefs and actions of the people in your audience.

16. Audience Motivation

Successful persuasive speeches appeal to the motives of the audience. You can increase your chances of successfully persuading your listeners through the following techniques:

- Using audience analysis to deduce listeners' motives, then shaping your message to specifically appeal to those motives
- Stressing how the changes in behavior or policy you advocate for in your speech will benefit the audience
- Establishing your credibility by illustrating a personal connection to the topic or demonstrating your expertise
- Aiming for modest results — it's unlikely that listeners will adopt an entirely new belief system as a result of your speech seeking to persuade them
- Establishing common ground with the members of your audience so that they will be more receptive to a challenging message

17. Appealing to Reason and Emotion

A persuasive speech relies on an argument. An argument is made up of two parts: a position the speaker takes for or against an idea or issue, and the evidence the speaker uses to support that position. The Greek philosopher Aristotle divided arguments into rational and emotional appeals. Emotional appeals, known as *pathos*, grab audience members' attention and inspire them to act. Appeals to reason, or *logos*, lay out a logical justification for the speaker's argument.

Speakers can generate pathos with vivid imagery and compelling stories that evoke shared values like courage, equality, and hope. Rhetorical devices like repetition and parallelism can also make an audience feel moved by your message.

Speakers can conjure logos by sharing facts and statistics that support main points, showing causal connections between concepts, or citing examples and drawing analogies that illustrate the thesis.

An argument that relies solely on logos may make sense, but it is unlikely to move your audience to act. Conversely, an argument based solely on pathos may sound good but actually be emotionally manipulative and misleading. Powerful persuasive messages balance pathos and logos.

18. Establishing Credibility

In addition to pathos and logos, successful arguments depend upon the audience's belief that the person delivering the message is worth listening to. Aristotle termed this necessary component of persuasion *ethos*. Today, it's also known as speaker credibility.

Even an argument that is emotionally and logically powerful will falter if the audience doubts the speaker's moral character, competence, or preparedness. You can use the following approaches to establish your credibility:

- Mentioning expertise or personal experience with the topic
- Demonstrating trustworthiness by finding common ground with audience members, revealing persuasive goals up front, and expressing interest in the welfare of the audience
- Being emotionally invested in the topic, which will inflect both your verbal and nonverbal delivery with passion and evoke sincerity

19. Maslow's Hierarchy of Needs

Successful persuasion appeals to an audience's motivations. Psychologist Abraham Maslow formulated a hierarchy of needs, which posits that fundamental physiological and safety needs must be fulfilled before higher-level needs can even be considered (see the figure on page 1056).

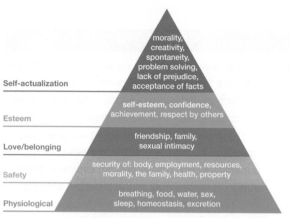

Self-actualization — morality, creativity, spontaneity, problem solving, lack of prejudice, acceptance of facts

Esteem — self-esteem, confidence, achievement, respect by others

Love/belonging — friendship, family, sexual intimacy

Safety — security of: body, employment, resources, morality, the family, health, property

Physiological — breathing, food, water, sex, sleep, homeostasis, excretion

20. Constructing Arguments

A persuasive speech depends on the power of its arguments. An argument has three parts:

1. Claims, or propositions, assert the speaker's conclusion.

2. Evidence substantiates a claim. Every claim needs evidence to support it.

3. Warrants are rationales that reinforce the link between the claim and the evidence.

20a. Types of Claims

A persuasive speech may stick to one type of claim or blend several types. There are three different kinds of claims:

CLAIMS OF FACT

These claims verify the truth of something and typically address questions for which competing answers exist (e.g., "Are rich people happier?"). Speculative claims of fact address questions whose answers are unknown (e.g., "Will climate change legislation help the economy?").

CLAIMS OF VALUE

Value claims try to show that something is right or wrong (e.g., whether the death penalty is ethical). Evidence for a claim of value is usually more subjective than the evidence offered to support a claim of fact.

CLAIMS OF POLICY

Policy claims endorse specific courses of action (e.g., "Body cameras should be worn by all police officers to reduce the use of excessive force during arrests"). These claims are prescriptive, meaning they argue that the proposed action will improve the status quo.

20b. Key Types of Evidence

Evidence is material intended to convince the audience a claim is valid. Some forms of evidence include examples, narratives, testimony, facts, and statistics. External evidence, or knowledge drawn from beyond the speaker's experience, is the most common form of evidence.

The audience's preexisting thoughts and beliefs can also be powerful evidence for a claim. Few strategies gratify audiences more than a reaffirmation of their beliefs, especially for claims of value and policy.

Finally, when a speaker's experience and opinions are relevant to a claim, that expertise can be used as evidence. However, audiences are often skeptical of claims supported solely by the speaker's testimony. Supplementing your expertise with external evidence is more likely to yield a persuasive message.

20c. Counterarguments

A one-sided message ignores opposing viewpoints; a two-sided message addresses opposing claims in order to weaken or refute them. As a general rule of thumb, a persuasive speech should contain a two-sided message. On the one hand, if your audience is aware of opposing viewpoints that your speech ignores, you risk losing credibility. On the other hand, it's impossible to review and refute every single possible counterargument. The best strategy is to focus on raising and refuting only the most important counterarguments your audience is likely to be familiar with.

20d. Effective Reasoning

Reasoning is the process of drawing logical conclusions from a body of evidence. Deductive reasoning begins with a general principle or case, is followed by an example of that case, and then concludes with a claim. If the audience accepts the general principle and the specific example, logic dictates that it must accept the conclusion.

GENERAL CASE
All dogs are mortal.

SPECIFIC CASE
Fido is a dog.

CONCLUSION
Therefore Fido is mortal.

Inductive reasoning begins with specific cases, or minor premises, then leads to a general conclusion those cases support. However strong such conclusions appear to be, they are not necessarily true. Many inductive arguments are in fact weak. An audience must decide if a conclusion reached through inductive reasoning is a valid one based on the evidence at hand.

SPECIFIC CASE 1
Papua New Guinea has recorded a rise in sea level.

SPECIFIC CASE 2
Key Largo has recorded a rise in sea level.

SPECIFIC CASE 3
New York City has recorded a rise in sea level.

CONCLUSION
Sea levels are rising worldwide.

Reasoning by analogy is a form of inductive reasoning in which the speaker presents two cases and implies that what is true of one is true of the other. Analogies presume that the circumstances underlying both cases are similar, if not identical — and for this reason, such arguments can have vulnerabilities.

Causal reasoning asserts that one event or issue is the cause of another (e.g., "Widespread online bullying, combined with the large amount of time teens spend online, has led to a nationwide increase in the number of teenagers diagnosed with anxiety disorders").

20e. Logical Fallacies

Logical fallacies are rationales for claims that may seem reasonable but are actually unsound — and usually false. Not only should you strive to avoid fallacious reasoning in your own speeches, but you should be able to identify it in others' speeches. While many logical fallacies exist, some of the most common are defined in the following table.

Logical Fallacy	Example
Begging the question An argument that assumes the conclusion it purports to prove instead of providing evidence.	People who don't study are doomed to fail their exams because studying is the only way to pass.
Bandwagoning An argument that incorrectly assumes that because an idea is popular, it is correct.	Because all of my friends like *Stranger Things*, it must be one of the best shows ever made.
Either-or fallacy An argument that implies there are only two alternatives when there are in fact more.	Since curbing carbon emissions by 75 percent would bankrupt the oil industry, Congress should not be allowed to regulate the industry at all.
Ad hominem An argument that attacks a person's credibility instead of attacking the associated argument.	We should spend less money on NASA and more money on education. After all, NASA's spokesperson was recently accused of tax fraud.
Red herring An argument that cites irrelevant evidence in support of its conclusion.	Less meat in our diet would make us healthier. For one, vegetable farming is easier on the environment than cattle ranching.

(continued)

Logical Fallacy	Example
Hasty generalization An argument in which a broad conclusion is drawn from too little evidence.	The exorbitant hospital bill for my uncle's appendectomy unquestionably proves that our health care system needs to be overhauled on the national level.
Slippery slope An argument based on an erroneous assumption that one action will lead inevitably to a chain of others.	Properly recycling old electronics will set a good example, leading to a new era where recycling has eliminated pollution entirely.
Appeal to tradition An argument that wrongly asserts that something is ideal just because it was popular in the past.	Hollywood should not introduce a new ratings system. After all, G, PG, PG-13, R, and NC-17 are the ratings we grew up with.
Non sequitur ("does not follow") An argument in which the rationale has nothing to do with the conclusion.	The Internet needs more restrictions on hate speech. Just look at how many teenagers are dropping out of high school.

21. Addressing Culture

An audience's cultural background affects its reaction to persuasive messages. Understanding the core values, cultural norms, and cultural premises of your audience is key to crafting effective emotional appeals.

Core values are beliefs shared by members of the same culture. Values such as individualism, hard work, and freedom are some you may recognize and believe in. Arguments that challenge core values tend to be unsuccessful.

Cultural norms are behavioral rules to which members of a group generally adhere. Persuasive messages that contradict cultural norms are rarely successful.

Cultural premises are beliefs about identity and relationships firmly embedded in a culture. Some cultural premises include the notion that wealth is worth pursuing and that science and technology improve our lives. Audiences who feel the very premises of their culture are being challenged are difficult to persuade.

22. Organizing Persuasive Speeches

The nature of your argument and its evidence, the response you want to elicit from your audience, and your audience's preconceived notions about your topic will all influence how you organize your speech.

22a. Problem-Solution Pattern

Some topics or claims inherently lend themselves to a particular organizational pattern. For example, the claim that the voting age should be raised implies that the current voting age represents a problem and that a higher age requirement represents a solution.

The problem-solution pattern is frequently used for persuasive speeches based on claims of policy. To use this pattern, organize your points to show the nature and significance of a problem before offering justification for a proposed solution, like so:

  I. Problem (what it is)
  II. Solution (how to fix the problem)

Complicated problems require more elaboration. In these cases, a three-point problem-cause-solution pattern may be used:

  I. Nature of the problem (why it's a problem, whom it affects, etc.)
  II. Cause(s) of the problem (how/when it began, why it persists)
  III. Solution to the problem (how it will work, how it differs from previous solution attempts)

When asserting a claim of policy, it might be necessary to demonstrate the proposal's feasibility. In these cases, you can employ a four-point problem-cause-solution-feasibility pattern that provides evidence for whether the solution you've proposed will actually work.

22b. Monroe's Motivated Sequence

In the mid-1930s, Purdue University professor Alan Monroe developed the motivated sequence pattern, a five-step organization for persuasion that is still widely used today. It's particularly effective when attempting to persuade an audience to take an action, such as buying a product, donating to a cause, or voting a particular way.

1. The attention step employs an example, statistic, quotation, or anecdote to make the topic relevant to the audience.

2. The need step shows how the topic applies to the psychological needs of the audience. This step also implies that your proposed solution and/or action will satisfy this need.

3. The satisfaction step identifies the solution and shows how the solution will satisfy the need established in the previous step.

4. The visualization step shows the audience what would happen if the solution were adopted. This imaginary success scenario is designed to focus attention on the benefits of the proposal (as opposed to its feasibility).

5. The action step exhorts the members of the audience to act on their acceptance of the speaker's message. This may include changing their way of thinking, renewing their commitment to the values they already possess, or adopting new behavior.

22c. Comparative Advantage Pattern

When your audience is not only aware of the problem your speech addresses but already agrees that a solution must be sought, it may be best to compare the advantages of different possible solutions. This pattern acknowledges the strengths of other solutions, then identifies weaknesses, and finally shows the advantages of the alternative.

22d. Refutation Pattern

When opposing viewpoints are vulnerable to criticism, the refutation pattern of organization can be optimal. Here, the speaker identifies opposing claims before showing how they are insufficient. Emphasizing objections to opposing arguments may even sway audience members who originally disagreed with you. Main points arranged in a refutation pattern follow this format:

Main Point I

State an opposing claim.

Main Point II

Demonstrate how the claim is faulty.

Main Point III

Present evidence for your own claim.

Main Point IV

Contrast your claim with the opposing claim, emphasizing your claim's superiority.

23. Identifying Audience Disposition

The way your listeners feel about your topic influences whether they will embrace or reject your appeals. Persuasion scholar Herbert Simon defines four audience types and suggests reasoning and organization strategies for each.

Audience Type	Possible Persuasive Strategies
Strongly opposed	• Address opposing viewpoints with the refutation pattern. • Emphasize points of agreement. • Use inductive reasoning. • Seek only a minor change in audience attitude. • If you must ask your audience to do something, hold off until the very end of your speech.

(continued)

Audience Type	Possible Persuasive Strategies
Skeptical or conflicted	• Address opposing viewpoints with the refutation pattern. • Present strong arguments supported by unbiased evidence.
Receptive	• Consider a narrative organization. • Reinforce audience sympathies with emotional appeals. • Stress commonality with the audience. • Clearly offer a call to action.
Uninformed or apathetic	• Capture the audience's attention. • Emphasize the topic's relevance to the audience. • Emphasize speaker credibility.

part 4

Citing Sources in Speeches

When you use ideas generated and facts gathered by others in a speech, you are obligated to credit your sources.

Acknowledging appropriate sources properly demonstrates the depth and quality of your research to your audience, which in turn bolsters your own credibility as a speaker who avoids plagiarism. Citing sources also allows your listeners to check your sources and do their own research.

24. Citing Sources

A verbal acknowledgment of a source within a speech is an oral citation. You should briefly offer the following information when orally citing a source:

- The author or origin of the source ("*New York Times* columnist Thomas Friedman . . ." or "According to the *National Education Association* website . . .")
- The type of source (TV interview, blog post, book, magazine, video, etc.)
- The title or a description of the source ("In the book *The Rise of Drones at Home* . . ." or "In an acclaimed memoir about overcoming substance abuse . . .")
- The date of the source ("An article published on *May 1st, 2022* . . ." or "According to a

revised report about the COVID-19 pandemic posted by the CDC on *July 12, 2022* . . .")

Keep oral citations as brief as possible to avoid disrupting the flow of your speech. However, you should maintain a formal written bibliography of all your sources.

24a. Establishing Trustworthy Sources

A skeptical audience will accept your supporting materials — examples, stories, testimony, facts, statistics — if, and only if, they believe the sources are credible. Aim to cite sources in a way that establishes their credibility. For example, if one of your sources is a Harvard professor, that fact could convince some of your listeners to accept the information from that source as reliable, and you should therefore weave this credential into your oral citation.

Source reliability refers to how trustworthy we consider a source to be, and it is often based in large part on the source's history of providing factual information. However, even reliable sources can be inaccurate. For example, a nurse might spot inaccuracies in a *New York Times* article about health care due to medical expertise, even though one might generally consider the *New York Times* reliable. Because no source is infallible, a claim supported by multiple sources will always seem more credible than a claim with only one source for support. The more controversial the claim, the more important it is to support that claim with a variety of sources.

Offering a source qualifier, or briefly noting why the source is qualified to address the topic, will bolster its credibility among skeptical listeners. For example, while making a claim about video games, one might introduce a source this way: "Former video games editor for *Wired* . . ."

24b. Dynamic Citation Delivery

Oral citation doesn't have to interrupt the flow of your speech. Varying the wording of your citations can make your delivery natural and keep audiences tuned in. For example, if you introduce one source with the phrase "According to . . . ," use another phrase for the next. "As reported by . . ."; "In the opinion of . . ."; and "*Wired* journalist Emily Dreyfuss writes that . . ." are just a few examples.

Leading with your claim places the most interesting information up front, and helps keep your speech organized in a way that helps the audience follow your logic. For example, you might begin a sentence with a claim that "Alcohol abuse can lead to colon cancer . . ." before revealing your source: "according to a new report by scientists at Carnegie Mellon University."

24c. Crediting Sources in Presentation Aids

Presentation aids that contain information drawn from research must also be labeled on the aid. If you reproduce copyrighted material such as photographs or infographics, put a copyright symbol (©) next to your citation(s). Use both oral and written citation in conjunction when the audience would benefit from both. For example, while pointing to a photograph labeled properly in its caption, you might also say, "This photo from *Life* magazine shows . . ."

25. Types of Sources and Sample Oral Citations

Below is a list of types of sources and sample oral citations.

Type of Source	What to Cite	Example
Book with *one or two* authors	First and last names, source qualifier(s), and date of publication	In the book *What We Know about Climate Change*, published in 2012, MIT meteorologist Kerry Emanuel argues that . . .
Book with *three or more* authors	First and last name of first author and "co-authors"	In the 1993 book *Captured Lives: Australian Captivity Narratives*, Kate Darian-Smith, professor of history at the University of Melbourne, and her two co-authors, both educators, show how . . .
Reference work (atlas, encyclopedia, almanac, etc.)	Title, date of publication, author or sponsoring organization, and source qualifier	According to 2014's *Almanac of American Politics*, a widely read survey of American races and political figures, Michael Barone and co–authors describe . . .

(continued)

Type of Source	What to Cite	Example
Print article	Same citation guidelines as a print book	In an article published in the May 2022 edition of the *New York Times*, Matthew Futterman, a veteran sports reporter, discusses the decision to bar Russian tennis players . . .
Online-only publication	Follow the same guidelines as for a book, but identify the source as an "online" publication	In a May 2, 2022, review for the online music blog *Pitchfork*, Olivia Horn gives her take on . . .
An organization's website	Site name, source qualifier, and, if applicable, the section of the site cited and its most recent update	On the Ebola section of its website, last updated May 26, 2022, the Centers for Disease Control, the foremost monitoring agency for disease outbreak in the world, reports that . . .
Blog	The blogger, source qualifier, affiliated website (if applicable), and date	In a May 23, 2015, post on his personal blog, Greg Mankiw, the chairman of the economics department at Harvard University, argues that . . .
TV or radio news program	The program, segment, reporter, source qualifier, and date aired	In a *60 Minutes* segment about TedTalks that aired on April 19, 2015, Lesley Stahl described . . .
Online video	The video source, program, segment, source qualifier, and date of publication, if applicable	In a lecture delivered at the 2010 Sewanee Writers' Conference and broadcast on the conference's YouTube channel on November 10, 2011, Robert Hass, U.S. Poet Laureate from 1995 to 1997, argued that . . .
Layperson or expert testimony	The person, source qualifier, context in which information was offered, and date information was offered	On March 26, 2015, in congressional testimony before the Senate Foreign Relations Committee, Ben Affleck, well-known filmmaker, actor, and founder of the Eastern Congo Initiative, testified as to the profound poverty endured by populations in Eastern Congo . . .
Interviews and personal communication	The person, source qualifier, date, and type of correspondence	In an email interview conducted on February 2, 2015, Austin, Texas, Police Chief Art Acevedo said . . .

part 5

Presentation Aids

Research has shown that audiences remember only about 30 percent of what they hear, but they remember more than 60 percent of what they hear *and* see. Using presentation aids not only helps audiences remember the points of your speech but also helps listeners visualize relationships among key concepts, rapidly evaluate data, and understand complex ideas. When visual aids look professional, they also bolster the speaker's credibility. However, presentation aids alone cannot make a speech work. No matter how great visual aids look, audiences are turned off by speakers who simply read information off the aids without adding anything new. Instead, aim to use aids as jumping-off points for engaging verbal information or argumentation.

26. Choosing a Presentation Aid

Presentation aids can include charts, diagrams, audio and video information, and props. Focus on selecting aids that illustrate your speech points most effectively.

26a. Props and Models

A prop is any physical object that enhances the audience's ability to visualize a main point. For example, a speech about fly-fishing might include a fishing rod, a fishing line, and a fishing net as props. A model is a three-dimensional, proportional representation of an object or process. For example, a doctor might use a human-sized skeleton as a model while explaining how a fracture affects movement.

Guidelines for using props and models include the following:

- If the aid might be distracting, keep it hidden until you are ready to use it.
- Make sure your aid is large enough for everyone in your audience to see.
- Practice incorporating the aid into your speech before actually giving the speech.

26b. Pictures, Diagrams, and Maps

A picture is any image (such as a photo or painting) that imparts information. For example, a photograph of a wrecked SUV might show the danger of texting and driving in a speech about auto safety. A diagram illustrates a process, showing how something works or how concepts are organized and related. For example, a diagram of a NASA rocket with each component labeled might supplement a speech about space flight. A map is an image that shows a geographic area or areas. A speech advocating for preservation of manatees might feature a map of Floridian waterways where both manatees and humans are active. In each case, the value of any picture, diagram, or map lies in its ability to efficiently convey information. Often this information is emotional, such as in the case of the wrecked SUV, or technical or numerical, as in the case of the rocket diagram.

26c. Graphs, Charts, and Tables

A graph represents relationships between variables. Most speakers use one of four types: a line graph, bar graph, pie graph, or pictogram.

A line graph plots one measurement along a horizontal axis and another measurement along a vertical axis, then connects each data point with a line. Line graphs can be powerful tools for representing trends that change over time.

A bar graph uses vertical or horizontal bars to compare quantities or magnitudes. Multidimensional bar graphs, in which differently colored or marked bars represent different kinds of information, allow audiences to easily compare two or more kinds of data in a single chart. When creating line and bar graphs, apply the following guidelines:

- Clearly label all graphs, including their axes.
- Begin the numerical axis at zero.
- Only compare like variables.
- Plot no more than two lines of data on one line graph.

A pie graph divides a whole into "slices" so that each slice corresponds to a percentage of the whole. Pie graphs are good at showing contrasts in proportion. When creating pie graphs, apply the following guidelines:

- Identify each slice and label it with its respective percentage.
- Limit the number of slices to a maximum of seven in order to reduce visual clutter.
- If possible, color each slice differently so that it's easy to distinguish between them.

A pictogram shows relationships and trends with icons or pictorial symbols. Pictograms add emotional impact to otherwise dry data. For example, a series of columns made up of missile icons stacked above different years might show how military spending has waxed or waned over time. When creating pictograms, clearly label your axes and indicate what variable each symbol represents.

Like a graph, a chart visually represents the relationship among data. A flowchart helps audiences visualize the flow of a complex process by animating its steps with boxes connected by arrows. A table allows audiences to rapidly examine and compare data by grouping it in columns and rows.

26d. Audio, Video, and Multimedia

An audio clip is a brief recording of music, sound, or speech. Video refers to excerpts from movies, television, online venues, or unpublished footage sources. A multimedia presentation combines any quantity of pictures, text, audio, and video data into a single production. Just as pictures can communicate complex information efficiently, audio, video, and multimedia presentation aids can also grab attention, add expressive power to main points, and make a speech engaging. When incorporating audio, video, and multimedia aids into a speech, remember to apply the following guidelines:

- Cue each clip to its appropriate starting point before the speech.
- Contextualize or preview the content of each clip for the audience before pressing *play*.
- After the clip has played, reiterate the reason why you showed it to the audience.

27. How to Present an Aid

There are many ways, both high-tech and low-tech, to present aids effectively. Whether you are using presentation slides, poster board, handouts, or another method for presenting data, images, or other visual aids, apply the following guidelines:

- Ensure that any technology you're using works and practice using it before the presentation.
- Deliver the speech while standing to the side of any visual aids, facing the audience.
- If you will need to direct your audience's attention to specific points within a visual, make sure you have a pointer, slide detail, or other tool or method to use.
- If you will need to create visual support during your presentation in response to audience comments or questions, be prepared with a whiteboard, flip chart, or other presentation aid.

part 6

Listening Effectively

Listening is the conscious act of receiving, understanding, interpreting, evaluating, and responding to messages. The act of audience listening is a vital component of any speech.

28. Selective Listening

Selective listening refers to the fact that audience members pay attention to certain messages and ignore others based on their background, level of attention, and interests. Many factors influence what grabs and holds an audience member's attention. Audience members pay attention both to what they think is important and to information to which they relate personally. When crafting a speech, it is helpful to keep in mind that audiences process unfamiliar information in terms of what is already familiar to them.

You can craft more successful messages using the following techniques:

- Appealing to the audience's interests, needs, attitudes, and values
- Emphasizing, in your speech introduction, what the audience stands to gain by listening
- Connecting new information to the audience's likely experiences
- Creating analogies that link new ideas to well-understood ones
- Repeating main points to better ensure audience comprehension
- Visually reinforcing your main points with presentation aids when appropriate

29. Listening to Foster Dialogue

A monologue imposes a speaker's message on the audience. By contrast, a dialogue is the respectful interchange of ideas between speaker and audience. In a dialogue, the speaker delivers the speech not to win the argument but to build a shared understanding with the audience, and the audience listens actively and empathetically.

When speaker and audience are engaged in a dialogue, a beneficial feedback loop of body language and verbal interchange can develop wherein the speaker's message is shaped by the audience's reaction, and vice versa. This shared connection between speaker and audience maximizes the impact of a message.

30. Overcoming Obstacles to Listening

Active listening, or listening that is focused and engaged, is impossible when the audience is

distracted. The following guidelines can improve your active listening as an audience member:

- Set a learning goal for each speech. For example: "In the next speech by a classmate, I will try to figure out why the speaker cares so much about the topic."
- Listen for the speaker's main points and note when the speaker mentions something that surprises you.
- Pay attention to nonverbal cues from the speaker.
- Try to discern the organizational pattern of the speech as it is delivered.

A listening distraction is anything competing for a listener's attention during a speech. External distractions, like ambulance sirens or the tapping sound texting makes when a phone is not in silent mode, come from the environment. Internal distractions, such as unrelated thoughts and feelings, come from within the listener. Speakers and audiences should try to anticipate and prepare for external distractions by arriving and setting up or taking a seat early. To reduce internal distractions, speakers and audiences should be rested, alert, and make a conscious effort to focus on the message of the speech.

When audience members focus on what they, rather than the speaker, will say next, it's a significant barrier to active listening. Similarly, audience members should avoid prematurely rejecting a speaker's message or tuning it out because they think the speaker has nothing to offer them. These tactics shut off communication. Even in cases of strong disagreement, letting a speaker finish before formulating a counterargument allows for an effective response.

Overconfidence or inattention may cause audience members to miss key information, only to realize later the speaker had something valuable to say. Audience members should always assume the speaker's message is important and pay attention accordingly.

31. Evaluating Evidence and Reasoning

Evaluating a speaker's evidence and reasoning is a vital part of active listening. To think critically about a speaker's message, audience members should do the following:

- Evaluate a speaker's evidence by asking if the sources seem credible and the facts cited seem accurate.
- Question the speaker's assumptions by looking for biases that might underlie the speaker's position and seeing if the evidence supports or contradicts those assumptions.
- Examine the speaker's reasoning by checking for fallacies or other examples of faulty logic.
- Consider alternative perspectives by trying to view the argument from all possible relevant points of view before assuming the speaker's perspective is valid.

32. Offering Feedback

To give the most useful feedback to a speaker, audience members should do the following:

- Be honest. Strive to be truthful, whether giving praise or criticism.
- Be compassionate. Begin criticism with a positive remark, and focus criticism on the speaker's message or delivery, rather than criticizing the speaker personally.
- Be specific. Neither blanket praise nor blanket criticism is helpful. Instead, focus your criticism or praise on individual techniques, main points, or parts of the speech that worked or didn't work.
- Allow for different delivery styles. Avoid negatively judging a message just because the speaker's style differs from yours.

part 7

Effective Group Communication

Most public speaking occurs in small groups involving anywhere from three to twenty people. These groups form in classrooms, offices, and even online discussion spaces. Small groups are also a common unit for giving group presentations. Therefore, learning how to work within a small group setting is vital to success both in school and in the workplace.

33. Setting an Agenda

A small group functions best when its agenda, or overall objective and schedule for meeting it, is clearly articulated and followed. Whether the group must make a decision or a presentation, setting an agenda can help the group resolve conflicts, focus, and stay on track.

34. Understanding Small Group Roles

Groups tend to succeed when individuals fulfill specific roles, and most members of a group will fulfill dual roles. Task roles are those that directly relate to the group's objectives. For example, during a group presentation, one person may be assigned to be the primary writer, another the primary speaker, and another the one responsible for presentation aids. In addition, group members may also adopt maintenance roles, or social roles within the group. For example, a "peacemaker" might excel at conflict resolution, a "comic reliever" might keep group morale up with intermittent jokes, and a "taskmaster" might keep the group focused.

Unfortunately, anti-group roles that undermine the agenda may also exist. A "blocker" might always undermine any idea, even if it is good, or someone might attempt to take credit for every idea, even if it belongs to the group as a whole. Group members should politely address anti-group problems at the outset to keep the group on track.

35. How to Frame Disagreements

When groups make decisions, conflict is inevitable, but it can also be quite positive. The best decisions usually emerge from a productive conflict in which group members challenge ideas by presenting counterexamples and considering alternatives to either strengthen the original idea or find a newer, better one. Such issues-based conflicts allow members to debate problems and brainstorm potential solutions. Alternatively, person-based conflict can also erupt, wherein members fight with each other for power, for credit, for less or more responsibility, and so on. Person-based conflicts waste time, reduce morale, and generally impede the group agenda.

36. Resisting Groupthink

For a group to be effective, members eventually need to establish consensus so that everyone can work together to achieve the group's objective. At the same time, groups must also avoid groupthink, which occurs when group members do not think critically about ideas merely to achieve consensus. Speak up if the following warning signs of groupthink occur:

- Individuals disagree on issues, but avoid hashing them out to spare each other's feelings.
- Participants who disagree with the rest of the group feel pressured to conform.
- Critical analysis of popular ideas is discouraged.
- Members spend more time justifying choices than testing them.

37. Group Decision Making

There are two methods of argument that generally help groups reach better decisions. Devil's advocacy occurs when members raise counterarguments, even when they are not sincerely held, merely to test the strength of a proposed idea. Dialectical inquiry occurs when members extend devil's advocacy to propose countersolutions to the original idea. These argumentation strategies expose weak assumptions that could prevent participants from making the best decision. Group leaders should encourage both methods of argument.

Print Resources

1. A Book with One Author

A book with one author serves as a general model for most MLA citations. Include author, title, publisher, and date of publication.

Robinson, Marilynne. *Jack*. Farrar, Straus and Giroux, 2020.

2. A Book with Multiple Authors

King, Stephen, and Peter Straub. *Black House*. Random House, 2001.

3. Two or More Works by the Same Author

Multiple entries should be arranged alphabetically by title. The author's name appears at the beginning of the first entry, but is replaced by three hyphens and a period in all subsequent entries.

Ward, Jesmyn. *Sing, Unburied, Sing*. Scribner, 2017.

---. *Salvage the Bones*. Bloomsbury, 2011.

---. *Where the Line Bleeds*. Agate, 2008.

4. Author and Editor Both Named

Vidal, Gore. *The Selected Essays of Gore Vidal*. Edited by Jay Parini, Vintage Books, 2009.

Alternately, to cite the editor's contribution, start with the editor's name.

Parini, Jay, editor. *The Selected Essays of Gore Vidal*. By Gore Vidal, Vintage Books, 2009.

5. Anthology

Oates, Joyce Carol, editor. *Telling Stories: An Anthology for Writers*. W. W. Norton, 1997.

Selection from an anthology:

Irving, Washington. "Rip Van Winkle." *American Literature & Rhetoric*, edited by Robin Aufses, et al., Bedford, Freeman & Worth, 2021, pp. 494–509.

6. Translation

Ferrante, Elena. *My Brilliant Friend*. Translated by Ann Goldstein, Europa Editions, 2011.

7. Entry in a Reference Work

Because most reference works are alphabetized, you should omit page numbers.

Lounsberry, Barbara. "Joan Didion." *Encyclopedia of the Essay*, edited by Tracy Chevalier, Fitzroy, 1997.

For a well-known encyclopedia, use only the edition and year of publication. When an article is not attributed to an author, start the entry with article's title.

> "Gilgamesh." *The Columbia Encyclopedia*. 5th ed., 1993.

8. Sacred Text

Unless a specific published edition is being cited, sacred texts should be omitted from the Works Cited list.

> *The New Testament*. Translated by Richmond Lattimore, North Point Press, 1997.

9. Article in a Journal

The title of the journal should be followed by the volume, issue, and year of the journal's publication, as well as the page range of the article.

> Marshall, Sarah. "Remote Control: Tonya Harding, Nancy Kerrigan, and the Spectacles of Female Power and Pain." *The Believer*, vol. 12, no. 1, 2014, pp. 1–10.

10. Article in a Magazine

In a weekly:

> Schjeldahl, Peter. "A Pairing of Josef Albers and Giorgio Morandi. *The New Yorker*, 1 February 2021, pp. 76–77.

In a monthly:

> Shulevitz, Judith. "The Brontës' Secret." *The Atlantic*, June 2016, pp. 38–41.

11. Article in a Newspaper

If you are citing a local paper that does not contain the city name in its title, add the city name in brackets after the newspaper title. When citing an article that does not appear on consecutive pages, list the first page followed by a plus sign. The edition needs to be included only if it is listed on the paper's masthead. For an opinion piece written by a named author, include the label "Op-ed" at the end of the entry if it is not clear from the title that it is an opinion piece.

> Krugman, Paul. "The Economy Is About to Take Off." *The New York Times*, 28 May 2021, p. A19.

12. Review

In a weekly:

> St. Félix, Doreen. "Social Contract." Review of *Mare of Easttown*, HBO Max, *The New Yorker*, 10 May 2021, p. 74.

In a monthly:

> Simpson, Mona. "Imperfect Union." Review of *Mrs. Woolf and the Servants*, by Alison Light, *The Atlantic*, Jan./Feb. 2009, pp. 93–101.

Electronic Resources

13. Article from a Database Accessed through a Subscription Service

Apply the normal rules for citing a journal article, but include the name of the subscription service in italics and the digital object identifier (doi), if available.

> Morano, Michele. "Boy Eats World." *Fourth Genre: Explorations in Nonfiction*, vol. 13, no. 2, 2011, pp. 31–35. *Project MUSE*, https://doi.org/10.1353/fge.2011.0029.

14. Article in an Online Magazine

Follow the author name and article title with the name of the magazine in italics, the date published, and the URL of the article.

> Schuman, Rebecca. "This Giant Sculpture of Kafka's Head Perfectly Encapsulates His Strange Relationship to Prague." *Slate*, 24 May 2016, slate.com/blogs/browbeat/2016/05/24/this_giant_moving_sculpture_of_kafka_s_head_is_the_perfect_tribute_to_kafka.html.

15. Article in an Online Newspaper

> Kelly, John. "The Secret to Keeping the Norwegian Royals Safe in World War II? The U.S. Secret Service." *The Washington Post*, 30 May 2020, www.washingtonpost.com/local/atlantic-crossing-secret-service/2021/05/29/862da36c-bfb7-11eb-83e3-0ca705a96ba4_story.html.

16. Online Review

> Stevens, Dana. "The New *It* Has Too Much Insane Clown, Not Enough Posse." Review of *It*, directed by Andrés Muschietti. *Slate*, 16 Oct. 2017, slate.com/arts/2017/09/the-new-adaptation-of-stephen-kings-it-reviewed.html.

17. Entry in an Online Reference Work

> "Eschatology." *Merriam-Webster*, 7 Apr. 2016, www.merriam-webster.com/dictionary/eschatology.

18. Work from a Website

> "Wallace Stevens (1879–1955)." *Poetry Foundation*, 2015, www.poetryfoundation.org/bio/wallace-stevens.

19. Entire Website

Website with editor:

> Dutton, Dennis, editor. *Arts and Letters Daily*. Chronicle of Higher Education, 2020, www.aldaily.com.

Website without editor:

> Academy of American Poets. *poets.org*. 2021, www.poets.org/.

Personal website:

> Valdez Quade, Kirstin. Home page, 2021, kirstinvaldezquade.com/.

20. Entire Web Log (Blog)

Benkkabou, Nagrisse, editor. *My Moroccan Food*. www.mymoroccanfood.com.

21. Social Media Post

List the author's full display name — that is, how it appears on the account, regardless of whether it's the person's real name — followed by the screen name or handle in brackets if it is significantly different from the display name. In the title position, use the caption of the post, the full text of the post (if it's brief), or the first few words of the post followed by an ellipsis (if it's long). Follow the capitalization and style of the post exactly and include any hashtags. If there is no text on the post, use a description of the photo or video as the title.

President Biden [@POTUS]. "I believe this is our moment to rebuild our economy from the bottom up and the middle out." *Twitter*, 27 May 2021, twitter.com/POTUS/status/1398062543466291200?s=20.

Brooklyn Nets [@brooklynnets]. Photo of James Harden, Game 3, Tonight 8:30pm. *Instagram*, 27 May 2020, www.instagram.com/p/CPaucADL1FR/?utm_source=ig_web_copy_link.

Lincoln Center [@lincolncenter] "BRB, watching this excerpt from Ballet Hispánico's "'CARMEN.maquia'" on repeat." 😊 #dancer #fyp #lincolncenter #ballet." *TikTok*, 7 May 2021, www.tiktok.com/@lincolncenter/video/6959623118910475526.

Richardson, Heather Cox. "Sunday, June 13, 2021." *Facebook*, 13 June 2021, www.facebook.com/heathercoxrichardson/posts/335806744581231.

22. Entry in a Wiki

"Pre-Raphaelite Brotherhood." *Wikipedia: The Free Encyclopedia*, Wikimedia Foundation, 25 Nov. 2013, en.wikipedia.org/wiki/Pre-Raphaelite_Brotherhood.

Other Sources

23. Film and Video

Follow the film title with the director, notable performers, the distribution company, and the date of release. For films viewed on the web, follow this with the URL of the website used to view the film. If citing a particular individual's work on the film, you may begin the entry with his or her name before the title.

Viewed in a theater:

The Hurt Locker. Directed by Kathryn Bigelow, performances by Jeremy Renner, Anthony Mackie, Guy Pearce, and Ralph Fiennes, Summit, 2009.

Viewed on the web (use original distributor and release date):

Fincher, David. "Mank." *Netflix*, 13 Nov. 2020, www.netflix.com.

24. Interview

Include the name of the interviewer if it is someone of note.

Personal interview:

> Tripp, Lawrence. Personal interview, 14 Apr. 2014.

In print:

> Dylan, Bob. "Who Is This Bob Dylan?" Interview by Tom Junod. *Esquire*, 23 Jan. 2014, pp. 124+.

On the radio:

> Thompson, Ahmir. "Questlove." Interview by Terry Gross. *Fresh Air*, NPR, 27 Apr. 2016.

On the web:

> Thompson, Ahmir. "Questlove." Interview by Terry Gross. *Fresh Air*, NPR, 27 Apr. 2016, www.npr.org/2016/04/27/475721555/questlove-on-prince-doo-wop-and-thefood-equivalent-of-the-mona-lisa.

25. Lecture or Speech

Viewed in person:

> Smith, Anna Deavere. "On the Road: A Search for American Character." Jefferson Lecture in the Humanities, John F. Kennedy Center for the Performing Arts, Washington, 6 Apr. 2015. 44th Jefferson Lecture.

Viewed on the web:

> Batuman, Elif. Lowell Humanities Series. Boston College. 13 Oct. 2010. www.frontrow.bc.edu/program/batuman.

26. Podcast

> Hobbes, Michael, and Sarah Marshall. "Princess Diana Part 4, The Divorce." *You're Wrong About*, 2 Nov. 2020, podcasts.apple.com/us/podcast/princess-diana-part-4-the-divorce/id1380008439?i=1000497028549.

27. Work of Art or Photograph

In a museum:

> Thomas, Mickalene. *A-E-I-O-U and Sometimes Y.* 2009, National Museum of Women in the Arts, Washington, D.C.

On the web:

> Thiebaud, Wayne. *Three Machines.* 1963, De Young Museum, San Francisco, art.famsf.org/wayne-thiebaud/three-machines-199318.

In print:

> Clark, Edward. *Navy CPO Graham Jackson Plays "Goin' Home."* 1945, *The Great LIFE Photographers*, Bulfinch, 2004, pp. 78–79.

28. Map or Chart

In print:

"U.S. Personal Savings Rate, 1929–1999." *Credit Card Nation: The Consequences of America's Addiction to Credit*, by Robert D. Manning, Basic, 2000, p. 100.

On the web:

"1914 New Balkan States and Central Europe Map." *National Geographic*, www.natgeomaps.com/hm-1914-new-balkan-states-and-central-europe.

29. Cartoon or Comic Strip

In print:

Flake, Emily. Cartoon. *The New Yorker*, 27 May 2021, p. 52.

On the web:

De Adder, Michael. "Doubling Down on Stupid," *The Washington Post*, 25 May 2021, www.washingtonpost.com/opinions/2021/05/25/doubling-down-stupid/.

30. Advertisement

In print:

Advertisement for Pittsburgh International Jazz Festival. *Jazz Times*, May 2021, p. 21.

On the web:

Advertisement for eBay authenticity guarantee. *Yahoo Sports*, 25 Nov. 2020, www.sports.yahoo.com.

Vocabulary and Word Roots

If your parents asked you to consent to a nonsensical plan to wake up everybody in the house with a light-sensor alarm clock, would you resent it, or be too sentimental to object?

The above sentence may not make much sense, except as an illustration of how word roots connect many words with related meanings. How many words in the preceding two sentences have as their basis the Latin root *sent* or *sens*, meaning "to feel"?

A *root* is the origin of a word, often from a different language. Recognizing the roots of words can help you understand their meanings. The words *consent, nonsensical, sensor, resent, sentimental, sentence,* and *sense* may all be familiar to you. But the root, meaning "to feel," might help you understand the meaning of an unfamiliar word, like *sentient*.

Many roots form new words by adding *prefixes* and/or *suffixes* to the root. The addition of the prefix *in-* and the suffix *-itive* turn the root *sens* into the word *insensitive*.

Below are some common roots, their meanings, and words derived from these roots.

Root	Meaning	Words
-audi- (Latin)	to hear	audible, auditory, audiovisual
-bene- (Greek)	good, well	benevolent, beneficial, benefit
-bio- (Greek)	life	biology, autobiography, biotech
-duc(t)- (Latin)	to lead, to make	conduct, education, induce
-gen- (Greek)	race, kind	genetic, regenerate, genre
-geo- (Greek)	earth	geography, geode, geometry
-graph- (Greek)	to write	graphite, autograph, paragraph
-jur-, -jus- (Latin)	law	injustice, jury, jurisdiction
-log(o)- (Greek)	word, thought	logical, sociology, dialogue
-luc- (Latin)	light	translucent, elucidate, lucid
-manu- (Latin)	hand	manuscript, manual, manufacture
-mit-, -mis- (Latin)	to send	transmit, mission, permission
-path- (Greek)	to feel, to suffer	sympathy, telepathy, pathos
-phil- (Greek)	love	philosophy, Francophile, philanthropy
-photo- (Greek)	light	photosynthesis, photocopy, telephoto
-port- (Latin)	to carry	transportation, portable, important
-psych- (Greek)	soul	psyche, psychiatry, psychic
-scrib-, -script- (Latin)	to write	transcription, scripture, unscripted
-sent-, -sens- (Latin)	to feel	sensitive, consensual, sentient
-tele- (Greek)	far away	television, telekinesis, telepathy
-tend- (Latin)	to stretch	extend, contending, distended
-terr- (Latin)	earth	terrain, extraterrestrial, disinter
-vac- (Latin)	empty	vacuum, vacation, vacuous
-vid-, -vis- (Latin)	to see	invisible, video, visor

Glossary / Glosario

Please note that this glossary/glosario is a general resource for your reference. It contains all of the key terms found in the book and has additional academic vocabulary you may find useful throughout the school year.

English

Español

A

absent parent See **archetypal characters**.

padres ausentes Ver **personajes arquetípicos.**

accuracy (p. 103) How true or correct the information in a source is.

precisión Qué tan verdadera o correcta es la información de una fuente.

act The major subunit into which the action of a play is divided. The number of acts in a play typically ranges between one and five, and the acts are usually further divided into scenes.

acto Subunidad principal en que se divide la acción de una obra. El número de actos de una obra de teatro varía entre uno y cinco y los actos generalmente se dividen en escenas.

acting To interpret and portray a character through inflections, gestures, facial expressions, and reactions.

actuar Interpretar y representar un personaje a través de inflexiones, gestos, expresiones faciales y reacciones.

active listening (p. 5) Listening that is focused and engaged.

escuchar activamente Escuchar de manera enfocada y participativa.

adjective A word that describes a noun or pronoun.

adjetivo Palabra que describe a un sustantivo o pronombre.

adverb A word that describes a verb (usually ending in –ly).

adverbio Palabra que describe a un verbo (con frecuencia termina en –mente).

alliteration Repetition of the same consonant sounds in a sequence of words.

aliteración Repetición de los mismos sonidos consonantes en una secuencia de palabras.

allusion (p. 50) Brief reference to a person, an event, or a place (real or fictitious) or to a work of art.

alusión Breve referencia a una persona, evento o lugar (real o ficticio) o a una obra de arte.

analogy A comparison between two seemingly dissimilar things. Often, an analogy uses something simple or familiar to explain something complex or unfamiliar.

analogía Comparación entre dos cosas que parecen diferentes. Las analogías usan algo sencillo o conocido para explicar algo complejo o poco conocido.

analysis See **expository strategies**.

análisis Ver **estrategias expositivas**.

anecdote A brief story used to illustrate a point or claim.

anécdota Historia breve que ilustra un punto o afirmación.

annotation (p. 20) Taking notes directly on a text.

anotación Tomar apuntes directamente sobre un texto.

antagonist (p. 248) The character who opposes the protagonist; while not necessarily an enemy, the antagonist creates or intensifies a conflict for the protagonist. An evil antagonist is a villain.

antagonista Personaje que se opone al protagonista; si bien no es necesariamente un enemigo, el antagonista crea o intensifica un conflicto para el protagonista. El antagonista malvado es un villano.

archetype Patterns of plot, setting, and character that recur regularly, with the creators oftentimes not fully aware that they are repeating long-established patterns.

arquetipo Patrones de trama, escena y personaje que ocurren de manera regular y repetitiva. Los creadores no siempre están plenamente conscientes de que repiten patrones que fueron establecidos hace mucho tiempo.

archetypal characters (p. 860)

The Absent Parent: Many heroes are orphans — Cinderella, Harry Potter, Anne Shirley from *Anne of Green Gables* — and sometimes the hero is reunited with a parent at some point in the journey.

The Companion: A character, sometimes an animal or magical creature, who assists the hero on the journey and who often provides friendship and support as needed. Sometimes this character is included for humorous effect and oftentimes lets the heroes show their true selves.

The Damsel in Distress: A common archetype of a character — often a woman, but not always — who needs to be rescued by the hero.

The Mentor: A guide and teacher who provides valuable information, instruction, or weapons to the hero and encourages the hero to start on the journey.

A Monster or Dragon: Often one of the antagonists the hero faces on the journey and represents evil, or a wilderness that the hero civilizes.

The Shadow: Often the chief antagonist that the hero must defeat or tame in the end before the hero can complete the journey. The name "the Shadow" implies that this character is in some way a reflection of the hero, sharing traits and characteristics with the hero, but in a more sinister form.

The Tempter/Temptress: A character who tries to prevent the hero from completing the journey by presenting temptations such as money, fame, sex, or other appeals.

The Trickster: Usually the protagonist of their own story, but occasionally a supporting character in a hero's journey tale. The trickster is clever, sometimes a thief, and is always on the lookout for a new or easier way to do things. Tricksters intentionally break the rules, and their actions sometimes lead to good things happening and sometimes to disaster.

personajes arquetípicos

Padres ausentes: muchos héroes son huérfanos — Cenicienta, Harry Potter, Anne Shirley de *Anne of Green Gables* — y en ocasiones el héroe se reencuentra con uno de sus padres en algún punto del viaje.

El acompañante: personaje, a veces un animal o un ser mágico, que ayuda al héroe en su viaje y que brinda amistad y apoyo según sea necesario. En ocasiones este personaje aparece para dar un efecto humorístico y otras veces deja que los héroes muestren su verdadera naturaleza.

La damisela en apuros: arquetipo común de un personaje, generalmente (aunque no siempre) una mujer que debe ser rescatada por el héroe.

El mentor: guía y maestro que ofrece información, instrucciones o armas valiosas al héroe y lo anima a emprender el viaje.

El monstruo o dragón: uno de los antagonistas que los héroes enfrentan en el viaje y que representa el mal o un lugar salvaje que el héroe civiliza.

La sombra: antagonista principal que el héroe debe derrotar o conquistar antes de completar el viaje. Es conocido como "la sombra" porque este personaje es una reflexión más oscura del héroe.

El tentador/la tentadora: Personaje que intenta evitar que el héroe complete el viaje y para ello presenta tentaciones como dinero, fama, sexo u otras atracciones.

El embaucador: normalmente protagoniza su propia historia, pero a veces es un personaje secundario en un cuento del viaje del héroe. El embaucador es astuto, a veces es un ladrón, y siempre está buscando maneras más fáciles de hacer las cosas. Rompe intencionalmente las reglas y sus acciones a veces conducen a resultados positivos y a veces son desastrosas.

archetypal plots (p. 857)

The Hero's Journey: An archetypal plot that evolves in three stages: the Call to Adventure, the Road of Trials, and the Return. In the Call to Adventure, the hero is asked to take on a challenge far from home. In the Road of Trials, the hero endures tests of strength, resourcefulness, and endurance. In the Return, the hero returns home after surviving the trials, changed in many ways.

Trickster Tale: An archetypal plot that evolves in three stages: Crossing the Boundary, Resolving the Conflict, and Creating Change. Whether it is breaking a social taboo, moving between heaven and earth, gods and mortals, or man and animals, the first step of any trickster tale is a transgression of social norms. By crossing the boundary, the Trickster has created some sort of conflict, which must be resolved. The Trickster often finds a clever way of achieving victory. Usually the result of crossing the boundary and resolving the conflict is that the Trickster generates progress or creates change.

archetypal settings (p. 863)

The Castle: A place of safety that holds the treasure the hero seeks, or the damsel who needs rescuing. It may represent home or some other powerful place.

The Garden: A place where humans live in harmony with nature. It is a symbol of innocence and security.

The Maze or Labyrinth: A puzzling dilemma or great uncertainty represented by a maze or confusing and disorientating space that the hero must navigate.

The Threshold: A place that symbolizes the movement between the known and the unknown worlds and is the last place the hero sees before fully committing to the journey.

The Underworld/Innermost Cave: Many heroes travel to dark settings from which they must emerge, symbolically conquering death. Sometimes this is an actual Underworld, or it could be a dark, confining space like a cave, den, dungeon, or lair.

trama arquetípica

El viaje del héroe: trama arquetípica que evoluciona en tres etapas: la llamada a la aventura, las pruebas y el retorno. En la llamada a la aventura, el héroe debe enfrentar un desafío lejos de casa. En las pruebas, el héroe enfrenta pruebas de fuerza, ingenio y resistencia. En el retorno, el héroe regresa a casa después de sobrevivir a las pruebas y ha cambiado de muchas maneras.

Cuento del embaucador: trama arquetípica que evoluciona en tres etapas: cruzar el límite, resolver el conflicto y generar un cambio. Ya sea que rompa un tabú social, se mueva entre cielo y tierra, dioses y mortales, o humanos y animales, el primer paso en el cuento del embaucador es una transgresión a las normas sociales. Al cruzar el límite, el embaucador crea algún tipo de conflicto, que debe ser resuelto. El embaucador encuentra maneras astutas de salir airoso. Normalmente, el resultado de cruzar el límite y resolver el conflicto es que el embaucador genera progreso o un cambio.

escenarios arquetípicos

El castillo: lugar seguro que contiene el tesoro que busca el héroe o a la damisela que debe ser rescatada. Puede representar el hogar u otro lugar poderoso.

El jardín: lugar donde los humanos viven en armonía con la naturaleza. Es un símbolo de inocencia y seguridad.

El laberinto: dilema confuso o gran incertidumbre representada por un laberinto o un espacio confuso y desorientador que el héroe debe navegar.

El umbral: lugar que simboliza el movimiento entre mundos conocidos y desconocidos y es el último lugar que el héroe ve antes de comprometerse completamente con el viaje.

El submundo/La cueva más interna: muchos héroes viajan a escenarios oscuros de los cuales deben emerger, como si conquistaran la muerte de manera simbólica. En ocasiones es un viaje al verdadero inframundo o puede ser un espacio oscuro y confinado como una cueva, una guarida, un calabozo o una madriguera.

The Wasteland: A place that is in many ways the opposite of the garden; it symbolizes loneliness and despair.

The Wilderness or Forest: A place that can symbolize the unknown world, where the laws of nature rule instead of the laws of humanity.

El yermo: lugar que de muchas maneras es lo contrario del jardín; simboliza la soledad y la desesperación.

El bosque o mundo salvaje: lugar que simboliza el mundo desconocido en el cual rigen las leyes de la naturaleza en lugar de las leyes de la humanidad.

---

argument To persuade through a process of reasoned inquiry. A persuasive discourse resulting in a coherent and considered movement from a claim to a conclusion.

argumento Persuadir a través de un proceso de indagación razonada. Un discurso persuasivo resulta en una transición coherente de una afirmación a una conclusión.

---

artistic license (p. 139) When a writer may embellish or add detail to assist readers in connecting with the story.

licencia artística Cuando un escritor exagera o agrega detalles para ayudar a los lectores a conectar con la historia.

---

assertion (p. 470) A statement that presents a claim or thesis.

aseveración Enunciado que presenta una afirmación o tesis.

---

assonance The repetition of internal vowel sounds in nearby words that do not end the same.

asonancia Repetición de vocales internas en palabras cercanas que no tienen la misma terminación.

---

audience (p. 26) The listener, viewer, or reader of a text. Most texts are likely to have multiple audiences.

público Lector, espectador o lector de un texto. La mayoría de los textos están destinados a más de un público.

---

author (p. 25) See **speaker.**

autor Ver **orador.**

---

authority (p. 103) Who wrote it? Who published it? What gives them ability to speak on the subject? Is the person an expert — by education or experience? If the information is from a website, what can you learn from the "About Us" page? Is there a physical address? Is there an editorial staff?

autoridad ¿Quién lo escribió? ¿Quién lo publicó? ¿Quién le dio la autoridad de hablar de este tema? ¿La persona es experta? ¿Por educación o por experiencia? Si es de un sitio web, ¿qué se puede saber a partir de la sección "Acerca de" del sitio? ¿Tiene una dirección física? ¿Hay personal editorial?

B

background information (p. 26) See **context.**

antecedentes Ver **contexto.**

---

bias (p. 103) A prejudice or preconceived notion that prevents a person from approaching a topic in a neutral or an objective way. While you can be biased *toward* something, the most common usage has a negative connotation.

sesgo Prejuicio o noción preconcebida que impide a una persona acercarse a un tema de manera neutral u objetiva. Si bien se puede tener un sesgo *a favor* de algo, el término generalmente se usa con una connotación negativa.

---

blank verse See **iambic pentameter** and **meter.**

verso blanco Ver **pentámetro yámbico** y **métrica.**

---

blocking (p. 135) The actions of the people in a story. In drama, this refers to the movements and gestures and expressions of actors on stage. In fiction and narrative, it refers to the descriptions of those movements, gestures, and expressions.

bloqueo Acciones de las personas de un cuento. En la dramaturgia, esto se refiere a los movimientos, gestos y expresiones de los actores en el escenario. En la ficción y narrativa, se refiere a las descripciones de estos movimientos, gestos y expresiones.

---

brackets ([ ]) (p. 115) Brackets are most often used to change a pronoun or to change the verb tense. They signal that the word in brackets has been changed and is not part of the original quotation.

corchetes ([ ]) Los corchetes se usan para cambiar un pronombre o cambiar el tiempo de un verbo. Señalan que la palabra en corchetes ha cambiado y no es parte de la cita original.

C

cast of characters In drama, a list of the characters in a play.

elenco de personajes En la dramaturgia, la lista de personajes de una obra.

castle See **archetypal settings**.

castillo Ver **escenarios arquetípicos**.

catharsis The emotional release felt by the audience at the end of a tragic drama. The term comes from Aristotle's *Poetics*, in which he explains this frequently felt relief in terms of a purification of the emotions caused by watching the tragic events. (*Catharsis* means "purgation" or "purification" in Greek.)

catarsis Liberación emocional que experimenta el público al final de un drama trágico. El término nace de la obra *Poética*, de Aristóteles, en la cual explica este alivio habitual en términos de la purificación de emociones que se desencadenan al presenciar eventos trágicos. (*Catarsis* significa "purgar" o "purificar" en griego).

cause and effect See **expository strategies**.

causa y efecto Ver **estrategias expositivas**.

challenge (p. 10) To disagree respectfully with others' ideas.

desafiar Expresar desacuerdo con ideas ajenas de manera respetuosa.

character (p. 25) A person depicted in a narrative. While this term generally refers to human beings, it can also include animals or inanimate objects that are given human characteristics. See also **archetypal characters**.

personaje Persona retratada en una narrativa. Si bien el término se refiere a seres humanos, también incluye animales u objetos inanimados a los cuáles se les asignan rasgos humanos. Ver también **personajes arquetípicos**.

characterization The method by which the author builds, or reveals, a character; it can be direct or indirect. Indirect characterization means that an author shows rather than tells us what a character is like through what the character says, does, or thinks or through what others say about the character. Direct characterization occurs when a narrator tells the reader who a character is by describing the background, motivation, temperament, or appearance of a character.

caracterización Método empleado por el autor para construir o revelar un personaje; puede ser directo o indirecto. La caracterización indirecta significa que el autor nos muestra, en lugar de decirnos, cómo es el personaje a través de su forma de hablar, de lo que hace o piensa o a través de lo que otros dicen sobre el personaje. La caracterización directa es cuando el narrador le dice al lector quién es el personaje a través de descripciones de sus antecedentes, motivaciones, temperamento o aspecto.

citing sources (p. 116) Showing where the source material came from.

citar fuentes Mostrar la fuente donde se origina el material.

claim (p. 392) Also called an assertion or proposition, a claim states the argument's main idea or position. A claim differs from a topic or subject in that a claim has to be arguable.

afirmación También conocida como aseveración o proposición, la afirmación establece la idea o postura principal del argumento. La afirmación es diferente de un tema o subtema ya que debe ser debatible.

clarity (p. 9) A clearer understanding of ideas.

claridad Entendimiento claro de las ideas.

classification See **expository strategies**.

clasificación Ver **estrategias expositivas**.

clause A group of words containing both a subject and a verb.

> **dependent clause** A clause that does not make sense when it stands alone.

> **independent clause** A clause that can stand by itself and still make sense.

> **subordinate clause** A group of words containing a subject and a verb that is less important and dependent on another group of words containing a subject and a verb.

climax See **plot**.

clincher (p. 91) The conclusion of a speech or essay that sums up the main points and makes a strong, memorable point.

coherence (p. 87) The quality of a paragraph where the ideas flow logically, one thought leading to the next.

colon (:) A form of punctuation that introduces an example.

comedy A happy play in which the protagonist experiences some sort of success. Comedies are often humorous, but not always, and have a happy ending.

comic hero A character in a comedy who is a simple or common person, with an endearing trait, who experiences some sort of success, whether it is finding love or achieving greatness.

comma (,) (p. 80) A form of punctuation that shows separations within a sentence. Commas are used to set off subordinate clauses, phrases, or items in a list.

comma splice (p. 81) Occurs when a writer connects two independent clauses with only a comma.

companion See **archetypal characters**.

comparison See **expository strategies**.

complex sentence See **sentence**.

compound sentence See **sentence**.

compound-complex sentence See **sentence**.

concede and refute (p. 392) See **concession** and **refutation**.

---

cláusula Grupo de palabras que contiene un sujeto y un verbo.

> **cláusula dependiente** Cláusula que no tiene sentido por sí sola.

> **cláusula independiente** Cláusula que tiene sentido y se sostiene por sí sola.

> **cláusula subordinada** Grupo de palabras que contiene un sujeto y un verbo que es menos importante y es dependiente de otro grupo de palabras que tienen un sujeto y un verbo.

clímax Ver **trama**.

punto clave Conclusión de un discurso o ensayo que resume los puntos más importantes y dice algo fuerte y memorable.

coherencia Calidad de un párrafo donde las ideas fluyen de manera lógica y un pensamiento conduce al siguiente.

dos puntos (:) Signo de puntuación que presenta un ejemplo.

comedia Obra teatral divertida donde el protagonista experimenta alguna forma de éxito. Las comedias suelen ser (aunque no siempre) humorísticas y tienen un final feliz.

héroe de la comedia Personaje de una comedia que es una persona común o sencilla con algún rasgo enternecedor, que experimenta cierto tipo de éxito, ya sea encontrar el amor o lograr la grandeza.

coma (,) Signo de puntuación que muestra separaciones dentro de una oración. Se usa para marcar cláusulas subordinadas, frases u objetos de una lista.

empalme de coma Sucede cuando un escritor conecta dos cláusulas independientes solamente con una coma.

acompañante Ver **personajes arquetípicos**.

comparación Ver **estrategias expositivas**.

oración compleja Ver **oración**.

oración compuesta Ver **oración**.

oración compuesta compleja Ver **oración**.

conceder y refutar Ver **concesión** y **refutación**.

concession An acknowledgment that an opposing argument may be true or reasonable. In a strong argument, a concession is usually accompanied by a refutation challenging the validity of the opposing argument.

concesión Reconocimiento de que un argumento opuesto puede ser cierto o razonable. En un argumento fuerte, la concesión va acompañada de una refutación que cuestiona la validez del argumento opuesto.

conclusion (p. 85) A sentence or paragraph that comments on the significance of the information presented, summarizes the information presented, and/or brings closure to a writer's ideas.

conclusión Oración o párrafo que comenta el significado de la información presentada, resume la información presentada y/o cierra las ideas del escritor.

conflict (p. 136) The tension, opposition, or struggle that drives a plot. External conflict is the opposition or tension between two characters or forces. Internal conflict occurs within a character. Conflict usually arises between the protagonist and the antagonist in a story.

conflicto Tensión, oposición o lucha que impulsa la trama. El conflicto externo es la oposición o tensión entre dos personajes o fuerzas. El conflicto interno ocurre dentro de un personaje. El conflicto normalmente surge entre el protagonista y el antagonista de una historia.

conjunction (p. 79) Words that connect things. Examples include *for*, *and*, and *but*.

conjunción Palabras que conectan cosas. Algunos ejemplos son *para*, *y* y *pero*.

connotation (p. 72) Refers to meanings or associations that readers have with a word beyond its dictionary definition, or denotation. Connotations are often positive or negative, and they often greatly affect the author's tone. See also **denotation**.

connotación Se refiere a los significados o asociaciones que los lectores tienen con una palabra más allá de su definición en el diccionario o su **denotación**. Las connotaciones pueden ser positivas o negativas, y pueden afectar el tono del autor. Ver también **denotación**.

consensus (p. 11) Finding areas of agreement with others.

consenso Encontrar puntos de acuerdo con otras personas.

content (p. 90) The information presented in an argument.

contenido Información presentada en un argumento.

context (p. 24) The circumstances, atmosphere, attitudes, and events surrounding a text.

contexto Circunstancias, ambiente, actitudes y eventos que rodean a un texto.

context clues (p. 26) Determining the definition of a word by looking at the familiar words nearby in a sentence or paragraph. See also **context**.

claves del contexto Determinar la definición de una palabra a partir de las palabras *conocidas* que la rodean en un párrafo u oración. Ver también **contexto**.

contrast See **expository strategies**.

contraste Ver **estrategias expositivas**.

coordination The use of a dependent word or clause to connect two ideas of equal importance.

coordinación Uso de una palabra o cláusula dependiente para conectar dos ideas de igual importancia.

costume Clothing and other items that an actor can wear or carry as part of the portrayal of a character.

disfraz Ropa y otros artículos que un actor puede llevar puesta o cargar al interpretar un personaje.

counterargument (p. 118) An opposing argument to the one a writer is putting forward. Rather than ignoring a counterargument, a strong writer will usually address it through the process of concession and refutation.

contraargumento Argumento opuesto al que presenta un escritor. En lugar de ignorar un contraargumento, un escritor habilidoso normalmente responde a través del proceso de concesión y refutación.

couplet See **stanza**.

pareado Ver **estrofa**.

credibility (p. 99) The quality of a source that is believable.

credibilidad Calidad de una fuente que es creíble.

cumulative sentence See **sentence**.

oración acumulativa Ver **oración**.

currency (p. 103) How recently a source was written or published.

actualidad Qué tan reciente es la escritura o publicación de una fuente.

D

damsel in distress See **archetypal characters**.

damisela en apuros Ver **personajes arquetípicos**.

dash (—) A form of punctuation that adds another thought to a sentence — like a bridge. It can also be used to interject a thought — an interruption, really — into a sentence.

guion largo (—) Signo de puntuación que añade un pensamiento a una oración — como un puente. También sirve para interponer un pensamiento — una interrupción, en realidad — en una oración.

debatable (p. 467) Something that reasonable people might disagree about. See also **debate**.

debatible Algo sobre lo cual la gente razonable puede estar en desacuerdo. Ver también **debate**.

debate (p. 7) A discussion about a certain topic, in which conflicting arguments are presented and all parties assume their opinion is the right one.

debate Discusión sobre cierto tema en la cual se presentan argumentos en conflicto y todas las partes suponen que su opinión es la correcta.

delivery (p. 92) The way that information is presented.

presentación Manera en que se entrega la información.

denotation (p. 72) A word's dictionary definition. See also **connotation**.

denotación Definición de diccionario de una palabra. Ver también **connotación**.

dependent clause See **clause**.

cláusula dependiente Ver **cláusula**.

description See **expository strategies**.

descripción Ver **estrategias expositivas**.

detail A descriptive fact that explains how something looks, feels, tastes, sounds, etc.

detalle Dato descriptivo que explica el aspecto, sabor, olor, sonido y otras características de algo.

dialogue (p. 7) A conversation between two or more people.

diálogo Conversación entre dos o más personas.

diction (p. 47) An author or speaker's choice of words. Analysis of diction looks at these choices and what they add to the speaker's message. Formal diction (p. 48) is the use of more serious language, perhaps using longer or more obscure words, or words that are unlikely to offend. Informal diction (p. 48) is the use of language in a relaxed style, perhaps using slang terms or a conversational tone.

dicción La elección de palabras de un autor. El análisis de la dicción estudia estas decisiones y lo que añaden al mensaje del emisor. La dicción formal es el uso de un lenguaje más serio, posiblemente con palabras más largas y desconocidas o palabras que es poco probable que ofendan. La dicción informal es el uso de un lenguaje relajado, posiblemente con jerga o un tono similar a una conversación.

direct characterization (p. 134) See **characterization**.

caracterización directa Ver **caracterización**.

dissonance A deliberate use of inharmonious words, phrases, or syllables intended to create harsh sounding effects and that could be considered an opposite of assonance.

disonancia Uso intencional de palabras, frases o sílabas no armónicas para crear efectos sonoros duros que podrían ser considerados lo opuesto a la asonancia.

drama A story meant to be performed in a live setting.

drama Historia creada para ser presentada en un escenario en vivo.

dramatic irony (p. 258) See **irony**.

ironía dramática Ver **ironía**.

dramatis personae See **cast of characters**.

dramatis personae Ver **elenco de personajes**.

E

either-or (false dilemma) In this fallacy, the speaker presents two extreme options as the only possible choices.

o lo uno o lo otro (dilema falso) En esta falacia, el orador presenta dos opciones extremas como las únicas opciones posibles.

ellipses (. . .) (p. 115) The series of dots that signal that something is missing from a quote.

puntos suspensivos (. . .) Serie de puntos que señala que falta algo en una cita.

end rhyme See **rhyme**.

rima final Ver **rima**.

endearing trait A quality of a character in a comedy that makes that character dear or lovable.

rasgo enternecedor Rasgo de un personaje de una comedia que hace que un personaje sea querido o adorable.

enjambment A poetic technique in which one line ends without a pause and continues to the next line to complete its meaning; also referred to as a "run-on line."

encabalgamiento Técnica poética en la que un verso termina sin pausa y continúa en el verso siguiente para completar su significado; también conocido como "verso mal formado".

ethos (p. 395) See **rhetorical appeals**.

ethos Ver **apelaciones retóricas**.

example See **expository strategies**.

ejemplo Ver **estrategias expositivas**.

explanation (p. 85) Commentary that tells why the evidence you provided is important to the development of your ideas.

explicación Comentario que indica por qué la evidencia ofrecida es importante para el desarrollo de tus ideas.

exposition See **plot**.

exposición Ver **trama**.

expository strategies Also known as **methods of development**, these are ways of organizing a text.

estrategias expositivas También conocidas como **métodos de desarrollo**, estas son formas de organizar un texto.

analysis To understand something by investigating its parts.

análisis Entender algo mediante el estudio de sus partes.

cause and effect To show causal relationships.

causa y efecto Mostrar relaciones causales.

classification To analyze by sorting into categories.

clasificación Ordenar en categorías para analizar.

comparison and contrast To highlight similarities and differences.

comparación y contraste Resaltar similitudes y diferencias.

description To make something vivid and concrete.

descripción Hacer que algo sea vívido y concreto.

example To demonstrate with specifics.

ejemplo Demostrar con detalles específicos.

eye rhyme See **rhyme**.

rima visual Ver **rima**.

fable A story, usually short, that features animals with human characteristics and that often puts forward a lesson or a moral. "The Tortoise and the Hare" is one of the most widely known fables.

fábula Historia, generalmente corta, sobre animales con características humanas que a menudo presenta una lección o moraleja. "La liebre y la tortuga" es una de las fábulas más conocidas.

fairy tale Stories that feature magical creatures and lands, often with princesses, princes, and other royalty. These usually take the form of children's stories. "Cinderella" is one of the most recognizable fairy tales.

cuento de hadas Historias protagonizadas por criaturas y lugares mágicos, que a veces incluyen princesas, príncipes y otros miembros de la realeza. Generalmente son cuentos infantiles. "La Cenicienta" es uno de los cuentos de hadas más reconocibles.

falling action See **plot**.

acción ascendente Ver **trama**.

fiction A genre of literature that tells a story describing imaginary characters and events.

ficción Género literario que cuenta una historia que describe personajes y eventos imaginarios.

figurative language (figure of speech) (p. 50) Nonliteral language, often evoking strong imagery, sometimes referred to as a trope. Figures of speech often compare one thing to another either explicitly (using simile) or implicitly (using metaphor). Other forms of figurative language include personification, paradox, overstatement (hyperbole), understatement, metonymy, synecdoche, and irony.

lenguaje figurativo Lenguaje no literal que evoca imágenes fuertes, a veces conocido como tropo. El lenguaje figurativo compara explícitamente una cosa con otra (a través de un símil) o implícitamente (por medio de metáforas). Otras formas de lenguaje figurativo son: personificación, paradoja, exageración (hipérbole), atenuación, metonimia, sinécdoque e ironía.

flashback (p. 251) A section of plot that shows earlier parts of the story.

escena retrospectiva Sección de la trama que muestra partes previas de la historia.

foil One common type of supporting character, whose purpose is to contrast with a main character in order to highlight an aspect or trait.

florete Tipo común de personaje secundario, cuyo propósito es contrastar con un personaje principal para resaltar un aspecto o rasgo.

foreshadowing (p. 257) The introduction early in a story of verbal and dramatic hints that suggest what is to come later.

presagiar Introducción temprana de pistas verbales y dramáticas que insinúan lo que viene más adelante.

form Refers to the defining structural characteristics of a work, especially a poem (i.e., meter and rhyme scheme). Often poets work within set forms, such as the sonnet, that require adherence to fixed conventions.

forma Se refiere a las características estructurales que definen una obra, especialmente un poema (por ejemplo, esquema de métrica y rima). A menudo los poetas trabajan con formas establecidas, como el soneto, que requieren adherirse a convenciones fijas.

formal diction (p. 48) See **diction**.

dicción formal Ver **dicción**.

fragment (p. 83) An incomplete sentence. Usually fragments omit a subject, a verb/predicate, or both.

fragmento Oración incompleta. Los fragmentos generalmente omiten el sujeto, verbo/predicado o ambos.

free verse A form of poetry with lines that closely follow the natural rhythms of speech, not adhering to any specific pattern of rhyme or meter.

verso libre Forma de poesía con versos que siguen de cerca los ritmos naturales del habla, sin adherirse a un patrón específico de rima o métrica.

G

garden See **archetypal settings**.

jardín Ver **escenarios arquetípicos**.

genre A category of literary texts. Some literary genres include fiction, poetry, and drama.

género Categoría de textos literarios. Algunos géneros literarios son: ficción, poesía y drama.

gerund A noun made from a verb.

gerundio Sustantivo creado a partir de un verbo.

H

haiku A Japanese verse form of three unrhymed lines in five, seven, and five syllables. Its goal is to create a single, memorable image for the reader.

haiku Forma de poesía japonesa de tres versos sin rima con cinco, siete y cinco sílabas. Su objetivo es crear una imagen memorable y única para el lector.

hero's journey See **archetypal plots**.

viaje del héroe Ver **tramas arquetípicas**.

homonyms Words that are spelled and pronounced the same but have very different meanings. For example, the term "arms" could mean either body parts or weapons.

homónimos Palabras que se escriben y pronuncian igual, pero tienen significados muy diferentes. Por ejemplo, la palabra "banco" puede ser una institución financiera o un asiento.

homophones Words that sound the same but are spelled differently and have very different meanings. Some common homophones are *accept* and *except*, *lesson* and *lessen*, *then* and *than*, and *you're* and *your*.

homófonos Palabras que suenan igual, pero se escriben diferente y tienen significados diferentes. Algunos ejemplos de homófonos son: *tasa* y *taza*, *arrollo* y *arroyo* y *tuvo* y *tubo*.

hook (p. 91) An opening of an argument with the purpose of getting the audience's attention.

gancho Inicio de un argumento que tiene como fin obtener la atención del público.

hubris The Greek term for pride. In drama, hubris is the most common tragic flaw of a character. See also **tragic flaw**.

hubris Término griego que significa orgullo. En la dramática, *hubris* es el defecto trágico más común de un personaje. Ver también **falla trágica**.

hyperbole (p. 50) Deliberate exaggeration used for emphasis or to produce a comic or an ironic effect; an overstatement to make a point.

hipérbole Exageración intencional que se usa para enfatizar o producir un efecto cómico o irónico; una exageración para reforzar un punto.

hyphen (-) A hyphen connects words together, making them into one multi-word cluster.

guion (-) El guion conecta palabras y las convierte en un conjunto de palabras múltiples.

I

iambic pentameter An iamb, the most common metrical foot in English poetry, is made up of an unstressed syllable followed by a stressed one. Iambic pentameter, then, is a rhythmic meter containing five iambs. Unrhymed iambic pentameter is called blank verse. See also **meter**.

pentámetro yámbico El yambo, pie métrico más común en la poesía inglesa, se compone de una sílaba átona seguida de una acentuada. El pentámetro yámbico, por tanto, es una métrica rítmica de cinco yambos. Un pentámetro yámbico sin rima es un verso blanco. Ver también **métrica**.

imagery (p. 50) A description of how something looks, feels, tastes, smells, or sounds. Imagery may use literal or figurative language to appeal to the senses.

imágenes Descripción de cómo algo se ve, se siente, sabe, huele o suena. Las imágenes usan lenguaje literal o figurativo para a apelar a los sentidos.

imperative sentence See **sentence**.

oración imperativa Ver **oración**.

independent clause See **clause**.	**cláusula independiente** Ver **cláusula**.
indirect characterization (p. 134) See **characterization**.	**caracterización indirecta** Ver **caracterización**.
inference (p. 38) A conclusion drawn by looking at many pieces of evidence.	**inferencia** Conclusión que se saca a partir de muchos elementos de evidencia.
informal diction (p. 48) See **diction**.	**dicción informal** Ver **dicción**.
informed opinion (p. 96) A belief or judgment based on facts or knowledge.	**opinión informada** Creencia o juicio basado en hechos o conocimientos.
integrate (p. 113) To weave a quotation into your writing, which really comes down to putting it into context.	**integrar** Tejer una cita en tu escritura, lo cual realmente se reduce a colocarla en contexto.
internal rhyme See **rhyme**.	**rima interna** Ver **rima**.
interpretation (p. 38) An explanation of the meaning and significance of something.	**interpretación** Explicación del significado y la importancia de algo.
inversion Inverted order of words in a sentence (deviation from the standard subject-verb-object order).	**inversión** Orden invertido de las palabras en una oración (desviación del orden estándar sujeto-verbo-objeto).
irony (p. 258) An incongruity between expectation and reality.	**ironía** Incongruencia entre expectativa y realidad.
dramatic irony (p. 258) Tension created by the contrast between what a character says or thinks and what the audience or readers know to be true; as a result of this technique, some words and actions in a story or play take on a different meaning for the reader than they do for the characters.	**ironía dramática** Tensión creada por el contraste entre lo que dice o piensa un personaje y lo que el público o los lectores saben que es real; como resultado de esta técnica, algunas palabras y acciones de un cuento u obra adquieren un significado diferente para el lector que para los personajes.
situational irony (p. 258) A discrepancy between what is expected and what actually happens.	**ironía de la situación** Discrepancia entre lo que se espera y lo que ocurre en realidad.
verbal irony (p. 258) A figure of speech that occurs when a speaker or character says one thing but means something else, or when what is said is the opposite of what is expected, creating a noticeable incongruity. **Sarcasm** is verbal irony used derisively.	**ironía verbal** Figura retórica que ocurre cuando un orador o personaje dice una cosa, pero quiere decir otra, o cuando lo que se dice es opuesto de lo que se espera, lo cual crea una incongruencia notable. El **sarcasmo** es ironía verbal que se usa con fines de burla.

J

juxtaposition Placement of two things closely together to emphasize similarities or differences.	**yuxtaposición** Colocación cercana de dos cosas para resaltar similitudes o diferencias.

L

legend A story from the past that might have been real at one point but cannot be authenticated. The legend of King Arthur is one of the most famous legends.	**leyenda** Historia del pasado que pudo haber sido real en algún momento, pero no puede ser comprobada. La leyenda del Rey Arturo es una de las leyendas más famosas.

lighting (p. 717) An element of staging that can help establish setting or mood or convey transitions from one scene or setting to another.

iluminación Elemento escénico que ayuda a crear el escenario o ambiente o comunica transiciones entre escenas.

limited omniscient narrator (p. 254) A character or persona that tells a narrative and is usually privy to the thoughts and actions of only one character. See also **narrator**.

narrador omnisciente limitado Personaje o persona que cuenta una narrativa y tiene acceso a los pensamientos y acciones de un solo personaje. Ver también **narrador**.

loaded term (p. 74) A word that has very strong connotations. See also **connotation**.

término cargado Palabra con connotaciones muy fuertes. Ver también **connotación**.

logos (p. 395) See **rhetorical appeals**.

logos Ver **apelaciones retóricas**.

M

main idea (p. 31) The central point of a piece of writing or speech.

idea principal Punto central de un texto o discurso.

maze or labyrinth See **archetypal settings**.

laberinto Ver **escenarios arquetípicos**.

mentor See **archetypal characters**.

mentor Ver **personajes arquetípicos**.

metaphor (p. 50) Figure of speech that compares two things without using *like* or *as*.

metáfora Figura retórica que compara dos cosas sin usar la palabra *como*.

meter The formal, regular organization of stressed and unstressed syllables, measured in feet. A foot is distinguished by the number of syllables it contains and how stress is placed on the syllables — stressed (´) or unstressed (˘). There are five typical feet in English verse: iamb (˘ ´), trochee (´ ˘), anapest (˘ ˘ ´), dactyl (´ ˘ ˘), and spondee (´ ´). Some meters dictate the number of feet per line, the most common being tetrameter, pentameter, and hexameter, having four, five, and six feet, respectively. See also **iambic pentameter**.

métrica Organización formal regular de sílabas acentuadas y átonas, que se miden en pies. Un pie se distingue por el número de sílabas que contiene y por la manera en que se acentúan las sílabas: acentuadas (´) o átonas (˘). Hay cinco pies típicos en los versos en inglés: yambo (˘ ´), troqueo (´ ˘), anapesto (˘ ˘ ´), dáctilo (´ ˘ ˘) y espondeo (´ ´). Algunas métricas dictan el número de pies por verso, y los más comunes son el tetrámetro, el pentámetro y el hexámetro, que tienen cuatro, cinco y seis pies, respectivamente. Ver también **pentámetro yámbico**.

methods of development See **expository strategies**.

métodos de desarrollo Ver **estrategias expositivas**.

modifier An adjective, an adverb, a phrase, or a clause that modifies a noun, pronoun, or verb. The purpose of a modifier is usually to describe, focus, or qualify.

modificador Adjetivo, adverbio, frase o cláusula que modifica a un sustantivo, pronombre o verbo. El propósito de un modificador es describir, enfocar o calificar.

monologue In drama, a speech that a character gives to either themselves, the audience, or another character.

monólogo En la dramática, discurso que da un personaje a sí mismo, al público o a otro personaje.

monster or dragon See **archetypal characters**.

monstruo o dragón Ver **personajes arquetípicos**.

mood (p. 255) The feeling or atmosphere created by a text, related to the setting.

ambiente Sentimiento o atmósfera que crea un texto en relación con el escenario.

myth A traditional story of deep importance to a culture that tells the supernatural stories pertaining to early history, the actions of deities, or explanations of natural or social phenomena. A well-known myth is that of the Greek Heracles or the Roman Hercules.

mito Historia tradicional de gran importancia para una cultura que cuenta las historias sobrenaturales que pertenecen a la historia temprana, a las acciones de deidades, o explicaciones de fenómenos sociales o naturales. Un mito famoso es el mito griego de Heracles o del romano Hércules.

N

narration A mode of nonfiction that tells a true story; that part of fiction that is not dialogue and is told by a narrator.

narración Modo de no ficción que cuenta una historia real; aquella parte de la ficción que no es diálogo y es contada por un narrador.

narrator The character, or persona, that the author uses to tell a narrative, or story. Narrators may tell stories from several different points of view, including first person, second person (very rare), and third person.

narrador El personaje, o persona, que el autor usa para contar una narrativa o historia. Los narradores a veces cuentan historias desde distintos puntos de vista, como primera persona, segunda persona (poco común) y tercera persona.

near rhyme See **rhyme**.

rima cercana Ver **rima**.

noun A word that names a person, place, thing, or idea.

sustantivo Palabra que representa a una persona, lugar, cosa o idea.

O

object (p. 27) A word that identifies who or what receives the action described by a verb. See also **subject (of a sentence)** and **verb**.

objeto Palabra que identifica quién o qué recibe la acción descrita por un verbo. Ver también **sujeto (de una oración)** y **verbo**.

objectivity (p. 103) A quality of a source that discusses all sides of an issue, and attempts to handle it fairly.

objetividad Atributo de una fuente que reconoce todas las perspectivas de un tema e intenta analizarlo de manera justa.

objective narrator (p. 254) A character or persona that tells a narrative that reports actions and dialogue of the characters, and describes the setting, but does not move into the thoughts of any of the characters. See also **narrator**.

narrador objetivo Personaje o persona que cuenta una narrativa que reporta las acciones y el diálogo de los personajes y describe el escenario, pero no conoce los pensamientos de los personajes. Ver también **narrador**.

occasion (p. 26) The time, place, and situation in which a speech is given or a piece is written.

ocasión Tiempo, lugar y situación en la cual se escribe cierto discurso o texto.

octet See **stanza**.

octeto ver **estrofa**.

omniscient narrator (p. 254) A character or persona who tells a narrative and is privy to the thoughts and actions of all the characters in the story. See also **narrator**.

narrador omnisciente Personaje o persona que cuenta una narrativa y conoce los pensamientos de todos los personajes de la historia. Ver también **narrador**.

onomatopoeia Use of words that refer to sounds and whose pronunciations mimic those sounds.

onomatopeya Uso de palabras que se refieren a sonidos y cuya pronunciación imita dichos sonidos.

oxymoron A paradox made up of two seemingly contradictory words.

oxímoron Paradoja compuesta de dos palabras aparentemente contradictorias.

paradox A statement or situation that seems contradictory but reveals an ironic truth.

paradoja Afirmación o situación que parece contradictoria, pero revela una verdad irónica.

parallelism Similarity of structure in a pair or series of related words, phrases, or clauses.

paralelismo Similitud estructural en un par o serie de palabras, frases o cláusulas relacionadas.

paraphrase (p. 116) To communicate the meaning of a source using words and sentence structure that are distinct from the original.

paráfrasis Comunicar el significado de una fuente de manera más breve y clara que el original.

participle An adjective made from a verb.

participio Adjetivo formado a partir de un verbo.

passive voice A sentence employs passive voice when the subject doesn't act but rather is acted on.

voz pasiva Una oración emplea la voz pasiva cuando el sujeto no actúa, sino que se actúa sobre él.

pathos (p. 395) See **rhetorical appeals**.

pathos Ver **apelaciones retóricas**.

patterns of development See **expository strategies**.

patrones de desarrollo Ver **estrategias expositivas**.

persona Greek for "mask." The face or character that a speaker shows to an audience.

persona "Máscara" en griego. El rostro o personaje que un orador muestra al público.

personification (p. 50) Attribution of a lifelike quality to an inanimate object or an idea.

personificación Atribución de una cualidad humana a un objeto o idea inanimado.

Petrarchan sonnet See **sonnet**.

Soneto petrarquista Ver **soneto**.

phrase A group of words lacking either a subject or a verb.

frase Grupo de palabras que carecen de sujeto o de verbo.

plagiarism (p. 122) The act of representing someone else's words, ideas, or research as your own.

plagio Acto de representar palabras, ideas o investigaciones ajenas como propias.

plot (p. 251) The arrangement of events in a narrative. Almost always, a conflict is central to a plot, and traditionally a plot develops in accordance with the following model: exposition, rising action, climax, falling action, resolution. There can be more than one sequence of events in a work, although typically there is one major sequence along with other minor sequences. These minor sequences are called subplots. See also **archetypal plots**.

trama Orden de sucesos de una narrativa. Casi siempre, el conflicto está en el centro de la trama y tradicionalmente, la trama se desarrolla de acuerdo con el siguiente modelo: exposición, acción ascendente, clímax, acción descendente, resolución. Puede haber más de una secuencia de eventos en una obra, aunque típicamente hay una secuencia principal acompañada de otras secuencias menores. Las secuencias menores se llaman subtramas. Ver también **tramas arquetípicas**.

exposition (p. 252) A mode of nonfiction used to explain. In literature, exposition usually takes place at the beginning and is the part of the story in which the author provides background information about the characters, settings, or major ideas.

exposición Modo de no ficción que se usa para explicar. En la literatura, la exposición casi siempre está al inicio y es la parte de la historia donde el autor ofrece información sobre los antecedentes de los personajes, escenarios o ideas principales.

rising action (p. 252) The events, marked by increasing tension and conflict, that build up to a story's climax.

climax (p. 252) The place where the tension of the rising action has reached its most significant place.

falling action (p. 252) A section of plot that includes those events immediately after the climax, during which the characters normally deal only with the results of the choices made during the climax.

resolution (p. 252) The working out of a plot's conflicts, following the climax.

poetry A mode of literature that sometimes employs elements such as rhyme and meter to artfully express an idea, convey an experience, or describe a person or an object.

point of view (p. 253) The perspective from which a work is told. The most common narrative vantage points are:

first person point of view (p. 134) Told by a narrator who is a character in the story and self-references as "I." First person narrators are sometimes unreliable narrators because they don't always see the big picture or because they might be biased.

second person point of view Though rare, some stories are told using second person pronouns (*you*). This casts the reader as a character in the story.

third person limited omniscient point of view Told by a narrator who relates the action using third person pronouns (*he*, *she*, *it*). This narrator is usually privy to the thoughts and actions of only one character.

third person omniscient point of view Told by a narrator using third person pronouns. This narrator is privy to the thoughts and actions of all the characters in the story.

third person objective point of view Told by one who reports actions and dialogue of the characters, and describes the setting, but does not move into the thoughts of any of the characters.

acción ascendente Los eventos, marcados por un aumento en la tensión y conflicto, que conducen al clímax de la historia.

clímax Punto donde la tensión de la acción ascendente alcanza su momento más significativo.

acción descendente Sección de la trama que incluye los sucesos que siguen inmediatamente después del clímax, donde los personajes enfrentan únicamente los resultados de las decisiones tomadas durante el clímax.

resolución Desenlace de los conflictos de la trama tras el clímax.

poesía Modo literario que a veces emplea elementos como rima y métrica para expresar una idea, relatar una experiencia o describir un objeto de manera artística.

punto de vista Perspectiva desde la cual se cuenta una obra. Los puntos de vista narrativos más comunes son:

punto de vista en primera persona Contado por un narrador que es un personaje de la historia y se refiere a sí mismo como "yo". Los narradores en primera persona a veces son poco fiables porque no siempre ven el panorama completo o pueden estar sesgados.

punto de vista en segunda persona Aunque es poco común, algunas historias se cuentan a través de pronombres en la segunda persona: (*tú/usted*). Esto convierte al lector en personaje del cuento.

punto de vista del narrador omnisciente limitado en tercera persona Contado por un narrador que relata la acción a través de pronombres en tercera persona (*él, ella*). Este narrador normalmente conoce los pensamientos y acciones de un personaje únicamente.

punto de vista del narrador omnisciente en tercera persona Contado por un narrador que usa pronombres en tercera persona. Este narrador conoce los pensamientos y acciones de todos los personajes del cuento.

punto de vista del narrador en tercera persona Contado por una voz que reporta las acciones y diálogos de los personajes y describe el escenario, pero desconoce los pensamientos de los personajes.

prefix (p. 26) An element of a word that is attached to the beginning of a root in order to add meaning.

prefijo Elemento de una palabra que se coloca al inicio de la raíz para agregar significado.

preposition Words that express a relation of one thing to another.

preposición Palabras que expresan una relación entre una cosa y otra.

pronoun A word that takes the place of a noun.

pronombre Palabra que ocupa el sitio de un sustantivo.

prop All of the items actors interact with in a play.

utilería Todos los objetos con los cuales interactúan los actores de una obra.

propaganda The spread of ideas and information to further a cause. In its negative sense, propaganda is the use of rumors, lies, disinformation, and scare tactics to damage or promote a cause.

propaganda Esparcimiento de ideas e información para impulsar una causa. En el sentido negativo, la propaganda es el uso de rumores, mentiras, desinformación y tácticas de miedo para dañar o promover una causa.

prose A term that refers to written texts that are not poetry.

prosa Término que se refiere a textos escritos que no son poesía.

protagonist (p. 134) The main character who drives the action of the story; often a hero or heroine, but not always.

protagonista Personaje principal que impulsa la acción de la historia; a veces, pero no siempre, es un héroe o heroína.

pun A play on words that derives its humor from the replacement of one word with another that has a similar pronunciation or spelling but a different meaning. A pun can also derive humor from the use of a single word that has more than one meaning.

juego de palabras Chiste o idea que deriva su humor de la sustitución de una palabra con otra que tiene pronunciación u ortografía similar, pero distinto significado. Un juego de palabras también deriva su humor del uso de una palabra que tiene más de un significado.

punctuation Symbols used in writing to show to what extent ideas are connected or separated.

puntuación Símbolos de la escritura que muestran qué tan conectadas o separadas están las palabras.

purpose (p. 26) The goal the author or speaker wants to achieve.

propósito Objetivo que el autor u orador quiere alcanzar.

Q

qualitative evidence Evidence that is supported by reason, tradition, or precedent and cannot be represented in numbers.

evidencia cualitativa Evidencia respaldada por la razón, tradición o precedentes y que no puede ser representada en números.

quantitative evidence Evidence that can be measured, cited, counted, or otherwise represented in numbers — for instance, statistics, surveys, polls, and census information.

evidencia cuantitativa Evidencia que puede ser medida, citada, contada o representada de forma numérica de alguna u otra manera, por ejemplo, estadísticas, encuestas, estudios e información obtenida a través de censos.

quatrain See **stanza**.

cuarteto Ver **estrofa**.

R

reflection (p. 138) A key element of narrative, in which the author gives some perspective on what was learned from the event and thus signals to the reader the significance of the story.

reflexión Elemento clave de la narrativa, en el cual el autor da cierta perspectiva sobre lo que aprendió del suceso y, por tanto, señala el significado de la historia al lector.

refrain A line that is repeated at times within the work.	**estribillo** Verso que se repite dentro de la obra.
refutation The process of uncovering the weakness of a counterargument in order to support your own claim.	**refutación** Proceso de descubrir la flaqueza de un contraargumento con el fin de respaldar la afirmación propia.
relevance (p. 103) How closely related something is to the issue at hand.	**relevancia** Qué tan cercana es la relación de algo con el asunto en cuestión.
rhetoric (p. 388) Aristotle defined rhetoric as "the faculty of observing in any given case the available means of persuasion." In other words, it is the art of finding ways of persuading an audience.	**retórica** Aristóteles definió la retórica como "la facultad de observar en cualquier caso dado los medios de persuasión disponibles". Dicho de otra forma, es el arte de encontrar de maneras de persuadir al público.
rhetorical appeals (p. 395) Rhetorical techniques used to persuade an audience by emphasizing what they find most important or compelling. The three major appeals are to **ethos** (character), **logos** (reason), and **pathos** (emotion).	**apelaciones retóricas** Técnicas retóricas empleadas para persuadir al público al enfatizar aquello que les resulta más importante o convincente. Las tres apelaciones principales son al **ethos** (carácter), **logos** (razón) y **pathos** (emoción).
ethos (p. 395) Greek for "character." Speakers appeal to ethos to demonstrate that they are credible and trustworthy to speak on a given topic. Ethos is established by both who you are and what you say.	**ethos** "Carácter" en griego. Los oradores apelan al ethos para demostrar que son confiables y tienen credibilidad para hablar de cierto tema. El ethos se establece a través de quién eres y lo que dices.
logos (p. 395) Greek for "embodied thought." Speakers appeal to logos, or reason, by offering clear, rational ideas and using specific details, examples, facts, statistics, or expert testimony to back them up.	**logos** "Pensamiento encarnado" en griego. Los oradores apelan al logos, o razón, al ofrecer ideas claras y racionales y usar detalles, ejemplos, datos, estadísticas específicos o testimonios de expertos para respaldarlas.
pathos (p. 395) Greek for "suffering" or "experience." Speakers appeal to pathos to emotionally motivate their audience. More specific appeals to pathos might play on the audience's values, desires, and hopes, on the one hand, or fears and prejudices, on the other.	**pathos** "Experiencia" o "sufrimiento" en griego. Los oradores apelan al pathos para motivar al público de manera emotiva. Las apelaciones dirigidas específicamente al pathos actúan, por un lado, sobre los valores, deseos y esperanzas del público y, por el otro, a sus miedos o prejuicios.
rhetorical modes Different types of nonfiction texts. The primary rhetorical modes are argument, exposition, and narration.	**modos retóricos** Distintos tipos de textos de no ficción. Los principales modos retóricos son: argumento, exposición y narración.
rhetorical question Figure of speech in the form of a question posed for rhetorical effect rather than for the purpose of getting an answer.	**pregunta retórica** Manera de hablar a través de preguntas hechas por su efecto retórico más que con el fin de obtener una respuesta.

rhetorical situation (p. 390) The context surrounding a text, including who the speaker is, what the subject is, who the audience is, and the relationship among these three elements. The rhetorical situation also includes the author's purpose, and the occasion that has prompted the text. See also **rhetorical triangle**.

situación retórica Contexto que rodea un texto, incluyendo quién es el orador, cuál es el sujeto, quién es el público y la relación entre estos tres elementos. La situación retórica incluye el propósito del autor y la ocasión que ha motivado el texto. Ver también **triángulo retórico**.

rhetorical triangle (Aristotelian triangle) A diagram that illustrates the interrelationship among the speaker, audience, and subject in determining a text. See also **rhetorical situation**.

triángulo retórico (triángulo aristotélico) Diagrama que ilustra la interrelación entre el orador, el público y el sujeto al determinar un texto. Ver también **situación retórica**.

rhyme The poetic repetition of the same (or similar) vowel sounds or of vowel and consonant combinations.

rima La repetición poética del sonido de una misma vocal (o una similar) o de combinaciones de vocales y consonantes.

> **end rhyme** A rhyme at the end of two or more lines of poetry.

> **rima final** Rima al final de dos o más versos de poesía.

> **eye rhyme** Also called sight rhyme, a rhyme that works only because the words look the same.

> **rima visual** También conocida como rima de ojo, rima que solo funciona porque las palabras se ven parecidas.

> **internal rhyme** A rhyme that occurs within a line.

> **rima interna** Rima que ocurre dentro de un mismo verso.

> **near rhyme** Also called slant rhyme, a rhyme that pairs sounds that are similar but not exactly the same.

> **rima cercana** También conocida como rima inclinada, rima que agrupa sonidos que son similares, pero no son iguales.

rhyme scheme The pattern a rhyme follows. Not all poems have a rhyme scheme. See also **rhyme**.

esquema de rimas Patrón que sigue una rima. No todos los poemas siguen un esquema de rimas. Ver también **rima**.

root (p. 26) The origin of a word, often from a different language.

raíz El origen de una palabra, a menudo procedente de otro idioma.

run-on sentence (p. 81) A sentence that includes two independent clauses without any punctuation.

oración mal formada Oración que incluye dos cláusulas independientes sin puntuación de por medio.

S

satire The use of irony or sarcasm as a means of critique, usually of a society or an individual. See also **irony**.

sátira Uso de ironía o sarcasmo como medio de crítica, normalmente de una sociedad o individuo. Ver también **ironía**.

scene A minor subunit into which the action of a play is divided. Scenes typically divide the acts of a play.

escena Subunidad menor que divide la acción de una obra. Las escenas normalmente dividen los actos de una obra.

semicolon (;) (p. 80) A punctuation mark that puts together two sentences; usually the sentences share some meaning.

punto y coma (;) Signo de puntuación que une dos oraciones; normalmente, las oraciones comparten significado.

sentence Specific types of sentences discussed in this book include the following:

complex sentence (p. 76) A sentence that includes one independent clause and at least one dependent clause.

compound sentence (p. 76) A sentence that includes at least two independent clauses.

compound-complex sentence (p. 77) A sentence that includes two or more independent clauses and one or more dependent clauses.

cumulative sentence A sentence that completes the main idea at the beginning of the sentence and then builds and adds on.

imperative sentence A sentence used to command or enjoin.

simple sentence (p. 76) A sentence composed of one main clause without any subordinate clauses.

sentence variety (p. 48) The strategic use of long and short sentences in order to spice up writing and keep readers focused. See also **syntax**.

sestet See **stanza**.

set (p. 716) All of the scenery, furniture, and other structures that make up the setting onstage.

setting (p. 26) Where and when a story takes place. See also **archetypal settings**.

shadow See **archetypal characters**.

Shakespearean sonnet See **sonnet**.

signal word (p. 113) A word that signals that a quotation is about to begin. Common signal words include *says*, *argues*, and *recommends*.

simile (p. 50) A figure of speech used to explain or clarify an idea by comparing it explicitly to something else, using the words *like*, *as*, or *as though*.

simple sentence See **sentence**.

situational irony (p. 258) See **irony**.

oración Los tipos específicos de oración que se comentan en este libro son:

oración compleja Oración que incluye una cláusula independiente y al menos una cláusula dependiente.

oración compuesta Oración que incluye al menos dos cláusulas independientes.

oración compuesta compleja Oración que incluye dos o más cláusulas independientes y una o más cláusulas dependientes.

oración acumulativa Oración que completa la idea principal del inicio de la oración y luego continúa con más información.

oración imperativa Oración que se usa para dar una orden.

oración simple Oración compuesta de una cláusula principal sin cláusulas subordinadas.

variedad de oraciones Uso estratégico de oraciones largas y cortas para crear una escritura más dinámica y mantener la atención de los lectores. Ver también **sintaxis**.

sexteto Ver **estrofa**.

escenografía Todo el escenario, muebles y demás estructuras que componen la escena.

escenario El lugar y tiempo donde ocurre una historia. Ver también **escenarios arquetípicos**.

sombra Ver **personajes arquetípicos**.

soneto shakespeariano Ver **soneto**.

palabra señaladora Palabra que señala el inicio de una cita textual. Algunos ejemplos de palabras señaladoras son *dice*, *argumenta* y *recomienda*.

símil Figura retórica que explica o aclara una idea al compararla explícitamente con otra cosa a través de las palabras *como*, *tan*, o *como si*.

oración simple Ver **oración**.

ironía de la situación Ver **ironía**.

slant rhyme See **rhyme**.

SOAPS A mnemonic device that stands for Subject, Occasion, Audience, Purpose, and Speaker. It is a handy way to remember the various elements that make up the rhetorical situation.

soliloquy A type of monologue in which characters are in conversation with themselves.

sonnet A poetic form composed of fourteen lines in iambic pentameter that adheres to a particular rhyme scheme. The two most common types are the following:

Petrarchan sonnet Also known as the Italian sonnet, its fourteen lines are divided into an octet (8 lines) and a sestet (6 lines). The octet rhymes *abba*, *abba*; the sestet that follows can have a variety of different rhyme schemes: *cdcdcd*, *cdecde*, *cddcdd*.

Shakespearean sonnet Also known as the English sonnet, its fourteen lines are composed of three quatrains (4 lines) and a couplet (2 lines), and its rhyme scheme is *abab*, *cdcd*, *efef*, *gg*.

sound The musical quality of poetry, as created through techniques such as rhyme, enjambment, caesura, alliteration, assonance, onomatopoeia, and meter.

sources (p. 95) The viewpoints of others, whether written, spoken, or presented visually.

speaker (p. 25) The person or group who creates a text. This might be a politician who delivers a speech, a commentator who writes an article, an artist who draws a political cartoon, or even a company that commissions an advertisement.

stage directions In drama, instructions within the play intended for the director or actor in order to accurately portray the scene. See also **blocking**.

staging (p. 716) Refers to how the director chooses to portray the setting on stage, including the design of the set, the lighting, and the props.

---

rima inclinada Ver **rima**.

SOAPS Recurso mnemónico en inglés que significa Sujeto (Subject), Ocasión (Occasion), Público (Audience), Propósito (Purpose) y Orador (Speaker). Es útil para recordar los elementos que componen una situación retórica.

soliloquio Tipo de monólogo donde los personajes están en conversación consigo mismos.

soneto Forma poética compuesta de catorce versos escritos en pentámetro yámbico que adhiere a un esquema de rima particular. Los dos tipos más comunes son:

soneto petrarquista También conocido como soneto italiano, sus catorce versos se dividen en un octeto (8 versos) y un sexteto (6 versos). El octeto rima *abba*, *abba*; el sexteto que sigue puede tener una variedad de esquemas de rima: *cdcdcd*, *cdecde*, *cddcdd*.

soneto shakespeariano También conocido como soneto inglés, sus catorce versos están formados por tres cuartetos (4 versos) y una copla (2 versos), y su esquema de rima es *abab*, *cdcd*, *efef*, *gg*.

sonido Calidad musical de la poesía, creada a través de técnicas como rimas, encabalgamiento, cesura, aliteración, asonancia, onomatopeya y métrica.

fuentes Puntos de vista ajenos, ya sean escritos, orales o presentados en formato visual.

orador Persona o grupo que crea un texto. Puede ser un político que da un discurso, un comentarista que escribe un artículo, un artista que dibuja una caricatura política o incluso una empresa que encarga un anuncio.

dirección escénica En la dramática, instrucciones dentro de la obra para el actor o director con el fin de representar la escena con precisión. Ver también **bloqueo**.

puesta en escena Se refiere a la manera en qué el director elige retratar la escenografía sobre el escenario, lo cual incluye el diseño del escenario, la iluminación y la utilería.

stanza A group of lines separated from others, similar to paragraphs in prose. Stanzas within a poem usually have repetitive forms, often sharing rhyme schemes or rhythmic structures. A number of frequently used stanza types have specific names:

>**couplet** A two-line, rhyming stanza.
>
>**tercet** A three-line stanza.
>
>**quatrain** A four-line stanza.
>
>**sestet** A six-line stanza.
>
>**octet** An eight-line stanza.

style (p. 45) The way a literary work is written. Style is produced by an author's choices in diction, syntax, imagery, figurative language, and other literary elements.

subject (of a sentence) (p. 27) A word that identifies what or who exhibits the action or state of being expressed by a verb in a sentence. See also **verb** and **object**.

subject (of a text) The topic of a text. See also **text**.

subordination The use of a dependent word, clause, or idea to highlight the importance of another.

suffix (p. 26) An element of a word that is attached to the end of a root in order to add meaning.

summarize (p. 31) To present the main idea and the main supporting or relevant details that reinforce the main idea of a text.

support (supporting details) (p. 31) Information that reinforces the main idea in a text.

supporting or minor characters (p. 249) Characters that may add more depth to the story, or further complicate the conflict for the protagonist.

symbol (p. 257) A setting, an object, or an event in a story that carries more than literal meaning and therefore represents something significant to understanding the meaning of a work of literature.

---

estrofa Grupo de versos separados de otros, de manera similar a los párrafos en la prosa. Las estrofas de un poema tienen formas repetitivas y a veces comparten esquemas o estructuras rítmicos. Varios tipos de estrofas, que se usan comúnmente, tienen nombres específicos.

>**copla** Estrofa de dos versos que riman.
>
>**terceto** Estrofa de tres versos.
>
>**cuarteto** Estrofa de cuatro versos.
>
>**sexteto** Estrofa de seis versos.
>
>**octeto** Estrofa de ocho versos.

estilo Manera en qué está escrita una obra literaria. El estilo lo producen las decisiones del autor en cuanto a dicción, sintaxis, imágenes, lenguaje figurativo y otros elementos literarios.

sujeto (de una oración) Palabra que identifica qué o quién lleva a cabo la acción o estado que expresa el verbo de una oración. Ver también **verbo** y **objeto**.

sujeto (de un texto) Tema de un texto. Ver también **texto**.

subordinación Uso de una palabra, cláusula o idea dependiente para resaltar la importancia de otra.

sufijo Elemento de una palabra que se añade al final de una raíz para agregar significado.

resumir Presentar la idea principal y los principales detalles de apoyo para reforzar la idea central de un texto.

respaldar (detalles de apoyo) Información que refuerza la idea central de un texto.

personajes secundarios o de apoyo Personajes que dan mayor profundidad a la historia o complican aún más el conflicto del protagonista.

símbolo Escenario, objeto o evento en una historia cuyo significado es más que literal y por tanto representa algo significativo para entender el sentido de una obra literaria.

syntax (p. 48) The arrangement of words into phrases, clauses, and sentences. This includes word order (subject-verb-object, for instance, or an inverted structure); the length and structure of sentences (simple, compound, complex, or compound-complex); and such devices as parallelism, juxtaposition, and antithesis.

sintaxis Disposición de las palabras en frases, cláusulas y oraciones. Incluye el orden de las palabras (sujeto-verbo-objeto, por ejemplo, o una estructura invertida); la longitud y la estructura de las oraciones (simple, compuesta, compleja o compuesta compleja); y recursos como paralelismo, yuxtaposición y antítesis.

synthesis Combining two or more ideas in order to create something more complex in support of a new idea.

síntesis Combinar dos o más ideas para crear algo más complejo y respaldar una idea nueva.

T

tall tale Stories like legends, but including broad exaggerations, often for humorous effect. The tale of Paul Bunyan and his blue ox, Babe, might be one of the most widely shared tall tales.

relato exagerado Historias parecidas a leyendas, pero con exageraciones notables que en ocasiones tienen efectos humorísticos. El relato de Paul Bunyan y su buey azul, Babe, es uno de los relatos exagerados más conocidos.

tempter/temptress See **archetypal characters**.

tentador/tentadora Ver **personajes arquetípicos**.

tercet See **stanza**.

terceto Ver **estrofa**.

text (p. 18) While this term generally refers to the written word, in the humanities it has come to mean any cultural product that can be "read" — meaning not just consumed and comprehended, but also investigated. This includes fiction, nonfiction, poetry, political cartoons, fine art, photography, performances, fashion, cultural trends, and much more.

texto Si bien este término generalmente se refiere a la palabra escrita, en las humanidades significa cualquier producto cultural que puede ser "leído", es decir, que no solo puede ser consumido y comprendido, sino investigado. Esto incluye ficción, no ficción, poesía, caricaturas políticas, artes plásticas, fotografía, obras, moda, tendencias culturales y mucho más.

theme (p. 38) The underlying issues or ideas of a work.

tema Ideas o cuestiones subyacentes a una obra.

thesis statement The chief claim that a writer makes in any argumentative piece of writing, usually stated in one sentence.

enunciado de tesis Afirmación principal que plantea un escritor en cualquier texto de escritura argumentativa y que suele enunciarse en una oración.

threshold See **archetypal settings**.

umbral Ver **escenarios arquetípicos**.

tone (p. 45) A speaker's attitude toward the subject as conveyed by the speaker's stylistic and rhetorical choices.

tono Actitud de un orador hacia el sujeto transmitida por las decisiones estilísticas y retóricas del orador.

topic sentence (p. 85) A sentence that defines the topic that will be talked about in that paragraph.

oración temática Oración que define el tema del cual se hablará en el párrafo.

tragedy A serious dramatic work in which the protagonist experiences a series of unfortunate reversals due to some character trait, referred to as a **tragic flaw**.

tragedia Obra dramática seria en la cual el protagonista experimenta una serie de desafortunados reveces debido a un rasgo de su carácter, conocido como **falla trágica**.

tragic flaw A weakness in a hero's character that leads to their downfall. The most common tragic flaw is **hubris**, Greek for *pride*.	**falla trágica** Debilidad en el carácter de un héroe que conduce a su caída. La falla trágica más común es **hubris**, que en griego significa *orgullo*.
tragic hero The protagonist in a tragedy. This character has a **tragic flaw**, which leads to their downfall.	**héroe trágico** Protagonista de una tragedia. Este personaje tiene una **falla trágica**, que conduce a su caída.
transitions (p. 87) Words that signify a change in thought while keeping writing cohesive. Common transition words include *therefore*, *because of this*, and *for instance*.	**transiciones** Palabras que representan un cambio de pensamiento mientras mantienen la cohesión de la escritura. Algunas palabras de transición son: *por tanto*, *por ello* y *por ejemplo*.
trickster See **archetypal characters**.	**embaucador** Ver **personajes arquetípicos**.
trickster tales See **archetypal plots**.	**cuentos de embaucadores** Ver **tramas arquetípicas**.

U

understatement A figure of speech in which something is presented as less important, dire, urgent, good, and so on than it actually is, often for satiric or comical effect. Also called *litotes*, it is the opposite of hyperbole.	**atenuación** Figura retórica que presenta algo como menos importante, nefasto, urgente, bueno, etc. de lo que realmente es, en ocasiones con un efecto satírico o cómico. También se conoce como *litotes*; lo contrario de la hipérbole.
underworld or innermost cave See **archetypal settings**.	**inframundo o cueva más interna** Ver **personajes arquetípicos**.
unity (p. 87) Coherence in a text or portion of text that is about a single subject, with all statements and examples addressing that subject.	**unidad** Coherencia de un texto que trata de un solo sujeto, donde todas las afirmaciones y ejemplos se refieren a dicho sujeto.
unreliable narrator (p. 254) A narrator who is biased and doesn't give a full or an accurate picture of events in a narrative. Narrators may be unreliable because of youth, inexperience, madness, intentional or unintentional bias, or even a lack of morals. Authors often use this technique to distinguish the character's point of view from their own. Sometimes an author will use an unreliable narrator to make an ironic point. See also **narrator**.	**narrador poco fiable** Narrador sesgado o que no retrata fielmente los sucesos de una narrativa. Los narradores pueden ser poco fiables por juventud, inexperiencia, locura, sesgo intencional o accidental, o incluso por falta de escrúpulos. Los autores usan esta técnica para distinguir el punto de vista del personaje del punto de vista propio. A veces el autor usará un narrador poco fiable para hacer una observación irónica. Ver también **narrador**.

V

verb (p. 27) An action, state, or occurrence. See also **subject (of a sentence)** and **object**.	**verbo** Acción, estado o suceso. Ver también **sujeto (de una oración)** y **objeto**.
verbal irony (p. 258) See **irony**.	**ironía verbal** Ver **ironía**.
villanelle A form consisting of five three-line stanzas and a final quatrain, with the first and third lines of the first stanza repeating alternately in the following stanzas.	*villanelle* Forma que consiste en estrofas de tres a cinco versos y un cuarteto final, donde el primer y el tercer verso de la primera estrofa se repiten de manera alternada en las estrofas siguientes.

voice (p. 4) The unique ways that you communicate, whether through speech, writing, artwork, singing, and so on.

> **academic voice** A more formal voice used to communicate with and appeal to a wide variety of people from a range of backgrounds and cultures; a shared reflection of formal institutions.

voz Las formas únicas en que nos comunicamos, ya sea a través del habla, la escritura, el arte, el canto, etc.

> **voz académica** Voz formal que se usa para comunicar y dirigirse a una gran variedad de personas de distintos orígenes y culturas; un reflejo compartido de las instituciones formales.

W

wasteland See **archetypal settings**.

yermo Ver **escenarios arquetípicos**.

wilderness or forest See **archetypal settings**.

mundo salvaje o bosque Ver **escenarios arquetípicos**.

wit In rhetoric, the use of laughter, humor, irony, and satire in the confirmation or refutation of an argument.

ingenio En la retórica, uso de la risa, humor, ironía y sátira para confirmar o refutar un argumento.

Text Credits

The New York Times, April 23, 2021. Copyright © 2021 by The New York Times. All rights reserved. Used under license. https://www.nytimes/com.

Thomas Franck, "American students try harder if you pay them, economists found," *CNBC,* November 20, 2017. Copyright © 2017 by CNBC. Used with permission.

Neil Gaiman, "Good Boys Deserve Favors" from *Fragile Things: Short Fictions and Wonders.* Text (artwork) copyright © 2006 by Neil Gaiman. Reprinted by permission of Writers House LLC acting as agent for the author/illustrator.

Roxane Gay, "Peculiar Benefits," *the Rumpus*, May 16, 2012. Copyright © 2012 by Roxane Gay. Used with permission.

Nikki Giovanni, "The Cyclops in the Ocean" from *Those Who Ride the Night Winds.* Copyright © 1983 by Nikki Giovanni. Reprinted by permission of HarperCollins Publishers.

Nikki Giovanni, "Ego Tripping (there may be a reason why)" from *The Collected Poetry of Nikki Giovanni.* Copyright compilation © 2003 by Nikki Giovanni. Used by permission of HarperCollins Publishers.

Malcolm Gladwell, excerpt from *Blink: The Power of Thinking Without Thinking.* Copyright © 2005. Reprinted by permission of Little, Brown and Company an imprint of Hachette Book Group, Inc.

Beth Goder, "How To Say I Love You with Wikipedia" Copyright © 2019 by Beth Goder. Used with permission.

Suzette Hackney, "Simone Biles is a role model for prioritizing her own mental health over an Olympic medal," *USA Today*, July 27, 2021. Copyright © 2021 by USA Today. Used with permission.

Gareth Hinds, excerpt from *Romeo and Juliet.* Candlewick Press, 2013. Copyright © 2013 by Gareth Hinds. Reproduced by permission of the publisher, Candlewick Press, Somerville, MA.

Homer, Excerpts from THE ODYSSEY, translated by Robert Fitzgerald. Copyright © 1961, 1963 by Robert Fitzgerald. Copyright renewed 1989 by Benedict R.C. Fitzgerald, on behalf of the Fitzgerald children. Reprinted by permission of Farrar, Straus and Giroux. All rights reserved.

Dr. Dave Hone, "Why Zoos Are Good," *The Guardian*, August 19, 2014. Copyright © 2014 by Guardian News & Media Ltd 2021. Used with permission.

Langston Hughes, "Let America Be America Again," from *The Collected Poems of Langston Hughes*, edited by Arnold Rampersad with David Roessel, Associate Editor, copyright © 1994 by the Langston Hughes Estate. Used by permission of Alfred A. Knopf, an imprint of the Knopf Doubleday Publishing Group, a division of Penguin Random House LLC and reprinted by permission of Harold Ober Associates. All rights reserved.

Enrica Jang and Jason Strutz, *The Cask of Amontillado,* adapted from the Edgar Allan Poe short story. Copyright © 2016 by Action Lab Entertainment, Inc. Used with permission.

Ha Jin, "I Woke Up — Smiling" from *Facing Shadows*. Copyright © 1996 by Ha Jin. Reprinted by permission of Hanging Loose Press.

Lauren Kay Johnson, "Inheritance of War," *Drunken Boat* 24, December 15, 2016. Copyright © 2016 by Lauren Kay Johnson. All rights reserved. Used with permission.

Mindy Kaling, "Is Everyone Hanging Out Without Me? (Or, How I Made My First Real Friend)" from IS EVERYONE HANGING OUT WITHOUT ME? (AND OTHER CONCERNS), copyright © 2011 by Mindy Kaling. Used by permission of Crown Archetype, an imprint of Random House, a division of Penguin Random House LLC. All rights reserved.

Stephen King, "Stephen King's Guide to Movie Snacks," Copyright © 2008 by Stephen King. Originally appeared in *Entertainment Weekly,* July 27, 2008. Reprinted with permission. All rights reserved.

Alfie Kohn, "The Downside of 'Grit'," alfiekohn.org, April 6, 2014. Copyright © 2014 by Alfie Kohn. This article first appeared in the *Washington Post* and is adapted from the author's book *The Myth of the Spoiled Child.* For more information, please visit www.alfiekohn.org.

Raph Koster, *A Theory of Fun for Game Design.* Copyright © 2005 by Raph Koster. Republished with permission of O'Reilly Media. Permission conveyed through Copyright Clearance Center, Inc.

Kevin Leahy, "Simple Physics," *The Masters Review*. Copyright © 2021 by Kevin Leahy. Used with permission.

Daniel J. Levitin, "Want to learn faster? Stop multitasking and start daydreaming." Originally published in *The Guardian* October 24. Copyright © 2015 Daniel Levitin, used by permission of The Wylie Agency LLC.

Pippa Little, "Turning the Ship for Home and Then the Telling." Copyright © 2016 by Pippa Little. Permission granted by the author.

Justine Lloyd, "What is 'slacktivism' and can it change the world?" *The Lighthouse*, November 26, 2020. Copyright © 2020 by Justine Lloyd. Used with permission.

Layli Long Soldier, "Resolutions: I recognize" from *Whereas*. Copyright © 2017 by Layli Long Soldier. Reprinted with the permission of The Permissions Company, LLC on behalf of Graywolf Press, Minneapolis, Minnesota, graywolfpress.org.

Nelson Mandela, ed., "The Spider and the Crows" from *Favorite African Folktales.* Copyright © 2002 in this selection by Tafelberg Publishers Ltd. Used by permission of W. W. Norton & Company and by permission of Tafelberg Publishers.

Farhad Manjoo, excerpt from "Abolish Billionaires," *The New York Times,* February 6, 2019. Copyright © 2019 by The New York Times. All rights reserved. Used under license. https://nytimes.com/.

Nathaniel A. Marshall, "Harold's Chicken Shack #86" from *Wild Hundreds*. Copyright © 2015. Reprinted by permission of the University of Pittsburgh Press.

Rachel Martin, Taylor Haney, and Vince Pearson, from "On 'For Every Voice That Never Sang' Kishi Bashi Is Confident for a Changing World," April 14, 2021. ©2021 National Public Radio, Inc. originally published on npr.org. used with the permission of NPR. Any unauthorized duplication is strictly prohibited.

John Martz, "Beyond Slackvitism," *The Nib*, July 27, 2017. Copyright © 2017 by John Martz. Used with permission.

Amy McCready, "Does Paying Kids for Good Grades Pay Off?" *Positive Parenting Solutions*. Copyright © 2021 by Positive Parenting Solutions. Used with permission.

Robin McKie, "Is It Time to Shut Down the Zoos?" *The Guardian,* February 2, 2020. Copyright © 2020 by Guardian News and Media Ltd 2021. Used with permission.

Filippo Menczer and Thomas Hills, "Information Overload Helps Fake News Spread, and Social Media Knows It," *Scientific American,* December 1, 2020. Reproduced with permission. Copyright © 2020 by SCIENTIFIC AMERICAN, a Division of Springer Nature America, Inc. All rights reserved.

Katrina Miller, "Mystery Solved: How Plant Cells Know When to Stop Growing," *Wired*, July 8, 2021. Copyright © 2021 by Conde Nast. Used with permission.

Leigh Morrison, "A Point of View: Common Ground Does Not Spell Compromise," *The Inclusion Solution*, January 10, 2019. Copyright © 2019 by the Winters Group. Used with permission.

Siobhan Mullally, "The Realities of Slacktivism," *Alternatives Journal*, January 18, 2021. Copyright © 2021 by Alternatives Journal. Used with permission.

Julia Naughton, "What is love at first sight?" from *Explain That*, Felicity Lewis, ed. Copyright © 2021 by Penguin Random House Australia. Used with permission.

Garry Newman, "Why my videogame chooses your character's race and gender for you," *The Guardian*, April 13, 2016. Copyright © 2021 by Guardian News & Media Ltd 2021. Used with permission.

Viet Thanh Nguyen, "Viet Thanh Nguyen on being a refugee, an American — and a human being," *Financial Times*, February 3, 2017. Copyright © 2017 by Financial Times. Used under license from the Financial Times. All rights reserved.

Mishma Nixon, "Social Media Activism Can Work, but We Don't Need to Shame People Into It," *Teen Vogue*, March 2, 2021. Copyright © 2021 by Conde Nast Publications, Inc. Used with permission.

Norfolk Daily News Editorial, "All Athletes Should Agree Not to Protest or Become Political During Olympics," *Norfolk Daily News*, July 8, 2021. Copyright © 2021 by Norfolk Daily News. Used with permission.

Cirri Nottage, "OP-ED: The Case for LGBT-Inclusive Education," *NBC News*, June 9, 2016. Copyright © 2016 by Cirri Nottage. Used with permission.

Ifeanyi Nsofor, "Africans Mourn Chadwick Boseman: 'A Great Tree Has Fallen,'" Excerpts from *NPR*, were originally published on npr.org on September 1, 2020. Copyright © 2020 by National Public Radio, Inc. Used with the permission of NPR. Any unauthorized duplication is strictly prohibited.

Naomi Shihab Nye, "Kindness" from *Words Under the Words: Selected Poems* by Naomi Shihab Nye, copyright © 1995. Used with the permission of Far Corner Books.

Téa Obreht, "The Morningside," originally appeared in *The New York Times Magazine's Decameron Project*, July 7, 2020. Copyright © 2020 by Téa Obreht and The New York Times. Used with permission.

Tim O'Brien, "Ambush," from *The Things They Carried*. Copyright © 1990 by Tim O'Brien. Reprinted by permission of HarperCollins Publishers. All rights reserved.

David Oliver, "'Stan' culture needs to stop — or at least radically change. Here's why," *USA Today*. September 7, 2021. Copyright © 2021 by USA Today. All rights Reserved. Used with permission.

Larry Olmsted, "Sports Fans are Happier People," from *FANS*. © 2021 by Larry Olmsted. Reprinted by permission of Algonquin Books of Chapel Hill. All rights reserved. Used with permission.

Tochi Onyebuchi, "Samson and the Delilahs" from *Black Enough: Stories of Being Young & Black in America*. Copyright © 2019 by Tochi Onyebuchi. Used with permission.

Tommy Orange, "How Native American Is Native American Enough?" *BuzzFeed*, June 5, 2018. Copyright © 2018 by BuzzFeed. Used with permission.

Robert Pearl, "The Science of Regrettable Decisions," *Vox*, July 23, 2019. Copyright © 2019 by Vox Media, LLC. Located at https://www.vox.com/2019/7/23/20702987/brain-psychology-making-hard-decisions. Used with permission.

PETA, "Is There Such a Thing as a Reputable Roadside Zoo?" *PETA.org*, August 14, 2017. Copyright © 2017 by PETA. Used with permission.

David Polochanin, "We Already Know School Starts Too Early. It's Tim To Do Something About It," *Education Week*, October 2, 2018. Copyright © 2018 by David Polochanin. Used with permission.

Santha Rama Rau, "By Any Other Name," from *Gifts of Passage*. Copyright © 1951, 1952, 1954, 1955, 1957, 1958, 1960, 1961 by Vasanthi Rama Rau Bowers. Reprint Rights are granted by the Estate of Santha Rama Rau sole Proprietor Jai Bowers. All rights reserved. Used with permission.

Jonathan Rand, *Check, Please.* Copyright © 2003 Jonathan Rand. All rights reserved. Reprinted by permission of Playscripts, Inc. To purchase acting editions of this play, or to obtain stock and amateur performance rights, you must contact: Playscripts, Inc., website: http://playscripts.com, phone: 1-866-NEW-PLAY (639-7529).

Diane Ravitch, "We Shouldn't Pay Kids to Learn," *Forbes*, October 17, 2008. Copyright © 2008 by Forbes. All rights reserved. Used under license. https://forbes.com.

Liz Reisberg, "Foreign Language Study Should Be Mandatory!" *Inside Higher Education*, March 14, 2017. Copyright © 2017 by Liz Reisberg. Used with permission.

Jon Ronson, "How One Stupid Tweet Blew Up Justine Sacco's Life," *The New York Times*, February 12, 2015. Copyright © 2015 The New York Times. Used under license. All rights reserved. https://www.nytimes.com/.

Amy Rosen, "Why "Grit" May Be Everything for Success," *Entrepreneur*, August 7, 2015. Copyright © 2015 by Entrepreneur Media, Inc. Used with permission. https://www.entrepreneur.com/.

Brett Ryback, "A Roz by Any Other Name." Copyright © 2006 by Brett Ryback. Used with permission.

Erika L. Sanchez, "Learning To Love My Brown Skin," *RACKED*, January 7, 2016. Copyright © 2016 by Vox Media, LLC. Used with permission. All rights reserved. https://www.racked.com/2016/1/7/10723424/colorism-discrimination-mexico-beautyskin-lightening.

John Scalzi, "Straight White Male: The Lowest Difficulty Setting There Is," Whatever, May 15, 2012. Copyright © 2012 by John Scalzi. Used with permission.

David Sedaris, "Us and Them" from *Dress Your Family in Corduroy and Denim* by David Sedaris, copyright © 2004. Reprinted by permission of Little, Brown, an imprint of Hachette Book Group, Inc. All rights reserved.

William Shakespeare, Prologue from *Romeo and Juliet: The Graphic Novel*. Copyright © 2009 by Classical Comics, Ltd. Used with permission.

William Shakespeare, "Romeo and Juliet," glosses from *Romeo and Juliet*, 2nd Edition, Edited by G. Blakemore Evans, With contributions by Thomas Moisan, © Cambridge University Press 1984, 2003 (9780521825467). Reproduced with permission of the Licensor through PLSclear.

Selena Simmons-Duffin, "5 years later, researchers assess how children exposed to Zika are developing," by Selena Simmons-Duffin Originally

Index